Connecting with the Past

The D. C. Heath Document Sets for Western Civilization

to accompany

The Challenge of the West

Hunt • Martin • Rosenwein • Hsia • Smith

VOLUME II: FROM 1320

D. C. Heath and Company
Lexington, Massachusetts   Toronto

Address editorial correspondence to:

D. C. Heath and Company
125 Spring Street
Lexington, MA 02173

Published simultaneously in Canada.

Printed in the United States of America.

International Standard Book Number: 0-669-39679-6

10 9 8 7 6 5 4 3 2 1

Preface

Connecting with the Past: The D. C. Heath Document Sets in Western Civilization represents an exciting new way of supplying instructors with the source material they need for teaching the survey course by taking full advantage of modern technology. We hope that you not only will be pleased with the result, but will begin a real partnership with us in developing this project in the years to come.

For generations, most teachers have agreed that an essential dimension of training students in history is to allow them to read and interpret the fundamental material with which every working historian must grapple—the documents. Recognizing this need, educational publishers have long made available edited collections of documents and documentary extracts. Many textbooks have featured "sidebar" source readings and, in recent years, many instructors have braved the difficulties of securing permissions and assembled their own sets of primary and secondary reading material—"self-publishing" through copy shops. *Connecting with the Past* not only draws on all these ways of placing documents into students' hands, but also combines elements of all of them to uniquely widen your options.

First, *Connecting with the Past* is a large, two-volume anthology that can stand on its own as a Western Civilization reader; its contents range from the earliest creation myths of the ancient Near East to the fall of Communism. The documents have been chosen not only to offer students a generous selection of readings from classic texts in the Western cultural, intellectual, and political tradition, but also to provide rich insights into the lives of ordinary men and women who lived through the times that the seminal thinkers and artists interpreted in their writings. Juxtaposing private experiences with the milestones of Western culture has been a primary organizing principle in assembling these readings.

Second, we have planned this version of *Connecting with the Past* to coordinate closely with the structure of the Western Civilization textbook that D. C. Heath is publishing this year: *The Challenge of the West,* by Lynn Hunt and others. Every chapter of *Connecting with the Past* corresponds to one of the chapters in *The Challenge of the West,* so that students who are studying Western Civilization with the Hunt et al. textbook can easily find parallel, closely coordinated source readings in the equivalent chapter of *Connecting with the Past.* In this sense, *Connecting with the Past* can serve as a large *collection* of sidebars to *The Challenge of the West,* offering far more supplementary readings—and longer, more substantive ones—than ever could be accommodated within the textbook itself.

Minor exceptions to the chapter-by-chapter correlation with the Hunt et al. text do occur. For example, *The Challenge of the West* begins its treatment of the Enlightenment at the end of Chapter 18 and continues the discussion at the beginning of Chapter 19; *Connecting with the Past* concentrates its source materials on this topic in Chapter 19. And *Connecting with the Past*'s Chapter 29 corresponds to Chapters 29 and 30 of *The Challenge of the West.*

Third, *Connecting with the Past* is not, so to speak, a "finished product" that will stand unchanged until the next edition is published. Recent advances in custom publishing make it possible for D. C. Heath to offer instructors the opportunity to customize the anthology to suit their own courses. For details on how to customize *Connecting with the Past,* see the note that follows this preface. Feel free, as well, to discuss this matter with your D. C. Heath campus representative.

We look forward to working with you, and hope that you and your students enjoy *Connecting with the Past.*

James Miller, Ph.D.
Senior Editor, History
D. C. Heath and Company

Creating a Heath Custom Book Version of Connecting with the Past

You can easily create a *Heath Custom Book* version of *Connecting with the Past* by selecting portions of *Connecting with the Past* and adding your own original materials (such as course outlines), parts of other D. C. Heath ancillaries, and even selections from other sources. In this way you can provide your students with exactly those material you want them to have—no more, no less.

To learn how to do this, contact your D. C. Heath sales representative or call (800) 235–3565 and ask for a copy of our *D. C. Heath Custom Book Author's Guide.* Your custom books should be in your bookstore within six to eight weeks of our receiving your chosen materials.

Contents

CHAPTER 15
The Struggle for Faith and Power, 1494–1560   353

CHAPTER 16
Religious Warfare and Crises of Authority, 1560–1640   399

CHAPTER 18
New Societies and the Early Enlightenment, 1690-1740   469

CHAPTER 19
The Promise of a New Order, 1740–1787   485

CHAPTER 20
The Age of Revolutions, 1787-1799   519

CHAPTER 21
Napoleon, the Restoration, and The Revolutionary Legacy, 1799–1832   570

CHAPTER 23
Politics and Culture of the Nation-State, 1851–1871   632

CHAPTER 24
Empire, Industry, and Everyday Life, 1871–1894   662

CHAPTER 28
The Atomic Age, 1945–1962   781

CHAPTER 29
Contemporary Voices, The 1960s to the Present   811

13

The Collapse of Medieval Order, 1320–1430

The Black Death and Social Control

Documents A and B trace the social disintegration caused by the Black Death and the flagellant movement. Although it dates from a generation before the Black Death, a chronicle entry for the year 1310 (Document A) shows how frightening an outbreak of flagellantism could be to late medieval people; study this passage to understand the fear and hopes involved. Boccaccio's famous account of the plague in the *Decameron* rivals Thucydides' description of a similar disaster in fourth-century B.C. Athens (Set 3.1, Document E). Read Boccaccio's document for an understanding of both the epidemic itself and its social consequences.

The last three documents in this set address the issue of maintaining late medieval social control. In 1245, shortly before the Black Death struck, the London Guild of Spurriers (spur-makers) tightened regulations for bidding, excessive competition, and the taking of shortcuts in producing wares. Why? How would such behavior be regulated today? In Document D, the Statute of Laborers (1351), the English government responds to staggering population losses; read this document for an understanding of how drastically the plague altered social and economic relationships and how those in authority tried to maintain old hierarchies. Document E, from the Florentine archives, does not deal with the plague; still, how does this attempt to regulate townspeople's dress speak to the issue of social control?

A. Flagellants Come to Florence, 1310

In the said year [1310] a great marvel made its appearance. It began in Piedmont, advanced through Lombardy and the Genoese littoral, and spread thence to Tuscany and almost covered all Italy. Many people of the commoner sort, men and women and children without number, left their occupations and their cares behind them and, with the cross to point the way, went from place to place beating their bodies and crying *misericordia* ["God have mercy"] and turning people to penance by persuading them to make peace with one another. The Florentines and the inhabitants of a few other cities refused to let them enter their territory and drove them away saying that they were an augury of evil to the land.

B. Giovanni Boccaccio Describes the Black Death

"Dear ladies . . . here we tarry, as if, I think, for no other purpose than to bear witness to the number of the corpses that are brought here for internment. . . . And if we quit the church, we see dead or sick folk carried about, or we see those, who for their crimes were of late condemned to exile . . . but who, now . . . well knowing that their magistrates are a prey to death or disease, have returned, and traverse the city in packs, making it hideous with their riotous antics; or else we see the refuse of the people, fostered on our blood, becchini, as they call themselves, who for our torment go prancing about . . . making mock of our miseries in scurrilous songs. . . . Or go we home, what see we there? . . . where once were servants in plenty, I find none left but my maid, and shudder with terror, and feel the very hairs of my head to stand on end; and turn or tarry where I may, I encounter the ghosts of the departed. . . . None . . . having means and place of retirement as we have, stays here . . . or if any such there be, they are of those . . . who make no distinction between things honorable and their opposites, so they but answer the cravings of appetite, and, alone or in company, do daily and nightly what things soever give promise of most gratification. Nor are these secular persons alone, but such as live recluse in monasteries break their rule, and give themselves up to carnal pleasures, persuading themselves that they are permissible to them, and only forbidden to others, and, thereby thinking to escape, are become unchaste and dissolute.

C. Social Control Before the Black Death: English Guild Regulations, 1345

Be it remembered, that on Tuesday, the morrow of [the feast of] St. Peter's bonds, in the nineteenth year of the reign of King Edward III, the articles underwritten were read before John Hammond, mayor, Roger de Depham, recorder, and the other aldermen; and seeing that the same were deemed befitting, they were accepted and enrolled in these words.

In the first place, that no one of the trade of spurriers shall work longer than from the beginning of the day until curfew rings out at the church of St. Sepulcher, without Newgate; by reason that no man can work so neatly by night as by day. And many persons of the said trade, who compass how to practice deception in their work, desire to work by night rather than by day; and then they introduce false iron, and iron that has been cracked, for tin, and also they put gilt on false copper, and cracked.

And further, many of the said trade are wandering about all day, without working as all at their trade; and then, when they have become drunk and frantic, they take to their work, to the annoyance of the sick, and all their neighborhood as well, by reason of the broils that arise between them and the strange folk who are dwelling among them. And then they blow up their fires so vigorously, that their forges begin all at once to blaze, to the great peril of themselves and of all the neighborhood around. And then, too, all the neighbors are much in dread of the sparks, which so vigorously issue forth in all directions from the mouths of the chimneys in their forges.

By reason thereof it seems unto them that working by night should be put an end to, in order to avoid such false work and such perils; and therefore the mayor and the aldermen do will, by the assent of the good folk of the said trade and for the common profit, that from henceforth such time for working, and such false work made in the trade, shall be forbidden. And if any person shall be found in the said trade to do the contrary hereof, let him be amerced, the first time in forty pence, one half to go to the use of the Chamber of the Guildhall of London, and the other half to the use of the said trade; the second time, in half a mark; and the third time, in ten shillings, to the use of the same Chamber and trade; and the fourth time, let him forswear the trade forever.

Also, that no one of the said trade shall hang his spurs out on Sundays, or on any other days that are double feasts; but only a sign indicating his business; and such spurs as they shall so sell, they are to show and sell within their shops, without exposing them without or opening the doors or windows of their shops, on the pain aforesaid.

Also, that no one of the said trade shall keep a house or shop to carry on his business, unless he is free of the city; and that no one shall cause to be sold, or exposed for sale, any manner of old spurs for new ones, or shall garnish them or change them for new ones.

Also, that no one of the said trade shall take an apprentice for a less term than seven years, and such apprentice shall be enrolled according to the usages of the said city.

Also, that if any one of the said trade, who is not a freeman, shall take an apprentice for a term of years, he shall be amerced as aforesaid.

Also, that no one of the said trade shall receive the apprentice, serving man, or journeyman of another in the same trade, during the term agreed upon between his master and him, on the pain aforesaid.

Also, that no alien of another country, or foreigner of this country, shall follow or use the said trade, unless he is enfranchised before the mayor, aldermen, and chamberlain; and that, by witness and surety of the good folk of the said trade, who will go surety for him, as to his loyalty and his good behavior.

D. Social Control After the Black Death: The English Ordinance Concerning Laborers, 1351

The king to the sheriff of Kent, greeting. Because a great part of the people, and especially of workmen and servants, have lately died in the pestilence, many seeing the necessities of masters and great scarcity of servants, will not serve unless they may receive excessive wages, and others preferring to beg in idleness rather than by labor to get their living; we, considering the grievous incommodities which of the lack especially of ploughmen and such laborers may hereafter come, have upon deliberation and treaty with the prelates and the nobles and learned men assisting us, with their unanimous counsel ordained:

That every man and woman of our realm of England, of what condition he be, free or bond, able in body, and within the age of sixty years, not living in merchandize, nor exercising any craft, nor having of his own whereof he may live, nor land of his own about whose tillage he may occupy himself, and not serving any other; if he be required to serve in suitable service, his estate considered, he shall be bound to serve him which shall so require him; and take only the wages, livery, meed, or salary which were accustomed to be given in the places where he oweth to serve, the twentieth year of our reign of England, or five or six other common years next before. Provided always, that the lords be preferred before others in their bondmen or their land tenants, so in their service to be retained; so that, nevertheless, the said lords shall retain no more than be necessary for them. And if any such man or woman being so required to serve will not do the same, and that be proved by two true men before the sheriff, bailiff, lord, or constable of the town where the same shall happen to be done, he shall immediately be taken by them or any of them, and committed to the next gaol, there to remain under strait keeping, till he find surety to serve in the form aforesaid.

If any reaper, mower, other workman or servant, of what estate or condition he be, retained in any man's service, do depart from the said service without reasonable cause or license, before the term agreed, he shall have pain of imprisonment; and no one, under the same penalty, shall presume to receive or retain such a one in his service.

No one, moreover, shall pay or promise to pay to any one more wages, liveries, meed, or salary than was accustomed, as is before said; nor shall any one in any other manner demand or receive them, upon pain of doubling of that which shall have been so paid, promised, required or received, to him who thereof shall feel himself aggrieved; and if none such will sue, then the same shall be applied to any of the people that will sue; and such suit shall be in the court of the lord of the place where such case shall happen.

And if lords of towns or manors presume in any point to come against this present ordinance, either by them or by their servants, then suit shall be made against them in the form aforesaid, in the counties, wapentakes, and trithings, or such other courts of ours, for the penalty of treble that so paid or promised by them or their servants. And if any before this present ordinance hath covenanted with any so to serve for more wages, he shall not be bound, by reason of the said covenant, to pay more than at another time was wont to be paid to such a person; nor, under the same penalty, shall presume. to pay more.

Item. Saddlers, skinners, white tawyers, cordwainers, tailors, smiths, carpenters, masons, tilers, shipwrights, carters, and all other artificers and workmen, shall not take for their labor and workmanship above the same that was wont to be paid to such persons the said twentieth year, and other common years next preceding, as before is said, in the place where they shall happen to work; and if any man take more he shall be committed to the next gaol, in manner as before is said.

Item. That butchers, fishmongers, hostelers, brewers, bakers, poulterers, and all other sellers of all manner of victuals, shall be bound to sell the same victuals for a reasonable price, having respect to the price that such victuals be sold at in the places adjoining, so that the same sellers have moderate gains, and not excessive, reasonably to be required according to the distance of the place from which the said victuals be carried; and if any sell such victuals in any other manner, and thereof be convicted, in the manner and form aforesaid, he shall pay the double of the same that he so received to the party injured, or in default of him, to any other that will sue in this behalf. And the mayors and bailiffs of cities, boroughs, merchant towns, and others, and of the ports and maritime places, shall have power to inquire of all and singular, which shall in any thing offend against this, and to levy the said penalty to the use of them at whose suit such offenders shall be convicted. And in case the same mayors and bailiffs be negligent in doing execution of the premises, and thereof be convicted before our justices, by us to be assigned, then the same mayors and bailiffs shall be compelled by the same justices to pay the treble of the thing so sold to the party injured, or in default of him, to any other that will sue; and nevertheless they shall be grievously punished on our part.

And because many strong beggars, as long as they may live by begging, do refuse to labor, giving themselves to idleness and vice, and sometimes to theft and other abominations; none upon the said pain of imprisonment, shall, under the color of pity or alms, give anything to such, who are able to labor, or presume to favor them in their idleness, so that thereby they may be compelled to labor for their necessary living.

E. Florence Imposes Sumptuary Legislation, 1378

It is well known to all that the worthy men, Benozzo di Francesco di Andrea . . . [and fifteen others] . . . have been selected to discover ways and means by which money will accrue to the Commune. . . . Considering the Commune's need for revenue to pay current expenses . . . they have enacted . . . the following:

First, all women and girls, whether married or not, whether betrothed or not, of whatever age, rank, and condition . . . who wear—or who wear in future—any gold, silver, pearls, precious stones, bells, ribbons of gold or silver, or cloth of silk brocade on their bodies or heads . . . for the ornamentation of their bodies . . . will be required to pay each year . . . the sum of 50 florins . . . to the treasurer of the gabelle on contracts. . . . [The exceptions to this prohibition are] that every married woman may wear on her hand or hands as many as two rings. . . . And every married woman or girl who is betrothed may wear . . . a silver belt which does not exceed fourteen ounces in weight. . . .

So that the gabelle is not defrauded, and so that citizens—on account of clothing already made—are not forced to bear new expenditures, [the officials] have decreed that all dresses, gowns, coats, capes, and other items of clothing belonging to any women or girls above the age of ten years, which were made up to the present day and which are decorated in whatever manner, may be worn for ten years in the future without the payment of any *gabelle*. . . .

Document Set 13.1 References

A. Flagellants Come to Florence, 1310
   Giovanni Villani, *Chronicle*, in Kenneth R. Bartlett, ed., *The Civilization of the Italian Renaissance: A Sourcebook* (Lexington, Mass.: D. C. Heath, 1992), 40.
B. Giovanni Boccaccio Describes the Black Death
   Giovanni Boccaccio, *The Decameron*, ed. Edward Hutton (London, 1955), 1:13–14.
C. Social Control Before the Black Death: English Guild Regulations, 1345
   Articles of the Spurriers of London, in James Harvey Robinson, ed., *Readings in European History* (Boston: Ginn, 1904), 1:409–411.
D. Social Control After the Black Death: The English Ordinance Concerning Laborers, 1351
   Translations and Reprints from the Original Sources of European History (Philadelphia: University of Pennsylvania Press, 1898), 2/5:3–5.
E. Florence Imposes Sumptuary Legislation, 1378
   Gene Brucker, *The Society of Renaissance Florence* (New York: Harper & Row, 1971), 46–47.

DOCUMENT SET 13.2
Who Shall Rule the Church? The Great Schism

The crisis of the papacy tore at the heart of late medieval Western society. It was scandalous that the popes left Rome for Avignon and there built a bureaucracy that seemed much more interested in raising money and pursuing secular political goals than in guiding Christians safely to salvation. Things grew even worse after 1378, when two and then even three rival popes roared maledictions at each other and at their enemies' adherents.

Lay people at many levels tried to respond to this dangerous situation. One of the most important medieval political philosophers, Marsilius of Padua (1270–1336?), wrote *Defender of Peace* to argue the case of having the civil authority (here represented by the would-be Holy Roman Emperor, Louis of Bavaria) impose order on the church and bring peace to Christendom (Document A). What potential for the expansion of the secular state do you detect in his proposal—which the papacy furiously condemned in 1327 (Document B)?

In the East, meanwhile, the Byzantine Empire found itself increasingly beleaguered by encircling Ottoman Turkish forces. Although reunion with the Latin West appeared one possible way of getting aid, a Byzantine ambassador to the pope in 1339 insisted (Document C) that such a reunion could come only on the Eastern church's terms. What does this say for the papacy's claim to lead all Christendom?

Document D comes from the era of the Great Schism, when after 1378 Latin Christendom found itself divided between rival popes. An Avignon cleric called Nicholas Clamanges cited a long list of complaints against a worldly church establishment that, he charged, had lost sight of its real mission. But consider also how the church authorities might have handled the flood of business pouring into Avignon *without* becoming bureaucratic and materialistic.

The University of Paris took the lead in calling for a church council to settle the schism and put Christendom aright. Its 1393 plan appears in Document E. And when in 1415 such a council finally convened at Constance (Document F), the balance of power in the Church had apparently shifted against the papal monarchy. (How do you suppose Marsilius of Padua would have responded?) But such a shift did not become permanent. The early fifteenth-century councils like those at Constance and Basel (1431–1449) failed to head off arrangements between the papacy and the kings of western Europe.

Branding as heretical appeals to "future councils," popes like Pius II (*1458–1464) were able to kill off the conciliar movement, which by then had lost its prestige (Document G).

Drawing upon these documents and your reading of *The Challenge of the West*, prepare an analysis of the rise and fall of conciliarism. Why did it fail?

A. Marsilius of Padua Calls for Popular Sovereignty in Church and State, 1327

Only peace can furnish the necessary conditions for progress, for peace is the mother of all the higher arts. The evils of discord and strife have nearly all been described by Aristotle; but one great and important cause of trouble naturally escaped him,—a potent, hidden influence which interferes with the welfare not only of the empire but of all the governments of Europe. . . .

The power of making the laws should belong to the whole body of citizens, for there is no lawgiver among men superior to the people themselves. The argument that there are an infinite number of fools in the world may be met by pointing out that "foolish" is a relative term, and that the people know their own needs best and will not legislate against their own interests. Any particular class of people is, however, likely to be self-seeking, as is shown by the decrees of the popes and the clergy, where the self-interest of the lawmaker is only too apparent.

The actual administration must, nevertheless, be in the hands of a single person or group of persons. Perhaps a king is the best head for the state, but the monarch should be elected and not hold his office hereditarily, and should be deposed if he exceed his powers. . . .

The bishops of Rome have extended their jurisdiction not only over the clergy but, since the Donation of Constantine, over secular rulers as well. This is illustrated by the acts of the popes of the time (including the famous bull *Unam Sanctam*) and of the existing bishop of Rome, John XXII, who claims, both in Italy and Germany, to have supreme jurisdiction over the emperor and over the lesser princes and communities, even in purely temporal and feudal matters.

In its original meaning the "church" meant all

believers in Christ,—all those for whom he shed his blood. "Churchmen" then include all the faithful, whether they be priests or not. The assumed supremacy of the bishop of Rome is without foundation. Even if Peter was ever in Rome,—which is doubtful,—there is no reason to suppose that he handed down any exceptional power to the succeeding bishops.

B. Pope John XXII Condemns Marsilius's Heresy, 1327

(1) When Christ ordered the coin which was taken from the fish's mouth to be paid to the tax collector, he paid tribute to Caesar; and he did this not out of condescension or kindness, but because he had to pay it. From this it is clear that all temporal powers and possessions of the church are subject to the emperor, and he may take them as his own.

(2) That St. Peter had no more authority than the other apostles, and was not the head over the other apostles; and that Christ left behind no head of the church, and did not appoint anyone as his vicar.

(3) That the emperor has the right to make and depose popes and to punish them.

(4) That all priests, whether pope or archbishop or simple priest, are, in accordance with the appointment of Christ, of equal authority and jurisdiction.

(6) That the whole church together can not punish any man with coactive punishment, without the permission of the emperor.

The above articles are contrary to the holy scriptures and hostile to the catholic faith and we declare them to be heretical and erroneous, and the aforesaid Marsilius and John [of Jandun] to be open and notorious heretics, or rather heresiarchs.

C. The Byzantines Insist That Only an Ecumenical Council Can Restore Christian Unity, 1339

The emperor does not dare to manifest publicly that he desires union with you. If he did declare this, a great number of princes and men of the people, in the fear that he would renew the experience of Michael Palaeologus would seek an occasion to put him to death. . . . You have two means peacefully to realize the union. You can either convince the scholars, who in their turn will convince the people, or persuade both people and learned men at the same time. To convince the learned men is easy, since both they and you seek only the truth. But when the scholars return home they will be able to do absolutely nothing with the people. Some men will arise who, either from jealousy or from vainglory, and perhaps believing they act rightly, will teach all exactly the opposite of what you will have defined. They will say to the Greeks, "Do not let yourselves be seduced by these men who have sold themselves for gold and are swelled up with pride; let them say what they wish, do not change anything of your faith." And they will listen to them. . . .

To persuade therefore both the people and the learned men together there is only one way: a general council to be held in the East. For the Greeks admit that all that has been determined in a general council conforms to the faith. You will object, saying that already at Lyons a council to treat of union was held. But no one of the Greeks will accept that the Council of Lyons was ecumenical unless another council declares it so. The Greeks present at Lyons had been delegated neither by the four patriarchs who govern the Eastern church nor by the people, but by the emperor alone, who, without seeking to gain their consent, wanted to achieve union by force. Therefore send legates to the four patriarchs; under their presidency a general council will be held which will make union. And all of us who will have been present at this council will say to the people, "Here is what the Holy General Council has decreed. It is your duty to observe its decisions." And all will submit.

D. The Downfall of the Church: An Avignon Clergyman Exposes Avarice and Corruption

After the great increase of worldly goods, the virtues of our ancestors being quite neglected, boundless avarice and blind ambition invaded the hearts of the churchmen. As a result they were carried away by the glory of their position and the extent of their power, and soon gave way to the degrading effects of luxury. Three most exacting and troublesome masters had now to be satisfied. *Luxury* demands sundry gratifications,—wine, sleep, banquets, music, debasing sports, courtesans, and the like. *Display* requires fine houses, castles, towers, palaces, rich and varied furniture, expensive clothes, horses, servants, and the pomp of luxury. Lastly is *Avarice,* which carefully brings together vast treasures to supply the demands of the above-mentioned vices or, if these are otherwise provided for, to gratify the eye by the vain contemplation of the coins themselves.

So insatiable are these lords, and so imperious are their demands, that the Golden Age of Saturn, which we hear of in stories, should it now return, would hardly suffice to meet the requirements. Since it is impossible, however rich the bishop and ample his revenue, to satisfy these rapacious harpies with that alone, he must cast about for other sources of income.

For carrying on these exactions and gathering the gains into the camera, or Charybdis, as we may better call it, the popes appoint their *collectors* in every province,—those, namely, whom they know to be most skillful in extracting money, owing to peculiar energy, diligence, or harshness of temper, those, in short, who will neither spare nor except but would squeeze gold from a stone. To these the popes grant, moreover, the power of anathematizing any one, even prelates, and of expelling from the communion of the faithful every one who does not, within a fixed period, satisfy their demands for money. What ills these collectors have caused, and the extent to which poor churches and people have been oppressed, are questions best omitted, as we could never hope to do the matter justice. From this source come the laments of the unhappy ministers of the Church, which reach our ears, as they faint under the insupportable yoke,—yea, perish of hunger. Hence come suspensions from divine service, interdicts from entering a church, and anathemas, a thousandfold intensified in severity.

Such things were resorted to in the rarest instances by the fathers [i.e., by the early church], and then only for the most horrible of crimes; for by these penalties a man is separated from the companionship of the faithful and turned over to Satan. But nowadays these inflictions are so fallen in esteem that they are used for the lightest offense, often for no offense at all, so that they no longer bring terror but are objects of contempt.

To the same cause is to be ascribed the ruin of numerous churches and monasteries and the leveling to the ground, in so many places, of sacred edifices, while the money which was formerly used for their restoration is exhausted in paying these taxes. But it even happens, as some well know, that holy relics in not a few churches—crosses, chalices, feretories, and other precious articles—go to make up this tribute.

Who does not know how many abbots and other prelates, when they come to die, are, if they prove obnoxious to the papal camera on account of their poverty, refused a dignified funeral, and even denied burial, except perchance in some field or garden, or other profane spot, where they are secretly disposed of. Priests, as we all can see, are forced, by reason of their scanty means of support, to desert their parishes and their benefices and, in their hunger, seek bread where they may, performing profane services for lay-

men. Some rich and hitherto prosperous churches have, indeed, been able to support this burden, but all are now exhausted and can no longer bear to be cheated of their revenue.

E. The University of Paris Tries to Settle the Great Schism, 1393

The first way. Now the first way to end the schism is that both parties should entirely renounce and resign all rights which they may have or claim to have to the papal office. . . .

The second way. But if both cling tenaciously to their rights and refuse to resign, as they have done up to now, we would propose the way of arbitration. That is, that they should together choose worthy and suitable men, or permit such to be chosen in a regular and canonical way, and these shall have the full power and authority to discuss the case and decide it, and if necessary and expedient, and approved by those who according to the canon law have the authority [that is, the cardinals], they may also have the right to proceed to the election of a pope.

The third way. If the rival popes, after being urged in a brotherly and friendly manner, will not accept either of the above ways, there is a third way which we propose as an excellent remedy for this sacrilegious schism. We mean that the matter shall be left to a general council. This general council might be composed, according to canon law, only of prelates, or, since many of them are very illiterate, and many of them are bitter partisans of one or the other pope, there might be joined with the prelates an equal number of masters and doctors of theology and law from the faculties of approved universities. Or if this does not seem sufficient to anyone, there might be added besides one or more representatives from cathedral chapters and the chief monastic orders, in order that all decisions might be rendered only after most careful examination and mature deliberation.

F. The Council of Constance Imposes Reform, 1415–1417

This holy synod of Constance, constituting a general council for the extirpation of the present schism and the union and reformation of the Church of God in head and members, legitimately assembled in the Holy Ghost, to the praise of omnipotent God, in order that it may the more easily, safely, effectively, and freely bring about the union and reformation of the Church of God, hereby determines, decrees, ordains, and declares what follows:

It first declares that this same council, legitimately assembled in the Holy Ghost, forming a general council and representing the Catholic Church militant, has its power immediately from Christ, and every one, whatever his position or rank, even if it be the papal dignity itself, is bound to obey it in all those things which pertain to the faith, to the healing of the schism, and to the general reformation of the Church of God in head and members.

It further declares that any one, whatever his position, station, or rank, even if it be the papal, who shall contumaciously refuse to obey the mandates, decrees, ordinances, or instructions which have been, or shall be, issued by this holy council, or by any other general council legitimately summoned, which concern, or in any way relate to, the above-mentioned objects, shall, unless he repudiate his conduct, be subjected to condign penance and be suitably punished, having recourse, if necessary, to the resources of the law. . . .

A frequent celebration of general councils is an especial means for cultivating the field of the Lord and effecting the destruction of briers, thorns, and thistles, to wit, heresies, errors, and schism, and of bringing forth a most abundant harvest. The neglect to summon these fosters and develops all these evils, as may be plainly seen from a recollection of the past and a consideration of existing conditions. Therefore, by a perpetual edict, we sanction, decree, establish, and ordain that general councils shall be celebrated in the following manner, so that the next one shall follow the close of this present council at the end of five years. The second shall follow the close of that, at the end of seven years, and councils shall thereafter be celebrated every ten years in such places as the pope shall be required to designate and assign, with the consent and approbation of the council, one month before the close of the council in question, or which, in his absence, the council itself shall designate. Thus, with a certain continuity, a council will always be either in session, or be expected at the expiration of a definite time.

This term may, however, be shortened on account of emergencies, by the supreme pontiff, with the counsel of his brethren, the cardinals of the holy Roman Church, but it may not be hereafter lengthened. The place, moreover, designated for the future council may not be altered without evident necessity. If, however, some complication shall arise, in view of which such a change shall seem necessary, as, for example, a state of siege, a war, a pest, or other obstacles, it shall be permissible for the supreme pontiff, with the consent and subscription of his said brethren, or two thirds of them, to select another appropriate place near the first, which must be within the same country, unless such obstacles, or similar ones, shall exist throughout the whole nation. In that case, the council may be summoned to some appropriate neighboring place, within the bounds of another nation. To this the prelates, and others, who are wont to be summoned to a council, must betake themselves as if that place had been designated from the first. Such change of place, or shortening of the period, the supreme pontiff is required legitimately and solemnly to publish and announce one year before the expiration of the term fixed, that the said persons may be able to come together, for the celebration of the council, within the term specified. . . . [1417]

The holy council of Constance decrees and ordains that the supreme pontiff who shall next, by the grace of God, assume office, shall, in conjunction with this holy council, or with the deputies of the several "nations," reform the Church, before the council dissolves, in head and members, as well as the Roman curia, in accordance with justice and the proper organization of the Church, in all the respects enumerated below, and which are submitted by the "nations" as requiring reform:

The number, character, and nationality of the lords cardinals.

The reservations [of benefices] made by the apostolic see.

The annates, both the *servitia communia* and the *servitia minuta.*

The collation to benefices and expectative favors.

What cases are to be brought before the Roman curia and what not.

Appeals to the Roman curia.

The functions of the [papal] chancery and penitentiary.

Exemptions and incorporations made during the schism.

Benefices *in commendam.*

Confirmation of elections.

Income during vacancies.

The non-alienation of the possessions of the Roman church or other churches.

For what reasons and in what manner a pope shall be corrected or deposed.

The extirpation of heresy.

Dispensations.

The means of support of pope and cardinals.

Indulgences.

Tenths.

When the above-mentioned deputies shall have been appointed by the "nations," it shall be free to the others, with the permission of the pope, to return home. [1417]

G. Papal Monarchy Triumphant: Pope Pius II Forbids Appeals to Future Church Councils, 1459

The execrable and hitherto unknown abuse has grown up in our day, that certain persons, imbued with the spirit of rebellion, and not from a desire to secure a better judgment, but to escape the punishment of some offence which they have committed, presume to appeal from the pope to a future council, in spite of the fact that the pope is the vicar of Jesus Christ and to him, in the person of St. Peter, the following was said: "Feed my sheep" [John 21:16] and "Whatsoever thou shalt bind on earth shall be bound in heaven" [Matt. 16:18]. Wishing therefore to expel this pestiferous poison from the church of Christ and to care for the salvation of the flock entrusted to us, and to remove every cause of offence from the fold of our Saviour, with the advice and consent of our brothers, the cardinals of the holy Roman church, and of all the prelates, and of those who have been trained in the canon and civil law, who are at our court, and with our own sure knowledge, we condemn all such appeals and prohibit them as erroneous and detestable.

Document Set 13.2 References

A. Marsilius of Padua Calls for Popular Sovereignty in Church and State, 1327
Marsilius of Padua, *Defender of Peace*, in James Harvey Robinson, ed., *Readings in European History* (Boston: Ginn, 1904), 1:491–492.
B. Pope John XXII Condemns Marsilius's Heresy, 1327
O. J. Thatcher and E. H. McNeal, *A Source Book of Mediaeval History* (New York: Scribners, 1905), 324.
C. The Byzantines Insist That Only an Ecumenical Council Can Restore Christian Unity, 1339
Barlaam's address to the Pope, in Deno John Geanokoplos, ed., *Byzantium: Church, Society, and Civilization Seen Through Contemporary Eyes* (Chicago: University of Chicago Press, 1984), 220–221.
D. The Downfall of the Church: An Avignon Clergyman Exposes Avarice and Corruption
Nicholas Clamanges, *The Downfall of the Church*, in Robinson, 1:508–510.
E. The University of Paris Tries to Settle the Great Schism, 1393
Thatcher and McNeal, 326–327.
F. The Council of Constance Imposes Reform, 1415–1417
Council of Constance, in Robinson, 1:511–514.
G. Papal Monarchy Triumphant: Pope Pius II Forbids Appeals to Future Church Councils, 1459
Pius II, "Execrabilis," in Thatcher and McNeal, 332.

DOCUMENT SET 13.3
Spiritual Tensions

Battles over who should rule the church had no effect on popular piety. How deeply felt were the efforts of ordinary Christians to expiate their sins and placate divine wrath may be judged from the documents of this set.

William Langland (c. 1332–c. 1400), an English cleric in minor orders who shared the life of the London poor, composed the long allegorical poem *Piers Plowman* (in Document A translated into modern English prose), which criticized the clergy and spoke for the anxieties of ordinary people. Forming religious confraternities was one way that lay people could "pool" their devotions and increase their sense of security; one such organization from Norwich, England, is described in Document B.

Although most Christians managed to stay within prescribed bounds of belief and practice, heretical groups also thrived. In Italy most Franciscan friars made their compromises with "the world," but a minority, called *Fraticelli* ("little brothers"), continued to preach stringent asceticism and total poverty, and they were condemned as heretical. Document C shows how Florence in 1389 punished one of the Fraticelli. One of the traps that could lead one into heresy, indeed, was the belief that sacraments (like penance and communion) performed by sinful priests had no validity. This view, which if accepted would have undermined the whole institutional church (for who was to judge what priests were guilty?), was roundly condemned by churchmen like the author of a 1444 tract (Document D) against the heretical Waldensian movement.

To help to pull together this material and understand late medieval religious anxieties, consider also Document E, one of the sonnets of the great, restless Italian poet Petrarch (1304–1374). The poem describes the decision of Petrarch's brother to enter the especially strict Carthusian Order after his ladylove's death in 1343. No one in late-medieval Europe could ever forget the prospect of sudden death and judgment for one's sins; use the documents of this set and *The Challenge of the West* to evoke this melancholy foreboding and to analyze the means by which lay Christians sought to deal with it.

A. Piers Plowman Prefers Individual Piety to Reliance on the Church

And all this maketh me think upon my dream. And how the priest found no pardon like Do-well and thought that Do-well surpassed indulgences, saying mass two or three years for departed souls, and bishops' letters; and how Do-well shall be worthier received at the day of doom, and shall surpass all the pardons of St. Peter's church.

Now the pope hath power to grant people the power to pass into heaven without any penance. This is our belief, as learned men teach us. ("Whatsoever you shall bind on earth, it shall be bound in heaven," etc.) And so I truly believe (Lord forbid otherwise!) that pardon and penance and prayers indeed cause souls to be saved which have sinned deadly seven times. But to trust these three-year masses methinketh truly is not so safe for the soul, certes, as is Do-well.

Therefore, I counsel you, ye men who are rich on this earth and have three-year masses in trust of your treasure, be ye never the bolder to break the ten commandments; and especially, ye masters, mayors, judges, who are held for wise men and have the wealth of this world and can purchase pardon and the pope's bulls. At the dreadful doom when the dead shall rise and all come before Christ to render account,—how thou didst lead thy life here and didst keep his laws, and how thou didst do day by day, the doom will declare. And bagful of pardons there, or provincial letters,—or though ye be found in the fraternity of all the four monastic orders, and have doublefold indulgences,—except Do-well help you, I set your letters and pardons at the worth of a pea shell!

B. A Religious Confraternity in England Organizes Communal Devotion, 1389

In the first place with one assent it is ordained that all the brethren and sisters of this gild shall come together to the parish church of St. Simon and St. Jude, in Norwich, on the day of St. Katharine, to go in the procession with their candle, which is borne before them, and to hear the mass of St. Katharine in the aforesaid church; and at that mass every brother and sister shall offer a half-penny.

And also it is ordained that what brother or sister shall be absent at the procession aforesaid, or at mass, or at offering, he shall pay to the chattels of the gild two pounds of wax, but they may be excused reasonably.

And also it is ordained, that where a brother or a sister is dead, and every brother and sister shall come to *dirige*[1] and to mass; and at the mass, each shall offer a half-penny, and give a half-penny to alms; and for a mass to be sung for the soul of the dead, a penny. And at the *dirige*, every brother and sister that is lettered shall say, for the soul of the dead, *placebo* and *dirige*, in the place where they shall come together; and every brother and sister that is not lettered shall say for the soul of the dead, twenty times, the *Paternoster*, with *ave Maria*; and from the chattels of the gild shall there be two candles of wax, of sixteen pounds weight, about the body of the dead.

And also it is ordained, that if any brother or sister die out of the city of Norwich, within eight miles, six of the brethren that have the chattels of the gild in keeping, shall go to that brother or sister that is dead; and if it be lawful, they shall carry it to Norwich, or else it be buried there; and if the body be buried out of Norwich, all the brethren and sisters shall be warned to come to the foresaid church of St. Simon and St. Jude, and there shall be done for the soul of the dead all service, light and offering as if the body were there present. And what brother or sister be absent at *placebo* and *dirige*, or at mass, he shall pay two pounds of wax to the chattels of the gild, unless he be reasonably excused. And nevertheless he shall do for the dead as it is said before. . . .

And also it is ordained that if any brother or sister fall into poverty, through adventure of the world, his estate shall be helped by every brother and sister of the gild, with a farthing in the week.

And also it is ordained by common assent that if there be any discord between brothers and sisters, that discord shall be first showed to other brothers and sisters of the gild, and by them shall accord be made, if it may be skillfully. And if they cannot be so brought to accord, it shall be lawful to them to go to the common law, without any maintenance. And whoso does against this ordinance, he shall pay two pounds of wax to the light.

Also it is ordained, by common assent, that if any brother of this gild be chosen into office and refuse it, he shall pay two pounds of wax to the light of St. Katharine.

Also it is ordained, by common assent, that the brethren and sisters of this gild, in the worship of St. Katharine, shall have a livery of hoods in suit, and eat together in their gild day, at their common cost; and whoso fails, he shall pay two pounds of wax to the light.

Also it is ordained, by common assent, that no brother or sister shall be received into this gild but by the alderman and twelve brethren of the gild. . . .

C. One of the Florentine *Fraticelli* Is Burned at the Stake, 1389

This is the condemnation of Giovanni, called Fra Michele di Berti of Calci, in the territory of Pisa, a man of low condition, evil conversation, life, and reputation, and a heretic against the Catholic faith, against whom we have proceeded by means of inquisition. . . . It has come to our attention that this Giovanni . . . with the spirit and intent of being a heretic, had relations with the Fraticelli, called the Little Brothers of Poverty, heretics and schismatics and denounced by the Holy Roman Church, and that he joined that depraved sect in a place called the grotto of the *Dieci Yoffensi*, in which place they congregated and stayed. . . .

Now everything which I here describe, I who write both saw or heard. Fra Michele, having come into the courtyard, waited attentively to hear the condemnation. And the vicar [general of the bishop] spoke: "The bishop and the Inquisitor have sent me here to tell you that if you wish to return to the Holy Church and renounce your errors, then do so, in order that the people may see that the church is merciful." And Fra Michele replied, "I believe in the poor crucified Christ, and I believe that Christ, showing the way to perfection, possessed nothing. . . ." Having read his confession, the judge turned his back upon Fra Michele . . . and the guards seized him and with great force pushed him outside of the gate of the judge's palace. He remained there alone, surrounded by scoundrels, appearing in truth as one of the martyrs. And there was such a great crowd that one could scarcely see. And the throng increased in size, shouting: "You don't want to die!" And Fra Michele replied, "I will die for Christ." And the crowd answered: "Oh! You aren't dying for Christ! You don't believe in God!" And Fra Michele replied: "I believe in God, in the Virgin Mary, and in the Holy Church!" And someone said to him, "You wretch! The devil is pushing you from behind!" . . .

. . . And at the Mercato Nuovo, the shouts grew louder: "Repent, repent!" And he replied, "Repent of your sins; repent of your usury and your false mer-

---

[1] Various prayers in the Latin liturgy are named in this document.

chandising. . . ." And at the Piazza del Grano, there were many women in the windows of the houses who cried to him: "Repent, repent!" And he replied, "Repent of your sins, your usury, your gambling, your fornication. . . ." When he arrived at S. Croce, near the gate of the friars, the image of St. Francis was shown to him and he raised his eyes to heaven and said, "St. Francis, my father, pray to Christ for me. . . ."

And when he arrived at the gate near the place of execution, one of the faithful began to cry, "Remain firm, martyr of Christ, for soon you will receive the crown. . . ." And arriving at the place of execution, there was a great turmoil and the crowd urged him to repent and save himself and he refused. . . . And the guards pushed the crowd back and formed a circle of horsemen around the pyre so that no one could enter. I myself did not enter but climbed upon the river bank to see, but I was unable to hear. . . . And he was bound to the stake . . . and the crowd begged him to recant, except one of the faithful, who comforted him. . . . And they set fire to the wood . . . and Fra Michele began to recite the Te Deum. . . . And when he had said, "In your hands, O Lord, I commend my spirit," the fire burned the cords which bound him and he fell dead . . . to the earth.

And many of the onlookers said, "He seems to be a saint." Even his enemies whispered it . . . and then they slowly began to return to their homes. They talked about Michele and the majority said that he was wrong and that no one should speak such evil of the priests. And some said, "He is a martyr," and others said, "He is a saint," and still others denied it. And there was a greater tumult and disturbance in Florence than there had ever been. . . .

D. Are Sacraments Performed by an Unworthy Priest Valid?

Since the sin of adultery does not take from a king the royal dignity, if otherwise he is a good prince who righteously executes justice in the earth, so neither can it take the sacerdotal dignity from the priest, if otherwise he performs the sacraments rightly and preaches the word of God. Who doubts that a licentious king is more noble than a chaste knight, although not more holy? . . . No one can doubt that Nathaniel was more holy than Judas Iscariot; nevertheless Judas was more noble on account of the apostleship of the Lord, to which Judas and not Nathaniel was called.

But thou, heretic, wilt say: "Christ said to his disciples, 'Receive ye the Holy Ghost. Whosesoever sins ye remit, they are remitted unto them'; therefore the priest who does not receive the Holy Ghost because he is wicked cannot absolve." Even if a wicked priest has neither charity nor the Holy Ghost as a private man, nevertheless his priesthood is worthy as far as the efficacy of the sacraments goes, though he himself may be unworthy of the priesthood. . . .

For example, a red rose is equally red in the hands of an emperor or of a dirty old woman; likewise a carbuncle in the hand of a king or of a peasant; and my servant cleans the stable just as well with a rusty iron hoe as with a golden one adorned with gems. No one doubts that in the time of Elijah there were many swans in the world, but the Lord did not feed the prophet by swans, but by a black crow. It might have been pleasanter for him to have had a swan, but he was just as well fed by a crow. And though it may be pleasanter to drink nectar from a golden goblet than from an earthen vessel, the draught intoxicates just the same, wherever it comes from.

E. Petrarch Broods on Love and Death

Thy lady fair, whom thou didst love so well,
Hath from amongst us suddenly withdrawn,
And unto heav'n—that dare I hope—is gone;
Such pleasantness and softness round her fell.
'Tis therefore time, that in thy keeping dwell
Thy heart's two keys, which living she did own;
Thou shouldst pursue her, by straight path, anon,
And from thee all the weight of earth dispel.
Thou art from thy chief hinderance now freed,
And may'st whate'er remains lay down with ease,
And like unloaded pilgrims, may'st emerge.
Thou see'st now well, how every creature flees
Always to death, and how the soul hath need
To step, with lightness, to that perilous verge.

Document Set 13.3 References

A. Piers Plowman Prefers Individual Piety to Reliance on the Church
James Harvey Robinson, ed., *Readings in European History* (Boston: Ginn, 1904), 1:477.
B. A Religious Confraternity in England Organizes Communal Devotion, 1389
Translations and Reprints from the Original Sources of European History (Philadelphia: University of Pennsylvania Press, 1902), 34–35.
C. One of the Florentine *Fraticelli* Is Burned at the Stake, 1389
Alessandro D'Ancona in Gene Brucker, ed., *The Society of Renaissance Florence* (New York: Harper & Row, 1971), 253–257.
D. Are Sacraments Performed by an Unworthy Priest Valid?
Pilichdorfer, *Against the Wilderness*, in Robinson, 1:383–384.
E. Petrarch Broods on Love and Death
Petrarch, Sonnet 70, trans. C. B. Cayley.

DOCUMENT SET 13.4
Wycliffe, Hus, and Their Followers

This set continues to deal with lay concerns for religious safeguards as expressed in Set 13.3, but with a focus on how John Wycliffe in England and Jan Hus in Bohemia took stands that the church declared heretical.

Both Wycliffe (c. 1329–1384) and Hus (c. 1369–1415) were priests and university teachers who became deeply aware of abuses in the church through their sympathetic contacts with ordinary people. The ideas of Wycliffe, a generation older than Hus, probably became known to the latter through direct contacts between the universities of Oxford and Prague and also through the presence in Prague of Englishmen associated with the English-born queen of Bohemia. Wycliffe survived because the church, divided by schism, could not prevail on the English authorities (among whom he had many sympathizers) to hand him over. Hus was martyred by the Council of Constance, which although it had deposed popes, was not about to tolerate "Wycliffite" attacks on central church dogmas like transubstantiation (the doctrine that the priest transforms the communion bread and wine into the actual body and blood of Christ).

The central message of Wycliffe's and Hus's teaching was that the clergy could not mediate between the individual Christian and God. Document A is a brief extract from Wycliffe's voluminous writings on this theme, translated into modern English; in Document B, Hus writes from his prison cell in Constance to justify his position and protest against the council's attempt to silence him. In Document C the consequences of Hus's revolt become apparent: the Czech people rose in arms to resist their king, Sigismund, who had betrayed Hus and now was attempting to enforce the council's decrees on religious conformity. In this document a member of the Prague City Council, a moderate Hussite, describes how radical Hussites founded a community they called Tabor. His account combines sympathy for the persecuted with a rejection of the social and religious radicalism of the sectarians, who fervently believed they were ushering in the reign of God's righteousness on earth.

A. John Wycliffe Attacks the Clergy for Withholding the Gospel from the People

We should put on the armor of Christ, for the antichrist has turned these clergy to covetousness and worldly love, and has so blinded the people and decried the law of Christ that his servants be thick [many], and few be on Christ's side. And always they despise that men should know Christ's life, for by his life and his teaching should help arise on his side, and priests should be ashamed of their lives, and especially these high priests, for they reverse Christ both in word and deed.

And therefore the great Bishop of England, as men say, is ill-pleased that God's law be written in English for laymen; and he pursues a priest for writing to men this English, and summons him and persecutes him, so that he is hard pressed to cry out. And thus he pursues another priest by the help of Pharisees, for he preached Christ's gospel freely without distortions.

B. Jan Hus, on the Eve of His Execution, Writes "to the Entire Christian World," 1415

I, Master John Hus, in hope a servant of Jesus Christ, heartily desiring that Christ's faithful after my decease should have no occasion to be offended on account of my death by judging me as if I were an obstinate heretic; and taking Christ Jesus as witness, for Whose law I desire to die, write this as a memorial to the friends of truth.

First, that in the very many private hearings and later in the public hearings of the Council I protested my willingness to submit to instruction and direction, revocation and punishment, were I taught that anything I had written, taught, or said in reply was contrary to the truth. And fifty doctors, delegates of the Council, as they said, often rebuked by me even in the public hearing of the Council because of their false abstracting of the articles, were not willing to give me any private instruction; yea, they were not willing even to confer with me, saying: "You must stand by the decision of the Council." As for the Council, when I adduced in the public hearing Christ's Scripture or [the opinion] of the holy doctors, they either mocked me or said that I understood it wrongly, while the doctors said that I adduced it inappropriately. Also a certain cardinal, the highest in the Council and delegated by the Council, taking out a paper, said at a public hearing: "Look, a certain master of sacred theology presented me this argument: answer it!" It was an argument about the common essence which I had conceded to exist in divine things. Afterward, when he floundered, although he is reputed to be a most eminent doctor of theology, I spoke to him about the common created essence which is the first created being and is communicated to every individual creature. From this he wished to prove the remanence of the material bread. But being obviously reduced to the utmost lack of knowledge of the argument, he became silent.

Immediately thereafter an English doctor began to argue, but he similarly floundered, and another English doctor, who at a private hearing said to me that Wyclif had wished to destroy all knowledge and that in every one of his books and his treatises of logic he had committed errors; he, rising, began to argue about the multiplication of the body of Christ in the host. Failing in the argument, when they told him to keep still, he said: "Look! he [Hus] astutely deceives the Council! Beware, lest the Council be deceived as it was deceived by Berengar!"[1] When he became silent, someone began to argue noisily about the common created essence; but he was shouted down by the crowd. I, however, standing up, asked to be accorded a hearing, saying to him: "Argue boldly; I shall gladly answer you." But he likewise gave up and ill-temperedly added: "It is a heresy!"

What clamor then, what mocking, jeering, and reviling arose against me in that assembly is known to lords Wenceslas of Dubá and John of Chlum and his notary Peter, the most steadfast knights and lovers of God's truth. Hence even I, being often overwhelmed by such clamor, spoke these words: "I had supposed that in this Council would be greater reverence, piety, and discipline." Then they all listened because the king ordered silence. The cardinal presiding over the Council said: "You spoke more humbly in the castle!" I said: "Because then nobody shouted at me; while now all are shouting against me." And he added: "Look! the Council requests whether you are willing to submit to instruction." I said: "Most gladly am I willing, in accordance with my declaration." And he said: "Yea, this constitutes your instruction,

that the doctors declare the articles drawn from your books to be erroneous. You must revoke them and abjure those which were deposed against you by the witnesses." The king then said: "They will be shortly written for you, and you will reply." And the cardinal said: "This will be done at the next hearing." And immediately the Council rose up. God knows what great temptings I suffered afterward!

C. Lawrence of Brezová Describes the Founding of Tabor

In these times therefore the faithful Czechs, both clergy and laity, who favored communion in both kinds and devotedly promoted it, and who grieved at the unjust death of Master John Hus . . . suffered very great difficulties, tribulations, anguish, and torment throughout the Kingdom of Bohemia, at the hands of the enemies and blasphemers of the Truth. . . . For these enemies of the Truth hunted down priests and laymen who ardently supported the chalice in various parts of the realm and brought them to the men of Kutná Hora,[2] to whom they sold some for money. The Kutná Horans—Germans and cruel persecutors and enemies of the Czech—afflicted them with various blasphemies and diverse punishments, and inhumanly threw them—some alive, some first decapitated—into deep mine shafts, especially into the mine shaft near the church of St. Martin near the Kourim gate, which shaft the Kutná Horans called "Tabor." . . . In a short time more than 1,600 utraquists [those who took communion in both kinds] were killed . . . the executioners often being exhausted by the fatigue of slaughter. . . .

During this time certain Taborite priests were preaching to the people a new coming of Christ, in which all evil men and enemies of the Truth would perish and be exterminated, while the good would be preserved in five cities. . . . They urged that all those desiring to be saved from the wrath of Almighty God, which in their view was about to be visited on the whole globe, should leave their cities, castles, villages, and towns, as Lot left Sodom, and should go to the five cities of refuge. . . . And many simple folk . . . sold their property, taking even a low price, and flocked to these priests from various parts of the Kingdom of Bohemia and . . . Moravia, with their wives and children, and they threw their money at the feet of the priests.

---

[1] A French theologian (c. 999–1088) whose views denying transubstantiation were condemned by the church in the eleventh century.

[2] A rich mining town near Prague, inhabited by a mixed Czech-German population

Document Set 13.4 References

A. John Wycliffe Attacks the Clergy for Withholding the Gospel from the People
John Wycliffe, adapted from James Harvey Robinson, ed., *Readings in European History* (Boston: Ginn, 1904), 1:497–498.

B. Jan Hus, on the Eve of His Execution, Writes "to the Entire Christian World," 1415
M. Spinka, *John Hus and the Council of Constance* (New York: 1965), 293–294.

C. Lawrence of Brezová Describes the Founding of Tabor
Lawrence of Brezová in Howard Kaminsky, *A History of the Hussite Revolution* (Berkeley: University of California Press, 1967), 310–312.

DOCUMENT SET 13.5
Domination

The three documents of this set reflect upper-class views of the social hierarchy in late medieval society. Read them to extract the values they express.

Document A is an extract from the prologue to *The Canterbury Tales* of Geoffrey Chaucer, which introduces the characters who will subsequently tell their stories as they journey on a pilgrimage to the great shrine at Canterbury. Chaucer's Prologue sets before us the complete social hierarchy, and it should be read in its entirety, if possible. Read Document B—an extract from Christine de Pizan's (1364–c. 1430) *The Book of the City of Ladies*—for her views on how a "wise princess" should keep the women in her charge under control. Christine was an accomplished woman of her day, a professional writer patronized by the queen of France, and she understood well the secluded world of court women whose chain-of-command paralleled that of men of comparable rank. Finally consider the tournament, staged in 1390 during the Hundred Years' War, as described in the *Chronicles* of Sir John Froissart (1333?–1400). Such entertainments brought together men and women of the court and the town to enjoy a display of knightly prowess.

A. Geoffrey Chaucer Idealizes "a Truly Perfect, Gentle Knight"

A knight there was, and he a worthy man,
Who, from the moment that he first began
To ride about the world, loved chivalry,
Truth, honour, freedom and all courtesy.
Full worthy was he in his liege-lord's war,
And therein had he ridden (none more far)
As well in Christendom as heathenesse,
And honoured everywhere for worthiness.
    At Alexandria, he, when it was won;
Full oft the table's roster he'd begun
Above all nations' knights in Prussia.
In Latvia raided he, and Russia,
No christened man so oft of his degree.
In far Granada at the siege was he
Of Algeciras,[1] and in Belmarie.
At Ayas was he and at Satalye
When they were won; and on the Middle Sea
At many a noble meeting chanced to be.

1 Various campaigns against the Muslims in Southern Spain and North Africa are named here.

Of mortal battles he had fought fifteen,
And he'd fought for our faith at Tramissene
Three times in lists, and each time slain his foe.
This self-same worthy knight had been also
At one time with the lord of Palatye
Against another heathen in Turkey:
And always won he sovereign fame for prize.
Though so illustrious, he was very wise
And bore himself as meekly as a maid.
He never yet had any vileness said,
In all his life, to whatsoever wight.
He was a truly perfect, gentle knight.
But now, to tell you all of his array,
His steeds were good, but yet he was not gay.
Of simple fustian wore he a jupon
Sadly discoloured by his habergeon;
For he had lately come from his voyage
And now was going on this pilgrimage.

B. Christine de Pizan Advises "How the Wise Princess Will Keep the Women of Her Court in Good Order"

17. The sixth teaching: how the wise princess will keep the women of her court in good order.

Just as the good shepherd takes care that his lambs are maintained in health, and if any of them becomes mangy, separates it from the flock for fear that it may infect the others, so the princess will take upon herself the responsibility for the care of her women servants and companions, who she will ensure are all good and chaste, for she will not want to have any other sort of person around her. Since it is the established custom that knights and squires and all men (especially certain men) who associate with women have a habit of pleading for love tokens from them and trying to seduce them, the wise princess will so enforce her regulations that there will be no visitor to her court so foolhardy as to dare to whisper privately with any of her women or give the appearance of seduction. If he does it or if he is noticed giving any sign of it, immediately she should take such an attitude towards him that he will not dare to importune them any more. The lady who is chaste will want all her women to be so too, on pain of being banished from her company.

She will want them to amuse themselves with decent games, such that men cannot mock, as they do the games of some women, though at the time the men laugh and join in. The women should restrain themselves with seemly conduct among knights and squires and all men. They should speak demurely and sweetly and, whether in dances or other amusements, divert and enjoy themselves decorously and without wantonness. They must not be frolicsome, forward, or boisterous in speech, expression, bearing or laughter. They must not go about with their heads raised like wild deer. This kind of behaviour would be very unseemly and greatly derisory in a woman of the court, in whom there should be more modesty, good manners and courteous behaviour than in any others, for where there is most honour there ought to be the most perfect manners and behaviour. Women of the court in any country would be deceiving themselves very much if they imagined that it was more appropriate for them to be frolicsome and saucy than for other women. For this reason we hope that in time to come our doctrine in this book may be carried into many kingdoms, so that it may be valuable in all places where there might be any shortcoming.

We say generally to all women of all countries that it is the duty of every lady and maiden of the court, whether she be young or old, to be more prudent, more decorous, and better schooled in all things than other women. The ladies of the court ought to be models of all good things and all honour to other women, and if they do otherwise they will do no honour to their mistress nor to themselves. In addition, so that everything may be consistent in modesty, the wise princess will wish that the clothing and the ornaments of her women, though they be appropriately beautiful and rich, be of a modest fashion, well fitting and seemly, neat and properly cared for. There should be no deviation from this modesty nor any immodesty in the matter of plunging necklines or other excesses.

In all things the wise princess will keep her women in order just as the good and prudent abbess does her convent, so that bad reports about it may not circulate in the town, in distant regions or anywhere else. This princess will be so feared and respected because of the wise management that she will be seen to practise that no man or woman will be so foolhardy as to disobey her commands in any respect or to question her will, for there is no doubt that a lady is more feared and respected and held in greater reverence when she is seen to be wise and chaste and of firm behaviour. But there is nothing wrong or inconsistent in her being kind and gentle, for the mere look of the wise lady and her subdued reception is enough of a sign to correct those men and women who err and to inspire them with fear.

C. Sir John Froissart Describes the Pageantry of a Joust, 1390

The King of England and his three uncles had received the fullest information of the splendid feasts and entertainments made for Queen Isabella's public entry into Paris; and in imitation of it, they ordered grand tournaments and feasts to be holden in the city of London, where sixty knights should be accompanied by sixty noble ladies richly ornamented and dressed. The sixty knights were to tilt for two days; that is to say, on the Sunday after Michaelmas day, and the Monday following, in the year of grace 1390. They were to set out at two o'clock in the afternoon from the Tower of London with their ladies, and parade through the streets, down Cheapside, to a large square called Smithfield. There they were to wait on the Sunday the arrival of any foreign knights who might be desirous of tilting; and this feast of the Sunday was called the challengers'.

The same ceremonies were to take place on the Monday, and the sixty knights to be prepared for tilting courteously, with blunted lances, against all comers. The prize for the best knight of the opponents was a rich crown of gold, that for the tenants of the lists a very rich golden clasp. They were to be given to the most gallant tilter, according to the judgment of the ladies who should be present with the Queen of England, and the great barons, as spectators. On Tuesday the tournaments were to be continued by squires against others of the same rank who wished to oppose them. The prize for the opponents was a courser saddled and bridled, and for the tenants of the lists a falcon. Accordingly when Sunday came, about three o'clock, there paraded from the Tower of London, which is situated in the square of St. Catherine, on the banks of the Thames, sixty barbed coursers ornamented for the tournament, and on each was mounted a squire of honour. . . .

Document Set 13.5 References

A. Geoffrey Chaucer Idealizes "a Truly Perfect, Gentle Knight"
Geoffrey Chaucer, *Canterbury Tales*, trans., J. U. Nicolson (Garden City, N.Y.: Garden City Publishing Co., 1934), 2–3.
B. Christine de Pizan Advises "How the Wise Princess Will Keep the Women of Her Court in Good Order"
Christine de Pizan, *The Book of the City of Ladies*, in Sarah Lawson, trans., *Treasuries of the City of Ladies* (Penguin, 1985), 74–76.
C. Sir John Froissart Describes the Pageantry of a Joust, 1390
John Froissart, *The Chronicles of England, France and Spain* (London: Dutton, 1906), 481.

DOCUMENT SET 13.6
Violence and Revolt

The inverse of displays of upper-class authority, examined in Set 13.5, was the frequent eruption of lower-class violence. The fourteenth and early fifteenth centuries were an age of brutal conflict both between rival monarchies and within them. Document A describes an insurrection in the Byzantine city of Thessalonika (in present-day northern Greece) in 1346. How do you account for the religious coloration evidenced in this account of the rioters' behavior?

Froissart's account of a tournament (Set 13.5, Document C) presents one side of the Hundred Years' War; Documents B and C of this set show another aspect. How do you account for the brutality of the sack of Limoges, a French town, as Froissart describes it (Document B), or for the speculations in ransomed prisoners (Document C)? Draw upon *The Challenge of the West* in answering such questions. The English Peasant Rebellion of 1381 climaxed a long period of rural oppression—serfdom itself, compounded by taxation and the lords' desperate attempts to maintain their accustomed dominance in the face of a severe labor shortage after the Black Death. The law "against the excess of the villeins [serfs]" enacted in 1377 (Document D) shows how Parliament tried to control this explosive situation, and the short extract from the peasants' embattled leader, John Ball, evokes the rebels' elemental demand for justice and order.

A. An Urban Insurrection: The Zealot Revolt in Thessalonika, 1345

In Thessalonika, since the *protostrator,* as we said, was doubtful over which emperor to associate himself with and openly pondered the matter, something even more reprehensible occurred—he tolerated the so-called Zealots, who chose to fight on behalf of the Palaeologan emperor against the Emperor Cantacuzene and who were gradually increasing in numbers. He did this on the one hand lest he should seem openly favorable to the side of Emperor Cantacuzene. For his wife and daughter, who were in Byzantium, . . . caused him great indecision, lest on account of him they be subjected to many misfortunes. This also made him indifferent [toward the Zealots], the fact that not only the garrison of Thessalonika, which was not small, but also the powerful members of the citizenry had chosen the side of the Emperor Cantacuzene (citizens whom he

believed confidently would, whenever they might wish, suppress the Zealots).

And then, when the Zealots, on account of his [the *protostrator's*] neglect, became somewhat greater in number, and when they incited the people [*demos*] against the rich [*dynatoi*], and when the *protostrator* was recognized as doing the bidding of the Emperor Cantacuzene, the Zealots attacked in a mob and drove out from the city about a thousand people. A small crowd formed as a result of the skirmishing, in which a few even of the household of the *protostrator* were wounded, and they also captured some of the rich [*dynatoi*] who were unable to escape along with the others at the time of the first attack. After the Zealots had taken possession of the city, they rushed to the houses of the fugitives and razed them and seized their goods and did other things, things that men would do who were driven by poverty and urged on to reckless violence on account of the immense wealth [of the rich]. They came to such a point of murder and audacity that some dared even the most terrible things. Seizing the cross from the holy sanctuary, they used it as a banner and said they were fighting under it (although they were actually led by the enemy of the cross). And if someone was involved in legal dispute with another, he, seizing the cross, displayed it alongside his opponent's house as if the cross itself had given a signal. And at once, it was [deemed] necessary to raze the house to its foundation, since the people [*demos*] were driven by irrational force and hope of profit.

For two or three days Thessalonika was devoured as if by enemy soldiers, and nothing was done there which was not customary for captured cities. The victors, at night and during the day, roved around in groups, expressed themselves with cries and shouting, and plundered and carried away the property of the vanquished. The victims, lamenting, hid in intolerable places, accepting the situation as inescapable, [fearing] lest suddenly they might be killed. Since the revolt would cease when corrupt citizens were lacking, the Zealots, who from the poorest and most ignoble status had suddenly become rich and arrogant, seized everything for themselves, and either drew the middle class toward them or forced them (reluctantly) to accept them. Or the Zealots condemned wisdom and reasonableness as being "Cantacuzenism." In Thessalonika, then, such things were happening.

B. Sir John Froissart Describes the Sack of Limoges, 1370

[Having mined the town walls,] the miners set fire into their mine, and so the next morning, as the prince had ordained, there fell down a great piece of the wall and filled the moats, whereof the Englishmen were glad and were ready armed in the field to enter the town. the foot-men might well enter at their ease, and so they did, and ran to the gate and beat down the fortifying and barriers, for there was no defense against them: it was done so suddenly that they of the town were not aware thereof.

Then the prince, the duke of Lancaster, the earl of Cambridge, the earl of Pembroke, Sir Guichard d'Angle, and all the others, with their companies, entered into the city, and all other foot-men ready apparelled to do evil, and to pill and rob the city, and to slay men, women, and children; for so it was commanded them to do. It was a great pity to see the men, women, and children that kneeled down on their knees before the prince for mercy. But he was so inflamed with ire that he took no heed of them, so that none was heard, but all put to death as they were met withal, and such as were nothing culpable.

There was no pity taken of the poor people who wrought never no manner of treason, yet they bought it dearer than the great personages, such as had done the evil and trespass. There was not so hard a heart within the city of Limoges and if he had any remembrance of God, but that wept piteously for the great mischief that they saw before their eyen, for more than three thousand men, women, and children were slain that day. God have mercy on their souls, for I trow they were martyrs.

And thus entering into the city, a certain company of Englishmen entered into the bishop's palace, and there they found the bishop; and so they brought him to the prince's presence, who beheld him right fiercely and felly, and the best word that he could have of him was how he would have his head stricken off, and so he was had out of his sight. . . .

Thus the city of Limoges was pilled, robbed, and clean brent and brought to destruction.

C. War for Profit: An English Knight Speculates in Ransomed French Prisoners, 1376

A.D. 1376. To all persons who these letters shall see or hear, William de Beauchaumpe, greeting. Whereas Messire Thomas de Feltone is bound unto me, and obligated, in 4000 silver marks, by reason of the purchase of Messire Berard de la Bret, my prisoner, I do will and grant that the said Messire Thomas, his heirs, and his executors, shall be acquitted and discharged by these present letters; and that I myself, my heirs, and my executors, be ousted for ever hereby from all manner of action by reason of the said statute, or by reason of the purchase of the said Messire Berard, my prisoner.

D. King Richard II and John Ball: Two Views of the English Peasant Revolt, 1381

King Richard II:

At the grievous complaint of the lords and commons of the realm, as well men of holy church as other, made in this Parliament, of that in many lordships and parts of the realm of England, the villains and land tenants in villainage, who owe services and customs to their said lords, have now late withdrawn and do daily withdraw their services and customs due to their said lords; by comfort and procurement of other their counsellors, maintainers and abettors in the country, which have taken hire and profit of the said villains and land tenants by color of certain exemplifications made out of the book of Domesday of the manors and towns where they have been dwelling, and by virtue of the same exemplifications and their evil interpretations of the same, they affirm them to be quit and utterly discharged of all manner of serfdom, due as well of their body as of their said tenures, and will not suffer any distress or other justice to be made upon them; but do menace the servants of their lords of life and member, and, which is more, gather themselves together in great routs, and agree by such confederacy, that every one shall aid other to resist their lords with strong hand; and much other harm they do in sundry ways, to the great damage of their said lords and evil example to others to begin such riots; so that if due remedy be not the rather provided upon the same rebels, greater mischief, which God prohibit, may thereofspring through the realm. It is ordained and established that the lords which feel themselves grieved, shall have special commission under the great seal to the justices of the peace, or to other sufficient persons, to inquire of all such rebels, and of their offences, and their counsellors, procurers, maintainers and abettors, and to imprison all those that shall be thereof indicted before them, as well for the time past as for the time to come, without delivering them out of prison by mainprise, bail or otherwise, without assent of their lords, till they be attainted or acquitted thereof; and that the same justices have power to hear and determine as well at the king's suit as at the suit of the party.

And as to the said exemplifications, made and purchased as afore is said, which were caused to come in the Parliament, it is declared in the said Parliament that the same may not nor ought to avail, or hold place to the said villains or land tenants, as to the franchise of their bodies; nor to change the condition of their tenure and customs of old time due; nor to do prejudice to the said lords, to have their services and customs as they were wont of old time; and it is ordained that upon this declaration the said lords shall have letters patent under the great seal, as many and such as they shall need, if they the same require.

John Ball:

John Schep, som tyme Seynt Marie prest of York, and now of Colchester, greteth welle Johan Nameles,[1] and Johan the Mullere, and Johan Cartere, and biddeth hem that thei ware of gyle in borugh [i.e., who had entered the town by guile], and stondeth togiddir in Goddis name, and biddeth Peres Ploughman go to his werke, and chastise welle Hobbe the robber, and taketh with you Johan Trewman, and alle his felaws, and no mo, and loke scharpe you to on heved, and no mo.

Johan the Muller hath ygrownde [grown] smal, smal, smal;

The Kyngis sone of hevene [i.e., Jesus] shalle pay for alle.

Be ware or ye be wo.

Knoweth your frende fro youre foo,

Haveth ynowe [enough], and seythe "Hoo;"

And do welle and bettre, and fleth synne,

And seketh pees [peace], and holde therynne [there in].

And so biddeth Johan Trewman and alle his felawes.

Document Set 13.6 References

A. An Urban Insurrection: The Zealot Revolt in Thessalonika, 1345
John Cantacuzene, *Historia,* in Deno John Geanokoplos, ed., *Byzantium: Church, Society, and Civilization Seen Through Contemporary Eyes* (Chicago: University of Chicago Press, 1984), 271–272.

B. Sir John Froissart Describes the Sack of Limoges, 1370
John Froissart, *The Chronicles of England, France and Spain,* in James Harvey Robinson, ed., *Readings in European History* (Boston: Ginn, 1904), 1:472–473.

C. War for Profit: An English Knight Speculates in Ransomed French Prisoners, 1376
H. T. Riley, *Memorials of London* (1868), 392.

D. King Richard II and John Ball: Two Views of the English Peasant Revolt, 1381
Translations and Reprints from the Original Sources of European History (Philadelphia: University of Pennsylvania Press, 1898), 2/5:17–19.

[1] Johan [John] Nameles[s] and other names given here are allegorical names standing for members of various groups.

DOCUMENT SET 13.7
Fears of the Occult

It was not enough for late-medieval society to fear religious anxiety, status insecurity, sudden death, war, and lower-class violence; the occult world of black magic, alchemy, and witchcraft also fed the lurking sense of unease. In Document A, the University of Paris's Faculty of Theology paused amid its other labors in 1398 to crack down on the black arts it had learned were being practiced in its own citadel of learning. The Florentine authorities regarded with equal horror an alchemist who in 1402 defrauded some gullible citizens (Document B) and a woman who in 1427 used witchcraft to keep her lovers (Document C).

Perhaps the most celebrated accusation of witchcraft in these years was that lodged against Joan of Arc by her English and Burgundian captors, who burned her at the stake in 1431. Did they genuinely feel that her charismatic career resulted from a diabolical pact? Did they mean simply to discredit the nineteen-year-old "Maid"? Testifying to her inquisitors, Joan insisted on her divine inspiration, and two contemporaries testified to her bravery and her religious calling. Using *The Challenge of the West,* write a brief essay that puts her case into the perspective of fifteenth-century hopes, fears, and aspirations.

A. The University of Paris Condemns Magic, 1398

Considering the feat or principal operation and its makeup in itself and all its accompanying circumstances, namely, the great circle conscribed with divers unknown names and marked with various characters, the little wooden wheel raised on four wooden feet and a stake in the midst of the same great circle and the bottle placed upon the said wheel, above which bottle on a little paper scroll were written certain names, whose meaning is unknown to us, forsooth Garsepin, Oroth, Carmesine, Visoc, with the sign of the cross and certain characters interposed between the said names, and also thrones, earthen pots, a fire kindled, suffumigations, lights, swords and many other characters and figures and divers names and unknown words and also the naming or writing of four kings on four small paper wheels, for-

From *University Records and Life in the Middle Ages,* by Lynn Thorndike, pp. 260–266. Copyright © 1944 by Columbia University Press. Reprinted with permission of the publisher.

sooth, king Galtinus of the north, king Baltinus of the east, king Saltinus of the south, king Ultinus of the west, with certain characters written in red interposed between the names of the said kings; considering also the time and the suspect place and the behavior of those who were present at the said work and participated in it and the things they did after oaths had been taken by them many times as to making a legal division of the treasures to be found, also repeated after the declaration of the said work by the principal actor of that artifice, as appears from their confessions, from which it is learned that in a certain room in which were the said instruments, superstitious in themselves, with lights lit and suffumigations about the bottle and circles, in which were the said inscriptions and said characters, the said coworkers, stripped to the waist in their smallclothes, holding swords by their hilts each one before a throne, sometimes fixing the points in the earth and sometimes circling about with the said swords near the thrones and circles and bottle, raising the points of the swords to the sky, and sometimes placing their hands together with the hand of the protagonist over the bottle, which he called holy and in which, as they said, should come the spirit who would reveal and make known hidden treasures; in view of all the aforesaid and their accompaniments our deliberate conclusion is as follows, that not only those who use such figments and sorceries to find hidden treasure or learn and know things secret and occult, but also all professed Christians in possession of reason who voluntarily operate and employ such things in such manner are to be held superstitious in the Christian religion, are to be deemed idolaters, are to be deemed invokers of demons and strongly suspect in the faith.

To all devotees of the orthodox faith the chancellor of Paris and the faculty of theology in the dear university of Paris, our mother, with full honor of divine worship, to have hope in the Lord and not look upon vanities and false insanities. From olden darkness a foul flood of errors newly emerging has warned us to recall, that often catholic truth which escapes others is quite clear to those studious in sacred writ, since certainly every art has this property of being clear to those trained in it, so that thence comes that maxim, "Believe the man who is skilled in his art. . . .

Moreover, the first article is that by magic arts and sorceries and nefarious invocations to seek the intimacy and friendship and aid of demons is not idolatry. An error.

Second article, that to give or offer or promise to demons such-and-such a thing in order that they may fulfill a man's desire, or in their honor to kiss or carry something, is not idolatry. Error.

Third article, that to enter on a pact with demons, tacit or express, is not idolatry or a species of idolatry and apostasy. Error. . . .

Twenty-first article, that images of copper or lead or gold or white or red wax or other material baptized, exorcized and consecrated, or rather execrated, according to the said arts and on certain days, have marvelous virtues which are recited in the books of such arts. An error in faith, in natural philosophy, and in true astrology.

Twenty-second article, that to use such and believe in them is not idolatry and infidelity. An error.

Twenty-third article, that some demons are good, some benign, some omniscient, some neither saved nor damned. An error. . . .

Twenty-sixth article, that the intelligence which moves the heaven influences the rational soul just as the body of the heaven influences the human body. An error.

Twenty-seventh article, that our intellectual cogitations and inner volitions are caused immediately by the sky, and that by a magic tradition such can be known, and that thereby it is licit to pass certain judgment as to them. An error.

Twenty-eighth article, that by certain magic arts we can reach the vision of the divine essence or of the holy spirits. An error. . . .

B. An Alchemist Defrauds Some Florentines, 1402

. . . We condemn . . . Master Antonio di Luca of Messina in Sicily, a perpetrator of fraud and a man of evil condition. . . . He attempted to defraud the following men: Michele di Messer Vanni Castellani, Otto di Messer Mainardo Cavalcanti, Messer Tommaso of Città di Castello and Ser Francesco of Gubbio. . . . He had a conversation with Michele and Otto . . . and another with Messer Tommaso and Ser Francesco, saying to them: "If you wish, and if you furnish me the means, I will perform . . . an act of alchemy for you, in the following manner. I will transform and reduce copper from its color into a very white color [i.e., like silver]. . . . But to do this, I must have some gold, and the more the better, and we will place it on the fire and liquify it and then reduce

it to powder. With this powder, we will be able to transform the copper from its original color and state to a white substance."

Having no doubts about these words of Master Antonio but rather accepting them credulously, Tommaso, Michelino, Otto, and Ser Francesco . . . brought the abovementioned sums of money and hastily prepared the pots in the following manner. Michelino and Otto . . . brought 1,000 gold florins in an earthern cooking pot, with the intention of placing that pot on the fire to liquify these coins in a kiln which had been built by Master Antonio in his house. . . . When Michelino and Otto brought this pot holding the money to the kiln, Master Antonio instructed them to place the copper in certain receptacles so that they might be placed in the oven. Then, Master Antonio secretly took the pot containing the money and replaced it with another pot, similar in size and appearance. . . . Into that pot Master Antonio placed the following ingredients: sublimate silver, cinnabar, saltpeter, sulphur, and many other things, which he placed . . . upon the fire in the oven. But the pot containing the money he secretly took away . . . and hid it in an underground room of the house. . . .

Item, Tommaso and Ser Francesco brought a pot containing 400 florins to Master Antonio for the purpose of liquifying and pulverizing them . . . in an earthern oven. . . . And on a certain day . . . Master Antonio went to Tommaso's house, pretending to inspect the project and to see how it was progressing. . . . He secretly took the pot and hid it in the sleeves of his jacket, and replaced it in the oven with another pot in which he had put silver, saltpeter, sublimate silver, sulphur, cinnabar, and many other ingredients. . . .

Then, Master Antonio . . . had a conversation with Pierotto and Corsino . . . and said to them: "If you wish, and if you give me the means, I will make you an indigo dye so strong that it can be used a hundred times [for dyeing cloth] and it will be worth 60 florins or more. If we begin [this project], I want to make a large quantity. And so that you don't think that I will trick you, I will invest 200 florins of my own money, and you will invest 1,000 florins. And each of us will share the profit and loss according to his investment. It is necessary to place these florins in a pot on the fire to liquify them. . . . Then we shall mix this molten metal with other ingredients necessary to make the indigo dye." Pierotto and Corsino . . . told Master Antoni that they were willing if he would invest 200 florins. . . . So Master Antonio took some of the money which he had stolen and counted out 200 florins and gave it to Pierotto and Corsino. [Antonio was captured and imprisoned by the captain of the *popolo*.] To avoid paying the penalty for his crimes, he took his belt . . . and made a noose and placed it around his neck. Then he suspended himself from the iron bars of a prison window, and had he not been rescued by a prison guardian, we would have died. [Antonio was condemned to be burned at the stake; the sentence was executed.]

C. Florence Condemns a Witch, 1427

. . . We condemn . . . Giovanna called Caterina, daughter of Francesco called El Toso, a resident of the parish of S. Ambrogio of Florence . . . who is a magician, witch, and sorceress, and a practitioner of the black arts. . . . It happened that Giovanni Ceresani of the parish of S. Jacopo tra le Fosse was passing by her door and stared at her fixedly. She thought that she would draw the chaste spirit of Giovanni to her for carnal purposes by means of the black arts. . . . She went to the shop of Monna Gilia, the druggist, and purchased from her a small amount of lead . . . and then she took a bowl and placed the lead in it and put it on the fire so that the lead would melt. With this melted lead she made a small chain and spoke certain words which have significance for this magical and diabolical art (and which, lest the people learn about them, shall not be recorded). . . . All this which was done and spoken against Giovanni's safety by Giovanna was so powerful that his chaste spirit was deflected to lust after her, so that willynilly he went several times to her house and there he fulfilled her perfidious desire. . . .

In the time when Giovanna was menstruating, she took a little of her menses, that quantity which is required by the diabolical ceremonies, and placed it in a small beaker . . . and then poured it into another flask filled with wine . . . and gave it to Giovanni to drink. And on account of this and other things described above, Giovanni no longer has time for his affairs as he did in the past, and he has left his home and his wife and son . . . and does only what pleases Giovanna. . . .

Several years ago, Giovanna was the concubine of Niccolò di Ser Casciotto of the parish of S. Giorgio, and she had three children by him. Having a great affection for Niccolò, who was then in Hungary, she wanted him to return to her in Florence. . . . So she planned a diabolical experiment by invoking a demon, to the detriment of Niccolò's health. . . . She went to someone who shall not be identified . . . and asked him to go to another diabolical woman, a sorceress (whose name shall not be publicized, for the public good), and asked her to make for Giovanna a wax image in the form of a woman, and also some pins and other items required by this diabolical experiment. . . . Giovanna took that image and placed it in a chest in her house. When, a few days later, she had to leave that house and move to another, she left the image in the chest. Later it was discovered by the residents of the house, who burned it. . . .

She collected nine beans, a piece of cloth, some charcoal, several olive leaves which had been blessed and which stood before the image of the Virgin Mary, a coin with a cross, and a grain of salt. With these in her hand she genuflected . . . [before the image] and recited three times the Pater Noster and the Ave Maria, spurning the divine prayers composed for the worship of God and his mother the Virgin Mary. Having done this, she placed these items on a piece of linen cloth and slept over them for three nights. And afterwards, she took them in her hand and thrice repeated the Pater Noster and the Ave Maria. . . . And thus Giovanna knew that her future husband would not love her. And so it happened, for after the celebration and the consummation of the marriage, her husband Giovanni stayed with her for a few days, and then left her and has not yet returned. [Giovanna confessed to these crimes and was beheaded.]

D. Joan of Arc Faces Her Inquisitors, 1431

Joan [to her inquisitors]: When I was thirteen years old, I had a voice from God to help me govern my conduct. And the first time I was very fearful. And came this voice, about the hour of noon, in the summer-time, in my father's garden. . . . I heard the voice on the right-hand side . . . and rarely do I hear it without a brightness. . . . It has taught me to conduct myself well, to go habitually to church. . . . The voice told me that I should raise the siege laid to the city of Orleans . . . and me, I answered it that I was a poor girl who knew not how to ride nor lead in war.

Jean Pasquerel [priest, Joan's confessor]: "On the morrow, Saturday, I rose early and celebrated mass. And Joan went out against the fortress of the bridge where was the Englishman Classidas. And the assault lasted there from morning until sunset. In this assault . . . Joan . . . was struck by an arrow above the breast, and when she felt herself wounded she was afraid and wept. . . . And some soldiers, seeing her so wounded, wanted to apply a charm to her wound, but she would not have it, saying: "I would rather die than do a thing which I know to be a sin or against the will of God." . . . But if to her could be applied a remedy without sin, she was very willing to be cured. And they put on to her wound olive oil and lard. And after that had been applied, Joan made her confession to me, weeping and lamenting."

Count Dunois: "The assault lasted from the morning until eight . . . so that there was hardly hope of victory that day. So that I was going to break off and . . . withdraw. . . . Then the Maid came to me and required me to wait yet a while. She . . . mounted her horse and retired alone into a vineyard. . . . And in this vineyard she remained at prayer. . . . Then she came back . . . at once seized her standard in hand and placed herself on the parapet of the trench, and the moment she was there the English trembled and were terrified. The king's soldiers regained courage and began to go up, charging against the boulevard without meeting the least resistance."

Jean Pasquerel: "Joan returned to the charge, crying and saying: 'Classidas, Classidas, yield thee, yield thee to the King of Heaven; thou hast called me 'whore'; I take great pity on thy soul and thy people's! Then Classidas, armed from head to foot, fell into the river of Loire and was drowned. And Joan, moved by pity, began to weep much for the soul of Classidas and the others who were drowned in great numbers." . . .

Document Set 13.7 References

A. The University of Paris Condemns Magic, 1398
   Eduard Winkelmann, in Lynn Thorndike, ed., *University Records and Life in the Middle Ages* (New York: Columbia University Press, 1944), 261–266.
B. An Alchemist Defrauds Some Florentines, 1402
   Gene Brucker, ed., *The Society of Renaissance Florence* (New York: Harper & Row, 1971), 157–159.
C. Florence Condemns a Witch, 1427
   Brucker, 270–273.
D. Joan of Arc Faces Her Inquisitors, 1431
   Régine Pernoud, *Joan of Arc, By Herself and Her Witnesses* (New York: 1966), 30, 90–92.

DOCUMENT SET 13.8
Florence on the Eve of the Renaissance

Florence, where early humanism first became a coherent cultural movement towards the end of the fourteenth and the beginning of the fifteenth centuries, was one of the largest and richest cities in Europe. Some sense of the great city's resources on the eve of the Black Death emerges from Document A, the *Florentine Chronicle* of Giovanni Villani (who died in the Black Death along with perhaps a third of the population). Notice in particular the continuing presence of old aristocrats (magnates and knights), whose violent tendencies the commune kept in check, and the curious imbalance in the number of male and female babies baptized; how do you account for this? Above all, consider Villani's statistical precision and the wealth he describes; do you see any connection between mind-set and enterprise here?

Petrarch, a transitional figure between medieval piety and modern individualism (compare Set 13.3, Document G), was obsessed with his reputation. His "Letter to Posterity" (Document B) reflects some of the ambiguities of his character. He also felt acutely that he lived in a degenerate age—an attitude that made him a leader in the budding campaign to revive ancient standards of Latin eloquence, which we now call humanism.

Humanism was definitely an elite phenomenon, and to understand the Florentine elite we must keep in mind the turbulent, mercilessly exploited lower class, the *Ciompi,* or day laborers in the wool industry. Their uprising in 1378 was barely contained by the savage efforts of the combined forces of the city's upper and artisan classes; in Document C, the Ciompi explain their cause.

A climactic event in the emergence of Florence's characteristic brand of humanism was the city's lonely struggle against the despotic Milanese Galeazzo Visconti, who until 1402 seemed likely to bring most of northern and central Italy under his sway. His unexpected defeat—described in Document D by the Florentine humanist Coluccio Salutati and his associates to exalt Roman republicanism as the fitting ideal for Florence, breaking the long-medieval tradition of venerating Julius Caesar and imperial Rome.

The creation of appropriate works of public art was always a matter of concern for the Florentine commune and the elite who dominated it, as the 1424 letter (Document E) from the man of letters Leonardo Bruni attests. The occasion was the commissioning of a second set of bronze doors for the Florentine Baptistery, part of the city's cathedral. An enthusiastic humanist who in 1427–1444 served as the Florentine chancellor, Bruni wished to guide the artisan who would execute the work, and he had in mind more than a mere copy of traditional medieval iconography. The sculptor Lorenzo Ghiberti (c. 1378–1455), whose first set of doors had already been triumphantly completed, responded with one of the great masterpieces of early Florentine Renaissance art, the "Gates of Paradise." In what ways do you see Bruni articulating specifically humanist values?

A. Giovanni Villani Recounts "the Greatness and State and Magnificence of the Commune of Florence," c. 1338

Since we have spoken about the income and expenditure of the Commune of Florence in this period, I think it is fitting to mention this and other great features of our city, so that our descendants in days to come may be aware of any rise, stability, and decline in condition and power that our city may undergo, and also so that, through the wise and able citizens who at the time shall be in charge of its government, [our descendants] may endeavor to advance it in condition and power, seeing our record and example in this chronicle. We find after careful investigation that in this period there were in Florence about 25,000 men from the ages of fifteen to seventy fit to bear arms, all citizens. And among them were 1,500 noble and powerful citizens who as magnates gave security to the Commune. There were in Florence also some seventy-five full-dress knights. To be sure, we find that before the second popular government now in power was formed there were more than 250 knights; but from the time that the people began to rule, the magnates no longer had the status and authority enjoyed earlier, and hence few persons were knighted. From the amount of bread constantly needed for the city, it was estimated that in Florence there were some 90,000 mouths divided among men, women,

From *Medieval Trade in the Mediterranean World* by Lopez and Raymond, pp. 71–74. Copyright © 1955 by Columbia University Press. Reprinted with permission of the publisher.

and children, as can readily be grasped [from what we shall say] later; and it was reckoned that in the city there were always about 1,500 foreigners, transients, and soldiers, not including in the total the citizens who were clerics and cloistered monks and nuns, of whom we shall speak later. It was reckoned that in this period there were some 80,000 men in the territory and district of Florence. From the rector who baptized the infants—since he deposited a black bean for every male baptized in San Giovanni and a white bean for every female in order to ascertain their number—we find that at this period there were from 5,500 to 6,000 baptisms every year, the males usually outnumbering the females by 300 to 500. We find that the boys and girls learning to read [numbered] from 8,000 to 10,000, the children learning the abacus and algorism from 1,000 to 1,200, and those learning grammar and logic in four large schools from 550 to 600. . . .

The workshops of the *Arte della Lana* [the cloth guild] were 200 or more, and they made from 70,000 to 80,000 pieces of cloth, which were worth more than 1,200,000 gold florins. And a good third [of this sum] remained in the land as [the reward] of labor, without counting the profit of the entrepreneurs. And more than 30,000 persons lived by it. [To be sure,] we find that some thirty years earlier there were 300 workshops or thereabouts, and they made more than 100,000 pieces of cloth yearly; but these cloths were coarser and one half less valuable, because at that time English wool was not imported and they did not know, as they did later, how to work it.

The *fondachi* [warehouses] of the *Arte di Calimala*, dealing in French and Transalpine cloth, were some twenty, and they imported yearly more than 10,000 pieces of cloth, worth 300,000 gold florins. And all these were sold in Florence, without counting those which were reexported from Florence.

The banks of money-changers were about eighty. The gold coins which were struck amounted to some 350,000 gold florins and at times 400,000 [yearly]. And as for deniers of four petty each, about 20,000 pounds of them were struck yearly. . . .

Merchants and mercers were a large number; the shops of shoemakers, slipper makers, and wooden-shoe makers were so numerous they could not be counted. . . .

[Florence] within the walls was well built, with many beautiful houses, and at that period people kept building with improved techniques to obtain comfort and richness by importing designs of every kind of improvement. [They built] parish churches and churches of friars of every order, and splendid monasteries. And besides this, there was no citizen, whether commoner or magnate, who had not built or was not building in the country a large and rich estate with a very costly mansion and with fine buildings, much better than those in the city—and in this they all were committing sin, and they were called crazy on account of their wild expenses. And yet, this was such a wonderful sight that when foreigners, not accustomed to [cities like] Florence, came from abroad, they usually believed that all of the costly buildings and beautiful palaces which surrounded the city for three miles were part of the city in the manner of Rome—not to mention the costly palaces with towers, courts, and walled gardens farther distant, which would have been called castles in any other country. To sum up, it was estimated that within a six-mile radius around the city there were more than twice as many rich and noble mansions as in Florence.

B. Petrarch Writes to Posterity

Greeting.—It is possible that some word of me may have come to you, though even this is doubtful, since an insignificant and obscure name will scarcely penetrate far in either time or space. If, however, you should have heard of me, you may desire to know what manner of man I was, or what was the outcome of my labors, especially those of which some description or, at any rate, the bare titles may have reached you.

To begin with myself, then: the utterances of men concerning me will differ widely, since in passing judgment almost every one is influenced not so much by truth as by preference, and good and evil report alike know no bounds. I was, in truth, a poor mortal like yourself, neither very exalted in my origin, nor, on the other hand, of the most humble birth, but belonging, as Augustus Caesar says of himself, to an ancient family. As to my disposition, I was not naturally perverse or wanting in modesty, however the contagion of evil associations may have corrupted me.

My youth was gone before I realized it; I was carried away by the strength of manhood; but a riper age brought me to my senses and taught me by experience the truth I had long before read in books, that youth and pleasure are vanity,—nay, that the Author of all ages and times permits us miserable mortals, puffed up with emptiness, thus to wander about, until finally, coming to a tardy consciousness of our sins, we shall learn to know ourselves.

In my prime I was blessed with a quick and active body, although not exceptionally strong; and while I do not lay claim to remarkable personal beauty, I was comely enough in my best days. I was possessed of a clear complexion, between light and dark, lively eyes, and for long years a keen vision, which however deserted me, contrary to my hopes, after I reached my sixtieth birthday, and forced me, to my great annoyance, to resort to glasses. Although I had previously enjoyed perfect health, old age brought with it the usual array of discomforts.

My parents were honorable folk, Florentine in their origin, of medium fortune, or, I may as well admit it, in a condition verging upon poverty. They had been expelled from their native city, and consequently I was born in exile, at Arezzo, in the year 1304 of this latter age, which begins with Christ's birth, July the 20th, on a Monday, at dawn.... In my familiar associations with kings and princes, and in my friendship with noble personages, my good fortune has been such as to excite envy. But it is the cruel fate of those who are growing old that they can commonly only weep for friends who have passed away. The greatest kings of this age have loved and courted me. They may know why; I certainly do not. With some of them I was on such terms that they seemed in a certain sense my guests rather than I theirs; their lofty position in no way embarrassing me, but, on the contrary, bringing with it many advantages. I fled, however, from many of those to whom I was greatly attached; and such was my innate longing for liberty, that I studiously avoided those whose very name seemed incompatible with the freedom that I loved.

I possessed a well-balanced rather than a keen intellect,—one prone to all kinds of good and wholesome study, but especially inclined to moral philosophy and the art of poetry. The latter, indeed, I neglected as time went on, and took delight in sacred literature. Finding in that a hidden sweetness which I had once esteemed but lightly, I came to regard the works of the poets as only amenities.

Among the many subjects which interested me, I dwelt especially upon antiquity, for our own age has always repelled me, so that, had it not been for the love of those dear to me, I should have preferred to have been born in any other period than our own. In order to forget my own time, I have constantly striven to place myself in spirit in other ages, and consequently I delighted in history. The conflicting statements troubled me, but when in doubt I accepted what appeared most probable, or yielded to the authority of the writer.

C. The Ciompi Demand Their Place in the Commune, 1378

[July 21, 1378] When the *popolo* [ordinary working people] and the guildsmen had seized the palace [of the podestà, or chief magistrate], they sent a message to the Signoria [Florentine government] . . . that they wished to make certain demands by means of petitions, which were just and reasonable. . . . They said that, for the peace and repose of the city, they wanted certain things which they had decided among themselves . . . and they begged the priors to have them read, and then to deliberate on them, and to present them to their colleges. . . .

The first chapter [of the petition] stated that the Lana [cloth-merchants'] guild would no longer have a [police] official of the guild. Another was that the combers, carders, trimmers, washers, and other cloth workers would have their own [guild] consuls, and would no longer be subject to the Lana guild. Another chapter [stated that] the Commune's funded debt would no longer pay interest, but the capital would be restored [to the shareholders] within twelve years. . . . Another chapter was that all outlaws and those who had been condemned by the Commune . . . except rebels and traitors would be pardoned. Moreover, all penalties involving a loss of a limb would be cancelled, and those who were condemned would pay a money fine. . . . Furthermore, for two years none of the poor people could be prosecuted for debts of 50 florins or less. For a period of six months, no forced loans were to be levied. . . . And within that six months' period, a schedule for levying direct taxes [*estimo*] was to be compiled. . . .

The *popolo* entered the palace and [the podestà] departed, without any harm being done to him. They ascended the bell tower and placed there the emblem of the blacksmiths' guild, that is, the tongs. Then the banners of the other guilds, both great and small, were unfurled from the windows of the [palace of] the podestà, and also the standard of justice, but there was no flag of the Lana guild. Those inside the palace threw out and burned . . . every document which they found. And they remained there, all that day and night, in honor of God. Both rich and poor were there, each one to protect the standard of his guild.

The next morning the *popolo* brought the standard of justice from the palace and they marched, all armed, to the Piazza della Signoria, shouting: "Long live the *popolo minuto!*" [lit., "little people"] . . . Then they began to cry "that the Signoria should leave, and if they didn't wish to depart, they would be taken to their homes." Into the piazza came a certain Michele di Lando, a wool-comber, who was the son of Monna

Simona, who sold provisions to the prisoners in the Stinche . . . and he was seized and the standard of justice placed in his hands. . . . Then the *popolo* ordered the priors to abandon the palace. It was well furnished with supplies necessary [for defense] but they were frightened men and they left [the palace], which was the best course. Then the *popolo* entered, taking with them the standard of justice . . . and they entered all the rooms and they found many ropes which [the authorities] had bought to hang the poor people. . . . Several young men climbed the bell tower and rang the bells to signal the victory which they had won in seizing the palace, in God's honor. Then they decided to do everything necessary to fortify themselves and to liberate the *popolo minuto*. Then they acclaimed the wool-comber, Michele di Lando, as *signore* [lord] and standard-bearer of justice, and he was *signore* for two days. . . . Then [the *popolo*] decided to call other priors who would be good comrades and who would fill up the office of those priors who had been expelled. And so by acclamation, they named eight priors and the Twelve and the [Sixteen] standard-bearers. . . .

When they wished to convene a council, these priors called together the colleges and the consuls of the guilds. . . . This council enacted a decree that everyone who had been proscribed as a Ghibelline since 1357 was to be restored to Guelf status. . . . And this was done to give a part to more people, and so that each would be content, and each would have a share of the offices, and so that all of the citizens would be united. Thus poor men would have their due, for they have always borne the expenses [of government], and only the rich have profited.

. . . And they deliberated to expand the lower guilds, and where there had been fourteen, there would now be seventeen, and thus they would be stronger, and this was done. The first new guild comprised those who worked in the woolen industry: factors, brokers in wool and in thread, workers who were employed in the dye shops and the stretching sheds, menders, sorters, shearers, beaters, combers, and weavers. These were all banded together, some nine thousand men. . . . The second new guild was made up of dyers, washers, carders, and makers of combs. . . . In the third guild were menders, trimmers, stretchers, washers, shirtmakers, tailors, stockingmakers, and makers of flags. . . . So all together, the lower guilds increased by some thirteen thousand men.

The lord priors and the colleges decided to burn the old Communal scrutiny lists, and this was done. Then a new scrutiny was held. The Offices were divided as follows: the [seven] greater guilds had three priors; the fourteen [lower] guilds had another three, and the three new guilds had three priors. And so a new scrutiny was completed, which satisfied many who had never before had any share of the offices, and had always borne the expenses.

D. Coluccio Salutati Narrates Florence's Defense of Republican Liberty Against the Milanese Despotism, 1402

The following year, which was 1402, great battles were fought around Bologna. Even before the emperor's complete withdrawal, Galeazzo, elated by the way things were going for him, sent part of his forces into Bolognese territory, to overthrow if possible the new lord of that city. The arrival of these forces immediately put the city in great peril, for there were enough powerful exiles to make the castles and towns of the area rise up, and the citizens inside the city were not all happy about the government of the lord of Bologna either. The Florentines responded to the danger by sending the captain Bernardone with a large number of troops. They added more troops in time, as they learned of reinforcements sent to the enemy. Large forces were sent to the aid of Bologna by the lord of Padua and other allies, and the lord of Padua sent two of his sons along. All the forces of the Florentine people and of their allies, and all the forces of the enemy, were finally gathered around Bologna. Both sides made encampments around the city. . . .

Bologna after the return of the exiles received a civil government. A formal republic and formal liberty were restored. This indeed was what Galeazzo had promised the exiles. The pleasure only lasted two or three days, however. Then certain persons sent by the duke with a military force ran through the city shouting the name of Galeazzo, usurped the authority of the city's officials, and proclaimed the entire lordship of Milan. The people and the exiles were disappointed, but they had to bend their necks to the yoke of servitude.

When the Florentines heard that the army had been defeated and . . . that Bologna too had fallen, they were even more terrified, expecting the enemy from hour to hour. Without the general and the army, they seemed to despair completely. Had the enemy approached promptly to follow up his victory, the city could not have withstood him. The enemy, however, whether because of weariness or internal discord, let the time for action pass in useless settling down. . . .

. . .The enemy seemed to want to make peace after taking Bologna, and sent representatives to Venice to propose rather reasonable conditions. The Florentines suspected deception and fraud, and finally decided to agree to the peace and to the Venetian alliance at the same time, thinking that if the peace began at the same time as the alliance, the peace would be more durable and the conditions demanded by the Venetians less important. They instructed their representatives to sign, with the addition of a few corrections, peace with the enemy and an alliance with Venice.

While the city was just doing this, word came through that Galeazzo was dead. The death was first announced by Paolo Guinisi, lord of Lucca, but it was not considered a certainty. Later it was repeated as a certainty, but a deep secret. At once letters were sent to the representatives in Venice not to agree to the peace nor to the alliance. The Venetians learned of the duke's death only from the Florentine embassy, having heard nothing before. There had been signs, however, such as some forces sent towards Tuscany through Piacenza and Lunigiana being suddenly recalled. The leaders of the army, who were still before Bologna, had received orders not to move from the spot. It now proved that Galeazzo had become ill soon after Bologna was taken. He had died somewhat later of the same illness, at the Milanese castle of Marignano. These facts had been kept secret at first. Eventually they had to be made public, and there was a magnificent funeral. It also came out that Galeazzo, while he lay ill, had passionately desired peace with Florence. Hence the attempt to send a mission to Venice and to make a new peace. He realized that his sons were still young and were being left in the midst of great danger. So he was in a hurry to make peace before he would leave the world. This would have been accomplished, too, if he had lived just a little longer. His sudden death brought such a reversal of things that those who before had hardly any hope left for their own safety were now filled with high confidence, while those who had just considered themselves victorious lost all hope of being able to resist.

E. Leonardo Bruni Describes the Making of Ghiberti's Baptistery Doors, 1424

I consider that the twenty stories, which you have decided are to be chosen from the Old Testament, should have two qualities principally, being both resplendent and significant. By 'resplendent' I mean that they should delight the eye with the variety of their design; by 'significant' that they should be important enough to rest in the memory. With these two presuppositions in my mind, I have chosen according to my judgement twenty stories, which I am sending to you noted down on paper. It will be necessary for whoever does them to be well instructed about each story, so that he can render well both the persons and the actions which occur in it, and that he has a lightness of touch so that he can adorn them well. In addition to the twenty stories, I have made a note of eight prophets, as you see on the paper. Now I do not doubt that this work, as I have planned it, will succeed excellently. But I would very much like to be with whoever has the job of designing it, to make sure that he takes into account the whole significance of each story. I recommend myself to you.

Your Leonardo of Arezzo

Document Set 13.8 References

A. Giovanni Villani Recounts "the Greatness and State and Magnificence of the Commune of Florence," c. 1338
Giovanni Villani, *Chronicle*, in Robert S. Lopez and Irving W. Raymond, *Medieval Trade in the Mediterranean World* (New York: Columbia University Press, 1930s), 71–74.

B. Petrarch Writes to Posterity
Petrarch, *Letter to Posterity*, in James Harvey Robinson, ed., *Readings in European History* (Boston: Ginn, 1904), 1:524–526.

C. The Ciompi Demand Their Place in the Commune, 1378
Gene Brucker, ed., *The Society of Renaissance Florence* (New York: Harper & Row, 1971), 236–239.

D. Coluccio Salutati Narrates Florence's Defense of Republican Liberty Against the Milanese Despotism, 1402
Coluccio Salutati, *History of Florence*, in Kenneth R. Bartlett, ed., *The Civilization of the Italian Renaissance: A Sourcebook* (Lexington, Mass.: D. C. Heath, 1992), 99–102.

E. Leonardo Bruni Describes the Making of Ghiberti's Baptistery Doors, 1424
Leonardo Bruni to Niccolò da Uzzano in D. S. Chambers, *Patrons and Artists in the Italian Renaissance* (Columbia, S.C.: University of South Carolina Press, 1971), 48.

CHAPTER

14

Renaissance Europe, 1430–1493

DOCUMENT SET 14.1
Humanism

The Italian word *umanista* (humanist) was originally medieval student slang for a teacher of elementary subjects such as grammar and rhetoric, which a university student took before studying technical subjects like logic, law, and theology. In the fourteenth and fifteenth centuries, however, the prestige of the lowly humanities courses rose. As *The Challenge of the West* explains (Chapters 14 and 15), an educated, prosperous middle class was emerging, interested in classical literature and history. Moreover, governments increasingly felt it necessary to employ high officials who could speak and write elegant Latin.

The six documents in this set chart the humanities' rising prestige. In Document A, the fifteenth-century Florentine bookseller Vespasiano da Bisticci—who wrote short biographies of many of his eminent customers—sketches the character of the prominent humanist Nicolò Nicoli (d. 1437), whose inherited wealth let him live for the life of a collector and patron. Document B is an extract from an educational treatise by one of Renaissance Italy's great pedagogues, Battista Guarino (1370?–1460), who ran a boarding school for the sons of prominent families. Education in the humanities—which prepared one for a public career and enhanced family prestige—was overwhelmingly a male pursuit. Yet a few young women (often educators' daughters) also managed to get such training. One was Laura Cereta (d. 1499), whose outspoken *Defense of the Liberal Instruction of Women* (Document C) protests against male humanists' typical scorn for women's intellectual capacity.

Document D, Giovanni Pico della Mirandola's (1463–1494) famous *Oration on the Dignity of Man,* on the other hand, should be read as a vindication of the potential for human self improvement. A minor Italian princeling, Pico spent his entire short life feverishly pursuing wisdom, not only through well-known classical literature and philosophy but also through esoteric ancient magical lore and the mystical Hebrew *càbala.* He wrote his *Oration* to open a public debate on his ideas, but the pope condemned some of these ideas as heretical, and Pico died as a more orthodox Christian.

The final two documents throw additional light on fifteenth-century humanism. Document E records the determination of the city fathers of Ferrara to improve the teaching of grammar in that Italian city's schools. In Document F, the German scholar Conrad Celtes (1459–1508), who made a considerable stir by traveling from one German university to another propagating Italian-style humanism, receives a stinging rebuke from the undergraduates of the University of Ingolstadt in Bavaria.

Using these documents and also drawing upon *The Challenge of the West,* you should be able to write a brief essay on the program of Italian Humanism. What did the Humanists claim as the value of their type of education? How does it differ from what you have learned about medieval education? How would you evaluate humanist education from your late twentieth-century perspective?

A. Nicolò Nicoli Collects the Classics

Nicolò may justly be called the father and the benefactor of all students of letters, for he gave them protection and encouragement to work, and pointed out to them the rewards which would follow. If he knew of any Greek or Latin book which was not in Florence he spared neither trouble nor cost until he should procure it; indeed, there are numberless Latin books which the city possesses through his care. He gained such high reputation amongst men of letters that Messer Leonardo sent him his *Life of Cicero* and pronounced him to be the censor [i.e., foremost critic] of the Latin tongue.

He was a man of upright life who favored virtue and censured vice. He collected a fine library, not regarding the cost, and was always searching for rare books. He bought all these with the wealth which his father had left, putting aside only what was necessary for his maintenance. He sold several of his farms and spent the proceeds on his library. He was a devoted Christian, who specially favored monks and friars, and was the foe of evildoers. He held his books rather for the use of others than of himself, and all lettered students of Greek or Latin would come to him to borrow books, which he would always lend.... If he heard of students going to Greece or to France or elsewhere he would give them the names of books which they lacked in Florence, and procure for them the help of Cosimo de' Medici who would do anything for him. When it happened that he could only get the copy of a book he would copy it himself, either in current or shaped characters, all in the finest script, as may be seen in San Marco, where there are many books from his hand in one lettering or the other. He procured at his own expense the works of Tertullian and other [ancient] writers which were not in Italy. He also found an imperfect copy of Ammianus Marcellinus and wrote it out with his own hand. The *De Oratore* and the *Brutus* [by Cicero] were sent to Nicolò from Lombardy, having been brought by the envoys of Duke Filippo when they went to ask for peace in the time of Pope Martin. The book was found in a chest in a very old church; this chest had not been opened for a long time, and they found the book, a very ancient example, while searching for evidence concerning certain ancient rights. *De Oratore* was found broken up, and it is through the care of Nicolò that we find it perfect today. He also rediscovered many sacred works and several of Tully's [Cicero's] orations.

Through Nicolò Florence acquired many fine works of sculpture, of which he had great knowledge as well as of painting. A complete copy of Pliny did not exist in Florence, but when Nicolò heard that there was one in Lübeck, in Germany, he secured it by Cosimo's aid, and thus Pliny came to Florence. All the young men he knew in Florence used to come to him for instruction in letters, and he cared for the needs of all those who wanted books or teachers. He did not seek any office in Florence [although] he was made an official in the University; many times he was selected for some governorship, but he refused them all, saying that they were food for the vultures, and he would let these feed on them. He called vultures those who went into the alehouses and devoured the poor....

B. Battista Guarino Outlines a Course of Liberal Studies

... From the first, stress must be laid upon distinct and sustained enunciation, both in speaking and in reading. But at the same time utterance must be perfectly natural; if affected or exaggerated the effect is unpleasing. The foundation of education must be laid in Grammar. Unless this be thoroughly learnt subsequent progress is uncertain—a house built upon treacherous ground. Hence let the knowledge of nouns and verbs be secured early, as the starting point for the rest. The master will employ the devices of repetition, examination, and the correction of erroneous inflexions purposely introduced....

I have said that ability to write Latin verse is one of the essential marks of an educated person. I wish now to indicate a second, which is of at least equal importance, namely, familiarity with the language and literature of Greece. The time has come when we must speak with no uncertain voice upon this vital requirement of scholarship. I am well aware that those who are ignorant of the Greek tongue decry its necessity, for reasons which are sufficiently evident. But I can allow no doubt to remain as to my own conviction that without a knowledge of Greek Latin scholarship itself is, in any real sense, impossible....

Our scholar should make his first acquaintance with the Poets through Homer, the sovereign master of them all. For from Homer our own poets, notably Vergil, drew their inspiration; and in reading the *Iliad* or the *Odyssey* no small part of our pleasure is derived from the constant parallels we meet with. Indeed in them we see as in a mirror the form and manner of the *Aeneid* figured roughly before us, the incidents, not less than the simile or epithet which describe them, are, one might say, all there. In the same way, in his minor works Vergil has borrowed from Theocritus or Hesiod. After Homer has been attempted the way lies open to the other Heroic poets and to the Dramatists.

In reading of this wider range a large increase of vocabulary is gained, and in this the memory will be greatly assisted by the practice of making notes, which should be methodically arranged afterwards. . . .

But whilst a beginning is being thus made with Greek, continued progress must at the same time be secured in Latin. For instance the broader rules of grammar which sufficed in the earlier stages must give place to a more complete study of structure, such as we find in Priscian, and irregularities or exceptions, hitherto ignored, must be duly noted. At the same time the *Epistles* of Cicero will be taken in hand for purposes of declamation. Committed to memory they serve as one of the finest possible aids to purity, directness, and facility of style, and supply admirable matter in no less admirable form for adaptation to our own uses. Yet I would not be understood to claim the *Letters* of Cicero as alone offering a sufficient training in style. For distinction of style is the fruit of a far wider field of study. To quote Horace once more:

> *Of writing well, be sure, the secret lies*
> *In wisdom: therefore study to be wise.*

But we are now passing from the first, or elementary, to the second, or more advanced, stage of grammar which I called "Historice," which is concerned with the study of continuous prose authors, more particularly the Historians. Here we begin with a short but comprehensive view of general history, which will include that of the Roman people, by such writers as Justin or Valerius Maximus. The latter author is also valuable as affording actual illustrations of virtuous precepts couched in attractive style. The scholar will now devote his attention to the Historians in regular order. By their aid he will learn to understand the manners, laws and institutions of different types of nation, and will examine the varying fortunes of individuals and states, the sources of their success and failure, their strength and their weakness. Not only is such Knowledge of interest in daily intercourse but it is of practical value in the ordering of affairs.

Side by side with the study of history a careful reading of the poets will be taken in hand. The true significance of poetic fiction will now be appreciated. . . .

The course of study which I have thus far sketched out will prove an admirable preparation for that further branch of scholarship which constitutes Rhetoric, including the thorough examination of the great monuments of eloquence, and skill in the oratorial art itself. The first work to claim our attention in this subject is the *Rhetoric* of Cicero, in which we find all the points of Oratory concisely but comprehensively set forth. The other rhetorical writings of Cicero will follow, and the principles therein laid down must be examined in the light of his own speeches. Indeed the student of eloquence must have his Cicero constantly in his hand; the simplicity, the lofty moral standard, the practical temper of his writings render them a peculiarly noble training for a public speaker. Nor should the admirable Quintilian be neglected in this same connection.

It will be desirable also to include the elements of Logic in our course of studies, and with that the *Ethics* of Aristotle, and the Dialogues of Plato; for these are necessary aids to the proper understanding of Cicero.

C. Laura Cereta Defends the Liberal Education of Women

My ears are wearied by your carping. You brashly and publicly not merely wonder but indeed lament that I am said to possess as fine a mind as nature ever bestowed upon the most learned man. You seem to think that so learned a woman has scarcely before been seen in the world. You are wrong on both counts, Sempronius, and have clearly strayed from the path of truth and disseminate falsehood. I agree that you should be grieved; indeed, you should be ashamed, for you have ceased to be a living man, but have become an animated stone; having rejected the studies which make men wise, you rot in torpid leisure. Not nature but your own soul has betrayed you, deserting virtue for the easy path of sin.

You pretend to admire me as a female prodigy, but there lurks sugared deceit in your adulation. You wait perpetually in ambush to entrap my lovely sex, and overcome by your hatred seek to trample me underfoot and dash me to the earth. It is a crafty ploy, but only a low and vulgar mind would think to halt Medusa with honey. You would better have crept up on a mole than on a wolf. For a mole with its dark vision can see nothing around it, while a wolf's eyes glow in the dark. For the wise person sees by [force of] mind, and anticipating what lies ahead, proceeds by the light of reason. For by foreknowledge the thinker scatters with knowing feet the evils which litter her path.

I would have been silent, believe me, if that savage old enmity of yours had attacked me alone. For the light of Phoebus cannot be befouled even in the mud. But I cannot tolerate your having attacked my entire sex. For this reason my thirsty soul seeks revenge, my sleeping pen is aroused to literary struggle, raging anger stirs mental passions long chained by silence. With just cause I am moved to demonstrate how great a reputation for learning and virtue women have won by their inborn excellence, manifested in every age as knowledge, the [purveyor] of honor. Certain, indeed, and legitimate is our possession of this inheritance, come to us from a long eternity of ages past. . . .

D. Pico della Mirandola Exalts Human Dignity

. . . At last it seems to me I have come to understand why man is the most fortunate of creatures and consequently worthy of all admiration and what precisely is that rank which is his lot in the universal chain of Being—a rank to be envied not only by brutes but even by the stars and by minds beyond this world. It is a matter past faith and a wondrous one. Why should it not be? For it is on this very account that man is rightly called and judged a great miracle and a wonderful creature indeed. . . .

O supreme generosity of God the Father, O highest and most marvelous felicity of man! To him it is granted to have whatever he chooses, to be whatever he wills. Beasts as soon as they are born (so says Lucilius) bring with them from their mother's womb all they will ever possess. Spiritual beings, either from the beginning or soon thereafter, become what they are to be for ever and ever. On man when he came into life the Father conferred the seeds of all kinds and the germs of every way of life. Whatever seeds each man cultivates will grow to maturity and bear in him their own fruit. If they be vegetative, he will be like a plant. If sensitive, he will become brutish. If rational, he will grow into a heavenly being. If intellectual, he will be an angel and the son of God. And if, happy in the lot of no created thing, he withdraws into the center of his own unity, his spirit, made one with God, in the solitary darkness of God, who is set above all things, shall surpass them all. Who would not admire this our chameleon? Or who could more greatly admire aught else whatever? It is man who Asclepius of Athens, arguing from his mutability of character and from his self-transforming nature, on just grounds says was symbolized by Proteus in the mysteries. Hence those metamorphoses renowned among the Hebrews and the Pythagoreans. . . .

E. Ferrara Condemns Ignorant School Teachers

There exists at this time in this city a seminary of evil learning and ignorance. Our citizens desire to instruct their sons and their adolescents in good letters, and they are sunk in I know not what pit from which they can never extricate themselves. That is, certain barbarous teachers—who, far from knowing, never even saw, any good literature—have invaded our city, opened schools, and professed grammar. Citizens ignorant of these men's ignorance entrust their sons to them to be educated. They want them to learn and to graduate learned, but they learn those things which later they must unlearn. Lest this calamity and pest progress further, they decree that no one take scholars to train, nor hold a school, unless first he shall have demonstrated that he is acquainted with good literature or has been approved by the board of the Twelve Wise as suited to open a school. If anyone shall dare to do different, let him be ejected from the city as a pestiferous beast.

F. His Students Denounce the German Humanist Conrad Celtes as a Windbag

By your long and incessant scoldings, with which you frequently consume half the hour, you force us to make some reply in the name of truth. You accuse us of madness and charge that we are stupid barbarians, and you call wild beasts those whose fees support you. . . . This we might have borne with better grace, but for the fact that you yourself abound in the faults of which you accuse us. For what of the fact that, while you carp about us, you yourself are so torpid from dissipation that in private conversation your drowsy head droops to your elbow like a figure eight. You touch on many points in questions, but you speak neither plain argument nor cultured speech nor elegant Latin expositions; nor do you observe true coherence and order of speaking. Yet you have at hand the motto, "He teaches clearly who understands clearly." Either you lack understanding—a shameful thing in a doctor—or you think us unworthy of your learning, which is incredible. For you certainly experience daily studious auditors, sometimes learned men, calculated to adorn you with great praise. Or you dislike the labor of lecturing, as we clearly comprehend, understand and see. In this one point you both derogate from your own reputation and seem to us all deficient. But now we have clearly expressed ourselves on that point. Wherefore, if you are ready and willing to vindicate the name and dignity of a preceptor and doctor, to fulfill your professional duties, we will be more attentive. If first, as befits you, you clear yourself of the fault you impute to us, you will make us more diligent by your diligence, which has now long been lacking, if you can conquer and overcome your dislike of study and tardiness in work. If you do less, we shall have to take more stringent measures.

Document Set 14.1 References

A. Nicolò Nicoli Collects the Classics
   Vespasiano, *Lives,* in Kenneth R. Bartlett, ed., *The Civilization of the Italian Renaissance: A Sourcebook* (Lexington, Mass.: D. C. Heath, 1992), 89–90.

B. Battista Guarino Outlines a Course of Liberal Studies
   Battista Guarino, "On the Means of Teaching and Learning," in Bartlett, 283–288.

C. Laura Cereta Defends the Liberal Education of Women
   Laura Cereta, "In Defense of the Liberal Instruction of Women," in M. L. King and Albert Rabil, Jr., eds., *Selected Works By and About the Woman Humanists of Quattrocento Italy* (Binghamton, N.Y.: Medieval and Renaissance Texts and Studies, 1983), 81–84.

D. Pico della Mirandola Exalts Human Dignity
   Pico della Mirandola, "Oration on the Dignity of Man," in Bartlett, 130–133.

E. Ferrara Condemns Ignorant School Teachers
   Borsetti, *History of the Ferrara Schools,* in Lynn Thorndike, ed., *University Records and Life in the Middle Ages* (New York: Columbia University Press, 1944), 337.

F. His Students Denounce the German Humanist Conrad Celtes as a Windbag
   Thorndike, 366.

The Quattrocento Artist

Artist-patron relationships are of great importance in cultural history, tracing not only changes in taste but also attesting to the degree of control that patrons exercised over artists. The documents in this set testify to the varying conditions under which fifteenth-century artists worked. In Document A, for example, Duke Philip the Good of Burgundy offers with some deference his patronage to the famous Netherlands master Jan van Eyck (d. 1441). The extracts from Document B bespeak a far greater degree of patronly control over a commissioned work of art, in this case an altarpiece being executed at Avignon in the south of France. Document C, an order issued by Duke Galeazzo Maria Sforza of Milan in 1463, suggests something of that potentate's method of dealing with subordinates.

The last three documents all concern famous Italian Renaissance painters. Document D speaks much for the touchy relationship between the painter Andrea Mantegna (1431?–1506) and Duke Federico I of Mantua (who in this 1480 letter addresses the Duchess of Milan). In Document E, the neo-Platonist Florentine philosopher Marsilio Ficino writes to his patron, Lorenzo the Magnificent, describing an elaborate allegorical painting similar to Sandro Botticelli's masterpiece *La Primavera* (Spring), which was executed for the Medicis in 1477–1478. (Scholars debate whether Botticelli painted it under Ficino's direction.) Document F dates from 1550: it comes from Giorgio Vasari's collection of biographies of Renaissance painters and describes how in 1495–1497 Leonardo da Vinci painted his fresco *The Last Supper* in Milan.

Taken together, these documents offer insights into the artist's transition from relatively humble medieval artisan to "inspired genius." They will be particularly rewarding if you write a brief essay analyzing this transition, not only through the documents of this set but also through Sets 14.1, 14.4, and 14.5.

A. The Duke of Burgundy Extends His Patronage to Jan van Eyck

Jan van Eyck, former painter and equerry of the late Lord John, Duke of Bavaria, was known for his ability and craftsmanship by my said lord [Philip the Good] who had heard thereof from several of his people and which he knew to be true, being acquainted personally with the said Jan van Eyck. Confident of his loyalty and probity, my lord has retained said Jan as his painter and equerry, with the customary honors, prerogatives, franchises, liberties, rights, profits and usual emoluments pertaining to this position. And to the end that he shall be held to work for him in painting whenever it pleases him, my lord has ordered him to have and to take on his general receipt from Flanders, the sum of 100 parisis in Flemish money in two settlements yearly, half at Christmas and the other half at Saint John's, of which he wishes the first payment to be at Christmas 1425 and the other at Saint John's, and so from year to year and payment to payment, as long as it shall please him. Ordering to the masters of his household and his other officers that all his present honors, rights, prerogatives, profits and emoluments above mentioned they shall make and allow the said Jan to enjoy peaceably without prevention or disturbance; in addition ordering to his said receiver general of Flanders, present and future, that he shall pay, give and deliver every year the said sum of 100 Parisian pounds per year on the above declared terms to the said Jan, his painter and equerry, so all that is said on these matters may appear more plainly in the letters patent of my beforementioned lord, given in his city of Bruges, the 19th day of May in the year 1425. By virtue of that attestation is briefly given here to make payment for the term of Christmas 1425, and that which will follow to make a payment of 50 pounds on his quittance.

For the terms of St. John and Christmas 1426 together is made payment of 100 pounds on his quittance.

B. An Avignon Priest Contracts to Have an Altarpiece Painted, 1453

On the 25th day of April [1453], Master Enguerrand Quarton, of the diocese of Laon, painter, resident in Avignon, made a contract and agreement with the said Dominus Jean de Montagnac—both contracting parties being present—for painting an altarpiece according to the manner, form, and prescription contained and set forth article by article on a sheet of paper, which they passed over to me, written in French, whose tenor follows and is such:

Here follows the list of items of the altarpiece that Messer Jean de Montagnac has commissioned from Master Enguerrand, painter, to be placed in the church of the Carthusians, Villeneuve-les-Avignon, on the altar of the Holy City.

First: There should be the form of Paradise, and

in that Paradise should be the Holy Trinity, and there should not be any difference between the Father and the Son; and the Holy Ghost in the form of a dove; and Our Lady in front as it will seem best to Master Enguerrand; the Holy Trinity will place the crown on the head of Our Lady.

Item: The vestments should be very rich; those of Our Lady should be white-figured damask according to the judgement of said Master Enguerrand; and surrounding the Holy Trinity should be cherubim and seraphim. . . .

Item: On the left side will be Hell, and between Purgatory and Hell will be a mountain, and from the part of Purgatory below the mountain will be an angel comforting the souls of Purgatory; and from the part of Hell will be a very disfigured devil turning his back to the angel and throwing certain souls into Hell, given him by other devils.

Item: In Purgatory and Hell will be all the estates according to the judgement of said Master Enguerrand.

Item: Said altarpiece shall be made in fine oil colors and the blue should be fine blue of Acre, except that which will be put on the frame, that should be fine German blue, and the gold that will be used on the frame as well as around the altarpiece should be fine gold and burnished.

Item: Said Master Enguerrand will show all his knowledge and skill in the Holy Trinity and in the Blessed Virgin Mary, and will be governed by his conscience. . . .

A promise was given, I declare, by the same Master Enguerrand to execute these things faithfully and according to the foregoing description, from the next [feast of] St. Michael, for the next one continuous year, for the price of one hundred and twenty florins, each at the value of XXIII *sous* of the currency at Avignon. . . .

C. Galeazzo Maria Sforza Orders His Painter About

To Vincenzo of Brescia, painter

We want you when you receive these letters to come to us here, and bring with you the picture you received from Papi, our chamberlain as your model for a portrait of Our Lady. Come whether or not your own work is finished, because we want to employ you in other matters. Come at once with the said picture.

Milan, 3 March 1463

D. The Gonzagas Find Mantegna a Temperamental Artist

Most illustrious Excellency, I have received the portrait painting that Your Excellency sent me and have done my utmost to make Mantegna make a small reproduction in elegant form. He says this would almost be the work of a miniature-painter, and because he is not accustomed to painting small figures he would much rather do a Madonna, or something the length of a *braccia* [an arm] or a *braccia* and a half, if it were pleasing to Your Most illustrious Highness. My Lady, if I might know what Your Ladyship wants me to do, I shall endeavour to satisfy your wish, but usually these painters have a touch of the fantastic and it is advisable to take what they offer one; but if Your Ladyship is not served as quickly as you wished, I beseech you to excuse me; in your good grace etc.

E. The Philosopher Marsilio Ficino Suggests the Theme for Botticelli's *Primavera*

My immense love for you, excellent Lorenzo [patron of Botticelli], has long prompted me to make you an immense present. For anyone who contemplates the heavens, nothing he sets eyes upon seems immense but the heavens themselves. If, therefore, I make you a present of the heavens themselves what would be its price? But I would rather not talk of the price; for Love, born from the Graces, gives and accepts everything without payment; nor indeed can anything under heaven fairly balance against heaven itself.

The astrologers have it that the happiest man is he for whom Fate has so disposed the heavenly signs that Luna is not contrary in aspect to Mars and Saturn, that furthermore she is in a favourable aspect to Sol and Jupiter, Mercury and Venus. And just as the astrologers call happy the man for whom Fate has thus arranged the heavenly bodies, so the theologians deem him happy who has disposed his own self in a similar way. You may well wonder whether this is not asking too much—it certainly is much, but nevertheless, my gifted Lorenzo, go forward to the task with good cheer, for he who made you is greater than the heavens, and you too will be greater than the heavens as soon as you resolve to face them. We must not look for these matters outside ourselves, for all the heavens are within us and the fiery vigour in us testifies to our heavenly origin.

First Luna—what else can she signify in us but that continuous motion of the soul and of the body? Mars stands for speed, Saturn for tardiness, Sol for God, Jupiter for the Law, Mercury for Reason, and Venus for Humanity.

Onward, then, great-minded youth, gird yourself, and, together with me, dispose your own heavens. Your Luna—the continuous motion of your soul and body—should avoid the excessive speed of Mars and the tardiness of Saturn, that is, it should leave everything to the right and opportune moment, and should not hasten unduly, nor tarry too long. Furthermore, this Luna within you should continuously behold the Sun, that is God himself, from whom she ever receives the life-giving rays, for you must honour him above all things to whom you are beholden, and make yourself worthy of the honour. Your Luna should also behold Jupiter, the laws human and divine, which should never be transgressed—for a deviation of the laws by which all things are governed is tantamount to perdition. She should also direct her gaze on Mercury, that is on good counsel, reason and knowledge, for nothing should be said or done for which no plausible reason can be adduced. A man not versed in science and letters is considered blind and deaf. Finally she should fix her eyes on Venus herself, that is to say on Humanity. This serves us as an exhortation and a reminder that we cannot possess anything great on this earth without possessing the men themselves from whose favour all earthly things spring. Men, however, cannot be caught by any other bait but that of Humanity. Be careful, therefore, not to despise it, thinking perhaps that *humanitas* is of earthly origin.

For Humanity herself is a nymph of excellent comeliness, born of heaven and more than others beloved by God all highest. Her soul and mind are Love and Charity, her eyes Dignity and Magnanimity, the hands Liberality and Magnificence, the feet Comeliness and Modesty. The whole, then, is Temperance and Honesty, Charm and Splendour. Oh, what exquisite beauty! How beautiful to behold! My dear Lorenzo, a nymph of such nobility has been given wholly into your hands. If you were to unite with her in wedlock and claim her as yours she would make all your years sweet.

In fine, then, to speak briefly, if you thus dispose the heavenly signs and your gifts in this way, you will escape all the threats of fortune, and, under divine favour, will live happy and free from cares.

F. Leonardo da Vinci Paints *The Last Supper*

Leonard also executed in Milan, for the Dominicans of Santa Maria delle Grazie, a marvellous and beautiful painting of the Last Supper. Having depicted the heads of the apostles full of splendor and majesty, he deliberately left the head of Christ unfinished, convinced he would fail to give it the divine spirituality it demands. . . . It is said that the prior used to keep pressing Leonardo, in the most importunate way, to hurry up and finish the work, because he was puzzled by Leonardo's habit of sometimes spending half a day at a time contemplating what he had done so far; if the prior had had his way, Leonardo would have toiled like one of the laborers hoeing in the garden and never put his brush down for a moment. Not satisfied with this, the prior then complained to the duke [Ludovico Sforza], making such a fuss that the duke was constrained to send for Leonardo. . . . Leonardo, knowing he was dealing with a prince of acute and discerning intelligence, was willing (as he never had been with the prior) to explain his mind at length. . . . He explained that men of genius sometimes accomplish most when they work the least. . . . Leonardo then said that he still had two heads to paint: the head of Christ was one, and for this he was unwilling to look for any human model. . . . Then, he said, he had yet to do the head of Judas, and this troubled him since he did not think he could imagine the features that would form the countenance of a man who, despite all the blessings he had been given, could so cruelly steel his will to betray his own master and the creator of the world. However, added Leonardo, he would try to find a model for Judas, and if he did not succeed in doing so, why then he was not without the head of that tactless and importunate prior. The duke roared with laughter at this and said that Leonardo had every reason in the world for saying so.

Document Set 14.2 References

A. The Duke of Burgundy Extends His Patronage to Jan van Eyck
   Elizabeth G. Holt, *A Documentary History of Art* (New York: Doubleday, 1957), 1:303–304.
B. An Avignon Priest Contracts to Have an Altarpiece Painted, 1453
   Holt, 298, 301–302.
C. Galeazzo Maria Sforza Orders His Painter About
   D. S. Chambers, *Patrons and Artists in the Italian Renaissance* (Columbia, S. C.: University of South Carolina Press, 1971), 154.
D. The Gonzagas Find Mantegna a Temperamental Artist
   Federico I. Gonzaga, in Chambers, 120.
E. The Philosopher Marsilio Ficino Suggests the Theme for Botticelli's *Primavera*
   Marsilio Ficino, in Chambers, 98–99.
F. Leonardo da Vinci Paints *The Last Supper*
   Giorgio Vasari, *Artists of the Renaissance: A Selection from "Lives of the Artists,"* trans. George Bull (New York: Penguin, 1978), 187–188.

DOCUMENT SET 14.3
Family Life

All the documents in this set come from Florence, where the evolution of family life can be studied using an unusually rich collection of documents and literary works. Document A consists of extracts from letters from the widow Alessandra Strozzi to her son Filippo in 1464–1465; they reveal Alessandra (assuming the role normally taken by the family patriarch) negotiating a suitable match for her son—a process in which the bride had no say at all. They illustrate the extreme seriousness with which upper-class families took the business of continuing their lineage. Document B is taken from the diary kept by the head of the Panzone family. Noting his wife's death with genuine emotion, Luca di Matteo da Panzone incidentally reveals clues about family relationships and the public-private dichotomy of Florentine life. Document C, an extract from a similar record book kept by Bernardo Machiavelli (1475), tells part of the story of what happened when the servant girl in a respectable family became pregnant. Many details of Bernard's account have been omitted for reasons of space, including the outcome: fearing a public scandal, the Machiavelli family came up with a small dowry to marry Nencia off in her hometown, unusually lenient treatment. What happened when another young woman of modest circumstances committed a sexual transgression can be seen in Document D, an official court record. Keep in mind these records of private life when reading Document E, in which the humanist Francesco Barbaro comments on conjugal love, in a literary work that puts forward some ideas a bit in advance of their time.

A. Marriage Negotiations in the Strozzi Family

[April 20, 1464] . . . Concerning the matter of a wife [for Filippo], it appears to me that if Francesco di Messer Guglielmino Tanagli wishes to give his daughter, that it would be a fine marriage. . . . Now I will speak with Marco [Parenti, Alessandra's son-in-law], to see if there are other prospects that would be better. . . . Francesco Tanagli has a good reputation, and he has held office, not the highest, but still he has been in office. You may ask: "Why should he give her to someone in exile?" There are three reasons. First, there aren't many young men of good family who have both virtue and property. Secondly, she has only a small dowry, 1,000 florins, which is the dowry of an artisan. . . . Third, I believe that he will give her away, because he has a large family and he will need help to settle them. . . .

[August 17, 1465] . . . Sunday morning I went to the first mass at S. Reparata . . . to see the Adimari girl, who customarily goes to that mass, and I found the Tanagli girl there. Not knowing who she was, I stood beside her. . . . She is very attractive, well proportioned, as large or larger than Caterina [Alessandra's daughter]. . . . She has a long face, and her features are not very delicate, but they aren't like a peasant's. From her demeanor, she does not appear to me to be indolent. . . . I walked behind her as we left the church, and thus I realized that she was one of the Tanagli. . . .

[September 13, 1465] . . . Marco came to me and said that he had met with Francesco Tanagli, who had spoken very coldly, so that I understand that he had changed his mind. . . . I believe that this is the result of the long delay in our replying to him, both yours and Marco's. Now that this delay has angered him, and he has at hand some prospect that is more attractive. . . . I am very annoyed by this business. . . .

[Filippo Strozzi eventually married Fiametta di Donato Adimari, in 1466]

B. Luca di Matteo da Panzone Records His Wife's Death, 1447

November 5, 1445. I record that my wife Lucrezia, from whom I have eleven children alive today, died this day, Friday evening, two and one-half hours after sunset. This has caused me as much grief as though I were dying, for we have lived together for twenty years, one month, and eleven days. I pray to God most fervently that He pardon her. She died in labor; the child was apparently stillborn. But since the child was said to be breathing, it was baptized and named Giovanni. We buried it in the church of S. Simone.

We dressed my daughter Gostanza and Monna Caterina, the wife of Filippo di Ghezzi, with fourteen yards of cloth for a cloak, and a pair of veils and handkerchiefs. On Saturday morning at 11 o'clock, we held a vigil in our house with priests and friars. We buried her that day in S. Croce, in the vault of Messer Luca [Luca's grandfather] next to the fount of holy water. On the 8th, we had a mass said for her soul in S. Croce, with candles and as much pomp as possible. A large number of friends and relatives attended.

The loss of this woman was a grievous blow; she was mourned by the entire populace of Florence. She was a good woman, sweet-tempered and well-mannered, and was loved by everyone who knew her. I believe that her soul has gone to sit at the feet of God's servants. For she bore her final sufferings with patience and humility. She lay ill for two weeks after the child was born. May God with His great mercy make a place for her with angels.

On May 16, 1446, I, Luca da Panzano, ordered thirty masses of St. Gregory to be said, one each morning on consecutive days, for the salvation of my wife Lucrezia's soul. I commissioned my confessor, Fra Altaviano del Mangano, a friar of S. Croce in Florence [to say these masses]. Today I gave him two wax candles weighing a pound each to keep lighted during these masses. And for his services, I gave Fra Altaviano approximately one-half yard of Alexandria velvet.

C. The Machiavellis' Servant Girl Nencia Gets Pregnant, 1475

My wife told me that from certain signs which she had observed, our servant girl Lorenza, also called Nencia di Lazerino, had missed her period and that she appeared to be pregnant. . . . I told her to confront the girl alone and to use threats and persuasions to find out the truth from her. I had to go away, and upon my return in the evening, she told me that she had the girl alone in a room and that, after cajoling and threatening her, she had learned that the girl was pregnant by Niccolò di Alessandro Machiavelli. When asked how this had happened, she said that after we had returned from the country last year, on November 8, she had often gone at night through the window over the roof, and then through the little window next to the kitchen hearth to Niccolò's house to stay with him. . . .

The truth was that he, Niccolò, had never had anything to do with her. Francesco had done this, and his only fault had been his failure to tell me.

In reply, I complained bitterly of his [Niccolò's] injury to me, which would have been grave in any event, but which was even worse, since he was my neighbor . . . and a close blood relation. [I said] that I had never done anything similar to him or his father, and that I did not understand how he could have held me in such low esteem. For both here [in Florence] and at the villa, he was often in my company and had never said anything to me so that I might prevent my house from becoming a bordello. He should also consider the nature of this affair, for this girl was not

a slut but came from a good but impoverished family of Pistoia, and her father and brothers were men of some worth. I did not want the girl in my house any longer, and I had no choice but to inform Giovanni Nelli, who had given her to me, or to arrange for her father and mother to come for her. Niccolò replied that he was aware that he had injured me, but that it was Francesco who had harmed the girl, and that his error had been in not telling me. . . .

D. Monna Francesca Commits Infanticide, 1404

. . . We [the magistrates] condemn . . . Monna Francesca, the daughter of Cristofano Ciuti of Villa Caso, the wife of Cecco Arrighi of Ponte Boccio. . . . During the months of April, May, and June of the past year, Francesca lived at Montemurlo . . . on a farm belonging to Buonaccorso Strozzi. There she had conversations with a certain Jacopo of Romagna, Buonaccorso's servant, who told her that he wanted to take her for his wife. So Francesca, persuaded by his words and his arguments, allowed herself to become intimate with him on several occasions . . . so that she became pregnant by Jacopo. . . .

Then Francesca, knowing herself to be pregnant . . . promised to marry . . . Cecco Arrighi of Ponte Boccio . . . in the month of October. . . . Cecco did not realize that Francesca was pregnant by Jacopo . . . although she had been questioned by Cecco and his brothers about her swollen stomach. . . .

In the month of March of the present year, Francesca . . . gave birth to a healthy male child. . . . But inspired by an evil spirit and so that no one would know that she had given birth to that child, she threw him in the river . . . and as a result this son and creature of God was drowned.

[Francesca confessed. She was led through the streets of Pistoia on a donkey, with the corpse of her child tied to her neck, and was then burned to death.]

E. Francesco Barbaro Commends Conjugal Love

Now we shall speak of conjugal love, whose great power and high dignity almost always created—as we know from many great thinkers—a pattern of perfect friendship. I must omit a great many topics so that I may speak primarily about what is to be observed most. I should like a wife to love her husband with such great delight, faithfulness, and affection that he can desire nothing more in diligence, love, and goodwill. Let her be so close to him that nothing seems good or pleasant to her without her husband. Indeed, I think that true love will be of the greatest help in this matter. In all matters there is no better, no shorter path than being exactly what we seem to be. . . .

In the first place, let wives strive so that their husbands will clearly perceive that they are pensive or joyful according to the differing states of their husbands' fortunes. Surely congratulations are proper in times of good fortune, just as consolations are appropriate in times of adversity. Let them openly discuss whatever is bothering them, provided it is worthy of prudent people, and let them feign nothing, dissemble nothing, and conceal nothing. Very often sorrow and trouble of mind are relieved by means of discussion and counsel that ought to be carried out in a friendly fashion with the husband. If a husband shares all the pressures of her anxieties, he will lighten them by participating in them and make their burden lighter, but if her troubles are very great or deeply rooted, they will be relieved as long as she is able to sigh in the embrace of her husband. I would like wives to live with their husbands in such a way that they can always be in agreement, and if this can be done, then, as Pythagoras defines friendship, the two are united in one. Now that this could be accomplished more easily, the people of Crete, who have for several centuries now lived under our dominion, used to permit their daughters to marry only those men with whom as virgins they had expressed mutual signs of love. The Cretans believe that those men would be more beloved by their wives if they were loved by them even before marriage. They recall that nature has so arranged and usage proven that all actions require time with few exceptions. It certainly happens that we may touch something hot and we are not immediately burned, or sometimes wood that is thrown into a fire does not always burst into flame right away. Hence, they think it is necessary for the girl to choose a husband suited to her own personality, just as one does in forming a friendship. The Cretans believe that a couple cannot properly know each other or fall passionately in love immediately. Whether the custom is a good one, I leave it to everyone to decide, but I cannot deny that it is well suited to the joy and constancy of love. . . .

Document Set 14.3 References

A. Marriage Negotiations in the Strozzi Family
   Gene Brucker, ed., *The Society of Renaissance Florence* (New York: 1971), 37–40.

B. Luca di Matteo da Panzone Records His Wife's Death, 1447
   Panzone, *Diary*, in Brucker, 44–45.

C. The Machiavellis' Servant Girl Nencia Gets Pregnant, 1475
   Bernardo Machiavelli, *Libro di Ricordi*, in Brucker, 218–220.

D. Monna Francesca Commits Infanticide, 1404
   Brucker, 156–157.

E. Francesco Barbaro Commends Conjugal Love
   Francesco Barbaro, in Kenneth R. Bartlett, ed., *The Civilization of the Italian Renaissance: A Sourcebook* (Lexington, Mass.: D. C. Heath, 1992), 144–145.

DOCUMENT SET 14.4
Wealth

Urban Italy probably boasted the greatest concentration of wealth in fifteenth-century Europe; the documents in this set comment on that prosperity. Document A juxtaposes the assets and debts reported by a rich merchant against those of a humble worker in Florence in 1427—data compiled in connection with *Catasto* calculations of residents' wealth. Although not everyone filled out these precursors of an IRS form with scrupulous honesty, *Catasto* documents demonstrate typical disparities in economic standing. In Document B a rich patrician of the Ruccellai family reveals his thoughts on making, keeping, and wisely spending money; while reading this document, keep in mind what you have learned already about Florentines' ideas of family prestige.

Documents C and D come from Naples and Milan and attest to the diligence with which fifteenth-century merchants kept track of transactions. Double-entry bookkeeping was developed in Renaissance Italy; Document D gives a good example.

Studying these documents and reading Chapter 14 of *The Challenge of the West* should help you write a brief report on how wealth was gained and spent in Renaissance Italy.

A. A Rich Man and a Wool Carder Report Their Assets and Liabilities in the Florentine *Catasto*, 1427

The Declaration of Conte di Giovanni Compagni

[Figures are in florins, soldi, denari.]

Assets of Conte di Giovanni Compagni. . .

A house with furnishings which I inhabit, located in the parish of S. Trinita on the street of the Lungarno

    [not taxable]   0

A house in the parish of S. Trinita on the street of the Lungarno . . . which is rented to Niccolò and Tommaso Soderini for 24 florins per year, [capitalized] at 7 percent   342-17-2

A house on the Lungarno in that parish . . . rented to Giovanni di Simone Vespucci for 24 florins per year, [capitalized] at 7 percent   342-17-2

A house located in that street . . . rented to Michele di Piero Dini for 12 florins per year. . . .   171-8-9

Two shops . . . with courtyards and basements for selling wine, located in the parish of S. Agostino in the Via de' Terni . . . rented to Daddo di Zanobi, wineseller, for 20 florins per year. . . .   285-14-6

One-half of two-thirds of some shops in the palace of the Aretti of Pisa. . . . My share [of the rent] is 28 florins per year, more or less. . . .   400-0-0

A farm in the parish of S. Maria a Quarto . . . 238-11-6

A farm in the parish of S. Giorgio in the *contado* of Prato, with laborer's cottage, including several plots of vineyard and pieces of woodland adjacent to the farm. . . . Bartolomeo di Filippo cultivates this farm; he has borrowed 38 1/2 florins [from me] and he keeps a pair of oxen at his risk. . . . [The farm is valued at]   353-15-2

A small farm in the Valdimarina in the parish of S. Margherita a Torre with a villa and a laborer's cottage and olive trees and woods [valued at]139-13-0

A piece of woodland [valued at]   35-14-0

He [Conte] has invested in a shop of the Lana [woolen cloth manufacturers] guild in the company of Michele di Benedetto di Ser Michele, the sum of   2000-0-0

In another account with Michele in that shop, he is to receive   911-0-0

And in another account, he is to receive   66-0-0

Money which is owed to him by:

Francesco and Niccolò Tornabuoni	1130-0-0
Bartolomeo Peruzzi and company	335-5-0
Lorenzo di Messer Palla Strozzi and company	465-0-0
Michele Dini	75-0-0
Lorenzo di Messer Palla [Strozzi] and company	500-0-0
Michele di Benedetto di Ser Michele	325-0-0
Giovanni and Rinaldo Peruzzi and company	17-2-0

[Compagni estimated his holdings in *Monte* shares (communal bonds) and accrued interest at   4390-3-0

He also estimated that he would collect only 500 florins of some 1,079 florins owed to him by delinquent debtors.]   500-0-0

Obligations

Money owed to:

Creditors of Gino	39-0-0
Giovanni and Rinaldo di Rinieri Peruzzi	33-0-0

Lorenzo di Messer Palla [Strozzi] and company	118-18-6
Lorenzo di Messer Palla and company	45-11-0
Baldo, my servant	12-0-0
Marco di Bernardo and company, druggists	15-0-0
Monna Guida of the Mugello, my servant	10-0-0
[other obligations]	128-11-6

Personal exemptions:

Conte, aged 61	200-0-0
Monna Nanna, his wife	200-0-0
Ilarione, his son, aged 15	200-0-0
Giovanni, his son, aged 11	200-0-0
[Total estimated value of Conte's taxable assets]	
	13,039-6-3
[Total debts and exemptions]	1,202-1-0
[Net assets subject to taxation]	11,837-5-3 . . .

The Declaration of Biagio di Niccolò, Wool Carder

He owns one-third of a house in the parish of _____; his father bought it for 30 florins. . . . He lives in it.   0

One-half of a cottage located in the Via delle Romite. He receives 3 1/4 florins of rent

annually	46-0-0
Next to the cottage is a small piece of garden . . .	0-8-8

Obligations

He owes Braccio di Giovanni, cloth manufacturer	20-0-0

Personal exemptions:

Biagio di Niccolò	200-0-0
Monna Fiora, his wife	200-0-0
Gemma, his daughter, aged 9	200-0-0
Chola, his daughter, aged 5	200-0-0
He pays rent on the two-thirds of his house which he does not own . . .	14-5-0
[Biagio's taxable assets]	65-18-8
[His obligations and exemptions]	834-5-10

B. A Rich Florentine Comments on Getting and Keeping Wealth, c. 1460

Now I shall discuss the best way to invest money: whether it should be all in cash, or all in real estate and communal bonds, or some in one and some in the other. Now it is true that money is very difficult to conserve and to handle; it is very susceptible to the whims of fortune, and few know how to manage it.

But whoever possesses a lot of money and knows how to manage it is, as they say, the master of the business community because he is the nerve center of all of the trades and commercial activities. For in every moment of adverse fortune, in times of exile and those disasters which occur in the world, those with money will suffer less than those who are well provided with real estate. . . . I would not wish to deny, however, that real estate is more secure and more durable [than money], although occasionally it has been damaged and even destroyed by war, by enemies with fire and sword. Real estate holdings are particularly useful for minors and for others who have no experience in banking. . . . There is nothing easier to lose, nothing more difficult to conserve, more dangerous to invest, or more troublesome to keep, than money. . . . The prudent family head will consider all of his property, and will guard against having it all in one place or in one chest. If war or other disaster occur here, you might still be secure there; and if you are damaged there, then you may save yourself here. . . .

Let me warn you again that in our city of Florence, wealth is conserved only with the greatest difficulty. This is due to the frequent and almost continual wars of the Commune, which have required the expenditure of great sums, and the Commune's imposition of many taxes and forced loans. I have found no better remedy for defending myself than to take care not to gain enemies, for a single enemy will harm you more than four friends will help. I have always remained on good terms with my relatives and neighbors and the other residents of the district, so that whenever the taxes have been assessed, they have befriended me and taken pity on me. In this business, good friends and relatives are very useful. . . . So guard against making enemies or involving yourself in quarrels or disputes. And if someone with gall and arrogance tries to quarrel with you, you should treat him with courtesy and patience. . . .

With respect to good, honest, and virtuous friends, I again counsel you to serve them and be liberal with them. Lend to them, give to them, trust them. . . . And while being liberal and generous to friends, one should occasionally do the same to strangers, so that one will gain a reputation for not being miserly, and also will acquire new friends.

I have told you, my sons, how I have treated good friends, and also how I have treated the swindlers and beggars who daily petition me. Now I must tell you how to respond when, as happens every day, your close relatives make demands on you. It seems to me that one is obligated to help them, not so much with money, as with blood and sweat and whatever one can, even to sacrificing one's life for the honor of the family. One must know how to spend money and to acquire possessions. He who spends only in eating and dressing, or who does not know how to disburse money for the benefit and honor of his family, is certainly not wise. But in these matters, one must use good judgment, because it makes no sense to destroy one's own fortune in order to save that of a relative. . . .

Of necessity, the rich man must be generous, for generosity is the most noble virtue that he can possess, and to exercise it requires wisdom and moderation. Whoever wishes to be regarded as liberal must spend and give away his wealth, for which trait the rich are much liked. . . . But who gives beyond his means soon dissipates his fortune. But if you wish to acquire a reputation for liberality, consider well your resources, the times, the expenses which you must bear, and the qualities of men. According to your means, give to men who are in need and who are worthy. And whoever does otherwise goes beyond the rule of liberality, and does not acquire praise thereby. Whatever you give to the unworthy is lost, and whoever disburses his wealth beyond measure soon experiences poverty.

C. "On Commerce and the Perfect Merchant": A Neopolitan Businessman's Advice

The pen is an instrument so noble and excellent that it is absolutely necessary not only to merchants but also in any art, whether liberal, mercantile, or mechanical. And when you see a merchant to whom the pen is a burden or who is inept with the pen, you may say that he is not a merchant. And [a good merchant] not only must be skilled in writing but also must keep his records (scritture) methodically. And with these records we plan to deal in the present chapter. For no merchant ought to transact his business by heart, unless he were like King Cyrus, who could call by name every person in his entire army, which was innumerable. And in the same way Lucius Scipio, the Roman, and Cynea, the legate of Pyrrhus, the day after entering Rome, greeted every member of the senate by his name. But since this is not possible for everyone, we shall turn to the practice of [keeping] records. These not only preserve and keep in the memory [all] transactions, but they also are a means to avoid many litigations, quarrels, and scandals. And they also cause literate men to live thousands upon thousands of years. . . .

Mercantile records are the means to remember all that a man does, and from whom he must have, and to whom he must give, and the costs of wares, and the profits, and the losses, and every other transaction on which the merchant is at all dependent. And it should be noted that knowing how to keep good and orderly records teaches one how to draw contracts, how to do business, and how to obtain a profit. And undoubtedly a merchant must not rely upon memory, for such reliance has caused many persons to err. Of this speaks Averroes, the commentator. When he wished to chide Avicenna, who was relying upon his own intelligence, he said: "Two things cause men to err in natural matters, reliance upon [one's own] intelligence, and ignorance of logic."

Therefore the merchant ought to keep three books, that is, the ledger (quaderno), the journal (giornale), and the memorandum (memoriale). And the ledger ought to have its alphabetical [index] through which one may quickly find any account written in the said ledger. And it ought to be marked A; and on its first sheet [the merchant] ought to invoke the name of God and [to state] what it deals with and of how many sheets it consists. And he also will mark by the said [letter] A his journal, alphabetical [index], and memorandum.

In the journal you shall reconstruct methodically all [your] capital, item by item, and you shall carry it forward in the ledger. Then you shall be able, as you please, to begin your management with that capital and to do business with it. And when you have finished writing the said ledger, you shall settle all accounts opened in it, extract from them all balances (resti) to the debit or likewise to the credit, [and carry forward the balances] in the last sheet after the last account. Then, when you carry them forward in a new ledger, give every balance its separate account. And you shall mark that ledger by [the letter] B, also marking by the same [letter] the new journal, alphabetical [index], and memorandum [corresponding] to it. Always continue like that successively from one book to another, up to the last syllable of the alphabet, always invoking in the first sheet of a ledger the name of God, etc., as above.

In the memorandum you ought to note every evening or morning before you leave your home everything you have traded and transacted on that day because of your commerce or of [any] other necessary and incidental [expense]—such as sales, purchases, payments, receipts, remittances, orders of payment (assegnamenti), exchanges, expenses, promises, and any other business—before any account originates from it in the journal. For many things happen while [business] is transacted without making accounts in the journal.

And you should further note that you ought to keep always with you a small notebook (*libriccino piccolo delle ricordanze*) in which you shall note day by day and hour by hour even the minute [detail] of your transactions, so that later you may at your best convenience create accounts in the memorandum book or the journal. And always exert yourself to carry the accounts, or part of them, forward from the said memorandum into the journal the same day or the following one; then carry them forward in the ledger daily.

And at the end of every year you shall check the ledger against the accounts in the journal, making the trial balance (*bilancione*) of them, and carrying forward all profits or losses (*avanzi overo disavanzi*) in your capital account.

Further, you ought to keep two more books, one to copy the statements (*conti*) which are sent out, the other to copy the letters you sent, [including] even those of the smallest importance.

Also you must keep your writing desk in order, and note on all letters you receive where they come from, and of what year, and of what day according as you have received them daily. And then every month you shall make bundles of those letters, and you shall put away each bundle into the drawer of the proper class in your writing desk, together with all other records—such as contracts, instruments, chirographs, [bills of] exchange, statements, policies, etc.—keeping them there as true merchants are wont to do.

And for the sake of brevity let it be enough to have said this about the method [of keeping] books and records; for if I wanted to tell everything here in detail I would be too long-winded—and it is almost impossible to explain it, since one can hardly learn it from a book without oral instruction. And therefore I warn and encourage any merchant to take pleasure in knowing how to keep his books well and methodically. And whoever does not know [how to do this], let him get instruction, or else let him keep an adequate and expert young bookkeeper (*quaderniero*). Otherwise your commerce will be chaos, a confusion of Babel—of which you must beware if you cherish your honor and your substance.

D. Double-Entry Bookkeeping from Naples

1396

Alberico of Meda, maker of spurs, must give—Credited to the account of Marco Serrainerio on folio 6 on March 6—[for money] which he [Marco] paid to him

£ 9 s.– d.–

Item—[credited] to said Marco on folio 6 on March 11—[for money] deposited for Filippo, his [Alberico's] brother, in [the bank of] Paolino of Osnago

£ 15 s.– d.–

Item—[credited] to Giovanni of Dugnano, on folio 8 on March 24—[for money] which he [Giovannino] ordered to be given him [Alberico or Filippo?] in [the bank of] Andrea Monte

£ 18 s.– d.–

Item—[credited] to Marco Serrrainerio, on folio 6 on May 13—[for money] deposited in [the bank of] Mano, [son] of Ser Jacopo

£ 15 s.– d.–

Item—paid in his behalf on the aforesaid day to Pietrino Bazuella—posted in the cash account on folio 23   £ 10 s.– d.–

Item—for the [balance] posted to the credit account of the joint profit [of the partnership] on folio 20 on January 3, 1397

£ 4s.–8 d.–

1396

He [Alberico] must have—Debited to the account of Merceries on folio 15 on February 24—for 6 dozen fine jeweled spurs, at £ 4 s.10 imperial per dozen, amounting to

£ 27 s.– d.–

Item, posted as above, for 6 dozen small fine jeweled spurs, at s.54 per dozen   £ 16 s.4 d.–

Item, posted as above, for 6 dozen Cordovan spurs, at s.48 per dozen, amounting to £ 14 s.8 d.–

Item, posted as above, for 4 dozen spurs with a prick, at s.26 per dozen, amounting to £ 5 s.4 d.–

Item, posted as above, for 4 dozen quality spurs with thick arms, at s.23 per dozen £ 4. s.12 d.–

Item, posted as above, for 4 dozen spurs of medium quality, at s.20 per dozen   £ 4 s.– d.–

Total £ 71s.8

Document Set 14.4 References

A. A Rich Man and a Wool Carder Report Their Assets and
   Liabilities in the Florentine *Catasto,* 1427
   Gene Brucker, ed., *The Society of Renaissance Florence* (New
   York: Harper & Row, 1971), 6–8, 13.
B. A Rich Florentine Comments on Getting and Keeping
   Wealth, c. 1460
   Giovanni Rucellai, in Brucker, 24–27.
C. "On Commerce and the Perfect Merchant": A Neapolitan
   Businessman's Advice
   Benedetto Cotrugli, in Robert S. Lopez and Irving W.
   Raymond, *Medieval Trade in the Mediterranean World* (New
   York: Columbia University Press, 1930s), 375–377.
D. Double-Entry Bookkeeping from Naples
   Lopez and Raymond, 372–373.

Faith in the supernatural infused every aspect of fifteenth-century life. However worldly minded an individual may have appeared, thoughts about how such behavior might affect one's standing with God almost invariably arose. The documents in this set focus directly on three dimensions of religious experience. In Document A, Thomas à Kempis conveys a sense of the individual piety permeating the *Devoto Moderna,* the lay (opposed to monastic) movement that spread widely across northern Europe. Document B testifies to a very different kind of piety: that of Florentine intellectuals who tried to reconcile newly rediscovered Platonic philosophy with their Christian beliefs. The author of this commentary, Marsilio Ficino, was a kind of "philosopher in residence" to the Medici family; you have already encountered him in Document Set 14.2. You should also refer back to Document Set 3.3 for Plato's account of the conversation about love between Socrates and Diotima, upon which Ficino comments.

Document C is taken from the *Commentaries* of Pope Pius II, a set of memoirs completed in 1462. Pius here describes his vigorous reaction to a French challenge to papal authority in 1438—following which he enjoys a delightful summer vacation.

All three documents reveal challenges to the medieval church and to traditional church-centered devotion that were building up during the fifteenth century. Identify and explain as many of these challenges as you can.

A. Thomas à Kempis Expresses the Piety of the Devotio Moderna

Evil ought not be done for anything in the world, nor for the love of any human being; but yet for the benefit of one that is in need, a good work is sometimes freely to be left undone, or rather to be changed for what is better.

For by this means a good work is not lost, but changed into a better.

Without charity, the outward work provideth nothing; but whatever is done out of charity, be it ever so little and contemptible, it is all made fruitful, inasmuch as God regardeth more out of how much love a man doth a work, than how much he doth.

2. He doth much who loveth much.

He doth much who doth well what he hath to do.

He doth well, who regardeth rather the common good than his own will.

Oftentimes that seemeth to be charity which is rather carnality; for natural inclination, self-will, hope of reward, study of our own interests, will seldom be absent.

3. He that hath true and perfect charity, seeketh himself in nothing, but only desireth God to be glorified in all things.

And he envieth no man, for he loveth no joy for himself alone.

Neither doth he desire to rejoice in himself, but wisheth to find his blessedness above all good things in God.

He attributeth nothing of good to any man, but referreth it all to God, from whom, as from their fountain, all things proceed, and in whom, as in their end, all the Saints repose in fruition.

Oh, if one had but a spark of real charity, truly would he feel that all earthly things are full of vanity!

B. Marsilio Ficino Attempts to Fuse Platonism and Christianity

". . . The beauty of any individual man, O Socrates, you will scorn if you compare it to that abstract concept of yours. You possess that concept not so much thanks to bodies as to your own soul. Therefore love that concept which your soul has created, and the soul itself, its creator, rather than that external beauty, which is defective and scattered.

"But what is it that I urge you to love in the soul? The beauty of the soul. The beauty of bodies is a light; the beauty of the soul is also a light. The light of the soul is truth, which is the only thing which your friend Plato seems to ask of God in his prayers:

Grant to me, O God, he says, *that my soul may become beautiful, and that those things which pertain to the body may not impair the beauty of the soul, and that I may think only the wise man rich.*

In this prayer Plato says that the beauty of the soul consists in truth and wisdom, and that it is given to men by God. Truth, which is given to us by God single and uniform, through its various effects acquires the names of various virtues. Insofar as it deals with divine things, it is called Wisdom (which Plato asked of God above all else); insofar as it deals with natural things, it is called Knowledge; with human things, Prudence. Insofar as it makes men equal, it is called Justice; insofar as it makes them invincible, Courage; and tranquil, Temperance. . . .

But we, my distinguished friends, shall love God not only without moderation, as Diotima is imagined as commanding, but God alone. For the Angelic Mind is to God as the vision of our eyes is to the sun. The eye desires not only light above all else, but light alone. If we do love bodies, souls, or angels, we shall not really be loving these things, but God in them. In loving bodies we shall really be loving the shadow of God; in souls, the likeness of God; in angels, the image of God. Thus in this life we shall love God in all things so that in the next we may love all things in God. For living in this way we shall proceed to the point where we shall see both God and all things in God, and love both Him, and all things which are in Him. And anyone who surrenders himself to God with love in this life will recover himself in God in the next life. Such a man will certainly return to his own Idea, the Idea by which he was created. There any defect in him will be corrected again; he will be united with his Idea forever. For the true man and the Idea of a man are the same. For this reason as long as we are in this life, separated from God, none of us is a true man, for we are separated from our own Idea or Form. To it, divine love and piety will lead us. Even though we may be dismembered and mutilated here, then, joined by love to our own Idea, we shall become whole men, so that we shall seem to have first worshipped God in things, in order later to worship things in God, and to worship things in God for this reason, in order to recover ourselves in Him above all, and in loving God we shall seem to have loved ourselves.

c. Pius II Tries to Restore Papal Power, Then Goes on Vacation, 1462

It was the sixteenth year of Charles's reign and the 1438th of the Incarnation of our Lord, when the prelates of France on July 7 presented the completed volume of the Pragmatic Sanction to this same Charles for his approval. Charles, apparently forgetting the divine grace which he had experienced through the Maid as well as the many benefits heaped upon him by the Apostolic See in sending the Cardinal of Santa Croce to reconcile the Burgundians with him, approved these impious and unjust enactments and commanded that they should be observed throughout his dominions on pain of most severe punishment.

This decree of the King together with the constitutions of the prelates received the name of the Pragmatic Sanction. The numerous envoys sent to France by the Apostolic See during the lives of Eugenius. Nicholas, and Calixtus to obtain its annulment accomplished nothing. It was twenty-four years before it was completely wiped out under Pius II.[1] As a result of this law the prelates of France, who thought they were going to be free, were reduced to the most abject servitude and became practically slaves of the laity. They were forced to give evidence in the French parliament in individual cases; to confer benefices at the pleasure of the king or other princes and powerful nobles; to advance to the priesthood minors, ignoramuses, monsters, and libertines; to remit the punishment of those they had condemned for misdeeds and to absolve the excommunicated without their making atonement. No independent right of censure was left them. Anyone who brought to France an apostolic letter opposing the Pragmatic Sanction was condemned to death. Cases concerning bishops, metropolitan churches, marriages, and heresy were investigated in parliament and the insolence of the laity ran riot in France, to such an extent that the most holy Body of Christ, when, as often happened, it was being carried in procession to be worshipped by the people or taken as viaticum for the sick, was ordered to halt by the supreme authority of the king. Bishops and other prelates and priests deserving of respect were haled off to public prisons: estates of the Church and all property of the clergy were confiscated on flimsy pretexts of the decision of a secular judge and given over to the laity. Thus many acts of folly were brought about by the Pragmatic Sanction and either enforced or permitted by an ungrateful king.

Meantime, when the summer was over, Pius, who had been invited by Giovanni, Cardinal of San Sisto, to visit the monastery of Subiaco over which he presided, set out with four cardinals on a trip for pleasure and refreshment. They crossed the Aniene at Tivoli, followed along its left bank, and spent the first night at Vicovaro, which some think means Varro's town and some Varus's. It lies on a high cliff and is triangular in shape. Two sides are protected by precipitous rocks divided on one side by a never-failing stream and on the other jutting out into the current of the Aniene. The third side is defended by a lofty tower, a strongly fortified citadel, and an artificial moat. It still retains traces of its early splendor. A good part of the wall constructed of huge blocks of

---

[1] Pius refers to himself throughout in the third person.

stone such as we see in ancient works is still standing, lying about are numerous columns and broken statues that yet give evidence of the talent of their sculptors. Francesco Orsini, when prefect of the city, began a noble chapel of gleaming white marble and adorned it with fine statues and flowers, works of art by no means despicable for our times. Death prevented his completing his work and his successors, who are contesting their inheritance by force of arms, have not yet put the finishing touches to it.

Pius granted the town indulgence that the chapel might be completed. He lodged in a house overlooking the Aniene which commanded a most delightful view, as did also the mountain on the other side of the river which was covered with forests still green and leafy. The land down by the river was either meadows or vineyards; the hills were clothed halfway up with vines and the rest of the way with acorn-bearing oaks.

From here they went to San Clemente some two miles distant. The people worship there with the greatest reverence and the monks are celebrated for their sanctity. The ground where the monastery stands is level but behind it the cliffs above the Aniene fall to such a depth that the eye can hardly see the water at their base. The Pope entered the chapel and prayed. Then after blessing the monks he continued his journey, . . .

Document Set 14.5 References

A. Thomas à Kempis Expresses the Piety of the Devotio Moderna
   Thomas à Kempis, *The Imitation of Christ,* ch. 15.
B. Marsilio Ficino Attempts to Fuse Platonism and Christianity
   Marsilo Ficino, in Kenneth R. Bartlett, ed., *The Civilization of the Italian Renaissance: A Sourcebook* (Lexington, Mass.: D. C. Heath, 1992), 122–125.
C. Pius II Tries to Restore Papal Power, Then Goes on Vacation, 1462
   Memoirs of a Renaissance Pope: Commentaries of Pius II: An Abridgement, trans. Florence A. Gragg, ed. Leona C. Gabel (New York: Capricorn, 1962), 210–212.

DOCUMENT SET 14.6
The State as a Work of Art

The nineteenth-century Swiss historian Jacob Burckhardt, who originated the idea of the Renaissance, used the expression "the state as a work of art" to refer to a key feature of Renaissance politics. As Chapter 14 of *The Challenge of the West* explains, this expression refers to the essentially contrived character of Renaissance state-building, which often involved imposing new forms of rule or nurturing new loyalties. The three documents of this set all speak to Renaissance state-building.

Document A is an ambassador's dispatch to the princely government of Milan (itself a newly created state) describing the Duke of Burgundy's use of the elaborate ritual of his Order of the Golden Fleece to win the loyalty of his nobles. The dispatch (partly written in cipher, indicated here in italics) also testifies to the new institutions and practices of diplomacy, a fifteenth-century Italian innovation. Document B records the sort of civic ritual that the Florentine Republic used to reinforce loyalty to the state. In Document C, Lorenzo the Magnificent, the head of the Medicis at the end of the fifteenth century and a prince in all but name, recalls the cost to his family of staging the lavish displays necessary to demonstrate its power and generosity—and finds it all worthwhile. (Detailed investigation of the Medici family's banking enterprises shows that overspending and neglect of business interests in favor of politics were already undermining the Medici fortune even as Lorenzo was making himself the virtual ruler of Florence.)

After examining these documents, consider afresh what Burckhardt meant by calling the Renaissance state an essentially "artistic creation." Consider also the evidence that you encountered in Sets 14.1 through 14.4.

A. The Duke of Burgundy Presides Over the Order of the Golden Fleece, 1461

For the rest, the ceremonies of the Golden Fleece have been celebrated. In these the Duke of Burgundy exemplified three themes: worship, lofty solemnity, ritual. Worship: the Duke remained most devoutly on his knees throughout the divine service, which lasted until two o'clock in the afternoon, constantly contemplating the arms and insignia of King Alfonso, [of Aragon, died 1458] which he had before his eyes as a mirror of the human condition. Lofty solemnity: in

that he has such revered princes who acknowledge him their Duke, Father, Lord, although he honors them in sharing the bond of brotherhood. Ritual: in the cult, divine and human, of the Highest.

The ordering of the celebration was as follows. In the stalls of the choir sat at the head and on the right the lord Duke, and along both sides of the choir were ranged the insignia, names, and titles of all the princes, barons, and knights of the Order. All wore the vestments of the Golden Fleece, scarlet hoods and scarlet mantels that reached to the feet and were fringed with gold, and had about their necks the collar of the Golden Fleece. In the stalls of those absent sat their proxies; in the stalls of the deceased were hung black cloths displaying their insignia, names, and titles. I was given the first place on the left side, beneath the head of the barons on that side. At the offertory, *Golden Fleece*, chief of the Duke's heralds, ceremoniously called the roll of the Order by name and title, except that there was announced the suspension of the Duke of Alençon on account of his being a prisoner, until his case, if indeed there was a case, is considered by the Order. Subsequently *Orléans'* name was called, *as Duke of Orléans and Count of Blois, but he was not given the accustomed title of Duke of Milan, at which point the Duke of Burgundy gave me a significant glance.*

The church, which is very large, was splendidly hung with arras depicting with magnificent artistry the Apocalypse. The choir was similarly embellished, with hangings of cloth of gold depicting various stories from the Old and New Testament. The altar, as a thing divine, was adorned with religious objects: namely, first a very large cross containing a piece of the True Cross; then eighteen images, of gold not silver, of the length of an arm; and in the middle the holy Fleur-de-Lys, more than an arm's length tall and almost as wide, which contained holy relics and was crusted with jewels, precious both in their quantity and quality. Of singers, heralds, and such appurtenances, there was an infinite number, all superbly contributing to the ceremonies.

The banquet hall, which is of the size of that of the most illustrious lady, the Duchess, but with a higher ceiling, was completely hung with tapestries of cloth of gold, as above, marvellous works depicting the whole story of how the golden fleece was sent down from heaven to Gideon as a sign that he was to undertake the salvation of the people of Israel. Behind the dais where sat the princes were silken hangings and other adornments of gold. Opposite was a display of plate, very rich and all of vessels of gold and silver gilt, four unicorn horns arranged in order of size like organ pipes, and many vessels of crystal and of other precious stones. This plate remained untouched that day because so much of it does the Duke have that there was plenty of additional plate for the dinner service.

At the banquet the Duke sat at the middle of the board with the others ranged on either side in accordance with their seniority in the Order. On the extreme right was my lord [Charles] of Charolais; at the other end [Antoine], the Bastard of Burgundy, both sons of the Duke. Each of the princes of the Golden Fleece had his own service, and the banquet consisted of fifty courses, each served by fifty servitors and the courses borne through the hall in a grand procession of trumpeters and other musicians, with the other nobles then being served. These ceremonies were held on May 2.

The number of the princes of the Order is established by the constitution at thirty-one. There are two main bases of the Order: a vow to defend Holy Church, and a vow to maintain all honor, morality, and good custom without stain, these vows being part of the articles of the Order, of which articles I hope to be able to obtain a copy because I think they are worthy and useful. Stemming from these vows is the requirement *that all members of the Order be in league, confraternity, and identity of wills with each other. The Duke of Burgundy finds this brotherhood of great value to him because he has their aid and counsel.*

To supply the places of the deceased members, six of them, many secret councils were held, as is customary, and according to what they themselves have told me, I believe that at present they will elect five *new members, unless they change their minds. I believe that, in honor of the late King of Aragon, they will not fill his place until they elect another King, and I think they are reserving the place for King Ferrante, if matters permit. This is my judgment of the situation.*

Considering then the nature of this Order of the Golden Fleece and the honor and prestige that it confers, I confess to have within me a strong desire for Count Galeazzo to be elected to it. Nonetheless since I do not know how Your Excellency feels about the matter and since I also do not know whether, in this procedure, indication of a desire to be elected does a service or disservice, I have contented myself with offering a certain indication, or rather a very small one. However, what I have been able to do, acting with discretion, I have done, such as calling upon these princes in order to speak with them about Your

Excellency and to describe your manners and modes of government, your justice, liberality, the grace and authority that all universally find in you, and similar things, and to explain how in these customs, with great and marvelous loftiness of spirit and intelligence, has been reared, and made knight, Count Galeazzo.

I believe that by these means I aroused the right feeling among these princes, and if the obstacle of the Duke of Orléans did not stand in the way, which I do not like to believe, I am not without some thought that they may have elected Count Galeazzo, although neither I nor others know for certain because it is a custom of the Order never to announce the names of outsiders who are chosen until they consent to become members, and this is for the honor of the Order. This is my view of the matter, reserving always the judgment of Your Excellency. Would that thus it was, because it would seem to me that in this honorable way, and without incurring the dislike of any lord in the world, you would acquire a league with the Duke of Burgundy and with the other lords of the Order without expense etc., which league could some time come in very handy, however things turn out. I can well assure Your Excellency that you have a greater reputation in these parts than—speaking always with permission—has had any other who has been Duke of Milan. Should Count Galeazzo be elected, the news will be brought to Your Excellency by a worthy emissary, to whom, if Your Excellency agrees, it will be well to pay high honors, etc. However, I offer no assurance about all this, for I would not want to send Your Excellency unbaked dough [i.e. opinion masquerading as fact]. However, as I say, I have some hopes about the matter, and therefore I would strongly suggest that Count Galeazzo become acquainted, through letters and a little something more, with the son of the Duke of Burgundy. I humbly recommend myself to Your Excellency. Given as above.

B. Florentines Celebrate a Communal Ritual

When springtime comes and the whole world rejoices, every Florentine begins to think about organizing a magnificent celebration on the feast day of St. John the Baptist [June 24]. . . . For two months in advance, everyone is planning marriage feasts or other celebrations in honor of the day. There are preparations for the horse races, the costumes of the retinues, the flags and the trumpets; there are the pennants and the wax candles and other things which the subject territories offer to the Commune. Messengers are sent to obtain provisions for the banquets, and horses come from everywhere to run in the races. The whole city is engaged in preparing for the feast, and the spirits of the young people and the women [are animated] by these preparations. . . . Everyone is filled with gaiety; there are dances and concerts and songfests and tournaments and other joyous activities. Up to the eve of the holiday, no one thinks about anything else.

Early on the morning of the day before the holiday, each guild has a display outside of its shops of its fine wares, its ornaments and jewels. There are cloths of gold and silk sufficient to adorn ten kingdoms. . . . Then at the third hour, there is a solemn procession of clerics, priests, monks, and friars, and there are so many [religious] orders, and so many relics of saints, that the procession seems endless. [It is a manifestation] of great devotion, on account of the marvelous richness of the adornments . . . and clothing of gold and silk with embroidered figures. There are many confraternities of men who assemble at the place where their meetings are held, dressed as angels, and with musical instruments of every kind and marvelous singing. They stage the most beautiful representations of the saints, and of those relics in whose honor they perform. They leave from S. Maria del Fiore [the cathedral] and march through the city and then return.

Then, after midday, when the heat has abated before sunset, all of the citizens assemble under [the banner of] their district, of which there are sixteen. Each goes in the procession in turn, the first, then the second, and so on with one district following the other, and in each group the citizens march two by two, with the oldest and most distinguished at the head, and proceeding down to the young men in rich garments. They march to the church of St. John [the Bapistery] to offer, one by one, a wax candle weighing one pound. . . . The walls along the streets through which they pass are all decorated, and there are . . . benches on which are seated young ladies and girls dressed in silk and adorned with jewels, pearls, and precious stones. This procession continues until sunset, and after each citizen has made his offering, he returns home with his wife to prepare for the next morning.

Whoever goes to the Piazza della Signoria on the morning of St. John's Day witnesses a magnificent, marvelous, and triumphant sight, which the mind can scarcely grasp. Around the great piazza are a hundred towers which appear to be made of gold. Some were brought on carts and others by porters. . . . [These towers] are made of wood, paper, and wax [and dec-

orated] with gold, colored paints, and with figures. . . . Next to the rostrum of the palace [of the Signoria] are standards . . . which belong to the most important towns which are subject to the Commune: Pisa, Arezzo, Pistoia, Volterra, Cortona, Lucignano. . . .

First to present their offering, in the morning, are the captains of the Parte Guelfa, together with all of the knights, lords, ambassadors, and foreign knights. They are accompanied by a large number of the most honorable citizens, and before them, riding on a charger covered with a cloth . . . is one of their pages carrying a banner with the insignia of the Parte Guelfa. Then there follow the abovementioned standards, each one carried by men on horseback . . . and they all go to make their offerings at the Baptistery. And these standards are given as tribute by the districts which have been acquired by the Commune of Florence. . . . The wax candles, which have the appearance of golden towers, are the tribute of the regions which in most ancient times were subject to the Florentines. In order of dignity, they are brought, one by one, to be offered to St. John, and on the following day, they are hung inside the church and there they remain for the entire year until the next feast day. . . . Then come . . . an infinite number of large wax candles, some weighing 100 pounds and others 50, some more and some less . . . carried by the residents of the villages [in the *contado*] which offer them. . . .

Then the lord priors and their colleges come to make their offerings, accompanied by their rectors, that is, the podestà, the captain [of the *popolo*], and the executor. . . . And after the lord [priors] come those who are participating in the horse race, and they are followed by the Flemings and the residents of Brabant who are weavers of woolen cloth in Florence. Then there are offerings by twelve prisoners who, as an act of mercy, have been released from prison . . . in honor of St. John, and these are poor people. . . . After all of these offerings have been made, men and women return home to dine. . . . [There follows a description of the horse race which takes place in the afternoon.]

C. Lorenzo de' Medici Totals up the Medicis' Spending on Public Display

To do as others had done, I held a joust in the Piazza S. Croce at great expense and with great pomp. I find we spent about 10,000 ducats. . . . Piero, our father, departed this life on July 2 . . . having been much tormented with gout. He would not make a will, but we drew up an inventory and found we possessed 237,988 scudi [a coin worth approximately a florin]. . . .

I find that from 1434 till now we have spent large sums of money, as appear in a small quarto notebook of the said year to the end of 1471. Incredible are the sums written down. They amount to 663,755 florins for alms, buildings, and taxes, let alone other expenses. But I do not regret this, for though many would consider it better to have a part of that sum in their purse, I consider that it gave great honor to our State, and I think the money was well expended, and am well pleased.

Document Set 14.6 References

A. The Duke of Burgundy Presides Over the Order of the Golden Fleece, 1461
   Paul M. Kendall and Vincent Ilardi, eds., *Dispatches with Related Documents of the Milanese Ambassadors to France and Burgundy, 1450–1483* (Athens, Ohio: Ohio University Press, 1971), 2:346–354.

B. Florentines Celebrate a Communal Ritual
   Gregorio Dati, in Gene Brucker, ed., *The Society of Renaissance Florence* (New York: Harper & Row, 1971), 75–78.

C. Lorenzo de' Medici Totals up the Medicis' Spending on Public Display
   Lorenzo de' Medici, in J. Ross, *Lives of the Early Medicis* (Boston: 1911), 134–135.

DOCUMENT SET 14.7
The End of the Byzantine Empire

The year 1453 is an epochal date in European history, marking the end of Christian Constantinople, which for a thousand years had stood as the capital of the eastern empire. Henceforth the city would be known as Istanbul, and its population would be islamicized.

Document A suggests one reason for this outcome: the Byzantine people's refusal to subject themselves to papal religious leadership in order to win Western support against the Turks. (How much aid the West would likely have sent even if the Byzantines had submitted to Rome is something that you should think about as you read *The Challenge of the West*.) The Turkish conquest of Constantinople is described—and the contrasting Muslim and Christian emotions evoked—in Documents B and C. Drawing upon these selections and the account in Chapter 14, write a brief account of the fall of Constantinople from the viewpoints of all three heirs of the ancient world: Orthodox Eastern Christianity, Latin Western Christianity, and Islam.

A. The Byzantines Reject the Council of Florence, 1439

At this time the schismatic party went to the Monastery of the Pantocrator, to the cell of Gennadios, the former George Scholarios, and asked him "What are we to do?" He was in seclusion in his cell, and taking a piece of paper he expressed his thoughts and counsel in writing. His words were: "Wretched Romans, how you have gone astray! You have rejected the hope of God and trusted in the strength of the Franks; you have lost your piety along with your city which is about to be destroyed. Lord have mercy on me. I testify before you that I am innocent of such transgression. Know, wretched citizens, what you are doing. Along with your impending captivity, you have forsaken the faith handed down from your fathers [*patroparadoton*] and assented to impiety. Woe unto you, when you are judged!" This and many other things he had written, he placed on the door of his cell; he secluded himself inside and what he wrote was read.

Then all the nuns, who believed themselves to be pure and dedicated servants of God in Orthodoxy, in accordance with their own sentiment and that of their teacher Gennadios, cried out the anathema, and along with them the abbots and confessors and the remaining priests and laymen. They condemned the doctrinal definition of the council [of Florence] and all those who had acquiesced to it, all those who were now acquiescing, and all who would do so in the future. The common and low-born people, leaving the courtyard of the monastery, entered into the taverns and, holding bottles of unwatered wine in their hands, anathematized the unionists and drank to the intercession of the icon of the Mother of God [the *Hodegetria*]. And they beseeched her to guard and aid the city now against Mehmed, as she had formerly done against Chosroës, Kaghan, and the Arabs. "We need neither the aid of the Latins nor Union. Keep the worship of the azymites far from us."

B. The Turks Exalt in the Fall of Constantinople

The fighting went on, day and night, for fifty days. On the fifty-first day the Sultan ordered free plunder. They attacked. On the fifty-first day, a Tuesday, the citadel was captured. There was good booty and plunder. Gold and silver and jewels and fine stuffs were brought and stacked in the camp market. They began to sell them. They made the people of the city slaves and killed their Emperor, and the gāzīs [soldiers] embraced their pretty girls. . . .

This victory was achieved by Sultan Mehmed Khan in the year 857 of the Hijira [1453].

C. The Byzantines Lament the Fall of Constantinople

And the entire City [its inhabitants and wealth] was to be seen in the tents of the [Turkish] camp, the city deserted, lying lifeless, naked, soundless, without either form or beauty. O City, City, head of all cities! O City, City, center of the four corners of the world! O City, City, pride of the Romans, civilizer of the barbarians! O City, second paradise planted toward the west, possessing all kinds of vegetation, laden with spiritual fruits! Where is your beauty, O paradise, where the beneficent strength of the charms of your spirit, soul, and body? Where are the bodies of the Apostles of my Lord, which were implanted long ago in the always-green paradise, having in their midst the purple cloak, the lance, the sponge, the reed, which, when we kissed them, made us believe that we were seeing him who was raised on the Cross? Where are the relics of the saints, those of the martyrs? Where the remains of Constantine the Great and the other emperors? Roads, courtyards, crossroads, fields, and vineyard enclosures, all teem with the relics of saints, with the bodies of nobles, of the chaste, and of male and female ascetics. Oh what a loss! "The dead bodies of thy servants, O Lord, have they given to be meat unto the fowls of the heaven, the flesh of thy saints unto the beasts of the earth round about New Sion and there was none to bury them [Psalm 78:2–3]."

O temple [Hagia Sophia]! O earthly heaven! O heavenly altar! O sacred and divine places! O magnificence of the churches! O holy books and words of God! O ancient and modern laws! O tablets inscribed by the finger of God! O Scriptures spoken by his mouth! O divine discourses of angels who bore flesh! O doctrines of men filled with the Holy Spirit! O

teachings of semi-divine heroes! O commonwealth! O citizens! O army, formerly beyond number, now removed from sight like a ship sunk into the sea! O houses and palaces of every type! O sacred walls! Today I invoke you all, and as if incarnate beings I mourn with you, having Jeremiah as [choral] leader of this lamentable tragedy!

Document Set 14.7 References

A. The Byzantines Reject the Council of Florence, 1439
   Ducas, *Historia Turcobyzantia, 1341–1462,* in Deno John Geanokoplos, ed., *Byzantium: Church, Society, and Civilization Seen Through Contemporary Eyes* (Chicago: University of Chicago Press, 1984), 225.
B. The Turks Exult in the Fall of Constantinople
   Naphtali Lewis, *Islam: From the Prophet Muhammed to the Capture of Constantinople* (New York: Walker, 1987), 145–146.
C. The Byzantines Lament the Fall of Constantinople
   Ducas, in Geanokoplos, 389.

DOCUMENT SET 14.8
Life in the Fifteenth-Century North

The documents in this chapter's final set can only hint at many important aspects of life north of the Alps. One way to read these six documents is to look for features that both recall late medieval life and point toward coming changes.

Document A is an account from the 1430s of the devastation that France suffered during the Hundred Years' War, a horrible experience that left the monarchy determined to consolidate its resources and overcome provincial disunity. Document B speaks to peacetime concerns in the ordinance of the Tailors' Guild in the English city of Exeter. It contrasts with much less settled conditions in Document C, which describes rural troubles that began when a Warwickshire gentleman, Henry Smith, converted common village lands to his private use in 1493, dispossessing the peasants. In Document D we return to France, where the "Spider King" Louis XI (1423–1483) is described in the memoirs of the observant French statesman Philippe de Commynes. Anything but a glamorous monarch, Louis ruthlessly gathered under tight central control the lands nominally subject to the French crown.

Document E originated in Germany but would exert a baleful influence throughout early modern Europe: an extract from the *Malleus Maleficarum* ("The Hammer of Witches") published with papal encouragement in 1486 by two Dominican friars, cataloging the alleged practices of witches and giving directions for their detection. (Notice how this document assumes that the accused is likely to be a woman.) Publication of the *Malleus Maleficarum* marked the onset of an obsessive, officially organized campaign against witchcraft that would convulse the West for 200 years. Equally disturbing (although it dates from the early sixteenth century), Document F, also from Germany, illustrates all too well the rampant antisemitism sweeping through that country's cities in the fifteenth century.

Using these documents in conjunction with your textbook, sketch out some elements of the popular "mentality" (a favorite historian's word) of north Europeans in this century marked by a waning of medieval culture and the first stirrings of the early modern era. Focus particularly on Europeans' anxieties—the changes and tensions in the air that convinced people that times were "out of joint" and evil forces were running rampant. Consider as well the evidence that you have extracted from Chapter 14's earlier sets. You will then have a good sense of European life on the eve of the Reformation.

A. France Emerges from the Hundred Years' War

. . . In his time, owing to the long wars which had raged within and without, the lethargy and cowardliness of the officers and commanders who were under him, the destruction of all military discipline and order, the rapacity of the troopers, and the general dissolution into which all things had fallen, such destruction had been wrought that from the river Loire to the Seine—even to the Somme,—the farmers were dead or had fled, and almost all the fields had for many years lain without cultivation or any one to cultivate them. A few districts might indeed be excepted, where if any agriculture remained, it was because they were far from cities, towns, or castles, and in consequence the constant excursions of the despoilers could not be extended to them. Lower Normandy, embracing the bishoprics of Bayeux and Coutances, which were under English rule, were far from the headquarters of the enemy, nor could they be easily reached by the depredators. They therefore remained somewhat better off in the matter of population and cultivators, but nevertheless were often afflicted by the greatest misfortunes, as will appear later.

We have ourselves beheld the vast regions of Champagne, Brie, Chartres, Perche, Beauvais, . . . Amiens, Abbeville, Soissons, Laon, and beyond toward Hainault, well-nigh deserted, untilled, without husbandmen, grown up to weeds and briers. In many places where fruit trees could flourish these had grown up into dense forests. The vestiges of such ruin, unless the divine clemency shall aid mere human endeavor, will, it is to be feared, last for long years to come.

If any kind of cultivation was still carried on in the regions enumerated, it could only be done close to cities, towns, or castles, no farther away than the watch could be seen, stationed on a high lookout, whence he could observe the robbers as they approached. He would then give the alarm by means of a bell, or a hunter's horn, to those in the fields or vineyard, so that they could betake themselves to a place of safety. This happened so frequently in many places that so soon as the oxen and plow animals were loosed, having heard the signal of the watch, they would, taught by long experience, rush to a place of safety in a state of terror. Even the pigs and sheep did the same.

B. The Tailors of Exeter Regulate Their Lives, 1466

To the worship of God and of our Lady Saint Mary, and of St. John the Baptist, and of all Saints; These be the ordinances made and established of the fraternity of the craft of tailors, of the city of Exeter, by assent and consent of the fraternity of the craft aforesaid gathered there together, for evermore to endure.

First, it is ordained, by virtue of the charter granted by our sovereign lord King Edward the Fourth, in the sixth year of his reign, that the master of the aforesaid craft for the time being, every Thursday shall be at the common hall, or else a deputy for him upon pain of two pounds of wax. And every warden that is absent without reasonable cause shall pay a pound of wax to the use and profit of the aforesaid fraternity; and that the aforesaid master and wardens be there every Thursday at nine of the clock, there to obtain and rule what may be for the welfare of the fraternity and craft aforesaid, and none to act without the other.

Also, it is ordained by the master and wardens and the common council aforesaid that every person who is privileged with the craft aforesaid who is of the value of £20 of goods and above, shall be of the masters' fellowship and clothing. And every person that is of the fellowship and the aforesaid craft shall pay, every year, for his feast, at Midsummer, 12d., and his offering; and for his clothing as it comes to, within a month from Midsummer day, upon pain of being put out of the aforesaid fraternity and craft for evermore. And every person that is so admitted shall pay a spoon of silver, weighing an ounce, and its fashioning.

Also, it is ordained that every out-brother, that is not privileged of the aforesaid fraternity and gild, shall pay every year 6d. at Midsummer. And if he refuse to pay this within a month from Midsummer, he is to be dismissed from the aforesaid fraternity and gild for evermore.

Also, it is ordained that all the fellowship of the bachelors shall hold their feast on St. John's day, in harvest. And every person that is a shop-holder of the aforesaid fellowship and craft shall pay to the aforesaid feast 8d. and his offering. And every servant that receiveth wages shall pay 6d. to the aforesaid feast. And every out-brother that is of the aforesaid fellow-ship shall pay, every year, 4d. And if any of the fellowship and craft aforesaid, refuse to pay this, then their names shall be certified to the master and wardens, that they may do correction therein, as belongeth to them to do, according to charter granted by the sovereign lord, the King Edward the Fourth, the sixth year of his reign, by assent and consent of the mayor, the bailiffs, and commons of the city of Exeter, for ever to endure.

Also, it is ordained by the aforesaid master and wardens and fellowship of the fraternity and craft aforesaid that every servant that is of the aforesaid craft that taketh wages to the value of 20s. and above shall pay 20d. to be a free sewer, to the use and profit of the aforesaid fraternity; that no man of the aforesaid craft set any new sewer to work above the space of fifteen days without bringing him before the master and wardens there to pay his 20d. to be made a free sewer, or else to find a surety.

Also it is ordained by the master and wardens aforesaid that if any person of the aforesaid craft who is bound to pay any debt over to the aforesaid master and wardens, breaks his day by the space of half a year, he shall forfeit his whole bond. Provided, always, that if any person or persons aforesaid have fallen into poverty, and will testify so by his oath, he shall be discharged of his bond and debt and shall have sustenance by the foresaid craft as may be thought, by their discretion, convenient and reasonable.

Also, it is ordained by the foresaid master and wardens that if any brother of the aforesaid fraternity and craft despise another, calling him knave, or whoreson, or stupid, or any other misname, he shall pay at the first fault, 12d.; at the second fault, 20d.; and at the third fault, to be put out of the fraternity and craft for evermore.

Also, it is ordained by the foresaid master and wardens and the whole fellowship, that if any brother of the aforesaid craft take any clothing of any lord, knight or gentlemen, outside of the city without leave of the master and wardens, at the first fault, 40s., and at the second fault to be put out of the fraternity and craft for evermore.

Also, it is ordained by the foresaid master and wardens that there shall be four quarter-days that every brother of this craft shall assemble at our common-hall. And every shop-holder shall spend 2d. for a breakfast, or send his money by a deputy. And at that the oath and the ordinances and constitutions shall be read. The first day shall be the next Thursday after Twelfth day, and the second day shall be the second Thursday after Easter, and the third day shall be the second Thursday after the feast of St. John the

Baptist, and the fourth day shall be the next Thursday after St. Michael's day. And at every of these foresaid days, after dinner there shall come all free sewers and take the remains of the meat and drink that the aforesaid master and shopholders leave; and each of them shall spend 1d. to the welfare of the aforesaid fraternity and gild.

Also, it is ordained by the master and wardens that at every coste of ale that is given into the aforesaid fraternity and gild, every shopholder shall spend thereto 1d., aud every free sewer one farthing, and he that cometh not shall send his money by the beadle, upon pain of one pound of wax.

Also, it is ordained by the master and wardens and all the whole craft, that from henceforth no man of the said craft shall hold more than three servants and one apprentice at the most, without license of the master and wardens for the time being, upon pain of 40s. and he that pleadeth for him that doth against this ordinance shall forfeit 20s.

Also, it is ordained by the master and wardens and all the whole craft, that every person of the said craft that taketh an apprentice shall bring him before the master and wardens, there to have his indenture enrolled, the master to pay 12d. for his enrollment. This is to be done within a twelvemonth and a day or else he is to lose his freedom of the craft for evermore.

Also, it is ordained by the master and wardens and the craft aforesaid that every apprentice of the said craft that is enrolled and truly serveth his covenant shall pay a silver spoon weighing an ounce and its fashioning, and shall give a breakfast to the foresaid master and wardens before the day that he is able to be made freeman of the city aforesaid; and if he pay not a spoon worth 4s., then 4s. in money for the same.

Also, it is ordained by the master and wardens and the whole fellowship that every person that shall be made free of the craft by redemption shall pay 20s. to his fine without any pardon; and when he is enabled, shall give a breakfast to the master and wardens, before he is admitted free man of the city. And every person so enabled from henceforth shall have, the first year, but one servant, the second year, two, the third, three, and an apprentice if he be able. And he that doeth against this ordinance shall forfeit, at the first fault, 20s. at the second offense, 40s., at the third offense, he shall be put out of the fraternity and craft for evermore.

C. Enclosures Disrupt Late Fifteenth-Century England

And the aforesaid jurors say that Henry Smith was recently seised in his demesne as of fee of 12 mes-

suages and 4 cottages, 640 acres of arable land to the annual value of 55*l* with appurtenances in Stretton super Street in the aforesaid county, and with each of the aforesaid messuages 40 acres of arable land, suitable for and ordinarily in cultivation, were accustomed to be let, farmed and occupied from time immemorial. Thus was the same Henry Smith seised on the 6th. December 9 Henry VII. He enclosed the messuages, cottages and lands with ditches and banks and he wilfully caused the same messuages and cottages to be demolished and laid waste and he converted them from the use of cultivation and arable husbandry into pasture for brute animals. Thus he holds them to this day, on account of which 12 ploughs that were employed in the cultivation of those lands are withdrawn and 80 persons, who similarly were occupied in the same cultivation, and who dwelled in the said messuages and cottages, were compelled to depart tearfully against their will. Since then they have remained idle and thus they lead a miserable existence, and indeed they die wretched. What is more to be lamented is [that] the church of Stretton on that occasion fell into ruin and decay, so that the Christian congregation, which used to gather there to hear the divine offices, is no longer held there and the worship of God is almost at an end. In the church animals are sheltered from the storms of the air and brute animals feed among the tombs of Christian bodies in the churchyard. In all things the church and burial-place are profaned to the evil example of others inclined to act in such a manner.

D. Louis XI of France Hunts and Schemes

Small hopes and comfort ought poor and inferior people to have in this world, considering what so great a king suffered and underwent, and how he was at last forced to leave all, and could not, with all his care and diligence, protract his life one single hour. I knew him, and was entertained in his service in the flower of his age and at the height of his prosperity, yet I never saw him free from labor and care.

Of all diversions he loved hunting and hawking in their seasons, but his chief delight was in dogs. . . . In hunting, his eagerness and pain were equal to his pleasure, for his chase was the stag, which he always ran down. He rose very early in the morning, rode sometimes a great distance, and would not leave his sport, let the weather be never so bad. And when he came home at night he was often very weary and generally in a violent passion with some of his courtiers or huntsmen; for hunting is a sport not always to be managed according to the master's direction; yet, in the opinion of most people, he understood it as well as any prince of his time. He was continually at these sports, lodging in the country villages to which his recreations led him, till he was interrupted by business; for during the most part of the summer there was constantly war between him and Charles, duke of Burgundy, while in the winter they made truces. . . .

When his body was at rest his mind was at work, for he had affairs in several places at once, and would concern himself as much in those of his neighbors as in his own, putting officers of his own over all the great families, and endeavoring to divide their authority as much as possible. When he was at war he labored for a peace or a truce, and when he had obtained it he was impatient for war again. He troubled himself with many trifles in his government which he had better have let alone; but it was his temper, and he could not help it. Besides, he had a prodigious memory, and he forgot nothing, but knew everybody, as well in other countries as in his own. . . .

I am of opinion that if all the days of his life were computed in which his joys and pleasures outweighed his pain and trouble, they would be found so few, that there would be twenty mournful ones to one pleasant. He lived about sixty-one years, yet he always fancied he should never outlive sixty, giving this for a reason, that for a long time no king of France had lived beyond that age. . . .

E. The *Malleus Maleficarum* Tells How to Torture a Suspected Witch

The method of beginning an examination by torture is as follows: First, the jailers prepare the implements of torture, then they strip the prisoner (if it be a woman, she has already been stripped by other women, upright and of good report). This stripping is lest some means of witchcraft may have been sewed into the clothing—such as often, taught by the Devil, they prepare from the bodies of unbaptized infants, [murdered] that they may forfeit salvation. And when the implements of torture have been prepared, the judge, both in person and through other good men zealous in the faith, tries to persuade the prisoner to confess the truth freely; but, if he will not confess, he bids attendants make the prisoner fast to the strappado or some other implement of torture. The attendants obey forthwith, yet with feigned agitation. Then, at the prayer of some of those present, the prisoner is loosed again and is taken aside and once more

persuaded to confess, being led to believe that he will in that case not be put to death.

Here it may be asked whether the judge, in the case of a prisoner much defamed, convicted both by witnesses and by proofs, nothing being lacking but his own confession, can properly lead him to hope that his life will be spared—when, even if he confess his crime, he will be punished with death.

It must be answered that opinions vary. Some hold that even a witch of very ill repute, against whom the evidence justifies violent suspicion, and who, as a ringleader of the witches, is accounted very dangerous, may be assured her life, and condemned instead to perpetual imprisonment on bread and water, in case she will give sure and convincing testimony against other witches; yet this penalty of perpetual imprisonment must not be announced to her, but only that her life will be spared, and that she will be punished in some other fashion, perhaps by exile. And doubtless such notorious witches, especially those who prepare witch-potions or who by magical methods cure those bewitched, would be peculiarly suited to be thus preserved, in order to aid the bewitched or to accuse other witches, were it not that their accusations cannot be trusted, since the Devil is a liar, unless confirmed by proofs and witnesses.

Others hold, as to this point, that for a time the promise made to the witch sentenced to imprisonment is to be kept, but that after a time she should be burned.

A third view is, that the judge may safely promise witches to spare their lives, if only he will later excuse himself from pronouncing the sentence and will let another do this in his place. . . .

But if, neither by threats nor by promises such as these, the witch can be induced to speak the truth, then the jailers must carry out the sentence, and torture the prisoner according to the accepted methods, with more or less of severity as the delinquent's crime may demand. And, while he is being tortured, he must be questioned on the articles of accusation, and this frequently and persistently, beginning with the lighter charges—for he will more readily confess the lighter than the heavier. And, while this is being done, the notary must write down everything in his record of the trial—how the prisoner is tortured, on what points he is questioned, and how he answers.

And note that, if he confesses under the torture, he must afterward be conducted to another place, that he may confirm it and certify that it was not due alone to the force of the torture.

But, if the prisoner will not confess the truth satisfactorily, other sorts of tortures must be placed before him, with the statement that, unless he will confess the truth, he must endure these also. But, if not even thus he can be brought into terror and to the truth, then the next day or the next but one is to be set for a *continuation* of the tortures—not a *repetition,* for they must not be repeated unless new evidences be produced.

The judge must then address to the prisoners the following sentence: We, the judge, etc., do assign to you, —, such and such a day for the continuation of the tortures, that from your own mouth the truth may be heard, and that the whole may be recorded by the notary.

And during the interval, before the day assigned, the judge, in person or through approved men, must in the manner above described try to persuade the prisoner to confess, promising her (if there is aught to be gained by this promise) that her life shall be spared.

The judge shall see to it, moreover, that throughout this interval guards are constantly with the prisoner, so that she may not be left alone; because she will be visited by the Devil and tempted into suicide.

F. "How the Jews Were Driven from Regensburg"

Among the Christians were a few
Felt pity for the wretched Jew;
These loved not God and felt no urge
To venerate the Holy Church.
But other men were free of blame;
Among them Thomas Fuchs I name . . .

By murder and usury, the Jews
Had done our city grave abuse.
Stirred by laments from young and old,
By pleas from all the land, I'm told,
The council acted. Otherwise,
Had council members shut their eyes
And left the Jews in impunity
They would have wrecked our community.
May our brave councillors be blessed
For having rid us of this pest.
God's purpose was behind their action,
For our Lord feels satisfaction
Whenever Jews are driven from
A famous city in Christendom.
God heeds the cries of honest folk

Excerpt from "How the Jews Were Driven from Regensberg" from Gerald Strauss, *Manifestations of Discontent in Germany on the Eve of the Reformation*, pp. 124–129. Reprinted by permission of Indiana University Press.

Oppressed beneath the Jewish yoke.
No craftsmen's income is too small
For Jews to demand it all.
He needs a suit, a pair of shoes?

Off he goes trudging to the Jews;
There he finds pewter, silver plate,
Velvet and linen stuffs, brocade,
The things that he himself not owns
Jews hold as pledges for their loans,
Or buy from highwayman and thief
To make their pile from Christian grief.
Stolen or found, cheap stuff or rare,
Look at the Jew's; you'll find it there.
He's got the cash to lend on it,
No questions asked, depend on it.
A piece worth fifty gulden when
Bought new, the Jew gets it for ten,
Holds on to it two weeks or three,
Then claims it as his property,
Converts his house into a store
With pants and coats stuffed roof to floor;
A cobbler can't sell a pair of shoes,
Townfolk buy only from the Jews.

But these misdeeds, though they are cursed
By all the world, are not their worst.
A graver crime and fouler deed
Lies on this Godforsaken breed.
Obstinate, blind, faithless toward
Their patient, kind, forgiving Lord,
They've always sinned, never repent,
As we learn from the Old Testament.
The five books of Moses, the Book of Kings
Show how the Jew to his habits clings;
They prove it to satiety:
Jews are a race without piety.
We're told by wise old Jeremiah
That they killed their prophets with sword and fire.
David, among their kings the first,
They sent to hell despised and cursed.
Moses, a demigod to Jews,
They covered with hatred and abuse.
No wonder, given such behavior,
They crucified God's son, our savior.
They're in the dark, can't see the clearing,
They'll never give their prophets hearing,
Must live forever in God's ban;
Who gives them aid is no Christian man.

Jewish malignity was foretold
by the prophet Isaiah in days of old;
And if further evidence you desire,
Ask Doctor Balthasar Hubmair

To tell you why it is that we
Treat the Jews with such hostility.
He'll waste no time convincing you
(By quoting God's own Gospel, too)
That there's no punishment too painful
For a tribe so openly disdainful
Not only of Christ, their adversary,
But of his mother, the Virgin Mary.
For a Christian there's no sin so great
As to merit a Jew's love, not his hate.
Unceasingly the Jewish swine
Scheme how to violate, malign,
Dishonor the pure Virgin Maid,
Our Christian solace, hope, and aid,
Whose son died on the cross that we
Might live in bliss eternally.
No city therefore can fare well
Until it's sent its Jews to hell.

Now listen and pay careful heed
To a horrendous, bestial deed
Of Christian blood shed without pity
By murderous Jews in our city.
It happened in Emperor Frederick's reign;
Six children they killed with dreadful pain.
Into a dungeon then they threw them
To hide the bodies, bleeding and gruesome.
But soon their crime was indicated,
All of the Jews incarcerated,
And the burghers resolved, for the Virgin's sake,
To burn the damned Jews at the stake.
But—though to tell it is a disgrace—
The Jews found help in an exalted place.
Our council spent what money it could
To keep the Jews from winning their suit,
But with the emperor to defend
Their case, the Jews won in the end.
This caused complaints and lamentations;
Citizens sent deputations
To ask why Jewish dogs who spilled
Pure Christian blood should not be killed.
As for the Jews, they caught the drift
Of things, made many a handsome gift
Where money counts; their silver and gold
Regained for them their old foothold.
The burghers would have burned the Jews,
But the emperor saw fit to refuse.
The might and glory of his crown
Served to keep Jews in our town.
Our councillors resented this intervention,
Which frustrated their good intention
Of just revenge on the blaspheming Jew
For the innocent children whom they slew.

The gold sent abroad also caused them grief;
It could have been used for poor relief.
Three years they wasted in vain appeal,
But the emperor adhered to his deal.
Nothing the councilors could say
Would change his mind; the Jews must stay.

For forty years we pressed our case
Against the murderous Jewish race.
Of money paid out, the total score
Was a hundred and thirty-five thousand gulden or
      more;
The city registers record it.
Our citizens could scarcely afford it,
While the Jews, who had much more to spend,
Bribed the emperor's courtiers to pretend
To Maximilian, double-tongued,
That the Jews of Regensburg had been wronged.
Money makes lies like truth appear,
And the facts were kept from the emperor's ear.
Thus matters stood, justice defied,
Until the day Maximilian died,
And God eliminated a few
Of our Jew-loving burghers, too,
Which left the Jews without a friend
Their horrid actions to defend.
That's all I'll say about them here,
Their stubborn blindness cost them dear.
We're free at last of their oppressions;
May God forgive them their transgressions.

Document Set 14.8 References

A. France Emerges from the Hundred Years' War
   French account, in James Harvey Robinson, ed., *Readings in European History* (Boston: Ginn, 1904), 1:474–475.
B. The Tailors of Exeter Regulate Their Lives, 1466
   Ordinances of the Gild of the Tailors, in *Smith's English Gilds* (Early English Text Society, 1870), 312–316.
C. Enclosures Disrupt Late Fifteenth-Century England
   Government report, in H. E. S. Fisher and A. R. J. Jurica, eds., *Documents in English Economic History* (London: G. Bell, 1977), 1:117.
D. Louis XI of France Hunts and Schemes
   Commynes, *Memoirs*, in James Harvey Robinson, ed., *Readings in European History* (Boston: Ginn, 1904), 1:481–483.
E. The *Malleus Maleficarum* Tells How to Torture a Suspected Witch
   Translations and Reprints from the Original Sources of European History (Philadelphia: University of Pennsylvania Press, 1898), 3/2:11–13.
F. "How the Jews Were Driven from Regensburg"
   Anonymous verse, in Gerald Strauss, *Manifestations of Discontent in Germany on the Eve of the Reformation* (Bloomington: University of Indiana Press, 1971), 124–129.

15

The Struggle for Faith and Power, 1494–1560

DOCUMENT SET 15.1
Wider Horizons in the Old World: The Portuguese Explore Africa and the East

Seeking to outflank middlemen and trade for gold at the source, fifteenth-century Portuguese adventurers explored farther and farther south along the coast of West Africa as they simultaneously learned the vital skill of tacking back north against winds and currents. As early as the mid-fifteenth century, they began establishing trading posts in West Africa. Document A, by a Venetian who sailed with the Portuguese as far as present-day Mauretania, describes how the Europeans were also discovering a lucrative trade in African slaves. This is one of the earliest sources documenting the European-African encounter and the Atlantic slave trade; read it for evidence of the attitudes on both sides.

Document B was written three-quarters of a century later. The Portuguese had by then rounded the Cape, reached India, and blazed a commercial route to Canton (Guangchou) in southern China. It is instructive reading for the mind-sets that it reveals.

A. The Portuguese Encounter Africans and the Slave Trade, 1455–1456

You should also know that behind this Cauo Bianco on the land, is a place called Hoden,[1] which is about

[1] Wadan, an important desert market about 350 miles east of Arguim. Later, in 1487, when the Portuguese were endeavouring to penetrate the interior they attempted to establish a trading factory at Wadan which acted as a feeder to Arguim, tapping the north-bound caravan traffic and diverting some of it to the west coast.

six days inland by camel. This place is not walled, but is frequented by Arabs, and is a market where the caravans arrive from Tanbutu [Timbuktu], and from other places in the land of the Blacks, on their way to our nearer Barbary. The food of the peoples of this place is dates, and barley, of which there is sufficient, for they grow in some of these places, but not abundantly. They drink the milk of camels and other animals, for they have no wine. They also have cows and goats, but not many, for the land is dry. Their oxen and cows, compared with ours, are small.

They are Muhammadans, and very hostile to Christians. They never remain settled, but are always wandering over these deserts. These are the men who go to the land of the Blacks, and also to our nearer Barbary. They are very numerous, and have many camels on which they carry brass and silver from Barbary and other things to Tanbuto and to the land of the Blacks. Thence they carry away gold and pepper, which they bring hither. They are brown complexioned, and wear white cloaks edged with a red stripe: their women also dress thus, without shifts. On their heads the men wear turbans in the Moorish fashion, and they always go barefooted. In these sandy districts there are many lions, leopards, and ostriches, the eggs of which I have often eaten and found good.

You should know that the said Lord Infante of Portugal [the crown prince, Henry the Navigator] has leased this island of Argin to Christians [for ten years], so that no one can enter the bay to trade with the Arabs save those who hold the license. These have dwellings on the island and factories where they buy and sell with the said Arabs who come to the coast to trade for merchandise of various kinds, such as woollen cloths, cotton, silver, and "alchezeli," that is, cloaks, carpets, and similar articles and above all, corn, for they are always short of food. They give in exchange slaves whom the Arabs bring from the land of the Blacks, and gold *tiber*. The Lord Infante therefore caused a castle to be built on the island to protect this trade for ever. For this reason, Portuguese caravels are coming and going all the year to this island.

These Arabs also have many Berber horses, which they trade, and take to the Land of the Blacks, exchanging them with the rulers for slaves. Ten or fifteen slaves are given for one of these horses, according to their quality. The Arabs likewise take articles of Moorish silk, made in Granata and in Tunis of Barbary, silver, and other goods, obtaining in exchange any number of these slaves, and some gold. These slaves are brought to the market and town of Hoden; there they are divided: some go to the mountains of Barcha, and thence to Sicily, [others to the said town of Tunis and to all the coasts of Barbary], and others again are taken to this place, Argin, and sold to the Portuguese leaseholders. As a result every year the Portuguese carry away from Argin a thousand slaves. Note that before this traffic was organized, the Portuguese caravels, sometimes four, sometimes more, were wont to come armed to the Golfo d'Argin, and descending on the land by night, would assail the fisher villages, and so ravage the land. Thus they took of these Arabs both men and women, and carried them to Portugal for sale: behaving in a like manner along all the rest of the coast, which stretches from Cauo Bianco to the Rio di Senega and even beyond. . . .

B. Portuguese Emissaries Reach China, 1517

God grant that these Chinese may be fools enough to lose the country; because up to the present they have had no dominion, but little by little they have gone on taking the land from their neighbours; and for this reason the kingdom is great, because the Chinese are full of much cowardice, and hence they come to be presumptuous, arrogant, cruel; and because up to the present, being a cowardly people, they have managed without arms and without any practice of war, and have always gone on getting the land from their neighbors, and not by force but by stratagems and deceptions; and they imagine that no one can do them harm. They call every foreigner a savage; and their country they call the kingdom of God. Whoever shall come now, let it be a captain with a fleet of ten or fifteen sail. The first thing will be to destroy the fleet if they should have one, which I believe they have not; let it be by fire and blood and cruel fear for this day, without sparing the life of a single person, every junk being burnt, and no one being taken prisoner, in order not to waste the provisions, because at all times a hundred Chinese will be found for one Portuguese. And this done, Nanto must be cleared, and at once they will have a fortress and provisions if they wish, because it will at once be in their power; and then with the whole fleet attack Aynācha, which lies at the bar of Tācoam, as I have already said above having a good port. Here the ships, which cannot enter the river, will be anchored, and whatever craft they may have will be burnt; and after it has been taken if it seem good the town can be burnt, in order to terrify the Chinese. . . .

Document Set 15.1 References

A. The Portuguese Encounter Africans and the Slave Trade, 1455–1456
   Alvise da Ca' da Mosto, "Description of Capo Bianco and the Islands Nearest to It," in J. H. Parry, *European Reconnaissance: Selected Documents* (New York: Walker, 1968), 59–61.
B. Portuguese Emissaries Reach China, 1517
   Letters from Canton, trans. and ed. D. Ferguson, *The Indian Antiquary* 31 (Jan. 1902): 10–30, in Perry, *European Reconnaissance*, 140.

DOCUMENT SET 15.2
New Worlds: America

Except for Brazil, the lands of the Western Hemisphere fell to explorers sent out by the Spanish rather than by the Portuguese crown. Document A, describing one of the earliest European contacts with Native Americans, is dated November 8, 1492. It is an extract from Christopher Columbus's log, entered one month after his first landfall in the Bahamas. Here he meets the native population of Cuba. In what ways does Columbus suggest what was to be the Indians' subsequent fate, and why?

By 1518, Spain had already done so thorough a job of carving out colonies in the Caribbean that Castilian adventurers like Hernando Cortés were itching to seek new lands to conquer. Mexico, which Cortés and his small band of soldiers attacked, was a sophisticated civilization and a highly organized state. Cortés's letters to Charles V reported the progress of his conquest, reflecting both admiration for the grandeur of Aztec urban civilization and disgust at the human sacrifices and cannibalism with which the Aztecs coerced their subjects. Evaluate his letters describing Tenochtitlán (today Mexico City) as a valuable source of early ethnography and a justification for imperialism.

The conduct of the new Spanish lords of the Caribbean was harshly criticized by Dominican friars like Fray Anton Montesino. Document C is taken from the famous account of another Dominican, Bartolomé de las Casas (1474–1566), who had first come to Hispaniola as a layman to join in its exploitation but was converted to becoming the Indians' defender by witnessing horrors such as Montesino here describes. Evaluate the source of the Dominicans' concerns and what they proposed to do to halt the atrocities.

Document D is an extract from a mid-sixteenth-century Venetian ambassador's report. The gold and silver pouring into Spain from the Americas astonished everyone, but its chief economic impact was to touch off sustained inflation throughout Europe as the Spanish monarchy turned its gold into money with which to settle the enormous debts that its wars and diplomacy incurred. Read this document for signs of the ambassador's understanding of what was occurring.

A. Christopher Columbus Reaches Land, 1492

It appears to me that it would be well to take some of these people . . . to the Sovereigns, in order that they might learn our language and we might learn what there is in this country. Upon return they may speak the language of the Christians and take our customs and Faith to their people. I see and know that these people have no religion whatever, nor are they idolaters, but rather, they are very meek and know no evil. They do not kill or capture others and are without weapons. They are so timid that a hundred of them flee from one of us. . . . They are very trusting; they believe that there is a God in Heaven, and they firmly believe that we come from Heaven. . . . Therefore, Your Highnesses must resolve to make them Christians. I believe that if this effort commences, in a short time a multitude of peoples will be converted to our Holy Faith, and Spain will acquire great domains and riches and all of their villages. Beyond doubt there is a very great amount of gold in this country. . . .

B. Hernando Cortez Approaches Tenochtitlán, 1521

This great city of Tenochtitlán is built on the salt lake. . . . It has four approaches by means of artificial causeways. . . . The city is as large as Seville or Cordoba. Its streets . . . are very broad and straight, some of these, and all the others, are one half land, and the other half water on which they go about in canoes. . . . There are bridges, very large, strong, and well constructed, so that, over many, ten horsemen can ride abreast. . . . The city has many squares where markets are held. . . . There is one square, twice as large as that of Salamanca, all surrounded by arcades, where there are daily more than sixty thousand souls, buying and selling . . . in the service and manners of its people, their fashion of living was almost the same as in Spain, with just as much harmony and order; and considering that these people were barbarous, so cut off from the knowledge of God and other civilized peoples, it is admirable to see to what they attained in every respect. [Second letter]

It happened . . . that a Spaniard saw an Indian . . . eating a piece of flesh taken from the body of an Indian who had been killed. . . . I had the culprit burned, explaining that the cause was his having killed that Indian and eaten him which was prohibited by Your Majesty, and by me in Your Royal name. I further made the chief understand that all the people . . . must abstain from this custom. . . . I came . . . to protect their lives as well as their property, and to teach them that they were to adore but one God . . . that they must turn from their idols, and the rites they had practised until then, for these were lies and deceptions which the devil . . . had invented. . . . I, likewise, had come to teach them that Your Majesty, by the will of Divine Providence, rules the universe, and that they also must submit themselves to the imperial yoke, and do all that we who are Your Majesty's ministers here might order them. . . . [Fifth letter]

C. Antón Montesino Preaches in Hispaniola

The Dominican friars had already pondered on the sad life and harsh captivity suffered by the natives on the island and had noticed the Spanish lack of concern for their fate except as a business loss which brought about no softening of their oppression. There were two kinds of Spaniards, one very cruel and pitiless, whose goal was to squeeze the last drop of Indian blood in order to get rich, and one less cruel, who must have felt sorry for the Indians; but in each case they placed their own interests above the health and salvation of those poor people. Of all those who used Indians, I knew only one man, Pedro de Rentería—of whom there will be much to say later, if God so wills—who was pious toward them. The friars, then, weighed these matters as well as the innocence, the inestimable patience and the gentleness of Indians, and deliberated on the following points among themselves. Weren't these people human beings? Wasn't justice and charity owed them? Had they no right to their own territory, their own kingdoms? Have they offended us? Aren't we under obligation to preach to them the Christian religion and work diligently toward their conversion? How is it that in fifteen or sixteen years their number has so decreased, since they tell us how crowded it was when they first came here? . . .

The most scholarly among them [the Dominicans] composed the first sermon on the subject by order of their superior, fray Pedro de Córdoba, and they all signed it to show that it represented common sentiment and not that of the preacher alone. They gave it to their most important preacher, Fray Antón Montesino, who was the second of

three preachers the Order had sent here. Fray Antón Montesino's talent lay in a certain sternness when reproaching faults and a certain way of reading sermons both choleric and efficient, which was thought to reap great results. So then, as a very animated speaker, they gave him that first sermon on such a new theme; the novelty consisting in saying that killing a man is more serious than killing a beetle. They set aside the fourth week of Advent for the sermon, since the Gospel according to St. John that week is "The Pharisees asked St. John the Baptist who he was and he said: *Ego vox clamantis in deserto.*" ["I am a voice crying in the wilderness."] The whole city of Santo Domingo was to be there, including the admiral Diego Columbus, and all the jurists and royal officials, who had been notified each and every one individually to come and hear a sermon of great importance. They accepted readily, some out of respect for the virtue of the friars; others, out of curiosity to hear what was to be said that concerned them so much, though had they known, they would have refused to come and would have censured the sermon as well.

At the appointed time fray Antón Montesino went to the pulpit and announced the theme of the sermon: *Ego vox clamantis in deserto.* After the introductory words on Advent, he compared the sterility of the desert to the conscience of the Spaniards who lived on Hispaniola in a state of blindness, a danger of damnation, sunk deep in the waters of insensitivity and drowning without being aware of it. Then he said: "I have come here in order to declare it unto you, I the voice of Christ in the desert of this island. Open your hearts and your senses, all of you, for this voice will speak new things harshly, and will be frightening." For a good while the voice spoke in such punitive terms that the congregation trembled as if facing Judgment Day. "This voice," he continued, "says that you are living in deadly sin for the atrocities you tyrannically impose on these innocent people. Tell me, what right have you to enslave them? What authority did you use to make war against them who lived at peace on their territories, killing them cruelly with methods never before heard of? How can you oppress them and not care to feed or cure them, and work them to death to satisfy your greed? And why don't you look after their spiritual health, so that they should come to know God, that they should be baptized, and that they should hear Mass and keep the holy days? Aren't they human beings? Have they no rational soul? Aren't you obligated to love them as you love yourselves? Don't you understand? How can you live in such a lethargical dream? You may rest assured that you are in no better state of salvation than the Moors [Muslims of Spain] or the Turks who reject the Christian Faith." The voice had astounded them all; some reacted as if they had lost their senses, some were petrified and others showed signs of repentance, but no one was really convinced. After his sermon, he descended from the pulpit holding his head straight, as if unafraid—he wasn't the kind of man to show fear—for much was at stake in displeasing the audience by speaking what had to be said, and he went on to his thin cabbage soup and the straw house of his Order accompanied by a friend. . . .

[Although the settlers request that the Dominicans apologize, Frey Montesino preaches again.]

　　To return to the subject: they left the church in a state of rage and again salted their meal that day with bitterness. Not bothering with the friars, since conversation with them had proved useless, they decided to tell the King [Ferdinand] on the first occasion that the Dominicans had scandalized the world by spreading a new doctrine that condemned them all to Hell because they used Indians in the mines, a doctrine that went against the orders of His Highness and aimed at nothing else but to deprive him of both power and a source of income. The King required an interview with the Castilian provincial of the Order—the friars of Hispaniola had not yet been granted a charter—and complained to him about his choice of friars, who had done him a great disservice by preaching against the state and causing disturbances all over the world. The King ordered him to correct this by threatening to take action. You see how easy it is to deceive a King, how ruinous to a kingdom it is to heed misinformation, and how oppression thrives where truth is not allowed a voice.

D. A Venetian Ambassador Reports on Spain's Apparent Wealth from the Gold of the Indies, 1559

From New Spain are obtained gold and silver, cochineal (little insects like flies), from which crim-

son dye is made, leather, cotton, sugar and other things; but from Peru nothing is obtained except minerals. The fifth part of all that is produced goes to the king, but since the gold and silver is brought to Spain and he has a tenth part of that which goes to the mint and is refined and coined, he eventually gets one-fourth of the whole sum, which fourth does not exceed in all four or five hundred thousand ducats, although it is reckoned not alone at millions, but at millions of pounds. Nor is it likely that it will long remain at this figure, because great quantities of gold and silver are no longer found upon the surface of the earth, as they have been in past years; and to penetrate into the bowels of the earth requires greater effort, skill and outlay, and the Spaniards are not willing to do the work themselves, and the natives cannot be forced to do so, because the Emperor has freed them from all obligation of service as soon as they accept the Christian religion. Wherefore it is necessary to acquire negro slaves, who are brought from the coasts of Africa, both within and without the Straits, and these are selling dearer every day, because on account of their natural lack of strength and the change of climate, added to the lack of discretion upon the part of their masters in making them work too hard and giving them too little to eat, they fall sick and the greater part of them die.

Document Set 15.2 References

A. Christopher Columbus Reaches Land, 1492
　　The Log of Christopher Columbus, trans. Robert H. Fuson (Camden, Maine: International Marine, 1987), 106–107.
B. Hernando Cortez Approaches Tenochtitlán, 1521
　　Letters of Cortes, trans. Francis A. MacNutt (New York: 1908), 1:256–257, 2:244.
C. Anton Montesino Preaches in Hispaniola
　　B. de Las Casas, *History of the Indies,* trans. and ed. Andrée Collard (New York: Harper & Row, 1971), 181–187.
D. A Venetian Ambassador Reports on Spain's Apparent Wealth from the Gold of the Indies, 1559
　　Michele Soriano, *Relazione di Spagna,* in *Translations and Reprints from the Original Sources of European History* (Philadelphia: University of Pennsylvania Press, 1898), 3/3:5–6.

DOCUMENT SET 15.3
New Worlds: The Cosmos

America, Africa, and the East were not the only "New Worlds" that Europeans encountered at the beginning of the sixteenth century. New vistas also opened as a handful of Western thinkers began to contemplate the universe anew. In his secret notebooks, the great artist and thinker Leonardo da Vinci (1452–1519) entered, at some unknown date, the cryptic speculations about the sun that form Document A. Exactly where Leonardo may have gotten his ideas (if they were not wholly original with him) is unclear, but it should be remembered that Leonardo was not formally trained in philosophy or science and hence was free, indeed scornful, of traditional learning based on ancient authority.

Nicholas Copernicus (1473–1543) differed from Leonardo in having received a thorough technical education in mathematics and astronomy, but he resembled the Italian artist in his wish to keep his speculations secret until they could be properly understood by the competent few. At some point in the early sixteenth century (experts differ as to the date), he set down his revolutionary thoughts about the cosmos in an unpublished manuscript known as the *Commentariolus* ("little commentary"), excerpted here as Document B. Copernicus proceeded to spend the rest of his life working out the mathematics to support his new hypothesis, while also carrying out the duties of a cathedral canon and administrator in a remote corner of what used to be called East Prussia. Notice Copernicus's reasoning in the *Commentariolus* and his profound awareness of the precedents of ancient Greek thought; all his life he thought himself merely the *corrector*, not the supplanter of Ptolemy. Copernicus was reluctant to publish his masterwork *On the Revolutions of the Heavenly Bodies,* in which he demonstrated his theories mathematically—probably he feared ridicule, and certainly he knew that only an expert could understand what he had to say. In 1542 a German scholar finally persuaded him to publish, and when the first copy came off the press in 1543, the author lay on his deathbed. The editor (Andreas Osiander) wrote a preface (Document C) that completely distorted what Copernicus meant the book to assert. The ways in which conventionally educated Europeans reacted to news that an obscure Polish astronomer had questioned the physical reality of Ptolemy's and Aristotle's universe may be gauged from Martin Luther's off-the-cuff remarks (Document D).

A. Leonardo da Vinci Speculates on the Cosmos

Demonstration that the Earth is a Star

In your discourse you must prove that the earth is a star much like the moon, and the glory of our universe; and then you must treat of the size of various stars according to the authors.

The sun does not move.

The sun has substance, shape, motion, radiance, heat, and generative power: and these qualities all emanate from it without its diminution.

The sun has never seen any shadow.

Praise of the Sun

If you look at the stars without their rays (as may be done by looking at them through a small hole made with the extreme point of a fine needle and placed so as almost to touch the eye), you will see these stars to be so minute that it would seem as though nothing could be smaller; it is in fact the great distance which is the reason of their diminution, for many of them are very many times larger than the star which is the earth with the water. Think, then, what this star of ours would seem like at so great a distance, and then consider how many stars might be set in longitude and latitude between these stars which are scattered throughout this dark expanse. I can never do other than blame many of those ancients who said that the sun was no larger than it appears; among these being Epicurus; and I believe that he reasoned thus from the effects of a light placed in our atmosphere equidistant from the centre; whoever sees it never sees it diminished in size at any distance. . . .

But I wish I had words to serve me to blame those who would fain extol the worship of men above that of the sun; for in the whole universe I do not see a body of greater magnitude and power than this, and its light illumines all the celestial bodies which are distributed throughout the universe. All vital force descends from it since the heat that is in living creatures comes from the soul (vital spark); and there is no other heat nor light in the universe. . . . And certainly those who have chosen to worship men as gods such as Jove, Saturn, Mars, and the like have made a very great error, seeing that even if a man were as large as our earth he would seem like one of the least of the stars which appears but a speck in the universe; and seeing also that men are mortal and subject to decay and corruption in their tombs.

The Spera and Marullo and many others praise the sun.

B. Nicholas Copernicus Explains His First Heliocentric Hypothesis, 1520s

Our ancestors assumed, I observe, a large number of celestial spheres for this reason especially, to explain the apparent motion of the planets by the principle of regularity. For they thought it altogether absurd that a heavenly body, which is a perfect sphere, should not always move uniformly. They saw that by connecting and combining regular motions in various ways they could make any body appear to move to any position.

Callippus and Eudoxus, who endeavored to solve the problem by the use of concentric spheres, were unable to account for all the planetary movements; they had to explain not merely the apparent revolutions of the planets but also the fact that these bodies appear to us sometimes to mount higher in the heavens, sometimes to descend; and this fact is incompatible with the principle of concentricity. Therefore it seemed better to employ eccentrics and epicycles, a system which most scholars finally accepted.

Yet the planetary theories of Ptolemy and most other astronomers, although consistent with the numerical data, seemed likewise to present no small difficulty. For these theories were not adequate unless certain equants were also conceived; it then appeared that a planet moved with uniform velocity neither on its deferent nor about the center of its epicycle. Hence a system of this sort seemed neither sufficiently absolute nor sufficiently pleasing to the mind.

Having become aware of these defects, I often considered whether there could perhaps be found a more reasonable arrangement of circles, from which every apparent inequality would be derived and in which everything would move uniformly about its proper center, as the rule of absolute motion requires. After I had addressed myself to this very difficult and almost insoluble problem, the suggestion at length came to me how it could be solved with fewer and much simpler constructions than were formerly used, if some assumptions (which are called axioms) were granted me. They follow in this order.

Assumptions

1. There is no one center of all the celestial circles or spheres.

2. The center of the earth is not the center of the universe, but only of gravity and of the lunar sphere.

3. All the spheres revolve about the sun as their mid-point, and therefore the sun is the center of the universe.

4. The ratio of the earth's distance from the sun to the height of the firmament is so much smaller than the ratio of the earth's radius to its distance from the sun that the distance from the earth to the sun is imperceptible in comparison with the height of the firmament.

5. Whatever motion appears in the firmament arises not from any motion of the firmament, but from the earth's motion. The earth together with its circumjacent elements performs a complete rotation on its fixed poles in a daily motion, while the firmament and highest heaven abide unchanged.

6. What appear to us as motions of the sun arise not from its motion but from the motion of the earth and our sphere, with which we revolve about the sun like any other planet. The earth has, then, more than one motion.

7. The apparent retrograde and direct motion of the planets arises not from their motion but from the earth's. The motion of the earth alone, therefore, suffices to explain so many apparent inequalities in the heavens.

Having set forth these assumptions, I shall endeavor briefly to show how uniformity of the motions can be saved in a systematic way. However, I have thought it well, for the sake of brevity, to omit from this sketch mathematical demonstrations, reserving these for my larger work. But in the explanation of the circles I shall set down here the lengths of the radii; and from these the reader who is not unacquainted with mathematics will readily perceive how closely this arrangement of circles agrees with the numerical data and observations.

Accordingly, let no one suppose that I have gratuitously asserted, with the Pythagoreans, the motion of the earth; strong proof will be found in my exposition of the circles. For the principal arguments by which the natural philosophers attempt to establish the immobility of the earth rest for the most part on the appearances; it is particularly such arguments that collapse here, since I treat the earth's immobility as due to an appearance.

C. Copernicus's Editor Distorts *De Revolutionibus,* 1543

To the Reader Concerning the Hypotheses of This Work:

There have already been widespread reports about the novel hypotheses of this work, which declares that the earth moves whereas the sun is at rest in the center of the universe. Hence certain scholars, I have no doubt, are deeply offended and believe that the liberal arts, which were established long ago on a sound basis, should not be thrown into confusion. But if these men are willing to examine the matter closely, they will find that the author of this work has done nothing blameworthy. For it is the duty of an astronomer to compose the history of the celestial motions through careful and expert study. Then he must conceive and devise the causes of these motions or hypotheses about them. Since he cannot in any way attain to the true causes, he will adopt whatever suppositions enable the motions to be computed correctly from the principles of geometry for the future as well as the past. The present author has performed both these duties excellently. For these hypotheses need not be true nor even probable. On the contrary, if they provide a calculus consistent with the observations, that alone is enough. Perhaps there is someone who is so ignorant of geometry and optics that he regards the epicycle of Venus as probable, or thinks that it is the reason why Venus sometimes precedes and sometimes follows the sun by forty degrees and even more. Is there anyone who is not aware that from this assumption it necessarily follows that the diameter of the planet at perigee should appear more than four times, and the body of the planet more than sixteen times, as great as at apogee? Yet this variation is refuted by the experience of every age. In this science there are some other no less important absurdities, which need not be set forth at the moment. For this art, it is quite clear, is completely and absolutely ignorant of the causes of the apparent nonuniform motions. And if any causes are devised by the imagination, as indeed very many are, they are not put forward to convince anyone that they are true, but merely to provide a reliable basis for computation. However, since different hypotheses are sometimes offered for one and the same motion (for example, eccentricity and an epicycle for the sun's motion), the astronomer will take as his first choice that hypothe-sis which is the easiest to grasp. The philosopher will perhaps rather seek the semblance of the truth. But neither of them will understand or state anything certain, unless it has been divinely revealed to him.

Therefore alongside the ancient hypotheses, which are no more probable, let us permit these new hypotheses also to become known, especially since they are admirable as well as simple and bring with them a huge treasure of very skillful observations. So far as hypotheses are concerned, let no one expect anything certain from astronomy, which cannot furnish it, lest he accept as the truth ideas conceived for another purpose, and depart from this study a greater fool than when he entered it. Farewell.

D. Martin Luther Hears About Copernicus

There was mention of a certain new astrologer who wanted to prove that the earth moves and not the sky, the sun, and the moon. This would be as if somebody were riding on a cart or in a ship and imagined that he was standing still while the earth and the trees were moving. [Luther remarked,] "So it goes now. Whoever wants to be clever must agree with nothing that others esteem. He must do something of his own. This is what that fellow does who wishes to turn the whole of astronomy upside down. Even in these things that are thrown into disorder I believe the Holy Scriptures, for Joshua commanded the sun to stand still and not the earth."

Document Set 15.3 References

A. Leonardo da Vinci Speculates on the Cosmos
   Selections from the Notebooks of Leonardo da Vinci, ed. Irma A. Richter (Oxford, England: Oxford University Press, 1977), 54–55.
B. Nicholas Copernicus Explains His First Heliocentric Hypothesis, 1520s
   Copernicus, "The Commentariolus," in Edward Rosen, *Three Copernican Treatises,* 3d. ed. (New York: Octagon, 1971), 57–59.
C. Copernicus's Editor Distorts *De Revolutionibus,* 1543
   Osiander, "Address to the Reader," Preface to Copernicus's *De Revolutionibus,* in Edward Rosen, ed., *Copernicus and the Scientific Revolution* (Melbourne, Fla.: Krieger, 1984), 195–196.
D. Martin Luther Hears About Copernicus
   Luther, *Table Talk,* in Rosen, *Copernicus and the Scientific Revolution,* 182–183.

The Dream of Renovation: Savonarola and the Christian Humanists

Girolamo Savonarola (1452–1498) was no humanist but a passionately committed Dominican moralist and preacher who in the 1490s exerted a magnetic spell over Florence, including many of its intellectuals and artists. A critic of the Medici regime, Savonarola was thrust into power by the French invasion of 1494, which he interpreted as God's judgment on a wicked society. His vision of Florence transformed into a just, godly community (Document A) bears strong resemblance to the kind of purified regime many Christian reformers would later try to impose on sixteenth-century cities. Was it a practical program?

The prince of humanists on the eve of the reformation was the Dutchman Desiderius Erasmus (1466–1536). Traveling to Italy in 1506, Erasmus saw for himself the corruption and pomp of the papacy and the devastation of the wars brought on in part by papal politics. The wonderfully wicked scene in Document B comes from a short Latin dialogue that Erasmus published anonymously in 1517. *Julius Excluded* enjoyed a huge success, much to the church's anger. What do you see in it that prefigures the critique reformers like Luther would soon launch against the Catholic church? Erasmus's greatest work of satire, *The Praise of Folly* (1509), like all great comedy, not only ridicules but also brings home enduring truths of human character. What elements of mockery and idealism do you see in the extract that forms Document C?

An equally devastating satire was published in 1515 by the German humanist Ulrich von Hutten, the *Letters of Obscure Men.* Occasioned by clerical attacks on a humanist who had tried to study the Hebrew scriptures and the mystical cabala, Hutten's *Letters* were written in the crabbed Latin style of old-fashioned scholastics and were intended to mock all conservative resistance to the new learning—and, incidentally, also the externals of traditional piety.

A. Savonarola Proposes to Make Florence Perfect

Every Florentine citizen who wants to be a good member of his city and to help her, as everyone should wish to do, must first of all believe that this council and this civil government were ordained by God. This is true, indeed, not only because all good government comes from God, but also and especially because of the providential care which God has recently manifested in preserving the city. No one who has lived here for the past three years and is not blind and devoid of judgment would deny that, but for the hand of God, this government would never have been created against so much and such powerful opposition, nor would it have maintained itself to this day among so many traitors and so few friends. God, however, demands of us that we ourselves use the intellect and the free will he has given us. He has made all that pertains to government imperfect at first, so that with his help we can improve it. This government is still imperfect and has many flaws. We have hardly more than the foundation. Every citizen, therefore, should strive to perfect it. It can be made perfect only if all or at least the majority are blessed with the following four virtues.

First, fear of God. . . .

Second, love of the common good. When they hold offices and other dignities, the citizens must put aside all private interests and all the special needs of their relatives and friends. They must think solely of the common good. . . .

Third, love of one another. The citizens must drop feuds and forget all past offenses. Hatred, bad feelings, and envy blind the eye of the intellect and do not let it see the truth. Sitting in councils and in public offices, anyone who is not well purged in this regard will make many mistakes. . . .

Fourth, justice. Justice purges the city of bad men, or makes them live in fear. The good and just endure in high authority because they are gladly elected to office by those who love justice. They are enlightened by God in legislation and in guiding the city to a happy state. Justice will make the city fill up with goodness because it always rewards goodness; and the good men, wanting to live where there is justice, will congregate there in great numbers. God, for justice also, will increase the city's empire, as he did that of the Romans. Because the Romans exercised strict and severe justice, He gave them imperial power over the whole world. He wanted justice to make his peoples righteous.

The Florentine citizens, if they deliberate and use rational judgment, will see that they require no other government than the one we have described. If they have faith, moreover, that it was given to them by God, and exercise the four virtues we have named, their government will doubtless be soon perfected. . . .

B. Erasmus Shuts Pope Julius II Out of Heaven

[In this opening scene, Pope Julius finds heaven's gate locked and St. Peter, the gatekeeper, less than friendly.]

Julius: How about opening the door, you, right away! If you wanted to do your job right you would have come to meet me—with the whole parade of angels, in fact.
Peter: Pretty bossy, all right. But first, you tell me who you are. . . .
Julius: Cut out the foolishness, if you have any sense. For your information, I am the famous Julius the Ligurian, and I trust you recognize the letters P.M., unless you have forgotton the alphabet altogether.
Peter: I take it they stand for Pestilential Maximum . . .
Julius: Oh, come on—they stand for Pontifex Maximus, the supreme Pontiff. . . . Why don't you cut out the nonsense and open the door, unless you would rather have it battered down? In a word—do you see what a retinue I have?
Peter: To be sure, I see thoroughly hardened brigands. But in case you don't know it, these doors you must storm with other weapons.
Julius: Enough talk, I say! Unless you obey right away, I shall hurl—even against you—the thunderbolt of excommunication, with which I once terrified the mightiest of kings, or for that matter whole kingdoms. You see the Bull already prepared for this purpose?
Peter: What damned thunderbolt, what thunder, what Bulls, what bombast are you talking about, pray? We never heard anything of those matters from Christ.

C. Erasmus Mocks the Externals of Piety

To this same class of fools belong those who beguile themselves with the silly but pleasing notion that if they look upon a picture or image of St. Christopher,—that huge Polyphemus,—they will not die that day; or that he who salutes an image of St. Barbara with the proper form of address will come back from battle safe; or that one who approaches St. Erasmus on certain days with wax candles and prayers will soon be rich. They have found a new Hercules in St. George,—a sort of second Hippolytus. They seem to adore even his horse, which is scrupulously decked out with gorgeous trappings, and additional offerings are constantly being made in the hope of gaining new favors. His bronze helmet one would think half divine, the way people swear by it.

And what shall I say of those who comfortably delude themselves with imaginary pardons for their sins, and who measure the time in purgatory with an hourglass into years, months, days, and hours, with all the precision of a mathematical table? There are plenty, too, who, relying upon certain magical little certificates and prayers,—which some pious impostor devised either in fun or for the benefit of his pocket,—believe that they may procure riches, honor, future happiness, health, perpetual prosperity, long life, a lusty old age,—nay, in the end, a seat at the right hand of Christ in heaven; but as for this last, it matters not how long it be deferred: they will content themselves with the joys of heaven only when they must finally surrender the pleasures of this world, to which they lovingly cling.

The trader, the soldier, and the judge think that they can clean up the Augean stable of a lifetime, once for all, by sacrificing a single coin from their ill-gotten gains. They flatter themselves that all sorts of perjury, debauchery, drunkenness, quarrels, bloodshed, imposture, perfidy, and treason can be compounded for by contract and so adjusted that, having paid off their arrears, they can begin a new score.

How foolish, or rather how happy, are those who promise themselves more than supernal happiness if they repeat the verses of the seven holy psalms! Those magical lines are supposed to have been taught to St. Bernard by a demon, who seems to have been a wag; but he was not very clever, and, poor fellow, was frustrated in his attempt to deceive the saint. These silly things which even I, Folly, am almost ashamed of, are approved not only by the common herd but even by the teachers of religion.

How foolish, too, for religious bodies each to give preference to its particular guardian saint! Nay, each saint has his particular office allotted to him, and is addressed each in his special way: this one is called upon to alleviate toothache; that, to aid in childbirth; others, to restore a stolen article, bring rescue to the shipwrecked, or protect cattle,—and so on with the rest, who are much too numerous to mention. A few indeed among the saints are good in more than one emergency, especially the Holy Virgin, to whom the common man now attributes almost more than to her Son.

And for what, after all, do men petition the saints except for foolish things? Look at the votive offerings which cover the walls of certain churches and with which you see even the ceiling filled; do you find any one who expresses his gratitude that he has escaped

Folly or because he has become a whit wiser? One perhaps was saved from drowning, another recovered when he had been run through by his enemy; another, while his fellows were fighting, ran away with expedition and success; another, on the point of being hanged, escaped, through the aid of some saintly friend of thieves, and lived to relieve a few more of those whom he believed to be overburdened with their wealth. . . .

These various forms of foolishness so pervade the whole life of Christians that even the priests themselves find no objection to admitting, not to say fostering, them, since they do not fail to perceive how many tidy little sums accrue to them from such sources. But what if some odious philosopher should chime in and say, as is quite true: "You will not die badly if you live well. You are redeeming your sins when you add to the sum that you contribute a hearty detestation of evil doers: then you may spare yourself tears, vigils, invocations, fasts, and all that kind of life. You may rely upon any saint to aid you when once you begin to imitate his life."

As for the theologians, perhaps the less said the better on this gloomy and dangerous theme, since they are a style of man who show themselves exceeding supercilious and irritable unless they can heap up six hundred conclusions about you and force you to recant; and if you refuse, they promptly brand you as a heretic,—for it is their custom to terrify by their thunderings those whom they dislike. It must be confessed that no other group of fools are so reluctant to acknowledge Folly's benefits toward them, although I have many titles to their gratitude, for I make them so in love with themselves that they seem to be happily exalted to the third heaven, whence they look down with something like pity upon all other mortals, wandering about on the earth like mere cattle. . . .

D. Ulrich von Hutten Pokes Fun at the "Obscure Men" Who Block Reform

Henricus Schaffsmulius to Master Ortuin Gratius, many salutations:
When I first went to the Curia you told me that I should write to you frequently and address any theological questions to you, for you wished to answer them more satisfactorily than could those about the papal court at Rome. I, therefore, wish now to ask your opinion in the case of one who should on Friday, which is the sixth day, or upon any other fast day, eat an egg in which there is a chick. For we were recently dining at an inn in the Campo Fiore, and were eating eggs. And I, opening my egg, discovered that there was a chick within; but upon showing it to my companion, he urged me to swallow it straightway before the host caught sight of it, for otherwise I should have to pay a Carolinus or a Julius for a fowl, since it is the custom here to pay for everything the host places on the table, because they will take nothing back. Now if he saw that there was a chick in the egg he would say, "You must pay me for a fowl,"—for he would charge for a little one just as much as he would for a big one.

And I immediately swallowed the egg and the chick at the same time, and afterwards it occurred to me that it was Friday, and I said to my companion, "You have caused me to commit a mortal sin in eating meat on Friday."

But he said that is was not a mortal sin, nor even a venial sin, since a chick may not be considered other than an egg until it is born. And he remarked that it is just the same in the case of cheese in which there are worms, and of the worms in cherries, and in peas, and young beans; but they are eaten on the sixth day, and even on the vigils of the apostles. But inn proprietors are such rascals that they sometimes say that these are meat in order to gain thereby.

Then I went out and thought about it, and, by Heaven, Master Ortuin, I am much disturbed, and I do not know what I ought to do about it. It is true that I might take counsel with a member of the papal court, but I know that they have bad consciences. As for myself, it seems to me that chicks in the egg are meat, because the matter is already formed and shaped into the members and body of an animal, and it has animal life. It is otherwise in the case of worms in cheese and in other comestibles, for worms are accounted to be fish, as I have heard from a physician, who is also a very able scientist.

I beseech of you earnestly to reply to my question. For if you hold that it is a mortal sin, then I wish to seek absolution before I go to Germany; for you probably know that our lord, Jacob Hochstraten, borrowed a thousand florins from the bank, and I believe he would want to make something out of the case; and may the devil take that John Reuchlin and those other poets and men of law, who are trying to fight the Church of God—that is to say, the theologians, who are the real backbone of the Church, as Christ said, "Thou art Peter, and upon this rock will I build my church."

May the Lord God preserve you. Farewell.
Written in the city of Rome.

Document Set 15.4 References

A. Savonarola Proposes to Make Florence Perfect
Savanarola, in "Draft Constitution for Florence," in R. Watkins, ed., *Humanism and Liberty* (Columbia, S.C.: University of South Carolina Press, 1978), 253–260.

B. Erasmus Shuts Pope Julius II Out of Heaven
Desiderius Erasmus, *The Julius Exclusus of Erasmus,* trans. Paul Pascal (Bloomington, Ind.: University of Indiana Press, 1968), 45–49.

C. Erasmus Mocks the Externals of Piety
Erasmus, *The Praise of Folly,* in James Harvey Robinson, ed., *Readings in European History* (Boston: Ginn, 1904), 2:41–43.

D. Ulrich von Hutten Pokes Fun at the "Obscure Men" Who Block Reform
Ulrich Von Hutten, "Letters of Obscure Men." in Robinson 2:47–49.

DOCUMENT SET 15.5
Luther

The origins of Luther's mission as a reformer lie not in humanist "new learning" or in the moralists' attack on abuses, but in Luther's own solitary struggle with his conscience. Confronting his apparent inability to feel that his conduct would satisfy God and atone for the sinfulness that he could never expunge from his innermost character, Luther came to interpret St. Paul's Epistle to the Romans to mean that God would "justify" (redeem) those who had faith in divine mercy, without regard for the merit of their own feeble efforts. Read Documents A (from Paul's Epistle) and B (Luther's own recollections much later in life) in the light of this struggle. His new understanding in many ways recalled St. Augustine's solution a thousand years earlier and very likely the Apostle Paul's original spiritual battle between Jesus' teachings and Jewish law. Only after having arrived at this decision was Luther impelled to become a public critic of the abuses of indulgence-selling, which can be followed in Documents C and D. In Document C the newly elected Archbishop of Mainz gives instructions for an indulgence-selling campaign designed to strengthen his financial position (not the safeguards that the actual sellers apparently disregarded); in Document D, Luther posts his Ninety-five Theses, which you should read with an eye to how Luther is already attacking the foundations of papal power.

Document E is an excerpt from Luther's pamphlet *The Freedom of a Christian,* composed and published in 1520. Unlike Latin treatises for the intellectual elite, this pamphlet was published in German and reached a broad public through the printing press. It popularized Luther's idea of justification by faith. How can it be said to undermine the entire structure of Catholicism: clergy, sacraments, rules, and good works?

In recent years scholars have debated the extent to which Luther's reformation "succeeded." Prime evidence in this controversy is the surviving sermon and "visitation" material. (The latter are records of parish inspections and examinations of individuals, which were carried out by higher church officials.) What signs do these sources reveal to you of changes in behavior among ordinary Christians "reformed" by Protestantism? Document F summarizes one of Luther's own sermons to his congregation; Document G comes from a visitation report in north-central Germany, 1594. Judging from this evidence, how would you assess the practical outcome of the Lutheran Reformation?

A. St. Paul Writes to the Christians at Rome on Justification by Faith

Now we know that what things soever the law saith, it saith to them who are under the law: that every mouth may be stopped, and all the world may become guilty before God. Therefore by the deeds of the law there shall no flesh be justified in his sight: for by the law is the knowledge of sin.

But now the righteousness of God without the law is manifested, being witnessed by the law and the prophets; even the righteousness of God which is by faith in Jesus Christ unto all and upon all them that believe: for there is no difference: for all have sinned, and come short of the glory of God; being justified freely by his grace through the redemption that is in Christ Jesus: whom God hath set forth to be a propitiation through faith in his blood, to declare his righteousness for the remission of sins that are past, through the forbearance of God; to declare, I say, at this time his righteousness: that he might be just, and the justifier of him which believeth in Jesus.

Where is boasting then? It is excluded. By what law? Of works? Nay: but by the law of faith. Therefore we conclude that a man is justified by faith without the deeds of the law.

B. Luther Discovers the True Meaning of Paul's *Epistle to the Romans*

I greatly longed to understand Paul's Epistle to the Romans and nothing stood in the way but that one expression, "the justice of God," because I took it to mean that justice whereby God is just and deals justly in punishing the unjust. My situation was that, although an impeccable monk, I stood before God as a sinner troubled in conscience, and I had no confidence that my merit would assuage him. Therefore I did not love a just and angry God, but rather hated and murmured against him. Yet I clung to the dear Paul and had a great yearning to know what he meant.

Night and day I pondered until I saw the connection between the justice of God and the statement that "the just shall live by his faith." Then I grasped that the justice of God is that righteousness by which through grace and sheer mercy God justifies us through faith. Thereupon I felt myself to be reborn and to have gone through open doors into paradise. The whole of Scripture took on a new meaning, and whereas before the "justice of God" had filled me with hate, now it became to me inexpressibly sweet in greater love. This passage of Paul became to me a gate to heaven. . . .

If you have a true faith that Christ is your Saviour, then at once you have a gracious God, for faith leads you in and opens up God's heart and will, that you should see pure grace and overflowing love. This it is to behold God in faith that you should look upon his fatherly, friendly heart, in which there is no anger nor ungraciousness. He who sees God as angry does not see him rightly but looks only on a curtain, as if a dark cloud had been drawn across his face.

C. Archbishop Albert of Mainz Gives His Instructions for Indulgence-Selling, 1517

Here follow the four principal graces and privileges, which are granted by the apostolic bull, of which each may be obtained without the other. In the matter of these four privileges preachers shall take pains to commend each to believers with the greatest care, and, in-so-far as in their power lies, to explain the same.

The first grace is the complete remission of all sins; and nothing greater than this can be named, since man who lives in sin and forfeits the favor of God, obtains complete remission by these means and once more enjoys God's favor: moreover, through this remission of sins the punishment which one is obliged to undergo in Purgatory on account of the affront to the divine Majesty, is all remitted, and the pains of Purgatory completely blotted out. And although nothing is precious enough to be given in exchange for such a grace,—since it is the free gift of God and a grace beyond price,—yet in order that Christian believers may be the more easily induced to procure the same, we establish the following rules, to wit:

In the first place every one who is contrite in heart, and has made oral confession, or at all events has the intention of confessing at a suitable time, shall visit at least the seven churches indicated for this purpose, that is to say, those in which the papal arms are displayed, and in each church shall say devoutly five Paternosters and five Ave Marias in honor of the five wounds of our Lord Jesus Christ, whereby our salvation is won, or one *Miserere* [the prayer beginning "Lord have mercy"], which Psalm is particularly well adapted for obtaining forgiveness of sins. . . .

Respecting, now, the contribution to the chest, for the building of the said church of the chief of the apostles, the penitentiaries and confessors, after they have explained to those making confession the full remission and privileges, shall ask of them, for how much money or other temporal goods they would conscientiously go without the said most complete remission and privileges; and this shall be done in order that hereafter they may be brought the more easily to contribute. And because the conditions and occupations of men are so manifold and diverse that we cannot consider them individually, and impose specific rates accordingly, we have therefore concluded that the rates should be determined according to the recognized classes of persons.

Kings and Queens and their offspring, archbishops and bishops, and other great rulers as well, provided they seek the places where the cross is raised, or otherwise present themselves, shall pay at least five and twenty Rhenish guilders in gold. Abbots and the great prelates of Cathedral churches, counts, barons, and others of the higher nobility, together with their consorts, shall pay for each letter of indulgence ten such guilders. Other lesser prelates and nobles, as also the rectors of celebrated places, and all others, who, either from permanent incomes or merchandise, or otherwise, enjoy a total yearly revenue of five hundred gold guilders, shall pay six such guilders. Other citizens and tradespeople and artisans, who have individual incomes and families of their own, shall pay one such guilder; others of less means only a half. And where it is impossible to adhere rigidly to the schedule above indicated, then we declare that the said kings, bishops, dukes, abbots, prelates, counts, barons, members of the higher nobility and rectors, together with all others above mentioned, shall place or caused to be placed in the chest a sum in accordance with the dictates of sound reason, proportionate to their magnificence or generosity, after they have listened to the advice and council of the sub-commissioners and penitentiaries and of their confessors, in order that they may fully obtain the grace and privileges. All other persons are confided to the discretion of the confessors and penitentiaries, who should have ever in view the advancement of this building, and should urge their penitents to a freer contribution, but should let no one go away without some portion of grace, because the happiness of Christian believers is here concerned not less than the interests of the building. And those that have no money, they shall supply their contribution with prayer and fasting; for the Kingdom of Heaven should be open to the poor not less than to the rich.

And although a married woman may not dispose

of the husband's goods against his will, yet she shall be able to contribute in this instance against the will of her husband of her dowry or of her own private property, which has come to her in a regular manner. Where she has no such possessions, or is prevented by her husband, she shall then supply such contribution with prayer; and the same we wish to have understood concerning sons who still remain under parental control. . . .

The second signal grace is a confessional letter containing the most extraordinarily comforting and hitherto unheard of privileges, and which also retains its virtue even after our bull expires at the end of eight years, since the bull says: "they shall be participators now and for ever." The meaning of the same preachers and confessors shall explain and bring unto all possible prominence; for there will be granted in the confessional letter, to those who buy: first, the power to choose a qualified confessor, even a monk from the mendicant orders, who shall absolve them first and foremost, with the consent of the persons involved, from all censures by whomsoever imposed; in the second place, from each and every crime, even the greatest, and as well from those reserved to the apostolic see, once in a lifetime and in the hour of death; third, in those cases which are not reserved, as often as necessary; fourth, the chosen confessor may grant him complete forgiveness of all sins once in life, and at the hour of death, as often as it may seem at hand, although death ensue not; and, fifth, transform all kinds of vows, excepting alone those solemnly taken, into other works of piety (as when one has vowed to perform the journey to the Holy Land, or to visit the holy Apostles at Rome, to make a pilgrimage to St. James at Compostella, to become a monk, or to take a vow of chastity); sixth, the confessor may administer to him the sacrament of the alter at all seasons, except on Easter day, and in the hour of death. . . .

The third most important grace is the participation in all the possessions of the church universal, which consists herein, that contributors toward the said building, together with their deceased relations, who have departed this world in a state of grace, shall from now and for eternity, be partakers in all petitions, intercessions, alms, fastings, prayers, in each and every pilgrimage, even those to the Holy Land; furthermore, in the stations at Rome, in the masses canonical hours, flagellations, and all other spiritual goods which have been brought forth or which shall be brought forth by the universal, most holy church militant or by any of its members. Believers will become participants in all these things who purchase confessional letters. Preachers and confessors must insist with great perseverance upon these advantages,

and persuade believers that they should not neglect to acquire these along with their confessional letter.

We also declare that in order to acquire these two most important graces, it is not necessary to make confession, or to visit the churches and altars, but merely to purchase the confessional letter. . . .

The fourth distinctive grace is for those souls which are in purgatory, and is the complete remission of all sins, which remission the pope brings to pass through his intercession to the advantage of said souls, in this wise; that the same contribution shall be placed in the chest by a living person as one would make for himself. It is our wish, however, that our subcommissioners should modify the regulations regarding contributions of this kind which are given for the dead, and that they should use their judgment in all other cases, where in their opinion modifications are desirable. It is furthermore not necessary that the persons who place their contributions in the chest for the dead should be contrite in heart and have orally confessed, since this grace is based simply on the state of grace in which the dead departed, and on the contribution of the living, as is evident from the text of the bull. Moreover, preachers shall exert themselves to give this grace the widest publicity, since through the same, help will surely come to departed souls, and the construction of the Church of St. Peter will be abundantly promoted at the same time. . . .

D. Luther Posts His Ninety-five Theses, 1517

1. Our Lord and Master Jesus Christ in saying "Repent ye" (*poenitentiam agite*) etc., intended that the whole life of believers should be penitence (*poenitentia*).

2. This word cannot be understood as sacramental penance (*poenitentia*), that is, of the confession and satisfaction which are performed under the ministry of priests.

3. It does not, however, refer solely to inward penitence (*poenitentia*); nay such inward penitence is naught, unless it outwardly produces various mortifications of the flesh.

4. The penalty (*poena*) thus continues as long as the hatred of self (that is, true inward penitence); namely, till our entrance into the kingdom of heaven.

5. The Pope has neither the will nor the power to remit any penalties except those which he has imposed by his own authority, or by that of the canons.

6. The Pope has no power to remit any guilt, except by declaring and warranting it to have been remitted by God; or at most by remitting cases reserved for himself; in which cases, if his power were despised, guilt would certainly remain.

7. Certainly God remits no man's guilt without at the same time subjecting him, humbled in all things, to the authority of his representative the priest.

8. The penitential canons are imposed only on the living, and no burden ought to be imposed on the dying, according to them.

9. Hence, the Holy Spirit acting in the Pope does well for us in that, in his decrees, he always makes exception of the article of death and of necessity.

10. Those priests act unlearnedly and wrongly who, in the case of the dying, reserve the canonical penances for purgatory. . . .

20. Therefore the Pope, when he speaks of the plenary remission of all penalties, does not mean really of all, but only of those imposed by himself.

21. Thus those preachers of indulgences are in error who say that by the indulgences of the Pope a man is freed and saved from all punishment.

22. For in fact he remits to souls in purgatory no penalty which they would have had to pay in this life according to the canons.

23. If any entire remission of all penalties can be granted to any one it is certain that it is granted to none but the most perfect, that is to very few.

24. Hence, the greater part of the people must needs be deceived by this indiscriminate and high-sounding promise of release from penalties. . . .

26. The Pope acts most rightly in granting remission to souls not by the power of the keys (which is of no avail in this case) but by the way of intercession.

27. They preach man who say that the soul flies out of Purgatory as soon as the money thrown into the chest rattles.[1]

28. It is certain that, when the money rattles in the chest, avarice and gain may be increased, but the effect of the intercession of the Church depends on the will of God alone.

29. Who knows whether all the souls in purgatory desire to be redeemed from it—witness the story told of Saints Severinus and Paschal?

30. No man is sure of the reality of his own contrition, much less of the attainment of plenary remission.

31. Rare as is a true penitent, so rare is one who truly buys indulgences—that is to say, most rare.

---

[1] This was the claim being made by the indulgence seller Tetzel in Luther's Saxony.

32. Those who believe that, through letters of pardon, they are made sure of their own salvation will be eternally damned along with their teachers.

33. We must especially beware of those who say that these pardons from the Pope are that inestimable gift of God by which man is reconciled to God.

34. For the grace conveyed by these pardons has respect only to the penalties of sacramental satisfaction, which are of human appointment.

35. They preach no Christian doctrine who teach that contrition is not necessary for those who buy souls [out of purgatory] or buy confessional licenses.

36. Every Christian who feels true compunction has of right plenary remission of punishment and guilt even without letters of pardon.

37. Every true Christian, whether living or dead, has a share in all the benefits of Christ and of the Church, given him by God, even without letters of pardon.

38. The remission, however, imparted by the Pope is by no means to be despised, since it is, as I have said, a declaration of the divine remission.

39. It is a most difficult thing, even for the most learned theologians, to exalt at the same time in the eyes of the people the ample effect of pardons and the necessity of true contrition.

40. True contrition seeks and loves punishment; while the ampleness of pardons relaxes it, and causes men to hate it, or at least gives occasion for them to do so.

41. Apostolic pardons ought to be proclaimed with caution, lest the people should falsely suppose that they are placed before other good works of charity.

42. Christians should be taught that it is not the wish of the Pope that the buying of pardons should be in any way compared to works of mercy.

43. Christians should be taught that he who gives to a poor man, or lends to a needy man, does better than if he bought pardons.

44. Because by works of charity, charity increases, and the man becomes better; while by means of pardons, he does not become better, but only freer from punishment.

45. Christians should be taught that he who sees any one in need, and, passing him by, gives money for pardons, is not purchasing for himself the indulgences of the Pope but the anger of God.

46. Christians should be taught that, unless they have superfluous wealth, they are bound to keep what is necessary for the use of their own households, and by no means to lavish it on pardons.

47. Christians should be taught that while they are free to buy pardons they are not commanded to do so.

48. Christians should be taught that the Pope, in granting pardons, has both more need and more desire that devout prayer should be made for him than that money should be readily paid.

49. Christians should be taught that the Pope's pardons are useful if they do not put their trust in them, but most hurtful if through them they lose the fear of God.

50. Christians should be taught that, if the Pope were acquainted with the exactions of the Preachers of pardons, he would prefer that the Basilica of St. Peter should be burnt to ashes rather than that it should be built up with the skin, flesh, and bones of his sheep.

51. Christians should be taught that as it would be the duty so it would be the wish of the Pope even to sell, if necessary, the Basilica of St. Peter, and to give of his own money to very many of those from whom the preachers of pardons extract money.

52. Vain is the hope of salvation through letters of pardon, even if a commissary—nay, the Pope himself—were to pledge his own soul for them.

53. They were enemies of Christ and of the Pope who, in order that pardons may be preached, condemn the word of God to utter silence in other churches.

54. Wrong is done to the Word of God when, in the same sermon, an equal or longer time is spent on pardons than on it.

55. The mind of the Pope necessarily is that, if pardons, which are a very small matter, are celebrated with single bells, single processions, and single ceremonies, the Gospel, which is a very great matter, should be preached with a hundred bells, a hundred processions, and a hundred ceremonies.

56. The treasures of the Church, whence the Pope grants indulgences, are neither sufficiently named nor known among the people of Christ.

57. It is clear that they are at least not temporal treasures, for these are not so readily lavished, but only accumulated, by many of the preachers.

58. Nor are they the merits of Christ and of the saints, for these, independently of the Pope, are always working grace to the inner man, and the cross, death, and hell to the outer man. . . .

67. Those indulgences, which the preachers loudly proclaim to be the greatest graces, are seen to be truly such as regards the promotion of gain.

68. Yet they are in reality most insignificant when compared to the grace of God and the piety of the cross. . . .

75. To think that the Papal pardons have such power that they could absolve a man even if—by an impossibility—he had violated the Mother of God, is madness.

76. We affirm on the contrary that Papal pardons cannot take away even the least of venial sins, as regards its guilt.

77. The saying that, even if St. Peter were now Pope, he could grant no greater graces, is blasphemy against St. Peter and the Pope.

78. We affirm on the contrary that both he and any other Pope has greater graces to grant, namely, the Gospel, powers, gifts of healing, etc. (1 Cor. xii.)

79. To say that the cross set up among the insignia of the Papal arms is of equal power with the cross of Christ, is blasphemy.

80. Those bishops, priests and theologians who allow such discourses to have currency among the people will have to render an account.

81. This license in the preaching of pardons makes it no easy thing, even for learned men, to protect the reverence due to the Pope against the calumnies, or, at all events, the keen questionings of the laity.

82. As for instance: Why does not the Pope empty purgatory for the sake of most holy charity and of the supreme necessity of souls—this being the most just of all reasons—if he redeems an infinite number of souls for the sake of that most fatal thing, money, to be spent on building a basilica—this being a very slight reason?

83. Again; why do funeral masses and anniversary masses for the deceased continue, and why does not the Pope return, or permit the withdrawal of, the funds bequeathed for this purpose, since it is a wrong to pray for those who are already redeemed?

84. Again; what is this new kindness of God and the Pope, in that, for money's sake, they permit an impious man and an enemy of God to redeem a pious soul which loves God, and yet do not redeem that same pious and beloved soul out of free charity on account of its own need?

85. Again; why is it that the penitential canons, long since abrogated and dead in themselves, in very fact and not only by usage, are yet still redeemed with money, through the granting of indulgences, as if they were full of life?

86. Again; why does not the Pope, whose riches are at this day more ample than those of the wealthiest of the wealthy, build the single Basilica of St. Peter with his own money rather than with that of poor believers?

87. Again; what does the Pope remit or impart to those who through perfect contrition have a right to plenary remission and participation?

88. Again; what greater good could the Church receive than if the Pope, instead of once, as he does now, were to bestow these remissions and participations a hundred times a day on any one of the faithful?

89. Since it is the salvation of souls, rather than money, that the Pope seeks by his pardons, why does he suspend the letters and pardons granted long ago, since they are equally efficacious? . . .

91. If all these pardons were preached according to the spirit and mind of the Pope, all these questions would be resolved with ease; nay, would not exist. . . .

E. Luther Explains the True Freedom of a Christian, 1520

One thing, and only one thing, is necessary for Christian life, righteousness, and freedom. That one thing is the most holy Word of God, the gospel of Christ . . . it is easy to see from what source faith derives such great power and why a good work or all good works together cannot equal it. No good work can rely upon the Word of God or live in the soul, for faith alone and the Word of God rule in the soul. Just as the heated iron glows like fire because of the union of fire with it, so the Word imparts its qualities to the soul. It is clear, then, that a Christian has all that he needs in faith and needs no works to justify him; and if he has no need of works, he has no need of the law; and if he has no need of the law, surely he is free from the law. . . . This is that Christian liberty, our faith, which does not induce us to live in idleness or wickedness but makes the law and works unnecessary for any man's righteousness and salvation.

F. Luther Preaches to His Congregation, 1528

The sermon on the 8th of November, 1528, was on the lord who forgave his servant: This lord, said Luther, is a type of the Kingdom of God. The servant was not forgiven because he had forgiven his fellow servant. On the contrary he received forgiveness before he had done anything whatever about his fellow servant. From this we see that there are two kinds of forgiveness. The first is that which we receive from God; the second is that which we exercise by bearing no ill will to any upon earth. But we must not overlook the two administrations, the civil and the spiritual, because the prince cannot and should not forgive. He has a different administration than Christ,

who rules over crushed and broken hearts. The Kaiser rules over scoundrels who do not recognize their sins and mock and carry their heads high. That is why the emperor carries a sword, a sign of blood and not of peace. But Christ's kingdom is for the troubled conscience. He says, "I do not ask of you a penny, only this, that you do the same for your neighbor." And the lord in the parable does not tell the servant to found a monastery, but simply that he should have mercy on his fellow servants.

But now what shall I say to you Wittenbergers? It would be better that I preach to you the *Sachsenspiegel* [the imperial law], because you want to be Christians while still practicing usury, robbing and stealing. How do people who are so sunk in sins expect to receive forgiveness? The sword of the emperor really applies here, but my sermon is for crushed hearts who feel their sins and have no peace. Enough for this gospel.

I understand that this is the week for the church collection, and many of you do not want to give a thing. You ungrateful people should be ashamed of yourselves. You Wittenbergers have been relieved of schools and hospitals, which have been taken over by the common chest, and now you want to know why you are asked to give four pennies. They are for the ministers, schoolteachers, and sacristans. The first labor for your salvation, preach to you the precious treasure of the gospel, administer the sacraments, and visit you at great personal risk in the plague. The second train children to be good magistrates, judges, and ministers. The third care for the poor. So far the common chest has cared for these, and now that you are asked to give four miserable pennies you are up in arms. What does this mean if not that you do not want the gospel preached, the children taught, and the poor helped? I am not saying this for myself. I receive nothing from you. I am the prince's beggar. But I am sorry I ever freed you from the tyrants and the papists. You ungrateful beasts, you are not worthy of the treasure of the gospel. If you don't improve, I will stop preaching rather than cast pearls before swine.

And now another point: couples to be blessed by the curate before a wedding should come early. There are stated hours: in summer, mornings at eight and afternoons at three; in winter, mornings at nine and afternoons at two. If you come later, I will bless you myself, and you won't thank me for it. And the invited guests should prepare themselves in good time for the wedding and let not Miss Goose wait for Mrs. Duck.

G. Lutheran Church Officials Inspect a Parish, 1594

First, gruesome cursing and blaspheming, as for instance "by God," "by God's Holy Cross," "by God's Passion, -death, -flesh, -blood, -heart, -hand," etc., "A Thousand Sacraments," "by the Baptism," "element," "star," "thunder and hail," "earth." Also dreadful swearing by various fears, epidemics, and injuries. These oaths are very common among young and old, women as well as men. People cannot carry on a friendly chat, or even address their children, without the use of these words. And none of them considers it a sin to swear.

Everyone is lax about going to church, both young and old. Many have not been seen by their pastor in a year or more. . . . Those who come to service are usually drunk. As soon as they sit down they lean their heads on their arms and sleep through the whole sermon, except that sometimes they fall off the benches, making a great clatter, or women drop their babies on the floor. . . . At times the wailing of babies is so loud that the preacher cannot make himself heard in the church.

The moment the sermon ends, everyone runs out. No one stays for the hymn, prayer, and blessing. They behave as if they were at a dance, not a divine service. . . . On Sunday afternoons, hardly ten or fifteen of 150 householders come to catechism practice, nor do they oblige their children and servants to attend. Instead they loaf at home, or sit about gossiping. . . . In many places catechism preaching on holiday afternoons has had to be abandoned for lack of auditors.

Document Set 15.5 References

A. St. Paul Writes to the Christians at Rome on Justification by Faith
Romans 3:19–28.

B. Luther Discovers the True Meaning of Paul's *Epistle to the Romans*
Martin Luther, in Roland H. Bainton, *Here I Stand* (Nashville, Tenn.: Abington Press, 1950; Mentor Books edition), 49–50.

C. Archbishop Albert of Mainz Gives His Instructions for Indulgence-Selling, 1517
Gerdes, *Introductio in Historian Evangelii Seculo,* in *Translations and Reprints from the Original Sources of European History* (Philadelphia: University of Pennsylvania Press, 1898), 2/6:4–9.

D. Luther Posts His Ninety-five Theses, 1517
Martin Luther, "Ninety-five Theses," in *Translations and Reprints,* 2/6:12–18.

E. Luther Explains the True Freedom of a Christian, 1520
Martin Luther, *The Freedom of a Christian,* in *Luther's Works,* American Edition (Philadelphia: 1957), 31:345, 349–350.

F. Luther Preaches to His Congregation, 1528
Martin Luther, Sermon of November 8, 1528, in 274–275.

G. Lutheran Church Officials Inspect a Parish, 1594
Report of Visitation in Nassau-Wiesbaden, in Gerald Strauss, *Luther's House of Learning* (Baltimore: Johns Hopkins University Press, 1978), 283–284.

The Reformation of the Common Man: The Peasants' War and the Anabaptists

One reason that historians often cite for the declining acceptability of Luther's message among ordinary people (Section 15.5, Documents F and G) is the crisis of the 1520s, during which many unlettered German men and women did in fact try to implement their understanding of the Gospel. Read Document A, an extract from the Twelve Articles that formed the basis of villagers' demand in the Peasants' War of 1525, looking for both the grievances and the peasants' idea of justice; compare Document B, in which the Zurich town council debates tithing with the aggrieved local peasantry.

Documents C to F all come from the Peasants' War. Read them to answer such questions as why did the fighting spread so far and so fast in the spring of 1525? Who were the peasants' leaders and what (if any) organizations did they possess? What roles did Thomas Müntzer and Martin Luther play?

Document G comes from the same south German town of Rothenburg that two years earlier had experienced the full brunt of the Peasants' War. Did this trauma have something to do with the ferocity with which the town executed the gentle pacifist Michael Sattler for preaching Anabaptist ideas? In what ways were these ideas judged subversive by the authorities?

The final document of the set (H) dates from after the Anabaptist debacle at Münster; Obbe Philips, a Dutch Anabaptist, found himself forced by circumstance to conclude that *all* Anabaptist idealism—whether pacifist or violent—was somehow fatally flawed. Why, on the basis of the evidence you have read, did he reach that conclusion?

After studying the documents in this set, write a brief essay assessing the peasants' insurgence and the Anabaptists as representatives of ordinary Germans in the Reformation Era.

A. The German Peasants Plead for Justice: The Twelve Articles

Peace to the Christian Reader and the Grace of God through Christ.

There are many evil writings put forth of late which take occasion, on account of the assembling of the peasants, to cast scorn upon the Gospel, saying: Is this the fruit of the new teaching, that no one should obey but all should everywhere rise in revolt, and rush together to reform, or perhaps destroy entirely, the authorities, both ecclesiastical and lay? The articles below shall answer these godless and criminal fault-finders, and serve in the first place to remove the reproach from the word of God and, in the second place, to give a Christian excuse for the disobedience or even the revolt of the entire Peasantry. In the first place the Gospel is not the cause of revolt and disorder, since it is the message of Christ, the promised Messiah, the Word of Life, teaching only love, peace, patience and concord. Thus, all who believe in Christ should learn to be loving, peaceful, long-suffering and harmonious. This is the foundation of all the articles of the peasants (as will be seen) who accept the gospel and live according to it. How then can the evil reports declare the Gospel to be a cause of revolt and disobedience? That the authors of the evil reports and the enemies of the Gospel oppose themselves to these demands is due not to the Gospel but to the Devil, the worst enemy of the Gospel, who causes this opposition by raising doubts in the minds of his followers; and thus the word of God, which teaches love, peace and concord, is overcome. In the second place, it is clear that the peasants demand that this Gospel be taught them as a guide in life, and they ought not to be called disobedient or disorderly. Whether God grant the peasants (earnestly wishing to live according to his word) their requests or no, who shall find fault with the will of the Most High? Who shall meddle in his judgments or oppose his majesty? Did he not hear the children of Israel when they called upon him and save them out of the hands of Pharaoh? Can he not save his own to-day? Yea, he will save them and that speedily. Therefore, Christian reader, read the following articles with care and then judge. Here follow the articles:

The First Article.—First, it is our humble petition and desire, as also our will and resolution, that in the future we should have power and authority so that each community should choose and appoint a pastor, and that we should have the right to depose him should he conduct himself improperly. The pastor thus chosen should teach us the Gospel pure and simple, without any addition, doctrine or ordinance of man. . . .

The Second Article.—According as the just tithe is established by the Old Testament and fulfilled in the New, we are ready and willing to pay the fair tithe of grain. The word of God plainly provides that in giving according to right to God and distributing to his people the services of a pastor are required. We will that for the future our church provost, whomsoever the community may appoint, shall gather and receive this tithe. From this he shall give to the pastor, elected by the whole community, a decent and sufficient maintenance for him and his (*im und den seynen*), as shall seem right to the whole community [*or*, with the knowledge of the community]. What remains over shall be given to the poor of the place, as the circumstances and the general opinion demand. Should anything farther remain, let it be kept, lest anyone should have to leave the country from poverty. Provision should also be made from this surplus to avoid laying any land tax on the poor. . . .

The Third Article.—It has been the custom hitherto for men to hold us as their own property, which is pitable enough, considering that Christ has delivered and redeemed us all, without exception, by the shedding of his precious blood, the lowly as well as the great. Accordingly, it is consistent with Scripture that we should be free and wish to be so. Not that we would wish to be absolutely free and under no authority. God does not teach us that we should lead a disorderly life in the lusts of the flesh, but that we should love the Lord our God and our neighbor. We would gladly observe all this as God has commanded us in the celebration of the communion. He has not commanded us not to obey the authorities, but rather that we should be humble, not only towards those in authority, but towards everyone. We are thus ready to yield obedience according to God's law to our elected and regular authorities in all proper things becoming to a Christian. We, therefore, take it for granted that you will release us from serfdom, as true Christians, unless it should be shown us from the Gospel that we are serfs.

The Fourth Article.—In the fourth place it has been the custom heretofore, that no poor man should be allowed to touch venison or wild fowl, or fish in flowing water, which seems to us quite unseemly and unbrotherly, as well as selfish and not agreeable to the word of God. In some places the authorities preserve the game to our great annoyance and loss, recklessly permitting the unreasoning animals to destroy to no purpose our crops, which God suffers to grow for the use of man, and yet we must remain quiet. This is neither godly nor neighborly. For when God created man he gave him dominion over all the animals, over the birds of the air and over the fish in the water. Accordingly it is our desire if a man holds possession of waters that he should prove from satisfactory documents that his right has been unwittingly acquired by purchase. . . .

The Fifth Article.—In the fifth place we are aggrieved in the matter of wood-cutting, for the noble folk have appropriated all the woods to themselves alone. If a poor man requires wood he must pay double for it, [*or perhaps*, two pieces of money]. . . .

The Sixth Article.—Our sixth complaint is in regard to the excessive services demanded of us, which are increased from day to day. We ask that this matter be properly looked into so that we shall not continue to be oppressed in this way, and that some gracious consideration be given us, since our forefathers were required only to serve according to the word of God.

The Seventh Article.—Seventh, we will not hereafter allow ourselves to be farther oppressed by our lords, but will let them demand only what is just and proper according to the word of the agreement between the lord and the peasant. The lord should no longer try to force more services or other dues from the peasant without payment, but permit the peasant to enjoy his holding in peace and quiet. The peasant should, however, help the lord when it is necessary, and at proper times, when it will not be disadvantageous to the peasant, and for a suitable payment.

The Eighth Article.—In the eighth place, we are greatly burdened by holdings which cannot support the rent exacted from them. The peasants suffer loss in this way and are ruined; and we ask that the lords may appoint persons of honor to inspect these holdings, and fix a rent in accordance with justice, so that the peasant shall not work for nothing, since the laborer is worthy of his hire.

The Ninth Article.—In the ninth place, we are burdened with a great evil in the constant making of new laws. We are not judged according to the offence, but sometimes with great ill will, and sometimes much too leniently. In our opinion we should be judged according to the old written law, so that the case shall be decided according to its merits, and not with partiality.

The Tenth Article.—In the tenth place, we are aggrieved by the appropriation by individuals of meadows and fields which at one time belonged to a community. . . .

The Eleventh Article.—In the eleventh place we will entirely abolish the due called *Todfall* [a payment owed upon a peasant's death by his heirs], and will no longer endure it, nor allow widows and orphans to be thus shamefully robbed against God's will, and in violation of justice and right, as has been done in many places, and by those who should shield and protect them. . . .

Conclusion.—In the twelfth place it is our conclusion and final resolution, that if any one or more of the articles here set forth should not be in agreement with the word of God, as we think they are, such article we will willingly recede from, when it is proved really to be against the word of God by a clear explanation of the Scripture. . . . For this we shall pray God, since he can grant this, and he alone. The peace of Christ abide with us all.

B. The Zurich City Council and Local Peasants Debate the Justice of Tithes, 1525

The peasants would not be peaceful and held a commune at Kloten and at Gossau, and would gladly have freed themselves from the tithe. But the lords of Zürich ordered that the tithe should be paid as before [issuing a mandate to that effect of 7 June 1525] . . . Such a mandate was unwelcome to the self-seeking crowd and many wanted to blame the preachers. They had taught that a Christian was free, etc. [arguing that] "the tithe in the New Testament is not divine law, etc." However, each Christian was to give what he was obliged to pay, and what had grown up of old . . . There was a public discussion about this dispute on the tithe, and an assembly of all the priests of the town and countryside of Zürich was held. The countryfolk also sent representatives to this meeting, intending that the peasants would be freed from the tithe, or, at the very least, the small tithe. But the lords of Zürich would not allow this, and after discussion issued an explanatory mandate . . . as follows:

Mandate of July 1, 1525: it has come to the notice of our lords, the Mayor, Council, and Great Council, that there is some misunderstanding among you about the tithe. Some think that when the seven crops—that is, corn, rye, oats, barley, wheat, wine, and hay (where this is customarily tithed)—have been paid, the small tithe and others are remitted. Our lords reply that all communes have received recent instructions (and since their reply to the communes is quite clear there can be no misunderstanding). Before the very eyes of our lords and of the priests of town and countryside, [the communes] dropped the articles they had written down, (for all the communes agreed to uphold the Word of God and clearly said that the disturbance about the tithe had arisen from the divisive preaching of the priests), and requested our lords . . . to deliberate whether the articles had any foundation and to remit those without foundation in the Word of God. Our lords therefore told the

envoys that they should return home, and that they would deliberate on the articles as soon as business allowed . . . and, with the advice of master Ulrich Zwingli and other learned and knowledgeable men, they would weigh the matter thoroughly and see what they could redress according to the Word of God. Nonetheless, one should pay the tithe and rents due to various ecclesiastical and secular persons, according to the content of the last mandate issued on this matter.

Whereupon one person was deputed from each guild to sit in judgment on the peasant articles and to consider thoroughly what could be conceded. After lengthy discussion, the mandate was confirmed, that all rents and tithes should be paid as was obligatory by custom, even the small tithe except that wherever two crops were grown annually in a field, [for example,] the aftermath of hay, or turnips after hemp, or millet after winter barley, etc., only the first crop would be tithed and the second would be free, such as the second crop of hay, turnips, etc.

[The Zürich town council, however, first issued a mandate on the peasant articles and the tithe on 14 August 1525.]... We do not doubt that you have all been informed that some disagreement and dispute have arisen over the tithe, because of the conflicting sermons of our preachers, and misunderstanding on the part of some of our surrounding subjects (in our view out of self-interest). For this reason, some areas, namely, those from the county of Kyburg, the territory of Eglisau, of Grüningen, Greifensee, Andelfingen, Bülach, Neuamt, and Rümlang, appeared before us in the person of their envoys, together with their pastors and preachers, to discuss and negotiate extensively and in detail over the tithe. Finally, the envoys of the communes were told that such disturbance arose in their midst only on account of their priests and their conflicting preaching and that they had been instructed and taught by them. Therewith the matter was referred to us [the council] for a decision according to the Word of God, and to remit those articles which were not grounded in it.

Since we heard, saw, and felt that there were some who, out of self-seeking, persisted in their disobedience, from which great disadvantage might ensue for us and all of you in the eyes of God, our fellow confederates and other neighbors on our borders who receive tithes in our territories, so we nominated certain councillors and biblical scholars to read through and search the holy Scripture with especial diligence and industry. And we can find in no part of the divine Word, either according to God or the law, that anyone is obliged to give the tithe or to supply it, or [obliged] to renounce it. Thus, it is unfitting for us or any judge to refuse any holders, ecclesiastical or lay their tithes where they have been rendered and received in peaceful possession for many hundreds of years according to praiseworthy ancient tradition and good credentials, and thus to take or remove their property from them. But for many reasons which are godly, Christian, and founded in Scripture, we have decided, adjudged, and affirmed what we wish to be observed this year and each year henceforth:

1. All those who have holdings in our territories . . . whether they be residents or not, shall be bound and obliged to give the great tithe, not only on the seven crops . . . but also on all other items on which each commune or parish has been accustomed to pay the great tithe, wherever and to whom, secular and lay, it was previously given, without alteration or diminution.

2. On the small tithe, since it is unbecoming for us to wrest any possessions, inheritances, or estates from the hands of either natives or foreigners within our territories, we further declare that each parish and commune should deliver and pay the small tithe, together with whatever belonged to it of old, they have habitually rendered, this year and every year henceforth, without dimunition or alteration, but with this concession, that whenever anyone sows a field once during the year, a tithe should be given from it, but any further sowings during the year shall be free. Whoever transgresses the above provisions and is arraigned shall be punished with temporal penalties over and above what he may expect from God, so that he will chose to obey us as his sovereign authority, according to divine Scripture.

3. Nonetheless we will see to it with the help of Almighty God that the ecclesiastical tithes remaining in our lands which we administer shall be restored to a proper use according to the content of the divine Word, i.e. that pastors will be afforded a suitable competency, and that the remainder will be deployed in good time according to the will of God.

4. We are also willing to help to negotiate genuinely over the small tithe, so that where there is anyone, either native or foreigner, who has purchased a small tithe on a deed of redemption, then the parishes or communes may redeem it. But where there is neither a letter of purchase nor a sealed attestation, and the possession is only vested in peaceful ownership and praiseworthy tradition without a deed of redemption, we will apply ourselves amicable and do the best we can, so that the parishes and communes may achieve a reasonable redemption . . .

The peasants were not at all content with this explanation or in agreement with it. They had promised [earlier] . . . that they would commit their lives and goods for the Word of God, [believing that] their evangelical freedom would bring them some advantage. Many took the tithe into their own barns and were later punished for it. They laid all the blame for this on the preachers, since some of them were said to have proclaimed that the tithe was not demanded in the New Testament. Yet since they were ancient traditions, usages, and customs bequeathed to us, no Christian should refuse to pay them, but give the cloak as well as the coat. But this proposal vexed the peasants, who withdrew in great hatred of the preachers, where previously they would have given their right arm for the Gospel.

C. The Peasants' War Engulfs Rothenburg, 1525

Through the preachers here in Rothenburg,—namely, Caspar Cristian, a priest, and Brother Melchior, who married the blind monk's sister and held the wedding in Schwarzman's house,—also especially through the efforts of Hans Rotfuchs, the blind monk himself, and another fellow who gave himself out for a peasant, and through certain citizens here in Rothenburg who adhere to the heresy of Luther and Carlstadt,[1] it has come about that bad, false teaching has greatly got the upper hand, owing also to the dissimulation and concessions of some of the town authorities. Dr. Andreas Carlstadt has appeared in person, preached here, and asked to be received as a burgher.

On March 21, a Tuesday, thirty or forty peasants got together in a mob in Rothenburg, bought a kettledrum, and marched about the town, a part going to Pretheim and a part toward Orenbach. They got together again on Thursday and on Friday, as many as four hundred.

The working classes in the town now begin to revolt. They cease to obey the authorities and form a committee of thirty-six to manage affairs. Cunz Eberhardt and George Bermeter are meanwhile dispatched to learn what the peasants are doing; but the peasants will give no reply, for they say that they have not all got together yet. A letter is received from Margrave Casimir [of Brandenburg]. This is read to the community. He offers to aid the town authorities and if necessary come in person to reëstablish peace and harmony. The community and their committee of thirty-six treat this scornfully and do not accept the offer.

---

[1] Carlstadt was another preacher of reforms, originally an ally of Luther but later an opponent.

March 24. This evening between five and six o'clock some one knocked off the head of Christ's image on a crucifix and struck off the arms.

March 25. The town councils are in great danger and anxiety, for they are oppressed by the community and its committee of thirty-six.

March 27. The councilors are forced to pledge their obedience to the community, for they are taken out one by one, guarded by members of the committee of thirty-six. Each thought he was going to be killed, but after taking the pledge he was secretly sent home without his companions' knowledge.

March 26. Chrischainz, the baker, knocked the missal out of the priest's hand in the chapel of our Lady and drove away the priest from mass. To-day the peasants let themselves be seen in the field outside the Galgenthor.

The following Monday, while the priest was performing service in the parish church and chanting "Adjuva nos, deus salutaris noster" [Save us, Lord our salvation!], Ernfried Kumpf addressed him rudely, saying that if he wished to save himself he would better leave the altar. Kumpf then knocked the missal on to the floor and drove the scholars out of the choir.

On Tuesday eight hundred peasants came together. Those who would not join them willingly they forced to do so or took their property, as happened to a peasant at Wettring.

On Friday the peasants all gathered, as many as two thousand strong, and camped near Neusitz. Lorenz Knobloch went out to them, and they promised to make him a captain. The same day some of the peasants were sent into the town to give a report of their demands and plans. Meanwhile representatives of the emperor and of the Swabian League arrive with a hope of making peace, but they ride away without accomplishing anything, as did those from Nuremberg.

On this same day all the artisans were to lay all their complaints and demands before a committee. The taxes, wages, and methods of weighing were discussed. The peasants encamped near Santhof. Friday, April 7, Kueplein, during the sermon, threw the lighted oil lamps about the church. Some of the peasants came into Rothenburg and the neighboring towns, everywhere plundering cupboards and cellars.

On Good Friday all services were suspended in the churches of Rothenburg, for there was neither chanting nor preaching except that Dr. John Teuschel preached against emperor, kings, princes, and lords, ecclesiastical and lay, with foul abuse and slander, on the ground that they were hindering God's word.

On Saturday the blind monk, Hans Rotfuchs, spoke contemptuously of the holy sacrament, calling it idolatry and heresy.

On Holy Easter there was neither singing nor preaching. . . .

April 18. The reforms of the committee are proclaimed. The younger priests may, and should, marry, and may enjoy their benefices for three years. The old priests shall have theirs for life. There is a struggle between Kueplein and his followers, on the one hand, who want to destroy a picture of the Virgin, and the pious old Christians, on the other, who wish to protect it. Some knives are drawn.

April 19. The peasants take three casks of wine from the priest at Scheckenpach and drink it up.

April 20. The women here in Rothenburg take eleven measures of grain from the house of Conrad Volemar. George Bermeter [one of the revolutionists] is chosen burgomaster.

On the same day, Thursday after Easter, the women run up and down Hafengasse with forks and sticks, declaring that they will plunder all the priests' houses, but are prevented.

Friday. All priests are forced to become citizens, otherwise they would have lost all their goods. They are to take their share of guard duty and work on the fortifications.

On Wednesday (April 26) Lorenz Knobloch was hewn to pieces by the peasants at Ostheim, and then they pelted one another with the fragments. They said he was a traitor and that he wanted to mislead them. Divine retribution! He had said he would not die until he had killed three priests, but, thank God, not one fell into his hands.

April 30. The monastery of Anhausen was plundered and burned in the night, also that near Dinkelsbühl. The peasants also attacked the monastery of Schwarzach, and the castle of Reichelsberg was burned.

May 6. Early in the morning the great bell rang three times, summoning the people to hear a message from Margrave Casimir, brought by three noblemen, and inviting all to take refuge in Rothenburg under his protection. The greater part refused, and some were noted by the margrave's representative, and afterward lost their heads.

Monday. The peasants approach Neuhaus, and next day plunder and burn.

In Rothenburg the citizens are summoned to decide whether, like the neighboring towns of Heilbronn, Dinkelsbühl, and Wimfen, they will aid the peasants. The majority decide to send them guns and pikes, powder and lead.

May 12. The clergy forced to take arms like the rest. All monks are compelled to lay aside their cowls and the nuns their veils.

May 15. The bell summoned the community. In spite of the protests of the old Christians, they are forced to obey the majority, and Rothenburg that day fell away from the empire and joined the peasants. In the meantime a gallows was erected in the market place as a warning, according to their ideas of brotherhood. Supplies were sent to the camp.

May 15. The peasants attack the castle of Würzburg and scale the walls, but are all killed. The peasants attempt to get possession of Rothenburg by conspiracy, but are ejected without bloodshed.

May 21. Certain Hohenlohe peasants burn their lord's castle.

On the next Monday Margrave Casimir proceeds with his forces to subdue and punish the peasants. Hans Krelein the older, priest at Wernitz, was beheaded, with four peasants, at Leutershausen. Seven have their fingers cut off. Likewise at Neuenstat eighteen burghers and peasants are beheaded. At Kitzingen fifty-eight have their eyes put out and are forbidden to enter the town again.

On Friday before Whitsuntide the forces of the Swabian League slay four thousand peasants at Königshofen.

On Monday after Whitsunday eight thousand peasants are slaughtered by the troops of the League near Büttart and Sulzdorf. In all these battles the League lost not over one hundred and fifty men.

On June 6 messengers are sent from Rothenburg to Casimir to ask for pardon. Next day others are sent to the League, but they are told that they must surrender unconditionally.

On Thursday following, after the League had retaken the town of Würzburg, they beheaded sixty-two.

After the League had attacked Bamberg they beheaded twenty-one.

On Friday after Corpus Christi, mass was once more chanted in Rothenburg, as formerly.

June 17. Vespers, complines, and matins are once more sung.

On June 23 Dr. John Teuschel and the blind monk Hans are taken and shut up, but several others, including Dr. Andreas Carlstadt, who had done most to stir up trouble, secretly escape.

On the eve of Peter and Paul's day Margrave Casimir rides into Rothenburg with four hundred horsemen, a thousand footmen, and two hundred wagons full of arms and equipments.

Next day four hundred foot soldiers belonging to the margrave and the League divide into two parts. One went to the village of Orenbach, which they plundered, and burned the church to the ground. The other went to Pretheim, a fine village. This they plundered, killing a number of people, including the innkeeper, behind a table. They burned the village, including the church, and carried off six hundred head of cattle and thirty carts full of plunder.

June 30. The citizens of Rothenburg are summoned to the market place by a herald and surrounded by pikemen. They are accused of deserting the empire and joining the peasants, and are threatened with the vengeance they deserve.

The names of a number of citizens are read off, and they are beheaded on the spot. Their bodies are left on the market place all day. Some got away through the ring of soldiers: Lorenz Diem, the sexton, Joseph Schad, a tanner, Fritz Dalck, a butcher, and others, but were nevertheless executed.

July 1. Fifteen more are beheaded in the market place, including the blind monk. All the bodies are left on the market place all day, then buried. All of these died without confession or the last sacrament, and did not even ask for it.

D. A Peasant Band Pressures a Reluctant Community, 1525

Dear brothers in Christ, our friendly greetings. You have probably heard that our assembly has met at Rappertsweiler on the hill and that we have entered a Christian undertaking. . . . We have heard that some in Hofsteig speak ill of our Christian undertaking, which displeases and disturbs us, and we once again hope that you, the magistrate and entire community, will do as many other Christian people have done and support and not oppose us, and will confirm this in writing. If that does not happen, we must suppose that what has been reported to us is true, and that we will neither tolerate nor endure. Therefore, dear brothers and neighbors, think it over carefully and aid us in our Christian enterprise, and we will commit our lives, honor, and goods to you as Christian brothers. You should do the same for us. Dated in haste at Tettnang on the Tuesday after Invocavit, anno 25.

E. Thomas Müntzer Exhorts His Parishioners, 1525

May the pure fear of God be with you, dear brothers. How long are you going to slumber, how long are you going to resist God's will . . . ? If you are unwilling to suffer for the sake of God, then you will have to be martyrs for the devil. . . . The whole of

Germany, France, Italy is awake; the master wants to set the game in motion, the evildoers are for it. At Fulda four abbeys were laid waste during Easter week, the peasants in the Klettgau and the Hegau in the Black Forest have risen, three thousand strong. . . .

Even if there are only three of you whose trust in God is imperturbable and who seek his name and honor alone, you need have no fear of a hundred thousand. So go to it, go to it, go to it! The time has come, the evildoers are running like scared dogs! . . . Pay no attention to the cries of the godless . . . they will whimper and wheedle like children. Show no pity, as God has commanded in the words of Moses, Deuteronomy 7:[1–5] . . . Alert the villages and towns and especially the mineworkers and other good fellows who will be of use. We cannot slumber any longer.

. . . The time has come. Let Balthasar and Barthel Krump, Valentin and Bischof lead the dance! Let this letter go out to the miners . . .

Go to it, go to it, while the fire is hot. Hammer away ding-dong on the anvils of Nimrod [i.e. the princes and lords], cast down their tower to the ground! As long as they live it is impossible for you to rid yourselves of the fear of men . . . Go to it, go to it, while it is day. God goes before you; follow, follow . . .

This is what God says, "You should have no fear. You should not shrink from this great host; it is not your fight, but the Lord's." . . .

Mühlhausen, in the year 1525.

Thomas Müntzer, a servant of God against the godless.

F. Luther Rages "Against the Murdering and Robbing Bands of Peasants"

In my preceding pamphlet [on the "Twelve Articles"] I had no occasion to condemn the peasants, because they promised to yield to law and better instruction, as Christ also demands (Matt. vii. 1). But before I can turn around, they go out and appeal to force, in spite of their promises, and rob and pillage and act like mad dogs. From this it is quite apparent what they had in their false minds, and that what they put forth under the name of the gospel in the "Twelve Articles" was all vain pretense. In short, they practice mere devil's work, and it is the arch-devil himself who reigns at Mühlhausen,[1] indulging in nothing but rob-

---

[1] Thomas Münzer

bery, murder, and bloodshed; as Christ says of the devil in John viii. 44, "he was a murderer from the beginning." Since, therefore, those peasants and miserable wretches allow themselves to be led astray and act differently from what they declared, I likewise must write differently concerning them; and first bring their sins before their eyes, as God commands (Isa. lviii. 1; Ezek. ii. 7), whether perchance some of them may come to their senses; and, further, I would instruct those in authority how to conduct themselves in this matter.

With threefold horrible sins against God and men have these peasants loaded themselves, for which they have deserved a manifold death of body and soul.

First, they have sworn to their true and gracious rulers to be submissive and obedient, in accord with God's command. . . . But since they have deliberately and sacrilegiously abandoned their obedience, and in addition have dared to oppose their lords, they have thereby forfeited body and soul, as perfidious, perjured, lying, disobedient wretches and scoundrels are wont to do. . . .

Second, they cause uproar and sacrilegiously rob and pillage monasteries and castles that do not belong to them, for which, like public highwaymen and murderers, they deserve the twofold death of body and soul. It is right and lawful to slay at the first opportunity a rebellious person, who is known as such, for he is already under God's and the emperor's ban. Every man is at once judge and executioner of a public rebel; just as, when a fire starts, he who can extinguish it first is the best fellow. Rebellion is not simply vile murder, but is like a great fire that kindles and devastates a country; it fills the land with murder and bloodshed, makes widows and orphans, and destroys everything, like the greatest calamity. Therefore, whosoever can, should smite, strangle, and stab, secretly or publicly, and should remember that there is nothing more poisonous, pernicious, and devilish than a rebellious man. Just as one must slay a mad dog, so, if you do not fight the rebels, they will fight you, and the whole country with you.

Third, they cloak their frightful and revolting sins with the gospel, call themselves Christian brethren, swear allegiance, and compel people to join them in such abominations. Thereby they become the greatest blasphemers and violators of God's holy name, and serve and honor the devil under the semblance of the gospel, so that they have ten times deserved death of body and soul, for never have I heard of uglier sins. And I believe also that the devil foresees the judgment day, that he undertakes such an unheard-of measure; as if he said, "It is the last and therefore it shall be the worst; I'll stir up the dregs and knock the very bottom out." May the Lord restrain him! Lo, how mighty a prince is the devil, how he holds the world in his hands and can put it to confusion: who else could so soon capture so many thousands of peasants, lead them astray, blind and deceive them, stir them to revolt, and make them the willing executioners of his malice. . . .

And should the peasants prevail (which God forbid!),—for all things are possible to God, and we know not but that he is preparing for the judgment day, which cannot be far distant, and may purpose to destroy, by means of the devil, all order and authority and throw the world into wild chaos,—yet surely they who are found, sword in hand, shall perish in the wreck with clear consciences, leaving to the devil the kingdom of this world and receiving instead the eternal kingdom. For we are come upon such strange times that a prince may more easily win heaven by the shedding of blood than others by prayers.

G. Rothenburg Condemns the Anabaptist Michael Sattler, 1527

"In regard to the articles relating to me and my brethren and sisters, hear this brief answer:

"First, that we have acted contrary to the imperial mandate, we do not admit. For the same says that the Lutheran doctrine and delusion is not to be adhered to, but only the gospel and the Word of God. This we have kept. For I am not aware that we have acted contrary to the gospel and the Word of God. I appeal to the words of Christ.

"Secondly, that the real body of Christ the Lord is not present in the sacrament, we admit. For the Scripture says: Christ ascended into heaven and sitteth on the right hand of his Heavenly Father, whence he shall come to judge the quick and the dead, from which it follows that, if he is in heaven and not in the bread, he may not be eaten bodily.

"Thirdly, as to baptism we say infant baptism is of no avail to salvation. For it is written [Rom. 1:17] that we live by faith alone. Again [Mark 16:16]: He that believeth and is baptized shall be saved. Peter says the same [I, ch. 3:21]: Which doth also now save you in baptism (which is signified by that [Ark of Noah]), not the putting away of the filth of the flesh but rather the convenant of a good conscience with God by the resurrection of Jesus Christ. . . .

[He goes on to deny having insulted the Blessed Virgin.]

"Sixthly, we hold that we are not to swear before the authorities, for the Lord says [Matt. 5:34]: Swear not, but let your communication be, Yea, yea; nay, nay.

"Seventhly, when God called me to testify of his Word and I had read Paul and also considered the unchristian and perilous state in which I was, beholding the pomp, pride, usury, and great whoredom of the monks and priests, I went and took unto me a wife, according to the command of God; for Paul well prophesies concerning this to Timothy [I, ch. 4:3]: In the latter time it shall come to pass that men shall forbid to marry and command to abstain from meats which God hath created to be received with thanksgiving.

"Eighthly, if the Turks should come, we ought not to resist them. For it is written [Matt. 5:21]: Thou shalt not kill. We must not defend ourselves against the Turks and others of our persecutors, but are to beseech God with earnest prayer to repel and resist them. . . .

"In conclusion, ministers of God, I admonish you to consider the end for which God has appointed you, to punish the evil and to defend and protect the pious. Whereas, then, we have not acted contrary to God and the gospel, you will find that neither I nor my brethren and sisters have offended in word or deed against any authority. Therefore, ministers of God, if you have neither heard nor read the Word of God, send for the most learned men and for the sacred books of the Bible in whatsoever language they may be and let them confer with us in the Word of God. If they prove to us with the Holy Scriptures that we err and are in the wrong, we will gladly desist and recant and also willingly suffer the sentence and punishment for that of which we have been accused; but if no error is proven to us, I hope to God that you will be converted and receive instruction."

Upon this speech the judges laughed and put their heads together, and the town clerk of Ensisheim said: "Yes, you infamous, desperate rascal of a monk, should we dispute with you? The hangman will dispute with you, I assure you!"

Michael said: "God's will be done."

The town clerk said: "It were well if you had never been born."

Michael replied: "God knows what is good."

The town clerk: "You archheretic, you have seduced pious people. If they would only now forsake their error and commit themselves to grace!"

Michael: "Grace is with God alone."

One of the prisoners also said: "We must not depart from the truth."

The town clerk: "Yes, you desperate villain, you archheretic, I say, if there were no hangman here, I would hang you myself and be doing God a good service thereby."

Michael: "God will judge aright."

[While the judges were deliberating, Sattler was mocked and insulted by the soldiers guarding him.]

The judges having returned to the room, the sentence was read. It was as follows: . . . [J]udgment is passed that Michael Sattler shall be delivered to the executioner, who shall lead him to the place of execution and cut out his tongue, then forge him fast to a wagon and thereon with red-hot tongs twice tear pieces from his body; and after he has been brought outside the gate, he shall be plied five times more in the same manner. . . .

After this had been done in the manner prescribed, he was burned to ashes as a heretic. His fellow brethren were executed with the sword, and the sisters drowned. His wife, also after being subjected to many entreaties, admonitions, and threats, under which she remained steadfast, was drowned a few days afterward. Done the 21st day of May, A.D. 1527.

H. The Anabaptist Obbe Philips Sorrowfully Recants

Just as John Matthijs was truly Enoch with the true commission and apostolic office, so he also came to his end and received his reward according to his works. Melchior died in prison and did not come out again as the prophets and prophetesses had predicted, and all his intentions with all his following toppled to the ground and came to nothing more. John Matthijs, as an apostle and Enoch, was beaten before the gates of Münster in a skirmish or hostile encounter, for he daily strode there in his armor and with his musket like a wild man out of his senses. He was so fierce and bloodthirsty that he brought various people to their deaths; yea, and he was so violent that even his enemies for their part were terrified of him, and when finally in a tumult they became too powerful for him, they were so incensed that they did not just kill him like other people but hacked and chopped him into little pieces, so that his brethren had to carry him in a basket when the tumult was over. Yet some of the brethren insisted that, following the prophecy of Enoch and Elijah, he would be resurrected on the fourth day and before all people he would rise up to heaven or be carried away by a cloud. So blind with such frightful blindness were some of them smitten. . . .

O how many times were some of us so distressed to death that the heart in our bodies turned cold, and we did not know where to turn, nor what best to do; the whole world pursued us to death with fire, water, sword, and bloody tyranny for our belief. The prophecies deceived us on all sides and the letter of the Scriptures took us prisoner. . . .

. . . I shall be silent about all the false commissions, prophecies, visions, dreams, revelations, and unspeakable spiritual pride which immediately from the first hour stole in among the brethren. For those baptized one day cried on the morrow about all the godless, that they must be rooted out. And actually, as soon as anyone was baptized, he was at once a pious Christian and slandered all people and admitted no one on earth to be good but himself and his fellow brethren. Was that not a great and terrible pride? And who can express the great wrangling and dissension among the congregations, of debating and arguing about the Tabernacle of Moses, the cloven claw, about the commission, the armor of David, about the thousand-year Kingdom of Christ on earth, about the incarnation, baptism, belief, Supper, the promised David, second marriage, free will, predestination, the conscious sin unto death. And all this occurred with ban, condemnations, blasphemy, slander, the blackening of reputation, backbiting, judging, and adjudication, [the labeling of others] as heretical, godless, papistical, Lutheran, Zwinglian. And this the brethren did among each other, the one as much as the other, the one this and the other that. . . .

Document Set 15.6 References

A. The German Peasants Plead for Justice: The Twelve Articles
Translations and Reprints from the Original Sources of European History (Philadelphia: University of Pennsylvania Press, 1898), 2/6:25–30.

B. The Zurich City Council and Local Peasants Debate the Justice of Tithes, 1525
Johannes Stumpf, *Reformation Chronicle*, in Tom Scott and Bob Scribner, eds., *The German Peasants' War* (Atlantic Highlands, N.J.: Humanities Press International, 1991), 111–113.

C. The Peasants' War Engulfs Rothenburg, 1525
Michael Eisenhart, in James Harvey Robinson, ed., *Readings in European History* (Boston: Ginn, 1904), 2:106.

D. A Peasant Band Pressures a Reluctant Community, 1525
Captain and Councillors in Tettnang, in Scott and Scribner, 135.

E. Thomas Müntzer Exhorts His Parishioners, 1525
Müntzer, open letter, in Scott and Scribner, 238.

F. Luther Rages "Against the Murdering and Robbing Bands of Peasants"
Martin Luther, in Robinson, 2:106–108.

G. Rothenburg Condemns the Anabaptist Michael Sattler, 1527
Martyrs' Mirror, excerpted in Library of Christian Classics, vol. 25: *Spiritual and Anabaptist Writers*, ed. G. H. Williams (Philadelphia: Westminster Press, n.d.), 138–144.

H. The Anabaptist Obbe Philips Sorrowfully Recants
"Obbe Philips: A Confession," trans. C. T. Lievstro, Library of Christian Classics, 25:221–225.

DOCUMENT SET 15.7
Calvin and the Radicals

In many respects John Calvin (1509–1564) was the heir of the Christian humanist reformers; indeed, he began his career as a humanist, editing Seneca. In his *Institutes of the Christian Religion* (first published in 1536 and revised and expanded several times during his lifetime), Calvin emphatically rejected the charge of "innovator," raised by his Catholic opponents to discredit him (Document A). In the case of Document B, an extract from the *Institutes* in which Calvin spells out his doctrine of predestination, the reformer would likewise have indignantly rejected the label "innovator." Judging from this evidence, why was it so important for sixteenth-century reformers of all camps to insist that they were not innovators but, rather, their opponents were?

Documents C to E all refer to the rigorous regime over which Calvin presided at Geneva. Assess its aims and methods in indoctrinating and coercing (where necessary) the people of Geneva. Would you have liked to live there? Consider your answer both from a twentieth-century perspective and from that of the sixteenth century. In what ways does this regime show Calvin to be an heir of humanism—and, perhaps, of Savonarola (see Set 15.4, Document A)?

Both in Geneva and in east-central Europe the Calvinist movement bore the brunt of defending theological orthodoxy against a growing array of radical critics who attacked such ideas as the Trinity (that is, the teaching that Christianity's One God consisted of three equal manifestations, Father, Son, and Holy Spirit). The Spanish physician Miguel Servetus (1511–1553) was one of the principal preachers of the antitrinitarian position (that God, the Father, is the sole God and that Jesus, the Son, was a man mystically raised to something approaching divinity). Servetus's arguments were difficult to refute without simply reverting to the decrees of ancient church bodies like the fourth-century Council of Nicaea (see Chapter 7). Document F details the charges that the Genevan authorities made against him when Servetus was discovered in that city. Calvin approved the death sentence but tried in vain to have it carried out in a less horrifying manner than burning at the stake, which was Servetus's eventual fate. Document G suggests how readily Servetus's ideas, as well as other radical and Anabaptist teachings, spread in the late sixteenth century in Poland-Lithuania, where central authority was generally too weak (and usually disinclined) to persecute. The Polish-Lithuanian commonwealth, indeed, became a kind of test case for the variety of ways in which complex Christian teachings were understood by unsophisticated lay people (such as were the local gentry, who decided what faith would be preached in their local parish church). The author of this document, Andrzej Lubieniecki, was a nobleman who belonged to a sect that eventually coalesced in a communistic community at the little town of Raków, Poland. What, in your opinion, were the sources of these radical ideas, and how do they relate to the impulses set in motion by Servetus?

A. Calvin Rejects the Charge of "Innovation," 1536

[Our detractors call our teaching] new, and lately forged they cavil that it is doubtful and uncertain; they demand by what miracle it is confirmed; they ask whether it be meet that it should prevail against the consent of so many holy fathers and the most ancient customs; they press upon us to confess it to be schismatical, which moveth war against the Church, or that the true Church hath lain dead through the many ages in which no such thing hath been heard of. Last of all, they say that they need no arguments, for (say they) it may be judged by its fruits of what sort it is, which, namely, hath bred so big a heap of sects, so many turmoils of sedition, so great licentiousness of vices. Truly, full easy it is for them to triumph over a forsaken cause among the credulous and ignorant multitude, but if we might also have our turn to speak, verily this sharp haste would soon be cooled wherewith they do, licentiously and with full mouth, foam against us.

First, whereas they call it new, they do great wrong to God, whose holy word deserves not to be accused of newness. To them indeed I nothing doubt that it is new, to whom Christ is new, and his gospel is new. But they that know the preaching of Paul to be old, and that Jesus Christ died for our sins and rose again for our justification, shall find nothing new among us. Secondly, that it hath long lain hidden, unknown, and buried,—that is the fault of the ungodliness of men. Sith it is by the bountifulness of God restored to us, it ought at least, by right of full restitution, to receive the title of ancient.

They may mock at the uncertainty of our teachings, but if they were driven to steal their own doctrine with their own blood and with the loss of their lives, men might see how much they set by it. Far other is our faith, which dreadeth neither the terrors of death nor yet the very judgment seat of God. . . .

As for the dilemma into which they would drive us, to compel us to confess that either the Church hath lain dead a certain time, or that we have controversy against the real Church: truly the Church of Christ hath lived and shall live so long as Christ shall reign at the right hand of the father. . . . But they err not a little from the truth when they acknowledge no church but that which they see with the present eye, and when they affirm that the form of the Church is always to be seen; for they set the true form of the Church in the see of Rome and in the order of their prelates. We, on the contrary side, affirm both that the Church may consist of no visible form, and that the form itself is not contained in that outward splendor which they foolishly admire, but hath a far other indication, namely, the pure teaching of the word of God and the right ministration of the sacraments. . . .

Thus, O King, is the venomous injustice of slanders so largely spread abroad that you should not too easily believe their reports. . . . Your mind, though it be now turned away and estranged from us, yea, even inflamed against us, yet we trust that we shall be able to recover the favor thereof. But if the whisperings of the malicious do so possess your ears that there is no place for accused men to speak for themselves; and if those outrageous furies do still, with your winking at them, exercise cruelty, with prisoning, tormenting, mutilating, and burning,—then shall we indeed, as sheep appointed to the slaughter, be brought to all extremities, yet so that in our patience we shall possess our soul and wait for the strong hand of the Lord, which shall without doubt be present in time and stretch forth itself armed, both to deliver the poor out of affliction and to take vengeance on the despisers which now triumph with so great assuredness.

The Lord, the King of kings, establish your throne with righteousness and your seat with equity, most noble King.

At Basel, the tenth day before the Kalends of September.

B. Calvin Explains Predestination

Therefore we say that the Scripture shows that God, by His eternal and immutable counsel once for all determined both those whom He desired one day to admit to salvation and those whom He would give back to destruction. We affirm that this counsel as to the elect is founded upon His gratuitous mercy, without any respect to human merit; but to those whom He had handed over to damnation, by His just and blameless though incomprehensible judgment, the way of life is closed.

In the case of the elect we regard calling as an evidence of election, and justification another token of its manifestation, until they arrive in glory, where its fulness shall be found. Just as God seals His elect by calling and justification, so by shutting out the rejected ones either from the knowledge of His name or the sanctification of His spirit He makes known to them the judgment that awaits them.

C. Calvin Plans the Regeneration of Geneva, 1537

Our Lord established excommunication as a means of correction and discipline, by which those who led a disordered life unworthy of a Christian, and who despised to mend their ways and return to the strait way after they had been admonished, should be expelled from the body of the church and cut off as rotten members until they come to themselves and acknowledge their fault. . . . We have an example given by St. Paul (1 Tim. i and 1 Cor. v), in a solemn warning that we should not keep company with one who is called a Christian but who is, none the less, a fornicator, covetous, an idolater, a railer, a drunkard, or an extortioner. So if there be in us any fear of God, this ordinance should be enforced in our Church.

To accomplish this we have determined to petition you [i.e. the town council] to establish and choose, according to your good pleasure, certain persons [namely, the elders] of upright life and good repute among all the faithful, likewise constant and not easy to corrupt, who shall be assigned and distributed in all parts of the town and have an eye on the life and conduct of every individual. If one of these see any obvious vice which is to be reprehended, he shall bring this to the attention of some one of the ministers, who shall admonish whoever it may be who is at fault and exhort him in a brotherly way to correct his ways. If it is apparent that such remonstrances do no good, he shall be warned that his obstinacy will be reported to the church. Then if he repents, there is in that alone excellent fruit of this form of discipline. If he will not listen to warnings, it shall be time for the minister, being informed by those who have the matter in charge, to declare publicly to the congregation the efforts which have been made to bring the sinner to amend, and how all has been in vain.

Should it appear that he proposes to persevere in

his hardness of heart, it shall be time to excommunicate him; that is to say, that the offender shall be regarded as cast out from the companionship of Christians and left in the power of the devil for his temporal confusion, until he shall give good proofs of penitence and amendment. In sign of his casting out he shall be excluded from the communion, and the faithful shall be forbidden to hold familiar converse with him. Nevertheless he shall not omit to attend the sermons in order to receive instruction, so that it may be seen whether it shall please the Lord to turn his heart to the right way.

The offenses to be corrected in this manner are those named by St. Paul above, and others like them. When others than the said deputies—for example, neighbors or relatives—shall first have knowledge of such offenses, they may make the necessary remonstrances themselves. If they accomplish nothing, then they shall notify the deputies to do their duty.

This then is the manner in which it would seem expedient to us to introduce excommunication into our Church and maintain it in its full force; for beyond this form of correction the Church does not go. But should there be insolent persons, abandoned to all perversity, who only laugh when they are excommunicated and do not mind living and dying in that condition of rejection, it shall be your affair to determine whether you should long suffer such contempt and mocking of God to pass unpunished. . . .

If those who agree with us in faith should be punished by excommunication for their offenses, how much more should the Church refuse to tolerate those who oppose us in religion? The remedy that we have thought of is to petition you to require all the inhabitants of your city to make a confession and give an account of their faith, so that you may know who agree with the gospel and who, on the contrary, would prefer the kingdom of the pope to the kingdom of Jesus Christ.

D. Genevan Children Learn Calvinist Doctrine

Concerning the Lord's Supper.

The minister. Have we in the supper simply a signification of the things above mentioned, or are they given to us in reality?

The child. Since Jesus Christ is truth itself there can be no doubt that the promises he has made regarding the supper are accomplished, and that what is figured there is verified there also. Wherefore according as he promises and represents I have no doubt that he makes us partakers of his own substance, in order that he may unite us with him in one life.

The minister. But how may this be, when the body of Jesus Christ is in heaven, and we are on this earthly pilgrimage?

The child. It comes about through the incomprehensible power of his spirit, which may indeed unite things widely separated in space.

The minister. You do not understand then that the body is enclosed in the bread, or the blood in the cup?

The child. No. On the contrary, in order that the reality of the sacrament be achieved our hearts must be raised to heaven, where Jesus Christ dwells in the glory of the Father, whence we await him for our redemption; and we are not to seek him in these corruptible elements.

The minister. You understand then that there are two things in this sacrament: the natural bread and wine, which we see with the eye, touch with the hand and perceive with the taste; and Jesus Christ, through whom our souls are inwardly nourished?

The child. I do. In such a way moreover that we have there the very witness and so say a pledge of the resurrection of our bodies; since they are made partakers in the symbol of life.

E. Geneva Suppresses Catholic Piety, 1546

[August 31, 1546]. The sister of Sr. Curtet, Lucresse, to whom remonstrances have been made on account of her going with certain monies to have masses said at Nessy by the monks of St. Claire. Questioned whether she has no scruples as to what she says. Replied that her father and mother have brought her up to obey a different law from the one now in force here: however she does not despise the present law. Asked as to when was the festival of St. Felix, she replied that it was yesterday. Asked if she had not fasted, she replied that she fasted when it pleased her. Asked if she did not desire to pray to a single God; said that she did. Asked if she did not pray to St. Felix; said that she prayed to St. Felix and other saints who interceded for her. She is very obstinate. Decision that she be sent to some minister of her choice every sermon day and that the Lord's supper be withheld from her. *Calvin present.*

F. Calvin's Secretary Presses the Orthodox Case Against the Antitrinitarian Michael Servetus

Nicholas de la Fontaine asserts that he has instituted proceedings against Michael Servetus, and on this account he has allowed himself to be held prisoner in criminal process.

1. In the first place that about twenty-four years ago the defendant commenced to annoy the churches of Germany with his errors and heresies, and was condemned and took to flight in order to escape the punishment prepared for him.

2. *Item,* that on or about this time he printed a wretched book, which has infected many people.

3. *Item,* that since that time he has not ceased by all means in his power to scatter his poison, as much by his construction of biblical text, as by certain annotations which he has made upon Ptolemy.

4. *Item,* that since that time he has printed in secrecy another book containing endless blasphemies.

5. *Item,* that while detained in prison in the city of Vienne [in France], when he saw that they were willing to pardon him on condition of his recanting, he found means to escape from prison.

Said Nicholas demands that said Servetus be examined upon all these points.

And since he is able to evade the question by pretending that his blasphemies and heresies are nought else than good doctrine, said Nicholas proposes certain articles upon which he demands said heretic be examined.

6. To wit, whether he has not written and falsely taught and published that to believe that in a single essence of God there are three distinct persons, the Father, the Son, and the Holy Ghost, is to create four phantoms, which cannot and ought not to be imagined.

7. *Item,* that to put such distinction into the essence of God is to cause God to be divided into three parts, and that this is a threeheaded devil, like to Cerberus, whom the ancient poets have called the dog of hell, a monster, and things equally injurious. . . .

9. *Item,* whether he does not say that our Lord Jesus Christ is not the Son of God, except in so much as he was conceived of the Holy Ghost in the womb of the virgin Mary.

10. *Item,* that those who believe Jesus Christ to have been the word of God the Father, engendered through all eternity, have a scheme of redemption which is fanciful and of the nature of sorcery.

11. *Item,* that Jesus Christ is God, insomuch as God has caused him to be such. . . .

27. *Item,* that the soul of man is mortal, and that the only thing which is immortal is an elementary breath, which is the substance that Jesus Christ now possesses in heaven and which is also the elementary and divine and incorruptible substance of the Holy Ghost. . . .

32. *Item,* that the baptism of little children is an invention of the Devil, an infernal falsehood tending to the destruction of all Christianity. . . .

37. *Item,* that in the person of M. Calvin, minister of the word of God in the Church of Geneva, he has defamed with printed book the doctrine which he preached, uttering all the injurious and blasphemous things which it is possible to invent. . . .

G. Radical Sects Proliferate in Poland-Lithuania

. . . Within a period so short [1562–1572], and in a corner of the world so small as this our land, we saw a mass of various worships the like of which could have been seen but in heathen times: Roman Catholics, Greeks or Armenians, Jewish, Tartar, Karaimian.

There were many tritheists who, rejecting the word Holy Trinity, worshipped three divine beings: God the Father, God the Son, and the Holy Ghost. Such were the Wilno group, the Lithuania and Podlasie groups, and others [in Lithuania].

There were ditheists, who did not recognize the Holy Ghost as a person and claimed the Son and Father were one in essence, out of the Father. Others said that the Son had been born of the Holy Ghost centuries back, and thought him a minor being.

And those were most markedly split in two.

For there were those who baptized infants, and whose leaders were . . . [several named]; and of them, there is no trace. And second were those who did not baptize infants, and whose leaders were . . . [several named], they too are gone or have been dispersed among other denominations.

Then there were those in the Kujawia [in Poland] who held that Jesus had been with the Father for ages; they baptized adults, differed from the ones above in the instruction of exculpation, and followed a rigorous discipline among themselves; their leaders were then . . . [several named].

Besides them were the Dutch Neo-baptists who had come to settle in [West] Prussia, whose ideas they shared and tried to inculcate in the group; they did not fare well either.

There were those who introduced and propagated Moravian communism[1] and concepts, whom the Moravians themselves were helping to bring in; but they accomplished little, and are not heard of any more.

There were also those who spoke of the Scripture as a dead letter and a daub of printer's ink and, wishing to imitate Schwenkfeld[2], held that dreams, visions, and ideas were the things most necessary in religious practice and for salvation; and to them, sins not contravening civil law did not preclude attendance in churches, temples, and synagogues—as offenses committed in body did not matter if spirits were pure.

There were those who condemned all officiating at any religious service, claiming that nobody was fit to officiate or instruct unless he had had a divine revelation and had either witnessed miracles or performed them. Such were . . . [names listed]; and they too were wiped out by the Lord Jesus.

There were also those who were loutish themselves, walked, lay, and labored in uncouth manner—claiming their ways to be favored by God; and, preening themselves because of them, thought other people undeserving of eternal life. They too are gone and are not seen any more.

There were those who incited godly and honest men to relinquish their offices, put away their arms, refuse litigation regardless of the wrong sustained, and who forbade the repeating of an oath. Many decent men left their offices and sold their estates or scattered their possessions.

But also there were some whose transgression was the worst—and whom Satan strew most thickly throughout Lithuania, White Russia [Belarus], Podlasie, Wolynia [northern Ukraine], and the Ukraine—for they did not believe in Jesus Christ. Some mingled together the Old Testament and the Gospel; others placed the Old Testament above the Gospel and introduced Judaism. And of those, some had taken to celebrate the Sabbath, or did not eat dishes not eaten by Jews. But they too were routed by Jesus Christ through his servants, and moreover wiped out so completely that none remained in our lands.

But God's will was done in the last days of [King Sigismund] Augustus' reign [1569–1572], sapping the strength of all the sects or else destroying them. For when people got weary of controversies and quarrels, of the public bickering going on in the Diets and in the synods held nearly every year, there were men who came out to say they had sickened of all worldly affairs and wished to go away some place in a band so as to live together, practice their religion, and await death in peace. At that time, Mr. Sienieński [a Polish nobleman] founded [the town of] Raków, to which flocked people of the same faith—noblemen, burghers, ministers, and countless others, foreigners and scholars. There was no peace, day or night, for three years (1569–1572), for the various debates went on without respite, until, finally, a fair number were converted through the arguments propounded, while the remainder, unconvinced, went on their way and later perished. The ones who stayed on in Raków were those known as Christians; they continued to live together in peace, having elaborated their doctrine and humbled their hearts, or—as they called it—yielded them to the Lord Jesus. Among them were scores of ministers later assigned to different places: ten were brought by Mr. Kiszka to his Podlasie estates in Lithuania, the Wojewoda Sieniawski took some to Ruthenia [the western Ukraine], Prince Zbaraski had others go to Wolynia, and various noblemen also distributed them throughout their estates.

Document Set 15.7 References

A. Calvin Rejects the Charge of "Innovation," 1536
   John Calvin, letter to Francis I, in James Harvey Robinson, ed., *Readings in European History* (Boston: Ginn, 1904), 2:124–126.
B. Calvin Explains Predestination
   John Calvin, *Institutes of the Christian Religion*, in *Translations and Reprints from the Original Sources of European History* (Philadelphia: University of Pennsylvania Press, 1898), 3/2:7–8.
C. Calvin Plans the Regeneration of Geneva, 1537
   John Calvin's Proposal to Geneva Town Council, in Robinson, 2:130–132.
D. Genevan Children Learn Calvinist Doctrine
   John Calvin, *The Genevan Catechism*, in *Translations and Reprints*, 3/2:8–9.
E. Geneva Suppresses Catholic Piety, 1546
   Geneva Consistory on Heresy Case, in *Translations and Reprints*, 3/2:9.
F. Calvin's Secretary Presses the Orthodox Case Against the Antitrinitarian Michael Servetus
   Nicholas de la Fontaine, in *Translations and Reprints*, 3/2:12–15.
G. Radical Sects Proliferate in Poland-Lithuania
   Andrew Lubieniecki, *Polonoeutychia*, in Stanislaw Kot, *Socinianism in Poland*, trans. E. M. Wilbur (Boston: Starr King, 1957), xv–xvii.

---

[1] A reference to religious and social radicals who established a Hussite- and Anabaptist-influenced community in Moravia (modern Czech Republic) that practiced communism.

[2] Casper Schwenkfeld (1489–1561) was a nobleman who founded a spiritualist movement in Germany that dissented equally from the Lutherans and the Zwinglians; his followers formed small, secret brotherhoods.

DOCUMENT SET 15.8
The Catholic Reformers

This document set, as well as the whole tradition of Erasmian reform (Set 15.4), shows that critics within the Catholic church were conscious of abuses well before Luther appeared. The author of the excerpt in Document A, Gasparo Contarini (1483–1542), a clergyman from a noble Venetian family, remained within the Catholic church and eventually became cardinal. He advocated making concessions that would induce at least the moderate Protestant reformers to return, but his viewpoint did not prevail. Document A, taken from his book *On the Office of Bishops* (1516), appealed to the clergy to root out superstition and encourage "true piety." The Spaniard St. Ignatius de Loyola (1491–1556), the founder of the Jesuit Order, demanded of his followers unswerving obedience to the pope and—as Document B shows—intense devotion, though not asceticism to the point of damaging health. What stand does Loyola take on the great doctrinal issues of the day? The Jesuits were later to become famous for their insistence that individuals could exercise free will to choose repentance and good works, and thus merit salvation; what evidence do you see for this in Loyola's rules?

Document C is an extract from the Council of Trent's final decrees. The Council condemned heresy in terms calculated to draw the sharpest possible line between Catholicism and Protestant "heresy." What evidence for this do you see in Document C? Compare the Council of Trent's approach to thirteenth-century efforts to tighten up church discipline (Set 12.2). Do you see any common threads, and if so, what are they?

A. Gasparo Contarini Attacks Superstition and Impiety, 1516

The other sin . . . is superstition which is what I might call an exaggeration [*excessus*] of religion. . . . Therefore let all superstition be diligently destroyed, so that when the saints dwelling in heaven are invoked or their relics are venerated or likenesses of the Lord, the Most Blessed Virgin, and other saints are depicted in the churches everything be done with the greatest propriety and in good order. Such practices ought to lead the people to the worship of the one God as if they were leading them step by step by hand, so to speak. But if any abuse in these matters does creep in, it will be well for the prudent Bishop and ecclesiastic to do away with it gradually, lest, if we are carried along hastily or without consideration, we destroy the very worship of God, faith in the sacraments, and also the hierarchical order of the Church as heretics have done. Consequently, let the people often be taught that in all things God must be loved and worshipped; also, that all exists because of God without whom nothing has been made; and that the saints themselves are nothing. Thus, let every action and thought proceed from Him and to Him finally return, as the Alpha and Omega. If men have recourse to the saints, let them know why they are doing it and in addition what has been most wisely decreed and explained by the Councils. But if anyone, either because of avarice or for some other reason, should make wrong use of relics or sacred images, let such plagues at once be kept far from the Church of God and let a heavy penalty be imposed, lest Christian purity be corrupted by these perversions.

When the error of superstition and the sin of impiety have been avoided, the people can be easily kept in the right religious path. Nevertheless, let the Bishop take care that everyone frequent the sacraments of Penance and the Eucharist at least at the proper times, and let him inquire about this of the priests in charge of the districts of the city and the villages. If anyone fails in this obligation, let the Bishop first endeavor, having summoned the offender before him, to call him back to his duty and the right path of piety by persuasion and gentle rebuking. But if he observes that anyone obstinately persists in his wrongdoing and refuses to be corrected, then let him judge him guilty before others and subject to the ecclesiastical fines and censures, lest others also be infected by contact with the evil of that man.

Further, let the Bishop attend to the education of the young people, and let him not allow, as far as he is able, the souls of boys from their youth to be corrupted by the licentiousness of poets and other authors of this kind. If the young drink in such wantonness in their childhood years, it will be almost impossible to summon them again at a maturer age to greater virtue. . . .

B. St. Ignatius Loyola Codifies the Rules for Thinking with the Catholic Church

In order to think truly, as we ought, in the church militant, the following rules are to be observed.

Laying aside all private judgment, we ought to keep our minds prepared and ready to obey in all things the true Spouse of Christ our Lord, which is our Holy Mother, the Hierarchical Church.

The second is to praise confession made to a priest, and the reception of the Most Holy Sacrament, once a year, and what is much better once a month, and much better still every eight days, always with the requisite and due dispositions.

The third is to praise the frequent hearing of Mass, also hymns, psalms, and long prayers, both in and out of the church, and likewise the hours ordained at fixed times for all the Divine Office, for prayers of any kind, and all the canonical hours.

The fourth, to praise greatly religious orders, and a life of virginity and continency, and not to praise the married state as much as any of these.

The fifth is to praise the vows of religion, of Obedience, Poverty, and Chastity, and vows to perform other works of perfection and supererogation; and it is to be noticed that as a vow is made in matters more nearly approaching evangelical perfection, so in matters which depart from it a vow ought not to be made, *e.g.,* to become a merchant or to enter the marriage state. &c.

The sixth is to praise the relics of saints, showing veneration to the relics, and praying to the saints, and to praise likewise the Stations, pilgrimages, indulgences, jubilees, Bulls of the *Cruciata* [crusade], and candles lighted in churches.

The seventh is to praise the precepts with regard to fasts and abstinences, as those of Lent, Ember days, Vigils, Fridays, and Saturdays; likewise not only interior but also exterior penances.

To praise the building and the ornaments of churches; and also images, and to venerate them according to what they represent.

Finally, to praise all the precepts of the Church, keeping our minds ready to seek reasons to defend, never to impugn them. . . .

To attain the truth in all things, we ought always to hold that we believe what seems to us white to be black, if the Hierarchical Church so defines it; believing that between Christ our Lord the Bridegroom and the Church His Bride there is one and the same Spirit, which governs and directs us to the salvation of our souls; for our Holy Mother the Church is guided and ruled by the same Spirit and Lord that gave the Ten Commandments.

Although it is very true that no one can be saved without being predestined, and without having faith and grace, we must be very careful in our manner of speaking and treating of all this subject.

We ought not habitually to speak of much of Predestination; but if sometimes mention be made of it in any way, we must so speak that the common people may not fall into error, as happens sometimes when they say: "It is already fixed whether I am to be saved or damned, and there cannot be any other result whether I do good or ill"; and, becoming slothful in consequence, they neglect works conducive to their salvation, and to the spiritual profit of their souls.

In the same way it is to be noticed that we must take heed lest by speaking much with great earnestness on Faith, without any distinction or explanation, occasion be given to the people to become slothful and sluggish in good works, whether it be before or after that faith is formed in charity.

In like manner we ought not to speak or to insist on the doctrine of Grace so strongly, as to give rise to that poisonous teaching that takes away free-will. Therefore, we may treat of Faith and Grace, as far as we may with the help of God, for the greater praise of His Divine Majesty; but not in such a way, especially in these dangerous times of ours, that works or free-will receive any detriment, or come to be accounted for nothing.

Although it is above all things praiseworthy to greatly serve God our Lord out of pure love, yet we ought much to praise the fear of His Divine Majesty, because not only is filial fear a pious and most holy thing, but even servile fear, when a man does not rise to anything better and more useful, is of great help to him to escape from mortal sin; and, after he has escaped from it, he easily attains to filial fear, which is altogether acceptable and pleasing to God our Lord, because it is inseparable from Divine love.

C. The Council of Trent Decrees Reform and Condemns Protestant Doctrine

The universal Church has always understood that the complete confession of sins was instituted by the Lord, and is of divine right necessary for all who have fallen into sin after baptism; because our Lord Jesus Christ, when about to ascend from earth to heaven, left priests, his own vicars, as leaders and judges, before whom all the mortal offenses into which the faithful of Christ may have fallen should be carried, in order that, in accordance with the power of the keys, they may pronounce the sentence of forgiveness or of retention of sins. For it is manifest that priests could not have exercised this judgment without knowledge of the case. . . .

This holy Council enjoins on all bishops and others who are charged with teaching, that they instruct the faithful diligently concerning the intercession and invocation of saints, the honor paid to relics, and the legitimate use of images. Let them teach that the saints, who reign together with Christ, offer up their own prayers to God for men; that it is good and useful suppliantly to invoke them, and to have recourse to their prayers and aid in obtaining benefits from God, through his Son, Jesus Christ our Lord, who is our sole Redeemer and Saviour; and that those persons think impiously who deny that the saints, who enjoy eternal happiness in heaven, are to be invoked; or who assert that the saints do not pray for men, or that the invocation of them to pray for each of us individually is idolatry; or who declare that it is repugnant to the word of God, and opposed to the honor of the "one mediator of God and men, Christ Jesus," or that it is foolish to supplicate, orally or mentally, those who reign in heaven. . . .

If any one saith that the New Testament does not provide for a distinct, visible priesthood; or that this priesthood has not any power of consecrating and offering up the true body and blood of the Lord, and of forgiving and retaining sins, but is only an office and bare ministry of preaching the gospel; or that those who do not preach are not priests at all; let him be anathema. . . .

If any one saith that by sacred ordination the Holy Ghost is not given, and that vainly therefore do the bishops say, "Receive ye the Holy Ghost"; or that a character is not imprinted by that ordination; or that he who has once been a priest can again become a layman; let him be anathema. . . .

If any one saith that in the Catholic Church there is not a hierarchy instituted by divine ordination, consisting of bishops, priests, and ministers; let him be anathema.

If any one saith that the sacraments of the new law were not all instituted by Jesus Christ, our Lord; or that they are more or less than seven, to wit, baptism, confirmation, the eucharist, penance, extreme unction, orders, and matrimony; or even that any one of these seven is not truly and properly a sacrament; let him be anathema. . . .

In order that the faithful may approach and receive the sacraments with greater reverence and devotion of mind, this Holy Council enjoins on all bishops that, not only when they are themselves about to administer them to the people they shall first explain, in a manner suited to the capacity of those who receive them, the efficacy and use of those sacraments, but they shall endeavor that the same be done piously and prudently by every parish priest; and this even in the vernacular tongue, if need be, and if it can be conveniently done.

Such instruction shall be given in accordance with the form which will be prescribed for each of the sacraments by this holy Council in a catechism, which the bishops shall take care to have faithfully translated into the vulgar tongue, and to have expounded to the people by all parish priests. They shall also explain in the said vulgar tongue, during the solemnization of mass, or the celebration of the divine offices, on all festivals or solemnities, the sacred oracles and the maxims of salvation; and, setting aside all unprofitable questions, they shall endeavor to impress them on the hearts of all, and to instruct their hearers in the law of the Lord. . . .

It is to be desired that those who undertake the office of bishop should understand what their portion is, and comprehend that they are called, not to their own convenience, not to riches or luxury, but to labors and cares, for the glory of God. For it is not to be doubted that the rest of the faithful also will be more easily excited to religion and innocence if they shall see those who are set over them not fixing their thoughts on the things of this world, but on the salvation of souls and on their heavenly country. Wherefore this holy Council, being minded that these things are of the greatest importance towards restoring ecclesiastical discipline, admonishes all bishops that, often mediating thereon, they show themselves conformable to their office by their actual deeds and the actions of their lives; which is a kind of perpetual sermon; but, above all, that they so order their whole conversation that others may thence be able to derive examples of frugality, modesty, continency, and of that holy humility which so much commends us to God.

Wherefore, after the example of our fathers in the Council of Carthage, this Council not only orders that bishops be content with modest furniture, and a frugal table and diet, but that they also give heed that in the rest of their manner of living, and in their whole house, there be nothing seen which is alien to this holy institution, and which does not manifest simplicity, zeal toward God, and a contempt of vanities.

It strictly forbids them, moreover, to strive to

enrich their own kindred or domestics out of the revenues of the Church; seeing that even the canons of the apostles forbid them to give to their kindred the property of the Church, which belongs to God; but if their kindred be poor, let them distribute to them thereof as poor, but not misapply or waste the Church's goods for their sakes: yea, this holy Council, with the utmost earnestness, admonishes them completely to lay aside all this human and carnal affection towards brothers, nephews, and kindred, which is the seed plot of many evils in the Church. And what has been said of bishops, the same is to be observed by all who hold ecclesiastical benefices, whether secular or regular, each according to the nature of his rank. . . .

Document Set 15.8 References

A. Gasparo Contarini Attacks Superstition and Impiety, 1516
Contarini, *De Officio Episcopi,* in John C. Olin, ed., *The Catholic Reformation: Savoranola to Ignatius Loyola* (New York: Harper & Row, 1969), 105–106.

B. St. Ignatius Loyola Codifies the Rules for Thinking with the Catholic Church
Loyola, *Spiritual Exercises,* trans. Burns and Oates, 4th ed. (1908).

C. The Council of Trent Decrees Reform and Condemns Protestant Doctrine
Acts of the Council of Trent, in Robinson, 2:156–161.

DOCUMENT SET 15.9
The Triumph of the State

Document A, an extract from an early sixteenth-century description of the French monarchy by Claude de Seyssel, *The Grand Monarchy of France,* sets forth a very traditional view of how kings and subjects ought to relate to one another. Point out elements in his description that might have been written in the Middle Ages. How realistic does such a political order seem under sixteenth-century conditions? Specifically, how would Seyssel's views be received by his near contemporary, Niccolò Machiavelli (1469–1527)? An extract from Machiavelli's *The Prince* appears as Document B. Why did Machiavelli's ideas so shock his contemporaries, even though the practices he described were commonplace? How would you evaluate Emperor Charles V's instructions to his high official Matthias Held, bearing in mind Seyssel's remarks on how a ruler ought to behave and Machiavelli's observations on how princes actually acted?

The Peace of Augsburg in 1555 ended Catholic resistance to legalizing Lutheranism (not Calvinism or radical Protestantism) within the Holy Roman Empire. How would you evaluate the provisions, excerpted in Document D, from the standpoint of "reasons of state"? What decisions did the Peace leave to the princes?

A. Claude de Seyssel Describes the Traditional Values of the French Monarchy

The authority and power of the king in France is regulated and restrained by three checks . . . the first is Religion, the second, Justice and the third, Police. . . .

With regard to the first, it is an indisputable fact that the French have always been, and still are . . . pious and god-fearing . . . For that reason it is both proper and necessary that whoever is king should make it known to the people by example and by visible and outward signs that he is a zealot, an observer of the Faith and of the Christian religion, and that he is resolved to use his power to sustain and strengthen it . . . so long as the king respects . . . the Christian religion he cannot act as a tyrant. If he is guilty of such an act, it is permissible for a prelate or any other devout man of religion who respects the people, to remonstrate with and to upbraid him, and for a simple preacher to rebuke and accuse him publicly as well as in private. . . .

Justice, which is the second check . . . indubitably carries more weight in France than in any other country in the world, especially because of the institution of the *Parlements,* whose principal rose is to bridle the absolute power which kings might seek to use. . . . In the matter of distributive justice the king has always been subject to these courts, so that in civil cases an individual may gain satisfaction and justice indiscriminately against the king or against his subjects. As far as criminal cases are concerned, royal pardons and remissions are so contested, and those who obtain them are the subject of such violent argument that, lacking hope and confidence in such remissions, few people dare to act in an ill-advised, much less in a thoroughly odious manner. . . . Besides, justice is that much more powerful because those who are deputed to administer it have permanent possession of their offices and the king has no power to remove them, save in the event of forfeiture. . . .

The third check is that of Police, by which is intended those many ordinances that have been promulgated, and subsequently confirmed and approved from time to time, by the kings themselves, which help to preserve the kingdom as a whole and the rights of the individuals who compose it. . . .

Regarding the monarchical state, since everything depends upon the monarch it appears that no other remedy for abuse is required, no other means of maintaining order is necessary than that the king should be good. Because he commands the entire obedience of his subjects he can, without difficulty, enforce the observance and maintenance of good laws, ordinances and customs, he can correct and annul those which are not beneficial or completely faultless, and he can make new laws if necessary; by living in a law-abiding way himself he can induce his subjects to follow his example and . . . do what is right. . . .

B. Niccolò Machiavelli Asks "Whether It Is Prudent for a Prince to Keep His Promises," 1513

Every one understands how praiseworthy it is in a prince to keep faith, and to live uprightly and not craftily. Nevertheless we see, from what has taken place in our own days, that princes who have set little store by their word, but have known how to overreach men by their cunning, have accomplished great things, and in the end got the better of those who trusted to honest dealing.

Be it known, then, that there are two ways of contending,—one in accordance with the laws, the other by force; the first of which is proper to men, the second to beasts. But since the first method is often ineffectual, it becomes necessary to resort to the second. A prince should, therefore, understand how to use well both the man and the beast. . . . But inasmuch as a prince should know how to use the beast's nature wisely, he ought of beasts to choose both the lion and the fox; for the lion cannot guard himself from the toils, nor the fox from wolves. He must therefore be a fox to discern toils, and a lion to drive off wolves.

To rely wholly on the lion is unwise; and for this reason a prudent prince neither can nor ought to keep his word when to keep it is hurtful to him and the causes which led him to pledge it are removed. If all men were good, this would not be good advice, but since they are dishonest and do not keep faith with you, you in return need not keep faith with them; and no prince was ever at a loss for plausible reasons to cloak a breach of faith. Of this numberless recent instances could be given, and it might be shown how many solemn treaties and engagements have been rendered inoperative and idle through want of faith among princes, and that he who has best known how to play the fox has had the best success.

It is necessary, indeed, to put a good color on this nature, and to be skilled in simulating and dissembling. But men are so simple, and governed so absolutely by their present needs, that he who wishes to deceive will never fail in finding willing dupes. One recent example I will not omit. Pope Alexander VI had no care or thought but how to deceive, and always found material to work on. No man ever had a more effective manner or asseverating, or made promises with more solemn protestations, or observed them less. And yet, because he understood this side of human nature, his frauds always succeeded. . . .

In his efforts to aggrandize his son the duke [Caesar Borgia], Alexander VI had to face many difficulties, both immediate and remote. In the first place, he saw no way to make him ruler of any state which did not belong to the Church. Yet, if he sought to take for him a state of the Church, he knew that the duke of Milan and the Venetians would withhold their consent, Faenza and Rimini [towns in the province of Romagna] being already under the protection of the latter. Further, he saw that the forces of Italy, and those more especially of which he might

have availed himself, were in the hands of men who had reason to fear his aggrandizement,—that is, of the Orsini, the Colonnesi [Roman noble families] and their followers. These, therefore, he could not trust. . . .

And since this part of his [Caesar Borgia's] conduct merits both attention and imitation, I shall not pass it over in silence. After the duke had taken Romagna, finding that it had been ruled by feeble lords, who thought more of plundering than of governing their subjects,—which gave them more cause for division than for union, so that the country was overrun with robbery, tumult, and every kind of outrage,—he judged it necessary, with a view to rendering it peaceful, and obedient to his authority, to provide it with a good government. Accordingly he set over it Messer Remiro d' Orco, a stern and prompt ruler, who, being intrusted with the fullest powers, in a very short time, and with much credit to himself, restored it to tranquillity and order. But afterwards the duke, apprehending that such unlimited authority might become odious, decided that it was no longer needed, and established the center of the province a civil tribunal, with an excellent president, in which every town was represented by its advocate. And knowing that past severities had generated ill feeling against himself, in order to purge the minds of the people and gain their good will, he sought to show them that any cruelty which had been done had not originated with him, but in the harsh disposition of this minister. Availing himself of the pretext which this afforded, he one morning caused Remiro to be beheaded, and exposed in the market place of Cesena with a block and bloody ax by his side. The barbarity of this spectacle at once astounded and satisfied the populace.

C. Monarchy in Practice: Charles V Secretly Instructs Vice-Chancellor Mathias Held, 1536

In addition to the instructions which you, Messire Mathias Held, our dear and faithful councillor and Vice-Chancellor of the Empire, have already received, drawn up in German, and relating to the business for which we have sent you to Germany, we think it essential to confide in you the following secret instructions, which you are to impart confidentially to the king, our good brother [Ferdinand I] and to the most reverend cardinal of Trent, without, however, allowing the matter to reach the ears of any one else.

First you shall inform my lord, our brother concerning what you saw and heard of public matters up to the time of your departure, and of the existing relation with the pope, the Venetians, an other powers of Italy, as well as with the kings of France and of England. Of these matters we shall say no more here since we do not wish to lengthen this instruction unduly, and are, morever, expecting more exact information of the status of affairs. You will also speak of the conditions in Flanders, and of various other matters which can be more advantageously communicated by you than written.

The information which you might otherwise convey to our brother, as to the policy which we desire and are in a position to adopt, cannot well be formulated without learning first what action the said king of France will take in regard to peace and the conditions which we have offered in the case of Milan. These you have seen, and of them you have a copy. We must, moreover, learn what further violence the said king will resort to. Inform our brother of the measures we have taken to learn as soon as possible if matters can be arranged. He must, moreover, be made aware of the measures which the pope, the Venetians and the other powers will take should the king of France obstinately continue the war. It is further very essential to learn the aim and intentions of the electors, princes and estates of the Empire in respect to the matters with which you are commissioned, not only as regards the question of the faith, but concerning the sympathy and assistance which we may expect and hope from them. You must exercise the greatest diligence and prudence in this matter, and inform us of the disposition which you find.

In view of the ill-will which the king of France has always shown, and the frequent negotiations for peace which have come to naught, we are inclined to doubt whether any results will be reached in the present case, hence it is especially important that you should make every effort to learn what can be done to gain the favor and assistance of Germany in case of the continuance of the war.

It must always be kept in mind that the division in Germany is at bottom entirely due to the controversy in regard to our holy religion. This prevents Germany from being united as it should be in obedience to us and the holy Empire. This encourages the king of France, moreover, to persist in the war, and furnishes him an obvious excuse for impeding, in a most unwarrantable fashion, the meeting of the council.[1] The confusion may even become worse in view of the said king's favorable attitude towards the

Turks, should no means be found to restore peace. This point must be emphasized in Germany, and some agreement ought to be reached as to the measures which should be adopted in case the pope, through the influence of the said king of France or through fear on the part of the Holy Father of losing his authority in the kingdom of France, should refuse to consent to the calling of the council, on the ground of the war between us and the king of France, or for other reasons. To say the truth it would seem, in spite of the evil deeds of the king of France, which are notorious and proven beyond the chance of doubt, that the Holy Father does not care to take any measure against the king, but that he will, in a word, remain neutral until he discovers which is in the wrong, as if the king of France had committed no offences up to the present and our actions belonged in the same category as his. He would seem to excuse himself and escape responsibility on the ground that he ought to arbitrate between us as a father and that, especially, he fears the loss of his authority in France. He may in this way be simply disguising the partiality which he constantly showed towards France before he became pope.

It is, however, none the less true that, in spite of the anxiety caused by the attitude of the Holy Father and the obstinacy of the king of France, we do not wish to use our power in any way against the apostolic authority and dignity [the papacy], or do anything prejudicial, directly or indirectly, to the essentials of our religion or the holy Catholic institutions. But we see clearly that should the pope continue to maintain his attitude of indifference or dissimulation, and not frankly consent to a council, it is all the more necessary that some means should be devised as soon as possible to prevent an increase of confusion in Germany, which will cause the destruction both of religion and the imperial authority. Owing to this disorder we are prevented from doing anything for Christianity itself or towards the defence against the Turks, whom the king of France is constantly encouraging. Our power is thus paralyzed to an extent which manifestly jeopardizes our realms and estates and those of our brother.

For these reasons, while maintaining the great secrecy which the affair demands, you should confer very particularly with my lord our brother, as to whether there be any way of celebrating the council, should Germany consent, even if the said pope and king of France should not agree to it, and as to how this may be done and with what certainty. This would seem to be a plan based upon perfect right and reason, and all the more, because the Holy Father has already promised a council and pledged himself expressly for

---

[1] That is, an ecumenical council to settle issues raised by the Reformation.

the king of France. The principal need of a council is, moreover, for the German nation. The king of Portugal will consent to and support the plan, as will probably the king of Poland, and the most of the powers of Italy. As for England, since it is utterly schismatic, the pope and the king of France cannot validly allege against the legitimacy of the council the fact that that country was not included.

Should the resort to a council in Germany, with the approbation of all or the greater part of that nation, prove impracticable, it should be determined whether there is not some other expedient, for example, to assure those who have fallen from the faith that no further coercion will be used if they will but sincerely conform with the other members of Germany in maintaining peace at home and in cooperating with our said brother and ourselves, or might not the treaty of Nuremberg by modified, or such a new one drawn up as the change of times and altered circumstances might dictate. Or may it not be advisable to call a national assembly in Germany and adjust, or neglect, such matters as may not be essential to our holy religion. Or let some other expedient be devised so that the imperial, Roman authority be not sacrificed, as well as our said brother and ourselves, even should it not supply a remedy in the matter of religion. For we can but wait until God grants such remedy as he shall judge fitting to his holy service, since he knows the regret with which our said brother and we behold the sad state of affairs, and that our aim and desire is to serve him and apply ourselves to cure the existing evils so soon as any means shall offer themselves.

We are thus placed in a difficult and critical position, for we cannot have peace if our enemy does not consent, for, as it is well known, he is as obstinate as he is powerful, and regards neither God nor good faith, placing his chief hope in the division of Germany and the difference in religious matters which exists there, as well as in the approach of the Turk, whom, as it is reported, he spares no efforts to encourage. In view of this it behooves our brother to turn his attention to this matter, since everything is at stake, and to find some way of settling his difficulties in Hungary, and any other complications in which he may be involved. For it would be quite impossible for us to lend him any assistance, being, as we are, far in arrears for the outlays we have been forced to make in the past. Our kingdoms and countries are so surcharged with burdens that we do not know where we are to look for the absolutely necessary means of continuing this war. This is one of the chief motives which induces us to return to our Spanish kingdoms in order to take council there as to what may be done.

D. The Triumph of State Interests: The German Princes Conclude the Peace of Augsburg, 1555

. . . In order that . . . peace, which is especially necessary in view of the divided religions, as is seen from the causes before mentioned, and is demanded by the sad necessity of the Holy Roman Empire of the German nation, may be the better established and made secure and enduring between his Roman Imperial Majesty and us, on the one hand, and the electors, princes, and estates of the Holy Empire of the German nation on the other, therefore his Imperial Majesty, and we, and the electors, princes, and estates of the Holy Empire will not make war upon any estate of the empire on account of the Augsburg Confession and the doctrine, religion, and faith of the same, nor injure nor do violence to those estates that hold it, nor force them, against their conscience, knowledge, and will, to abandon the religion, faith, church usages, ordinances, and ceremonies of the Augsburg Confession, where these have been established, or may hereafter be established, in their principalities, lands, and dominions. Nor shall we, through mandate or in any other way, trouble or disparage them, but shall let them quietly and peacefully enjoy their religion, faith, church usages, ordinances, and ceremonies, as well as their possessions, real and personal property, lands, people, dominions, governments, honors, and rights. . . .

On the other hand, the estates that have accepted the Augsburg Confession shall suffer his Imperial Majesty, us, and the electors, princes, and other estates of he Holy Empire, adhering to the old religion, to abide in like manner by their religion, faith, church usages, ordinances, and ceremonies. They shall also leave undisturbed their possessions, real and personal property, lands, people, dominions, government, honors, and rights, rents, interest, and tithes. . . .

But all others who are not adherents of either of the above-mentioned religions are not included in this peace, but shall be altogether excluded. . . .

No estate shall urge another estate, or the subjects of the same, to embrace its religion.

But when our subjects and those of the electors, princes, and estates, adhering to the old religion or to the Augsburg Confession, wish, for the sake of their religion, to go with wife and children to another place in the lands, principalities, and cities of the electors, princes, and estates of the Holy Empire, and settle there, such going and coming, and the sale of property and goods, in return for reasonable compensation for serfdom and arrears of taxes, . . . shall be everywhere unhindered, permitted, and granted. . . .

Document Set 15.9 References

A. Claude de Seyssel Describes the Traditional Values of the French Monarchy
De Seyssel, *La Monarchie de France,* in J. H. Shennan, *Government and Society in France, 1461–1661* (London: George Allen & Unwin, 1969), 77–78.

B. Niccolò Machiavelli Asks "Whether It Is Prudent for a Prince to Keep His Promises," 1513
Machiavelli, *The Prince,* trans. N. H. Thomson, in James Harvey Robinson, ed., *Readings in European History* (Boston: Ginn, 1904), 2:10–13.

C. Monarchy in Practice: Charles V Secretly Instructs Vice-Chancellor Mathias Held, 1536
Translations and Reprints from the Original Sources of European History (Philadelphia: University of Pennsylvania Press, 1898), 2/6:31–34.

D. The Triumph of State Interests: The German Princes Conclude the Peace of Augsburg, 1555
"The Religious Peace of Augsburg," in Robinson, 2:114–116.

DOCUMENT SET 15.10
Courtiers and Patrons

Amid the Reformation era's wars and doctrinal disputes, court life throughout Europe was becoming more refined, though not notably more moral. The great model for courtly behavior—it was translated into most European languages—was *The Courtier,* a series of dialogues written by the Italian diplomat Baldassare Castiglione (1478–1529). An extract appears as Document A. What conclusion do you draw from the *tone* of the dialogue—the rather light-hearted bantering, the advice that the "perfect courtier" adopt the pose of "nonchalance" even when he performs difficult feats, and the apparently equal participation of men and women in the conversation?

A very different view of court life came from the *Heptameron* of Marguerite de Navarre (1492–1549), the queen of Navarre and sister of Francis I, who spent most of her life at the French court. A gifted writer and woman of strong, rather unorthodox, religious convictions, Marguerite in the *Heptameron* tells a series of stories. In the one excerpted here, a nobleman has attempted to rape a princess, a woman of great beauty and virtue, but she fights off her assailant with the assistance of her lady-in-waiting. After hearing the story, the male and female characters in *Heptameron* comment: Hircain claims that male honor justifies even murder, to which the noblewoman Nomerfide responds with horror.

Still another classic literary account of court life comes from Thomas More's *Utopia* (1516). Scholars still debate the meaning of More's famous book, describing an imaginary land of "nowhere" (Utopia) and contrasting it with the injustices of sixteenth-century life. But the passage quoted here as Document C seems to have a clear meaning: in it More expresses his own ambivalence about serving King Henry VIII at court because he will not be able to give his king truly honest advice. (As it happened, More did become a royal servitor but was beheaded in 1535 because he refused to support Henry's break with Rome.)

Document D offers still another perspective on court life. As noted in Set 14.2, the treatment of Renaissance artists ranged from peremptory to highly deferential. In the sixteenth century the trend toward regarding *some* artists as inspired geniuses continued. Michelangelo (1475–1564) was unquestionably regarded with awe—often mixed with exasperation—by his contemporaries, including the cardinal who sent him this obsequious letter.

After examining these documents and using *The Challenge of the West* for background, prepare an analysis of the place of courts and artistic patronage in early sixteenth-century life. It would also be helpful to consider Set 15.9.

A. Baldassare Castiglione Describes the Perfect Courtier

Messer Federico replied: "Get Marquess Febus to tell you, who has often seen them in France; and perhaps they were done to him."

Marquess Febus replied: "I have seen nothing of the kind done in France that is not also done in Italy; but every thing that is good among the Italians in the way of dress, sports, banquets, handling arms, and everything else that befits a Courtier— they have gotten it all from the French."

"I do not say," replied messer Federico, "that very fine and modest cavaliers are not also to be found among the French, and I myself have known many that are truly worthy of every praise. Still, there are some who are careless; and, generally speaking, it strikes me that the customs of the Spaniards suit the Italians better than do those of the French, because the calm gravity that is peculiar to the Spaniards is, I think, far more suited to us than the ready vivacity we see in the French in almost all their movements: which is not unbecoming to them, nay, is charming, because it is so natural and proper to them as not to appear an affectation on their part. There are indeed many Italians who devote every effort to imitating that manner; and they do nothing but shake their heads as they speak, bowing clumsily to the side; and when they pass through town they walk so fast that their lackeys cannot keep up with them. By way of such manners they deem themselves to be good Frenchmen and to have the free manner of the French, which actually happens rarely save in those who have been reared in France and have acquired the manner from childhood.

"The same is true of knowing many languages, which is something I very much approve of in the Courtier, especially Spanish and French, because intercourse with both of these nations is very frequent in Italy, and they have more in common with us than any of the others; and their two princes, being very powerful in war and most magnificent in peace, always have their courts full of noble cavaliers, who are then spread abroad in the world; and we do indeed have occasion to hold converse with them.". . .

"Now I would not go on to speak in any more detail of things too well known, such as that our Courtier ought not to profess to be a great eater or drinker, or be dissolute in any bad habit, or be vile or disorderly in his way of life, or have certain peasant ways that bespeak the hoe and the plow a thousand miles away; because a man of this sort not only may not hope to become a good Courtier, but no suitable job can be given him other than tending sheep.

"And, to conclude, I declare that it would be well for the Courtier to know perfectly all we have said befits him, so that everything possible may be easy for him, and that everyone may marvel at him and he at no one. It is understood however, that in this there is to be no proud and inhuman rigidity, such as some have who refuse to show any wonder at all at what others do, because they think they are able to do much better, and by their silence they scorn those things as unworthy of any mention; and act as if they wished to show that no one is their equal, let alone able to undersand the profundity of their knowledge. The Courtier must avoid these odious ways, and praise the good achievements of others with kindness and good will; and, although he may feel that he is admirable and much superior to all others, yet he ought not to appear to think so.

"But because such complete perfection as this is very rarely, and perhaps never, found in human nature, a man who feels himself wanting in some particular ought not to lose confidence in himself or the hope of reaching a high mark, even though he cannot attain to that perfect and highest excellence to which he aspires. For in every art there are many ranks besides the highest that are praiseworthy, and he who aims at the summit will seldom fail to mount more than half the way. Therefore if our Courtier knows himself to be excellent in something besides arms, I would have him with propriety derive profit and honor from it; and let him have the discretion and good judgment to know how to bring people adroitly and opportunely to see and hear what he considers himself to excel in, always seeming to do this without ostentation, casually as it were, and rather when begged by others than because he wishes it. And in everything that he has to do or say, let him, if possible, always come prepared and ready, but give the appearance that all is done on the spur of the moment. But, as for those things in which he feels himself to be mediocre, let him touch on them in passing, without dwelling much upon them, though in such a way as to cause others to think that he knows much more about them than he lays claim to know: like certain poets who have sometimes suggested the most subtle things in philosophy or other sciences, when probably they understood very little about them. Then, in those things wherein he knows himself to be totally ignorant, I would never have him claim ability in any way or seek to gain fame by them; on the contrary, when need be, let him confess openly that he knows nothing."

"That," said Calmeta, "is not what Nicoletto would have done, who, being an excellent philosopher, but with no more knowledge of law than of flying, when a certain mayor of Padua decided to give him a lectureship in law, was never willing (although many students so urged him) to undeceive that mayor and confess his ignorance; saying always that he did not agree with the opinion of Socrates in this matter, and that it was not for a philosopher ever to declare himself ignorant in anything."

"I do not say," replied messer Federico, "that the Courtier, unrequired by others, should venture of himself to confess his own ignorance; for I too dislike this folly of accusing and depreciating oneself. And sometimes therefore I laugh to myself at certain men who are so ready, without any coercion, to tell of certain things, which, even though they may have happened through no fault of theirs, yet imply a certain disgrace; like a cavalier you all know, who, every time mention was made of the battle fought against King Charles in the Parmesan, would begin at once to tell how he had fled, making it clear that on that day he had seen and heard nothing else; or, whenever a certain famous joust was mentioned, would always tell how he had fallen; and in his conversation he often appeared to try to create the occasion for telling how one night, when he was on his way to speak with a certain lady, he had gotten a sound beating.

"I would not have our Courtier say such silly things; but rather, should the occasion arise when he might show his ignorance in something, then I think he ought to avoid it; and if compelled by necessity, then he ought openly to confess his ignorance rather than expose himself to that risk. And in this way he will escape the censure that many nowadays deserve who (out of I know not what perverse instinct or imprudent judgment) are always attempting things of which they are ignorant and avoiding things they know how to do. And, in proof of this, I know a very excellent musician who has abandoned music and given himself over entirely to composing verses, and, thinking himself very great at that, has made himself the laughingstock of everyone, and by now has lost even his music. Another, one of the first painters of the world, scorns that art wherein he is most rare, and has set about studying philosophy; in which he comes up with such strange notions and new chimeras that, for all his art as a painter, he would never be able to paint them. And countless instances like these are to be found.

"There are of course some who know their own excellence in one thing and yet make a profession of something else, though something in which they are not ignorant; and every time they have an occasion to show their worth in the thing wherein they feel they have talent, they give evidence of their considerable ability. And it sometimes happens that the company, seeing this ability of theirs in something that is not their profession, think they must be able to do far better in what is their profession. Such an art, when accompanied by good judgment, does not displease me in the least."

B. Marguerite de Navarre Observes Honor and Sexuality at Court

"And that, Ladies, is a story that should strike fear into the hearts of any man who thinks he can help himself to what doesn't belong to him. The Princess's virtue and the good sense of her lady-in-waiting should inspire courage in the hearts of all women. . . ."

"In my opinion," said Hircan, "the tall lord of your story lacked nerve, and didn't deserve to have his memory preserved. What an opportunity he had! He should never have been content to eat or sleep till he'd succeeded. And one really can't say that his love was very great, if there was still room in his heart for the fear of death and dishonor."

"And what," asked Nomerfide, "could the poor man have done with two women against him?"

"He should have killed the old one, and when the young one realized there was no one to help her, he'd have been half-way there!"

"Kill her!" Nomerfide cried. "You wouldn't mind him being a murderer as well, then? If that's what you think, we'd better watch out we don't fall into your clutches!"

"If I'd gone that far," he replied, "I'd consider my honor ruined if I didn't go through with it!"

C. Sir Thomas More and His Fictional Friend, Just Back from Utopia, Discuss the Advice that a Courtier Can Safely Give His King

"Do not you think that if I were about any king, proposing good laws to him, and endeavoring to root out all the cursed seeds of evil that I found in him, I should either be turned out of his court or at least be laughed at for my pains? For instance, what could it signify if I were about the King of France, and were called into his Cabinet Council, where several wise men, in his hearing, were proposing many expedients, as by what arts and practices Milan may be kept, and Naples, that had so oft slipped out of their hands, recovered; how the Venetians, and after them the rest of Italy, may be subdued; and then how Flanders, Brabant, and all Burgundy, and some other kingdoms which he has swallowed already in his designs, may be added to his empire. One proposes a league with the Venetians, to be kept as long as he finds his account in it, and that he ought to communicate councils with them, and give them some share of the spoil, till his success makes him need or fear them less, and then it will be easily taken out of their hands. Another proposes the hiring the Germans, and the securing the Switzers by pensions. Another proposes the gaining the Emperor by money, which is omnipotent with him. Another proposes a peace with the King of Aragon, and, in order to cement it, the yielding up the King of Navarre's pretensions. Another thinks the Prince of Castile is to be wrought on, by the hope of an alliance; and that some of his courtiers are to be gained to the French faction by pensions. The hardest point of all is what to do with England: a treaty of peace is to be set on foot, and if their alliance is not to be depended on, yet it is to be made as firm as possible; and they are to be called friends, but suspected as enemies: therefore the Scots are to be kept in readiness, to be let loose upon England on every occasion: and some banished nobleman is to be supported underhand (for by the league it cannot be done avowedly) who had a pretension to the crown, by which means that suspected prince may be kept in awe.

"Now when things are in so great a fermentation, and so many gallant men are joining councils, how to carry on the war, if so mean a man as I should stand up, and wish them to change all their councils, to let Italy alone, and stay at home, since the Kingdom of France was indeed greater than could be well governed by one man; that therefore he ought not to think of adding others to it: and if after this, I should propose to them the resolutions of the Achorians, a people that lie on the southeast of Utopia, who long ago engaged in war, in order to add to the dominions of their prince another kingdom, to which he had some pretensions by an ancient alliance. This they conquered, but found that the trouble of keeping it was equal to that by which it was gained; that the conquered people were always either in rebellion or exposed to foreign invasions, while they were obliged to be incessantly at war, either for or against them, and consequently could never disband their army; that in the meantime they were oppressed with taxes, their money went out of the kingdom, their blood was spilt for the glory of their King, without procuring the least advantage to the people, who received not the smallest benefit from it even in time of peace; and that their manners being corrupted by a long war, robbery and murders everywhere abounded, and their laws fell into contempt; while their King, distracted with the care of two kingdoms, was the less able to apply his mind to the interests of either.

"When they saw this, and that there would be no end to these evils, they by joint councils made an humble address to their King, desiring him to choose which of the two kingdoms he had the greatest mind to keep, since he could not hold both; for they were too great a people to be governed by a divided king, since no man would willingly have a groom that should be in common between him and another. Upon which the good prince was forced to quit his new kingdom to one of his friends (who was not long after dethroned), and to be contented with his old one. To this I would add that after all those warlike attempts, the vast confusions, and the consumption both of treasure and of people that must follow them; perhaps upon some misfortune, they might be forced to throw up all at last; therefore it seemed much more eligible that the King should improve his ancient kingdom all he could, and make it flourish as much as possible; that he should love his people, and be beloved of them; that should live among them, govern them gently, and let other kingdoms alone, since that which had fallen to his share was big enough, if not too big for him. Pray how do you think would such a speech as this be heard?"

"I confess," said I, "I think not very well."

D. A Cardinal Respectfully Addresses "My Dearest Michelangelo," 1518

We have received your letter dated the eighth, to which we reply that we are vastly pleased to hear of the diligence you have shown, and that one Hieronimo of Porto Venere has promised on good security to deliver the marble for the tomb of Pope Julius of happy memory, because as you know we want to see the said tomb finished. We are very sorry to hear that you have been ill, but thank God for restoring you to health as you write and as we have understood from Leonardo [Sellaio], the bearer of your letter. We beg you to take care to regain your strength and keep well, both for your own sake and so that we may see the completion of the said tomb. We wait with eagerness to see the two figures ready at the time you have promised. Be of good spirit and do not be carried away by any passion; we put more trust in your slightest word than whatever the rest may say to the contrary. We know your good faith, and believe in it as much as we possibly can, and as we have said at other times, want you to take every care for your safety, because we love you from the heart and want to do everything we can for you.

Farewell. Rome, 23 October 1518
Your Cardinal San Pietro ad Vincula

To the discreet Michelangelo, the excellent sculptor, our most dear friend

Document Set 15.10 References

A. Baldassare Castiglione Describes the Perfect Courtier
Castiglione, *The Courtier*, trans. Charles S. Singleton (Garden City, N.Y.: Anchor Books, 1962), 134–138.
B. Marguerite de Navarre Observes Honor and Sexuality at Court
Marguerite de Navarre, *Heptameron*, trans., P. A. Chilton (Harmondsworth: Penguin, 1984), 96–97.
C. Sir Thomas More and His Fictional Friend, Just Back from Utopia, Discuss the Advice that a Courtier Can Safely Give His King
Thomas More, "Dialogue of Counsel" in *Utopia* (New York: Colonial Press, 1901), 22–24.
D. A Cardinal Respectfully Addresses "My Dearest Michelangelo," 1518
Cardinal Leonardo Grosso della Rovere to Michelangelo, in D. S. Chambers, *Patrons and Artists in the Italian Renaissance* (Columbia, S.C.: University of South Carolina Press, 1971), 35.

16

Religious Warfare and Crises of Authority, 1560–1640

DOCUMENT SET 16.1
Rebellion and Civil War

Chapter 15 of *The Challenge of the West* analyzed the authoritarian bent of institutions in most European states during the era of struggles over religion known as the Reformation. Set 16.1 traces the backlash against this authoritarianism.

Reflecting the clarity and dispassion characteristic of the genre, the Venetian ambassador's report on France in 1559 (Document A) sets forth the social and political order of that kingdom on the eve of the great upheavals of the Wars of Religion, 1560–1598. What mutual relationships bound the various strata of French society together, and what differences separated them? Going by this report, would you expect the nobility to oppose royal authoritarianism? On whom would the monarchy tend to depend for support? Why, according to the ambassador, was it proving difficult to maintain religious unity?

Document B describes one of the most notorious events of the Wars of Religion, the St. Bartholomew's Day massacre of 1572. The author of this selection, Charlotte de Mornay (1550–1606), is an example of the many able and intellectually sophisticated Huguenot noblewomen who strongly influenced the religious choices of their families and friends. In 1572 she was a young widow (her first husband had died in the wars before he was twenty), and she was planning to spend the winter with her sister. Later she married Philippe de Mornay, a French Protestant political leader. Read this document bearing in mind the picture of the French state that you are evolving from your other source readings—especially Document C, an extract from the *Vindiciae contra*

Tyrannos (1579). The most likely author of this anonymously published work was the Huguenot leader François Hotman. The word *tyranny* is often used indiscriminately; what does it mean here, and how does Hotman's idea of tyranny compare with the traditional concept of French monarchy? What implications do you see in Hotman's call for resistance to tyranny? With Document D we are witnessing the other great European revolution of the 1550s to 1570s, the Dutch revolt. The author, a former official in Antwerp, fled to Germany in 1567 after witnessing the events of the previous year, described here. What concerns for the social order does he express? How do you reconcile his evident conservatism with his support for rebels against the Spanish crown? Can a conservative become a revolutionary?

Document E takes us to Eastern Europe, where Tsar Ivan IV (known as "The Terrible," *1533–1584) was throwing Russia into turmoil with his attack on the noble boyar class. One of his councillors, Prince Andrei Kurbsky, broke with Ivan in 1564 and fled to Poland-Lithuania (with which Russia was then at war), denouncing the tsar as a bloodthirsty tyrant. Kurbsky's defection drove Ivan to even more gory repression at home. The ensuing exchange of letters between Kurbsky and Ivan, which was published at the time, is regarded as authentic by most historians. How does the picture of tyranny and the resistance to it compare with similar conflicts in the sixteenth-century West? How do you regard Ivan's account (largely accurate) of how as a young boy he was dominated and mistreated by a boyar conspiracy?

A. A Venetian Ambassador Sketches the Hierarchy in France, 1558

The inhabitants of the kingdom are divided into four classes of persons, viz: nobles; men of the long robe; peasantry; and clergy. The nobles, under which designation are included lords and princes, do not dwell in the cities, but in the villages, in their castles, and for the most part give little attention to letters, but are either soldiers or follow the court, leaving the management of the house and the revenues to their wives.

The French are, generally speaking, suspicious, high spirited and impatient of restraint, wherefore it is noticeable that in war, after the first dash is over, they are almost useless. They are more liberal away from home than at home; nevertheless, whoever accommodates himself to their moods will find them for the most part courteous. They avoid labor in so far as they are able, and above all it is a peculiarity of the Frenchman that he reflects little, and therefore very many of their conclusions are hastily arrived at; whence it often happens that they have no sooner finished an undertaking than they perceive its error and repent of it; but the strength of the kingdom is great enough to overcome all these errors.

There is no special burden upon the nobility beyond that which arises from their feudal holdings, which is to go to war at their own expense with such a number of horsemen as may be determined by the conditions of their investiture, in default of which they are condemned to pay money, and now the burden has become so great by reason of continued warfare that the nobility of France is seen to be almost wholly impoverished.

This militia is called the *arrière-ban*, because those who compose it are the last who are obliged to go to war and are for the defence of the kingdom. They are able to bring out about 16,000 horse, and they do not all come out at one time, but only that part for which an immediate need is felt; and from the fact that it is a very inferior soldiery, since the lords do not themselves go to war, but send their retainers and these badly equipped, it is understood that the king intends to do away with the obligation to send men to war and substitute a proportionate money payment, with which he may increase the number of his men-at-arms.

The second class embraces those who are called men of the long robe, and is divided into two groups. The first, which is the better bred, is made up of those who occupy judicial positions and all the other officials of the palace and those as well who manage the finances and accounts of the king. All these offices his majesty sells for the lifetime of the purchaser, and their honor and advantage is so great that they are bought at high prices. They enjoy also many important privileges, as though they were nobles, and easily secure the same for their descendants.

The other group is that of the merchants, who have personally no way of gaining a share in any sort of distinction, but if they wish to give a certain position to their sons they have them made doctors, whereby a judicial career is open to them equally with the members of the former group; and it may be said moreover that in them principally the wealth of France is to be found. No special burden is laid upon this class beyond the maintenance of 50,000 infantry for four months, for the defence of the kingdom in time of war, which contribution has been for some time so modified that all the inhabitants of the cities and other walled places now contribute to it. But because the greater part of these who have offices from the king are exempt by special privilege, the burden has come to rest wholly upon those who are least able to bear it.

The third class is the peasantry, who are extremely poor, principally on account of the heavy taxes which they pay to the king, since they are obliged to pay an ordinary *taille* of four millions of francs; and also on account of the *aides,* which amount to six hundred thousand; in addition to this a million francs to augment the number of men-at-arms; and, outside of all this, in times of war, the *taille* has at times been increased in amount two millions of francs; to which burdens those peasants alone contribute who work the soil. The assessments are made first upon the provinces, are then distributed by villages, and the peasants arrange the further *per capita* assessment, each one being responsible for the others, in such a way that the king actually receives the whole amount that he has demanded.

The fourth class is the clergy, in which are comprised the 117 bishoprics, 15 archbishoprics and 1230 abbacies, besides an infinite number of priories and benefices, which altogether amount in value to six million francs of income, and in ordinary time the king levies upon these an annual tax of four-tenths; and sometimes, in case of war, even up to six-tenths. But from the fact that the assessment is made very loosely and upon an estimate of incomes as they existed many years ago, they do not render more than 300,000 francs for each tenth. The disposition of all these benefices belongs to the king, except in the case of those which become vacant through the death of those prelates who die at the Roman court, and these belong to the pope. The authority for this disposition was first granted by pope Leo; then enlarged by Clement and finally confirmed by pope Julius II; nor shall I omit to say that these benefices are for the most part awarded with little respect for sacred things and by simple favor, or to recompense benefits conferred, with little consideration for the personality of the applicant; in such a way that whoever has served the king in war or otherwise desires no better thing by way of being rewarded than with benefices; wherefore it is a common thing to see a man who yesterday was a soldier or merchant, today a bishop or abbot: and if he has a wife and cannot assume ecclesiastical garb he is allowed to put his benefice under the name of another and retain the revenues for himself. And it is on this account, as well as through the evil tendencies of the time, that heresy has increased to such an extent in this realm, that they say there are at present 400,000 Lutherans,[1] so united by intercourse and mutual understanding that it is with great difficulty that any method may be found of remedying this state of affairs.

B. Charlotte de Mornay Describes the St. Bartholomew's Day Massacre

While I was still in bed, one of my kitchen servants, who was of the religion [Huguenot] and was coming from the city, came very terrified to find me. She told me that people were being killed everywhere. . . . Looking from my windows into Saint Antoine Street where I lived, I saw that everyone was very agitated, and several guards were wearing white crosses in their hats [to identify themselves as Catholics]. . . . I sent my daughter, who was then three and a half years old, in the arms of a servant to Mister de Perreuze . . . one of my closest relatives and friends, who let her in the back gate, received her, and sent word to ask if I would come, saying I would be welcome. I accepted his offer and left myself. . . . There was sedition all over the city. It was then eight in the morning, and I had no sooner left my lodgings than the servants of the Duke of Guise came in, called my host to find me, and looked for me everywhere. Finally, they sent to my mother telling her that if I wanted to bring them 100 *écus*, they would spare my life and my goods. . . . After having thought a little, I decided it was not a good idea to let it be known where I was or to go to find them, but I begged my mother to let them know that she did not know where I was and to offer them the sum that they were

demanding. Having heard nothing from me, they pillaged by lodgings. . . .

[Mister de Perreuze] was obliged to hide us . . . me with one of my servants in a hollow of the roof vaulting; the rest of our people were disguised and hidden as well as possible. Inside the vaulting, at the top of the attic, I heard the strange cries of men, women, and children who were being massacred in the streets, and having left my daughter below, I was in such perplexity and almost despair that, without fearing that I offended God, I would sooner have thrown myself out the window than to fall alive into the hands of the populace and see my daughter massacred—something I feared more than my death. . . . [After fleeing from one house to another, she hid for five days in the home of a grain merchant, then took a boat out of Paris, where she was stopped because she did not have a passport. She narrowly escaped capture and certain death by posing as a servant and hiding in the house of a vineyard worker. Throughout the ordeal, she steadfastly refused to go to mass in order to save herself.]

C. A Huguenot Leader Justifies Resistance to Tyranny

A king, we have said, is someone who has obtained the kingdom in due form, either by descent or by election, and who rules and governs in accordance with the law. Since a tyrant is the opposite of a king, it follows either that he has seized authority by force or fraud, or that he is a king who rules a kingdom freely given him in a manner contrary to equity and justice and persists in that misrule in violation of the laws and compacts to which he took a solemn oath. A single person can, of course, be both of these at once. The former is commonly called a "tyrant without title," the latter, "a tyrant by conduct." But it sometimes happens that a kingdom occupied by force is governed justly; a kingdom legally conveyed, unjustly. And since justice is here more important than inheritance, and performance more important than title to possession, it appears that a ruler who performs his office badly is more properly a tyrant than one who did not receive his office in due form. Similarly, a Pope who enters office illegally is called an "intruder," one who governs badly, an "abuser." . . .

In sum, a king promotes the public interest, a tyrant seeks his own. But since men are only human, no king can have the public interest in view on every question, and no tyrant can exist for long who seeks his own advantage in all respects whatever. Therefore,

---

[1] "Lutherans" was the label that Roman Catholics in the sixteenth century often applied to all Protestants, irrespective of confession. Here, these "Lutherans" were in fact mostly Calvinists.

if the public interest is generally uppermost we may speak of a king and of a kingdom, and if the ruler's interest generally predominates, we speak of a tyrant and a tyranny. . . .

The next question is whether a tyrant may be lawfully resisted and, if so, by whom and by what means. And we shall begin by considering tyranny without title, as it is commonly called. Suppose, then, that a Ninus invades a people over which he has no legal claim and which has not done him any injury; or that a Caesar subjugates the Roman Republic, his fatherland; or that a Popelus uses murder and deceit in an attempt to make the kingdom of Poland hereditary rather than elective; or that a Bruenhilde takes over the entire government of France for herself and her Protadius; or that an Ebroinus, encouraged by Theodoric's negligence, seizes the governorships of the kingdom and enslaves the people. What is the law in all these cases?

In the first place, nature instructs us to defend our lives and also our liberty, without which life is hardly life at all. If this is the instinct of nature implanted in dogs against the wolf, in bulls against the lion, in pigeons against the falcon, and in chickens against the hawk, how much stronger must it be in man against another man who has become a wolf to man. To fight back is not only permitted, but enjoined, for it is nature herself that seems to fight here.

Next, there is the law of peoples (*jus gentium*), which distinguishes countries and establishes boundaries that everyone is obligated to defend against any person whatsoever. . . . An Alexander pillaging a country may be opposed no less than the vagabond who steals a cloak; an invader battering the ramparts of a city, no less than the burglar breaking into buildings.

Last and most important is the civil law, which is the legislation that societies establish for their particular needs, so that here is one and there another kind of government, some being ruled by one man, others by a few, and still others by all. Some peoples deny political authority to women, others admit them; with some, kings are chosen from a particular line, among others the choice is free; and so forth. If anyone tries to break this law through force or fraud, resistance is incumbent upon all of us, because the criminal does violence to that association to which we owe everything we have, because he subverts the foundations of the fatherland to which we are bound—by nature, by the laws, and by our oath. Therefore, if we do not resist, we are traitors to our country, deserters of human society, and contemners of the law.

Thus, the law of nature, the law of peoples, and civil law command us to take arms against tyrants without title, nor is there any legal scruple to detain us—no oath or compact whatsoever, entered into either publicly or privately. Therefore, when this kind of tyranny occurs, anyone may act to drive it out, including private individuals. . . .

D. Jacob van Wesenbeke Analyzes the Drift Toward Rebellion in the Netherlands, 1566

All people were made to hope that the States General of the country would be called to draft a definitive and good ordinance concerning religion. Such an ordinance, intended to be really binding, to restore calm, to bring no harm to the country and give satisfaction to the inhabitants had been awaited, longed for and yearned for by every one. Shortly afterwards the hope and the satisfaction of the population turned to sadness, hatred and suspicion, because it was discovered that at court men had secretly devised a moderation or new edict which was sent to His Majesty in Spain. And although it had been hoped that the States General would be convoked thereupon, as had been asked in the petition of the nobles and had moreover been promised them, some persons schemed so ingeniously and successfully that it was resolved to present this moderation, not to the States General convoked for that purpose but to the provincial States of every province one after the other and, in the same order, to the provincial councils. Learning this many people feared and concluded that no good would arise from such a procedure and that things would grow worse every day, for they were far from confident that the result would come up to the hope deeply cherished by the people. No one, it was feared, would like to be subjected to such private consultation and the population continued to favour the convocation of the States General as an alternative acceptable to everybody. This suspicion, this distrust and this embitterment greatly increased and took root in people's hearts when they saw clearly, that some provincial States were ordered to meet separately (according to the aforementioned plan) in the presence of their governors or other knights of the Order or lords of high rank who were sent there to persuade them to accept the proposed moderation.

Excerpt from "The Revolt of the Netherlands" from Kossman and Mellink, eds., *Texts Concerning the Revolt of the Netherlands*, Cambridge University Press, 1975, pp. 66–69. Reprinted with the permission of Cambridge University Press.

Moreover, people's perplexity and despair about the results were complete when it was found that the provincial States were left so little liberty in convoking the meeting that only a few selected members were summoned and many, who also belonged there, were omitted and in several places people were even excluded who usually attended the meetings. Moreover, discussion was almost impossible; members were not allowed the usual time or means to deliberate and consult others, and were made to swear that they would not notify anyone of the proceedings or inform any members of the councils in the town they came from except the magistrates. In short the approval of States meeting in such circumstances was generally considered to be an extorted rather than a free and frank opinion. People who attended the discussions in the States of Artois, Hainault, Namur and Tournay know that this was the way it went.

A further important reason for scandal and discontent was the fact that the States were first convoked in the provinces which were least accustomed to show that they have some freedom and were most subject to the inquisition and the persecutions, while in the provinces which were most influenced by the novel developments, possessed the greatest privileges and had through words and deeds most boldly defended the freedom of the country, the States were not convoked at all. This was the case . . . above all [in] Brabant, the principal and most important province. As to the province second in importance, Flanders, this was only convoked after the States mentioned previously had met and passed judgment. And though every attempt was made to keep secret the contents of the new edict as well as the opinion of the States assembled to discuss it (which made things look even more suspicious to the common people), there were nevertheless some people who succeeded in discovering part of the truth and got to know still more about it when the States and Members of Flanders, told of the limitations prescribed for their meeting, with the utmost difficulty obtained at first four days' and later eight days' delay. And it became known that these States had given their approval to the new edict (though with some restrictions and conditions added by the secular States) without having, in the old way, convoked and heard all their members and councillors. All this caused a violent commotion among the people. Many different booklets and pamphlets were immediately written and distributed in various places arguing that the new edict was illegal, that it was no better than all the previous edicts, that the inquisition was still in force, that all this was the work of the adherents of Cardinal

Granvelle, some of them mentioned by name, and of the inquisitors who wanted to cause bloody disturbances, that it was done contrary to the promise made to the nobles and to the freedom of the country, that this way of assembling the States was an innovation never before witnessed, that this could not therefore be called approval of the edict and that it was entirely null. People were earnestly exhorted to oppose it forcefully and not to allow the enemies of the country to deceive the king and the governess and to give them false information any longer but to arrest and punish them. All this was accompanied by yet more strong and violent arguments and exclamations. It proved impossible to stop the flood of publications by prohibiting them, for the more the court issued edicts against them, the more the number of such booklets and writings increased. One complained that the commonalty was deprived of its liberty to explain and to discover the truth openly, whether in the councils of the provinces and the towns or in clear remonstrances and writings, although on this depended the prosperity of the country. People wrote that these outrages would very soon have all sort of evil consequences and suggested that the men who thus wanted to keep the king and the country in servitude, were afraid that their treachery would be revealed if the States General were convoked in the proper fashion and allowed to give their opinion freely. Soon, because of the refusal and delay in convoking the States, the commotion, embitterment and grumbling that had existed among the people before the nobles presented their petition, began anew.

This, however, was much more serious than before because the inhabitants, made much more hard-hearted and embittered by the course of events, gave up all hope of improvement and redress since the distinguished assembly and well-founded petition of the nobles as well as the promises made to them had been of no avail, and because they saw clearly that it was not the intention of the court to convoke the States General, or, if it was its intention, that there would be people to prevent it from being brought about although the meeting of the States General was considered by all sensible people to be the only remedy against the troubles. What else could be concluded when neither the supplication of the nobles, nor the desire of various provinces and towns intimated long before, nor the consent of many of the most important lords, including those who sat in the council and agreed to it and thought it necessary, had succeeded in persuading the court to do it? There seemed nothing left to give them hope that the promises given to the nobles might be kept, or that the inhabitants might be released from the hated persecutions and odious inquisition, or might be given some relief or exemption from the slavery and servitude of their consciences which they had been enduring for such a long time. Despair made those who dissented in religion more obdurate and made them prefer to oppose the government openly and confess their belief frankly, rather than to remain for ever oppressed and subdued. This was the reason why they started to hold their meetings and services each day more openly, thus getting so many more adherents. The others too now became embittered and opposed to the way in which the matter was being dealt with, and began to turn against the doctrines of the authorities who, in their opinion, were the cause of all these troubles, commotions and outrages.

E. Prince Andrei Kurbsky and Ivan the Terrible Trade Accusations, 1564

Kurbsky to Ivan IV: To the tsar, exalted above all by God, who appeared (formerly) most illustrious, particularly in the Orthodox faith, but who has now, in consequence of our sins, been found to be the contrary of this. If you have understanding, may you understand this with your leprous conscience—such a conscience as cannot be found even amongst the godless peoples. And I have not let my tongue say more than this on all these matters in turn; but because of the bitterest persecution from your power, with much sorrow in my heart will I hasten to inform you of a little. . . .

What evil and persecution have I not suffered from you! What ills and misfortunes have you not brought upon me! And what iniquitous tissues of lies have you not woven against me! But I cannot now recount the various misfortunes at your hands which have beset me owing to their multitude and since I am still filled with the grief of my soul. But, to conclude, I can summarize them all [thus]: of everything have I been deprived; I have been driven from the land of God without guilt [*lit.* in vain], hounded by you. I did not ask [for aught] with humble words, nor did I beseech you with tearful plaint; nor yet did I win from you any mercy through the intercession of the hierarchy. You have recompensed me with evil for good and for my love with implacable hatred. My blood, spilled like water for you, cries out against you to my Lord. God sees into [men's] hearts—in my

mind have I ardently reflected and my conscience have I placed as a witness [against myself], and I have sought and pried within my thoughts, and, examining myself [*lit.* turning myself around], I know not now—nor have I ever found—my guilt in aught before you. In front of your army have I marched—and marched again; and no dishonor have I brought upon you; but only brilliant victories, with the help of the angel of the Lord, have I won for your glory, and never have I turned the back of your regiments to the foe. But far more, I have achieved most glorious conquests to increase your renown. And this, not in one year, nor yet in two—but throughout many years have I toiled with much sweat and patience; and always have I been separated from my fatherland, and little have I seen my parents, and my wife have I not known; but always in far distant towns have I stood in arms against your foes and I have suffered many wants and natural illnesses, of which my Lord Jesus Christ is witness. Still more, I was visited with wounds inflicted by barbarian hands in various battles and all my body is already afflicted with sores. But to you, O tsar, was all this as nought; rather do you show us your intolerable wrath and bitterest hatred, and, furthermore, burning stoves.[2]

Ivan IV to Kurbsky: Wherefore, O Prince, if you regard yourself to have piety, have you lost your soul? What will you give in its place on the day of the terrible judgment? Even if you should acquire the whole world, death will reach you in the end! Why have you sold your soul for your body's sake? Is it because you were afraid of death at the false instigation of your demons and influential friends and counselors? . . .

Are you not ashamed before your slave Vaska Shibanov,[3] who preserved his piety and, having attached himself to you with a kiss of the cross, did not reject you before the tsar and the whole people, though standing at the gate of death, but praised you and was all too ready to die for you? But you did not emulate his devotion: on account of a single angry word of mine, have you lost not only your own soul, but the souls of all your ancestors: for, by God's will, had they been given as servants to our grandfather, the great tsar, and they gave their souls to him and served him up to their death, and ordered you, their children, to serve the children and grandchildren of our grandfather. But you have forgotten everything and traitorously, like a dog, have you transgressed the oath and have gone over to the enemies of

Excerpt from Chapter 33 of *Medieval Russia's Epics, Chronicles, and Tales,* Serge A Zenovsky, ed., E. P. Dutton, 1963, pp. 289–291, 296–298. Reprinted by permission.

[2] An allusion to one of Ivan's favorite methods of torture.
[3] Kurbsky's servant, whom Ivan tortured to death without forcing him to betray Kurbsky.

Christianity, and, not considering your wrath, you utter stupid words, hurling, as it were, stones at the sky.
. . .

It had pleased God to take away our mother, the pious Tsarina Helen, from the earthly kingdom to the kingdom of heaven. My brother George, who now rests in heaven, and I were left orphans and, as we received no care from anyone, we laid our trust in the Holy Virgin, and in the prayers of all the saints, and in the blessing of our parents. When I was in my eighth year, our subjects acted according to their will, for they found the empire without a ruler, and did not deign to bestow their voluntary attention upon us, their master, but were bent on acquiring wealth and glory, and were quarreling with each other. And what have they not done! How many boyars, how many friends of our father and generals they have killed! And they seized the farms and villages and possessions of our uncles, and established themselves therein. The treasure of our mother they trod underfoot and pierced with sharp sticks, and transferred it to the great treasure, but some of it they grabbed themselves; and that was done by your grandfather Mikhaylo Tuchkov. The Princes Vasily and Ivan Shuysky took it upon themselves to have me in their keeping, and those who had been the chief traitors of our father and mother they let out of prison, and they made friends with them. Prince Vasily Shuysky with a Judas crowd fell in the court belonging to our uncle upon our father confessor Fedor Mishurin, and insulted him, and killed him; and they imprisoned Prince Ivan Fedorovich Byelsky and many others in various places, and armed themselves against the realm; they ousted metropolitan Daniel from the metropolitan see and banished him: and thus they improved their opportunity, and began to rule themselves...

Document Set 16.1 References

A. A Venetian Ambassador Sketches the Hierarchy in France, 1558
Giovanni Sorano, in *Reports of the Venetian Ambassadors,* in *Translations and Reprints from the Original Sources of European History* (Philadelphia: University of Pennsylvania Press, 1902), 3/2:16–19.

B. Charlotte de Mornay Describes the St. Bartholomew's Day Massacre
Memoires de Madame de Mornay (Paris: J. Nenouard, 1868–1869), 1:59–62. Translated by Lynn Hunt.

C. A Huguenot Leader Justifies Resistance to Tyranny
Julian H. Franklin, *Constitutionalism and Resistance in the Sixteenth Century* (New York: Pegasus, 1969), 185–197 passim.

D. Jacob van Wesenbeke Analyzes the Drift Toward Rebellion in the Netherlands, 1566
Van Wesenbeke in E. H. Kossman and A. F. Mellink, eds., *Texts Concerning the Revolt in the Netherlands* (Cambridge: Cambridge University Press, 1974), 66–69.

E. Prince Andrei Kurbsky and Ivan the Terrible Trade Accusations, 1564
Serge A. Zenkovsky, ed. and trans., *Medieval Russia's Epics, Chronicles, and Tales* (New York: E. P. Dutton, 1963), 289–299.

DOCUMENT SET 16.2
Alternatives to Wars of Religion

Secular governments' insistence on unity of belief was the primary reason why differences in religion escalated into civil war or degenerated into persecutions. Overwhelmingly, sixteenth-century men and women felt their convictions strongly enough to believe that theirs was the only true path prescribed by God. Read the documents in this set with the question in mind of how faith in the correctness of one's "inner" religious vision was giving way as the sixteenth century wore on and as the consequences of religious wars became ever more appalling.

The French nobleman Michel de Montaigne (1533–1592) was the first great writer of the literary essay (a term he invented), devoted to the examination of one's own character and experiences. Particularly at the outset of his literary career, he was deeply influenced by the ancient philosophical tradition of skepticism, with its radical doubt of all received wisdom. During the civil wars, Montaigne conformed to Catholicism because it was the traditional religion of France, but he never expressed serious conviction. In Document A he characteristically exposes the frailty of human understanding, and its vulnerability to prejudice and subjective experience.

Jean Bodin (c. 1530–1596), one of the foremost political philosophers of the era, unequivocally rejected the right of revolution, which Hotman and other Huguenot writers (Set 16.1, Document 4) had advocated. In Document B, an extract from his *Six Books of the Republic* (1676), Bodin argued that every state should have a sovereign authority which could never be divided or ended and which no subject could legally or morally oppose. Yet in another work, the *Colloquium Heptaplomeres* (1587), the nominally Catholic Bodin presented seven men differing radically in religion (including a Jew, a Muslim, and an ancient Epicurean) and concluded that they must live together in peace. (Lest you give Bodin too much credit as an advanced-thinking liberal, however, compare his views on witchcraft: Set 16.7, Document A.) In what respects—and why—was Bodin making a case for substituting a religion of obedience to the sovereign, peace-keeping state for a religion of obedience to God?

Unlike most of the rest of sixteenth-century Europe, the Polish-Lithuanian commonwealth experienced neither serious religious persecution nor civil war, although all the religious currents of the age flowed through it. In 1572–1573, facing a potentially

devastating crisis with the dying-out of the national dynasty and with rival religious interests vying to elect as their next king someone favorable to their viewpoint, the commonwealth's nobility instead pledged to maintain religious toleration among themselves. The Warsaw Confederation of 1573 (excerpted here as Document C) formalized this agreement; thereupon the Poles elected the candidate Henry of Valois, whose hands (unbeknownst in Warsaw) were drenched with the blood of St. Bartholomew's. At the same time, however, they placed severe limitations on royal power—restrictions so onerous that the new king fled Poland as soon as word arrived that he had succeeded to the French crown as Henry III. In what ways do you think that the Poles' determination to modify authoritarian government—a step that Jean Bodin greatly disapproved—reflected a response to the sixteenth-century experience with religious warfare? Comment also on the fact that the Warsaw Confederation's guarantee of religious liberty was limited to the nobility.

In the final reading of this set (Document D), the Venetian Republic in 1606 reacts to a papal interdict, a prohibition against holding any Catholic services (including giving last rites to the dying) in Venice until the republic brought its foreign policy into alignment with Rome's. As you will recall from Set 12.3, Document E, the papacy had used such a threat in 1309 to humble Venice. What was different in 1606? The Venetian Republic was strongly Catholic, but it would not allow the papacy to dictate its policies. How did its defiance of the papacy raise the issue of religious wars and reflect the growing power of the state?

A. Michel de Montaigne Ponders the Fallibility of Human Understanding

I do not know what to say about it, but it is evident from experience that so many interpretations disperse the truth and shatter it. Aristotle wrote to be understood; if he did not succeed, still less will another man, less able, and not treating his own ideas. By diluting the substance we allow it to escape and spill it all over the place; of one subject we make a thousand, and, multiplying and subdividing, fall back into Epicurus' infinity of atoms. Never did two men judge alike about the same thing, and it is impossible to find two opinions exactly alike, not only in different men, but in the same man at different times. Ordinarily I find subject for doubt in what the commentary has not deigned to touch on. I am more apt to trip on flat ground, like certain horses I know which stumble more often on a smooth road.

Who would not say that glosses increase doubts and ignorance, since there is no book to be found, whether human or divine, with which the world busies itself, whose difficulties are cleared up by interpretation? The hundredth commentator hands it on to his successor thornier and rougher than the first one had found it. When do we agree and say, "There has been enough about this book; henceforth there is nothing more to say about it"?

This is best seen in law practice. We give legal authority to numberless doctors, numberless decisions, and as many interpretations. Do we therefore find any end to the need of interpreting? Do we see any progress and advance toward tranquillity? Do we need fewer lawyers and judges than when this mass of law was still in its infancy? On the contrary, we obscure and bury the meaning; we no longer find it except hidden by so many enclosures and barriers.

Men do not know the natural infirmity of their mind: it does nothing but ferret and quest, and keeps incessantly whirling around, building up and becoming entangled in its own work, like our silkworms, and is suffocated in it. *A mouse in a pitch barrel* [Erasmus]. It thinks it notices from a distance some sort of glimmer of imaginary light and truth; but while running toward it, it is crossed by so many difficulties and obstacles, and diverted by so many new quests, that it strays from the road, bewildered. . . .

It is more of a job to interpret the interpretations than to interpret the things, and there are more books about books than about any other subject: we do nothing but write glosses about each other. The world is swarming with commentaries; of authors there is a great scarcity.

Is it not the chief and most reputed learning of our times to learn to understand the learned? Is that not the common and ultimate end of all studies?

Our opinions are grafted upon one another. The first serves as a stock for the second, the second for the third. Thus we scale the ladder, step by step. And thence it happens that he who has mounted highest has often more honor than merit; for he has only mounted one speck higher on the shoulders of the next last.

How often and perhaps how stupidly have I extended my book to make it speak for itself! Stupidly, if only for this reason, that I should have remembered what I say of others who do the same: that these frequent sheep's eyes at their own work testify that their heart thrills with love for it, and that even the rough, disdainful blows with which they beat it are only the love taps and affectations of maternal fondness; in keeping with Aristotle, to whom self-appreciation and self-depreciation often spring from the same sort of arrogance. For as for my excuse, that I ought to have more liberty in this than others, precisely because I write of myself and my writings as of my other actions, because my theme turns in upon itself—I do not know whether everyone will accept it.

I have observed in Germany that Luther has left as many divisions and altercations over the uncertainty of his opinions, and more, as he raised about the Holy Scriptures.

Our disputes are purely verbal. I ask what is "nature," "pleasure," "circle," "substitution." The question is one of words, and is answered in the same way. "A stone is a body." But if you pressed on: "And what is a body?"—"Substance."—"And what is substance?" and so on, you would finally drive the respondent to the end of his lexicon. We exchange one word for another word, often more unknown. I know better what is man than I know what is animal, or mortal, or rational. To satisfy one doubt, they give me three; it is the Hydra's head.

Socrates asked Meno what virtue was. "There is," said Meno, "the virtue of a man and a woman, of a magistrate and of a private individual, of a child and of an old man." "That's fine," exclaimed Socrates; "we were in search of one virtue, and here is a whole swarm of them."

B. Jean Bodin Defines Sovereignty

Sovereignty is that absolute and perpetual power vested in a commonwealth which in Latin is termed *majestas* . . . The term needs careful definition, because although it is the distinguishing mark of a commonwealth, and an understanding of its nature fundamental to any treatment of politics, no jurist or political philosopher has in fact attempted to define it. . . .

I have described it as *perpetual* because one can give absolute power to a person or group of persons for a period of time, but that time expired they become subjects once more. Therefore even while they enjoy power, they cannot properly be regarded as sovereign rulers, but only as the lieutenants and agents of the sovereign ruler, till the moment comes when it pleases the prince or the people to revoke the gift. The true sovereign remains always seized of his power. Just as a feudal lord who grants lands to another retains his eminent domain over them, so the ruler who delegates authority to judge and command, whether it be for a short period, or during pleasure, remains seized of those rights of jurisdiction actually exercised by another in the form of a revocable grant, or precarious tenancy. For this reason the law requires the governor of a province, or the prince's lieutenant, to make a formal surrender of the authority committed to him, at the expiration of his term of office. In this respect there is no difference between the highest officer of state and his humblest subordinate. If it were otherwise, and the absolute authority delegated by the prince to a lieutenant was regarded as itself sovereign power, the latter could use it against his prince who would thereby forfeit his eminence, and the subject could command his lord, the servant his master. This is a manifest absurdity, considering that the sovereign is always excepted personally, as a matter of right, in all delegations of authority, however extensive. . . .

C. The Polish-Lithuanian Nobles Promise Mutual Religious Toleration, 1573

We, the Spiritual and Temporal Counselors, the Gentry and the other Estates of the one and indivisible Republic, from Old and New Poland, from the Grand Duchy of Lithuania, etc.—and from the Cities of the Crown (declare):

"... Whereas there is a great dissidence in affairs of the Christian Religion within our Country, and to prevent any sedition for this reason among the people—like what we see clearly in other Kingdoms—we promise each other, on behalf of ourselves and our descendants, for perpetuity, under oath and pledging our faith, honor and consciences, that we who are *dissidentes de religione*[1] will keep peace between ourselves, and neither shed blood on account of differences of faiths or kinds of churches, nor punish one another by confiscation of goods, deprivation of honor, imprisonment or exile. . . ."

D. Venice Rejects the Papal Interdict, 1606

It has come to our knowledge that on the 17th of April last past, by the order of the most holy father, Pope Paul V, there was published and posted up in Rome a so-called brief, which was fulminated against us, our senate, and the whole of our state; and that one was addressed to you, the tenor and contents whereof were similar to those of the other. We there-

[1] Dissidents in religion—Catholics, Orthodox, and Protestants.

fore find ourselves constrained to preserve in peace and tranquility the state which God has given us to rule; and, in order to maintain our authority as a prince, who in temporal matters recognizes no superior saving the Divine Majesty, we, by these our public letters, do protest before the Lord God and the whole world that we have not failed to use every possible means to make his Holiness understand our most valid and irrefragable case; first, by means of our ambassador residing at the court of his Holiness; then, by letters of ours in answer to briefs addressed to us by his Holiness; and, lastly, by a special ambassador sent to him to this effect. But having found the ears of his Holiness closed against us and seeing that the brief aforesaid is published contrary to all right reason and contrary to the teaching of the divine Scriptures, the doctrine of the holy fathers, and the sacred canons, to the prejudice of the secular authority given us by God, and of the liberty of our state, inasmuch as it would cause disturbance in the quiet possession which, by divine Grace, under our government our faithful subjects hold of their properties, their honor and their lives, and occasion a most grave and universal scandal throughout the state; We do not hesitate to consider the said brief not only as unsuitable and unjust, but as null and void and of no worth or value whatever, and being thus invalid, vain, and unlawfully fulminated, *de facto nullo juris ordine servato*, we have thought fit to use in resisting it the remedies adopted by our ancestors and by other sovereign princes against such pontiffs as, in using the power given them by God to the use of edifying, have overstepped their due limits. . . . And we pray the Lord God to inspire him [the pope] with a sense of the invalidity and nullity of his brief and of the other acts committed against us, and the He, knowing the justice of our cause, may give us strength to maintain our reverence for the holy apostolic see, whose most devoted servants we and our predecessors, together with this republic, have been and ever shall be.

Document Set 16.2 References

A. Michel de Montaigne Ponders the Fallibility of Human Understanding
Montaigne, *Essays*, trans. Donald Frame (Stanford, Cal.: Stanford University Press, 1957), 817, 818–819.
B. Jean Bodin Defines Sovereignty
Bodin, *Six Books of the Republic*, abridged and edited by M. J. Toole (Oxford, England: Basil Blackwell, 1956), 25.
C. The Polish-Lithuanian Nobles Promise Mutual Religious Toleration, 1573
Manfred Kridl, ed. and trans., *For Your Freedom and Ours* (New York: Unger, 1943), 32–33.
D. Venice Rejects the Papal Interdict, 1606
Translations and Reprints from the Original Sources of European History (Philadelphia: University of Pennsylvania Press, 1898), 4/4:32–33.

DOCUMENT SET 16.3
The Greatness and Tragedy of Spain

Spain was the greatest power in sixteenth-century Europe. Yet it became badly overstretched by wars and international commitments, and by the early seventeenth century stood on the brink of a long descent. This set offers some basis for reflecting on Spain's greatness and impending decline.

Document A is another of those Venetian ambassadorial reports that historians find so useful for grasping the character of sixteenth-century political figures and understanding the mentality of the age. What is your assessment of the young Philip II, judging by this report?

The Spanish Inquisition, for all its fervent Catholicism, was primarily an instrument of state policy, intended to unify Spain and crush all manifestations of religious dissent. From Document B you can get some idea of how the Inquisition worked and what befell someone accused of being a "Lutheran" (which could mean any kind of Christian religious heterodoxy). Note that the person accused in this extract is a *converso*—an individual of converted Jewish parentage. Such people were primary targets of inquisitorial suspicion.

The destruction of the Spanish Armada in its futile attempt to defeat English intervention in the Netherlands and to crush the Dutch Republic's revolt is described in Document C in words that were spread throughout Europe in the Fugger Newsletters—one of the first instances of what we would today call journalism. The great Spanish novel of Miguel de Cervantes (1547–1616), *Don Quixote,* is often interpreted as a satire on the decline of medieval chivalry; like all great comedies, it not only pokes fun but also expresses great sympathy with the essential human condition. Document D is an extract from very early in *Don Quixote.* What elements of satire do you detect?

The final document in this set comes from the early seventeenth century. The foremost statesman of this era, the count-duke of Olivares (1587–1645), who served Philip IV as prime minister, tried valiantly to stem the monarchy's decline by instituting administrative reforms and by squeezing money out of the provinces despite their protests about local liberties. Document E is an extract of Olivares' plan for "union of arms" that would bring all Iberia together. This plan instead provoked both Portugal and Catalonia to rebel in 1640 and led to the count-duke's downfall a year later.

Using *The Challenge of the West* and the documents of this set, write a brief analysis of the strengths and weaknesses of the Spanish monarchy from the mid-sixteenth century to the mid-seventeenth century.

A. The Venetian Ambassador Suriano Takes the Measure of Philip II, 1559

. . . Although his actions display that royal dignity and gravity which are natural and habitual to him, he is none the less agreeable for this; on the contrary, his courtesy toward all seems only the more striking. His pleasing figure, his manly air, and his suavity of speech and manner serve to enhance the pleasing effect. He is slight in stature, but so well built, so admirably proportioned, and dressed with such taste and discernment that one could hardly imagine anything more perfect. . . .

Although the king resembles his father in his face and speech, in his attention to his religious duties, and in his habitual kindness and good faith, he nevertheless differs from him in several of those respects in which the greatness of rulers, after all, lies. The emperor was addicted to war, which he well understood; the king knows but little of it and has no love for it. The emperor undertook great enterprises with enthusiasm; his son avoids them. The father was fond of planning great things and would in the end realize his wishes by his skill; his son, on the contrary, pays less attention to augmenting his own greatness than to hindering that of others. The emperor never allowed himself to be influenced by threats or fear, while the king has lost some of his dominions owing to unreasonable apprehensions. The father was guided in all matters by his own opinion; the son follows the opinions of others.

In the king's eyes no nation is superior to the Spaniards. It is among them that he lives, it is they that he consults, and it is they that direct his policy; in all this he is acting quite contrary to the habit of his father. He thinks little of the Italians and Flemish and still less of the Germans. Although he may employ the chief men of all the countries over which he rules, he admits none of them to his secret counsels, but utilizes their services only in military affairs, and then perhaps not so much because he really esteems them, as in the hope that he will in this way prevent his enemies from making use of them.

B. The Spanish Inquisition Interrogates a Converso "Lutheran" and Sends Him to an *Auto Da Fé,* 1559

Sentencing of Pedro de Cazalla for Lutheranism in 1559 by the Valladolid tribunal.

The accused " . . . having confessed to us that for four years he had communicated with a certain person who had been his friend for fourteen years and who had instructed him in [the Lutheran explanation] of justification . . . [this friend] had suggested to him that there was no need to stop at the denial of purgatory, and from this inferred the uselessness of indulgences and things conceded by the Pope . . . [It was pointed out that] Pedro de Cazalla was descended from converted Jews on both sides . . . [and had] instructed and indoctrinated many others about the passion and merits of our redeemer, Jesus Christ, who had justified all sinners without recourse to works, penance. . . .

"Item . . . Cazalla believed in faith alone without works . . . penance, fasts, prayers . . . [none of the latter being] meritorious nor profitable for sinner's salvation, saying they were only justified by Christ's passion and merits.

"Item . . . believed there was no purgatory in the next life . . . and held the same error about the sacrifices, offerings, prayers, and aids in the Catholic Church for the deceased . . . [considering] all such aids superfluous and without effect.

"Item . . . believed that Christians who had faith did not have to have recourse to the saints, saying that the saints' intercession . . . had no effect concerning the salvation of sinners.

"Item . . . believed that the Apostolic Roman Catholic Church had no power or authority to force any Christians to observe its precepts, fast, vigils, celebrations, nor prohibit or make [special] distinctions about foods.

"Item, [he asserted] that the Pope or other eminence . . . had no power to excommunicate or absolve any Christian by means of indulgences, jubilees, and pardons . . . which were worthless . . . concerning the pardoning of sins.

"Item, [he denounced monasticism].

"Item . . . believed that oral confession . . . is not necessary, nor is a sacrament, nor is useful for the pardon and absolution of sins . . . [instead Cazalla recommended a kind of mental confession to God, directly and alone].

"Item . . . believed that the Catholic Church should have no more than two sacraments (cf. the nun Guevara, from the same group), baptism and communion in memory of the passion and [last] supper of the savior while the others . . . were not sacraments [this seems to be a quasi-Zwinglian view of the Eucharist, which testified to the book-smugglers' diligence in getting other than Lutheran Protestant works into Spain. Ed.] . . . .

"Item . . . believed that the . . . Eucharist of the consecrated host and chalice is not . . . Christ . . . nor sacramental, but only spiritual through the faith of the recipient and [He is] not really or corporeally [present] as our Holy Catholic faith and mother church has taught us. [This probably can be interpreted in several Protestant ways. Ed.]

"Item . . . believed that all Christians, priests and laymen, could administer and receive the . . . Eucharist under both kinds, of bread and of wine . . . [Classic statement of priesthood of all believers. Ed.]

"Item . . . Cazalla had made communion . . . with many others . . . according to the Lutheran usage . . . many times in diverse places, while hearing and preaching before this supper a sermon about the sect and errors of Luther in which [Lutheranism] was praised as the truth.

" . . . Item, in Cazalla's house were such [heretical] meetings held and . . . [he owned and loaned out] the heretical books of Luther and Calvin, and many other heretics.

"Item . . . declaring our definitive sentence that he is an apostate heretical Lutheran [Cazalla is sentenced to relaxation, confiscation of all goods, etc.]. . . ."

Auto de fe at Valladolid, May 21, 1559, attended by Don Carlos and the Regent, Princess Juana, Philip II's son and sister respectively; the King had not yet returned from the Netherlands.

"This *auto* was held in the Plaza de San Francisco on a very large platform [there follows a very minute, detailed description of the local arrangements for the occasion and the social eminence of the onlookers, including high clergy as well as laymen] . . . before the *auto* began a letter from the Holy Office was read imploring the princes [Carlos and Juana] and others . . . to aid the Inquisition [and the true faith generally] to punish and extirpate all errors, heresy, and apostacy . . . and Don Carlos and Princess Juana swore [to do as much] on the Gospels and the Cross . . . which all received with great admiration, joy, and contentment. Friar Melchor de Cano [the noted Dominican supporter of the tribunal and the ongoing scholastic revival of Thomism in Spain. Ed.] began to read the sentences in a very impressive manner . . . [fifteen burnt, sixteen reconciled]. . . . "

"Continuation of this *auto,* pp. 449–452. "Agustin de

Cazalla, Francisco de Vivero, and Alonso de Pérez [to be burnt] passed by the Princes' platform to the heretics'. The Bishop of Palencia and the grandly apparelled ponifical representative . . . formally degraded [unfrocked] these three clerics.

". . . Cazalla, at this, gave great indications of contrition with tears before all; . . . Vivero was smiling while Pérez displayed no feelings at the moment of this humiliation. Cazalla went down on his knees before the Princes saying in tear [he pleaded for his several relations arrested and sentenced with him, especially for an aged sister; otherwise he seemed to collapse pathetically] . . . [the executions start] Cazalla [, hysterical], proclaiming his belief in the Holy Mother Church of Rome for which he is dying . . . Vivero, Pérez, and Antonio Herrezuelo silent . . . Cazalla in a great voice said he died for having been Lutheran . . . but was repenting . . . and all those dying with him were dying for his doctrine, and by his inducement and great sympathy persuaded Herrezuelo to convert to Christ's faith [i.e., Cazalla's repudiation of his "Lutheranism" drove the latter to also deny it and revert to Catholicism; Herrezuelo subsequently went back on this recantation]. . . . the others did not show any feelings or demonstrate repentance.

. . . and thus were burnt alive . . . .

"Tuesday, the next day, dawn came to the Plaza and the scaffold. . . ."

C. The Fugger Newsletters Comment on the Destruction of the Armada

Report from England about the Spanish Armada, received in Augsburg from Hamburg on the 19th day of November 1588.

The Armada of the King of Spain set sail from Portugal with one hundred and thirty-five ships, to wit: four galleasses from Naples, four galleons from Portugal, ten vessels with victuals, fourteen Venetian ships, among them several galleons. The remainder was made up of other large and small craft. The Armada arrived in Corunna on the 5th day of July, from whence it intended to sail for Flanders, there to join forces with the Duke of Parma and invade England. At that time the English Armada was in Plymouth Port.

After they had been under sail from Corunna eight days they arrived in Ostend and thereupon lay south of the shores of England, where for four or five days they had various skirmishes with the English Armada. On that occasion the English took two ships. On one of these there was Don Pedro di Mendoza, whom they took prisoner and so to the loss of four Portuguese galleons which remained England. Storms south of England caused them stranded on the French coast. They then proceeded and cast anchor off Calais, since they could no longer get as far as Dunkirk. They wished to wait for the Duke of Parma in Calais, but he sent word that he could not be ready under eight days. Thereupon the admiral sent reply that he would again set sail for Spain. Meanwhile the English sent forth against the Spanish Armada several burning ships, so that they were forced to cut their moorings and to retire hastily. Each ship left two anchors behind and four of the largest galleasses were stranded and wrecked off Calais. The following day at eight o'clock, the two Armadas had a further encounter, heavily bombarding each other for eight hours. In this battle the Spanish lost four ships, namely two Portuguese galleasses, a vessel from Biscay and one other. All four went to the bottom of the sea. Three large Venetian craft remained behind off the coast of Flanders and were in great peril of going under. The inhabitants of Flushing took two of these ships, and the third was shipwrecked. One of them had on board the Colonel commanding the garrison of Seville. According to the prisoners' report the Spaniards lost four thousand men in the battle off Calais, amongst them the Commander-in-Chief of the cavalry at Naples and Seville. The Spaniards are said to have left one hundred and twenty ships, although others could count only one hundred and ten. The big galleon, which the Duke of Florence had sent, was not to be seen anywhere after the battle.

Hereafter the Armada made off and was pursued by the English for five days as far as Scotland. When they counted their men there they found that they had already lost eight thousand, most of whom had been killed or died of disease. From thence they set sail for Ireland without taking provisions on board. Off Ireland they lost two ships, the *San Sebastian* and the *San Mathias*, which had four hundred and fifty-six men on board. Lacking fresh water, the fleet threw many horses and mules overboard off Ireland. When they sailed away from Ireland, the Commander-in-Chief, the Duke of Medina Sidonia, ordered each one of his captains to set his course for Corunna or the first Spanish port. They thus sailed together throughout ten days. Then the storm separated the Duke of Medina Sidonia with twenty-seven of his ships from them and no one knew where they had gone. The last time the Armada was assembled it counted no more than seventy-eight ships. Of the big galleasses not one was left. Two of the Duke of Medina Sidonia's ships ran ashore. Only two or three of the men were saved. They say that the Chief Admiral had left on board only five-and-twenty more barrels of wine, but little bread and no water. His masts had been so weakened by firing that he could not carry full canvas. . . .

From Middleburg, the 14th day of November 1588.

It is said that news has arrived from Ireland that a further nine ships of the Spanish Armada have perished there. Sixteen hundred men are reported to be still alive, to whom the Irish are lending help. For that reason the Queen of England has dispatched thither six hundred men who are to take up hostilties against these people. From Sicily there comes information that the General Duke of Medina in Seville organized there a great procession to celebrate his return. Ninety ships of the Armada are missing, and every one has been forbidden to mourn his friends who were lost with the Armada. A forty days' fast has been ordered, hoping that thereby the return home of the missing ships will be obtained.

D. Don Quixote, Gone Mad, Turns Knight-Errant

In fine, he gave himself up so wholly to the reading of Romances, that a-Nights he would pore on 'till 'twas Day, and a-Days he would read on 'till 'twas Night; and thus by sleeping little, and reading much, the Moisture of his Brain was exhausted to that Degree, that at last he lost the Use of his Reason. A world of disorderly Notions, pick'd out of his Books, crouded into his Imagination; and now his Head was full of nothing but Inchantments, Quarrels, Battles, Challenges, Wounds, Complaints, Amours, Torments, and abundance of Stuff and Impossibilities; insomuch, that all the Fables and fantastical Tales which he read, seem'd to him now as true as the most authentick Histories. He would say, that the *Cid Ruy liaz* was a very brave Knight, but not worthy to stand in Competition with the *Knight of the Burning Sword,* who with a single Backstroke had cut in sunder two fierce and mighty Giants. He liked yet better *Bernardo del Carpio,* who at *Roncesvalles* depriv'd of Life the inchanted *Orlando,* having lifted him from the Ground, and choak'd him in the Air, as *Hercules* did *Antoeus* the Son of the Earth. . . .

Having thus lost his Understanding, he unluckily stumbled upon the oddest Fancy that ever enter'd into a Madman's Brain; for now he thought it convenient and necessary, as well for the Increase of his own Honour, as the Service of the Publick, to turn Knight-Errant, and roam through the whole World arm'd Cap-a-pee, and mounted on his Steed, in quest of Adventures; that thus imitating those Knight-Errants of whom he had read, and following their Course of Life, redressing all manner of Grievances, and exposing himself to Danger on all Occasions, at last, after a happy Conclusion of his Enterprizes, he might purchase everlasting Honour and Renown. Transported with these agreeable Delusions, the poor Gentleman already grasp'd in Imagination the Imperial Sceptre of *Trapizonde,* and, hurry'd away by his mighty Expectations, he prepares with all Expedition to take the Field.

The first Thing he did was to scour a Suit of Armour that had belong'd to his Great-Grandfather, and had lain Time out of Mind carelessly rusting in a Corner.

E. The Conde-Duque Olivares Attempts to Unify Iberia

Today, the common people look on the various nationals as if they were little better than enemies, and this happens in all the kingdoms. If Castile can be seen as feudatory of Aragon, and Aragon of Castile, Portugal of both and both of Portugal, and the same for all the kingdoms of Spain, those of Italy and Flanders being brought into a close relationship, then the blindness and separation of hearts which has existed hitherto must necessarily be ended by the close natural bond of a union of arms. For when the Portuguese see the Castilians and the Castilians the Portuguese, they will know that each sees the friend and feudatory of the other, who will help him with his blood and his men in time of need.

This closer union would bring immediate relief to Castile, while going a long way towards solving that problem of imperial defence which first brought home the need for more adequate co-operation among the provinces of the Monarchy.

Document Set 16.3 References

A. The Venetian Ambassador Suriano Takes the Measure of
Philip II, 1559
James Harvey Robinson, ed., *Readings in European History*
(Boston: Ginn, 1904), 2:168–169.
B. The Spanish Inquisition Interrogates a Converso "Lutheran"
and Sends Him to an *Auto Da Fé*, 1559
Paul Hauban, ed. and trans., *The Spanish Inquisition* (New
York: John Wiley, 1969), 70–76.
C. The Fugger Newsletters Comment on the Destruction of the
Armada
G. T. Matthews, ed., *The Fugger Newsletters* (New York:
G. P. Putnam's Sons, 1959), 161–163.
D. Don Quixote, Gone Mad, Turns Knight-Errant
Miguel de Cervantes, *Don Quixote*, Ozell's revision of the
translation of Peter Motteux (New York: Modern Library,
1930), 3–4.
E. The Conde-Duque Olivares Attempts to Unify Iberia
J. H. Elliott, *The Revolt of the Catalans: A Study in the
Decline of Spain (1598–1640)* (Cambridge: Cambridge
University Press, 1903), 206.

DOCUMENT SET 16.4
England from Elizabeth to the Early Stuarts

William Shakespeare (1564–1616) expressed with incomparable eloquence the generally accepted ideas of his day. In the extracts from his play *Troilus and Cressida* (Document A), set in the time of the Trojan War, he puts into the mouth of Ulysses a magnificent defense of social hierarchy. In what ways does this reflect sixteenth-century ideas of authority and deference? Can you also find such ideas expressed in Elizabeth I's speech to Parliament quoted in Document B? Notice here how the queen recognizes the mutual dependence of crown and Parliament; do you think her remarks are sincere?

Social policy in Elizabethan and early Stuart England depended heavily on the willingness of local authorities to accept responsibility for maintaining order. Read Document C for insights into what their obligations were; do you see any echo of ideas expressed in Documents A and B?

Documents D and E show two sides of the battle for individual conscience in late sixteenth-century England. In Document D, Jesuit Robert Johnson faces the gallows in 1582; what line does he draw between loyalty to the crown and his understanding of his duty to God, and how do the authorities respond? In Document F, the important Puritan writer William Perkins, a Cambridge divine, urges his noble patron (and all readers of his book) to listen closely to the voice of conscience. In Puritan teaching, it was through conscience that God called sinners to repentance and into the body of the elect. Compare the two examples of appeal to conscience across the religious divide.

The Stuarts were to find it impossible to govern England arbitrarily after they inherited the crown with James I's accession in 1603. Elizabeth, who understood the craft of ruling better than most of her colleagues among Europe's crowned heads, offered her cousin James VI of Scotland (who would become James I of England after her death) some shrewd advice on how to behave as a monarch. Her advice was prompted by news of a palace conspiracy against James in 1592. How well does this counsel (in Document F) fit with the ideas of governance and deference expressed elsewhere in this set? James's own notion of his prerogatives appears in Document G, a report on a church conference at which the new king had to listen to an English Puritan clergyman recall his many clashes with the Scottish Presbyterians. James's son Charles I (*1625–1649) tried to rule by combining heavy-handed arbitrariness, after dispens-

ing with Parliament, and wooing ordinary English people's loyalty away from the strict Puritan regimen. His decree in favor of Sunday sports (Document H) was typical of the Stuarts' claim to have the interests of humble subjects at heart.

The final document (I) returns us to the voice of conscience. The lay Puritan John Winthrop had to search his soul deeply before deciding that emigration to America was the right course for him. Ultimately he decided to go, and he became one of the leaders of Massachusetts Bay Colony. What considerations passed through this prominent gentleman's mind, and what did he hope that emigration would accomplish? How did his decision reflect tensions within Tudor-Stuart England?

A. William Shakespeare Defends the Social Order

The heavens themselves, the planets and this center,
Observe degree, priority, and place,
Insisture, course, proportion, season, form,
Office, and custom, in all line of order.
And therefore is the glorious planet Sol [the sun]
In noble eminence enthroned and sphered
Amidst the other, whose medicinable eye
Corrects the ill aspécts of planets evil,
And posts like the commandment of a king,
Sans check to good and bad. But when the planets
In evil mixture to disorder wander,
What plagues and what portents, what mutiny,
What raging of the sea, shaking of earth,
Commotion in the winds, frights, changes, horrors,
Divert and crack, rend and deracinate,
The unity and married calm of states
Quite from their fixure! Oh, when degree is shaked,
Which is the ladder to all high designs,
The enterprise is sick! How could communities,
Degrees in schools and brotherhoods in cities,
Peaceful commerce from dividable shores,
The primogenitive and due of birth,
Prerogative of age, crowns, scepters, laurels,
But by degree, stand in authentic place?
Take but degree away, untune that string,
And hark, what discord follows! Each thing meets
In mere oppugnancy. The bounded waters
Should lift their bosoms higher than the shores,
And make a sop of all this solid globe.
Strength should be lord of imbecility,

And the rude son should strike his father dead.
Force should be right, or rather, right and wrong,
Between whose endless jar justice resides,
Should lose their names, and so should justice too.
Then everything includes itself in power,
Power into will, will into appetite,
And appetite, a universal wolf,
So doubly seconded with will and power,
Must make perforce a universal prey,
And last eat up himself. . . .

B. The Young Elizabeth I Beguiles Her Subjects

Now, if ever any person had either the gift or the style to win the hearts of people, it was this Queen. . . . Every motion seemed a well guided action; her eye was set upon one, her ear listened to another, her judgment ran upon a third, to a fourth she addressed her speech; her spirit seemed to be everywhere, and yet so entire in her self, as it seemed to be nowhere else.

. . . She was a Lady, upon whom nature had bestowed, and well placed, many of her fairest favors; of stature average, slender, straight, and amiably composed; of such state in her carriage, as every motion of her seemed to bear majesty.

. . . In life, she was most innocent; in desire, moderate; in purpose, just; of spirit, above credit and almost capacity of her sex; of divine wit, as well for depth of judgment, as for quick conceit and speedy expedition; of eloquence, as sweet in the utterance, so ready and easy to come to the utterance; of wonderful knowledge both in learning and affairs; skilfull not only in Latin and Greek, but also in diverse other foreign languages: none knew better the hardest art of all others, that is, of commanding men.

C. Parliament Imposes Compulsory Poor Rates, 1572

And forasmuch as charity would that poor, aged and impotent persons should as necessarily be provided for, as the said rogues, vagabonds and sturdy beggars repressed, and that the said aged, impotent and poor people should have convenient habitations and abiding places throughout this realm to settle themselves upon, to the end that they nor any of them should hereafter beg or wander about; It is therefore enacted . . . that the justices of peace of . . . the shires of England and Wales . . . and all other justices of the peace, mayors, sheriffs, bailiffs, and other officers of all and every city, borough, riding and franchises within this realm . . . shall at or before the . . . feast of St. Bartholomew [August 24] next coming . . . make diligent search and enquiry of all aged, poor, impotent and decayed persons born within their . . . divisions and limits, or which were there dwelling within three years next before this present parliament, which live or of necessity be compelled to live by alms . . . and shall . . . make a register book containing [their] names and surnames . . . And when the number of the said poor people forced to live upon alms be by that means truly known, then the said justices . . . and other officers shall within like convenient time devise and appoint, within every their said several divisions, meet and convenient places by their discretions to settle the same poor people for their habitations and abidings, if the parish within the which they shall be found shall not or will not provide for them; and shall also within like convenient time number all the said poor people within their said several limits, and thereupon (having regard to the number) set down what portion the weekly charge towards the relief and sustentation of the said poor people will amount unto within every their said several divisions and limits; and that done, they . . . shall be their good discretions tax and assess all and every the inhabitants, dwelling in all and every city, borough, town, village, hamlet and place known within the said limits and divisions, to such weekly charge as they and every of them shall weekly contribute towards the relief of the said poor people, and the names of all such inhabitants taxed shall also enter into the said register book together with their taxation, and also shall be their discretion within every their said divisions and limits appoint or see collectors for one whole year to be appointed of the said weekly portion, which shall collect and gather the said proportion, and make delivery of so much thereof, according to the discretion of the said justices . . . and other officers, to the said poor people, as the said justices . . . and other officers shall apoint them: and also shall appoint the overseers of the said poor people by their discretions, to continue also for one whole year; and if they do refuse to be overseers, then every of them so refusing to forfeit ten shillings for every such default . . .

D. An English Jesuit Goes to the Gallows, 1582

Johnson. I am a Catholic, and am condemn'd for conspiring the queen's death at Rheims, with the other company who were condemn'd with me. I protest, that as for some of them with whom I was condemn'd to have conspired withal, I did never see them before we met at the barr, neither did I ever write unto them, or receive letters from them: and as for any treasons, I am not guilty in deed nor thought . . .

Sheriff. Dost thou acknowledge the queen for lawful queen? Repent thee, and notwithstanding thy traitorous practices, we have authority from the queen to carry thee back.

Johnson. I do acknowledge her as lawful as Queen Mary was. I can say no more; but pray to God to give her grace, and that she may now stay her hand from shedding of innocent blood.

Sheriff. Dost thou acknowledge her supreme head of the church in ecclesiastical matters?

Johnson. I acknowledge her to have as full and great authority as ever Queen Mary had; and more with safety and conscience I cannot give her.

Sheriff. Thou art a traitor most obstinate.

Johnson. If I be a traitor for maintaining this faith, then all the kings and queens of this realm heretofore, and all our ancestors, were traitors, for they maintain'd the same.

Sheriff. What! You will preach treason also, if we suffer you!

Johnson. I teach but the Catholic religion.

Hereupon the rope was put about his neck, and he was willed to pray, which he did in Latin. They willed him to pray in English, that they might witness with him; he said, "I pray that prayer which Christ taught, in a tongue I well understand." A minister cried out, "Pray as Christ taught": to whom Mr. Johnson replied, "What! do you think Christ taught in English?" He went on, saying in Latin his *Pater, Ave,* and Creed, and *In manus tuas,*[1] etc. And so the cart was drawn away, and he finish'd this life as the rest did . . .

E. A Puritan Searches His Conscience: William Perkins, 1586

Sir, I pray you consider with me an especial point of God's word, carefully to be weighed. It is this: (a) Many professors of Christ, in the day of grace, persuade themselves that they are in the estate of grace, and so the true church esteemeth of them too; yet when the day of grace is past, they contrariwise shall find themselves to be in the estate of damnation, remediless. A doleful case, yet a most resolute truth, and the reason is plain. Men that live in the church are greatly annoyed with a fearful security and deadness

of heart, by which it comes to pass that they think it enough to make a common protestation of the faith, not once in all their lifetimes examining themselves whether they be in the estate of grace before the eternal God or not. (b) And indeed it is a grace peculiar to the man elect, to try himself whether he be in the estate of grace or not.

F. Elizabeth I Advises James VI on Ruling

The dear care, my dear brother, that ever I carried, from your infancy, of your prosperous estate and quiet, could not permit [me to] hear of so many, yea so traitorous attempts, without unspeakable dolour and unexpressful woe. . . . To redouble crimes so oft, I say with your pardon, most to your charge, which never durst have been renewed if the first had received the condign reward; for slacking of due correction engenders the bold minds for new crimes. And if my counsels had as well been followed as they were truly meant, your subjects had now better known their king, and you no more need of further justice. You find by sour experience what this neglect hath bred you.

I hear of so uncouth a way taken by some of your conventions, yea, agreed to by yourself, that I must [wonder] how you will be clerk to such lessons. Must a king be prescribed what councillors he will take as if you were their ward? Shall you be obliged to tie or undo what they list make or revoke? O Lord, what strange dreams hear I, that would God they were so, for then at my waking I should find them fables. If you mean, therefore, to reign, I exhort you to show you worthy the place, which never can be surely settled without a steady course held to make you loved and feared. I assure myself many have escaped your hands more for dread of your remissness than for love of the escaped; so oft they see you cherishing some men for open crimes, and so they mistrust more their revenge than your assurance. My affection for you best lies on this, my plainness, whose patience is too much moved with these like everlasting faults.

And since it so likes you to demand my counsel, I find so many ways your state so unjointed, that it needs a skilfuller bonesetter than I to join each part in his right place. But to fulfil your will, take, in short, these few words: For all whose you know the assailers of your courts, the shameful attempters of your sacred decree, if ever you pardon I will never be the suitor. Who to peril a king were inventors or actors, they should crack a halter if I were king. Such is my charity. Who under pretence of better[ing] your

---

[1] *Pater,* etc.: Catholic prayers, in Latin.

estate, endangers the king, or needs will be his school-masters, if I might appoint their university they should be assigned to learn first to obey; so should they better teach you next. I am not so unskilful of a kingly rule that I would wink at no fault, yet would be open-eyed at public indignity. Neither should all have the whip though some were scourged. But if, like a toy, of a king's life so oft endangered nought shall follow but a scorn, what sequel I may doubt of such contempt I dread to think and dare not name. The rest I bequeath to the trust of your faithful servant, and pray the Almighty God to inspire you in time, afore too late, to cut their combs whose crest may danger you. I am void of malice. God is judge. I know them not. Forgive this too too long a writing.

G. James I Tells the Presbyterians: "No Bishop, No King"

At which speech his Majesty was somewhat stirred, yet, which is admirable in him, without passion or show thereof; thinking that they aimed at a Scottish presbytery which, saith he, as well agreeth with a monarchy as God and the devil. "Then Jack and Tom and Will and Dick shall meet and at their pleasure censure me and my council and all our proceedings. Then Will shall stand up and say it must be thus; then Dick shall reply and say, 'Nay, marry, but we will have it thus.' " . . .

"I will tell you a tale. After that the religion restored by King Edward the Sixth was soon overthrown by the succession of Queen Mary here in England, we in Scotland felt the effect of it. Whereupon Master Knox writes to the queen regent [2] (of whom, without flattery, I may say that she was a virtuous and moderate lady), telling her that she was supreme head of the Church, and charged her, as she would answer it before God's tribunal, to take care of Christ, his Evangel, and of suppressing the popish prelates, who withstood the same. But how long, trow ye, did this continue? Even so long, till by her authority, by the popish bishops were repressed. He [Knox] himself and his adherents were brought in and well settled, and by these means made strong enough to undertake the matters of reformation themselves. Then, lo, they began to make small account of her supremacy, nor would longer rest upon her authority, but took the cause into their own hand; according to that more light wherewith they were illuminated, made a further reformation of religion. How they used that poor lady, my mother, is not unknown, and with grief I may remember it; who, because she had not been otherwise instructed, did desire only a private chapel wherein to serve God, after her manner, with some few selected persons; but her supremacy was not sufficient to obtain it at their hands. And how they dealt with me in my minority you all know; it was not done secretly, and though I would, I cannot conceal it. . . . But if once you [my lords the bishops] were out, and they in place, I know what would become of my supremacy. No bishop, no king, as before I said."

H. Charles I Allows Sunday Sports, 1633

Our dear father of blessed memory, [James I], in his return from Scotland, coming through Lancashire, found that his subjects were debarred from lawful recreations upon Sundays after evening prayers ended and, upon holydays; and he prudently considered that if these times were taken from them, the meaner sort, who labor hard all the week, should have to recreations at all to refresh their spirits; and after his return he further saw that his loyal subjects in all other parts of his kingdom did suffer in the same kind, though perhaps not in the same degree; and did therefore, in his princely wisdom, publish a declaration to all his loving subjects concerning lawful sports to be used at such times . . . in the year 1618. . . .

Our pleasure likewise is, that the bishop of that diocese take the like strait order with all the Puritans and precisians within the same, either constraining them to conform themselves or to leave the county, according to the laws of our kingdom and canons of our Church, and so to strike equally on both hands against the contemners of our authority and adversaries of our Church; and as for our good people's lawful recreation, our pleasure likewise is, that after the end of divine service our good people be not disturbed, letted, or discouraged from any lawful recreation, such as dancing, either men or women; archery for men, leaping, vaulting, or any other such harmless recreation, nor from having of May-games, Whitsunales, and Morris-dances, and the setting up of Maypoles and other sports therewith used, so as the same be had in due and convenient time, without impediment or neglect of divine service; and that women shall have leave to carry rushes to the church for the decorating of it, according to their old custom; but withal we do here account still as prohibited all

---

[2] Mary Queen of Scots' mother

unlawful games to be used upon Sundays only, as bear and bull baitings, interludes, and at all times in the meaner sort of people by law prohibited, bowling.

I. John Winthrop Ponders a Puritan Migration to New England, 1629

1. It will be a service to the Church of great consequence to carry the gospel into those parts of the world, to help on the coming of the fullness of the Gentiles, and to raise a bulwark against the kingdom of Antichrist which the Jesuits labor to rear up in those parts.

2. All other churches of Europe are brought to desolation, and our sins, for which the Lord begins already to frown upon us and to cut us short, do threaten evil times to be coming upon us; and who knows but that God hath provided this place to be a refuge for many whom he means to save out of the general calamity, and seeing the Church hath no place left to fly into but the wilderness, what better work can there be than to go and provide tabernacles and food for her against she comes thither?

3. This land grows weary of her inhabitants, so as man, who is the most precious of all creatures, is here more vile and base than the earth we tread upon, and of less price among us than an horse or a sheep; masters are forced by authority to entertain servants, parents to maintain their own children; all towns complain of the burden of their poor, though we have taken up many unnecessary—yea, unlawful—trades to maintain them, and we use the authority of the law to hinder the increase of our people, as by urging the statute against cottages and inmates, and thus it is come to pass that children, servants, and neighbors, especially if they be poor, are counted the greatest burdens, which, if things were right, would be the chiefest earthly blessings.

4. The whole earth is the Lord's garden, and he hath given it to the sons of men with a general commission (Gen. i. 28) to increase and multiply, and replenish the earth and subdue it, which was again renewed to Noah; the end is double and natural, that man might enjoy the fruits of the earth and God might have his due glory from the creature. Why then should we stand here striving for places of habitation, etc. (many men spending as much labor and cost to recover or keep sometimes an acre or two of land as would procure them many, and as good or better, in another country), and in the meantime suffer a whole continent as fruitful and convenient for the use of man to lie waste without any improvement?

5. We are grown to that height of intemperance in all excess of riot as no man's estate almost will suffice to keep sail with his equals; and who fails herein must live in scorn and contempt. Hence it comes that all arts and trades are carried in that deceitful and unrighteous course as it is almost impossible for a good and upright man to maintain his charge and live comfortably in any of them.

6. The fountains of learning and religion are so corrupted as (besides the insupportable charge of their education) most children (even the best wits and of fairest hopes) are perverted, corrupted, and utterly overthrown by the multitude of evil examples and the licentious government of those seminaries where men strain at gnats and swallow camels, use all severity for maintenance of caps and other accompliments, but suffer all ruffianlike fashions and disorder in manners to pass uncontrolled.

7. What can be a better work and more honorable and worthy a Christian than to help raise and support a particular church while it is in its infancy, and join his forces with such a company of faithful people as by a timely assistance may grow strong and prosper, and for want of it may be put to great hazard, if not wholly ruined? . . .

Document Set 16.4 References

A. William Shakespeare Upholds the Social Order
Shakespeare, *Troilus and Cressida,* Act I, Scene 3, lines 85–124.
B. The Young Elizabeth I Beguiles Her Subjects
Sir John Hayward in Alan Glover, ed., *Gloriana's Glass* (London: Nonesuch Press, 1953), 57–58.
C. Parliament Imposes Compulsory Poor Rates, 1572
H. E. S. Fisher and A. R. J. Jurica, eds., *Documents in English Economic History* (London: G. Bell, 1977), 2:427–428.
D. An English Jesuit Goes to the Gallows, 1582
Richard Johnson, Scaffold Speech, in Lacey Baldwin Smith and Jean Reeder Smith, eds., *The Past Speaks,* 2d ed. (Lexington, Mass.: D. C. Heath, 1993), 1:305–306.
E. A Puritan Searches His Conscience: William Perkins, 1586
Perkins, Letter, in Smith and Smith, 1:311–312.
F. Elizabeth I Advises James VI on Ruling
John Bruce, *Letters of Queen Elizabeth and James VI of Scotland* (London: Camden Society, 1849), orig. series, 46:75–76.
G. James I Tells the Presbyterians: "No Bishop, No King"
James I, 1604, in James Harvey Robinson, ed., *Readings in European History* (Boston: Ginn, 1904), 2:218–219.
H. Charles I Allows Sunday Sports, 1633
Declaration of Sports, in Robinson, 2:228–230.
I. John Winthrop Ponders a Puritan Migration to New England, 1629
Winthrop, "Reasons to be Considered . . .," in Robinson, 2:225–226.

DOCUMENT SET 16.5
Recovering from the Wars of Religion: France from Henry IV to Richelieu

The Edict of Nantes (Document A) must be read against the background of Set 16.1 and Set 16.2. Henry IV, formerly the Huguenots' leader and now having succeeded to the French crown, made a political decision to switch religions in order to be accepted as France's legitimate king, yet he conceded important rights to his former Huguenot followers. How well did these rights guarantee the Huguenots' status as a protected minority? In what respects does the Edict accord with Bodin's ideas on undivided sovereignty as the only solution to a society suffering an authority crisis (compare Set 16.2, Document B)?

The remaining documents in the set all reflect various strategies attempted in the early seventeenth century for reestablishing order in the land. The law of 1604 known as the Paulette regularized the sale of offices by royal officials, a practice that had been going on de facto for a very long time. Considering the implications of this practice—bestowing life-time rights to important judicial and other state offices for a fee—how do you suppose that such a law, as enacted by men like Henry IV and his minister Sully, could be the means of ending political disorder? In Document D, the great royal minister Cardinal Richelieu (1585–1642) recalls in his *Memoirs* the disastrous state of French affairs at the time he was summoned to power by Louis XIII (1624). Notice in particular his remarks about the aristocracy and the Huguenots. Why was he so determined to break these adversaries? Why too, in Document E, should Richelieu's regime have been so concerned to put down false claims of nobility—continuing a policy that nobles in the Estates General had demanded in 1614? It may be easier to understand the motivation behind Document F, the edict that Richelieu had the king promulgate ordering the demolition of nobles' castles. Likewise it was at Richelieu's instigation that in 1635 Louis XIII established the French Academy (Document G); what political and social purpose do you see in this measure? Considering all these documents together and drawing upon *The Challenge of the West,* write a brief essay on the consolidation of royal authority in early seventeenth-century France, keeping in mind this country's social background.

A. Henry IV Promises the Huguenots Limited Toleration: the Edict of Nantes, 1598

Among the infinite benefits which it has pleased God to heap upon us, the most signal and precious is his granting us the strength and ability to withstand the fearful disorders and troubles which prevailed on our advent in this kingdom. The realm was so torn by innumerable factions and sects that the most legitimate of all the parties was fewest in numbers. God has given us strength to stand out against this storm; we have finally surmounted the waves and made our port of safety,—peace for our state. For which his be the glory all in all, and ours a free recognition of his grace in making use of our instrumentality in the good work. . . . We implore and await from the Divine Goodness the same protection and favor which he has ever granted to this kingdom from the beginning. . . .

We have, by this perpetual and irrevocable edict, established and proclaimed and do establish and proclaim:

I. First, that the recollection of everything done by one party or the other between March, 1585, and our accession to the crown, and during all the preceding period of troubles, remain obliterated and forgotten, as if no such things had ever happened.

III. We ordain that the Catholic Apostolic and Roman religion shall be restored and reestablished in all places and localities of this our kingdom and countries subject to our sway, where the exercise of the same has been interrupted, in order that it may be peaceably and freely exercised, without any trouble or hindrance; forbidding very expressly all persons, of whatsoever estate, quality, or condition, from troubling, molesting, or disturbing ecclesiastics in the celebration of divine service, in the enjoyment or collection of tithes, fruits, or revenues of their benefices, and all other rights and dues belonging to them; and that all those who during the troubles have taken possession of churches, houses, goods or revenues, belonging to the said ecclesiastics, shall surrender to them entire possession and peaceable enjoyment of such rights, liberties, and sureties as they had before they were deprived of them.

VI. And in order to leave no occasion for troubles or differences between our subjects, we have permitted, and herewith permit, those of the said religion called Reformed to live and abide in all the cities and places of this our kingdom and countries of our sway, without being annoyed, molested, or compelled to do anything in the matter of religion contrary to their consciences, . . . upon conditions that they comport themselves in other respects according to that which is contained in this our present edict.

VII. It is permitted to all lords, gentlemen, and other persons making profession of the said religion called Reformed, holding the right of high justice [or a certain feudal tenure], to exercise the said religion in their houses.

IX. We also permit those of the said religion to make and continue the exercise of the same in all villages and places of our dominion where it was established by them and publicly enjoyed several and divers times in the year 1597, up to the end of the month of August, notwithstanding all decrees and judgments to the contrary.

XIII. We very expressly forbid to all those of the said religion its exercise, either in respect to ministry, regulation, discipline, or the public instruction of children, or otherwise, in this our kingdom and lands of our dominion, otherwise than in the places permitted and granted by the present edict.

XIV. It is forbidden as well to perform any function of the said religion on our court or retinue, or in our lands and territories beyond the mountains, or in our city of Paris, or within five leagues of the said city.

XVIII. We also forbid all our subjects, of whatever quality and condition, from carrying off by force or persuasion, against the will of their parents, the children of the said religion, in order to cause them to be baptized or confirmed in the Catholic Apostolic and Roman Church; and the same is forbidden to those of the said religion called Reformed, upon penalty of being punished with special severity.

XXI. Books concerning the said religion called Reformed may not be printed and publicly sold, except in cities and places where the public exercise of the said religion is permitted.

XXII. We ordain that there shall be no difference or distinction made in respect to the said religion, in receiving pupils to be instructed in universities, colleges, and schools; or in receiving the sick and poor into hospitals, retreats and public charities.

XXIII. Those of the said religion called Reformed shall be obliged to respect the laws of the Catholic Apostolic and Roman Church, recognized in this our kingdom, for the consummation of marriages contracted, or to be contracted, as regards to the degrees of consanguinity and kinship.

B. The Sale of Offices Is Regulated: the Paulette, 1604

Henry, by the grace of God, king of France and Navarre, etc. Having never desired anything more than the opportunity to indicate to our subjects in general and to our officers in particular the effects of our favour we have recently listened with a good deal of satisfaction to the supplications and remonstrances which have been made to us by a number of the chief and most senior officers of this kingdom seeking to persuade us to introduce some regulation into the practice of resignation of office so that they should not be forced, when they are elderly and consequently more capable of exercising them worthily, to resign their offices in favour of younger and less experienced men in order to avoid the loss of such a large sum as the value of their offices entails: consequently, recognizing the considerable interest of our officers, the good which we will do in this kingdom by keeping offices in the hands of those most skilled in affairs and their readiness to pay the four *deniers per livre* tax on the estimated value of their offices which we will collect annually from those who are prepared to raise the said tax in order to redeem themselves from the severity of the forty day rule.

For all these reasons after having deliberated over this matter in our council, in which were a number of princes of the royal blood, officers of our crown and other *seigneurs* and notable personages who have judged this proposal just and advantageous to our officers and worthy of the affection that we have for our subjects; with their advice and in conformity with the decree already issued on this matter, and with our certain knowledge, full power and royal authority we have by this present declaration . . . decreed and declared . . . that hence-forward, the officers of our kingdom, whether judicial, financial or of any other kind, whatever their station . . . who are subject to the forty day rule . . . shall be dispensed from the rigour of the forty days which each of these officers must survive after his resignation, counting from the day and date of the receipt of money paid into the *Parties Casuelles,* by the annual payment of four *deniers per livre* of the estimated value of their offices by those who wish voluntarily to avail themselves of this favour and dispensation . . . in return for this money, if they should die during the year, their offices will not be declared vacant and obtainable for our profit, but will be kept in favour of their resignees as far as those offices which are subject to suppression are concerned; and as for those which are not subject to suppression, they will go to the widows and heirs who may dispose of them as they see fit and to their own profit, as something belonging to them; . . . all officers who will have paid the said tax shall enjoy the said favour and dispensation during the year for which they have paid, their guarantee being simply the receipt for the money contributed for the said annual right of dispensation duly signed by *maître* Charles Paulet, a secretary of our chamber. . . .

C. Richelieu Assesses the State of France in 1624

At the time when your Majesty resolved to admit me both to your council and to an important place in your confidence for the direction of your affairs, I may say that the Huguenots shared the state with you; that the nobles conducted themselves as if they were not your subjects, and the most powerful governors of the provinces as if they were sovereign in their offices.

I may say that the bad example of all these was so injurious to this realm that even the best regulated *parlements* were affected by it, and endeavored, in certain cases, to diminish your royal authority as far as they were able in order to stretch their own powers beyond the limits of reason.

I may say that every one measured his own merit by his audacity; that in place of estimating the benefits which they received from your Majesty at their proper worth, all valued them only in so far as they satisfied the extravagant demands of their imagination; that the most arrogant were held to be the wisest, and found themselves the most prosperous.

I may also say that the foreign alliances were unfortunate, individual interests being preferred to those of the public; in a word, the dignity of the royal majesty was so disparaged, and so different from what it should be, owing to the malfeasance of those who conducted your affairs, that it was almost impossible to perceive its existence.

It was impossible, without losing all, to tolerate longer the conduct of those to whom your Majesty had instrusted the helm of state; and, on the other had, everything could not be changed at once without violating the laws of prudence, which do not permit the abrupt passing from one extreme to another.

The sad state of your affairs seemed to force you to hasty decisions, without permitting a choice of time or of means; and yet it was necessary to make a choice of both, in order to profit by the change which necessity demanded from your prudence.

Thoughtful observers did not think that it would be possible to escape all the rocks in so tempestuous a period; the court was full of people who censured the temerity of those who wished to undertake a reform; all well knew that princes are quick to impute

to those who are near them the bad outcome of the undertakings upon which they have been well advised; few people consequently expected good results from the change which it was announced that I wished to make, and many believed my fall assured even before you Majesty had elevated me.

Notwithstanding these difficulties which I represented to your Majesty, knowing how much kings may do when they make good use of their power, I ventured to promise you, with confidence, that you would soon get control of your state, and that in a short time your prudence, your courage, and the benediction of God would give a new aspect to the realm.

I promised your Majesty to employ all my industry and all the authority which it should please you to give me to ruin the Huguenot party, to abase the pride of the nobles, to bring back all your subjects to their duty, and to elevate your name among foreign nations to the point where it belongs.

D. Bogus Claims of Nobility Are Forbidden, 1614–1634

His Majesty is most humbly entreated to ensure . . . that those who have taken advantage of the times to give themselves unjustly the title of nobleman and to enjoy the privileges appertaining thereto should be deprived to their title and declared *roturiers;* and so that non-nobles should not infiltrate into the ranks of the nobility an exact register should be drawn up of all the noblemen in the kingdom, together with their coats of arms and an account of the honours and ancient lineage of their families. . . . In future letters of knighthood should be bestowed only upon persons of worth whose public service greatly merits such a reward . . . it should be lawful for the nobility to take part in wholesale trading without forfeiture of nobility, this without prejudice to the custom of Brittany. Also, only noblemen ought to hold the rank of port-captain.

Louis XIII forbids fraudulent claims of nobility, 1634

We forbid any of our subjects to usurp the status of nobility, to take the title of esquire and to bear coats of arms if they are not of a noble house and extraction, under pain of a fine of 2,000 *livres.*

E. The Demolition of Feudal Castles Is Ordered, 1626

Whereas formerly the assemblies of the estates of this realm and those of notable persons chosen to give advice to ourselves, and to the late king, our very honorable lord and father, on important affairs of this realm, and likewise the assembly of the estates of the province of Brittany held by us in the year 1614, have repeatedly requested and very humbly supplicated our said lord and father and ourselves to cause the demolition of many strongholds in divers places of this realm, which, being neither on hostile frontiers nor in important passes or places, only serve to augment our expenses by the maintenance of useless garrisons, and also serve as retreats for divers persons who on the least provocation disturb the provinces where they are located; . . .

For these reasons, we announce, declare, ordain, and will that all the strongholds, either towns or castles, which are in the interior of our realm or provinces of the same, not situated in places of importance either for frontier or defense or other considerations of weight, shall be razed and demolished; even ancient walls shall be destroyed so far as it shall be deemed necessary for the well-being and repose of our subjects and the security of this state, so that our said subjects henceforth need not fear that the said places will cause them any inconvenience, and so that we shall be freed from the expense of supporting garrisons in them.

F. Louis XIII Establishes the French Academy, 1635

When God called us to the headship of the state we cherished the purpose not only of putting an end to the disorders caused by the civil wars which had so long distracted the realm, but we also aimed to adorn the state with all the ornaments appropriate to the oldest and most illustrious of existing monarchies. Although we have labored without intermission to realize this purpose, it has been impossible hitherto fully to accomplish it. . . . [But now] the confusion has at last given way to good order, which we have reëstablished by the best of all means, namely, by reviving commerce, enforcing military discipline in our armies, adjusting the taxes, and checking luxury. Every one is aware of the part that our very dear and beloved cousin, the cardinal, duke of Richelieu, has had in the accomplishment of all these things.

Consequently when we communicated our intention to him, he represented to us that one of the most glorious proofs of the happiness of a realm is that the sciences and arts flourish within it, and that letters as well as arms are held in esteem, since these constitute one of the chief ornaments of a powerful state; that, after so many memorable exploits, we had now only to add the agreeable to the essential, and to adorn the useful. He believed that we could not do better than to commence with the most noble of all arts, namely, eloquence. The French language, which has suffered much hitherto from neglect on the part of those who might have rendered it the most perfect of modern tongues, is now more capable than ever of taking its high place, owing to the great number of persons who possess a special knowledge of the advantages which it enjoys and who can augment these advantages. The cardinal informed us that, with a view of establishing fixed rules for the language, he had arranged meetings of scholars whose decisions in these matters had met with his hearty approval, and that in order to put these decisions into execution and render the French language not only elegant but capable of treating all the arts and sciences, it would only be necessary to perpetuate these gatherings. This could be done with great advantage should it please us to sanction them, to permit rules and regulations to be drawn up for the order of procedure to be observed, and to reward those who compose the association by some honorable marks of our favor.

For these reasons, and in view of the advantages which our subjects may derive from the said meetings, acceding to the desires of our said cousin:

We do permit, by our special favor, power, and royal authority, and do authorize and approve by these presents, signed by our hand, the said assemblies and conferences. We will that they continue hereafter in our good city of Paris, under the name of the *French Academy;* that our said cousin shall be designated as its head and protector; that the number of members be limited to forty persons. . . .

Document Set 16.5 References

A. Henry IV Promises the Huguenots Limited Toleration: the Edict of Nantes, 1598
   Edict of Nantes, excerpted in James Harvey Robinson, ed., *Readings in European History* (Boston: Ginn, 1904), 2:183–185.
B. The Sale of Offices Is Regulated: the Paulette, 1604
   J. H. Shennan, ed. and trans., *Government and Society in France, 1461–1661* (London: G. Allen and Unwin, 1969), 137–138.
C. Richelieu Assesses the State of France in 1624
   Richelieu, "Political Testament," in Robinson, 2:268–269.
D. Bogus Claims of Nobility Are Forbidden, 1614–1624
   Edict of Louis XIII, January 1634, in Shennan, 107.
E. The Demolition of Feudal Castles Is Ordered, 1626
   Edict of Louis XIII, in Robinson, 2:270.
F. Louis XIII Establishes the French Academy, 1635
   Letters Patent Establishing the French Academy, in Robinson, 2:271.

DOCUMENT SET 16.6
The Ultimate War of Religion: The Thirty Years' War

The three documents in this set have been chosen to illustrate aspects of the climactic struggle of the religious confessions born of the Reformation, the Thirty Years' War of 1618–1648.

Document A is an extract from the novel *Simplicissimus* by H. J. C. von Grimmelshausen (c. 1622–1676), the introduction to which was discussed at the beginning of *The Challenge of the West,* Chapter 16. The present extract, from later in the novel, describes how soldiers spent much of their time scrounging for food. (Grimmelshausen wrote from personal experience, having served in the Imperial Army; his book was published in 1669.) Document B describes the horrors of the siege, capture, and destruction of Magdeburg, a Protestant city in north-central Germany, by the Imperial forces. (The Catholic General Tilly did not order the massacre and burning of the city; these acts were the results of undisciplined soldiers running amuck.) In Document C, the pope, having heard that an end to the war had finally been negotiated, condemned the peace as injurious to people's interests. Write an essay drawing upon these documents and *The Challenge of the West,* placing the Thirty Years' War in its social and political context as a watershed event.

A. Simplicissimus Endures

. . . Truth to tell, a musketeer is a miserable creature who has to live this way in a garrison and who has to get by on dry bread—and not half enough of that. He's no better than a prisoner who is prolonging his poor life with the bread and water of tribulation. In fact, a prisoner is better off, for he does not have to stand watch, go the rounds, or do sentry duty; he stays quietly in bed and has just as much hope as a sad garrison trooper of getting out of his prison in time. There were a few who, by various means, had it a little better; but none of these ways of getting a bite more to eat were to my liking. In their misery, a few troopers took on wives (some of these formerly were two-bit sluts) who could increase their income by such work as sewing, washing, spinning, or by selling second-hand clothing or other junk, or even by stealing. Among the women was a female ensign who drew her pay like a corporal! Another was a midwife, and she was given many a good meal for herself and her husband. Another took in laundry and ironing; she washed shirts, socks, nightshirts, and other apparel for the bachelors among the officers and men, and she had quite a reputation. Others sold tobacco and furnished pipes for those who needed them. Still others sold brandy; it was generally thought that they were adulterating it with water distilled by their own bodies—but that didn't change the color of the liquor in the least! Another was a seamstress who was able to earn money through hemstitching and embroidery. Still another could pick a living off the field; in the winter she dug up snails, in the spring she picked salad herbs, in summer she took the young out of birds' nests, and in fall she could gather hundreds of other tidbits. Some sold kindling wood, which they carried to market like donkeys; others peddled still other merchandise. To earn my keep that way was not for me, since I already had a wife. Some of the men made a living by gambling (which they could do better than professional sharps), and by means of false dice and cards they got what they wanted from their simple-minded fellow soldiers. I despised such a trade. Others worked at building fortifications or at other odd jobs; for this I was too lazy. Some carried on a trade, but I had learned none. If a musician had been needed I could have served, but this starvation district got along on pipes and drums. Some took over others' guard duty and stood watch day and night. I would rather have starved than wear out my body that way. Some made both ends meet by going on raids, but I wasn't even permitted to step outside of the gate. Some could "organize" things better than a general; I hated such actions like sin. To make it brief, no matter where I turned, I could pick up nothing with which to fill my stomach. And what made me maddest was having to take it when the gang said, "You're a doctor and yet don't know how to cure starvation?"

Finally, necessity made me juggle a couple of good-sized carp out of the moat into my hands as I stood on the rampart; but as soon as the colonel heard of it I was in dutch and he forbade further prestidigitation on pain of hanging. At last, others' misfortune turned out to be my luck. Having cured a few cases of jaundice and fever—these patients must have had special faith in me—I was allowed to wander out of the fortress to gather (so I said) medicinal roots and herbs. But instead I set snares for rabbits and was lucky to catch two the first night. These I took to the colonel and he gave me not only a thaler as a present but also permission to go out after rabbits when I was off duty. Since the country was rather deserted and nobody was catching these animals, which had multiplied over the years, I had grist in my mill again, especially as it seemed that rabbits turned up everywhere or that I could charm them into my snares. When the officers saw that they could trust me, I was allowed to go raiding with the others, and I resumed the life of Soest, except that I could not be in charge. For that, one had to know all the roads and byways and the course of the Rhine.

B. Magdeburg Is Destroyed, 1631

So the General Pappenheim collected a number of his people on the ramparts by the New Town, and brought them from there into the streets of the city. Von Falckenberg [an emissary of Gustavus Adolphus] was shot, and fires were kindled in different quarters; then indeed it was all over with the city, and further resistance was useless. Nevertheless some of the soldiers and citizens did try to make a stand here and there, but the imperial troops kept bringing on more and more forces—cavalry, too—to help them, and finally they got the Kröckenthor open and let in the whole imperial army and the forces of the Catholic League,—Hungarians, Croats, Poles, Walloons, Italians, Spaniards, French, North and South Germans.

Thus it came about that the city and all its inhabitants fell into the hands of the enemy, whose violence and cruelty were due in part to their common hatred of the adherents of the Augsburg Confession, and in part to their being imbittered by the chain shot which had been fired at them and by the derision and insults that the Magdeburgers had heaped upon them from the ramparts.

Then was there naught but beating and burning, plundering, torture, and murder. Most especially was every one of the enemy bent on securing much booty. When a marauding party entered a house, if its master had anything to give he might thereby purchase respite and protection for himself and his family till the next man, who also wanted something, should come along. It was only when everything had been brought forth and there was nothing left to give that the real trouble commenced. Then, what with blows and threats of shooting, stabbing, and hanging, the poor people were so terrified that if they had had anything left they would have brought it forth if it had been buried in the earth or hidden away in a thousand castles. In this frenzied rage, the great and splendid city that had stood like a fair princess in the land was now, in its hour of direst need and unutterable distress and woe, given over to the flames, and thousands of innocent men, women, and children, in the midst of a horrible din of heartrending shrieks and cries, were tortured and put to death in so cruel and shameful a manner that no words would suffice to describe, nor no tears to bewail it. . . .

Thus in a single day this noble and famous city, the pride of the whole country, went up in fire and smoke; and the remnant of its citizens, with their wives and children, were taken prisoners and driven away by the enemy with a noise of weeping and wailing that could be heard from afar, while the cinders and ashes from the town were carried by the wind to Wanzleben, Egeln, and still more distant places. . . .

In addition to all this, quantities of sumptuous and irreplaceable house furnishings and movable property of all kinds, such as books, manuscripts, paintings, memorials of all sorts, . . . which money could not buy, were either burned or carried away by the soldiers as booty. The most magnificent garments, hangings, silk stuffs, gold and silver lace, linen of all sorts, and other household goods were bought by the army sutlers for a mere song and peddled about by the cart load all through the archbishopric of Magdeburg and in Anhalt and Brunswick. Gold chains and rings, jewels, and every kind of gold and silver utensils were to be bought from the common soldiers for a tenth of their real value. . . .

C. Pope Innocent X Condemns the Peace of Westphalia, 1648

Consumed by zeal for the house of the Lord, we are especially concerned with the endeavor everywhere to maintain the integrity of the orthodox faith and the authority of the Catholic Church, so that the ecclesiastical rights of which we have been appointed guardian by our Saviour shall not in any way be impaired by those who seek their own interest rather than God's, and that we may not be accused of negligence when we shall render account to the Sovereign Judge. Accordingly it is not without deep pain that we have learned that by several articles in the peace concluded at Osnabrück, August 6, 1648, between our very dear son in Christ, Ferdinand, king of the Romans and emperor elect, his allies and adherents, on the one hand, and the Swedes, with their allies and adherents, on the other, as well as in that peace which was likewise concluded at Münster in Westphalia on the twenty-fourth day of October of this same year 1648, between the same Ferdinand, king of the Romans, etc., and our very dear son in Jesus Christ, Louis, the very Christian king of the French, his allies and adherents, great prejudice has been done to the Catholic religion, the divine service, the roman apostolic see, the ecclesiastical order, their jurisdictions, authority, immunities, liberties, exemptions, privileges, possessions, and rights; since by various articles in one of these treaties of peace the ecclesiastical possessions which the heretics formerly seized are abandoned to them and to their successors, and the heretics, called those of the Augsburg Confession, are permitted the free exercise of their heresy in various districts. They are promised places in which they may build temples for their worship and are admitted with the Catholics to public offices and positions. . . . Many other things have been done too shameful to enumerate and very prejudicial to the orthodox religion and the Roman see. . . .

[Accordingly] we assert and declare by these presents that all the said articles in one or both of the said treaties which in any way impair or prejudice in the slightest degree, or that can be said, alleged, understood, or imagined to be able in any way to injure or to have injured the Catholic religion, divine worship, the salvation of souls, the said Roman apostolic see, the inferior churches, the ecclesiastical order or estate, their persons, affairs, possessions, jurisdictions, authorities, immunities, liberties, privileges, prerogatives, and rights whatsoever,—all such provisions have been, and are of right, and shall perpetually be, null and void, invalid, iniquitous, unjust, condemned, rejected, frivolous, without force or effect, and no one is to observe them, even when they be ratified by oath . . .

Document Set 16.6 References

A. Simplicissimus Endures
   J. J. C. von Grimmelshausen, *Simplicius Simplicissimus,* trans. George Schutz Behrend (Indianapolis: Bobbs-Merrill, 1965), 220–222.
B. Magdeburg Is Destroyed, 1631
   Contemporary Account, in James Harvey Robinson, ed., *Readings in European History* (Boston: Ginn, 1904), 2:211–212.
C. Pope Innocent X Condemns the Peace of Westphalia, 1648
   Innocent X, in Robinson, 2:214.

DOCUMENT SET 16.7
The Witchcraft Hysteria

This and Set 16.8 should be read together as you ask why and how the early seventeenth century saw the climax of Europe's bloody obsession with witchcraft and, simultaneously, several major breakthroughs in what has become known as the Scientific Revolution.

Ask, for example, how the rational political philosopher Jean Bodin could also have written Document A, a ferocious call upon magistrates to do their duty in prosecuting witchcraft. When you read Documents B through D, consider how accusations of witchcraft, once set in motion, could engulf whole communities in hysteria. Was there any validity to the accusations, or anything that victims might have done to attract suspicion? Do you see evidence here of systematic misogyny (hatred of women) at work? How did those in authority respond? You should also look back at Set 14.8, Document E—the infamous fifteenth-century witch-hunters' handbook, *Malleus Maleficarum.*

A. Jean Bodin Insists That Magistrates Have a Duty to Prosecute Witchcraft, 1580

There are two means by which states are maintained in their weal and greatness—reward and penalty: the one for the good, the other for the bad. And, if the distribution of these two be faulty, nothing else is to be expected than the inevitable ruin of the state. . . .

But those greatly err who think that penalties are established only to punish crime. I hold that this is the least of the fruits which accrue therefrom to the state. For the greatest and the chief is the appeasing of the wrath of God, especially if the crime is directly against the majesty of God, as is this one. . . . Now, if there is any means to appease the wrath of God, to gain his blessing, to strike awe into some by the punishment of others, to preserve some from being infected by others, to diminish the number of evildoers, to make secure the life of the well-disposed, and to punish the most detestable crimes of which the human mind can conceive, it is to punish with the utmost rigor the witches. . . . [Bodin lists fifteen horrid crimes of which every witch is guilty; in default of proof, presumption is enough to merit death.]

Now, it is not within the power of princes to pardon a crime which the law of God punishes with the penalty of death—such as are the crimes of witches.

Moreover, princes do gravely insult God in pardoning such horrible crimes committed directly against his majesty, seeing that the pettiest prince avenges with death insults against himself. Those too who let the witches escape, or who do not punish them with the utmost rigor, any rest assured that they will be abandoned by God to the mercy of the witches. And the country which shall tolerate this will be scourged with pestilences, famines, and wars; and those which shall take vengeance on the witches will be blessed by him and will make his anger to cease. Therefore it is that one accused of being a witch ought never to be folly acquitted and set free unless the calumny of the accuser is clearer than the sun, inasmuch as the proof of such crimes is so obscure and so difficult that not one witch in a million would be accused or punished if the procedure were governed by the ordinary rules. . . .

B. An Eyewitness Describes the Witch-Hysteria at Trier, 1589

Inasmuch as it was popularly believed that the continued sterility of many years was caused by witches through the malice of the Devil, the whole country rose to exterminate the witches. This movement was promoted by many in office, who hoped wealth from the persecution. And so, from court to court throughout the towns and villages of all the diocese, scurried special accusers, inquisitors, notaries, jurors, judges, constables, dragging to trial and torture human beings of both sexes and burning them in great numbers. Scarcely any of those who were accused escaped punishment. Nor were there spared even the leading men in the city of Trier. For the Judge, with two Burgomasters, several Councilors and Associate Judges, canons of sundry collegiate churches, parish-priests, rural deans, were swept away in this ruin. So far, at length, did the madness of the furious populace and of the courts go in this thirst for blood and booty that there was scarcely anybody who was not smirched by some suspicion of this crime.

Meanwhile notaries, copyists, and innkeepers grew rich. The executioner rode a blooded horse, like a noble of the court, and went clad in gold and silver; his wife vied with noble dames in the richness of her array. The children of those convicted and punished were sent into exile; their goods were confiscated;

plowman and vintner failed—hence came sterility. A direr pestilence or a more ruthless invader could hardly have ravaged the territory of Trier than this inquisition and persecution without bounds: many were the reasons for doubting that all were really guilty. This persecution lasted for several years; and some of those who presided over the administration of justice gloried in the multitude of the stakes, at each of which a human being had been given the flames.

At last, though the flames were still unsated, the people grew impoverished, rules were made and enforced restricting the fees and costs of examinations and examiners, and suddenly, as when in war funds fail, the zeal of the persecutors died out.

C. A French Witch Confesses, 1652

Asked how long she has been in subjugation to the devil.

—Says that it has been about twenty-five or twenty-six years, that her lover also then made her renounce God, Lent, baptism, that he has known her carnally three or four times, and that he has given her satisfaction. . . .

Asked if the devil did not advise her to steal from Elisabeth Dehan and to do harm to her.

—Said that he advised her to steal from her and promised that he would help her; but urged her not to do harm to her; and that is because she [Elisabeth Dehan] had cut the wood in her [Suzanne Gaudry's] fence and stirred up the seeds in her garden, saying that her lover told her that she would avenge herself by beating her.

D. The Toll of a Witch-Hunt at Bonn

Those burned are mostly male witches of the sort described. There must be half the city implicated: for already professors, law-students, pastors, canons, vicars, and monks have here been arrested and burned. His Princely Grace has seventy wards who are to become pastors, one of whom, eminent as a musician, was yesterday arrested; two others were sought for, but have fled. The Chancellor and his wife and the Private Secretary's wife are already executed. On the eve of Our Lady's Day there was executed here a maiden of nineteen who bore the name of being the fairest and most blameless of all the city, and who from her childhood had been brought up by the Bishop himself. A canon of the cathedral, named Rotenbahn, I saw beheaded and burned. Children of three or four years have devils for their paramours. Students and boys of noble birth, of nine, ten, eleven, twelve, thirteen, fourteen years, have here been burned. In fine, things are in such a pitiful state that one does not know with what people one may talk and associate.

Document Set 16.7 References

A. Jean Bodin Insists That Magistrates Have a Duty to Prosecute Witchcraft, 1580
   Jean Bodin, "De la Démonomanie des Sorciers," in *Translations and Reprints from the Original Sources of European History* (Philadelphia: University of Pennsylvania Press, 1902), 3/2:5–6.
B. An Eyewitness Describes the Witch-Hysteria at Trier, 1589
   Linden, *Gesta Tevirorum*, in *Translations and Reprints*, 3/2:13–14.
C. A French Witch Confesses, 1652
   J. Français, *L'Eglise et la Sorcellerie* (Paris: 1910), 236–251, quoted in Alan Kors and Edward Peters, eds., *Witchcraft in Europe* (Philadelphia: University of Pennsylvania Press, 1972), 266–275.
D. The Toll of a Witch-Hunt at Bonn
   Duren, Letter, in *Translations and Reprints*, 3/2:18–19.

DOCUMENT SET 16.8
An Intellectual Revolution

Copernicus, as we saw in Set 15.3, set the agenda for what we now call the Scientific Revolution; the problems raised by his heliocentric theory had to be answered. Notice in Document A how Galileo's epoch-making observations of the moons of Jupiter in 1610 suggested confirmation of some Copernican ideas while also casting doubt on some of Aristotle's ancient ideas about the incorruptibility of the heavens. Even more explicitly, the German astronomer Johann Kepler (Document B) saw Galileo's discoveries as a vindication of the Copernican vision.

Sir Francis Bacon (1561–1629), the English politician and author of *Novum Organum* (1620), from which Document C is taken, was an ambitious, grasping, obsequious courtier, fully convinced of his own unparalleled genius. He was not a scientist and can hardly be called a philosopher. His greatness lay in his insistence that experiment, not authority, should guide scientific inquiry; no one ever attacked medieval philosophy and its Aristotelian foundations so relentlessly, nor called so vigorously for science to exploit nature for humanity's benefit. To what extent does Bacon's onslaught seem to you characteristic of the Scientific Revolution? And how do you react to Bacon's argument that there is no conflict between science and religion? Bear in mind that Protestants (and especially Puritans, of which company Bacon was not) tended to be less fearful than Catholics that scientific inquiry would undermine religious truths.

René Descartes (1596-1650), whose *Discourse on Method,* 1637, is excerpted in Document D, was one of the great philosophical minds of the seventeenth century. His "method" rested on radical doubt of all sensory evidence while he searched for and ultimately found a new principle of knowledge based on the realization that he could trust the fact of his own existence as a thinking being. The extract in Document D explains how Descartes arrived at his fundamental insight. He had to be especially wary of being identified as a Copernican, but his support of rationalism (particularly in France) was tremendously important in undermining Aristotelianism and scholasticism, which by the seventeenth century had become identified merely with citing ancient authority and predetermined propositions.

The dangers that anyone in Catholic Europe, including Descartes, faced in endorsing Copernicus's theories is apparent from Galileo's ordeal before the Papal Inquisition (Document D) after he had ridiculed Aristotelianism in his *Dialogue of the Two-World Systems* (1632).

A. Galileo Turns His Telescope on Jupiter, January–March 1610

On the seventh day of January in this present year 1610, at the first hour of night, when I was viewing the heavenly bodies with a telescope, Jupiter presented itself to me; and because I had prepared a very excellent instrument for myself, I perceived (as I had not before, on account of the weakness of my previous instrument) that beside the planet there were three starlets, small indeed, but very bright. Though I believed them to be among the host of fixed stars, they aroused my curiosity somewhat by appearing to lie in an exact straight line parallel to the ecliptic, and by their being more splendid than others of their size. Their arrangement with respect to Jupiter and each other was the following:

East   *   *   O   *   *West*

that is, there were two stars on the eastern side and one to the west . . . on January eighth—led by what, I do not know—I found a very different arrangement. The three starlets were now all to the west of Jupiter, closer together, and at equal intervals from one another as shown in the following sketch:

East   O   *   *   *   *West*

At this time, though I did not yet turn my attention to the way the stars had come together, I began to concern myself with the question how Jupiter could be east of all these stars when on the previous day it had been west of two of them. . . .

On the tenth of January, however, the stars appeared in this position with respect to Jupiter:

East   *   *   O   *West*

that is, there were but two of them, both easterly, the third (as I supposed) being hidden behind Jupiter. As at first, they were in the same straight line with Jupiter and were arranged precisely in the line of the zodiac. Noticing this, and knowing that there was no way in which such alterations could be attributed to Jupiter's motion, yet being certain that these were still the same stars I had observed (in fact no other was to be found along the line of the zodiac for a long way on either side of Jupiter), my perplexity was now transformed into amazement. I was sure that the apparent changes belonged not to Jupiter but to the observed stars, and I resolved to pursue this investigation with greater care and attention.

And thus, on the eleventh of January, I saw the following disposition:

East　　　 *　 *　 O　　　 *West* . . .

I had now decided beyond all question that there existed in the heavens three stars wandering about Jupiter as do Venus and Mercury about the sun, and this became plainer that daylight from observations on similar occasions which followed. Nor were there just three such stars; four wanderers complete their revolutions about Jupiter, and of their alterations as observed more precisely later on we shall give a description here. Also I measured the distances between them by means of the telescope, using the method explained before. Moreover I recorded the times of the observations, especially when more than one was made during the same night—for the revolutions of these planets are so speedily completed that it is usually possible to take even their hourly variations. [Galileo continues to make similar observations until March 2, noting the changes in the "stars" adjacent to Jupiter.] . . .

Such are the observations concerning the four Medicean planets recently first discovered by me, and although from this data their periods have not yet been reconstructed in numerical form, it is legitimate at least to put in evidence some facts worthy of note. Above all, since they sometimes follow and sometimes precede Jupiter by the same intervals, and they remain within very limited distances either to east or west of Jupiter, accompanying that planet in both its retrograde and direct movements in a constant manner, no one can doubt that they complete their revolutions about Jupiter and at the same time effect all together a twelve-year period about the center of the universe. That they also revolve in unequal circles is manifestly deduced from the fact that at the greatest elongation from Jupiter it is never possible to see two of these planets in conjunction, whereas in the vicinity of Jupiter they are found united two, three, and sometimes all four together. It is also observed that the revolutions are swifter in those planets which describe smaller circles about Jupiter, since the stars closest to Jupiter are usually seen to the east when on the previous day they appeared to the west, and vice versa, while the planet which traces the largest orbit appears upon accurate observation of its returns to have a semimonthly period.

Here we have a fine and elegant argument for quieting the doubts of those who, while accepting with tranquil mind the revolutions of the planets about the sun in the Copernican system, are mightily disturbed to have the moon alone revolve about the earth and accompany it in an annual rotation about the sun. Some have believed that this structure of the universe should be rejected as impossible. But now we have not just one planet rotating about another while both run through a great orbit around the sun; our own eyes show us four stars which wander around Jupiter as does the moon around the earth, while all together trace out a grand revolution about the sun in the space of twelve years. . . .

B. Johann Kepler Speculates on the Implications of Galileo's Discoveries

. . . I rejoice that I am to some extent restored to life by your work. If you had discovered any planets revolving around one of the fixed stars, there would now be waiting for me chains and a prison amid Bruno's innumerabilities, I should rather say, exile to his infinite space. Therefore, by reporting that these four planets revolve, not around one of the fixed stars, but around the planet Jupiter, you have for the present freed me from the great fear which gripped me as soon as I had heard about your book from my opponent's triumphal shout.

Wackher of course had once more been seized by deep admiration for that dreadful philosophy. What Galileo recently saw with his own eyes, it had many years before not only proposed as a surmise, but thoroughly established by reasoning. It is doubtless with perfect justice that those men attain fame whose intellect anticipates the senses in closely related branches of philosophy. Theoretical astronomy, at a time when it had never set foot outside Greece, nevertheless disclosed the characteristics of the Arctic Zone. Who then would not rank it in nobility above Caesar's experience of learning from the water-clocks that the nights on the coasts of Britain are a little shorter than the nights in Rome, or above the Dutchmen's spending the winter in the north, an expedition which was indeed wonderful, but which would have been impossible without that theoretical knowledge? Who does not honor Plato's myth of Atlantis, Plutarch's legend of the gold-colored islands beyond Thule, and Seneca's prophetic verses about the forthcoming discovery of a New World, now that the evidence for such a place has finally been furnished by that Argonaut from Florence? Columbus himself keeps his readers uncertain whether to admire his intellect in divining the New World from the direction of the winds, more than his courage in facing unknown seas and the boundless ocean, and his good luck in gaining his objective.

In my own field too, the prodigies will naturally be Pythagoras, Plato, and Euclid. Borne aloft by the preeminence of their reason, they argued that God could not have done otherwise than to arrange the world on the model of the five regular solids. But they mistook the pattern. On the other hand, the plaudits of the average man will go to Copernicus who, equipped with a mind that was not average, yet drew a picture of the universe virtually as it is seen by the eye. But he brought to light only the bare facts. Trailing far behind the ancients will be Kepler. From the visual outlook of the Copernican system he rises, as it were, from the facts to the causes, and to the same explanation as Plato from on high had set forth deductively so many centuries before. He shows that the Copernican system of the world exhibits the reason for the five Platonic solids. It is not an act of folly or jealousy to set the ancients above the moderns; the very nature of the subject demands it. For the glory of the Creator of this world is greater than that of the student of the world, however ingenious. The former brought forth the structural design from within himself, whereas the latter, despite strenuous efforts, scarcely perceives the plan embodied in the structure. Surely those thinkers who intellectually grasp the causes of phenomena, before these are revealed to the senses, resemble the Creator more closely than the others, who speculate about the causes after the phenomena have been seen.

Therefore, Galileo, you will not envy our predecessors their due praise. What you report as having been quite recently observed by your own eyes, they predicted, long before you, as necessarily so. Nevertheless, you will have your own fame. Copernicus and I, as a Copernican, pointed out to the ancients the mistaken way in which they considered the five solids to be expressed in the world, and we substituted the authentic and true way. Similarly, you correct and, in part, unsettle Bruce's doctrine, borrowed from Bruno. These men thought that other celestial bodies have their own moons revolving around them, like our earth with its moon. But you prove that they were talking in generalities. Moreover, they supposed it was the fixed stars that are so accompanied. Bruno even expounded the reason why this must be so. The fixed stars, forsooth, have the quality of sun and fire, but the planets, of water. By an indefeasible law of nature these opposites combine. The sun cannot be deprived of the planets; the fire, of its water; nor in turn the water, of the fire. Now the weakness of his reasoning is exposed by your observations. In the first place, sup-

pose that each and every fixed star is a sun. No moons have yet been seen revolving around them. Hence this will remain an open question until this phenomenon too is detected by someone equipped for marvelously refined observations. At any rate, this is what your success threatens us with, in the judgment of certain persons. On the other hand, Jupiter is one of the planets, which Bruno describes as earths. And behold, there are four other planets around Jupiter. Yet Bruno's argument made this claim not for the earths, but for the suns.

Meanwhile I cannot refrain from contributing this additional feature to the unorthodox aspects of your findings. It is not improbable, I must point out, that there are inhabitants not only on the moon but on Jupiter too or (as was delightfully remarked at a recent gathering of certain philosophers) that those areas are now being unveiled for the first time. But as soon as somebody demonstrates the art of flying, settlers from our species of man will not be lacking. Who would once have thought that the crossing of the wide ocean was calmer and safer than that of the narrow Adriatic Sea, Baltic Sea, or English Channel? Given ships or sails adapted to the breezes of heaven, there will be those who will not shrink from even that vast expanse. Therefore, for the sake of those who, as it were, will presently be on hand to attempt this voyage, let us establish the astronomy, Galileo, you of Jupiter, and me of the moon. . . .

C. Francis Bacon Announces the March of Progress

The discoveries which have hitherto been made in the sciences are such as lie close to vulgar notions, scarcely beneath the surface. In order to penetrate into the inner and further recesses of nature, it is necessary that both notions and axioms derived from things by a more sure and guarded way, and that a method of intellectual operation be introduced altogether better and more certain. . . .

There is no soundness in our notions, whether logical or physical. Substance, quality, action, passion, essence itself are not sound notions; much less are heavy, light, dense, rare, moist, dry, generation, corruption, attraction, repulsion, element, matter, form, and the like; but all are fantastical and ill-defined. . . .

There are and can be only two ways of searching into and discovering truth. The one flies from the senses and particulars to the most general axioms, and from these principles, the truth of which it takes for settled and immovable, proceeds to judgment and the discovery of middle axioms. And this way is now in fashion. The other derives axioms from the senses and particulars, rising by a gradual and unbroken ascent, so that it arrives at the most general axioms last of all. This is the true way, but as yet untried. . . .

It is not to be forgotten that in every age natural philosophy has had a troublesome adversary and hard to deal with,—namely, superstition and the blind and immoderate zeal of religion. For we see among the Greeks that those who first proposed to man's uninitiated ears the natural causes for thunder and for storms were thereupon found guilty of impiety. Nor was much more forbearance shown by some of the ancient fathers of the Christian Church to those who, on most convincing grounds (such as no one in his senses would now think of contradicting), maintained that the earth was round and, of consequence, asserted the existence of the antipodes.

Moreover, as things now are, to discourse of nature is made harder and more perilous by the summaries and systems of the schoolmen; who, having reduced theology into regular order as well as they were able, and fashioned it into the shape of an art, ended in incorporating the contentious and thorny philosophy of Aristotle, more than was fit, with the body of religion. . . .

Lastly, some are weakly afraid lest a deeper search into nature should transgress the permitted limits of sobermindedness; wrongfully wresting and transferring what is said in Holy Writ against those who pry into sacred mysteries to the hidden things of nature, which are barred by no prohibition. Others, with more subtlety, surmise and reflect that if secondary causes are unknown everything can be more readily referred to the divine hand and rod,—a point in which they think religion greatly concerned; which is, in fact, nothing else but to seek to gratify God with a lie. Others fear from past example that movements and changes in philosophy will end in assaults on religion; and others again appear apprehensive that in the investigation of nature something may be found to subvert, or at least shake, the authority of religion, especially with the unlearned.

But these two last fears seem to me to savor utterly of carnal wisdom; as if men in the recesses and secret thoughts of their hearts doubted and distrusted the strength of religion, and the empire of faith over the senses, and therefore feared that the investigation of truth in nature might be dangerous to them. But if the matter by truly considered, natural philosophy is, after the word of God, at once the surest medicine against superstition and the most approved nourishment for faith; and therefore she is rightly given to religion as her most faithful handmaid, since

the one displays the will of God, the other his power. . . .

D. René Descartes Conceives a New Method of Reasoning

I was then in Germany, attracted thither by the wars in that country, which have not yet been brought to a termination; and as I was returning to the army from the coronation of the Emperor, the setting in of winter arrested me in a locality where, as I found no society to interest me, and was besides fortunately undisturbed by any cares or passions, I remained the whole day in [a stove-heated room,] with full opportunity to occupy my attention with my own thoughts. Of these one of the very first that occurred to me was, that there is seldom so much perfection in works composed of many separate parts, upon which different hands have been employed, as in those completed by a single master. Thus it is observable that the buildings which a single architect has planned and executed, are generally more elegant and commodious than those which several have attempted to improve, by making old walls serve for purposes for which they were not originally built. Thus also, those ancient cities which, from being at first only villages, have become, in course of time, large towns, are usually but ill laid out compared with the regularly constructed towns which a professional architect has freely planned on an open plain; so that although the several buildings of the former may often equal or surpass in beauty those of the latter, yet when one observes their indiscriminate juxtaposition, there a large one and here a small, and the consequent crookedness and irregularity of the streets, one is disposed to allege that chance rather than any human will guided by reason, must have led to such an arrangement. . . .

It is true . . . that it is not customary to pull down all the houses of a town with the single design of rebuilding them differently, and thereby rendering the streets more handsome; but it often happens that a private individual takes down his own with the view of erecting it anew, and that people are even sometimes constrained to this when their houses are in danger of falling from age, or when the foundations are insecure. With this before me by way of example, I was persuaded that it would indeed be preposterous for a private individual to think of reforming a state by fundamentally changing it throughout, and overturning it in order to set it up amended; and the same I thought was true of any similar project for reforming the body of the Sciences, or the order of teaching them established in the Schools [scholastic philosophy]: but as for the opinions which up to that time I had embraced, I thought that I could not do better than resolve at once to sweep them wholly away, that I might afterwards be in a position to admit either others more correct, or even perhaps the same when they had undergone the scrutiny of Reason. I firmly believed that in this way I should much better succeed in the conduct of my life, than if I built only upon old foundations, and leant upon principles which, in my youth, I had taken upon trust. . . .

Among the branches of Philosophy, I had, at an earlier period, given some attention to Logic, and among those of the Mathematics to Geometrical Analysis and Algebra,—three arts or Sciences which ought, as I conceived, to contribute something to my design. But, on examination, I found that, as for Logic, its syllogisms and the majority of its other precepts are of avail rather in the communication of what we already know . . . than in the investigation of the unknown; and although this Science contains indeed a number of correct and very excellent precepts, there are, nevertheless, so many others, and these either injurious or superfluous, mingled with the former, that it is almost quite as difficult to effect a severance of the true form the false as it is to extract a Diana or a Minerva form a rough block of marble. . . . By these considerations I was induced to seek some other Method which would comprise [their] advantages . . . and be exempt from their defects. And as a multitude of laws often only hampers justice, so that a state is best governed when, with few laws, these are rigidly administered; in like manner, instead of the great number of precepts of which Logic is composed, I believed that the four following would prove perfectly sufficient for me, provided I took the firm and unwavering resolution never in a single instance to fail in observing them.

The *first* was never to accept anything for true which I did not clearly know to be such; that is to say, carefully to avoid precipitancy and prejudice, and to comprise nothing more in my judgment than what was presented to my mind so clearly and distinctly as to exclude all ground of doubt.

The *second,* to divide each of the difficulties under examination into as many parts as possible, and as might be necessary for its adequate solution.

The *third,* to conduct my thoughts in such order that, by commencing with objects the simplest and easiest to know, I might ascend by little and little, and, as it were, step by step, to the knowledge of the more complex; assigning in thought a certain order even to those objects which in their own nature do not stand in a relation of antecedence and sequence.

And the *last,* in every case to make enumerations so complete, and reviews so general, that I might be assured that nothing was omitted.

The long chains of simple and easy reasonings by means of which geometers are accustomed to reach the conclusions of their most difficult demonstrations, had led me to imagine that all things, to the knowledge of which man is competent, are mutually connected in the same way, and that there is nothing so far removed from us as to be beyond our reach, or so hidden that we cannot discover it, provided only we abstain from accepting the false for the true, and always preserve in our thoughts the order necessary for the deduction of one truth from another. . . .

E. Galileo Faces the Inquisition

I, Galileo, son of the late Vincenzo Galilei, Florentine, aged seventy years . . . have been pronounced by the Holy Office [of the Inquisition] to be vehemently suspected of heresy, that is to say, of having held and believed that the Sun is the center of the world and immovable and that the Earth is not the center and moves: . . . with sincere heart and unfeigned faith I abjure, curse, and detest the aforesaid errors and heresies.

Document Set 16.8 References

A. Galileo Turns His Telescope on Jupiter, January–March 1610
Stilman Drake, ed., *Discoveries and Opinions of Galileo* (Garden City, N.Y.: Doubleday, 1957), 51–57.

B. Johann Kepler Speculates on the Implications of Galileo's Discoveries
Edward Rosen, ed., *Kepler's Conversation with Galileo's Sidereal Messenger* (New York: Johnson Reprint Co., 1965), 36–39.

C. Francis Bacon Announces the March of Progress
Bacon, *Novum Organum,* in James Harvey Robinson, ed., *Readings in European History* (Boston: Ginn, 1904), 2:601–603.

D. René Descartes Conceives a New Method of Reasoning
Descartes, *Discourse on Method,* trans. John Veitch (Edinburgh, 1873), 11–14, 17–20.

E. Galileo Faces the Inquisition
Giorgio de Santillana, *The Crime of Galileo* (Chicago: University of Chicago Press, 1955), 292–293, 312.

17

Rebellion and State Building, 1640–1690

DOCUMENT SET 17.1
The English Revolution

The two documents of this set starkly contrast the two sides, parliament and king, at the outset of the English Civil War. By an eleven-vote margin the House of Commons enacted the Grand Remonstrance (Document A) in November 1641, a time of rising tension between Parliament, in which radical Puritans were gaining the upper hand, and Charles I, who was ever more determined to resist. Open civil war was only nine months away. Read the document for an understanding of how positions had hardened on both sides: not everything in the Grand Remonstrance was strictly true.

Document B comes from the end of the Civil War. Charles had been defeated and eventually put on trial for his life—as "Charles Stuart, Esq.," not as King Charles I—before Parliament, which claimed to "have the supreme power in the nation." How do you react to Charles's insistence that he had become the persecuted defender of tradition and law?

A. Parliament Confronts the King: The Grand Remonstrance, 1641

The Commons in this present Parliament assembled, having with much earnestness and faithfulness of affection and zeal to the public good of this kingdom, and His Majesty's honour and service for the space of twelve months, wrestled with great dangers and fears, the pressing miseries and calamities, the various distempers and disorders which had not only assaulted, but even overwhelmed and extinguished the liberty, peace and prosperity of this kingdom, the comfort

and hopes of all His Majesty's good subjects, and exceedingly weakened and undermined the foundation and strength of his own royal throne, do yet find an abounding malignity and opposition in those parties and factions who have been the cause of those evils, and do still labour to cast aspersions upon that which hath been done, and to raise many difficulties for the hindrance of that which remains yet undone, and to foment jealousies between the king and Parliament, that so they may deprive him and his people of the fruit of his own gracious intentions, and their humble desires of procuring the public peace, safety and happiness of this realm.

For the preventing of those miserable effects which such malicious endeavours may produce, we have thought good to declare the root and the growth of these mischievous designs: the maturity and ripeness to which they have attained before the beginning of the Parliament: the effectual means which have been used for the extirpation of those dangerous evils, and the progress which hath therein been made by His Majesty's goodness and the wisdom of the Parliament: the ways of obstruction and opposition by which that progress hath been interrupted: the courses to be taken for the removing those obstacles, and for the accomplishing of our most dutiful and faithful intentions and endeavours of restoring and establishing the ancient honour, greatness and security of this Crown and nation.

The root of all this mischief we find to be a malignant and pernicious design of subverting the fundamental laws and principles of government, upon which the religion and justice of this kingdom are firmly established. The actors and promoters hereof have been:

1. The Jesuited papists, who hate the laws, as the obstacles of that change and subversion of religion which they so much long for.

2. The bishops, and the corrupt part of the clergy, who cherish formality and superstition as the natural effects and more probable supports of their own ecclesiastical tyranny and usurpation.

3. Such councillors and courtiers as for private ends have engaged themselves to further the interests of some foreign princes or states to the prejudice of His Majesty and the state at home. . . .

In the beginning of His Majesty's reign the [Catholic] party began to revive and flourish again. . . .

[There follows a long list of protests against arbitrary and excessive taxation.]

37. The Court of Star Chamber hath abounded in extravagant censures, not only for the maintenance and improvement of monopolies and other unlawful taxes, but for divers other causes where there hath been no offence, or very small; whereby His Majesty's subjects have been oppressed by grievous fines, imprisonments, stigmatising, mutilations, whippings, pillories, gags, confinements, banishments; after so rigid a manner as hath not only deprived men of the society of their friends, exercise of their professions, comfort of books, use of paper or ink, but even violated that near union which God hath established between men and their wives, by forced and constrained separation. . . .

48. Titles of honour, judicial places, sergeantships at law, and other offices have been sold for great sums of money, whereby the common justice of the kingdom hath been much endangered, not only by opening a way of employment in places of great trust, and advantage to men of weak parts, but also by giving occasion to bribery, extortion, partiality, it seldom happening that places ill-gotten are well used. . . .

51. The bishops and the rest of the clergy did triumph in the suspensions, excommunications, deprivations, and degradations of divers painful, learned and pious ministers, in the vexation and grievous oppression of great numbers of His Majesty's good subjects.

52. The [ecclesiastical court of] High Commission grew to such excess of sharpness and severity as was not much less than the Romish Inquisition, and yet in many cases by the archbishop's power was made much more heavy, being assisted and strengthened by authority of the Council Table.

53. The bishops and their courts were as eager in the country; although their jurisdiction could not reach so high in rigour and extremity of punishment, yet were they no less grievous in respect of the generality and multiplicity of vexations, which lighting upon the meaner sort of tradesmen and artificers did impoverish many thousands.

54. And so afflict and trouble others, that great numbers to avoid their miseries departed out of the kingdom, some into New England and other parts of America, others into Holland. . . .

B. Charles I Defies Parliament, 1649

Having already made my protestations, not only against the illegality of this pretended court, but also, that no earthly power can justly call me (who am your king) in question as a delinquent, I would not any more open my mouth upon this occasion, more than to refer myself to what I have spoken, were I in this case alone concerned: but the duty I owe to God in the preservation of the true liberty of my people will not suffer me at this time to be silent: for, how can any freeborn subject of England call life or anything he possesseth his own, if power without right daily make new, and abrogate the old fundamental laws of the land which I now take to be the present case? Wherefore when I came hither, I expected that you would have endeavored to have satisfied me concerning these grounds which hinder me to answer to your pretended impeachment. But since I see that nothing I can say will move you to it (though negatives are not so naturally proved as affirmatives) yet I will show you the reason why I am confident you cannot judge me, nor indeed the meanest man in England: for I will not (like you) without showing a reason, seek to impose a belief upon my subjects.

There is no proceeding just against any man, but what is warranted, either by God's laws or the municipal laws of the country where he lives. Now I am most confident this day's proceeding cannot be warranted by God's laws; for, on the contrary, the authority of obedience unto kings is clearly warranted, and strictly commanded in both the Old and New Testament, which, if denied, I am ready instantly to prove.

And for the question now in hand, there it is said, that "where the word of a king is, there is power; and who may say unto him, what dost thou?" Eccles. viii. 4. Then for the law of this land, I am no less confident, that no learned lawyer will affirm that an impeachment can lie against the king, they all going in his name: and one of their maxims is, that the king can do no wrong. Besides, the law upon which you ground your proceedings, must either be old or new: if old, show it; if new, tell what authority, warranted by the fundamental laws of the land, hath made it, and when. But how the House of Commons can erect a court of judicature, which was never one itself (as is well known to all lawyers) I leave to God and the world to judge. And it were full as strange, that they should pretend to make laws without king or Lords' House, to any that have heard speak of the laws of England.

And admitting, but not granting, that the people of England's commission could grant your pretended power, I see nothing you can show for that; for certainly you never asked the question of the tenth man in the kingdom, and in this way you manifestly wrong even the poorest ploughman, if you demand not his free consent; nor can you pretend any color for this your pretended commission, without the consent at least of the major part of every man in England of whatsoever quality or condition, which I am sure you never went about to seek, so far are you from having it. Thus you see that I speak not for my own right alone, as I am your king, but also for the true liberty of all my subjects, which consists not in the power of government, but in living under such laws, such a government, as may give themselves the best assurance of their lives, and property of their goods. . . . Then for anything I can see, the higher house is totally excluded; and for the House of Commons, it is too well known that the major part of them are detained or deterred from sitting; so as if I

had no other, this were sufficient for me to protest against the lawfulness of your pretended court. Besides all this, the peace of the kingdom is not the least in my thoughts; and what hope of settlement is there, so long as power reigns without rule or law, changing the whole frame of that government under which this kingdom hath flourished for many hundred years? (nor will I say what will fall out in case this lawless, unjust proceeding against me do go on) and believe it, the commons of England will not thank you for this change; . . . and by this time it will be too sensibly evident, that the arms I took up were only to defend the fundamental laws of this kingdom against those who have supposed my power hath totally changed the ancient government.

Thus, having showed you briefly the reasons why I cannot submit to your pretended authority, without violating the trust which I have from God for the welfare and liberty of my people, I expect from you either clear reasons to convince my judgment, showing me that I am in an error (and then truly I will answer) or that you will withdraw your proceedings. . . .

Document Set 17.1 References

A. Parliament Confronts the King: The Grand Remonstrance, 1641
   Lacey Baldwin Smith and Jean Reeder Smith, eds., *The Past Speaks: Sources and Problems in English History*, 2d ed. (Lexington, Mass.: D. C. Heath, 1993), 1:341–343.
B. Charles I Defies Parliament, 1649
   Charles I, in Smith and Smith, 1:349–350.

Radical voices began to echo as soon as king and Parliament clashed in 1641. The anonymous *A Glimpse of Sion's Glory* shows that radical millennial ideas appealed even to respectable middle-class Puritans.

In 1649, the end of the Civil War raised the urgent question of what kind of government should succeed the monarchy. In May 1649 *An Agreement of the Free People of England* (Document B) was published containing a defense of four Levellers (army and lower-class radicals) accused of treason for publishing seditious pamphlets. The tone was moderate, but the demands extreme for the time. To assess how radical the Levellers were, see Document C, an account of a debate between two army officers, Colonel Thomas Rainsborough (a radical) and General Henry Ireton (a conservative). How do Ireton's sentiments reflect mainstream contemporary values?

As *The Challenge of the West* makes clear, the English Revolution brought women into considerable prominence in the radical sects. In Document D, feisty Susannah Parr recalls her difficulties with the (male) elders of her congregation. Among other insights, notice how she speaks of the procedure (normal in Puritan congregations) of having a prospective new member publicly reveal the private experiences in which she had received assurance of God's grace—that is, her "conversion experience." What is significant in her minister's criticism of her "censoriousness"? Notice that the minister who criticized her was himself of extremely radical (Quaker) leanings.

Oliver Cromwell (1599–1658), the leader of the parliamentary army, became England's military dictator. He has always been a controversial figure. Edward Hyde (later named the Earl of Clarendon), a member of parliament who early turned against the Revolution and lived to write its history, paid an eloquent tribute to his opponent Cromwell in the extract from his *History of the Rebellion* that forms Document E.

One of the noblest spirits among the English revolutionaries was the Puritan poet John Milton (1608–1674), who served the parliamentary cause and the Commonwealth as a pamphleteer and Latin secretary. But a proposal to censor controversial religious and political books brought forth in 1644 one of Milton's most eloquent efforts, the essay *Areopagitica,* defending freedom of expression. It is

difficult to extract a short passage from this moving plea; the excerpt in Document F, however, makes a powerful statement that it is precisely out of the clash of ideas that a new, freer, and more glorious England shall arise.

Using these documents and relying on *The Challenge of the West,* write a brief analysis of the mid-seventeenth century English Revolution as a battlefield of political and religious ideas.

A. A Puritan Visionary Catches "A Glimpse of Sion's Glory," 1641

Rev. 19.6: *And I heard as it were the voice of a great multitude, and as the voice of many waters, and as the voice of mighty thunderings, saying: Hallelujah, for the Lord God Omnipotent reigneth.*

At the pouring forth of the first vial, there was a voice saying: *Babylon is fallen, it is fallen.* At the pouring forth of the sixth, John hears a voice as the voice of many waters, and as the voice of thunderings, saying: *Hallelujah, the Lord God Omnipotent reigneth,* immediately following the other. Babylon's falling is Sion's raising. Babylon's destruction is Jerusalem's salvation. The fourth vial was poured upon the sun, which is yet doing, namely upon the emperor and that house of Austria, and will be till that house be destroyed. . . . This is the work that is in hand. As soon as ever this is done, that Antichrist is down, Babylon fallen, then comes in Jesus Christ reigning gloriously; then comes in this *Hallelujah, the Lord God Omnipotent reigneth.* . . . It is the work of the day to cry down Babylon, that it may fall more and more; and it is the work of the day to give God no rest till he sets up Jerusalem as the praise of the whole world. Blessed is he that dasheth the brats of Babylon against the stones. Blessed is he that hath any hand in pulling down Babylon. And beautiful likewise are the feet of them that bring glad tidings unto Jerusalem, unto Zion, saying, *The Lord God Omnipotent reigneth.* This is the work of this exercise: to show unto you how, upon the destruction of Babylon, Christ shall reign gloriously, and how we are to further it. . . .

From whence came this hallelujah? *I heard as it were the voice of a great multitude, and as the voice of many waters.* By waters we are to understand people: the voice of many waters, of many people. . . .

The voice, of Jesus Christ reigning in his Church, comes first from the multitude, the common people. The voice is heard from them first, before it is heard from any others. God uses the common people and the multitude to proclaim that the Lord God Omnipotent reigneth. As when Christ came at first the poor receive[d] the Gospel—not many wise, not many noble, not many rich, but the poor—so in the reformation of religion, after Antichrist began to be discovered, it was the common people that first came to look after Christ. . . . The business, brethren, concerning the Scots, it is a business in the issue whereof we hope there will be great things. Where began it? At the very feet, at the very soles of the feet. You that are of the meaner rank, common people, be not discouraged; for God intends to make use of the common people in the great work of proclaiming the kingdom of his Son. . . .

Though the voice of Christ's reign came first from the multitude; yet it comes but in a confused manner, as the noise of many waters. Though the multitude may begin a thing, and their intention may be good in it, yet it is not for them to bring it to perfection: that which they do commonly is mixed with much confusion and a great deal of disorder. . . . After the beginning of this confused noise among the multitude, God moves the hearts of great ones, of noble, of learned ones; and they come in to the work, and their voice is as the voice of mighty thundering, a voice that strikes terror, and hath a majesty in it to prevail. . . . This is the work of the day, for us to lift up our voice to heaven, that it might be mighty to bring forth more and more the voice of our Parliament as a voice of thunder, a terrible voice to the Antichristian party, that they may say, *The Lord God Omnipotent reigneth.* And let us not be discouraged, for our prayers, though they be poor and mean, and scattered, they may further the voice of thunderings. . . .

Though Christ's kingdom be for a while darkened, Christ shall reign gloriously. That is implied. It is revealed to John as a great wonder, as a glorious thing. Why, did not Christ reign before? Yes, but not in that manner that now he is to reign: the kingdom of Christ hath been exceedingly darkened in the world: though it now begins to appear a little more brightly, it hath been exceedingly darkened. . . .

You see that the Saints have little now in the world; now they are the poorest and the meanest of all; but then when the adoption of the sons of God shall come in the fulness of it, the world shall be theirs; for the world is purchased for them by Jesus Christ. *Not only heaven shall be your kingdom, but this world bodily.* . . .

B. The Levellers Demand a Thorough-Going Revolution: The Agreement of the People

We the free People of England . . . agree to ascertain our Government, to abolish all arbitrary Power, and to set bounds and limits both to our Supreme, and all Subordinate Authority. . . .

I. That the Supreme Authority of England and the Territories therewith incorporate, shall be and reside henceforward in a Representative of the People consisting of four hundred persons, but no more; in the choice of whom (according to naturall right) all men of the age of one and twenty yeers and upwards (not being servants, or receiving alms, or having served the late King in Arms or voluntary Contributions) shall have their voices; and be capable of being elected to that Supreme Trust. . . .

VIII. . . . That the next and al future Representatives, shall continue in full power for the space of one whole year: and that the people shall of course, chuse a Parliament once every year. . . .

X. That we do not impower or entrust our said representatives to continue in force, or to make any Lawes, Oaths, or Covenants, whereby to compell by penalties or otherwise any person to any thing in or about matters of faith, Religion or Gods worship or to restrain any person from the profession of his faith, or exercise of Religion according to his Conscience, nothing having caused more distractions, and heart burnings in all ages, then persecution and molestation for matters of Conscience in and about Religion.

C. Major Rainsborough and Major General Ireton Debate the Levellers' Demands at Putney

Rainsborough: For my part, I think we cannot engage one way or other in the army if we do not think of the people's liberties. If we can agree where the liberty and freedom of the people lies, that will do all.

Ireton: I cannot consent so far. As I said before: when I see the hand of God destroying king, and Lords, and Commons too, [or] any foundation of human constitution, when I see God hath done it, I shall, I hope, comfortably acquiesce in it. But . . . if the principle upon which you move this alteration, or the ground upon which you press that we should make this alteration, do destroy all kind of property or whatsoever a man hath by human constitution, [I cannot consent to it]. The law of God doth not give me property, nor the law of Nature, but property is of human constitution. I have a property and this I shall enjoy. Constitution founds property. If either the thing itself that you press or the consequence [of] that you press [do destroy property], though I shall acquiesce in having no property, yet I cannot give my heart or hand to it; because it is a thing evil in itself and scandalous to the world, and I desire this army may be free from both. . . .

D. Susanna Parr, Independent, Searches Her Soul and Is Disciplined by Her Congregation, 1650s

They who desired admission into the society were sometimes desired in a private meeting to speak what experience they had of the work of grace upon their souls. After which we were every one of us, both men and women, to declare our thoughts of what was spoken; it being laid down as a ground, that we must have an account of a change from a natural and legal estate, into an estate of grace and believing, of those whom we admitted into communion with us. I among the rest did according to my weak measure declare myself against that which I thought would not stand for grace. I was so far from delighting in this work as that it was a trouble to me, an employment from which I would willingly have been freed. I conceived it more needful for myself to study the Word, and compare my own heart with the rule, than to be so taken up about the condition of others. But this was our principle: we were to keep the house of God pure, we were set as porters at the door; it was our duty, we were not to be wanting at such times; yea, it was our liberty that we, who were to have communion with those who came to be admitted, should give in our assent or dissent in reference to their admission. I did therefore at such times declare my thoughts as well as the rest, but left the determination to themselves, as it appears in Ganicle, who was admitted though I was at the first against his admission. I mention him because he was brought by Mr. Eveleigh as an instance of my censoriousness. I was blamed for disliking him whom they said was one of the most eminent among them, and yet it was not long after before he discovered himself, by renouncing the principles of Christianity and turning Quaker. He, in speaking out his experiences, pretended unto much joy and ravishment of spirit, but (the Lord knows) when he spake of such enjoyments, he spake as a stranger that never intermeddled with this joy, never declaring any powerful effect thereof, but only that which was only but a Balaam's wish. I the

rather instance in him because he was the first that kindled the fire of contention, which then brake out in that manner as it is not quenched to this day; here began the quarrel on their part. When I was called by the Elder to give in my thoughts concerning a person proposed, he most disorderly intercepted me, for which there was not the least admonition given him: but not long after, his folly was made manifest by his casting off the very form of godliness. This is one and the chief one of those persons whom I disliked, though approved of by the church. If I be contentious for opposing such a one, let me be contentious still; though none among them will witness for me, yet he doth, he stands to this day as a sad witness between me and them, whether I were contentious in my oppositions, or they infallible in their determinations. Besides, as for some who continue among them, if you look for distinguishing characters they are scarcely visible, much less easy to be discerned.

E. A Great, Bad Man: The Earl of Clarendon Pays Tribute to His Opponent Cromwell

He was one of those men . . . [who] could never have done half that mischief without great parts of courage and industry and judgment. And he must have had a wonderful understanding in the natures and humours of men, and as great a dexterity in the applying them, who from a private and obscure birth (though of a good family), without interest of estate, alliance, or friendships, could raise himself to such a height, and compound and knead such opposite and contradictory tempers, humours, and interests into a consistence that contributed to his designs and to their own destruction, whilst himself grew insensibly powerful enough to cut off those by whom he had climbed in the instant that they projected to demolish their own building. . . . Without doubt, no man with more wickedness ever attempted anything, or brought to pass what he desired more wickedly, more in the face and contempt of religion and moral honesty; yet wickedness as great as his could never have accomplished those trophies without the assistance of a great spirit, an admirable circumspection and sagacity, and a most magnanimous resolution.

When he appeared first in the Parliament, he seemed to have a person in no degree gracious, no ornament of discourse, none of those talents which use to reconcile the affections of the standers-by; yet as he grew into place and authority, his parts seemed to be renew[ed], as if he had concealed faculties till he had occasion to use them; and when he was to act the part of a great man, he did it without any indecency through the want of custom.

After he was confirmed and invested Protector by the humble Petition and Advice, he consulted with very few upon any action of importance, nor communicated any enterprise he resolved upon with more than those who were to have principal parts in the execution of it; nor to them sooner than was absolutely necessary. What he once resolved, in which he was not rash, he would not be dissuaded from, nor endure any contradiction of his power and authority, but extorted obedience from them who were not willing to yield to it. . . .

In all other matters which did not concern the life of his jurisdiction, he seemed to have great reverence for the law, and rarely interposed between party and party. And as he proceeded with this kind of indignation and haughtiness with those who were refractory and dared to contend with his greatness, so towards those who complied with his good pleasure, and courted his protection, he used a wonderful civility, generosity, and bounty.

To reduce three nations, which perfectly hated him, to an entire obedience to all his dictates; to awe and govern those nations by an army that was indevoted to him and wished his ruin; was an instance of a very prodigious address. But his greatness at home was but a shadow of the glory he had abroad. It was hard to discover which feared him most, France, Spain, or the Low Countries, where his friendship was current at the value he put upon it. And as they did all sacrifice their honour and their interest to his pleasure, so there is nothing he could have demanded that either of them would have denied him. . . .

F. John Milton Sees a Free England Rising in Majesty

Methinks I see in my mind a noble and puissant Nation rousing herself like a strong man after sleep, and shaking her invincible locks. Methinks I see her as an Eagle muing her mighty youth, and kindling her undazl'd eyes at the full midday beam, purging and unscaling her long abused sight at the fountain itself of heav'nly radiance, while the whole noise of timorous and flocking birds, with those also that love the twilight, flutter about, amaz'd at what she means, and in their envious gabble would prognosticat a year of sects and schisms.

What should ye doe then, should ye suppresse all this flowry crop of knowledge and new light sprung up and yet springing daily in this City, should ye set an *Oligarchy* of twenty ingrossers over it, to bring a

famin upon our minds again, when we shall know nothing but what is measur'd to us by their bushel? Beleeve it, Lords and Commons, they who counsell ye to such a suppressing doe as good as bid ye suppresse yourselves; and I will soon shew how. If it be desir'd to know the immediat cause of all this free writing and free speaking, there cannot be assign'd a truer then your own mild and free and human government; it is the liberty, Lords and Commons, which your own valorous and happy counsels have purchast us, liberty which is the nurse of all great wits; this is that which hath rarify'd and enlightn'd our spirits like the influence of heav'n; this is that which hath enfranchis'd, enlarg'd and lifted up our apprehensions degrees above themselves. Ye cannot make us now lesse capable, lesse knowing, lesse eagerly pursuing of the truth, unlesse ye first make your selves, that made us so, lesse the lovers, lesse the founders of our true liberty. We can grow ignorant again, brutish, formall, and slavish, as ye found us; but you then must first become that which ye cannot be, oppressive, arbitrary, and tyrannous, as they were from whom ye have free'd us. That our hearts are now more capacious, our thoughts more erected to the search and expectation of greatest and exactest things, is the issue of your owne vertu propagated in us; ye cannot suppresse that unlesse ye reinforce an abrogated and mercilesse law, that fathers may dispatch at will their own children. . . .

Document Set 17.2 References

A. A Puritan Visionary Catches "A Glimpse of Sion's Glory," 1641
   Hanserd Knollys or Thomas Goodwin, "A Glimpse of Sion's Glory," in Lacey Baldwin Smith and Jean Reeder Smith, eds., *The Past Speaks*, 2d ed., (Lexington, Mass.: D. C. Heath, 1993), 1:351–353.
B. The Levellers Demand a Thorough-Going Revolution: The Agreement of the People
   William Haller and Godfrey Davies, eds. *The Leveller Tracts, 1647–1653* (New York: Columbia University Press, 1944), 318–328.
C. Major Rainsborough and Major General Ireton Debate the Levellers' Demands at Putney
   Thomas Rainsborough and Henry Ireton, in Smith and Smith, 1:385.
D. Susanna Parr, Independent, Searches Her Soul and Is Disciplined by Her Congregation, 1650s
   Elspeth Graham et al., eds., *Her Own Life: Autobio-graphical Writings by Seventeeth-Century English Women* (London: Routledge, 1989), 108–109.
E. A Great, Bad Man: The Earl of Clarendon Pays Tribute to His Opponent Cromwell
   Clarendon, *History of the Rebellion*, in James Harvey Robinson, ed., *Readings in European History* (Boston: Ginn, 1904), 2:249–250.
F. John Milton Sees a Free England Rising in Majesty
   Milton, *Areopagitica* (London: Oxford University Press, 1875), 49–50.

The anonymous pamphlet excerpted in Document A recites grievances that had grown steadily in English minds at all social levels under the dictatorship of Oliver Cromwell. Drawing on your understanding of the Commonwealth (as informed by Set 17.2 and *The Challenge of the West*), consider the nature and gravity of the complaints that this pamphleteer sets forth. What picture of a stable, peaceful England does the author seem to invoke? And does it persuade you?

Sir William Petty (1623–1687) is one of the first European thinkers who merits being called an economist in the modern sense. In 1672 he wrote *Political Arithmetic* as an inquiry into how an understanding of national statistics can help guide state policy. Petty enjoyed considerable favor (including being named to the Royal Society) under Charles II. Compared to the oceans of statistics in which governments now find themselves awash, the data at the Stuarts' disposal were obviously puny. In what ways could the kind of information catalogued in Document B (Petty's Table of Contents) be of use in designing policy? Notice the jumble of significant and (to us) fantastic topics; what does this reveal about the late seventeenth-century mind?

Documents C and D come from the Glorious Revolution, the overthrow of the Stuarts in 1688–1689 and the installation of a regime willing to recognize Parliament's ultimate control of England's political destiny. Sir John Evelyn (1620–1706), a diarist who seemed to be everywhere and in contact with everyone in late seventeenth-century England, in Document C records the fall of James II very much from the perspective of a member of the politically active Anglican elite. The Bill of Rights (Document D) enshrined the Glorious Revolution's outcome and takes its place next to Magna Carta and the U.S. Bill of Rights as a statement of fundamental liberties in the English-speaking world. Using *The Challenge of the West* to supplement your fund of information, analyze the outcome of the Glorious Revolution using these materials. Consider, in particular, the willingness of the elite to close ranks before Catholics or lower-class radicals found an opening to exploit.

Document E should be read—or better, sung—partly for fun and partly as a wry comment on the continuities of local authority despite revolutionary upheavals. (It has a very catchy tune, and recordings exist.) The verses were composed anonymously sometime in the early eighteenth century, and "the vicar of Bray" remains Britain's proverbial political opportunist.

A. A Call for the Stuarts' Restoration, 1659

If we take a view of the several pretensions, carried on in the nation apart, we shall find the most considerable to be the Roman Catholic, the Royalist, the Presbyterian, the Anabaptist, the Army, the Protectorian, and that of the Parliament.

1. 'Tis the Roman Catholic's aim not only to abrogate the penal laws, and become capable of all employments in the Commonwealth, but to introduce his religion, to restore the rights of the Church, and utterly eradicate all that he esteems heresy.

2. 'Tis the Royalist's desire to bring in the king as a conqueror, to recover their losses in the late war, be rendered capable of civil employments, and have the former government of the Church.

3. 'Tis the Presbyterian's desire to set up his discipline, to have the covenant reënforced, and only such as take it to be employed in church or state; to be indemnified in reference to what they have done, and secured of what they possess.

4. 'Tis the wish of the baptized churches that there might be no ecclesiastical government of any kind, nor ministerial function, or provision for it; and that only persons so minded should be capable of employment; likewise to be indemnified for what they have done.

5. 'Tis the aim of the Army to govern the nation, to keep themselves from being disbanded, or engaged in war, to secure their pay, and to be indemnified for all past action.

6. 'Tis the desire of the family of the late Protector to establish the heir of the house, that they may rule him, and he the nation, and so both preserve and advance themselves.

7. 'Tis the wish of the present Parliament (as far as they have one common design) to continue themselves in absolute power by the specious name of a popular government; to new-model and divide, and, at last, take down, the Army; and, finally, under the pretences of a committee of Parliament, or council of state, set up an oligarchy resembling that of the Thirty Tyrants in Athens.

Lastly, 't is the general interest of the nation to establish the ancient fundamental laws, upon which every one's propriety and liberty are built, to settle religion, to procure a general indemnity for all actions past, to revive their languishing and almost dead trade, gain an alliance with our neighbour states; to put the government in such hands as, besides present force, can plead a legal title to it; into the hands of such with whose private interest that of the public not only consists, but in which 't is necessarily involved, which likewise does least contradict the aims of particular parties; lastly, the hands of such whose counsel is fit to direct in matters of deliberation, and courage fit to vindicate the injuries of the nation.

From which premises we may conclude that the pretensions of no party now on foot in the nation are attainable; or, if attained, are consistent with the good of other parties, or of the nation; or, in fine, with their own; and from hence likewise one would be apt to conclude that the ruin of the public is inevitable; there being no door of hope left open to receive, no method visible to unite, such distant and incompatible ends.

But, notwithstanding all this, 't is not impossible —no, nor hard—to find an expedient that shall evacuate all these difficulties; not only establish the general concernment, but (exorbitant passion only retrenched) satisfy the real interest of every party— nay, single person—in the nation.

Now to the cheerful reception of such an overture, I suppose there is no need to persuade, nor even to admonish, that words and names, however rendered odious, ought not to frighten us from our certain benefit and dearest interest. All that is demanded here is that if , upon serious consideration, the proposal be found reasonable, men would be so kind to themselves as to receive it. The assertion I doubt not to make most plain and evident, and therefore shall as plainly pronounce it. 'T is this: the calling in the king is the certain and only means for the preservation of the kingdom, and also of the rights and interests of all single persons in it.

B. Sir William Petty Searches Statistics for the Key to Progress and Stability, 1672

The scope of this essay is concerning people and colonies, and to make way for another essay concerning the growth of the City of London. I desire in this first essay to give the world some light, concerning the number of people in England, with Wales, and in Ireland; as also, of the number of houses and families wherein they live and of acres they occupy.

2. How many live upon their lands, how many upon their personal estates and commerce, and how many upon art and labour; how many upon alms, how many upon offices and public employments, and how many as cheats and thieves; how many are impotents, children and decrepit old men.

3. How many upon the poll-taxes in England do pay extraordinary rates, and how many at the level.

4. How many men and women are prolific, and how many of each are married or unmarried.

5. What the value of people are in England, and what in Ireland, at a medium, both as members of the church or commonwealth, or as slaves and servants to one another; with a method how to estimate the same in any other country or colony.

6. How to compute the value of land in colonies, in comparison to England and Ireland.

7. How 10,000 people in a colony may be, and planted to the best advantage.

8. A conjecture in what number of years England and Ireland may be fully peopled, as also all America, and lastly the whole habitable earth.

9. What spot of the earth's globe were fittest for a general and universal emporium, whereby all the people thereof may best enjoy one another's labours and commodities.

10. Whether the speedy peopling of the earth would make first, for the good of mankind. Secondly, to fulfill the revealed will of God. Thirdly, to what prince or state the same would be most advantageous.

11. An exhortation of all thinking men to salve the Scriptures and other good histories, concerning the number of people in all ages of the world, in the great cities thereof, and elsewhere.

12. An appendix concerning the different number of sea-fish and wild-fowl at the end of every thousand years, since Noah's flood.

13. An hypothesis of the use of those spaces (of about 8,000 miles through) within the globe of our earth, supposing a shell of 150 miles thick.

14. What may be the meaning of glorified bodies, in case the place of the Blessed shall be without the convex of the orb of the fixed stars, if that the whole system of the world was made for the use of our earth's men.

C. Sir John Evelyn Records the Glorious Revolution in His Diary, January 1689

1689. 15th January. I visited the archbishop of Canterbury, where I found the bishops of St. Asaph, Ely, Bath and Wells, Peterborough, and Chichester, the earls of Aylesbury and Clarendon, Sir George Mackenize Lord-Advocate of Scotland, and then came in a Scotch archbishop, etc. After prayers and dinner, divers serious matters were discoursed, concerning the present state of the public, and sorry I was to find there was as yet no accord in the judgments of those of the Lords and Commons who were to convene; some would have the princess made queen without any more dispute, others were for a regency; there was a Tory party (then so called), who were for inviting his Majesty again upon conditions; and there were republicans who would make the Prince of Orange like a stadtholder [an elected chief prince, as in the Dutch Republic]. The Romanists were busy among these several parties to bring them into confusion: most for ambition or other interest, few for conscience and moderate resolutions. I found nothing of all this in this assembly of bishops, who were pleased to admit me into their discourses; they were all for a regency, thereby to salve their oaths, and so all public matters to proceed in his Majesty's name, by that to facilitate the calling of a Parliament, according to the laws in being. Such was the result of this meeting. . . .

The great convention being assembled the day before, falling upon the question about the government, resolved that King James having by the advice of the Jesuits and other wicked persons endeavoured to subvert the laws of church and state, and deserted the kingdom, carrying away the seals, etc., without any care for the management of the government, had by demise abdicated himself and wholly vacated his right; they did therefore desire the Lords' concurrence to their vote, to place the crown on the next heir, the Prince of Orange, for his life, then to the princess, his wife, and if she died without issue, to the Princess of Denmark (Anne), and she failing, to the heirs of the prince, excluding forever all possibility of admitting a Roman Catholic. . . .

29th. The votes of the House of Commons being carried up by Mr. Hampden, their chairman, to the Lords, I got a station by the prince's lodgings at the door of the lobby to the House, and heard much of the debate, which lasted very long. Lord Derby was in the chair (for the House was resolved into a grand committee of the whole House); after all had spoken, it came to the question, which was carried by three voices against a regency, which 51 were for, 54 against; the minority alleging the danger of dethroning kings, and scrupling many passages and expressions in the vote of the Commons, too long to set down particularly. Some were for sending to his Majesty with conditions; others that the king could do no wrong, and that the maladministration was

chargeable on his ministers. There were not more than eight or nine bishops, and but two against the regency; the archbishop was absent, and the clergy now began to change their note, both in pulpit and discourse, on their old passive obedience, so as people began to talk of the bishops being cast out of the House. In short, things tended to dissatisfaction on both sides; add to this, the morose temper of the Prince of Orange, who showed little countenance to the noblemen and others, who expected a more gracious and cheerful reception when they made their court. The English army also was not so in order, and firm to his interest, nor so weakened but that it might give interruption. Ireland was in an ill posture as well as Scotland. Nothing was yet done towards a settlement. God of His infinite mercy compose these things, that we may be at last a nation and a church under some fixed and sober establishment. . . .

D. Parliament Enacts the English Bill of Rights, 1689

Whereas the said late King James II having abdicated the government, and the throne being thereby vacant, his Highness the prince of Orange (whom it hath pleased Almighty God to make the glorious instrument of delivering this kingdom from popery and arbitrary power) did (by the device of the lords spiritual and temporal, and diverse principal persons of the Commons) cause letters to be written to the lords spiritual and temporal, being Protestants, and other letters to the several counties, cities, universities, boroughs, and Cinque Ports [five port towns on the English Channel, having special privileges], for the choosing of such persons to represent them, as were of right to be sent to parliament, to meet and sit at Westminster upon the two and twentieth day of January, in this year 1689, in order to such an establishment as that their religion, laws, and liberties might not again be in danger of being subverted; upon which letters elections have been accordingly made.

And thereupon the said lords spiritual and temporal and Commons, pursuant to their respective letters and elections, being now assembled in a full and free representation of this nation, taking into their most serious consideration the best means for attaining the ends aforesaid, do in the first place (as their ancestors in like case have usually done), for the vindication and assertion of their ancient rights and liberties, declare:

1. That the pretended power of suspending laws, or the execution of laws, by regal authority, without consent of parliament is illegal.

2. That the pretended power of dispensing with the laws, or the execution of law by regal authority, as it hath been assumed and exercised of late, is illegal.

3. That the commission for erecting the late court of commissioners for ecclesiastical causes, and all other commissions and courts of like nature, are illegal and pernicious.

4. That levying money for or to the use of the crown by pretense of prerogative, without grant of parliament, for longer time or in other manner than the same is or shall be granted, is illegal.

5. That it is the right of the subjects to petition the king, and all commitments and prosecutions for such petitioning are illegal.

6. That the raising or keeping a standing army within the kingdom in time of peace, unless it be with consent of parliament, is against law.

7. That the subjects which are Protestants may have arms for their defense suitable to their conditions, and as allowed by law.

8. That election of members of parliament ought to be free.

9. That the freedom of speech, and debates or proceedings in parliament, ought not to be impeached or questioned in any court or place out of parliament.

10. That excessive bail ought not to be required, nor excessive fines imposed, nor cruel and unusual punishments inflicted.

11. That jurors ought to be duly impaneled and returned, and jurors which pass upon men in trials for high treason ought to be freeholders.

12. That all grants and promises of fines and forfeitures of particular persons before conviction are illegal and void.

13. And that for redress of all grievances, and for the amending, strengthening, and preserving of the laws, parliament ought to be held frequently.

E. The "Vicar of Bray" Achieves Stability, c. 1725

In good King *Charles's* golden days,
    When Loyalty no harm meant;
A Furious High-Church Man I was,
    And so I gain'd Preferment.[1]
Unto my Flock I daily Preach'd,
    Kings are by God appointed,

And Damn'd are those who dare resist,
    Or touch the Lord's Anointed.
        And this is Law, I will maintain
        Unto my Dying Day, Sir,
        That whatsoever King shall Reign,
        I will be Vicar of *Bray*, Sir!

When Royal *James* possest the Crown,
    And Popery grew in fashion,
The Penal Law I hooted down,
    And read the Declaration:
The Church of *Rome*, I found would fit,
    Full well my Constitution,
And I had been a Jesuit,
    But for the Revolution.
        And this is Law, etc.

When *William* our Deliverer came,
    To heal the Nation's Grievance,
I turned the Cat in Pan again,
    And swore to him Allegiance;
Old Principles I did revoke,
    Set Conscience at a distance,
Passive Obedience is a Joke,
    A Jest is Non-resistance.
        And this is Law, etc.

When glorious *Ann* became our
        Queen,
    The Church of *England's* Glory,
Another face of things was seen,
    And I became a Tory:
Occasional Conformists base,
    I Damn'd, and Moderation,
And thought the Church in
        danger was,
    From such Prevarication.
        And this is Law, etc.

When *George* in Pudding time[2]
        came o'er,
    And Moderate Men looked big, Sir,
My Principles I chang'd once more,
    And so became a Whig, Sir:
And thus Preferment I procur'd,
    From our Faith's Great Defender,
And almost every day abjur'd
    The Pope, and the Pretender.
        And this is Law, etc.

The Illustrious House of *Hannover*,
    And Protestant Succession,

---

[1] Appointment to office

[2] A lucky or favorable time

To these I lustily will swear,
    Whilst they can keep possession:
For in my Faith, and Loyalty,
    I never once will falter,
But *George*, my Lawful King shall be,
    Except the Times shou'd alter,
        And this is Law, etc.

Document Set 17.3 References

A. A Call for the Stuarts' Restoration, 1659
Contemporary Pamphlet, Quoted in James Harvey Robinson, ed., *Readings in European History* (Boston: Ginn, 1904), 2:251–252.

B. Sir William Petty Searches Statistics for the Key to Progress and Stability, 1672
Petty, "Concerning the Encrease of People and Colonies," in Lacey Baldwin Smith and Jean Reeder Smith, eds., *The Past Speaks*, 2d ed. (Lexington, Mass.: D. C. Heath, 1993), 1:413.

C. Sir John Evelyn Records the Glorious Revolution in His Diary, January 1689
Evelyn, *Diary*, in Walter L. Arnstein, *The Past Speaks*, 2d ed. (Lexington, Mass.: D. C. Heath, 1993), 2:3–10 passim.

D. Parliament Enacts the English Bill of Rights, 1689
The Statutes, rev. ed. (London: Eyre and Spotiswoode, 1871), 2:10–12.

E. The "Vicar of Bray" Achieves Stability, c. 1725
Anonymous Poem, in Arnstein, 2:22.

DOCUMENT SET 17.4
Summing Up the English Revolution: Baxter, Milton, Hobbes, and Locke

The authors of the four selections in this set are among the foremost names of mid to late seventeenth-century English thought. Their commentaries offer a valuable perspective on England's fate in these revolutionary decades.

Richard Baxter (1615–1691) was one of England's notable Puritan voices as a preacher during the Civil War. He was most influential, however, as a spokesman for defeated Puritanism after the Restoration, when he was hounded out of his position for being too vocal a nonconformist. His advice (Document A) on how a good Protestant ought to behave in the world, taken from his 1673 book *A Christian Directory,* is a classic summary of what we now call the Protestant Ethic: hard work reveals godliness. Countless English nonconformists took this path with particular vigor after the fall of the Puritan regime shut them out of the political realm.

Milton's *Paradise Lost,* the great blind poet's epic interpretation of God's purpose, was also composed after Puritanism had ceased to be England's established faith. The passage quoted as Document B is the famous opening invocation. Since God had apparently "spit in our faces"—as one Puritan, shocked by events after 1659, put it—Milton's courageous reassurance that God indeed had "ways" that could be justified was no small comfort.

Thomas Hobbes (1588–1679), one of the greatest philosophical minds of Western culture, wrote *Leviathan* (1651) as a reflection on the turmoil set in motion by the fall of traditional authority in England. He surpasses even Machiavelli as a realistic analyst of why human beings form and maintain civil societies. What echoes of the Civil War era do you see in the extract from *Leviathan* that appears as Document C?

John Locke (1632–1704), a more comfortable, less daring, and more influential thinker than Hobbes, wrote his *Second Treatise of Government* (Document D) early in the 1680s and published it in 1689. It is notable for refuting Robert Filmer's thoroughly traditional justification of government as patriarchy writ large. Instead, Locke saw government as a pragmatic contract for guaranteeing life, liberty, and property. His was the right book at the right time; he perfectly vindicated the Glorious Revolution. It became virtual holy writ for eighteenth-century Americans.

A. Richard Baxter Justifies the Puritan Ethic, 1673

Every man that is able, must be steadily and ordinarily employed in such work as is serviceable to God, and to the common good. . . . Everyone that is a member of a church or commonwealth must employ their parts to the utmost for the good of the church and commonwealth, public service is God's greatest service. To neglect this, and to say, I will pray and meditate, is as if your servant should refuse your greatest work, and to tie himself to some lesser easy part; and God has commanded you some way or another to labour for your daily bread, and not to live as drones on the sweat of others only. Innocent Adam was put into the Garden of Eden to dress it, and fallen man must eat his bread in the sweat of his brow (Genesis 3:19). And he that will not work must be forbidden to eat (2 Thes. 3:6, 10 and 12). And indeed, it is necessary for ourselves, for the health of our bodies, which will grow diseased with idleness. And for the health of our souls, which will fail if the body fail. And man in flesh must have work for his body as well as his soul. And he that will do nothing but pray and meditate, it's like will (by sickness or melancholy) be disabled ere long to pray or meditate, unless he have a body extraordinary strong . . .

It gloryeth God, by showing the excellency of faith, when we contemn the riches and honor of the world, and live above the worldling's life, accounting that a despicable thing, which he accounts his happiness, and loses his soul for . . . When seeming Christians are worldly and ambitious as others, and make as great matter of the gain, and wealth and honour, it shows that they do but cover the base and sordid spirit of worldlings, with the visor of the Christian name . . .

As labour is thus necessary so understand how needful a state a calling is, for the right performance of your labours. A calling is a stated course of labour. This is very needful for these reasons: (1) Out of a calling a man's labours are but occasional or inconstant, so more time is spent in idleness than labour; (2) A man is best skilled in that which he is used to; (3) And he will be best provided for it with instruments and necessaries; (4) Therefore he does it better than he could do any other work, and so wrongs not others, but attains more the end of his labour; (5) And he does it more easily, when a man unused and unskilled and unfurnished, toils himself much in doing little; (6) And he will do his work more orderly, when another is in continual confusion, and his business knows not its time and place, but one part contradicts another. Therefore some certain calling or trade of life is best for everyman . . .

The first and principal thing to be intended in the choice of a trade or calling for yourselves or children is the service of God, and the public good. And, therefore, *ceteris paribus* [other things being equal], that calling which most conduces to the public good is to be preferred. The callings most useful to the public good are the magistrate, the pastor, the teacher of the church, schoolmaster, physician, lawyer, etc., husbandmen (ploughmen, graziers and shepherds); and next to them are mariners, clothiers, booksellers, tailors and such others that are employed about things most necessary to mankind. And some callings are employed about matters of so little use, as tobacco-sellers, lace-sellers, feather-makers, periwig-makers, and many more such, that he that may choose better, should be loath to take up with one of these, though possibly in itself it may be lawful. It is a great satisfaction to an honest mind, to spend his life in doing the greatest good he can, and a prison and a constant calamity, to be tied to spend one's life in doing little good at all to others, though he should grow rich by it . . .

If thou be called to the poorest laborious calling, do not carnally murmur at it; because it is wearisome to the flesh, nor imagine that God accepts the less of thy work and thee. But cheerfully follow it, and make it the matter of thy pleasure and joy that thou art still in thy heavenly master's services, though it be the lowest thing. And that He who knows what is best for thee, has chosen this for thy good, and tries and values thy obedience to Him the more, by how much the meaner work thou stoopest to at His command. But see that thou do it all in obedience to God, and not merely for thy own necessity. Thus every servant must serve the Lord, in serving their master, and from God expect their chief reward . . .

In doing good to others we do good to ourselves: because we are living members of Christ's body, and by love and communion feel their joys, as well as pains.

Good works are comfortable evidence that faith is sincere, and that the heart dissembles not with God.

Good works are much to the honour of religion, and consequently of God, and much tend to men's conviction, conversion and salvation.

B. John Milton Justifies God's Ways to Man, 1663

Of man's first disobedience, and the fruit
Of that forbidden tree, whose mortal taste
Brought death into the world, and all our woe,
With loss of Eden, till one greater Man
Restore us, and regain the blissful seat,
Sing, Heavenly Muse, that on the secret top
Of Oreb, or of Sinai, didst inspire
That shepherd, who first taught the chosen seed,
In the beginning how the Heavens and Earth
Rose out of Chaos; or if Sion hill
Delight thee more, and Siloa's brook that flowed
Fast by the oracle of God, I thence
Invoke thy aid to my adventurous song,
That with no middle flight intends to soar
Above the Aonian mount, while it pursues
Things unattempted yet in prose or rhyme.
And chiefly thou, O Spirit, that dost prefer
Before all temples the upright heart and pure,
Instruct me, for thou know'st; thou from the first
Wast present, and with mighty wings outspread
Dove-like sat'st brooding on the vast abyss
And mad'st it prégnant: what in me is dark
Illumine, what is low raise and support;
That to the highth of this great argument
I may assert Eternal Providence,
and justify the ways of God to men. . . .

C. Thomas Hobbes Justifies the State as Leviathan, 1651

Hereby it is manifest, that during the time men live without a common power to keep them all in awe, they are in that condition which is called war; and such a war, as is of every man, against every man. For war, consisteth not in battle only, or the act of fighting; but in a tract of time, wherein the will to contend by battle is sufficiently known: and therefore the notion of *time,* is to be considered in the nature of war; as it is in the nature of weather. For as the nature of foul weather, lieth not in a shower or two of rain; but in an inclination thereto of many days together: so the nature of war, consisteth not in actual fighting; but in the known disposition thereto, during all the time there is no assurance to the contrary. All other time is peace.

Whatsoever therefore is consequent to a time of war, where every man is enemy to every man; the same is consequent to the time, wherein men live without other security, than what their own strength, and their own invention shall furnish them withal. In such condition, there is no place for industry; because the fruit thereof is uncertain: and consequently no culture of the earth; no navigation, nor use of the commodities that may be imported by sea; no commodious building; no instruments of moving, and removing, such things as require much force; no knowledge of the face of the earth; no account of time; no arts; no letters; no society; and which is worst of all, continual fear, and danger of violent death; and the life of man, solitary, poor, nasty, brutish, and short.

It may seem strange to some man, that has not well weighed these things; that nature should thus dissociate, and render men apt to invade, and destroy one another: and he may therefore, not trusting to this inference, made from the passions, desire perhaps to have the same confirmed by experience. Let him therefore consider with himself, when taking a journey, he arms himself, and seeks to go well accompanied; when going to sleep, he locks his doors; when even in his house he locks his chests; and this when he knows there be laws, and public officers, armed, to revenge all injuries shall be done him; what opinion he has of his fellow-subjects, when he rides armed; of his fellow citizens, when he locks his doors; and of his children, and servants, when he locks his chests. Does he not there as much accuse mankind by his actions, as I do by my words? But neither of us accuse man's nature in it. The desires, and other passions of man, are in themselves no sin. No more are the actions, that proceed from those passions, till they know a law that forbids them: which till laws be made they cannot know: nor can any law be made, till they have agreed upon the person that shall make it.

It may peradventure be thought, there was never such a time, nor condition of war as this; and I believe it was never generally so, over all the world: but there are many places, where they live so now. For the savage people in many places of America, except the government of small families, the concord whereof dependeth on natural lust, have no government at all; and live at this day in that brutish manner, as I said before. Howsoever, it may be perceived what manner of life there would be, where there were no common power to fear, by the manner of life, which men that have formerly lived under a peaceful government, use to degenerate into, in a civil war.

But though there had never been any time, wherein particular men were in a condition of war one against another; yet in all times, kings, and persons of sovereign authority, because of their independency, are in continual jealousies, and in the state and posture of gladiators; having their weapons pointing, and their eyes fixed on one another; that is, their forts, garrisons, and guns upon the frontiers of their kingdoms; and continual spies upon their neighbours; which is a posture of war. But because they uphold thereby, the industry of their subjects; there does not follow from it, that misery, which accompanies the liberty of particular men.

To this war of every man, against every man, this also is consequent; that nothing can be unjust. The notions of right and wrong, justice and injustice have there no place. Where there is no common power, there is no law: where no law, no injustice. Force, and fraud, are in war the two cardinal virtues. Justice, and injustice are none of the faculties neither of the body, nor mind. If they were, they might be in a man that were alone in the world, as well as his senses, and passions. They are qualities, that relate to men in society, not in solitude. It is consequent also to the same condition, that there be no propriety, no dominion, no *mine* and *thine* distinct; but only that to be every man's, that he can get; and for so long, as he can keep it. And thus much for the ill condition, which man by mere nature is actually placed in; though with a possibility to come out of it, consisting partly in the passions, partly in his reason.

The passions that incline men to peace, are fear of death; desire of such things as are necessary to commodious living; and a hope by their industry to obtain them. And reason suggesteth convenient articles of peace, upon which men may be drawn to agreement. These articles, are they, which otherwise are called the Laws of Nature. . .

D. John Locke Justifies the Glorious Revolution as the Essence of the Social Contract, 1690

87. Man being born, as has been proved, with a Title to perfect Freedom, and an uncontrouled enjoyment of all the Rights and Privileges of the Law of Nature, equally with any other Man, or Number of Men in the World, hath by Nature a Power, not only to preserve his Property, that is, his Life, Liberty and Estate, against the Injuries and Attempts of other Men; but to judge of, and punish the breaches of that Law in others, as he is perswaded the Offence deserves, even with Death it self, in Crimes where the heinousness of the Fact, in his Opinion, requires it. But because no *Political Society* can be, nor subsist without having in it self the Power to preserve the Property, and in order thereunto punish the Offences of all those of that Society; there, and there only is *Political Society*, where every one of the Members hath quitted this natural Power, resign'd it up into the

hands of the Community in all cases that exclude him not from appealing for Protection to the Law established by it. And thus all private judgement of every particular Member being excluded, the Community comes to be Umpire, by settled standing Rules, indifferent, and the same to all Parties; and by Men having Authority from the Community, for the execution of those Rules, decides all the differences that may happen between any Members of that Society, concerning any matter of right; and punishes those Offences, which any Member hath committed against the Society, with such Penalties as the Law has established: Whereby it is easie to discern who are, and who are not, in *Political Society* together. Those who are united into one Body, and have a common establish'd Law and Judicature to appeal to, with Authority to decide Controversies between them, and punish Offenders, *are in Civil Society* one with another: but those who have no such common Appeal, I mean on Earth, are still in the state of Nature, each being, where there is no other, Judge for himself, and Executioner; which is, as I have before shew'd it, the perfect *state of Nature.*

88. And thus the Commonwealth comes by a Power to set down, what punishment shall belong to the several transgressions which they think worthy of it, committed amongst the Members of that Society, (which is the *power of making Laws*) as well as it has the power to punish any Injury done unto any of its Members, by any one that is not of it, (which is the *power of War and Peace;*) and all this for the preservation of the property of all the Members of that Society, as far as is possible. But though every Man who has enter'd into civil Society, and is become a member of any Commonwealth, has thereby quitted his power to punish Offences against the Law of Nature, in prosecution of his own private Judgment; yet with the Judgment of Offences which he has given up to the Legislative in all Cases, where he can Appeal to the Magistrate, he has given a right to the Commonwealth to imploy his force, for the Execution of the Judgments of the Commonwealth, whenever he shall be called to it; which indeed are his own Judgments, they being made by himself, or his Representative. And herein we have the original of the *Legislative* and *Executive Power* of Civil Society, which is to judge by standing Laws how far Offences are to be punished, when committed within the Commonwealth; and also to determin, by occasional Judgments founded on the present Circumstances of the Fact, how far Injuries from without are to be vindicated, and in both these to imploy all the force of all the Members when there shall be need.

89. Where-ever therefore any number of Men are so united into one Society, as to quit every one his Executive Power of the Law of Nature, and to resign it to the publick, there and there only is a *Political, or Civil Society.* And this is done where-ever any number of Men, in the state of Nature, enter into Society to make one People, one Body Politick under one Supreme Government, or else when any one joyns himself to, and incorporates with any Government already made. For hereby he authorizes the Society, or which is all one, the Legislative thereof to make Laws for him as the publick good of the Society shall require; to the Execution whereof, his own assistance (as to his own Decrees) is due. And this *puts Men* out of a State of Nature *into* that of a *Commonwealth,* by setting up a Judge on Earth, with Authority to determine all the Controversies, and redress the Injuries, that may happen to any Member of the Commonwealth; which Judge is the Legislative, or Magistrates appointed by it. And where-ever there are any number of Men, however associated, that have no such decisive power to appeal to, there they are still *in the state of Nature.*

90. Hence it is evident, that *Absolute Monarchy,* which by some Men is counted the only Government in the World, is indeed *inconsistent with Civil Society,* and so can be no Form of Civil Government at all. For the *end of Civil Society,* being to avoid, and remedy those inconveniencies of the State of Nature, which necessarily follow from every Man's being Judge in his own Case, by setting up a known Authority, to which every one of that Society may Appeal upon any injury received, or Controversie that may arise, and which every one of the Society ought to obey; where-ever any persons are, who have not such an Authority to Appeal to, for the decision of any difference between them, there those persons are still *in the state of Nature.* And so is every *Absolute Prince* in respect of those who are under his *Dominion.*

91. For he being suppos'd to have all, both Legislative and Executive Power in himself alone, there is no Judge to be found, no Appeal lies open to any one, who may fairly, and indifferently, and with Authority decide, and from whose decision relief and redress may be expected of any Injury or Inconveniency, that may be suffered from the Prince or by his Order: So that such a Man, however intitled, *Czar,* or *Grand Signior,* or how you please, is as much *in the state of Nature,* with all under his Dominion, as he is with the rest of Mankind. For where-ever any two Men are, who have no standing

Rule, and common Judge to Appeal to on Earth for the determination of Controversies of Right betwixt them, there they are still *in the state of Nature,* and under all the inconveniencies of it, with only this woful difference to the Subject, or rather Slave of an Absolute Prince: That whereas, in the ordinary State of Nature, he has a liberty to judge of his Right, and according to the best of his Power, to maintain it; now whenever his Property is invaded by the Will and Order of his Monarch, he has not only no Appeal, as those in Society ought to have, but as if he were degraded from the common state of Rational Creatures, is denied a liberty to judge of, or to defend his Right, and so is exposed to all the Misery and Inconveniencies that a Man can fear from one, who being in the unrestrained state of Nature, is yet corrupted with Flattery, and armed with Power.

92. For that thinks *absolute Power purifies Mens Bloods,* and corrects the baseness of Humane Nature, need read but the History of this, or any other Age to be convinced of the contrary. He that would have been insolent and injurious in the Woods of *America,* would not probably be much better in a Throne; where perhaps Learning and Religion shall be found out to justifie all, that he shall do to his Subjects, and the Sword presently silence all those that dare question it. For what the *Protection of Absolute Monarchy* is, what kind of Fathers of their Countries it makes Princes to be, and to what a degree of Happiness and Security it carries Civil Society where this sort of Government is grown to perfection, he that will look into the late Relation of *Ceylon,* may easily see.

Document Set 17.4 References

A. Richard Baxter Justifies the Puritan Ethic, 1673
   Baxter, *A Christian Directory: Or a Summa of Practical Theologie and Cases of Conscience,* in H. E. S. Fisher and A. R. J. Jurica, eds., *Documents in English Economic History* (London: G. Bell, 1977), 1:519–521.
B. John Milton Justifies God's Ways to Man, 1663
   Milton, *Paradise Lost,* book I, lines 1–26.
C. Thomas Hobbes Justifies the State as Leviathan, 1651
   Hobbes, *The Leviathan,* 252–257.
D. John Locke Justifies the Glorious Revolution as the Essence of the Social Contract, 1690
   Locke, *Second Treatise on Government,* §§ 87–92.

DOCUMENT SET 17.5
Louis XIV's France: State, Court, and Subjects

Taxation and the threat—or outbreak—of popular revolt were the two fundamental realities of life in seventeenth century France. The letter quoted as Document A was a report by the royal governor of Guyenne province about 1645, conveying typical details in such cases. And although the nobility was exempt from paying the *taille* and other onerous exactions, it often felt keenly the need to hold down commoners' taxes as Document B—an appeal to the government in 1661—reveals. It is obvious why these nobles should want to see the price of offices reduced, but why were they concerned about the welfare of the lower classes?

Louis XIV was one of the handful of kings who took the trouble to write extensive, self-serving memoirs, a task he undertook for the benefit of his heir. Document C is an excerpt from the king's recollections of his early years. Judging by other evidence in the set and from what you have learned from *The Challenge of the West,* how do you evaluate the case he makes for authoritarian royal government?

Another famous set of memoirs of Louis XIV's reign was written by the Duc de Saint-Simon (1675–1755) (Document D). An acute though acerbic observer of the Sun King's court in its later years, after 1695, Saint-Simon was as eager as anyone to gain royal favor. In interpreting his remarks, we must remember that they describe the king in his pious old age. A somewhat younger Louis appears in Document E, a letter written by Elizabeth Charlotte, Duchess of Orleans, the German wife of Louis's brother. During her fifty years at the French court she wrote about forty long letters per week. Why, as this letter seems to indicate, should Louis's every act have influenced the behavior of court nobles?

Not everything that went on at the Versailles court turned on matters of etiquette and place. Louis XIV's chief minister, Jean-Baptiste Colbert (1619–1683), was busy supervising the revival of French finances and encouraging industry and colonization. The anonymous pamphlet excerpted in Document F was written at Colbert's behest in 1664 to argue the advantages of colonial trade and to urge the foundation of the French East India Company. Why does it make so much of the Dutch success, and why, when translated into English, did it cause alarm in England?

A. A Tax Revolt Brews, 1645

I learned at Grenade in a letter from the aldermen [*jurats*] of Bordeaux that a revolt was feared there as a result of the rumour of a new imposition of the *sou* per *livre* tax, and upon receiving this news I set out at once for Bordeaux. Yesterday in letters sent by the same aldermen and by the first president [of the *parlement* of Bordeaux] I learned that Monsieur de Lanson (the *intendant*) whom the people suspected of being at Bordeaux to supervise this imposition, had left the town on the advice of the *parlement* and had been accompanied by the aldermen, as he himself wished, as far as the boat that was to take him to Bourg . . . With God's help I shall reach Bordeaux in two days and do all that I can to maintain order and stifle a sedition which could flare up and spread very easily in this province because of the extraordinary expense of supporting soldiers which it has borne for five months and is still sustaining, the difficulty of paying *tailles* and other royal revenues, the discontent of the office-holders in the *parlement* and in the *présidial* courts because of the half-yearly arrangements [*semestres*], the separation of jurisdictions and the establishment of new tribunals with which they are threatened.

B. The Nobility of Troyes Plead for a Reduction Both in the Price of Offices and in Taxes, 1651

Now to come to the matter of the reformation of justice in your kingdom, Your Majesty is entreated to listen to the general complaints of the whole of France, concerning venality and the excessive price of judicial and financial offices, which is the cause of the widespread corruption discernible in those who exercise them. . . . The cause of this immensely high cost of offices may be traced to that enemy of the state, the *paulette*, palotte [sic] now called the annual due which in the manner of a canker is gradually undermining and consuming all the families of this kingdom, and therefore the nobility begs His Majesty most humbly to revoke the wretched annual due immediately and forever, with orders forbidding its re-establishment under any pretext whatsoever.

And may this be done on the last day of next December since the officers have not paid any loans nor made any advance payments since it has been continued and re-established this last time and all the nobility of the kingdom are entreated to unite in order to secure this present article, for it has an interest in seeing the prices of offices reduced and restored if possible to what they were in our fathers' time fifty or sixty years ago when a nobleman of the *robe* could call three or four of his children into public offices; now only tax-farmers can do that and it is even impossible for a nobleman who follows the profession of arms to place any of his children (although they are capable) into offices of the *robe* because of their excessive and enormous price, and truly it is monstrous to witness this great superfluity and cost of office, not previously heard of nor even contemplated and unlikely to be believed by posterity.

We are therefore now obliged most humbly to entreat Your Majesty to re-establish the ancient order, which obtained before the time of Louis XII; under that régime when a judicial office became vacant whether in the sovereign courts, on the royal benches or in subordinate jurisdictions, the officers in the place concerned elected three suitable persons capable of exercising the vacant office and the king conferred it upon one of the three, who did not have to spend a single *denier;* and because such offices had cost nothing their holders rendered justice freely and without fees (*épices*), content with the honour of being judges. Moreover, His Majesty's conscience was clear before God and his people.

C. Louis XIV Recalls the Problems He Faced at the Outset of His Reign

From my early infancy the very name of *rois fainéants* or *maires du palais*[1] displeased me when mentioned in my presence. But I must point out the state of affairs: grievous disturbances throughout the kingdom before and after my majority; a foreign war in which these troubles at home had lost to France thousands and thousands of advantages; a Prince of my blood and of great name at the head of my enemies; many Cabals in the State; the Parliaments still in the possession and enjoyment of a usurped authority; at my Court very little disinterested fidelity and, on this account, my subjects, though outwardly most submissive, as much a responsibility and cause of misgiving to me as the most rebellious; a minister re-established in power despite so many factions, very

skilful and very adroit, but whose views and methods were naturally very different from mine, whom, nevertheless, I could not gainsay, nor abate the least portion of his credit, without running the risk of again raising against him by some misleading appearance of disgrace those very storms which had been allayed with so much difficulty. I myself was still very young, though I had reached the majority of kings, which the State laws anticipate in order to avoid still greater evils, but not the age at which mere private persons begin to regulate freely their own affairs. I only knew to its full extent the greatness of my burden, without having yet learned my own capabilities. . . .

I made a beginning by casting my eyes over all the different parties in the State, not indifferently, but with the glance of experience, sensibly touched at seeing nothing which did not invite and urge me to take it in hand, but carefully watching what the occasion and the state of affairs would permit. Everywhere was disorder. . . .

The finances, which give movement and action to the great organisation of the monarchy, were entirely exhausted, so much so that we could hardly find the ways and means. Much of the most necessary and most privileged expenses of my house and my own privy purse were in arrears beyond all that was fitting, or maintained only on credit, to be a further subsequent burden. At the same time a prodigality showed itself among public men, masking on the one hand their malversations by every king of artifice, and revealing them on the other in insolent and daring luxury, as though they feared I might take no notice of them.

The Church, apart from its usual troubles, after lengthy disputes on matters of the schools, a knowledge of which they allowed was unnecessary to salvation for any one, with points of disagreement augmenting day by day through the heat and obstinacy of their minds, and ceaselessly involving fresh human interests, was finally threatened with open schism by men who were all the more dangerous because they were capable of being very serviceable and greatly deserving, had they themselves been less opinionated. . . .

The least of the ills affecting the order of Nobility was the fact of its being shared by an infinite number of usurpers possessing no right to it, or one acquired by money without any claim from service rendered. The tyranny exercised by the nobles over their vassals and neighbours in some of my provinces could no longer be suffered or suppressed save by making severe and rigorous examples. The range for dueling—somewhat modified by the exact observance of the latest regulations, over which I was

1 "Do-nothing kings" and mayors of the palace: terms dating from the time of the weak Merovingian kings of France and their Carolingian successors.

always inflexible—was only noticeable in a now well advanced recovery from so inveterate an ill, so that there was no reason to despair of the remedy.

The administration of Justice itself, whose duty it is to reform others, appeared to me the most difficult to reform. An infinity of things contributed to this state of affairs: the appointments filled haphazard or by money rather than by selection and merit; scant experience and less knowledge on the part of some of the judges; the regulations referring to age and service almost everywhere eluded; chicanery firmly established through many centuries, and fertile in inventing means of evading the most salutary laws. And what especially conduced to this was the fact that these insatiable gentry loved litigation and fostered it as their own peculiar property, applying themselves only to prolong and to add to it. Even my Council, instead of supervising the other jurisdictions, too often only introduced disorder by issuing a strange number of contrary regulations, all in my name and as though by my command, which rendered the confusion far more disgraceful.

All this collection of evils, their consequences and effects, fell principally upon the people, who in addition, were loaded with impositions, some crushed down by poverty, others suffering want from their own laziness since the peace, and needing above all to be alleviated and occupied. . . .

D. The Duke of Saint-Simon Characterizes Louis XIV

The king's great qualities shone more brilliantly by reason of an exterior so unique and incomparable as to lend infinite distinction to his slightest actions; the very figure of a hero, so impregnated with a natural but most imposing majesty that it appeared even in his most insignificant gestures and movements, without arrogance but with simple gravity; proportions such as a sculptor would choose to model; a perfect countenance and the grandest air and mien ever vouchsafed to man; all these advantages enhanced by a natural grace which enveloped all his actions with a singular charm which has never perhaps been equaled. He was as dignified and majestic in his dressing gown as when dressed in robes of state, or on horseback at the head of his troops.

He excelled in all sorts of exercise and liked to have every facility for it. No fatigue nor stress of weather made any impression on that heroic figure and bearing; drenched with rain or snow, pierced with cold, bathed in sweat or covered with dust, he was always the same. I have often observed with admiration that except in the most extreme and exceptional weather nothing prevented his spending considerable time out of doors every day.

A voice whose tones corresponded with the rest of his person; the ability to speak well and to listen with quick comprehension; much reserve of manner adjusted with exactness to the quality of different persons; a courtesy always grave, always dignified, always distinguished, and suited to the age, rank, and sex of each individual, and, for the ladies, always an air of natural gallantry. So much for his exterior, which has never been equaled nor even approached.

In whatever did not concern what he believed to be his rightful authority and prerogative, he showed a natural kindness of heart and a sense of justice which made one regret the education, the flatteries, the artifice which resulted in preventing him from being his real self except on the rare occasions when he gave way to some natural impulse and showed that,—prerogative aside, which choked and stifled everything,—he loved truth, justice, order, reason,—that he loved even to let himself be vanquished.

Nothing could be regulated with greater exactitude than were his days and hours. In spite of all his variety of places, affairs, and amusements, with an almanac and a watch one might tell, three hundred leagues away, exactly what he was doing. . . . Except at Marly, any man could have an opportunity to speak to him five or six times during the day; he listened, and almost always replied, "I will see," in order not to accord or decide anything lightly. Never a reply or a speech that would give pain; patient to the last degree in business and in matters of personal service; completely master of his face, manner, and bearing; never giving way to impatience or anger. If he administered reproof, it was rarely, in few words, and never hastily. He did not lose control of himself ten times in his whole life, and then only with inferior persons, and not more than four or five times seriously. . . .

Louis XIV's vanity was without limit or restraint; it colored everything and convinced him that no one even approached him in military talents, in plans and enterprises, in government. Hence those pictures and inscriptions in the gallery of Versailles which disgust every foreigner; those opera prologues that he himself tried to sing; that flood of prose and verse in his praise for which his appetite was insatiable; those dedications of statues copied from pagan sculpture, and the insipid and sickening compliments that were continually offered to him in person and which he swallowed with unfailing relish; hence his distaste for all merit, intelligence, education, and, most of all, for all independence of character and sentiment in others; his mistakes of judgment in matters of importance; his familiarity and favor reserved entirely for those to whom he felt himself superior in acquirements and ability; and, above everything else, a jealously of his own authority which determined and took precedence of every other sort of justice, reason, and consideration whatever.

E. The Duchess of Orleans Describes the Court of Louis XIV

Although I had not hurt myself or fallen on my head, he would not rest until he had personally examined my head on all sides . . . he also led me back to my room and even stayed with me for a while to see whether I might become dizzy. . . . I must say that even now the King still shows me his favor every day. . . . This is also the reason that I am now very much à la mode; whatever I say or do, whether it be good or awry, is greatly admired by the courtiers, to the point that when I decided to wear my old sable in this cold weather to keep my neck warm, everyone had one made from the same pattern, and sables have become quite the rage. This makes me laugh, for five years ago the very people who now admire and wear this fashion so laughed at me and made so much fun of me with my sable that I could no longer wear it. This is what happens at this court: if the courtiers imagine that someone is in favor it does not matter what the person does, one can be certain that the courtiers approve of it; but if they imagine the contrary, they will think that person ridiculous, even if he has come straight from heaven.

F. Colbert Sponsors a Pamphlet on "The Advantages of Overseas Trade"

Now of all commerces whatsoever throughout the whole world, that of the East Indies is one of the most rich and considerable. From thence it is (the sun being kinder to them, than to us) that we have our merchandise of greatest value and that which contributes the most not only to the pleasure of life but also to glory, and magnificence. From thence it is that we fetch our gold and precious stones and a thousand other commodities (both of a general esteem and a certain return) to which we are so accustomed that it is impossible for us to be without them, as silk, cinnamon, pepper, ginger, nutmegs, cotton cloth, oüate (vulgarly [cotton] wadding), porcelain, woods for dyeing, ivory, frankincense, bezoar [an antidote for poisons], etc. So that having an absolute necessity

upon us, to make use of all these things, why we should not rather furnish ourselves, than take them from others, and apply that profit hereafter to our own countrymen, which we have hitherto allowed to strangers, I cannot understand.

Why should the Portuguese, the Hollanders, the English, the Danes, trade daily to the East Indies possessing there, their magazines, and their forts, and the French neither the one nor the other? . . . To what end is it *in fine* that we pride ourselves to be subjects of the prime monarch of the universe, if being so, we dare not so much as show our heads in those places where our neighbors have established themselves with power? . . .

What has it been, but this very navigation and traffic that has enabled the Hollanders to bear up against the power of Spain, with forces so unequal, nay, and to become terrible to them and to bring them down at last to an advantageous peace? Since that time it is that this people, who had not only the Spaniards abroad, but the very sea and earth at home to struggle with, have in spite of all opposition made themselves so considerable, that they begin now to dispute power and plenty with the greatest part of their neighbors. This observation is no more than truth, their East India Company being known to be the principal support of their state and the most sensible cause of their greatness.

Document Set 17.5 References

A. A Tax Revolt Brews, 1645
   Letter of the duc d'Epernan [governor of Guyenne] to Seguier, in J. H. Shennan, ed. and trans., *Government and Society in France, 1461–1661* (London: G. Allen and Unwin, 1969), 151.
B. The Nobility of Troyes Plead for a Reduction Both in the Price of Offices and in Taxes, 1651
   Cahier of the Remonstrances of the Nobility in the Bailiwick of Troyes, in Shennan, 154–155.
C. Louis XIV Recalls the Problems He Faced at the Outset of His Reign
   Louis XIV, *Memoirs*, trans. Herbert Wilson (Port Washington, N.Y.: Kennikat), 41–45.
D. The Duke of Saint-Simon Characterizes Louis XIV
   James Harvey Robinson, ed., *Readings in European History* (Boston: Ginn, 1904), 2:285–286.
E. The Duchess of Orleans Describes the Court of Louis XIV
   A Woman's Life in the Court of Sun King: Letters of Liselotte von der Pfalz, 1652–1722 (Elisabeth Charlotte, Duchesse d'Orleans), trans. Elborg Forster (Baltimore: Johns Hopkins University Press, 1984), 17–18.
F. Colbert Sponsors a Pamphlet on "The Advantages of Overseas Trade"
   Colbert, "A Discourse . . . ," trans. R. L'Estrange (London: 1664), in Geoffrey Symcox, ed., *War, Diplomacy, and Imperialism, 1618–1763* (New York: Walker, 1974), 257–260.

DOCUMENT SET 17.6
Louis XIV's France: Religion and Sensibility

Religion was taken seriously in Louis XIV's France. Not only did memories of the sixteenth-century wars of religion still fester; the monarchy was also acutely aware that religious heterodoxy could have serious political implications. Louis himself grew more pious as he aged, and the court followed suit. But religious controversies were exceedingly convoluted. Royal Catholicism did not mean accepting papal dictation to France's "Gallican" church. An intense controversy grew up within French Catholicism over Jansenism, pitting the strongly pro-papal Jesuit order against what the papacy had declared to be an almost Protestant heresy, of which the royal government also disapproved without bowing to the Jesuits and Rome.

The documents of this set explore various dimensions of the religious and social tensions coursing through the French elite. Document A is an extract from *The Provincial Letters* (1656–1657) of Blaise Pascal (1623–1662). One of the great mathematical minds of the ages, Pascal suffered from intense religious anxiety, which we will explore further in Set 17.8. He joined the Jansenists, a religious movement within Catholicism that stressed deep piety and came close to agreeing with the Calvinist doctrine of predestination. The Jansenists' great enemy was the Jesuit Order, which they had accused of making religion too "easy" by encouraging well-born sinners to interpret their transgressions in a favorable light. Pascal's *Provincial Letters,* purporting to be the correspondence of a country gentleman, ridiculed the Jesuit position mercilessly.

In 1685 Louis made one of the great mistakes of his reign, revoking the Edict of Nantes on the wildly misinformed grounds that practically no Huguenots remained in France. As a consequence, more than 50,000 Huguenot families who refused to convert to Catholicism were expelled from the Kingdom. The magnitude of this mistake became apparent at once, and the Duc de Saint-Simon commented bitterly on it in his *Memoirs* (Document B).

The novels of the Countess de Lafayette (1634–1693) are an excellent barometer of the sensibilities of Louis XIV's court. Her *Princess of Cleves*, excerpted in Document C, balances sensuality and propriety exquisitely, while also making one more contribution to that perennially belabored topic of court life, "What is true nobility?" Molière (1622–1673), the great playwright, wrote comedies

satirizing both religious hypocrisy and social climbing; his *Bourgeois gentilhomme* (1671), on the latter subject, is excerpted in Document D, a scene in which the soberly bourgeois Mme. Jourdain expresses her doubts about her rich husband's foolish aspirations to buy his way into the nobility.

What was the reality, meanwhile, of French Catholicism at the grassroots? In Document E a reform-minded Catholic clergyman suggests that a century of Counter-Reformation had done little to make ordinary rural parishioners behave in a seemly, pious manner.

Pulling together the material in this set, use these documents and *The Challenge of the West* to write a brief analysis of the anxieties and aspirations of France's middle class and elite. Considering also the materials in Set 17.5 will enhance your analysis.

A. Blaise Pascal Satirizes Jesuitical Reasoning

"Show me, with all your directing of the intention," returned I, "that it is allowable to fight a duel."

"Our great Hurtado de Mendoza," said the [Jesuit] father, "will satisfy you on that point in a twinkling. 'If a gentleman,' says he, in a passage cited by Diana, 'who is challenged to fight a duel, is well known to have no religion, and if the vices to which he is openly and unscrupulously addicted are such as would lead people to conclude, in the event of his refusing to fight, that he is actuated, not by the fear of God, but by cowardice, and induce them to say of him that he was a *hen,* and not a man—*gallina, et non vir;* in that case he may, to save his honor, appear at the appointed spot—not, indeed, with the express intention of fighting a duel, but merely with that of defending himself, should the person who challenged him come there unjustly to attack him. His action in this case, viewed by itself, will be perfectly indifferent; for what moral evil is there in one stepping into a field, taking a stroll in expectation of meeting a person, and defending one's self in the event of being attacked? And thus the gentleman is guilty of no sin whatever; for in fact it cannot be called accepting a challenge at all, his intention being directed to other circumstances, and the acceptance of a challenge consisting in an express intention to fight, which we are supposing the gentleman never had.'"

"You have not kept your word with me, sir," said

I. "This is not, properly speaking, to permit duelling; on the contrary, the casuist is so persuaded that this practice is forbidden, that, in licensing the action in question, he carefully avoids calling it a duel."

"Ah!" cried the monk, "you begin to get knowing on my hand, I am glad to see. I might reply, that the author I have quoted grants all that duellists are disposed to ask. But since you must have a categorical answer, I shall allow our Father Layman to give it for me. He permits duelling in so many words, provided that, in accepting the challenge, the person directs his intention solely to the preservation of his honor or his property: 'If a soldier or a courtier is in such a predicament that he must lose either his honor or his fortune unless he accepts a challenge, I see nothing to hinder him from doing so in self-defence.' The same thing is said by Peter Hurtado, as quoted by our famous Escobar; his words are: 'One may fight a duel even to defend one's property, should that be necessary; because every man has a right to defend his property, though at the expense of his enemy's life!'"

I was struck, on hearing these passages, with the reflection that while the piety of the king appears in his exerting all his power to prohibit and abolish the practice of duelling in the State, the piety of the Jesuits is shown in their employing all their ingenuity to tolerate and sanction it in the Church. But the good father was in such an excellent key for talking, that it would have been cruel to have interrupted him; so he went on with his discourse.

"In short," said he, "Sanchez (mark, now, what great names I am quoting you!) Sanchez, sir, goes a step further; for he shows how, simply by managing the intention rightly, a person may not only receive a challenge, but give one. And our Escobar follows him." . . .

B. The Duke of Saint-Simon Deplores the Revocation of the Edict of Nantes

The revocation of the Edict of Nantes, without the slightest pretext or necessity, and the various proscriptions that followed it, were the fruits of a frightful plot, in which the new spouse was one of the chief conspirators, and which depopulated a quarter of the realm; ruined its commerce; weakened it in every direction; gave it up for a long time to the public and avowed pillage of he dragoons; authorized torments and punishments by which many innocent people of both sexes were killed by thousands; ruined a numerous class; tore in pieces a world of families; armed relatives against relatives, so as to seize their property and leave them to die of hunger; banished our manufactures to foreign lands; made those lands flourish and overflow at the expense of France, and enabled them to build new cities; gave to the world the spectacle of a prodigious population proscribed without crime, stripped, fugitive, wandering, and seeking shelter far from their country; sent to the galleys nobles, rich old men, people much esteemed for their piety, learning, and virtue, people carefully nurtured, weak, and delicate;—and all solely on account of religion; in fact, to heap up the measure of horror, filled the realm with perjury and sacrilege, in the midst of the echoed cries of these unfortunate victims of error, while so many others sacrificed their conscience to their wealth and their repose, and purchased both by simulated abjuration, from which without pause they were dragged to adore what they did not believe in, and to receive the divine body of the Most Holy whilst remaining persuaded that they were only eating bread which they ought to abhor!

Such was the general abomination born of flattery and cruelty. From torture to abjuration, and from that to communion, there was often only a space of twenty-four hours; and executioners were the guides of the converts and their witnesses. . . . The king received from all sides detailed news of these conversions. It was by thousands that those who had abjured and taken the communion were counted; ten thousand in one place, six thousand in another,—all at once and instantly. The king congratulated himself on his power and his piety. He believed himself to have brought back the days of the apostles, and attributed to himself all the honor. The bishops wrote panegyrics of him; the Jesuits made the pulpit resound with his praise. All France was filled with horror and confusion; and yet there was never such triumph and joy, such boundless laudation of the king.

C. Madame de Lafayette's *Princess of Cleves* Suggests the Proper Values for a Young Noblewoman

Now there appeared at the Court a beauty. All eyes were upon her and she must indeed have been a paragon to be so much admired in a place where lovely women were the rule. She belonged to the same family as the Vidame de Chartres, and was one of the greatest heiresses in France. Her father had died young, leaving her to be brought up by his widow, Madame de Chartres, a good, noble, and distinguished person. For some years after her husband's death she left the Court and devoted herself to her daughter's education, not only cultivating her mind and caring for her beauty, but also trying to make her good and give her a real love of virtue. Most mothers think that they can best protect their children by never speaking of love in their presence, but Madame de Chartres had different ideas; she often described it to her daughter, minimizing none of its charm so that the girl should more readily understand what she told her of its dangers. She told her that men were not very sincere, not very faithful and not above deceit; she spoke of the unhappiness that love affairs can bring to a family, and then, on the other hand, she showed her the life of a good woman—happy, serene, and enjoying the particular glamor that attaches to noble birth when there is also virtue. She impressed upon her that this virtue can only be kept by vigilance and by following the one line of conduct which can make a woman happy—that is to say, loving her husband and being loved by him.

D. Mme. Jourdain Has Her Doubts

M. Jourdain: Shut up, saucebox. You're always sticking your oar in the conversation. I have enough property for my daughter; all I need is honor; and I want to make her a marquise.

Mme Jourdain: Marquise?

M. Jourdain: Yes, marquise.

Mme Jourdain: Alas, God forbid!

M. Jourdain: It's something I've made up my mind to.

Mme Jourdain: As for me, it's something I'll never consent to. Alliances with people above our own rank are always likely to have very unpleasant results. I don't want to have my son-in-law able to reproach my daughter for her parents, and I don't want her children to be ashamed to call me their grandma. If she should happen to come and visit me in her grand lady's carriage, and if by mistake she should fail to salute some one of the neighbors, you can imagine how they'd talk. "Take a look at that fine Madame la Marquise showing off," they'd say. "She's the daughter of Monsieur Jourdain, and when she was little, she was only too glad to play at being a fine lady. She wasn't always so high and mighty as she is now, and both her grandfathers sold dry goods besides the

Porte Saint Innocent. They both piled up money for their children, and now perhaps they're paying dear for it in the next world; you don't get so rich by being honest." Well, I don't want that kind of talk to go on; and in short, I want a man who will feel under obligation to my daughter, and I want to be able to say to him: "Sit down there, my boy, and eat dinner with us."

M. Jourdain: Those views reveal a mean and petty mind, that wants to remain forever in its base condition. Don't answer back to me again. My daughter will be a marquise in spite of everyone; and if you get me angry, I'll make her a duchess.

E. Catholic Priest Noël Chomel Denounces Dancing on Holy Days

During these holy days, the air is filled with the worst sort of filth; impudence knows no bounds; and because of negligence great enough to make one cry, even the most moderate persons approve what on other occasions they would judge to be a scandal and an atrocious crime. . . . To see the lewd and violent gyrations of the girls mixed in dance with the young men, does it not seem that one is watching bacchantes and savages rather than Christians?

Document Set 17.6 References

A. Blaise Pascal Satirizes Jesuitical Reasoning
Pascal, *Provincial Lettes*, Thomas M'Cree, trans. (New York: Modern Library, 1941), 406–408.

B. The Duke of Saint-Simon Deplores the Revocation of the Edict of Nantes
James Harvey Robinson, ed., *Readings in European History* (Boston: Ginn, 1904), 2:291–293.

C. Madame de Lafayette's *Princess of Cleves* Suggests the Proper Values for a Young Noblewoman
Mme. de Lafayette, *The Princess of Cleves*, trans. Nancy Mitford (Westport, Conn.: Greenwood, 1977), 11–12.

D. Mme. Jourdain Has Her Doubts
Molière, *Le Bourgeois Gentilhomme*, in Morris Bishop, trans., *Eight Plays by Molière* (New York: Modern Library, 1957), 372.

E. Catholic Priest Noël Chomel Denounces Dancing on Holy Days
Paul T. Hoffman, *Church and Community in the Diocese of Lyon 1500–1780* (New Haven, Conn.: Yale University Press, 1984), 88.

Varieties of Liberty on the Continent

Seventeenth-century Poland-Lithuania was one of the great exceptions to the era's trend toward more authoritarian—or at least better organized—states. The right of the commonwealth's nobility to elect a king and hold him in obedience to a contentious parliament typified Poland-Lithuania's "golden freedom." Jan Chrzyzostom Pasek, a Polish nobleman of middling fortune and great but untutored literary skill, left fascinating memoirs of his experiences that have only recently been translated into English. His uproarious account of the royal election of 1669 (Document A), out of which a weak national candidate named Michał Wiśniowiecki (*1669–1673) was elected king despite lavish bribery by a French-sponsored candidate, gives a vivid picture of "gentry democracy" at work.

The expulsion of the Huguenots from France (Set 17.6, Document B) provided a great opportunity for the Protestant powers of Europe not only to demonstrate their liberality but also to gain industrious new subjects. Energetic at crushing the liberties of his own burgher- and noble-dominated provincial legislatures, Brandenburg's great elector Frederick William (*1640–1688) eagerly welcomed the Huguenot refugees to his lands (Document B). Some of their descendants, still bearing French names, remained prominent in the Prussian aristocracy until the twentieth century. In view of his otherwise repressive policies, what do you make of the Great Elector's welcome to the Huguenots?

Another citadel of liberty (as contemporaries would have expressed it) in seventeenth-century Europe was the Dutch Republic, then at the peak of a prosperity that was the envy of the rest of the continent. One foreigner who understood the connection was Sir William Temple (1628–1699), an English essayist and diplomat. Do you agree with his assessment? It may help to recall that the republic had a stormy history, including several French invasions and a violent mob uprising in 1672.

The latter event profoundly shook the great Dutch-Jewish philosopher Baruch Spinoza (1632–1677), who was personally close to the de Witt brothers, important Dutch leaders lynched by the mob. Spinoza recognized that civil society poised precariously above a cauldron of violence; in Document D he pleads for moderation of the passions (a central theme of his philosophy) and for the tempering of free thought with responsibility for maintaining legitimate authority.

A. Golden Freedom: The Polish Nobility Elects a King, 1669

The election of the king took place then. Announcements went out to the districts from the archbishop, urging *ordines Reipublicae* [the estates of the Commonwealth] to accomplish a speedy election, tendering the wish that the election be carried off *per deputatos* [by the deputies]. But the provinces refused their assent and, indeed, ordered everyone to horse as if for war. . . .

But when the sessions of the Diet began, divers men were of divers minds: this one'll be king, that one will, yet no one mentioned the one whom God himself had forseen. All those who sent deputies were scheming and hoping that things would turn out as they'd planned. While he, our future king, expects nothing, knowing the likelihood to be nil. The French deputies, as if cowed, work in secret, but the Neuburg and Lorraine deputies work openly. Not a word about a Polish candidate. The others are handing out money, giving it away, wining, dining, making promises; while he bestows nothing on anybody, promises nothing, requests nothing: and yet he carries off the crown. . . .

[At first the French candidate, the Duke of Lorraine, appeared to have the upper hand, although his supporters had to fight some serious brawls with advocates of other candidates—all very colorfully described.]

As this is going on, [the nobles from the province of] Wielkopolska now gives a shout: *"Vivat rex!"* Several from our delegation dash over to see whom they are cheering; they returned with the news that it was Charles of Lorraine. In Łęczyce and Kujawy they were saying, "we don't need a rich man for, upon becoming the king of Poland, he'll be rich. We don't need anyone related to other royalty, for 'tis a *periculum libertatis,* [danger to liberty] but we need a *virum fortem,* a *virum bellicosum* [a strong, bellicose man]. Were Czarniecki[1] here, he'd surely have sat on the throne; but as God took him from us, let us elect his disciple, let us elect [Alexander] Polanowski."

This is going on here; meanwhile I, *per curiositatem* [out of curiosity] dashed over to the deputies from Sandomierz, they were standing the closest to us, and what should I find but that they prefer some-

---

[1] A notable magnate, recently deceased

one *de sanguine gentis* [of native blood], and they're saying: "We have not far to look for a king, he's in our midst. Recalling the virtue and decency, and the many services to this country of the deceased Prince [Jeremi] Wiśniowiecki, right and fitting would it be to pay our debt of gratitude to his *posteritas*. Here is Prince Michał Wiśniowiecki; why should we not elect him? Is he not from an ancient family of great princes? Is he not worthy of the crown?"

And he is sitting there among the gentry, humble as pie, wincing, saying nothing. I rush back to my own delegation and say: "Gentlemen, already several delegations are putting forth a Piast."[2] Our Kraków lordship inquires: "Who is it?" Say I: "Polanowski and Wiśniowiecki." And meanwhile there's a roar from Sandomierz: "*Vivat Piast!*" Debicki, the chamberlain, hurls his cap into the air, yelling at the top of his voice: "*Vivat Piast! Vivat Rex Michael!*" And now our Kraków deputies too: "*Vivat Piast!*" A few of us run off to the other provincial delegations with the news, shouting "*Vivat Piast!*" Those from Łęczyce and Kujawy, thinking it's for their Polanowski, at once started shouting too; other delegations too. Returning to my own, they're now taking his arm, they're leading him to the assembly.

Our Kraków officers *negant, contradicunt,* [do not wish it, oppose it] (having taken a great deal of money from others and made big promises), in particular, Pisarski and Lipski who were saying: "For God's sake, what are we doing? Have we gone mad? Wait! This cannot be." Our Kraków lordship has now withdrawn from us, the nominee being his kinsman; there he is, next to the candidate. Many other senators are coming toward us. Some protest, others remain silent. Pisarski says to me (he nonetheless held me in esteem); "My dear fellow, what think you of this situation?" I reply: "I think what God has put in my heart: "*Vivat Rex Michael!*" Where upon, I ride out of the line and dash after Sandomierz; in all haste the squadrons with their standards follow after me, only Pisarski, slamming his cap on his head, rode off to the side.

We led Wiśniowiecki then to the assembly. Now come the *gratulationes* [congratulations], now was there rejoicing for men of good will, heartache for the evildoers.

B. The Great Elector Welcomes French Huguenot Refugees to Brandenburg

In view of the sympathy which we ought to, and do, feel for our brethren of the reformed evangelical religion in France, who have been driven by persecution to leave their homes and settle in other countries, we, Frederick William, etc., desire by this edict to offer them a free and safe refuge in all our lands and possessions and to specify what rights, privileges, and prerogatives we are graciously minded to grant them. . . .

3. . . . We particularly specify the towns of Stendal, Werben, Rathenow, Brandenburg, and Frankfurt in the electorate of Brandenburg, Magdeburg, Halle, and Calbe in the duchy of Magdeburg, and Königsberg in Prussia, as places where living is cheap and opportunities for trade and other means of support abundant; and we command herewith that when any of the said French people of the reformed evangelical religion make their appearance, they shall be well received in the said towns, and that every opportunity and assistance shall be given them in establishing themselves there. They shall, moreover, be free to establish themselves in any other place in our lands and dominions outside the above-mentioned towns which shall seem to them more convenient for the purposes of their trade or calling.

4. They shall be permitted to bring with them any furniture, merchandise, or other moveable property free of all duties or imposts of any kind whatever. . . .

6. In towns or other places where there are unoccupied or waste lands or properties, we ordain that these shall be given over to our said French brethren of the reformed evangelical religion, free of all and every incumbrance, to hold and enjoy for themselves and their posterity. We further ordain that the necessary materials for the cultivation of these lands shall be furnished them gratis. . . .

7. So soon as any of our said French brethren of the reformed evangelical religion shall have settled themselves in any town or village, they shall be invested, without payment of any kind, with all the rights, benefits, and privileges of citizenship enjoyed or exercised by our subjects who live and were born in said town or village.

8. If any of them shall desire to establish manufactories of cloth, stuffs, hats, or other articles, we will not only bestow on them all the necessary permissions, rights, and privileges, but will further aid

---

[2] A native-born candidate

them, so far as is in our power, with money and requisite materials.

9. Those who wish to settle in the country shall be given a certain amount of land to cultivate, shall be furnished with the requisite utensils and materials and encouraged in every way, as has been done in the case of certain families who have come from Switzerland to settle in our country. . . .

11. In every town where our said French brethren in the faith are established, we will support a special preacher and set apart a proper place where they may hold their services in the French language, and with such usages and ceremonies as are customary in the reformed evangelical churches in France.

12. As for the members of the French nobility who have placed themselves under our protection and entered our service, they enjoy the same honors, dignities, and prerogatives as our own subjects of noble birth, and several of them have been given some of the most important offices at our court as well as in our army; and we are graciously disposed to show like favor to all such of the French nobility as may in future present themselves to us.

Given at Potsdam, the 29th of October, 1685.

Frederick William, Elector.

C. Sir William Temple Observes Liberty and Prosperity in the Dutch Republic

In this city of Amsterdam is the famous bank, which is the greatest treasure, either real or imaginary, that is known any where in the world. The place of it is a great vault under the Stadthouse, made strong with all the circumstances of doors and locks, and other appearing cautions of safety, that can be: and it is certain, that whoever is carried to see the bank, shall never fail to find the appearance of a mighty real treasure, in bars of gold and silver, plate, and infinite bags of metals, which are supposed to be all gold and silver, and may be so for aught I know. But, the Burgomasters only having the inspection of this bank, and no man ever taking any particular account of what issues in and out, from age to age, it is impossible to make any calculation, or guess, what proportion the real treasure may hold to the credit of it. Therefore the security of the bank lies not only in the effects that are in it, but in the credit of the whole town or state of Amsterdam, whose stock and revenue is equal to that of some kingdoms; and who are bound to make good all monies that are brought into their bank: the tickets or bills hereof make all the usual great payments, that are made between man and

man in the town; and not only in most other places of the United Provinces, but in many other trading parts of the world. So as this bank is properly a general cash, where every man lodges money, because he esteems it safer, and easier paid in and out, than if it were in his coffers at home; and the bank is so far from paying any interest for what is there brought in, that money in the bank is worth something more in common payments, than what runs current in coin from hand to hand; no other money passing in the bank, but in the species of coin the best known, the most ascertained, and the most generally current in all parts of the Higher as well as the Lower Germany. . . .

It is certain, that, in no town, strength, beauty, and convenience are better provided for, nor with more unlimited expence, than in this, by the magnificence of their public buildings, as the Stadthouse and Arsenals; the number and spaciousness, as well as order and revenues, of their many hospitals; the commodiousness of their canals, running through the chief streets of passage; the mighty strength of their bastions and ramparts; and the neatness, as well as convenience, of their streets, so far as can be compassed in so great a confluence of industrious people; all which could never be achieved without a charge much exceeding what seems proportioned to the revenue of one single town. . . .

[At the beginning of the next chapter Temple notes that the Dutch must import all their raw materials:]. Nor has Holland grown rich by any native commodities, but by force of industry; by improvement and manufacture of all foreign growths; by being the general magazine of Europe, and furnishing all parts with whatever the market wants or invites; and by their seamen being, as they have properly been called, the common carriers of the world.

Since the ground of trade cannot be deduced from havens, or native commodities (as may well be concluded from the survey of Holland, which has the least and the worst; and of Ireland, which has the most and the best, of both) it were not amiss to consider, from what other source it may be more naturally and certainly derived: for, if we talk of industry, we are still as much to seek, what it is that makes people industrious in one country, and idle in another. I conceive the true original and ground of trade to be, great multitude of people crowded into small compass of land, whereby all things necessary to life become dear, and all men, who have possessions, are induced to parsimony; but those, who have none, are forced to industry and labour, or else to want. Bodies, that are vigorous, fall to labour; such, as are not, supply that defect by some sort of inventions or ingenuity. These customs arise first from necessity, but increase by imitation, and grow in time to be habitual in a country; and where-ever they are so, if it lies upon the sea, they naturally break out into trade, both because whatever they want of their own, that is necessary to so many men's lives, must be supplied from abroad; and because, by the multitude of people, and smallness of country, land grows so dear, that the improvement of money that way is inconsiderable, and so turns to sea, where the greatness of the profit makes amends for the venture.

This cannot be better illustrated, than by its contrary, which appears no where more than in Ireland; where, by the largeness and plenty of the food, and scarcity of people, all things necessary to life are so cheap, that an industrious man, by two days labour, may gain enough to feed him the rest of the week; which I take to be very plain ground of the laziness attributed to the people: for men naturally prefer ease before labour, and will not take pains, if they can live idle: though when, by necessity, they have been inured to it, they cannot leave it, being grown a custom necessary to their health, and to their very entertainment: nor perhaps is the change harder, from constant ease to labour, than from constant labour to ease.

This account of the original of trade agrees with the experience of all ages, and with the constitutions of all places, where it has most flourished in the world, as Tyre, Carthage, Athens, Syracuse, Agrigentum, Rhodes, Venice, Holland; and will be so obvious to every man, that knows and considers the situation, the extent, and the nature, of all those countries, that it will need no enlargement upon the comparisons.

By these examples, which are all of commonwealths, and by the decay and dissolution of trade in the six first, when they came to be conquered, or subjected to arbitrary dominions, it might be concluded, that there is something, in that form of government, proper and natural to trade, in a more peculiar manner. But the height it arrived to at Bruges and Antwerp, under their Princes, for four or five descents of the house of Burgundy, and two of Austria, shews, it may thrive under good Princes and legal monarchies, as well as under free States. Under arbitrary and tyrannical power it must of necessity decay and dissolve, because this empties a country of people, whereas the others fill it; this extinguishes industry, whilst men are in doubt of enjoying themselves what they get, or leaving it to their children; the others encourage it, by securing men of both: one fills a country with soldiers, and the other with merchants; who were never known yet to live well together, because they cannot trust one another. And as trade cannot live with mutual trust among private men; so it cannot grow or thrive, to any great degree, without a confidence both of public and private safety, and consequently a trust in the government, from an opinion of its strength, wisdom, and justice; which must be grounded either upon the personal virtues and qualities of a Prince, or else upon the constitutions and orders of a State.

D. Baruch Spinoza Balances Freedom of Thought and Political Authority

Of the Functions of Supreme Authorities

The right of the supreme authorities is limited by their power; the most important part of that right is, that they are, as it were, the mind of the dominion, whereby all ought to be guided; and accordingly, such authorities alone have the right of deciding what is good, evil, equitable or iniquitous, that is, what must be done or left undone by the subjects severally or collectively. And, accordingly, they have the sole right of laying down laws, and of interpreting the same, whenever their meaning is disputed, and of deciding whether a given case is in conformity with or violation of the laws; and, lastly, of waging war, and of drawing up and offering propositions for peace, or of accepting such when offered.

As all these functions, and also the means required to execute them, are matters which regard the whole body of the dominion, that is, are affairs of state, it follows that affairs of state depend on the direction of him only who holds supreme dominion. And hence it follows that it is the right of the supreme authority alone to judge the deeds of every individual, and demand of him an account of the same; to punish criminals, and decide questions of law between citizens, or appoint jurists acquainted with the existing laws, to administer these matters on its behalf; and, further, to use and order all means to war and peace, as to found and fortify cities, levy soldiers, assign military posts, and order what it would have done, and, with a view to peace, to send and give audience to ambassadors; and, finally, to levy the costs of all this.

Since, then, it is the right of the supreme authority alone to handle public matters, or choose officials to do so, it follows that that subject is a pretender to the dominion, who, without the supreme council's knowledge, enters upon any public matter, although he believe that his design will be to the best interest of the commonwealth.

But it is often asked, whether the supreme authority is bound by laws, and, consequently, whether it can do wrong. Now as the words "law" and "wrong-doing" often refer not merely to the laws of a commonwealth, but also to the general rules which concern all natural things, and especially to the general rules of reason, we cannot, without qualification, say that the commonwealth is bound by no laws, or can do no wrong. For were the commonwealth bound by no laws or rules, which removed, the commonwealth were no commonwealth, we should have to regard it not as a natural thing, but as a chimera. A commonwealth then does wrong, when it does, or suffers to be done, things which may be the cause of its own ruin; and we can say that it then does wrong, in the sense in which philosophers or doctors say that Nature does wrong; and in this sense we can say, that a commonwealth does wrong, when it acts against the dictate of reason. For a commonwealth is most independent when it acts according to the dictate of reason; so far, then, as it acts against reason, it falls itself, or does wrong. And we shall be able more easily to understand this if we reflect that when we say, that a man can do what he will with his own, this authority must be limited not only by the power of the agent, but by the capacity of the object. If, for instance, I say that I can rightfully do what I will with this table, I do not certainly mean that I have the right to make it eat grass. So, too, though we say, that men depend not on themselves, but on the commonwealth, we do not mean, that men lose their human nature and put on another; nor yet that the commonwealth has the right to make men wish for this or that, or (what is just as impossible) regard with honor things which excite ridicule or disgust. But it is implied that there are certain intervening circumstances which supposed, one likewise supposes the reverence and fear of the subjects towards the commonwealth, and which abstracted, one makes abstraction likewise of that fear and reverence, and therewith of the commonwealth itself. The commonwealth, then, to maintain its independence, is bound to preserve the causes of fear and reverence, otherwise it ceases to be a commonwealth. For the person or persons that hold dominion can no more combine with the keeping up of majesty the running with harlots drunk or naked about the streets, or the performances of a stage-player, or the open violation or contempt of laws passed by themselves, than they can combine existence with non-existence. But to proceed to slay and rob subjects, ravish maidens, and the like, turns fear into indignation and the civil state into a state of enmity.

We see, then, in what sense we may say, that a commonwealth is bound by laws and can do wrong. But if by "law" we understand civil law, and by "wrong" that which, by civil law, is forbidden to be done, that is, if these words be taken in their proper sense, we cannot at all say that a commonwealth is bound by laws or can do wrong. For the maxims and motives of fear and reverence which a commonwealth is bound to observe in its own interest, pertain not to civil jurisprudence, but to the law of Nature, since they cannot be vindicated by the civil law, but by the law of war. And a commonwealth is bound by them in no other sense than that in which in the state of Nature a man is bound to take heed that he preserve his independence and be not his own enemy, lest he should destroy himself; and in this taking heed lies not the subjection, but the liberty of human nature. But civil jurisprudence depends on the mere decree of the commonwealth, which is not bound to please any but itself, nor to hold anything to be good or bad, but what it judges to be such for itself. And, accordingly, it has not merely the right to avenge itself, or to lay down and interpret laws, but also to abolish the same, and to pardon any guilty person out of the fullness of its power.

Contracts or laws, whereby the multitude transfers its rights to one council or man, should without doubt be broken, when it is expedient for the general welfare to do so. But to decide this point, whether, that is, it be expedient for the general welfare to break them or not, is within the right of no private person, but of him only who holds dominion; therefore of these laws he who holds dominion remains sole interpreter. Moreover, no private person can by right vindicate these laws, and so they do not really bind him who holds dominion. Notwithstanding, if they are of such a nature that they cannot be broken without at the same time weakening the commonwealth's strength, that is, without at the same time changing to indignation the common fear of most of the citizens, by this very fact the commonwealth is dissolved, and the contract comes to an end; and therefore such contract is vindicated not by the civil law, but by the law of war. And so he who holds dominion is not bound to observe the terms of the contract by any other cause than that, which bids a man in the state of Nature to beware of being his own enemy, lest he should destroy himself.

Of the Best State of a Dominion

We have shown that man is then most independent when he is most led by reason, and, in consequence, that that commonwealth is most powerful and most independent which is founded and guided by reason. But, as the best plan of living, so as to assure to the utmost self-preservation, is that which is framed according to the dictate of reason, therefore it follows that that in every kind is best done, which a man or commonwealth does, so far as he or it is in the highest degree independent. For it is one thing to till a field by right, and another to till it in the best way. One thing, I say, to defend or preserve oneself, and to pass judgment by right, and another in defend or preserve oneself in the best way, and to pass the best judgment; and, consequently, it is one thing to have dominion and care of affairs of state by right, and another to exercise dominion and direct affairs of state in the best way. And so, as we have treated of the right of every commonwealth in general, it is time to treat of the best state of every dominion.

Now the quality of the state of any dominion is easily perceived from the end of the civil state, which end in nothing else but peace and security of life. And therefore that dominion is the best, where men pass their lives in unity, and the laws are kept unbroken. For it is certain, that seditions, wars, and contempt or breach of the laws are not so much to be imputed to the wickedness of the subjects, as to the bad state of a dominion. For men are not born fit for citizenship, but must be made so. Besides, men's natural passions are everywhere the same; and if wickedness more prevails, and more offenses are committed in one commonwealth than in another, it is certain that the former has not enough pursued the end of unity, nor framed its laws with sufficient forethought; and that, therefore, it has failed in making quite good its right as a commonwealth. For a civil state, which has not done away with the causes of seditions, where war is a perpetual object of fear, and where, lastly, the laws are often broken, differs but little from the mere state of Nature, in which every one lives after his own mind at the great risk of his life.

But as the vices and inordinate license and contumacy of subjects must be imputed to the commonwealth, so, on the other hand, their virtue and constant obedience to the laws are to be ascribed in the main to the virtue and perfect right of the commonwealth. And so it is deservedly reckoned to Hannibal as an extraordinary virtue, that in his army there never arose a sedition.

Of a commonwealth, whose subjects are but hindered by terror from taking arms, it should rather be said, that it is free from war, than that it has peace. For peace is not mere absence of war, but is a virtue that springs from force of character: for obedience is the constant will to execute what, by the general decree of the commonwealth, ought to be done. Besides, that commonwealth whose peace depends on the sluggishness of its subjects, that are led about like sheep to learn but slavery, may more properly be called a desert than a commonwealth.

When, then, we call that dominion best, where men pass their lives in unity, I understand a human life, defined not by mere circulation of the blood, and other qualities common to all animals, but above all by reason, the true excellence and life of the mind.

But be it remarked that, by the dominion which I have said is established for this end, I intend that which has been established by a free multitude, not that which is acquired over a multitude by right of war. For a free multitude is guided more by hope than fear; a conquered one, more by fear than by hope: inasmuch as the former aims at making use of life, the latter but at escaping death. The former, I say, aims at living for its own ends, the latter is forced to belong to the conqueror; and so we way that this is enslaved, but that free. And, therefore, the end of a dominion, which one gets by right of war, is to be master, and have rather slaves than subjects. And although between the dominion created by a free multitude, and that gained by right of war, if we regard generally the right of each, we can make no essential distinction; yet their ends, as we have already shown, and further the means to the preservation of each are very different.

But what means a prince, whose sole motive is lust of mastery, should use to establish and maintain his dominion the most ingenious Machiavelli has set forth at large, but with what design one can hardly be sure. If, however, he had some good design, as one should believe of a learned man, it seems to have been to show, with how little foresight many attempt to remove a tyrant, though thereby the causes which make the prince a tyrant can in no wise be removed, but, on the contrary, are so much the more established, as the prince is given more cause to fear, which happens when the multitude has made an example of its prince, and glories in the parricide as in a thing well done. Moreover, he perhaps wished to show how cautious a free multitude should be of entrusting its welfare absolutely to one man, who, unless in his vanity he thinks he can please everybody, must be in daily fear of plots, and so is forced to look chiefly after his own interest, and, as for the multitude, rather to plot against it than consult its good. And I am the more led to this opinion concerning that most far-seeing man, because it is known that he was favorable to liberty, for the maintenance of which he has besides given the most wholesome advice.

Document Set 17.7 References

A. Golden Freedom: The Polish Nobility Elects a King, 1669
Jan Chrzysostom Pasek, *Memoirs of the Polish Baroque,* trans. Catherine Leach (Berkeley and Los Angeles: University of California Press, 1976), 210–211, 214–215.

B. The Great Elector Welcomes French Huguenot Refugees to Brandenburg
Frederick William, Edict, in James Harvey Robinson, ed., *Readings in European History* (Boston: Ginn, 1904), 2:316–317.

C. Sir William Temple Observes Liberty and Prosperity in the Dutch Republic
The Works of Sir William Temple (London: 1814), 1:119–121, 183–185.

D. Baruch Spinoza Balances Freedom of Thought and Political Authority
Spinoza, "A Political Treatise," in *The Philosophy of Spinoza Selected from His Chief Works,* ed. Joseph Ratner (New York: Modern Library, 1927), 324–332.

DOCUMENT SET 17.8

Regaining Coherence: Faith and Rationalism at the End of the Seventeenth Century

". . . All coherence gone," lamented John Donne (1572–1631), the English metaphysical poet of the early seventeenth century, thinking of how Copernican astronomy had destroyed the world-picture of European tradition without having established any new basis for understanding God's universe. But by the late seventeenth century, a new sense of coherence began to gain ground.

One manifestation of the intense spiritual uneasiness wrought by the challenge of a new cosmology—with its assumption that the universe must be a terrifying place of almost infinite dimensions, with God's earth a mere speck of cosmic dust whirling through the void—was the tortured conscience of Blaise Pascal, whom we have already met (Set 17.6). His *Pensées* (Thoughts), a jumble of notes found after his death in 1662, are excerpted as Document A. Notice his famous wager on God's existence; how close do you think Pascal came to atheism?

Thomas Hobbes, probably England's greatest philosophical mind in the seventeenth century, took a decidedly pessimistic view of humanity (Document B). Convinced that careful education could temper the passions, John Locke viewed humanity more optimistically (Document C). Does this, too, bespeak a growing faith in reason?

Sir Isaac Newton (1642–1729) formulated the laws of classical physics that framed the modern world-view until supplemented by Einstein's theory of relativity in the early twentieth century. Newton's epochal work at last provided rigorous mathematical confirmation of the Copernican universe and by the early eighteenth century had helped convince educated Europeans that God had indeed created a reasonable, ordered, and comprehensible universe that, figuratively speaking, ran like clockwork. As we shall see in *The Challenge of the West*'s Chapters 18 and 19, Newton's world-view underlay the eighteenth-century Enlightenment. Document D, taken from Newton's masterpiece, *Principia mathematica* (1687), shows the extent to which, for Newton, modern scientific method had already come into focus, leaving behind the scholastic practice of deducing conclusions from theory or authority and substituting a *quantitative* for the traditionally *qualitative* approach to unraveling nature's secrets.

Newton remained a devout theist; indeed, he devoted enormous energy throughout his career to trying to predict when the world would end by uncovering secret patterns in the numbers given in biblical texts. But did he see theological implications in his laws of physics? Document E, his response to an English theologian named Bentley who tried to draw such conclusions, suggested that Newton was cautiously neutral about the ultimate meaning of his discoveries—an attitude that most modern scientists would heartily endorse.

A. Blaise Pascal Wagers on God's Existence

199. Let us imagine a number of men in chains, and all condemned to death, where some are killed each day in the sight of the others, and those who remain see their own fate in that of their fellows, and wait their turn, looking at each other sorrowfully and without hope. It is an image of the condition of men. . . .

205. When I consider the short duration of my life, swallowed up in the eternity before and after, the little space which I fill, and even can see, engulfed in the infinite immensity of spaces of which I am ignorant, and which know me not, I am frightened, and am astonished at being here rather than there; for there is no reason why here rather than there, why now rather than then. Who has put me here? By whose order and direction have this place and time been allotted to me? *Memoria hospitis unius diei praetereuntis.*

206. The eternal silence of these infinite spaces frightens me. . . .

229. This is what I see and what troubles me. I look on all sides, and I see only darkness everywhere. Nature presents to me nothing which is not matter of doubt and concern. If I saw nothing there which revealed a Divinity, I would come to a negative conclusion; if I saw everywhere the signs of a Creator, I would remain peacefully in faith. But, seeing too much to deny and too little to be sure, I am in a state to be pitied; wherefore I have a hundred times wished that if a God maintains nature, she should testify to

Him unequivocally, and that, if the signs she gives are deceptive, she should suppress them altogether; that she should say everything or nothing, that I might see which cause I ought to follow. Whereas in my present state, ignorant of what I am or of what I ought to do, I know neither my condition nor my duty. My heart inclines wholly to know where is the true good, in order to follow it; nothing would be too dear to me for eternity.

I envy those whom I see living in the faith with such carelessness, and who make such a bad use of a gift of which it seems to me I would make such a different use.

230. It is incomprehensible that God should exist, and it is incomprehensible that He should not exist; that the soul should be joined to the body, and that we should have no soul; that the world should be created, and that it should not be created, etc.; that original sin should be, and that it should not be. . . .

346. Thought constitutes the greatness of man.

347. Man is but a reed, the most feeble thing in nature; but he is a thinking reed. The entire universe need not arm itself to crush him. A vapour, a drop of water suffices to kill him. But, if the universe were to crush him, man would still be more noble than that which killed him, because he knows that he dies and the advantage which the universe has over him; the universe knows nothing of this.

All our dignity consists, then, in thought. By it we must elevate ourselves, and not by space and time which we cannot fill. Let us endeavour, then, to think well; this is the principle of morality.

348. *A thinking reed.*—It is not from space that I must seek my dignity, but from the government of my thought. I shall have no more if I possess worlds. By space the universe encompasses and swallows me up like an atom; by thought I comprehend the world.

. . . If there is a God, He is infinitely incomprehensible, since, having neither parts nor limits, He has no affinity to us. We are then incapable of knowing either what He is or if He is. This being so, who will dare to undertake the decision of the question? Not we, who have no affinity to Him. . . .

. . . But you must wager. It is not optional. You are embarked. Which will you choose then? Let us see. Since you must choose, let us see which interests you least. You have two things to lose, the true and the good; and two things to stake, your reason and your will, your knowledge and your happiness; and your nature has two things to shun, error and misery. Your reason is no more shocked in choosing one rather than the other, since you must of necessity choose. This is one point settled. But your happiness? Let us weigh the gain and the loss in wagering that

God is. Let us estimate these two chances. If you gain, you gain all; if you lose, you lose nothing. Wager, then, without hesitation that He is.— "That is very fine. Yes, I must wager; but I may perhaps wager too much."—Let us see. Since there is equal risk of gain and loss, if you had only to gain two lives, instead of one, you might still wager. But if there were three lives to gain, you would have to play (since you are under the necessity of playing), and you would be imprudent, when you are forced to play, not to chance you life to gain three at a game where there is an equal risk of loss and gain. But there is an eternity of life and happiness. And this being so, if there were an infinity of chances, of which one only would be for you, you would still be right in wagering one to win two, and you would act stupidly, being obliged to play, by refusing to stake one life against three at a game in which out of an infinity of chances there is one for you, if there were an infinity of an infinitely happy life to gain. But there is here an infinity of an infinitely happy life to gain, a chance to gain against a finite number of chances of loss, and what you stake is finite. It is all divided; wherever the infinite is and there is not an infinity of chances of loss against that of gain, there is no time to hesitate, you must give all. And thus, when one is forced to play, he must renounce reason to preserve his life, rather than risk it for infinite gain, as likely to happen as the loss of nothingness.

For it is no use to say it is uncertain if we will gain, and it is certain that we risk, and that the infinite distance between the *certainty* of what is staked and the *uncertainty* of what will be gained, equals the finite good which is certainly staked against the uncertain infinite. It is not so, as every player stakes a certainty to gain an uncertainty, and yet he stakes a finite certainty to gain a finite uncertainty, without transgressing against reason. There is not an infinite distance between the certainty staked and the uncertainty of the gain; that is untrue. In truth, there is an infinity between the certainty of gain and the certainty of loss. But the uncertainty of the gain is proportioned to the certainty of the stake according to the proportion of the chances of gain and loss. Hence it comes that, if there are as many risks on one side as on the other, the course is to play even; and then the certainy of the stake is equal to the uncertainty of the gain, so far is it from fact that there is an infinite distance between them. And so our proposition is of infinite force, when there is the finite to stake in a game where there are equal risks of gain and loss, and the infinite to gain. This is demonstrable: and if men are capable of any truths, this is one.

B. Thomas Hobbes Takes a Bleak View of Humanity's Natural State

. . . In the nature of man, we find three principal causes of quarrel. First, competition; secondly, diffidence; thirdly, glory.

The first, maketh men invade for gain; the second, for safety; and the third, for reputation. The first use violence, to make themselves masters of other men's persons, wives, children, and cattle; the second, to defend them; the third, for trifles, as a word, a smile, a different opinion, and any other sign of undervalue, either direct in their persons, or by reflection in their kindred, their friends, their nation, their profession, or their name.

Hereby it is manifest, that during the time men live without a common power to keep them all in awe, they are in that condition which is called war; and such a war, as is of every man, against every man. For war, consisteth not in battle only, or the act of fighting; but in a tract of time, wherein the will to contend by battle is sufficiently known: . . . so the nature of war, consisteth not in actual fighting; but in the known disposition thereto, during all the time there is no assurance to the contrary. All other time is peace.

Whatsoever therefore is consequent to a time of war, where every man is enemy to every man; the same is consequent to the time, wherein men live without other security, than what their own strength, and their own invention shall furnish them withal. In such condition, there is no place for industry; because the fruit thereof is uncertain; and consequently no culture of the earth; no navigation, nor use of the commodities that may be imported by sea; no commodious building; no instruments of moving, and removing, such things as require much force; no knowledge of the face of the earth; no account of time; no arts; no letters; no society; and which is worst of all, continual fear, and danger of violent death; and the life of man, solitary, poor, nasty, brutish, and short . . .

The desires, and other passions of man, are in themselves no sin. No more are the actions, that proceed from those passions, till they know a law that forbids them: which till laws be made they cannot know: nor can any law be made, till they have agreed upon the person that shall make it . . .

To this war of every man, against every man, this also is consequent; that nothing can be unjust. The notions of right and wrong, justice and injustice have there no place. Where there is no common power, there is no law; where no law, no injustice. Force, and fraud, are in war the two cardinal virtues. Justice, and injustice are none of the faculties neither of the body, nor mind . . . They are qualities, that relate to men in society, not in solitude. It is consequent also to the same condition, that there be no propriety, no dominion, no *mine* and *thine* distinct; but only that to be every man's, that he can get; and for so long, as he can keep it. And thus much for the ill condition, which man by mere nature is actually placed in; though with a possibility to come out of it, consisting partly in the passions, partly in his reason.

The passions that incline men to peace, are fear of death; desire of such things as are necessary to commodious living; and a hope by their industry to obtain them. . . .

C. John Locke Views More Hopefully the Natural Human Condition

. . . The first capacity of human intellect is that the mind is fitted to receive the impressions made on it, either through the senses by outward objects or by its own operations when it reflects on them. This is the first step a man makes towards the discovery of anything and the groundwork whereupon to build all those notions which ever he shall have naturally in this world. All those sublime thoughts which tower above the clouds and reach as high as heaven itself take their rise and footing here; in all that great extent wherein the mind wanders in those remote speculations it may seem to be elevated with, it stirs not one jot beyond those ideas which sense or reflection have offered for its contemplation. . . .

D. Sir Isaac Newton Explains the Rules for Reasoning in Natural Science, 1687

Rule I

We are to admit no more causes of natural things than such as are both true and sufficient to explain their appearances.

To this purpose the philosophers say that Nature does nothing in vain, and more is in vain when less will serve; for Nature is pleased with simplicity, and affects not the pomp of superfluous causes.

Rule II

Therefore to the same natural effects we must, as far as possible, assign the same causes.

As to respiration in a man and in a beast; the descent of stones in *Europe* and in *America;* the light of our culinary fire and of the sun; the reflection of light in the earth, and in the planets.

Rule III

The qualities of bodies, which admit neither intensification nor remission of degrees, and which are found to belong to all bodies within the reach of our experiments, are to be esteemed the universal qualities of all bodies whatsoever.

For since the qualities of bodies are only known to us by experiments, we are to hold for universal all such as universally agree with experiments; and such as are not liable to diminution can never be quite taken away. We are certainly not to relinquish the evidence of experiments for the sake of dreams and vain fictions of our own devising; nor are we to recede from the analogy of Nature, which is wont to be simple, and always consonant to itself. We no other way know the extension of bodies than by our senses, nor do these reach it in all bodies; but because we perceive extension in all that are sensible, therefore we ascribe it universally to all others also. That abundance of bodies are hard, we learn by experience; and because the hardness of the whole arises from the hardness of the parts, we therefore justly infer the hardness of the undivided particles not only of the bodies we feel but of all others. That all bodies are impenetrable, we gather not from reason, but from sensation. The bodies which we handle we find impenetrable, and thence conclude impenetrability to be an universal property of all bodies whatsoever. That all bodies are movable, and endowed with certain powers (which we call the inertia) of persevering in their motion, or in their rest, we only infer from the like properties observed in the bodies which we have seen. The extension, hardness, impenetrability, mobility, and inertia of the whole, result form the extension, hardness, impenetrability, mobility, and inertia of the parts; and hence we conclude the least particles of all bodies to be also all extended, and hard and impenetrable, and movable, and endowed with their proper inertia. And this is the foundation of all philosophy. Moreover, that the divided but contiguous particles of bodies may be separated from one another, is matter of observation; and, in the particles that remain undivided, our minds are able to distinguish yet lesser parts, as is mathematically demonstrated. But whether the parts so distinguished, and not yet divided, may, by the powers of Nature, be actually divided and separated from

one another, we cannot certainly determine. Yet, had we the proof of but one experiment that any undivided particle, in breaking a hard and solid body, suffered a division, we might by virtue of this rule conclude that the undivided as well as the divided particles may be divided and actually separated to infinity.

Lastly, if it universally appears, by experiments and astronomical observations, that all bodies about the earth gravitate towards the earth, and that in proportion to the quantity of matter which they severally contain; that the moon likewise, according to the quantity of its matter, gravitates towards the earth; that, on the other hand, our sea gravitates towards the moon; and all the planets one towards another; and the comets in like manner towards the sun; we must, in consequence of this rule, universally allow that all bodies whatsoever are endowed with a principle of mutual gravitation. For the argument from the appearances concludes with more force for the universal gravitation of all bodies than for their impenetrability; of which, among those in the celestial regions, we have no experiments, nor any manner of observation. Not that I affirm gravity to be essential to bodies: by their *vis insita* [force of inertia] I mean nothing but their inertia. This is immutable. Their gravity is diminished as they recede from the earth.

Rule IV

In experimental philosophy we are to look upon propositions inferred by general induction from phenomena as accurately or very nearly true, notwithstanding any contrary hypotheses that may be imagined, till such time as other phenomena occur, by which they may either be made more accurate, or liable to exceptions.

This rule we must follow, that the argument of induction may not be evaded by hypotheses.

E. Newton Declines to Derive Wider Implications from His Discoveries

The Hypothesis of deriving the Frame of the World by mechanical Principles from Matter evenly spread through the Heavens, being inconsistent with my System, I had considered it very little before your Letters put me upon it, and therefore trouble you with a Line or two more about it, if this comes not too late for your Use.

In my former I represented that the diurnal Rotations of the Planets could not be derived from Gravity, but required a divine Arm to impress them. And tho' Gravity might give the Planets a Motion of Descent towards the Sun, either directly or with some little Obliquity, yet the transverse Motions by which they revolve in their several Orbs, required the divine Arm to impress them according to the Tangents of their Orbs. I would now add, that the Hypothesis of Matter's being at first evenly spread through the Heavens, is, in my Opinion, inconsistent with the Hypothesis of innate Gravity, without a Supernatural Power to reconcile them, and therefore it infers a Deity. For if there be innate Gravity, it is impossible now for the Matter of the Earth and all the Planets and Stars to fly up from them, and become evenly spread throughout all the Heavens, without a Supernatural Power; and certainly that which can never be hereafter without a Supernatural Power, could never be heretofore without the same Power.

You queried, whether Matter evenly spread throughout a finite space, of some other Figure than spherical, would not in falling down towards a central Body, cause that Body to be of the same Figure with the whole Space, and I answered, yes. But in my Answer it is to be supposed that the Matter descends directly downwards to that Body, and that that Body has no diurnal Rotation.

This, Sir, is all I would add to my former Letters.

Document Set 17.8 References

A. Blaise Pascal Wagers on God's Existence
   Pascal, *Pensées,* trans. W. F. Trotter (New York: Modern Library, 1941), 73–82.
B. Thomas Hobbes Takes a Bleak View of Humanity's Natural State
   Hobbes, *Leviathan,* in Lacey Baldwin Smith and Jean Reeder Smith, eds., *The Past Speaks,* 2d ed. (Lexington, Mass.: D. C. Heath, 1993), 1:377–378.
C. John Locke Views More Hopefully the Natural Human Condition
   Locke, *Essay Concerning Human Understanding,* in Smith and Smith, 1:410–411.
D. Sir Isaac Newton Explains the Rules for Reasoning in Natural Science, 1687
   Newton, *Principia Mathematica,* trans. Andrew Motte (1729), rev. Florian Cajori (Berkeley and Los Angeles: University of California Press, 1947), 398–400.
E. Newton Declines to Derive Wider Implications from His Discoveries
   Isaac Newton's Papers and Letters on Natural Philosophy and Related Documents, I. Bernard Cohen, ed. (Cambridge, Mass.: Harvard University Press, 1978), 310–312.

18

New Societies and the Early Enlightenment, 1690–1740

The Rise of the European Colonial Empires

In 1700, according to Document A of this set, the English Parliament severely restricted the import of various kinds of Asian cloth. Besides attesting to the expansion of world-wide trading links by the early eighteenth century, in what ways does this legislation reflect mercantilist concerns? Why import *any* of the banned goods if they were simply to be warehoused under lock and key?

Slave trading and the creation of slave-labor plantation economies were central to the rise of eighteenth-century colonial empires. In Document B a Dutch sea captain explains the details of slaving in West Africa. In Document C a West African named Olaudah Equiano narrates a victim's experience. Converted to Christianity and literate in English, he had the rare good luck eventually to become emancipated and settle in London, where in the late eighteenth century he published his moving description of what it meant to be enslaved.

England's Virginia colony developed full-fledged black slavery by the beginning of the eighteenth century, distinguishing such hereditary bondage from the temporary loss of freedom endured by white indentured servants. A 1705 law (Document D) enacted by the Virginia legislature authorized local sheriffs to hunt down runaway black slaves. The harshest conditions of slavery, however, prevailed on the large plantations of Brazil, the West Indies, and South Carolina, on which sugar was raised and milled for export under conditions that effectively worked the slaves to death. A Swiss traveler in the mid eighteenth century left a description of the French colony of Saint-Domingue

(today Haiti) that makes clear why the colony's labor supply had to be constantly replenished with fresh bodies from Africa (Document E). Such accounts moved a French priest, the Abbé Raynal, in 1780 to call for liberation of the West Indian slaves by any means possible, including violent insurrection (Document F).

Of foreign lands, the French Baron de Montesquieu (1689–1755) in reality knew only England well. He published his *Persian Letters* (Document G) in 1721, knowing practically nothing about Persia, to debunk French customs of which he disapproved by having exotic foreigners express amazement at them. In writing the *Letters* he demonstrated that European ways of life were neither natural nor inevitable. What, in your opinion, is the value of considering Montesquieu's satire in the context of Europe's increasingly aggressive encounter with the wider world?

A. Parliament Imposes Import Controls and Forbids Smuggling, 1700

Whereas it is most evident, that the continuance of the trade to the East Indies, in the same manner and proportions as it hath been for two years last past, must inevitably be to the great detriment of this kingdom, by exhausting the treasure thereof, and melting down the coin, and taking away the labor of the people, whereby very many of the manufacturers of this nation are become excessively burdensome and chargeable to their respective parishes, and others are thereby compelled to seek for employment in foreign parts: for remedy whereof be it enacted . . . That from and after [September 29, 1701] all wrought silk, bengalls,[1] and stuffs mixed with silk or herba, of the manufacture of Persia, China, or East India, and all calicoes, painted, dyed, printed, or stained there, which are or shall be imported into this kingdom, shall not be worn, or otherwise used within this kingdom of England, dominion of Wales, or town of Berwick upon Tweed, but under such limitations as are herein after mentioned and expressed.

II. And for the better effecting the same, be it enacted . . . that all such . . . [goods] which are or shall be imported into this kingdom[2] shall, after entry thereof, be forthwith carried and put into such warehouse or warehouses, as shall be for that purpose approved of by the commissioners of his Majesty's customs for the time being. . . .

III. And for preventing all clandestine importing or bringing into this kingdom . . . any of the aforesaid goods hereby prohibited, or intended to be prohibited, from being worn or used in England; be it further enacted by the authority aforesaid, That if any person or persons, or bodies corporate, from and after [September 29, 1701], shall import or bring into any port of or in this kingdom . . . other than the port of London, any of the aforesaid prohibited goods, or into the port of London, and shall not make due entries of such goods so imported, or brought in, the same shall be, and is hereby adjudged, deemed, accounted, and taken to be clandestine running thereof, and such person or persons, or bodies corporate so offending therein, and their abettors, shall not only forfeit and lose the said goods so clandestinely run, as aforesaid, but also the sum of fine hundred pounds. . . .

IV. And be it further enacted, That if any question or doubt shall arise where the said goods were manufactured, the proof shall lie upon the owner or owners thereof, and not upon the prosecutor; any law, usage, or custom to the contrary notwithstanding.

V. And be it further enacted by the authority aforesaid, That if any action, bill, plaint, suit, or information, shall be commenced, or prosecuted against any person or persons, for any seizure, or other thing to be made or done, in pursuance or in execution of any thing before in this act contained,

such person or persons, so sued in any court whatsoever, may plead the general issue, and give this act and the special matter in evidence, for their excuse or justification. . . .

VI. And for preventing clandestinely carrying out of the said warehouses any of the said goods hereby prohibited, and by this act intended for exportation, as aforesaid; be it further enacted by the authority aforesaid, That the warehouse-keeper or warehouse-keepers shall keep one or more book or books, wherein he or they shall fairly enter or write down an exact, particular, and true account of all and every chest, bale, and number of pieces therein contained, of such of the aforesaid goods only, which shall be brought into, and carried out of, his or their said warehouse or warehouses, and the days and times when the same shall be so brought in and carried out; and shall every six months in the year transmit in writing an exact account thereof, upon oath, to the said commissioners, together with an exact account how much shall be remaining in his or their said warehouse or warehouses respectively; and the said commissioners are hereby impowered and injoined, within one month after the same shall be transmitted to them, as aforesaid, to appoint one or more person or persons to inspect the said book or books, warehouse or warehouses, and examine the said accounts, and to lay a true account of the same before the Parliament. . . .

VIII. Provided always, and be it further enacted, That it shall and may be lawful to and for the proprietor or proprietors of the said goods so lodged in any warehouse or warehouses, as aforesaid, to affix one lock to every such warehouse or warehouses, the key of which shall remain in the custody of the said proprietor or proprietors; and that he or they may view, sort, or deliver the said goods, in order for exportation, as aforesaid, in the presence of the said warehouse-keeper or warehouse-keepers, who is and are hereby obliged, at seasonable times, to give attendance for that purpose. . . .

B. The Dutch Captain Willem Bosman Describes Trading for Slaves in Guinea, c. 1700

Not a few in our country fondly imagine that parents here sell their children, men their wives, and one brother the other. But those who think so, do deceive themselves; for this never happens on any other account but that of necessity, or some great crime; but most of the slaves that are offered to us, are prisoners of war, which are sold by the victors as their booty.

---

[1] A type of cloth imported from Bengal, India
[2] Scotland and Ireland are excluded from the law.

When these slaves come to Fida, they are put in prison all together; and when we treat concerning buying them, they are all brought out together in a large plain; where, by our surgeons, whose province it is, they are thoroughly examined, even to the smallest member, and that naked both men and women, without the least distinction or modesty. . . .

The invalids and the maimed being thrown out, as I have told you, the remainder are numbered, and it is entered who delivered them. In the meanwhile, a burning iron, with the arms or name of the companies, lies in the fire, with which our are marked on the breast. This is done that we may distinguish them from the slaves of the English, French, or others (which are also marked with their mark), and to prevent the Negroes exchanging them for worse, at which they have a good hand. I doubt not but this trade seems very barbarous to you, but since it is followed by mere necessity, it must go on; but we yet take all possible care that they are not burned too hard, especially the women, who are more tender than the men.

We are seldom long detained in the buying of these slaves, because their price is established, the women being one fourth or fifth part cheaper than the men. The disputes which we generally have with the owners of these slaves are, that we will not give them such goods as they ask for them, especially the *boesies* [cowry shells] (as I have told you, the money of this country) of which they are very fond, though we generally make a division on this head, in order to make one part of the goods help off another; because those slaves which are paid for in *boesies,* cost the company one half more than those bought with other goods. . . .

When we have agreed with the owners of the slaves, they are returned to their prison; where, from that time forwards, they are kept at our charge, cost us two pence a day a slave; which serves to subsist them, like our criminals, on bread and water: so that to save charges, we send them on board our ships with the very first opportunity, before which their masters strip them of all they have on their backs; so that they come to us stark-naked, as well women as men: in which condition they are obliged to continue, if the master of the ship is not so charitable (which he commonly is) as to bestow something on them to cover their nakedness.

You would really wonder to see how these slaves live on board; for though their number sometimes amounts to six or seven hundred, yet by the careful management of our masters of ships, they are so [well] regulated, that it seems incredible. And in this particular our nation exceeds all other Europeans; for as the French, Portuguese, and English slave-ships are always foul and stinking; on the contrary, our are for the most part clean and neat.

The slaves are fed three times a day with indifferent good victuals, and much better than they eat in their own country. Their lodging place is divided into two parts; one of which is appointed for the men, the other for the women, each sex being kept apart. Here they lie as close together as it is possible for them to be crowded. . . .

C. The West African Olaudah Equiano Is Brought Aboard a Slave Ship

The first object which saluted my eyes when I arrived on the coast was the sea, and a slave ship, which was then riding at anchor, and waiting for its cargo. These filled me with astonishment, which was soon converted into terror, which I am yet at a loss to describe nor the then feelings of my mind. When I was carried on board I was immediately handled, and tossed up, to see if I were sound by some of the crew; and I was now persuaded that I had got into a world of bad spirits, and that they were going to kill me. Their complexions too differing so much from ours, their long hair, and the language they spoke, which was very different from any I had ever heard, united to confirm me in this belief. Indeed, such were the horrors of my views and fears at the moment, that, if ten thousand worlds had been my own, I would have parted with them all to have exchanged my condition with that of the meanest slave in my own country. When I looked around the ship too, and saw a large furnace or copper boiling, and a multitude of black people of every description chained together, every one of their countenances expressing dejection and sorrow, I no longer doubted of my fate; and, quite overpowered with horror and anguish, I fell motionless on the deck and fainted. When I recovered a little, I found some black people about me, who, I believed were some of those who brought me on board, and had been receiving their pay; they talked to me in order to cheer me, but all in vain. I asked them if we were not to be eaten by those white men with horrible looks, red faces, and long hair? They told me I was not; and one of the crew brought me a small portion of spirituous liquor in a wine glass; but, being afraid of him, I would not take it out of his hand. One of the blacks therefore took it from him, and gave it to me, and I took a little down my palate, which, instead of reviving me, as they thought it would, threw me into the greatest consternation at the strange feeling it produced, having never tasted any such liquor before. Soon after this, the blacks who brought me on board went off, and left me abandoned to despair. I now saw myself deprived of any chance of returning to my native country, or even the least glimpse of hope of gaining the shore, which I now considered as friendly; and I even wished for my former slavery, in preference to my present situation, which was filled with horrors of every kind, still heightened by my ignorance of what I was to undergo. I was not long suffered to indulge my grief; I was soon put down under the decks, and there I received such a salutation in my nostrils as I had never experienced in my life; so that, with the loathsomeness of the stench, and crying together, I became so sick and low that I was not able to eat, nor had I the least desire to taste any thing. I now wished for the last friend, Death, to relieve me; but soon, to my grief, two of the white men offered me eatables; and, on my refusing to eat, one of them held me fast by the hands, and laid me across, I think, the windlass, and tied my feet, while the other flogged me severely. . . .

D. Virginia Prescribes the Laws of Slavery

It shall be lawful for any person or persons whatsoever, to kill and destroy such slaves by such ways and means as he, she, or they shall think fit, without accusation or impeachment of any crime for the same: And if any slave, that hath run away and lain out as aforesaid, shall be apprehended by the sheriff, or any other person, upon the application of the owner of the said slave, it shall and may be lawful for the county court, to order such punishment to the said slave, either *by dismembering,* or any other way, not touching his life, as they in their discretion shall think fit, for the reclaiming any such incorrigible slave, and terrifying others from the like practices.

E. A Swiss Traveler Observes Plantation Slave Labor in Saint-Domingue, 1785

They were about a hundred men and women of different ages, all occupied in digging ditches in a cane-field, the majority of them naked or covered with rags. The sun shone down with full force on their heads. Sweat rolled from all parts of their bodies. Their limbs, weighed down by the heat, fatigued with the weight of their picks and by the resistance of the clayey soil baked hard enough to break their imple-

ments, strained themselves to overcome every obstacle. A mournful silence reigned. Exhaustion was stamped on every face, but the hour of rest had not yet come. The pitiless eye of the Manager patrolled the gang and several foremen armed with long whips moved periodically between them, giving stinging blows to all who, worn out by fatigue, were compelled to take a rest—men or women, young or old.

F. The Abbé Reynal Calls for a Black Liberator of America

If self-interest alone prevails with nations and their masters, there is another power. Nature speaks in louder tones than philosophy or self-interest. Already are there established two colonies of fugitive negroes, whom treaties and power protect from assault. Those lightnings announce the thunder. A courageous chief only is wanted. Where is he, that great man whom Nature owes to her vexed, oppressed and tormented children? Where is he? He will appear, doubt it not; he will come forth and raise the sacred standard of liberty. This venerable signal will gather around him the companions of his misfortune. More impetuous than the torrents, they will everywhere leave the indelible traces of their just resentment. Everywhere people will bless the name of the hero who shall have reestablished the rights of the human race; everywhere will they raise trophies in his honour.

G. Montesquieu's Imaginary Persian Observes European Ways

The King of France is the most powerful ruler in Europe. . . . He has been known to undertake or sustain major wars with no other funds but what he gets from selling honorific titles, and by miracle of human vanity, his troops are paid, his fortresses supplied, and his fleets equipped.

Moreover, this king is a great magician. He exerts authority even over the minds of his subjects; he makes them think what he wants. If there are only a million crowns in the exchequer, and he needs two million, all he has to do is persuade them that one crown is worth two, and they believe it [Montesquieu is referring here to currency debasement]. . . .

You must not be amazed at what I tell you about this prince: there is another magician, stronger than he, who controls his mind as completely as he controls other people's. This magician is called the Pope. He will make the king believe that three are only one [the doctrine of the trinity], or else that the bread one eats is not bread, or that the wine one drinks not wine [the sacrament of communion], and a thousand other things of the same kind.

Document Set 18.1 References

A. Parliament Imposes Import Controls and Forbids Smuggling, 1700
Walter Arnstein, ed., *The Past Speaks*, 2d ed. (Lexington, Mass.: D. C. Heath, 1993), 2:62–63.
B. The Dutch Captain Willem Bosman Describes Trading for Slaves in Guinea, c. 1700
Bosman, *"A New and Accurate Description . . ."* (London: 1721), in David Northrup, ed., *The Atlantic Slave Trade* (Lexington, Mass.: D. C. Heath, 1994) 72–73.
C. The West African Olaudah Equiano Is Brought Aboard a Slave Ship
The Interesting Narrative of the Life of Olaudah Equiano (London: 1793), in Northrup, 77–78.
D. Virginia Prescribes the Laws of Slavery
A. Leon Higginbotham, Jr., *In the Matter of Color: Race and the American Legal Process (The Colonial Period)* (New York: Oxford University Press, 1978), 56.
E. A Swiss Traveler Observes Plantation Slave Labor in Saint-Domingue, 1785
Girod-Chantrans, in C. L. R. James, *The Black Jacobins*, 2d ed. (New York: Vintage Books, 1963), 10.
F. The Abbé Reynal Calls for a Black Liberator of America
Abbé Reynal, *Philosophical and Political History . . .*, in James, 25.
G. Montesquieu's Imaginary Persian Observes European Ways
Montesquieu, *Persian Letters*, trans. C. J. Betts (Harmondsworth, England: Penguin, 1973), 72–73.

DOCUMENT SET 18.2
Modernizing Muscovite Russia

The emergence of Russia as a major political and military power, and as a society westernizing on orders from the tsar, was one of the most significant changes in eighteenth-century Europe. Yet the Russia that Peter the Great (*1685–1725) painfully pushed onto the European stage remained a highly distinctive country, still deeply influenced by its old Muscovite past. For example, serfdom had gained the force of law in the Muscovite Code of Law of 1649 (Document A), more than a generation before Peter's time. Serfdom depended on the power conceded to landlords to prevent their peasants from migrating to escape debts, and it permitted landlords to recover peasants at any time. Determined as well to force the nobility into life-long service, Peter tightened the bonds of serfdom to assure his bureaucrats and army officers a stable income from their estates.

Peter turned the Russian Orthodox church into an arm of the government—for example, by abolishing the office of patriarch and substituting a committee of laymen called the Holy Synod—so that the old church had lost its independence by the late seventeenth century. Popular sentiment was probably on the side of the sectarians called Old Believers, who resisted the liturgical and organizational changes accepted by the official state church. To gauge the Old Believers' state of mind, read Document B, an extract from the autobiography of the Archpriest Avvakum (1620–1682), a passionate opponent of the new order who eventually died at the stake. The struggle between schismatics and the state continued throughout Peter's reign—and for a very long time thereafter—but the supremacy of the state was never in doubt.

Peter's most visible internal reforms featured the creation of a European-looking capital city—St. Petersburg—and a Western-style ruling class. Documents C to F all comment on aspects of this transformation: building St. Petersburg, legislation ordering officials to wear German-style clothes and to shave (a practice repugnant to traditional Russian males, who regarded cutting the beard as an affront to the presumably bewhiskered God the Father), and the advancement of technically skilled foreign recruits like the Scottish general Alexander Gordon.

Using these documents and relying also on the *Challenge of the West,* prepare an analysis of Peter's aims and methods in modernizing Muscovite Russia.

A. The Muscovite Law Code of 1649 Prescribes the Rules of Serfdom

1. Any peasants of the Sovereign and labourers of the crown villages and black volosts [administrative areas] who have fled from the Sovereign's crown villages and from the black volosts . . . are to be brought to the crown villages of the Sovereign and to the black volosts to their old lots according to the registers of inquisition with wives and children and with all their peasant property without term of years.

2. Also should there be any lords holding an estate by inheritance of service who start to petition the Sovereign about their fugitive peasants and labourers and say that their peasants and labourers who have fled from them live in the crown villages of the Sovereign and in black volosts or among the artisans in the artisan quarters of towns or among the musketeers, cossacks or among the gunners, or among any other serving men in the towns . . . [there follows a long list of all the possible places to which fugitives might have fled] then those peasants and labourers in accordance with law and the [right of] search are to be handed over according to the inquisition registers which the officers handed in to the Service Tenure Department.

20. But if any people come to anyone in an estate held by inheritance or service and say that they are free and those people want to live under them as peasants or as labourers, then those people to whom they come are to question them: who are those free people, and where is their birthplace and under whom did they live and where have they come from, and are they not somebody's runaway people, peasants and labourers, and whether they have charters of manumission. And if any say they do not have charters of manumission on them, those holding estates by service and inheritance are to get to know genuinely about such people, are they really free people; and after genuinely getting to know, to take them the same year to be registered. . . .

22. And if any peasants' children deny their fathers and mothers they are to be tortured.

B. The Archpriest Avvakum Defends the Old Believers' Faith and Practices

Thus having remained ten weeks in Pafnutiev in chains, they took me again to Moscow, and in the room of the Cross the bishops held disputation with me. They led me to the Cathedral church, and after the Elevation of the Host they sheared me and the deacon Theodore, and then they cursed us and I cursed them back. And I was heavy at heart for the Mass. And after I had stayed for a time at the patriarchal court, they took us by night to Ugresha,[1] to the monastery of St. Nicholas—and the enemies of God shaved off my beard. . . .

And poor Prince Ivan Vorotynsky came there without the tsar to pray, and he asked to be admitted to my prison cell. But they would not let the hapless man in. I could only, looking through the window, weep over him. My sweet friend feared God, he was Christ's orphan. Christ will not cast him away. Thus always was Christ on our side, and all the boyars were good to us, only the devil was malicious and what could we have done if Christ had left us? They beat my dear Prince Ivan Khovansky with rods and they burnt Isaiah, and the lady Theodosia Morozova they brought to ruin, and they killed her son and tortured her and her sister Eudoxia, beating them with rods; and they parted her from her children and divorced her from her husband, and him they say, Prince Peter Urusov, they married to another wife. But what was there to do? Let them torture those dear ones, they will go to their heavenly bridegroom. In every wise God will cause to pass this troublesome time and will call to himself the bridegroom to his heavenly palace, he the true Sun, our Light and our Hope. . . .

I will tell you yet more of my wanderings when they brought me out of the Pafnutiev Monastery in Moscow and placed me in the guesthouse, and after many wanderings they set me down in the Miracle Monastery, before the patriarchs of all Christendom, and the Russian Nikonites sat there like so many foxes. I spoke of many things in Holy Writ with the patriarchs. God did open my sinful mouth and Christ put them to shame. The last word they spoke to me was this: "Why," said they, "art thou stubborn? The folk of Palestine, Serbia, Albania, the Wallachians, they of Rome and Poland, all these do cross themselves with three fingers, only thou standest out in thine obstinacy and dost cross thyself with two fingers; it is not seemly." And I answered them for Christ thus: "O you teachers of Christendom, Rome

fell away long ago and lies prostrate, and the Poles fell in the like ruin with her, being to the end the enemies of the Christian. And among you orthodoxy is of mongrel breed; and no wonder—if by the violence of the Turkish Mohmut you have become impotent, and henceforth it is you who should come to us to learn. By the gift of God among us there is autocracy; till the time of Nikon, the apostate, in our Russia under our pious princes and tsars the Orthodox faith was pure and undefiled, and in the church was no sedition. Nikon, the wolf, together with the devil, ordained that men should cross themselves with three fingers, but our first shepherds made the sign of the cross and blessed men as of old with two fingers, according to the tradition of our holy fathers, Meletina of Antioch, Theodoret, the blessed Bishop of Cyrene, Peter of Damascus and Maxim the Greek; and so too did our own synod of Moscow, at the time of the Tsar Ivan, bid them, putting their fingers together in that wise, make the sign of the cross and give the blessing, as of old the holy fathers Melety and others taught. Then in the time of Ivan [IV] the Tsar, there were the standard-bearers, Gury and Varsanophy, wonder-workers of Kazan, and Phillip the Abbot of Solovki among the Russian saints. And the patriarchs fell to thinking, and our people began to howl like wolf cubs and to belch out words against their fathers saying, "Our Russian holy men were ignorant, and they understood nothing, they are unlearned folk," said they. "How can one trust them? they have no letters." O Holy God! How hast thou suffered so great reviling of thy holy ones? I, miserable one, was bitter in my heart, but I could do nothing. I abused them as hard as I could . . . them, poor things! Woe to the hapless followers of Nikon! They have perished of their own wickedness and their stubbornness of soul!

Then they brought us from the Vorobiev hills to the guest-house of the Andreevsky Monastery to the Savin suburb, and as though we were robbers, followed after us and left us not, nay, even when we relieved nature. It was both pitable and laughable, as though the devil had blinded them.

Then again we were taken to the St. Nickolas Monastery at Ugresha. And there the tsar sent to me the officer Yury Lutokhin, that I might bless him, and we had much converse concerning this and that.

Then again they brought me to Moscow, to the guesthouse of the Nikolsky Monastery, and they demanded of us yet again a statement of the true faith. After that there were sent more than once to me gentlemen of the bedchamber, diverse persons, Artemon and Dementy. And they spake to me in the name of the tsar; "Archpriest!" they said, "I see thy life that it

---

[1] A village in the vicinity of Moscow.

is pure and undefiled and pleasing unto God, I and the tsarina and our children, be entreated of us." The envoy wept as he spake, and for him I weep always. I was exceeding sorry for him. And again he spake: "I beg of thee, hearken to me. Be thou reconciled with the patriarchs." And I said, "Even if God will that I should die, I will not be joined together with apostates. Thou art my tsar, but they, what have they to do with thee? They have lost their tsar and they have come here to gobble you up. I—say I—will not cease to uplift my hands to heaven until God give thee over to me."

The last word I got from the tsar was, "Wherever," said he, "thou shalt be, do not forget us in thy prayers." And I, sinful one, now, as far as I may, pray to God for him.

XV. Banishment to Pustozersk

After scourging my friends, but not me, they banished me to Pustozersk. And I sent from Pustozersk to the tsar two letters, the first not long but the other longer, what I had said to him, that I wrote also in the letters, and also certain signs of God, which had appeared to me in my prison. Who reads will understand. Also a letter written by the deacon was sent to Moscow by me and the brotherhood as a gift to the True Believers.

C. Peter the Great Founds St. Petersburg

In the year 1703 the tsar took the field early, cantoned his troops in the month of March, and about the 20th of April brought the army together; then marched and invested another small but important place called Nyen-Chance, which surrendered on the 14th of May. The commodious situation of this place made the tsar resolve to erect on it a considerable town, with a strong citadel, consisting of six royal bastions, together with good outworks; this he soon put into execution and called it St. Petersburg, which is now esteemed so strong that it will be scarcely possible for the Swedes ever to take it by force.

As he was digesting the scheme of this, his favorite town, which he designed not only for the place of his residence but the principal harbor of his shipping, as having a communication with the sea by the river Nyen; having duly observed and sounded it all over, he found it would be a very natural project to erect a fort in the isle opposite to the island of Ratusary; which for a whole league over to the land is not above four feet deep. This is a most curious work scarcely to be matched. He went about it in winter, in the month of November, when the ice was so strong that it could bear any weight, causing it to carry materials such as timber, stone, etc. The foundation was thus laid; trees of about thirty feet in length and about fifteen inches thick were taken and joined artfully together into chests ten feet high; these chests were filled with stones of great weight, which sunk down through the sea, and made a very solid foundation, upon which he raised his fort, called Cronstat. . . .

About two hundred fathoms distant from the island Ratusary there is also erected another strong fort, with a tolerable small town, called Cronburgh, where sea officers are commonly lodged. Betwixt Cronstat and Cronburgh is all sea, deep only in the middle, about thirty fathoms broad, so that ships of great burden can pass only one after another. These two forts secure St. Petersburg from any insult by sea, and make it perhaps one of the best and safest harbors in the known world. . . . The work gave no small umbrage to the Swedes. In carrying materials for it there were upwards of eight thousand horses destroyed and near as many men.

D. Peter the Great Orders Certain Subjects to Wear Western Dress and to Shave, 1701–1705

Peter's Decree on Wearing German Clothes, 1701

[All ranks of the service nobility, leading merchants, military personnel, and inhabitants of Moscow and the other towns, except the clergy] are to wear German clothes and hats and footwear and to ride in German saddles; and their wives and children without exception are also so to dress. Henceforth nobody is to wear [traditional] Russian or cossack clothes or to ride in Russian [i.e., Tatar-style] saddles; nor are craftsmen to make such things or to trade in them. And if contrary to this the Great Sovereign's decree some people wear such Russian or cossack clothes and ride in Russian Saddles, the town gate-keepers are to exact a fine from them, [so much] for those on foot and [much more] from those on horseback. Also, craftsmen who make such things and trade in them will be, for their disobedience, severely punished.

Peter's Decree on Shaving, 1705

All courtiers and officials in Moscow and all the other towns, as well as leading merchants and other townsmen, except priests and deacons, must henceforth by this the Great Sovereign's decree shave their beards and mustaches. And whosoever does not wish to do so, but to go about with [traditional Russian] beard and mustache, is to pay a [hefty] fine, according to his rank. . . . And the Department of Land Affairs [in Moscow] is to give [such persons] a badge in receipt, as will the government offices in the other towns, which badges they must wear. And from the peasants a [small] toll is to be exacted every day at the town gates, without which they cannot enter or leave the town. . . .

E. A Frenchman Describes the Enforcement of Peter's Decree on Dress

The tsar labored at the reform of fashions, or, more properly speaking, of dress. Until that time the Russians had always worn long beards, which they cherished and preserved with much care, allowing them to hang down on their bosoms, without even cutting the moustache. With these long beards they wore the hair very short, except the ecclesiastics, who, to distinguish themselves, wore it very long. The tsar, in order to reform that custom, ordered that gentlemen, merchants, and other subjects, except priests and peasants, should each pay a tax of one hundred rubles a year if they wished to keep their beards; the commoners had to pay one kopeck each. Officials were stationed at the gates of the towns to collect that tax, which the Russians regarded as an enormous sin on the part of the tsar and as a thing which tended to the abolition of their religion.

These insinuations, which came from the priests, occasioned the publication of many pamphlets in Moscow, where for that reason alone the tsar was regarded as a tyrant and a pagan; and there were many old Russians who, after having their beards shaved off, saved them preciously, in order to have them placed in their coffins, fearing that they would not be allowed to enter heaven without their beards. As for the young men, they followed the new custom with the more readiness as it made them appear more agreeable to the fair sex.

From the reform in beards we may pass to that of clothes. Their garments, like those of the Orientals, were very long, reaching to the heel. The tsar issued an ordinance abolishing that costume, commanding all the boyars (nobles) and all those who had positions at the court to dress after the French fashion, and likewise to adorn their clothes with gold or silver according to their means.

As for the rest of the people, the following method was employed. A suit of clothes cut accord-ing to the new fashion was hung at the gate of the city, with a decree of enjoining upon all except peasants to have their clothes made on this model, under penalty of being forced to kneel and have all that part of their garments which fell below the knee cut off, or pay two grives every time they entered the town with clothes in the old style. Since the guards at the gates executed their duty in curtailing the garments in a sportive spirit, the people were amused and readily abandoned their old dress, especially in Moscow and its environs, and in the towns which the tsar oftenest visited.

The dress of the women was changed, too. English hairdressing was substituted for the caps and bonnets hitherto worn: bodices, stays, and skirts, for the former undergarment. . . .

The same ordinance also provided that in the future women, as well as men, should be invited to entertainments, such as weddings, banquets, and the like, where both sexes should mingle in the same hall, as in Holland and England. It was likewise added that these entertainments should conclude with concerts and dances, but that only those should be admitted who were dressed in English costumes. His Majesty set the example in all these changes.

F. The Scottish General Alexander Gordon Describes Peter the Great

This great emperor came in a few years to know to a farthing the amount of all his revenues, as also how they were laid out. He was at little or no expense about his person, and by living rather like a private gentleman than a prince he saved wholly that great expense which other monarchs are at in supporting the grandeur of their courts. It was uneasy for him to appear in majesty, which he seldom or never did, but when absolutely necessary, on such occasions as giving audience to ambassadors or the like; so that he had all the pleasure of a great emperor and at the same time that of a private gentleman.

He was a lover of company, and a man of much humor and pleasantry, exceedingly facetious and of vast natural parts. He had no letters; he could only read and write, but had a great regard for learning and was at much pains to introduce it into the country. He rose early; the morning he gave to business till ten or eleven o'clock at the farthest; all the rest of the day, and a great part of the night, to diversion and pleasure. He took his bottle heartily, so must all the company; for when he was merry himself he loved to see everybody so; though at the same time he could not endure habitual drinkers, for such he thought unfit for business.

When he paid a visit to a friend he would pass almost the whole night, not caring to part with good company till past two o'clock in the morning. He never kept guards about his person. . . . He never could abide ceremony, but loved to be spoke to frankly and without reserve.

Document Set 18.2 References

A. The Muscovite Law Code of 1649 Prescribes the Rules of Serfdom
Code of 1649, in Thomas G. Barnes and Gerald D. Feldman, eds., *Renaissance, Reformation, and Absolutism, 1400–1650* (Berkeley and Los Angeles: University of California Press, 1972), 148–151.

B. The Archpriest Avvakum Defends the Old Believers' Faith and Practices
Avvakum, in Serge A. Zinkovsky, ed. and trans., *Medieval Russia's Epics, Chronicles, and Tales* (New York: E. P. Dutton, 1963), 358–359, 362–364.

C. Peter the Great Founds St. Petersburg
Alexander Gordon, *History,* in James Harvey Robinson, ed., *Readings in European History* (Boston: Ginn, 1904), 2:309.

D. Peter the Great Orders Certain Subjects to Wear Western Dress and to Shave, 1701–1705
Laws of Peter I, in James Cracraft, ed., *Major Problems in the History of Imperial Russia* (Lexington, Mass.: D. C. Heath, 1994), 110–111.

E. A Frenchman Describes the Enforcement of Peter's Decree on Dress
Jean Rousset (Ivan Nestesuranoi), in Robinson, 2:310–311.

F. The Scottish General Alexander Gordon Describes Peter the Great
Gordon, in Robinson, 2:308–309.

DOCUMENT SET 18.3
Before the Industrial Revolution: Life and Death in Eighteenth-Century Europe

Spanning a larger chronology than Chapter 8, the documents of this set illustrate important aspects of life in Europe before industrialization (beginning in the mid-eighteenth century and extending well into the next century) transformed society forever.

Document A serves as a reminder of the way in which middle-class English families ate at the end of the seventeenth century. Such a diet was not only characteristic of well-off urbanites but also of the country gentry and prosperous yeomen and tenant farmers. The contrast with the presumably more fastidious French diet is apparent from the writer's comments. Left unsaid is how such fare differed from that consumed by poor tenants, farm laborers, and continental peasants; typically they made do with a monotonous diet of porridge, bread, beer or ale, and sometimes root vegetables like carrots—and a bit of meat on only the rarest of occasions.

Between 1709 and 1720, Mr. and Mrs. Edmund Williamson, gentry in the English county of Bedfordshire, took the trouble to record their family's births and deaths. The terse entries speak for themselves. But they should be weighed against statistics like those tabulated in Document C. These statistics come from eighteenth-century Norway, where sufficiently careful records were being kept (by church and state officials) to permit modern demographers to measure gross trends. What patterns do you notice? What differences do you see between patterns for farmers (rural people with substantial holdings) and cotters (the rural poor)? What do such statistics suggest to you about marriage, reproduction, and premarital sexuality?

Urban crime, to judge from Document D, was not an easily manageable problem even before our own disorderly times. Henry Fielding (1707–1754), the English novelist who wrote *Tom Jones,* was also a London magistrate who founded the forerunner of the modern police force. His *Inquiries into the Causes of Robbers* repays close reading for his analysis of the demoralization and class conflict that he saw as "root causes" of crime—certainly a modern explanation.

The final two documents of this set provide an interesting contrast. Both are reports by traveling, carefully inquiring Englishmen dating from the late eighteenth century. Arthur Young (1741–1820) was an English agricultural expert whose travels through France are an extremely valuable source for under-standing the society of that country on the eve of revolution; his contrasting descriptions (Document E) of prosperous and backward regions are a reminder of the unevenness of change and of the dangers of generalizing too broadly. William Coxe (1747–1828), a clergyman and historian, published in 1783 an account of his extensive travels in Poland (Document F), in which he sympathetically pondered the plight of the desperately poor, enserfed peasantry, utterly dependent on a land-owning nobility that had only recently begun to experiment with freeing their villages from bondage.

A. A French Visitor Comments on the Middle-Class English Diet, About 1695

The English eat a great deal at dinner; they rest a while, and to it again, till they have quite stuffed their paunch. Their supper is moderate: gluttons at noon and abstinent at night. I always heard they were great flesh-eaters, and I found it true. I have known several people in England that never eat any bread, and universally they eat very little: they nibble a few crumbs, while they chew the meat by whole mouthfuls. Generally speaking, the English tables are not delicately served. There are some noblemen that have both French and English cooks, and these eat much after the French manner. But among the middling sort of people . . . they have ten or twelve sorts of common meats, which infallibly take their turns at their tables, and two dishes are their dinners; a pudding, for instance, and a piece of roast beef: another time they will have a piece of boiled beef, and then they salt it some days beforehand, and besiege it with five or six heaps of cabbage, carrots, turnips, or some other herbs or roots, well prepared and salted, and swimming in butter: a leg of roast or boiled mutton, dished up with the same dainties, fowls, pigs, ox-tripes, and tongues, rabbits, pigeons, all well moistened with butter, without larding. Two of these dishes, always served up one after the other, make the usual dinner of a substantial gentleman, or wealthy citizen. When they have boiled meat, there is sometimes one of the company that will have the broth; this is a kind of soup with a little oatmeal in it, and some leaves of thyme or sage, or other such small herbs. They bring up this in as many porringers as there are people that desire it; those that please crumble a little bread into it, and this makes a king of *potage*. The pudding is a dish very difficult to be described, because of the several sorts there are of it; flour, milk, eggs, butter, sugar, suet, marrow, raisins, &c., &c. are the most common ingredients of a pudding. They bake them in an oven, they boil them with meat; they make them fifty several ways. Blessed be he that invented pudding, for it is a manna that hits the palates of all sorts of people; a manna, better than that of the wilderness, because the people are never weary of it. Ah, what an excellent thing is an English pudding! To come in pudding-time, is as much as to say, to come in the most lucky moment in the world. Give an Englishman a pudding, and he shall think it a noble treat in any part of the world. The dessert they never dream of, unless it be a piece of cheese. Fruit is brought only to the tables of the great, and of a small number even among them. It would be unjust to take, in a rigorous sense, all that I have said of these common dishes; for the English eat everything that is produced naturally, as well as any other nation. I say naturally, in opposition to the infinite multitude of your made dishes; for they dress their meat much plainer than we do.

B. Edmund Williamson and His Second Wife Record Births and Deaths, 1709–1720

1709

March 29. My wife fell into labor and a little after 9 in the morning was delivered of a son. Present: aunt Taylor, cousin White, sister Smith, cousin Clarkson, widow Hern, Mrs. Howe, midwife, Mr[s]. Wallis, nurse, Mrs. Holms, Eleanor Hobbs, servants.
April 4. He was baptised by Doctor Battle by the name of John. . . .
[April] 16. The child died about 1 o'clock in the morning.

1711

Sept. 17. My said wife was delivered of a son just before 4 in the morning. Present: Mrs. Thomas Molyneux's lady and maid, Mrs. Mann, midwife, Margaret Williamson, nurse, Susan Nuthall, servant.
Oct. 4. He was baptised by Mr. Trabeck by the name of Talbot after my grandmother's name. Sir John Talbot and John Pulteny esquire were gossips,[1] with my sister Smith godmother. . . .

1713

June 9. About 8 at night my said wife began her labor.
[June] 10. Half an hour after 1 in the morning was brought to bed of a son. Present: Mrs. Molyneux, Mrs. Bisset, Mrs. Mann, midwife, Nurse Williamson, Susan Nuthall and Betty Ginger, servants.
[June] 30. Baptised by Mr. Mompesson of Mansfield by the name of Edmond. . . .

1715

March 7. My said wife was brought to bed of a daughter 10 minutes before 6 in the morning. Present: Mrs. Molyneux, Mrs. Mann, midwife, Nurse Williamson, Mary Evans, Mary Cole and Mary Wheeler, servants.
[March] 29. Was baptised by Dr. Mandivel, chancellor of Lincoln, by the name of Christian.

1716

March 9. My wife was delivered of a daughter at 7 at night. Present: aunt Taylor, Mrs. Molyneux, Mrs. Oliver, Mrs. Mann, midwife, Mary Smith, nurse, Jane Kensey, and Mary Wheeler, servants.
[March] 31. Was baptised by Mr. Widmore, the reader of St. Margaret's, by the name of Elizanna. . . . Registered in St. Margaret's, Westminster, as all the rest were.
April 27. Died, was buried in the new chapel yard in the Broadway.

1718

Jan. 21. [Mrs. Williamson:] I was brought to bed of a son about 2 in the morning, Mrs. Mann, midwife, nurse Chatty, dry-nurse, present; Mrs. Taylor, Mrs. White and Mrs. Molyneux, Jane Beadle; servants: Mary Wells, Jane Griffith, Edmond Kinward. He was baptised by Mr. Widmore, reader of St. Margaret's, Westminster, by the name of Francis. . . .

1719

Feb. 21. [Mrs. Williamson:] I was brought to bed of a son between 6 and 7 in the evening, Mrs. Mann, midwife, nurse Chatty, dry-nurse; present: aunt Taylor, Mrs. Molyneux and Jane Beadle; servants: Rebecca Shippy, Betty Hall and Mathew Dowect.
March 7. He was baptised by Mr. Widmore, reader of St. Margaret's, Westminster, by the name of William. . . .
[N.d.] Died and buried at Hadley.

1720

June. My wife brought to bed of a daughter, but the child did not live a minute.
July 21. My wife died and was buried at Isleworth.
Sept. 9. [Francis] died of the smallpox at Nurse Ward's in Hampstead, and was buried at Hadley.

---

[1] Godfathers

C. Vital Statistics from Eighteenth-Century Norway

Comparative Demographic Profile, Eastern Norwegian Towns, Eighteenth Century

Median Age at Marriage, First Marriages, Both Sexes.

Men		Farmers	Cottars[2]	Miners/Ironworkers
Ullensaker	1733–1789	29.1	28.6	—
Nesodden	Information lacking			
Bø	1727–1815	26.3	27.6	26.5
Sandsvær	1750–1801	29.2	29.2	27.1
Rendalen	1733–1780	28.2	33.3	—
Women				
Ullensaker	1733–1789	26.0	28.6	—
Nesodden	1710–1800	25.4	31.0	—
Bø	1727–1815	22.8	26.9	24.8
Sandsvær	1750–1780	24.7	27.8	26.3
Rendalen	1733–1780	24.5	30.5	—

Remarriage for Social Groups. Percentage. Both Sexes.

	Men				*Women*			
	Ullensaker 1733– 1789	Bø 1727– 1815	Sandsvær 1750– 1801	Ullensaker 1790– 1839	Ullensaker 1733– 1789	Bø 1727– 1815	Sandsvær 1750– 1801	Ullensaker 1790– 1839
Farmers	54	69	48	44	37	45	39	33
Cottars	67	70	50	55	39	36	26	25
Miners	—	67	67	—	—	14	31	—
Total	59	69	54	49	38	39	33	30

Permanent Celibacy. Percentage of Age Groups 45–49, 50–54 Not Married, Both sexes.

	Ullensaker	Nesodden	Bø	Sandsvær	Rendalen
Men	5.7	11.4	4.5	6.6	18.5
Women	4.3	10.3	9.8	9.9	10.7

Percentage of Brides That Had First Birth Before or 0–7 Months After the Wedding.

		Farmers	Cottars	Miners/Ironworkers
Ullensaker	1733–1789	26	58	—
Nesodden	1710–1800	29	49	—
Bø	1727–1815	33	47	67
Sandsvær	1750–1801	33	60	53
Rendalen	1733–1780	45	61	—

[2] A cottar is a tenant renting land from a farmer or landlord.

Survivors per 1,000 Liveborn Babies at Different Age. Different Social Groups.

		1 Year	5 Years	10 Years	15 Years
Ullensaker	Farmers	802	637	593	569
	Cottars	724	565	511	470
Bø	Farmers	811	704	676	652
	Cottars	804	705	655	626
	Ironworkers	800	700	663	625
Sandsvær	Farmers	835	737	704	690
	Cottars	833	755	722	710
	Miners	737	600	570	558
Rendalen	Farmers	879	811	755	730
	Cottars	841	732	620	588

Expected Numbers of Years Still to Live at the Age of 0. Both Sexes.

		1727–49	1750–69	1770–89	1790–1815
Bø	Women	38.3	39.2	41.8	41.7
	Men	36.6	37.3	39.7	39.6

Average Number of Children per Family. Different Social Groups and Total.

	Farmers	Cottars	Miners	Total
Ullensaker	4.31	3.51	—	3.91
Nesodden	No information			
Bø	4.90	3.60	—	4.20
Sandsvær	4.44	3.10	3.95	3.86
Rendalen	5.02	2.78	—	3.85

D. Henry Fielding Studies London's Crime Wave, 1751

The great increase of robberies within these few years is an evil which to me appears to deserve some attention; and the rather as it seems (though already become so flagrant) not yet to have arrived to that height of which it is capable, and which it is likely to attain; for diseases in the political, as in the natural body, seldom fail going on to their crisis, especially when nourished and encouraged by faults in the constitution. In fact, I make no doubt, but that the streets of this town, and the roads leading to it, will shortly be impassable without the utmost hazard; nor are we threatened with seeing less dangerous gangs of rogues among us, than those which the Italians call the banditti. . . .

I cannot help thinking it high time to put some stop to the farther progress of such impudent and audacious insults, not only on the properties of the subject, but on the national justice, and on the laws themselves. The means of accomplishing this (the best which suggest themselves to me I shall submit to the public consideration after having first inquired into the causes of the present growth of this evil, and whence we have great reason to apprehend its farther increase. . . .

First then, I think, that the vast torrent of luxury,

which of late years hath poured itself into this nation, hath greatly contributed to produce, among many others, the mischief I here complain of. I am not here to satirize the great, among whom luxury is probably rather a moral than a political evil. But vices no more than diseases will stop with them; for bad habits are as infectious by example, as the plague itself by contact. In free countries, at least, it is a branch of liberty claimed by the people to be as wicked and as profligate as their superiors. Thus while the nobleman will emulate the grandeur of a prince, and the gentleman will aspire to the proper state of the nobleman, the tradesman steps from behind his counter into the vacant place of the gentleman. Nor doth the confusion end here; it reaches the very dregs of the people, who aspiring still to a degree beyond that which belongs to them, and not being able by the fruits of honest labor to support the state which they affect, they disdain the wages to which their industry would entitle them; and abandoning themselves to idleness, the more simple and poor-spirited betake themselves to a state of starving and beggary, while those of more art and courage become thieves, sharpers [swindlers], and robbers. . . .

But the expense of money, and loss of time, with their certain consequences, are not the only evils which attend the luxury of the vulgar; drunkenness is almost inseparably annexed to the pleasures of such people. A vice by no means to be construed as a spiritual offense alone, since so many temporal mischiefs arise from it; amongst which are very frequently robbery, and murder itself. . . .

The drunkenness I here intend [refer to] is that acquired by the strongest intoxicating liquors, and particularly by that poison called *Gin*; which I have great reason to think is the principal sustenance (if it may be so called) of more than a hundred thousand people in this metropolis. Many of these wretches there are who swallow pints of this poison within the twenty-four hours; the dreadful effects of which I have the misfortune every day to see, and to smell too. But I have no need to insist on my own credit, or on that of my informers; the great revenue arising from the tax on this liquor (the consumption of which is almost wholly confined to the lowest order of people) will prove the quantity consumed better than any other evidence.

E. Arthur Young Tours France to Observe Agricultural Practices, 1787

9th. Enter a different country, with the new province of Quercy, which is part of Guienne; not near so beautiful as Limosin, but, to make amends, it is far better cultivated. Thanks to maize [American corn], which does wonders! Pass Noailles, on the summit of a high hill, the chateau of the Marshal Duke of that name.—Enter a calcareous country, and lose chestnuts at the same time.

In going down to Souillac, there is a prospect that must universally please: it is a bird's-eye view of a delicious little valley sunk deep amongst some very bold hills that enclose it; a margin of wild mountain contrasts the extreme beauty of the level surface below, a scene of cultivation scattered with fine walnut trees; nothing can apparently exceed the exuberant fertility of this spot.

Souillac is a little town in a thriving state, having some rich merchants. They receive staves from the mountains of Auvergne by their river Dordonne, which is navigable eight months in the year; these they export to Bourdeaux and Libourn; also wine, corn, and cattle, and import salt in great quantities. It is not in the power of an English imagination to figure the animals that waited upon us here, at the Chapeau Rouge. Some things that called themselves by the courtesy of Souillac women, but in reality walking dung-hills.—But a neatly dressed clean waiting girl at an inn will be looked for in vain in France.—34 miles.

10th. Cross the Dordonne by a ferry; the boat well contrived for driving in at one end, and out at the other, without the abominable operation, common in England, of beating horses till they leap into them; the price is as great a contrast as the excellence; we paid for an English whisky, a French cabriolet, one saddle-horse, and six persons, no more than 50 sous (2s. Id.) I have paid half-a-crown a wheel in England for execrable ferries, passed over at the hazard of the horses' limbs.—This river runs in a very deep valley between two ridges of high hills: extensive views, all scattered with villages and single houses; an appearance of great population. Chestnuts on a calcareous soil, contrary to the Limosin maxim.

Pass Payrac, and meet many beggars, which we had not done before. All the country, girls and women, are without shoes or stockings; and the ploughmen at their work have neither sabots [wooden shoes] nor feet to their stockings. This is a poverty that strikes at the root of national prosperity; a large consumption among the poor being of more consequence than among the rich: the wealth of a nation lies in its circulation and consumption; and the case of poor people abstaining from the use of manufactures of leather and wool ought to be considered as an evil of the first magnitude. It reminded me of the misery of Ireland. Pass Pont-de-Rodez, and come to high land, whence we enjoyed an immense and singular prospect of ridges, hills, vales, and gentle slopes, rising one beyond another in every direction, with few masses of wood, but many scattered trees. At least forty miles are tolerably distinct to the eye, and without a level acre; the sun, on the point of being set, illumined part of it, and displayed a vast number of villages and scattered farms. The mountains of Auvergne, at the distance of 100 miles, added to the view. Pass by several cottages, exceedingly well built of stone and slate or tiles, yet without any glass to the windows; can a country be likely to thrive where the great object is to spare manufactures? Women picking weeds into their aprons for their cows, another sign of poverty I observed, during the whole way from Calais.—30 miles.

F. An English Traveler Comments on the Consequences of Serfdom in Eighteenth-Century Poland

Peasants belonging to individuals are at the absolute disposal of their master, and have scarcely any positive security, either for their properties or their lives. Until 1768 the Statutes of Poland only exacted a fine from a lord who killed his slave; but in that year a decree passed, that the murder of a peasant was a capital crime; yet, as the law in question requires such an accumulation of evidence as is seldom to be obtained, it has more appearance of protection than the reality.

How deplorable must be the state of that country, when a law of that nature was thought requisite to be enacted, yet is found incapable of being enforced. The generality, indeed, of the Polish nobles are not inclined either to establish or give efficacy to any regulations in favour of the peasants, whom they scarcely consider as entitled to the common rights of humanity. A few nobles, however, of benevolent hearts and enlightened understandings, have acted upon different principles, and have ventured upon the expedient of giving liberty to their vassals. The event has showed this project to be no less judicious than humane, no less friendly to their own interests than to the happiness of their peasants: for it appears that in the districts, in which the new arrangement has been introduced, the population of their villages is considerably increased, and the revenues of their estates augmented in a triple proportion.

The first noble who granted freedom to his peasants was [Andrzej] Zamoiski, formerly great chancellor, who in 1760 enfranchised six villages in the palatinate of Masovia. These villages were, in 1777, visited by the author of the Patriotic Letters [advocating political reform], from whom I received the following information: on inspecting the parish-registers of births from 1750 to 1760, that is, during the ten years of slavery immediately preceding their enfranchisement, he found the number of births 434; in the first ten years of their freedom, from 1760 to 1770, 620; and from 1770 to the beginning of 1777, 585 births.

By these extracts it appeared that

During the first period there were only 43 births
second period   62 each year.
third period   77

If we suppose an improvement of this sort to take place throughout the kingdom, how great would be the increase of national population!

The revenues of the six villages, since their enfranchisement, have been augmented in a much greater proportion than their population. In their state of vassalage Zamoiski was obliged, according to the custom of Poland, to build cottages and barns for his peasants, and to furnish them with feed, horses, ploughs, and every implement of agriculture; since their attainment of liberty they are become so easy in their circumstances, as to provide themselves with all these necessaries at their own expence; and they likewise cheerfully pay an annual rent, in lieu of the manual labour, which their master formerly exacted from them. By these means the receipts of this particular estate have been nearly tripled.

Document Set 18.3 References

A. A French Visitor Comments on the Middle-Class English Diet, About 1695
   M. Missor's Memoirs and Observations in His Travels Over England, trans. J. Ozell (1719), in H. E. S. Fisher and A. R. J. Jurica, eds., *Documents in English Economic History* (London: G. Bell, 1977), 1:455–456.

B. Edmund Williamson and His Second Wife Record Births and Deaths, 1709–1720
   Edmond Williamson, "An Account of the Birth of My Children by My Second Wife (1709–1720)," in Walter Arnstein, ed., *The Past Speaks,* 2d ed. (Lexington, Mass.: D. C. Heath, 1993), 2:33–34.

C. Vital Statistics from Eighteenth-Century Norway
   Bonnie G. Smith, *Changing Lives: Women in European History Since 1700* (Lexington, Mass.: D. C. Heath, 1989), 16–17.

D. Henry Fielding Studies London's Crime Wave, 1751
   Henry Fielding, *An Inquiry into the Causes of the Late Increase of Robbers* (1751), in Arnstein, 2:43–44.

E. Arthur Young Tours France to Observe Agricultural Practices, 1787
   Arthur Young, *Travels in France,* in James Harvey Robinson, ed., *Readings in European History* (Boston: Ginn, 1904),

F. An English Traveler Comments on the Consequences of Serfdom in Eighteenth-Century Poland
   William Coxe, *Travels into Poland . . .* (London, 1785; reprinted New York: Arno Press, 1971), 115–117.

19

The Promise of a New Order, 1740–1787

DOCUMENT SET 19.1
Fundamental Values of the Enlightenment

There is no better way to begin inquiring into the nature of the Enlightenment than with Document A, the essay "What is Enlightenment" by the German philosopher Immanual Kant (1724–1804). With one of the world's greatest minds, Kant formulated a philosophy of daunting complexity, aimed at refuting both skepticism and mechanistic materialism. His university lectures and essays, such as the one quoted here, are far more accessible to the general reader.

As Chapters 18 and 19 of the *Challenge of the West* explain, an essential quality of the Enlightenment movement was its *sociability,* and all the remaining selections of this set is one way or another comment on this quality. Salons in a few key cities, for example, were indispensable to the flow of ideas among the well-born or well-connected men and women committed to thinking "without prejudice." Document B offers extracts from a single letter (August 7, 1765) of Mme. Marie Thérèse Geoffrin, a Parisian hostess who corresponded tirelessly with "enlightened" writers and political leaders all over Europe. One of her most faithful correspondents was the king of Poland, Stanislaw August Poniatawski (*1764–1794), to whom she wrote long letters at least once a month between 1765 and 1777. The letter quoted here suggests the range of her concerns.

The word *philosopher* normally suggests someone of lofty intellect, accustomed to commune with abstract ideas (a definition that would fit Kant perfectly). But in the eighteenth century the French word *philosophe*—which literally translates as "philosopher"—actually meant something quite different. The

essay by Denis Diderot (1713–1774) entitled "The Philosopher," written for that great compendium of Enlightenment ideas, the *Encyclopedia* (of which he was editor), applies this designation to any enlightened person devoted passionately to the life of reason (Document C). Evaluate his portrait of the Enlightenment *philosophe.* Does such an individual strike you as a professional or academic thinker? Notice particularly Diderot's stress on living usefully and sociably within the practical world. An excellent example of a man who lived by such a creed was the Marquis de Condorcet (1773–1794), a mathematician and *Encyclopedia* contributor who eventually took part in the French Revolution. Jailed by the extremist Jacobin party, he escaped the guillotine only by committing suicide. Hiding out before his arrest, Condorcet wrote one of the Enlightenment's great confessions of faith (Document D).

Two contrasting perspectives on Enlightenment sociability appear in the last two documents. The famous portrait painter Elizabeth Vigée-Lebrun (1755–1842), who worked for Marie Antoinette and numerous other wealthy patrons, supported herself by her work but evidently knew how to relax after hours with the most "amiable" and reasonable of Parisian company (Document E). On the other hand, that strange, contorted genius Jean-Jacques Rousseau (1712–1757) hated the sophisticated urban scene. As he relates in his *Confessions* (Document F), he left Paris "forever" in 1756 to live in the countryside, away from the corruptions, temptations, and deceitful habitués of the salon life. In fact, his rural exile was not permanent, and Rousseau had largely himself to blame for his unhappiness. But his account is a useful corrective to other Enlightenment figures' seemingly irrepressible attraction to the world of witty repartée.

A. Immanuel Kant Asks, "What Is Enlightenment?"

Enlightenment is man's release from his self-incurred tutelage. Tutelage is man's inability to make use of his understanding without direction from another. Self-incurred is this tutelage when its cause lies not in lack of reason but in lack of resolution and courage to use it without direction from another. *Sapere aude!*[1] "Have courage to use your own reason!"—that is the motto of enlightenment.

Laziness and cowardice are the reasons why so great a portion of mankind, after nature has long since discharged them from external direction . . . , nevertheless remains under lifelong tutelage, and why it is so easy for others to set themselves up as their guardians. It is so easy not to be of age. If I have a book which understands for me, a pastor who has a conscience for me, a physician who decides my diet, and so forth, I need not trouble myself. I need not think, if I can only pay—others will readily undertake the irksome work for me.

That the step is competence is held to be very dangerous by the far greater portion of mankind (and by the entire fair sex)—quite apart from its being arduous—is seen to by those guardians who have so kindly assumed superintendence over them. After the guardians have first made their domestic cattle dumb and have made sure that these placid creatures will not dare take a single step without the harness of the cart to which they are tethered, the guardians then show them the danger which threatens if they try to go alone. Actually, however, this danger is not so great, for by falling a few times they would finally learn to walk alone. But an example of this failure makes them timid and ordinarily frightens them away from all further trials.

For any single individual to work himself out of the life under tutelage which has become almost his nature is very difficult. He has come to be fond of this state, and he is for the present really incapable of making use of his reason, for no one has ever let him try it out. Statutes and formulas, those mechanical tools of the rational employment or rather misem-

ployment of his natural gifts, are the fetters of an everlasting tutelage. Whoever throws them off makes only an uncertain leap over the narrowest ditch because he is not accustomed to that kind of free motion. Therefore, there are few who have succeeded by their own exercise of mind both in freeing themselves from incompetence and in achieving a steady pace. . . .

B. Mme. Geoffrin Writes to the King of Poland

I am sending to you a banker named Claudel who is returning to Warsaw. He will have with him a printed memoir on a new kind of mill. The more I have learned about it, the more I see that this machine is very well-known. Your Majesty is best advised to invite a miller to come from France; he will know how to set it up and show how to use it, and use of it can spread from there.

Prince Sulkowski [a Polish nobleman] met Mr. Hennin at my salon. Mr. Hennin had been for a long time in Warsaw, and they talked together about Poland. I see with pain that it has a very bad government [Stanislaw was elected king only in 1764]; it seems almost impossible to make it better. . . .

I sent you the catalogue of the diamonds of Madame de Pompadour [King Louis XV's mistress had died recently and her diamonds were auctioned off] . . .

Do not forget, my dear son, to send the memoir on commerce to Mr. Riancourt when he returns. . . .

I cannot report any news yet on your project for paintings; I am very sad about the death of poor Carle Vanloo [a leading French painter who died in July 1765]. It was a horrible loss for the arts.

C. Denis Diderot, in the *Encyclopedia*, Defines "the Philosopher"

There is nothing which costs less to acquire nowadays than the name of *Philosopher*; an obscure and retired life, some outward signs of wisdom, with a little reading, suffice to attach this name to persons who enjoy the honor without meriting it.

Others in whom freedom of thought takes the place of reasoning, regard themselves as the only true philosophers, because they have dared to overturn the consecrated limits placed by religion, and have broken the fetters which faith laid upon their reason. Proud of having gotten rid of the prejudices of edu-

---

[1] "Dare to know!" was the motto adopted in 1736 by the Society of the Friends of Truth, an important circle in the German Enlightenment.

cation, in the matter of religion, they look upon others with scorn as feeble souls, servile and pusillanimous spirits, who allow themselves to be frightened by the consequences to which irreligion leads, and who, not daring to emerge for an instant from the circle of established verities, nor to proceed along unaccustomed paths, sink to sleep under the yoke of superstition. But one ought to have a more adequate idea of the philosopher, and here is the character which we give him:

Other men make up their minds to act without thinking, nor are they conscious of the causes which move them, not even knowing that such exist. The philosopher, on the contrary, distinguishes the causes to what extent he may, and often anticipates them, and knowingly surrenders himself to them. In this manner he avoids objects that may cause him sensations that are not conducive to his well being or his rational existence, and seeks those which may excite in him affections agreeable with the state in which he finds himself. Reason is in the estimation of the philosopher what grace is to the Christian. Grace determines the Christian's action; reason the philosopher's.

Other men are carried away by their passions, so that the acts which they produce do not proceed from reflection. These are the men who move in darkness; while the philosopher, even in his passions, moves only after reflection. He marches at night, but a torch goes on ahead.

The philosopher forms his principles upon an infinity of individual observations. The people adopt the principle without a thought of the observations which have produced it, believing that the maxim exists, so to speak, of itself; but the philosopher takes the maxim at its source, he examines its origin, he knows its real value, and only makes use of it, if it seems to him satisfactory.

Truth is not for the philosopher a mistress who vitiates his imagination, and whom he believes to find everywhere. He contents himself with being able to discover it wherever he may chance to find it. He does not confound it with its semblance; but takes for true that which is true, for false that which is false, for doubtful that which is doubtful, and for probable that which is only probable. He does more—and this is the great perfection of philosophy; that when he has no real grounds for passing judgment, he knows how to remain undetermined.

The world is full of persons of understanding, even of much understanding, who always pass judgment. They are guessing always, because it is guessing to pass judgment without knowing when one has proper grounds for judgment. They misjudge of the capacity of the human mind; they believe it is possible to know everything, and so they are ashamed not to be prepared to pass judgment, and they imagine that understanding consists in passing judgment. The philosopher believes that it consists in judging well: he is better pleased with himself when he has suspended the faculty of determining, than if he had determined before having acquired proper grounds for his decision. . . .

The philosophic spirit is then a spirit of observation and of exactness, which refers everything to its true principles; but it is not the understanding alone which the philosopher cultivates; he carries further his attention and his labors.

Man is not a monster, made to live only at the bottom of the sea or in the depths of the forest; the very necessities of his life render intercourse with others necessary; and in whatsoever state we find him, his needs and his well-being lead him to live in society. To that reason demands of him that he should know, that he should study and that he should labor to acquire social qualities.

Our philosopher does not believe himself an exile in the world; he does not believe himself in the enemy's country; he wishes to enjoy, like a wise economist, the goods that nature offers him; he wishes to find his pleasure with others; and in order to find it, it is necessary to assist in producing it; so he seeks to harmonize with those with whom chance or his choice has determined he shall live; and he finds at the same time that which suits him: he is an honest man who wishes to please and render himself useful. . . .

D. The Marquis de Condorcet Predicts the March of Progress

The aim of the book that I have undertaken to write, and what it will prove, is that man by using reason and facts will attain perfection. Nature has set no limits to the perfection of the human faculties. The perfectibility of mankind is truly indefinite; and the progress of this perfectibility, henceforth to be free of all hindrances, will last as long as the globe on which nature has placed us. Doubtless his progress will be more or less rapid, but it will never retrograde, at least as long as the globe occupies its present place in the system of the universe; and unless the general laws that govern this system bring to pass a universal cataclysm, or such changes as will prevent man from maintaining his existence, from using his faculties, and from finding his needed resources. . . .

Since the period when alphabetical writing flourished in Greece the history of mankind has been linked to the condition of man of our time in the most enlightened countries of Europe by an unbroken chain of facts and observations. The picture of the march and progress of the human mind is now revealed as being truly historical. Philosophy no longer has to guess, no longer has to advance hypothetical theories. It now suffices to assemble and to arrange the facts, and to show the truths that arise from their connection and from their totality. . . .

If man can predict with almost complete certainty those phenomena whose laws he knows; and if, when he does not know these laws, he can, on the basis of his experience in the past, predict future events with assurance why then should it be regarded as chimerical to trace with a fair degree of accuracy the picture of man's future on the basis of his history? The sole foundations for belief in the natural sciences is the principle that universal laws, known or unknown, which regulate the universe are necessary and constant. Why then should this principle be less true for the development of the intellectual and moral faculties of man than it is for the other operations of nature? Finally, since beliefs, based on past experience under like conditions, constitute the only rule according to which the wisest men act, why then forbid the philosopher to support his beliefs on the same foundations, as long as he does not attribute to them a certainty not warranted by the number, the constancy, and the accuracy of his observations. . . .

E. The Painter Elisabeth Vigée-Lebrun Describes an Artist's Life and Pleasures

The business of the day over, twelve or fifteen amiable people would gather to finish their evening in their hostess's home. The relaxed and easy gaiety that reigned over these light evening meals gave them a charm that formal dinners could never have. A sort of confidence and intimacy spread among the guests; and because well-bred people can always eliminate stiffness, it was in these suppers that Parisian high society showed itself superior to the rest of Europe.

At my house, for instance, we gathered about nine o'clock. We never talked of politics, but of literature or recounted the story of the day. Sometimes we amused ourselves with charades and sometimes [authors] read us a few of their verses. At ten we seated ourselves; my suppers were the simplest, composed always of a fowl, a fish, vegetables, and salad; but it mattered little, we were gay, amiable, hours passed as if they were minutes, and at about midnight, everyone departed.

One evening my brother was reading me the *Travels of Anacharis.* When he got to the place where a description of a Greek dinner appears, it explained how to make several sauces. I called my cook and we decided to have such and such a sauce for the fowl and another for the eels. As I was expecting very pretty women [for dinner], I decided to dress all of us in Greek fashions. My studio, full of everything necessary to drape my models, would furnish enough clothes, and the Count de Parois also had a superb collection of Etruscan vases. The charming Madame de Bonneuil arrived, then Madame Vigée, my sister-in-law, and soon both had been transformed into veritable Athenians. Lebrun-Pindar entered; we removed his hair powder, and I put a crown of laurel on his head. I also found costumes for Monsieur de Riviere, Guinguene, and Chaudet, the famous sculptor.

Besides the two dishes that I have already mentioned, we ate a cake of honey and raisins, and two plates of vegetables. We also drank a bottle of old wine from Cyprus that someone had given me as a guest. We spent a long time at dinner where Lebrun recited us several odes of Anacreon that he translated himself. I don't believe I ever had a more amusing evening.

F. Jean-Jacques Rousseau Leaves Paris, "Never to Live in a City Again," 1756

It was on the 9th of April, 1756, that I left Paris, never to live in a city again, for I do not reckon the brief periods for which I afterwards stayed in Paris, London and other cities, only when passing through them, or against my will. Madame d'Epinay took us all three in her carriage; her farmer took charge of my small amount of luggage, and I was installed in my new home the same day. I found my little retreat arranged and furnished simply, but neatly and even tastefully. The hand which had attended to these arrangements conferred upon them in my eyes an inestimable value, and I found it delightful to be the guest of my friend, in a house of my own choice, which she had built on purpose for me. Although it was cold, and there was still some snow on the ground, the earth was beginning to show signs of vegetation: violets and primroses could be seen, the buds were beginning to open on the trees, and the night of my arrival was marked by the first song of the nightingale, which made itself heard nearly under my window, in a wood adjoining the house. When I awoke, after a light sleep, forgetting my change of abode, I thought that I was still in the Rue de Grenelle, when suddenly this warbling made me start, and in my delight I exclaimed, "At last all my wishes are fulfilled!" My first thought was to abandon myself to the impression caused by the rural objects by which I was surrounded. Instead of beginning to set things in order in my new abode, I began by making arrangements for my walks; there was not a path, not a copse, not a thicket, not a corner round my dwelling, which I had not explored by the following day. The more I examined this charming retreat, the more I felt that it was made for me. This spot, solitary rather than wild, transported me in spirit to the end of the world. It possessed those impressive beauties which are rarely seen in the neighbourhood of cities; no one, who had suddenly been transported there, would have believed that he was only four leagues from Paris. . . .

. . . Although for some years I had visited the country pretty frequently, I had rarely enjoyed it; and those excursions, always taken in the company of pretentious persons, and always spoiled by a feeling of restraint, only whetted my appetite for country pleasures, and, the nearer the glimpse I had of them, the more I felt the want of them. I was so weary of salons, waterfalls, groves, flower-gardens, and their still more wearisome exhibitors; I was so tired of stitching, pianos, sorting wool, making bows, foolish witticisms, insipid affectations, trifling story-tellers, and big suppers that, when I caught a glimpse of a simple thorn-bush, a hedge, a barn, or a meadow; when I inhaled, while passing through a hamlet, the fragrance of a savoury chervil omelette; when I heard from a distance the rustic refrain of the *bisquières* [female goatherds], I wished all rouge, furbelows, and ambergris [perfume] at the devil; and, regretting the good-wife's homely dinner and the native wine, I should have been delighted to slap the face of M. le chef and M. le maître, who forced me to dine at my usual supper-hour, and to sup at a time when I am usually asleep; above all, I should have liked to slap MM. les laquais [the servants], who devoured with their eyes the morsels I ate, and, if I was not prepared to die of thirst, sold me their master's adulterated wine at ten times the price I should have paid for wine of a better quality at an inn.

Behold me, then, at last, in my own house, in a pleasant and solitary retreat, able to spend my days in the independent, even, and peaceful life, for which I felt that I was born. Before describing the effect of this situation, so new to me, upon my heart, it behoves me to recapitulate its secret inclinations, that the progress of these new modifications may be better followed up in its origin. . . .

Document Set 19.1 References

A. Immanuel Kant Asks, "What Is Enlightenment?" L. W. Beck, ed. and trans., *Immanuel Kant on History* (Indianapolis: Bobbs-Merrill, 1963), 3–4.
B. Mme. Geoffrin Writes to the King of Poland Charles de Mouy, ed., *Correspondance inédite due roi Stanislaw-Auguste Poniatowski et de Madam Geoffrin (1764–1777)* (Geneva: Satine, 1970, reprint of 1875 edition, 164–168. Translated by Lynn Hunt.
C. Denis Diderot, in the *Encyclopedia*, Defines "the Philosopher" Diderot, *Encyclopedia*, in *Translations and Reprints from the Original Sources of European History* (Philadelphia: University of Pennsylvania Press, 1898), 6/3:20–22.
D. The Marquis de Condorcet Predicts the March of Progress Condorcet, *Esquisse d'un Tableau historique des progrès de l'esprit humain*, in J. Salwyn Schapiro, ed., *Liberalism: Its Meaning and History* (Princeton, N.J.: D. Van Nonstrand, 1958), 103–104.
E. The Painter Elisabeth Vigée-Lebrun Describes an Artist's Life and Pleasures Elisabeth Vigée-Lebrun, *Souvenirs* (Paris: Des Femmes, 1984), 1:85–88, in Bonnie Smith, *Changing Lives: Women in European History Since 1700* (Lexington Mass.: D. C. Heath, 1989), 31.
F. Jean-Jacques Rousseau Leaves Paris, "Never to Live in a City Again," 1756 Rousseau, *Confessions* (London: Dent, 1904), 2:54, 62–63.

DOCUMENT SET 19.2
Breaking with Traditional Religion

"Crush the infamous thing" was the battle cry of Voltaire (1694–1778), the archetypal man of the Enlightenment. The target of his wrath was institutional religion, which backed its ancient dogmas with the power to destroy dissenters' lives. He professed a religion devoid—so he claimed—of "superstition" and revelation, but instead envisioned a benevolent "divine clockmaker" who had set the universe in motion according to Newton's reasonable laws. Such a faith was called deism, and from its lofty heights Voltaire pleaded that reasonable people of all religious backgrounds could agree on simple truths and practice universal toleration (Document A). A similar hope and faith, together with a passionate cry against "blind religious zeal," breathes from every pore of Diderot's *Encyclopedia* article "Fanaticism," (Document B).

The minority touched by the Enlightenment faced two major untraditional choices. The German-born Baron d'Holbach (1723–1789) broke entirely with Christianity, insisting that science had proved that human beings were simply living machines (Document C). Rousseau followed the more mainstream Enlightenment impulse to dissolve Christianity into deism, combined with his own brand of nature worship (Document D).

The vast majority of Europeans continued to adhere to traditional religion, though, as we shall see, eighteenth-century cultural currents had their effects here, too. In Great Britain and North America the rapid emergence of Methodism at mid-century testified to the hunger ordinary people felt for an emotionally satisfying form of Christianity. John Wesley, the father of Methodism, was not an Enlightenment figure, but in examining Document E, look for evidence of concerns that he shared with the *philosophes*. Among the Jews of Poland-Lithuania, the eighteenth century saw the rapid rise of a movement called Hasidism, which interpreted Judaic law in a less formal, more joyful sense. Document F, written by the twentieth-century Jewish philosopher Martin Buber, recreates oral-tradition tales relating to the Baal Shem Tov, the rabbi and faith-healer most influential in revitalizing eastern European Judaism at the grass roots. Remember, however, that Judaism itself was the target of sophisticated scorn by Enlightenment intellectuals like Voltaire (Document G), for whom the Jews' religion was simply one more archaic "superstition."

A. Voltaire Pleads for Toleration

One does not need great art and skilful eloquence to prove that Christians ought to tolerate each other—nay, even to regard all men as brothers. Why, you say, is the Turk, the Chinese, or the Jew my brother? Assuredly; are we not all children of the same father, creatures of the same God?

But these people despise us and treat us as idolaters. Very well; I will tell them that they are quite wrong. It seems to me that I might astonish, at least, the stubborn pride of a Mohammedan or a Buddhist priest if I spoke to them somewhat as follows:

This little globe, which is but a point, travels in space like many other globes; we are lost in the immensity. Man, about five feet high, is certainly a small thing in the universe. One of these imperceptible beings says to some of his neighbours, in Arabia or South Africa: "Listen to me, for the God of all these worlds has enlightened me. There are nine hundred million little ants like us on the earth, but my ant-hole alone is dear to God. All the others are eternally reprobated by him. Mine alone will be happy."

They would then interrupt me, and ask who was the fool that talked all this nonsense. I should be obliged to tell them that it was themselves. I would then try to appease them, which would be difficult. . . .

B. Diderot Excoriates "Fanaticism"

FANATICISM, noun (philosophy) is blind and passionate zeal born of superstitious opinions, causing people to commit ridiculous, unjust, and cruel actions, not only without any shame or remorse, but even with a kind of joy and comfort. *Fanaticism*, therefore, is only superstition put into practice. . . . The particular causes of *fanaticism* are to be found:

1) In the nature of dogmas. If they are contrary to reason, they overthrow sound judgment and subject everything to imagination whose abuses are the greatest of all evils. . . . Obscure dogmas produce a multitude of interpretations thereby creating the dissension of the sects. Truth does not make any *fanatics*. It is so clear that it hardly allows any contradiction; it so penetrates the mind that the most demented people cannot diminish its enjoyment. . . .

5) In the intolerance of one religion is regard to others, or of one sect among several of the same reli-

gion, because all hands join forces against the common enemy. . . .

6) In persecution, which arises essentially from intolerance. . . .

Fanaticism has done much more harm to the world than impiety. What do impious people claim? To free themselves of a yoke, while *fanatics* want to extend their chains over all the earth. Infernal zealomania! Have we ever seen sects of unbelievers gather into mobs and march with weapons against the Divinity? Their souls are too weak to spill human blood.

C. Baron d'Holbach Denounces Intellectual Conservatism and Questions the Idea of the Soul

Man's ignorance has endured so long, he has taken such slow, irresolute steps to ameliorate his condition, only because he has neglected to study nature, to scrutinize her laws, to search out her resources, to discover her properties. His sluggishness finds its account in permitting himself to be guided by precedent, rather than to follow experience which demands activity; to be led by routine, rather than by his reason which exacts reflection. Hence may be traced the aversion man betrays for everything that swerves from these rules to which he has been accustomed; hence his stupid, his scrupulous respect for antiquity, for the most silly, the most absurd institutions of his fathers; hence those fears that seize him, when the most advantageous changes are proposed to him, or the most probable attempts are made to better his condition. He dreads to examine, because he has been taught to hold it a profanation of something immediately connected with his welfare; he credulously believes the interested advice, and spurns at those who wish to show him the danger of the road he is traveling.

This is the reason why nations linger on in the most scandalous lethargy, groaning under abuses transmitted from century to century, trembling at the very idea of that which alone can remedy their misfortunes. . . .

The more man reflects, the more he will be convinced that the soul, very far from being distinguished from the body, is only the body itself considered relatively to some of its functions, or to some of the modes of existing or acting of which it is susceptible, whilst it enjoys life. Thus, the soul in man is considered relatively to the faculty he has of feeling, of thinking, and of acting in a mode resulting from his peculiar nature; that is to say, from his properties,

from his particular organization, from the modifications, whether durable or transitory, which the beings who act upon him cause his machine to undergo. . . .

An organized being may be compared to a clock, which, once broken, is no longer suitable to the use for which it was designed. To say that the soul shall feel, shall think, shall enjoy, shall suffer after the death of the body, is to pretend that a clock, shivered into a thousand pieces, will continue to strike the hour and have the faculty of marking the progress of time. Those who say that the soul of man is able to subsist notwithstanding the destruction of the body, evidently support the position that the modification of a body will be enabled to conserve itself after the subject is destroyed; but this is completely absurd.

D. Rousseau Advocates a Deistic Religion of Feeling

Christianity is a purely spiritual religion, occupied solely with heavenly things; the country of a Christian is not of this world. He does his duty, it is true, but he does it with a profound indifference as to the good or ill success of his efforts. Provided he has nothing to reproach himself with, it matters little to him whether things go well or ill here below. If the state is flourishing, he scarcely dares enjoy the public felicity; he fears to become proud of the glory of his country. If the state degenerates, he blesses the hand of God which lies heavy upon his people. . . .

Should the depository of this [political] power abuse it, he regards this abuse as the rod with which God punishes his children. People would have scruples about driving out the usurper: it would be necessary to disturb the public repose, to use violence, to shed blood; all this accords ill with the gentleness of the Christian, and, after all, what matters it whether one is a slave or free in this vale of misery? The essential thing is to go to paradise, and resignation is but one more means to accomplish it.

Should some foreign war supervene, the citizens march to combat without difficulty. None among them think of flying; they do their duty, but without passion for victory; they know better how to die than to win. Whether they are victors or vanquished, what matters it? Does not Providence know better than they what they need? . . .

But I am in error in speaking of a Christian republic; each of these words excludes the other. Christianity preaches only servitude and dependence. Its spirit is too favorable to tyranny not to be taken advantage of by it. Christians are made to be slaves: they know it and do not care; this short life has too little value in their eyes. . . .

There is, however, a profession of faith purely civil, of which it is the sovereign's [i.e. the people's] duty to decide upon the articles, not precisely as dogmas of religion, but as sentiments of sociality without which it is impossible to be a good citizen or a faithful subject. Without being able to oblige any one to believe them, the sovereign can banish from the state whoever does not believe them; the sovereign should banish him, not as impious, but as unsocial, as incapable of loving law and justice sincerely, and of sacrificing at need his life to his duty. If any one, having publicly acknowledged these dogmas, conducts himself as if he did not acknowledge them, he should be punished with death; he has committed the greatest of crimes,—he has lied before the law.

The dogmas of civil religion should be simple, few in number, announced with precision, without explanation or commentary. The existence of a powerful, intelligent, benevolent, prescient, and provident Divinity, the life to come, the happiness of the just, the punishment of the wicked, the sacredness of the social contract and the law,—these are the positive dogmas.

As to the negative dogmas, I limit them to one,—intolerance: it enters into the religions which we have excluded. Those who make a distinction between civil intolerance and theological intolerance deceive themselves, to my mind. These two intolerances are inseparable. It is impossible to live in peace with people whom one believes to be damned, to love them is to hate God, who punishes them; they must be redeemed or else tortured. Wherever theological intolerance is admitted, it must have some civil effects; and as soon as it has them the sovereign is no more a sovereign even in temporal matters. From that time priests are the true masters; kings are but their officers.

E. John Wesley Explains Methodism

1. About ten years ago my brother [Charles Wesley] and I were desired to preach in many parts of London. We had no view therein but, so far as we were able (and we knew God could work by whomsoever it pleased Him) to convince those who would hear, what true Christianity was, and to persuade them to embrace it.

2. The points we chiefly insisted upon were four: First, that orthodoxy or right opinions is, at best, but a very slender part of religion, if it can be allowed to be any part of it at all; that neither does religion consist in negatives, in bare harmlessness of any kind, nor merely in externals in doing good or using the means of grace, in works of piety (so called) or of charity:

that it is nothing short of or different from the mind that was in Christ, the image of God stamped upon the heart, inward righteousness attended with the peace of God and joy in the Holy Ghost.

Secondly, that the only way under heaven to this religion is to repent and believe the gospel, of (as the apostle words it) repentance toward God and faith in our Lord Jesus Christ.

Thirdly, that by this faith, he that worketh not, but believeth in Him that justifieth the ungodly, is justified freely by His grace, through the redemption which is in Jesus Christ.

And lastly, that being justified by faith we taste of the heaven to which were are going; we are holy and happy; we tread down sin and fear, and sit in heavenly places with Christ Jesus. . . .

4. Immediately . . . [those who accepted this new way] were surrounded with difficulties. All the world rose up against them; neighbors, strangers, acquaintances, relations, friends began to cry out amain, "Be not righteous overmuch: why shouldst thou destroy thyself? Let not much religion make thee mad.". . .

You are supposed to have the faith that "overcometh the world." To you, therefore, it is not grievous:

I. Carefully to abstain from doing evil; in particular:
1. Neither to buy nor sell anything at all on the Lord's day.
2. To taste no spiritous liquor, no dram of any kind, unless prescribed by a physician.
3. To be at a word [to be honest] both in buying and selling.
4. To pawn nothing, no, not to save life.
5. Not to mention the fault of any behind his back, and to stop those short that do.
6. To wear no needless ornaments, such as rings, earrings, necklaces, lace, ruffles.
7. To use no needless self-indulgence, such as taking snuff or tobacco, unless prescribed by a physician.

II. Zealously to maintain good works; in particular:

1. To give alms of such things as you possess, and that to the uttermost of your power.
2. To reprove all that sin in your sight, and that in love and meekness of wisdom.
3. To be patterns of diligence and frugality, of self-denial, and taking up the cross daily.

III. Constantly to attend on all the ordinances of God; in particular:

1. To be at church and at the Lord's table every week, and at every public meeting of the bands.

2. To attend the ministry of the word every morning unless distance, business or sickness prevent.
3. To use private prayer every day; and family prayer, if you are at the head of a family.
4. To read the scriptures, and meditate therein, at every vacant hour. And
5. To observe, as days of fasting or abstinence, all Fridays in the year. . . .

F. Hasidism Spreads Through East European Jewry: Tales of the Baal Shem

The disciples of the Baal Shem heard that a certain man had a great reputation for learning. Some of them wanted to go to him and find out what he had to teach. The master gave them permission to go, but first they asked him: "And how shall we be able to tell whether he is a true zaddik?"

The Baal Shem replied. "Ask him to advise you what to do to keep unholy thoughts from disturbing you in your prayers and studies. If he gives you advice, then you will know that he belongs to those who are of no account. For this is the service of men in the world to the very hour of their death; to struggle time after time with the extraneous, and time after time to uplift and fit it into the nature of the Divine Name." . . .

The Sermon

Once they asked the Baal Shem to preach after the prayer of the congregation. He began his sermon, but in the middle of it he was shaken with a fit of trembling, such as sometimes seized him while he was praying. He broke off and said: "O, Lord of the world, you know that I am not speaking to increase my own reputation . . . " Here he stopped again, and then the words rushed from his lips. "Much have I learned, and much have I been able to do, and there is no one to whom I could reveal it." And he said nothing further.

Like Locusts

Rabbi Mikhal of Zlotchov told:

"Once when we were on a journey with our teacher, Rabbi Israel Baal Shem Tov, the Light of the Seven Days, he went into the woods to say the Afternoon Prayer. Suddenly we saw him strike his head against a tree and cry aloud. Later we asked him about it. He said: "While I plunged into the holy spirit I saw that in the generations which precede the coming of the Messiah, the rabbis of the hasidim will multiply like locusts, and it will be they who delay

redemption, for they will bring about the separation of hearts and groundless hatred."

Before the Coming of the Messiah

The Baal Shem said:

"Before the coming of the Messiah there will be great abundance in the world. The Jews will get rich. They will become accustomed to running their houses in the grand style and moderation will be cast to the winds. Then the lean years will come; want and a meagre livelihood, and the world will be full of poverty. The Jews will not be able to satisfy their needs, grown beyond rhyme or reason. And then the labor which will bring forth the Messiah, will begin.". . . After prayer, the Baal Shem asked him: "Did you go to the bath yesterday?" He answered "No." Then the Baal Shem said: "It has already come to pass, and after this there is nothing more."

G. Voltaire Sneers at Judaism

. . . the Hebrews have ever been vagrants, or robbers, or slaves, or seditious. They are still vagabonds upon the earth, and abhorred by men, yet affirming that heaven and earth and all mankind were created for them alone. . . .

You ask, what was the philosophy of the Hebrews? The answer will be a very short one—they had none. Their legislator himself does not anywhere speak expressly of the immortality of the soul, nor of the rewards of another life. Josephus and Philo believe the soul to be material; their doctors admitted corporeal angels. . . . The Jews, in the latter times of their sojourn at Jerusalem, were scrupulously attached to nothing but the ceremonials of their law. The man who had eaten pudding or rabbit would have been stoned; while he who denied the immortality of the soul might be high-priest. . . .

Their law must appear, to every polished people, as singular as their conduct; if it were not divine, it would seem to be the law of savages beginning to assemble themselves into a nation; and being divine, one cannot understand how it is that it has not existed from all ages, for them, and for all men. . . .

In this law it is forbidden to eat eels, because they have no scales; and hares, because they chew the cud, and have cloven feet. Apparently, the Jews had hares different from ours. The griffin is unclean, and four-footed birds are unclean, which animals are somewhat rare. Whoever touches a mouse or a mole is unclean. The women are forbidden to lie with horses or asses. The Jewish women must have been subject to this sort of gallantry. The men are forbidden to offer up their seed to Moloch; and here the term seed is not metaphorical. It seems that it was customary, in the deserts of Arabia, to offer up this singular present to the gods; as it is said to be used in Cochin and some other countries of India, for the girls to yield their virginity to an iron Priapus in a temple. These two ceremonies prove that mankind is capable of everything. The Kaffirs, who deprive themselves of one testicle, are a still more ridiculous example of the extravagance of superstition.

Another law of the Jews, equally strange, is their proof of adultery. A woman accused by her husband must be presented to the priests, and she is made to drink of the waters of jealousy, mixed with wormwood and dust. If she is innocent, the water makes her more beautiful; if she is guilty, her eyes start from her head, her belly swells, and she bursts before the Lord. . . .

It is true that, considering the carnage that was made of them under some of the Roman emperors, and the slaughter of them so often repeated in every Christian state, one is astonished that this people not only still exists, but is at this day no less numerous than it was formerly. Their numbers must be attributed to their exemption from bearing arms, their ardor for marriage, their custom of contracting it in their families early, their law of divorce, their sober and regular way of life, their abstinence, their toil, and their exercise.

Their firm attachment to the Mosaic law is no less remarkable, especially when we consider their frequent apostasies when they lived under the government of their kings and their judges; and Judaism is now, of all the religions in the world, the one most rarely abjured—which is partly the fruit of the persecutions it has suffered. Its followers, perpetual martyrs to their creed, have regarded themselves with progressively increasing confidence, as the fountain of all sanctity; looking upon us as no other than rebellious Jews, who have abjured the law of God, and put to death or torture those who received it from His hand. . . .

Document Set 19.2 References

A. Voltaire Pleads for Toleration
   Voltaire, *Essay on Toleration*, J. McCabe, trans. (New York: Putnam's, 1912).
B. Diderot Excoriates "Fanaticism"
   Stephen J. Gendzier, ed. and trans., *Denis Diderot's The Encyclopedia: Selections* (New York: Harper and Row, 1967), 104–106.
C. Baron d'Holbach Denounces Intellectual Conservatism and Questions the Idea of the Soul
   d'Holbach, *The System of Nature*, in *Translations and Reprints frm the Original Sources of European History* (Philadelphia: University of Pennsylvania Press, 1898), 3/1:26–27.
D. Rousseau Advocates a Deistic Religion of Feeling
   James Harvey Robinson, ed., *Readings in European History* (Boston: Ginn, 1904), 2:384–386.
E. John Wesley Explains Methodism
   John Wesley, *A Plain Account of the People Called Methodists (1749)*, in Walter Arnstein, ed., *The Past Speaks*, 2d ed. (Lexington, Mass.: D. C. Heath, 1993), 2:87–89.
F. Hasidism Spreads Through East European Jewry: Tales of the Baal Shem
   Martin Buber, *Tales of the Hasidim: The Early Masters*, Olga Marx, trans. (New York: Schocken, 1947), 66–67, 82–83.
G. Voltaire Sneers at Judaism
   Richard Levy, ed., *Antisemitism in the Modern World* (Lexington, Mass.: D. C. Heath, 1992), 40–43.

DOCUMENT SET 19.3
In Search of an Enlightened Society

"Reasonableness" and "usefulness" were the Enlightenment's watchwords in weighing the political institutions of the age, and by these standards the status quo (except in Britain) was usually found wanting. In his masterpiece *The Spirit of the Laws,* Montesquieu looked for rules by which a polity could be designed to best fit its geography and population (Document A). From his knowledge of England, he developed exceedingly influential advice—heeded by the framers of the United States Constitution—that liberty is best safeguarded by dividing authority within the state (Document B). Without ever visiting Pennsylvania, Voltaire decided that the moderate and tolerant regime established there by William Penn was the ideal society for Europeans to emulate (Document C). Rousseau redefined the social-contract theory of government (see Chapter 17 for Hobbes's and Locke's versions of it) to incorporate the universal moral law, which he called the General Will, under which human beings acknowledged their interdependence (Document D).

Even the institution of marriage was examined according to Enlightenment criteria. The first English feminist, Mary Astell, was sufficiently ahead of her time to argue in her anonymously published *Reflections upon Marriage* (1700) that celibacy as an alternative to marriage could give upper-class women some measure of independence. (Astell was quite conventional in her conservative and Tory-Anglican politics.)

A. Montesquieu Speculates on the Optimal Sizes of Various Kinds of States

It is natural for a republic to have only a small territory; otherwise it cannot long subsist. In an extensive republic there are men of large fortunes, and consequently of less moderation; there are trusts too considerable to be placed in any single subject; he has interests of his own; he soon begins to think that he may be happy and glorious by oppressing his fellow-citizens; and that he may raise himself to grandeur on the ruins of his country.

In an extensive republic the public good is sacrificed to a thousand private views; it is subordinate to exceptions, and depends on accidents. In a small one the interest of the public is more obvious, better understood, and more within the reach of every citizen; abuses have less extent, and, of course, are less protected.

A monarchical state ought to be of moderate extent. Were it small, it would form itself into a republic; were it very large, the nobility, possessed of great estates, far from the eye of the prince, with a private court of their own, and secure, moreover, from sudden executions by the laws and manners or the country—such a nobility, I say, might throw off their allegiance, having nothing to fear from too slow and too distant a government.

A large empire supposes a despotic authority in the person who governs. It is necessary that the quickness of the prince's resolutions should supply the distance of the places they are sent to; that fear should prevent the remissness of the distant governor or magistrate; that the law should be derived from a single person, and should shift continually, according to the accidents which necessarily multiply in a state in proportion to its extent.

B. Montesquieu Advocates the Separation of Powers

In every government there are three sorts of power: the legislative; the executive in respect to things dependent on the law of nations; and the executive in regard to matters that depend on the civil law.

By virtue of the first, the prince or magistrate enacts temporary or perpetual laws, and amends or abrogates those that have been already enacted. By the second, he makes peace or war, sends or receives embassies, establishes the public security, and provides against invasions. By the third, he punishes criminals, or determines the disputes that arise between individuals. The latter we shall call the judiciary power, and the other simply the executive power of the state.

The political liberty of the subject is a tranquillity of mind arising from the opinion each person has of his safety. In order to have this liberty, it is requisite the government be so constituted as one man need not be afraid of another.

When the legislative and executive powers are united in the same person, or in the same body of magistrates, there can be no liberty; because apprehensions may arise, lest the same monarch or senate should enact tyrannical laws, to execute them in a tyrannical manner.

Again, there is no liberty, if the judiciary power be not separated from the legislative and executive. Were it joined with the legislative, the life and liberty of the subject would be exposed to arbitrary control; for the judge would be then the legislator. Were it joined to the executive power, the judge might behave with violence and oppression.

There would be an end of everything, were the same man or the same body, whether of the nobles or of the people, to exercise those three powers, that of enacting laws, that of executing the public resolutions, and of trying the causes of individuals.

Most kingdoms in Europe enjoy a moderate government because the prince who is invested with the two first powers leaves the third to his subjects. In Turkey, where these three powers are united in the Sultan's person, the subjects groan under the most dreadful oppression.

In the republics of Italy, where these three powers are united, there is less liberty than in our monarchies. Hence their government is obliged to have recourse to as violent methods for its support as even that of the Turks; witness the state inquisitors, and the lion's mouth into which every informer may at all hours throw his written accusations.

C. Voltaire Sees Utopia Among the Pennsylvania Quakers

About this time there appeared on the scene the illustrious William Penn, who established the power of the Quakers in America, and who would have secured them respectability in Europe if men were able to respect virtue when it lies beneath a ridiculous exterior. . . .

. . . He founded [in Pennsylvania] the city of Philadelphia, today [ca. 1755] a very flourishing one. He began by making an alliance with the Americans, his neighbors. This is the only treaty between these peoples and the Christians that was never sworn to and has never been broken. The new sovereign was also the legislator of Pennsylvania; he enacted wise laws, none of which has since been altered. The first is to mistreat no one for his religion, and to regard all those who believe in a God as brothers.

Hardly had he established his government, when a number of American merchants arrived to people this colony. The natives of the country, instead of fleeing into the forests, gradually got used to the peaceable Quakers; to the degree that they hated the other Christians, conquerors and destroyers of America, they loved these newcomers. Before long, delighted with the gentleness of their neighbors, a great crowd of these supported savages came to ask William Penn if he would receive them as his vassals. It was quite a new sort of spectacle: a sovereign whom everyone familiarly *thee'd* and *thou'd*, and spoke to with one's hat on; a government without priests, a people without weapons, citizens all of them equals—magistrates excepted—and neighbors free from jealousy.

William Penn could boast of having brought forth on this earth the Golden Age that everyone talks so much about, and that probably never was, except in Pennsylvania . . .

D. Rousseau Proclaims the Sovereignty of the People, United by the General Will

Since no man has any natural authority over his fellowmen, and since force is not the source of right, conventions remain as the basis of all lawful authority among men. [Book I, Chapter 4].

Now, as men cannot create any new forces, but only combine and direct those that exist, they have no other means of self-preservation than to form by aggregation a sum of forces which may overcome the resistance, to put them in action by a single motive power, and to make them work in concert.

This sum of forces can be produced only by the combination of many; but the strength and freedom of each man being the chief instruments of his preservation, how can he pledge them without injuring himself, and without neglecting the cares which he owes to himself? This difficulty, applied to my subject, may be expressed in these terms.

"To find a form of association which may defend and protect with the whole force of the community the person and property of every associate, and by means of which each, coalescing with all, may nevertheless obey only himself, and remain as free as before." Such is the fundamental problem of which the social contract furnishes the solution. . . .

If then we set aside what is not of the essence of the social contract, we shall find that it is reducible to the following terms: "Each of us puts in common his person and his whole power under the supreme direction of the general will, and in return we receive every member as an indivisible part of the whole." [Book I, Chapter 6].

But the body politic or sovereign, deriving its existence only from the contract, can never bind itself, even to others, in anything that derogates from the original act, such as alienation of some portion of itself, or submission to another sovereign. To violate the act by which it exists would be to annihilate itself, and what is nothing produces nothing. [Book I, Chapter 7].

It follows from what precedes, that the general will is always right and always tends to the public advantage; but it does not follow that the resolutions of the people have always the same rectitude. Men always desire their own good, but do not always discern it; the people are never corrupted, though often deceived, and it is only then that they seem to will what is evil. [Book II, Chapter 3.]

The public force, then, requires a suitable agent to concentrate it and put it in action according to the directions of the general will, to serve as a means of communication between the state and the sovereign, to effect in some manner in the public person what the union of soul and body effects in a man. This is, in the State, the function of government, improperly confounded with the sovereign of which it is only the minister.

What, then, is the government? An intermediate body established between the subjects and the sovereign for their mutual correspondence, charged with the execution of the laws and with the maintenance of liberty both civil and political. [Book III, Chapter 1.]

It is not sufficient that the assembled people should have once fixed the constitution of the state by giving their sanction to a body of laws; it is not sufficient that they should have established a perpetual government, or that they should have once for all provided for the election of magistrates. Besides the extraordinary assemblies which unforeseen events may require, it is necessary that there should be fixed and periodical ones which nothing can abolish or prorogue; so that, on the appointed day, the people are rightfully convoked by the law, without needing for that purpose any formal summons. [Book III, Chapter 13.]

So soon as the people are lawfully assembled as a sovereign body, the whole jurisdiction of the government ceases, the executive power is suspended, and the person of the meanest citizen is as sacred and inviolable as that of the first magistrate, because where the represented are, there is no longer any representative. [Book III, Chapter 14.]

These assemblies, which have as their object the maintenance of the social treaty, ought always to be opened with two propositions, which no one should be able to suppress, and which should pass separately by vote. The first: "Whether it pleases the sovereign to maintain the present form of government." The second: "Whether it pleases the people to leave the administration to those at present entrusted with it."

I presuppose here what I believe I have proved, viz., that there is in the State no fundamental law which cannot be revoked, not even this social compact; for if all the citizens assembled in order to break the compact by a solemn agreement, no one can doubt that it could be quite legitimately broken. [Book III, Chapter 18.]

E. Mary Astell Considers the Institution of Marriage

Tis true, thro' Want of Learning, and of that Superior Genius which Men as Men lay claim to, she was ignorant of the *Natural Inferiority* of our Sex, which our Masters lay down as a Self-Evident and Fundamental Truth. She saw nothing in the Reason of Things, to make this either a Principle or a Conclusion, but much to the contrary. . . .

That the Custom of the World has put Women, generally speaking, into a State of Subjection, in not deny'd; but the Right can no more be prov'd from the Fact, than the Predominancy of Vice can justifie it. . . .

The Domestic Sovereign [husband] is without Dispute Elected, and the Stipulations and Contract are mutual, is it not then partial in Men to the last degree, to contend for, and practise that Arbitrary Dominion in their Families, which they abhor and exclaim against in the State? For if Arbitrary Power is evil in itself, and an improper Method of Governing Rational and Free Agents, it ought not to be Practis'd any where; Nor is it less, but rather more mischievous in Families than in Kingdoms, by how much 100000 Tyrants are worse than one.

Document Set 19.3 References

A. Montesquieu Speculates on the Optimal Sizes of Various Kinds of States
Montesquieu, *The Spirit of Laws*, book VIII, chap. 16–20 passim, in *Translations and Reprints from the Original Sources of European History* (Philadelphia: University of Pennsylvania Press, 1902), 3/1:4–5.
B. Montesquieu Advocates the Separation of Powers
Montesquieu, *The Spirit of Laws*, trans. T. Nugent (New York: Hafner, 1949), 151–152.
C. Voltaire Sees Utopia Among the Pennsylvania Quakers
Voltaire, *Philosophical Letters*, trans. Ernest Dilworth (Indianapolis: Bobbs-Merrill, 1961), 16, 18–19.
D. Rousseau Proclaims the Sovereignty of the People, United by the General Will
Jean-Jacques Rousseau, *The Social Contract*, in *Translations and Reprints*, 1/6:14–16.
E. Mary Astell Considers the Institution of Marriage
Mary Astell, *Reflections Upon Marriage*, in Bridget Hill, ed., *The First English Feminist: Reflections Upon Marriage and Other Writings by Mary Astell* (New York: St. Martin's, 1986), 71, 72, 76.

DOCUMENT SET 19.4
Inculcating Enlightenment

Education and the proper upbringing of children were obviously the keys to securing a truly enlightened society; otherwise the superstitious violence and ignorance of the masses would always threaten the well-bred from below and give the state a perfect excuse to maintain despotism. Rousseau pondered the problem of educating children in the spirit of generous humanitarianism and wrote a much-discussed didactic novel on the subject, *Emile,* excerpted in Document A. Unfortunately, his own record on raising children leaves much to be desired. He placed all of his illegitimate offspring in foundling homes, where they vanished without a trace, the sad fate of most abandoned children in this era. His lachrymose, self-justifying account of this episode forms a memorable passage in his *Confessions* (Document B). In a more practical vein, the Polish writer Stanislaw Konarski (1700–1773) advanced in 1773 a moderate pedagogical program for the Noble's College founded in Warsaw to train young boys from the gentry in the enlightened spirit that, it was hoped, would enable the Commonwealth from its century-long decline (Document C).

A. Rousseau Recommends Learning a Virtuous Trade

If you cultivate the arts whose success depends upon the reputation of the artist, if you turn your attention to those employments which are obtained only by favor, of what use will it all be to you, when, rightly disgusted with the world, you disdain the means without which you cannot hope to succeed? You have studied diplomacy and the interests of princes? Good; but what will you do with this knowledge, unless you know how to conciliate the ministers, the ladies of the court, the heads of the bureaus; unless you possess the secret of pleasing them; unless all find in you the rascal that suits their purposes? You are architect or painter? Good; but it is necessary that you should make your talent known. Do you expect to go straightway and exhibit your work at the salon? Alas! that doesn't happen so easily! It is necessary to be in the Academy; it is necessary to be a favorite in order to obtain even a dark corner of the wall. Give up your model and your brush, take a cab and go from door to door; it is in this way that you will acquire celebrity. But you ought to know that all these illustrious doors have Swiss or porters who understand only by motions, and whose ears are in their hands. Do you wish to impart what you have learned, and become a teacher of geography, or mathematics, or languages, or music, or drawing? For that it is necessary to find pupils, and consequently somebody to recommend you. Remember, it contributes more toward success to be plausible than to be able, and that, if you know no trade but your own, you will never by anything but a dunce.

See then how little solidity all these brilliant resources possess, and how many other resources are necessary in order to derive any advantage from them. And then, what will become of you in this cowardly abasement? Reverses, instead of instructing you, debase you. More than ever the creature of public opinion, how will you elevate yourself above those prejudices, arbiters of your lot? How will you despise baseness and the vices of which you have need for your subsistence? You were dependent only on wealth, and now you are dependent on wealth; you have only deepened your slavery and surcharged it with your poverty. You are poor without becoming free; it is the worst state into which a man can fall.

But instead of resorting for a livelihood to those high knowledges which are made for nourishing the soul and not the body, if you resort, in time of need, to your hands and the use which you know how to make of them, all difficulties vanish, all artifices become useless. Your resources are always ready at the moment their use is required; probity and honor are no longer an obstacle to living; you have no need to be a coward and a liar before the great, to bend and cringe before rascals, a vile pander to all the world, a borrower or a thief, which are almost the same thing when one has nothing. The opinion of others concerns you not; you have your court to make to no one, no fool to flatter, no Swiss to knuckle to, no courtier to fee, or what is worse, to worship. That rogues manage the affairs of the great is of no consequence to you. That does not prevent you in your obscure life from being an honest man and having bread. You enter the first shop whose trade you have learned: "Master, I need work." "Journeyman, go there and get to work." Before the dinner hour arrives you have earned your dinner. If you are diligent and sober, before eight hours have passed you will have wherewith to live eight hours more. You will have lived free, sound, true, industrious and just. To gain it thus is not to lose one's time.

B. Rousseau Places His Own Children in a Foundling Home

While philosophising upon the duties of man, an event occurred which made me reflect more seriously upon my own. Thérèse [Rousseau's mistress] became pregnant for the third time. Too honest towards myself, too proud in my heart to desire to belie my principles by my actions, I began to consider the destination of my children and my connection with their mother, in the light of the laws of nature, justice, and reason, and of that religion—pure, holy and eternal, like its author—which men have polluted, while pretending to be anxious to purify it, and which they have converted, by their formulas, into a mere religion of words, seeing that it costs men little to prescribe what is impossible, when they dispense with carrying it out in practice.

If I was wrong in my conclusions, nothing can be more remarkable than the calmness with which I abandoned myself to them. If I had been one of those low-born men, who are deaf to the gentle voice of Nature, in whose heart no real sentiment of justice or humanity ever springs up, this hardening of my heart would have been quite easy to understand. But is it possible that my warm-heartedness, lively sensibility, readiness to form attachments, the powerful hold which they exercise over me, the cruel heartbreakings I experience when forced to break them off, my natural goodwill towards all my fellow-creatures, my ardent love of the great, the true, the beautiful and the just; my horror of evil of every kind, my utter inability to hate or injure, or even to think of it; the sweet and lively emotion which I feel at the sight of all that is virtuous, generous, and amiable; is it possible, I ask, that all these can ever agree in the same heart with the depravity which, without the least scruple, tramples underfoot the sweetest of obligations? No! I feel and loudly assert—it is impossible. Never, for a single moment in his life, could Jean Jacques have been a man without feeling, without compassion, or an unnatural father. I may have been mistaken, never hardened. If I were to state my reasons, I should say too much. Since they were strong enough to mislead me, they might mislead many others, and I do not desire to expose young people, who may read my works, to the danger of allowing themselves to be misled by the same error. I will content myself with observing, that my error was such that, in handing over my children to the State to educate, for want of means to bring them up myself, in deciding to fit them for becoming workmen and peasants rather than adventurers and fortune-hunters, I thought that I was behaving like a citizen and a father, and considered myself a member of Plato's Republic. More than once since then, the regrets of my heart have told me that I was wrong; but, far from my reason having given me the same information, I have often blessed Heaven for having preserved them from their father's lot, and from the lot which threatened them as soon as I should have been obliged to abandon them. If I had left them with Madame d'Epinay or Madame de Luxembourg, who, from friendship, generosity, or some other motive, expressed themselves willing to take charge of them, would they have been happier, would they have been brought up at least as honest men? I do not know; but I do know that they would have been brought up to hate, perhaps to betray, their parents; it is a hundred times better that they have never known them.

My third child was accordingly taken to the Foundling Hospital, like the other two. The two next were disposed of in the same manner, for I had five altogether. This arrangement appeared to me so admirable, so rational, and so legitimate, that, if I did not openly boast of it, this was solely out of regard for the mother; but I told all who were acquainted with our relations. I told Grimm and Diderot. I afterwards informed [several other friends]. . . . In a word, I made no mystery of what I did, not only because I have never known how to keep a secret from my friends, but because I really saw no harm in it. All things considered, I chose for my children what was best, or, at least, what I believed to be best for them. I could have wished, and still wish, that I had been reared and brought up as they have been. . . .

C. Stanislaw Konarski Establishes a Program of Enlightened Education in Poland, 1753

If it were possible to eliminate from our schools corporal punishment this should be very desirable. Let us then at least behave in such a way as to take care lest the schools earn the name of "torture chambers" and "children's shambles", and the teachers the name of floggers, whippers, executioners and butchers. Therefore, one should follow that important counsel urging moderation which is given to educators by wise persons, and always observe the principles recommended by mere prudence: *viz.,* the boys should not be flogged for negligence in their school duties or assignments, etc., or even for more frequently occurring excesses, outbursts of anger or even slight disrespect of religion in church, for arrogant answers, improper fulfillments of some duty, or some other offense, but solely and exclusively for obstinacy, stubbornness and headstrongness. When one says for obstinacy and headstrongness in evil, the concept of the cause is very wide and contains much in itself. But where this cause is actually absent, one should refrain from flogging, and instead appeal rather to reason, double one's watchfulness, admonish, chastise, and in general try all other means tending to the improvement of youth, namely, to the extirpation of laziness, lying or any other wickedness. . . .

Well born lads should refrain from the practices of deceitfulness into which youth so easily falls; as from the worst disgrace, the deepest shame, and the gravest evil. For lying is the proof of a false, perverted and unworthy nature, and whosoever falls into this loathsome habit loses his reputation for the whole of life. He will never get free from it. . . . A youth of good character and honest spirit will always tell the truth even though he be afraid of what it entails; for lying is worse than losing a good name. He will prefer to suffer rather than compromise his own credit and the Divine patience. . . .

One of the greatest benefits of the school should be the habit engendered in the student of reading good books: books treating of life, history, public questions, books about literature and the sciences. Reading alone can make men learned and great in their nation, and those who take good books for their tutors need no others. . . . It is also clear that when one leaves school the only way to make up for time ill-used there is by reading. And what hope is there that he who does not form a love for books while at school will find time for them, when out in the world and facing so many distractions? Whoever while young learns to love books will certainly not forsake them the rest of his days. . . .

The youth should have often in mind their country for which they were born; learning from earliest days to love her, and not disappointing the hopes she entertains of them. They should school themselves in good habits and a life worthy of great sons of their nations. They should keep ever before their eyes the name and honor of their own families, whose ornament and strength they must become. Above all they should ground themselves in the love of our Holy Faith, for which their fathers shed their blood: as also, in godly fear, in Christian duties and excellence, without which no one can be of use either to himself or to the commonwealth.

We do not wish that students should find the studies in the college a burden, or too severe a business. If the truth be told there is nothing so hard that it does not become easy, if only one gets under it!

Document Set 19.4 References

A. Rousseau Recommends Learning a Virtuous Trade
   Jean-Jacques Rousseau, *Emile*, book 3, in *Translations and Reprints from the Original Sources of European History* (Philadelphia: University of Pennsylvania Press, 1898), 1/6:18–20.

B. Rousseau Places His Own Children in a Foundling Home
   Jean-Jacques Rousseau, *Confessions* (London: Dent, 1904), 1:8–9.

C. Stanislaw Konarski Establishes a Program of Enlightened Education in Poland, 1753
   Konarski, *Ordinationes (School Regulations)*, in Manfred Kridl, ed. and trans., *For Your Freedom and Ours* (New York: Unger, 1943), 51–55.

Enlightened Despotism in Central and Eastern Europe

Enlightened despotism, a term sanctioned by long usage among historians, may be a contradiction in terms. But it does refer usefully to a specific phenomenon: the efforts of the bureaucratic monarchies of continental Europe to enact Enlightenment-inspired reforms while maintaining or enhancing their own totalitarian power. In different ways, Austria, Prussia, and Russia all pursued such aims.

Thus Document A shows Holy Roman Emperor Joseph II (*1780–1790) removing by decrees-from-above in 1781 and 1782 the worst disabilities traditionally borne by Jews in the Habsburg lands. The extracts here show influence of the Enlightenment—and also the deep-rooted antisemitism of Austria's gentile population. Prussia's Frederick II (*1740–1786), the archetypal enlightened despot and friend of Voltaire, in 1752 instructed one of his officials in the proper implementation of a mercantilist policy for Prussia, drawing on the Enlightenment idea of promoting socially useful innovations (Document B). And Russia's Catherine the Great (*1762–1796), a German-born ruler of great intelligence, energy, and ruthlessness, in 1767 filled her instructions to her Legislative Commission with Enlightenment precepts. All this, however, was lost on the enserfed peasantry, the vast majority of Russia's population. For their view of justice, see Document D, a pathetic 1774 petition from the Upper Volga region to "Peter III," the name that the Cossack rebel Pugachev adopted. See also Document E, an extract from a book that a genuine Russian admirer of the Enlightenment, the nobleman Alexander Radishchev, tried to publish in 1790—only to find himself exiled to Siberia as a subversive by Catherine.

A. Joseph II Emancipates the Austrian Jews

In order to make the Jews more useful, the discrimination hitherto observed in relation to their clothing is abolished in its entirety. Consequently the obligation for the men to wear yellow armbands and the women to wear yellow ribbons is abolished. If they behave quietly and decently, then no one has the right to dictate to them on matters of dress.

Within two years the Jews must abandon their own language. . . . Consequently the Jews may use their own language only during religious services.

Those Jews who do not have the opportunity to send their children to Jewish schools are to be compelled to send them to Christian schools, to learn reading, writing, arithmetic and other subjects.

Jewish youth will also be allowed to attend the imperial universities.

To prevent the Jewish children and the Jews in general suffering as a result of the concessions granted to them, the authorities and the leaders of the local communities must instruct the subjects in a rational manner that the Jews are to be regarded like any other fellow human-beings and that there must be an end to the prejudice and contempt which some subjects, particularly the unintelligent, have shown towards the Jewish nation and which several times in the past have led to deplorable behaviour and even criminal excesses. On the other hand the Jews must be warned to behave like decent citizens and it must be emphasised in particular that they must not allow the beneficence of His Majesty to go to their heads and indulge in wanton and licentious excesses and swindling.

B. Frederick the Great Demands an Industrial Policy for Prussia

To Privy Finance Councillor Faesch

Since I have seen from your report of the ninth that you are of the opinion that except for the few factories listed by you, which in themselves are very good and necessary, we need no more factories in this country, but have more than enough, I cannot refrain from informing you that I must conclude that you can have made only a very superficial survey and examination of the extracts and balance sheets of imports and exports sent in by the Cameral; certainly, if you had looked attentively at the rubrics in them of imports from foreign countries, you would easily have seen from the details specified in them how very many objects there are which at present we have to get from abroad, and that we could spare ourselves that necessity by setting up our own factories here or sometimes by extending beginnings already made. The example of silk alone will make my ideas clearer to you. We have made a small beginning in setting up silk factories here, but they are still very far from sufficient to meet all our domestic demand for silken goods of all kinds, much less to meet the demands of neighboring countries; so that we are forced to use a very considerable quantity of foreign silks, importing them, and sending the money for them abroad. I cannot accept it if you object that you could not see this out of the Cameral extracts; if you had only taken the total or sum cost of the imported foreign silks and had reckoned out, taking approximate prices, how much this worked out to per piece and ell and then how many pieces can be made in a year on one frame and how many frames we are still short of, you would have seen that we are still lacking in a considerable number of such frames, which could be established here with assurance of success. The same attention would have shown you that we still have in our provinces no vellum factories, or not nearly enough, yet the consumption of vellum is so large that big sums of money have to go out of the country for it.

Besides these examples, you would have found a hundred more similar things for which we have at present no factories and will gradually have to establish them. I therefore require you to go through the extracts (which are being returned to you) again, with closest attention, and report accordingly. You must pay special attention to the question of which factories are particularly advantageous to each province and whether there are too many of any kind in some province, in which case they must be established in another, in which they are lacking. You appeal, indeed, to the order issued by the Cameral President that shortage of factories is the Camera's business; but when you consider with how many different questions the President is charged, whereas the Fifth Department has no other business, you will see yourself that it is its duty to work on the question with all attention.

FRIEDRICH

Potsdam, August 11, 1752

C. Catherine the Great Gives Directions to the Legislative Commission, 1767

. . . 6. Russia is a European state.

7. This is clearly demonstrated by the following observations: the alterations which Peter the Great undertook in Russia succeeded with greater ease because the manners which prevailed at that time, and had been introduced amongst us by a mixture of different nations and the conquest of foreign territories, were quite unsuitable to the climate. Peter the First, by introducing the manners and customs of Europe among the *European* people in his domains, found at that time such means [success] as even he himself did not expect. . . .

9. The Sovereign is absolute; for there is no other authority but that which centers in his single person that can act with a vigor proportionate to the extent of such a vast Dominion. . . .

13. What is the true end of Monarchy? Not to deprive people of their natural liberty but to correct their actions, in order to attain the Supreme Good. . . .

15. The intention and end of Monarchy is the glory of the Citizens, of the State, and of the Sovereign. . . .

66. All laws which aim at the extremity of rigor, may be evaded. It is moderation which rules a people, and not excess of severity.

67. Civil liberty flourishes when the laws deduce every punishment from the peculiar nature of every crime. The application of punishment ought not to proceed from the arbitrary will or mere caprice of the Legislator, but from the nature of the crime. . . .

68. Crimes are divisible into four classes: against religion, against manners [morality], against the peace, against the security of the citizens. . . .

74. I include under the first class of crimes [only] a direct and immediate attack upon religion, such as sacrilege, distinctly and clearly defined by law. . . . In order that the punishment for the crime of sacrilege might flow from the nature of the thing, it ought to consist in depriving the offender of those benefits to which we are entitled by religion; for instance, by expulsion from the churches, exclusion from the society of the faithful for a limited time, or for ever. . . .

76. In the second class of crimes are included those which are contrary to good manners.

77. Such [include] the corruption of the purity of morals in general, either publick or private; that is, every procedure contrary to the rules which show in what manner we ought to enjoy the external conveniences given to man by Nature for his necessities, interest, and satisfaction. The punishments of these crimes ought to flow also from the nature of the thing [offense]: deprivation of those advantages which Society has attached to purity of morals, [for example,] monetary penalties, shame, or dishonor . . . expulsion from the city and the community; in a word, all the punishments which at judicial discretion are sufficient to repress the presumption and disorderly behavior of both sexes. In fact, these offenses do not spring so much from badness of heart as from a certain forgetfulness or mean opinion of one's self. To this class belong only the crimes which are prejudicial to manners, and not those which at the same time violate publick security, such as carrying off by force and rape; for these are crimes of the fourth class.

78. The crimes of the third class are those which violate the peace and tranquillity of the citizens. The

punishments for them ought also to flow from the very nature of the crime, as for instance, imprisonment, banishment, corrections, and the like which reclaim these turbulent people and bring them back to the established order. Crimes against the peace I confine to those things only which consist in a simple breach of the civil polity.

79. The penalties due to crimes of the fourth class are peculiarly and emphatically termed Capital Punishments. They are a kind of retaliation by which Society deprives that citizen of his security who has deprived, or would deprive, another of it. The punishment is taken from the nature of the thing, deduced from Reason, and the sources of Good and Evil. A citizen deserves death when he has violated the public security so far as to have taken away, or attempted to take away, the life of another. Capital punishment is the remedy for a distempered society. If publick security is violated with respect to property, reasons may be produced to prove that the offender ought not in such a case suffer capital punishment; but that it seems better and more conformable to Nature that crimes against the publick security with respect to property should be punished by deprivation of property. And this ought inevitably to have been done, if the wealth of everyone had been common, or equal. But as those who have no property are always most ready to invade the property of others, to remedy this defect corporal punishment was obliged to be substituted for pecuniary. What I have here mentioned is drawn from the nature of things, and conduces to the protection of the liberty of the citizens. . . .

348. The rules of Education are the fundamental institutes which train us up to be citizens. . . .

350. It is impossible to give a general education to a very numerous people and to bring up all the children in schools; for that reason, it will be proper to establish some general rules which may serve by way of advice to all parents.

351. Every parent is obliged to teach his children the fear of God as the beginning of all Wisdom, and to inculcate in them all those duties which God demands from us in the Ten Commandants and in the rules and traditions of our Orthodox Eastern Greek religion.

352. Also to inculcate in them the love of their Country, and to ensure they pay due respect to the established civil laws, and reverence the courts of judicature in their Country as those who, by the appointment of God, watch over their happiness in this world.

353. Every parent ought to refrain in the presence of his children not only from actions but even from words that tend to injustice and violence, as for instance, quarreling, swearing, fighting, every sort of cruelty, and such like behavior; and not to allow those who are around his children to set them such bad examples. . . .

511. A Monarchy is destroyed when a Sovereign imagines that he displays his power more by changing the order of things than by adhering to it, and when he is more fond of his own imaginations than of his will, from which the laws proceed and have proceeded.

512. It is true there are cases where Power ought and can exert its full influence without any danger to the State. But there are cases also where it ought to act according to the limits prescribed by itself.

513. The supreme art of governing a State consists in the precise knowledge of that degree of power, whether great or small, which ought to be exerted according to the different exigencies of affairs. For in a Monarchy the prosperity of the State depends, in part, on a mild and condescending government. . . .

522. Nothing more remains now for the Commission to do but to compare every part of the laws with the rules of this Instruction.

D. Serfs Petition "Peter III," 1774

Most brilliant and autocratic Great Sovereign Peter Fedorovich, Autocrat of Little and White Russia, etc., etc.!

This declaration comes from the Guselinkova part of the village of Spasskoe in Kungurskii district, in the name of an entire community through its authorized representatives, Kornilo Prokopov'ev Shiriaev and Ustin Ananienich Medvidev. It addresses the following points:

1. By the grace of God, we have heard that Your Imperial Majesty—from the southern part of the country, in Orenburg province—has great strength. We praised God that our beautiful sun of old, after having been concealed beneath the soil, now rises from the east and wishes to radiate mercy on us, Your most humble and loyal slaves. We peasants bow to the ground [before You] in total unanimity.

2. We slaves, all the peasants in this community, most humbly petition for tsarist mercy from the military officers and do not wish to oppose [them]. Your Majesty did not declare his anger and punishment toward us, and we request that the commanding officers spare us of the destructive sword and that they obey Your Majesty's orders.

3. We also nourish the great hope that his tsarist majesty will mercifully spare us of vicious, wild, poi-

sonous animals and break off the sharp claws of the miscreants, the aristorcrats and officers—like those in the Iugov state factories, Mikhail Ivanovich Bashmakov, also (in the city of Kungurov) Ivan Sidorovich Nikonov, Aleksei Semenovich Elchanov, and Dmitrii Popov. . . . These magnates make us indignant through their order that whoever invokes the name of the great Peter Fedorovich ["Peter III"] is a great evildoer and [to be punished] with death.

4. Therefore we slaves, all peasants, have sent reliable people to discover the truth about Your Majesty and to bow down before Your military commanders, not to resist them. Therefore, if you please, give them encouragement so that we slaves know of Your Tsarist Majesty's health, for which we slaves would have great jubilation.

5. Show Your merciful judgment upon our most humble petition, so that we suffer no damages from Your armies.

E. Alexander Radishchev Learns About Serfdom from a Serf, 1790

[Village of Liubani.] . . . A few steps from the road I saw a peasant ploughing a field. The weather was hot. I looked at my watch. It was twenty minutes before one. I had set out on Saturday. It was now Sunday. The ploughing peasant, of course, belonged to a landed proprietor, who would not let him pay [dues in money or kind (obrok)]. The peasant was ploughing very carefully. The field, of course, was not part of his master's land. He turned the plough with astonishing ease.

"God help you," I said, walking up to the ploughman, who, without stopping, was finishing the furrow he had started. "God help you," I repeated.

"Thank you, sir," the ploughman said to me, shaking the earth off the ploughshare and transferring it to a new furrow.

"You must be a Dissenter [Old Believer], since you plough on a Sunday."

"No, sir, I make the true sign of the cross," he said, showing me the three fingers together. "And God is merciful and does not bid us starve to death, so long as we have strength and a family."

"Have you no time to work during the week, then, and can you not have any rest on Sundays, in the hottest part of the day, at that?"

"In a week, sir, there are six days, and we go six times a week to work on the master's fields; in the evening, if the weather is good, we haul to the master's house the hay that is left in the woods; and on holidays the women and girls go walking in the woods, looking for mushrooms and berries. God grant," he continued, making the sign of the cross, "that it rains this evening. If you have peasants of your own, sir, they are praying to God for the same thing."

"My friend, I have no peasants, and so nobody curses me. Do you have a large family?"

"Three sons and three daughters. The eldest is nine years old."

"But how do you manage to get food enough, if you have only the holidays free?"

"Not only the holidays: the nights are ours, too. If a fellow isn't lazy, he won't starve to death. You see, one horse is resting; and when this one gets tired, I'll take the other; so the work gets done."

"Do you work the same way for your master?"

"No, sir, it would be a sin to work the same way. On his fields there are a hundred hands for one mouth, while I have two for seven mouths: you can figure it out for yourself. No matter how hard you work for the master, no one will thank you for it. The master will not pay our head [soul] tax; but, though he doesn't pay it, he doesn't demand one sheep, one hen, or any linen or butter the less. The peasants are much better off where the landlord lets them pay a commutation tax [obrok] without the interference of the steward. It is true that sometimes even good masters take more than three rubles a man; but even that's better than having to work on the master's fields. Nowadays it's getting to be the custom to let [lease] villages to [noble] tenants, as they call it. But we call it putting our heads in a noose. A landless tenant skins us peasants alive; even the best ones don't leave us any time for ourselves. In the winter he won't let us do any carting of goods and won't let us go into town to work; all our work has to be for him, because he pays our head tax. It is an invention of the Devil to turn your peasants over to work for a stranger. You can make a complaint against a bad steward, but to whom can you complain against a bad tenant?"

"My friend, you are mistaken; the laws forbid them to torture people."

"Torture? That's true; but all the same, sir, you would not want to be in my hide." Meanwhile the ploughman hitched up the other horse to the plough and bade me good-bye as he began a new furrow.

The words of this peasant awakened in me a multitude of thoughts. I thought especially of the inequality of treatment within the peasant class. I compared the [state] peasants with the [proprietary] peasants. They both live in villages; but the former pay a fixed sum, while the latter must be prepared to pay whatever their master demands. The former are judged by their equals; the latter are dead to the law, except, perhaps, in criminal cases. A member of society becomes known to the government protecting him, only when he breaks the social bonds, when he becomes a criminal! This thought made my blood boil.

Document Set 19.5 References

A. Joseph II Emancipates the Austrian Jews
   T. C. W. Blanning, *Joseph II and Enlightened Despotism* (London: Longman, 1970), 142–144.
B. Frederick the Great Demands an Industrial Policy for Prussia
   Frederick the Great in C. A. Macartney, ed., *The Hadsburg and Hohenzollern Dynasties in the Seventeenth and Eighteenth Centuries* (New York: Harper and Row, 1970), 346–347.
C. Catherine the Great Gives Directions to the Legislative Commission, 1767
   Catherine II, *The Grand Instruction to the Commissioners Appointed to Frame a New Code of Laws for the Russian Empire*, in James Cracraft, ed., *Major Problems in the History of Imperial Russia* (Lexington, Mass.: D. C. Heath, 1994), 200–205.
D. Serfs Petition "Peter III," 1774
   Petition From Serfs in Kungurskii District to Peter III, in Gregory Freeze, ed. and trans., *From Supplication to Revolution* (New York: Oxford University Press, 1988), 84–85.
E. Alexander Radishchev Learns About Serfdom from a Serf, 1790
   Radishchev, *A Journey from St. Petersburg to Moscow*, in Cracraft, 212–213.

Financial and administrative troubles dominated Louis XVI's reign from his accession in 1774 to the onset of the Revolution in 1789. Authoritarian reform figured prominently among the strategies by which the monarchy tried to escape the consequences of hundreds of years of traditional muddling along. Jacques Turgot (1727–1781), a man with connections to the philosophes who served as Louis's principal reforming minister from 1774 to 1776, tried to overhaul finances and abolish guilds (Documents A and B), before political intrigues and the unpopularity of belt-tightening forced him out. The Genevan banker Jacques Necker (1732–1804), who followed Turgot from 1777 to 1781, managed to achieve piecemeal reforms (Document C).

Arbitrary state power remained a reality in French life, though it was under strong challenge from public opinion. The right of the royal government to jail an individual indefinitely under a secret order—*Lettre de Cachet*—was, for example, protested by the lower courts (Document D). And, as we shall see in Chapter 20, absolute monarchy itself was increasingly rejected by the French public.

A. Turgot Outlines His Reform Program to Louis XVI, 1774

Compiègne, August 24, 1774.

Sire:

Having just come from the private interview with which your Majesty has honored me, still full of the anxiety produced by the immensity of the duties now imposed upon me, agitated by all the feelings excited by the touching kindness with which you have encouraged me, I hasten to convey to you my respectful gratitude and the devotion of my whole life.

Your Majesty has been good enough to permit me to place on record the engagement you have taken upon you to sustain me in the execution of those plans of economy which are at all times, and to-day more than ever, an indispensable necessity. . . . At this moment, sire, I confine myself to recalling to you these three items:

No bankruptcy.

No increase of taxes.

No loans.

No *bankruptcy,* either avowed or disguised by illegal reductions.

No *increase of taxes;* the reason for this lying in the condition of your people, and, still more, in that of your Majesty's own generous heart.

No *loans;* because every loan always diminishes the free revenue and necessitates, at the end of a certain time, either bankruptcy or the increase of taxes. In times of peace it is permissible to borrow only in order to liquidate old debts, or in order to redeem other loans contracted on less advantageous terms.

To meet these three points there is but one means. It is to reduce expenditure below the revenue, and sufficiently below it to insure each year a saving of twenty millions, to be applied to redemption of the old debts. Without that, the first gunshot will force the state into bankruptcy.

The question will be asked incredulously, "On what can we retrench?" and each one, speaking for his own department, will maintain that nearly every particular item of expense is indispensable. They will be able to allege very good reasons, but these must all yield to the absolute necessity of economy. . . .

These are the matters which I have been permitted to recall to your Majesty. You will not forget that in accepting the place of comptroller general I have felt the full value of the confidence with which you honor me; I have felt that you intrust to me the happiness of your people, and, if it be permitted to me to say so, the care of promoting among your people the love of your person and of your authority.

At the same time I feel all the danger to which I expose myself. I foresee that I shall be alone in fighting against abuses of every kind, against the power of those who profit by these abuses, against the crowd of prejudiced people who oppose themselves to all reform, and who are such powerful instruments in the hands of interested parties for perpetuating the disorder. I shall have to struggle even against the natural goodness and generosity of your Majesty, and of the persons who are most dear to you. I shall be feared, hated even, by nearly all the court, by all who solicit favors. They will impute to me all the refusals; they will describe me as a hard man because I shall have advised your Majesty that you ought not to enrich even those that you love at the expense of your people's subsistence.

And this people, for whom I shall sacrifice myself, are so easily deceived that perhaps I shall encounter their hatred by the very measures I take to defend them against exactions. I shall be calumniated (having, perhaps, appearances against me) in order to deprive me of your Majesty's confidence. I shall not regret losing a place which I never solicited. I am ready to resign it to your Majesty as soon as I can no longer hope to be useful in it. . . .

Your Majesty will remember that it is upon the faith of your promises made to me that I charge myself with a burden perhaps beyond my strength, and it is to yourself personally, to the upright man, the just and good man, rather than to the king, that I give myself.

I venture to repeat here what you have already been kind enough to hear and approve of. The affecting kindness with which you condescended to press my hands within your own, as if sealing my devotion, will never be effaced from my memory. It will sustain my courage. It has forever united my personal happiness with the interest, the glory, and the happiness of your Majesty. It is with these sentiments that I am, sire, etc.

B. Turgot Decrees the Abolition of Guilds

In almost all the towns the exercise of the different arts and trades is concentrated in the hands of a small number of masters, united in corporations, who alone can, to the exclusion of all other citizens, make or sell the articles belonging to their particular industry. Any person who, by inclination or necessity, intends following an art or trade can only do so by acquiring the mastership [i.e. freedom of the corporation] after a probation as long and vexatious as it is superfluous. By having to satisfy repeated exactions, the money he had so much need of in order to start his trade or open his workshop has been consumed in mere waste. . . .

Citizens of all classes are deprived both of the right to choose the workmen they would employ, and of the advantages they would enjoy from competition operating toward improvements in manufacture and reduction in price. Often one cannot get the samplest work done without its having to go through the hands of several workmen of different corporations, and without enduring the delays, tricks, and exaction which the pretensions of the different corporations, and the caprices of their arbitrary and mercenary directors, demand and encourage. . . .

Among the infinite number of unreasonable regulations, we find in some corporations that all are excluded from them except the sons of masters, or those who marry the widows of masters. Others reject all those whom they call "strangers,"—that is, those born in another town. In many of them for a young man to be married is enough to exclude him from the apprenticeship, and consequently from the mastership. The spirit of monopoly which has dictated the making of these statutes has been carried out to the excluding of women even from the trades the most suitable to their sex, such as embroidery, which they are forbidden to exercise on their own account. . . .

God, by giving to man wants, and making his recourse to work necessary to supply them, has made the right to work the property of every man, and this property is the first, the most sacred, the most imprescriptible of all. . . .

It shall be free to all persons, of whatever quality or condition they may be, even to all foreigners, to undertake and to exercise in all our kingdom, and particularly in our good city of Paris, whatever kind of trade and whatever profession of art or industry may seem good to them; for which purpose we now extinguish and suppress all corporations and communities of merchants and artisans, as well as all masterships and guild directories. We abrogate all privileges, statutes, and regulations of the said corporations, so that none of our subjects shall be troubled in the exercise of his trade or profession by any cause or under any pretext whatever.

C. Necker Reviews His Administration, 1781

The review I take of my past administration occasions, it is true, neither remorse nor repentance: possibly I may even find in it some actions the remembrance of which will shed a happy influence over the remainder of my days; possibly I may think that, if it had not been for the revival and support of public confidence, the enemies of the king, who relied on the effects of the former disorder and low state of public credit in France, might have gained advantages that have escaped them; possibly I may think that if, in the first years of the war, I had been obliged to furnish the resources of a prudent government to taxes or rigorous operations, the poor would have been very unhappy, and the other classes of citizens would have taken alarm.

Yet, to balance these pleasing recollections, I shall always behold the empty shadow of the more lively and pure satisfactions that my administration was deprived of; I shall have always present to my mind those benefits of every kind which it would have been so easy to have effected if the fruits of so many solicitudes, instead of being appropriated solely to the extraordinary expenses of the state, could have been applied daily to augment the happiness and prosperity of the people.

Alas! what might not have been done under other circumstances! It wounds my heart to think of it! I labored during the storm; I put the ship, as it were, afloat again, and others enjoy the command of her in the days of peace! But such is the fate of men; that Providence which searches the human heart and finds even in the virtues on which we pride ourselves some motives which are not perhaps pure enough in its sight, takes a delight in disappointing the most pardonable of all passions, namely, that of the love of glory and of the good opinion of the public....

I regret, and I have made no secret of it, that I was interrupted in the middle of my career, and that I was not able to finish what I had conceived for the good of the state and for the honor of the kingdom. I have not the hypocritical vanity to affect a deceitful serenity, which would be too nearly allied to indifference to deserve a place among the virtues. That moment will be long present to my mind when, some days after my resignation, being occupied in assorting and classifying my papers, I came across those that contained my various ideas for future reforms, and more especially the plans I had formed for ameliorating the salt tax, for the suppression of every custom-house in the interior parts of the kingdom, and for the extension of the provincial administrations:—I could proceed no farther, and pushing away all these notes by a kind of involuntary motion, I covered my face with my hands, and a flood of tears overpowered me.

D. A French Court Protests a *Lettre de Cachet*, 1770

Sire:

Your Court of Excises, having been impeded in the administration of justice by illegal acts which cannot have emanated from your Majesty personally, have determined that a very humble and very respectful protest should be made to you concerning the matter....

Certain agents of the "farm" arrested an individual named Monnerat without observing any of the restrictions imposed by law. Shortly afterwards an order from your Majesty was produced in virtue of which the man was taken to the prison of Bicêtre and held there for twenty months. Yet it is not the excessive length of the imprisonment that should most deeply touch your Majesty. There exist in the fortress of Bicêtre subterranean dungeons which were dug long ago to receive certain famous criminals who, after having been condemned to death, saved themselves by exposing their accomplices. It would seem that they were condemned to a life which would have made death the preferable alternative. While it was desired that their cells should be absolutely dark, it was necessary to admit enough air to sustain life. Accordingly hollow pillars were constructed which established some connection with the outer air without letting in any light. The victims that are cast into these damp cells, which necessarily become foul after a few days, are fastened to the wall by a heavy chain and are supplied with nothing but a little straw, and bread and water. Your Majesty will find it difficult to believe that a man simply *suspected* of smuggling should be kept in such a place of horror for more than a month.

According to the testimony of Monnerat himself, and the deposition of a witness, it appears that after emerging from his subterranean cell, which he calls "the black dungeon," he was kept for a long time in another less dark. This precaution was taken for the welfare of the prisoner, since experience has shown—perhaps at the cost of a number of lives—that it is dangerous to pass too suddenly from the black dungeon to the open air and the light of day.

Monnerat, upon being released from prison, brought suit for damages against the farmers general. Up to that point the question was one of an individual. But the arrest was illegal in form and the imprisonment a real injustice. If this man was a smuggler, he should have been punished according to the laws, which are very severe in this matter. But when your Majesty grants an order for the imprisonment of one suspected of smuggling, it is not your intention to have the suspected person kept in confinement for nearly two years waiting for proofs of his guilt. Now Monnerat has always maintained, both during and since his imprisonment, that he was not even the person for whom the order was obtained....

According to the prevailing system, whenever the farmer of the revenue has no proof of smuggling except such as the courts would regard as suspicious and insufficient, he resorts to your Majesty's orders, called *lettres de cachet*, in order to punish the offense....

The result is, sire, that no citizen in your kingdom can be assured that his liberty will not be sacrificed to a private grudge; for no one is so exalted that he is safe from the ill will of a minister, or so insignificant that he may not incur that of a clerk in the employ of the farm. The day will come, sire, when the multiplicity of the abuses of the *lettres de cachet* will lead your Majesty to abolish a custom so opposed to the constitution of your kingdom and the liberty which your subjects should enjoy.

Document Set 19.6 References

A. Turgot Outlines His Reform Program to Louis XVI, 1774
   Turgot, Letter, in James Harvey Robinson, ed., *Readings in European History* (Boston: Ginn, 1904), 2:386–388.
B. Turgot Decrees the Abolition of Guilds
   Preamble to Turgot's Edict Abolishing Guilds, in Robinson, 2:389.
C. Necker Reviews His Administration, 1781
   Necker, *A Treatise on the Administration of the Finances of France*, in Robinson, 2:390–391.
D. A French Court Protests a *Lettre de Cachet*, 1770
   Robinson, 2:362–364.

DOCUMENT SET 19.7
Britain and America in the Age of the Atlantic Revolutions

Foreigners admired the unwritten British Constitution, under which the king reigned but did not rule and Parliament, in which the crown had an important part, made the laws. But the reality was not as pretty as the theory. Politics was by our standards blatantly corrupt; where voting took place (which was not everywhere in the country), electoral procedures could be almost ludicrously unfair, as one member of Parliament complacently related in the letter quoted as Document A. The court—a term that also embraced the nation's banking system and political patronage network—seemed a cesspool of shady dealing and backstabbing to the opposition politician Lord Chesterfield (1694–1773) in his famous letters of advice to his son (Document B). George III, immortalized in the American Declaration of Independence as a tyrant, considered himself a faithful participant in the British constitutional system and sincerely tried to do well by his country (Document C).

The American colonists, however, regarded Parliament's plan of extending effective British sovereignty over the hitherto rather autonomous outposts as not only destructive of their liberties but also as a threat to involve a virtuous New World in the corrupt politics of the old. Britain's great empire builder William Pitt (1708–1788), who disapproved of coercing the Americans for fear of driving them to rebellion, clearly understood that the colonists were fighting the same battle against a corrupt political system that British reformers at home were waging—a struggle that would not succeed until at least the 1830s (Document D).

Declaring independence in 1776, the American revolutionaries raised their original rather local quarrel with the British Parliament into a universal cause: the right of a people to create a new government for themselves if their old one becomes oppressive (Document E). The author of the Declaration, Thomas Jefferson (1723–1826), was a man of the Enlightenment, equally at home among the intellectuals of Europe and the farmers of Virginia. His *Notes on the State of Virginia* (1781–1782), intended for foreign readers, was written while he was American minister to France. It is part of the extensive contemporary literature explaining America to Europeans (Document F). Notice his thoughts on slavery, an institution that deeply embarrassed him but on which he was economically dependent.

The most profound work of political philosophy ever written by Americans, *The Federalist,* originated as a series of political pieces in support of ratifying the new United State Constitution in 1776 to 1787. James Madison, the chief draftsman of that document and author of *The Federalist No. 51* (Document G), makes a compelling argument for dispersing power among rival branches of government and for exploiting the natural failings of human nature to ensure the survival of free institutions. This was a stunning break from the traditions of Western political thought going back to Plato and Aristotle, which held that only human virtue could ensure good government.

The readings in Sets 19.1 to 19.7 should be considered as a group in evaluating the meaning of the Enlightenment. Supplement your analysis by consulting *The Challenge of the West,* Chapters 18 and 19. Who were the men and women of the Enlightenment? How did they stand in relation to ordinary people? What were their ideals? What were their religious and philosophical principles, and in what ways did these ideals represent something new in history? How did they approach the age-old problems of governing human society? Do you consider them idealistic benefactors of humanity, élitist dreamers, or subverters of tradition—or are any such generalizations valid?

A. Sir George Selwyn's Supporters Get "Shopped," 1761

Two of my voters were murdered yesterday by an experiment which we call shopping, that is, locking them up and keeping them dead drunk to the day of election. Mr. Snell's agents forced two single Selwyns into a post chaise, where, being suffocated with the brandy that was given them and a very fat man that had the custody of them, they were taken out stone dead. Here follows a hanging; in short, it is one roundeau of delights.

B. Lord Chesterfield Warns His Son About Courts, 1749

You will soon be at Courts, where though you will not be concerned, yet reflection and observation upon what you see and hear there may be of use to you when hereafter you may come to be concerned in courts yourself. Nothing in courts is exactly as it appears to be,—often very different, sometimes directly contrary. Interest, which is the real spring of everything there, equally creates and dissolves friendship, produces and reconciles enmities; or rather, allows of neither real friendships nor enmities; for as Dryden very justly observes, "Politicians neither love nor hate." This is so true that you may think you connect yourself with two friends to-day and be obliged to-morrow to make your option between them as enemies. Observe therefore such a degree of reserve with your friends as not to put yourself in their power if they should become your enemies, and such a degree of moderation with your enemies as not to make it impossible for them to become your friends.

Courts are unquestionably the seats of politeness and good breeding; were they not so, they would be the seats of slaughter and desolation. Those who now smile upon and embrace, would affront and stab each other, if manners did not interpose; but ambition and avarice, the two prevailing passions at courts, found dissimulation more effectual than violence; and dissimulation introduced that habit of politeness which distinguishes the courtier from the country gentleman. In the former case the strongest body would prevail; in the latter, the strongest mind.

A man of parts and efficiency need not flatter everybody at court, but he must take great care to offend nobody personally, it being in the power of very many to hurt him who cannot serve him. Homer supposes a chain let down from Jupiter to the earth to connect him with mortals. There is at all courts a chain which connects the prince of the minister with the page of the backstairs or the chambermaid. The king's wife, or mistress, has an influence over him; a lover has an influence over her; the chambermaid or the valet de chambre has an influence over both; and so *ad infinitum*. You must therefore not break a link of that chain by which you hope to climb up to the prince.

C. George III Upholds the British Constitution, 1760

. . . Born and educated in this country, I glory in the name of Briton; and the peculiar happiness of my life will ever consist in promoting the welfare of a people, whose loyalty and warm affection to me, I consider as the greatest and most permanent security of my throne; and I doubt not but their steadiness in these principles will equal the firmness of my invariable resolution, to adhere to and strengthen this excellent constitution in church and state, and to maintain the toleration inviolable. The civil and religious rights of my loving subjects are equally dear to me with the most valuable prerogatives of my crown: and, as the surest foundation of the whole, and the best means to draw down the divine favor on my reign; it is my fixed purpose to countenance and encourage the practice of true religion and virtue. . . .

[The king describes recent successes of British arms in the Seven Years' War.]

Gentleman of the House of Commons, The greatest uneasiness which I feel at this time is, in considering the uncommon burthens necessarily brought upon my faithful subjects: I desire only such supplies as shall be requisite to prosecute the war with advantage, be adequate to the necessary services, and that they may be provided for in the most sure and effectual manner: you may depend upon the faithful and punctual application of what shall be granted.

I have ordered the proper estimates for the ensuing year to be laid before you; and also an account of the extraordinary expenses, which, from the nature of the different and remote operations, have been unavoidably incurred.

It is with peculiar reluctance that I am obliged, at such a time, to mention any thing which personally regards myself; but, as the grant of the greatest part of the civil list revenues is now determined, I trust in your duty and affection to me, to make the proper provision for supporting my civil government with honor and dignity: on my part, you may be assured of a regular and becoming economy.

My Lords, and gentlemen, The eyes of all Europe are upon you. From your resolutions the Protestant interest hopes for protection; as well as all our friends, for the preservation of their independency; and our enemies fear the final disappointment of their ambitious and destructive views. Let these hopes and fears be confirmed and augmented, by the vigor, unanimity, and dispatch, of your proceedings.

In this expectation I am the more encouraged, by a pleasing circumstance, which I look upon as one of the most auspicious omens of my reign. That happy extinction of divisions, and that union and good harmony which continue to prevail amongst my subjects, afford me the most agreeable prospect: the natural disposition and wish of my heart are to cement and promote them: and I promise myself, that nothing will arise on your part, to interrupt or disturb a situation so essential to the true and lasting felicity of this great people.

D. William Pitt Links American Resistance and British Reform, 1775

This resistance to your arbitrary system of taxation might have been foreseen; it was obvious from the nature of things and of mankind, and, above all, from the Whiggish spirit flourishing in that country. The spirit which now resists your taxation in America is the same which formerly opposed loans, benevolences, and ship money in England; the same spirit which called all England on its legs, and by the Bill of Rights vindicated the English constitution; the same spirit which established the great, fundamental, essential maxim of your liberties, that no subject of England shall be taxed but by his own consent.

This glorious spirit of Whiggism animates three millions in America, who prefer poverty with liberty to gilded chains and sordid affluence, and who will die in the defense of their rights as men, as free men. What shall oppose this spirit, aided by the congenial flame glowing in the breast of every Whig in England, to the amount, I hope, of double the American numbers? Ireland they have to a man. In that country, joined it is with the cause of the colonies, and placed at their head, the distinction I contend for is and must be observed. This country superintends and controls their trade and navigation, but they tax themselves. And this distinction between external and internal control is sacred and insurmountable; it is involved in the abstract nature of things. Property is private, individual, absolute. Trade is an extended and complicated consideration; it reaches as far as ships can sail or winds can blow; it is a great and various machine. To regulate the numberless movements of the several parts and combine them into effect for the good of the whole, requires the superintending wisdom and energy of the supreme power in the empire. But this supreme power has no effect towards internal taxation, for it does not exist in that relation; there is no such thing, no such idea in this constitution, as a supreme power operating upon property. Let this distinction then remain forever ascertained: taxation is theirs, commercial regulation is ours. As an American, I would recognize to England her supreme right of regulating commerce and navigation; as an Englishman by birth and principle, I recognize to the Americans their supreme unalienable right in their property,—a right which they are justified in the defense of to the last extremity. To maintain this principle is the common cause of the Whigs on the other side of the Atlantic and on this. "'Tis liberty to liberty engaged," that they will defend themselves, their families, and their country. In this great cause they are immovably allied: it is the alliance of God and nature,—immovable, eternal, fixed as the firmament of heaven.

E. The United States Declares Independence, 1776

When, in the course of human events, it becomes necessary for one people to dissolve the political bands which have connected them with another, and to assume, among the powers of the earth, the separate and equal station to which the laws of nature and of nature's God entitle them, a decent respect to the opinions of mankind requires that they should declare the causes which impel them to the separation.

We hold these truths to be self-evident: That all men are created equal; that they are endowed by their Creator with certain unalienable rights; that among these are life, liberty, and the pursuit of happiness; that, to secure these rights, governments are instituted among men, deriving their just powers from the consent of the governed; that whenever any form of government becomes destructive of these ends, it is the right of the people to alter or to abolish it, and to institute new government, laying its foundation on such principles, and organizing its powers in such form, as to them shall seem most likely to effect their safety and happiness. Prudence, indeed, will dictate that governments long established should not be changed for light and transient causes; and accordingly all experience hath shown that mankind are more disposed to suffer, while evils are sufferable, than to right themselves by abolishing the forms to which they are accustomed. But when a long train of abuses and usurpations, pursuing invariably the same object, evinces a design to reduce them under absolute despotism, it is their right, it is their duty, to throw off such government, and to provide new guards for their future security. Such has been the patient sufferance of these colonies; and such is now the necessity which constrains them to alter their former systems of government. The history of the present King of Great Britain is a history of repeated injuries and usurpations, all having in direct object the establishment of an absolute tyranny over these states. To prove this, let facts be submitted to a candid world. . . .

F. Thomas Jefferson Describes Virginia to European Readers

Query XIII: Constitution

This constitution [of the state of Virginia] was formed when we were new and unexperienced in the science of government. It was the first too which was formed in the whole United States. No wonder then that time and trial have discovered very capital defects in it.

1. The majority of the men in the state, who pay and fight for its support, are unrepresented in the legislature, the roll of freeholders intitled to vote, not including generally the half of those on the roll of the militia, or of the tax-gatherers.

2. Among those who share the representation, the shares are very unequal. . . .

3. The senate, is by its constitution, too homogeneous with the house of delegates. . . .

Query XIV: Laws

[In this section Jefferson advocates emancipating the slaves, educating girls of former slave families to age eighteen and boys to twenty-one, and then sending them away to unspecified colonies.]

It will probably be asked, Why not retain and incorporate the blacks into the state, and thus save the expence of supplying, by importation of white settlers, the vacancies they will leave? Deep rooted prejudices entertained by the whites; ten thousand recollections, by the blacks of the injuries they have sustained; new provocations; the real distinctions which nature has made; and many other circumstances, will divide us into parties, and produce convulsions which will probably never end.

G. James Madison Meditates on Why Limited Government Is Necessary

To what expedient than shall we finally resort for maintaining in practice the necessary partition of power among the several departments, as laid down in the constitution? The only answer that can be given is, that as all these exterior provisions are found to be inadequate, the defect must be supplied, by so contriving the interior structure of the government, as that its several constituent parts may, by their mutual relations, be the means of keeping each other in their proper places. . . .

. . . [T]he great security against a gradual concentration of the several powers in the same department, consists in giving to those who administer each department, the necessary constitutional means, and personal motives, to resist encroachments of the oth-

ers. The provision for defense must in this, as in all other cases, be made commensurate to the danger of attack. Ambition must be made to counteract ambition. The interest of the man must be connected with the constitutional right of the place. It may be a reflection on human nature, that such devices should be necessary to control the abuses of government. But what is government itself but the greatest of all reflections on human nature? If men were angels, no government would be necessary. If angels were to govern men, neither external nor internal controls on government would be necessary. In framing a government which is to be administered by men over men, the great difficulty lies in this: You must first enable the government to control the governed; and in the next place, oblige it to control itself. A dependence on the people is no doubt the primary control on the government; but experience has taught mankind the necessity of auxiliary precautions.

This policy of supplying by opposite and rival interests, the defect of better motives, might be traced through the whole system of human affairs, private as well as public. We see it particularly displayed in all the subordinate distributions of power; where the constant aim is to divide and arrange the several offices in such a manner as that each may be a check on the other; that the private interest of every individual, may be a sentinel over the public rights. These inventions of prudence cannot be less requisite in the distribution of the supreme powers of the state.

Document Set 19.7 References

A. Sir George Selwyn's Supporters Get "Shopped," 1761
   Selwyn, in Lewis B. Namier, *The Structure of Politics at the Accession of George III* (New York: St. Martin's, 1968), 78.

B. Lord Chesterfield Warns His Son About Courts, 1749
   Edward Gilpin Johnson, ed., *The Best Letters of Lord Chesterfield* (Chicago: McClure, 1890), 131–133.

C. George III Upholds the British Constitution, 1760
   George III, in Walter Arnstein, ed., *The Past Speaks*, 2d ed. (Lexington, Mass.: D. C. Heath, 1993), 2:94, 95.

D. William Pitt Links American Resistance and British Reform, 1775
   William Pitt, in James Harvey Robinson, ed., *Readings in European History* (Boston: Ginn, 1904), 2:354–355.

E. The United States Declares Independence, 1776
   The Declaration of Independence.

F. Thomas Jefferson Describes Virginia to European Readers
   Thomas Jefferson, *Notes on the State of Virginia*, in Harvey C. Mansfield, Jr., ed., *Thomas Jefferson: Selected Writings* (Arlington Heights, Ill.: AHM, 1979), 28–29, 37.

G. James Madison Meditates on Why Limited Government Is Necessary
   James Madison, *The Federalist*, No. 51, February 6, 1778.

DOCUMENT SET 19.8
The Agricultural Revolution and Early Industrialization in Britain

The intellectual revolution of the Enlightenment coincided with another fundamental change of direction in the Western world: the beginnings of industrialization.

In cause-effect relationships that scholars still debate, rising population in the eighteenth century created demand for both more food and more manufactured goods. Eastern England was a particularly important center of improvements in agriculture that helped boost productivity, but the "improving" landlords who enclosed traditional village lands and evicted tenants exacted a high price for the progress they wrought. Document A juxtaposes Arthur Young's approving judgment and the victims' protests.

Besides marking the American Declaration of Independence, the year 1776 was epoch-making also for the publication of Adam Smith's *The Wealth of Nations,* the first fully modern treatise on capitalism and the market economy. Document B offers two key passages from this massive book: Smith's famous demonstration of the efficiency of mass production in the case of pins, and his argument for absolute advantage and specialization in international trade. It was in letting the efficiencies of the marketplace work their effects through such mechanisms as these, Smith argued, that the "invisible hand" of competition would function to humanity's natural advantage. Documents C and D suggest how the freeing of the "invisible hand" worked in practice, as the city of Manchester arose from an obscure village to a thriving industrial town in just a generation, while "Luddites"—displaced and despairing artisans—tried to halt mechanization by destroying machinery.

The eighteenth century saw the birth of an idea that most Westerners now take for granted: progress. From the days of ancient Israel and Greece, the key to understanding history had been the notion that humanity had degenerated from an Age of Gold (or Garden of Eden) to its present state of corruption. The Enlightenment and the promise of more abundant production held out the hope that humanity's path might lead upward, not downward. But as the eighteenth century was about to close, the English clergyman and economist Robert Malthus (1766–1834) published a somber correction to his century's optimism, the *Essay on Population* (Document E), which argued that the natural increase of population outstrips the increase in the means of subsistence. Whether Malthus was right in the long run is a question still to be answered.

A. Two Views of Enclosure, Late Eighteenth Century

1. Arthur Young, 1771

As I shall presently leave Norfolk it will not be improper to give a slight review of the husbandry which has rendered the name of this county so famous in the farming world. Pointing out the practices which have succeeded so nobly here, may perhaps be of some use to other countries possessed of the same advantages, but unknowing in the art to use them.

From forty to fifty years ago, all the northern and western, and a part of the eastern tracts of the county, were sheep walks, let [leased] so low as from 6*d.* to 1*s.* and 2*s.* an acre. Much of it was in this condition only thirty years ago. The great improvements have been made by means of the following circumstances.

First. By inclosing without the assistance of parliament.

Second. By a spirited use of marl and clay.

Third. By the introduction of an excellent course of crops.

Fourth. By the culture of turnips well hand-hoed.

Fifth. By the culture of clover and ray-grass.

Sixth. By landlords granting long leases.

Seventh. By the country being divided chiefly into large farms.

The Course of Crops

After the best managed inclosure, and the most spirited conduct in marling, still the whole success of the undertaking depends on this point: No fortune will be made in Norfolk by farming, unless a judicious course of crops be pursued. That which has been chiefly adopted by the Norfolk farmers is,

1. Turnips.
2. Barley.
3. Clover: or clover and ray-grass.
4. Wheat.

Large Farms

If the preceding articles are properly reviewed, it will at once be apparent that no small farmers could effect such great things as have been done in Norfolk. Inclosing, marling, and keeping a flock of sheep large enough for folding, belong absolutely and exclusively to great farmers. . . . Nor should it be forgotten that the best husbandry in Norfolk is that of the largest farmers. . . . Great farms have been the soul of the Norfolk culture: split them into tenures of an hundred pounds a year, you will find nothing but beggars and weeds in the whole county.

2. A PETITION AGAINST ENCLOSURE

A Petition of the hereunder-signed small Proprietors of Land and Persons entitled to Rights of Common [at Raunds, Northamptonshire].

That the petitioners beg leave to represent to the House that, under the pretence of improving lands in the same parish, the cottages and other persons entitled to right of common on the lands intended to be enclosed, will be deprived of an inestimable privilege, which they now enjoy, of turning a certain number of their cows, calves, and sheep, on and over the said lands; a privilege that enables them not only to maintain themselves and their families in the depth of winter, when they cannot, even for their money, obtain from the occupiers of other lands the smallest portion of milk or whey for such necessary purpose, but in addition to this, they can now supply the grazier with young or lean stock at a reasonable price, to fatten and bring to market at a more moderate rate for general consumption, which they conceive to be the most rational and effectual way of establishing public plenty and cheapness of provision; and they further conceive, that a more ruinous effect of this enclosure will be the almost total depopulation of their town, now filled with bold and hardy husbandmen, from among whom, and the inhabitants of other open parishes, the nation has hitherto derived its greatest strength and glory, in the supply of its fleets and armies, and driving them, from necessity and want of employ, in vast crowds, into manufacturing towns, where the very nature of their employment, over the loom or the forge, soon may waste their strength, and consequently debilitate their posterity, and by imperceptible degrees obliterate that great principle of obedience to the Laws of God and their country, which forms the character of the simple and artless villagers, more equally distributed through the open counties, and on which so much depends the good order and government of the state. These are some of the injuries to themselves as individuals, and of the ill consequences to the public, which the petitioners conceive will follow from this, as they have already done from many enclosures, but which they did not think they were entitled to lay before the House (the constitutional patron and protector of the poor) until it unhappily came to their own lot to be exposed to them through the Bill now pending.

B. Adam Smith Presents the Case for Economic Efficiency

To take an example, therefore, from a very trifling manufacture; but one in which the division of labour has been very often taken notice of, the trade of the pin-maker; a workman not educated to this business (which the division of labour has rendered a distinct trade), nor acquainted with the use of the machinery employed in it (to the invention of which the same division of labour has probably given occasion), could scarce, perhaps, with his utmost industry, make one pin in a day, and certainly could not make twenty. But in the way in which this business is now carried on, not only the whole work is a peculiar trade, but it is divided into a number of branches, of which the greater part are likewise peculiar trades. One man draws out the wire, another straights it, a third cuts it, a fourth points it, a fifth grinds it at the top for receiving the head; to make the head requires two or three distinct operations; to put it on, is a peculiar business, to whiten the pins is another; it is even a trade by itself to put them into the paper; and the important business of making a pin is, in this manner, divided into about eighteen distinct operations, which, in some manufactories, are all performed by distinct hands, though in others the same man will sometimes perform two or three of them. I have seen a small manufactory of this kind where ten men only were employed, and where some of them consequently performed two or three distinct operations. But though they were very poor, and therefore but indifferently accommodated with the necessary machinery, they could, when they exerted themselves, make among them about twelve pounds of pins in a day. There are in a pound upwards of four thousand pins of a middling size. Those ten persons, therefore, could make among them upwards of forty-eight thousand pins in a day. Each person, therefore, making a tenth part of forty-eight thousand pins, might be considered as making four thousand eight hundred pins in a day. But if they had all wrought separately and independently, and without any of them having been educated to this peculiar business, they certainly could not each of them have made twenty, perhaps not one pin in a day; that is, certainly, not the two hundred and fortieth, perhaps not the four thousand eight hundredth part of what they are at present capable of performing, in consequence of a proper division and combination of their different operations.

In every other art and manufacture, the effects of the division of labour are similar to what they are in this very trifling one: though, in many of them, the labour can neither be so much subdivided, nor reduced to so great a simplicity of operation. The division of labour, however, so far as it can be introduced, occasions, in every art, a proportionable increase of the productive powers of labour. The separation of different trades and employments from one another, seems to have taken place, in consequence of this advantage. This separation too is generally carried furthest in those countries which enjoy the highest degree of industry and improvement; what is the work of one man in a rude state of society, being generally that of several in an improved one. . . .

. . . As every individual, therefore, endeavours as much as he can both to employ his capital in the support of domestic industry, and so to direct that industry that its produce may be of the greatest value; every individual necessarily labours to render the annual revenue of the society as great as he can. He generally, indeed, neither intends to promote the public interest, nor knows how much he is promoting it. By preferring the support of domestic to that of foreign industry, he intends only his own security; and by directing that industry in such a manner as its produce may be of the greatest value, he intends only his own gain, and he is in this, as in many other cases, led by an invisible hand to promote an end which was no part of his intention. Nor is it always the worse for the society that it was no part of it. By pursuing his own interest he frequently promotes that of the society more effectually than when he really intends to promote it. I have never known much good done by those who affected to trade for the public good. It is an affectation, indeed, not very common among merchants, and very few words need be employed in dissuading them from it. . . .

The natural advantages which one country has over another in producing particular commodities are sometimes so great, that it is acknowledged by all the world to be in vain to struggle with them. By means of glasses, hotbeds, and hotwalls, very good grapes can be raised in Scotland, and very good wine too can be made of them at about thirty times the expence for which at least equally good can be brought from foreign countries. Would it be a reasonable law to prohibit the importation of all foreign wines, merely to encourage the making of claret and burgundy in Scotland? But if there would be a manifest absurdity in turning towards any employment, thirty times more of the capital and industry of the country, than would be necessary to purchase from foreign countries an equal quantity of the commodities wanted, there must be an absurdity, though not altogether so glaring, yet exactly of the same kind, in turning towards any such employment a thirtieth, or even a three hundredth part more of either. Whether the

advantages which one country has over another, be natural or acquired, is in this respect of no consequence. As long as the one country has those advantages, and the other wants them, it will always be more advantageous for the latter, rather to buy of the former than to make. It is an acquired advantage only, which one artificer has over his neighbour, who exercises another trade; and yet they both find it more advantageous to buy of one another, than to make what does not belong to their particular trades. . . .

C. Manchester Becomes a Thriving Industrial City, 1795

. . . No exertions of the masters or workmen could have answered the demands of trade without the introduction of *spinning machines.*

These were first used by the country people on a confined scale, twelve spindles being thought a great matter; while the awkward posture required to spin on them was discouraging to grown up people, who saw with surprise children from nine to twelve years of age manage them with dexterity, whereby plenty was brought into families formerly overburthened with children, and the poor weavers were delivered from the bondage in which they had lain from the insolence of spinners. . . .

The improvements kept increasing, till the capital engines for twist were perfected, by which thousands of spindles are put in motion by a water wheel, and managed mostly by children, without confusion and with less waste of cotton than by the former methods. But the carding and slubbing preparatory to twisting required a greater range of invention. The first attempts were in carding engines, which are very curious, and now brought to a great degree of perfection; and an engine has been contrived for converting the carded wool to slubbing, by drawing it to about the thickness of candlewick preparatory to throwing it into twist. . . .

These machines exhibit in their construction an aggregate of clock-maker's work and machinery most wonderful to behold. The cotton to be spun is introduced through three sets of rollers, so governed by the clock-work, that the set which first receives the cotton makes so many revolutions than the next in order, and these more than the last which feed the spindles, that it is drawn out considerably in passing through the rollers; being lastly received by spindles, which have every one on the bobbin a fly like that of a flax wheel; . . .

Upon these machines twist is made of any fineness proper for warps; but as it is drawn length way of the staple, it was not so proper for weft; wherefore on the introduction of fine callicoes and muslins, mules were invented, having a name expressive of their species, being a mixed machinery between jennies and the machines for twisting, and adapted to spin weft as fine as could be desired. . . .

These mules carry often to a hundred and fifty spindles, and can be set to draw weft to an exact fineness up to 150 hanks in the pound, of which muslin has been made, which for a while had a prompt sale; but the flimsiness of its fabric has brought the finer sorts into discredit, and a stagnation of trade damped the sale of the rest. . . .

The prodigious extension of the several branches of the Manchester manufactures has likewise greatly increased the business of several trades and manufactures connected with or dependent upon them. The making of paper at mills in the vicinity has been brought to great perfection, and now includes all kinds, from the strongest parcelling paper to the finest writing sorts, and that on which banker's bills are printed. To the ironmongers shops, which are greatly increased of late, are generally annexed smithies, where many articles are made, even to nails. A considerable iron foundry is established in Salford, in which are cast most of the articles wanted in Manchester and its neighborhood, consisting chiefly of large cast wheels for the cotton machines; cylinders, boilers, and pipes for steam engines; cast ovens, and grates of all sizes. This work belongs to Batemen and Sharrard, gen[tle]men every way qualified for so great an undertaking. Mr. Sharrard is a very ingenious and able engineer, who has improved upon and brought the steam engine to great perfection. . . .

The tin-plate workers have found additional employment in furnishing many articles for spinning machines; as have also the braziers in casting wheels for the motion-work of the rollers used in them; and the clock-makers in cutting them. Harness-makers have been much employed in making bands for carding engines, and large wheels for the first operation of drawing out the cardings, whereby the consumption of strong curried leather has been much increased. . . .

Within the last twenty or thirty years the vast increase of foreign trade has caused many of the Manchester manufacturers to travel abroad, and agents or partners to be fixed for a considerable time on the continent, as well as foreigners to reside at Manchester. And the town has now in every respect assumed the style and manners of one of the commercial capitals of Europe. . . .

D. Yorkshire Luddites Resist Machinery

Sir,

Information has just been given in, that you are a holder of those detestable Shearing Frames, and I was desired by my men to write to you, and give you fair warning to pull them down, and for that purpose I desire that you will understand I am now writing to you, you will take notice that if they are not taken down by the end of next week, I shall detach one of my lieutenants with at least 300 men to destroy them, and further more take notice that if you give us the trouble of coming thus far, we will increase your misfortunes by burning your buildings down to ashes. . . . We hope for assistance from the French Emperor in shaking off the Yoke of the Rottenest, wickedest and most Tyrannical Government that ever existed. . . . We will never lay down our arms till the House of Commons passes an act to put down all the machinery hurtfull [sic] to the Commonality and repeal that to the Frame Breakers. . . .

Signed by the General of the Army of Redressers,
Ned Ludd, Clerk

E. Robert Malthus Doubts Human Perfectibility, 1798

I have read some of the speculations on the perfectibility of man and of society with great pleasure. I have been warmed and delighted with the enchanting picture which they hold forth. I ardently wish for such happy improvements. But I see great, and, to my understanding, unconquerable difficulties in the way to them. These difficulties it is my present purpose to state; declaring, at the same time, that so far from exulting in them, as a cause of triumphing over the friends of innovation, nothing would give me greater pleasure than to see them completely removed. . . .

I think I may fairly make two postulata.

First, That food is necessary to the existence of man.

Secondly, That the passion between the sexes is necessary, and will remain nearly in its present state. . . .

Assuming, then, my postulata as granted, I say, that the power of population is indefinitely greater than the power in the earth to produce subsistence for man.

Population, when unchecked, increases in a geometrical ratio. Subsistence only increases in an arithmetical ratio. A slight acquaintance with numbers will show the immensity of the first power in comparison of the second.

By that law of our nature which makes food necessary to the life of man, the effects of these two unequal powers must be kept equal.

This implies a strong and constantly operating check on population from the difficulty of subsistence. This difficulty must fall some where; and must necessarily be severely felt by a large portion of mankind. . . .

The ultimate check to population appears then to be a want of food arising necessarily from the different ratios according to which population and food increase. But this ultimate check is never the immediate check, except in cases of actual famine.

The immediate check may be stated to consist in all those customs, and all those diseases which seem to be generated by a scarcity of the means of subsistence; and all those causes, independent of this scarcity, whether of a moral or physical nature, which tend prematurely to weaken and destroy the human frame.

In every country some of these checks are, with more or less force, in constant operation; yet, notwithstanding their general prevalence, there are few states in which there is not a constant effort in the population to increase beyond the means of subsistence. This constant effort as constantly tends to subject the lower classes of society to distress, and to prevent any great permanent melioration of their condition.

These effects, in the present state of society, seem to be produced in the following manner. We will suppose the means of subsistence in any country just equal to the easy support of its inhabitants. The constant effort toward population, which is found to act even in the most vicious societies, increases the number of people before the means of subsistence are increased. The food, therefore, which before supported eleven millions, must now be divided among eleven millions and a half. The poor consequently must live much worse, and many of them be reduced to severe distress. The number of laborers also being above the proportion of work in the market, the price of labor must tend to fall, while the price of provisions would at the same time tend to rise. The laborer therefore must do more work to earn the same as he did before. During this season of distress, the discouragements to marriage and the difficulty of rearing a family are so great, that the progress of population is retarded. In the meantime, the cheapness of labor, the plenty of laborers, and the necessity of an increased industry among them, encourage cultivators to employ more labor upon their land, to turn up fresh soil, and to manure and improve more completely what is already in tillage, till ultimately the means of subsistence may become in the same proportion to the population as at the period from which we set out. The situation of the laborer being then again tolerably comfortable, the restraints to population are in some degree loosened; and, after a short period, the same retrograde and progressive movements, with respect to happiness, are repeated. . . .

Document Set 19.8 References

A. Two Views of Enclosure, Late Eighteenth Century
   A. Young, *The Farmer's Tour*, 1771, in A. E. Bland, P. E. Brown, and R. H. Tawney, eds., *English Economic History: Selected Documents* (London: G. Bell, 1915), 530–532.
B. Adam Smith Presents the Case for Economic Efficiency
   Adam Smith, *The Wealth of Nations*, Edwin Cannan, ed. (New York: Modern Library, 1937), 4–5, 423, 425–426.
C. Manchester Becomes a Thriving Industrial City, 1795
   John Aikin, *A Description of the Country from Thirty to Forty Miles Round Manchester*, in Walter Arnstein, ed., *The Past Speaks*, 2d ed. (Lexington, Mass.: D. C. Heath, 1993), 2:148–149.
D. Yorkshire Luddites Resist Machinery
   G. D. H. Cole and A. W. Filson, eds., *British Working Class Documents: Selected Documents 1789–1875* (London: Macmillan, 1951), 113–115.
E. Robert Malthus Doubts Human Perfectibility, 1798
   Malthus, *An Essay on the Principle of Population*, in Arnstein, 2:144–146.

CHAPTER

20

The Age of Revolutions,
1787–1799

DOCUMENT SET 20.1
France Observed: The Eve of the Revolution

Arthur Young (1741–1820), an English agricultural expert known for his advocacy of improved farming methods, traveled extensively in France in the late 1780s. His book *Travels in France,* which he published between 1792 and 1794, has long been recognized by historians as an important primary source.

In the excerpts that follow, dating from October 1787, Young comments on the lively debate that erupted among educated French people after the announcement of certain proposals for political reform by Louis XVI's minister Calonne—reforms that would have increased taxation of the politically privileged nobility in order to head off bankruptcy of the monarchy. He also vividly describes the city of Paris, which within two years would be the epicenter of revolution.

As you read Young's observations, see if you can discern where his sympathies lie, what he forecasts for France, and how he assesses the response to Calonne's proposals in the circles he frequented: the well-educated middle class and nobility. As you read the other documents in this chapter about the Revolution, bear in mind his description of life in Paris.

A. Arthur Young Visits France on the Eve of the Revolution

October 17, 1787. . . . Dined to-day with a party whose conversation was entirely political. Monsieur de Calonne's *Requête au Roi* is come over, and all the world are reading and disputing on it. It seems, however, generally agreed that, without exonerating himself from the charge of the agiotage, he has thrown no inconsiderable load on the shoulders of the Archbishop of Toulouse, the present premier, who will be puzzled to get rid of the attack. But both these ministers were condemned on all hands in the lump as being absolutely unequal to the difficulties of so arduous a period. One opinion pervaded the whole company, that they are on the eve of some great revolution in the government: that everything points to it: the confusion in the finances great; with a *deficit* impossible to provide for without the states-general of the kingdom, yet no ideas formed of what would be the consequence of their meeting: no minister existing, or to be looked to in or out of power, with such decisive talents as to promise any other remedy than palliative ones: a prince on the throne, with excellent dispositions, but without the resources of a mind that could govern in such a moment without ministers: a court buried in pleasure and dissipation; and adding to the distress instead of endeavouring to be placed in a more independent situation: a great ferment amongst all ranks of men, who are eager for some change, without knowing what to look to or to hope for: and a strong leaven of liberty, increasing every hour since the American revolution—altogether form a combination of circumstances that promise e'er long to ferment into motion if some master hand of very superior talents and inflexible courage is not found at the helm to guide events, instead of being driven by them. It is very remarkable that such conversation never occurs but a bankruptcy is a topic: the curious question on which is, *would a bankruptcy occasion a civil war and a total overthrow of the government?* The answers that I have received to this question appear to be just: such a measure conducted by a man of abilities, vigour, and firmness would certainly not occasion either one or the other. But the same measure, attempted by a man of a different character, might possibly do both. All agree that the states of the kingdom cannot assemble without more liberty being the consequence; but I meet with so few men that have any just ideas of freedom that I question much the species of this new liberty that is to arise. They know not how to value the privileges of THE PEOPLE: as to the nobility and the clergy, if a revolution added anything to their scale I think it would do more mischief than good. . . .

October 25, 1787. This great city [Paris] appears to be in many respects the most ineligible and inconvenient for the residence of a person of small fortune of any that I have seen; and vastly inferior to London. The streets are very narrow, and many of them crowded, nine-tenths dirty, and all without foot-pavements. Walking, which in London is so pleasant and so clean that ladies do it every day, is here a toil and a fatigue to a man and an impossibility to a well-dressed woman. The coaches are numerous, and, what are much worse, there are an infinity of one-horse cabriolets which are driven by young men of fashion and their imitators, alike fools, with such rapidity as to be real nuisances, and render the streets exceedingly dangerous without an incessant caution. I saw a poor child run over and probably killed, and have been myself many times blackened with the mud of the kennels. This beggarly practice of driving a one-horse booby hutch about the streets of a great capital flows either from poverty or wretched and despicable economy; nor is it possible to speak of it with too much severity. If young noblemen at London were to drive their chaises in streets without foot-ways, as their brethren do at Paris, they would speedily and justly get very well thrashed or rolled in the kennel. This circumstance renders Paris an ineligible residence for persons, particularly families, that cannot afford to keep a coach; a convenience which is as dear as at London. The *fiacres*, hackney-coaches, are much worse than at that city; and chairs there are none, for they would be driven down in the streets. To this circumstance also it is owing that all persons of small or moderate fortune are forced to dress in black, with black stockings; the dusky hue of this in company is not so disagreeable a circumstance as being too great a distinction; too clear a line drawn in company between a man that has a good fortune and another that has not. With the pride, arrogance, and ill-temper of English wealth this could not be borne; but the prevailing good humour of the French eases all such untoward circumstances. Lodgings are not half so good as at London, yet considerably dearer. If you do not hire a whole suite of rooms at a hotel, you must probably mount three, four, or five pair of stairs, and in general have nothing but a bed-chamber. After the horrid fatigue of the streets, such an elevation is a delectable circumstance. You must search with trouble before you will be lodged in a private family as gentlemen usually are at London, and pay a higher price. Servants' wages are about the same as at that city. It is to be regretted that Paris should have these disadvantages, for in other respects I take it to be a most eligible residence for such as prefer a great city. The society for a man of letters, or who has any scientific pursuit, cannot be exceeded. The intercourse between such men and the great, which, if it is not upon an equal footing, ought never to exist at all, is respectable. Persons of the highest rank pay an attention to science and literature, and emulate the character they confer. I should pity the man who expected, without other advantages of a very different nature, to be well received in a brilliant circle at London because he was a fellow of the Royal Society. But this would not be the case with a member of the Academy of Sciences at Paris; he is sure of a good reception everywhere. Perhaps this contrast depends in a great measure on the difference of the governments of the two countries. Politics are too much attended to in England to allow a due respect to be paid to anything else; and should the French establish a freer government, academicians will not be held in such estimation when rivalled in the public esteem by the orators who hold forth liberty and property in a free parliament.

Document Set 20.1 References

A. Arthur Young Visits France on the Eve of the Revolution
Arthur Young, *Travels in France*, in James Harvey Robinson, ed., *Readings in European History* (Boston: Ginn, 1904), 2:402–404.

DOCUMENT SET 20.2
The Estates-General Convenes, 1788–1789

Forced to summon the Estates-General to deal with its financial crisis, the royal government invited the three estates of each province to elect representatives and draw up proposals for restoring France to fiscal solvency and to political and social harmony. The *cahiers,* statements of grievances and programs of reform that resulted from these elections, offer revealing insights into the state of mind of French clergy, nobles, and commoners as the Revolution was beginning to unfold.

The *cahier* that appears as Document A was prepared by the Third Estate (commoners) of the Carcassonne district in southern France. Is it a revolutionary manifesto? How do you explain its tone and the nature of the changes it demands? In what ways does it foreshadow the turmoil about to engulf France?

Documents B and C were written from very different perspectives: Madame de Campan, one of Marie Antoinette's ladies-in-waiting, and the English traveler Arthur Young. Both accounts mention the activities of count de Mirabeau (1749–1791), a colorful, ambitious, rather unscrupulous, but highly perceptive nobleman long known for his radical antipathy to the royal regime, who sided with the Third Estate. (During the Revolution itself, Mirabeau would attempt to persuade the king and queen to become constitutional monarchs, but they never trusted him.)

Young also mentions the Abbé Sieyès, the Third Estate's great spokesman, an extract from whose famous *What Is the Third Estate?* forms Document D. "What is the Third Estate? It is nothing? What does it wish to be? Everything." This, in briefest form, is Sieyès's argument. Emmanuel Joseph Sieyès (1748–1836), a French clergyman (hence his title *abbé*) of noble birth but reforming sympathies, was elected as a Third Estate delegate from Paris after he had gained a wide reputation as a brilliant writer against legal privileges. As the Revolution took a radical turn in the early 1790s, however, Sieyès dropped from public view, resurfacing as a shrewd moderate on the eve of Napoleon Bonaparte's ascendancy.

What Is the Third Estate? is Sieyès most important contribution to the unfolding of the French Revolution, articulating the aspirations of the French middle class for personal dignity and a political role commensurate with its wealth and education. How are these aspirations expressed in the reading? In what ways can Sieyès be described as a democrat?

In evaluating the documents in this set, consider the point of view of the writers, the state of the public mood that each reports, and the concerns on which each writer focuses.

After studying these documents, write an essay analyzing the events accompanying the opening of the Estates-General. Rely on *The Challenge of the West,* Chapter 20, for essential information.

A. A Third Estate *Cahier*

The third estate of the electoral district of Carcassonne, desiring to give to a beloved monarch, and one so worthy of our affection, the most unmistakable proof of its love and respect, of its gratitude and fidelity, desiring to cooperate with the whole nation in repairing the successive misfortunes which have overwhelmed it, and with the hope of reviving once more its ancient glory, declares that the happiness of the nation must, in their opinion, depend upon that of its king, upon the stability of the monarchy, and upon the preservation of the orders which compose it and of the fundamental laws which govern it.

Considering, too, that a holy respect for religion, morality, civil liberty, and the rights of property, a speedy return to true principles, a careful selection and due measure in the matter of the taxes, a strict proportionality in their assessment, a persistent economy in government expenditures, and indispensable reforms in all branches of the administration, are the best and perhaps the only means of perpetuating the existence of the monarchy;

The third estate of the electoral district of Carcassonne very humbly petitions his Majesty to take into consideration these several matters, weigh them in his wisdom, and permit his people to enjoy, as soon as may be, fresh proofs of that benevolence which he has never ceased to exhibit toward them and which is dictated by his affection for them.

In view of the obligation imposed by his Majesty's command that the third estate of this district should confide to his paternal ear the causes of the ills which afflict them and the means by which they may be remedied or moderated, they believe that they are fulfilling the duties of faithful subjects and zealous citizens in submitting to the consideration of the nation, and to the sentiments of justice and affection which his Majesty entertains for his subjects, the following:

1. Public worship should be confined to the Roman Catholic apostolic religion, to the exclusion of all other forms of worship; its extension should be promoted and the most efficient measures taken to reestablish the discipline of the Church and increase its prestige.

2. Nevertheless the civil rights of those of the king's subjects who are not Catholics should be confirmed, and they should be admitted to positions and offices in the public administration, without however extending this privilege—which reason and humanity alike demand for them—to judicial or police functions or to those of public instruction.

3. The nation should consider some means of abolishing the annates and all other dues paid to the holy see, to the prejudice and against the protests of the whole French people. . . .

[The holding of multiple church positions should be prohibited, monasteries reduced in numbers, and holidays suppressed or decreased.]

7. The rights which have just been restored to the nation should be consecrated as fundamental principles of the monarchy, and their perpetual and unalterable enjoyment should be assured by a solemn law, which should so define the rights both of the monarch and of the people that their violation shall hereafter be impossible.

8. Among these rights the following should be especially noted: the nation should hereafter be subject only to such laws and taxes as it shall itself freely ratify.

9. The meetings of the Estates General of the kingdom should be fixed for definite periods, and the subsidies judged necessary for the support of the state and the public service should be voted for no longer a period than to the close of the year in which the next meeting of the Estates General is to occur.

10. In order to assure to the third estate the influence to which it is entitled in view of the number of its members, the amount of its contributions to the public treasury, and the manifold interests which it has to defend or promote in the national assemblies, its votes in the assembly should be taken and counted by head.

11. No order, corporation, or individual citizen may lay claim to any pecuniary exemptions. . . . All taxes should be assessed on the same system throughout the nation.

12. The due exacted from commoners holding fiefs should be abolished, and also the general or particular regulations which exclude members of the third estate from certain positions, offices, and ranks which have hitherto been bestowed on nobles either for life or hereditarily. A law should be passed declaring members of the third estate qualified to fill all such offices for which they are judged to be personally fitted.

13. Since individual liberty is intimately associated with national liberty, his Majesty is hereby petitioned not to permit that it be hereafter interfered with by arbitrary orders for imprisonment. . . .

14. Freedom should be granted also to the press, which should however be subjected, by means of strict regulations, to the principles of religion, morality, and public decency. . . .

60. The third estate of the district of Carcassonne places its trust, for the rest, in the zeal, patriotism, honor, and probity of its deputies in the National Assembly in all matters which may accord with the beneficent views of his Majesty, the welfare of the kingdom, the union of the three estates, and the public peace.

B. The Opening of the Estates-General, from a Frenchwoman's Memoirs

The Estates General opened May 4 [1789]. For the last time the queen appeared in royal magnificence. . . . The first session of the Estates was held next day. The king delivered his address with assurance and dignity. The queen told me that he gave the matter much attention, and rehearsed his speech frequently in order to be quite master of the intonations of his voice. His Majesty gave public indications of his attachment and deference for the queen, who was applauded; but it was easy to see that the applause was really meant for the king alone.

From the very early sessions it was clear that Mirabeau would prove very dangerous to the government. It is alleged that he revealed at this time to the king, and more particularly to the queen, a part of the plans he had in mind, and the conditions upon which he would abandon them. He had already exhibited the weapons with which his eloquence and audacity furnished him, in order that he might open negotiations with the party he proposed to attack. This man played at revolution in order to gain a fortune. The queen told me at this time that he asked for an embassy,—Constantinople, if I remember rightly. He was refused with that proper contempt which vice inspires, but which policy would doubtless best have disguised, if the future could have been foreseen.

The general enthusiasm which prevailed during the early sessions of the Assembly, the discussions among the deputies of the third estate and nobility, and even of the clergy, filled their Majesties and those attached to the cause of monarchy with increasing alarm. . . . The deputies of the third estate arrived at Versailles with the deepest prejudices against the court. The wicked sayings of Paris never fail to spread throughout the provinces. The deputies believed that the king indulged in the pleasures of the table to a shameful excess. They were persuaded that the queen exhausted the treasury of the state to gratify the most unreasonable luxury.

Almost all wished to visit the Little Trianon.[1] The extreme simplicity of this pleasure house did not correspond with their ideas. Some insisted that they be shown even the smallest closets, on the ground that some richly furnished apartments were being concealed from them. At last they designated one which they declared was said to be decorated throughout with diamonds and twisted columns set with sapphires and rubies. The queen could not get these silly ideas out of her head and told the king about them. He thought from the description of the room furnished to the guards in the Trianon, that the deputies had in mind the decoration of imitation diamonds in the theater at Fontainebleau constructed in Louis XV's reign.

C. The Opening of the Estates-General from an English Perspective

The king, court, nobility, clergy, army, and parliament [*parlements*] are nearly in the same situation. All these consider with equal dread the ideas of liberty now afloat, except the first, who, for reasons obvious to those who know his character, troubles himself little, even with circumstances that concern his power the most intimately. . . .

The business going forward at present in the pamphlet shops of Paris is incredible. I went to the Palais Royal to see what new things were published, and to procure a catalogue of all. Every hour produces something new. Thirteen came out to-day, sixteen yesterday, and ninety-two last week.

Nineteen-twentieths of these productions are in favor of liberty, and commonly violent against the clergy and the nobility. I have to-day bespoke many of this description that have reputation; but inquiring for such as had appeared on the other side of the question, to my astonishment I find there are but two or three that have merit enough to be known.

But the coffee-houses in the Palais Royal present yet more singular and astonishing spectacles: they are

not only crowded within, but other expectant crowds are at the doors and windows, listening *à gorge déployé* [with gaping mouths] to certain orators, who from chairs or tables harangue each his little audience. The eagerness with which they are heard, and the thunder of applause they receive for every sentiment of more than common hardiness or violence against the present government, cannot easily be imagined. I am all amazement at the ministry permitting such nests and hotbeds of sedition and revolt, which disseminate amongst the people every hour principles that by and by must be opposed with vigor; and therefore it seems little short of madness to allow the propagation at present.

Everything conspires to render the present period in France critical. The want of bread is terrible; accounts arrive every moment from the provinces of riots and disturbances, and calling in the military to preserve the peace of the markets. . . .

June 15. This has been a rich day, and such a one as ten years ago none could believe would ever arrive in France; a very important debate being expected on what, in our House of Commons, would be termed the state of the nation. My friend, Monsieur Lazowski, and myself were at Versailles at eight in the morning. We went immediately to the hall of the states to secure good seats in the gallery; we found some deputies already there, and a pretty numerous audience collected. The room is too large; none but stentorian lungs or the finest, clearest voices can be heard. However, the very size of the apartment, which admits two thousand people, gave a dignity to the scene. It was indeed an interesting one. The spectacle of the representatives of twenty-five millions of people, just emerging from the evils of two hundred years of arbitrary power, and rising to the blessings of a freer constitution, assembled with open doors under the eye of the public, was framed to call into animated feelings every latent spark, every emotion of a liberal bosom; to banish whatever ideas might intrude of their being a people too often hostile to my own country, and to dwell with pleasure on the glorious idea of happiness to a great nation.

Monsieur l'Abbé Sieyès opened the debate. He is one of the most zealous sticklers for the popular cause; carries his ideas not to a regulation of the present government, which he thinks too bad to be regulated at all, but wishes to see it absolutely overturned,—being in fact a violent republican: this is the character he commonly bears, and in his pamphlets he seems pretty much to justify such an idea. He speaks ungracefully and uneloquently, but logically,—or rather reads so, for he read his speech, which was prepared. His motion, or rather string of

---

[1] A simple little pleasure house in a secluded part of the gardens at Versailles, much beloved by the queen.

motions, was to declare themselves the representatives known and verified of the French nation, admitting the right of all absent deputies [the nobility and clergy] to be received among them on the verification of their powers.

Monsieur de Mirabeau spoke without notes for near an hour, with a warmth, animation, and eloquence that entitles him to the reputation of an undoubted orator. He opposed the words "known" and "verified," in the proposition of Abbé Sieyès, with great force of reasoning, and proposed in lieu that they should declare themselves simply *Représentatives du peúple Françoise* [Representatives of the French People]; that no *veto* should exist against their resolves in any other assembly; that all [existing] taxes are illegal, but should be granted during the present sessions of the states, and no longer; that the debt of the king should become the debt of the nation, and be secured on funds accordingly. Monsieur de Mirabeau was well heard, and his proposition much applauded.

In regard to their general method of proceeding, there are two circumstances in which they are very deficient. The spectators in the galleries are allowed to interfere in the debates by clapping their hands, and other noisy expressions of approbation: this is grossly indecent; it is also dangerous; for, if they are permitted to express approbation, they are, by parity of reason, allowed expressions of dissent, and they may hiss as well as clap; which it is said they have sometimes done: this would be to overrule the debate and influence the deliberations.

Another circumstance is the want of order among themselves. More than once to-day there were a hundred members on their legs at a time, and Monsieur Bailly[2] absolutely without power to keep order.

D. The Abbé Sieyès Asks, "What Is the Third Estate?"

What is necessary that a nation should subsist and prosper? Individual effort and public functions.

All individual efforts may be included in four classes: 1. Since the earth and the waters furnish crude products for the needs of man, the first class, in logical sequence, will be that of all families which devote themselves to agricultural labor. 2. Between the first sale of products and their consumption or use, a new manipulation, more or less repeated, adds to these products a second value more or less composite. In this manner human industry succeeds in perfecting the gifts of nature, and the crude product increases two-fold, ten-fold, one hundred-fold in value. Such are the efforts of the second class. 3. Between production and consumption, as well as between the various stages of production, a group of intermediary agents establish themselves, useful both to producers and consumers; these are the merchants and brokers: the brokers who, comparing incessantly the demands of time and place, speculate upon the profit of retention and transportation; merchants who are charged with distribution, in the last analysis, either at wholesale or at retail. This species of utility characterizes the third class. 4. Outside of these three classes of productive and useful citizens, who are occupied with real objects of consumption and use, there is also need in a society of a series of efforts and pains, whose objects are directly useful or agreeable to the individual. This fourth class embraces all those who stand between the most distinguished and liberal professions and the less esteemed services of domestics.

Such are the efforts which sustain society. Who puts them forth? The Third Estate.

Public functions may be classified equally well, in the present state of affairs, under four recognized heads; the sword, the robe, the church and the administration. It would be superfluous to take them up one by one, for the purpose of showing that everywhere the Third Estate attends to nineteen-twentieths of them, with this distinction; that it is laden with all that which is really painful, with all the burdens which the privileged classes refuse to carry. Do we give the Third Estate credit for this? That this might come about, it would be necessary that the Third Estate should refuse to fill these places, or that it should be less ready to exercise their functions. The facts are well known. Meanwhile they have dared to impose a prohibition upon the order of the Third Estate. They have said to it: "Whatever may be your services, whatever may be your abilities, you shall go thus far; you may not pass beyond!" Certain rare exceptions, properly regarded, are but a mockery, and the terms which are indulged in on such occasions, one insult the more.

If this exclusion is a social crime against the Third Estate; if it is a veritable act of hostility, could it perhaps be said that it is useful to the public weal? Alas! who is ignorant of the effects of monopoly? If it discourages those whom it rejects, is it not well known that it tends to render less able those whom it favors? Is it not understood that every employment from which free competition is removed, becomes dearer and less effective?

---

[2] The presiding officer

In setting aside any function whatsoever to serve as an appanage for a distinct class among citizens, is it not to be observed that it is no longer the man alone who does the work that it is necessary to reward, but all the unemployed members of that same caste, and also the entire families of those who are employed as well as those who are not? Is it not to be remarked that since the government has become the patrimony of a particular class, it has been distended beyond all measure; places have been created, not on account of the necessities of the governed, but in the interests of the governing, etc., etc.? Has not attention been called to the fact that this order of things, which is basely and—I even presume to say—beastly respectable with us, when we find it in reading the History of Ancient Egypt or the accounts of Voyages to the Indies,[3] is despicable, monstrous, destructive of all industry, the enemy of social progress; above all degrading to the human race in general, and particularly intolerable to Europeans, etc., etc.? But I must leave these considerations, which, if they increase the importance of the subject and throw light upon it, perhaps, along with the new light, slacken our progress.

It suffices here to have made it clear that the pretended utility of a privileged order for the public service is nothing more than a chimera; that with it all that which is burdensome in this service is performed by the Third Estate; that without it the superior places would be infinitely better filled; that they naturally ought to be the lot and the recompense of ability and recognized services, and that if privileged persons have come to usurp all the lucrative and honorable posts, it is a hateful injustice to the rank and file of citizens and at the same time a treason to the public weal.

Who then shall dare to say that the Third Estate has not within itself all that is necessary for the information of a complete nation? It is the strong and robust man who has one arm still shackled. If the privileged order should be abolished, the nation would be nothing less, but something more. Therefore, what is the Third Estate? Everything; but an everything shackled and oppressed. What would it be without the privileged order? Everything, but an everything free and flourishing. Nothing can succeed without it, everything would be infinitely better without the others.

It is not sufficient to show that privileged persons, far from being useful to the nation, cannot but enfeeble and injure it; it is necessary to prove further that the noble order does not enter at all into the social organization; that it may indeed be a burden upon the nation, but that it cannot of itself constitute a nation.

In the first place, it is not possible in the number of all the elementary parts of a nation to find a place for the *caste* of nobles. I know that there are individuals in great number whom infirmities, incapacity, incurable laziness, or the weight of bad habits render strangers to the labors of society. The exception and the abuse are everywhere found beside the rule. But it will be admitted that the less there are of these abuses, the better it will be for the State. The worst possible arrangement of all would be where not alone isolated individuals, but a whole class of citizens should take pride in remaining motionless in the midst of the general movement, and should consume the best part of the product without bearing any part in its production. Such a class is surely estranged to the nation by its indolence.

The noble order is not less estranged from the generality of us by its civil and political prerogatives.

What is a nation? A body of associates, living under a common law, and represented by the same legislature, etc.

Is it not evident that the noble order has privileges and expenditures which it dares to call its rights, but which are apart from the rights of the great body of citizens? It departs there from the common order, from the common law. So its civil rights make of it an isolated people in the midst of the great nation. This is truly *imperium in imperio* [a state within the state].

In regard to its political rights, these also it exercises apart. It has its special representatives, which are not charged with securing the interests of the people. The body of its deputies sit apart; and when it is assembled in the same hall with the deputies of simple citizens, it is nonetheless true that its representation is essentially distinct and separate: it is a stranger to the nation, in the first place, by its origin, since its commission is not derived from the people; then by its object, which consists of defending not the general, but the particular interest.

The Third Estate embraces then all that which belongs to the nation; and all that which is not the Third Estate, cannot be regarded as being of the nation. What is the Third Estate? It is the whole.

---

[3] The reference here is to a widely read book of the time describing the caste system in India.

Document Set 20.2 References

A. A Third Estate *Cahier*
Commissioners of Carcassonne, in James Harvey Robinson, ed., *Readings in European History* (Boston: Ginn, 1904), 2:397–399.

B. The Opening of the Estates-General, from a Frenchwoman's Memoirs
Mme. de Campan, *Memoirs,* in Robinson, 2:400–402.

C. The Opening of the Estates-General from an English Perspective
Arthur Young, *Travels in France,* in Robinson, 2:402–404.

D. The Abbé Sieyès Asks, "What Is the Third Estate?"
Emmanuel Joseph Sieyès, "What is the Third Estate?" in *Translations and Reprints from the Original Sources of European History* (Philadelphia: University of Pennsylvania Press, 1898), 6:32–35.

DOCUMENT SET 20.3
Popular Uprisings: Bastille Day, 1789, and the Women's March on Versailles

The attack on July 14, 1789, on the Bastille, the medieval fortress from which royal forces had traditionally dominated Paris, by the aroused people of the city is one of the Revolution's most famous events. The attack occurred as rumors swirled about the city of a royal *coup d'état* and as ordinary Parisians endured a summer of rapidly rising food prices and a shortage of bread (a consequence of several years of poor harvests). After rioters had seized the Bastille and begun to demolish it, a few aged prisoners were liberated, and the severed head of the fortress's erstwhile governor was paraded about the city, much to the disgust of the English observer whose account is excerpted in Document A.

Fears of a counterrevolutionary coup did not end with the fall of the Bastille. In early October 1789 the people of Paris again had reason to fear that the royal family, still resident at Versailles (where the National Assembly also sat), was plotting to bring in troops to occupy the city and restore the old order. Crowds of Parisians, outraged working-class women prominent among them, accordingly converged on Versailles, joined later by the middle-class National Guard, commanded by Lafayette. (Maillard, mentioned in the documents, was a young man who had taken a leading role in the assault on the Bastille.) After some violence and the threat of even more severe action, the people and the National Guard "persuaded" the king, queen, and National Assembly to move to the city, seething with discontent and danger. The accounts in Document B, both taken from memoirs published many years later, dramatically narrate the scene.

As you read these documents, consider why masses of ordinary Parisians decided to take matters into their own hands by attacking the Bastille and threatening violence to the royal family itself. Compare these accounts to those documenting later outbreaks of popular fury during the course of the Revolution. Bear in mind the social and political bias of the writers—in Document A an English traveler and in Document B a series of French royalists.

Finally, consider why (apart from its obvious dramatic quality) the anniversary of the fall of the Bastille is modern France's national holiday, much as the Fourth of July is ours. What does Bastille Day continue to symbolize?

A. An English Traveler Witnesses the Fall of the Bastille

July 14. A Canadian Frenchman, whom we found in the crowd and who spoke good English, was the first who intimated to us that it had been resolved to attack the Bastille. We smiled at the gentleman, and suggested the improbability of undisciplined citizens taking a citadel which had held out against the most experienced troops in Europe; little thinking it would be actually in the hands of the people before night. From the commencement of the struggle on Sunday evening there had been scarcely any time in which the firing of guns had not been heard in all quarters of the city, and, as this was principally produced by exercising the citizens in the use of the musket, in trying cannon, etc., it excited, except at first, but little alarm. Another sound equally incessant was produced by the ringing of bells to call together the inhabitants in different parts of the city. These joint sounds being constantly iterated, the additional noise produced by the attack on the Bastille was so little distinguished that I doubt not it had begun a considerable time, and even been completed, before it was known to many thousands of the inhabitants as well as to ourselves.

We ran to the end of the Rue St. Honoré. We here soon perceived an immense crowd proceeding towards the Palais Royal with acceleration of an extraordinary kind, but which sufficiently indicated a joyful event, and, as it approached we say a flag, some large keys, and a paper elevated on a pole above the crowd, in which was inscribed *"La Bastille est prise et les portes sont ouvertes."* ["The Bastille is taken and the gates are open."] The intelligence of this extraordinary event thus communicated, produced an impression upon the crowd really indescribable. A sudden burst of the most frantic joy instantaneously took place; every possible mode in which the most rapturous feelings of joy could be expressed, were everywhere exhibited. Shouts and shrieks, leaping and embracing, laughter and tears, every sound and every gesture, including even what approached to nervous and hysterical affection, manifested, among the promiscuous crowd, such an instantaneous and unanimous emotion of extreme gladness as I should suppose was never before experienced by human beings. . . .

The crowd passed on to the Palais Royal, and in a few minutes another succeeded. Its approach was also announced by loud and triumphant acclamations, but, as it came nearer, we soon perceived a different character, as though bearing additional testimony to the fact reported by the first crowd, the impression by it on the people was of a very different kind. A deep and hollow murmur at once pervaded them, their countenances expressing amazement mingled with alarm. We could not at first explain these circumstances; but as we pressed more to the centre of the crowd we suddenly partook of the general sensation, for we then, and not till then, perceived two bloody heads raised on pikes, which were said to be the heads of the Marquis de Launay, Governor of the Bastille, and of Monsieur Flesselles, *Prévôt des Marchands.* It was a chilling and a horrid sight! An idea of savageness and ferocity was impressed on the spectators, and instantly checked those emotions of joy which had before prevailed. Many others, as well as ourselves, shocked and disgusted at this scene, retired immediately from the streets. . . .

The night approached; the crowd without continued agitated. Reports of a meditated attack upon the city that night by a formidable army under the command of the Count d'Artois and the Maréchal Broglie were in circulation, and gained such credit as to induce the inhabitants to take measures for opposing them. Trees were cut down and thrown across the principal approaches to the city; the streets were impaved, and the stones carried to the tops of houses which fronted the streets through which the troops might pass (for the fate of Pyrrhus was not unknown to the French) and the windows in most parts of the city were illuminated. The night passed with various indications of alarm; guns were firing continually; the tocsin sounded unceasingly; groups of agitated citizens passed hastily along, and parties of the *Milice Bourgeoise* [citizens' militia] (for such was the name already assumed by those who had taken arms the day before) paraded the streets. . . .

I went (July 15) and was led by the sound of an approaching crowd towards the end of the Rue St. Honoré, and there I witnessed a most affecting spectacle. The Bastille had been scarcely entered and the opposition subdued, when an eager search began to find out and liberate every unhappy captive immured within its walls. Two wretched victims of the detestable tyranny of the old Government had just been discovered and taken from some of the most obscure dungeons of this horrid castle, and were at this time conducted by the crowd to the Palais Royal. One of these was a little feeble old man, I could not learn his history; he exhibited an appearance of childishness and fatuity; he tottered as he walked, and his countenance exhibited little more than the smile of an idiot. . . . The other was a tall and rather robust old man; his countenance and whole figure interesting in the highest degree; he walked upright, with a firm and steady gait; his hands were folded and turned upwards, he looked but little at the crowd; the character of his face seemed a mixture of surprise and alarm, for he knew not whither they were leading him, he knew not what fate awaited him; his face was directed towards the sky, but his eyes were but little open. . . . He had a remarkably high forehead, which, with the crown of his head, was completely bald; but he had a very long beard, and on the back of his head the hair was unusually abundant. . . . His dress was an old greasy reddish tunic; the colour and the form of the garb were probably some indication of what his rank had been; for we afterwards learned that he was a Count d'Auche, that he had been a major of cavalry, and a young man of some talent, and that the offence for which he had sustained this long imprisonment had been his having written a pamphlet against the Jesuits. Every one who witnessed this scene probably felt as I did, an emotion which partook of horror and detestation of the Government which could so obdurately as well as unjustly expose human beings to such sufferings; and of pity for the miserable individuals before us. . . .

It had been reported that the King was to come to Paris on the Thursday (July 16), and great crowds filled the streets through which it was expected he would pass: but his coming did not take place till the Friday (July 17). We were very desirous of witnessing the spectacle of the monarch thus, I might almost say, led captive. The spectacle was very interesting, though not from the artificial circumstances which have usually given distinction to royal processions. The impression made on the spectator was not the effect of any adventitious splendour of costly robes or glittering ornaments—the appearance of the King was simple, if not humble; the man was no longer concealed in the dazzling radiance of the sovereign. . . . The streets were lined with the armed bourgeois, three deep—forming a line, as we were assured, of several miles extent. The procession began to pass the place where we were at a quarter past three. The first who appeared were the city officers and the police guards; some women followed them, carrying green branches of trees which were fancifully decorated; then more officers; then the Prévôt des Marchands and different members of the city magistracy. Many of the armed bourgeois followed on horseback; then some of the King's officers, some on horseback and some on foot; then followed the whole body of the Etats Généraux [Estates General] on foot, the noblesse, clergy, and Tiers-Etats [Third Estate], each in their peculiar dresses. That of the noblesse was very beautiful; they wore a peculiar kind of hat with large white feathers, and many of them were tall, elegant young men. The clergy, especially the bishops and some of the higher orders, were most superbly dressed; many of them in lawn dresses, with pink scarfs and massive crosses of gold hanging before them. The dress of the Tiers-Etats was very ordinary, even worse than that of the inferior order of gownsmen at the English universities. More of the King's officers followed; then the King in a large plain coach with eight horses. After this more bourgeois; then another coach and eight horses with other officers of state; than an immense number of the bourgeois, there having been, it was said, two hundred thousand of them in arms. The countenance of the King was little marked with sensibility, and his general appearance by no means indicated alarm. He was accustomed to throw his head very much back on his shoulders, which, by obliging him to look upwards, gave a kind of stupid character to his countenance by increasing the apparent breadth of his face, by preventing that variation of expression which is produced by looking about. He received neither marks of applause nor insult from the populace, unless their silence could be construed into a negative sort of disrespect. Nor were any insults shown to the noblesse or clergy, except in the instance of the Archbishop of Paris, a very tall thin man. He was very much hissed, the popular clamour having been excited against him by a story circulated of his having encouraged the King to use strong measures against the people, and of his attempting to make an impression on the people by a superstitious exposure of a crucifix. He looked a good deal agitated, and whether he had a leaden eye or not I know not, but it certainly loved the ground. The warm and enthusiastic applause of the people was reserved for the Tiers-Etat. . . . *Vivent les Tiers-Etats! Vive la Liberté!* ["Long live the Third Estate! Long live liberty!] were loudly iterated as they passed. . . .

On the Saturday (July 18) we visited more of the public places, but the most interesting object, and which attracted the greatest number of spectators, was the Bastille. We found two hundred workmen busily employed in the destruction of this castle of despotism. We saw the battlements tumble down amidst the applauding shouts of the people. I observed a number of artists taking drawings of what from this time was to have no existence but on paper. . . .

And this reminds me of our having a second time seen the other prisoner, the feeble old man. He was placed conspicuously at a window opposite the house where we saw the King pass, and at that time he was brought forward and made to wave his hat, having a three coloured cockade on it.

B. The Women's March on Versailles, October 5–6, 1789[1]

The March to Versailles

(a) On Sunday, October 4, the people resorted to acts of violence in the public promenades against officers of the army and other individuals who were pointed out to them as aristocrats. There was in Paris an extreme agitation. The symptoms of a violent insurrection were alarmingly manifest in the evening. Monday, the fifth, as early as morning, one saw women, a species of furies, running the streets, crying out that there was no bread at the baker's. They were soon joined by a considerable number of men in the Place de l'Hôtel de Ville. Their first operation was to hang on a lamp-post a baker accused of having sold bread under weight. This man was saved by M. De Gouvion, a major of the national guard. These maniacs wanted to get into the town hall; there they turned the papers in some of the offices topsy-turvy, threatening to set fire to them; but they were prevented from executing their project. They loaded the most atrocious insults on MM. Bailly, de La Fayette, and the members of the commune; and this circumstance proves better than any amount of reasoning that the authorities who then governed Paris had no connection with the insurgents who directed this disorder.

(b) [Maillard] was occupied with a crowd of women · . . . he took away their torches, and nearly lost his life in thus opposing their project. He told them that they could go in a deputation to the commune to demand justice and present their situation, which was that all demanded bread. But they replied that the commune was made up of bad citizens, all deserving to be hanged to the lamp-post, MM. Bailly and La Fayette first of all . . . these women would not listen to reason, and after having put in ruin the Hôtel de Ville, they wanted to go to the National Assembly to find out what had been decreed previous to this day of the fifth of October. . . . [Maillard secured] a drum at the

---

[1] Extracts, listed here as (a) to (j), are identified at the end of the selection.

door of the Hôtel de Ville, where the women had already assembled in great numbers. Detachments of them departed for various districts to recruit other women, to whom they gave rendezvous at the Place Louis XV. Maillard saw several men place themselves at their head, and make to them harangues calculated to excite sedition . . . they took the route to Versailles, having before them eight or ten drummers. The women at that time might have numbered six or seven thousand.

At Versailles

(c) They [the mob of women] consented to do what he [Maillard] wished. In consequence the cannons were placed behind them and the said women were invited to sing *Vive Henri IV!* while entering Versailles and to cry "Long live the King!" This they ceaselessly did in the midst of the people of the city, who awaited them, crying, "Long live our Parisiennes!" They arrived at the door of the National Assembly. . . .

After some debating among these women, fifteen were found to enter with him to the bar of the National Assembly. . . . He asked the president, M. Mounier, for permission to speak. This being accorded him, he said that two or three persons whom they had encountered on the way, and who were riding in a carriage from the court, had told him that an *abbé* attached to the Assembly had given a miller two hundred livres to stop making flour, and had promised him a like sum every week. The National Assembly vigorously demanded his name, but Maillard was unable to give it. . . . The Assembly still persisting in its desire to know the name of the man denounced, M. de Robespierre, deputy from Artois, took the floor and said that . . . the Abbé Grégoire could throw some light on the subject. . . . Maillard then asked for the floor and said it was also essential that they end the disorder and uncertainty which had spread through the capital upon the arrival of the regiment of Flanders in Versailles. This regiment should be sent away because the citizens feared that they would start a revolution. M. Mounier replied that they would inform the king of this in the evening when he returned from the hunt, which was where he was said to be.

(d) Maillard and the women who accompanied him appeared to be drunk. "Where is our Comte de Mirabeau?" these women asked repeatedly. "We want to see our Comte de Mirabeau!" Some of them showed a piece of black and moldy bread and added, "We will make the Austrian [Marie Antoinette] swallow it and we will cut her throat." The number of women gradually increased. They entered pell-mell into the seats of the deputies and carried on loud conversations with those in the tribunes. Some surrounded the desk of the secretaries, others the chair of the president. They obliged the president and several of the deputies to receive their grimy and unpleasant kisses.

(e) After the return of the king to the palace, several *gardes du corps* [members of the palace guard] and other persons in service at the court, who had been searching for the king in all directions, found themselves in the grand avenue in the midst of these brigands of both sexes, and were assailed with insults and musket shots. Several balls fired at them struck the walls of the hall of the National Assembly.

The insults and indignities, together with the musket shots fired by the first column of brigands, had given just cause for uneasiness at the court. The king's guard, the regiment of Flanders, and the national guard of Versailles were ordered to take to arms. The guards at the gate closed the grills, and the king's guards, stationed outside, received orders not to touch their sabers or pistols, and to avoid everything that might irritate the people. The *gardes du corps* conformed to this order with such resignation that they could have been peaceably massacred one after the other if only their enemies had dared to attempt it.

(f) A deputation of eight women was introduced into the palace. They were conducted to M. de Saint-Priest, the minister of Paris, of whom they demanded bread. "When you had only one king," dryly replied Saint-Priest, "you did not lack for bread; now that you have twelve hundred, go ask them for it." The women were then admitted to the council room; they repeated to the king the request they had proffered to M. de Saint-Priest. "You should know my benevolence," replied the king. "I am going to order that all the bread in Versailles be brought and given to you." This response appeared to satisfy these women. Most of them were there in good faith, knowing, nothing of the projects of the conspirators. Forcibly dragged to Versailles, they had had it dinned into their ears that the people were dying of hunger and that the only means of ending the famine was to address themselves to the king and the National Assembly. They believed they were fulfilling the purpose of their expedition in obtaining a decree on sustenance from the Assembly, and having it sanctioned by the king. These women, enchanted with the way they had been received, left the council room, crying, "Long live the King! Long live the *gardes du corps!*"

(g) The people, who had given quarter to the *gardes du corps*, did not, for all that, lose sight of the principal object of their enterprise. They demanded, with shrieks, that the king come to Paris; they said that if the royal family would come to Paris to live there would be no lack of provisions. M. de La Fayette seconded this desire with all his might in the council which was then held in the presence of Their Majesties. Finally, the king, fatigued, solicited, and pressed by all, gave his word that he would depart at midday. This promise flew from mouth to mouth; the acclamations of the people and a fusillade of musketry were the results.

His Majesty appeared then for the second time on the balcony to confirm to the people the promise he had just given to M. de La Fayette. At this second appearance, the joy of the populace was unrestrained. A voice demanded "the queen on the balcony." This princess, who was never greater nor more magnanimous than at moments when danger was most imminent, unhesitatingly presented herself on the balcony, holding M. le Dauphin by one hand and Madame Royale by the other. At that a voice cried out, "No children!" The queen, by a backward movement of her arms, pushed the children back into the room, and remained alone on the balcony, folding her hands on her breast, with a countenance showing calmness, nobility, and dignity impossible to describe, and seemed thus to wait for death. This act of resignation astonished the assassins so much and inspired so much admiration in the coarse people that a general clapping of hands and cries of "Bravo! Long live the queen!" repeated on all sides, disconcerted the malevolent. I saw, however, one of these madmen aim at the queen, and his neighbor knock down the barrel of the musket with a blow of his hand, nearly massacring this brigand who was doubtless one of those who had made the irruption of the morning.

The Return to Paris

(h) One saw first the mass of the Parisian troops file by. Each soldier carried a loaf on the end of his bayonet. Then came the fishwives, drunk with fury, joy and wine, holding branches of trees ornamented with ribbons, sitting astride the cannon, mounted on the horses of the *gardes du corps,* and wearing their hats. Some disported cuirasses before and behind, and others were armed with sabers and muskets. They were accompanied by the multitude of brigands and Paris laborers. . . . They halted from time to time to fire new salvos, while the fishwives descended from their horses and cannon to march around the carriage of the king. They embraced the soldiers and roared out songs to the refrain of "Here is the baker, the baker's wife, and the baker's little boy!" The horror of a cold, somber, rainy day; the infamous militia splattering through the mud; the harpies, monsters with human faces; the captive monarch and his family ignominiously dragged along surrounded by guards; all formed such a frightful spectacle, such a mixture of shame and anguish, that to this very day I cannot think of it without my senses being completely overwhelmed.

At times the queen was in a state of passive endurance difficult to describe. Her son was on her knees; he suffered hunger and asked for food. Unable to fulfill his desires, Marie Antoinette pressed him to her heart, weeping. She exhorted him to suffer in silence. The young prince became resigned. . . .

(i) As soon as the royal family entered the Hôtel de Ville, the king had to listen to two harangues by M. Bailly, and to denunciations against his ministers. Then an official report of the sitting was drawn up and publicly read by M. Bailly. But as it cited some words of the king's discourse inexactly, the queen interrupted him with the presence of mind which was one of the fine traits of her character. He had forgotten one of the most touching parts of the discourse of the king. The queen recalled to him gracefully that His Majesty had said, "I have relied upon the attachment and fidelity of my people, and have placed myself in the midst of my subjects with complete confidence." . . .

After this the family re-entered the carriage in the midst of acclamations and betook themselves, with a part of the national guard. to the palace of the Tuileries. Monsieur and Madame went to the Luxembourg.

(j) The Comte de Mirabeau announced [to the Assembly] that the king was about to depart for Paris. In eagerness to hold their sessions in the midst of the tumult of the capital, they declared themselves inseparable from the monarch, and carried to him this declaration as a proof of their zeal for his interests. In reality, it was an express approbation of the violation of his liberty.

Document Set 20.3 References

A. An English Traveler Witnesses the Fall of the Bastille
   Edward Rigby, in J. M. Thompson, ed., *English Witnesses of the French Revolution* (Oxford, England: Basil Blackwell, 1938), 55–60.
B. The Women's March on Versailles, October 5–6, 1789
   E. L. Higgins, *The French Revolution as Told by Contemporaries* (Boston, Houghton Mifflin, 1938), 122–125, 129–131.

DOCUMENT SET 20.4
The Regeneration of France

Revolt engulfed the French countryside in the summer of 1789, as peasants panicked at the twin specters of their lords' reasserting age-old domination over villagers and landless riffraff invading the villages to seize the peasants' own property. Desperately hoping to stave off the violence and shocked at the consequences of Old Regime "abuses," the reformers in the National Assembly abolished what it called feudalism. It also decided to create for France a written constitution, the opening section of which (drawn up shortly thereafter) was the Declaration of the Rights of Man and Citizen, one of the Western world's basic statements of human rights. It appears as Document A.

Having made France a constitutional monarchy, the National Assembly in February 1790 summed up the reforms it enacted and looked forward optimistically (Document B). Two personal account follow (Documents C and D), from September 1790 and March 1791, respectively, in which English travelers express their skepticism about the reforms. Note in particular their remarks about how changes in dress reflected political attitudes and about the currency depreciation that occurred with the fall in value of *assignats*—notes of obligation issued by the government payable out of the proceeds of sales of nationalized church property. (Document D alludes to Edmund Burke's critique of the French Revolution.) Finally, in Document E, an early French feminist, Olympe de Gouges, demands that the "regeneration of France" be extended in a direction few male reformers even considered: to achieve the political equality of men and women. Compare her Declaration of the Rights of Woman and Citizen to the Declaration of the Rights of Man and Citizen.

Extract from these accounts a picture of the ideals and the realities of reform-oriented politics in this early phase of the French Revolution. Who appears to have been benefiting the most from reform, and why? In what ways to these documents reveal a historical turning point? And do you agree with the qualifications on absolute human rights set out in the Declaration of the Rights of Man?

A. Declaration of Rights of Man and Citizen

The representatives of the French people, organized as a National Assembly, believing that the ignorance, neglect, or contempt of the rights of man are the sole cause of public calamities and of the corruption of governments, have determined to set forth in a solemn declaration the natural, inalienable, and sacred rights of man, in order that this declaration, being constantly before all the members of the social body, shall remind them continually of their rights and duties; in order that the acts of the legislative power, as well as those of the executive power, may be compared at any moment with the objects and purposes of all political institutions and may thus be more respected; and, lastly, in order that the grievances of the citizens, based hereafter upon simple and incontestable principles, shall tend to the maintenance of the constitution and redound to the happiness of all. Therefore the National Assembly recognizes and proclaims, in the presence and under the auspices of the Supreme Being, the following rights of man and of the citizen:

ARTICLE 1. Men are born and remain free and equal in rights. Social distinctions may be founded only upon the general good.

2. The aim of all political association is the preservation of the natural and imprescriptible rights of man. These rights are liberty, property, security, and resistance to oppression.

3. The principle of all sovereignty resides essentially in the nation. No body nor individual may exercise any authority which does not proceed directly from the nation.

4. Liberty consists in the freedom to do everything which injures no one else; hence the exercise of the natural rights of each man has no limits except those which assure to the other members of the society the enjoyment of the same rights. These limits can only be determined by law.

5. Law can only prohibit such actions as are hurtful to society. Nothing may be prevented which is not forbidden by law, and no one may be forced to do anything not provided for by law.

6. Law is the expression of the general will. Every citizen has a right to participate personally, or through his representative, in its formation. It must be the same for all, whether it protects or punishes. All citizens, being equal in the eyes of the law, are equally eligible to all dignities and to all public positions and occupations, according to their abilities, and without distinction except that of their virtues and talents.

7. No person shall be accused, arrested, or imprisoned except in the cases and according to the forms prescribed by law. Any one soliciting, transmitting, executing, or causing to be executed, any arbitrary order, shall be punished. But any citizen summoned or arrested in virtue of the law shall submit without delay, as resistance constitutes an offense.

8. The law shall provide for such punishments only as are strictly and obviously necessary, and no one shall suffer punishment except it be legally inflicted in virtue of a law passed and promulgated before the commission of the offense.

9. As all persons are held innocent until they shall have been declared guilty, if arrest shall be deemed indispensable, all harshness not essential to the securing of the prisoner's person shall be severely repressed by law.

10. No one shall be disquieted on account of his opinions, including his religious views, provided their manifestation does not disturb the public order established by law.

11. The free communication of ideas and opinions is one of the most precious of the rights of man. Every citizen may, accordingly, speak, write, and print with freedom, but shall be responsible for such abuses of this freedom as shall be defined by law.

12. The security of the rights of man and of the citizen requires public military forces. These forces are, therefore, established for the good of all and not for the personal advantage of those to whom they shall be intrusted.

13. A common contribution is essential for the maintenance of the public forces and for the cost of administration. This should be equitably distributed among all the citizens in proportion to their means.

14. All the citizens have a right to decide, either personally or by their representatives, as to the necessity of the public contribution; to grant this freely; to know to what uses it is put; and to fix the proportion, the mode of assessment and of collection and the duration of the taxes.

15. Society has the right to require of every public agent an account of his administration.

16. A society in which the observance of the law is not assured, nor the separation of powers defined, has no constitution at all.

17. Since property is an inviolable and sacred right, no one shall be deprived thereof except where public necessity, legally determined, shall clearly demand it, and then only on condition that the owner shall have been previously and equitably indemnified.

B. The National Assembly Addresses the French People, February 11, 1790

The National Assembly, as it progresses in its work, is receiving upon every hand the felicitations of the provinces, cities, and villages, testimonials of the public satisfaction and expressions of grateful appreciation; but murmurs reach it as well, from those who are affected or injured by the blows aimed at so many abuses and prejudices. While occupied with the welfare of all, the Assembly is solicitous in regard to individual ills. It can forgive prejudice, bitterness, and injustice, but it feels it to be one of its duties to warn you against the influence of calumny, and to quiet the empty terrors which some are vainly trying to arouse in you. To what have they not resorted in order to mislead and discourage you? They pretend to be unaware of the good that the National Assembly has accomplished; this we propose to recall to your mind. Objections have been raised against what has been done; these we propose to meet. Doubts and anxiety have been disseminated as to what we propose to do in the future; this we will explain to you.

What has the Assembly accomplished? In the midst of storms, it has, with a firm hand, traced the principles of a constitution which will assure your liberty forever. The rights of man had been misconceived and insulted for centuries; they have been reestablished for all humanity in that declaration, which shall serve as an everlasting war cry against oppressors and as a law for the legislators themselves. The nation had lost the right to decree both the laws and the taxes; this right has been restored to it, while at the same time the true principles of monarchy have been solemnly established, as well as the inviolability of the august head of the nation and the heredity of the throne in a family so dear to all Frenchmen.

Formerly you had only the Estates General; now you have a National Assembly of which you can never be again deprived. In the Estates General the several orders, which were necessarily at odds and under the domination of ancient pretensions, dictated the decrees and could check the free action of the national will. These orders no longer exist; all have disappeared before the honorable title of *citizen*. All being citizens alike, you demanded citizen-defenders and, at the first summons, the National Guard arose, which, called together by patriotism and commanded by honor, has everywhere maintained or established order and watches with untiring zeal over the safety of each for the benefit of all.

Privileges without number, irreconcilably at enmity with every good, made up our entire public law. These have been destroyed, and at the word of this Assembly the provinces which were the most jealous of their own privileges applauded their disappearance, feeling that they gained rather than lost thereby. A vexatious feudal system, powerful even in its ruin, covered the whole of France; it has now disappeared, never to return. In the provinces you were subject to a harassing administration; from this you have been freed. Arbitrary commands threatened the liberty of the citizens; they have been done away with. You desired a complete organization of the municipalities; this you have just received, and the creation of these bodies, chosen by your votes, offers, at this moment, a most imposing spectacle. At the same time the National Assembly has finished the task of a new division of the kingdom, which alone might serve to remove the last trace of former prejudices, substitute for provincial selfishness the true love for one's country, and serve as the basis of a just system of representation. . . .

This, Frenchmen, is our work, or rather yours, for we are only your organ, and you have enlightened, encouraged, and sustained us in our labors. What a glorious period is this which we at last enjoy! How honorable the heritage which you may transmit to your posterity! Raised to the rank of citizens; admissible to every form of employment; enlightened censors of the administration when it is not actually in your hands; certain that all will be done by you and for you; equally before the law; free to act, to speak, to write; owing no account to individuals but always to the common will;—what condition more happy! Is there a single citizen worthy of the name who would dare look back, who would rebuild once more the ruins which surround us, in order again to contemplate the former structure?

Yet what has not been said and done to weaken the natural impressions which such advantages should produce upon you? It is urged that we have destroyed everything; everything must, then, be reconstructed. But what is there which need be so much regretted? If we would know, let those be questioned in regard to the objects of reform or destruction who did not profit by them; let even men of good faith be questioned who did profit by them. But let us leave one side those who, in order to ennoble the demands of purely personal interests, now choose as the objects of their commiseration the fate of those to whom they were formerly quite indifferent. We may then judge if each subject of reform does not enjoy the approval of all of those whose opinions should be considered.

Some say that we have acted too precipitately, as many others proclaim that we have been too deliberate. Too much precipitation! Does not every one

know that only by attacking and overthrowing all the abuses at the same time can we hope to be freed from them without danger of their return; that then, and then only, every one becomes interested in the reestablishment of order; that slow and partial reforms have always resulted in no reform at all, and that an abuse preserved becomes the support, and before long the means of restoring all those which we thought to have destroyed?

Our meetings are said to be disorderly; what of that, if the decrees which proceed from them are wise? We are indeed far from wishing to hold up for your admiration the details of all our debates. More than once they have been a source of annoyance to us, but at the same time we have felt that it was very unjust to take advantage of this disorder; and indeed this impetuosity is the almost inevitable effect of the first conflict which has perhaps ever been fought by every right principle against every form of error.

We are accused of having aspired to a chimerical perfection. A curious reproach indeed, which, if one looks at it closely, proves to be only an ill-disguised desire for the perpetuation of the abuses. The National Assembly has not allowed itself to be influenced by motives of servile interest or pusillanimity. It has had the courage, or rather the sense, to believe that useful ideas, essential to the human race, were not destined simply to adorn the pages of a book, and that the Supreme Being, when he granted the attribute of perfectibility to man, did not forbid him to apply this peculiar appanage of his nature to the social organization, which has become the most comprehensive of his interests and almost the most important of his needs.

It is impossible, some say, to regenerate an old and corrupt nation. Let such objectors learn that there is nothing corrupt but those who wish to perpetuate corrupting abuses, and that a nation becomes young again the moment it resolves to be born anew in liberty. Behold the regeneration! How the nation's heart already beats with joy and hope, and how pure, elevated, and patriotic are its sentiments! With what enthusiasm do the people daily solicit the honor of being allowed to take the oath of citizen!—but why consider so despicable a reproach? Shall the National Assembly be reduced to excuse itself for not having rendered the French people desperate?

But we have done nothing for the people, their pretended friends cry on all sides. Yet it is the people's cause which is everywhere triumphant. Nothing done for the people! Does not every abuse which is abolished prepare the way for, and assure to them, relief? Is there an abuse which does not weigh upon the people? They do not complain—it is because the excess of their ills has stifled complaint. They are now unhappy,—say better that they are still unhappy,—but not for long; that we swear.

We have destroyed the power of the executive—no, say rather the power of the ministers, which, in reality, formerly destroyed or often degraded the executive power. We have enlightened the executive power by showing it its true rights; we have, above all, ennobled it by bringing it to the true source of its power, the power of the people. The executive power is now without force,—against the constitution and the law, that is true, but in support of them it will be more powerful than ever before.

The people are aroused,—yes, for its defense, and with reason. But, it is urged, in several places there have been unfortunate occurrences. Should the National Assembly be reproached for these? Should disasters be attributed to it which it mourns, which it would have prevented and arrested by the force of its decrees, and which the hereafter indissoluble union between the two powers and the irresistible action of all the national forces will doubtless check?

We have exceeded our powers. The reply is simple. We were incontestably sent to make a constitution; this was the wish and the need of the whole of France. But was it possible to create a constitution and form an even imperfect body of constitutional decrees, without the plentitude of power which we have exercised? We will say more: without the National Assembly France was lost; without the recognition of the principle which has governed all our decrees, of submitting the decision of every matter to a majority of votes, freely cast, it is impossible to conceive, we will not say a constitution, but even the prospect of destroying permanently the least of the abuses. This principle embodies an eternal truth and has been recognized throughout France. It receives recognition in a thousand ways in the numerous ratifications which oppose the swarm of libels reproaching us for exceeding our powers. These addresses, felicitations, compliments, and patriotic resolutions,—what a conclusive confirmation do they constitute of those powers which some would contest!

These, Frenchmen, are the reproaches which have been directed against your representatives in the mass of culpable writings in which a tone of civic grief is assumed. But then authors flatter themselves in vain that we are to be discouraged. Our courage is redoubled; you will not long wait for the results. . . . We will pursue our laborious task, devoting ourselves to the great work of drawing up the constitution—your work as well as ours. We will complete it, aided by the wisdom of all France.

C. An English Traveler Comments on the State of Affairs in Paris, September 1790

You are well able to judge how strange the contrast must be between Paris governed, and Paris governing; but it is so strange in so many ways, that I own I find great difficulty in attempting to answer your question of what strikes me most, for I am quite perplexed by the number and variety of ridiculous and absurd things, which I hear and see everywhere, and every day. The common people appear to me to be exactly as gay as I remember them, though it is undoubtedly true that the greater part of them is starving for want of employment, especially the tradesmen; and notwithstanding they all talk the highest language in favour of the Revolution, they laugh at the National Assembly without scruple, and say they had rather have Aristocratical Louis, than Democratical Assignats. The streets are crowded with newsmen and hawkers, crying about libels of all sorts from morning till night, exactly in the manner you must have observed in Dublin; nothing is too indecent or abusive. There being an end of the police, it is not possible to imagine any kind of bawdy print that is not publicly stuck up in the Palais Royal, and on the Boulevards: the Attorney General's blood would boil at the sight of such audacious bawdery. The object seems to be everywhere to mark a contempt for all former regulations. At the *spectacle,* they have introduced monks and nuns and crucifixes on the stage; and the actors are violently applauded, merely for wearing these forbidden garments. The *parterre* is more riotous than twenty English upper galleries put together; a few nights ago Richard Coeur de Lion was acted, and a women of fashion was absolutely forced to leave the house, because she clapped with too much violence while the famous song of *O Richard, O mon roi!* was singing; a hundred fellows started up together roaring *à bas la femme en éventail blanc* ["down with the woman with the white fan": Marie Antoinette], and would not suffer the actors to proceed till this *Aristocrate* left the house. . . . Nothing can be more tiresome than all their new plays and operas; they are a heap of hackneyed public sentiments on general topics of the rights of men and duties of Kings, just like Sheridan's grand paragraphs in the *Morning Post* [a London newspaper]: these are applauded to the skies. I do not know whether you have heard that many of the Petits Maitres [young gentlemen], in order to show their attachment to the Democracy, have sacrificed their curls, *toupées,* and *queues:* [i.e., their powdered wigs];

some of them go about with cropped locks like English farmers without any powder, and others wear little black scratch wigs, both these fashions are called *Têtes à la Romaine* ["Roman heads"], which is a comical name for such folly. I must not forget that I have seen several wear gold earrings with their black scratches. . . . I understand from everybody whom I have seen that nothing can be more changed than the whole of their manners. The *Democrates* out of the Assembly are very few indeed among the people of any distinction, and the *Aristocrates* are melancholy and miserable to the last degree; this makes the society at Paris very gloomy; the number of deserted houses is immense, and if it were not for the Deputies, the Ambassadors, and some refugees from Brussels, there would be scarcely a gentleman's coach to be seen in the streets. You have certainly been informed of the principles of the two clubs, the *Enragées,* whose name is easily understood, and the *Quatre Vingt Neuf,* the latter is something like our armed neutrality . . . ; for this club acting together, can give a majority either to the *côté gauche or droite*[1] in the Assembly. . . . I have never been at this club of 1789, although they admit English members of Parliament, because I understand nothing is done publicly excepting the recital of speeches and motions intended for the Assembly; and with these I have been sufficiently tired at the Assembly itself. I have been there several times, and it is not possible to imagine so strange a scene; the confusion at times surpasses all that ever has been known since government appeared in the world. . . . They have no regular forms of debate on ordinary business; some speak from their seats, some from the floor, some from the table, and some from the tribunes or desks; . . . they speak without preparation, and I thought many of them acquitted themselves well enough in that way, where only a few sentences were to be delivered; but on these occasions the riot is so great that it is very difficult to collect what is said. I am certain that I have seen above a hundred in the act of addressing the Assembly together, all persisting to speak, and as many more replying in different parts of the House, sentence by sentence; then the President claps his hands on both ears and roars order, as if he was calling a coach; sometimes he is quite driven to despair; he beats his table, his breast; . . . wringing his hands is quite a common action, and I really believe he swears. . . . At last he seizes a favourable moment of

quiet, either to put the question or to name who ought to speak; then five hundred reclamations all at once renew the confusion, which seldom ends till the performers are completely hoarse, and obliged to give way to a fresh set. On great occasions the speakers deliver their speeches from the tribune, and these are always written speeches, or so generally, that I believe Mirabeau and Maury and Barnave are the only exceptions; and even these often read their speeches. Nothing can be more fatiguing than these readings, which entirely destroy all the spirit and interest of debate. . . . I heard Mirabeau and Maury both speak a few sentences in the midst of one of the riots I have mentioned, and I preferred Maury, whose manner is bold and unaffected, and his voice very fine; Mirabeau appeared to me to be full of affectation, and he has a bad voice, but he is the most admired speaker. There are four galleries which contain above twice the number admitted into the gallery in England, and here a most extraordinary scene is exhibited; for the galleries approve and disapprove by groaning and clapping, exactly as if the whole was a *spectacle.* . . . While the orators are reading their speeches, the Assembly frequently shows a most singular degree of patience such as I am certain the English House of Commons is not capable of. . . . Dulness and monotony are borne in perfect silence; and during such speeches, the President generally amuses himself with reading some pamphlets or newspapers. . . . I forgot to mention one circumstance that had a most comical effect. The *Huissiers* ["sergeants at arms"] of the Assembly walk up and down the room during times of great tumult, bellowing silence as loud as they can hollow, and endeavouring to persuade the disorderly orators to sit down.

I went to Court this morning at the Tuilleries, and a most gloomy Court it was; many of the young people of the first fashion and rank wear mourning always for economy. . . . The King seemed well, but I thought his manner evidently humbled since I was introduced to him before; he now bows to everybody, which was not a Bourbon fashion before the Revolution. The Queen looked very ill; the Dauphin was with her, and she appeared anxious to shew him. They say here that he is her shield; she never stirs out without him.

D. Another Englishman Comments on the Paris Scene, March 1791

There is one point upon which all parties seem to be agreed—that the restoration of the ancient form of government is become totally impracticable, from

---

[1] The left or the right. The custom of grouping the more liberal or radical members on the left and the more conservative ones on the right, from which comes the designation of "left wing" or "right wing" in modern politics, dates from the French Revolution.

any quarter or by any means whatsoever. The three descriptions of persons *in the Kingdom,* the most interested in the event, are the Sovereign, the Nobility, and the Clergy; but it is evident that their exertions alone, unaided by foreign Powers, are absolutely inadequate to the accomplishment of it. That loyalty and attachment to their Sovereign, which were formerly the characteristics of this nation, exist no longer. The mental imbecility of the present King, and the profligacy of some branches of the royal family, have implanted contempt and aversion so deeply in the bulk of the people that his present melancholy state of captivity and humiliation, so far from creating a spirit of indignation against those who have usurped his authority, has afforded a subject of ridicule and triumph to a great majority of the nation. In regard to the nobility, their dispersion, their want of concert, of pecuniary resources and of a leader, but chiefly the circumstances of their estates being at the mercy of their enemies, all concur to prevent them from forming or carrying into execution any enterprize of much magnitude and moment. The respect that used to be paid to the character and functions of the clergy has long been dwindling away, and the influence which that body derived from their great territorial possessions, now act as an instrument against them. Not only inasmuch as their estates have been wrested from them, but also as the individuals who have purchased those estates under the national faith are now materially interested in protecting them, *by every means,* against any invasion of their newly acquired rights, and the possibility of their ever reverting to their original possessors. With respect to the prospect of any *external* interference, you, Sir, are better able to judge of that than I can be. I am, however, firmly persuaded that no serious apprehensions on that head are entertained here. The ruling party, indeed, do not rely on the three millions of men (now trained to arms) alone—they assert they have a more effectual pledge for the non-intervention of foreign Powers, in possessing the persons of the King, and of such of the Aristocratical party as have not chosen to expatriate themselves, both of whom they would not scruple to deliver up to the fury of an exasperated populace on the first appearance of a foreign invasion. . . .

There is no assertion of Mr. [Edmund] Burke's more true than this—that the French have shown themselves much more skilful in destroying than in erecting. As I am convinced that no man in this country, *even at this moment,* has any clear notion of the new order of things that is to arise in the place of the old, it is therefore needless to enter into any discussion of the numerous speculative theories that now swarm in the nation, which have no other foundation than the heated imaginations of their fabricators.

No party in the National Assembly seems to be actuated by an adherence to a regular well-defined system, which is, I think, pretty clearly proved by the contradictory decrees that are every day issuing out to answer the emergency of the moment. And even if there was a system, there does not appear to be any man of abilities so transcendent, or of patriotism so unsuspected, as to be capable of giving direction and energy to the movements of any compact *concentrated* body of individuals. This is a circumstance which separates the French Revolution from every preceding one in any other country, and renders it impossible to discern a clue to the present and future operations of that body, in whom all authority is at present centered. . . .

In the meantime they avoid rendering themselves obnoxious and unpopular, by throwing the execution of everything that is either odious or absurd in their own numerous decrees on the King and his ministers. They have stripped royalty of everything that could make it either respectable or amiable, and by perpetually separating the *function* from the *person* of the monarch, they insensibly confound him in the general mass of citizens. Indeed their affectation is carried to so ridiculous a pitch, that I am rather surprised that we do not hear of the *pouvoir executif's* [executive power] looking out of the window, or going to bed to *its* wife.

In the midst of all this wretched scene of political confusion, it is strongly suspected that several members of the National Assembly have enriched themselves by stock-jobbing and other arts, and Mirabeau in particular. That arch-patriot is now living in great magnificence, and indulges his ruling passion for buying up valuable books with unexampled profusion.

As you may have been perhaps surprised that the late discussion of the question of Regency should have appeared to be a matter of such urgency, I think it necessary to remark that the King's health, not from extreme sensibility, but from want of exercise, and from indulging too freely in the pleasures of the table, has suffered so much that it is not expected his Majesty can survive many years.

I must not omit to mention two circumstances that have struck me greatly in my present residence in this capital—the tranquillity which now appears to subsist in it, and the little interruption that the newly-created paper money has had to encounter in its circulation. Excepting a greater number of men in military uniforms parading the streets, all the common occupations of life proceed as smoothly and regularly as if no event of consequence had occurred, and the public amusements are followed with as much avidity as in the most quiet and flourishing periods of the monarchy. In regard to the *Assignats,* although they are now at a discount of 7 per cent and are expected to fall lower, no person seems to murmur at taking them in payment, or to express any doubts of their validity.

E. Olympe de Gouges Issues Her Declaration of the Rights of Woman and Citizen

The mothers, daughters, and sisters, representatives of the nation, demand to be constituted a national assembly. Considering that ignorance, disregard of or contempt for the rights of women are the only causes of public misfortune and of governmental corruption, they have resolved to set forth in a solemn declaration, the natural, inalienable and sacred rights of woman. . . .

1. Woman is born free and remains equal in rights to man. . . .

3. The principle of all sovereignty resides essentially in the Nation, which is none other than the union of Woman and Man. . . .

4. Liberty and Justice consist of rendering to persons those things that belong to them; thus, the exercise of woman's natural rights is limited only by the perpetual tyranny with which man opposes her; these limits must be changed according to the laws of nature and reason. . . .

10. No one should be punished for their opinions. Woman has the right to mount the scaffold; she should likewise have the right to speak in public, provided that her demonstrations do not disrupt public order as established by law.

Document Set 20.4 References

A. Declaration of Rights of Man and Citizen
James Harvey Robinson, ed., *Readings in European History* (Boston: Ginn, 1904), 2:409–411.
B. The National Assembly Addresses the French People, February 11, 1790
Address of the French Assembly, in James Harvey Robinson, ed., *Readings in European History* (Boston: Ginn, 1904), 2:417–422.
C. An English Traveler Comments on the State of Affairs in Paris, September 1790
Lord Morington, in J. M. Thompson, ed., *English Witnesses of the French Revolution* (Oxford, England: Basil Blackwell, 1938), 93–96.
D. Another Englishman Comments on the Paris Scene, March 1791
George Hammond, in Thompson, 110–112.
E. Olympe de Gouges issues her Declaration of the Rights of Woman and Citizen
Susan Grooge Bell and Karen M. Offen, eds., *Women, the Family, and Freedom: The Debate in Documents* (Stanford, Cal.: Stanford University Press, 1983), 1:105–106.

DOCUMENT SET 20.5
The Fall of the French Monarchy

Louis XVI never accepted his new role as a limited monarch, and in April 1791 he tried unsuccessfully to flee to the Holy Roman Empire, hoping to rally *émigré* forces with the backing of Europe's conservative monarchies. The Parisian people's reaction to the royal flight, dating from June 1791, appears in Document A.

Document B is a vehement piece by the editor of the radical newspaper *The Friend of the People,* Jean-Paul Marat. It was written after the moderate majority in the National Assembly had attempted to overlook the king's flight; a petition protesting the assembly's position was prepared by the more radical political clubs (including the Jacobins and the Cordeliers, mentioned by Marat) and circulated among the Parisians. When the petitioners assembled on July 17, 1791, they clashed violently with the middle-class National Guard commanded by the marquis de Lafayette, a liberal royalist famous for his participation in the American Revolution.

Document C is a secret letter that Louis wrote to the king of Prussia in December 1791, revealing his continuing hopes for a foreign-backed counterrevolution.

Antimonarchical sentiment continued to mount in 1792, particularly after France declared war on the Holy Roman Emperor, the *émigrés'* chief foreign patron. The mood of patriotic exaltation and revolutionary fervor, and the sentiments of ordinary French men and women, are captured in Document D, excerpts from a book by the English traveler Richard Twiss, who visited Paris in the summer of 1792.

Document E is a letter from a member of the National Guard to a friend in Rennes, describing the tumultuous events of August 10, 1792, to which Richard Twiss (Document D) also alluded. Fearing (with some justification) that recent military defeats had resulted from treason by royalist French military officers and by the king himself, a crowd of 20,000 Parisians and *fédérés* (volunteers from the provinces sent to help defend Paris) attacked the Tuileries Palace, where Louis and his family had resided until recently taking refuge with the National Assembly. About 390 of the attackers and 600 Swiss mercenaries defending the Tuileries died in the fighting and the subsequent massacre. As a result of this violent uprising, the French monarchy was "suspended" and Louis XVI deprived of his powers. (As we will see in the next group of documents, the monarchy would be abolished in September, and in January 1793 the king executed.)

One of the centers of radical agitation in Paris was the Jacobin Club, whose overwhelmingly middle-class members consistently looked favorably upon the revolutionary fervor of the Parisian masses. One of the most prominent Jacobins was Maximilian Robespierre; by the summer of 1792 he was a prominent and vocal radical in the Legislative Assembly, the successor to the National Assembly. The Jacobin Club, described by an English observer in Document F, was itself a tumultuous debating forum open to pressure from ordinary Parisians, both male and female, and even to colorful foreigners like Théroigne de Méricourt, a Luxembourg-born young woman known for her passionate republicanism and her prominence in the August 10 events.

Read these documents not only for their descriptions of tumultuous events but also with an eye to the motivations of the participants: the king, fearful of his safety yet unwilling to reconcile himself to the loss of his absolutist power; the moderate middle class and noble reformers, trying to keep control of an increasingly dangerous situation; ordinary Parisians, oppressed by rising prices and increasing unemployment, yet conscious of the power they could unleash in a violent uprising; and radical journalists like Marat and politicians like Robespierre, who proclaimed themselves the voices of the people. Keep in mind, too, the ceaseless political agitation, the disappearance of censorship, and the marked tendency toward political leveling, all of which Twiss describes accurately, if not approvingly.

A. Parisians React to the King's Flight, 1791

It was not until ten o'clock in the morning that the municipal government announced, by firing a cannon thrice, the unexpected event of the day. But for three hours the news had already been passing from mouth to mouth and was circulating in all quarters of the city. During these three hours many outrages might have been committed. The king had gone. This news produced a moment of anxiety, and everybody ran in a crowd to the palace of the Tuileries to see if it were true; but every one turned almost immediately to the hall where the National Assembly met, declaring that their king was in there and that Louis XVI might go where he pleased.

Then the people became curious to visit the apartments vacated by the royal family; they traversed them all, and we questioned the sentinels we found there, "Where, and how, could he have escaped? How could this fat royal person, who complained of the meanness of his lodging, manage to make himself invisible to the sentries,—he whose girth would stop up any passage?" The soldiers of the guard had nothing to say to this. We insisted: "This flight is not natural; your commanders must have been in the plot. . . . for while you were at your post Louis XVI left his without your knowing it and yet passing close to you." These reflections, which naturally suggested themselves, account for the reception which made Lafayette pale when he appeared in the Place de Grève and passed along the quays. He took refuge in the National Assembly, where he made some confessions that did little to restore him to popular favor.

Far from being "famished for a glimpse of the king," the people proved, by the way in which they took the escape of Louis XVI, that they were sick of the throne and tired of paying for it. If they had known, moreover, that Louis XVI, in his message, which was just then being read in the National Assembly, complained "that he had not been able to find in the palace of the Tuileries the most simple conveniences of life," the people might have been roused to some excess; but they knew their own strength and did not permit themselves any of those little exhibitions of vengeance which are natural to irritated weakness.

They contented themselves with making sport, in their own way, of royalty and of the man who was invested with it. The portrait of the king was taken down from its place of honor and hung on the door. A fruit woman took possession of Antoinette's bed and used it to display her cherries, saying, "It's the nation's turn now to be comfortable." A young girl refused to let them put the queen's bonnet on her head and trampled on it with indignation and contempt. They had more respect for the dauphin's study,—but we should blush to report the titles of the books which his mother had selected.

The streets and public squares offered a spectacle of another kind. The national force deployed itself everywhere in an imposing manner. The brave Santerre alone enrolled two thousand pikemen in this *faubourg.* These were not the "active" citizens and the royal bluecoats, that were enjoying the honors of the celebration. The woolen caps reappeared and eclipsed the bearskins. The women contested with the men the duty of guarding the city gates, saying, "It was the women who brought the king to Paris and the men who let him escape." But do not boast too loudly, ladies; it was not much of a present, after all.

The prevailing spirit was apathy in regard to kings in general and contempt for Louis XVI in particular. This showed itself in the least details. On the Place de Grève the people broke up a bust of Louis XVI, which was illuminated by that celebrated lantern which had been a source of terror to the enemies of the Revolution. When will the people execute justice upon all these bronze kings, monuments of our idolatry? In the Rue St. Honoré they forced a dealer to sacrifice a plaster head which somewhat resembled Louis XVI. In another shop they contented themselves with putting a paper band over his eyes. The words "king," "queen," "royal," "Bourbon," "Louis," "court," "Monsieur," "the king's brother," were effaced wherever they were found on pictures or on the signs over shops and stores.

B. Marat Attacks the Moderate Royalists, July 1791

O credulous Parisians! can you be duped by these shameful deceits and cowardly impostures? See if their aim in massacring the patriots was not to annihilate your clubs! Even while the massacre was going on, the emissaries of Mottier [Lafayette] were running about the streets mixing with the groups of people and loudly accusing the fraternal societies and the club of the Cordeliers of causing the misfortunes. The same evening the club of the Cordeliers, wishing to come together, found the doors of their place of meeting nailed up. Two pieces of artillery barred the entrance to the Fraternal Society, and only those conscript fathers who were sold to the court were permitted to enter the Jacobin Club, by means of their deputy's cards.

Not satisfied with annihilating the patriotic associations, these scoundrels violate the liberty of the press, annihilate the Declaration of Rights—the rights of nature. Cowardly citizens, can you hear this without trembling? They declare the oppressed, who, in order to escape their tyranny, would make a weapon of his despair and counsel the massacre of his oppressors, a disturber of the public peace. They declare every citizen a disturber of the public peace who cries, in an uprising, to the ferocious satellites to lower or lay down their arms, thus metamorphosing into crimes the very humanity of peaceful citizens, the cries of terror and natural self-defense.

Infamous legislators, vile scoundrels, monsters satiated with gold and blood, privileged brigands who traffic with the monarch, with our fortunes, our rights, our liberty, and our lives! You thought to strike terror into the hearts of patriotic writers and paralyze them with fright at the sight of the punishments you inflict. I flatter myself that they will not soften. As for *The Friend of the People,* you know that for a long time your decrees directed against the Declaration of Rights have been waste paper to him. Could he but rally at his call two thousand determined men to save the country, he would proceed at their head to tear out the heart of the infernal Mottier in the midst of his battalions of slaves. He would burn the monarch and his minions in his palace, and impale you on your seats and bury you in the burning ruins of your lair.

C. Louis XVI Appeals to the King of Prussia

Paris, December 3, 1791

My Brother:

I have learned through M. du Moustier of the interest which your Majesty has expressed not only in my person but also in the welfare of my kingdom. In giving me these proofs, the attitude of your Majesty has, in all cases where your interest might prove advantageous to my people, excited my lively appreciation. I confidently take advantage of it at this time when, in spite of the fact that I have accepted the new constitution, seditious leaders are openly exhibiting their purpose of entirely destroying the remnants of the monarchy. I have just addressed myself to the emperor, the empress of Russia, and to the kings of Spain and Sweden; I am suggesting to them the idea of a congress of the chief powers of Europe, supported by an armed force, as the best means of checking seditious parties, of establishing a more desirable order of things, and of preventing the evil which afflicts us from reaching the other states of Europe.

I trust that your Majesty will approve my ideas, and that you will maintain the most absolute secrecy about the proposition I am making to you. You will easily understand that the circumstances in which I find myself force me to observe the greatest caution. That is why no one but the baron of Breteuil is informed of my plans, and your Majesty may therefore communicate to him anything you wish....

Your good brother,
Louis

D. An Englishman in Paris, Summer 1792

In every one of the towns between Calais and Paris a full-grown tree (generally a poplar) has been planted in the market place, with many of its boughs and leaves; these last being withered, it makes but a dismal appearance; on the top of this tree or pole is a red woollen or cotton night-cap, which is called the *Cap of Liberty,* with streamers about the pole, or red, blue and white ribbands. I saw several statues of saints, both within and without the churches (and in Paris likewise) with similar caps, and several crucifixes with the national cockade of ribbands tied to the left arm of the image on the cross, but not one with the cockade in its proper place; the reason of which I know not....

The churches in Paris are not much frequented on the week-days, at present; I found a few old women on their knees in some of them, hearing mass; and, at the same time, at the other end of one of these churches commissaries were sitting and entering the names of volunteers for the army. The iron rails in the churches which part the choir from the nave, and also those which encompass chapels and tombs, are all ordered to be converted into heads for pikes....

Hitherto cockades of silk had been worn, the *aristocrats* wore such as were of a paler blue and red than those worn by the *democrats,* and the former were even distinguished by their carriages, on which a cloud was painted upon the arms, which entirely obliterated them (of these I saw above thirty in the evening *promenade* in the *Bois de Boulogne*), but on the 30th of July, every person was compelled by the people to wear a linen cockade, without any distinction in the red and blue colours....

I went once to Versailles; there is hardly anything in the palace but the bare walls, a very few of the looking-glasses, tapestry, and large pictures remaining, as it has now been near two years uninhabited. I crossed the great canal on foot; there was not a drop of water in it....

I went several times to the National Assembly; the *Tribunes,* or *Galleries* (of which there are three) entered warmly, by applauses and by murmurs and hisses, into the affairs which were treated of....

All the coats of arms which formerly decorated the gates of *Hôtels* are taken away, and even seals are at present engraven with cyphers only. The *Chevaliers de St. Louis* still continue to wear the cross, or the ribband, at the buttonhole; all other orders of knighthood are abolished. No liveries are worn by servants, that badge of slavery is likewise abolished; and also all corporation companies, as well as every other monopolizing society, and there are no longer any *Royal* tobacco or salt shops. . . .

Books of all sorts are printed without any *approbation* or *privilege.* Many are exposed on stalls, which are very improper for the public eye. One of them was called the *Private Life of the Queen,* in two volumes, with obscene prints. The book itself is contemptible and disgusting, and might as well have been called, the *Woman of Pleasure.* Of books of this sort I saw above thirty, with plates. Another was a subject not fit even to be mentioned. I read a small pamphlet, entitled "*Le Christ-Roi,* or a Parallel of the Sufferings of Louis XVI etc." I can say nothing in favor of it. . . .

The common people are in general much better clothed than they were before the Revolution, which may be ascribed to their not being so grievously taxed as they were. . . . All those ornaments, which three years ago were worn of silver, are now of gold. All the women of lower class, even those who sit behind green-stalls, etc., wear gold earrings, with large drops, some of which cost two or three *louis,* and necklaces of the same. Many of the men wear plain gold earrings: those worn by officers and other gentlemen are usually as large as a half-crown piece. Even children of two years old have small gold drops in their ears. The general dress of the women is white linen and muslin gowns, large caps which cover all their hair, excepting just a small triangular piece over the forehead, pomatumed, or rather plaistered and powdered, without any hats; neither do they wear any stays, but only *corsets* (waistcoats or jumps). Tight lacing is not known here, nor yet high and narrow heeled shoes. Because many of the ladies *ci-devant* of quality[1] have emigrated or ran away, and those which remain in Paris keep within doors, I saw no face that was painted, excepting on the stage. Most of the men wear coats made like great-coats, or in other words, long great-coats without any coat; this in fine weather and in the middle of summer made them appear to me like invalides. There is hardly any possibility of distinguishing the rank of either man or woman by their dress at present, or rather, there are no ranks to distinguish. The nation in general is much improved in cleanliness, and even in politeness. The French no longer look on every Englishman as a lord, but as their equal. There are no beggars to be seen about the streets in Paris, and when the chaise stopped for fresh horses, only two or three old and infirm people surrounded it and solicited charity, whereas formerly the beggars used to assemble in hundreds. I did not see a single pair of *sabots* (wooden-shoes) in France this time. The table of the peasants is also better supplied than it was before the revolution. . . .

Before the 10th [of August] I saw several dancing parties of the *Poissardes* and *sansculottes* in the beer-houses, on the *Quai des Ormes* and the *Quai St. Paul,* and have played the favourite and animating air of *ça ira,* on the fiddle, to eight couple of dancers: the ceiling of these rooms (which open into the street) is not above ten feet high, and on this ceiling (which is generally white washed) are the numbers 1, 2, to 8, in black, and the same in red, which mark the places where the ladies and gentlemen are to stand. When the dance was concluded, I requested the ladies to salute me (*m'embrasser*) which they did, by gently touching my cheek with their lips. . . .

I saw many thousands of these men [National Guard] from my windows, on the way to the *Tuileries,* early on *the* Friday morning [August 10th]; their march was at the rate of perhaps five miles an hour, without running or looking aside; and this was the pace they used when they carried heads upon pikes, and when they were in pursuit of important business, rushing along the streets like a torrent, and attending wholly and solely to the object they had in view. On such occasions, when I saw them approaching, I turned into some cross street till they were passed, not that I had anything to apprehend, but the being swept along with the crowd, and perhaps trampled upon. I cannot express what I felt on seeing such immense bodies of men so vigorously actuated by the same principle. I also saw many thousands of volunteers going to join the armies at the frontiers, marching along the *Boulevarts,* almost at the same pace, accompanied as far as *Barriers* by their women, who were carrying their muskets for them; some with large sausages, pieces of cold meat, and loaves of bread, stuck on the bayonets, and all laughing, or singing *ça ira* [a famous revolutionary song].

E. A Parisian Describes the Uprising on August 10, 1792

Paris—11 August 1792—Year 4 of Liberty We are all tired out, doubtless less from spending two nights under arms than from heartache. Men's spirits were stirred after the unfortunate decree which whitewashed Lafayette. Nevertheless, we had a quiet enough evening; a group of *fédérés* from Marseille gaily chanted patriotic songs in the Beaucaire café, the refreshment room of the National Assembly. It was rumoured "Tonight the tocsin will ring, the alarm drum will be beaten. All the *faubourgs* will

---

[1] That is, aristocratic women

burst into insurrection, supported by 6,000 *fédérés.*"
At 11 o'clock we go home, at the same instant as the drums call us back to arms. We speed from our quarters and our battalion, headed by two pieces of artillery, marches to the palace. Hardly have we reached the garden of the Tuileries than we hear the alarm cannon. The alarm drum resounds through all the streets of Paris. People run for arms from all over the place. Soon the public squares, the new bridge, the main thoroughfares, are covered with troops. The National Assembly, which had finished its debate early, was recalled to its duties. It only knew of some of the preparations which had been made for the *Journée* [uprising] of 10 August. First the commandant of the palace wishes to hold the mayor a hostage there, then he sends him to the mayor's office. The people fear a display of his talents! In the general council of the Commune it is decreed that, according to the wishes of the forty-eight sections, it is no longer necessary to recognise the constituted authorities if dethronement is not immediately announced and new municipal bodies, keeping Pétion and Manuel[2] at their head, entrusted with popular authority. However, the *faubourgs* [subdivisions of the city] organised themselves into an army and placed in their centre Bretons, Marseillais and Bordelais, and all the other *fédérés*. More than 20,000 men march across Paris, bristling with pikes and bayonets. Santerre had been obliged to take command of them. The National Assembly are told that the army has broken into the palace. All hearts are frozen. Discussion is provoked again by the question of the safety of the king, when it is learned that Louis XVI seeks refuge in the bosom of the Assembly.

Forty-eight members are sent to the palace. The royal family places itself in the middle of the deputation. The people fling bitter reproaches at the king and accuse him of being the author of his troubles. Hardly was the king safe than the noise of cannon-fire increased. The Breton *fédérés* beat a tattoo. Some officers suggested retreat to the commander of the Swiss guards. But he seemed prepared and soon, by a clever tactic, captured the artillery which the National Guard held in the courtyard. These guns, now turned on the people, fire and strike them down. But soon the conflict is intensified everywhere. The Swiss, surrounded, overpowered, stricken, then run out of ammunition. They plea for mercy, but it is impossible to calm the people, furious at Helvetian treachery.

The Swiss were cut to pieces. Some were killed in the state-rooms, others in the garden. Many died on the Champs-Elysees. Heavens! That Liberty should cost Frenchmen blood and tears! How many victims there were among both the People and the National Guard! The total number of dead could run to 2,000. All the Swiss who had been taken prisoner were escorted to the Place de Grève. There they had their brains blown out. They were traitors sacrificed to vengeance. What vengeance! I shivered to the roots of my being. At least 47 heads were cut off. The Grève was littered with corpses, and heads were paraded on the ends of several pikes. The first heads to be severed were those of seven *chevaliers du poignard* [noblemen], slain at eight o'clock in the morning on the Place Vendôme. Many Marseillais perished in the journée of 10 August. Their second-in-command was killed, so was the commander of the Bretons.

The bronze statues in the Place Royale, Place Vendôme, Place Louis XIV, Place Louis XV, are thrown to the ground. The Swiss are pursued everywhere. The National Assembly, the department and the municipality are in permanent session. . . . People are still far from calm and it will be difficult to reestablish order. However, we see peace starting to reappear. The king and his family have passed the night in the porter's lodging of the National Assembly.

Tonight the National Assembly has decreed [the creation of] the National Convention. The electors are gathered in primary assemblies to select deputies. They only need to be twenty-five years old and have a residence qualification. It appears that the *coup* of 10 August has forestalled one by the aristocracy. One realizes now that the Swiss are the victims of their credulity, that they hoped for support, but that the rich men who should have fought with them dared not put in an appearance. We have been told that there are 8,000 royalist grenadiers in Paris. These 8,000 citizens seem to have stayed at home. Only one equestrian statue has been preserved in the capital: that of Henri IV.[3]

F. The Jacobin Club, Summer 1792

The hall in which the Jacobins meet, is fitted up nearly in the same style with that of the National Assembly. The tribune, or pulpit from which the members speak, is opposite to that in which the pres-

---

2 The incumbent municipal authorities

3 Henry IV was regarded as the "people's king," and his statues and tomb were spared from the destruction visited upon public monuments to other French kings during the Revolution.

ident is seated: there is a table for the secretaries and galleries for a large audience of both sexes, in the one as in the other. Men are appointed, who walk through the hall to command, or rather solicit, silence when the debate becomes turbulent at the club of Jacobins, in the same manner as the huissiers do at the National Assembly, and usually with as little effect: the bell of the president, and voices of the huissiers, are equally disregarded in stormy debates at both Assemblies.

I have been told that some of the most distinguished members in point of talent and character, have lately withdrawn from this society, and that it is not now on such a respectable footing as it has been. Roberspierre [sic], who was a member of the Constituent Assembly, and of course cannot be of the present, has great sway in the club of Jacobins, by which means his influence in the Assembly, and in the common council of Paris, is very considerable.

There was not, properly speaking, a debate at the Jacobins to-day, but rather a series of violent speeches against him. I understand indeed, that of late the speakers are generally of one opinion; for Roberspierre's [sic], partisans raise such a noise when any one attempts to utter sentiments opposite to what he is known to maintain, that the voice of the speaker is drowned, and he is obliged to yield the tribune to another orator whose doctrine is more palatable.

There were abundance of women in the galleries; but as there were none in the body of the hall where the members are seated, I was surprised to see one enter and take her seat among them: she was dressed in a kind of English riding-habit, but her jacket was the uniform of the national guards. On enquiry, I was informed that the name of this amazon is Mademoiselle Theroigne: she distinguished herself in the action of the 10th, by rallying those who fled, and attacking a second time at the head of the Marseillois.

She seems about one or two and thirty, is somewhat above the middle size of women, and has a smart martial air, which in a man would not be disagreeable.

I walked home about nine: the night was uncommonly dark; by way lay across the Carousel, along the Pont Royal to the fauxbourg St. Germain. I have frequently come the same way alone from the Caffé de Foy in the Palais Royal after it was dark. I never was attacked, nor have I heard of a single street robbery, or house-breaking, since I have been in Paris.

This seems to me very remarkable, in the ungovernable state in which Paris may be supposed to be since the 10th of this month.

Document Set 20.5 References

A. Parisians React to the King's Flight, 1791
   Prudhomme, *Révolutions de Paris,* in James Harvey Robinson, ed., *Readings in European History* (Boston: Ginn, 1904), 2:428–430.
B. Marat Attacks the Moderate Royalists, July 1791
   Marat, *The People's Friend,* in Robinson, 2:431–432.
C. Louis XVI Appeals to the King of Prussia
   Louis XVI, Letter, Dec. 3, 1791, in Robinson, 2:438–439.
D. An Englishman in Paris, Summer 1792
   Richard Twiss, "A Trip to Paris," in J. M. Thompson, ed., *English Witnesses of the French Revolution* (Oxford, England: Basil Blackwell, 1938), 111–112.
E. A Parisian Describes the Uprising on August 10, 1792
   Letter, in D. G. Wright, ed., *Revolution and Terror in France, 1789–1795* (Essex, England: Longman, 1974), 112–114.
F. The Jacobin Club, Summer 1792
   Théroigne de Méricourt, in Thompson, 180–181.

DOCUMENT SET 20.6
From the September Massacres to the King's Execution, September 1792–January 1793

The military situation remained critical at the beginning of September 1792, the Prussian army continuing to march toward Paris and its commander threatening the city with harsh punishment should the French royal family suffer harm. This was the background of the September massacres, one of the bloodiest uprisings of the Revolution, in which Parisian crowds attacked the places of confinement where many royalists were being held, slaughtering several thousand of them. The massacres are described by an English political agent in Document A.

On September 21, 1792, France's new supreme governing body, the Convention, formally abolished the monarchy and declared France a republic (Document B); by the end of the year, it was urging the people of foreign nations to throw off monarchical oppression (Document C). Republicanism had thus become an ideology justifying the extension of French influence abroad, and a dramatic change in French military fortunes at this time made such expansion a very real possibility.

Louis XVI was by now an imprisoned individual, "Citizen Capet," but while he lived he remained the embodiment of all that the Republic was determined to uproot; moreover, most French men and women who supported the Republic were convinced that he had been guilty of systematic treason ever since the Revolution had begun. In January 1793 he was tried by the Convention, which narrowly voted for his execution. Politically stupid but personally a mild-mannered and ineffectual man who had wished all his subjects well, Louis displayed great courage at the guillotine, an event dramatically described by the English Catholic clergyman who was with him at the end (Document E). As a result of the king's execution, Great Britain declared war on France. Most of Europe was now aflame with an ideological war between republican France and the international forces of counterrevolution.

In reading these documents, consider both the fears and fury of the Parisian people at the prospect of a successful counterrevolution and the motivations of middle-class republican politicians. Under these circumstances, how do you explain the king's execution?

A. An Englishman Witnesses the September 1792 Massacres in Paris

About one o'clock on Sunday fore-noon [September 4] three signal guns were fired, the Tocsin was rung, and one of the Municipality on horseback proclaimed in different parts of the city, that the enemy was at the gates, Verdun was besieged, and could only hold out a few days. The inhabitants were therefore ordered to assemble in their respective sections, and from thence to march to the Champ de Mars, where they were to select an army of sixty thousand men.

The first part of this proclamation was put in execution, but the second was totally neglected; for I went to the Champ de Mars myself where I only saw M. Péthion, who on finding no one there returned home. During the time the officer of the Municipality was making the proclamation, two others attended at the bar of the National Assembly to acquaint them with the steps that had been taken by the direction of the Conseil de la Commune. The Assembly applauded their conduct, and immediately passed a decree, directing that those who refused their arms to those that wished to serve, or objected serving themselves, should be deemed traitors and worthy of death, that all horses of luxury should be seized for the use of the army, and that those who refused to obey the orders of the present executive power should be punished with death. It concluded by decreeing that twelve members of the National Assembly should be added to the other six that at present compose the executive power. As soon as these decrees were passed, the carriages and horses of gentlemen were seized in the streets (agreeable to the spirit of the decree). Their owners were obliged to walk home, and the horses in general were sent to the École Militaire, and the carriages were put under the care of different guards. The proceedings with the beating of drums, firing of cannon, and the marching up and down of armed men of course created no little agitation in the minds of the people. That however was nothing to the scene of horror that ensued soon after. A party at the instigation of some one or other declared they would not quit Paris, as long as the prisons were filled with Traitors (for they called those so, that were confined in the different Prisons and Churches), who might in the absence of such a number of Citizens rise and not only effect the release of His Majesty, but make an entire counter-revolution. To prevent this, a large body of sans-culottes attended by a number of Marseillais and Brestois, the hired assassins of a Party, proceeded to the Church de Carmes, rue de Vaugirard, where amidst the acclamations of a savage mob they massacred a number of refractory Priests, all the Vicaires de Saint Sulpice, the directors of the Seminaries, and the Doctors of the Sorbonne, with the *ci-devant* [former] Archbishop of Arles, and a number of others, exceeding in all one hundred and seventy, including those that had been confided there since the tenth. After this they proceeded to the Abbaye, where they massacred a vast number of prisoners, amongst whom were also many respectable characters. These executioners increasing in number, different detachments were sent to the Châtelet, the prison de la Force, de Ste Pélagie, and the prisons of the Conciergerie. At all these places a most horrid massacre took place, none were exempted but debtors and many of these fell victims to the fury of the people. During this sad scene, the more humane, which were but few in number, hurried to the National Assembly to obtain their interference for stopping such melancholy outrages. They immediately decreed that six of their members should go and see if it was possible to prevent such cruelties. With difficulty these members arrived at the Abbaye; when there one of them got upon a chair to harangue the people, but neither he nor the others could make themselves heard, and with some risk, they made their escape. Many of the Municipality attended at the different prisons, and endeavoured to quell the fury of the people, but all in vain; they therefore proposed to the mob a plan of establishing a kind of Court of justice in the prisons, for the immediate trial of the remaining offenders. They caught at this, and two of the Municipality with a detachment of the mob, about two on Monday morning, began this strange Court of justice. The gaoler's list was called for, those that were confined for forging assignats, or theft, with the unhappy people that were any way suspected to be concerned in the affair of the 10th, were in general massacred; this form took place in nearly all the prisons in Paris. But early on Monday morning a detachment with seven pieces of cannon went to attack Bicêtre. It is reported that these wretches charged their cannon with small stones and such other things, and fired promiscuously among the prisoners. I cannot however vouch for this, they have however not finished their cruelties there yet, and it is now past six o'clock Tuesday evening. To be convinced of what I could not believe, I made a visit to the prison of the Abbaye about seven o'clock on Monday evening, for the slaughter had not ceased.

This prison, which takes its name from an adjoining Abbaye, stands in a narrow street, which was at this time from a variety of lights, as light as day: a single file of men armed with swords, or piques, formed a lane of some length, commencing from the prison door. This body might consist of about fifty; these people were either Marseillais, Brestois, or the National Guards of Paris, and when I saw them seemed much fatigued with their horrid work. For besides the irregular massacre that continued till two o'clock on Monday morning, many of them delighted with their strange office continued their services when I left them, which was about nine on Monday evening.

Two of the Municipality were then in the prison with some of the mob distributing their justice. Those they found guilty were seemingly released, but only to be precipitated by the door on a number of piques, and then among the savage cries of *vive la nation* ["long live the nation!"], to be hacked to pieces by those that had swords and were ready to receive them. After this their dead bodies were dragged by the arms or legs to the Abbaye, which is distant from the prison about two hundred yards; here they were laid up in heaps till carts could carry them away. The kennel was swimming with blood, and a bloody track was traced from the prison to the Abbaye door where they had dragged these unfortunate people.

I was fortunate enough to be present when five men were acquitted. Such a circumstance, a bystander told me, had not happened in the operations of this horrid tribunal; and these inconsistent murderers seemed nearly as much pleased at the acquittal of a prisoner as they were at his condemnation. The Governor of the Invalides happened to be one of those I saw acquitted, the street rung with acclamations of joy, but the old man was so feeble with fear, and suspense, and so overcome with the caresses of his daughter, who was attending to know his fate, that they both sunk lifeless into the arms of some of the spectators, who carried them to the Hospital des Invalides. The same congratulations attended the others that were acquitted and the same those that were condemned. Nothing can exceed the inconsistency of these people. After the general massacre of Sunday night many of the dead bodies were laid on the Pont-neuf to be claimed, a person in the action of stealing a handkerchief from one of the corpses was hacked to pieces on the spot, by the same people who had been guilty of so much cruelty and injustice.

One of the Municipality was fortunate enough for that night to save some of the women, but many of these underwent the same mock trial next day; and the Princess Lamballe, after having been butchered in the most shocking manner, had her head severed from her body, which these monsters carried about, while others dragged her body through many of the streets. It is even said they attempted to carry it to the Queen, but the Guards would not permit that. Mademoiselle de Tourzelles was also reported to have been murdered, but I understand that she and Madame de Ste Brice were saved from the fury of the people, and carried *à la section des droits de l'homme.* Many other women of family were killed and others escaped. Major Bauchman of the Swiss Guards was beheaded on the Place de Carouzel early on Monday morning. Mr Montmorin, Governor of Fontainebleau and nephew of Mr Montmorin late Minister, who was killed at the Abbaye, had been regularly tried and acquitted on Friday, but not being released was also massacred at the Conciergerie. Monsieur d'Affry was acquitted by the people and escaped. In all it is supposed they have murdered four thousand, some say seven, but I think that exaggerated.

By what I can understand it was late on Sunday evening before Mr Péthion took any steps to prevent the progress of this unexampled outrage, and the National Guards of course made no opposition to such irregularities. The Mayor however at last sent to the Temple the Commandant General of the National Guards, and I am happy to inform you that in the midst of all this confusion, though there was a crowd in the street, yet the court of the Temple was quiet. The Section du Marais has sworn not to permit any violence to be exercised against the prisoners in that place, and the National Assembly have also appointed six of their members as a safe-guard to the sacred persons of Their Majesties, and a number of the Municipality also attend. A motion was made last week to confine Their Majesties in separate apartments; that right was however found to rest with the Municipality, and I have the pleasure of saying that Their Most Christian Majesties still enjoy the comfort of being together, and were, not an hour ago, in perfect good health.

I ask pardon for giving such a detailed account of such uncommon barbarity, which I am sure must be as disagreeable for you to read as it is for me to commit such acts to paper, but they ought to be particularized to the eternal disgrace of a people who pretend to be the most civilized among the nations of Europe.

B. The Convention Debates the Abolition of the Monarchy, September 21, 1792

The citizens chosen by the French people to form the National Convention having assembled to the number of three hundred and seventy one, and having examined the credentials of the members, declare that the National Convention is organized. . . .

M. Manuel. Representatives of the sovereign people: the task which devolves upon you demands the power and wisdom of gods themselves. When Cineas entered the Roman senate he thought he beheld an assembly of kings. Such a comparison would be an insult to you. Here we see an assembly of philosophers occupied in preparing the way for the happiness of the world. I move that the president of France have his residence in the national palace, that the symbols of law and power be always at his side, and that every time that he opens a session all the citizens shall rise. This act of homage to the sovereignty of the people will constantly recall to us our rights and duties.

M. Simon. I move that the Assembly declare that they will never deliberate except in the presence of the people.

The President. Your motion, having no relation to the previous motion, I cannot give the floor to those who wish to support or oppose your proposition until the Assembly has passed upon the motion of Monsieur Manuel.

M. Mathieu. I am doubtful whether the discussion suggested by Monsieur Manuel should take precedence in our deliberations. Our predecessors lost much time in determining the exact dimensions of the chair of the former king. We do not wish to commit the same error. . . .

M. Chabot. Representatives of the people: I oppose the motion made by Citizen Manuel. I am astonished that Citizen Manuel, after having repudiated every idea of any comparison with kings, should propose to make one of our members like a king. The French nation, by sending to the Convention two hundred members of the legislative body who have individually taken an oath to combat both kings and royalty, has made itself quite clear as to its desire to establish a popular government. It is not only the *name* of king that it would abolish but everything which suggests preeminence, so that there will be no president of France. You cannot look for any other kind of dignity than associating with the *sans-culottes* who compose the majority of the nation. Only by making yourselves like your fellow-citizens will you acquire the necessary dignity to cause your decrees to be respected. . . .

M. Tallien. I am much astonished to hear this discussion about ceremonials. . . . Outside of this hall the president of the Convention is a simple citizen. If you want to speak to him, you can go and look for him on the third or the fifth floor. There is where virtue has its lodging. . . .

The Assembly unanimously rejected the motion of Monsieur Manuel.

M. Tallien. I move that before everything else the Assembly take a solemn pledge not to separate till it has given the French people a government established on the foundations of liberty and equality. I move that the members take an oath to make no laws which depart from this standard, and that this oath shall constantly guide the representatives of the people in their work. Those who shall perjure themselves shall be immolated to the just vengeance of the people. . . . [*Applause.*]

M. Merlin. I move that we do not take any oaths. Let us promise the people to save them. Let us go to work.

M. Couthon. . . . I am not afraid that, in the discussion which is about to take place, any one will dare to speak of royalty again; it is fit only for slaves, and the French would be unworthy of the liberty which they have acquired should they dream of retaining a form of government branded by fourteen centuries of crime. But it is not royalty alone that must be eliminated from our constitution, but every kind of individual power which tends to restrict the rights of the people and violate the principles of equality. . . .

M. Philippeaux. There is a still more pressing subject; that is, to furnish the organs of the law the necessary power to maintain public tranquillity. I move that you maintain provisionally in power all the authorities now in existence. . . .

M. Camus. The most essential thing is to order that the taxes continue to be collected, for you know that they have to be voted at the opening of every new legislature.

The motions of Messieurs Philippeaux and Camus were unanimously passed. . . .

M. Collot d'Herbois. You have just taken a wise resolution, but there is one which you cannot postpone until the morrow, or even until this evening, or indeed for a single instant, without being faithless to the wish of the nation,—that is the abolition of royalty. [*Unanimous applause.*]

M. Quinette. We are not the judges of royalty; that belongs to the people. Our business is to make a concrete government, and the people will then choose between the old form where there was royalty and that which we shall submit to them. . . .

M. Grégoire. Assuredly no one of us would ever propose to retain in France the fatal race of kings; we all know but too well that dynasties have never been anything else than rapacious tribes who lived on nothing but human flesh. It is necessary completely to reassure the friends of liberty. We must destroy this talisman, whose magic power is still sufficient to stupefy many a man. I move accordingly that you sanction by a solemn law the abolition of royalty.

The entire Assembly rose by a spontaneous movement and passed the motion of Monsieur Grégoire by acclamation.

M Bazire. I rise to a point of order. . . . It would be a frightful example for the people to see an Assembly commissioned with its dearest interests voting in a moment of enthusiasm. I move that the question be discussed.

M. Grégoire. Surely it is quite unnecessary to discuss what everybody agrees on. Kings are in the moral order what monsters are in the physical. Courts are the workshops of crimes, the lair of tyrants. The history of kings is the martyrology of nations. Since we are all convinced of the truth of this, why discuss it? I demand that my motion be put to vote, and that later it be supplied with a formal justification worthy of the solemnity of the decree.

M. Ducos. The form of your decree would be only the history of the crimes of Louis XVI, a history already but too well known to the French people. I demand that it be drawn up in the simplest terms. There is no need of explanation after the knowledge which has been spread abroad by the events of August 10.

The discussion was closed. There was a profound silence. The motion of Monsieur Grégoire, put to vote, was adopted amidst the liveliest applause:

"The National Convention decrees that royalty is abolished in France."

C. The French Convention Appeals to Foreign Nations to Destroy Monarchy, December 15, 1792

The French people to the people of   ; brothers and friends:

We have conquered our liberty and we shall maintain it. We offer to bring this inestimable blessing to you, for it has always been rightly ours, and only by a crime have our oppressors robbed us of it. We have driven out your tyrants. Show yourselves free men and we will protect you from their vengeance, their machinations, or their return.

From this moment the French nation proclaims the sovereignty of the people, the suppression of all civil and military authorities which have hitherto governed you and of all that taxes which you bear, under whatever form, the abolition of the tithe, of feudalism, of seigniorial rights and monopolies of every kind, of serfdom, whether real or personal, of hunting and fishing privileges, of the *corvée*, the salt tax, the tolls and local imposts, and, in general, of all the various kinds of taxes with which you have been loaded by your usurpers; it also proclaims the abolition among you of all noble and ecclesiastical corporations and of all prerogatives and privileges opposed to equality. You are, from this moment, brothers and friends; all are citizens, equal in rights, and all are alike called to govern, to serve, and to defend your country.

D. The Execution of Louis XVI, as Witnessed by an Attending Priest

The unfortunate Louis XVI, foreseeing to what lengths the malice of his enemies was likely to go, and resolved to be prepared at all events, cast his eyes upon me, to assist him in his last moments, if condemned to die. He would not make any application to the ruling party, nor even mention my name without my consent. The message he sent me was touching beyond expression, and worded in a manner which I shall never forget. A King, though in chains, had a right to command, but he commanded not. My attendance was requested merely as a pledge of my attachment for him, and as a favour, which he hoped I would not refuse. But as the service was likely to be attended with some danger for me, he dared not to insist, and only prayed (in case I deemed the danger to be too great) to point out to him a clergyman worthy of his confidence, but less known than I was myself, leaving the person absolutely to my choice. . . . Being obliged to take my party upon the spot, I resolved to comply with what appeared to be at that moment the call of Almighty God; and committing to His providence all the rest, I made answer to the most unfortunate of Kings, that whether he lived or died, I would be his friend to the last. . . .

The King finding himself seated in the carriage, where he could neither speak to me nor be spoken to without witness, kept a profound silence. I presented him with my breviary, the only book I had with me, and he seemed to accept it with pleasure: he appeared anxious that I should point out to him the psalms that were most suited to his situation, and he recited them attentively with me. The gend'armes, without speaking, seemed astonished and confounded at the tranquil piety of their monarch, to whom they doubtless never had before approached so near.

The procession lasted almost two hours; the streets were lined with citizens, all armed, some with pikes and some with guns, and the carriage was surrounded by a body of troops, formed of the most desperate people of Paris. As another precaution, they had placed before the horses a number of drums, intended to drown any noise or murmur in favour of the King; but how could they be heard? Nobody appeared either at the doors or windows, and in the street nothing was to be seen, but armed citizens—citizens, all rushing towards the commission of a crime, which perhaps they detested in their hearts.

The carriage proceeded thus in silence to the Place de Louis XV, and stopped in the middle of a large space that had been left round the scaffold: this space was surrounded with cannon, and beyond, an armed multitude extended as far as the eye could reach. As soon as the King perceived that the carriage stopped, he turned and whispered to me, "We are arrived, if I mistake not." My silence answered that we were. One of the guards came to open the carriage door, and the gend'armes would have jumped out, but the King stopped them, and leaning his arm on my knee, "Gentlemen," said he, with the tone of majesty, "I recommend to you this good man; take care that after my death no insult be offered to him— I charge you to prevent it.". . . . As soon as the King had left the carriage, three guards surrounded him, and would have taken off his clothes, but he repulsed them with haughtiness: he undressed himself, untied his neckcloth, opened his shirt, and arranged it himself. The guards, whom the determined countenance of the King had for a moment disconcerted, seemed to recover their audacity. They surrounded him again, and would have seized his hands. "What are you attempting?" said the King, drawing back his hands. "To bind you," answered the wretches. "To bind *me*," said the King, with an indignant air. "No! I shall never consent to that: do what you have been ordered, but you shall never bind me. . . "

The path leading to the scaffold was extremely rough and difficult to pass; the King was obliged to lean on my arm, and from the slowness with which he proceeded, I feared for a moment that his courage might fail; but what was my astonishment, when arrived at the last step, I felt that he suddenly let go my arm, and I saw him cross with a firm foot the breadth of the whole scaffold; silence, by his look alone, fifteen or twenty drums that were placed opposite to me; and in a voice so loud, that it must have been heard at the Pont Tournant, I heard him pronounce distinctly these memorable words: *I die innocent of all the crimes laid to my charge; I pardon those who have occasioned my death; and I pray to God that the blood you are going to shed may never be visited on France.*

He was proceeding, when a man on horseback, in the national uniform, and with a ferocious cry, ordered the drums to beat. Many voices were at the same time heard encouraging the executioners. They seemed reanimated themselves, in seizing with violence the most virtuous of Kings, they dragged him under the axe of the guillotine, which with one stroke severed his head from his body. All this passed in a moment. The youngest of the guards, who seemed about eighteen, immediately seized the head, and shewed it to the people as he walked round the scaffold; he accompanied this monstrous ceremony with the most atrocious and indecent gestures. At first an awful silence prevailed; at length some cries of "Vive la République!" were heard. By degrees the voices multiplied, and in less than ten minutes this cry, a thousand times repeated, became the universal shout of the multitude, and every hat was in the air.

Document Set 20.6 References

A. An Englishman Witnesses the September 1792 Massacres in Paris
J. M. Thompson, ed., *English Witnesses of the French Revolution* (Oxford, England: Basil Blackwell, 1938), 190–195.

B. The Convention Debates the Abolition of the Monarchy, September 21, 1792
National Convention, in James Harvey Robinson, ed., *Readings in European History* (Boston: Ginn, 1904), 2:446–449.

C. The French Convention Appeals to Foreign Nations to Destroy Monarchy, December 15, 1792
National Convention, in Robinson, 2:449–450.

D. The Execution of Louis XVI, as Witnessed by an Attending Priest
Henry Essex Edgeworth de Firmont, in Thompson, 229–231.

DOCUMENT SET 20.7
Terror and the Terrorists

The Reign of Terror, which held France in its grip through most of 1793 and the spring and summer of 1794, will always remain one of the most controversial aspects of the Revolution. To many, indeed, it is the very essence, whether for good or evil. Was it a reflection of the mass savagery and class resentment? Did it represent an honest attempt to uproot the abuses of the Old Regime and substitute the Enlightenment-inspired ideals of republican citizenship? Was it an expression of abstract theorizing run wild or an attempt by totalitarian-minded fanatics to impose despotism in the name of liberty? Or was it the pragmatic response of desperate leaders faced with a series of military, economic, and political emergencies? The documents in this set will help you evaluate the Terror. Keep in mind that despite the thousands of "aristocrats" (which could mean anyone out of sympathy with the Revolution), clergy, and moderate politicians executed during the Reign of Terror, the majority of those whose heads fell under the guillotine were ordinary people found guilty of violating harsh ordinances designed to prevent inflation, black-marketeering, hoarding, draft evasion, and petty crime.

In Document A, Maximilian Robespierre, the leading figure of the Committee of Public Safety, which directed the Terror as well as the French government itself, speaks for himself in February 1794. (Five months later his political opponents would join forces to guillotine him before he could destroy them.)

A particularly graphic example of the Terror at work was the fate meted out to the city of Lyons, where popular discontent with the war and with economic dislocations precipitated an uprising against the national government in late 1793. After Revolutionary armed forces crushed this grass-roots counterrevolution, the Paris authorities installed a Temporary Commission in the city, directing it to use all necessary means to instill a more nationally oriented kind of revolutionary patriotism. The commission's instructions for purging the city of abuses are excerpted in Document B.

After studying these documents, analyze the ideals and realities that could drive leaders like Robespierre and the Lyons revolutionary authorities to such fanaticism in their determination to uproot "fanaticism," consulting *The Challenge of the West* for background information.

A. Robespierre Appeals for Republican Virtue, February 1794

We desire an order of things where all base and cruel passions and enchained by the laws, all beneficent and generous feelings awakened by them; where ambition is the desire to deserve glory and to be useful to one's country; where distinctions arise only from equality itself; where the citizen is subject to the magistrate, the magistrate to the people, the people to justice; where the country secures the welfare of each individual, and each individual proudly enjoys the prosperity and glory of his country; where all minds are enlarged by the constant interchange of republican sentiments and by the need of earning the respect of a great people; where industry is an adornment to the liberty that ennobles it, and commerce is the source of public wealth, not simply of monstrous riches for a few families.

We wish to substitute in our country morality for egotism, probity for a mere sense of honour, principle for habit, duty for etiquette, the rule of reason for the tyranny of custom, contempt for vice for contempt for misfortune, pride for insolence, large-mindedness for vanity, the love of glory for the love of money, good men for good company, merit for intrigue, talent for conceit, truth for show, the charm of happiness for the tedium of pleasure, the grandeur of man for the triviality of grand society, a people magnanimous, powerful and happy for a people lovable, frivolous and wretched—that is to say, all the virtues and miracles of the Republic for all the vices and puerilities of the monarchy.

We wish in a word to fulfil the course of nature, to accomplish the destiny of mankind, to make good the promises of philosophy, to absolve Providence from the long reign of tyranny and crime. May France, once illustrious among peoples of slaves, eclipse the glory of all free peoples that have existed, become the model to the nations, the terror of oppressors, the consolation of the oppressed, the ornament of the universe; and in sealing our work with our blood, may we ourselves see at least the dawn of universal felicity gleam before us! That is our ambition. That is our aim.

B. The Terror Reaches Lyons, November 1793

The goal of the Revolution is the happiness of the people.

Paragraph I: Concerning the Revolutionary Spirit

The Revolution is made for the people; the happiness of the people is its goal; love of the people is the touchstone of the revolutionary spirit.

It is easy to understand that by "the people" we do not mean that class privileged by its riches which has usurped all the pleasures of life and all its assets from society. "The people" is the universality of French citizens; "the people" is above all the immense class of the poor, that class which gives men to the *Patrie*, defenders to our frontiers, which maintains society by its labors, embellishes it by its talents, which adorns it and honors it by its virtues. The Revolution would be a political and moral monstrosity if its end was to assure the happiness of a few hundred individuals and to consolidate the misery of twenty-four million citizens. . . .

Republicans, to be worthy of that name, begin by feeling your dignity. Hold high your head with pride and let men read in your eyes that you know who you are and what the Republic is. Do not be mistaken, to be truly republican each citizen must experience within himself a revolution equal to that which has changed the face of France. There is nothing, absolutely nothing, in common between the slave of a tyrant and the inhabitant of a free state: the customs of the latter, his principles, his sentiments, his actions must all be new. You were oppressed; you must crush your oppressors. You were the slaves of superstition; you must no longer worship anything except liberty; you must have no other morality than that of nature. You were strangers to military offices; henceforth all Frenchmen are soldiers. You lived in ignorance; to assure the conquest of your rights, you must be instructed. You knew no *Patrie* [Fatherland], never had its sweet voice echoed in your hearts; today, you must know nothing apart from it; you must see it, hear it, and adore it in everything. The magistrate is vigilant, the farmer sows his fields, the soldier fights, the citizen breathes only for the *Patrie!* Its sacred image mingles in all his actions, adds to his pleasures, rewards him for his pains. Long live the Republic! Long live the people! There is his rallying cry, the expression of his joy, the solace of his sorrows. Any

man to whom this enthusiasm is foreign, who knows other pleasures, other cares than the happiness of the people . . . any man who doesn't feel his blood boil at the very name of tyranny, slavery, or opulence; any man who has tears to shed for the enemies of the people, who doesn't reserve all his compassion for the victims of despotism, and for the martyrs of liberty, all such men who dare to call themselves Republicans have lied against nature and in their hearts. Let them flee the soil of liberty: they will soon be recognized and will water it with their impure blood. The Republic wants only free men within its bosom; it is determined to exterminate all others and to recognize as its children only those who know how to live, fight and die for it. . . .

Paragraph III: The Revolutionary Tax on the Rich

The expenses of the war must be defrayed, and the costs of the Revolution met. Who will come to the help of the *Patrie* in its need if it is not the rich? If they are aristocrats, it is just that they should pay for a war to which they and their supporters alone have given rise; if they are patriots, you will be anticipating their desires by asking them to put their riches to the only use fit for Republicans; that is to say, a purpose useful to the Republic. Thus, nothing can excuse you from establishing this tax promptly. No exemptions are necessary; any man who has more than he needs must participate in this extraordinary assistance. This tax must be proportioned to the great needs of the *Patrie*, so you must begin by deciding in a grand and truly revolutionary manner the sum that each individual must put in common for the public welfare. This isn't a case for mathematical exactitude nor for the timid scruple which must be employed to apportion the public taxes; it is an extraordinary measure which must exhibit the character of the times which compel it. Operate, then, on a large scale; take all that a citizen has that is unnecessary; for superfluity is an evident and gratuitous violation of the rights of the people. Any man who has more than his needs cannot use it, he can only abuse it; thus, if he is left what is strictly necessary, all the rest belongs to the Republic and to its unfortunate members. . . .

Paragraph V: The Eradication of Fanaticism

Priests are the sole cause of the misfortunes of France; it is they who for thirteen hundred years have raised, by degrees, the edifice of our slavery and have adorned it with all the sacred baubles which could conceal flaws from the eye of reason. . . .

First of all, Citizens, relations between God and man are a purely private matter and, to be sincere, have no need of display in worship and the visible

D. I. Wright, *The French Revolution: Introductory Documents,* © D. I. Wright, 1992. Reprinted by permission of the author.

monuments of superstition. You will begin by sending to the treasury of the Republic all the vases, all the gold and silver ornaments which may flatter the vanity of priests but which are nothing to the truly religious man and to the Being whom he claims to honour....

... The Republican has no other divinity than his *Patrie*, no other idol than liberty. The Republican is essentially religious because he is good, just, and courageous; the patriot honors virtue, respects age, consoles misfortune, comforts indigence and punishes treachery. What better homage for the Divinity! The patriot isn't foolish enough to claim to worship him by practices useless to humanity and bad for himself; he does not condemn himself to an apparent celibacy in order to give himself up the more freely to debauchery. Worthy son of nature and useful member of society, he gives happiness to a virtuous wife and raises his numerous children according to the severe principles of morality and republicanism....

Republicans . . . be on guard, you have great wrongs to expiate; the crimes of the rebellious Lyonnais are yours.... Regain then, and promptly, in liberty's way, all the ground that you have lost, and win again by your virtues and patriotic efforts the esteem and confidence of France. The National Convention, the representatives of the people, are watching you and your magistrates; the account that they demand of you will be all the stricter because you have faults to be pardoned. And we, who are intermediaries between them and you, we whom they have charged to watch over you and instruct you, we swear that our glance will not leave you for an instant and that we will use with severity all the authority committed to us and that we will punish as treachery what in other circumstances you might have called dilatoriness, weakness or negligence. The time for half-measures and for beating about the bush is past. Help us to strike great blows or you will be the first to feel them. *Liberty or death:* reflect and choose.

[Signed by the Commission and approved by the deputies on mission, Collot d'Herbois and Fouché, members of the Committee of Public Safety.]

Document Set 20.7 References

A. Robespierre Appeals for Republican Virtue, February 1794
M. J. Sydenham, *The French Revolution* (New York: Capricorn Books, 1965), 207–208.
B. The Terror Reaches Lyons, November 1793
Temporary Committee of Republican Surveillance in Lyons, in D. I. Wright, ed., *The French Revolution: Introductory Documents* (Newcastle, Australia: University of Queensland Press, 1974), 194–197.

DOCUMENT SET 20.8
The Sans-Culottes

Much of the impetus driving the Terror came from the Parisian artisans and shopkeepers who called themselves *sans-culottes* (ordinary working folk who did not wear the knee breeches [*culottes*] and silk stockings that were standard dress for eighteenth-century gentlemen). It was they who dominated the "sections," or neighborhood political bodies, into which the city had been divided, fretted about the rising price of bread, poured into the streets in revolutionary riot, and demanded that the Revolution leaders destroy every vestige of the Old Regime. Most were neither rich nor penniless but respectable and hard working. The newspaper article excerpted in Document A gives an idealized portrait, but one that nevertheless captures the readiness to resort to violence in defense of the Revolution.

The economic realities that such ordinary people faced are apparent from the statistical tables in Document B, a modern historian's calculations of typical wages and the cost of living in Paris during the Revolution. These figures lend weight to the petition that one Parisian section, dominated by *sans-culottes*, presented to the Convention in May 1793, demanding strict price controls and a crackdown on profiteers (Document C.). The Convention's response, the law known as the Maximum-General (Document D), was passed in September 1793 in an ultimately futile attempt to fix wages and the prices of various staple goods for urban working people. (What is *not* covered in the legislation is also noteworthy.)

The information contained in these documents, as well as others in this collection, should help you write a brief essay defining the *sans-culottes* and explaining why they should not be considered simply a mob of wild-eyed, lower-class fanatics—the view of them that conservative French and most English-speaking historians generally held until fairly recently.

A. A Contemporary Definition of a *Sans-Culotte*

A *sans culotte*, you rogues? He is someone who always goes about on foot, who has not got the millions you would all live to have, who has no castles, no valets to wait on him, and who lives simply with his wife and children, if he has any, on the fourth or fifth story. He is useful because he knows how to till a field, to forge iron, to use a saw, to roof a house, to make shoes, and to spill his blood to the last drop for the safety of the Republic. . . .

In the evening he goes to the assembly of his Section, not powdered and perfumed and nattily booted, in the hope of being noticed by the citizenesses in the galleries, but ready to support sound proposals with all his might and ready to pulverize those which come from the despised faction of politicians.

Finally, a *sans culotte* always has his sabre well-sharpened, ready to cut off the ears of all opponents of the Revolution.

B. Prices and Wages in Paris, 1789–1793

Percentage of Income Spent on Bread by Parisian Workers, 1789
(in *sous*)

Occupation	Daily Wage	Effective Daily Earnings[1]	Expenditure on Bread as Percentage of Income			
			At 9 s.	At 14-1/2 s.	At 13-1/2 s.	At 12 s.
Laborer in Réveillon's factory	25 s.	15 s.	60	97	90	80
Builder's laborer	30 s.	18 s.	50	80	75	67
Journeyman mason	40 s.	24 s.	37	60	56	50
Journeyman locksmith, carpenter, etc.	50 s.	30 s.	30	48	45	40
Sculptor, goldsmith	100 s.	60 s.	15	24	22-1/2	20

[1] In computing 'effective' earnings, allowance has been made for the numerous unpaid Feast Days of the *ancien régime*. Here these are assumed to number 111 per year (G. M. Jaffé, *Le Mouvement ouvrier à Paris pendant la Révolution française*, pp. 26–27). Further allowance should also be made for sickness.

Hypothetical Budgets of Parisian Workers, June 1789 and June 1791
(in *sous*)

Budget of a Builder's Laborer (wage, 30 s.; effective income, 18 s.)		Budget of a Journeyman Carpenter, or Locksmith (wage, 50 s.; effective income, 30 s.)	
June 1789	*June 1791*	*June 1789*	*June 1791*
4 lb. bread 14-1/2 s.	4 lb. bread 8 s.	4 lb. bread 14-1/2 s.	4 lb. bread 8 s.
Rent 3 s.	Rent 3 s.	Rent 3 s.	Rent 3 s.
	1/2 liter wine 4 s.	1/2 liter wine 5 s.	1 liter wine 8 s.
	1-1/4 lb. meat 2-1/2 s.	1/2 lb. meat 5 s.	1/2 lb. meat 5 s.
Balance for oil, vegetables, clothing, etc. 1/2 s.	Balance 1/2 s.	Balance 2-1/2 s.	Balance 6 s.
Total 18 s.	18 s.	30 s.	30 s.

Hypothetical Budgets of Parisian Workers, June 1790 and June 1793
(in *sous*)

Budget of a Journeyman Carpenter		Budget of a Journeyman Locksmith	
June 1790 (wage, 50 s.; effective income, 30 s.)	*June 1793* (wage, 80 s.; effective income, 57 s.)	*June 1790* (wage, 50 s.; effective income, 30 s.)	*June 1793* Wage, 110 s.; effective income, 78 s.)
4 lb. bread 11 s.	4 lb. bread 12. s.	4 lb. bread 11 s.	4 lb. bread 12 s.
Rent 3 s.	Rent 6 s.	Rent 3 s.	Rent 6 s.
1 liter wine 10 s.	1-1/2 liters wine 24 s.	1 liter wine 10 s.	1-1/2 liters wine 24 s.
1/2 lb. meat 5 s.	1/2 lb. meat 9 s.	1/2 lb. meat 5 s.	1 lb. meat 18 s.
Balance for vegetables, oil, clothing, etc. 1 s.	Balance 6 s.	Balance 1 s.	Balance 18 s.
Total 30 s.	57 s.	30 s.	78 s.

C. A Parisian Section of *Sans-Culotte* Petitions the Convention About Economic Grievances, May 1793

Representatives of the people: For far too long entire families belonging to our brothers have languished and perished from need; for far too long the high price of essential commodities has deprived a host of citizens of their subsistence. We must now put a brake on the insatiable greed of those infamous egoists who traffic in the blood of the unfortunate and make public misery the basis of their private fortunes.

D. I. Wright, *The French Revolution: Introductory Documents*, © D. I. Wright, 1992. Reprinted by permission of the author.

Since it is true that these monopolists are moved neither by the sight of the sufferings of their equals, nor by the cries of the indigent, nor by the lamentations of their victims, since nothing can move those hearts of steel, representatives of the people, let national justice break forth and set limits to their crimes.

We demand that you put an end to our sufferings. So that we shall be able to eat, as is necessary to maintain life, we demand that you fix the price of essential commodities and proportion their cost to the value of a man's labour so that they may be easily within the reach of all. We demand that this beneficent law should extend over the whole Republic.

If at the very moment when the people is rising [the insurrection against the Girondins], our section comes again to address you, it is in the hope that in once more laying down its arms before you, and in rendering up to you the exercise of its sovereignty, you will make use of it for the happiness of the people. Pay heed, then, to its voice, and forestall the unfortunate excesses to which despair and rage may bring it, with you the first victim.

D. The Maximum-General Attempts to Control Prices, September 29, 1793

The National Convention, having heard the report of its Commission on the drafting of a law fixing a *maximum* for essential goods and merchandise, decrees as follows:

Article 1. The articles which the National Convention has judged to be essential, and of which it has believed it should fix the maximum or highest price are: fresh meat, salt meat and bacon, butter, sweet oil, cattle, salt fish, wine, brandy, vinegar, cider, beer, firewood, charcoal, coal, candles, lamp oil, salt, soda, soap, potash, sugar, honey, white paper, hides, iron, cast iron, lead, steel, copper, hemp, flax, wools, fabrics, linen cloth, the raw materials used for manufacture, clogs, shoes, colza and rape, tobacco.

2. Among the articles listed above, the *maximum* price of first quality firewood, charcoal and coal is the same as in 1790, plus one-twentieth. The law of 19 August on the fixing by departments of the price of firewood, coal and peat is revoked.

The *maximum* or the highest price of twist tobacco is 20 *sous* per livre . . . that of smoking tobacco is 10 *sous*; that of a livre of salt is two *sous*; that of soap is 25 *sous*.

3. The maximum price of all other goods and merchandise listed in article 1 shall be, over the whole extent of the Republic, until September next, their price in 1790 as stated by the market price lists or the current prices in each department, plus one-third, deduction being made for fiscal and other fees to which they were then subject, under whatever name they may have existed.

4. The tables of the *maximum* or highest price of each of the goods, listed in article 1 shall be drafted by each district administration, posted within a week of the receipt of this law, and sent to the department.

5. The *procureur-général-syndic* shall, within the following fortnight, forward copies to both the Provisional Executive Council and the National Convention.

6. The Commissaries of the National Convention are charged with dismissing *procureurs* of communes, *procureurs-syndics*, and *procureurs-généraux-syndics* who shall not have fulfilled the arrangements detailed in the foregoing articles within the time prescribed, each so far as his responsibility extends.

7. Everyone who sells or buys the merchandise listed in article 1 above the *maximum* determined and posted in each department shall pay, jointly and severally, through the municipal police, a fine of double the value of the object sold, payable to the informant. Their names shall be inscribed on the list of suspect persons and they shall be treated as such. The buyer shall not be subject to the above penalty if he denounces the seller's breach, and each merchant shall be required to have a list bearing the *maximum* or highest price of his goods conspicuous in his shop.

8. The *maximum* or highest rate with respect to salaries, wages, manual labour and day-labour in each place shall be fixed, beginning from the publication of this law, until September next, by general and communal councils, at the 1790 rate plus one-half.

9. Municipalities may requisition and punish, with three days detention, as the circumstances require, workmen, manufacturers and various kinds of labourers who refuse their ordinary work without legitimate cause. . . .

[Articles 10–16 deal with technical, administrative matters.]

17. For the duration of the war, all exportation of essential merchandise or goods is prohibited over every frontier under any name or commission whatever, salt excepted.

18. The above listed articles destined for export and intercepted in contravention [of the law] within two leagues of the frontier on this side, and without a permit from the municipality of the driver's place [of residence], shall be confiscated with the conveyances, beasts of burden, or vessels transporting them, for the benefit of those who stop them. There shall be a penalty of ten years imprisonment for the contraveners, owners and drivers.

19. So that the crews of neutral or Frenchified ships may not abuse the favour of hospitality by taking away from maritime cities and places victuals and provisions beyond their needs, they shall appear before the municipality which shall cause all that they need to be purchased for them.

20. The present decree shall be despatched by special messenger.

Document Set 20.8 References

A. A Contemporary Definition of a *Sans Culotte*
Newspaper account, in D. G. Wright, ed., *Revolution and Terror in France, 1789–1795* (London: Longman, 1974), 116.

B. Prices and Wages in Paris, 1789–1793
George Rudé, *The Crowd in the French Revolution* (New York: Oxford University Press, 1959), 251–252.

C. A Parisian Section of *Sans-Culotte* Petitions the Convention About Economic Grievances, May 1793
D. I. Wright, ed., *The French Revolution: Introductory Documents* (Newcastle, Australia: University of Queensland Press, 1974), 172.

D. The Maximum-General Attempts to Control Prices, September 29, 1793
D. I. Wright, 190–192.

DOCUMENT SET 20.9
Revolutionary Women, Counterrevolutionary Peasants, and Volunteer Soldiers

Olympe de Gouges, the pioneer feminist who in 1791 wrote the Declaration of the Rights of Woman and Citizen, eventually found herself aligned with the wrong political faction and in the summer of 1793 was arrested by the Committee of Public Safety. Protesting her innocence and the fervor of her republican sentiments, she managed to have her "Political Testament" (Document A) posted by her supporters on walls around Paris before she went bravely to her death at the guillotine.

The *sans-culottes* women who petitioned the Convention in August 1793 (Document B) were not the educated daughters of the privileged old order like Olympe de Gouges, but their sturdy patriotism and sense of shared grievances with their working-class husbands, brothers, and sons points to an equally fervent republican enthusiasm.

Not all ordinary French men and women were revolutionaries. The peasants of the Vendée region in western France rose in a savage counterrevolution against the Republic in 1793. Although they objected vehemently to the persecution of "nonjuring" priests who had refused to become salaried state functionaries, their grievances were not merely religious; they also resisted economic and political dominance by staunchly republican local townspeople. Extracts from various accounts by the military and political authorities charged with putting down the Vendéan revolt form Document C. Is it valid to compare the rebel bands with modern left-wing guerrilla insurgencies?

The final reading in this group, Document D, is a letter written in March 1794 by Theobald Wolf Tone, an Irish patriot who had fled to France to join the international republican crusade against the Old Regime and to help liberate his native land from English rule. His description of the enthusiasm of young men in volunteering for the army suggests how republicanism had spread among ordinary people, at least in towns. Note the credit that he gives to the volunteers' girlfriends in inspiring enlistments.

In reading these documents, consider the factors inspiring revolutionary enthusiasm—or the lack of it— among ordinary French men and women. Do you see any specifically feminist consciousness as motivating revolutionary women? And how might Wolf Tone's perceptions by shaped by his view of appropriate gender relations?

A. Olympe de Gouges Faces Death, Summer of 1793

My son, the wealth of the whole world, the universe in servitude at my feet, the daggers of assassins raised at me, nothing can extinguish the love of country that burns in my soul; nothing could make me betray my conscience. Men deranged by passions, what have you done and what incalculable evils are you perpetrating on Paris and on the whole of France? You are risking everything; you flatter yourselves into thinking that it is only a question of a great purge to save the public; let the departments, infused with terror, blindly adopt your horrible measures.

If, by a last effort, I can save the public welfare, I want even my persecutors, as they destroy me by their furor, to be jealous of my kind of death. And if one day French women are pointed out to future generations perhaps my memory will equal that of the Romans. I have predicted it all; I know that my death is inevitable; but it is glorious for a well-intentioned soul, when an ignominious death threatens all good citizens, to die for a dying country!

I will my heart to the nation, my integrity to men (they have need of it). To women, I will my soul; my creative spirit to dramatic artists; my disinterestedness to the ambitious; my philosophy to those who are persecuted; my intelligence to all fanatics; my religion to atheists; my gaiety to women on the decline; and all the poor remains of an honest fortune to my son, if he survives me.

Frenchmen, those are my last words, listen to what I am saying and reach down into the bottom of your hearts: do you recognize the austere virtues and the unselfishness of a republican? Answer me: who has loved and served the nation more—you or I? People, your reign is over if you fail to stop yourselves at the edge of this abyss. You have never been grander or more sublime than in the majestic calm you have kept during this bloody storm. If you can preserve this calm and this august kind of supervision, you will save Paris, the whole of France, and republican government.

B. Revolutionary Parisian Women Petition the Convention, August 1793

Citizen legislators: Justly indignant at the endless jobbery which has occurred in the Ministry . . . we come to demand of you the execution of constitutional laws. We did not accept the principles of the Constitution so that anarchy and the rule of schemers might be prolonged indefinitely. The premeditated war has lasted long enough. It is time for the children of liberty to sacrifice themselves for the *Patrie* and not for the ambition and pride of a heap of rogues at the head of our armies. Let us see by the dismissal of all nobles that you are not among their defenders. Hurry, and convince all France by your actions that we have not brought the representatives of a great people from all corners of the Republic, with great show, simply to put on a moving performance in the *Champ de Mars.* Prove that this Constitution, which we have seen accepted, is a reality and will indeed bring about our happiness. It is not sufficient to tell the people that its happiness is drawing near; it must feel its effects. Four years' experience of misfortune has taught it to mistrust the fine promises made to it endlessly. . . .

Believe us, legislators, four years of misfortune have taught us enough to be able to discern ambition under the very mask of patriotism; we no longer believe in the virtue of those men who are reduced to praising themselves. More than words is now necessary to convince us that ambition does not reign in your committees. Organize the government along the lines required by the Constitution. In vain do you tell us that this step will bring about the fall of France . . . we shall see only the fall of the schemers. In a Paris where the laws are strictly observed, do you expect us to believe that the enemies of the *Patrie* have no official defenders among you? Dismiss all nobles without exception; if there are some men of good faith among them, they will prove it by making a voluntary sacrifice for the happiness of their *Patrie.*

Don't be afraid of disorganizing the army; the more talented a general is, the more urgent it is to replace him if he is ill-intentioned. Don't do patriots the injustice of saying that there aren't men among them able to command our armies. Let us have some of these fine soldiers whose talents and deserts have been sacrificed to the ambition and pride of that formerly privileged caste. If, under the reign of despotism, their crime won preference, under that of liberty, virtue must sweep it away. You have made a decree according to which all suspects must be arrested; but we ask you, isn't this law derisory while these very suspects must execute it?

Legislators! Thus is the people mocked! There is the equality which was to be the basis of its happiness; there is its thanks for the countless evils it has suffered so patiently! It will not be said that this people, reduced to despair, was obliged to seek justice for itself; you will render justice by dismissing all guilty administrators, and by creating extraordinary tribunals in a sufficient number so that the people, before leaving for the frontiers, may say: "I am easy about the fate of my wife and children, for I have seen all domestic conspirators perish under the sword of the law."

Decree these measures, legislators, and the *levée en masse,* and you will have saved the *Patrie!*

C. Peasants of the Vendée Region Resist the Revolution, 1793

Wednesday, 13 March, toward 5 P.M., a large number of men in a band, armed with guns, hooks, forks, scythes, etc., all wearing white cockades and decorated with small, square, cloth medals, on which are embroidered different shapes, such as crosses, little hearts pierced with pikes, and other signs of that kind, appeared in the bourg of St. Pierre. All these fellows shouted, "Long live the King and our Good Priests! We want our King, our priests and the old regime!" And they wanted to kill off all the Patriots, especially the present witnesses. All that troop, which was of a frightening size, cast itself at the Patriots, who were assembled to resist their attempt, killed many, made many of them prisoners, and dispersed the rest.

The generals could never form the Vendéans into a permanent army or keep them under arms; it was never possible to make them remain to guard the cities they took; nor could anyone make them camp or subject them to military discipline. Accustomed to an active life, they could not stand the idleness of the camp. They went to battle eagerly, but were no less prompt to return home; they often fought with courage, but they were never soldiers.

The army was not at all permanent; it only formed on the chief's convocation. These orders were transmitted rapidly by couriers designated in each commune, and always ready to leave. The peasants gathered at the sound of the tocsin, the parish commandant gave the orders to them, the number of men needed, the day and the place of the rendezvous, and the time the expedition would last, which was hardly ever more than four or five days. The group formed, the priests officiated, built up enthusiasm with their preaching, disturbed indulgences and absolutions, and then the expedition got under way. When the appointed time had run out, the peasant felt free to go home, regardless of what was happening, and soon there was no army left.

What made the Vendéans fearsome in the beginning was their way of making war. They fought without order, in squads or crowds, often as individual snipers, hiding behind hedgerows, spreading out, then rallying, in a way that astonished their enemies, who were entirely unprepared for these maneuvers; they were seen to run up to cannons and steal them from under the eyes of the gunners, who hardly expected such audacity. They marched to combat, which they called *aller au feu* [to go to the fire], when they were called by their parish commandants, chiefs taken from their ranks and named by them, centurions, so to speak, who had more of their confidence than did the generals chance had given them; in battle, as at the doors of their churches on Sunday, they were surrounded by the acquaintances, their kinfolk and their friends; they did not separate except when they had to fly in retreat. After the action, whether victors or vanquished, they went back home, took care of their usual tasks, in fields or shops, always ready to fight.

D. Theobald Wolf Tone Comments on Army Volunteers' Enthusiasm, March 1794

Went to-day to the Church of St. Roch, to the *Fête de la Jeunesse* [Festival of Youth]; all the youth of the district, who have attained the age of sixteen, were to present themselves before the municipality, and receive their arms, and those who were arrived at twenty-one were to be enrolled in the list of citizens, in order to ascertain their right of voting in the assemblies. The church was decorated with the national colours, and a statue of Liberty, with an altar blazing before her. At the foot of the statue the municipality were seated, and the sides of the church were filled with a crowd of spectators, the parents and friends of the young men, leaving a space vacant in the centre of [for?] the procession. It consisted of the État-Major of the sections composing the district, of the National Guards under arms, of the officers of the sections, and, finally, of the young men who were to be presented. The guard was mounted by veterans of the troops of the line, and there was a great pile of muskets and of sabres before the municipality. When the procession arrived, the names of the two classes were enrolled, and, in the meantime, the veterans distributed the arms amongst the parents and friends and mistresses of the young men. When the enrolment was finished, an officer pronounced a short address to the youths of sixteen, on the duty which they owed to their country, and the honour of bearing arms in her defence, to which they were about to be admitted. They then ran among the crowd of spectators, and received their firelocks and sabres; some from their fathers, some from their mothers, and many, I could observe, from their lovers. When they were armed, their parents and mistresses embraced them, and they returned to their station. It is impossible to conceive anything more interesting than the spectacle was at that moment; the pride and pleasure in the countenance of the parents; the fierté of the young soldiers; and, above all, the expression in the features of so many young females, many of them beautiful, and all interesting from the occasion. I was in an enthusiasm. I do not at all wonder at the miracles which the French army has wrought in the contest for their liberties.

Document Set 20.9 References

A. Olympe de Gouges Faces Death, Summer of 1793
Marie Olympe de Gouges, *Politische Schriften in Auswahl*, Margarete Wolters and Clara Sutor, eds. (Hamburg: Helmut Buske Verlag, 1979), 202–206; adapted in Bonnie Smith, *Changing Lives: Women in European History Since 1700* (Lexington, Mass.: D. C. Heath, 1989), 108–109.

B. Revolutionary Parisian Women Petition the Convention, August 1793
D. I. Wright, ed., *The French Revolution: Introductory Documents* (Newcastle, Austrailia: University of Queensland Press, 1974), 184–185.

C. Peasants of the Vendée Region Resist the Revolution, 1793
Contemporary Accounts in Charles Tilly, *The Vendée: A Study in Counter Revolution* (Cambridge, Mass.: Harvard University Press, 1964), 317, 331, 332, 334.

D. Theobald Wolf Tone Comments on Army Volunteers' Enthusiasm, March 1794
J. M. Thompson, ed., *English Witnesses of the French Revolution* (Oxford, England: Basil Blackwell, 1938), 263–264.

DOCUMENT SET 20.10
Toussaint L'Ouverture and the Slave Revolt in Haiti

The greatest black revolutionary of the era of the French Revolution was Pierre Dominique Toussaint L'Ouverture (1746?–1803), born a slave in the French West Indian colony of Saint-Domingue, now the Republic of Haiti. His master gave him the opportunity to gain literacy and some knowledge of the outside world. When the French Revolution began, Toussaint rose to leadership among the black people—the vast majority of the colony's population—who found themselves struggling for liberation amid other contending groups: white planters generally aligned with Revolutionary France, mixed-blood (mulatto) people who sought some political autonomy, and royalist officials who from time to time were willing to use either mulattos or blacks against the white planters. At first Toussaint threw his lot with the royalists and the Spanish authorities in neighboring Santo Domingo (now the Dominican Republic), but even as a soldier ostensibly loyal to the French king in 1793, his objective was some form of freedom for the blacks (Document A). By 1797 he was in a position to warn the authorities in Paris that he and his formerly enslaved followers would use any means possible to prevent the restoration of slavery (Document B).

Recognized by the French Republic as its representative in Saint-Domingue, Toussaint drove out occupying British and Spanish forces, but in 1800 he refused to submit to Napoleon Bonaparte, who was bent on restoring slavery. He was captured and taken to France, where he died, but ultimately Napoleon's armies failed to subjugate Haiti. As you read these two documents, look for indications that Toussaint and other black leaders in Haiti had come to understand both the language and the ideas of the French Revolution to assert their own human rights.

A. Toussaint L'Ouverture Leads the Haitian Blacks as a French Royalist

Brothers and friends. I am Toussaint L'Ouverture, my name is perhaps known to you. I have undertaken vengeance. I want Liberty and Equality to reign in San Domingo. I work to bring them into existence. Unite yourselves to us, brothers, and fight with us for the same cause, etc.

> Your very humble and very obedient servant.
> Toussaint L'Ouverture,
> General of the Armies of the
> King, for the Public Good.

B. Toussaint L'Ouverture Leads the Haitian Blacks as a Republican General

The impolitic and incendiary discourse of Vaublanc has not affected the blacks nearly so much as their certainty of the projects which the proprietors of San Domingo are planning: insidious declarations should not have any effect in the eyes of wise legislators who have decreed liberty for the nations. But the attempts on that liberty which the colonists propose are all the more to be feared because it is with the veil of patriotism that they cover their detestable plans. We know that they seek to impose some of them on you by illusory and specious promises, in order to see renewed in this colony its former scenes of horror. Already perfidious emissaries have stepped in among us to ferment the destructive leaven prepared by the hands of liberticides. But they will not succeed. I swear it by all that liberty holds most sacred. My attachment to France, my knowledge of the blacks, make it my duty not to leave you ignorant either of the crimes which they meditate or the oath that we renew, to bury ourselves under the ruins of a country revived by liberty rather than suffer the return of slavery.

It is for you, Citizens Directors, to turn from over our heads the storm which the eternal enemies of our liberty are preparing in the shades of silence. It is for you to enlighten the legislature, it is for you to prevent the enemies of the present system from spreading themselves on our unfortunate shores to sully it with new crimes. Do not allow our brothers, our friends, to be sacrificed to men who wish to reign over the ruins of the human species. But no, your wisdom will enable you to avoid the dangerous snares which our common enemies hold out for you. . . .

I send you with this letter a declaration which will acquaint you with the unity that exists between the proprietors of San Domingo who are in France, those in the United States, and those who serve under the English banner. You will see there a resolution, unequivocal and carefully constructed, for the restoration of slavery; you will see there that their determination to succeed has led them to envelop themselves in the mantle of liberty in order to strike it more deadly blows. You will see that they are counting heavily on my complacency in lending myself to their perfidious views by my fear for my children. It is not astonishing that these men who sacrifice their country to their interests are unable to conceive how many sacrifices a true love of country can support in a better father than they, since I unhesitatingly base the happiness of my children on that of my country, which they and they alone wish to destroy.

I shall never hesitate between the safety of San Domingo and my personal happiness; but I have nothing to fear. It is to the solicitude of the French Government that I have confided my children. . . . I would tremble with horror if it was into the hands of the colonists that I had sent them as hostages; but even if it were so, let them know that in punishing them for the fidelity of their father, they would only add one degree more to their barbarism, without any hope of ever making me fail in my duty. . . . Blind as they are! They cannot see how this odious conduct on their part can become the signal of new disasters and irreparable misfortunes, and that far from making them regain what in their eyes liberty for all has made them lose, they expose themselves to a total ruin and the colony to its inevitable destruction. Do they think that men who have been able to enjoy the blessing of liberty will calmly see it snatched away? They supported their chains only so long as they did not know any condition of life more happy than that of slavery. But to-day when they have left it, if they had a thousand lives they would sacrifice them all rather than be forced into slavery again. But no, the same hand which has broken our chains will not enslave us anew. France will not revoke her princi-

ples, she will not withdraw from us the greatest of her benefits. She will protect us against all our enemies; she will not permit her sublime morality to be perverted, those principles which do her most honour to be destroyed, her most beautiful achievement to be degraded, and her Decree of 16 Pluviôse which so honors humanity to be revoked. *But if, to re-establish slavery in San Domingo, this was done, then I declare to you it would be to attempt the impossible: we have known how to face dangers to obtain our liberty, we shall know how to brave death to maintain it.*

This, Citizens Directors, is the morale of the people of San Domingo, those are the principles that they transmit to you by me.

My own you know. It is sufficient to renew, my hand in yours, the oath that I have made, to cease to live before gratitude dies in my heart, before I cease to be faithful to France and to my duty, before the god of liberty is profaned and sullied by the liberticides, before they can snatch from my hands that sword, those arms, which France confided to me for the defence of its rights and those of humanity, for the triumph of liberty and equality.

Document Set 20.10 References

A. Toussaint L'Ouverture Leads the Haitian Blacks as a French Royalist
   Toussaint, Letter, in C. L. R. James, *The Black Jacobins*, 2d ed. (New York: Vintage Books, 1963), 125.
B. Toussaint L'Ouverture Leads the Haitian Blacks as a Republican General
   Toussaint, Letter, in James, 195–197.

DOCUMENT SET 20.11
Burke, Paine, and Wollstonecraft

Intellectually the most subtle contemporary critic of the French Revolution was the Irish-born British politician Edmund Burke (1729–1797). A member of the House of Commons who had supported the American colonists against the claims of Parliament, Burke almost from the outset refused to expect anything positive to result from the French Revolution. Answering the inquiry of one of the many English supporters of the Revolution, Burke in 1790 published his book-length *Reflections on the Revolution in France.* Document A is a series of short extracts from this book. Burke's central argument is that societies and states are created over long periods of historical evolution and that human attempts to impose sweeping change in accordance with abstract ideals like "the rights of man" will lead to disaster. Burke's attack stimulated an equally eloquent response: *The Rights of Man* by Thomas Paine (1737–1809), a man of working-class origins and deep faith in the right and duty of ordinary people to take the lead in securing a just society (Document B). Paine had emerged as a political prophet in the American Revolution by encouraging the rebellious colonists to declare their independence in *Common Sense* (1776). After writing *The Rights of Man,* he emigrated to France and was elected to the Convention, but he ran afoul of Robespierre and barely survived the Reign of Terror. Eventually he settled in the United States.

The first great English feminist, Mary Wollstonecraft (1759–1797), also contested Burke's view of the French Revolution. In 1792 she published her best-known book, *Vindication of the Rights of Woman,* extracts of which appear as Document C. Taking as her starting point a Paine-like faith in the reality and defensibility of universal human rights, she drew the logical conclusion that women as well as men had inalienable political and social rights and should exercise these rights on the basis of genuine equality. Further, she demanded that women cease to abase themselves by living according to masculine notions of feminine propriety. Like Paine, she went to live in France and survived the Terror, dying in childbirth in 1797.

The three documents in this set debate the very foundations of the modern Western world's faith that human rights should be the basis on which civil society is organized. Do you tend to agree more with Burke or with Paine? Whichever side you take, summarize as fully and persuasively as you can the argu-

ment of the other side. Is it possible that in the heat of argument both overstate their case and that their disagreement is not as fundamental as it may seem? What evidence can you add from the history of the French Revolution to substantiate or refute the arguments of all three writers? How successful, in other words, *was* the French Revolution in securing human rights for all men and women?

A. Edmund Burke Condemns the Revolution

Is it because liberty in the abstract may be classed amongst the blessings of mankind that I am seriously to felicitate a madman, who has escaped from the protecting restraint and wholesome darkness of his cell, on his restoration to the enjoyment of light and liberty? . . . I should therefore suspend my congratulations on the new liberty of France, until I was informed how it had been combined with government. . . . The effect of liberty to individuals is, that they may do what they please; we ought to see what it will please them to do, before we risk congratulations, which may be soon turned into complaints. . . . The French Revolution is the most astonishing that has hitherto happened in the world. . . . Everything seems out of nature in this strange chaos of levity and ferocity. . . . It cannot, however, be denied, that to some this strange scene . . . inspired no other sentiments than those of exultation and rapture. . . .

You will observe that, from Magna Carta to the Declaration of Right, it has been the uniform policy of our [British] constitution to claim and assert our liberties, as an entailed inheritance derived to us from our forefathers, and to be transmitted to our posterity; as an estate specially belonging to the people of this kingdom; without any reference whatever to any other more general or prior right. By this means our constitution preserves a unity in so great a diversity of its parts. We have an inheritable crown; an inheritable peerage; and a House of Commons and a people inheriting privileges, franchises, and liberties, from a long line of ancestors. . . . Inheritance furnishes a sure principle of conservation and a sure principle of transmission; without at all excluding a principle of improvement. It leaves acquisition free; but it secures what it acquires. . . . In this choice of inheritance we have given to our frame of polity the image of a relation in blood; binding up the constitution of our country with our dearest domestic ties; adopting our fundamental laws into the bosom of our family affections; keeping inseparable, and cherishing with the warmth of all their combined and mutually reflected charities, our state, our hearths, our sepulchers, and our altars. . . .

We procure reverence to our civil institution on the principle upon which nature teaches us to revere individual men; on account of their age, and on account of those from whom they are descended. All your sophisters cannot produce anything better adapted to preserve a rational and manly freedom than the course that we have pursued, who have chosen our nature rather than our speculations, our breasts rather an our inventions, for the great conservatories and magazines of our rights and privileges. . . . After I had read over the list of the persons and descriptions selected into the [Third Estate], nothing which they afterwards did could appear astonishing. Among them, indeed, I saw some of known rank; some of shining talents; but of any practical experience in the state, not one man was to be found. . . . When the National Assembly has completed its work, it will have accomplished its ruin. . . . The person, whom they persevere in calling their king, has not power left to him by the hundredth part sufficient to hold together this collection of republics. . . .

It is no wonder, therefore, that with these ideas of everything in their constitution and government at home, either in church or state, as illegitimate and usurped or at best as a vain mockery, they look abroad with an eager and passionate enthusiasm. Whilst they are possessed by these notions, it is vain to talk to them of the practice of their ancestors, the fundamental laws of their country, the fixed form of a constitution, whose merits are confirmed by the solid test of long experience, and an increasing public strength and national prosperity. They despise experience as the wisdom of unlettered men; and as for the rest, they have wrought under ground a mine that will blow up, at one grand explosion, all examples of antiquity, all precedents, charters, and acts of parliament. They have "the rights of men." Against these there can be no prescription; against these no agreement is binding; these admit to temperament and no compromise: anything withheld from their full demand is so much of fraud and injustice. Against these their rights of men let no government look for security. . . .

Far am I from denying . . . the *real* rights of men. In denying their false claims of right, I do not mean to injure those which are real, and are such as their pretended rights would totally destroy. . . . Whatever each man can separately do, without trespassing upon others, he has a right to do for himself. . . .

Government is not made in virtue of natural rights, which may and do exist in total independence of it; and exist in much greater clearness, and in a much greater degree of abstract perfection: but their abstract perfection is their practical defect. By having a right to everything they want everything. Government is a contrivance of human wisdom to provide for human wants. Men have a right that these wants should be provided for by this wisdom. Among these wants is to be reckoned the want, out of civil society, of a sufficient restraint upon their passions. . . . This can only be done by a power out of themselves: and not, in the exercise of its function, subject to that will and to those passions which it is its office to bridle and subdue. In this sense the restraints on men, as well as their liberties, are to be reckoned among their rights. . . . This it is which makes the constitution of a state, and the due distribution of its powers, a matter of the most delicate and complicated skill. It requires a deep knowledge of human nature. . . . What is the use of discussing a man's abstract right to food or medicine? The question is upon the method of procuring and administering them. In that deliberation I shall always advise to call in the aid of the farmer and the physician, rather than the professor of metaphysics. . . .

The science of constructing a commonwealth, or renovating it, or reforming it, is, like every other experimental science, not to be taught *a priori*. . . . The science of government being therefore so practical in itself, and intended for such practical purposes, a matter which requires experience, and even more experience than any person can gain in his whole life, however sagacious and observing he may be, it is with infinite caution that any man ought to venture upon pulling down an edifice, which has answered in any tolerable degree for ages the common purposes of society. . . .

But now all is to be changed. All the pleasing illusions, which made power gentle and obedience liberal, which harmonized the different shades of life, and which, by a bland assimilation, incorporated into politics the sentiments which beautify and soften private society, are to be dissolved by this new conquering empire of light and reason. All the decent drapery of life is to be rudely torn off. All the superadded ideas, furnished from the wardrobe of a moral imagination, which the heart owns, and the understanding ratifies, as necessary to cover the defects of our naked, shivering nature, and to raise it to dignity in our own estimation, are to be exploded as a ridiculous, absurd, and antiquated fashion. . . .

On this scheme of things, a king is but a man, a queen is but a woman; a woman is but an animal, and an animal not of the highest order. . . . On the scheme of this barbarous philosophy, which is the offspring of cold hearts and muddy understandings, and which is as void of solid wisdom as it is destitute of all taste and elegance, laws are to be supported only by their own terrors, and by the concern which each individual may find in them from his own private speculations, or can spare to them from his own private interests. In the groves of their academy, at the end of every vista, you see nothing but the gallows. . . .

Society is indeed a contract. Subordinate contracts for objects of mere occasional interest may be dissolved at pleasure—but the state ought not to be considered as nothing better than a partnership agreement in a trade of pepper and coffee, calico or tobacco, or some other such low concern, to be taken up for a little temporary interest, and to be dissolved by the fancy of the parties. It is to be looked on with other reverence; because it is not a partnership in things subservient only to the gross animal existence of a temporary and perishable nature. It is a partnership in all science; a partnership in all art; a partnership in every virtue, and in all perfection. As the ends of such a partnership cannot be obtained in many generations, it become a partnership not only between those who are living, but between those who are living, those who are dead, and those who are to be born.

Each contract of each particular state is but a clause in the great primeval contract of eternal society, linking the lower with the higher natures, connecting the visible and invisible world, according to a fixed compact sanctioned by the inviolable oath which holds all physical and all moral natures, each in their appointed place. This law is not subject to the will of those, who by an obligation above them, and infinitely superior, are bound to submit their will to that law. . . . But if . . . the law is broken, nature is disobeyed, and the rebellious are outlawed, cast forth, and exiled from this world of reason, and order, and peace, and virtue, and fruitful penitence, into the antagonist world of madness, discord, vice, confusion, and unavailing sorrow.

B. Thomas Paine Defends the Revolution

To George Washington,
President of the United States of America
Sir,

I present you a small treatise in defense of those principles of freedom which your exemplary virtue hath so eminently contributed to establish. That the Rights of Man may become as universal as your benevolence can wish, and that you may enjoy the happiness of seeing the New World regenerate the Old, is the prayer of

Sir,
Your much obliged, and
Obedient humble servant,
Thomas Paine

From the part Mr. Burke took in the American Revolution, it was natural that I should consider him a friend to mankind; and as our acquaintance commenced on that ground, it would have been more agreeable to me to have had cause to continue in that opinion, than to change it.

At the time Mr. Burke made his violent speech last winter in the English Parliament against the French Revolution and the National Assembly, I was in Paris, and had written to him but a short time before, to inform him how prosperously matters were going on. Soon after this, I saw his advertisement of the pamphlet he intended to publish. . . .

Among the incivilities by which nations or individuals provoke and irritate each other, Mr. Burke's pamphlet on the French Revolution is an extraordinary instance. Neither the people of France, nor the National Assembly, were troubling themselves about the affairs of England, or the English Parliament; and that Mr. Burke should commence an unprovoked attack upon them, both in Parliament and in public, is a conduct that cannot be pardoned on the score of manners, nor justified on that of policy. . . .

Not sufficiently content with abusing the National Assembly, a great part of his work is taken up with abusing Dr. Price (one of the best-hearted men that lives), and the two societies in England known by the name of the Revolution Society, and the Society for Constitutional Information.

Dr. Price had preached a sermon on the 4th of November, 1789, being the anniversary of what is called in England the Revolution, which took place in 1688. Mr. Burke, speaking of this sermon, says, "The political divine proceeds dogmatically to assert that,

by the principles of the Revolution, the people of England have acquired three fundamental rights:
1. To choose our own governors.
2. To cashier them for misconduct.
3. To frame a government for ourselves.

Dr. Price does not say that the right to do these things exists in this or in that person, or in this or in that description of persons, but that it exists in the *whole;* that it is a right resident in the nation. Mr. Burke, on the contrary, denies that such a right exists in the nation, either in whole or in part, or that it exists any where; and, what is still more strange and marvelous, he says, "that the people of England utterly disclaim such a right, and that they will resist the practical assertion of it with their lives and fortunes."

That men should take up arms, and spend their lives and fortunes, *not* to maintain their rights, but to maintain they have *not* rights, is an entirely new species of discovery, and suited to the paradoxical genius of Mr. Burke.

The English Parliament of 1688 did a certain thing, which, for themselves and their constituents, they had a right to do, and which it appeared right should be done: But, in addition to this right, which they possessed by delegation, *they set up another right by assumption,* that of binding and controlling posterity to the end of time. . . .

There never did, there never will, and there never can exist a parliament, or any description of men, or any generation of men, in any country, possessed of the right or the power of binding and controlling posterity to the "end of time," or of commanding forever how the world shall be governed, or who shall govern it; and therefore, all such clauses, acts or declarations, by which the makers of them attempt to do what they have neither the right nor the power to do, nor the power to execute, are in themselves null and void.

Every age and generation must be as free to act for itself, *in all cases,* as the ages and generation which preceded it. The vanity and presumption of governing beyond the grave, is the most ridiculous and insolent of all tyrannies. . . .

It was not against Louis XVI, but against the despotic principles of the government, that the nation revolted. These principles had not their origin in him, but in the original establishment, many centuries back; and they were become too deeply rooted to be removed, and the Augean stable of parasites and plunderers too abominably filthy to be cleansed, by anything short of a complete and universal revolution. . . . There were, if I may so express it, a thousand despotisms to be reformed in France, which had grown up under the hereditary despotism of the monarchy, and became so rooted as to be in a great measure independent of it. . . .

Not one glance of compassion, not one commiserating reflection, that I can find throughout his book, has he [Burke] bestowed on those who lingered out the most wretched of lives, a life without hope, in the most miserable of prisons.

It is painful to behold a man employing his talents to corrupt himself. Nature has been kinder to Mr. Burke than he is to her. He is not affected by the reality of distress touching his heart, but by the showy resemblage of it striking his imagination. He pities the plumage, but forgets the dying bird. . . .

More of the citizens fell in this struggle than of their opponents; but four or five persons were seized by the populace, and instantly put to death; the governor of the Bastille, and the mayor of Paris, who was detected in the act of betraying them; and afterwards Foulon, one of the new ministry, and Berthier, his son-in-law, who had accepted the office of intendant of Paris. Their heads were struck upon spikes, and carried about the city; and it is upon this mode of punishment that Mr. Burke builds a great part of his tragic scenes. . . .

These outrages are not the effect of the principles of the revolution, but of the degraded mind that existed before the revolution, and which the revolution is calculated to reform. Place them then to their proper cause, and take the reproach of them to your own side. . . .

Mr. Burke, with his usual outrage, abuses the *Declaration of the Rights of Man,* published by the National Assembly of France, as the basis on which the constitution of France is built. This he calls "paltry and blurred sheets of paper about the rights of man."

Does Mr. Burke mean to deny that *man* has any rights? If he does, then he must mean that there are no such things as rights any where, and that he has none himself; for who is there in the world but man? But if Mr. Burke means to admit that man has rights, the question then will be, what are those rights, and how came man by them originally? . . .

The duty of man is not a wilderness of turnpike gates, through which he is to pass by tickets from one to the other. It is plain and simple, and consists but of two points. His duty to God, which every man must feel, and with respect to his neighbor, to do as he would be done by. . . .

Hitherto we have spoken only (and that but in part) of the natural rights of man. We have now to consider the civil rights of man, and to show how the one originates from the other. Man did not enter into society to become *worse* than he was before, nor to have fewer rights than he had before, but to have those rights better secured. His natural rights are the foundation of all his civil rights. . . .

In casting our eyes over the world, it is extremely easy to ditinguish the governments which have arisen out of society, or out of the social compact, from those which have not: but to place this in a clearer light than what a single glance may afford, it will be proper to take a review of the several sources from which the governments have arisen, and on which they have been founded.

They may be all comprehended under three heads. First, superstition. Secondly, power. Thirdly, the common interests of society, and the common rights of man.

The first was a government of priestcraft, the second of conquerors, and the third of reason. . . .

We have now to review the governments which arise out of society, in contradistinction to those which arose out of superstition and conquest.

It has been thought a considerable advance toward establishing the principles of freedom, to say, that government is a compact between those who govern and those who are governed: but this cannot be true, because it is putting the effect before the cause, for as a man must have existed before governments existed, there necessarily was a time when governments did not exist, and consequently there could originally exist no governments to form such a compact with.

The fact therefore must be, that the *individuals themselves,* each in his own personal and sovereign right, *entered into a compact with each other* to produce a government: and this is the only mode in which governments have a right to arise, and the only principle on which they have a right to exist. . . . The constitution of a country is not the act of its government, but of the people constituting a government. . . .

The authority of the present [National] Assembly [of France] is different to what the authority of future assemblies will be. The authority of the present one is to form a constitution; the authority of future assemblies will be to legislate according to the principles and forms prescribed in that constitution; and if experience should hereafter show that alterations, amendments, or additions are necessary, the constitution will point out the mode by which such things shall be done, and not leave it to the discretionary power of the future government. . . .

The Constitution of France says, that every man who pays a tax of sixty *sous* per annum (2*s.* and 6*d.* English) is an elector. What article will Mr. Burke place against this? Can anything be more limited, and at the same time more capricious, than what the qualifications are in England? . . .

The French Constitution says, that the number of representatives for any place shall be in a ratio to the number of taxable inhabitants or electors. What article will Mr. Burke place against this? The county of Yorkshire, which contains near a million souls, sends two county members; and so does the county of Rutland, which contains not a hundredth part of that number. . . .

The French Constitution says, there shall be no game laws; that the farmer on whose land wild game shall be found (for it is by the produce of those lands they are fed) shall have a right to what he can take. That there shall be no monopolies of any kind, that all trades shall be free, and every man free to follow any occupation by which he can procure an honest livelihood, and in any place, town, or city, throughout the nation. What will Mr. Burke say to this? . . .

The French Constitution says, *there shall be no titles;* and of consequence, all that class of equivocal generation, which in some countries is called "*aristocracy,*" and in others "*nobility,*" is done away, and the *peer* is exalted into *man.*

Titles are but nicknames, and every nickname is a title. The thing is perfectly harmless in itself, but it marks a sort of foppery in the human character which degrades it. . . .

The French Constitution has reformed the condition of the clergy. It has raised the income of the lower and middle classes, and taken from the higher. None is now less than twelve hundred *livres* (fifty pounds sterling), nor any higher than about two or three thousand pounds. What will Mr. Burke place against this? . . .

The French Constitution has abolished tithes, that source of perpetual discontent between the tithe-holder and the parishioner. . . .

The French Constitution hath abolished or renounced *toleration,* and *intolerance* also, and hath established UNIVERSAL RIGHT OF CONSCIENCE. . . .

Persecution is not an original feature in *any* religion; but it is always the strongly marked feature of all law-religions, or religions established by law. Take away the law-establishment, and every religion reasumes its original benignity. In America, a Catholic priest is a good citizen, a good character, and a good neighbor; an Episcopal minister is of the same description: and this proceeds, independently of the men, from there being no law-establishment in America. . . .

By the French Constitution, the nation is always named before the king. The third article of the Declaration of Rights says, "*The nation is essentially the source* (or fountain) *of all sovereignty.*" Mr. Burke argues, that, in England, a king is the fountain—that he is the fountain of all honor. . . . In contemplating the French Constitution, we see in it a rational order of things. . . .

One of the first works of the National Assembly, instead of vindictive proclamations, as has been the case with other governments, published a Declaration of the Rights of Man, as the basis on which the new Constitution was to be built. . . .

. . . We see the solemn and majestic spectacle of a nation opening its commission, under the auspices of its Creator, to establish a government; a scene so new, and so transcendently unequalled by any thing in the European world, that the name of a revolution is diminutive of its character, and it rises into a regeneration of man.

What are the present governments of Europe, but a scene of iniquity and oppression? What is that of England? Do not its own inhabitants say? It is a market where every man has his price, and where corruption is common traffic, at the expense of a deluded people? No wonder, then, that the French Revolution is traduced. . . .

Notwithstanding the nonsense, for it deserves not better name, that Mr. Burke has asserted about hereditary rights, and hereditary succession, and that a nation has not a right to form a government for itself; it happened to fall in his way to give some account of what government is. "*Government,*" say he, "*is a contrivance of human wisdom.*" . . .

Admitting that government is a contrivance of human *wisdom,* it must necessarily follow, that hereditary succession, and hereditary rights (as they are called), can make no part of it, because it is impossible to make wisdom hereditary; and on the other hand, *that* cannot be a wise contrivance, which in its operation may commit the government of a nation to the wisdom of an idiot. The ground which Mr. Burke now takes, is fatal to every part of his cause. . . .

What were formerly called revolutions, were little more than a change of persons, or an alteration of local circumstances. . . . But what we now see in the world, from the revolutions of America and France, is a renovation of the natural order of things, a system of principles as universal as truth and the existence of man, and combining moral with political happiness and national prosperity. . . .

Government on the old system is an assumption of power for the aggrandizement of itself; on the new, a delegation of power, for the common benefit of society. The former supports itself by keeping up a system of war; the latter promotes a system of peace, as the true means of enriching a nation. The one encourages national prejudices; the other promotes universal society, as the means of universal commerce. The one measures its prosperity, by the quantity of revenue it extorts; the other proves its excellence, by the small quantity of taxes it requires. . . . The representative system takes society and civilization for its basis; nature, reason, and experience for its guide. . . .

Never did so great an opportunity offer itself to England, and to all Europe, as is produced by the two revolutions of America and France. By the former, freedom has a national champion in the western world; and by the latter, in Europe. When another nation shall join France, despotism and bad government will scarcely dare to appear. To use a trite expression, the iron is becoming hot all over Europe. The insulted German and the enslaved Spaniard, the Russ and the Pole are beginning to think. The present age will hereafter merit to be called the Age of Reason, and the present generation will appear to the future as the Adam of a new world.

C. Mary Wollstonecraft Defends Women's Rights

My own sex, I hope, will excuse me, if I treat them like rational creatures, instead of flattering their *fascinating* graces, and viewing them as if they were in a state of perpetual childhood, unable to stand alone. I earnestly wish to point out in what true dignity and human happiness consists—I wish to persuade women to endeavor to acquire strength, both of mind and body, and to convince them that the soft phrases, susceptibility of heart, delicacy of sentiment, and refinement of taste, are almost synonymous with epithets of weakness, and that those beings who are only the objects of pity will soon become objects of contempt.

Dismissing those soft pretty feminine phrases, which the men condescendingly use to soften our slavish dependence, and despising that weak elegancy of mind, exquisite sensibility, and sweet docility of manners, supposed to be the sexual characteristics of the weaker vessel, I wish to shew that elegance is inferior to virtue, that the first object of laudable ambition is to obtain a character as a human being, regardless of the distinction of sex.

Youth is the season for love in both sexes; but in those days of thoughtless enjoyment provision should be made for the more important years of life, when reflection takes place of sensation. The woman who has only been taught to please will soon find that her charms are oblique sunbeams and that they cannot have much effect on her husband's heart when they are seen every day, when the summer is passed and gone. Will she then have sufficient native energy to look into herself for comfort, and cultivate her dormant faculties? or, is it not more rational to expect that she will try to please other men?

Why must the female mind be tainted by coquettish arts to gratify the sensualist and prevent love from subsiding into friendship, or compassionate tenderness, when there are not qualities on which friendship can be built? Let the honest heart shew itself, and *reason* teach passion to submit to necessity; or, let the dignified pursuit of virtue and knowledge raise the mind above those emotions. . . .

If then women are not a swarm of ephemeron triflers, why should they be kept in ignorance under the specious name of innocence? . . . As to the argument respecting the subjection in which the sex has ever been held, it retorts on man. The many have always been enthralled by the few; and monsters, who scarcely have shown any discernment of human excellence, have tyrannized over thousands of their fellow-creatures. . . . China is not the only country where a living man has been made a God. *Men* have submitted to superior strength to enjoy with impunity the pleasure of the moment; *women* have only done the same, and therefore till it is proved that the courtier, who servilely resigns the birthright of a man, is not a moral agent, it cannot be demonstrated that woman is essentially inferior to man because she has always been subjugated.

Document Set 20.11 References

A. Edmund Burke Condemns the Revolution
   Burke, Reflections on the *Revolution in France* (1790), in Peter Viereck, ed., Conservatism (Princeton, N.J.: Van Nostrand, 1956), 111–115.
B. Thomas Paine Defends the Revolution
   Paine, *The Rights of Man*, in Walter L. Arnstein, ed., *The Past Speaks*, 2d ed. (Lexington, Mass.: D. C. Heath, 1993), 2:127–133.
C. Mary Wollstonecraft Defends Women's Rights
   Wollstonecraft, *A Vindication of the Rights of Women* (1792), ed. Carol H. Poston (New York: W. W. Norton, 1975), 9–10, 27, 31.

Napoleon, the Restoration, and the Revolutionary Legacy, 1799–1832

Napoleonic State-Building

Napoleon Bonaparte justified his seizure and retention of power by arguing that he had become the sole guarantor of order, the consolidator of the Revolution, and France's protector against implacable, vengeful foreign powers. Consider how plausible was his claim as you read the selections that follow. In Document A he reports to his rubber-stamp legislative body on the last day of 1804, less than a month after he had crowned himself emperor. Document B, an extract from the Civil Code, focuses on one dimension of his consolidation of order—making a legal reality of the idea of separate male and female spheres, with the latter at a definite disadvantage. The regime's effort to indoctrinate the young is apparent in Document C, a slightly revised version of a catechism dating back to the late seventeenth century. Finally, in Document D, a Napoleonic court lady, the Countess de Rémusat (1780–1821), speculates after the regime's downfall on the readiness of formerly republican French citizens to accept Napoleon's rule.

A. Napoleon Justifies His Assumption of Imperial Authority, December 31, 1804

Five years after Bonaparte had become the head of the French government he sums up the general situation in France in a statement which he laid before the Legislative Body, December 31, 1804.

The internal situation of France is today as calm as it has even been in the most peaceful periods. There is no agitation to disturb the public tranquillity, no suggestion of those crimes which recall the Revolution. Everywhere useful enterprises are in progress, and the general improvements, both public and private, attest the universal confidence and sense of security. . . .

A plot conceived by an implacable government was about to replunge France into the abyss of civil war and anarchy. The discovery of this horrible crime stirred all France profoundly, and anxieties that had scarcely been calmed again awoke. Experience has taught that a divided power in the state is impotent and at odds with itself. It was generally felt that if power was delegated for short periods only it was so uncertain as to discourage any prolonged undertakings or wide-reaching plans. If vested in an individual for life, it would lapse with him, and after him would prove a source of anarchy and discord. It was clearly seen that for a great nation the only salvation lies in hereditary power, which can alone assure a continuous political life which may endure for generations, even for centuries. . . .

After prolonged consideration, repeated conferences with the members of the Senate, discussion in the councils, and the suggestions of the most prudent advisers, a series of provisions was drawn up which regulate the succession to the imperial throne. These provisions were decreed by a *senatus consultus* of the 28th Floréal last. The French people, by a free and independent expression, then manifested its desire that the imperial dignity should pass down in a direct line through the legitimate or adopted descendants of

Napoleon Bonaparte, or through the legitimate descendants of Joseph Bonaparte, or of Louis Bonaparte.

From this moment Napoleon was, by the most unquestionable of titles, emperor of the French. No other act was necessary to sanction his right and consecrate his authority. But he wished to restore in France the ancient forms and recall those institutions which divinity itself seems to have inspired. He wished to impress the seal of religion itself upon the opening of his reign. The head of the Church, in order to give the French a striking proof of his paternal affection, consented to officiate at this august ceremony. What deep and enduring impressions did this leave on the mind of Napoleon and in the memory of the nation! What thoughts for future races! What a subject of wonder for all Europe!

In the midst of this pomp, and under the eye of the Eternal, Napoleon pronounced the inviolable oath which assures the integrity of the empire, the security of property, the perpetuity of institutions, the respect for law, and the happiness of the nation. The oath of Napoleon shall be forever the terror of the enemies of France. If our borders are attacked, it will be repeated at the head of our armies, and our frontiers shall never more fear foreign invasion.

The principles safeguarded by the coronation oath are those of our legislation. Hereafter there will be fewer laws to submit to the Legislative Body. The civil code has fulfilled the expectations of the public; all citizens are acquainted with it; it serves as their guide in their various transactions, and is everywhere lauded as a benefaction. A draft of a criminal code has been completed for two years and has been subjected to the criticism of the courts; at this moment it is being discussed for the last time by the council of state. The code of procedure and the commercial code are still where they were a year ago, for pressing cares have diverted the emperor's attention elsewhere.

New schools are being opened, and inspectors have been appointed to see that the instruction does not degenerate into vain and sterile examinations. The *lycées* and the secondary schools are filling with youth eager for instruction. The polytechnic school is peopling our arsenals, ports, and factories with useful citizens. Prizes have been established in various branches of science, letters, and arts, and in the period of ten years fixed in his Majesty for the award of these prizes there can be no doubt that French genius will produce works of distinction.

The emperor's decrees have reëstablished commerce on the left bank of the Rhine. Our manufacturers are improving, although the mercenaries subsidized by the British government vaunt, in their empty declamations, her foreign trade and her precarious resources scattered about the seas and in the Indies, while they describe our shops as deserted and our artisans as dying of hunger. In spite of this, our industries are striking root in our own soil and are driving English commerce far from our shores. Our products now equal theirs and will soon compete with them in all the markets of the world.

Religion has resumed its sway, but exhibits itself only in acts of humanity. Adhering to a wise policy of toleration, the ministers of different sects who worship the same God do themselves honor by their mutual respect; and their rivalry confines itself to emulation in virtue. Such is our situation at home.

B. The Napoleonic Code Takes Notice of Women and the Family

Of the Rights and Respective Duties of Husband and Wife

212. Husband and wife mutually owe to each other fidelity, succor, and assistance.
213. The husband owes protection to his wife, the wife obedience to her husband.
214. The wife is obliged to live with her husband, and to follow him wherever he may think proper to dwell; the husband is bound to receive her, and to furnish her with everything necessary for the purposes of life, according to his means and condition.
215. The wife can do no act in law without the authority of her husband. . . .

Of Causes of Divorce

229. The husband may demand divorce for cause of adultery on the part of his wife.
230. The wife may demand divorce for cause of adultery on the part of her husband, where he shall have kept his concubine in their common house.

Of the Effects of Divorce

298. In the case of divorce allowed at law for cause of adultery, the guilty party can never marry his or her accomplice. The adulterous wife shall be condemned by the same judgment, and upon the requisition of the public ministry, to confinement in a house of correction for a certain period, which shall not be less than three months, nor exceed two years.

C. The Imperial Catechism Indoctrinates the Young

Question. What are the duties of Christians toward those who govern them, and what in particular are our duties towards Napoleon I, our emperor?

Answer. Christians owe to the princes who govern them, and we in particular owe to Napoleon I, our emperor, love, respect, obedience, fidelity, military service, and the taxes levied for the preservation and defense of the empire and of his throne. We also owe him fervent prayers for his safety and for the spiritual and temporal prosperity of the state.

Question. Why are we subject to all these duties toward our emperor?

Answer. First, because God, who has created empires and distributes them according to his will, has, by loading our emperor with gifts both in peace and in war, established him as our sovereign and made him the agent of his power and his image upon earth. To honor and serve our emperor is therefore to honor and serve God himself. Secondly, because our Lord Jesus Christ himself, both by his teaching and his example, has taught us what we owe to our sovereign. Even at his very birth he obeyed the edict of Caesar Augustus; he paid the established tax; and while he commanded us to render to God those things which belong to God, he also commanded us to render unto Caesar those things which are Caesar's.

Question. Are there not special motives which should attach us more closely to Napoleon I, our emperor?

Answer. Yes, for it is he whom God has raised up in trying times to reëstablish the public worship of the holy religion of our fathers and to be its protector; he has reëstablished and preserved public order by his profound and active wisdom; he defends the state by his mighty arm; he has become the anointed of the Lord by the consecration which he has received from the sovereign pontiff, head of the Church universal.

Question. What must we think of those who are wanting in their duties toward our emperor?

Answer. According to the apostle Paul, they are resisting the order established by God himself and render themselves worthy of eternal damnation.

D. Mme. de Rémusat Considers Why the French Submitted to Napoleon

I can understand how it was that men worn out by the turmoil of the Revolution, and afraid of that liberty which had long been associated with death, looked for repose under the dominion of an able ruler on whom fortune was seemingly resolved to smile. I can conceive that they regarded his elevation as a decree of destiny and fondly believed that in the irrevocable they should find peace. I may confidently assert that those persons believed quite sincerely that Bonaparte, whether as consul or emperor, would exert his authority to oppose the intrigues of faction and would save us from the perils of anarchy.

None dared to utter the word "republic," so deeply had the Terror stained that name; and the government of the Directory had perished in the contempt with which its chiefs were regarded. The return of the Bourbons could only be brought about by the aid of a revolution; and the slightest disturbance terrified the French people, in whom enthusiasm of every king seemed dead. Besides, the men in whom they had trusted had one after the other deceived them; and as, this time, they were yielding to force, they were at least certain that they were not deceiving themselves.

The belief, or rather the error, that only despotism could at that epoch maintain order in France was very widespread.

It became the mainstay of Bonaparte; and it is due to him to say that he also believed it. The factions played into his hands by imprudent attempts which he turned to his own advantage. He had some grounds for his belief that he was necessary; France believed it, too; and he even succeeded in persuading foreign sovereigns that he constituted a barrier against republican influences, which, but for him, might spread widely. At the moment when Bonaparte placed the imperial crown upon his head there was not a king in Europe who did not believe that he wore his own crown more securely because of that event. Had the new emperor granted a liberal constitution, the peace of nations and of kings might really have been forever secured.

Document Set 21.1 References

A. Napoleon Justifies His Assumption of Imperial Authority, December 31, 1804
   Napoleon Bonaparte, in James Harvey Robinson, ed., *Readings in European History* (Boston: Ginn, 1904), 2:491–494.
B. The Napoleonic Code Takes Notice of Women and the Family
   Napoleon Bonaparte, *Of the Rights and Respective Duties of Husband and Wife*, in Geoffrey Bruun, ed., *Napoleon and His Empire* (New York: D. Van Nostrand, 1972), 123–124.
C. The Imperial Catechism Indoctrinates the Young
   Imperial Catechism (April 1806), in Robinson, 2:509–510.
D. Mme. de Rémusat Considers Why the French Submitted to Napoleon
   de Rémusat, in Robinson, 2:490–491.

DOCUMENT SET 21.2
The Napoleonic Wars

Though consolidator of order in France, Napoleon abroad increasingly played the role of conqueror. By the end of his reign, most of the nationalities that had fallen under imperial domination and had become the battleground of his wars were ready to take back their pre-revolutionary rulers.

Document A, a letter from Johanna Schopenauer, the mother of the German philosopher Artur Schopenauer and herself a successful novelist, describes the danger to civilians who found themselves trapped in the midst of fighting—admittedly, not a statistically likely prospect. But the depredations of French soldiers on the loose in foreign lands was feared in every occupied territory.

The defeat of an old-regime power by the Napoleonic army could lead to salutary internal reforms. After the overthrow of Prussia at the Battle of Jena, in October 1807, the king of what was left of that state was compelled to take steps that his predecessor, Frederick the Great, had never dared: he abolished serfdom and tried to build the kingdom's economy by freeing nobles from the obligation to support their peasants in times of adversity (Document B). Napoleon himself proposed to reward Spain for receiving him as the country's "deliverer" in 1808 by establishing a thoroughly up-to-date, post-feudal regime (Document C). Unfortunately for the emperor and his imperial troops, most ordinary Spaniards regarded their French occupiers as impious bloodsuckers. One of the liberal Spanish aristocrats who fought the French occupation forces (and also rejected the reactionary Spanish king's attempt to bring absolutism) recognized the Spanish people as the main driving force of the liberation movement (Document D).

The crowning act of what the ancient Greeks would have called Napoleon's *hubris*—his overweening, fatal pride—was the French invasion of Russia in 1812. Far from rising to welcome the French as liberators, Russia's serfs remained faithful to their tsar and to Orthodoxy, and no French victory on the battlefield could overcome the Russian army's most valuable allies, Russia's vast distances and harsh winter climate. In the end Napoleon suffered a horrible defeat, described in Document E by a liberal Frenchman who witnessed the tragedy, Benjamin Constant.

A. A Woman Witnesses the French Occupation of Jena, 1806

The dreadful cry was heard in the streets, "the French are coming!" Hundreds of men rushed by to the market-place, which is not far from us. Now all hope was gone: we clasped each other's hands in silence. The cannons again roared, nearer and nearer, awfully near. The floor shook, and the windows rattled. How near death was to us! We no longer heard any single report, but the hissing and rattling of the balls and small-shot which flew over our house and onto the houses and the ground fifty paces from us, without our being hurt thereby: God's angel protected us. Peace and calm were suddenly restored to my heart, I drew my Adela to my bosom, and sat down with her on a sofa, hoping that a ball might kill us both,—at all events that neither might have to weep over the other. Never was the thought of death nearer to me, and never was it less formidable. Throughout the day, and even at that sad moment, Adela did not lose her self-composure. Not a tear did she shed, nor a cry did she utter: when her feelings became overpowering she drew herself nearer to me, kissed me, drew me close to her, and begged me not to distress myself. Even now she was quite still; but I felt her delicate limbs tremble with a feverish chill, and heard her teeth striking against each other. I kissed her and begged her to compose herself, for if we died we should die together; she ceased to tremble, and looked affectionately up in my face. It was nearly eight o'clock. I insisted on it that we should sit down properly to dinner; none of us had tasted anything all day but a few cups of broth and a glass or two of wine, and had endured this distracting anxiety besides. Just as we had seated ourselves at dinner, there was a cry of fire, and a column of flames, like Mont Blanc, burst forth. We saw plainly that it was not quite close to us, but there was a cry—"the castle's on fire!" and again, "the city is set fire to in four places!" There was no wind; we put our trust in God, and were more calm.

Soon after an attempt was made to force open the front door. Sophy and Conta ran down, and persuaded the ferocious men,—how, I cannot to tell,—to come under the window. They demanded bread and wine quickly; both were handed to them out of the window. They were merry; they sang, and drank Sophy's health; she was obliged to drink theirs in return, and then they went away. This was repeated several times. We had all crowded into a small back parlour not to let any light be seen: I had laid Adela on a bed; I sat down on it with a purse containing a few crowns in my hand. Now we heard their wild voices down-stairs:—"Du pain, du vin, vite, nous montons!" [Bread! Wine! Quick, we're coming up!"] and Sophy and Conta bid them welcome in a most amiable manner. Sophy said,—she had been waiting for them a long while, and had cooked in readiness, so they had better be quiet. The table and all was ready, and thereupon she set out the bread and wine, and roast meat before them. Conta, who passed for her husband, did his part: the savages became tame; they ate, drank, and got quite tipsy. Just fancy their hideous faces, their bloody swords drawn, the white smocks they wore on such occasions, all sprinkled with blood, their savage merriment and conversation, and hands dyed red with blood. I had only a momentary glance from the stairs at them: they were ten or twelve in number. Sophy was joking, and laughing with them below. One grasped her round the waist. Then Sophy fetched Adela, who spoke to them very respectfully, and begged them to leave, because she was very sleepy; the wretches yielded to the child's request and went off.

B. The Prussian Reform Edict of 1807 Abolishes Serfdom

We, Frederick William, by the grace of God king of Prussia, etc., etc., hereby make known and proclaim that: Since peace has been established we have been occupied before everything else with the care for the depressed condition of our faithful subjects and the speediest revival and greatest possible improvement in this respect. We have considered that, in face of the prevailing want, the means at our disposal would be insufficient to aid each individual, and even if they were sufficient, we could not hope to accomplish our object; and that, moreover, in accordance with the imperative demands of justice and with the principles of a judicious economic policy, it behooves us to remove every obstacle which has hitherto prevented the individual from attaining such a state of prosperity as he was capable of reaching. We have further considered that the existing restrictions, both on the possession and enjoyment of landed property and on the personal condition of the agricultural laborer, especially interfere with our benevolent purpose and disable a great force which might be applied to the restoration of agriculture,—the former, by their prejudicial influence upon the value of landed property and the credit of the proprietor; the latter, by dimin-

ishing the value of labor. We desire, therefore, to reduce both kinds of restrictions so far as the common well-being demands, and we accordingly ordain the following.

1. Every inhabitant of our states is competent, without any limitation on the part of the state, to own or mortgage landed property of every kind. The noble may therefore own not only noble, but also non-noble, citizen and peasant lands of every kind, and the citizen and peasant may possess not only citizen, peasant, and other non-noble, but also noble tracts of land without in any case needing special permission for any acquisition whatever, although henceforth, as before, every change of ownership must be announced to the authorities. All privileges which are possessed by noble over citizen inheritances are entirely abolished. . . .

2. Every noble is henceforth permitted, without any derogation from his station, to engage in citizen occupation, and every citizen or peasant is allowed to pass from the citizen into the peasant class or from the peasant into the citizen class. . . .

10. From the date of this ordinance no new relation of serfdom, whether by birth or marriage, or by assuming the position of a serf, or by contract, can be created.

11. With the publication of the present ordinance the existing relations of serfdom of those serfs, with their wives and children, who possess their peasant holdings by inheritance, or in their own right, or by perpetual leases, or of copyhold, shall cease entirely, together with all mutual rights and duties.

12. From Martinmas, one thousand eight hundred and ten (1810), all serfdom shall cease throughout our whole realm. From Martinmas, 1810, there shall be only free persons, as is already the case upon the royal domains in all our provinces,—free persons, however, still subject, as a matter of course, to all obligations which bind them, as free persons, by reason of the possession of an estate or by virtue of a special contract.

To this declaration of our supreme will every one whom it may concern, and in particular our provincial authorities and other officials, are exactly and dutifully to conform, and the present ordinance is to be universally made known.

C. Napoleon Offers the Spanish Enlightened Reforms, 1808

To date from the publication of the present decree, feudal rights are abolished in Spain.

All personal obligations, all exclusive fishing

rights and other rights of similar nature on the coast or on rivers and streams, all feudal monopolies (*banalités*) of ovens, mills, and inns are suppressed. It shall be free to every one who shall conform to the laws to develop his industry without restraint.

The tribunal of the Inquisition is abolished, as inconsistent with the civil sovereignty and authority.

The property of the Inquisition shall be sequestered and fall to the Spanish state, to serve as security for the bonded debt.

Considering that the members of the various monastic orders have increased to an undue degree and that, although a certain number of them are useful in assisting the ministers of the altar in the administration of the sacraments, the existence of too great a number interferes with the prosperity of the state, we have decreed and do decree as follows:

The number of convents now in existence in Spain shall be reduced to a third of their present number. This reduction shall be accomplished by uniting the members of several convents of the same order into one.

From the publication of the present decree, no one shall be admitted to the novitiate or permitted to take the monastic vow until the number of the religious of both sexes has been reduced to one third of that now in existence. . . .

All regular ecclesiastics who desire to renounce the monastic life and live as secular ecclesiastics are at liberty to leave their monasteries. . . .

In view of the fact that the institution which stands most in the way of the internal prosperity of Spain is that of the customs lines separating the provinces, we have decreed and do decree what follows:

To date from January 1 next, the barriers existing between the provinces shall be suppressed. The custom houses shall be removed to the frontiers and there established.

D. The Spanish Nobleman Manuel García Herreros Credits the People with Liberating Their Country, 1811

What, gentlemen, would become of the Spanish nation if that revolution which we consider holy had been entrusted solely to the aristocracy? . . . When the nation was invaded and caught by surprise by those hordes of innumerable vandals, would the nobility have been able by itself to reconquer liberty? Was it not the people who with their awe-inspiring effort . . . tried to break the chains with which the tyrant endeavored to tie us to the chariot of his tri-

umphs? . . . Some will say to me that noblemen have equally contributed to our cause and that they have rendered great services to the fatherland. I am glad of it. I do not doubt that the nobility has done its duty. But, gentlemen, how insufficient . . . would have been all the efforts and sacrifices if the salvation of the fatherland had depended exclusively on them!

E. A Frenchman Recalls the Retreat from Moscow

On the 25th of November [1812] there had been thrown across the river temporary bridges made of beams taken from the cabins of the Poles. . . . At a little after five in the afternoon the beams gave way, not being sufficiently strong; and as it was necessary to wait until the next day, the army again abandoned itself to gloomy forebodings. It was evident that they would have to endure the fire of the enemy all the next day. But there was no longer any choice; for it was only at the end of this night of agony and suffering of every description that the first beams were secured in the river. It is hard to comprehend how men could submit to stand, up to their mouths in water filled with ice, rallying all the strength which nature had given them, added to all that the energy of devotion furnished, and drive piles several feet deep into a miry bed, struggling against the most horrible fatigue, pushing back with their hands enormous blocks of ice which threatened to submerge and sink them. . . .

The emperor awaited daylight in a poor hut, and in the morning said to Prince Berthier, "Well, Berthier, how do we get out of this?" He was seated in his room, great tears flowing down his cheeks, which were paler than usual and the prince was seated near him. They exchanged words, and the emperor appeared overcome by his grief, leave to the imagination what was passing in his soul.

When the artillery and baggage wagons passed, the bridge was so overweighted that it fell in. Instantly a backward movement took place, which crowded together all the magnitude of stragglers who were advancing in the rear of the artillery, like a flock being herded. Another bridge had been constructed, as if the sad thought had occurred that the first might give way, but the second was narrow and without a railing; nevertheless it seemed at first a very valuable makeshift in such a calamity. But how disasters follow one upon another! The stragglers rushed to the second bridge in crowds. But the artillery, the baggage wagons,—a word, all the army supplies,—had been in front on the first bridge when it broke down. . . . Now, since it was urgent that the artillery should pass first, it rushed impetuously toward the only road to safety which remained. No one can describe the scene of horror which ensued; for it was literally over a road of trampled human bodies that conveyances of all sorts reached the bridge. On this occasion one could see how much brutality and cold-blooded ferocity can be produced in human minds by the instinct of self-preservation. . . . As I have said, the bridge had no railing; and crowds of those who forced their way across fell into the river and were engulfed beneath the ice. Others, in the fall, tried to stop themselves by grasping the planks of the bridge, and remained suspended over the abyss until, their hands crushed by the wheels of the vehicles, they lost their grasp and went to join their comrades as the waves closed over them. Entire caissons with drivers and horses were precipitated into the water. . . .

Officers harnessed themselves to sleds to carry some of their companions who were rendered helpless by their wounds. They wrapped these unfortunates as warmly as possible, cheered them from time to time with a glass of brandy when they could procure it, and lavished upon them the most touching attention. There were many who behaved in this unselfish manner, of whose names we are ignorant; and how few returned to enjoy in their own country the remembrance of the most heroic deeds of their lives!

On the 29th the emperor quitted the banks of the Beretina and we slept at Kamen, where his Majesty occupied a poor wooden building which the icy air penetrated from all sides through the windows, for nearly all the glass was broken. We closed the openings as well as we could with bundles of hay. A short distance from us, in a large lot, were penned up the wretched Russian prisoners whom the army drove before it. I had much difficulty in comprehending the delusion of victory which our poor soldiers still kept up by dragging after them this wretched luxury of prisoners, who could only be an added burden, as they required constant surveillance. When the conquerors are dying of famine, what becomes of the conquered? These poor Russians, exhausted by marches and hunger, nearly all perished that night. . . .

[Napoleon secretly decided to leave his stricken army and return to France as quickly as possible.] The emperor left in the night. By daybreak the army had learned the news, and the impression it made cannot be depicted. Discouragement was at its height, and many soldiers cursed the emperor and reproached him for abandoning them.

This night, the 6th [of December], the cold increased greatly. Its severity may be imaged, as birds were found on the ground frozen stiff. Soldiers seated themselves with their heads in their hands and bodies bent forward in order thus to feel less the emptiness of their stomachs. . . . Everything had failed us. Long before reaching Wilna [Vilnius, today in Lithuania], the horses being dead, we received orders to burn our carriages and all their contents.

Document Set 21.2 References

A. A Woman Witnesses the French Occupation of Jena, 1806
   Johanna Schopenauer, *Youthful Life and Pictures of Travel* (London: Longman, Brown, Green, and Longmans, 1847), 1:279–288.

B. The Prussian Reform Edict of 1807 Abolishes Serfdom
   Edict of Frederick William (1807), in James Harvey Robinson, ed., *Readings in European History* (Boston: Ginn, 1904), 2:520–521.

C. Napoleon Offers the Spanish Enlightened Reforms, 1808
   Decrees Affecting Spain, in Robinson, 2:512–513.

D. The Spanish Nobleman Manuel García Herreros Credits the People with Libertating Their Country, 1811
   Herreros, in Gabriel H. Lovett, *Napoleon and the Birth of Modern Spain* (New York: New York University Press, 1965), 2:447.

E. A Frenchman Recalls the Retreat from Moscow
   Constant, *Memoirs*, in Robinson, 2:515-518.

DOCUMENT SET 21.3
Restoration, Conservatism, and Counter-Revolution on the Continent

In evaluating the success of the peace settlement and the political restoration of 1814–1815, keep in mind the nature of the Napoleonic regime in France and the reaction of conquered peoples to occupation by French troops (Sets 21.1 and 21.2).

Restored to the French throne, Louis XVIII (*1814–1824) granted a "constitutional charter" whose wording indicates that times had changed since pre-revolutionary absolutism. Read Document A with an eye to the concessions that Louis XVI's brother thought it necessary to offer, and contrast this with the hopes that the rulers of Russia, Prussia, and Austria professed in subscribing to the Holy Alliance (Document B).

In Germany, opposition to the reactionary restoration governments ran strongest in the university communities, stirring with ideas of nationalism. The Carlsbad Decrees of 1819 (Document C) were enacted by the German Confederation in response to book-burning demonstrations and the assassination of a reputed Russian spy by a student. Yet so bureaucratic was the spirit with which measures such as these were enforced that they elicited a spirited protest from one of Germany's leading conservative theorists, Joseph Görres (Document D).

A. Louis XVIII Grants France a Constitutional Charter, 1814

Louis by the Grace of God, King of France and Navarre—to all those to whom these presents come, salutation. Divine Providence in recalling us to our estates after a long absence has imposed grave responsibilities upon us. Peace was the first necessity of our subjects, and we have unceasingly occupied ourselves with this. That peace, so essential to France and to the rest of Europe has been signed. A constitutional charter was demanded by the existing condition of the kingdom, we promised this and now publish it. We have taken into consideration the fact that although the whole authority in France resides in the person of the king, our predecessors have not hesitated to modify the exercise of this in accordance with the differences of the times. It was thus that the communes owed their enfranchisement to Louis the Fat, the confirmation and extension of their rights to Saint Louis and Philip the Fair, and that the judicial system was established and developed by the laws of Louis XI, Henry II, and Charles IX. It was in this way

finally that Louis XIV, regulated almost every portion of the public administration by various ordinances which have never been surpassed in wisdom. We, like the kings our predecessors, have had to consider the effects of the ever increasing progress of knowledge, the new relations which this progress has introduced into society, the direction given to the public mind during half a century and the serious troubles resulting therefrom. We have perceived that the wish of our subjects for a constitutional charter was the expression of a real need, but in yielding to this wish we have taken every precaution that this charter should be worthy of us and of the people whom we are proud to rule. Able men taken from the first bodies of the state were added to the commissioners of our council to elaborate this important work. While we recognize that the expectations of enlightened Europe ought to be gratified by a free monarchical constitution, we have had to remember that our first duty toward our peoples was to preserve for their own interest the rights and prerogatives of our crown. We hope that, taught by experience, they may be convinced that the supreme authority can alone give to institutions which it establishes the power, permanence and dignity with which it is itself clothed. That, consequently, when the wisdom of kings freely harmonizes with the wish of the peoples, a constitutional charter may long endure, but that when concessions are snatched with violence from a weak government, public liberty is not less endangered than the throne itself.

We have sought the principles of the constitutional charter in the French character and in the venerable monuments of past centuries. Thus we perceived in the revival of the peerage a truly national institution which binds memories to hope, by uniting ancient and modern times. We have replaced by the chamber of deputies, those ancient assemblies of the March Field and May Field, and those chambers of the third estate which so often exhibited at once proof of their zeal for the interests of the people, and fidelity and respect for the authority of kings. In thus endeavoring to renew the chain of time which fatal excesses had broken, we effaced from our memory, as we would we might blot out from history, all the evils which have afflicted the country during our absence. Happy to find ourselves again in the bosom of our great family, we could only respond to the love of which we receive so many testimonies by uttering words of peace and consolation. The dearest wish of our heart is that all the French may live like brothers, and that no bitter memory should ever trouble the security which ought to follow the solemn act which we grant them to-day.

Confident in our intentions, strong in our conscience, we engage ourselves before the assembly which listens to us to be faithful to this Constitutional Charter, with the intention of swearing to maintain it with added solemnity before the altars of Him who weighs in the same balance kings and nations.

For these reasons we have voluntarily and by the free exercise of our royal authority granted and do grant, concede and accord, as well for us as for our successors forever, the Constitutional Charter as follows:

B. Alexander I, Francis I, and Frederick William III Sign the Holy Alliance

Their majesties, the Emperor of Austria, the King of Prussia and the Emperor of Russia, in view of the great events which the last three years have brought to pass in Europe and in view especially of the benefits which it has pleased Divine Providence to confer upon those states whose governments have placed their confidence and their hope in Him alone, having reached the profound conviction that the policy of the powers, in their mutual relations, ought to be guided by the sublime truths taught by the eternal religion of God our Savior, solemnly declare that the present act has no other aim than to manifest to the world their unchangeable determination to adopt no other rule of conduct, either in the government of their respective countries or in their political relations with other governments, than the precepts of that holy religion, the precepts of justice, charity and peace. These, far from being applicable exclusively to private life, ought on the contrary directly to control the resolutions of princes and to guide their steps as the sole means of establishing human institutions and of remedying their imperfections. Hence their majesties have agreed upon the following articles:

ARTICLE I.—Comformably to the words of Holy Scripture which command all men to look upon each other as brothers, the three contracting monarchs will continue united by the bonds of a true and indissoluble fraternity and, regarding themselves as compatriots, they shall lend aid and assistance to each other on all occasions and in all places, viewing themselves, in their relations to their subjects and to their armies, as fathers of families, they shall direct them in the same spirit of fraternity by which they are animated for the protection of religion, peace and justice.

ARTICLE II.—Hence the sole principle of conduct, be it between the said government or their subjects, shall be that of rendering mutual service, and testifying by unceasing good-will, the mutual affection with which they should be animated. Considering themselves all as members of one great Christian nation, the three allied princes look upon themselves as delegates of Providence called upon to govern three branches of the same family, viz: Austria, Russia and Prussia. They thus confess that the Christian nation, of which they and their people form a part, has in reality no other sovereign than He alone to whom belongs by right the power, for in Him alone are to be found all the treasures of love, of knowledge and of infinite wisdom, that is to say God, our Divine Saviour Jesus Christ, the word of the Most High, the word of life. Their majesties recommend, therefore, to their peoples, as the sole means of enjoying that peace which springs from a good conscience and is alone enduring, to fortify themselves each day in the principles and practice of those duties which the Divine Saviour has taught to men.

ARTICLE III.—All those powers who wish solemnly to make avowal of the sacred principles which have dictated the present act, and who would recognize how important it is to the happiness of nations, too long agitated, that these truths should hereafter exercise upon human destiny all the influence belonging to them, shall be received into this Holy Alliance with as much cordiality as affection.

Engrossed in three copies and signed at Paris, year of grace, 1815, September $\frac{14}{26}$.

	FRANCIS,
Signed	FREDERICK WILLIAM,
	ALEXANDER.

C. The Carlsbad Decrees Crack Down on the German Universities, 1819

1. A special representative of the ruler of each state shall be appointed for each university with appropriate instructions and extended powers, and who shall reside in the place where the university is situated. . . .

The function of this agent shall be to see to the strictest enforcement of existing laws and disciplinary regulations; to observe carefully the spirit which is shown by the instructors in the university in their public lectures and regular courses, and, without directly interfering in scientific matters or in the methods of teaching, to give a salutary direction to the instruction, having in view the future attitude of the students. Lastly, they shall devote unceasing attention to everything that may promote morality, good order and outward propriety among the students. . . .

2. The confederated governments mutually pledge themselves to remove from the universities or other public educational institutions all teachers who, by obvious deviation from their duty or by exceeding the limits of their functions, or by the abuse of their legitimate influence over the youthful minds, or by propagating harmful doctrines hostile to the public order or subversive of existing governmental institutions, shall have unmistakably proved their unfitness for the important office intrusted to them. . . .

No teacher who shall have been removed in this manner shall be again appointed to a position in any public institution of learning in another state of the Union.

3. Those laws which have for a long period been directed against secret and unauthorized societies in the universities, shall be strictly enforced. These laws apply especially to that association established some years since under the name Universal Students' Union (*Allgemeine Burschenschaft*), since the very conception of the society implies the utterly unallowable plan of permanent fellowship and constant communication between the various universities. The duty of especial watchfulness in this matter should be impressed upon the special agents of the government.

The governments mutually agree that such persons as shall, after the publication of the present decree, be shown to have remained in secret or unauthorized associations or shall have entered such associations, shall not be admitted to any public office.

4. No student, who shall be expelled from a university by a decision of the University Senate, which was ratified or prompted by the agent of the government, or who shall have left the institution in order to escape expulsion, shall be received in any other university. Nor, in general, shall any student be admitted to another university without a satisfactory certificate of his good conduct at the university he has left.

D. The German Catholic Conservative Joseph Görres Condemns Both Nationalistic Agitation and Bureaucratic Repression

After a violent party struggle of four years, a blind and foolish opposition to the claims of the age, and partial concessions to them on the one hand, and exaggerations of various descriptions on the other, things have at length come to such a pass, that the minds of men throughout all Germany are in a state of the most violent excitation; and that disposition has become universally prevalent, which is usually seen to precede great catastrophes in history. What the most active, the most crafty and deceitful demagogues, with all their intrigues, could never of themselves have effected from below, has been successfully accomplished by the dexterous co-operation of those who have taken the business in hand by the long arm of the lever from above; and thus the peaceful, the tranquilly disposed, the sober-minded and moderate people of Germany, have been agitated in all their elements and all their depths, and worked up to the utmost degree of bitterness and rage. And that these agitators may, with the utmost justice, lay claim to the greatest part of the honour of this achievement, they are now preparing with the utmost joy and alacrity to supply, in a short space, what little may yet be wanting to give the last finish to the whole; that the work, in all its parts, may exhibit the hand of a master. As whenever the agitated passions seemed in any measure to subside, they have always, at the suitable moment, supplied new incentives to discontent and irritation; as with inimitable dexterity they have contrived to find out the weak side of every one, and availed themselves of every occurrence of the times to apply its sharp edge to the sore, or yet imperfectly cicatrised places; they have thus actually discovered a secret for rousing the whole body of the people, so that a common feeling of discontent prevails from one end of the country to the other; and the governments are at this time entangled in a hopeless contest with all that is good and noble and energetic, and are lost in errors from which they will never be able to extricate themselves by the ways they have hitherto pursued. As in a sultry and oppressive summer heat, when the sky begins to overcast, the dread of the dark and boding tempest is unable to extinguish the inward longing of nature for the refreshing coolness which follows in its train; in like manner public opinion has now almost reconciled itself to all that is most dreadful in events, if they only promise to relieve us from our present ignominy, and open to us a source of pure hope in the heavens, the face of which is now obscured by a vapour which veils every happy star from our sight. Hence those birds of presage, harbingers of the approaching tempest, the youths who, to remove out of the way the base and unworthy in its organs, devote themselves to death, fill it not with alarm, nor was it surprised when the discovery of a great and widespread conspiracy for the establishment of a German Republic was announced from Berlin, because the experience of the last age has sufficiently inculcated the knowledge of the universal law in nature, that every extreme has a necessary and inevitable tendency to produce its opposite. Only one thing amidst the alarm created by the breaking open of trunks and boxes, the going and coming of gendarmes and police agents, the precaution which seemed to have been taken, purposely, as it were, to trample on all judicial forms, the trouble and uneasiness given to peaceable men, whom the least tact or knowledge of the world would at once have acquitted beforehand, the examinations and sealings of papers, arrests, and discharges from arrest; only one thing was wondered at in the midst of all these fearful movements, that, while searching for traces of secret conspiracies carried on in the dark, these profound politicians should see nothing of a good conspiracy, which spreads its extensive ramifications over all Germany, throughout every rank and age and sex; which sits murmuring by every hearth, which raises its voice aloud in markets and highways, which is easily perceived in all its members without any sign, and which, without secret heads, and without impulse from a common centre, works constantly in concert and with the very best understanding to promote one common end; which stares with many thousand open eyes into the most hidden recesses, and which has many thousand arms constantly at command; that conspiracy, namely, in which the irritated feelings, the disappointed hopes, the wounded pride, the sufferings and oppression of the nation, have associated themselves together against the rigid obstinacy of arbitrary power, the mechanism of lifeless forms, the devouring poison of despotic maxims of government unconsciously acted on, the fruit of the corruption of the times, and the blindest prejudices, and which conspiracy, powerful and formidable to a degree that no former one ever yet reached, and growing every day in power and activity, is so sure of attaining its object, that the danger will not certainly arise from the tardiness, but from the excessive rapidity of its progress.

Document Set 21.3 References

A. Louis XVIII Grants France a Constitutional Charter, 1814
   Constitutional Charter, June 4–10, 1814, in *Translations and Reprints from the Original Sources of European History* (Philadelphia: University of Pennsylvania Press, 1897), 1/3:2–3.
B. Alexander I, Francis I, and Frederick III Sign the Holy Alliance
   The Holy Alliance, September 1815, in *Translations and Reprints*, 1/3:9–10.
C. The Carlsbad Decrees Crack Down on the German Universities, 1819
   P. A. G. von Meyer, *Corpus Juris Confoederationis Germanicae*, in *Translations and Reprints*, 1/4:16–17.
D. The German Catholic Conservative Joseph Görres Condemns Both Nationalistic Agitation and Bureaucratic Repression
   Görres, in J. G. Legge, *Rhyme and Revolution in Germany* (London: Constable, 1918), 46–48.

DOCUMENT SET 21.4
Nationalism

As we have just seen, nationalism posed an explosive challenge to the Restoration political system. Nationalist sentiment in the first half of the nineteenth century could appear in different contexts, ranging from intolerant chauvinism to rather gentle nostalgia for traditional culture. Johann Fichte (1762–1814), a German philosopher, became an outspoken proponent of the first kind of nationalism (Document A), which alarmed the liberal-minded German-Jewish poet and voluntary exile from the fatherland Heinrich Heine (1797–1856, Document B). The Italian nationalist and republican Guiseppe Mazzini (1805–1872), a life-long revolutionary, espoused a brand of nationalism whose compatibility with liberal principles seems at times ambiguous (Document C).

Among the Czechs, the recovery of national traditions and the creation of a modern literary language were led by a few philologists, historians and journalists. Jan Kollár (1793–1852), who combined all three of these occupations, pushed the awakening Czech nationalism in the direction of pan-Slavism: the idea that all Slavic nations should ally themselves, preferably under Russian leadership (Document D). A considerably less apocalyptic sort of nationalism was embodied in the 1855 novel *Granny* by Božena Němcová, the most popular woman novelist in nineteenth century Bohemia. In the scene quoted as Document E, an old woman and her granddaughters commune with nature while one of the girls tells the story of a female prophet, the Sibyl.

A. Johann Fichte Wants Germans to Think in German

Further, if I should use in speaking to the German, instead of the words Popularity (*Popularität*) and Liberality (*Liberalität*), the expressions 'striving for favour among the great mob' and 'not having the mind of a slave,' which is how those words must be literally translated, he would at first not obtain the clear and lively sensual image such as the Roman of old days certainly obtained. The latter saw every day with his own eyes the flexible politeness of an ambitious candidate to all and sundry, and saw outbursts of the slave-mind also; and those words represented these things to him in a living fashion. The change in the form of government and the introduction of Christianity took away even from the Roman of later days these sights and shows; and then, too, his own

language was beginning to die away to a great extent in his own mouth, this being more especially due to Christianity, which was alien to him and which he could neither ward off nor incorporate with himself. How could this language, already half dead in its own home, have been transmitted alive to a foreign people? And how should it now be capable of transmission to us Germans? Further, with regard to the sensual image of a mental thing that lies in both those expressions, there is in Popularity even at the very beginning something base, which became perverted to a virtue in the mouth of the nation, owing to their corruption and their constitution. The German never falls into this perversion so long as it is presented to him in his own language. But when Liberality is translated by saying that a man has not 'the soul of a slave,' or, to bring it into accordance with modern custom, 'a lackey's way of thinking,' he answers once more that when this is said it means very little too.

. . . Now supposing that what those . . . foreign words must really be intended to man, if they mean anything at all, had been expressed to the German in his own words and in his own circle of sensual images as follows: . . . *Leutseligkeit* (condescension or affability), and *Edelmut* (noble-mindedness), he would have understood us; but the base associations we have named could never have been slipped into those designations. In the range of German speech a wrapping-up in incomprehensibility and darkness of the kind mentioned arises either from clumsiness or evil design; it can be avoided, and the means always ready to hand is to translate into right and true German. But in the Romance languages this incomprehensibility is natural and primitive and there is no means of avoiding it, for [those using] these languages are not in possession of any living language at all by which they might examine the dead one, and if one looks at the matter closely, are entirely without a mother tongue.

B. Heinrich Heine Worries About German Nationalism's Ultimate Direction, c. 1830

Christianity has to a certain degree moderated that brutal lust of battle, such as we find it among the ancient Germanic races who fought, not to destroy, nor yet to conquer, but merely from a fierce demoniac love of battle itself; but it could not altogether eradicate it. And when once that restraining talisman, the cross, is broken, then the smouldering ferocity of those ancient warriors will again blaze up; then again will be heard the deadly clang of that frantic Berserker wrath, of which the Norse poets say and sing so much. That talisman is rotten with decay, and the day will surely come when it will crumble and fall. Then the ancient stone gods will arise from out the ashes of dismantled ruins, and rub the dust of a thousand years from their eyes; and finally Thor, with his colossal hammer, will leap up and with it shatter into fragments the Gothic cathedrals. . . . . Smile not at my advice as the counsel of a visionary warning you against Kantians, Fichteans and natural philosophers. Scoff not at the dreamer who expects in the material world a revolution similar to that which has already taken place in the domain of thought. The thought goes before the deed, as the lightening precedes the thunder. True, the German thunder is German, is rather awkward, and comes rolling along rather tardily; but come it surely will, and when ye once hear a crash the like of which in the world's history was never heard before, then know that the German thunderbolt has reached its mark. At this crash the eagles will fall dead in mid air, and the lions in Africa's most distant deserts will cower and sneak into their most royal dens. A drama will be enacted in Germany in comparison with which the French Revolution will appear a harmless idyl.

. . . That hour will come. As on the raised benches of an amphitheatre the nations will group themselves around Germany to behold the great tournament. . . . Ye have more to fear from emancipated Germany than from the whole Holy Alliance, with all its Croats and Cossacks.

C. Guiseppe Mazzini Envisions Italian National Unity

LIBERTY—EQUALITY—HUMANITY—
INDEPENDENCE—UNITY

Young Italy is a brotherhood of Italians who believe in a law of *progress* and *duty*, and are convinced that Italy is destined to become one nation, convinced also that she possesses sufficient strength within herself to become one, and that the ill success of her former efforts is to be attributed not to the weakness, but to the misdirection of the revolutionary elements within her,—that the secret force lies in constancy and unity of effort. They join this association with the firm intention of consecrating both thought and action to the great aim of reconstituting Italy as one independent sovereign nation of free men and equals. . . .

The aim of the association is *revolution*; but its labors will be essentially educational, both before and after the day of revolution; and it therefore declares the principles upon which the national education should be conducted, and from which alone Italy may hope for safety and regeneration. . . .

Young Italy is *republican* and *unitarian*[1]—republican, because theoretically every nation is destined, by the law of God and humanity, to form a free and equal community of brothers; and the republican government is the only from of government that ensures this future: Because all true sovereignty resides essentially in the nation, the sole progressive and continuous interpreter of the supreme moral law; . . . because the monarchical element being incapable of sustaining itself alone by the side of the popular element, it necessarily involves the existence of the intermediate element of an aristocracy,—the source of inequality and corruption to the whole nation; because both history and the nature of things teach us that elective monarchy tends to generate anarchy, and hereditary monarchy tends to generate despotism; because, when monarchy is not—as in the Middle Ages—based upon the belief, now extinct, in right divine, it becomes too weak to be a bond of unity and authority in the State; because the inevitable tendency of the series of progressive transformations taking place in Europe is toward the enthronement of the republican principle, and because the inauguration of the monarchical principle in Italy would carry along with it the necessity of a new revolution shortly after.

Our Italian tradition is essentially republican; our great memories are republican; the whole history of our national progress is republican; whereas the introduction of monarchy amongst us was coeval [coincided] with our decay, and consummated our ruin by its constant servility to the foreigner and antagonism to the people as well as to the unity of the nation.

While the populations of the various Italian states would cheerfully unite in the name of a principle which could give no umbrage to local ambition, they would not willingly submit to be governed by one man,—the offspring of one of those States; and their several pretensions would necessarily tend to federalism.

If monarchy were once set up as the aim of the Italian insurrection, it would, by a logical necessity,

---

1 That is, Italy must not become a mere federation.

draw along with it all the obligations of the monarchical system, concessions to foreign courts, trust in and respect for diplomacy, and the repression of that popular element, by which alone our salvation can be achieved. By intrusting the supreme authority to monarchists whose interest it would be to betray us, we should infallibly bring the insurrection to naught. . . .

Young Italy is *unitarian,* because, without unity there is no true nation; because, without unity there is no real strength; and Italy, surrounded as she is by powerful, united, and jealous nations, has need of strength above all things; because federalism, by reducing her to the political impotence of Switzerland, would necessarily place her under the influence of one of the neighboring nations; because federalism, by reviving the local rivalries now extinct, would throw Italy back upon the Middle Ages; . . . because federalism, by destroying the unity of the great Italian family, would strike at the root of the great mission Italy is destined to accomplish for humanity; because Europe is undergoing a progressive series of transformations, which are gradually and irresistibly guiding European society to form itself into vast and united masses; because the entire work of internal civilization in Italy will be seen, if rightly studied, to have been tending for ages toward unity.

The means by which Young Italy proposes to reach its aim are education and insurrection, to be adopted simultaneously and made to harmonize with each other. Education must ever be directed to teach, by example, word, and pen, the necessity of insurrection. Insurrection, whenever it can be realized, must be so conducted as to render it a means of national education. Education, though of necessity secret in Italy, will be public outside of Italy. . . .

Insurrection, by means of guerrilla bands, is the true method of warfare for all nations desirous of emancipating themselves from a foreign yoke. This method of warfare supplies the want—inevitable at the commencement of the insurrection—of a regular army; it calls the greatest number of elements into the field, and yet may be sustained by the smallest number. It forms the military education of the people and consecrates every foot of the native soil by the memory of some warlike deed. Guerrilla warfare opens a field of activity for every local capacity, forces the enemy into an unaccustomed method of battle, avoids the evil consequences of a great defeat, secures the national war from the risk of treason, and has the advantage of not confining it within any defined and determinate basis of operations. It is invincible, inde-

structible. The regular army, recruited with all possible solicitude and organized with all possible care, will complete the work begun by the war of insurrection.

All the members of Young Italy will exert themselves to diffuse these principles of insurrection. The association will develop them more fully in its writings, and will explain from time to time the ideas and organization which should govern the period of insurrection.

D. Jan Kollár Beholds the Glorious Slavic Future, 1824

It is true that we came somewhat late, but so much the younger we are. . . .

Everywhere the Slavs like a mighty flood will extend their limits; the language which the Germans wrongly consider a mere speech of slaves will resound in places and even in the mouths of its rivals. The sciences will flow through Slav channels; our people's dress, their manners and their song will be fashionable on the Seine and on the Elbe. Oh, that I was not born in that great age of Slav dominion; or that I may not rise from the grave to witness it.

E. The Novelist Božena Němcová Appeals to the Czechs to Preserve Their Native Tongue, 1855

"The Sibyl foretold that great misery would come on the Czech lands, that there would be wars and famine and plague. But the worst of all would be when father wouldn't understand son, or son father, or brother brother, and when neither word nor bond would be worth anything. That would be the worst of all, she said, and then the Czech earth would be scattered under the hooves of horses."

"You remembered it well. But God forbid it should ever come true," said Granny with a sigh.

"Oh, Granny, sometimes I'm so afraid I can't tell you! You wouldn't like the Czech earth to be scattered under the hooves of horses, either, would you?"

"Silly girl, or course I wouldn't! Don't we pray every day for the well-being of the Czech earth? Isn't this land our mother? Well, then, if I should see my mother falling into distress, do you think I could be indifferent? What would you do, if somebody was trying to kill your mother?"

"We should scream and cry," said the boys and Adelka.

"Ah, you're children," said Granny with a smile.

"We should have to go to her help, shouldn't we, Granny?" said Babbie, and her eyes were burning.

"That's it, child, that's it, that's the right of it! Screaming and crying don't help," said the old woman, and laid her hand upon her granddaughter's head.

"But, Granny, we're only little, how could we help?" asked John, who was annoyed that he should be dismissed as a mere child.

"Don't you remember what I told you about little David, who killed great Goliath? You see, even a little person can do much, if he has faith in God, you remember that. When you grow up and go out into the world you'll get to know evil and good, you'll be led astray and brought into temptation. Then remember your Granny, and the things she told you when she was out walking with you. You know that I left the good living the Prussian king offered me, and chose to work till I dropped rather than let my children be turned into foreigners and estranged from me. You must love your country like a mother, too, love her above all things, and work for her like good

sons and daughters, and then the prophecy that frightens you will never be fulfilled. I shan't see you grow to be men, but I hope you'll remember your Granny's words," she concluded in a trembling voice.

"I'll never, never forget them," whispered Babbie, hiding her face in the old woman's lap.

Document Set 21.4 References

A. Johann Fichte Wants Germans to Think in German
Fichte, in J. G. Legge, *Rhyme and Revolution in Germany* (London: Constable, 1918), 78–79.

B. Heinrich Heine Worries About German Nationalism's Ultimate Direction, c. 1830
Heine, *Religion and Philosophy in Germany,* in Legge, 58–59.

C. Guiseppe Mazzini Envisions Italian National Unity
Mazzini's Instructions to Members of Young Italy, in James Harvey Robinson and Charles Beard, eds., *Readings in Modern European History* (Boston: Ginn, 1909), 2:115–118.

D. Jan Kollár Beholds the Glorious Slavic Future, 1824
Kollár, in Hans Kohn, *Panslavism* (New York: Random House, 1960), 9.

E. The Novelist Božena Němcová Appeals to the Czechs to Preserve Their Native Tongue, 1855
Nemcová, *Granny: Scenes from Country Life,* Edith Pargeter, trans. (Westport, Conn.: Greenwood, 1976), 195–196.

DOCUMENT SET 21.5
Liberalism and Democracy

It is perhaps natural from our perspective to identify nineteenth century liberalism and democracy as a single phenomenon, but the two should be distinguished. James Mill (1773–1836), a distinguished British philosopher and the father of the even more celebrated John Stuart Mill (see Set 23.4, Document C), pondered deeply the question of government's proper role in assuring the just and efficient functioning of society. Document A—an extract from his essay on government for the *Encyclopaedia Britannica*—demonstrates that he was more concerned with limiting the state's coercive power than with broadening participation in it. Likewise, the Russian officers and noblemen who formed the Decembrist conspiracy that tried to topple the tsarist government in 1825 were motivated by liberal sentiments (Document B) but spoke for such a tiny sliver of Russian society that their aims could not possibly have been sustained by the formal establishment of democratic institutions even had their coup d'etat succeeded. Liberal enthusiasm ran high in German towns in 1830, as the minor German novelist Corvin related in the scene describing the Prussian-ruled Rhineland town of Mainz (Document C): but note the middle-class focus of this account, the antagonism between citizens and the officer corps, and the general ineffectualness of the bourgeois liberal patriots.

Alexis de Tocqueville (1805–1859), a French nobleman of moderately liberal sympathies and great insight into nineteenth-century social change, published the masterful study *Democracy in America* in 1835 after spending several years in the United States studying prison reforms at the request of the French government. Tocqueville understood that the political democracy then emerging in Jacksonian America prefigured what was likely to occur in Europe, too. How well the restless, rootless ambitions of people in democratic communities would tolerate individuality and what Tocqueville considered the natural inequalities of human talents disturbed him greatly (Document D).

A. James Mill States the Case for Classical Liberalism

Of the laws of nature on which the condition of man depends, that which is attended with the greatest number of consequences is the necessity of labor for obtaining the means of subsistence, as well as the means of the greatest part of our pleasures. This is no doubt the primary cause of government; for if nature had produced spontaneously all the objects which we desire, and in sufficient abundance for the desires of all, there would have been no source of dispute or of injury among men, nor would any man have possessed the means of ever acquiring authority over another.

The results are exceedingly different when nature produces the objects of desire not in sufficient abundance for all. The source of dispute is then exhaustless, and every man has the means of acquiring authority over others in proportion to the quantity of those objects which he is able to possess. In this case the end to be obtained through government as the means, is to make that distribution of the scanty materials of happiness which would insure the greatest sum of it in the members of the community taken altogether, preventing every individual or combination of individuals from interfering with that distribution or making any man to have less than his share.

When it is considered that most of the objects of desire and even the means of subsistence are the product of labor, it is evident that the means of insuring labor must be provided for as the foundation of all. The means for the insuring of labor are of two sorts: the one made out of the matter of evil, the other made out of the matter of good. The first sort is commonly denominated force, and under its application the laborers are slaves. This mode of procuring labor we need not consider, for if the end of government be to produce the greatest happiness of the greatest number, that end cannot be attained by making the greatest number slaves.

The other mode of obtaining labor is by allurement, or the advantage which it brings. To obtain all the objects of desire in the greatest possible quantity, we must obtain labor in the greatest possible quantity; and to obtain labor in the greatest possible quantity, we must raise to the greatest possible height the advantage attached to labor. It is impossible to attach to labor a greater degree of advantage than the whole of the product of labor. Why so? Because if you give more to one man than the produce of his labor, you can do so only by taking it away from the produce of some other man's labor. The greatest possible happiness of society is therefore attained by insuring to every man the greatest possible quantity of the produce of his labor.

How is this to be accomplished? For it is obvious

that every man who has not all the objects of his desire, has inducement to take them from any other man who is weaker than himself: and how is he to be prevented? One mode is sufficiently obvious, and it does not appear that there is any other: the union of a certain number of men to protect one another. The object, it is plain, can best be attained when a great number of men combine and delegate to a small number the power necessary for protecting them all. This is government.

With respect to the end of government, or that for the sake of which it exists, it is not conceived to be necessary on the present occasion that the analysis should be carried any further. What follows is an attempt to analyze the means.

Two things are here to be considered: the power with which the small number are entrusted, and the use which they are to make of it. With respect to the first there is no difficulty. The elements out of which the power of coercing others is fabricated are obvious to all. Of these we shall therefore not lengthen this article by any explanation. All the difficult questions of government relate to the means of restraining those in whose hands are lodged the powers necessary for the protection of all from making a bad use of it.

Whatever would be the temptations under which individuals would lie if there was no government, to take the objects of desire from others weaker than themselves, under the same temptations the members of the government lie, to take the objects of desire from the members of the community, if they are not prevented from doing so. Whatever, then, are the reasons for establishing government, the very same exactly are the reasons for establishing securities that those entrusted with the powers necessary for protecting others, make use of them for that purpose solely, and not for the purpose of taking from the members of the community the objects of desire.

B. The Decembrists Proclaim Russia's Liberation, 1825

1. The abolition of the previous government.
2. The establishment of a temporary [government] until the formation of a permanent [one] by elected deputies.
3. Freedom of the press, and hence the abolition of censorship.
4. Freedom of worship to all faiths.
5. Abolition of property rights over persons [i.e., the abolition of serfdom].
6. Equality before the law of all estates and, there-

fore, abolition of Military Tribunals and all types of Judicial Commissions.

C. A Liberal Recalls the German Reaction to the 1830 Revolutions

The people of Mayence [Mainz] were at this time very much excited. The revolution of July 1830 had stirred up old sympathies with France, whilst, on the other hand, German patriots were of the opinion that the Germans had also outgrown the 'paternal,' despotic government, and were desirous of a constitution. Many young men in the city put on the French cockade and sang the 'Marseillaise,' and applauded in the theatre at every sentence expressing hatred of tyrants and love of liberty. Several pieces were prohibited on this account by the government of the fortress; for instance, *The Dumb Girl of Portici*, because, when the soldiers were repulsed by the people in the market-place, the audience cried bravo like mad, and sang the 'Marseillaise.' *William Tell* was also prohibited for similar reasons.[1] For a time this excitement found an outlet in the enthusiasm for the Poles. All the young ladies at their harps were singing 'Poland's cause is not yet lost,' when it was lost already[2] and the exiled Poles were received everywhere like conquering heroes. Everybody did his best to do them honour; and the women were wildly enthusiastic about them. Many a rascal put on a Polish uniform and spoke broken German, as it helped him better through the country than even a passport from the chief of police himself would have done.

We officers also caught this enthusiasm, for we admired the bravery the Poles had shown. Some Polish officers were not only received in a friendly manner in our casino, but even chummed with Prussian comrades. This, however, came to an end when our superiors discovered or received information from Berlin that the Poles after all had committed high treason, and that it was therefore improper for Prussian officers to associate with them.

It was, however, inevitable that we should meet them at public balls and other places of amusement; and as they had nothing else to do, they were to be found everywhere, and mostly drunk. It seemed to be an affair of honour with the Mayence citizens not to

---

[1] *The Dumb Girl of Portici* and *William Tell* were popular operas, each romanticizing popular uprisings of centuries past.
[2] "Poland's Cause Is Not Yet Lost" is the Polish national anthem.

suffer a sober Pole in their city. I, at least, never saw one.

The Polish enthusiasm was followed by the black, red, and gold fever. The old German colours were then the badge of Liberalism, and he who laid claim to the title of a patriot wore a cockade of these colours. The German Confederation looked, however, with a very suspicious eye on these aspirations; the princes were perfectly satisfied with the existing state of things; they wanted no change, and as they had the military power in their hands, they used it to suppress all demonstrations. The soldiers, therefore, became very unpopular, and conflicts between officers and citizens occurred frequently. Officers were insulted, and made use of their arms; and the excitement grew from day to day. One of these conflicts took place at a casino ball. Young citizens, sitting at the same table with Prussian officers, began to sing Liberal songs, and proposed corresponding toasts. The officers behaved very well; in order not to create any disturbance they even touched the glasses of the young citizens with theirs, if requested; but once, when the young men presumed too much on this forbearance of the officers, one of the latter rose and proposed a toast to the King of Prussia, by his look compelling one of the loudest to join him in it. . . .

The order was given to all guards to arrest every one wearing the German colours, and that the soldiers might be acquainted with them, a black, red, and gold cockade was pasted in every guard-book. This measure did much to increase the excitement instead of quelling it, as was intended. The persons arrested were conveyed to the citadel, where an officer on special duty had to receive and dispose of them. . . .

As I must needs always put my nose foremost, wanting to show my contempt in some striking manner, one Friday, when thousands were assembled for the concert in the new 'Anlage' I appeared there with my little dog, Hélène, which proudly wore a large German cockade attached to its little stump of a tail. The joke was immensely applauded by all officers, both Prussian and Austrian, and my colonel laughed much about it, but warned me to take care lest my little dog should be killed. I told him, however, that I was ready to defend my dog's tail with my life. At that time neither my colonel nor myself imagined that both of us, and even the King of Prussia, would one day wear this then despised cockade.

D. Alexis de Tocqueville Ponders America's Emerging Democracy, 1840

The equality of conditions leads by a still straighter road to several of the effects which I have here described. When all the privileges of birth and fortune are abolished, when all professions are accessible to all, and a man's own energies may place him at the top of any one of them, an easy and unbounded career seems open to his ambition, and he will readily persuade himself that he is born to no vulgar destinies. But this is an erroneous notion, which is corrected by daily experience. The same equality which allows every citizen to conceive these lofty hopes, renders all the citizens less able to realize them; it circumscribes their powers on every side, while it gives freer scope to their desires. Not only are they themselves powerless, but they are met at every step by immense obstacles, which they did not at first perceive. They have swept away the privileges of some of their fellow-creatures which stood in their way; but they have opened the door to universal competition: the barrier has changed its shape rather than its position. When men are nearly alike, and all follow the same track, it is very difficult for any one individual to walk quick and cleave a way through the dense throng which surrounds and presses him. This constant strife between the propensities springing from the equality of conditions and the means it supplies to satisfy them, harasses and wearies the mind.

It is possible to conceive men arrived at a degree of freedom which should completely content them; they would then enjoy their independence without anxiety and without impatience. But men will never establish any equality with which they can be contented. Whatever efforts a people may make, they will never succeed in reducing all the conditions of society to a perfect level; and even if the unhappily attained that absolute and complete depression, the inequality of minds would still remain, which, coming directly from the hand of God, will for ever escape the laws of man. However democratic then the social state and the political constitution of a people may be, it is certain that every member of the community will always find out several points about him which command his own position; and we may foresee that his looks will be doggedly fixed in that direction. When inequality of conditions is the common law of society, the most marked inequalities do not strike the eye; when everything is nearly on the same level, the slightest are marked enough to hurt it. Hence the desire of equality always becomes more insatiable in proportion as equality is more complete.

Among democratic nations men easily attain a certain equality of conditions; they can never attain the equality they desire. It perpetually retires from before them, yet without hiding itself from their sight, and in retiring draws them on. At every moment they think they are about to grasp it; it escapes at every moment from their hold. They are near enough to see its charms, but too far off to enjoy them; and before they have fully tasted its delights, they die. . . .

In democratic ages enjoyments are more intense than in the ages of aristocracy, and especially the number of those who partake in them is larger. But, on the other hand, it must be admitted that man's hopes and his desires are often blasted, the soul is more stricken and perturbed, and care itself more keen.

Document Set 21.5 References

A. James Mill States the Case for Classical Liberalism
   Mill, "Essay on Government," in C. A. Burtt, ed., *The English Philosophers from Bacon to Mill* (New York: Modern Library, 1939), 858–859.
B. The Decembrists Proclaim Russia's Liberation, 1825
   Sergei Petrovich Trubetskoi's Proclamation, in Marc Raeff, ed., *The Decembrist Movement* (Englewood Cliffs, N.J.: Prentice-Hall, 1966), 101.
C. A Liberal Recalls the German Reaction to the 1830 Revolutions
   Corvin, in J. G. Legge, *Rhyme and Revolution in Germany* (London: Constable, 1918), 103–104.
D. Alexis de Tocqueville Ponders America's Emerging Democracy, 1840
   de Tocqueville, *Democracy in America,* (Boston: C. C. Little & J. Brown, 1841), vol. 2, chap. 13.

DOCUMENT SET 21.6
Romanticism and Domesticity

The cultural movement called romanticism has always been recognized as one of the keys to understanding the European mentality in the first half of the nineteenth century. The ideology of domesticity has come into focus only in recent years as we have understood more about the changing status of nineteenth century women. Yet it is difficult to conceive of the cluster of attitudes known as domesticity being taken very seriously in any but a romantic cultural climate, and it is therefore appropriate to consider the two phenomena from the same vantage point.

Anna Louise Germaine Necker, better known as Mme. de Staël (1766–1817), was the daughter of the Swiss banker Necker who had tried to rescue French finances before the Revolution (Set 19.6). A woman of great energy and intelligence, she maintained salons all over Europe during the revolutionary era and enraged Napoleon with her moderate liberalism. She gained first-hand knowledge of the new literary currents in Germany that she labeled *romanticism* (a word she coined) and acquainted all Europe with these in her book (*On Germany*, published despite Napoleonic censorship in 1810, Document A). The French writer known by the penname Stendhal (1783–1842), the author of such romantic novels as *The Red and the Black* (1830), also produced penetrating art criticism that extended the concept of romanticism to painting. In his review of the Salon (art exhibition) of 1824 (Document B), he explicitly contrasts romanticism with classicism to the latter's detriment.

In Germany, the composer Ludwig van Beethoven (1770–1827) invented musical romanticism virtually single-handed. Bettina von Arnim (1785–1859), a young noblewoman who also knew the poet Goethe, met Beethoven in 1810, managed to get the great musician (always ready to confide in a sympathetic woman) to open his heart to her, and conveyed his thoughts to Goethe in a famous letter (Document C). Johann Wolfgang von Goethe (1749–1832), a universal genius, defies categorization. He professed to despise romanticism as "all that is sick," but his great poetic drama *Faust* is romantic to its core. In the extract quoted in Document D, the aged Doctor Faust confides to his pedantic associate Wagner his divided soul and his longing for regeneration and godlike power in poetry of matchless eloquence.

Romantics reveled in the misery of being—or

imagining themselves—"outsiders." The French poet Alfred de Musset (1810–1857) delineated the feelings of his "lost" generation of men and women after the turmoil of the Napoleonic age and sought distraction in feverish love affairs and idealistic causes (Document D). The author of the novel *Frankenstein*, Mary Wollstonecraft Shelley (1797–1851), whose mother died soon after giving birth to her, was an authentic "outsider." She lived with the rebellious English poet Percy Shelley and shared his wandering life until his early death in 1822. *Frankenstein* (1818) is a romantic allegory of the genius who attempts to benefit humanity but ends by incurring disaster; the monster whom the mad scientist Frankenstein creates is a mirror of suffering, outcast humanity (Document E).

Mary Wollstonecraft Shelley, Bettina von Arnim, and Mme. de Staël were anything but advocates of domesticity; neither was George Sand, the pen name of the woman novelist who numbered Alfred de Musset among her numerous lovers. These women stand in sharp contrast to the ideals of womanhood praised by Mrs. Sarah Stickney Ellis, an Englishwoman who embodied the outlook of domesticity. Read Document G not only to understand the values Mrs. Ellis considered normative for respectable family women, but also to observe how she shared her age's preoccupation with emotion and its search for lofty causes to which the noblehearted individual could sacrifice him- or herself. It is also useful to contrast Mrs. Ellis's vision of middle-class women redeeming society with the reality of an English cotton-spinner's life (Document H).

Sets 21.4 through 21.6 lend themselves to consideration as a group. Study *The Challenge of the West*'s account of how and why the concept of *ideology* emerged in post-revolutionary Europe. Turning to the documents illustrating nationalism, liberalism, romanticism, and domesticity, how do these movements succeed as ways to explain character or organize society? How do they draw on one another for underlying assumptions, and how do they reinforce—or contradict—one another? Be sure to consult your textbook for supporting evidence and examples.

A. Mme. de Staël Discovers German Romanticism, 1813

The word *romantic* has been lately introduced in Germany, to designate that kind of poetry which is derived from the songs of the Troubadours; that which owes its birth to the union of chivalry and Christianity. If we do not admit that the empire of literature has been divided between paganism and Christianity, the north and the south, antiquity and the middle ages, chivalry and the institutions of Greece and Rome, we shall never succeed in forming a philosophical judgment of ancient and of modern taste. . . .

The new school maintains the same system in the fine arts as in literature, and affirms that Christianity is the source of all modern genius; the writers of this school also characterize, in a new manner, all that in Gothic architecture agrees with the religious sentiments of Christians. It does not follow however from this, that the moderns can and ought to construct Gothic churches; neither art nor nature admit of repetition: it is only of consequence to us, in the present silence of genius, to lay aside the contempt which has been thrown on all the conceptions of the middle ages; it certainly does not suit us to adopt them, but nothing is more injurious to the development of genius, than to consider as barbarous everything that is original.

B. Stendahl Describes the Salon of 1824

We are at the dawn of a revolution in the fine arts. The huge pictures composed of thirty nude figures inspired by antique statues and the heavy tragedies in verse in five acts are, without a doubt, very respectable works; but in spite of all that may be said in their favor, they have begun to be a little boring. If the painting of *The Battle of the Romans and the Sabines* [by the neo-classical painter Jacques Louis David] were to appear today, we would find that its figures were without passion and that in any country it is absurd to march off to battle with no clothes on. . . . The romantic in all the arts is that which shows the men of today and not those who probably never existed in those heroic times so distant from us. . . . That which may console *romanticism* for the attacks of the [newspaper] *Journal des débats* is that good sense applied to the arts has made immense progress in the last four years and particularly among the leaders of society.

C. Bettina von Arnim Describes Beethoven to Goethe, 1810

. . . Who among us could replace this genius? from whom could we expect a similar achievement? All human activity is like the pendulum of a clock that comes and goes for him: he alone is free and produces of his own free will, as he wishes, the uncreated and the unexpected. What matters then his traffic with the world, to him whom the rising sun finds already engaged upon the hallowed task of every day and who hardly lifts his eyes at sunset to glance about him; he who forgets to feed his body and whom the torrent of his inspiration keeps far removed from the platitudes of daily life? He has told me himself: "From the moment when I open my eyes I begin to groan, for what I see goes against my religion, and I must despise the world which does not sense that music is a more sublime revelation than all wisdom and all philosophy; it is the wine that inspires and leads to fresh creations, and I am the Bacchus who presses for mankind this wine of magnificence, it is I who makes them spiritually drunk; and when they find themselves with an empty stomach once more, they have in their intoxication fished in all sorts of things that they bring back with them onto the dry shore. I have no friend, I have to live alone with myself; but I know well that God is closer to me in my art than to all others, and I advance with him without fear, having recognized and understood him every time. Nor do I feel anxious about my music which could have no adverse destiny: he who freely opens his mind and his feelings shall be forever exempt from all the misery in which the others drag along."

All these things Beethoven said to me when I saw him for the first time. A great sentiment of veneration took hold of me on hearing him thus reveal his thoughts to me who must have seemed to him so puny. I was the more surprised since I had been assured that he was misanthropic and would engage in conversation with no one. Nobody wanted to introduce me to him; I had to seek him out for myself. He owns three apartments in which he hides in turn; one in the country, one in town, the third in the *bastion*; it was there, in the third, that I was to find him. I went in unannounced; he was at the piano; I told him my name. He received me affectionately and asked me at once whether I would like to hear a song he had just put to music. And then he started to sing *Kennst du das Land* . . . ["Knowst thou the land," one of Mignon's songs from Goethe's *Wilhelm Meister*] in a voice so powerful and penetrating that its melancholy took possession of me.—"Is it not beautiful?" he asked me enthusiastically. "Wonderful." "I shall sing it a second time." He rejoiced at my delightful approval. "Most humans," he said to me, "are moved by something good, but they are in no way artistic natures; artists are made of fire; they do not weep." And he began once me to sing another song of yours, which he had composed in the last few days. . . .

D. Goethe's Faust Meditates on Human Aspiration

Faust

Oh, happy the man with any hope
of rising out of error's ocean!
You need just what you do not know,
and what you really know is worthless.
But let us not embitter this blessed hour
with melancholy thoughts.
See how the green-encircled huts
shine in the glow of the evening sun.
The day is over; the sun yields and hastens
onward to quicken new life. Oh, that wings
could lift me from the earth to follow,
struggling in the sun-wake! I would see
beneath my feet the silent world
glowing in the eternal evening;
each peak on fire, each valley calm,
the silver brooks flowing to golden rivers.
And the wild mountain with its gorges
could not check my godlike flight.
Already the ocean with its sun-warmed bays
broadens beneath my astonished eye.
Yet finally the sun appears to sink;
and a new instinct awakens.
I hurry onward to drink his eternal light,
the day before me, and the night behind,
the sky above, the waves below—
a splendid dream until the sun fades out.
Ah, if only the wings that raise the spirit
might be brothered by strong earthly wings!
Man is born with a desire
that drives his feeling upward, onward,
when overhead, lost in blue space,
the skylark sings his quavering song;
when over craggy fir-topped heights
he sees the out-spread eagle soaring,
or the crane struggling homeward
over lakes and swampy moors.

Wagner

I've often had strange whims myself,
but never such an urge as that.

You soon get bored with fields and forests;
I'll never envy any bird his flight.
How differently the spirit's pleasures bear us,
from page to page, through volume after volume.
Then winter nights are cheerful and friendly,
warm delight steals through the bones,
and ah, when you unroll some precious parchment,
Heaven itself comes down to you!

Faust

You know the one impulse only.
It's better if you never learn the other.
Alas, there are two souls that live in me
and one would like to leave its brother;
one with gripping organs clings to earth
with a rough and hearty lust;
the other rises powerfully from the dirt
up toward the region of the great forefathers.
If there are lordly spirits in the air
roaming between the earth and sky,
let them come down from the golden atmosphere
and lead me to a new, more vivid life!
Yes, if I had a magic cloak to carry me
to foreign lands, I would not trade it
for the richest robes, or for the mantle of a king.

E. Alfred de Musset Moans for His "Lost Generation" of Romantics, 1836

During the wars of the Empire, while the husbands and brothers were in Germany, the anxious mothers brought forth an ardent, pale, nervous generation. Conceived between two battles, educated amidst the noises of war, thousands of children looked about them with a somber eye while testing their puny muscles. From time to time their blood-stained fathers would appear, raise them on their gold-laced bosoms, then place them on the ground and remount their horses. . . .

Then there seated itself on a world in ruins an anxious youth. All the children were drops of burning blood which had inundated the earth; they were born in the bosom of war, for war. For fifteen years they had dreamed of the snows of Moscow and of the sun of the pyramids. They had not gone beyond their native towns; but they were told that through each gate of these towns lay the road to a capital of Europe. They had in their heads all the world; they beheld the earth, the sky, the streets and the highways; all these were empty, and the bells of parish churches resounded faintly in the distance.

Pale phantoms, shrouded in black robes, slowly traversed the country; others knocked at the doors of houses, and when admitted, drew from their pockets large well-worn documents with which they drove out the tenants. From every direction came men still trembling with the fear which had seized them when they fled twenty years before. All began to urge their claims, disputing loudly and crying for help; it was strange that a single death should attract so many crows.

Three elements entered into the life which offered itself to these children: behind them a past forever destroyed, moving uneasily on its ruins with all the fossils of centuries of absolutism; before them the aurora of an immense horizon, the first gleams of the future; and between these two worlds—something like the Ocean which separates the old world from Young America, something vague and floating, a troubled sea filled with wreckage, traversed from time to time by some distant sail or some ship breathing out a heavy vapor; the present, in a word, which separates the past from the future, which is neither the one nor the other, which resemble both, and where one can not know whether, at each step, one is treading on a seed or a piece of refuse.

It was in this chaos that choice must be made; this was the aspect presented to children full of spirit and of audacity, sons of the Empire and grandsons of the Revolution.

A feeling of extreme uneasiness began to ferment in all young hearts. Condemned to inaction by the powers which governed the world, delivered to vulgar pedants of every kind, to idleness and to ennui [restless boredom] the youth saw the foaming billows which they had prepared to meet, subside. All these gladiators, glistening with oil, felt in the bottom of their souls an insupportable wretchedness. The richest became libertines; those of moderate fortune followed some profession and resigned themselves to the sword or to the robe. The poorest gave themselves up with cold enthusiasm to great thoughts, plunged into the frightful sea of aimless effort. As human weakness seeks association and as men are herds by nature, politics became mingled with it. There were struggles with the *garde du crops* on the steps of the legislative assembly; at the theater, Talma wore a peruke which made him resemble Caesar; every one flocked to the burial of a liberal deputy.

The customs of students and artists, those customs so free, so beautiful, so full of youth, began to experience the universal change. Men in taking leave of women whispered the word which wounds to the death: contempt. They plunged into the dissipation of wine and courtesans. Students and artists did the same; love was treated as glory and religion: it was an old illusion. The grisette, that class so dreamy, so romantic, so tender, and so sweet in love, abandoned herself to the counting-house and to the shop.

Then they formed into two camps; on the one side the exalted spirits, sufferers, all the expansive souls who had need of the infinite, bowed their heads and wept; they wrapped themselves in unhealthy dreams and there could be seen nothing but broken reeds on an ocean of bitterness. On the other side the men of the flesh remained standing, inflexible in the midst of positive joys, and cared for nothing except to count the money they had acquired. It was only a sob and a burst of laughter, the one coming from the soul, the other from the body. . . .

F. Mary Wollstonecraft Shelley's Frankenstein Confronts His Monster

It was nearly noon when I arrived at the top of the ascent. For some time I sat upon the rock that overlooks the sea of ice. A mist covered both that and the surrounding mountains. Presently a breeze dissipated the cloud, and I descended upon the glacier. The surface is very uneven, rising like the waves of a troubled sea, descending low, and interspersed by rifts that sink deep. The field of ice is almost a league in width, but I spent nearly two hours in crossing it. The opposite mountain is a bare perpendicular rock. From the side where I now stood. Montanvert was exactly opposite, at the distance of a league; and above it rose Mount Blanc, in awful majesty. I remained in a recess of the rock, gazing on this wonderful and stupendous scene. The sea, or rather the vast river of ice, wound among its dependent mountains, whose aerial summits hung over its recesses. Their icy and glittering peaks shone in the sunlight over the clouds. My heart, which was before sorrowful, now swelled with something like joy; I exclaimed—"Wandering spirits, if indeed ye wander, and do not rest in your narrow beds, allow me this faint happiness, or take me, as your companion, away from the joys of life."

As I said this, I suddenly beheld the figure of a man, at some distance, advancing towards me with super-human speed. He bounded over the crevices in the ice, among which I had walked with caution; his stature, also, as he approached, seemed to exceed that of man. I was troubled: a mist came over my eyes, and I felt a faintness seize me; but I was quickly restored by the cold gale of the mountains. I perceived, as the shape came nearer (sight tremendous and abhorred!) that it was the wretch whom I had created. I trembled with rage and horror, resolving to wait his approach, and then close with him in mortal combat. He approached; his countenance bespoke bitter anguish, combined with disdain and malignity, while its unearthly ugliness rendered it almost too horrible for human eyes. But I scarcely observed this; rage and hatred had at first deprived me of utterance, and I recovered only to overwhelm him with words expressive of furious detestation and contempt.

"Devil," I exclaimed, "do you dare approach me? and do not you fear the fierce vengeance of my arm wreaked on your miserable head? Begone, vile insect! or rather, stay, that I may trample you to dust! and, oh! that I could, with the extinction of your miserable existence, restore those victims whom you have so diabolically murdered!"

"I expected this reception," said the daemon. "All men hate the wretched; how, then, must I be hated, who am miserable beyond all living things! Yet you, my creator, detest and spurn me, thy creature, to whom thou art bound by ties only dissoluble by the annihilation of one of us. You purpose to kill me. How dare you sport thus with life? Do your duty towards me, and I will do mine towards you and the rest of mankind. If you will comply with my conditions, I will leave them and you at peace; but if you refuse, I will glut the maw of death, until it be satisfied with the blood of your remaining friends."

"Abhorred monster! fiend that thou art! the tortures of hell are too mild a vengeance for thy crimes. Wretched devil! you reproach me with your creation; come on, then, that I may extinguish the spark which I so negligently bestowed."

My rage was without bounds; I sprang on him, impelled by all the feelings which can arm one being against the existence of another.

He easily eluded me, and said—

"Be calm! I entreat you to hear me, before you give vent to your hatred on my devoted head. Have I not suffered enough that you seek to increase my misery? Life, although it may only be an accumulation of anguish, is dear to me, and I will defend it. Remember, thou hast made me more powerful than thyself; my height is superior to thine; my joints more supple. But I will not be tempted to set myself in opposition to thee. I am thy creature, and I will be even mild and docile to my natural lord and king, if thou wilt also perform thy part, the which thou owest me. Oh, Frankenstein, be not equitable to every other, and trample upon me alone, to whom thy justice, and even thy clemency and affection, is most due. Remember, that I am thy creature; I ought to be thy Adam; but I am rather the fallen angel, whom thou drivest from joy for no misdeed. Everywhere I see bliss, from which I alone am irrev-

ocably excluded. I was benevolent and good; misery made me a fiend. Make me happy, and I shall again be virtuous."

G. Middle-Class Domesticity: Sarah Stickney Ellis Speaks of English Women's Moral Sensibilities and Social Duties, 1838

One of the noblest features in her national character . . . is the domestic character of England—the home comforts, and fireside virtues for which she is so justly celebrated. These I hope to be able to speak of without presumption, as intimately associated with, and dependent upon, the moral feelings and habits of the women of this favored country. . . .

In looking around, then, upon our "nation of shop-keepers," we readily perceive that by dividing society into three classes, as regards what is commonly called rank, the middle class must include so vast a portion of the intelligence and moral power of the country at large, that it may not improperly be designated the pillar of our nation's strength, its base being the important class of the laborious poor, and its rich and highly ornamental capital, the ancient nobility of the land. In no other country is society thus beautifully proportioned, and England should beware of any deviation from the order and symmetry of her national column. . . .

Perhaps it may be necessary to be more specific in describing the class of women to which this work relates. It is, then, strictly speaking, to those who belong to that great mass of the population of England which is connected with trade and manufactures;—or, in order to make the application more direct, to that portion of it who are restricted to the services of from one to four domestics,—who, on the one hand, enjoy the advantages of a liberal education, and, on the other, have no pretension to family rank. . . .

It is from the class of females above described, that we naturally look for the highest tone of moral feeling, because they are at the same time removed from the pressing necessities of absolute poverty, and admitted to the intellectual privileges of the great: and thus, while they enjoy every facility in the way of acquiring knowledge, it is their still higher privilege not to be exempt from the domestic duties which call forth the best energies of the female character.

"What shall I do to gratify myself—to be admired—or to vary the tenor of my existence?" are not the questions which a woman of right feelings asks on first awaking to the avocations of the day.

Much more congenial to the highest attributes of woman's character, are inquiries such as these: "How shall I endeavor through this day to turn the time, the health, and the means permitted me to enjoy, to the best account? Is any one sick, I must visit their chamber without delay, and try to give their apartment an air of comfort, by arranging such things as the wearied nurse may not have thought of. Is any one about to set off on a journey, I must see that the early meal is spread, to prepare it with my own hands, in order that the servant, who was working late last night, may profit by unbroken rest. Did I fail in what was kind or considerate to any of the family yesterday; I will meet her this morning with a cordial welcome, and show, in the most delicate way I can, that I am anxious to atone for the past. Was any one exhausted by the last day's exertion, I will be an hour before them this morning, and let them see that their labor is so much in advance. Or, if nothing extraordinary occurs to claim my attention, I will meet the family with a consciousness that, being the least engaged of any member of it, I am consequently the most at liberty to devote myself to the general good of the whole, by cultivating cheerful conversation, adapting myself to the prevailing tone of feeling, and leading those who are least happy, to think and speak of what will make them more so."...

Above all other characteristics of the women of England, the strong moral feeling pervading even their most trifling and familiar actions, ought to be mentioned as most conducive to the maintenance of that high place which they so justly claim in the society of their native land.... The women of England are not surpassed by those of any other country for their clear perception of the right and the wrong of common and familiar things, for their reference to principle in the ordinary affairs of life, and for their united maintenance of that social order, sound integrity, and domestic peace, which constitute the foundation of all that is most valuable in the society of our native land.

Much as I have said of the influence of the domestic habits of my country-women, it is, after all, to the prevalence of religious instruction, and the operation of religious principle upon the heart, that the consistent maintenance of their high tone of moral character is to be attributed.... Women are said to be more easily brought under this influence than men; and we consequently see, in places of public worship, and on all occasions in which a religious object is the motive for exertion, a greater proportion of women than of men....

If ... all was confusion and neglect at home—filial appeals unanswered—domestic comforts uncalcu-lated—husbands, sons, and brothers referred to servants for all the little offices of social kindness, in order that the ladies of the family might hurry away at the appointed time to some committee-room, scientific lecture, or public assembly: however laudable the object for which they met, there would be sufficient cause why their cheeks should be mantled with the blush of burning shame ... which those whose charity has not begun at home, ought never to appropriate to themselves.

It is a widely mistaken notion to suppose that the sphere of usefulness recommended here, is a humiliating and degraded one.... With [some women] it is a favorite plea, brought forward in extenuation of their own uselessness, that they have no influence—that they are not leading women—that society takes no note of them....

It is not to be presumed that women *possess* more moral power than men; but happily for them, such are their early impressions, associations, and general position in the world, that their moral feelings are less liable to be impaired by the pecuniary objects which too often constitute the chief end of man, and which, even under the limitations of better principle, necessarily engage a large portion of his thoughts....

H. Working-Class Domestic Reality: The Wife of a Cotton Spinner Describes Her Home Life

Her husband is a fine spinner, at Mr. ———, where he has been from 1816, has five children. Her eldest daughter, now going on fourteen, has been her father's piecer for three years. At her present age, her labor is worth 4s. 6d. a week, and has been worth as much for these last four months; before, it was worth less. At present her husband's earnings and her daughter's together amount to about 25s. a week—at least she sees no more than 25s. a week; and before his daughter could piece for him, and when he had to pay for a piecer in her stead, he only brought home 19s. or 20s. a week.

Rent of house, 3s. 6d. a week.

Breakfast is generally porridge, bread and milk, lined with flour or oatmeal. On Sunday, a sup of tea and bread and butter.—*Dinner*, on week days, potatoes and bacon, and bread, which is generally white. On a Sunday, a little flesh meat; no butter, egg, or pudding.—*Tea-time*, every day, tea, and bread and butter; nothing extra on Sunday at tea.—*Supper*, oatmeal porridge and milk; sometimes potatoes and milk. Sunday, sometimes a little bread and cheese for supper: never have this on week days. Now and then buys eggs when they are as low as a halfpenny apiece, and fries them to bacon.

They never taste any other vegetables than potatoes; never use any beer or spirits; now and then may take a gill of beer when ill, which costs a penny. Perhaps she and her husband may have two gills a week. Her husband never drinks any beer or spirits that she knows of beyond this. The house consists of four rooms, two on each floor; the furniture consists of two beds in the same room, one for themselves, the other for the children; have four chairs, one table in the house, boxes to put clothes in, no chest of drawers, two pans and a tea kettle for boiling, a gridiron and frying-pan, half-a-dozen large and small plates, four pair of knives and forks, several pewter spoons. They subscribe 1*d.* a week for each child to a funeral society for the children. Two of the children go to school at 3*d.* a week each: they are taught reading for this, but not writing. Have a few books, such as a Bible, hymn-book, and several small books that the children have got as prizes at the Sunday School. Four children go to Stott's Sunday School.

QUESTION. Does your daughter, who pieces for her father, seem much fatigued when she comes home at night?

ANSWER. No, she does not seem much fatigued. She is coming of an age that perhaps she may be. She has a good appetite. Hears her complain of headache sometimes; does not hear her complain of not sleeping

Q. Do you think that people in your own way of life, spinners and such like, and their families, are better off than yourselves, or worse off, or just about the same?

A. Well, some's better, some's worse, some's the same. It is according to their work—whether they work upon fine or coarse work.

Q. I want to know whether the most are like off to yourselves. Now, at Mr. — mill, are most of the parents of children as well off, or better off, than yourself?

A. Well, they are most of them at his mill as well off as we ourselves, because it is one of the best mills in the town. There is not many better than his.

In answer to questions concerning herself, she said she should be forty years old on Whitsun Monday: that at fourteen years old she began frame-tenting, and worked at it for two years every day, from six in the morning till eight in the evening— sometimes from half-past five in the morning. She then went to stretching, at which she worked till twenty-five years old: at that she worked fourteen hours a day regularly every day. At twenty-five years old she married, and has staid at home ever since. Her father was a bleacher, her mother a spinner. Has eight brothers and sisters; but can't give no idea whether her brothers and sisters are bigger or less than her parents, because her mother took them all away to America when she was a child.

Q. Should you say you were as healthy a woman now, as if you had not been a frame tenter or a stretcher?

A. Well, I don't know but what I am. I have not my health very well at present. I do not know that work injured it.

Q. How many different mills were you in when you were young?

A. In four mills. Has heard different language at some from others; some very bad, some very well. A child may pick up much bad in mills. Better to put a child in a mill than let it run in the streets; it won't get as much harm in a mill.

Q. Do girls run a chance of being bad by living in mills; in short, to be unchaste?

A. I can't say. I never see'd nothing of bad wherever I worked. It is according to their own endeavors a good deal.

Consumption by the week, of different articles, by her husband, herself, and five children.	£	s.	d.
Butter, 1 1/2 lb. at 10*d*.	0	1	3
Tea, 1 1/2 oz.	0	0	4-1/2
Bread she makes herself: buys 24 lb. of flour—flour, barm, salt, and baking, cost	0	4	6
Half a peck of oatmeal	0	0	6-1/2
Bacon, 1 1/2 lb.	0	0	9
Potatoes, two score a week, at 8*d*. a score	0	1	4
Milk, a quart a day, at 3*d*. a quart	0	1	9
Flesh meat on Sunday, about a pound	0	0	7
Sugar, 1 1/2 lb. a week, at 6*d*.	0	0	9
Pepper, mustard, salt, and extras, say	0	0	3
Soap and candles	0	1	0
Coals	0	1	6
Rent	0	3	6
	£0	18	1
Alleged total of weekly income	£1	5	0
Deduct foregoing expenses	0	18	1
Leaves for clothing, sickness of seven persons, schooling, etc. a surplus of	£0	6	11

Document Set 21.6 References

A. Mme. de Staël Discovers German Romanticism, 1813
de Staël, *Concerning Germany,* in Howard E. Hugo, ed., *The Portable Romantic Reader* (New York: Viking, 1957), 64, 66.

B. Stendahl Describes the Salon of 1824
Stendahl, in Elizabeth Gilmore Holt, ed., *The Triumph of Art for the Public: The Emerging Role of Exhibitions and Critics* (Princeton, N.J.: Princeton University Press, 1983), 261, 279.

C. Bettina von Arnim Describes Beethoven to Goethe, 1810
von Arnim, Letter to Goethe, in Eugen Weber, *Movements, Currents, Trends: Aspects of European Thought in the Nineteenth and Twentieth Centuries* (Lexington, Mass.: D. C. Heath, 1992), 127–128.

D. Goethe's Faust Meditates on Human Aspiration
Johann Wolfgang von Goethe, *Faust,* trans. C. F. MacIntyre (New York: New Directions, 1949), 31–32.

E. Alfred de Musset Moans for His "Lost Generation" of Romantics, 1836
de Musset, in Hugo, 93–99.

F. Mary Wollstonecraft Shelley's Frankenstein Confronts His Monster, 1818
Shelley, *Frankenstein,* "I Am the Fallen Angel," in Hugo, 276–280.

G. Middle-Class Domesticity: Sarah Stickney Ellis Speaks of English Women's Moral Sensibilities and Social Duties, 1838
Sarah Stickney Ellis, *The Women of England: Their Social Duties and Domestic Habits,* in Walter Arnstein, ed., *The Past Speaks,* 2d ed. (Lexington, Mass.: D. C. Heath, 1993), 2:172–175.

H. Working-Class Domestic Reality: The Wife of a Cotton Spinner Describes Her Home Life
Reports from Factory Commissioners, *Parliamentary Paper* (1833), in Arnstein, 2:178–180.

DOCUMENT SET 21.7
Industrialization, Urbanization, and Revolution, 1832–1852

You have already caught a glimpse of industrial working class life in Document H of the preceding set. Such conditions alarmed governments, conservatives, and well-meaning middle-class reformers alike. For example, the successful industrialist Robert Owen tried to discover how society could reap the benefits of the factory system without paying the price of appalling degradation, and in a scheme for curbing human greed he thought he found it (Document A). How, in contrast, would you suppose the British economist David Ricardo (Document B) would respond to Owen's proposal—and Owen to Ricardo's "Iron Law of Wages"?

Document C originates in the inquiries that British authorities (including parliamentary committees) conducted into the consequences of industrialization. How can you explain the interest that these representatives of the dominant classes took in the conditions endured by working people?

Calls for another kind of reform also grew overwhelming in post-revolutionary Britain, demanding at last the overhaul of the country's medieval system of land-based political representation that the rise of manufacturing cities like Manchester had rendered totally anachronistic. Conservatives fought the reform, but support for it crossed class lines. Lord John Russell (1792–1878), destined to be one of Victorian Britain's great political figures, presented the ministry's Reform Bill in 1832 (Document D). What do you make of this nobleman's decision to defend middle-class and industrialists' interest in parliamentary reform?

A. Robert Owen Hopes to Temper the "Principle of Gain," 1815

The immediate effects of this manufacturing phenomenon were a rapid increase of the wealth, industry, population, and political influence of the British Empire; and by the aid of which it has been enabled to contend for five-and-twenty years against the most formidable military and *immoral* power [France] that the world perhaps every contained.

These important results, however, great as they really are, have not been obtained without accompanying evils of such a magnitude as to raise a doubt whether the latter do not preponderate over the former.

Hitherto, legislators have appeared to regard manufactures, only in one point of view, as a source of national wealth.

The other mighty consequences which proceed from extended manufactures *when left to their natural progress,* have never yet engaged the attention of any legislature. Yet the political and moral effects to which we allude, well deserve to occupy the best faculties of the greatest and the wisest statesmen.

The general diffusion of manufactures throughout a country generates a new character in its inhabitants; and as this character is formed upon a principle quite unfavorable to individual or general happiness, it will produce the most lamentable and permanent evils, unless its tendency be counteracted by legislative interference and direction. . . .

The acquisition of wealth, and the desire which it naturally creates for a continued increase, have introduced a fondness for essentially injurious luxuries among a numerous class of individuals who formerly never thought of them, and they have also generated a disposition which strongly impels its possessors to sacrifice the best feelings of human nature to this love of accumulation. To succeed in this career, the industry of the lower orders, from whose labor this wealth is now drawn, has been carried by new competitors striving against those of longer standing, to a point of real oppression, reducing them by successive changes, as the spirit of competition increased and the ease of acquiring wealth diminished, to a state more wretched than can be imagined by those who have not attentively observed the changes as they have gradually occurred. In consequence, they are at present in a situation infinitely more degraded and miserable than they were before the introduction of these manufactories, upon the success of which their bare subsistence now depends. . . .

The effects of this principle of gain, unrestrained, are still more lamentable on the working classes, those who are employed in the operative parts of the manufactures; for most of these branches are more or less unfavorable to the health and morals of adults. Yet parents do not hesitate to sacrifice the well-being of their children by putting them to occupations by which the constitution of their minds and bodies is rendered greatly inferior to what it might and ought to be under a system of common foresight and humanity. . . .

The children now find they must labor incessantly for their bare subsistence: they have not been used to innocent, healthy, and rational amusements; they are not permitted the requisite time, if they had been previously accustomed to enjoy them. They know not what relaxation means, except by the actual cessation from labor. They are surrounded by others similarly circumstanced with themselves; and thus passing on from childhood to youth, they become gradually initiated, the young men in particular, but often the young females also, in the seductive pleasures of the pot-house and inebriation: for which their daily hard labor, want of better habits, and the general vacuity of their minds, tend to prepare them. . . .

The employer regards the employed as mere instruments of gain, while these acquire a gross ferocity of character, which, if legislative measures shall not be judiciously devised to prevent its increase, and ameliorate the condition of this class, will sooner or later plunge the country into a formidable and perhaps inextricable state of danger.

B. David Ricardo Defines the "Iron Law of Wages," 1817

LABOUR, like all other things which are purchased and sold, and which may be increased or diminished in quantity, has its natural and its market price. The natural price of labour is that price which is necessary to enable the labourers, one with another, to subsist and to perpetuate their race, without either increase or diminution.

The power of the labourer to support himself, and the family which may be necessary to keep up the number of labourers, does not depend on the quantity of money which he may receive for wages, but on the quantity of food, necessaries, and conveniences become essential to him from habit, which that money will purchase. The natural price of labour, therefore, depends on the price of the food, necessaries, and conveniences required for the support of the labourer and his family. With a rise in the price of food and necessaries, the natural price of labour will rise; with the fall in their price, the natural price of labour will fall.

With the progress of society the natural price of labour has always a tendency to rise, because one of the principal commodities by which its natural price is regulated, has a tendency to become dearer, from the greater difficulty of producing it. As, however, the improvements in agriculture, the discovery of new markets, whence provisions may be imported, may for a time counteract the tendency to a rise in the price of necessaries, and may even occasion their natural price to fall, so will the same causes produce the correspondent effects on the natural price of labour.

The natural price of all commodities, excepting raw produce and labour, has a tendency to fall, in the progress of wealth and population; for though, on one hand, they are enhanced in real value, from the rise in the natural price of the raw material of which they are made, this is more than counterbalanced by the improvements in machinery, by the better division and distribution of labour, and by the increasing skill, both in science and art, of the producers.

The market price of labour is the price which is really paid for it, from the natural operation of the proportion of the supply to the demand; labour is dear when it is scarce, and cheap when it is plentiful. However much the market price of labour may deviate from its natural price, it has, like commodities, a tendency to conform to it.

It is when the market price of labour exceeds its natural price, that the condition of the labourer is flourishing and happy, that he has it in his power to command a greater proportion of the necessaries and enjoyments of life, and therefore to rear a healthy and numerous family. When, however, by the encouragement which high wages give to the increase of population, the number of labourers is increased, wages again fall to their natural price, and indeed from a reaction sometimes fall below it.

When the market price of labour is below its natural price, the condition of the labourers is most wretched: then poverty deprives them of those comforts which custom renders absolute necessaries. It is only after their privations have reduced their number, or the demand for labour has increased, that the market price of labour will rise to its natural price, and that the labourer will have the moderate comforts which the natural rate of wages will afford.

Notwithstanding the tendency of wages to conform to their natural rate, their market rate may, in an improving society, for an indefinite period, be constantly above it; for no sooner may the impulse, which an increased capital gives to a new demand for labour be obeyed, than another increase of capital may produce the same effect; and thus, if the increase of capital be gradual and constant, the demand for labour may give a continued stimulus to an increase of people.

C. Charles Harris, Age 12, Testifies to a Parliamentary Inquiry About His Work

I am twelve years old. I have been in the mill twelve months. I attend to a drawing machine. We begin at six o'clock and stop at half past seven. We don't stop work for breakfast. We do sometimes. This week we have not. Nothing has been said to me by Mr. Oldacres or the overlooker, or anybody else, about having any questions asked me. I am sure of that. The engine always stops for dinner. It works at tea time in the hot weather; and then we give over at half past seven instead of eight, which is the general time. We have generally about twelve hours and a half of it. On Saturday we begin at six and give over at four. I get 2s. 6d. a week. I have a father and mother, and give them what I earn. I have worked overhours for two or three weeks together about a fortnight since. All the difference was, we worked breakfast time and tea time, and did not go away till eight. We are paid for such overhours at the rate of 2d. for three hours. I have always that for myself.

What do you do with it?

I save it for clothes sometimes. I put it into a money club for clothes. I have worked nine hours over in one week. I got for that 5 1/2 d. I gave it my mother, and she made it up to 6d. and put it into the money club. She always puts by 6d. a week from my wages for that.

Then your mother gets what you earn by the overhours, don't she?

No; I gets it for myself.

Do you work overhours or not, just as you like?

No; them as works must work. . . .

If overhours are put on next week, shall you be glad or sorry?

It won't signify. I shall be neither glad nor sorry. Sometimes mother gives me a halfpenny to spend.

What do you do with it?

I saves it to buy shoes. Have never saved above a shilling for that; mother put more to it, and bought me a pair. . . .

Don't you play sometimes after work's over?

Yes, sometimes.

Well, are you not sorry to lose that?

No, I don't mind about it. I am quite sure I don't. I am sometimes tired when I have been at work long hours. I am not tired now; I have been at work all day except dinner; it is now five o'clock. I am sure I had rather work as I do than lose any of my wages. I go to school of a Sunday sometimes. I went first about a month ago. I have been every Sunday since. I can only read in the alphabet yet. I mean to go regular. There is no reason why I should not. I wants to be a scholar.

D. Lord John Russell Urges Parliamentary Reform, 1831

. . . Allow me to imagine, for a moment, a stranger from some distant country, who should arrive in England to examine our institutions. All the information he would have collected would have told him that this country was singular for the degree which it had attained in wealth, in science, and in civilization. He would have learned that in no country have the arts of life been carried further, nowhere the inventions of mechanical skill been rendered more conducive to the comfort and prosperity of mankind. He would have made himself acquainted with its fame in history, and, above all, he would have been told that the proudest boast of this celebrated country was its political freedom. If, in addition to this, he had heard that once in six years this country, so wise, so renowned, so free, chose its representatives to sit in the great council where all the ministerial affairs were discussed and determined, he would not be a little curious to see the process by which so important and solemn an operation was effected.

What, then, would be his surprise, if he were taken by his guide, whom he had asked to conduct him to one of the places of election, to a green mound, and told that this green mound sent two members to parliament; or to be taken to a stone wall with three niches in it, and told that these three niches sent two members to parliament; or, if he were shown a green park with many signs of flourishing vegetable life but none of human habitation, and told that this green park sent two members to parliament? But his surprise would increase to astonishment if he were carried into the north of England, where he would see large flourishing towns, full of trade and activity, containing vast magazines of wealth and manufactures, and were told that these places had no representatives in the assembly which was said to represent the people.

Suppose him, after all, for I will not disguise any part of the case,—suppose him to ask for a specimen of popular election, and to be carried for that purpose to Liverpool; his surprise would be turned to disgust at the gross venality and corruption which he would find to pervade the electors. After seeing all this, would he not wonder that a nation which had made such progress in every kind of knowledge, and which valued itself for its freedom, should permit so absurd and defective a system of representation any longer to prevail? . . .

I repeat that the confidence of the country in the construction and constitution of the House of Commons is gone—and gone forever. I would say more: I affirm that it would be easier to transfer the flourishing manufactories of Leeds and Manchester to Gatton and Old Sarum than to reëstablish the confidence and sympathy between this House and those whom it calls its constituents. I end this argument, therefore, by saying that if the question be one of right, right is in favor of reform; if it be a question of reason, reason is in favor of reform; if it be a question of policy and expediency, policy and expediency speak loudly for reform.

Document Set 21.7 References

A. Robert Owen Hopes to Temper the "Principle of Gain," 1815
Robert Owen, *Observations on the Effect of the Manufacturing System* (1815), in Walter Arnstein, ed., *The Past Speaks,* 2d ed. (Lexington, Mass.: D. C. Heath, 1993), 2:150–151.

B. David Ricardo Defines the "Iron Law of Wages," 1817
David Ricardo, *Principles of Political Economy and Taxation,* in Pierro Sraffa and M. H. Dobb, eds., *Works and Correspondence of David Ricardo* (Cambridge: Cambridge University Press, 1951), 93–95.

C. Charles Harris, Age 12, Testifies to a Parliamentary Inquiry About His Work
Report of Commissioners, in James Harvey Robinson and Charles Beard, eds., *Readings in Modern European History* (Boston: Ginn, 1909), 2:282–283.

D. Lord John Russell Urges Parliamentary Reform, 1831
Russell, Address to House of Lords, in Edward Cheyney, ed., *Readings in English History* (Boston: Ginn, 1908), 681–682.

22

Industrialization, Urbanization, and Revolution, 1832–1852

DOCUMENT SET 22.1
Industrialization Continues

As *The Challenge of the West* explains, the central trend of the years leading up to the revolution of 1848 was the spread of industrialization across the Continent and the accumulation of resulting, intractable social problems. Sets 22.1 through 22.3 all focus on aspects of this trend; Sets 22.4 through 22.8 all explore the mid-century revolutions.

As industrialization reached Germany, its progress was facilitated by the customs union (or common market, as we would say today) formed in 1834 under Prussian leadership, the *Zollverein*. Economic unity, liberals hoped, would hasten German political union. The German economist Friedrich List (1789–1846), originally a follower of Adam Smith and a naturalized U.S. citizen, became best known for advocating a "national" economic system of protective tariffs and other measures to strengthen the national state that he hoped to see arise in his native land (Document A). Would Smith have approved? Certainly the German poet Hoffmann von Fallersleben (1798–1878), author of the German national anthem, in the early 1840s saw in economic union the only hope for his country (Document B).

Reports are legion of Europeans' amazement at being able to speed along at 30 miles per hour on the railroads that were beginning to unite distant cities in the 1830s and 1840s. It is particularly interesting, however, to see how non-Westerners reacted to the newfangled system. Muhammad as-Saffar prepared for the sultan of Morocco the report cited in Document C.

A horrifying event of the 1840s was the Irish pota-

to famine, which cost several million lives and drove other millions of Irish to exile in Britain and North America (Document D). The starvation could have been alleviated had British landowners been willing to accept the repeal of tariffs (Corn Laws) that kept foreign grain out of Britain and the price of British grain high. The great liberal reformer Richard Cobden (1804–1865) demanded repeal, not only to relieve the starving Irish but also to lower the price of bread to English workers. Examining his argument (Document E), what strands of idealism and practicality do you detect? In what ways would repeal benefit middle-class industrialists? (Hint: see Ricardo's *Iron Law of Wages,* Set. 21.7, Document B.)

A. The German Economist Friedrich List Grows More Nationalist than Liberal, 1841

. . . The State is not merely justified in imposing, but bound to impose, certain regulations and restrictions on commerce (which is in itself harmless) for the best interests of the nation. By prohibitions and protective duties it does not give directions to individuals how to employ their productive powers and capital (as the popular school[1] sophistically alleges); it does not tell the one, 'You must invest your money in the building of a ship, or in the creation of a manufactory;' or the

---

[1] The laissez-faire economists

other, 'You must be a naval captain or a civil engineer:' it leaves it to the judgment of every individual how and where to invest his capital, or to what vocation he will devote himself. It merely says, 'It is to the advantage of our nation that we manufacture these or the other goods ourselves; but as by free competition with foreign countries we can never obtain possession of this advantage, we have imposed restrictions on that competition, so far as in our opinion is necessary, to give those among us who invest their capital in these new branches of industry, and those who devote their bodily and mental powers to them, the requisite guarantees that they shall not lose their capital and shall not miss their vocation in life; and further to stimulate foreigners to come over to our side with their productive powers. In this manner, it does not in the least degree restrain private industry; on the contrary, it secures to the personal, natural, and moneyed powers of the nation a greater and wider field of activity. It does not thereby do something which its individual citizens could understand better and do better than it; on the contrary, it does something which the individuals, even if they understood it, would not be able to do for themselves.

The allegation of the school, that the system of protection occasions unjust and anti-economical encroachments by the power of the State against the employment of the capital and industry of private individuals, appears in the least favourable light if we consider that it is the *foreign* commercial regulations which allow such encroachments on *our* private industry to take place, and that only by the aid of the system of protection are we enabled to counteract those injurious operations of the foreign commercial policy. If the English shut out our corn [grain] from their markets, what else are they doing than compelling our agriculturists to grow so much less corn than they would have sent out to England under systems of free importation? If they put such heavy duties on our wool, our wines, or our timber, that our export trade to England wholly or in great measure ceases, what else is thereby effected than that the power of the English nation restricts proportionately our branches of production? In these cases a direction is evidently given by *foreign legislation* to *our* capital and *our* personal productive powers, which but for the regulations made by it they would scarcely have followed. It follows from this, that were we to disown giving, by means of *our* own legislation, a direction to our own national industry in accordance with our own national interests, we could not prevent foreign nations from regulating our national industry after a fashion which corresponds with their own real or presumed advantage, and which in any case operates disadvantageously to the development of our own productive powers. . . .

The system of the school suffers, as we have already shown the preceding chapters . . . , from three main defects: firstly, from boundless *cosmopolitanism*, which neither recognises the principle of nationality, nor takes into consideration the satisfaction of its interests; secondly, from a dead *materialism*, which everywhere regards chiefly the mere exchangeable value of things without taking into consideration the mental and political, the present and the future interests, and the productive powers of the nation; thirdly, from a *disorganising particularism* and *individualism*, which, ignoring the nature and character of social labour and the operation of the union of powers in their higher consequences, considers private industry only as it would develop itself under a state of free interchange with society (i.e. with the whole human race) were that race not divided into separate national societies.

Between each individual and entire humanity, however, stands THE NATION, with its special language and literature, with its peculiar origin and history, with its special manners and customs, laws and institutions, with the claims of all these for existence, independence, perfection, and continuance for the future, and with its separate territory; a society which, united by a thousand ties of mind and of interests, combines itself into one independent whole, which recognises the law of right for and within itself, and in its united character is still opposed to other societies of a similar kind in their national liberty, and consequently can only under the existing conditions of the world maintain self-existence and independence by its own power and resources. As the individual chiefly obtains by means of the nation and in the nation mental culture, power of production, security, and prosperity, so is the civilisation of the human race only conceivable and possible by means of the civilisation and development of the individual nations.

Meanwhile, however, an infinite difference exists in the condition and circumstances of the various nations: we observe among them giants and dwarfs, well-formed bodies and cripples, civilised, half-civilised, and barbarous nations; but in all of them, as in the individual human being, exists the impulse of self-preservation, the striving for improvement which is implanted by nature. It is the task of politics to civilise the barbarous nationalities, to make the small and weak ones great and strong, but, above all, to secure to them existence and continuance. It is the task of national economy to accomplish *the econom-*

ical development of the nation, and to prepare it for admission into the universal society of the future. . . .

By its Zollverein, the German nation first obtained one of the most important attributes of its nationality. But this measure cannot be considered complete so long as it does not extend over the whole coast, from the mouth of the Rhine to the frontier of Poland, including *Holland* and *Denmark*. A natural consequence of this union must be the admission of both these countries into the German Bund, and consequently into the German nationality, whereby the latter will at once obtain what it is now in need of, namely, fisheries and naval power, maritime commerce and colonies. Besides, both these nations belong, as respects their descent and whole character, to the German nationality. The burden of debt with which they are oppressed is merely a consequence of their unnatural endeavours to maintain themselves as independent nationalities, and it is in the nature of things that this evil should rise to a point when it will become intolerable to those two nations themselves, and when incorporation with a larger nationality must seem desirable and necessary to them.

Belgium can only remedy by means of confederation with a neighbouring larger nation her needs which are inseparable from her restricted territory and population. . . .

B. Hoffmann von Fallersleben Gives Proper Credit for German Economic Unification

The Zollverein

Leather, salmon, eels and matches,
   Cows and madder, paper, shears,
Ham and cheese and boots and vetches,
   Wool and soap and yarns and beers;

Gingerbread and rags and fennels,
   Nuts, tobacco, glasses, flax,
Leather, salt, lard, dolls and funnels,
   Radish, rape, rep, whisky, wax;

Articles of home consumption,
   All our thanks are due to you!
You have wrought without presumption
   What no intellect could do;

You have made the German Nation
   Stand united, hand in hand,
More than the Confederation
   Ever did for Fatherland.

C. A Moroccan Visitor Comments on the Railroad

When we were about to depart, the chief started the engine, and it carried along whatever was joined to it at a speed we had never experienced, almost like a bird flying through the air. We covered the distance between Orléans and Paris in two and a half hours. When we looked at the sides of the road, we could not see what was there; it looked like an endless ribbon moving along with us, and we could not distinguish the rocks or anything. We tried as hard as we could to read the signs at the side of the road that measured off the miles—even though they were marked on white rocks in heavy black letters the height of a finger—but we were unable to fix our eyes on them because of our speed. They claim that if this road of iron extended from Marseille to Paris, it would take only a day and a night to cover the [entire] distance.

D. Richard Cobden Denounces the Corn Laws, 1838

With all sincerity I declare that I am for the total repeal of those taxes which affect the price of bread and provisions of every description, and I will not allow it to be said without denying it, that the three millions of people who have petitioned the House for the total repeal of those taxes are not sincere in their prayer. What are those taxes upon food? They are taxes levied upon the great body of the people, and the honorable gentlemen opposite, who show such sympathy for the working classes after they have made them paupers, cannot deny my right to claim on their behalf that those taxes should be a primary consideration.

I have heard them called protections; but taxes they are, and taxes they shall be in my mouth, as long as I have the honor of a seat in this House. The bread tax is a tax primarily levied upon the poorer classes; it is a tax, at the lowest estimate, of 40 per cent above the price we should pay if there were a free trade in corn [i.e. grain]. The report upon the hand-loom weavers puts down 10*s.* as the estimated weekly earnings of a family, and states that in all parts of the United Kingdom that will be found to be not an unfair estimate of the earnings of every laborer's family. It moreover states, that out of 10*s.* each family expends 5*s.* on bread. The tax of 40 per cent is therefore a tax of 2*s.* upon every laboring man's family earning 10*s.* a week, or 20 per cent upon their earnings. How does it operate as we proceed upwards in society? The man with 40s. a week pays an income tax of 5 per cent; the man of £250 a year pays but 1 per cent; and the nobleman or millionaire with an income of £200,000 a year, and whose family consumes no more bread than that of the agricultural laborer, pays less than one halfpenny in every £100. . . .

I will state generally, that, from both the manufacturing and agricultural districts, there was the most unimpeachable testimony that the condition of the great body of her Majesty's laboring subjects had deteriorated woefully within the last ten years, and more especially so within the three years last past; and furthermore, that in proportion as the price of the food of the people had increased, just so had their comforts been diminished. When they who sit in high places are oppressive and unjust to the poor, I am glad to see that there are men amongst us who, like Nathan of old, can be found to come forward and exclaim, "Thou art the man!" The religious people of the country have revolted against the infamous injustice of the bread tax, which is condemned by the immutable morality of the Scriptures. They have prepared and signed a petition to this House, in which they declare that these laws are a violation of the will of the Supreme Being, whose providence watches over his famishing children.

E. Famine Devastates Ireland

I did not see a child playing in the streets or on the roads; no children are to be seen outside the doors but a few sick and dying children . . . In the districts which are now being depopulated by starvation, coffins are only used for the more wealthy. The majority were taken to the grave without any coffin, and buried in their rags: in some instances even the rags are taken from the corpse to cover some still living body.

. . . On arriving at Cappagh, in the first house I saw a dead child lying in a corner of the house, and two children, pale as death, with their heads hanging down upon their breasts sitting by a small fire. The father had died on the road coming home from work. One of the children, a lad seventeen years of age, had been found, in the absence of his mother, who was looking for food, lying dead, with his legs held out of the fire by the little child which I then saw lying dead. Two other children had also died. The mother and the two children still alive had lived on one dish of barley for the last four days. On entering another house the doctor said, "Look there, Sir, you can't tell whether they are boys or girls." Taking up a skeleton child, he said, "here is the way it is with them all; their legs swing and rock like the legs of a doll, they have the smell of mice."

Document Set 22.1 References

A. The German Economist Friedrich List Grows More Nationalist than Liberal, 1841
List, *The National System of Political Economy*, trans. Sampson S. Lloyd (London: Longmans, 1904), 135–136, 141–143.
B. Hoffmann von Fallersleben Gives Proper Credit for German Economic Unification
von Fallersleben, "The Zollverein," in J. G. Legge, *Rhyme and Revolution in Germany* (London: Constable, 1918), 189.
C. A Moroccan Visitor Comments on the Railroad
Muhammad as-Saffar, in Susan Gilson Miller, ed. and trans., *Disorienting Encounter: Travels of a Moroccan Scholar in France in 1845–1846* (Berkeley: University of California Press, 1992), 115–116.
D. Richard Cobden Denounces the Corn Laws, 1838
Cobden, in James Harvey Robinson and Charles Beard, eds., *Readings in Modern European History* (Boston: Ginn, 1909), 2:287–288.
E. Famine Devastates Ireland
W. Steuart Trench, *Realities of Irish Life* (London: Longmans, Green, 1847).

DOCUMENT SET 22.2
Urbanization and the Middle-Class Reformers

The introduction to *The Challenge of the West's* Chapter 22 describes the devastation caused by Europe's great cholera epidemic in the early 1830s: read Document A as an illustration of how the British authorities tried (in vain) to keep their islands free of the disease, and observe the kind of restrictions imposed on citizens in the emergency.

Investigating and regulating the poor continued to preoccupy persons of means ·or authority. The English journalist Henry Mayhew (1812–1887) became famous for his verbatim records of poor peoples' experiences, such as the interview in 1849 with a woman who performed "sweated" (what we would call "sweatshop") labor in her home (Document B). In Belgium, Zoé Gatti de Gamond was moved by the plight of poor working women to hope that a utopian socialist community might relieve their powerlessness (Document C). Prostitution, because of its association with disease and crime, as well as for moral reasons, was a favorite target of concern to the authorities; Document D shows how the Viennese police in 1852 defined who was a prostitute and how she should be dealt with.

One of the most powerful voices in defense of the powerless—the poor, children, and abandoned women—was the great English novelist Charles Dickens (1812–1870). The more historians uncover about the social history of Victorian England, the more they recognize the essential accuracy of his reportage, as in the passage from *Oliver Twist* quoted as Document C. And lest one think of Dickens's board members as mere caricatures, consider the advice of that humorless social scientist Herbert Spencer (1820–1903), published in his *Social Statics* in 1851 (Document F).

A. Britain Tries to Keep Out the Cholera, 1831

To effect the prevention of the introduction of the disorder, the most active co-operation not only of the local authorities along the coast in the measures of the government, but likewise the 'exercise of the utmost caution by all the inhabitants of such parts of the country, becomes indispensably necessary. The quarantine regulations established by the government are sufficient, it is confidently hoped, to prevent the disorder from being communicated through any intercourse with the continent in the regular channel of trade or passage, but they cannot guard against its introduction by means of its secret and surreptitious intercourse which is known to exist between the coast of England and the opposite shores.

By such means this fatal disorder, in spite of all quarantine regulations, and of the utmost vigilance on the part of the government, might be introduced into the united kingdom; and it is clear that this danger can only be obviated by the most strenuous efforts on the part of all persons of any influence, to put a stop to such practices; the utmost exertions should be used to effect this end. The magistrates, the clergy, and all persons resident on the coast, it is hoped, will endeavour to impress upon the population of their different districts (and particularly of the retired villages along the sea shore), the danger to which they expose themselves in engaging in illicit intercourse with persons coming from the continent; and should appeal to their fears in warning them of the imminent risk which they incur by holding any communication with smugglers, and others who may evade the quarantine regulations.

To meet the other objects adverted to in the introduction,—namely, to prepare for the possible contingency of the country being visited by this disorder, as well as to assist in its prevention, it is recommended that in every town and village, commencing with those on the coast, there should be established a local Board of Health, to consist of the chief and other magistrates, the clergyman of the parish, two or more physicians or medical practitioners, and three or more of the principal inhabitants: and one of the medical members should be appointed to correspond with the Board of Health in London.

Every large town should be divided into districts, having a district committee of two or three members, one of whom should be of the medical profession, to watch over its health, and to give the earliest information to the Board of Health in the town, whose instructions they will carry into effect.

As the most effectual means of preventing the spreading of any pestilence has always been found to be the immediate separation of the sick from the healthy, it is of the utmost importance that the very first cases of cholera which may appear, should be made known as early as possible; concealment of the sick would not only endanger the safety of the public, but (as success in the treatment of the cholera has been found mainly to depend on medical assistance having been given in the earliest stage of the disease) would likewise deprive the patient of his best chance of recovery. . . .

It is recommended that those who may fall victims to this formidable disease, should be buried in a detached ground in the vicinity of the house that may have been selected for the reception of cholera patients. By this regulation it is intended to confine as much as possible every source of infection to one spot; on the same principle all persons who may be employed in the removal of the sick from their own houses, as well as all those who may attend upon cholera patients in the capacity of nurses, should live apart from the rest of the community. . . .

B. Henry Mayhew Describes "Sweated Labor" in London in the 1840s

I do the "looping." The looping consists in putting on the lace work down the front of the coats. I puts it on. That's my living; I wish it was not. I get 5d. for the looping of each coat; that's the regular price. It's three hours' work to do one coat, and work fast to do it as it's done now. I'm a particular quick hand. I have to find my own thread. It cost 1 1/2d. for a reel of cotton; that will do five coats. If I sit down between eight and nine in the morning, and work till twelve at night—I never enters my bed afore—and then rise between eight and nine again (that's the time I sit down to work on account of doing my own affairs first), and then work on till eleven, I get my four coats done by that time, and some wouldn't get done till two. It's an hour's work going and coming, and waiting to be served at the piece-master's, so that at them long hours it takes me a day and a half hard work to get four coats looped. When I first touched this work I could do eight in the same time, and be paid better; I had 7d. then instead of 5d.; now the work in each is nearly double in quantity, that it is.

I've got two boys both at work, one about fifteen, earning 3s. per week, and I have got him to keep and clothe. The week before last I bought him a top coat—it cost me 6s.—for fear he should be laid up, for he's such bad health. The other boy is eighteen years, and earns 9s. a week. He's been in work about four months, and was out six weeks. At the same time I had no work. Oh, it was awful then! I have been paying 1s. 6d. a week off a debt for bread and things I was obliged to get on credit then.

My last boy is only nine years of age, and him I have entirely to keep [support]. He goes to the charity school. It lets him have one coat and trousers and shoes and stockings every year. He wears a pinafore

now to save his coat. My eldest boy is like a hearty man to every meal. If he hadn't got me to manage for him, may be he'd spend all his earnings in mere food. I get my second bread, and I go as far as Nassau-street to save two or three halfpence. Butter we *never* have. A roast of meat none of us ever sees. A cup of tea, a piece of bread, and an onion, is generally all I have for my dinner, and sometimes I haven't even an onion.

C. A Belgian Woman Attacks Poverty, c. 1840

The most direct cause of women's misfortune is poverty; demanding their freedom means above all demanding reform in the economy of society which will eradicate poverty and give everyone education, a minimum standard of living, and the right to work. It is not only that class called "women of the people" for whom the major source of all their misfortunes is poverty, but rather women of all classes.

From that comes the subjection of women, their narrow dependence on men, and their reduction to a negative influence. Men have thus materialized love, perverted the angelic nature of women, and created a being who submits to their caprices, their desires—a domesticated animal shaped to their pleasures and to their needs. Using their powers, they have split women into the appearance of two classes; for the privileged group, marriage, the care of the household, and maternal love; for the other, the sad role of seduced woman and of the misfortunate one reduced to the last degree of misery and degradation. Everywhere oppression and nowhere liberty.

The question is not to decide whether it is fitting to give women political rights or to put them on an equal footing with men when it comes to admission to employment. Rather the question exists above all in the question of poverty; and to make women ready to fill political roles, it is poverty above all that must be effaced. Nor can the independence of women be reconciled with the isolation of households, which prevents even the working woman from being independent.

The system of Fourier, imperceptibly and smoothly introducing associations within society, resolves all the difficulties in the position of women; without changing legislation or proclaiming new rights, it will regenerate them, silence the sources of corruption and reform with one blow education and morals with the single fact that results naturally from the associational principles of his system: a common education and the independence of women assured by the right to work; independence rendered possible by the association of households, attractive and harmonious work, and the multiplication of wealth.

D. The Police Regulate Prostitution in Vienna, 1852

Instructions for Police Treatment of Prostitutes, 1852

1. Under the designation prostitute is understood to be every woman who seeks business by exposing her body for sale in lewdness.
2. Under what circumstances the prostitute is officially conducted to the criminal court and what penalties in all other cases remain under police jurisdiction is determined by penal law.
3. The prostitute falls into the realm of police correction when she:
a. walks the streets, that is, she walks in such a way as to enlist business from men;
b. loiters for the same end on doorsteps in allies or in open spaces;
c. has her residence in a house or part of the city in which are gathered such women of a conduct similar to those of a bordello or in a region known for its lewd manners;
d. lures people in a shameless way from a window or from an openair part of the house, or otherwise offends public decency, and not only in a criminal way.
4. Every one who is defined under these as a streetwalker and who is held in detention is subject to the following proceedings:
a. a medical examination;
b. an inquiry into her present situation, and
c. her past, in order to
d. conduct an investigation into her methods of earning a living and her personal relationships.
5. Should such a female qualify as a prostitute and be found ill, she must first of all go to the hospital or according to the circumstances to an investigatory hospital and after a successful cure further investigation will be undertaken.

E. Charles Dickens Describes the Philanthropic Workhouse, 1841

The members of this board were very sage, deep, philosophical men; and when they came to turn their attention to the workhouse, they found out at once, what ordinary folks would never have discovered— the poor people like it! It was a regular place of public entertainment for the poorer classes; a tavern where there was nothing to pay; a public breakfast, dinner, tea, and supper all the year round; a brick and mortar Elysium, where it was all play and no work. "Oho!" said the board, looking very knowing; "we are the fellows to set this to rights; we'll stop it all, in no time," So, they established the rule, that all poor people should have the alternative (for they would compel nobody, not they), or being starved by a gradual process in the house, or by a quick one out of it. With this view, they contracted with the water-works to lay on an unlimited supply of water; and with a corn-factor [grain merchant] to supply periodically small quantities of oatmeal; and issue three meals of thin gruel a day, with an onion twice a week, and half a roll on Sundays. They made a great many other wise and humane regulations, having reference to the ladies, which it is not necessary to repeat; kindly undertook to divorce poor married people, in consequence of the great expense of a suit in Doctors' Commons; and, instead of compelling a man to support his family, as they had theretofore done, took his family away from him, and made him a bachelor! There is no saying how many applicants for relief, under these last two heads, might have started up in all classes of society, if it had been coupled with the workhouse; but the board were long-headed men, and had provided for this difficulty. The relief was inseparable from the workhouse and the gruel; and that frightened people.

F. Herbert Spencer Condemns Charity, 1851

In common with its other assumptions of secondary offices, the assumption by a government of the office of Reliever-general to the poor, is necessarily forbidden by the principle that a government cannot rightly do anything more than protect. In demanding from a citizen contributions for the mitigation of distress-contributions not needed for the due administration of men's rights—the state is, as we have seen, reversing its function, and diminishing that liberty to exercise the faculties which it was instituted to maintain. Possibly, . . . some will assert that by satisfying the wants of the pauper, a government is in reality extending his liberty to exercise his faculties. . . . But this statement of the case implies a confounding of two widely-different things. To enforce the fundamental law—to take care that every man has freedom to do all that he wills, provided he infringes not the equal freedom of any other man—this is the special purpose for which the civil power exists. Now insuring to each the right to pursue within the specified limits the objects of his desires without let or hindrance, is quite a separate thing from insuring him satisfaction. . . .

Pervading all nature we may see at work a stern discipline, which is a little cruel that it may be very kind. That state of universal warfare maintained throughout the lower creation, to the great perplexity of many worthy people, is at bottom the most merciful provision which the circumstances admit of. . . . The poverty of the incapable, the distresses that come upon the imprudent, the starvation of the idle, and those shoulderings aside of the weak by the strong, which leave so many "in shallows and in miseries," are the decrees of a large, farseeing benevolence. It seems hard that an unskilfulness which with all its efforts he cannot overcome, should entail hunger upon the artizan. It seems hard that a labourer incapacitated by sickness from competing with his stronger fellows, should have to bear the resulting privations. It seems hard that widows and orphans should be left to struggle for life or death. Nevertheless, when regarded not separately, but in connection with the interests of universal humanity, these harsh fatalities are seen to be full of the highest beneficence—the same beneficence which brings to early graves the children of diseased parents, and singles out the low-spirited, the intemperate, and the debilitated as the victims of an epidemic. . . .

Document Set 22.2 References

A. Britain Tries to Keep Out the Cholera, 1831
   Annual Register, 1831, 357–360.
B. Henry Mayhew Describes "Sweated Labor" in London in the 1840s
   Adapted from Henry Mayhew, *The Morning Chronicle Survey of Labour and the Poor: The Metropolitan Districts* (Sussex, England: Caliban, 1980), 1:157–159.
C. A Belgian Woman Attacks Poverty, c. 1840
   Adapted from Zoé Gatti de Gamond, *Fourier et son système* (Paris: Capelle, 1841–1842), 247–266, in Bonnie Smith, *Changing Lives: Women in European History Since 1700* (Lexington, Mass.: D. C. Heath, 1989), 174–175.
D. The Police Regulate Prostitution in Vienna, 1852
   Josef Schrank, *Die Prostitution in Wien* (Wien: Genossenschafts-Buchdruckerei, 1886), 316, in Smith, 150–151.
E. Charles Dickens Describes the Philanthropic Workhouse, 1841
   Charles Dickens, *Oliver Twist,* 24–25.
F. Herbert Spencer Condemns Charity, 1851
   Herbert Spencer, *Social Statics,* in J. Salwyn Schapiro, ed., *Liberalism: Its Meaning and History* (New York: Van Nostrand Reinhold, 1958), 136–137.

DOCUMENT SET 22.3
Early Socialist Critics of Industrialization

We have already encountered in Set 22.2 (Document C) a Belgian follower of Charles Fourier (1772–1837), whose schemes to found ideal communities combined shrewd and crazy ideas in about equal measure. Fourier was one of the "utopian" socialists, a term coined with negative connotations by Karl Marx to characterize those whose hopes to rescue humanity from the evils of economic competition rested on pious good will rather than on Marx's "scientific" analysis of class warfare. The prince of all utopian socialists was Henri de Saint-Simon (1790–1825), a descendant of the famous Duc de Saint-Simon of Louis XIV's day. In 1831 his followers published the short summary of his ideas that is excerpted as Document A.

Saint-Simon and Fourier were regarded primarily as harmless cranks by all but their numerous followers; not so Pierre Joseph Proudhon (1809–1865), a socialist writer of worker origins who in 1840 published a book with the alarming title *What Is Property?* and answered the question: "theft" (Document B). Proudhon did not want to abolish private property entirely, only to redistribute it so as to ensure the working class its rightful share of the wealth it produced—a program that Marx would attack savagely as a compromise with bourgeois values. But Proudhon remained more typical of early socialism in the 1840s than Marx; the Swiss writer Gottfried Keller (1819–1890) describes in Document C (1843) German "communists" who were closer to Proudhon than to Marx.

One early socialist who actually tried to mobilize workers was Flora Tristan, who combined Fourierist utopianism with feminism but managed also to win male workers' confidence and understood their lives better than most middle-class utopians (Document D).

Reading the "utopians" should throw into relief the boldness, radicalism, historical grounding, and ruthless intellectual clarity of Karl Marx (1818–1883) and Friedrich Engels (1820–1895), co-authors of the *Communist Manifesto* (Document E, 1847).

A. His Disciples Expound "The Doctrine of Saint-Simon," 1829

A new science, a science as *positive* as any that deserves the title, has been created by SAINT-SIMON: this science is that of the *human race*; its method is the same employed by astronomy and physics; the facts within it are grouped within a series of homogeneous classes, linked to each other within an order of *generalization* and *particularization*, in such a way as to bring out the special *proclivity* of each, that is to say, to demonstrate the law of *increase* and *decrease* to which all must submit.

A primary application of this science proves the tendency of the human race toward *universal association,* or, in other words, the constant diminution of *antagonism,* explained in succession by these words: *families, castes, cities, nations,* HUMANITY; whence results that societies, originally organized for *war,* tend to blend into a *peaceful* UNIVERSAL ASSOCIATION.

A general picture of the development of the human race, including Jewish monotheism, Greek and Roman polytheism, and Christianity up to the present, demonstrates with proof this law of PROGRESS.

Up to now, man has exploited man. Masters and slaves; patrician, plebeian; lords, serfs; owners, farmers; idlers and workers—behold the progressive history of humanity up to our day. Behold our future with UNIVERSAL ASSOCIATION: *to each according to his capacity, to each capacity according to its productivity,* behold the new law which replaces that of *conquest* and of BIRTH: man no longer exploits man; but man, linked to man, exploits the natural world delivered to his power.

Ah! What do our lawyers, political journalists, economists come to tell us today? Does not their science prove to us that wealth and misery shall always be *hereditary;* that wealth is a necessary *attribute* of idleness? Does it not also prove that the sons of the poor are as free as those of the rich? Free! When one needs bread! That they are all *equal before the law?* Equal before the law? When one has the right to live without working, and the other—if he doesn't work, has only the right to die.

They repeat to us without end that property is the foundation of the social order; we too proclaim this eternal truth. But who shall be the property owner? Shall it be the *lazy, ignorant,* IMMORAL son of a deceased man, or shall it be rather the man capable of fulfilling his social function with dignity? They claim that all privileges of birth have been destroyed. Ah! What is the transmission of a fortune from father to son, with no other reason than the link of blood, if it is not the most *immoral* of all privileges—that of *living in society without working,* and there to be rewarded above and beyond one's labor?

A sad science, which would have maintained slavery, which would have stopped JESUS from preaching human *brotherhood,* fearful that His words might have resounded in the ears of a slave; a sad science that in an age even more distant would have proclaimed the validity of cannibalism!

Yes, all our political theorists have their eyes on the past, even those who claim themselves to be worthy of the future; and when we have announced to them the arrival of the reign of WORK, and that the reign of idleness is over, they have treated us as dreamers; they tell us that sons have always inherited from their fathers, like a pagan saying that a free man has always owned slaves. But humanity has proclaimed through JESUS, NO MORE SLAVERY! Through SAINT-SIMON it now cries: *to each according to his capacity, to each capacity according to its productivity,* NO MORE INHERITANCE!

All the members of the body social are men, but all too are *artists, scholars,* or *businessmen;* in other words, all *feel, think,* or *act.* This triple aspect of human life provides the occasion for a triple division in general and specialized education. This is the conception which serves as a foundation for education in the future, for which we have sketched the principal developments in summary fashion.

B. Pierre-Joseph Proudhon Asks, "What Is Property?" 1840

If I were called upon to answer the following question: *What is slavery?* and I replied: *It is murder,* my meaning would be comprehended immediately. There would be no need for amplification to demonstrate that the power to deprive a man of his thought, will, and personality is the power of life and death and that to make a man a slave is to kill him. Why, therefore, may I not meet this other question: *What is property?* by replying: *It is theft,* without feeling certain I shall be misunderstood, although this second proposition is no more than a transformation of the first?

I am taking it upon myself to discuss property, the essential principle of our government and our institutions. I am within my rights. I may be deceived in the conclusion to which my researchers lead me. I am within my rights. It pleases me to state my conclusion at the outset. I am still within my rights.

Such and such an author preaches that property is a civil right, generated by labor and sanctioned by law. Another maintains that it is a natural right which derives its origin from work. Both these doctrines, contradictory though they may appear, are endorsed and promoted. It is my contention that neither labor, nor business, nor law can create property: that it is an effect without a cause. Should I be reproved for this?

Yet I hear murmurs arising!

—*Property is theft!* This is the slogan of '93! This is the rallying cry of revolution.

Reader, reassure yourself. I am not an instrument of discord, a seditious incendiary. I am anticipating history a little; I am revealing a truth the march of which we are attempting in vain to halt. I proclaim the preamble of our future constitution. If our prepossessions would permit us to consider it, the definition *Property is theft,* which you deem heretical, might prove a lightning rod to deflect the thunderbolt. But how many interests, how many prejudices stand in the way! Philosophy, alas, will not alter the progress of events. Destiny will fulfill itself regardless of prophecy. . . .

C. Swiss Writer Gottfried Keller Discovers the Communist Movement in Germany, 1843

A vexed and pessimistic mood. And added to this comes the pernicious ferment and discontent of communism and its impudent and open expression. Reflecting on this soon to be important social question leaves one at a loss what to think. One thing appears to me certain, viz., that there is more misery in the world than ever and that communism has and is gaining many adherents.

. . . One of its apostles, the journeyman tailor Weitling who has written a book about it with spirit and fire—*Guarantees of Harmony and Freedom*—has been arrested here. His arrest has aroused dissatisfaction amongst the liberal party because it was carried out with aristocratic high-handedness, and because the free press was insulted at the same time by a midnight inquisition. Meanwhile I can see no good side to the communism of Weitling and his friends, as it consists on the one hand of chimeras which it is impossible to realise without augmenting the existing misery, . . . and on the other hand appears to me to be only the consequence of a growing passion for luxury and ease. But indeed it seems to me to be chiefly animated by a short-sighted and covetous envy of the rich of this world. They do not merely want, as Weitling clearly says, to eat, they want to eat abundantly, luxuriously and well. They want their turn. O ye fools and blind! Did you demand perfectly equal education by the state, state recognition of the right to live, state provision for the unemployable—then I am with you body and soul! But away from me with your utterly fanatical world-storming ideas! To the mad-house with you if you are sincere, and to the Devil if you are tempted by the belly you honour!

D. Flora Tristan Tries to Rouse the Lyon Silkweavers, 1844

Yesterday I saw the silk workers.—What men! There you have serious, reasonable, fearless workers.—There should be 10,000 workers of this temper in the city of Lyon.—I spent three very satisfying hours at this meeting.—That is what I call talking to workers—in other words, chatting with them—letting them expose their needs themselves; one of them is to give me some notes on the board of arbitration (*prud'hommes*)—but this institution is a veritable hoax for the worker! and in Paris not one politician speaking about the arbitrators knows what is happening in Lyon.— It was really a touching sight, all these heads of workshops, husbands, fathers of families; intelligent, educated men, already from thirty to forty years of age, who have come to listen to a woman's voice, thank her for her sympathy; each one telling her his troubles, his tribulations, the injustices, the thefts that the masters perpetrate on the poor, ignorant workers incapable of defending their interests.—Oh yes! What goes on here is a subject and sight worthy of attention.—There is in it the germ of a new order of things—here are men who no longer have confidence in other men, not in deputies, scholars, priests, or kings; they know that all these so-called superior men are . . . egotists without feelings, without fraternity for the working class.—These workers know that all rich men are their enemies—and that scholars do not concern themselves with them—and so these men, guided by their good sense, have said to themselves: there is a woman who comes to us in order to serve us, it is God who sends her, let us go and listen to her; and all of them come, no matter what their party.—There I am, without having premeditated it, in the role of Woman-Guide, just as I too had instinctively conceived of it.—What I am doing at this moment—the results that I obtain—speak more in favor of the superiority of woman than everything that could be written and said on the question.—The problem is resolved by actual deed—the mathematical proof; thus the first person in all humankind who really speaks to the unpolished, ignorant people is a woman! I consider the Chalon affair[1] wholly an act of God; it is He who made me

say:—"Sirs, I am traveling through France to speak to the workers and not to the bourgeois. Yes, it is a woman who will have been the first to have the wholly religious idea of speaking to the workers!"—and see what happens—man in the person of the royal prosecutor forbids me to speak to the workers.—"Sir," I said to him, "since this worker's union troubles you so much, I can dispense with their written adherence and will be satisfied with speaking to them."—"Madame, I cannot permit you to do it. To speak to the workers is too dangerous." Man thinks that the word of life is dangerous—and see what a difference, woman is impelled to propagate that word of life.—Woman is life and man is its limitations.—That is why woman is superior to man. These silk workers, heads of their shops, are the best thing I have encountered here; they have their own ideas—they combine to form a society—an "organized coalition"—they are very capable men and a year from now they will have brought into their association all of their intelligent counterparts in the city. Once these men have understood my little book, we shall see. . . .

The following day I saw the journeymen carpenters, the "Gavots." Well! I am forced to say that I found those men very backward—out of fifty men present there, only two had read my little book—without comprehending it.—However, I tried to get them to talk; but no one understood what is meant by "right to work."—I explained, and in the end they understood and then seemed very astonished that this right had not been thought of sooner.—The conversation touched on important questions and as soon as these men were at ease with me I saw that four of five of them were very intelligent.—One said to me: "what harms us, madame, is that we are kept from discussing political matters in our meetings; we would be able to exchange views as we are now doing with you."—The observation of this young man was very sensible—well, two elders intervened and argued against the ideas that the young journeymen had just expressed.—The workers must not talk politics, the police forbid it and if we talk politics they will have our society dissolved.—I found myself in a very critical position for I could not let pass the obscurantist doctrines of the two old journeymen and yet I knew very well that I risked being arrested in *flagrante delicto* if a police spy was present.—No matter, I did not recoil before the principle and I made a spirited address to them to make them understand that it was their duty as citizens, as brothers, and as progressive men to be concerned with questions of social economy, so-called political, that such matters entered into even household affairs—and that

---

[1] where she faced a large and hostile bourgeois audience

particular questions depended on general questions.—All the young were of my opinion and the old journeymen stuck in their obsolete ideas did not dare to contradict me.—So you see, the crudest and most ignorant men are capable of being instructed and very quickly.—There is thus but one course of action, and that is to talk to them.—It was agreed that they would come and take fifteen little books, that they would study them together, and that before my departure we would have another meeting in order to be able to have a discussion with knowledge of the facts.

When I arrived among these men my heart was wrung upon seeing their state of ignorance. On leaving I said to myself: well, I must not despair of anyone, all are capable of seeing and hearing.

E. Marx and Engels Announce That "A Specter Is Haunting Europe," 1847

A specter is haunting Europe—the specter of communism. All the powers of old Europe have entered into a holy alliance to exorcise this specter: Pope and Czar, Metternich and Guizot, French Radicals and German police-spies. . . .

Communism is already acknowledged by all European powers to be itself a power.

It is high time that Communists should openly, in the face of the whole world, punish their views, their aims, their tendencies, and meet this nursery tale of the specter of communism with a Manifesto of the party itself. . . .

The history of all hitherto existing society is the history of class struggles. . . .

Modern industry has established the world market, for which the discovery of America paved the way. This market has given an immense development to commerce, to navigation, to communication by land. This development has, in its turn, reacted on the extension of industry; and in proportion as industry, commerce, navigation, railways extended, in the same proportion the bourgeoisie developed, increased its capital, and pushed into the background every class handed down from the Middle Ages. . . .

The bourgeoisie, historically, has played a most revolutionary part.

The bourgeoisie, wherever it has got the upper hand, has put an end to all feudal, patriarchal, idyllic relations. It has pitilessly torn asunder the motley feudal ties that bound man to his "natural superiors," and has left remaining no other nexus between man and man than naked self-interest, than callous "cash

payment." It has drowned the most heavenly ecstasies of religious fervor, of chivalrous enthusiasm, of philistine sentimentalism, in the icy water of egotistical calculation. It has resolved personal worth into exchange value, and in place of the numberless indefeasible chartered freedoms, has set up that single, unconscionable freedom—Free Trade. In a word, for exploitation, veiled by religious and political illusions, it has substituted naked, shameless, direct, brutal exploitation.

The bourgeoisie has stripped of its halo every occupation hitherto honored and looked up to with reverent awe. It has converted the physician, the lawyer, the priest, the poet, and the man of science into its paid wage-laborers.

The bourgeoisie has torn away from the family its sentimental veil and has reduced the family relation to a mere money relation. . . .

The bourgeoisie has subjected the country to the rule of the towns. It has created enormous cities, greatly increased the urban population as compared with the rural, and thus rescued a considerable part of the population from the idiocy of rural life. . . .

The bourgeoisie, during its rule of scarcely one hundred years, has created more massive and more colossal productive forces than have all preceding generations together. . . .

But not only has the bourgeoisie forged the weapons that bring death to itself; it has also called into existence the men who are to wield those weapons—the modern working class—the proletariat.

In proportion as the bourgeoisie, *i.e.*, capital, develops, in the same proportion the proletariat, the modern working class, develops—a class of laborers, who live only so long as they find work, and who find work only so long as their labor increases capital. These laborers, who must sell themselves piecemeal, are a commodity, like every other article of commerce, and are consequently exposed to all the vicissitudes of competition, to all the fluctuations of the market. . . .

Of all the classes that stand face to face with the bourgeoisie today, the proletariat alone is a really revolutionary class. The other classes decay and finally disappear in the face of modern industry; the proletariat is its special and essential product. . . .

The socialist and communist systems properly so called, those of Saint Simon, Fourier, Owen and others, spring into existence in the early undeveloped period, described above, of the struggle between proletariat and bourgeoisie. . . .

Such fantastic pictures of future society, painted at a time when the proletariat is still in a very undeveloped state and has but a fantastic conception of its own position, correspond with the first instinctive yearnings of that class for a general reconstruction of society.

But these socialist and communist publications contain also a critical element. They attack every principle of existing society. . . .

The Communists fight for the attainment of the immediate aims, for the enforcement of the momentary interests of the working class; but in the movement of the present, they also represent and take care of the future of that movement. . . .

The Communists turn their attention chiefly to Germany, because that country is on the eve of a bourgeois revolution that is bound to be carried out under more advanced conditions of European civilization, and with a much more developed proletariat, than that of England was in the seventeenth, and of France in the eighteenth century, and because the bourgeois revolution in Germany will be but the prelude to an immediately following proletarian revolution.

In short, the Communists everywhere support every revolutionary movement against the existing social and political order of things.

In all these movements they bring to the fore, as the leading question in each, the property question, no matter what its degree of development at the time.

Finally, they labor everywhere for the union and agreement of the democratic parties of all countries.

The Communists disdain to conceal their views and aims. They openly declare that their ends can be attained only by the forcible overthrow of all existing social conditions. Let the ruling classes tremble at a Communistic revolution. The proletarians have nothing to lose but their chains. They have a world to win.

WORKING MEN OF ALL COUNTRIES, UNITE!

Document Set 22.3 References

A. His Disciples Expound "The Doctrine of Saint-Simon," 1829
   The Doctrine of Saint-Simon in Howard E. Hugo, ed., *The Portable Romantic Reader* (New York: Viking, 1957), 505–507.
B. Pierre Joseph Proudhon Asks, "What Is Property?," 1840
   Pierre Joseph Proudhon, *What Is Property?* in Geoffrey Bruun, ed., *Revolution and Reaction, 1848–1852* (Princeton, N.J.: D. Van Nostrand, 1958), 109–110.
C. Swiss Writer Gottfried Keller Discovers the Communist Movement in Germany, 1843
   Keller, in J. G. Legge, *Rhyme and Revolution in Germany* (London: Constable, 1918), 145.
D. Flora Tristan Tries to Rouse the Lyons Silkweavers, 1844
   Tristan, *Le Tour de France*, in Doris and Paul Beik, eds. and trans., *Flora Tristan, Utopian Feminist: Her Travel Diaries and Personal Crusade* (Bloomington: Indiana University Press, 1993), 135–137.
E. Marx and Engels Announce That "A Specter Is Haunting Europe," 1847
   Karl Marx and Friedrich, *The Communist Manifesto*, in Arthur P. Mendel, *The Essential Works of Marxism* (New York: Bantam, 1961), 13–17, 19, 23, 40–44.

DOCUMENT SET 22.4
The Revolution of 1848: France

It is striking to note the parallels between the *Communist Manifesto*'s 1847 warning of the "specter haunting Europe" and Heinrich Heine's article of five years earlier using a similar phrase to describe the Parisian bourgeoisie (Document A). Keep in mind this pervasive fear as you read the documents in this and subsequent sets on the 1848 Revolution. Notice, for example, the French provisional government's quick effort to head off trouble with the debt-ridden, unemployed workers (Document B) and the women workers' petition to the same authorities in March 1848 (Document C). Tocqueville felt the tension in his walk through revolutionary Paris soon after Louis Phillippe's fall (Document D), and it blazed out with full fury on the Paris barricades as the bourgeois National Guard and the workers fought it out in June 1848, as described in a letter by a middle-class Parisian woman. (Document E).

A. Heinrich Heine Diagnoses the Dread of the French Bourgeoisie, 1842

The Parisian bourgeoisie are obsessed by a nightmare apprehension of disaster. It is not fear of a republic but an instinctive dread of communism, of those sinister fellows who would swarm like rats from the ruin of the present regime. No, the French bourgeoisie would not be alarmed by a republic of the earlier variety, nor even by a little Robespierrism. They would easily reconcile themselves to that form of government and stand watch over the Tuileries regardless whether the building housed a Louis Phillippe or a Committee of Public Safety. For what the bourgeoisie want above all is order and protection—protection of their existing property rights—and these are objectives that a republic should be able to guarantee as surely as a monarchy. But as already noted these shopkeepers sense instinctively that today a republic might no longer represent the principles of the seventeen nineties. It might become the instrument through which a new unacknowledged power would seize control, a proletarian party preaching community of goods. The bourgeoisie are therefore conservative by external necessity, not by inward conviction. Their politics are motivated by fear.

Will this restraining fear persist very long? May not the national giddiness confuse these cautious heads some day or other and send them spinning once more into the whirlpool of revolution? I do not know. It is possible. In fact the election returns in Paris are a constant reminder that it is more than possible, it is probable. The French have short memories and easily forget even the dangers they have the best reasons to fear. This explains why they so often appear as the actors, nay more, as the principal protagonists, in the vast tragedy which the dear Lord has staged on Earth. . . .

B. The Liberal Provisional Government of France Decrees the Right to Work, February 25, 1848

The provisional government of the French republic decrees that the Tuileries shall serve hereafter as a home for the veterans of labor.

The provisional government of the French republic pledges itself to guarantee the means of subsistence of the workingman by labor.

It pledges itself to guarantee labor to all citizens.

It recognizes that workingmen ought to enter into associations among themselves in order to enjoy the advantage of their labor.

The provisional government returns to the workingmen, to whom it rightfully belongs, the million which was about to fall due upon the civil list.

The provisional government of the French republic decrees that all articles pledged at the pawn shops since the first of February, consisting of linen, garments, or clothes, etc., upon which the loan does not exceed ten francs, shall be given back to those who pledged them. The minister of finance is ordered to meet the payments incidental to the execution of the present edict.

The provisional government of the republic decrees the immediate establishment of national workshops. The minister of public works is charged with the execution of the present decree. . . .

C. Women Workers Petition the Republic, March 1848

Sirs,

The women workers exercising the trade (*état*) of rabbit fur cutters for the hat industry, two or three thousand in number, all diligent and mothers of families, have the honor of showing that this trade (*état*), which is only practiced by women, gives them the wherewithal to live, to feed their children, and to give a trade (*état*) to their daughters, enabling them according to their ability to earn 10 to 12 francs per week, although now they are reduced to earning 50 or 75 centimes a day, which makes it impossible for them to earn their livelihood or that of their families. This state of things, Sirs, arises from machines which have been adopted by the richest owners . . . and which cause us the greatest injury, . . . aggravate our already sad position, and snatch bread from our mouths. In addition, for fifteen years, ten thousand foreign workers have arrived to bring misery to a trade (*état*), which once flourished but which now is almost extinct.

For these reasons, the petitioners . . . beg the provisional government, from which all justice arises, to look with compassion on their unfortunate fate and to restore their livelihood by stopping these machines. . . . It is their most ardent wish and they have complete confidence that your humanity and your justice will not fail them and will protect them against the egotism of the wealthy cutters.

D. Tocqueville Walks Through Paris in February 1848

I spent the whole afternoon in walking about Paris. Two things in particular struck me: the first was, I will not say the mainly, but the uniquely and exclusively popular character of the revolution that had just taken place; the omnipotence it had given to the people properly so-called—that is to say, the classes who work with their hands—over all others. The second was the comparative absence of malignant passion, or, as a matter of fact, of any keen passion—an absence which at once made it clear that the lower orders had suddenly become masters of Paris.

Although the working classes had often played the leading part in the events of the First Revolution, they had never been the sole leaders and masters of the State. . . . The Revolution of July [1830] was effected by the people, but the middle class had stirred it up and led it, and secured the principal fruits of it. The Revolution of February, on the contrary, seemed to be made entirely outside the *bourgeoisie* and against it.

In the great concussion, the two parties of which the social body in France is mainly composed had, in a way, been thrown more completely asunder, and the mass of the people, which had stood alone, remained in sole possession of power. Nothing more novel had been known in our annals. . . .

Throughout this day, I did not see in Paris a single one of the former agents of the public authority: not a soldier, not a gendarme, not a policeman; the National Guard itself had disappeared. The people alone bore arms, guarded the public buildings, watched, gave orders, punished; it was an extraordinary and terrible thing to see in the sole hands of those who possessed nothing, all this immense town, so full of riches, or rather this great nation: for, thanks to centralization, he who reigns in Paris governs France. Hence the terror of all the other classes was extreme; I doubt whether at any period of the revolution it had been so great, and I should say that it was only to be compared to that which the civilized cities of the Roman Empire must have experienced when they suddenly found themselves in the power of the Goths and Vandals. As nothing like this had ever been seen before, many people expected acts of unexampled violence. For my part I did not once partake of these fears. What I saw led me to predict strange disturbances in the near future—singular crises. But I never believed that the rich would be pillaged; I knew the men of the people in Paris too well not to know that their first movements in times of revolution are usually generous, and that they are best pleased to spend the days immediately following their triumph in boasting of their victory, laying down the law, and playing at being great men. During that time it generally happens that some government or other is set up, the police returns to its post, and the judge to his bench; and when at last our great men consent to step down to the better known and more vulgar ground of petty and malicious human passion, they are no longer able to do so, and are reduced to live simply like honest men. Besides, we have spent so many years in insurrections that there has arisen among us a kind of morality peculiar to times of disorder, and a special code for days of rebellion. According to these exceptional laws, murder is tolerated and havoc permitted, but theft is strenuously forbidden; although this, whatever one may say, does not prevent a good deal of robbery from occurring upon those days, for the simple reason that society in a state of rebellion cannot be different from that at any other time, and it will always contain a number of rascals who as far as they are concerned, scorn the morality of the main body, and despise its point of honour when they are unobserved. What reassured me still more was the reflection that the victors had been as much surprised by success as their adversaries were by defeat: their passions had not had time to take fire and become intensified in the struggle; the Government had fallen undefended by others, even by itself. It had long been attacked, or at least keenly censured, by the very men who at heart most deeply regretted its fall. . . .

For the first time in sixty years, the priests, the old aristocracy and the people met in a common sentiment—a feeling of revenge, it is true, and not of affection; but even that is a great thing in politics, where a community of hatred is almost always the foundation of friendships. The real, the only vanquished, were the middle class; but even this had little to fear. Its reign had been exclusive rather than oppressive; corrupt, but not violent; it was despised rather than hatred. Moreover, the middle class never forms a compact body in the heart of the nation, a part very distinct from the whole; it always participates a little with all the others, and in some places merges into them. This absence of homogeneity and of exact limits makes the government of the middle class weak and uncertain, but it also makes it intangible, and, as it were, invisible to those who desire to strike it when it is no longer governing. . . .

E. On the Barricades: The National Guard and the Workers Fight It Out, June 1848

On the night of Friday to Saturday the twenty-fourth, the National Guards captured and recaptured two barricades in the narrow rue de la Tixanderie which ran alongside the Hôtel de Ville. The insurgents held all the houses in this dirty little street and were firing from all the windows and ventilators at the National Guard. The oil lanterns, which even at that time were hung on cables down the middle of the small streets to provide illumination, had all be shattered by bullets. But it was the month of June and the nights so bright that there was light enough for fighting. In [my brother] Arthur's company there were

five killed and twenty-six wounded. . . . Since the National Guards were divided from the rebels only by the height of the barricades and the thickness of the stones, they were able to hurl insults at them while reloading, and if the weapons of that time had been more accurate and those firing them had had a better eye they would have killed your uncle, for they aimed at him and shouted, 'You there, the little starveling with the pale face! We'll make you a bit paler yet!' They hated him because he was not wearing a uniform and this showed that he was a volunteer. They shouted at Alexandre Maugeret, who was next to him and wore spectacles: 'We'll close all your four eyes for you!' And at M. Berger, the professor of rhetoric who was very big and fat: 'Hey, you, there's enough of you for four bullets!' And at M. Pront, who was very tall and had white hair: 'We'll cut the old one down to size!'

Document Set 22.4 References

A. Heinrich Heine Diagnoses the Dread of the French Bourgeoisie, 1842
Heine, in Geoffrey Bruun, ed., *Revolution and Reaction, 1848–1852* (Princeton, N.J.: D. Van Nostrand, 1958), 108–109.
B. The Liberal Provisional Government of France Decrees the Right to Work, February 25, 1848
French Decrees, in James Harvey Robinson, ed., *Readings in European History* (Boston: Ginn, 1904), 2:560–561.
C. Women Workers Petition the Republic, March 1848
Lettre des coupeuses de poil de lapin à Messieurs les Membres du Gouvernement Provisoire (Paris: Archives Nationales de France, F/12 4898, 1848).
D. Tocqueville Walks Through Paris in February 1848
Alexis de Tocqueville, *Recollections*, J. P. Mayer, trans. (New York: Columbia University Press, 1949), 73–77.
E. On the Barricades: The National Guard and the Workers Fight It Out, June 1848
Mlle. Bary, in G. Daveau, *1848: The Making of a Revolution* (New York: Random House, 1967), 144–145.

DOCUMENT SET 22.5
The Revolution of 1848: Germany

Compare the account of Berlin's March 1848 uprising (Document A) with what you have learned in Set 22.4 of the early stages of the Paris insurrection. And see Document B for the fears and resentments with which German artisans regarded the "creeping capitalism" that was destroying their lives—sentiments voiced at an artisans' congress in the spring of 1848.

A complicating factor faced by the German liberals who attempted to assume power, one which their French opposite-numbers were spared, was nationalist conflict. The Frankfurt Parliament that set about writing a constitution for a united Germany had to contend with clashing German-Danish and German-Polish territorial claims. How one prominent deputy representing Berlin reacted to Polish demands that the future Germany give back territory annexed by Frederick the Great in the partitions of Poland may be grasped from Document C, an extract from the Frankfurt parliamentary journal.

In the end it all failed. Nationalist rivalries did not go away. Social conflicts proved just as implacable as in France, giving the Right its opening to restore order. The king of Prussia refused to become emperor of a united, liberal Germany, scorning "a crown from the gutter" (Document D), Germany would be united under other circumstances.

A. An Eyewitness Describes the Berlin Uprising, March 1848

On Thursday, 16th March, late in the afternoon, I was in the Square in front of the Opera House by the bronze statue of Blücher. Round about stood people talking eagerly. Any one who came along joined one of the groups automatically. The King's promises were eagerly discussed. The news of the revolution in Vienna and of the flight of Metternich encouraged and inflamed opinion among the people. Should Berlin remain behind Vienna and be content with the meagre concessions of the Government? We had no hated Minister who embodied the old system so completely in his own person as Metternich did, and whose dismissal we could demand as a satisfaction for freedom. . . . But they had something before their eyes that continually insulted, injured, and enraged them. 'Away with the soldiers!'—the people concentrated their demands in these words, and the cry grew more and more violent. So it was on that afternoon. . . . The crowd pressed forward, and there was

no obstacle between them and the soldiers. There were not many people shouting out or making an uproar; the great majority were gobemouches and idle spectators. In front there was a struggle. We saw one of the police with the white band on his arm run into the Guard-house. It may be that those who were threatening him wanted to follow him, or that the officer thought himself in danger—there was a short roll of drums and, as no one moved from the spot—a volley. Two were killed and several wounded. Then the horrified people scattered in all directions, yelling, groaning, and cursing. The soldiers did not advance any further. I was driven towards the side of the Prince of Prussia's palace. For although the crowd had taken to flight the crush was very great. When we came to a stand, an old, well-dressed man at my side flung his hat on the ground, either in wrath or in the reactions of fright, and wrung his hands aloft. 'Prussians fire on Prussians,' he cried, and the tears ran down his cheeks. The sight made an indelible impression on me. . . .

The populace had, doubtless, during all these days done many improper things, but when one considered fairly the excitement and restlessness which were so continually renewed by the quick and constant succession of tidings from France, Austria, and all the German cities, it had really committed no deed of violence, no revolutionary breach of the law. The Berlin people had not even yet conceived the idea of a contest with the military. . . . In all the encounters which had hitherto taken place, the only weapons made use of by the rioters were boards from the gutter-crossings and paving-stones from the street. This dominating trait of peaceableness revealed itself on Friday the 17th of March when it was strong enough to restrain every outburst of passion . . ., in spite of the previous day's casualties, which seemed to cry for vengeance, Berlin remained quiet. No gatherings in the streets either by day or night. In out-of-the-way alleys where neither police nor soldiers were to be seen, nothing stirred. No insurrectionary councils were held in church, factory, or beer-house. No suspicious figures either Polish or French were seen distributing five-franc pieces amongst the workers. Berlin was wrapped in the deepest calm. . . .

In the unusually warm and sunny March of that year the 18th was one of the most beautiful days with a sky of cloudless blue and sunshine like May. The citizens of Berlin were making ready between noon and two o'clock to give the King a great demonstration of loyalty on the Castle Square. When the high school classes closed at noon, the town was still intoxicated with joy. Not till three o'clock did I hear in the Rosenthalstrasse, where I was then living, wild shouting, tumult and cries for weapons. The people were rushing to the Haack Market, some terrified, some snorting with fury. The most defiant were brandishing bludgeons, crowbars, or hatchets in their hands. The fateful doings on the Castle Square were recounted with the most fanciful exaggerations: the infantry had shot down and the dragoons sabred the citizens waiting to shout 'Long live the King!' Many were killed and wounded. And to establish the truth of this—who in such an hour would have thought of it? Gusts of panic alternated with bursts of fury. Anger and hate filled all hearts. If the military wanted a fight, now they should have it! . . . Everywhere torn up pavement, gangways lifted from their places, overturned wagons and handcarts! . . .

. . . When dusk set in, the air began to be filled with low wailing and the clang of ringing bells. They sounded from every church all the evening—all through the night. Sometimes there was a short space of silence and then the tocsin began again. From the attic windows in front we could see right away over the Weidendamme Bridge and on the other side to the Linden. The moon shone calm and full in the sky. The greater part of the troops were moving gradually away from our part of the street towards the Halle Gate. . . . But neither in our house nor the next, which we communicated with across a little courtyard wall, was there a single weapon. It was not discipline or courage or clever leadership—it was the unarmed condition of the people which gave the troops the advantage from the very start. On the other hand the populace refused the soldiers any kind of food or drink. . . .

Morning dawned at last; in its early light the troops were withdrawn to barracks and the cannon rolled away from the streets. . . . From the Französischestrasse onwards the pavement of the roadway had been torn up for a great distance. We climbed over the ruins of the first barricade at the Taubenstrasse. I had been under artillery fire. From here on to the Leipzigerstrasse the effects of the fight were seen in the burst and shattered windows, the doors torn off their hinges, the ravaged pavement, the smashed up carriages and omnibuses. The dead and wounded had long before been carried into the houses. There were few people in the street. With wan and distorted faces they talked in low voices to each other of the scenes of terror they had come through. Beyond the Leipzigerstrasse the soldiers had not advanced, and here, towards one in the morning, the lasts shots had been fired. It had taken them almost ten hours to get this length from the Linden. Of their losses nothing was known; regarding their exhaustion, anger and brutality, where they had forced their way into houses, all accounts agreed.

B. The Weavers of Brunswick Protest Against Capitalism

Germans! In complete confidence we turn to you with the request that you consider carefully and act justly. It is too well known to require much explanation that through government blunders and lawlessness the capitalists were permitted to enter our trade at will and to manufacture with the aid of their financial resources the products of our trade, frequently by the use of machinery. They did not care that thousands of shops and families were ruined and thus exposed to want and starvation. Proof of this can be seen in Silesia and Saxony, for after the Silesians were deprived of their bread, were they not fed with grapeshot? Was this then the only salvation of the state existing by the grace of God? It is sad that we have always had such governments, for surely they must have recognized so grave an injustice, and yet they did not act accordingly. . . . Fortunately we Germans have finally put an end to laws which are senseless and harmful to the people. As for the fact that the weaver trade has until now been a free occupation, we must put an end to that too, since from it has certainly sprung the greatest cause of our calamity. The evidence proves it.

C. A German Liberal Nationalist Refuses to Acknowledge Polish Self-Determination

Wilhelm Jordan (Berlin): It were inhuman and barbarous to lock one's breast to all sympathy at the sight of the long passion of such a people, and I am far removed from such want of feeling. But it is one thing to be thrilled by a tragedy, and another to seek as it were to undo the tragedy. . . . To seek to re-establish Poland simply because her fall fills us with well founded grief, that I call a piece of weak-minded sentimentality. (Bravo from the Right, hisses from the Left.) It is a pleasant change for me once in a way to hear this tone from this side of the house. (Laughter.) . . . You say, 'Political sagacity counsels, justice demands, humanity insists on the re-establishment to a free Poland.' . . . We are to declare war against

Russia, in order to wring from Russia the independence of Poland. It is a crusade against Russia that is preached to us. . . . Hatred between nations is a barbarism that is incompatible with the culture of the nineteenth century, is downright nonsense. Certainly, the Russian people are not hateful! . . . Our hatred can only be directed against the system under which Russia groans. . . . I say, 'The policy which calls to us "Set Poland free, cost you what it may!" is a shortsighted policy, a policy of self-forgetfulness, a policy of weakness, a policy of fear, a policy of cowardice.' It is high time for us, once and for all to awake from this dreamy self-forgetfulness, in which we have raved over all possible nationalities, while we ourselves cowered in shameful bondage and were stamped upon by all the world, to awake to a wholesome national egotism, to say the word right out for once, which in every question places the welfare and honour of the fatherland uppermost. I admit without prevarication, our right is none other than the right of the stronger, the right of conquest. Yes, we have made conquests. . . . In the West we have only been conquered; in the East we have had the great misfortune ourselves to make conquests, and thereby have given whole swarms of German poets occasion for moving Jeremiads over the various nationalities which have had to succumb to the pressure of the German race. (Laughter from the Right, hisses from the Left.) Yes, gentlemen, you will perhaps hiss me still more, for I have the courage to set my face against a commonplace over which German Liberals have been fussing for nigh a generation. I have the courage to defend an act of cabinet policy dating from a time when there was no other policy, because the political and national consciousness was astir nowhere but in the brain of Absolutism; yes, I have the courage to tax with ignorance or falsification of history those who regard the partition of Poland in a light so desperately dark, that they have no other designation for it than that of an infamous scandal. (Prolonged hissing from the Left.) . . . Prussia can treat the accusation quite calmly when she is charged with complicity in the murder of a people. She can maintain a proud silence, and allow her work to speak for her; for this affords eloquent testimony that she has worked more effectively for the reanimation, or rather creation, of a new Polish nation than those fine gentlemen who turn up like stormy petrels wherever there is a chance of stirring up a war or an insurrection, in order to win the chance, amid the general shock, of raising a new conflict. . . . I am persuaded that in you the principle still lives: 'Freedom for all, but the strength and welfare of the fatherland above everything!' (Prolonged and tempestuous applause.)

D. Frederick William IV Rejects the German Crown, 1849

To my People:

Taking as a pretense the interests of Germany, the enemies of the fatherland have raised the standard of revolt, first in the neighboring Saxony, then in several districts of south Germany. To my deep chagrin, even in parts of our own land some have permitted themselves to be seduced into following this standard and attempting, in open rebellion against the legal government, to overturn the order of things established by both divine and human sanction. In so serious and dangerous a crisis I am moved publicly to address a word to my people.

I was not able to return a favorable reply to the offer of a crown on the part of the German National Assembly, because the Assembly has not the right, without the consent of the German governments, to bestow the crown which they tendered me, and, moreover, because they offered the crown upon condition that I would accept a constitution which could not be reconciled with the rights and safety of the German states.

I have exhausted every means to reach an understanding with the German National Assembly. . . . Now the Assembly has broken with Prussia. The majority of its members are no longer those men upon whom Germany looked with pride and confidence. The greater part of the deputies voluntarily left the Assembly when they saw that it was on the road to ruin, and yesterday I ordered all the Prussian deputies who had not already withdrawn to be recalled. The other governments will do the same.

A party now dominates the Assembly which is in league with the terrorists. While they urge the unity of Germany as a pretense, they are really fighting the battle of godlessness, perjury, and robbery, and kindling a war against monarchy; but if monarchy were overthrown it would carry with it the blessings of law, liberty, and property. The horrors committed in Dresden, Breslau, and Elberfeld under the banner of German unity afford a melancholy proof of this. New horrors are occurring and are in prospect.

While such crimes have put an end to the hope that the Frankfort Assembly can bring about German unity, I have, with a fidelity and persistence suiting my royal station, never lost hope. My government has taken up with the more important German states the work on the German constitution begun by the Frankfort Assembly. . . .

This is my method. Only madness or deception will dare, in view of these facts, to assert that I have

C. Czech Leader František Palacký Seeks National Self-Determination Within the Habsburg Monarchy

I am unable, gentlemen, to accept your invitation for my own person, nor can I send any other "trustworthy patriot" in my stead. Permit me to give you, as briefly as possible, my reasons.

The object of your assembly is to establish a federation of the German nation in place of the existing federation of princes, to guide the nation to real unity, to strengthen the sentiment of German national consciousness and in this manner expand the power and strength of the German Reich. . . . I am not a German. . . . I am a Czech of Slavonic blood. . . . That nation is a small one, it is true, but from time immemorial it has been a nation by itself and depends upon its own strength. . . . If, . . . anyone asks that, over and above this heretofore existing bond between princes, the Czech nation should now unite with the German nation, that is at the very least a novel demand, devoid of any historical or juridical basis, a demand to which I, so far as I personally am concerned, would not feel justified in acceding until I receive an express and authentic mandate to do so. . . .

The second reason which prevents me from taking part in your deliberations is the fact that, according to all I have so far learnt of your aims and intentions as publicly proclaimed, it is your irrevocable desire and purpose to undermine Austria as an independent empire and indeed to make her impossible for all time to come—an empire whose preservation, integrity and consolidation is, and must be, a great and important matter not only for my nation but also for the whole of Europe, indeed for humanity and civilization itself. . . .

You know that in the Southeast of Europe, along the frontiers of the Russian Empire there live many nations widely differing in origin, in language, in history and in customs—Slavs, Wallachians, Magyars, and Germans, not to speak of Turks and Albanians—none of whom is sufficiently powerful of itself to offer successful defiance to the superior neighbor on the East forever. They could only do so if a close and firm tie bound them all together as one. The vital artery of this necessary union of nations is the Danube. The fulcrum of power of such a union must never be moved from this river if the union is to be effective and to remain so. Assuredly if the Austrian state had not existed for ages it would have been incumbent upon us in the interests of Europe and indeed of humanity to endeavor to create it as soon as possible. . . .

. . . in the unhappy blindness that has long afflicted her, Austria has long failed to recognize the real juridical and moral basis of her existence, and has denied it; the fundamental rule, that is, that all the nationalities and all the religions under her sceptre should enjoy complete equality of rights and respect in common. The rights of nations are in truth the rights of nature. No nation on earth has the right to demand that its neighbors should sacrifice themselves for its benefit, no nation is under an obligation to deny or sacrifice itself for the good of its neighbor. Nature knows neither dominant nor subject nations. If the bond which unites a number of diverse nations in a single political entity is to be firm and enduring, no nation must have cause to fear that the union will cost it any of the things it holds most dear. On the contrary, each must have the certain hope that in the central authority it will find defence and protection against possible violations by neighbors of the principles of equality. Then will every nation do its best to delegate to that central authority such powers as will enable it successfully to provide the aforesaid protection. I am convinced that even now it is not too late for this fundamental rule of justice, this *sacra ancora* for a vessel in danger of foundering, to be publicly and sincerely proclaimed in the Austrian Empire and energetically carried out in all sectors with the consent and support of all. . . .

. . . I must briefly express my conviction that those who ask that Austria, and with her Bohemia should unite on national lines with Germany, are demanding that she should commit suicide—a step lacking either moral or political sense. . . .

D. The Croats Take Vienna, October 31–November 2, 1848

31ST OCTOBER

The night has passed over quietly. No certain information can be obtained respecting the Hungarians until near noon, when the fog has cleared off. The *rappel* [an alarm sounded by drum-beat] is again beaten, and the alarm-bells rung.

A proclamation is issued, signed by Messenhauser and Fenneberg, calling upon the people to lay down their arms, as the Hungarians are defeated. Who has ordered the bells to be rung and the alarm to be beaten? . . .

I again went up the tower of St. Stephen's; there was dreadful confusion. . . . Several now entered the apartment of the watchman's wife, and taking a clean sheet hoisted it in place of a white flag. Soon afterwards came other people, exclaiming that we were all dead men, that the proletarians and military deserters would not allow the white flag to be hoisted, and would butcher all whom they should find on the tower as the perpetrators of the act. We left the tower to take care of itself and repaired to a neighbouring wine-shop. It was awful to hear the crowd under a gateway, amidst scornful laughter and the noise of artillery, shouting the song *Gott exhalte unsern Kaiser* ["God Save Our Emperor," the Habsburg anthem], and in the pauses hooting and uttering the bitterest imprecations on the House of Hapsburg. In the vaulted wine-room, which was lighted with gas, we found a large assemblage of persons. . . . A glass door suddenly opened, and a new guest rushed in, exclaiming, 'The soldiers are here!' There was a deathlike silence: at last a man called out, 'When they come, we shall bid them good-evening.'

. . . On my return across the square 'Am Hofe,' I saw some men of gigantic figure—grenadiers—working with sledge-hammers by torchlight: they had destroyed the lamp-post on which Latour[1] had been hung, and were now working to shatter and root up the stump of the post; close by lay the pile of iron: at every stroke the crowd raised a loud hurrah. All trace of the barbarous act was to be swept from the earth; and yet who knows how many of the very people who now stood by shouting, were equally vociferous at the sight of the murder?

The houses were illuminated up to the fifth story, and everywhere white flags—curtains, sheets, etc.,—were hung out upon poles. Many of the honest citizens had tied white handkerchiefs round their left arms as emblems of peace. They conversed with the soldiers, who were drawn up in all the streets, and I continually heard expressions of compassion when the latter related the hardships they had suffered.

A great body of flames was rising from the Burg,—the library and church of the Augustines were on fire. . . .

I was in a cigar-shop, when a dark-featured soldier entered and demanded cigars; a handful were given him. 'Do you also come from Windischgrätz?' said the shopwoman's little son. '*Nix deutsch!*' ["No speak German"] answered the soldier as he walked away.

'When you grow older, you can also learn Croatian,' said the mother to her boy, who understood nothing of what had passed. Poor child, he will indeed learn it, for from this very evening the word has gone forth, *Nix deutsch!*

Those people in the streets who were able to speak Czechish and Croatian thought themselves lucky, and entered into eager conversation with the soldiers; but as soon as any one began to talk in 'good Viennese,' he received the general answer, *Nix deutsch!*

1st November.
There is quite a new population in the streets, a general unmasking. On every side the little attentions to dress, smart gloves and the like, are again to be seen,—luxuries which for weeks have been wholly unknown; and what a quantity of beards and long locks have fallen since yesterday! The German and Calabrian hats are exchanged for the ordinary, tasteless cylinder.

2nd November.
This afternoon Jellachich entered the city in triumph on his charger, surrounded by his staff, and accompanied by the Sereczans and Red-mantles. The Sereczans kept continually shouting'. 'Vivat, vivat, vivat!' and I am pained to say that the cry was echoed by the people around. The Viennese have learned all kinds of exclamations, Eljen, Zivio, Eviva,[2] etc. . . . Ladies in particular were waving their white handkerchiefs from every window, and saluting Jellachich, who bowed courteously on every side. He is a powerful man, with a countenance that bears the traces of an eventful life. The appearance of the Red-mantles is a mixture of the gipsy and the bandit: they wear a red cap on the head, and a long red cloak reaching nearly to the ground, with a hood of the same colour. A red jacket trimmed with lace, which in the officers' dress is of gold, an ornamental belt round the waist, in which are stuck pistols and a dagger, tight-fitting yellow trousers and red laced boots, compose the costumes of the Sereczans. . . .

The German flag has everywhere disappeared, and the black and yellow [the Habsburg colors] standard floats from St. Stephen's tower. No one passes without looking up at it, and many appear to regard this as the hardest measure Windischgrätz has inflicted on them: they loved the German colours though they were unable to stand by them. The statue of the Emperor Joseph, whose hand was the last to part with the German flag, now holds a black and yellow one in its place.

---

[1] The Habsburg minister brutally lynched by the Viennese in September 1848

[2] Shouts of triumph in Hungarian, Serbo-Croatian, and Italian

ourselves suddenly transferred to the year 1800, with all our habits, expectations, requirements, and standard of living formed upon the luxuries and appliances collected round us in 1850. In the first year of the century we should find ourselves eating bread at 1s. 10 1/2d. the quartern [four pound] loaf, and those who could not afford this price driven to short commons, to entire abstinence, or to some miserable substitute. We should find ourselves grumbling at heavy taxes laid on nearly all the necessaries and luxuries of life. . . . receiving our Edinburgh letters in London a week after they were written, and paying thirteen pence-halfpenny for them when delivered, exchanging the instantaneous telegraph for the slow and costly express by chaise and pair; . . . and relapsing from the blaze of light which gas now pours along our streets, into a perilous and uncomfortable darkness made visible by a few wretched oil lamps scattered at distant intervals.

But these would by no means comprise the sum total, nor the worst part, of the descent into barbarism. We should find our criminal law in a state worthy of Draco; executions taking place by the dozen; the stealing of five shillings punishable and punished as severely as rape or murder; slavery and the slave trade flourishing in their palmiest atrocity. We should find the liberty of the subject at the lowest ebb; freedom of discussion and writing always in fear and frequently in jeopardy; religious rights trampled under foot; Catholics, slaves and not citizens; Dissenters still disabled and despised. Parliament was unreformed; public jobbing flagrant and shameless; gentlemen drank a bottle where they now drink a glass, and measured their capacity by their cups; and the temperance medal was a thing undreamed of. Finally, the *people* in those days were little thought of, where they are now the main topic of discourse and statesmanship; steamboats were unknown, and a voyage to America occupied eight weeks instead of ten days; and while in 1850, a population of nearly 30,000,000 paid £50,000,000 of taxes, in 1801 a population of 15,000,000 paid no less than £63,000,000.

We have ample means of showing by indisputable facts that wealth has been *diffused* as well as increased during the period under review; that so far from "the rich having become richer and the poor poorer," as is so often and so inconsiderately asserted, the middle classes have advanced faster than the great, and the command over the comforts and luxuries of life, even among peasants and artisans, is far greater now than at any former period. . . .

In the first place let us look at the savings banks, which are entirely the growth of this century, the first having been established about 1806, and which are confined to the savings of the peasant and artisan class, of domestic servants, and of the humbler portion of the middle class. . . .

Let us now collect together a few facts showing the increase in the consumption of those articles of necessity, or luxury, which are used indiscriminately *among all classes.*

We have no means of comparing the amount of butchers' meat consumed now with that consumed at the beginning of the century, but the price we know has fallen from 5s.8d. to 3s.4d. a stone. . . . During the latter part of the 18th century rye and barley bread were very extensively used in many parts of England, the former being . . . the habitual food of one-seventh of the population; it is now unknown, except in Durham, while the use of wheaten bread is almost universal among the poorer classes.

In the use of coffee, tea, and sugar also, a marked advance has taken place. . . .

The truth is, that the relief to the population generally, and to the working classes especially, which has been given by the remission of taxation, has been something quite unprecedented. . . . If a poor man is content to live, as wise and great men have often thought it well to live, in health and comfort, but with strict frugality . . . he may escape taxation almost entirely. . . .

In no one point is the half-century we have just closed more distinguished from its predecessors than in the share of PUBLIC ATTENTION AND SYMPATHY WHICH THE CONDITION OF THE POORER CLASSES HAS OBTAINED. Formerly the lower orders were regarded, even by the kindly disposed, simply as hewers of wood and drawers of water. . . . The idea of studying them, of raising them, of investigating into the operation of the causes which affected them for good or evil, had scarcely taken rise. There was kindness, there was charity, there was sympathy toward the poor as *individuals,* but not any interest in their conditions as a class. We are far from considering the multiplication of charitable institutions as a . . . source of unalloyed good to the indigent and industrious of the community, but it at least shows the increase of sympathy towards them on the part of the rich. . . . In the metropolis alone the charitable institutions reach 491 in number, and have an annual income of £1,765,000. Of those 109 were established in the last, and no less than 294 in the present century.

But a far stronger proof of the general interest now taken in the working classes, is to be found in the various commissions that have of late years been issued to inquire into the state of the people in various occupations. Wherever there was a rumor of an abuse, a tyranny, or an injustice, a representation was made in Parliament, and an investigation immediately took place. We have had a factory commission, a children's employment commission, a commission to inquire into the condition of those employed in mines and manufactures, and a commission to inquire into the employment of women and children in agriculture. We have had inspectors of mines and inspectors of factories appointed. . . .

On the novel and extraordinary attention which is now being paid to SANITARY MATTERS we can look with . . . unmingled satisfaction. . . . Our progress since 1800 has been far from contemptible. The population is less crowded than it was, and roomier dwellings are constantly in process of erection. The average number of individuals in a house which was 5.67 in 1801 had fallen to 5.44 in 1841; and the census which is to be taken this year, will, we have no doubt, show a still further diminution. . . . Many removable causes of premature death yet remain, but the four or five years which the last half-century has added to the average duration of life are a hopeful earnest of what may yet be done to prolong it, now that the subject has awakened public interest, and that administrative exertions are conducted under the guidance of scientific skill.

We hope we [have] succeeded in satisfying those who [have] followed our facts and figures that the national advance in wealth and all the material appliances of civilization . . . has not been turned solely to the benefit of the more favored children of fortune, but that all classes of the community, the humbler as well as the richer, have participated in the blessings of the change. Indeed, it scarcely could be otherwise. The cheapness of the necessaries and of the commoner, and therefore more indispensable comforts of daily life, *must* redound more especially to the advantage of those whose income is most exclusively devoted to the purchase of those needful articles. A reduction in the price of bread, meat, coffee, sugar, and calico, affects the comforts of the poor man far more immediately and extensively than that of the rich or the easy classes. . . . The only way in which our conclusion could be shown to be erroneous, would be by proving that the wages of labor had fallen to an equal or a greater ratio; but this, it is well know, is far from having been generally the case. . . . While unquestionably wages have fallen considerably in a few departments of industry, this fall has been confined to those departments in which a change in the machinery employed has taken place, and in which the artisans have obstinately refused to accommodate themselves to the new state of things, and have continued to overstock an impoverished and

doomed employment, as in the case of plain handloom weaving; or to those where senseless *strikes* have introduced supernumerary hands or new mechanism into the trade, as in the cases of coarse cotton spinners and of the London tailors; or to those where the easiness and collateral conveniences of the occupation have attracted to it excessive numbers, as in the case of needlework. In these branches wages have undoubtedly fallen, and the hours of work have become in some instances longer; but the general tendency in most departments of industry has been the reverse;—a desire for shorter hours has been of late rapidly spreading. The hours of labor in factories have been reduced for adults from 74 to 60 a week, and for children from 72 to 40, shops are beginning to be closed much earlier, and great, and in some cases already successful, efforts are making to secure a weekly half-holiday for the generality of tradespeople. All these, where not pursued by illegitimate means, are steps in the right direction. . . .

[He praises the development of steam ocean transport.] But this advance is nothing compared to that which has taken place in LOCOMOTION BY LAND within the last twenty years. It is here that our progress has been most stupendous—surpassing all previous steps since the creation of the human race. . . . At the period at which we write, the whole of England is traversed by almost countless railways in every direction. . . . In 1850, [the normal speed of transportation] is habitually forty miles an hour, and *seventy* for those who like it. We have reached in a single bound from the speed of a horse's canter, to the utmost speed comparable with the known strength and coherence of brass and iron.

Now, who have specially benefited by this vast invention? The rich, whose horses and carriages carried them in comfort over the known world?—the middle classes to whom stage coaches and mails were an accessible mode of conveyance?—or the poor, whom the cost of locomotion condemned often to an almost vegetable existence? Clearly the latter. The railroad is the Magna Charter [sic] of their motive freedom. How few among the last generation ever stirred beyond their own village? How few among the present will die without visiting London? . . .

But even the rapid augmentation of our locomotive speed shrinks into nothing when compared to that which has taken place in the last five years in the transmission of intelligence. . . . In 1850, for a sum varying from 5s. to 12s. 6d., any private individual may send a message or summon a friend [by telegraph], the distance of many hundred miles in a space of time reckoned by seconds rather than by minutes. . . .

I concede, nevertheless, that, like the Emperor, I have many conquests to make. I would, like him, conquer, for the sake of harmony, the warring parties and bring into the great popular current the wasteful and conflicting eddies. I would conquer, for the sake of religion, morality, and material ease, that portion of the population, still very numerous, which, in the midst of a country of faith and belief, hardly knows the precepts of Christ; which, in the midst of the most fertile country of the world, is hardly able to enjoy the primary necessities of life. We have immense uncultivated districts to bring under cultivation, roads to open, harbors to construct, rivers to render navigable, canals to finish, and our network of railroads to bring to completion. . . .

This is what I understand by the empire, if the empire is to be reëstablished. These are the conquests which I contemplate, and all of you who surround me, who, like myself, wish the good of our common country, you are my soldiers.

C. Karl Marx Sardonically Dissects *The Eighteenth Brumaire of Louis Bonaparte*

Hegel remarks somewhere that all great, world-historical facts and personages occur, as it were, twice. He has forgotten to add: the first time as tragedy, the second as farce. Caussidière for Danton, Louis Blanc for Robespierre, the Mountain of 1848 to 1851 for the Mountain of 1793 to 1795, the Nephew for the Uncle. And the same caricature occurs in the circumstances in which the second edition of the Eighteenth Brumaire is taking place.

Men make their own history, but they do not make it just as they please; they do not make it under circumstances chosen by themselves, but under circumstances directly found, given and transmitted from the past. The tradition of all the dead generations weighs like a nightmare on the brain of the living. And just when they seem engaged in revolutionising themselves and things, in creating something entirely new, precisely in such epochs of revolutionary crisis they anxiously conjure up the spirits of the past to their service and borrow from them names, battle slogans and costumes in order to present the new scene of world history in this time-honoured disguise and this borrowed language. Thus Luther donned the mask of the Apostle Paul, the Revolution of 1789 to 1814 draped itself alternately as the Roman Republic and the Roman Empire, and the Revolution of 1848 knew nothing better to do than to parody, in turn, 1789 and the revolutionary tradition of 1793 to 1795. In like manner the beginner who has learnt a new language always translates it back into his mother tongue, but he has assimilated the spirit of the new language and can produce freely in it only when he moves in it without remembering the old and forgets in it his ancestral tongue. . . .

The February Revolution was a sudden attack, a taking of the old society by surprise, and the people proclaimed this unhoped for stroke as a world-historical deed, opening the new epoch. On December 2 the February Revolution is conjured away by a card-sharper's trick, and what seems overthrown is no longer the monarchy; it is the liberal concessions that were wrung from it by century-long struggles. Instead of *society* having conquered a new content for itself, the state only appears to have returned to its oldest form, to the shamelessly simple domination of the sabre and the cowl. . . .

Let us recapitulate in their general outlines the phases that the French Revolution has gone through from February 24, 1848, to December 1851. . . .

It could not be otherwise. The February days originally intended an electoral reform, by which the circle of the politically privileged among the possessing class itself was to be widened and the exclusive domination of the aristocracy of finance overthrown. When it came to the actual conflict, however, when the people mounted the barricades, the National Guard maintained a passive attitude, the army offered no serious resistance and the monarchy ran away, the republic appeared to be a matter of course. Every party construed it in its own sense. Having been won by the proletariat by force of arms, the proletariat impressed its stamp on it and proclaimed it to be a social republic. . . .

During the June days all classes and parties had united in the *party of order* against the proletarian class as the *party of anarchy*, of socialism, of communism. They had "saved" society from "*the enemies of society.*" They had given out the watchwords of the old society, "*property, family, religion, order,*" to their army as pass words and proclaimed to the counter-revolutionary crusaders: "In this sign you will conquer!" From that moment, as soon as one of the numerous parties which had gathered under this sign against the June insurgents seeks to hold the revolutionary battle field in its own interests, it goes down before the cry: "Property, family, religion, order." . . .

The history of the *Constituent National Assembly* since the June days is the *history of the domination and the liquidation of the republican section of the bourgeoisie,* of that section which is known by the names of tricolour republicans, pure republicans, political republicans, formalist republicans, etc. . . .

The republican bourgeois section, which had long regarded itself as the legitimate heir of the July monarchy, thus found itself successful beyond its hopes; it attained power, however, not as it had dreamed under Louis Philippe, through a liberal revolt of the bourgeoisie against the throne, but through a rising of the proletariat against capital, a rising laid low with grape-shot. What it had pictured to itself as the *most revolutionary* happening, turned out in reality to be the *most counter-revolutionary.* The fruit fell into its lap, but it fell from the tree of knowledge, not from the tree of life.

The exclusive *rule of the bourgeois republicans lasted* only from June 24 to December 10, 1848. It is summed up the *drafting of a republican Constitution* and in the *state of siege of Paris.* . . .

I have worked out elsewhere the significance of the election of December 10. I will not revert to it here. It is sufficient to remark here that it was a *reaction of the peasants,* who had had to pay the costs of the February Revolution, against the remaining classes of the nation, a *reaction of the countryside against the town.* It met with great approval in the army, for which the republicans of the *National* had provided neither glory nor additional pay, among the big bourgeoisie, which hailed Bonaparte as a bridge to monarchy; among the proletarians and petty bourgeois, who hailed him as a scourge for Cavaignac [the general who had crushed the workers' uprising in June 1848]. I shall have an opportunity later of going more closely into the relationship of the peasants to the French Revolution.

The period from December 20, 1848, until the dissolution of the Constituent Assembly in May, 1849, comprises the history of the downfall of the bourgeois republicans. After having founded a republic for the bourgeoisie, driven the revolutionary proletariat out of the field and reduced the democratic petty bourgeoisie to silence for the time being, they are themselves thrust aside by the mass of the bourgeoisie, which justly impounds this republic as *its property.* This bourgeois mass was, however, *royalist.* . . .

Before we finish with this period we must still cast a retrospective glance at the two powers, one of which annihilates the other on December 2, 1851, whereas from December 10, 1848, until the exit of the Constituent Assembly they lived in conjugal relations. We mean Louis Bonaparte, on the one hand, and the party of the royalist coalition, the Party of Order, of the big bourgeoisie, on the other. On his entry into the presidency, Bonaparte at once formed a ministry of the Party of Order, at the head of which he placed Odilon Barrot, the old leader, *nota bene,* of the most liberal section of the parliamentary bourgeoisie. . . .

Document Set 22.8 References

A. Louis Napoleon Bonaparte Runs for President, November 1848
   Louis Napoleon, Campaign Statement, in James Harvey Robinson, ed., *Readings in European History* (Boston: Ginn, 1904), 2:562–563.
B. Emperor-to-be Napoleon III Promises Peace and Prosperity, November 1852
   Louis Napoleon's Bordeaux Address, in Robinson, 2:563–564.
C. Karl Marx Sardonically Dissects *The Eighteenth Brumaire of Louis Bonaparte*
   Karl Marx, *The Eighteenth Brumaire of Louis Bonaparte* (New York: International Publishers, n.d.), 13, 16, 18–19, 22, 23, 25, 31, 32.

C. Garibaldi and Victor Emanuel Meet, 1861

26 October

My head is in a whirl. I'm still full of what I have seen, and I write. . . .

A white house at a cross-roads, horsemen in red and horsemen in black mingled together, Garibaldi on foot; poplar trees shedding their pale dead leaves over the heads of regulars marching towards Teano. With my eyes I see the living soldiers, but in my imagination the great dead Romans of the second civil war, Sulla and Sertorius, who met at this very spot. Their figures loom gigantic as the mountains of Samnium in the distance, but perhaps they were really no bigger than the living men I see before me. What elements are lacking to bring about another civil war [between monarchists and republicans]?

All of a sudden, quite near, there is a roll of drums and the royal fanfare of Piedmont. All leap on their horses. At that moment a peasant, but half-clothed in skins, turned towards the Venafro mountains and, shading his eyes with his hand, stared hard, perhaps to read the time from some shadow cast by distant crags. Then, a cloud of dust swirled up, there was galloping and shouted commands and then: '*Viva! Viva! The King! The King!*'

Everything went black for an instant and I could hardly see Garibaldi and Victor Emmanuel clasp hands or hear the immortal greeting: 'Hail, to the King of Italy!' It was midmorning, Garibaldi talked with bare head, while the King stroked the neck of his handsome grey horse who arched her neck under his caresses like an Arab princess. Perhaps Garibaldi felt sad, for he looked sad as Victor Emmanuel spurred his horse and rode away with himself on the King's left. Behind them followed a very large mixed cavalcade. Garibaldi's charger, Saïd, perhaps felt his master less masterful in the saddle, for he snorted and pulled to the side as though he wanted to carry him away into the desert, away to the Pampas, far away from this procession of Great Ones.

27 October

If rumour is right everything is understandable. Was King Victor cold in his attitude when he met Garibaldi? True it is that Francis II is his cousin and that he had invited him to join in his great war against the enemies of Italy and that he had admonished him. Also there exists a certain letter! Francis wouldn't or couldn't heed and it was fortunate for Italy that he refused. He was as obstinate and impotent as his father and he now pays the price for both of them.

Perhaps then a certain aloof dignity of Victor Emmanuel's when he met Garibaldi was due to delicate reserve? Or are those right who think he was meditating on the strange fate of kings? However, all this is only gossip, which will pass as the wind passes without trace. Up to now one hears nothing but of the greatness of Garibaldi and knows nothing of those watching for the sun that is yet to rise.

D. The Neapolitans Have Second Thoughts About Unification, 1862

Neapolitans have now accepted, quite rightly, that administrative reforms must be postponed a little. Italy still has no real capital, no proper frontier to the northeast, and is still occupied in part by an enemy Power; hence national unity must come first. Progressive reforms will follow, as indeed was implied in the government's acceptance of the plebiscite in southern Italy; but first the government must be helped to make the nation.

Patriotism, which many would say was the highest ideal of all, comes absolutely new to most Neapolitans. Former governments carefully fostered a local loyalty and increased the general antagonism between north and south. It was this selfish isolation, practiced by Italian rulers who lived under Austrian protection, which largely explains how Austria managed to dissolve the common front and end the revolution of 1848–9. Only five years ago, if I asked someone if he was an Italian, he would answer: "No, I am a Neapolitan"; and, apart from Neapolitans, also Calabrians and Sicilians each thought of themselves as quite separate peoples. Even though these southern provinces belonged to a single kingdom, they contained a veritable Babel of different *patois*.

Today things have changed. You will now be answered: "I am an Italian from Naples"—or from Messina, Brindisi, or Maida. Everyone is now an Italian and feels it. In 1860, after Garibaldi's arrival at Naples, people at first saw in him just a new, easier master replacing the old; and many of the common people would cry "Long live united Italy," and then ask us "What is *Italy,* and what does *united* mean?" But during May and June of this year, 1862, I have spoken to many people—sailors, peasants, and those delightful layabouts who would now be humiliated to be called *lazzaroni*—and all of them know about Italian unity. They speak about it together, and think of Rome. About Venice they say that "it is at the other end, as it were, the Reggio of northern Italy." Anyone who knows Neapolitans, and who remembers how indifferent they used to be to everything, will recognize that a striking progress has been made.

E. Feminist Anna Mozzoni Considers Women's Place in United Italy, 1864

The revision of the Civil Code by the Italian Parliament has placed in my mind the following argument: woman, excluded by worn out customs from the councils of state, has always submitted to the law without participating in the making of it, has always contributed her resources and work to the public good and always without any reward.

For her, taxes but not an education; for her, sacrifices but not employment; for her, strict virtue but not honor; for her, the struggle to maintain the family but not even control of her own person; for her, the capacity to be punished but not the right to be independent; strong enough to be laden with an array of painful duties, but sufficiently weak not to be allowed to govern herself.

I begin with the principles that all rights and all duties have as their foundation and rationale to serve as the force which gives the conscience its ostensible legitimacy. This principle holds for each human being of whatever sex and I do not see for what reason this faculty should be in one case exercised freely and sometimes with force and in the other case buried and entirely suffocated. This occurs so much that in the miserable conditions in which society has cast her, woman, deprived of half her wealth, weakened because of the degrading work actually given her, finds herself dragged down to the fatal necessity to destroy herself through trade in her unhappy body.

Humanity and the nation, civilization and morality, need women on their side.

Document Set 23.1 References

A. An Italian Noblewoman Expresses Her Liberal Nationalism, 1850
Nassau William Senior, *Journals Kept in France and Italy from 1848 to 1852* (London: 1871), 2:289–292.
B. Garibaldi Describes His Invasion of Sicily, 1860
Guiseppe Garibaldi, *Memoirs,* in James Harvey Robinson and Charles Beard, eds., *Readings in Modern European History* (Boston: Ginn, 1909), 2:126–127.
C. Garibaldi and Victor Emanuel Meet, 1861
G. C. Abba, *The Diary of One of Garibaldi's Thousand,* E. R. Vincent, trans. (Westport, Conn.: Greenwood, 1962), 160–161.
D. The Neapolitans Have Second Thoughts About Unification, 1862
Maxime du Camp, *Revue des Deux Mondes,* in Denis Mack Smith, ed., *The Making of Italy, 1796–1870* (New York: Harper and Row, 1968), 368.
E. Feminist Anna Mozzoni Considers Women's Place in United Italy, 1864
Adapted from Mozzoni, *La Liberazione Della Donna,* ed. Franca Pieroni Bartolotti (Milan: G. Mazzotta, 1975), 34, 57–58, in Bonnie Smith, *Changing Lives: Women in European History Since 1700* (Lexington, Mass.: D. C. Heath, 1989), 257.

In the aftermath of 1848, Prussian conservatives thought they saw an opportunity to capitalize on the antagonism between workers and industrialists by winning the former's support for a program of neo-absolutism (Document A). But as the decade of the 1850s wore on and industrialization advanced despite conservative qualms, the need arose for some other strategy to balance Prussian pre-eminence with German nationalism. Otto von Bismarck (1815–1898) ruthlessly accomplished that feat, not according to some preconceived plan but through brilliant improvisation—overpowering the Prussian liberals, browbeating his king, provoking wars with Denmark, Austria, and France, finding allies when he could, and dropping them whenever necessary. His letters to his wife (Document B) reveal his literary flair and mental convolutions, and his recollections of how he had constantly to overcome the scruples of King William I (Document C) are a reminder of how precarious is the fit among image, myth, and historical truth.

Until Bismarck destroyed Second-Empire France in 1870, the chief loser in the struggle to reorganize Central Europe was the Habsburg monarchy. Yet both Bismarck and the Magyar nationalists found it advantageous to allow Austria to reorganize and remain a great power. How difficult it still was to govern the hybrid new state is suggested by the text of the *Ausgleich* (Agreement) of 1867, creating the Austro-Hungarian dual monarchy (Document D).

The German word *Realpolitik* has become lodged in the English vocabulary to describe the pursuit of political objectives by unsentimental, realistic, and pragmatic policies. Consulting *The Challenge of the West* as a resource, use the documents of sets 23.1 and 23.2 to analyze the context of Realpolitik in the reorganizing of Germany and Italy in the 1850s and 1860s.

A. The Conservative Prussian Popular Union Bids for Working-Class Support Against the Liberals, 1861

Protection and esteem for honest labor, for every property, right, and estate. No favor and exclusive domination for capital. No surrender of handicraft and landed property to the false teachings and usurious artifices of the times. Freedom through the participation of the subject in legislation and through the autonomy and self-government of corporations and communities. Freedom through the maintenance of the protective order. No turn to bureaucratic absolutism and social servitude as the result of an unrestrained and licentious anarchy, and no imitation of the political and social institutions which have led France to Caesarism. Development of our constitution in the spirit of German freedom, in love and devotion to king and fatherland.

B. Bismarck Writes Candidly to His Wife and Sister

Half an hour ago a cabinet courier woke me with war and peace. Our policy drifts more and more into the Austrian wake; and when we have once fired a shot on the Rhine, it is over with the Italian-Austrian war, and in its place a Prussian-French comes on the scene, in which Austria, after we have taken the burden from her shoulders, stands by us, or fails to stand by us just so far as her own interests require. She will certainly not allow us to play a very brilliant victor's part.

As God wills! After all, everything here is only a question of time, nations and individuals, folly and wisdom, war and peace; they come and go like the waves, but the sea remains. There is nothing on this earth but hypocrisy and jugglery; and whether fever or grapeshot tear off this fleshly mask, a likeness will, after all, turn up between a Prussian and an Austrian, which will make it difficult to distinguish them. The stupid, and the clever too, look pretty much alike when their bones are well picked. With such views, a man certainly gets rid of his specific patriotism.

C. Bismarck Stiffens the King's Resolve, 1863

In the beginning of October [1863] I went as far as Jüterbogk [a town south of Berlin] to meet the King, who had been at Baden-Baden for September 30, his wife's birthday, and waited for him in the still unfinished railway station, filled with third-class travellers and workmen, seated in the dark on an overturned wheelbarrow. My object in taking this opportunity for an interview was to set his Majesty at rest about a speech made by me in the Budget Commission on September 30, which had aroused some excitement, and which, though not taken down in shorthand, had still been reproduced with tolerable accuracy in the newspapers.

For people who were less embittered and blinded by ambition, I had indicated plainly enough the direction in which I was going. Prussia—such was the point of my speech—as a glance at the map will show, could no longer wear unaided on its long narrow figure the panoply which Germany required for its security; that must be equally distributed over all German peoples. We should get no nearer the goal by speeches, associations, decisions of majorities; we should be unable to avoid a serious contest, a contest which could only be settled by blood and iron. In order to secure our success in this, the deputies must place the greatest possible weight of blood and iron in the hands of the King of Prussia, in order that according to his judgment he might throw it into one scale or the other. I had already given expression to the same idea in the House of Deputies in 1849, in answer to Schramm on the occasion of an amnesty debate.

Roon [the minister of war], who was present, expressed his dissatisfaction with my remarks on our way home, and said, among other things, that he did not regard these 'witty digressions' as advantageous for our cause. For my part, I was torn between the desire of winning over members to an energetic national policy, and the danger of inspiring the King, whose own disposition was cautious, and shrank from violent measures, with mistrust in me and my intentions. My object in going to meet him at Jüterbogk was to counteract betimes the probable effect of press criticisms.

I had some difficulty in discovering from the curt answers of the officials the carriage in the ordinary train, in which the King was seated by himself in an ordinary first-class carriage. The after-effect of his intercourse with his wife was an obvious depression, and when I begged for permission to narrate the events which had occurred during his absence, he interrupted me with the words: 'I can perfectly well see where all this will end. Over there, in front of the Opera House, under my windows, they will cut off your head, and mine a little while afterwards.'

I guessed, and it was afterwards confirmed by witnesses, that during his week's stay in Baden his mind had been worked upon with variations in the theme of Polignac, Strafford, and Lewis XVI. When he was silent, I answered with the short remark, '*Et après, Sire.*' '*Après*, indeed; we shall be dead,' answered the King. 'Yes,' I continued, 'then we shall be dead; but we must all die sooner or later, and can we perish more honourably? I, fighting for my King's cause, and your Majesty sealing with your own blood your rights as King by the grace of God; whether on the scaffold or the battlefield, makes no difference to the glory of sacrificing life and limb for the rights assigned to you by the grace of God. Your Majesty must not think of Lewis XVI; he lived and died in a condition of mental weakness, and does not present a heroic figure in history. Charles I, on the other hand, will always remain a noble historical character, for after drawing his sword for his rights and losing the battle, he did not hesitate to confirm his royal intent with his blood. Your Majesty is bound to fight, you cannot capitulate; you must, even at the risk of bodily danger, go fourth to meet any attempt at coercion.'

As I continued to speak in this sense, the King grew more and more animated, and began to assume the part of an officer fighting for kingdom and fatherland. In presence of external and personal danger he possessed a rare and absolutely natural fearlessness, whether on the field of battle or in the face of attempts on his life; his attitude in any external danger was elevating and inspiring. The ideal type of the Prussian officer who goes to meet certain death in the service with the simple words, 'At your orders,' but who, if he has to act on his own responsibility, dreads the criticism of his superior officer or of the world more than death, even to the extent of allowing his energy and correct judgment to be impaired by the fear of blame and reproof—this type was developed in him to the highest degree. Hitherto, on his journey, he had only asked himself whether, under the superior criticism of his wife and public opinion in Prussia, he would be able to keep steadfast on the road on which he was entering with me. The influence of our conversation in the dark railway compartment counteracted this sufficiently to make him regard the part which the situation forced upon him more from the standpoint of the officer. He felt as though he had been touched in his military honour, and was in the position of an officer who has orders to hold a certain position to the death, no matter whether he perishes in the task or not. This set him on a course of thought which was quite familiar to him; and in a few minutes he was restored to the confidence which he had lost at Baden, and even recovered his cheerfulness. To give up his life for King and Fatherland was the duty of an officer; still more that of a King, as the first officer in the land. As soon as he regarded his position from the point of view of military honour, it had no more terror for him than the command to defend what might prove a desperate position would have for any ordinary Prussian officer. This raised him above the anxiety about the criticism which public opinion, history, and his wife might pass on his political tactics. He fully entered into the part of the first officer in the Prussian monarchy, for whom death in the service would be an honourable conclusion to the task assigned him. The correctness of my judgment was confirmed by the fact that the King, whom I had found at Jüterbogk weary, depressed, and discouraged, had, even before we arrived at Berlin, developed a cheerful, I might almost say joyous and combative disposition, which was plainly evident to the ministers and officials who received him on his arrival. . . .

D. Austria and Hungary Strike a Compromise, 1867

Article 1. The following affairs are declared common to Austria and Hungary:

a. Foreign affairs, including diplomatic and commercial representation abroad, as well as measures relating to international treaties, reserving the right of the representative bodies of both parts of the empire [Reichsrat and Hungarian Diet] to approve such treaties, in so far as such approval is required by the Constitution.

b. Military and naval affairs. . . .

c. The finances, with reference to matters of common expense. . . .

Article 2. Besides these, the following affairs shall not indeed be administered in common, but shall be regulated upon uniform principles to be agreed upon from time to time:

1. Commercial affairs. . . .

2. Legislation concerning indirect taxes which stand in close relation to industrial production.

3. The establishment of a monetary system and monetary standards.

4. Regulations concerning railway lines which affect the interests of both parts of the empire.

5. The establishment of a system of defense.

Article 3. The expenses of affairs common to both Austria and Hungary shall be borne by the two parts of the empire in proportion to be fixed from time to time by an agreement between the two legislative bodies (Reichsrat and Diet), approved by the emperor. If an agreement can not be reached between the two representative bodies, the proportion shall be fixed by the emperor, but for the term of one year only. The method of defraying its quota of the common expense shall belong exclusively to each of the parts of the empire.

Nevertheless, joint loans may be made for affairs of common interest. . . .

The decision as to whether a joint loan shall be made is reserved for legislation by each of the two parts of the empire.

Article 4. The contribution towards the expense of the present public debt shall be determined by an agreement between the two parts of the empire.

Article 5. The administration of common affairs shall be conducted by a joint responsible ministry, which is forbidden to direct at the same time the administration of joint affairs and those of either part of the empire.

The regulation of the management, conduct, and internal organization of the joint army shall belong exclusively to the emperor.

Article 6. The legislative power belongings to the legislative bodies of each of the two parts of the empire [Reichsrat and Hungarian Diet] shall be exercised by them, in so far as it relates to joint affairs, by means of delegations. . . .

Article 11. The delegations shall be convened annually by the emperor, who shall determine the place of their meeting. . . .

Article 13. The powers of the delegations shall extend to all matters concerning common affairs.

All other matters shall be beyond their power.

Article 14. The projects of the government shall be submitted by the joint ministry to each of the delegations separately.

Each delegation shall also have the right to submit projects concerning affairs which are within its competence.

Article 15. For the passage of a law concerning matters within the power of the delegations the agreement of both delegations shall be necessary, or in default of such agreement, a vote of the full assembly of the two delegations sitting together; in either case the approval of the emperor shall be necessary.

Article 16. The right to hold the joint ministry to its responsibility shall be exercised by the delegations. . . .

Article 19. Each delegation shall act, deliberate and vote in separate session. . . .

Article 21. The delegates and substitutes from the Reichsrat shall receive no instructions from their electors. . . .

Article 27. The session of the delegation shall be closed, after the completion of its work, by the president with the consent of the emperor or by his order.

Article 29. The sessions of the delegation shall be as a rule public.

Exceptionally the public may be excluded if it is so decided by the assembly in secret session, upon the request of the president or of not less than five members.

Every decision, however, shall be made in public session. . . .

Document Set 23.2 References

A. The Conservative Prussian Popular Union Bids for Working-Class Support Against the Liberals, 1861
The Prussian Popular Union, in Theodore S. Hamerow, *Restoration, Revolution, Reaction: Economics and Politics in Germany, 1815–1871* (Princeton, N.J.: Princeton University Press, 1966), 246.

B. Bismarck Writes Candidly to His Wife and Sister
Otto von Bismarck, *Prince Bismarck's Letters to His Wife, His Sister, and Others,* Fitzhugh Maxse, trans. (New York: Scribner, 1878), 131–132.

C. Bismarck Stiffens the King's Resolve, 1863
Otto von Bismarck, *Memoirs,* A. J. Butler, trans. (New York: Howard Fertig, 1966), 1:312–316.

D. Austria and Hungary Strike a Compromise, 1867
Austrian Law, in Herbert F. Wright, ed., *The Constitution of the States at War, 1914–1918* (Washington, D.C.: Government Printing Office, 1919), 4–10.

DOCUMENT SET 23.3
Currents of Reform: Russia

Serfdom by the nineteenth century had become the bane of Russia's existence: a drag on economic modernization and an ever-present powder-keg ready to blow society apart in a popular revolution, yet essential to support the nobility on which the tsarist autocracy depended in turn. The government faced the delicate problems of abolishing serfdom without relinquishing control over the unpredictable peasant masses or impoverishing its ruling class. Meanwhile, young people of relatively privileged birth and education tried to survive in a society too backward to afford opportunities routinely open to Westerners. The result was a world familiar to readers of the great nineteenth-century Russian social novel: wonderful talkers, unable to do much to infuse their lives in society with justice and purpose. Artistically undistinguished, Nikolai Gavrilovich Chernyshevsky's (1828–1889) novel *What Is To Be Done?* (1864) impressed several generations of Russians with the earnestness of its high-minded young characters debating how they should lead better lives than autocratic Russia made possible. In the scene quoted in Document A, one of the heroes opens by telling Vera, his partner in a "phony marriage," about his plans to support her. *Fathers and Sons* (or, more accurately translated, *Fathers and Children*), the 1862 novel of the incomparably more gifted Ivan Turgenev (1818–1883), outraged both conservatives and radicals with its picture of the "nihilist" hero Bazarov, a medical student who rejects the idealism of an older generation of well-born "Westernizers" for the sake of unsentimental service to the people (Document B).

One of Russia's idealistic men of principle—and Turgenev's friend—Alexander Herzen (1812–1870), a nobleman's illegitimate son, lived much of his life in Western exile, from which vantage point he published an "underground" newspaper that even the tsar relied upon for accurate information. Herzen tried as well to interpret Russian society to puzzled Westerners. Document C shows how he responded to the French historian Jules Michelet's condemnation of Russia (characteristic of Western liberals and radicals) as a dark land of unenlightened despotism; note Herzen's sympathetic attempt to understand the peasant mentality.

When the abolition of serfdom finally came, it was by fiat from above; Tsar Alexander II (*1856–1881) made it clear in 1861 that Russia could avoid rural revolution only by taking this plunge (Document D).

Yet the terms of emancipation deeply disappointed the peasantry, as can be seen from an 1862 peasant petition from the Volga region to the relatively liberal Grand Duke Konstantin Nikolaevich (Document E).

Life went on. Document F, an extract from the childhood reminiscences of the great Russian mathematician Sonya Kovalevsky (1850–1891), relates an incident in which her cold, distant army officer father punishes her for the offense of reading too much. Fathers such as General Krukofsky represented a common nineteenth-century model of familial law and order, all too common in Russia and the West alike.

A. Nikolai Chernyshevsky Asks, "What Is to Be Done?"

"I will find employment in my profession, though it will not pay me much; but there will be time left to attend to patients, and, taking all things together, we shall be able to live."

"Yes, dear friend, we shall need so little; only I do not wish to live by our labor. I too will live by my labor; isn't that fair? I should not live at your expense."

"Who told you that, dear Verochka?"

"Oh! he asks who told me! Your books are full of such thoughts."

"In my books? At any rate I never said such a thing to you. When, then, did I say so?"

"When? Haven't you always told me that everything rests on money?"

"Well?"

"And do you really consider me so stupid that I cannot understand books and draw conclusions from premises?"

"Everything rests on money, you say, Dmitry Sergeich; consequently, whoever has money has power and freedom, say your books; then, as long as woman lives at man's expense, she will be dependent on him, will she not? You thought that I could not understand that, and would be your slave? I know that you intend to be a good and benevolent despot, but I do not intend that you should be a despot at all. And now this is what we will do. You shall cut off arms and legs and administer drugs; I, on the other hand, will give lessons on the piano."

B. Ivan Turgenev Defines the Nihilist and Offends All Russia, 1861

"What is Bazarov?" Arcadii smiled, "I'll tell you just what Bazarov is—would you like me to, Uncle?"

"Do oblige me, Nephew."

"He is a nihilist."

"How?" Nicholai Petrovich asked, while his brother lifted up his knife with a pat of butter at its tip and arrested his hand in midair.

"He's a nihilist," Arcadii repeated.

"A nihilist," his father uttered. "That comes from the Latin, *nihil*, meaning *nothing*, if I am any judge; the word, then, designates a man who . . . who recognizes nothing?"

"Say: one who respects nothing," Pavel Petrovich interjected and went back to buttering his bread.

"One who regards everything from a critical point of view," Arcadii commented.

"But isn't that all one?" his uncle queried.

"No, it's not. A nihilist is a man who does not accede to any authority, who does not accept a single principle on faith, no matter how great the aura of respect which surrounds that principle."

"Well, and is that a good thing?" Pavel Petrovich cut him short.

"That all depends on the person, Uncle. One man may find it a very good thing for him, while another may find it very bad."

"So, that's how things are. Well, now, I can see that's outside our province. We who belong to an older age, we go upon the assumption that without principles"—he gave the word a soft pronunciation, after the French manner, while Arcadii, on the contrary, gave it a harsh sound, placing the accent on the first syllable—"principles accepted on faith, as you said, a man cannot take a step, cannot draw a breath. *Vous avez changé tout cela*—you have changed all that. May God grant you good health and a general's rank, but as for us, we will merely look on and admire you, Messieurs *les*—what was that term you used?"

"Nihilists," Arcadii told him, enunciating the word clearly.

"Yes. Before we had the Hegelists, but now we have the nihilists. We'll see how you'll manage to exist in a void, in a vacuum; but right now please ring, brother Nicholai—it's time for my cocoa."

C. Alexander Herzen Describes the Realities of Russian Peasant Life to Jules Michelet

"The Russian," you say, "is a liar and a thief; he is lying and always stealing, and quite innocently, for it is his nature."

I shall not stop to call attention to the sweeping nature of this observation, but should like to be allowed to put to you this simple question: who, now, is the deceived, the robbed, the dupe? Heavens above, it is the landowner, the government official, the steward, the judge, the police officer: in other words, the sworn foes of the peasant, whom he looks upon as apostates, as traitors, as half-Germans. Deprived of every possible means of defense the peasant resorts to cunning in dealing with his oppressors; he deceives them, and his is perfectly right in doing so. Cunning, Monsieur, is, in the words of a great thinker [Hegel], the irony of brute force.

Through his horror of private property in land, as you have so well observed, through his listless, careless temperament, the Russian peasant, I say, has seen himself gradually and silently caught in the toils of the German bureaucracy and of the landowners' power. He has submitted to this humiliating yoke with the resignation of despair, I agree, but he has never *believed* in either the rights of the landowner, or the justice of the law-courts, or the fair-dealing of the administration. For nearly two hundred years the peasant's whole life has been nothing but a dumb, passive opposition to the existing order of things. He submits to oppression, he endures it, but he dips his hand in nothing that goes on outside the village communes.

The idea of the Tsar still enjoys prestige among the peasants; it is not the Tsar Nicholas that the people venerates; it is an abstract idea, a myth, a providence, an avenger, a representative of justice in the people's imagination.

After the Tsar, only the clergy could possibly have a moral influence on Orthodox Russia. The higher clergy alone represent old Russia in governing spheres; the clergy have never shaved their beards, and by that fact have remained on the side of the people. The people listen with confidence to a monk. But the monks and the higher clergy, occupied exclusively, as they say, with life beyond the grave, care little for the people. The *Pop* [priest] has lost all influence through his cupidity, his drunkenness, and his inti-

From *My Past and Thoughts* by Alexander Herzen pp. 1648, 1659–79. Copyright © 1968 by Chatto and Windus, Ltd. Reprinted by permission of Random House, Inc.

mate relations with the police. Here, too, the peasants respect the idea but not the person.

As for the sectaries [Old Believers] they hate both person and idea, both *Pop* and Tsar.

Apart from the Tsar and the clergy every element of government and society is utterly alien, essentially antagonistic to the people. The peasant finds himself in the literal sense of the word an outlaw. The law-court takes good care not to protect him, and his share in the existing order of things is entirely confined to the twofold tribute that lies heavily upon him and is paid in his sweat and his blood. Poor disinherited man, he instinctively understands that the whole system is ordered not for his benefit but to his detriment, and that the whole problem of the government and the landowners is to wring out of him as much labor and as much money as possible. Since he understands this and is gifted with a supple and resourceful intelligence, he deceives them all and in everything. It could not be otherwise; if he spoke the truth it would already be an assent on his side, an acceptance of their power over him; if he did not rob them (observe that to conceal part of the produce of his own labor is considered theft in a peasant) he would thereby be fatally recognizing the lawfulness of their exactions, the rights of the landowners and the justice of the law-courts. . . .

The life of the Russian peasantry has hitherto been confined to the commune. It is only in relation to the commune and its members that the peasant recognizes that he has rights and duties. Outside the commune he recognizes no duties and everything seems to him to be based upon violence. The baneful side of his nature is his submitting to that violence, and not his refusing in his own way to recognize it and his trying to protect himself by guile. There is much more uprightness in lying before a judge set over him by unlawful authority than in a hypocritical show of respect for the verdict of a jury packed by a prefect, whose revolting iniquity is as clear as daylight. The people respect only those institutions which reflect their innate conception of law and right. . . .

The Russian autocracy is entering upon a new phase. Having grown out of [the] anti-national revolution [of Peter the Great], it has accomplished its mission. It has created a colossal empire, a numerous army, a centralized government. Without principles, without tradition, it has no more to do; it is true that it undertook another task—to bring Western civilization into Russia; and it was to some extent successful in doing that while it still persisted in its fine role of civilizing government.

That role it has now abdicated.

The government, which had broken with the people in the name of civilization, has lost no time a hundred years later in breaking with civilization in the name of absolutism.

It did so as soon as the tri-colored specter of liberalism began to be visible through its civilizing tendencies: it tried then to return to nationalism, to the people. That was impossible—the people and the government had nothing in common any longer; the former had grown away from the latter, while the government thought it could discern rising from deep within the masses the still more terrible specter of the Red Cock. All things considered liberalism was still less dangerous than another Pugachev, but the panic and distaste of liberal ideas had become such that the government was no longer capable of making its peace with civilization.

D. Alexander II Tells the Russian Nobility Why Emancipation Must Come

". . . For the removal of certain unfounded reports, I consider it necessary to declare to you that I have not at present the intention of annihilating serfdom, but certainly, as you yourselves know, the existing manner of possessing serfs cannot remain unchanged. It is better to abolish serfdom from above than to await the time when it will begin to abolish itself from below. I request you, gentlemen, to consider how this can be put into execution, and to submit my words to the nobility for their consideration."

E. Peasants Complain About Mistreatment Since Emancipation, 1862

Your Imperial Excellency! Most gracious sire! Grand Duke Konstantin Nikolaevich!

Most magnanimous prince, given by God for the welfare of people in the Russian Empire! The countless acts of mercy and humanitarianism of Your Imperial Excellency toward the loyal subjects have emboldened us to fall to your feet and plead:

Show you steadfast and just protection of oppressed humanity! Following the example of our fathers, grandfathers and ancestors, we have always and without complaint obeyed the laws of Russian monarchs and the authority of its rulers. Hence, as peasants in the hamlet of Blagoveshchenskoe and three villages (Avdot'evka, Aleksandrovka and Uspenskaia) in Balashov District of Saratov province, we and our families, while under the authority of the squire, a retired colonel, Prince Vasil'chikov, have always enjoyed the blessings of the all-merciful God: fertile land.

The monarch's mercy—which has no precedent in the chronicles of all peoples in the universe—has now changed the attitude of our squire, who has reduced us 1,500 peasants to a pitiable condition. . . . [sic] After being informed of the Imperial manifesto on the emancipation of peasants from serfdom in 1861 (which was explained to us by the constable of township 2 of Balashov District), we received this [news] with jubilation, as a special gift from heaven, and expressed our willingness to obey the square's will in every respect during the coming two-year [transition] period [and to remain] on the fertile land which we occupy, where we could realise our life. . . . [sic]

But from this moment, our squire ordered that the land be cut off from the entire township. But this is absolutely intolerable for us: it not only denies us profit, but threatens us with a catastrophic future. He began to hold repeated meetings and [tried to] force us to sign that we agreed to accept the above land allotment. But, upon seeing so unexpected a change, and bearing in mind the gracious manifesto, we refused. Then Prince Vasil'chikov, with terrible threats, went to the city of Saratov, and soon afterwards the squires, Prince Prozorovskii, Golitsyn, Colonel Globbe, and the peace arbitrator Baishev came to our township office. After assembling the entire township, they tried to force us into making illegal signatures accepting the land cut-offs. But when they saw that this did not succeed, they had a company of soldiers sent in and said that they had been sent—by the Tsar!—to restore peace between us and the squires. We heard this and, despite the unsuitability of the land, we were ready to accept it—at first as 3 dessiatines per soul, than later 4 dessiatines.[1] But we did not give the demanded signatures, suspecting here a scheme by the squires' accomplices. Then [Col.] Globbe came from their midst, threatened us with exile to Siberia, and ordered the soldiers to strip the peasants and to punish seven people by flogging in the most inhuman manner. They still have not regained consciousness.

These inhuman acts and intolerable oppression have forced us to fall to the sacred feet of Your Imperial Excellency: 1,500 voices most humbly ask for just, most august defense, which can save weeping families from certain death, and [we ask] that You issue a decree [on our case].

[1] A dessiatine equalled 2.7 acres.

F. Mathematician Sonya Kovalevsky Recalls Her Family Life and Oppressive Father

In such cases, the governess had recourse to the most extreme measures: she sent me to my father with orders to relate my guilt to him myself. I feared this more than all other punishments.

In reality father was not at all severe with us; but I saw him rarely—only at dinner. He never permitted himself the slightest familiarity with us except when one of the children was ill. Then he was completely changed. We simply adored him at such times, and retained the memory of them for a long while. But on ordinary occasions, when all were well, he stuck to the rule that "a man must be severe," and therefore was very sparing of his caresses.

Hence, when the governess used to say, "Go to your father; make your boast to him of how you have been behaving," I felt genuine despair. I cried and resisted, but the governess was implacable, and taking me by the hand, she led me, or, to speak more correctly, she dragged me through the long suite of rooms to the door of the study, left me to my fate, and went away.

I knock, but very softly. Several moments, which seem to me interminable, elapse.

There is nothing to be done; I knock again.

"Who's there? Come in," calls father's voice at last from the study.

I enter, but halt in the semi-darkness on the threshold. Father sits at his writing-table with his back to the door, and does not see me.

"Who's there? What's wanted?" he cries impatiently.

"It is I, papa. Margarita Frantzovna has sent me," I gulp out in reply.

Then for the first time father divines what is the matter.

"Ah, ah! you have been naughty again, of course," he says, trying to communicate to his voice as stern an intonation as possible. "Come, tell your story. What have you been doing?"

After I told it, he responded, "What a horrid, naughty little girl you are. I am very much displeased with you," he says, and pauses because he does not know what else to say. "Go, stand in the corner," he pronounces judgment at last, because, out of all his pedagogic wisdom, his memory has retained nothing beyond the fact that naughty children are made to stand in the corner.

And so you may picture to yourself how I, a big girl of twelve—I, who a few minutes previously had been going through the most complicated dramas with the heroine of a romance perused on the sly,—I am obliged to go and stand in the corner like a foolish little child.

Document Set 23.3 References

A. Nikolai Chernyshevsky Asks, "What Is to Be Done?"
N. G. Chernyshevsky, *What Is To Be Done? Tales About New People,* trans. Benjamin R. Tucker and Ludmilla B. Tucker (New York: Random House, 1960), 108–109.

B. Ivan Turgenev Defines the Nihilist and Offends All Russia, 1861
Ivan Turgenev, *Fathers and Sons,* trans. Bernard Guilbert Guerney (New York: Modern Library, 1961), 29–31.

C. Alexander Herzen Describes the Realities of Russian Peasant Life to Jules Michelet
Herzen, in James Cracraft, ed., *Major Problems in the History of Imperial Russia* (Lexington, Mass.: D. C. Heath, 1994), 330–333.

D. Alexander II Tells the Russian Nobility Why Emancipation Must Come
Alexander II, Address to Moscow marshals, in A. Rambaud, *History of Russia from the Earliest Times to 1882* (Boston: 1886), 3:221.

E. Peasants Complain About Mistreatment Since Emancipation, 1862
Petition from peasants in Balashov District (Saratov Province) to Grand Duke Konstantin Nikolaevich 25 Jan. 1862, in Gregory Freeze, ed. and trans., *From Supplication to Revolution* (New York: Oxford University Press, 1988), 171–172.

F. Mathematician Sonya Kovalevsky Recalls Her Family Life and Oppressive Father
Adapted from Kovalevsky, *Her Recollections of Childhood,* Isabel Hapgood, trans. (New York: Century, 1895), 46–49, in Bonnie Smith, *Changing Lives: Women in European History Since 1700* (Lexington, Mass.: D. C. Heath, 1989), 188–189.

DOCUMENT SET 23.4
Currents of Reform: Western and Central Europe

In 1867 Parliament enacted the second great Reform Bill of nineteenth-century Britain, extending the suffrage to lower middle-class and better-off working-class males. This did not represent the complete realization of the People's Charter demands (Set 22.7, Document A), but it did move Britain a long way toward a democratic political culture, with mass parties competing for popular votes. Documents A and B show how two liberal members of Parliament, both known for their devotion to the classic nineteenth-century liberal dogma of limited government, argued on opposite sides of this issue. How could a liberal oppose suffrage extension? Document C shows the suffrage debate drawn out to its logical conclusion: the great liberal theorist John Stuart Mill argued for granting political rights to women. But his was a position too far in advance of the times to merit serious consideration.

The establishment of universal manhood suffrage in the North German Confederation (1866)—Bismarck's stepping stone to what would become the German Empire of 1871—meant that the era of mass politics was also dawning in Central Europe. Granted, the North German (and later the Imperial German) parliament did not ultimately govern, as Parliament did in Britain. But the breakthrough was sufficiently wide to make it plausible for German socialists to draw up the Eisenach Program in 1869 (Document D), a significant step toward turning revolutionary socialism into a reformist movement for social democracy.

A. British Liberal John Bright Supports Suffrage Extension, 1866

Well, then, there is this question that will not sleep—the question of the admission of the people of this country to the rights which are guaranteed to them, and promised to them by everything that we comprehend as the Constitution of this United Kingdom. . . .

I have always thought that it was one of the great objects of statesmen in our time not to separate the people into sections and classes, but rather to unite them all in one firm and compact body of citizenship, equally treated by the law, and equally loyal to the law and to the government of the country. . . .

. . . Sir, I protest against . . . the theory that the people of this country have an unreasonable and violent desire to shake or overturn institutions which they may not theoretically approve of. . . . I am perfectly content to live under the institutions which the intelligence, and the virtue, and the experience of my countrymen fairly represented in Parliament shall determine upon. . . .

The House of Commons is in reality the only guarantee we have for freedom. If you looked at any other country, and saw nothing but a monarch, he might be a good king and might do his best, but you would see that there is no guarantee for freedom—you know not who will be his successor. If you saw a country with no crown, but with a handful of nobles, administering the government of the country, you would say there is no guarantee there for freedom, because a number of individuals acting together have not the responsibility, or the feeling of responsibility, that one man has, and they do things which one man would not dare to do. . . . It is only the existence of that House which makes the institution they are so fond of safe and permanent at all—and they are afraid that the five millions somehow or other will get into it. Now, I beg to tell them that the five millions will get into it, though they may not get into it all at once; and perhaps few men desire that they should, for I am opposed myself to great and violent changes, which create needless shocks, and which are accepted, if they are accepted, with great alarm.

But I will undertake to say that some portion, a considerable and effective portion, of those five millions will before many years are passed be freely allowed to vote for members of the House of Commons. It is not the democracy which these gentlemen are always afraid of that is the peril of this country. It was not democracy in 1832 that was the peril. It was the desperate antagonism of the class that then had power to the just claims and rights of the people. . . .

England has long been famous for the enjoyment of personal freedom by her people. They are free to think, they are free to speak, they are free to write; and England has been famed of late years, and is famed now the world over, for the freedom of her industry and the greatness and the freedom of her commerce. I want to know then why it is that her people should not be free to vote.

B. British Liberal Robert Lowe Opposes Suffrage Extension, 1867

If the working classes, in addition to being a majority in the boroughs, get a redistribution of the seats in their favor, it will follow that their influence will be enormously increased. They will then urge the House of Commons to pass another Franchise Bill, and another Redistribution Bill to follow it. . . . No one can tell where it will stop, and it will not be likely to stop until we get equal electoral districts and a qualification so low that it will keep out nobody. There is another matter with which my honorable friend has not dealt. I mean the point of combination among the working classes. To many persons there appears great danger that the machinery which at present exists for strikes and trade unions may be used for political purposes.

I come now to the question of the representatives of the working classes. It is an old observation that every democracy is in some respect similar to a despotism. As courtiers and flatterers are worse than despots themselves, so those who flatter and fawn upon the people are generally very inferior to the people, the objects of their flattery and adulation. We see in America, where the people have undisputed power, that they do not send honest, hard-working men to represent them in Congress, but traffickers in office, bankrupts, men who have lost their character and been driven from every respectable way of life, and who take up politics as a last resource.

Now, Sir, democracy has yet another tendency, which it is worth while to study at the present moment. It is singularly prone to the concentration of power. Under it individual men are small and the government is great. That must be the character of a government which represents the majority, and which absolutely tramples down and equalizes everything except itself. And democracy has another strong peculiarity. It looks with the utmost hostility on all institutions not of immediate popular origin, which intervene between the people and the sovereign power which the people have set up.

Now, look what was done in France. Democracy has left nothing in that country between the people and the emperor except a bureaucracy which the emperor himself has created. In America it has done almost the same thing. You have there nothing to break the shock between the two great powers of the State. The wise men who framed the constitution tried to provide a remedy by dividing functions as much as possible. They assigned one function to the President, another to the Senate, a third to the Congress, and a fourth to the different States. But all

their efforts have been in vain, and you see how two hostile camps have arisen, and the terrible duel which is now taking place between them. . . .

I have now, Sir, traced as well as I can what I believe will be the natural results of a measure which, it seems to my poor imagination, is calculated, if it should pass into law, to destroy one after another those institutions which have secured for England an amount of happiness and prosperity which no country has ever reached or is ever likely to attain. Surely the heroic work of so many centuries, the matchless achievements of so many wise heads and strong hands, deserve a nobler consummation than to be sacrificed at the shrine of revolutionary passion or the maudlin enthusiasm of humanity. But if we do fall, we shall fall deservedly. Uncoerced by any external force, not borne down by any internal calamity, but in the full plethora of our wealth and the surfeit of our too exuberant prosperity, with out own rash and inconsiderate hands, we are about to pluck down on our own heads the venerable temple of our liberty and our glory. History may tell of other acts as signally disastrous, but of none more wanton, none more disgraceful.

C. British Liberal John Stuart Mill Advocates Extending Political Reform to Women's Rights, 1869

It will be said, the rule of men over women differs from all these others in not being a rule of force: it is accepted voluntarily; women make no complaint, and are consenting parties to it. In the first place, a great number of women do not accept it. Ever since there have been women able to make their sentiments known by their writings (the only mode of publicity which society permits to them), an increasing number of them have recorded protests against their present social condition: and recently many thousands of them, headed by the most eminent women known to the public, have petitioned Parliament for their admission to the parliamentary suffrage. The claim of women to be educated as solidly, and in the same branches of knowledge, as men, is urged with growing intensity, and with a great prospect of success; while the demand for their admission into professions and occupations hitherto closed against them, becomes every year more urgent. . . .

But if the principle is true, we ought to act as if we believed it, and not to ordain that to be born a girl instead of a boy, any more than to be born black instead of white, or a commoner instead of a nobleman, shall decide the person's position through all life—shall interdict people from all the more elevated social positions, and from all, except a few, respectable occupations. . . .

At present, in the more improved countries, the disabilities of women are the only case, save one, in which laws and institutions take persons at their birth, and ordain that they shall never in all their lives be allowed to compete for certain things. The one exception is that of royalty. . . . All other dignities and social advantages are open to the whole male sex: many indeed are only attainable by wealth, but wealth may be striven for by any one, and is actually obtained by many men of the very humblest origin. The difficulties, to the majority, are indeed insuperable without the aid of fortunate accidents; but no male human being is under any legal ban: neither law nor opinion superadd artificial obstacles to the natural ones. . . .

Neither does it avail anything to say that the nature of the two sexes adapt them to their present functions and position, and renders these appropriate to them. Standing on the ground of common sense and the constitution of the human mind, I deny that any one knows, or can know, the nature of the two sexes, as long as they have only been seen in their present relation to one another. . . . What is now called the nature of women is an eminently artificial thing—the result of forced repression in some directions, unnatural stimulation in others. . . .

One thing we may be certain of—that what is contrary to women's nature to do, they never will be made to do by simply giving their nature free play. The anxiety of mankind to interfere in behalf of nature, for fear lest nature should not succeed in effecting its purpose, is an altogether unnecessary solicitude. What women by nature cannot do, it is quite superfluous to forbid them from doing. What they can do, but not so well as the men who are their competitors, competition suffices to exclude them from; since nobody asks for protective duties and bounties in favor of women; it is only asked that the present bounties and protective duties in favor of men should be recalled. If women have a greater natural inclination for some things than for others, there is no need of laws or social inculcation to make the majority of them do the former in preference to the latter. Whatever women's services are most wanted for, the free play of competition will hold out the strongest inducements to them to undertake. . . .

Those who attempt to force women into marriage by closing all other doors against them . . . are afraid, not lest women should be unwilling to marry, for I do not think that any one in reality has that apprehension; but lest they should insist that marriage should be on equal conditions; lest all women of spirit and capacity should prefer doing almost anything else, not in their own eyes degrading, rather than marry, when marrying is giving themselves a master, and a master too of all their earthly possessions. . . . looking to the laws alone, society would be a hell upon earth. Happily there are both feelings and interests which in many men exclude, and in most, greatly temper, the impulses and propensies which lead to tyranny: and of those feelings, the tie which connects a man and his wife affords, in a normal state of things, incomparably the strongest example. The only tie which at all approaches to it, that between him and his children, tends, in all save exceptional cases, to strengthen, instead of conflicting with, the first. Because this is true; because men in general do not inflict, nor women suffer, all the misery which could be inflicted and suffered if the full power of tyranny with which the man is legally invested were acted on; the defenders of the existing form of the institution think that all its iniquity is justified, and that any complaint is merely quarrelling with the evil which is the price paid for every great good. . . .

D. Social Democracy: German Socialists Draw Up the Eisenach Program, 1869

1. The Social-Democratic Labour party aims at the establishment of a free Democratic State.

2. Every member of the party pledges himself to insist with all his might on the following principles:—

(a) The present political and social conditions are in the highest degree unjust and therefore to be opposed with the utmost energy.

(b) The struggle for the emancipation of the working-classes is not a struggle for class privileges and prerogatives, but for equal rights and equal duties and for the abolition of all class domination.

(c) The economic dependence of the worker on the capitalist is the basis of his servitude in all its forms, and the Social-Democratic party aims, by the abolition of the present method of production (the wages system) at assuring, by means of co-operative labour, that every worker shall receive the full product of his work.

(d) Political freedom is the indispensable basis of the economic emancipation of the working-classes. The social question is therefore inseparable from the political question; its solution depends upon the solution of the political question and is only possible in a democratic State.

(e) In consideration of the fact that the political

and economic emancipation of the working-class is only possible if this class wages war in common and united, the Social-Democratic Labour party adopts a united organisation which yet makes it possible for every one of its members to make his influence felt for the benefit of the whole.

(f) Considering that the emancipation of labour is neither a local nor a national but a social question, which embraces all countries in which there is a modern society, the Social-Democratic Labour party regards itself, as far as the laws of association permit, as a branch of the "International," and adopts its aims.

3. The following are to be regarded as the most urgent questions of propaganda:—

(a) Equal universal and direct suffrage by secret ballot for all men over twenty, in the elections for the Reichstag, the Diets of the several Federal States, the provincial and local assemblies, and all other representative bodies. The deputies are to be paid salaries.

(b) The introduction of direct legislation (Initiative and Referendum) by the people.

(c) Abolition of all privileges of class, property, birth, and creed.

(d) Substitution of a National Militia for standing armies.

(e) Separation of Church and State and secularisation of schools.

(f) Compulsory education in Elementary Schools and gratuitous instruction in all public educational establishments.

(g) Independence of the Courts, introduction of the jury system, industrial courts, public and oral procedure, and gratuitous jurisdiction.

(h) Abolition of all legal restriction of the Press, the right of association and combination, the introduction of a normal working day, the restriction of female labour, and the abolition of child labour.

(i) Abolition of all indirect taxation and the introduction of a single direct progressive income tax and a tax on inheritance.

(j) State help for co-operative undertakings and State credit for free productive co-operative associations, with democratic guarantees.

Document Set 23.4 References

A. British Liberal John Bright Supports Suffrage Extension, 1866
   The Speeches of John Bright, M.P., in Walter Arnstein, ed., *The Past Speaks,* 2d ed. (Lexington, Mass.: D. C. Heath, 1993), 2:230–233.

B. British Liberal Robert Lowe Opposes Suffrage Extension, 1867
   Robert Lowe, speech, in James Harvey Robinson and Charles Beard, eds., *Readings in Modern European History* (Boston: Ginn, 1909), 2:251–254.

C. British Liberal John Stuart Mill Advocates Extending Political Reform to Women's Rights, 1869
   Mill, *The Subjection of Women,* in Arnstein, 2d ed., 2:186–189.

D. Social Democracy: German Socialists Draw Up the Eisenach Program, 1869
   August Bebel, *My Life* (London: 1912; reprinted New York: Howard Fertig, 1973), 167–170.

DOCUMENT SET 23.5
Science and Religion in the Age of Darwin

The theory of evolution had been in gestation for a generation. Charles Darwin (1809–1882) supplied the crucial element in explaining how biological evolution worked—natural selection. His summary of that explanation and his thoughts on its wider implications, taken from the conclusion to his seminal *Origin of Species* (1859), appear as Document A. Still, his argument horrified orthodox Christians such as Anglican bishop Samuel Wilberforce (1805–1873; Document B). Likewise, the great Victorian poet Alfred Tennyson (1809–1892), later ennobled as Lord Tennyson, ruminated in his long series of elegies *In Memoriam* (1842) on the transience of life. Contemplating nature "red in tooth and claw" and the geological evidence for the extinction of whole species, he wondered whether the Christian hope of redemption and immortality was really plausible (Document C). Tennyson at least hoped it was.

The French thinker Auguste Comte (1798–1857) would have answered Tennyson with an emphatic no. Comte insisted that intellectual and social evolution had left behind all justification for theological speculation; society had now reached the state where "positive" facts could be gathered and rationally organized. His theory of positivism (Document D) had a political application. Subjecting everything to scrutiny, positivists challenged those who held the reins of government by tradition alone, as well as those committed to change society through revolution. Rather, government should be entrusted to those qualified to understand social laws—more precisely, to bureaucrats.

Originally thought to have vaguely liberal leanings, Pope Pius IX (*1846–1878) was frightened by the revolution of 1848 into becoming a rigid conservative, utterly rejecting all talk of "evolution" and "progress." His *Syllabus of Errors* of 1864 (excerpted in Document E) listed many modern ideas, each of which he emphatically rejected and condemned.

A. Charles Darwin Defends His Theory of Natural Selection

I have now recapitulated the facts and considerations which have thoroughly convinced me that species have been modified, during a long course of descent. This has been effected chiefly through the natural selections of numerous successive, slight, favourable variations; aided in an important manner by the inherited effects of the use and disuse of parts; and in

an unimportant manner, that is in relation to adaptive structures, whether past or present, by the direct action of external conditions, and by variations which seem to us in our ignorance to arise spontaneously. . . . But as my conclusions have lately been much misrepresented, and it has been stated that I attribute the modification of species exclusively to natural selection, I may be permitted to remark that in the first edition of this work, and subsequently, I placed in a most conspicuous position—namely, at the close of the Introduction—the following words: "I am convinced that natural selection has been the main but not the exclusive means of modification." This has been of no avail. Great is the power of steady misrepresentation; but the history of science shows that fortunately this power does not long endure.

It can hardly be supposed that a false theory would explain, in so satisfactory a manner as does the theory of natural selection, the several large classes of facts above specified. It has recently been objected that this is an unsafe method of arguing; but it is a method used in judging of the common events of life, and has often been used by the greatest natural philosophers. The undulatory theory of light has thus been arrived at; and the belief in the revolution of the earth on its own axis was until lately supported by hardly any direct evidence. It is no valid objection that science as yet throws no light on the far higher problem of the essence or origin of life. Who can explain what is the essence of the attraction of gravity? No one now objects to following out the results consequent on this unknown element of attraction; notwithstanding that Leibnitz formerly accused Newton of introducing "occult qualities and miracles into philosophy."

I see no good reason why the views given in this volume should shock the religious feelings of any one. It is satisfactory, as showing how transient such impressions are, to remember that the greatest discovery ever made by man, namely, the law of the attraction of gravity, was also attacked by Leibnitz, "as subversive of natural, and inferentially of revealed, religion." A celebrated author and divine has written to me that "he has gradually learnt to see that it is just as noble a conception of the Deity to believe that He created a few original forms capable of self-development into other and needful forms, as to believe that He required a fresh act of creation to supply the voids caused by the action of His laws." . . .

. . . The chief cause of our natural unwillingness to admit that one species has given birth to clear and distinct species, is that we are always slow in admitting great changes of which we do not see the steps. The difficulty is the same as that felt by so many geologists, when Lyell first insisted that long lines of inland cliffs had been formed, and great valleys excavated, by the agencies which we see still at work. The mind cannot possibly grasp the full meaning of the term of even a million years; it cannot add up and perceive the full effects of many slight variations, accumulated during an almost infinite number of generations. . . .

Authors of the highest eminence seem to be fully satisfied with the view that each species has been independently created. To my mind it accords better with what we know of the laws impressed on matter by the Creator, that the production and extinction of the past and present inhabitants of the world should have been due to secondary causes, like those determining the birth and death of the individual. When I view all beings not as special creations, but as the lineal descendants of some few beings which lived long before the first bed of the Cambrian system was deposited, they seem to me to become ennobled. Judging from the past, we may safely infer that not one living species will transmit its unaltered likeness to a distant futurity. And of the species now living very few will transmit progeny of any kind to a far distant futurity; for the manner in which all organic beings are grouped, shows that the greater number of species in each genus, and all the species in many genera, have left no descendants, but have become utterly extinct. We can so far take a prophetic glance into futurity as to foretell that it will be the common and widely-spread species, belonging to the larger and dominant groups within each class, which will ultimately prevail and procreate new and dominant species. As all the living forms of life are the lineal descendants of those which lived long before the Cambrian epoch, we may feel certain that the ordinary succession by generation has never once been broken, and that no cataclysm has desolated the whole world. Hence we may look with some confidence to a secure future of great length. And as natural selection works solely by and for the good of each being, all corporeal and mental endowments will tend to progress towards perfection.

It is interesting to contemplate a tangled bank, clothed with many plants of many kinds, with birds singing on the bushes, with various insects flitting about, and with worms crawling through the damp earth, and to reflect that these elaborately constructed forms, so different from each other, and dependent upon each other in so complex a manner, have all been produced by laws acting around us. . . . Thus, from the war of nature, from famine and death, the most exalted object which we are capable of conceiving, namely, the production of the higher animals, directly follows. There is grandeur in this view of life, with its several powers, having been originally breathed by the Creator into a few forms or into one; and that, whilst this planet has gone cycling on according to the fixed law of gravity, from so simple a beginning endless forms most beautiful and most wonderful have been and are being evolved.

B. Bishop Wilberforce Argues Against Darwin

The conclusion, then, to which Mr. Darwin would bring us is, that all the various forms of vegetable and animal life with which the globe is now peopled, or of which we find the remains preserved in a fossil state in the great earth-museum around us, which the science of geology unlocks for our instruction, . . . "have descended from some one primordial form into which life was first breathed by the Creator." This is the theory which really pervades the whole volume. Man, beast, creeping thing, and plant of the earth, are all the lineal and direct descendants of some one individual *ens*, whose various progeny have been simply modified by the action of natural and ascertainable conditions into the multiform aspect of life which we see around us. This is undoubtedly at first sight a somewhat startling conclusion to arrive at. To find that mosses, grasses, turnips, oaks, worms, and flies, mites and elephants, infusoria and whales, tadpoles of to-day and venerable saurians, truffles and men, are all equally the lineal descendants of the same aboriginal common ancestor. . . .—This, to say the least of it, is no common discovery—no very expected conclusion. . . .

We come then to these conclusions. All the facts presented to us in the natural world tend to show that none of the variations produced in the fixed forms of animal life, when seen in its most plastic condition under domestication, give any promise of a true transmutation of species; first, from the difficulty of accumulating and fixing variations within the same species; secondly, from the fact that these variations, though most serviceable for man, have no tendency to improve the individual beyond the standard of his own specific type, and so to afford matter, even if they were infinitely produced, for the supposed power of natural selection on which to work; whilst all variations from the mixture of species are barred by the inexorable law of hybrid sterility. Further, the embalmed records of 3,000 years show that there has been no beginning of transmutation in the species of our most familiar domesticated animals; and beyond this, that in the countless tribes of animal life around us, down to its lowest and most variable species, no one have ever discovered a single instance of such transmutation being now in prospect; no new organ has ever been known to be developed—no new natural instinct to be formed—whilst, finally, in the vast museum of departed animal life which the strata of the earth imbed for our examination, whilst they contain far too complete a representation of the past to be set aside as a mere imperfect record, yet afford no one instance of any such change as having ever been in progress, or give us anywhere the missing links of the assumed chain, or the remains which would enable now existing variations, by gradual approximations to shade off into unity. . . .

Few things have more deeply injured the cause of religion than the busy fussy energy with which men, narrow and feeble alike in faith and in science, have bustled forth to reconcile all new discoveries in physics with the word of inspiration. For it continually happens that some larger collection of facts, or some wider view of the phenomena of nature, alter the whole philosophic scheme; whilst revelation has been committed to declare an absolute agreement with what turns out after all to have been a misconception or an error. We cannot, therefore, consent to test the truth of natural science by the word of revelation. But this does not make it the less important to point out on scientific grounds scientific errors, when those errors tend to limit God's glory in creation, or to gainsay the revealed relations of that creation to Himself. To both these classes of error, though, we doubt not, quite unintentionally on his part, we think that Mr. Darwin's speculations directly tend.

C. Alfred Tennyson Contemplates "Nature Red in Tooth and Claw"

The wish, that of the living whole
　　No life may fail beyond the grave,
　　Derives it not from what we have
The likest God within the soul?

Are God and Nature then at strife
　　That Nature lends such evil dreams?
　　So careful of the type she seems,
So careless of the single life;

That I, considering everywhere
　　Her secret meaning in her deeds
　　And finding that of fifty seeds
She often brings but one to bear,

I falter where I firmly trod,
　　And falling with my weight of cares
　　Upon the great world's altar-stairs
That slope thro' darkness up to God,

I stretch lame hands of faith, and grope,
　　And gather dust and chaff, and call
　　To what I feel is Lord of all,
And faintly trust the larger hope.

'So careful of the type?' but no.
　　From scarped cliff and quarried stone
　　She cries, 'A thousand types are gone:
I care for nothing, all shall go.

'Thou makest thine appeal to me:
　　I bring to life, I bring to death:
　　The spirit does but mean the breath:
I know no more.' And he, shall he,

Man, her last work, who seem'd so fair,
　　Such splendid purpose in his eyes,
　　Who roll'd the psalm to wintry skies,
Who built him fanes of fruitless prayer,

Who trusted God was love indeed
　　And love Creation's final law—
　　Tho' Nature, red in tooth and claw
With ravine, shriek'd against his creed—

Who loved, who suffer'd countless ills,
　　Who battled for the True, the Just.
　　Be blown about the desert dust,
Or seal'd within the iron hills?

No more? A monster then, a dream,
　　A discord. Dragons of the prime,
　　That tare each other in their slime,
Were mellow music match'd with him.

O life as futile, then, as frail!
　　O for thy voice to soothe and bless!
　　What hope of answer, or redress?
Behind the veil, behind the veil.

D. August Comte Charts a Positivist Future for Society

Positivism will lay down a definite basis for the reorganization of society. It will offer a general system of education for the adoption of all civilized nations, and by this means will supply in every department of public and private life fixed principles of judgment and of conduct.

The primary object, then, of positivism is twofold: to generalize our scientific conceptions, and to systematize the art of social life.

This will lead us to another question. The regenerating doctrine cannot do its work without adherents; in what quarter should be hope to find them? Now, with individual exceptions of great value, we cannot expect the adhesion of any of the upper classes in society. They are all more or less under the influence of baseless metaphysical theories and of aristocratic self-seeking. They are absorbed in blind political agitation and in disputes for the possession of the useless remnants of the old theological and military system. Their action only tends to prolong the revolutionary state indefinitely, and can never result in true social renovation.

E. Pope Pius IX Catalogues Some Errors of the Day

15. Every man is free to embrace and profess the religion he shall believe true, guided by the light of reason.

18. Protestantism is nothing more than another form of the same true Christian religion, in which it is possible to be equally pleasing to God as in the Catholic Church.

20. The ecclesiastical power must not exercise its authority without the permission and assent of the civil government.

39. The commonwealth is the origin and source of all rights, and possesses rights which are not circumscribed by any limits.

41. The civil power, even when exercised by an unbelieving sovereign, possesses an indirect and negative power over religious affairs.

43. The civil power has a right to break, and to declare and render null, the conventions (commonly called *Concordats*) concluded with the Apostle See, relative to the exercise of rights pertaining to the ecclesiastical immunity, without the consent of the Holy See, and even contrary to its protests.

44. The civil authority may interfere in matters relating to religion, morality, and spiritual government.

47. The most approved theory of civil society requires that popular schools open to the children of all classes, and, generally, all public institutes intended for instruction in letters and philosophy, and for conducting the education of the young, should be freed from all ecclesiastical authority, government, and interference, and should be completely subject to the civil and political power, in conformity with the will of rulers and the prevalent opinions of the age. . . .

53. The laws for the protection of religious establishments, and securing their rights and duties, ought to be abolished; nay, more, the civil government may lend its assistance to all who desire to quit the religious life they have undertaken, and to break their vows. The government may also suppress religious orders.

55. The Church ought to be separated from the State, and the State from the Church.

63. It is allowable to refuse obedience to legitimate princes; nay, more, to rise in insurrection against them.

79. Moreover, it is false that the civil freedom granted to every mode of worship, and the full power given to all of overtly and publicly manifesting their opinions and their ideas, whatsoever their nature, conduce more easily to corrupt the morals and minds of the people, and facilitate the propagation of the pest of indifferentism.

80. The Roman Pontiff can and ought to reconcile himself to, and agree with, progress, liberalism, and civilization, as lately introduced.

Document Set 23.5 References

A. Charles Darwin Defends His Theory of Natural Selection
Charles Darwin, *The Origin of Species and the Descent of Man* (New York: Modern Library, n.d.), 367–368, 373–374.

B. Bishop Wilberforce Argues Against Darwin
Wilberforce, *The Quarterly Review*, Vol. 108 (1860), in Walter Arnstein, ed., *The Past Speaks*, 2d ed. (Lexington, Mass.: D. C. Heath, 1993), 2:215–217.

C. Alfred Tennyson Contemplates "Nature Red in Tooth and Claw"
Alfred Tennyson, *In Memoriam*, nos. 55, 56.

D. August Comte Charts a Positivist Future for Society
Adapted from *Auguste Comte and Positivism: The Essential Writings*, ed. Gertrud Lenzer (Chicago: University of Chicago Press, 1975), 318.

E. Pope Pius IX Catalogues Some Errors of the Day
Pius IX, Syllabus of 1864, in James Harvey Robinson and Charles Beard, eds., *Readings in Modern European History* (Boston: Ginn, 1909), 2:178–180.

DOCUMENT SET 23.6
Warfare in the Mid-Nineteenth Century

Six major wars[1] in the Western world and several smaller-scale clashes justified calling the years 1851–1871 an age of "Blood and Iron," to borrow a phrase made famous by the instigator of three of those wars, Bismarck. Europe had seen no significant fighting since 1815, so a generation reared to think of war as glorious found itself horrified by the bloodshed that advances in firepower now made possible. Napoleon III and Francis Joseph, for example, were both so literally sickened by viewing the carnage at Solferino in 1859 that they quickly made peace.

The young Russian aristocrat and artillery officer Leo Tolstoy (1828–1910) took part in the defense of Sebastopol and soon thereafter published his first book, *Sebastopol Sketches* (Document A), a powerful exposé of the gruesomeness of conflict, the moral failings of the officer class, and the stoic endurance of peasant conscripts. The horrors of the Crimean War were recorded on the British side (Document B) by William Howard Russell (1821–1907), one of the first great war correspondents—an occupation made possible by the invention of the telegraph and the rise of the popular newspaper. Tennyson's famous tribute "The Charge of the Light Brigade" (Document C), though it did not reflect firsthand witness, did express the British public's revulsion against the war's mismanagement while still breathing with romantic exultation in death-defying heroism. More significantly, the Crimean War opened a wide sphere of moral endeavor for nineteenth-century women (an experience repeated in the American Civil War). Florence Nightingale (1820–1910) led a group of volunteer women to the Crimea, shocking polite society because of fears that nurses among soldiers would become prostitutes. Nightingale's devoted service in alleviating suffering and her exposure of the shockingly high mortality rates made her a heroine and nursing a respected female profession. Document D is an extract from her 1858 book *Introducing Female Nurses into Military Hospitals*.

Bismarck witnessed some of the major battles of his wars, including Königgrätz (or Sadowa), where in 1866 Prussia decisively defeated Austria. His description, in a letter to his wife, constitutes Document E, reflecting his somber realization of what the victory

had—and had not—accomplished. How does it fit with what you know of Bismarck's character and aims?

Any description of the meaning of war for mid nineteenth-century Western civilization must include Abraham Lincoln's two-minute oration at the dedication of the military cemetery at Gettysburg in 1863 (Document F).

A. Leo Tolstoy Describes the Siege of Sevastopol, 1854–1855

Prince Galtzine met in constantly increasing numbers wounded men borne on stretchers, others dragging themselves along on foot or supporting each other, and talking noisily.

"When they fell upon us, brothers," said the bass voice of a tall soldier who carried two muskets on his shoulder—"when they fell upon us, shouting 'Allah! allah!' they pushed one another on. We killed the first, and others climbed over them. There was nothing to be done; there were too many of them—too many of them!"

"You come from the bastion?" asked Galtzine, interrupting the orator.

"Yes, your Excellency."

"Well, what happened there? Tell me."

"This happened, your Excellency—*his strength* surrounded us; he climbed on the ramparts and had the best of it, your Excellency."

"How? the best of it? But you beat them back?"

"Ah yes, beat them back! But when all *his strength* came down upon us, *he* killed our men, and no help for it!"

The soldier was mistaken, for the trenches were ours; but, strange but well-authenticated fact, a soldier wounded in a battle always believes it a lost and a terribly bloody one.

"I was told, nevertheless, that you beat him back," continued Galtzine, good-naturedly; "perhaps it was after you came away. Did you leave there long ago?"

"This very moment, your Excellency. The trenches must belong to him; he had the upper-hand—"

"Why, aren't you ashamed of yourselves? Abandon the trenches! It is frightful," said Galtzine, irritated by the indifference of the man.

"What could be done when *he* had the *strength*."

---

[1] The Crimean War, the Austro-French War of 1859, the American Civil War, the Danish War of 1864, the Seven Weeks' War, and the Franco-Prussian War

"Ah, your Excellency," said a soldier borne on a stretcher, "why not abandon them, when he has killed us all? If we had the *strength* we would never have abandoned them! But what was to be done? I had just stuck one of them when I was hit—Oh, softly, brothers, softly! Oh, for mercy's sake!" groaned the wounded man.

"Hold on; far too many are coming back," said Galtzine, again stopping the tall soldier with the two muskets. "Why don't you go back, hey? Halt!"

The soldier obeyed, and took off his cap with his left hand.

"Where are you going to?" sternly demanded the prince, "and who gave you permission, good-for—" But coming nearer, he saw that the soldier's right arm was covered with blood up to the elbow.

"I am wounded, your Excellency."

"Wounded! where?"

"Here, by a bullet," and the soldier showed his arm; "but I don't know what hit me a crack there." He held his head down, and showed on the back of his neck locks of hair glued together by coagulated blood.

"Whose gun is this?"

"It is a French carbine, your Excellency; I brought it away. I wouldn't have come away, but I had to lead that small soldier, who might fall down;" and he pointed to an infantryman who was walking some paces ahead of them leaning on his gun and dragging his left leg with difficulty.

Prince Galtzine was cruelly ashamed of his unjust suspicions, and conscious that he was blushing, turned around. Without questioning or looking after the wounded any more, he directed his steps towards the field-hospital. Making his way to the entrance with difficulty through soldiers, litters, stretcher-bearers who came in with the wounded and went out with the dead, Galtzine entered as far as the first room, took one look about him, recoiled involuntarily, and precipitately fled into the street. What he saw there was far too horrible!

B. An English Reporter Reports on the Bloody Storming of Sevastopol

On the 9th September Sebastopol was in flames! The fleet, the object of so much diplomatic controversy, and of so many bloody struggles, had disappeared in the deep! One more great act of carnage was added to the tremendous but glorious tragedy, of which the whole world, from the most civilized nations down to the most barbarous hordes of the East, was the anxious and excited audience.

Amid shouts of victory and cries of despair—in frantic rejoicing and passionate sorrow—a pall of black smoke, streaked by the fiery flashings of exploding fortresses, descended upon the stage, . . .

In the middle of the day there was a council of the allied generals, and at two o'clock it became generally known that the allies would assault the place at noon on the 8th, after a vigorous cannonade and bombardment. The hour was well selected, as it had been ascertained that the Russians were accustomed to indulge in a siesta about that time.

The weather changed suddenly on the 7th September, and on the morning of the 8th it became bitterly cold. A biting wind right from the north side of Sebastopol blew intolerable clouds of harsh dust into our faces. The sun was obscured, and the sky became of a leaden, wintry gray.

The French were reënforced by five thousand Sardinians, who marched up from the Tchernaya. It was arranged that the French should attack the Malakoff at noon, and, as soon as their attack succeeded, we were to assault the Redan. At five minutes before twelve o'clock, the French, like a swarm of bees, issued forth from their trenches close to the Malakoff, scrambled up its face, and were through the embrasures in the twinkling of an eye. They crossed the seven meters of ground which separated them from the enemy at a few bounds; they drifted as lightly and quickly as autumn leaves before the wind, battalion after battalion, into the embrasures, and in a minute or two after the head of their column issued from the ditch the tricolor was floating over the Korniloff Bastion. The musketry was very feeble at first,—indeed, our allies took the Russians by surprise, and very few of the latter were in the Malakoff; but they soon recovered themselves, and from twelve o'clock till past seven in the evening the French had to meet and repulse the repeated attempts of the enemy to regain the work, when, weary of the fearful slaughter of his men, who lay in thousands over the exterior of the works, and despairing of success, the Muscovite general withdrew his exhausted legions, and prepared, with admirable skill, to evacuate the place.

As the alarm of the English assault on the Redan circulated, the enemy came rushing up from the barracks in the rear of the Redan, increasing the force and intensity of their fire, while our soldiers dropped fast. The Russians were encouraged to maintain their ground by the immobility of our soldiers and the weakness of a fusillade, from the effects of which the enemy were well protected. In vain the officers, by voice and act, by example and daring valor, tried to urge our soldiers on to clear the works. The men, most of whom belonged to regiments which had suffered in the trenches and were acquainted with the traditions of June 18, had an impression that the Redan was extensively mined, and that if they advanced they would all be blown up; yet, to their honor be it recorded, many of them acted as became the men of Alma and Inkermann, and, rushing confusedly to the front, were swept down by the enemy's fire.

Every moment our men were diminishing in numbers, while the Russians were arriving in swarms from the town, and rushing down from the Malakoff, which had been occupied by the French. The struggle that ensued was short, desperate, and bloody. Our soldiers, taken at every disadvantage, met the enemy with the bayonet too, and isolated combats occurred, in which the brave fellows who stood their ground had to defend themselves against three or four adversaries at once. In this mêlée the officers, armed only with their swords, had but little chance; nor had those who carried pistols much opportunity of using them in such a close and sudden contest. They fell like heroes, and many a gallant soldier with them. The bodies of English and Russians inside the Redan, locked in an embrace which death could not relax, but had rather cemented all the closer, were found next day as evidences of the terrible animosity of the struggle.

The scene in the ditch was appalling, although some of the officers have assured me that they and the men were laughing at the precipitation with which many brave and gallant fellows did not hesitate to plunge headlong upon the mass of bayonets, muskets, and sprawling soldiers,—the ladders were all knocked down or broken, so that it was difficult for the men to scale the other side, and the dead, the dying, the wounded, and the uninjured were all lying in piles together. . . .

C. Tennyson Commemorates the Futile Valor of the Light Brigade

Half a league, half a league,
　　Half a league onward,
All in the valley of Death
　　Rode the six hundred.
"Forward, the Light Brigade!
Charge for the guns," he said:
Into the valley of Death
　　Rode the six hundred.

"Forward, the Light Brigade!"
Was there a man dismay'd?

Not tho' the soldier knew
　　Some one had blunder'd:
Theirs not to make reply,
Theirs not to reason why,
Theirs but to do and die:
Into the valley of Death
　　Rode the six hundred.

Cannon to right of them,
Cannon to left of them,
Cannon in front of them
　　Volley'd and thunder'd;
Storm'd at with shot and shell,
Boldly they rode and well,
Into the jaws of Death,
Into the mouth of Hell
　　Rode the six hundred.

Flash'd all their sabres bare,
Flash'd as they turn'd in air
Sabring the gunners there,
Charging an army, while
　　All the world wonder'd:
Plunged in the battery-smoke
Right thro' the line they broke;
Cossack and Russian
Reel'd from the sabre-stroke
　　Shatter'd and sunder'd.
Then they rode back, but not,
　　Not the six hundred.

Cannon to right of them,
Cannon to left of them,
Cannon behind them
　　Volley'd and thunder'd;
Storm'd at with shot and shell,
While horse and hero fell,
They that had fought so well
Came thro' the jaws of Death,
Back from the mouth of Hell,
All that was left of them,
　　Left of six hundred.

When can their glory fade!
O the wild charge they made!
　　All the world wonder'd.
Honor the charge they made!
Honor the Light Brigade,
　　Noble six hundred!

D. Florence Nightingale Nurses the Crimean War Wounded, 1858

There is no doubt that the admission of women to ward service is beset with difficulties. Nurses are careful, efficient, often decorous, and always kind, sometimes drunken, sometimes unchaste.

The nurses should be strong, active women, of unblemished character, and should be irreversibly dismissed for the first offence of unchastity, drunkenness, or dishonesty, or proved impropriety of any kind.

Their rules should be simple, very definite, should leave them at the absolute disposal of the surgeon. Their dress should be uniform.

Give them plenty to do, and great responsibility-two effectual means of steadying women.

"In quietness and in confidence shall be your strength." Quietness has been from the beginning of its publicity the one thing wanted in this work. I know the fuss, which from its beginning surrounded it, was abhorrent to us: but the work, which is all we care for, has throughout suffered from it. One hospital, naval, military, or civil, nursed well, and gradually training a few nurses, would do more good to the cause than an endless amount of meetings, testimonials, pounds, and speeches. This never will, never can be a popular work. Few good ones are, without the stern fructifying element of moral restraint and influence; and though the streams of this are many, its source is one. Hearts are not touched without Religion. Religion was not given us from above in impressions and generalities, but in habits of thought and action, in love of God and of mankind, carried into action.

E. Bismarck Witnesses the Battle of Königgrätz, 1866

... It goes well with us—at least, if we are not excessive in our demands and do not think that we have conquered the world, we shall achieve a peace that is worth while. But we are as easily elated as we are cast down, and I have the thankless task of pouring water into the intoxicating wine, and making it plain that we do not live alone in Europe but with three neighbors.

The Austrians have taken a stand in Moravia, and we are at present so rash as to propose that to-morrow our headquarters shall be on the spot they now occupy. Prisoners are still coming in, and one hundred and eighty cannon have arrived since the 3d. If they bring on their southern army, we shall, with God's gracious aid, beat that, too. Confidence is everywhere. Our soldiers are dears [*Unsere Leute sind zum Küssen*],—every one of them so heroic, quiet, obedient, and decent, though with empty stomachs, wet clothes, wet camp, little sleep, and no soles to their shoes! They are friendly to all, with no plundering or burning, but paying what they can, and eating moldy bread. There must be a goodly stock of fear of God among our common men, otherwise things could not be as they are. It is hard to get news of acquaintances; we are scattered miles apart, and do not know where to send, and have no one to send. There are men enough, of course, but no horses. ...

The king exposed himself a great deal on the 3d, and it was a good thing that I was with him, for the warnings of others did not influence him, and no one else would have dared to talk to him as I did the last time,—and it did the job,—when a knot of ten cuirassiers and fifteen horses of the sixth cuirassier regiment were trampling about us in bloody confusion and the shells buzzed around disagreeably near his Majesty. The worst of them happily did not go off. I should, however, rather have had him too venturesome than to have him show himself overprudent. He was delighted with his troops, and with good reason, so that he did not seem to notice the whizzing and din about him. He was as composed as if he were on the Kreuzberg, and kept finding a new battalion to thank and say good-night to, until we were nearly within the firing line again. But so much was said to him of his recklessness that he will be more careful in the future, so your mind may be at rest on that score. I can hardly believe yet that the battle has really taken place. ...

F. Abraham Lincoln Eulogizes the Union Dead at Gettysburg, 1863

Four score and seven years ago our fathers brought forth on this continent, a new nation, conceived in Liberty, and dedicated to the proposition that all men are created equal.

Now we are engaged in a great civil war, testing whether that nation, or any nation so conceived and so dedicated, can long endure. We are met on a great battle-field of that war. We have come to dedicate a portion of that field, as a final resting place for those who here gave their lives that that nation might live. It is altogether fitting and proper that we should do this.

But, in a larger sense, we can not dedicate—we can not consecrate—we can not hallow—this ground. The brave men, living and dead, who struggled here, have consecrated it, far above our poor power to add or detract. The world will little note, nor long remember what we say here, but it can never forget what they did here. It is for us the living, rather, to be dedicated here to the unfinished work which they who fought here have thus far so nobly advanced. It is rather for us to be here dedicated to the great task remaining before us—that from these honored dead we take increased devotion to that cause for which they gave the last full measure of devotion—that we here highly resolve that these dead shall not have died in vain—that this nation, under God, shall have a new birth of freedom—and that government of the people, by the people, for the people, shall not perish from the earth.

Document Set 23.6 References

A. Leo Tolstoy Describes the Siege of Sevastopol, 1854–1855
Tolstoy, *Sevastopol Sketches,* Frank D. Millet, trans. (Ann Arbor: University of Michigan Press, 1961), 65–69.
B. An English Reporter Reports on the Bloody Storming of Sevastopol
William Howard Russell, in James Harvey Robinson and Charles Beard, eds., *Readings in Modern European History* (Boston: Ginn, 1909), 2:391–394.
C. Tennyson Commemorates the Futile Valor of the Light Brigade
Alfred Tennyson, "The Charge of the Light Brigade."
D. Florence Nightingale Nurses the Crimean War Wounded, 1858
Nightingale, *Introducing Female Nurses into Military Hospitals,* in Lucy Ridgely Seymer, ed. *Selected Writings of Florence Nightingale* (New York: Macmillan, 1954), 17–19.
E. Bismarck Witnesses the Battle of Königgrätz, 1866
Otto von Bismarck, letter, in James Harvey Robinson, ed. *Readings in European History* (Boston: Ginn, 1904), 2:582–583.
F. Abraham Lincoln Eulogizes the Union Dead at Gettysburg, 1863
Abraham Lincoln, The Gettysburg Address.

DOCUMENT SET 23.7
The Franco-Prussian War

The documents of this set can be considered along with those of earlier sets in this chapter in analyzing the propensity of nineteenth-century Europeans to use war to settle differences among states, as well as the growing fragility of modern societies in the face of war.

Bismarck's account of the famous episode in which he waved "a 'red rag' [before] the Gallic Bull," maneuvering France into declaring war against Prussia in 1870, is in Document A. The memoirs of a very different kind of political figure, the "Red Virgin" Louise Michel (1830–1905), described the siege of Paris and the Commune from the viewpoint of a veteran revolutionary and feminist (Document B). How does her account compare with Karl Marx's famous analysis, *Civil War in France* (Document C)?

A. Bismarck Reveals How He Edited the Ems Telegram

All considerations, conscious and unconscious, strengthened my opinion that war could only be avoided at the cost of the honor of Prussia and of the national confidence in her. Under this conviction I made use of the royal authorization communicated to me through Abeken to publish the contents of the telegram; and in the presence of my two guests [General Moltke and General Roon] I reduced the telegram by striking out words, but without adding or altering anything, to the following form:

"After the news of the renunciation of the hereditary prince of Hohenzollern had been officially communicated to the imperial government of France by the royal government of Spain, the French ambassador at Ems made the further demand of his Majesty the king that he should authorize him to telegraph to Paris that his Majesty the king bound himself for all future time never again to give his consent if the Hohenzollerns should renew their candidature. His Majesty the king thereupon decided not to receive the French ambassador again, and sent to tell him, through the aid-de-camp on duty, that his Majesty had nothing further to communicate to the ambassador."

The difference in the effect of the abbreviated text of the Ems telegram as compared with that produced by the original was not the result of stronger words, but of the form, which made this announcement appear decisive, while Abeken's version would

only have been regarded as a fragment of a negotiation still pending and to be continued at Berlin.

After I had read out the concentrated edition to my two guests, Moltke remarked: "Now it has a different ring; in its original form it sounded like a parley; now it is like a flourish of trumpets in answer to a challenge." I went on to explain: "If, in execution of his Majesty's order, I at once communicate this text, which contains no alteration in or addition to the telegram, not only to the newspapers, but also by telegraph to all our embassies, it will be known in Paris before midnight, and not only on account of its contents, but also on account of the manner of its distribution, will have the effect of a red rag upon the Gallic bull.

"Fight we must if we do not want to act the part of the vanquished without a battle. Success, however, depends essentially upon the impression which the origination of the war makes upon us and others; it is important that we should be the ones attacked, and the Gallic insolence and touchiness will bring about this result if we announce in the face of Europe, so far as we can without the speaking tube of the Reichstag, that we fearlessly meet the public threats of France."

This explanation brought about in the two generals a revulsion to a more joyous mood, the liveliness of which surprised me. They had suddenly recovered their pleasure in eating and drinking and spoke in a more cheerful vein. Roon said, "Our God of old still lives, and will not let us perish in disgrace." Moltke so far relinquished his passive equanimity that, glancing up joyously toward the ceiling and abandoning his usual punctiliousness of speech, he smote his hand upon his breast and said, "If I may but live to lead our armies in such a war, then the devil may come directly afterwards and fetch away the old carcass."

B. A Radical Woman Recalls the Siege and the Paris Commune

In Montmartre, in the Eighteenth Arrondissement, we organized the Montmartre Vigilance Committee. Few of its members still survive, but during the Siege the committee made the reactionaries tremble. Every evening, we would burst out onto the streets from our headquarters at 41, chaussée Clignancourt, sometimes simply to talk up the Revolution, because the time for duplicity had passed. We knew how little the reactionary regime, in its death throes, valued its promises and the lives of its citizens, and the people had to be warned. . . .

The members of the men's Montmartre Vigilance Committee were remarkable persons. Never have I seen minds so direct, so unpretentious, and so elevated. Never have I seen individuals so clearheaded. I don't know how this group managed to do it. There were no weaknesses. Something good and strong supported people.

The women were courageous also, and among them, too, there were some remarkable minds. I belonged to both committees, and the leanings of the two groups were the same. Sometime in the future the women's committee should have its own history told. Or perhaps the two should be mingled, because people didn't worry about which sex they were before they did their duty. That stupid question was settled. . . .

Ultimately the Montmartre Vigilance Committees were mowed down, like all revolutionary groups. The rare members still alive know how proud we were there and how fervently we flew the flag of the Revolution. Little did it matter to those who were there whether they were beaten to the ground unnoticed in battle or died alone in the sunlight. It makes no difference how the millstone moves so long as the bread is made.

Everything was beginning, or rather, beginning again, after the long lethargy of the Empire. The first organization of the Rights of Women had begun to meet on the rue Thévenot with Mmes Jules Simon, André Léo, and Maria Deraismes. At the meetings of the Rights of Women group, and at other meetings, the most advanced men applauded the idea of equality. I noticed—I had seen it before, and I saw it later—that men, their declarations notwithstanding, although they appeared to help us, were always content with just the appearance. This was the result of custom and the force of old prejudices, and it convinced me that we women must simply take our place without begging for it. The issue of political rights is dead. Equal education, equal trades, so that prostitution would not be the only lucrative profession open to a woman—that is what was real in our program. The Russian revolutionaries are right; evolution is ended and now revolution is necessary or the butterfly will die in its cocoon.

Heroic women were found in all social positions. At the professional school of Mme Poulin, women of all social levels organized the Society for the Victims of the War. They would have preferred to die rather than surrender, and dispensed their efforts the best way they could, while demanding ceaselessly that Paris continue to resist the Prussian siege. . . .

. . . [B]efore dawn on March 18 the Versailles reactionaries sent in troops to seize the cannon now held by the National Guard. One of the points they moved toward was the Butte of Montmartre, where our cannon had been taken. The soldiers of the reactionaries captured our artillery by surprise, but they were unable to haul them away as they had intended, because they had neglected to bring horses with them.

Learning that the Versailles soldiers were trying to seize the cannon, men and women of Montmartre swarmed up the Butte in a surprise maneuver. Those people who were climbing believed they would die, but they were prepared to pay the price.

The Butte of Montmartre was bathed in the first light of day, through which things were glimpsed as if they were hidden behind a thin veil of water. Gradually the crowd increased. The other districts of Paris, hearing of the events taking place on the Butte of Montmartre, came to our assistance.

The women of Paris covered the cannon with their bodies. When their officers ordered the soldiers to fire, the men refused. The same army that would be used to crush Paris two months later decided now that it did not want to be an accomplice of the reaction. They gave up their attempt to seize the cannon from the National Guard. They understood that the people were defending the Republic by defending the arms that the royalists and imperialists would have turned on Paris in agreement with the Prussians. When we had won our victory, I looked around and noticed my poor mother, who had followed me to the Butte of Montmartre, believing that I was going to die.

On this day, the eighteenth of March, the people wakened. If they had not, it would have been the triumph of some king; instead it was a triumph of the people. The eighteenth of March could have belonged to the allies of kings, or to foreigners, or to the people. It was the people's. . . .

Several of our side perished. Turpin, who was wounded near me on the eighteenth in the predawn attack on 6, rue des Rosiers, died at Lariboisière several days later. He told me to commend his wife to Georges Clemenceau, the mayor of the Eighteenth Arrondissement, and I carried out his dying wish.

I have never heard Clemenceau's testimony at the inquiry into the events of March 18; we weren't able to read newspapers when he gave his evidence. Clemenceau's indecisiveness, for which people reproach him, comes from the illusion he holds that he should wait for parliamentarianism to bring progress. But parliamentarianism is dead, and Clemenceau's illusion is some kind of infection he caught from the Bordeaux Assembly. When that assembly became the Versailles government, he fled from it. Properly, his place is in the streets, and when his anger is finally roused, he will go there. That is what remains of his revolutionary temperament. His indignation at some infamy will bring him out of his illusions, as he came out of the Bordeaux Assembly. . . .

If the reaction had had as many enemies among women as it did among men, the Versailles government would have had a more difficult task subduing us. Our male friends are more susceptible to faintheartedness than we women are. A supposedly weak woman knows better than any man how to say: "It must be done." She may feel ripped open to her very womb, but she remains unmoved. Without hate, without anger, without pity for herself or others, whether her heart bleeds or not, she can say, "It must be done." Such were the women of the Commune. During Bloody Week, women erected and defended the barricade at the Place Blanche—and held it till they died. . . .

C. Karl Marx Sees in the Commune the Model of Coming Communist Revolutions

The direct antithesis to the empire was the Commune. The cry of "social republic" with which the Revolution of February was ushered in by the Paris proletariat, did but express a vague aspiration after a republic that was not only to supersede the monarchical form of class rule, but class rule itself. The Commune was the positive form of that republic. . . .

The Commune was formed of the municipal councillors, chosen by universal suffrage in the various wards of the town, responsible and revocable at short terms. The majority of its members were naturally working men, or acknowledged representatives of the working class. The Commune was to be a working, not a parliamentary body, executive and legislative at the same time. Instead of continuing to be the agent of the Central Government, the police was at once stripped of its political attributes, and turned into the responsible and at all times revocable agent of the Commune. So were the officials of all other branches of the administration. From the members of the Commune downwards, the public service had to be done at *workmen's wages*. The vested interests and the representation allowances of the high dignitaries of state disappeared along with the high dignitaries themselves. Public functions ceased to be the private property of the tools of the Central Government. Not only municipal administration, but the whole initiative hitherto exercised by the state was laid into the hands of the Commune. . . .

[N]o sooner do the working men anywhere take the subject into their own hands with a will, than uprises at once all the apologetic phraseology of the mouthpieces of present society. . . . The Commune, they exclaim, intends to abolish property, the basis of all civilisation! Yes, gentlemen, the Commune intended to abolish that class property which makes the labour of the many the wealth of the few. It aimed at the expropriation of the expropriators. It wanted to make individual property a truth by transforming the means of production, land and capital, now chiefly the means of enslaving and exploiting labour, into mere instruments of free and associated labour. But this is communism, "impossible" communism! . . .

The working class did not expect miracles from the Commune. They have no ready-made utopias to introduce *par decret du peuple* [by decree of the people]. They know that in order to work out their own emancipation, and along with it that higher form to which present society is irresistibly tending by its own economical agencies, they will have to pass through long struggles, through a series of historic processes, transforming circumstances and men. They have no ideals to realise, but to set free the elements of the new society with which old collapsing bourgeois society itself is pregnant. In the full consciousness of their historic mission, and with the heroic resolve to act up to it, the working class can afford to smile at the coarse invective of the gentlemen's gentlemen with the pen and inkhorn, and at the didactic patronage of well-wishing bourgeois-doctrinaires, pouring forth their ignorant platitudes and sectarian crotchets in the oracular tone of scientific infallibility.

When the Paris Commune took the management of the revolution in its own hands; when plain working men for the first time dared to infringe upon the governmental privilege of their "natural superiors," and, under circumstances of unexampled difficulty, performed their work modestly, conscientiously, and efficiently—performed it at salaries the highest of which barely amounted to one-fifth of what, according to high scientific authority is the minimum required for a secretary to a certain metropolitan school-board—the old world writhed in convulsion of rage at the sight of the Red Flag, the symbol of the Republic of Labour, floating over the Hôtel de Ville. . . .

Document Set 23.7 References

A. Bismarck Reveals How He Edited the Ems Telegram
Otto von Bismarck, *Memoirs,* in James Harvey Robinson and
Charles Beard, eds., *Readings in Modern European History*
(Boston: Ginn, 1909), 2:158–159.

B. A Radical Woman Recalls the Siege and the Paris Commune
Louise Michel, in Bullitt Lowry and Elizabeth Ellington
Guner, eds., *The Red Virgin: Memoirs of Louise Michel*
(Alabama: University of Alabama Press, 1981), 58–59, 63–65,
67.

C. Karl Marx Sees in the Commune the Model of Coming
Communist Revolutions
Karl Marx and V. I. Lenin, *The Civil War in France: The Paris
Commune* (New York: International Publishers, 1940, 1968),
56–57, 61–62.

Empire, Industry, and Everyday Life, 1871–1894

DOCUMENT SET 24.1
Imperialist Expansion and Diplomatic Equilibrium

The two themes of this chapter are closely linked. As long as Bismarck's diplomacy could maintain order— and as long as Germany was content with the security that the Iron Chancellor's system ensured—the Continent remained at peace. Most of the great powers pursued their ambitions for territorial growth overseas. Only as the nineteenth century was reaching its end did imperialist clashes begin to threaten the equilibrium at home. Imperialist expansion confirmed in Europeans the comfortable sense of their superiority that the idea of progress had already kindled in them. The English explorer and conqueror of Africa Henry M. Stanley (1841–1904) had much advice on how to prove one's superiority by controlling both Africans and military men (Document A). His exploits and those of the other explorers that he reported as a journalist captured the public imagination, but he and other prominent figures also entered the emerging urban popular culture of music-hall songs. In the early 1890s the song quoted in Document B regularly brought down the house at the London "Gaiety." Meanwhile, the gospel of imperialism was being preached in the emerging mass circulation press with arguments like those in Document C's front-page editorial. How effective do you judge such appeals?

Bismarck pushed defeated France to pursue imperial glory abroad, hoping (vainly) that they would forget the loss of Alsace-Loraine. To isolate France, Bismarck first made an alliance with former enemy Austria-Hungary in 1879 and then extended it in the Triple Alliance of Germany, Austria-Hungary, and Italy in 1882 (Document D). The treaty was defensive, but

many contemporaries thought otherwise because its provisions were secret. To check Russian and Austrian ambitions in the Balkans, Bismarck had meanwhile entered into the Three Emperors' League in 1881. When this expired in 1887, Germany and Russia substituted the Reinsurance Treaty (Document E), attempting to guarantee Russia against attack by Austria-Hungary. But this arrangement was unwelcome to Germany's new ruler, William II (*1888–1918), because it implied a less than totally supportive attitude toward Germanic Austria-Hungary. The Reinsurance Treaty lapsed in 1891, after Bismarck had been dismissed by the new Kaiser. The next year Bismarck's old nightmare came true: France broke its twenty-year isolation by signing a military convention with Russia (Document F), thereby threatening to encircle Germany on both sides.

Imperialist expansion and power politics were heady experiences. How would you evaluate the somber message of Rudyard Kipling (1865–1936), the Indian-born British poet who both celebrated British patriotism and satirized aspects of imperialism in his "Recessional"—a poem written for Queen Victoria's "Diamond Jubilee" in 1897 (Document G)?

A. Sir Henry Stanley Sums Up Imperialist Attitudes

Some explorers say: "One must not run through a country, but give the people time to become acquainted with you, and let their worst fears subside."

Now on the expedition across Africa I had no time to give, either to myself or to them. The river bore my heavy canoes downward; my goods would never have endured the dawdling requirement by the system of teaching every tribe I met who I was. To save myself and my men from certain starvation, I had to rush on and on, right through. But on this expedition, the very necessity of making roads to haul my enormous six-ton wagons gave time for my reputation to travel ahead of me. My name, purpose, and liberal rewards for native help, naturally exaggerated, prepared a welcome for me, and transformed my enemies of the old time into workmen, friendly allies, strong porters, and firm friends. I was greatly forbearing also; but, when a fight was inevitable, through open violence, it was sharp and decisive. Consequently, the natives rapidly learned that though everything was to be gained by friendship with me, wars brought nothing but ruin.

When a young white officer quits England for the first time, to lead blacks, he has got to learn to unlearn a great deal. We *must* have white men in Africa; but the raw white is a great nuisance there during the first year. In the second year, he begins to mend; during the third year, if his nature permits it, he has developed into a superior man, whose intelligence may be of transcendent utility for directing masses of inferior men.

My officers were possessed with the notion that my manner was "hard," because I had not many compliments for them. That is the kind of pap which we may offer women and boys. Besides, I thought they were superior natures, and required none of that encouragement, which the more childish blacks almost daily received.

B. Stanley Comes in for Some Satire

Oh, I went to find Emin Pasha, and started away for
    fun,
With a box of weeds and a bag of beads, some
    tracts and a Maxim gun . . .
I went to find Emin, I did, I looked for him far and
    wide;
I found him right, I found him tight, and a lot of folks
    beside,
Away through Darkest Africa, though it cost me lots
    of tin,
For without a doubt I'd find him out, when I went to
    find Emin!

C. A French Popular Newspaper Argues for Imperialism, 1883

The future and wealth of France depend above all on the extension and prosperity of our colonies. . . . When factories produce more than consumers need, work must stop for a time, and workers, condemned to inactivity for a more or less long period, must live off their savings and suffer without there being any possibility to institute a remedy for the evil. . . . The reasons for the abnormal situation can be boiled down to a lack of markets for our products. . . . Once the French genius is put to colonization . . . we will find a draining of our overflow of our factories, and at the same time we will be able to secure, at the source of production, the primary materials needed in our factories.

D. Bismarck Isolates France: The Triple Alliance, 1882

Article I. The High Contracting Parties mutually promise peace and friendship, and will enter into no alliance or engagement directed against any one of their States.

They engage to proceed to an exchange of ideas on political and economic questions of a general nature which may arise, and they further promise one another mutual support within the limits of their own interests.

Article II. In case Italy, without direct provocation on her part, should be attacked by France for any reason whatsoever, the two other Contracting Parties shall be bound to lend help and assistance with all their forces to the Party attacked.

This same obligation shall devolve upon Italy in case of any aggression without direct provocation by France against Germany.

Article III. If one, or two, of the High Contracting Parties, without direct provocation on their part, should chance to be attacked and to be engaged in a war with two or more Great Powers nonsignatory to the present Treaty, the *casus foederis* [activation of the alliance] will arise simultaneously for all the High Contracting Parties.

Article IV. In case a Great Power nonsignatory to the present Treaty should threaten the security of the states of one of the High Contracting Parties, and the threatened Party should find itself forced on that account to make war against it, the two others bind themselves to observe towards their Ally a benevolent neutrality. Each of them reserves to itself, in this case, the right to take part in the war, if it should see fit, to make common cause with its Ally.

Article V. If the peace of any of the High Contracting Parties should chance to be threatened under the circumstances foreseen by the preceding Articles, the High Contracting Parties shall take counsel together in ample time as to the military measures to be taken with a view to eventual coöperation.

They engage henceforward, in all cases of common participation in a war, to conclude neither armistice, nor peace, nor treaty, except by common agreement among themselves.

Article VI. The High Contracting Parties mutually promise secrecy as to the contents and existence of the present Treaty.

E. Bismarck Takes No Chances: The Reinsurance Treaty, 1887

The Imperial Courts of Germany and of Russia, animated by an equal desire to strengthen the general peace by an understanding destined to assure the defensive position of their respective States, have resolved to confirm the agreement established between them by a special arrangement, in view of the expiration on June 15/27, 1887, of the validity of the secret Treaty and Protocol, signed in 1881 and renewed in 1884 by the three Courts of Germany, Russia, and Austria-Hungary....

Article I. In case one of the High Contracting Parties should find itself at war with a third great Power, the other would maintain a benevolent neutrality towards it, and would devote its efforts to the localization of the conflict. This provision would not apply to a war against Austria or France in case this war should result from an attack directed against one of these two latter Powers by one of the High Contracting Parties.

Article II. Germany recognizes the rights historically acquired by Russia in the Balkan Peninsula, and particularly the legitimacy of her preponderant and decisive influence in Bulgaria and in Eastern Rumelia. The two Courts engage to admit no modification of the territorial status quo of the said peninsula without a previous agreement between them, and to oppose, as occasion arises, every attempt to disturb this status quo or to modify it without their consent.

Article III. The two Courts recognize the European and mutually obligatory character of the principle of the closing of the Straits of the Bosphorus and of the Dardanelles, founded on international law, confirmed by treaties, and summed up in the declaration of the second Plenipotentiary of Russia at the session of July 12 of the Congress of Berlin (Protocol 19).

They will take care in common that Turkey shall make no exception to this rule in favor of the interests of any Government whatsoever, by lending to warlike operations of a belligerent power the portion of its Empire constituted by the Straits. In case of infringement, or to prevent it if such infringement should be in prospect, the two Courts will inform Turkey that they would regard her, in that event, as putting herself in a state of war towards the injured Party, and as depriving herself thenceforth of the benefits of the security assured to her territorial status quo by the Treaty of Berlin.

Article IV. The present Treaty shall remain in force for the space of three years, dating from the day of the exchange of ratifications.

Article V. The High Contracting Parties mutually promise secrecy as to the contents and the existence of the present Treaty and of the Protocol annexed thereto....

F. Bismarck's Nightmare Comes True: The Franco-Russian Military Convention, 1892

(1) Draft of Military Convention

France and Russia, being animated by an equal desire to preserve peace, and having no other object than to meet the necessities of a defensive war, provoked by an attack of the forces of the Triple Alliance against the one or the other of them, have agreed upon the following provisions:

1. If France is attacked by Germany, or by Italy supported by Germany, Russia shall employ all her available forces to attack Germany.

If Russia is attacked by Germany, or by Austria supported by Germany, France shall employ all her available forces to fight Germany.

2. In case the forces of the Triple Alliance, or of one of the Powers composing it, should mobilize, France and Russia, at the first news of the event and without the necessity of any previous concert, shall mobilize immediately and simultaneously the whole of their forces and shall move them as close as possible to their frontiers.

3. The available forces to be employed against Germany shall be on the part of France, 1,300,000 men, on the part of Russia, 700,000 or 800,000 men.

These forces shall engage to the full, with all speed, in order that Germany may have to fight at the same time on the East and on the West.

4. The General Staffs of the Armies of the two countries shall coöperate with each other at all times in the preparation and facilitation of the execution of the measures above foreseen.

They shall communicate to each other, while there is still peace, all information relative to the armies of the Triple Alliance which is or shall be within their knowledge.

Ways and means of corresponding in times of war shall be studied and arranged in advance.

5. France and Russia shall not conclude peace separately.

6. The present Convention shall have the same duration as the Triple Alliance.

7. All the clauses above enumerated shall be kept rigorously secret. . . .

(2) General de Boisdeffre's interview with the Tsar regarding the Military Convention. "Mobilization is a declaration of war

Saint Petersburg, August 18, 1892

This morning, Tuesday, I received from the Minister of War a letter dated August 5/17, in which . . . he made known to me that the Emperor had approved in principle the project as a whole. [The draft of the Military Convention.] . . . The Emperor had evidently held that the basis of the entente would have to be precisely and officially fixed before his audience.

We have now, awaiting the exchange of ratifications with ministeries signatures, an official basis for a definite convention, a basis that can be considered as absolutely sure and decisive when one knows the reserve and the prudence of the Russian Government and the firmness of the Emperor in his engagements.

At eleven o'clock, I was received by the Emperor. His Majesty declared to me immediately that he had read, re-read, and studied the project of the convention, that he gave it his full approbation, taking it as a whole, and that he thanked the French Government for accepting some changes of wording that he had requested.

His Majesty added that the convention contained, to his mind, some political articles which he desired to have examined by the Minister of Foreign Affairs; that there might be, as a result, some minor changes of wording to be made. Finally, His Majesty repeated that the project gave him entire satisfaction and that everything seemed to him to be adjusted to the best interests of the two countries.

I did not believe it necessary to take up again the defence of the first text, since the new text had received the approval of the Government. I only said to the Emperor that the French Government had wished to testify once more through this concession to its confidence in him. The Emperor did not fail to tell me of his strong desire that we guard the secret absolutely. . . .

The Emperor spoke of his desire for peace. I remarked to him that we were no less pacific than His Majesty. "I know it," he responded. "You have given proof of it for twenty-two years." I believe, moreover, that at this moment, peace is not threatened. The German Emperor has enough internal troubles, and England has as many. Moreover, with our convention, I estimate that our situation will be favorable. I surely desire to have at least two more years of peace, for it is necessary for us to complete our armament, our railways, and to recover from want and from the cholera. In fine, it is necessary to hope that peace will be maintained for a long time yet, and let us wish for it.

The Emperor then spoke of mobilization under Article 2. I ventured to remark that mobilization was the declaration of war; that to mobilize was to oblige one's neighbor to do so also; that the mobilization entailed the execution of strategic transportation and of concentration. Without that, to allow the mobilization of a million men one one's frontier without doing the same simultaneously was to deny to one's self all possibility of stirring later. It would be like the situation an individual would be in if he had a pistol in his pocket and would allow his neighbor to point a gun at his forehead without drawing his own. "That is the way I understand it," the Emperor responded. . . .

G. Rudyard Kipling Cautions the Imperialist Generation

Recessional

God of our fathers, known of old—
Lord of our far-flung battle line—
Beneath whose awful hand we hold
Dominion over palm and pine—
　　Lord God of Hosts, be with us yet,
　　Lest we forget—lest we forget!

The tumult and the shouting die—
The Captains and the Kings depart—
Still stands thine ancient sacrifice,
An humble and a contrite heart.
　　Lord God of Hosts, . . .

Far-called, our navies melt away—
On dune and headland sinks the fire—
Lo, all our pomp of yesterday
Is one with Nineveh and Tyre!
　　Judge of the Nations, spare us yet,
　　Lest we forget . . .

If, drunk with sight of power, we loose
Wild tongues that have not Thee in awe—
Such boasting as the Gentiles use
Or lesser breeds without the Law—
    Lord God of Hosts, . . .

For heathen heart that puts her trust
In reeking tube and iron shard—
All valiant dust that builds on dust,
And guarding calls not Thee to guard,
For frantic boast and foolish word,
Thy Mercy on thy People, Lord!

Document Set 24.1 References

A. Sir Henry Stanley Sums Up Imperialist Attitudes
Henry Morgan Stanley, *Autobiography*, Dorothy Stanley, ed.
(New York: Houghton Mifflin, 1909), 342–343.

B. Stanley Comes in for Some Satire
Ernest Short, *Fifty Years of Vaudeville* (New York: Eyre and
Spotteswoode, 1946), 43.

C. A French Popular Newspaper Argues for Imperialism, 1883
Excerpt from the *Petit Journal* in William H. Schneider, *An
Empire for the Masses* (Westport, Conn.: Greenwood, 1982),
62.

D. Bismarck Isolates France: The Triple Alliance, 1882
First Treaty of Alliance Between Austria-Hungary, Germany,
and Italy, in William Henry Cooke and Edith Pierpont
Stickney, eds., *Readings in European International Relations*
(New York: Harper and Row, 1931), 8–9.

E. Bismarck Takes No Chances: The Reinsurance Treaty, 1887
The Reinsurance Treaty, 1887, in Cooke and Stickney, 21–22.

F. Bismarck's Nightmare Comes True: The Franco-Russian
Military Convention, 1892
Draft of Military Convention and Boisdeffre's Interview with
the Tsar, in Cooke and Stickney, 29–31.

G. Rudyard Kipling Cautions the Imperialist Generation
"Recessional," in Rudyard Kipling, *Barrack Room Ballads:
Recessional and Other Verse* (New York: Robert McBride,
1910).

DOCUMENT SET 24.2
The Emergence of Mass Society

A glittering symbol of the new urban mass society of late nineteenth-century Europe and North America was the department store. It fascinated people, not just as a giant commercial institution but also for its effect on that new species, the shopper. The prolific French realist novelist Emile Zola (1840–1902) wrote an entire novel about the department stores' transformation of Paris. The excerpt in Document A describes the owner's relationship to his female customers. What do you make of the religious metaphors and the antisemitism?

Immigration to the city—which occurred on a huge scale in the late nineteenth-century— was not confined to Europe. Vast numbers also crossed the Atlantic to North America, particularly from Austria-Hungary, Italy, and Russia. Among these was Rose Schneiderman (1882–1972), who came with her family from Russian Poland in 1890 (Document B). Quite soon she noticed how men and women adapted to the new mass culture. Adelheid Popp in Vienna—like Rose Schneiderman in America—eventually became an important labor leader, but her initiation into the crude ways of urban work clearly shocked this young woman who had grown up with the morality of village Catholicism (Document C). Notice in this case her mother's insistence that she overcome her squeamishness and earn her way.

Antisemitism constantly crops up in accounts of late nineteenth-century urban life. The baleful emergence of antisemitism as a mass political ideology dates from the 1880s (see also Set 24.3, Document E), and it fed on discontent whipped up by the middle-class merchants of cultural despair. Regrettably, one of these was the great composer Richard Wagner (1813–1883), who made his culural shrine at Bayreuth a hotbed of antisemitic propaganda such as the piece he published in his newspaper in 1878 (Document D). Notice Wagner's identification of Jewishness with the modernization that he professed to scorn.

A. Emile Zola Encounters the Department Store

It was for woman that the stores competed against each other, for woman whom they continually laid a trap with their sales, after having stunned her with their displays of goods. They had awakened in her flesh new desires, they were an immense temptation to which she succumbed fatally, first yielding to the purchases of a good housekeeper, then won over by coquettishness and finally devoured. In setting up things for sale, in democratizing luxury, the stores became a terrible agent of spending, ravaging households, exploiting the passion for ever more expensive fashions. And if, in the department store a woman was queen, adulated and flattered where she was weak, surrounded by kind attentions, she reigned there as a queen drunk with love, . . . who paid for every one of her follies with a drop of blood. Beneath his gallantry, Mouret [the owner] allowed himself the brutality of a jew selling something by the ounce; he raised a temple to her, he had her flattered by a legion of sales people, and created the rituals of a new cult; he thought of nothing but her, tried without rest to find even bigger seductions; and when he had emptied her pockets and wrecked her nerves, he was as full of a secret contempt as a man whose mistress had made the mistake of surrendering to him.

B. Russian-Born Rose Schneiderman Recalls the Immigrants' Experience in America

Mother had been here only a short time when I noticed that she looked older and more old-fashioned than father. It was so with most of our women, especially those who wore wigs or kerchiefs on their heads. So I thought that if I could persuade her to leave off her kerchief she would look younger and more up to date. So, one day, when we two were alone in the house, I asked her playfully to take off her kerchief and let me do her hair, just to see how it would look.

She consented reluctantly. She had never before in her married life had her hair uncovered before anyone. I was surprised how different she looked. I handed her our little mirror. She glanced at herself, admitted frankly that it looked well and began hastily to put on her kerchief.

"Mamma," I coaxed, "please don't put the kerchief on again—ever!"

At first she would not even listen to me. I began to coax and reason. I pointed out that wives often looked so much older because they were so old-fashioned, that the husbands were often ashamed to go out with them.

Mother put her finger on my lips.

"But father trims his beard," I still argued. Her

face looked sad. "Is that why," she said, "I too must sin?"

C. Working Life in Vienna, 1883: Adelheid Popp Finds Her First Job

I didn't give up hope, and one day I decided to put the few kreuzers I had for my lunch into the collection box for the Holy Father. On the same day I found a purse containing twelve guilders. I could scarcely contain my joy, and I thanked all the saints for this favor. It never occurred to me that some other poor devil might have been driven to despair by the loss of the purse. To me twelve guilders was such a great amount that I never thought that a poor person could have lost it. I didn't know anything about the responsibility of handing in things you found to the police. All I saw was the merciful hand of the saints in the purse lying in the way. That evening I joyously embraced my mother; I was so happy I couldn't speak; I could only get out the words "twelve guilders, twelve guilders." There was nothing but joy in our room now; and as if to crown our good luck, the next day I was summoned to report to a sandpaper and emery board factory, where I'd asked about work a few days earlier and they had taken down my name.

My new workplace was on the third floor of a building that was used exclusively for industrial purposes. Not having known the bustle of a factory, I had never felt so uncomfortable. Everything displeased me—the dirty, sticky work; the unpleasant glass dust; the crowd of people; the crude tone; and the whole way that the girls and even married women behaved.

The owner's wife—the "gracious lady," as she was called—was the actual manager of the factory, and she talked just like the girls. She was a nice-looking woman, but she drank brandy, took snuff, and made unseemly rude jokes with the workmen. The owner was very ill, and when he came himself, there was always a violent scene. I pitied him. He seemed to me to be so good and noble, and I gathered from the behavior and whole manner of his wife that he must be unhappy. At his instructions I received a different, much more pleasant job. Up to then my job had been to hang the papers, which were smeared with glue and sprinkled with glass, unto lines strung rather high across the workroom. This work exhausted me greatly, and the owner must have noticed that it wasn't suitable for me, because he instructed that from then on I was to keep count of the papers that were ready for processing. This work was clean and I

liked it a lot better. Of course when there wasn't anything to count, I had to do other kinds of work. . . .

They [the other working women] often spoke of a Herr Berger, who was the company's traveling representative and was expected back about then. All the women raved about him, so I was curious to see the man. I had been there for two weeks when he came. Everything was in a dither, and the only talk was of the looks of the traveler they so admired. Accompanied by the owner's wife, he came into the room where I worked. I didn't like him at all. That afternoon I was called into his office; Herr Berger sent me on an errand and made a silly remark about my "beautiful hands." It was already dark when I returned; I had to pass through an empty anteroom that wasn't lighted; it was half-dark since it got light only through the glass door leading into the workroom. Herr Berger was in the anteroom when I came. He took my by the hand and inquired sympathetically about my circumstance. I answered him truthfully and told of our poverty. He spoke a few words, taking pity on me and promising to use his influence to get me higher wages. Of course I was delighted with the prospect opening up to me, for I was getting only two and a half guilders a week, for which I had to work twelve hours a day. I stammered a few words of thanks and assured him that I would prove myself worthy of his solicitude. Before I even knew what was happening, Herr Berger had kissed me. He tried to calm my fright with the words, "It was just a fatherly kiss." He was twenty-six years old, and I was almost fifteen, so fatherliness was out of the question.

Beside myself, I hurried back to my work. I didn't know how I should interpret the incident; I thought the kiss was disgraceful, but Herr Berger had spoken so sympathetically and had held out the prospect of higher wages! At home I did tell of the promise, but I said nothing about it in front of my brother. But my mother and my brother were happy that I had found such an influential protector.

The next day I was overwhelmed with reproaches from one of my coworkers, a young blond girl whom I liked most of all. She reproached me for having taken her place with the traveler; up to now, if he had something to do or an errand to run, she had done it; he loved her, she protested through tears and sobs, and now I'd put an end to everything. The other girls joined in too; they called me a hypocrite, and the gracious lady herself asked me how I'd liked the kisses of the "handsome traveler." The incident of the previous evening had been observed through the glass door, and they interpreted it in a way very insulting to me.

I was defenseless against their taunts and sneers and longed for the hour when I could go home. It was Saturday, and when I received my wages, I went home with the intention of not returning Monday.

When I spoke of the matter at home, I was severely scolded. It was strange. My mother, who was always so intent on raising me to be a respectable girl, who always gave me instructions and warnings not to talk to men ("You should only allow yourself to be kissed by the man you're going to marry," she used to impress upon me)—in this instance my mother was against me. She said I was going too far. A kiss was nothing bad, and if I was getting more wages as a result, then it would be silly to give up my job. In the end she held my books responsible for my "overexcitement." My mother got so mad about my "pigheadedness" that all the splendid things I'd been lent—*The Book for Everyone [Das Buch Für Alle]*, *Over Land and Sea [Über Land und Meer]*, and *Chronicle of the Times [Chronik der Zeit]* (that's how far advanced I was in literature)—were thrown out the door. I collected them all again, but I didn't dare read in the evening, although I'd usually been allowed to read longer on Saturdays.

That was a sad Sunday! I was depressed, and what's more I was scolded the whole day. . . .

D. Richard Wagner Helps Define Modern Cultural Antisemitism, 1878

All of a sudden, there is "the modern world." This does not apparently refer to the world of today, the time in which we live, or—as modern German puts it so beautifully—"nowadays." No, in the heads of our latest culture bearers, it signifies a world that has never yet existed, namely a "modern" world such as the world has never known at any time. Thus, a new world that previous worlds do not even approach and that therefore must be measured completely and arbitrarily according to its own standards. To the Jews, who, as a national entity, until half a century ago stood completely outside our cultural strivings, this present-day world, which they have entered so suddenly and which they appropriate to themselves with increasing force, this world must in fact seem a wholly new and hitherto nonexistent one. . . .

It is extraordinary how difficult . . . seems to be for Jews [to learn proper German, as opposed to Yiddish]. We may suppose that they went too hastily to work in appropriating what was too alien to them and that their unripe knowledge of our language, that is, their jargon, may have led them astray. It belongs to another discussion to illuminate the character of language falsification and what we owe to Jewish journalism for the intrusion of "the modern" into our cultural development. To elaborate further on the present theme, however, we must point out the weighty destiny under which our language had to labor for so long and how it took the most ingenious instincts of our greatest poets and sages to restore it to its productive character. And how this remarkable, linguistic-literary process of development was encountered by decadents who frivolously abandon the deadly seriousness of their predecessors and proclaim themselves "Moderns." . . .

For the Moderns to explain what we ought to think about this term "modern" is not so easy, especially if they concede that it is something quite lamentable and even dangerous, particularly to us Germans. We will not suppose this because we are assuming that our Jewish fellow citizens mean well by us. Shall we, on this assumption, believe that they don't know what they are saying and only talk twaddle? It is useless here to trace the historical paths of the concept "modern," a term originally coined for the plastic arts of Italy to differentiate them from those of the classical age. It suffices that we have come to know the significance of "modishness" for the French national character. With an idiosyncratic pride, the Frenchman can call himself "modern," for the creates fashion and thereby dominates the external appearance of the entire world.

If, presently, the Jews, by dint of their "colossal efforts, in common with liberal Christians," are making us into articles of fashion, then let the God of their fathers reward them for "doing so well by us" poor German slaves of French fashion! For the time being, it still appears otherwise, however. For, in spite of all their power, they have no remedy for their lack of originality. And this applies particularly to the employment of that power that they insist none can deny them: "the power of the quill." They can deck themselves out with foreign feathers [quills], just as they can with the delicious names under which our new Jewish fellow citizens come to us—as surprising as they are enrapturing—and this while we poor old peasants and burghers have to satisfy ourselves forever with quite wretched names like "Schmidt," "Müller," "Weber," "Wagner," etc. . . .

Document Set 24.2 References

A. Emile Zola Encounters the Department Store
   Emile Zola, *Au Bonheur des Dames* (Paris: François
   Bernouard, 1928), 83–84. Translated by Bonnie G. Smith.

B. Russian-Born Rose Schneiderman Recalls the Immigrants'
   Experience in America
   Doris Weatherford, *Foreign and Female: Immigrant Women
   in America 1840–1930.* (New York: Schocken Books, 1986),
   235–236.

C. Working Life in Vienna, 1883: Adelheid Popp Finds Her First
   Job
   Alfred Kelly, trans. and ed., *The German Worker: Working-
   Class Autobiographies in the Age of Industrialization*
   (Berkeley and Los Angeles: University of California Press,
   1987), 123–126.

D. Richard Wagner Helps Define Modern Cultural Antisemitism,
   1878
   Richard Wagner, "Modern" in *Bayreuther Blätter* (March
   1878), 59–63.

The Emergence of Mass Politics

Urbanization, the growth of rudimentary literacy (enough to read the popular press), and the enfranchisement of most adult males were the essential prerequisites to the emergence of mass politics. After reading the documents of this set (keeping in mind also what you have learned from Sets 24.1 and 24.2), judge whether you consider this a positive or a negative trend (or a mixture of the two). Why?

We have already seen (Set 23.4, Document D) how socialists in Germany began to create a mass party with essentially reformist goals in 1869. This trend accelerated after the establishment of the new Reich; in 1875 the Social Democrats issued their Gotha Program (Document A). It alarmed Marx and Engels (Document B); analyze their grounds for objection. But the Social Democrats stirred up another enemy, too: Bismarck, who took alarm at their electoral success and outlawed the party in 1878. Bismarck also tried to steal the Socialists' thunder by proposing health, accident, and old age pension systems (Document C); laws to put these programs into effect were passed by 1883.

One of the many things that Queen Victoria disliked in Liberal Prime Minister William Ewarts Gladstone was his willingness to do some relatively dignified barnstorming at election time, most notably in his "Midlothian Campaign" among his Scottish constituents in 1880 (Document D). Popular politicking of a very different sort is represented by Document E, the speech in which Vienna's suave, popular mayor Karl Lueger announced his conversion from liberalism to antisemitism.

In 1864 Pius IX had condemned modern politics wholesale, along with virtually everything else in modern life (Set 23.5, Document E). A quarter-century later the next pope, Leo XIII, issued the encyclical *Rerum Novarum* that put the Catholic church on record in favor of certain kinds of social-welfare programs (Document F). Is this, however, a liberal program in either the nineteenth-century or twentieth-century sense of that term?

A. German Social Democracy Advocates Social Reform: The Gotha Program, 1875

1. Labor is the source of all wealth and of all civilization; and since it is only through society that generally productive labor is possible, the whole product of labor, where there is a general obligation to work, belongs to society,—that is, to all its members, by equal right, and to each according to his reasonable needs.

In the society of to-day the means of production are a monopoly of the capitalistic class; the dependence of the working class, which results from this, is the cause of misery and servitude in all its forms.

The emancipation of labor requires the conversion of the means of production into the common property of society and the social regulation of all labor and its application for the general good, together with the just distribution of the product of labor.

The emancipation of labor must be the work of the laboring class itself, opposed to which all other classes are reactionary groups.

2. Proceeding from these principles, the socialist labor party of Germany endeavors by every lawful means to bring about a free State and a socialistic society, to effect the destruction of the iron law of wages by doing away with the system of wage labor, to abolish exploitation of every kind, and to extinguish all social and political inequality.

The socialist labor party of Germany, although for the time being confining its activity within national bounds, is fully conscious of the international character of the labor movement, and is resolved to meet all the obligations which this lays upon the laborer, in order to bring the brotherhood of all mankind to a full realization.

The socialist labor party of Germany, in order to prepare the way for the solution of the social question, demands the establishment of socialistic productive associations with the support of the State and under the democratic control of the working people. These productive associations, for both industry and agriculture, are to be created to such an extent that the socialistic organization of all labor may result therefrom.

[In addition to the demand for universal suffrage for all above twenty years of age, secret ballot, freedom of the press, free and compulsory education, etc.,] the socialist labor party of Germany demands the following reforms in the present social organization: (1) the greatest possible extension of political rights and freedom in the sense of the above-mentioned demands; (2) a single progressive income tax, both State and local, instead of all the existing taxes, especially the indirect ones, which weigh heavily upon the people; (3) unlimited right of association;

(4) a normal working day corresponding with the needs of society, and the prohibition of work on Sunday; (5) prohibition of child labor and all forms of labor by women which are dangerous to health or morality; (6) laws for the protection of the life and health of workmen, sanitary control of workmen's houses, inspection of mines, factories, workshops, and domestic industries by officials chosen by the workmen themselves, and an effective system of enforcement of the same; (7) regulation of prison labor.

B. Marx and Engels Attack the Gotha Program

"The German Workers' Party, in order *to pave the way to the solution of the social question,* demands the establishment of producers' co-operative societies with state aid under the democratic control of the *toiling people.* The producers' co-operative societies *are to be called into being* for industry and agriculture in such dimensions *that the socialist organisation of the total labour will arise from them."*

After the Lassallean "iron law of wages," the remedy of the prophet. The way to it is "paved" in worthy fashion. In place of the existing class struggle appears a newspaper scribbler's phrase: "the social *question,"* to the *"solution"* of which one *"paves the way."* Instead of the revolutionary process of transformation of society, the "socialist organisation of the total labour" "arises" from the "state aid" that the state gives to the producers' co-operative societies and which the state, not the worker, *"calls into being."* This is worthy of Lassalle's imagination that one can build a new society by state loans just as well as a new railway!

From the remnants of a sense of shame, "state aid" has been put—under the democratic control of the "toiling people."

In the first place the majority of the "toiling people" in Germany consists of peasants and not of proletarians.

Secondly, "democratic" is in German *"volksherrschaftlich,"* ["by the rule of the people"]. But what does "control by the rule of the people of the toiling people" mean? And particularly in the case of a toiling people which, through these demands that it puts to the state, expresses its full consciousness that it neither rules nor is ripe for ruling! . . .

. . . The chief offence does not lie in having inscribed these specific nostrums in the programme, but in that in general a retrograde step from the standpoint of a class movement to that of a sectarian movement is being taken.

That the workers desire to establish the conditions of co-operative production on a social, and first of all on a national, scale in their own country, only means that they are working to revolutionise the present conditions of production, and has nothing in common with the foundation of co-operative societies with state aid. But as far as the present co-operative societies are concerned they are of value only in so far as they are the independent creations of the workers and not protégés either of the government or of the bourgeoisie.

I come now to the democratic section.

A. "The free basis of the state."

First of all, according to II, the German Workers' Party strives for the "free state."

Free state—what is this?

It is by no means the aim of the workers, who have got rid of the narrow mentality of humble subjects, to set the state free. In the German empire the "state" is almost as "free" as in Russia. Freedom consists in converting the state from an organ standing above society into one completely subordinated to it, and today also the forms of the state are more free or less free to the extent that they restrict the "freedom of the state."

The German Workers' Party—at least if it adopts the programme—shows that its socialist ideas are not even skin-deep, in that, instead of treating existing society (and this holds good of any future one) as the *basis* of the existing state (or of the future state in the case of future society) it treats the state rather as an independent entity that possesses its own *intellectual, moral and free basis.* . . .

C. Bismarck Demands That the State Protect Workers from Want and Socialism

Deputy Richter has called attention to the responsibility of the state for what it does, in the area now concerned. Well, gentlemen, I have a feeling that the state may also be responsible for its omissions. I am not of the opinion that *"laisser faire, laisser aller,"* "pure Manchesterism in politics," "as you make your bed, so you must lie," "every man for himself, and Devil take the hindmost," "to him that hath shall be given, and from him that hath not shall be taken away even that which he hath," have applicability in a state, especially a monarchical, paternalistic state; on the contrary, I believe that those who thus condemn the intervention of the state for the protection of the weaker are themselves suspect of wishing to exploit the strength they have, be it capitalistic, be it rhetorical, be it what it may, to gain a following, to oppress others, to build party dominance, and of becoming annoyed as soon as this understanding is disturbed by any influence of the government.

D. William E. Gladstone Campaigns in Midlothian, 1880

I am sorry to say we cannot reckon upon the aristocracy! We cannot reckon upon what is called the landed interest! We cannot reckon upon the clergy of the Established Church either in England or in Scotland! . . . We cannot reckon upon the wealth of the country, nor upon the rank of the country! . . . In the main these powers are against us . . . We must set them down among our most determined foes! But, gentlemen, above all these, and behind all these, there is the nation itself. And this great trial is now proceeding before the nation. The nation is a power hard to rouse, but when roused harder still and more hopeless to resist . . .

E. Ex-Liberal Karl Lueger Turns to Antisemitism, 1887

At this meeting the first speaker was the Hungarian anti-Semitic leader Dr. Komlossy, who was received with an ovation lasting several minutes, and, constantly interrupted by cries of assent, made a strongly anti-Semitic speech. . . . Lueger, as the second speaker, was meanwhile sitting near the chairman, Psenner, and asked him anxiously what he should speak on so as not to fall foul of Komlossy. Psenner's advice was that he could become the hero of the evening only if he outdid Komlossy in his anti-Semitism. Lueger appreciated this at once and, amid storms of applause, made a speech which, as Psenner said, set the seal on his transformation from a Democrat into an anti-Semite. . . .

(2) For my part, I like to ignore the small differences which might exist between one or other of the parties about the method of the struggle; I have very little regard for words and names, and much more for the cause. Whether Democrat or anti-Semite, the matter really comes to one and the same thing. The Democrats in their struggle against corruption come up against the Jews at every step, and the anti-Semites, if they want to carry out their economic programme, have to overcome not only the bad Jews but the bad Christians also. . . .

All my party comrades share my opinion that it is the first duty of a Democrat to take the side of the poor, oppressed people and to even harmful domination of a small fraction of the population. To be sure, the Manchester-Liberal papers have the habit of describing a Democrat in somewhat different terms. They claim, for instance, that it would be the duty of such a Democrat to come forward as an enemy of the Christian religion, to mock and ridicule its believers and priests. But we know that the motive of such a manoeuvre is solely to mislead the people, which we may deduce from the remarkable fact that were anybody to come forward against the Jewish religion and ridicule its doctrines and believers he would be branded by the same organs as a reactionary obscurantist. However, this strange conception can be seen even more clearly in an economic question. Quite shamelessly the Liberal organs threaten the confiscation of the property of the Church and claim that the goods of the "dead hand" are harmful. By this means an attempt is made to divert the attention of the people from the property of the "living hand" which, in my view, harms the people in the most grievous way. But what a yell of rage would go up from the Liberal press if one were to substitute the slogan "confiscation of Church property" with the slogan "confiscation of the goods of the conscious, living hand!" He who would dare this would risk at once being portrayed as injuring the sacred rights of property, as an anarchist, a communist who wanted to subvert the social order and destroy all existing things. And now I ask: is the title of property of the conscious, living hand stronger or more sacred than the title to the property of the Church? Surely not. And so it is more than extraordinary if one were to confiscate the property of the comparatively poor priests and through this help the rich of another denomination to increase their wealth!

F. Pope Leo XIII Looks at Modern Social Problems, 1891

Let it be laid down, in the first place, that humanity must remain as it is. It is impossible to reduce human society to a level. The socialists may do their utmost, but all striving against nature is vain. There naturally exist among mankind innumerable differences of the most important kind; people differ in capability, in diligence, in health, and in strength; an unequal fortune is a necessary result of inequality in condition. Such inequality is far from being disadvantageous either to individuals or to the community; social and public life can only go on by the help of various kinds of capacity and the playing of many parts; and each man, as a rule, chooses the part which peculiarly suits his case.

As regards bodily labor, even had man never fallen from "the state of innocence," he would not have been wholly unoccupied; but that which would then have been his free choice and delight became afterwards compulsory, and the painful expiation of his sin. "Cursed be the earth in thy work; in thy labor thou shall eat of it all the days of thy life." In like manner, the other pains and hardships of life will have no end or cessation on this earth; for the consequences of sin are bitter and hard to bear, and they must be with man as long as life lasts. To suffer and to endure, therefore, is the lot of humanity; let men try as they may, no strength and no artifice will ever succeed in banishing from human life the ills and troubles which beset it. If any there be who pretend differently,—who hold out to a hard-pressed people freedom from pain and trouble, undisturbed repose, and constant enjoyment,—they cheat the people and impose upon them; and their lying promises will only make the evil worse than before. There is nothing more useful than to look at the world as it really is,—and at the same time to look elsewhere for a remedy to its troubles.

The great mistake that is made in the matter now under consideration, is to possess one's self of the idea that class is naturally hostile to class; that rich and poor are intended by nature to live at war with one another. So irrational and so false is this view that the exact contrary is the truth. Just as the symmetry of the human body is the result of the disposition of the members of the body, so in a State it is ordained by nature that these two classes should exist in harmony and agreement, and should, as it were, fit into one another, so as to maintain the equilibrium of the body politic. Each requires the other; capital cannot do without labor, nor labor without capital. Mutual agreement results in pleasantness and good order; perpetual conflict necessarily produces confusion and violence.

Now, in preventing such strife as this, and in making it impossible, the efficacy of Christianity is marvelous and manifold. First of all, there is nothing more powerful than religion (of which the Church is the interpreter and guardian) in drawing rich and poor together, by reminding each class of its duties to the other, and especially of the duties of justice. Thus religion teaches the laboring man and the workman to carry out honestly and well all equitable agreements freely made; never to injure capital, or to attack the person of an employer; never to employ violence in representing his own cause, or to engage in riot or disorder; and to have nothing to do with men of evil principles, who work upon the people with artful promises, and raise foolish hopes which usually end in disaster and in repentance when too late.

Religion teaches the rich man and the employer that their work people are not their slaves; that they respect in every man his dignity as a man and as a Christian; that labor is nothing to be ashamed of, if we listen to right reason and to Christian philosophy, but is an honorable employment, enabling a man to sustain his life in an upright and creditable way; and that it is shameful and inhuman to treat men like chattels to make money by, or to look upon them merely as so much muscle or physical power.

If we turn now to things exterior and corporeal, the first concern of all is to save the poor workers from the cruelty of grasping speculators, who use human beings as mere instruments for making money. It is neither justice nor humanity so to grind men down with excessive labor as to stupefy their minds and wear out their bodies. Finally, work which is suitable for a strong man cannot reasonably be required from a woman or a child. And, in regard to children, great care should be taken not to place them in workshops and factories until their bodies and minds are sufficiently mature. For just as severe weather destroys the buds of spring, so too early an experience of life's hard work blights the young promise of a child's powers and makes any real education impossible.

We now approach a subject of very great importance, and one on which, if extremes are to be avoided, right ideas are absolutely necessary. Wages, we are told, are fixed by free consent; and therefore the employer, when he pays what was agreed upon, has done his part, and is not called upon for anything further. The only way, it is said, in which injustice could happen would be if the master refused to pay the whole of the wages, or the workman would not complete the work undertaken; when this happens the State should intervene, to see that each obtains his own,—but not under any other circumstances. . . .

Document Set 24.3 References

A. German Social Democracy Advocates Social Reform: The
Gotha Program, 1875
Gotha (1875) in James Harvey Robinson and Charles Beard,
eds., *Readings in Modern European History* (Boston: Ginn,
1909), 2:493–495.

B. Marx and Engels Attack the Gotha Program
Karl Marx and Friedrich Engels, *Critique of the Gotha
Program*, E. P. Dutt, ed. (New York: International Publishers,
1938), 16–17.

C. Bismarck Demands That the State Protect Workers from Want
and Socialism
Otto von Bismarck, Speech Before the Reichstag, in J. Salwyn
Shapiro, ed., *Liberalism: Its History and Meaning* (Princeton,
N.J.: Princeton University Press, 1958), 174.

D. William E. Gladstone Campaigns in Mildothian, 1880
Philip Magnus, *Gladstone* (New York: E. P. Dutton, 1964),
269–270.

E. Ex-Liberal Karl Lueger Turns to Antisemitism, 1887
Peter P. J. Pelzer, *The Rise of Political Antisemitism in
Germany and Austria* (New York: John Wiley, 1964), 169,
341–342.

F. Pope Leo XIII Looks at Modern Social Problems, 1891
Leo XIII, May 1891 Enclyclical, in Robinson and Beard,
2:502–505.

DOCUMENT SET 24.4
Nationalism, Revolution, and Repression: Russia

Activists who dreamed of building a just and progressive society in Russia had to go underground, in the 1860s and 1870s forming the Populist movement that tried but abysmally failed to revolutionize a peasantry distrustful of anyone with a modern education and gentry breeding. Frustrated, some Populists turned to terrorism; one group assassinated Tsar Alexander II in 1881, but this merely produced more repression. Populism remained, however, an enduring tradition; as late as 1917 it competed vigorously with various strains of Marxism for the loyalty of Russia's left-wing intelligentsia and popular masses.

Katarina Breshko-Breshkovskaya, born into the gentry in 1844, was an activist from the age of 26 until the fall of tsarism. In 1917 this "grandmother of the Russian Revolution" recalled her first experience of "going to the people" in 1870 (Document A). In Document B, the rationale of the small conspiratorial faction that broke off from the main populist movement and killed Alexander II may be gauged from the open letter that the faction sent to the dead tsar's son and successor, Alexander III, the day after the fatal bomb blast.

Fyodor Dostoyevsky (1821–1881) in his youth associated with utopian socialist circles in St. Petersburg and seemed destined to become a "progressive" journalist with a minor literary talent. But in 1849 he began ten years' soul-searing experience—a mock execution, prison and Siberian exile—that would leave him with an indelible sense of humanity's capacity for evil and regeneration. He returned a writer of unique, idiosyncratic genius: a political reactionary deeply sympathetic to the redemptive sufferings of ordinary people, an advocate of Christianity who struggled (apparently in vain) to believe in God, and a passionate Russian nationalist who denounced the revolutionaries of his day as "devils." That was the word that he used to entitle his anti-revolutionary novel *Besy* (1874), usually translated misleadingly as "The Possessed"; in an extract (Document C) the character Shatov expresses views close to Dostoyevsky's; Stavrogin is the more conventional liberal.

Antisemitism, which haunted the mass societies of late nineteenth-century western and central Europe, grew virulent in the Russian empire as well. Here its nest was in the villages and small towns where impoverished Jews and equally poor Russians, Ukrainians, and Poles competed endlessly to eke out a living. The struggle was punctuated by periodic mob violence (pogroms) against the Jews that was often incited or tolerated by the authorities. By the 1890s Zionism—the movement to gather scattered Jewry into a reconstituted national homeland—took its place beside socialism and emigration to America as strategies by which Jews hoped to protect themselves. The Russian Jew Leo Pinsker (1821–1891) published the pamphlet *Auto-Emancipation* (Document D) in 1882 as a Zionist appeal to western Jewry, but it found an audience chiefly in Russia. Pinsker argues that the emancipation and assimilation on which west European Jews counted were a delusion—that gentile society was inherently antisemitic and that Jews could never assimilate even if they wanted to. Does his argument implicitly accept the antisemites' reasoning?

Taking the readings in Set 24.4 as a group and using *The Challenge of the West* as an additional resource, consider the factors that made late nineteenth-century Russia both different from and similar to the western and central European societies of its time.

A. Populist Katarina Breshko-Breshkovskaya Recalls Her Upbringing and "Going to the People"

My father helped me think. He was a man of broad, liberal ideas. We read together many books of science and travel. Social science absorbed me. By 16, I had read much of Voltaire, Rousseau, and Diderot, and I knew by heart the French Revolution. I was not confined to Russian, for I spoke French from babyhood; my German governess soon taught me German, and at that time the world's best thought was not garbled by Russian censorship. So trained, I could hardly be called an ignorant fanatic. . . . and hands; I worked and ate with the peasants; I learned their speech; I traveled on foot, forging passports; I lived 'illegally.'

By night I did my organizing. You desire a picture? A low room with mud floor and walls. Rafters just over your head and a little higher an arch. The room was packed with men, women and children. Two big fellows sat up on the high brick stove, with their dangling feet knocking occasional applause. These people had been gathered by my host—a brave peasant whom I picked out—and he in turn had chosen only those whom Siberia could not terrify. When

I recalled their floggings, when I pointed to those who had been crippled for life, to women whose husbands died under the lash—those men would cry out so fiercely that the three or four cattle in the next room would begin to bellow loudly and have to be quieted. Then I told them they themselves were to blame. They had only the most wretched strips of land. To be free and live, the people must own the land. From my cloak I would bring a book of fables written to teach our principles and stir the love of freedom. And then far into the night the firelight showed a circle of great, broad faces and dilated eyes staring with all the reverence every peasant had for that mysterious thing—a book. These books, twice as effective as oral work, were printed in secrecy, at a heavy expense. But many of us had libraries, jewels, costly gowns and furs to sell. And new recruits kept adding to our fund. We had no personal expenses.

B. The Narodnik "Executive Committee" Writes an Open Letter to Alexander III After Assassinating His Father, 1881

Your Majesty: March 10, 1881

Although the Executive Committee understands fully the grief that you must experience at this moment, it believes that it has no right to yield to the feeling of natural delicacy which would perhaps dictate the postponements of the following explanation to another time. There is something higher than the most legitimate human feeling, and that is, duty to one's country,—the duty for which a citizen must sacrifice himself and his own feelings, and even the feelings of others. In obedience to this all-powerful duty we have decided to address you at once, waiting for nothing, as will wait for nothing the historical process that threatens us with rivers of blood and the most terrible convulsions. . . .

You are aware, your Majesty, that the government of the late Tsar could not be reproached with the lack of energy. It hanged the innocent and the guilty, and filled prisons and remote provinces with exiles. Scores of so-called "leaders" were captured and hanged, and died with the courage and tranquillity of martyrs; but the movement did not cease,—on the contrary it grew and strengthened. The revolutionary movement, your Majesty, is not dependent upon any particular individuals; it is a process of the social organism; and the scaffolds raised for its more energetic exponents are as powerless to save the outgrown order of things as the cross that was erected for the Redeemer was powerless to save the ancient world from the triumph of Christianity. The government, of course, may yet capture and hang an immense number of separate individuals, it may break up a great number of separate revolutionary groups; but all this will not change, in the slightest degree, the condition of affairs. . . .

A dispassionate glance at the grievous decade through which we have just passed will enable us to forecast accurately the future progress of the revolutionary movement, provided the policy of the government does not change. The movement will continue to grow and extend; deeds of a terroristic nature will increase in frequency and intensity. Meanwhile the number of the discontented in the country will grow larger and larger; confidence in the government, on the part of the people, will decline; and the idea of a revolution—of its possibility and inevitability—will establish itself in Russia more and more firmly. A terrible explosion, a bloody chaos, a revolutionary earthquake throughout Russia, will complete the destruction of the old order of things. . . .

From such a state of affairs there can be only two modes of escape: either a revolution,—absolutely inevitable and not to be averted by any punishments; or a voluntary turning of the supreme power to the people. In the interest of our native land, in the hope of preventing the useless waste of energy, in the hope of averting the terrible miseries that always accompany revolution, the Executive Committee approaches your Majesty with the advice to take the second course. Be assured, so soon as the supreme power ceases to rule arbitrarily, so soon as it firmly resolves to accede to the demands of the people's conscience and consciousness, you may, without fear, discharge the spies that disgrace the administration, send your guards back to their barracks, and burn the scaffolds that are demoralizing the people. The Executive Committee will voluntarily terminate its own existence, and the organizations formed about it will disperse, in order that their members may devote themselves to the work of promoting culture among the people of their native land. . . .

We set no conditions for you; do not let our proposition irritate you. The conditions that are prerequisite to a change from revolutionary activity to peaceful labor are created, not by us, but by history. These conditions are, in our opinion, two.

1. A general amnesty to cover all past political crimes; for the reason that they were not crimes but fulfillments of civil duty.

2. The summoning of representatives of the whole Russian people to examine the existing framework of social and governmental life, and to remodel it in accordance with the people's wishes.

We regard it as necessary, however, to remind you that the legalization of the supreme power, by the representatives of the people, can be valid only in case the elections are perfectly free. We declare solemnly, before the people of our native land and before the whole world, that our party will submit unconditionally to the decisions of a National Assembly elected in the manner above indicated, and that we will not allow ourselves, in future, to offer violent resistance to any government that the National Assembly may sanction.

C. Dostoyevsky Exalts the "God-Seeking" Russian Nation

Shatov bent forward in his chair again and again held up his finger for a moment.

"Not a single nation . . . has ever been founded on principles of science or reason. There has never been an example of it, except for a brief moment, through folly. Socialism is from its very nature bound to be atheism, seeing that it has from the very first proclaimed that it is an atheistic organisation of society, and that it intends to establish itself exclusively on the elements of science and reason. Science and reason have, from the beginning of time, played a secondary and subordinate part in the life of nations; so it will be till the end of time. Nations are built up and moved by another force which sways and dominates them, the origin of which is unknown and inexplicable: that force is the force of an insatiable desire to go on to the end, though at the same time it denies that end. It is the force of the persistent assertion of one's own existence, and a denial of death. . . . The object of every national movement, in every people and at every period of its existence is only the seeking for its god, who must be its own god, and the faith in him as the only true one. God is the synthetic personality of the whole people, taken from its beginning to its end. . . .

"I don't agree that you've not altered anything," Stavrogin observed cautiously. "You accepted them [my ideas] with ardour, and in your ardour have transformed them unconsciously. The very fact that you reduce God to a simple attribute of nationality. . . . "

He suddenly began watching Shatov with intense and peculiar attention, not so much his words as himself.

"I reduce God to the attribute of nationality?" cried Shatov. "On the contrary, I raise the people to God. And has it ever been otherwise? The people is the body of God. Every people is only a people so long as it has its own god and excludes all other gods on earth irreconcilably; so long as it believes that by its god it will conquer and drive out of the world all other gods. Such, from the beginning of time, has been the belief of all great nations, all, anyway, who have been specially remarkable, all who have been leaders of humanity. There is no going against facts. The Jews lived only to await the coming of the true God and left the world of the true God. The Greeks deified nature and bequeathed the world their religion, that is, philosophy and art. Rome deified the people in the State, and bequeathed the idea of the State to the nations. France throughout her long history was only the incarnation and development of the Roman god, and if they have at last flung their Roman god into the abyss and plunged into atheism, which, for the time being, they call socialism, it is solely because socialism is, anyway, healthier than Roman Catholicism. If a great people does not believe that the truth is only to be found in itself alone (in itself alone and in it exclusively); if it does not believe that it alone is fit and destined to raise up and save all the rest by its truth, it would at once sink into being ethnographical material, and not a great people. A really great people can never accept a secondary part in the history of Humanity, nor even one of the first, but will have the first part. A nation which loses this belief ceases to be a nation. But there is only one truth, and therefore only a single one out of the nations can have the true God, even though other nations may have great gods of their own. Only one nation is 'god-bearing,' that's the Russian people. . . .

D. Russian Zionist Leo Pinsker Appeals for "Auto-Emancipation"

That hoary problem, subsumed under the Jewish question, today, as ever in the past, provokes discussion. Like the squaring of the circle it remains unsolved, but unlike it, continues to be the ever-burning question of the day. That is because the problem is not one of mere theoretical interest: it renews and revives in everyday life and presses ever more urgently for solution.

This is the kernel of the problem, as we see it: *the Jews comprise a distinctive element among the nations under which they dwell, and as such can neither assimilate nor be readily digested by any nation.*

Text from *Modern Jewish History: A Source Reader* edited by Robert Chazan and Marc L. Raphael, Schocken Books, 1974, excerpts from pp. 161, 163, 165–166, 169, 170–171, 173–174. Random House, Inc.

Hence the solution lies in finding a means of so readjusting this exclusive element to the family of nations, that the basis of the Jewish question will be permanently removed....

A fear of the Jewish ghost has passed down the generations and the centuries. First a breeder of prejudice, later in the conjunction with other forces we are about to discuss, it culminated in Judeophobia.

Judeophobia, together with other symbols, superstitions, and idiosyncrasies, has acquired legitimacy among all the peoples of the earth with whom the Jews had intercourse. Judeophobia is a variety of demonopathy with the distinction that it is not peculiar to particular races but is common to the whole of mankind, and that this ghost is not disembodied like other ghosts but partakes of flesh and blood, must endure pain inflicted by the fearful mob who imagines itself endangered.

Judeophobia is a psychic aberration. As a psychic aberration it is hereditary, and as a disease transmitted for two thousand years it is incurable....

The Jews are aliens who can have no representatives, because they have no country. Because they have none, because their home has no boundaries within which they can be entrenched, their misery too is boundless. The *general law* does not apply to the Jews as true aliens, but there are everywhere *laws for the Jews*, and if the general law is to apply to them, a special and explicit bylaw is required to confirm it. Like the Negroes, like women, and unlike all free peoples, they must be *emancipated*. If, unlike the Negroes, they belong to an advanced race, and if, unlike women, they can produce not only women of distinction, but also distinguished men, even men of greatness, then it is very much the worse for them.

Since the Jew is nowhere at home, nowhere regarded as a native, he remains an alien everywhere. That he himself and his ancestors as well are born in the country does to alter this fact in the least.

When we are ill-used, robbed, plundered, and dishonored, we dare not defend ourselves, and, worse still, we take it almost as a matter of course. When our face is slapped, we soothe our burning cheek with cold water; and when a bloody wound has been inflicted, we apply a bandage. When we are turned out of the house which we ourselves built, we beg humbly for mercy, and when we fail to reach the heart of our oppressor we move on in search of another exile.

When an idle spectator on the road calls out to us: "You poor Jewish devils are certainly to be pitied," we are most deeply touched; and when a Jew is said to be an honor to his people, we are foolish enough to be proud of it. We have sunk so low that

we become almost jubilant when, as in the West, a small fraction of our people is put on an equal footing with non-Jews. But he who must be *put* on a footing stands but weakly. If no notice is taken of our descent and we are treated like others born in the country, we express our gratitude by actually turning renegades. For the sake of the comfortable position we are granted, for the fleshpots which we may enjoy in peace, we persuade ourselves, and others, that we are no longer Jews, but full-blooded citizens. Idle delusion! Though you prove yourselves patriots a thousand times, you will still be reminded at every opportunity of your Semitic descent. This fateful *memento mori* will not prevent you, however, from accepting the extended hospitality, until some fine morning you find yourself crossing the border and you are reminded by the mob that you are, after all, nothing but vagrants and parasites, without the protection of the law.

But even humane treatment does not prove that we are welcome. . . . Moreover, the belief in a Messiah, in the intervention of a higher power to bring about our political resurrection, and the religious assumption that we must bear patiently divine punishment, caused us to abandon every thought of our national liberation, unity, and independence. Consequently, we have renounced the idea of a nationhood and did so the more readily since we were preoccupied with out immediate needs. Thus we sank lower and lower. The people *without a country forgot their country*. Is it not high time to perceive the disgrace of it all?

Happily, matters stand somewhat differently now. The events of the last few years in *enlightened* Germany, in Romania, in Hungary, and especially in Russia, have effected what the far bloodiest persecutions of the Middle Ages could not. The national consciousness which until then had lain dormant in sterile martyrdom awoke the masses of the Russian and Romanian Jews and took form in an irresistible movement toward Palestine. Mistaken as this movement has proved to be by its results, it was, nevertheless, a right instinct to strike out for home. The severe trials which they have endured have now provoked a reaction quite different from the fatalistic submission to a divine condign punishment. Even the unenlightened masses of the Russian Jews have not entirely escaped the influences of the principles of modern culture. Without renouncing Judaism and their faith, they revolted against undeserved ill-treatment which could be inflicted with impunity only because the Russian Government regards the Jews as aliens. And the other European governments—why should they concern themselves with the citizens of a state in whose internal affairs they have no right to interfere?. . . .

If we would have a secure home, give up our endless life of wandering and rise to the dignity of a nation in our own eyes and in the eyes of the world, we must, above all, not dream of restoring ancient Judaea. We must not attach ourselves to the place where our political life was once violently interrupted and destroyed. The goal of our present endeavors must be not the "Holy Land," but a land of our own. We need nothing but a large tract of land for our poor brothers, which shall remain our property and from which no foreign power can expel us. There we shall take with us the most sacred possessions which we have saved from the shipwreck of our former country, the *God-idea* and the *Bible*. It is these alone which have made our old fatherland the Holy Land, and not Jerusalem or the Jordan. Perhaps the Holy Land will again become ours. If so, all the better, but *first of all*, we must determine—and this is the crucial point—what country is accessible to us, and at the same time adapted to offer the Jews of all lands who must leave their homes a secure and indisputed refuge, capable of productivization. . . .

Document Set 24.4 References

A. Populist Katarina Breshko-Breshkovskaya Recalls Her Upbringing and "Going to the People"
Katarina Breshko-Breshkovskaya in A. J. Sack, *The Birth of the Russian Democracy* (New York: Russian Information Bureau, 1918), 201–202.

B. The Narodnik "Executive Committee" Writes an Open Letter to Alexander III After Assassinating His Father, 1881
Letter of the Revolutionary Committee to Alexander III, in James Harvey Robinson and Charles Beard, eds., *Readings in Modern European History* (Boston: Ginn, 1909), 2:364–367.

C. Dostoyevsky Exalts the "God-Seeking" Russian Nation
Fyodor Dostoyevsky, *The Possessed*, Constance Garnett, trans. (New York: Modern Library, 1936), 253–255.

D. Russian Zionist Leo Pinsker Appeals for "Auto-Emancipation"
Pinsker, *Auto-Emancipation: An Appeal to His People by a Russian Jew* in Robert Chazan and Marc Lee Raphael, eds., *Modern Jewish History: A Source Reader* (New York: Schocken Books, 1974), 161, 163, 165–166, 169–171, 173–174.

DOCUMENT SET 24.5
The Dreyfus Case Rocks France

France's Third Republic (1870–1940) began life as a stopgap regime that conservatives would have transformed into a monarchy had they found a plausible king. In the 1890s it endured a particularly severe "mid-life crisis," the protracted scandal in which the assimilated Jewish officer Alfred Dreyfus (1859–1935) was wrongfully accused of spying for Germany. The Dreyfus Affair stirred up passions on both sides: rightwing defenders of the "honor" of the army determined to see Dreyfus's conviction stand even if it meant tolerating a miscarriage of justice, and liberals and radicals who saw in Dreyfus's frame-up a monstrous conspiracy to subvert the republic itself. Document A is the notorious *bordereau,* the document used in 1894 to convict Dreyfus of selling military secrets to the Germans, which was ultimately proved a forgery used to cover treasonous activity by other officers. By 1896–1898, when opponents of Dreyfus's conviction began to speak out, the Right's case against him broadened into an attack on Jews, liberals, and the legacy of 1789 in general, as may be judged from Document B, an editorial in the official Jesuit newspaper *Civilità Cattolica* in Rome. It was in the face of such right-wing propaganda that on January 6, 1898, the novelist Emile Zola published his stirring article "J'accuse," which made the case for Dreyfus and named the military men who had connived at his conviction (Document C). Zola himself risked punishment for slandering the army (he was sentenced to a year in jail but never served it), but he had rallied the Republic's defenders to a full-scale counterattack. Dreyfus had to endure another trial and re-conviction before a new president of the Republic in 1899 pardoned him.

The Dreyfus case is fascinating and complex. Use the documents in this set and the account in *The Challenge of the West*'s Chapters 24 and 25 as the starting point for further investigation. It will be particularly rewarding if you consider *L'Affaire* in the context of France's emergence as a modern mass society and of the resistance that modernization provoked among those who had never accepted the legitimacy of the French Revolution.

A. The Key Document in the Dreyfus Case: The "Bordereau"

I have no news to indicate that you wish to see me; however, I am sending you some interesting information.

1. A note on the hydraulic brake of the 120 mm. gun and on the way it was found to work.

2. A note on the supporting troops. Some modifications will be introduced by the new plan.

3. A note on the modification of artillery formations.

4. A note concerning Madagascar.

5. The provisional Firing Manual for Field Artillery [March 14, 1894].

This last document is extraordinarily difficult to procure, and I have it at my disposal only for a very few days. The Minister of War has issued a limited number to the corps, and the corps are responsible for them. Each officer who has a copy has to send it back after the maneuvers. If, therefore, you will take notes of whatever is of interest to you, and hold it at my disposal, I shall take it back. That is, unless you want me to have it copied in full and send you the copy. I am just off to the maneuvers.

B. The Jesuit Newspaper *Civilità Cattolica* Attacks Jews and Dreyfusards

The emancipation of the Jews was the corollary of the so-called principles of 1789, the yoke of which weighs on the neck of all Frenchmen. These French Jews grew in number by the immigration of German Jews, and now they total 130,000.

They got control of Masonry (Dreyfus is a Jew and a Mason as well), and Masonry is notoriously the master of the French State. This is the way they keep the Republic in their hands; it is more Hebrew than French. . . . Of 260 billions that constitute the wealth of France, the Jews possess 80. They direct home as well as foreign policy. The abandonment of Egypt [a reference to the concession to the British of De Lesseps' Suez Canal] was the work of these Jews who, at the behest of the government of London, corrupted the press, the government and parliament.

The condemnation of Dreyfus was a terrible blow for Israel. It branded the forehead of all Jews in the world, most of all in their French colonies. This mark they swore to wipe off. But how? With their usual subtlety, they invented a case of miscarriage of justice. the plot was hatched in Basle at the Zionist Congress, held under the pretext of discussing the deliverance of Jerusalem. The Protestants joined in common cause with the Jews and established a

Syndicate. The money came mostly from Germany. *Pecuniae obediunt omnia* is the principle of the Jews. They bought consciences and those newspapers which were for sale in every country of Europe. . . .

The Jew was created by God to serve as a spy wherever treason is in preparation. Moreover, ethnic solidarity ties the Jews to each other and prevents them from becoming loyal citizens in spite of naturalization. The Dreyfus affair reveals this fact clearly. Thus anti-Semitism will become, as it should, economic, political, and national. The Jews allege an error of justice. The true error was, however, that of the *Constituante* which accorded them French nationality. That law has to be revoked. . . . Not only in France, but in Germany, Austria, and Italy as well, the Jews are to be excluded from the nation.

Then the old harmony will be re-established and the peoples will again find their lost happiness.

C. Emile Zola Defends Dreyfus and the Republic, 1898

Dreyfus knows several languages: a crime. No compromising papers were found in his possession: a crime. He sometimes visited his native country: a crime. He is industrious and likes to find out about everything: a crime. He is calm: a crime. He is worried: a crime. . . .

I accuse Lieutenant-Colonel du Paty de Clam of having been the diabolical, but I would fain believe the unwitting, artisan of the miscarriage of justice, and thereafter of having defended his unhallowed work for three years by the most clumsy and culpable machinations.

I accuse General Mercier of having become, at all events through weakness, an accomplice in one of the greatest iniquities of the age.

I accuse General Billot of having had in his hands sure proofs of the innocence of Dreyfus and of having hushed them up, of having incurred the guilt of crimes against humanity and justice, for political ends and to save the face of the General Staff.

I accuse General de Boisdeffre and General Gonse of having been participators in the same crime, actuated, the one no doubt by clerical partisanship, the other, it may be, by that *esprit de corps* which would make the Army and the War Office the sacred Ark of the Covenant.

I accuse General de Pellieux and Major Ravary of conducting a disgraceful inquiry, by which I mean an inquiry characterized by the most monstrous partiality, of which we have, in the report of the latter of these two men, an imperishable monument of stupid audacity.

I accuse the three handwriting experts, MM. Belhomme, Varinard, and Couard, of drawing up misleading and lying reports, unless, indeed, a medical examination should reveal them to be suffering from some pathological abnormality of sight and judgment.

I accuse the War Office of conducting an abominable campaign in the Press, and particularly in the newspapers *l'Éclair* and *l'Echo de Paris*, in order to mislead public opinion and to conceal their own misdeeds.

I accuse the first Court-Martial of acting contrary to law by condemning as accused man on the strength of a secret document; and I accuse the second Court-Martial of having, in obedience to orders, concealed that illegality, and of committing in its turn the crime of knowingly acquitting a guilty man.

In bringing these charges, I am not unaware that I render myself liable to prosecution under Clauses 30 and 31 of the Act of the 29th of July, which deals with defamation of character in the public Press. But I do so of my own free will and with my eyes open.

As for those whom I accuse, I do not know them, I have never seen them. I entertain for them neither hatred nor ill-will. They are so far as I am concerned mere entities, spirits of social maleficence, and the action to which I have here committed myself is but a revolutionary means of hastening the explosion of Truth and Justice.

I have but one passion, and that is for light, and I plead in the name of that humanity which has so greatly suffered and has a right to happiness. My fiery protest is but the outcry of my soul. Let them drag me, then, into a Court of Justice and let the matter be thrashed out in broad daylight. I am ready.

Document Set 24.5 References

A. The Key Document in the Dreyfus Case: The "Bordereau"
Nicholas Halasz, *Captain Dreyfus* (New York: Simon and Schuster, 1955), 11.

B. The Jesuit Newspaper *Civilità Cattolica* Attacks Jews and Dreyfusards
Quoted in Halasz, 123.

C. Emile Zola Defends Dreyfus and the Republic, 1898
Extracts from Emile Zola, "J'Accuse" in Armand Charpentier, *The Dreyfus Case*, Lewis May, trans. (London: Geoffrey Bles, 1935), 142–144.

DOCUMENT SET 24.6
Realism, Impressionism, and Wagnerism

The arts in the nineteenth century were always a public matter. Novelists and poets, as we have frequently seen in these document sets, were often public figures who spoke out on the great questions of the day. Nationalist or patriotic sentiments permeated the music of some of the century's most important composers. Artistic movements often carried political overtones—even if they unfurled the banner of "art for art's sake," which was in itself a political statement.

Gustave Courbet (1819–1877), the great French realist painter, was a man of the Left: a republican, a friend of Proudhon, and a Communard who consequently suffered imprisonment and exile at the end of his life. Though he may not have painted with conscious political intent, viewers often reacted to his works positively or negatively depending on their attitudes toward socialism or the plight of the poor. How, then, do you respond to Courbet's own statement about his art (Document A)?

The great Impressionist painters—for example, Monet, Sisley, Manet, Renoir, and Cézanne—differed from the general pattern of nineteenth-century cultural life by trying to remain outside politics. Comparing Courbet's statement wth the attempt of the French art critic Emile Blémont to define Impressionism (Document B), do you detect any common purpose of trying to keep the arts apolitical? How might the Impressionists' attitude toward the nature of reality, an issue to which Blémont speaks directly, have implications for the artist's ability to interpret the society in which he or she worked?

Richard Wagner (1813–1883) was up to his neck in politics, a leftist and '48er in his younger years and an antisemitic nationalist in his old age (see Set 24.2, Document D). The magic of his art cut across lines of nationality and religion. The devoted Wagnerite whose account of hearing the master's works performed at Bayreuth is quoted in Document C was a Frenchman, and the musician whom Wagner handpicked to conduct his ambiguously Christian final music drama, *Parsifal,* was a Jew. The philosopher Friedrich Nietzsche (1844–1900) fell under Wagner's spell as a young man, but the spectacle of Wagner's summer festivals at Bayreuth, which attracted Europe's fashionable elite—along with Germany's prominent nationalists and antisemites—opened Nietzsche's eyes to the birth of a rather decadent cult of "Wagnerism" that to him embodied all that was wrong with late nineteenth-century European society (Document D).

The best way to understand painters and musicians is to look at their paintings and listen to their music. Having done this, however, investigating how these artists reflected and responded to the society and culture of their day will richly repay the effort.

A. Gustave Courbet Defines Realism

Without going into the greater or lesser or justification for an epithet that no one, I should hope, need really understand, I shall confine myself to a few words of explanation designed to put an end to present misunderstandings.

I have studied, without prejudice or theoretical views, the art of the ancients and the art of the moderns. I no more wanted to imitate the ones than to copy the others; nor did I intend to reach the idle end of *art for art's sake.* No! I simply wished to derive from a thorough acquaintance with tradition the reasoned and independent sense of my own individuality.

My purpose was to gain knowledge the better to act. To be in a position to translate and represent the ways, the ideas and the aspect of my time as I see them, to be not only a painter but also a man, in a word to practice a living art—that is my aim.

B. The Critic Emile Blémont Categorizes the Impressionists, 1876

What is an Impressionist painter? We have been given no satisfactory definition, but it seems that the artists who group themselves, or who are grouped, under this name pursue a similar end through different methods of work. Their aim is to reproduce with absolute sincerity, without contrivance or palliation, by a treatment simple and broad, the impression awakened in them by the aspects of reality.

Art is not for them a minute and punctilious imitation of what was once called "the beauties of nature." They are not concerned to reproduce more or less slavishly beings and things, or laboriously to reconstruct, minor detail by minor detail, a general picture. They do not imitate; they translate, they interpret, they apply themselves to extricate the consequence of the many lines and colors that the eye perceives in a view.

They are not analysts but synthesizers, and we believe that they are right in this; for if analysis is the scientific method par excellence, synthesis is the true method of operation for art. They have no other law than the necessary relations of things; they think, like Diderot, that the idea of beauty rests in the perception of these relations. And, as there are perhaps no two men in the world who perceive exactly the same relations in the same object, they see no reason to change, according to this or that convention, their personal and direct sensation of things.

In principle, in theory, we believe therefore that we can approve them wholeheartedly.

In practice, it is another matter. One does not always do what one wants to do, as it should be done; one does not always attain the end one sees clearly.

C. A French Wagnerite Makes the Pilgrimage to Bayreuth

I once experimented with myself in a way which I do not regret, but which I would not repeat for anything in the world, because it is most distressing. The series of performances which I was to attend consisted of *Parsifal*, the *Meistersinger, Tristan and Isolde*, and again *Parsifal*. I had devoted several weeks to a deep study of *Parsifal*, so that there could be not surprises in store for me; I knew the *Meistersinger*, which was also in the series, pretty well; but (and this is the important part of my experience) *I had not read a single note of "Tristan and Isolde,"* a few fragments of which I only knew from poor performances.

Now this is what happened; the two days of Parsifal were for me two days of the most pure and never-to-be-forgotten happiness; I was actually living among the Knights of the Grail, and I seemed to be in a dream as I strolled outside between the acts smoking cigarettes; the scenic illusion was as complete as possible and the happy impression it left upon me will never be effaced from my memory. I was more highly amused at the buffooneries (although somewhat coarse) of the Meistersinger than I had ever been at the Palais Royal; at the same time I was profoundly moved by the tender kindness of Sachs and his touching spirit of self-sacrifice. But as for Tristan, I understood nothing at all, nothing, nothing, absolutely nothing. Is that clear?

It takes a certain amount of courage to confess these things, especially when one has subsequently succeeded in penetrating the innumerable beauties of Tristan and Isolde; but I wish my sad example to be of service to others, and therefore it is necessary to relate it.

We must not go to Bayreuth, then, without first having made a serious preparatory study of the works which we are going to hear, and this study is just as necessary for the poetry as for the music. The more it is prolonged and intelligently conducted, the more pleasure we may promise ourselves from it.

I need scarcely say that I do not place in any class of admirers those unfortunate victims of snobbishness who go to Bayreuth because it is the fashion, or to show off their clothes, or to pose as intimate friends of the Wagner family, and get Herr Ernst to explain the work during the *entr'actes*. The symptoms of their disease—alas! incurable—are exceedingly simple; it is sufficient to sit down to the piano and improvise some utterly meaningless strains which you dignify with the name of *Leitmotive*; they immediately go into raptures. . . .

D. Friedrich Nietzche, Ex-Wagnerite, Lambastes Wagner

Wherein I Admire Wagner.

I believe that artists very often do not know what they are best able to do. They are much too vain. Their minds are directed to something prouder than merely to appear like little plants, which, with freshness, rareness, and beauty, know how to sprout from their soil with real perfection. The ultimate goodness of their own garden and vineyard is superciliously under-estimated by them, and their love and their insight are not of the same quality. Here is a musician who is a greater master than anyone else in the discovering of tones, peculiar to suffering, oppressed, and tormented souls, who can endow even dumb misery with speech. Nobody can approach him in the colours of late autumn, in the indescribably touching joy of a last, a very last, and all too short gladness; he knows of a chord which expresses those secret and weird midnight hours of the soul, when cause and effect seem to have fallen asunder and at every moment something may spring out of nonentity. He is happiest of all when creating from out the nethermost depths of human happiness, and, so to speak, from out man's empty bumper, in which the bitterest and most repulsive drops have mingled with the sweetest for good or evil at last. He knows that weary shuffling along of the soul which is no longer able either to spring or to fly, nay, which is no longer able to walk; he has the modest glance of concealed suffering, of understanding without comfort, of leave-taking without word or sign; verily as the Orpheus of all secret misery he is greater than anyone, and many a thing was introduced into art for the first time by him, which hitherto had not been given expression, had not even been thought worthy of art—the cynical revolts, for instance, of which only the greatest sufferer is capable, also many a small and quite microscopical feature of the soul, as it were the scales of its amphibious nature—yes indeed, he is the master of everything very small. But this he refuses to be! His tastes are much more in love with vast walls and with daring frescoes!... He does not see that his spirit has another desire and bent—a totally different outlook—that it prefers to squat peacefully in the corners of broken-down houses: concealed in this way, and hidden even from himself, he paints his really great masterpieces, all of which are very short, often only one bar in length—there, only, does he become quite good, great and perfect, perhaps there alone.—Wagner is one who has suffered much—and this elevates him above other musicians.—I admire Wagner wherever he sets *himself* to music.—

How I Got Rid of Wagner.

1.

Already in the summer of 1876, when the first festival at Bayreuth was at its height, I took leave of Wagner in my soul. I cannot endure anything double-faced. Since Wagner had returned to Germany, he had condescended step by step to everything that I despise—even to anti-Semitism. . . . As a matter of fact, it was then high time to bid him farewell: but the proof of this came only too soon. Richard Wagner, ostensibly the most triumphant creature alive; as a matter of fact, though, a cranky and desperate *décadent,* suddenly fell helpless and broken on his knees before the Christian cross. . . . Was there no German at that time who had the eyes to see, and the sympathy in his soul to feel, the ghastly nature of this spectacle? Was I the only one who *suffered* from it?—Enough, the unexpected event, like a flash of lightning, made me see only too clearly what kind of a place it was that I had just left,—and it also made me shudder as a man shudders who unawares has just escaped a great danger. As I continued my journey alone, I trembled. Not long after this I was ill, more than ill—I was *tired;*—tired of the continual disappointments over everything which remained for us modern men to be enthusiastic about, of the energy, industry, hope, youth, and love that are *squandered everywhere*; tired out of loathing for the whole world of idealistic lying and conscience-softening, which, once again, in the case of Wagner, had scored a victory over a man who was of the bravest; and last but not least, tired by the sadness of a ruthless suspicion—that I was now condemned to be ever more and more suspicious, ever more and more contemptuous, ever more and more *deeply* alone than I had been theretofore. For I had no one save Richard Wagner. . . . I was always *condemned* to the society of Germans. . . .

2.

Henceforward alone and cruelly distrustful of myself, I then took up sides—not without anger—*against myself* and *for* all that which hurt me and fell hard upon me: and thus I found the road to `that courageous pessimism which is the opposite of all idealistic falsehood, and which, as it seems to me, is also the road to *me—to my mission.* . . . That hidden and dominating thing, for which for long ages we have had no name, until ultimately it comes forth as our mission,—this tyrant in us wreaks a terrible revenge upon us for every attempt we make either to evade him or to escape him, for every one of our experiments in the way of befriending people to whom we do not belong, for every active occupation, however estimable, which may make us diverge from our principal object:—aye, and even for every virtue which would fain protect us from the rigour of our most intimate sense of responsibility. Illness is always the answer, whenever we venture to doubt our right to *our* mission, whenever we begin to make things too easy for ourselves. Curious and terrible at the same time! It is for our relaxation that we have to pay most dearly! And should we wish after all to return to health, we then have no choice: we are compelled to burden ourselves *more* heavily than we had been burdened before. . . .

Document Set 24.6 References

A. Gustave Courbet Defines Realism
   From the Catalog for the *Exhibition and Sale of 38 Paintings and a Drawing, from the Work of M. Gustave Courbet* in Eugen Weber, ed. and trans., *Movements, Currents, Trends: Aspects of European Thought in the Nineteenth and Twentieth Centuries* (Lexington, Mass.: D. C. Heath, 1992), 155–156.
B. The Critic Emile Blémont Categorizes the Impressionists, 1876
   Emile Blémont, *Le Rappel* (April 9, 1876) in Weber, 198–199.
C. A French Wagnerite Makes the Pilgrimage to Bayreuth
   Albert Lavaignac, *The Music Dramas of Richard Wagner* (New York: E. P. Dutton, 1891), 73–74.
D. Friedrich Nietzsche, Ex-Wagnerite, Lambastes Wagner
   "Nietzsche *Contra* Wagner" in *Nietzsche: Works*, ed. Oscar Levy (New York: Russell & Russell, 1964), 57–58, 73–75.

25

Modernity and the Road to War, 1894–1914

DOCUMENT SET 25.1
Revolution Again: Russia, 1900–1906

Sergei Witte (1849–1915) and V. I. Lenin (1870–1924) juxtapose two models of development open to Russia at the beginning of the twentieth century. Witte, one of the most capable and far-sighted ministers that tsarism ever produced, insisted that the regime could survive only by keeping Russia at peace and promoting foreign investment (Document A). He opposed the policies that led Russia into war with Japan, he helped extricate Russia from that conflict's consequences, and for his pains he was dismissed by Tsar Nicholas II. The Russo-Japanese War came close to shattering the tsarist regime in the Revolution of 1905, and it was the seemingly endless strain of World War I that finally brought down the empire, with power passing to the revolutionary party founded on the authoritarian, conspiratorial principles that Lenin enunciated in his 1903 pamphlet *What Is to Be Done?* (Document B). Only with the collapse of the Leninist regime at the end of the twentieth century has Witte reemerged as an admired precursor for those who would restore a market economy in Russia.

The 1905 Revolution was the "dress rehearsal" for 1917—for example, producing the first *soviets,* or workers' councils—and, more importantly, marked a fateful breach between tsardom and the Russian people. In the eyes of ordinary Russians, the autocracy never recovered from the moral stain of Bloody Sunday (Document C). And although he appointed Witte prime minister for a short while and promised in October 1905 to become a constitutional monarch, Nicholas II failed to keep the trust of Russia's growing middle class. The regime put its trust in the army

(Document D), which terrorized the peasantry into submission by "punitive raids" ("death squads" we would probably call these raiders today). Many industrialists as well as landlords thought they needed the heavy hand of repression to keep workers and peasants under control (Document E). As the experience of the ex-Soviet Union has recently reminded us, setting Russia on the road to a prosperous western-style civil society has always been a perilous undertaking.

A. Sergei Witte Tells Tsar Nicholas II What Russia Needs Most, 1900

Russia more than any other country needs a proper economic foundation for her national policy and culture. . . . International competition does not wait. If we do not take energetic and decisive measures so that in the course of the next decades our industry will be able to satisfy the needs of Russia and of the Asiatic countries which are—or should be—under our influence, then the rapidly growing foreign industries will break through our tariff barriers and establish themselves in our fatherland and the Asiatic countries mentioned above. . . . Our economic backwardness may lead to political and cultural backwardness as well.

B. V. I. Lenin Asks, *What Is to Be Done?*, 1903

The history of the revolutionary movement is so little known among us that the name "Narodnaya Volya" [People's Will, the original populist revolutionary movement of the earlier generation] is used to denote any idea of a militant centralized organisation which declares determined war upon tsarism. . . . [N]o revolutionary trend, if it seriously thinks of struggle, can dispense with such an organization. The mistake the Narodnaya Volya committed was not in striving to enlist *all* the discontented in the organisation and to direct this organisation to resolute struggle against autocracy; on the contrary, that was its great historical merit. The mistake was in relying on a theory which in substance was not a revolutionary theory at all, and the Narodnaya Volya members either did not know how, or were unable, to link their movement inseparably with the class struggle in the developing capitalist society. Only a gross failure to understand Marxism . . . could prompt the opinion that the rise of a mass, spontaneous working-class movement *relieves* us of the duty of creating as good an organisation of revolutionaries as the Zemlya i Volya[1] had, or, indeed, an incomparably better one. On the contrary, this movement *imposes* the duty upon us; for the spontaneous struggle of the proletariat will not become its genuine "class struggle" until this struggle is led by a strong organisation of revolutionaries.

We have always protested, and will, of course, continue to protest against *confining* the political struggle to conspiracy. But this does not, of course, mean that we deny the need for a strong revolutionary organisation. . . . In *form* such a strong revolutionary organisation in an autocratic country may also be described as a "conspiratorial" organisation, because the French word *conspiration* is the equivalent of the Russian word *zagovor* ("conspiracy"), and such an organisation must have the utmost secrecy. Secrecy is such a necessary condition for this kind of organisation that all the other conditions (number and selection of members, functions, etc.) must be made to conform to it. It would be extremely naïve indeed, therefore, to fear the charge that we Social-Democrats desire to create a conspiratorial organisation. . . .

The objection may be raised that such a powerful and strictly secret organisation, which concentrates in its hands all the threads of secret activities, an organisation which of necessity is centralised, may too easily rush into a premature attack, may thoughtlessly intensify the movement before the growth of political discontent, the intensity of the ferment and anger of the working class, etc., have made such an attack possible and necessary. Our reply to this is: Speaking abstractly, it cannot be denied, of course, that a militant organisation *may* thoughtlessly engage in battle, which *may* end in defeat entirely avoidable under other conditions. But we cannot confine ourselves to abstract reasoning on such a question, because every battle bears within itself the abstract possibility of defeat, and there is no way of *reducing* this possibility except by organised preparation for battle. If, however, we proceed from the concrete conditions at present obtaining in Russia, we must come to the positive conclusion that a strong revolutionary organisation is absolutely necessary precisely for the purpose of giving stability to the movement and of *safeguarding* it against the possibility of making thoughtless attacks. Precisely at the present time, when no such organisation yet exists, and when the revolutionary movement is rapidly and spontaneously growing, we *already observe* two opposite extremes (which, as it is to be expected, "meet"). These are: the utterly unsound Economism [concentrating on gaining economic improvements for the workers] and the preaching of moderation, and the equally unsound "excitative terror" which strives "artificially to call forth symptoms of the end of the movement, which is developing and strengthening itself, when this movement is as yet nearer to the start than the end. . ."[2]

Only a centralised, militant organisation that consistently carries out a Social-Democratic policy, that satisfies, so to speak, all revolutionary instincts and strivings, can safeguard the movement against making thoughtless attacks and prepare attacks that hold out the promise of success.

A further objection may be raised, that the views on organisation here expounded contradict the "democratic principle." . . .

. . . For the present, we shall examine more closely the "principle" that the Economists advance. Everyone will probably agree that "the broad democratic principle" presupposes the two following conditions: first, full publicity, and secondly, election to all offices. It would be absurd to speak of democracy without publicity, moreover, without a publicity that

---

[1] Land and Freedom, the most militant of the (Populist) revolutionary groups that arose out of Narodnaya Volya before 1881.

[2] Lenin here is quoting the veteran populist revolutionary Vera Zasulich.

is not limited to the membership of the organisation. We call the German Socialist Party a democratic organisation because all its activities are carried out publicly; even its party congresses are held in public. But no one would call an organisation democratic that is hidden from every one but its members by a veil of secrecy. What is the use, then, of advancing "the *broad* democratic principle" when the fundamental condition for this principle *cannot be fulfilled* by a secret organisation? "The broad principle" proves itself simply to be a resounding but hollow phrase. Moreover, it reveals a total lack of understanding of the urgent tasks of the moment in regard to organisation. Everyone knows how great the lack of secrecy is among the "broad" masses of our revolutionaries. We have heard the bitter complaints of B—v on this score and his absolutely just demand for a "strict selection of members" (*Rabocheye Dyelo*, No. 6, p. 42). Yet, persons who boast a keen "sense of realities" *urge*, in a situation like this, not the strictest secrecy and the strictest (consequently, more restricted) selection of members, but "the *broad* democratic principle"! This is what you call being wide of the mark.

Nor is the situation any better with regard to the second attribute of democracy, the principle of election. In politically free countries [Lenin cites Germany as an example], this condition is taken for granted. . . .

Try to fit this picture into the frame of our autocracy! Is it conceivable in Russia for all "who accept the principles of the Party programme and render the Party all possible support" to control every action of the revolutionary working in secret? Is it possible for all to elect one of these revolutionaries to any particular office, when, in the very interests of the work, the revolutionary *must* conceal his identity from nine out of ten of these "all"? Reflect somewhat over the real meaning of the high-sounding phrases [about democracy] . . . and you will realise that "broad democracy" in Party organisation, amidst the gloom of the autocracy and the domination of gendarmerie, is nothing more than a *useless and harmful toy*. It is a useless toy because, in point of fact, no revolutionary organisation has ever practised, or could practise, *broad* democracy, however much it may have desired to do so. It is a harmful toy because any attempt to practise "the broad democratic principle" will simply facilitate the work of the police in carrying out large-scale raids, will perpetuate the prevailing primitiveness, and will divert the thoughts of the practical workers from the serious and pressing task of training themselves to become professional revolutionar-

ies to that of drawing up detailed "paper" rules for election systems. Only abroad, where very often people with no opportunity for conducting really active work gather, could this "playing at democracy" develop here and there, especially in small groups. . . .

C. Before and After Bloody Sunday: Father Georgi Gapon First Petitions the Tsar and Then Denounces Him

I

Sire: We, workingmen and inhabitants of St. Petersburg of various classes, our wives and our children and our helpless old parents, come to Thee, Sire, to seek for truth and defense. We have become beggars; we have been oppressed; we are burdened by toil beyond our powers; we are scoffed at; we are not recognized as human beings; we are treated as slaves who must suffer their bitter fate and who must keep silence. We suffered, but we are pushed farther into the den of beggary, lawlessness, and ignorance. We are choked by despotism and irresponsibility, and we are breathless. We have no more power, Sire; the limit of patience has been reached. There has arrived for us that tremendous moment when death is better than the continuation of intolerable tortures. We have left off working, and we have declared to the masters that we shall not begin to work until they comply with our demands. We beg but little: we desire only that without which life is not life, but hard labor and eternal torture. The first request which we made was that our masters should discuss our needs with us; but this they refused, on the ground that no right to make this request is recognized by law. They also declared to be illegal our requests to diminish the working hours to eight hours daily, to agree with us about the prices for our work, to consider our misunderstandings with the inferior administration of the mills, to increase the wages for the labor of women and of general laborers, so that the minimum daily wage should be one ruble per day, to abolish overtime work, to give us medical attention without insulting us, to arrange the workshops so that it might be possible to work there, and not find in them death from awful draughts and from rain and snow. All these requests appeared to be, in the opinion of our masters and of the factory and mill administrations, illegal. Everyone of our requests was a crime, and the desire to improve our condition was regarded by them as impertinence, and as offensive to them.

Sire, here are many thousands of us, and all are human beings only in appearance. In reality in us, as in all Russian people, there is not recognized any human right, not even the right of speaking, thinking, meeting, discussing our needs, taking measures for the improvement of our condition. We have been enslaved, and enslaved under the auspices of Thy officials, with their assistance, and with their co-operation. Everyone of us who dares to raise a voice in defense of working-class and popular interests is thrown into jail or is sent into banishment. For the possession of good hearts and sensitive souls we are punished as for crimes. Even to pity a beaten man—a man tortured and without rights—means to commit a heavy crime. . . .

Russia is too great. Its necessities are too various and numerous for officials alone to rule. National representation is indispensable. It is indispensable that people should assist and should rule themselves. To them only are known their real necessities. Do not reject their assistance, accept it, order immediately the convocation of representatives of the Russian land from all ranks, including representatives from the workingmen. Let there be capitalists as well as workingmen—official and priest, doctor and teacher—let all, whatever they may be, elect their representatives. Let everyone be equal and free in the right of election, and for this purpose order that the elections for the Constitutional Assembly be carried on under the condition of universal, equal and secret voting. This is the most capital of our requests. In it and upon it everything is based. This is the principal and only plaster for our painful wounds, without which our wounds will fester and will bring us rapidly near to death. Yet one measure alone cannot heal our wounds. Other measures are also indispensable. Directly and openly as to a Father we speak to Thee, Sire, about them, in person, for all the toiling classes of Russia. . . .

II

With naive belief in thee as father of thy people, I was going peacefully to thee with the children of these very people. Thou must have known, thou didst know this. The innocent blood of workers, their wives and children, lies forever between thee, O soul destroyer, and the Russian people. Moral connection between thee and them may never be any more. The mighty river during its overflowing thou art already unable to stem by any half measures, even by a Zemsky Sobor (Popular Assembly). Bombs and dynamite, the terror by individuals and by masses, against thy breed and against the robbers of rightless people—all this must be and shall absolutely be. A sea of blood—unexampled—will be shed. Because of thee, because of thy whole family, Russia may perish.

Once for all, understand this and remember, better soon with all thy family abdicate the throne of Russia and give thyself up to the Russian people for trial. Pity thy children and the Russian lands, O thou offerer of peace for other countries and blood drunkard for thine own!

Otherwise let all blood which has to be shed fall upon thee, Hangman, and thy kindred!

GEORGE GAPON.

Postscriptum—Know that this letter is justifying document of the coming revolutionary terroristic occurrences in Russia. G. G.

D. Tsarist Troops Go on a Punitive Expedition, 1905

1. The Orders.

Moscow. An expedition is herewith ordered, to start on December 16, along the Kazan railroad visiting the stations Perovo, Lubertzy and Kolomna.

The commander of the expedition is to be *Colonel Rieman I.*

The expedition is to consist of the following units of the Semyonovski Life-Guards' Regiment:

9th Company, captain Shevetzov, Sub-Lieutenants Albertov II and Makarov.

10th Company, Captain Von Sievers I, Lieutenants Polivanov and Von-Vogt.

11th Company, Second-Captain Nazimov II, Sub-Lieutenants Scharnhorst and Romanovski.

12th Company, Captain Zykov and Lieutenant Shramtchenko.

14th Company, Captain Von Schimroth I, Sub-Lieutenants Von Krusenstern and Von Minnig.

15th Company, Captain Meyer, Sub-Lieutenants Falysev and Nikanorov.

2 guns.

2 machine-guns.

The aim of the expedition: to find the leaders, to annihilate the armed revolutionary militia.

General directions: *to make no prisoners and to act mercilessly.* Every house from which a shot has been fired to be destroyed by fire or by artillery.

Signed:

Commander of the Regiment, Aide-de-Camp, Colonel Mien.

Adjutant of the Regiment, Lieutenant Von Brummer. . . .

2. The Results.

Half a mile from the station Perovo, the soldier-train met on the side tracks a large number of peasants who were unloading what remained of the contents of a freight car. They paid little attention to the approaching train. True, they had been warned by the Perovo inhabitants that Cossacks were expected, but they did not believe it. Of what use could the Cossacks be now? The goods were nearly all removed; nobody had interfered from the beginning. Why should they care now when nothing remained? The peasants had come from a distance of a hundred versts.

Their good humor was dispelled by volleys from the windows of the slowly approaching train. The horses and many men fell, blood-stained, on the snow.

The shooting was furious; the soldiers sprang out of the cars and scattered over the tracks, firing upon the fleeing peasants. A group of peasants rushed to the left of them, through an open space. hoping to reach the nearby woods. Their hope was vain. The bullets were quicker, and many remained on the spot. Only a few reached the woods and escaped death. The number of the dead was 53-57.

When the expedition reached the station, Orlovski, the station-master's assistant, was on the platform. When he saw everybody driven away from the platform and the soldiers take possession of the apparatus, the signal devices and the management of the station, believing that there was nothing he could do, he went home to tell his wife that he was safe. He stayed at home about a quarter of an hour and returned to the station. He did not guess that those fifteen minutes were the last he would ever give to his wife. The next day his unfortunate widow received the mutilated, disfigured corpse of her husband.

The body was disfigured to such a degree that had it not been for the clothes it could not have been recognized. The face had been stabbed all over by bayonets. The eye sockets were pierced through to the brain. The chin, the cheeks and the nose were one bloody mask.

It was when Orlovski was approaching the station, after he had climbed the stairs that Colonel Rieman ordered him to be shot. Several bullets penetrated his body. When he fell down, he was still alive. The rest was done by bayonets. The soldiers lifted him into a car, and it was not till the next morning that the station employees brought the body to the young widow. . . .

E. Russian Manufacturers Protest Spontaneous Appropriations of Their Timber by Peasants, 1906

We, the undersigned, hold the authority of directors at the Fedor Shcherbakov & Sons Manufacturing Co., which owns 2,624 dessiatines[3] of arable land and forest near the villages of Aleshkov, Tarbushev, Rechitsy, Stoian'ev and Khakhlev (Kolomna District, Moscow Province). We are in full agreement with the compulsory alienation of whatever part of this property is needed by the peasants of these villages (on terms to be set by the State Duma and sanctioned by law). At the same time, we permit ourselves to ask you, as a representative of the State Duma (an institution which enjoys unquestioned moral prestige in the eyes of the population) to address an appropriate explanation to the peasant communities in the above villages. It should explain what manner of action (from the perspective of state interests) is desired from the peasant population regarding private land allotments until the agrarian question has been conclusively resolved in a legal manner.

The point is that, after more than forty years of peaceful coexistence with the peasants of the villages listed above, in December of last year the Rechitsy community began, without authorization, to take timber from company woods. Since then, despite the fact that the factory has taken no hostile actions against the illegal timbering, the peasants have caused ceaseless difficulties, even threatening to seize the fields that the company had planted. But this land incontestably belongs to the factory (on the basis of deeds), has been surveyed in the presence of the peasants, and put in the company's name. Seeing no end to the peasants' encroachments and wishing first to use all peaceful means to protect the company's proprietary rights until the land question has been resolved in a legal manner, we permit ourselves to address the above request, through your person, to the State Duma.

---

[3] One dessiatine equalled 2.7 acres.

Document Set 25.1 References

A. Sergei Witte Tells Tsar Nicholas II What Russia Needs Most, 1900
   Witte in Theodore Von Laue, *Why Lenin? Why Stalin?*, 2d. ed. (Philadelphia: Lippincott, 1971), 37–38.
B. V. I. Lenin Asks, *What Is to Be Done?*, 1903
   Lenin, *What Is to Be Done?* in Robert C. Tucker, ed. and trans., *The Lenin Anthology* (New York: W. W. Norton, 1975), 85–89.
C. Before and After Bloody Sunday: Father Georgi Gapon First Petitions the Tsar and Then Denounces Him
   A. J. Sack, *Birth of the Russian Democracy* (New York: Russian Information Bureau, 1918), 99–101, 103–104.
D. Tsarist Troops Go on a Punitive Expedition, 1905
   M. J. Olgin, *The Soul of the Russian Revolution* (New York: H. Holt and Company, 1917), 70, 162–163.
E. Russian Manufacturers Protest Spontaneous Appropriations of Their Timber by Peasants, 1906
   Petition from Kolomna Factory Managers to the Chairman of the Duma, 7 June 1906, in Gregory Freeze, ed. and trans., *From Supplication to Revolution* (New York: Oxford University Press, 1988), 254–255.

DOCUMENT SET 25.2

New Western Paths: Reformist Socialism, Democratic Feminism, and a Changing Liberalism

Many west Europeans feared a demographic crisis at the turn of the twentieth century. Family size appeared to be declining, the age of first marriage was rising slightly, and nationalists and militarists nervously contemplated the prospect of the next generation providing too few recruits. The French in particular dreaded their sluggish population growth compared to the explosive rise in the number of Germans. Everywhere there was talk of "national virility" being challenged. Increasing numbers of women were pursuing professional work, throwing themselves into public causes, and demanding the vote and other enhancements of their legal rights, while some highly visible "new women" attracted attention with their emancipated lifestyle. Most governments began assuming greater responsibility for the welfare of their citizens. Were there connections between these trends?

Documents A through C offer data on demographic trends at the turn of the century; it is particularly interesting to compare western and central Europe with such less developed societies as Russia and the Balkan nations. The anti-suffrage case that many educated and well-to-do women like Mrs. Humphrey Ward (1851–1920) argued in 1889—note her assumption that woman's sphere remained the world of domesticity and community service (Document D)—seemed old-fashioned to activists like radical suffragist Emmeline Pankhurst (1857–1928) in Britain (Document E) and socialist Clara Zetkin (1867–1933) in Germany (Document F). In what ways can the new feminists' activism be seen as a response to the challenges of mass society and the rise of mass politics?

The remaining documents reflect a variety of ways in which turn-of-the-century governments and (male-dominated) political movements responded to the public's sense that the state ought to assume broader social responsibilities. The motivation for the French legislation of 1913 on family allowances (Document G) seems obvious, but consider the implications of Article 2. In Document H, French socialist Alexandre Millerand (1859–1943) in 1896 proposes to reorient the party toward reforming "the anarchy of capitalism," implicitly abandoning talk of revolution. Three years later Millerand became the first socialist to join a European cabinet; he would become one of the Third Republic's leading statesmen, reaching the presidency in 1920. British social theorist Leonard Hobhouse (1864–1929) in 1911 called for a new definition of liberalism (Document I). Hobhouse's call to jettison liberalism's nineteenth-century *laissez-faire* prescriptions coincided with the enactment under two Liberal Party ministries, of social-reform laws providing for worker's compensation, old-age pensions, and health and unemployment insurance, paid for by higher taxes on the wealthy. Do you see any common ground emerging between Millerand's and Hobhouse's positions, and would it be fair to say that social democracy and liberalism were now converging? In what respects do they remain separate and antagonistic? And how would you evaluate the protest against the "new liberalism" by Georges Clemenceau (1841–1929), a fierce guardian of the old Jacobin tradition (Document J)?

A. Eastern and Western Europe Diverge in the Incidence of Unmarried People, c. 1900

Unmarried Population as Percentage of Total Population in Each Age Group

Europe (except Eastern Europe)

Country	Men			Women		
	20–24	*25–29*	*45–49*	*20–24*	*25–29*	*45–49*
Austria	93	51	11	66	38	13
Belgium	85	50	16	71	41	17
Denmark	88	50	9	75	42	13
Finland	84	51	14	68	40	15
France	90	48	11	58	30	12
Germany	91	48	9	71	34	10
Great Britain	83	47	12	73	42	15
Holland	89	53	13	79	44	14
Iceland	92	66	19	81	56	29
Ireland	96	78	20	86	59	17
Italy	86	46	11	60	30	11
Norway	86	54	11	77	48	18
Portugal	84	48	13	69	41	20
Sweden	92	61	13	80	52	19
Switzerland	91	58	16	78	45	17

Eastern Europe

Country	Men			Women		
	20–24	*25–29*	*45–49*	*20–24*	*25–29*	*45–49*
Greece	82	47	9	14	13	4
Hungary	81	31	5	36	15	4
Romania	67	21	5	20	8	3
Bulgaria	58	23	3	24	3	1
U.S.S.R.	51	18	3	28	9	4
Serbia	50	18	3	16	2	1

B. Population Trends, 1871–1911

	c.1871	c.1911	% increase
	(000,000)	(000,000)	
German Empire	41.1	64.9	57.8
France	36.1	39.6	9.7
Austria-Hungary*	35.8	49.5	38.3
United Kingdom	31.8	45.4	42.8
Italy	26.8	34.7	29.5
Spain	16.0	19.2	20.0

*not including Bosnia-Herzegovina

C. Live Births per 1,000 Inhabitants, 1908–1913

European Russia	45.6	Australia (1911-13)	28.1
Romania	43.1	Denmark	27.1
Serbia	38.2	Norway	26.0
Portugal	34.6	England	24.9
Italy	32.4	Sweden	24.4
Austria	31.9	USA	24.3
Germany	29.5	Ireland	23.3
Netherlands	29.1	France	19.5

D. Mrs. Humphrey Ward Opposes Woman Suffrage, 1889

We, the undersigned, wish to appeal to the common sense and the educated thought of men and women of England against the proposed extension of the Parliamentary suffrage to women.

While desiring the fullest possible development of the powers, energies, and education of women, we believe that their work for the State, and their responsibilities towards it, must always differ essentially from those of men, and that therefore their share in the working of the State machinery should be different from that assigned to men. Certain large departments of the national life are of necessity worked exclusively by men. To men belong the struggle of debate and legislation in Parliament; the working of the army and navy; all the heavy, laborious, fundamental industries of the State, such as those of mines, metals, and railways; the lead and supervision of English commerce, the service of that merchant fleet on which our food supply depends.

At the same time we are heartily in sympathy with all the recent efforts which have been made to give women a more important part in those affairs of the community where their interests and those of men are equally concerned; where it is possible for them not only to decide but to help in carrying out, and where, therefore, judgment is weighted by a true responsibility, and can be guided by experience and the practical information which comes from it. As voters for or members of School Boards, Boards of Guardians, and other important public bodies, women have now opportunities for public usefulness which must promote the growth of character, and at the same time strengthen among them the social sense and habit. But we believe that the emancipating process has now reached the limits fixed by the physical constitution of women, and by the fundamental difference which must always exist between their main occupations and those of men. The care of the sick and the insane; the treatment of the poor; the education of children: in all these matters, and others besides, they have made good their claim to larger and more extended powers. We rejoice in it. But when it comes to questions of foreign or colonial policy, or of grave constitutional change, then we maintain that the necessary and normal experience of women does not and can never provide them with such materials for sound judgment as are open to men.

In conclusion: nothing can be further from our minds than to seek to depreciate the position or the importance of women. It is because we are keenly alive to the enormous value of their special contribution to the community, that we oppose what seems to us likely to endanger that contribution. We are convinced that the pursuit of a mere outward equality with men is for women not only vain but demoralizing. It leads to a total misconception of women's true dignity and special mission. It tends to personal struggle and rivalry, where the only effort of both the great divisions of the human family should be to contribute the characteristic labour and the best gifts of each to the common stock.

E. Emmeline Pankhurst Radicalizes Suffragism

The contention of the old-fashioned suffragists, and of the politicians as well, has always been that an educated public opinion will ultimately give votes to women without any great force being exerted in behalf of the reform.... In the year 1906 there was an immensely large public opinion in favor of woman suffrage. But what good did that do the cause?

From the very first ... we made the public aware of the woman suffrage movement as it had never been before.... We threw away all our conventional notions of what was "ladylike" and "good form," and we applied to our methods the one test question, Will it help? Just as the [Salvation Army] took religion to the street crowds in such fashion that the church people were horrified, so we took suffrage to the general public in a manner that amazed and scandalised the other suffragists....

Women have concealed themselves for thirty-six hours in dangerous positions, under the platforms, in the organs, wherever they could get a vantage point. They waited starving in the cold, sometimes on the roof exposed to a winter's night, just to get a chance of saying in the course of a Cabinet Minister's speech, "When is the Liberal Government going to put its promises into practice?"

F. Clara Zetkin Offers Men and Women a Socialist Solution

It is not just the women workers who suffer because of the miserable payment of their labor. The males workers, too, suffer because of it. As a consequence of their low wages, the women are transformed from mere competitors into unfair competitors who push down the wages of men. Cheap women's labor eliminates the work of men and if the men want to continue to earn their daily bread, they must put up with low wages. Thus women's work is not only a cheap form of labor, it also cheapens the work of men and for that reason it is doubly appreciated by the capitalist, who craves profits. The economic advantages of the industrial activity of proletarian women only aid the tiny minority of the sacrosanct guild of coupon clippers and extortionists of profit.

Given the fact that many thousands of female workers are active in industry, it is vital for the trade unions to incorporate them into their movement. In individual industries where female labor plays an important role, any movement advocating better wages, shorter working hours, etc., would be doomed from the start because of the attitude of those women workers who are not organized. Battles which begin propitiously enough, ended up in failure because the employers were able to play off non-union female workers against those that are organized in unions. These non-union workers continued to work (or took up work) under any conditions, which transformed them from competitors in dirty work to scabs.

Certainly one of the reasons for these poor wages for women is the circumstances that female workers are practically unorganized. They lack the strength which comes with unity. They lack the courage, the feeling of power, the spirit of resistance, and the ability to resist which is produced by the strength of an organization in which the individual fights for everybody and everybody fights for the individual. Furthermore, they lack the enlightenment and the training which an organization provides.

G. The French Republic Encourages Big Families, 1913

Article 1—For large families allowances are a compulsory service for all *départements*, with the participation of the communes and the State.

Article 2—Every head of a family of French nationality, who is responsible for more than three legitimate or acknowledged children and whose resources are insufficient for their upbringing, receives an annual allowance for each child under thirteen years of age, after the third child under thirteen years of age.

Article 3—The rate of allowance is determined for each commune by the municipal council, subject to the approval of the General Council and the Minister of the Interior.

It may not be less than 60 francs per year per child, and not more than 90 francs; if the allowance exceeds 90 francs, the difference is the exclusive responsibility of the commune.

H. French Socialist Alexandre Millerand Seeks Socialist Reforms Through the Ballot Box, 1896

Is not the Socialistic idea completely summed up in the earnest desire to secure for every being, in the bosom of society, the unimpaired development of his personality? That necessarily implies two conditions, of which one is a factor of the other: first, individual appropriation of things necessary for the security and development of the individual, *i.e.* property; secondly, liberty, which is only a sounding and hollow word if it is not based on and safeguarded by property. . . .

The anarchy of capitalism has often been described. You may characterize it in one sentence, by stating that under it there is no security for any one. Farmers, merchants, manufacturers, intellectual as well as manual workers, are the prey of every chance. But it is this very excess of ill, whence collectivism holds that salvation will spring "Collectivism!" I have uttered the dreadful word whose magic incantation should arouse against us the millions of urban and rural workers whom "Socialism," certainly, no longer avails to terrify. Of the collectivist idea I will say but one thing; it is not the product of a dreamer's imagination, nor the outcome of a philosopher's conceptions, but the statement, pure and simple, of phenomena being unrolled before our eyes. Men do not and will not set up collectivism; it is setting itself up daily; it is, if I may be allowed the phrase, being secreted by the capitalist *régime*. Under the double influence of the progress of science, of which the development of machinery is only the translation into practice, and of the concentration of capital, we see the small proprietors being expropriated, labour and property being dissociated, and a new feudal class being set up, which is accumulating in its hands the ownership of the instruments of production, to become by a slow but implacable progress the absolute master of the economic, political, and moral life of the whole people, reduced by it to the modern form of slavery called the wages system. Collectivism declares that the wages system will be no more everlasting than were those previous modes of servitude and human exploitation called slavery and serfdom. Collectivism observes that the normal development of capitalistic society replaces individual property, the condition and safeguard of liberty, by the tyrannous monopoly of a minority. It does not rebel against this observed fact; it bows before it. It does not pretend to retrace the course of the centuries, nor decree the transformation of mankind; on the contrary, it adapts itself to its rules. Since it is a law of sociological evolution that all the means of production and exchange pass from the form of individual property to that of capitalistic property, it merely claims that in proportion as these vast capitalistic properties are formed beneath whose rays small property, individual property, withers and dies, in that proportion social property should replace capitalistic.

Here I seem to have my finger on the characteristic feature of the Socialist programme. In my view, whoever does not admit the necessary and progressive replacement of capitalistic property by social property, is not a Socialist. . . .

Socialism does aim at securing for every human being, by a beneficent and quite natural transformation, these two twin blessings, liberty and property, of which the capitalistic *régime* inevitably robs him. But in thus indicating the end which our party pursues, I have answered beforehand the ridiculous charge, so often made, that it expects its ideas to triumph only by violent revolution. . . . Resort to force?—for whom and against whom? Republicans before everything, we do not indulge the crazy idea of appealing to a pretender's sham prestige or a dictator's sword to secure the triumph of our doctrines. We appeal only to universal suffrage. It is the voter whom we want to set economically and politically free. We claim only the right of persuading him. I do not suppose any one will credit us with the absurd intention of taking revolutionary steps against the Senate; which a Radical Ministry, had it vacillated less, would have sufficed to reduce to reason. No, to realize the immediate reforms capable of relieving the lot of the working-class, and thus fitting it to win its own freedom, and to begin, as conditioned by the nature of things, the socialization of the means of production, it is necessary and sufficient for the Socialist party to endeavour to capture the Government through universal suffrage. . . .

I. Leonard Hobhouse Calls for an Activist Liberalism, 1911

. . . On all sides we find the State making active provision for the poorer classes and not by any means for the destitute alone. We find it educating the children, providing medical inspection, authorizing the feeding of the necessitous at the expense of the ratepayers, helping them to obtain employment through free Labour Exchanges, seeking to organize the labour market with a view to the mitigation of unemployment, and providing old age pensions for all whose incomes fall below thirteen shillings a week, without exacting any contribution. Now, in all this, we may well ask, is the State going forward blindly on the paths of broad and generous but unconsidered charity? Is it and can it remain indifferent to the effect on individual initiative and personal or parental responsibility? Or may we suppose that the wiser heads are well aware of what they are about, have looked at the matter on all sides, and are guided by a reasonable conception of the duty of the State and the responsibilities of the individual? Are we, in fact—for this is really the question—seeking charity or justice?

We said above that it was the function of the State to secure the conditions upon which mind and character may develop themselves. Similarly we may say now that the function of the State is to secure conditions upon which its citizens are able to win by their own efforts all that is necessary to a full civic efficiency. It is not for the State to feed, house, or clothe them. It is for the State to take care that the economic conditions are such that the normal man who is not defective in mind or body or will can by useful labour feed, house, and clothe himself and his family. The "right to work" and the right to a "living wage" are just as valid as the rights of person or property. That is to say, they are integral conditions of a good social order.

J. Old-Fashioned Liberal Georges Clemenceau Deplores the New Liberalism

I reject the omnipotence of the secular State, because I see it as a tyranny: others reject it because it is not *their* tyranny. . . . We made the French Revolution. Our fathers thought that it was to free themselves. Not at all, it seems it was only to change masters. . . . We have guillotined the King, long live the State-King. . . . We have dethroned the Pope: long live the State-Pope. . . . I know the State. It has a long history, full of murder and blood. . . . The State is by its nature implacable: it has no soul, no entrails, it is deaf to pity. . . . Because I am the enemy of the Emperor

and the Pope, I am the enemy of the omnipotent State, the sovereign master of humanity. Do you think that I have renounced that ancient vision of a divine Providence holding the keys of heaven and hell, that I have renounced the gospel of sweetness and charity preached on the Mount, in order to worship the State, that monster dripping with human blood, responsible for all the oppression under which humankind suffered, and is still suffering? I cannot do it.

Document Set 25.2 References

A. Eastern and Western Europe Diverge in the Incidence of Unmarried People, c. 1900
J. Hajnal, "European Marriage Patterns in Perspective" in D. V. Glass and D. E. C. Eversley, *Population in History: Essays in Historical Demography* (London: Edward Arnold, 1965), 102–103.

B. Population Trends, 1871–1911
M. Huber, *La Population de la France Pendant la Guerre* (Paris: P. U. F., 1931), 7.

C. Live Births per 1,000 Inhabitants, 1908–1913
Annuaire International de Statistique (La Have, 1917), 2:2.

D. Mrs. Humphrey Ward Opposes Woman Suffrage, 1889
Mrs. Humphrey Ward, "An Appeal Against Female Suffrage" in *The Nineteenth Century,* 148 (June 1889): 781–785.

E. Emmeline Pankhurst Radicalizes Suffragism
Emmeline Pankhurst, *Mrs. Pankhurst's Own Story* (New York: Hearst's International Library, 1914), 61, 62, 235.

F. Clara Zetkin Offers Men and Women a Socialist Solution
Clara Zetkin, "Women's Work and the Trade Unions" in Philip S. Foner, ed., *Clara Zetkin, Selected Writings* (New York: International Publishers, 1984), 54–56.

G. The French Republic Encourages Big Families, 1913
Law of July 14, 1913, in David Thompson, ed., *France: Empire and Republic, 1850–1940* (New York: Walker and Co., 1968), 285.

H. French Socialist Alexandre Millerand Seeks Socialist Reforms Through the Ballot Box, 1896
Millerand in R. C. K. Ensor, ed., *Modern Socialism* (New York: Scribner's, 1907), 49–51, 54.

I. Leonard Hobhouse Calls for an Activist Liberalism, 1911
Hobhouse, *Liberalism* (Reprinted Oxford: Oxford University Press, 1964), 83–84.

J. Old-Fashioned Liberal Georges Clemenceau Deplores the New Liberalism
Clemenceau in David Robin Watson, *Clemenceau, A Political Biography* (London: Eyre Methuen, 1974), 158–159.

DOCUMENT SET 25.3
Modernism and Positivist Science

The question of how art could—or should—represent reality had been opened by Impressionism (Set. 24.6), and the debate sharpened at the turn of the century. What *is* reality: that which is immediately perceived by the senses, or something less tangible? What larger generalizations can one draw from the sensory messages that one perceives? The debate coincided with social scientists' attempts to penetrate beneath the surface of the phenomena they investigated, be it hysterical behavior, economic enterprise, or a pattern of historical events. Enormously important scientific work was being done—the discovery, for example, of atomic structure and radiation, and the emergence of quantum and relativity theory—but how appropriate were the methods of the natural sciences to the social sciences, let alone to the artist's work?

Symbolism, the name applied to the principal cultural movement of the era, is a concept as elusive and multifaceted as the phenomena that symbolist writers sought to define. Jean Moréas (1856–1910), a Greek-born French poet of strongly classicist leanings, attempted as early as 1886 to use symbolist poetry "to clothe the Idea in a perceptible form" (Document A), while a painter who shared the symbolist impulse, Russian-born Wassily Kandinsky (1866–1944), strove to translate into artistic idiom the inherent internal order that he perceived within anarchism (Document B).

Friedrich Nietzsche, the philosopher whom we have already encountered as Wagner's disciple and critic (Set 24.6, Document D), cast a tremendous spell over the turn-of-the-century mind. Ironically, his influence rose only as he lay hopelessly insane (probably the victim of syphilis) for ten years before his death in 1900. Nietzsche's parable "The Madman" (Document C), written of course before the onset of his own madness, tragically foreshadows his fate as an uncomprehended prophet. His philosophic message revolved around the conviction that God had died, destroyed by positivist science and leaving humanity alone to define its values—a loss that the shallow, vulgar values of his day could not grasp.

The work of Sigmund Freud (1856–1939), Max Weber (1864–1920), and Marya Sklodowska Curie (1867–1934), three of the finest representatives of European science at the beginning of the twentieth century, brings into focus the problem that positivism had bequeathed. All three saw themselves as objective scientists. Trained as a medical man, Freud's early studies of hysteria led him to explore the world of the unconscious, to the development of psychoanalysis, and to the notoriety of destroying modern humanity's innocence (Document D). Weber, like Freud a man of enormous erudition, founded the discipline of historical sociology through his investigations of the ideas at the heart of capitalism and bureaucracy. Yet in his essay "The Vocation of Science" (Document E) he acknowledged the barrier that separates the artist's sweeping insights from what the scientist is granted to know. The letter that Marya Sklodowska wrote to her brother in 1893 while studying in Paris (Document F) attests to Weber's point that science is indeed a calling that can demand heroic self-sacrifice, but one that yields no ultimate truths explaining the human condition. Sklodowska later married Pierre Curie, discovered radium, and after half a lifetime's exposure to radiation died of leukemia. Science for her was an end for which she gave her life, and she was, Albert Einstein wrote, "of all celebrated beings, the only one whom fame has not corrupted."

A. A Symbolist Manifesto, 1886

We have already suggested the title of *Symbolism* as one that can most reasonably describe the present tendency of the creative spirit in art. This title can be maintained. . . .

Opposed to "teaching, declamation, false sensibility, objective description," symbolic poetry seeks to clothe the Idea in a perceptible form which, nevertheless, would not be an end in itself; rather, while serving to express the idea, it would remain subject to it. The Idea, in its turn, must not let itself be deprived of the sumptuous robes of external analogies; for the essential character of symbolic art consists in never going so far as to conceive the Idea in itself. Thus, in this art, the depiction of nature, the actions of men, all the concrete phenomena, could not show themselves as such: they are concrete appearances whose purpose is to represent their esoteric affinities with primordial Ideas. . . .

For the exact translation of its synthesis, Symbolism needs an archetypal and complex style: unpolluted words, firm periods to act as buttresses and alternate with others of undulating faintness, the significant pleonasm, the mysterious ellipsis, the suspended anacoluthe, every trope daring and multiform; lastly, good French—restored and modernized—the good, brisk, luxuriant French of the days before Vaugelas and Boileau-Despréaux, the speech of François Rabelais and of Philippe de Commines, of Villon, of Rutebeuf,[1] and of so many other writers who were free and ready to hurl the sharp terms of language like Thracian archers their sinuous arrows. . . .

B. Wassily Kandinsky Links Art and Anarchy

"Anarchy" is what many call the current state of painting. The same word is also used here and there to characterize the present state of music. People falsely use the term to denote planless disruption and disorder. Anarchy is really methodicalness and order, which is not established through external and ultimately futile force, but through a *sensation of the good*. In other words, limits are also established here, but these limits must be called *internal* and they will replace the external ones.

C. Friedrich Nietzsche Mourns the Death of God

The madman. Have you not heard of that madman who lit a lantern in the bright morning hours, ran to the market place, and cried incessantly, "I seek God! I seek God!" As many of those who do not believe in God were standing around just then, he provoked much laughter. Why, did he get lost? said one. Did he lose his way like a child? said another. Or is he hiding? Is he afraid of us? Has he gone on a voyage? or emigrated? Thus they yelled and laughed. The madman jumped into their midst and pierced them with his glances.

"Whither is God?" he cried. "I shall tell you. *We have killed him*—you and I. All of us are his murderers. But how have we done this? How were we able to drink up the sea? Who gave us the sponge to wipe away the entire horizon? What did we do when we unchained this earth from its sun? Whither is it moving now? Away from all suns? Are we not plunging continually? Backward, sideward, forward, in all directions? Is there any up or down left? Are we not straying as through an infinite nothing? Do we not feel the breath of empty space? Has it not become colder? Is not night and more night coming on all the while? Must not lanterns be lit in the morning? Do we not hear anything yet of the noise of the grave-

diggers who are burying God? Do we not smell anything yet of God's decomposition? Gods too decompose. God is dead. God remains dead. And we have killed him. How shall we, the murderers of all murderers, comfort ourselves? What was holiest and most powerful of all that the world has yet owned has bled to death under our knives. Who will wipe this blood off us? What water is there for us to clean ourselves? What festivals of atonement, what sacred games shall we have to invent? Is not the greatness of this deed too great for us? Must not we ourselves become gods simply to seem worthy of it? There has never been a greater deed; and whoever will be born after us—for the sake of this deed he will be part of a higher history than all history hitherto."

Here the madman fell silent and looked again at his listeners; and they too were silent and stared at him in astonishment. At last he threw his lantern on the ground, and it broke and went out. "I come too early," he said then; "my time has not come yet. This tremendous event is still on its way, still wandering—it has not yet reached the ears of man. Lightning and thunder require time, the light of the stars requires time, deeds require time even after they are done, before they can be seen and heard. This deed is still more distant from them than the most distant stars—*and yet they have done it themselves.*"

It has been related further that on that same day the madman entered divers churches and there sang his *requiem aeternam deo*. Led out and called to account, he is said to have replied each time, "What are the churches now if they are not the tombs and sepulchers of God?" . . .

D. Sigmund Freud Interprets a Viennese Woman's "Innocent" Dream

An intelligent and refined young woman, who in real life is distinctly reserved, one of those people of whom one says that "still waters run deep," relates the following dream: *"I dreamt that I arrived at the market too late, and could get nothing from either the butcher or the greengrocer woman."* Surely a guileless dream, but as it has not the appearance of a real dream I induce her to relate it in detail. Her report then runs as follows: *She goes to the market with her cook, who carries the basket. The butcher tells her, after she has asked him for something: "That is no longer to be obtained," and wants to give her something else, with the remark: "That is good, too." She refuses, and goes to the greengrocer woman. The latter tries to sell her a peculiar vegetable, which is bound up in bundles,*

---

[1] That is, the colorful literary French of the sixteenth century, before the imposition of the classical "rules" of the seventeenth and eighteenth centuries.

and is black in colour. She says: "I don't know that, I won't take it."

The connection of the dream with the preceding day is simple enough. She had really gone to the market too late, and had been unable to buy anything. *The meatshop was already closed,* comes into one's mind as a description of the experience. But wait, is not that a very vulgar phrase which—or rather, the opposite of which—denotes a certain neglect with regard to a man's clothing?[2] The dreamer has not used these words; she has perhaps avoided them; but let us look for the interpretation of the details contained in the dream.

When in a dream something has the character of a spoken utterance—that is, when it is said or heard, not merely thought—and the distinction can usually be made with certainty—then it originates in the utterances of waking life, which have, of course, been treated as raw material, dismembered, and slightly altered, and above all removed from their context. In the work of interpretation we may take such utterances as our starting-point. Where, then, does the butcher's statement, *That is no longer to be obtained,* come from? From myself; I had explained to her some days previously "that the oldest experiences of childhood are *no longer to be obtained* as such, but will be replaced in the analysis by 'transferences' and dreams." Thus, I am the butcher; and she refuses to accept these transferences to the present of old ways of thinking and feeling. Where does her dream utterance, *I don't know that, I won't take it,* come from? For the purposes of the analysis this has to be dissected. "I don't know that" she herself had said to her cook, with whom she had a dispute the previous day, but she had then added: *Behave yourself decently.* Here a displacement is palpable; of the two sentences which she spoke to her cook, she included the insignificant one in her dream; but the suppressed sentence, "Behave yourself decently!" alone fits in with the rest of the dream-content. One might use the words to a man who was making indecent overtures, and had neglected "to close his meat-shop." That we have really hit upon the trail of the interpretation is proved by its agreement with the allusions made by the incident with the greengrocer woman. A vegetable which is sold tied up in bundles (a longish vegetable, as she subsequently adds), and is also black: what can this be but a dream-combination of asparagus and black radish? I need not interpret asparagus to the initiated; and the other vegetable, too (think of the exclamation: "Blacky, save yourself!"), seems to

me to point to the sexual theme at which we guessed in the beginning, when we wanted to replace the story of the dream by "the meat-shop is closed." We are not here concerned with the full meaning of the dream; so much is certain, that it is full of meaning and by no means guileless.[3]

E. Max Weber Discerns the Limits of Art and Science

In the field of science only he who is devoted *solely* to the work at hand has "personality." And this holds not only for the field of science; we know of no great artist who has ever done anything but serve his work and only his work. As far as his art is concerned, even with a personality of Goethe's rank, it has been detrimental to take the liberty of trying to make his "life" into a work of art. And even if one doubts this, one has to be a Goethe in order to dare permit oneself such liberty. Everybody will admit at least this much: that even with a man like Goethe, who appears once in a thousand years, this liberty did not go unpaid for. In politics matters are not different, but we shall not discuss that today. In the field of science, however, the man who makes himself the impresario of the subject to which he should be devoted, and steps upon the stage and seeks to legitimate himself through "experience," asking: How can I prove that I am something other than a mere "specialist" and how can I manage to say something in form or in content that nobody else has ever said?—such a man is no "personality." Today such conduct is a crowd phenomenon, and it always makes a petty impression and debases the one who is thus concerned. Instead of this, an inner devotion to the task, and that alone, should lift the scientist to the height and dignity of the subject he pretends to serve. And in this it is not different with the artist.

In contrast with these preconditions which scientific work shares with art, science has a fate that pro-

2 Its meaning is: "Your fly is undone." (Trans.)

3 For the curious, I may remark that behind the dream there is hidden a phantasy of indecent, sexually provoking conduct on my part, and of repulsion on the part of the lady. If this interpretation should seem preposterous, I would remind the reader of the numerous cases in which physicians have been made the object of such charges by hysterical women, with whom the same phantasy has not appeared in a distorted form as a dream, but has become undisguisedly conscious and delusional.—With this dream the patient began her psychoanalytical treatment. It was only later that I learned that with this dream she repeated the initial trauma in which her neurosis originated, and since then I have noticed the same behaviour in other persons who in their childhood were victims of sexual attacks, and now, as it were, wish in their dreams for them to be repeated. [Freud's footnote]

foundly distinguishes it from artistic work. Scientific work is chained to the course of progress; whereas in the realm of art there is no progress in the same sense. It is not true that the work of art of a period that has worked out new technical means, or, for instance, the laws of perspective, stands therefore artistically higher than a work of art devoid of all knowledge of those means and laws—if its form does justice to the material, that is, if its object has been chosen and formed so that it could be artistically mastered without applying those conditions and means. A work of art which is genuine "fulfilment" is never surpassed; it will never be antiquated. Individuals may differ in appreciating the personal significance of works of art, but no one will ever be able to say of such a work that it is "outstripped by another work which is also 'fulfilment.'"

In science, each of us knows that what he has accomplished will be antiquated in ten, twenty, fifty years. That is the fate to which science is subjected; it is the very *meaning* of scientific work, to which it is devoted in a quite specific sense, as compared with other spheres of culture for which in general the same holds. Every scientific "fulfilment" raises new "questions"; it *asks* to be "surpassed" and outdated. Whoever wishes to serve science has to resign himself to this fact. Scientific works certainly can last as "gratifications" because of their artistic quality, or they may remain important as a means of training. Yet they will be surpassed scientifically—let that be repeated—for it is our common fate and, more, our common goal. We cannot work without hoping that others will advance further than we have. In principle, this progress goes on *ad infinitum.* And with this we come to inquire into the *meaning of* science. For, after all, it is not self-evident that something subordinate to such a law is sensible and meaningful in itself. Why does one engage in doing something that in reality never comes, and never can come, to an end? . . .

The fate of our times is characterized by rationalization and intellectualization and, above all, by the "disenchantment of the world." Precisely the ultimate and most sublime values have retreated from public life either into the transcendental realm of mystic life or into the brotherlines of direct and personal human relations. It is not accidental that our greatest art is intimate and not monumental, nor is it accidental that today only within the smallest and intimate circles, in personal human situations, in *pianissimo,* that something is pulsating that corresponds to the prophetic *pneuma,* which in former times swept through the great communities like a firebrand, welding them together. If we attempt to force and to "invent" a monumental style in art, such miserable monstrosities are produced as the many monuments of the last twenty years. If one tries intellectually to construe new religions without a new and genuine prophecy, then, in an inner sense, something similar will result, but with still worse effects. And academic prophecy, finally, will create only fanatical sects but never a genuine community.

To the person who cannot bear the fate of the times like a man, one must say: may he rather return silently, without the usual publicity build-up of renegades, but simply and plainly. The arms of the old churches are opened widely and compassionately for him. After all, they do not make it hard for him. . . .

F. Marya Sklodowska Devotes Her Life to Science, 1893

I have already rented my room on the sixth floor in a clean and decent street which suits me very well. Tell Father that in that place where I was going to take a room there was nothing free, and that I am very satisfied with this room. It should not be cold here, especially as the floor is of wood and not tiles. Compared to my last year's room it is a veritable palace.

I hardly need to say that I am delighted to be back in Paris. It was very hard for me to separate again from Father, but I could see that he was well, very lively, and that he could do without me—especially as you are living in Warsaw. As for me, it is my whole life that is at stake. It seemed to me, therefore, that I could stay on here without having remorse on my conscience.

Just now I am studying mathematics unceasingly, so as to be up to date when the courses begin. I have three mornings a week taken by lessons with one of my French comrades who is preparing for the examination I have just passed. Tell Father that I am getting used to this work, that it does not tire me as much as before, and that I do not intend to abandon it.

It seems that life is not easy for any of us. But what of that? We must have perseverance and above all confidence in ourselves. We must believe that we are gifted for something, and that this thing, at whatever cost, must be obtained.

It is difficult for me to tell you about my life in detail; it is so monotonous and, in fact, so uninteresting. Nevertheless I have no feeling of uniformity and I regret only one thing, which is that the days are so short and that they pass so quickly. One never notices what has been done; one can only see what remains to be done, and if one didn't like the work it would be very discouraging.

Document Set 25.3 References

A. A Symbolist Manifesto, 1886
From *Le Figaro* (September 18, 1886) in Eugen Weber, ed. and trans., *Movements, Currents, Trends: Aspects of European Thought in the Nineteenth and Twentieth Centuries* (Lexington, Mass.: D. C. Heath, 1992), 223–224.

B. Wassily Kandinsky Links Art and Anarchy
Kandinsky in Peter Jelavich, *Munich and Theatrical Modernism: Politics, Playwriting, and Performance 1890–1914* (Cambridge, Mass.: Harvard University Press, 1985), 231–232.

C. Friedrich Nietzsche Mourns the Death of God
Nietzsche, "The Madman" in Weber, 454–455.

D. Sigmund Freud Interprets a Viennese Woman's "Innocent" Dream
Freud, *The Interpretations of Dreams*, in *The Basic Writings of Sigmund Freud*, E. J. Brill, ed. and trans. (New York: Modern Library, 1938), 251–252.

E. Max Weber Discerns the Limits of Art and Science
Weber, in H. H. Gerth and C. Wright Mills, eds. and trans., *From Max Weber* (New York: Oxford University Press, 1958), 137–138, 155.

F. Marya Sklodowska Devotes Her Life to Science, 1893
Eve Curie, *Madame Curie*, Vincent Sheean, trans. (New York: Doubleday, Doran and Co., 1938), 115–116.

Drifting Toward War

With perhaps one exception (Jaurès), the authors of the documents in this set cannot be ranked among the more noble minds of Western civilization, but they were all taken very seriously by pre-World War I Europeans.

The German historian Heinrich von Treitschke (1834–1896) was one of the mid-nineteenth-century liberals who came to worship at Bismarck's shrine and emerged as a right-wing nationalist. Treitschke's lectures on politics (excerpted in Document A) were an annual event at the University of Berlin, delivered pompously before stamping, cheering benches of undergraduates and visiting junior army officers and government officials. He became a kind of academic William II. Indeed, the Kaiser probably owed some of his ideas to Professor Treitschke; with the speech quoted in Document B, for example, he dispatched a fleet to China in 1897 to demand restitution for some German missionaries who had been killed there. But Germany had no monopoly on inflammatory rhetoric. In France, Maurice Barrès (1862–1923), monarchist politician and literary stylist (he was a member of the French Academy), made sure that his generation never forgot that it must someday avenge the defeat of 1870 (Document C).

Fear that the pre-war generation was growing "soft" from years of peace and prosperity was not confined to the Right. Georges Sorel (1847–1922), a French engineer who in the early twentieth century turned to politics, rejected all talk of gradualism and social democracy. His 1908 book *Reflections on Violence* (Document D) argued that socialism could only come about through a disciplined uprising of the workers. Sorel found his most significant followers among discontented left-wing Western intellectuals— among them an Italian socialist newspaper editor named Benito Mussolini.

The mainstream in French socialism on the eve of the war was led by Jean Jaurès (1859–1914), a philosophy professor turned legislator. The Dreyfus affair had linked for him the causes of republicanism and democratic socialism; and although he was a devoted French patriot he also took seriously the internationalist side of socialism. In the weeks just before the outbreak of World War I he worked feverishly to unite Europe's socialist parties against the impending conflict, but on July 31, 1914, as he was returning to Paris from the Second International's headquarters in Germany, he was gunned down by a French super-patriot. Jaurès clearly understood what kind of war would be fought (Document E), and in a real sense he was its first casualty.

A. Heinrich von Treitschke Teaches a Generation of German Leaders

The next essential function of the State is the conduct of war. The long oblivion into which this principle had fallen is a proof of how effeminate the science of government had become in civilian hands. In our century this sentimentality was dissipated by Clausewitz, but a one-sided materialism arose in its place, after the fashion of the Manchester school, seeing in man a biped creature, whose destiny lies in buying cheap and selling dear. It is obvious that this idea is not compatible with war, and it is only since the last war [1870–71] that a sounder theory arose of the State and its military power.

Without war no State could be. All those we know of arose through war, and the protection of their members by armed force remains their primary and essential task. War, therefore, will endure to the end of history, as long as there is multiplicity of States. The laws of human thought and of human nature forbid any alternative, neither is one to be wished for. The blind worshipper of an eternal peace falls into the error of isolating the State, or dreams of one which is universal, which we have already seen to be at variance with reason.

Even as it is impossible to conceive of a tribunal above the State, which we have recognized as sovereign in its very essence, so it is likewise impossible to banish the idea of war from the world. It is a favourite fashion of our time to instance England as particularly ready for peace. But England is perpetually at war; there is hardly an instant in her recent history in which she has not been obliged to be fighting somewhere. The great strides which civilization makes against barbarism and unreason are only made actual by the sword. Between civilized nations also war is the form of litigation by which States make their claims valid. The arguments brought forward in these terrible law suits of the nations compel as no argument in civil suits can ever do. Often as we have tried by theory to convince the small States that Prussia alone can be the leader in Germany, we had to produce the final proof upon the battlefields of Bohemia and the [river] Main [in 1866].

Moreover war is a uniting as well as a dividing element among nations; it does not draw them together in enmity only, for through its means they learn to know and to respect each other's peculiar qualities.

It is important not to look upon war always as a judgment from God. Its consequences are evanescent; but the life of a nation is reckoned by centuries, and the final verdict can only be pronounced after the survey of whole epochs.

B. William II Offers Characteristic Bombast, 1897

The voyage on which you are starting and the task you have to perform have nothing essentially novel about them. They are the logical consequences of the political labors of my late grandfather and his great Chancellor,[1] and of our noble father's achievements with the sword on the battlefield. They are nothing more than the first effort of the reunited and reëstablished German Empire to perform its duties across the seas. In the astonishing development of its commercial interests the empire has attained such dimensions that it is my duty to follow the new German Hansa, and to afford it the protection it has a right to demand from the empire and the emperor. Our German brethren in holy orders, who have gone out to work in peace, and who have not shrunk from risking their lives in order to carry our religion to foreign soil and among foreign nations, have placed themselves under my protection, and we have now to give permanent support and safety to these brethren, who have been repeatedly harassed and often hard pressed.

For this reason, the enterprise which I have intrusted to you, and which you will have to carry out conjointly with the comrades and the ships already on the spot, is essentially of a defensive and not of an offensive nature. Under the protecting banner of our German war flag, the rights we are justified in claiming are to be secured to German commerce, German merchants, and German ships,—the same rights that are accorded by foreigners to all other nations. Our commerce is not new, for the Hansa was, in old times, one of the mightiest enterprises the world has ever seen, and the German towns were able to fit out fleets such as the broad expanse of the sea had hardly ever borne before.

The Hansa decayed, however, and could not but decay, for the one condition, namely imperial protection, was wanting. Now things are altered. As the first preliminary condition, the German Empire has been created. As the second preliminary condition, German commerce is flourishing and developing, and it can develop and prosper securely only if it feels safe under the power of the empire. Imperial power means naval power, and they are so mutually dependent that the one cannot exist without the other.

As a sign of imperial and of naval power, the squadron, strengthened by your division, will now have to act in close intercourse and good friendship with all the comrades of the foreign fleets out there, for the protection of our home interests against everybody who tries to injure Germany. That is your vocation and your task. May it be clear to every European out there, to the German merchant, and, above all, to the foreigner whose soil we may be on, and with whom we shall have to deal, that the German Michael[2] has planted his shield, adorned with the eagle of the empire, firmly on that soil, in order, once and for all, to afford protection to those who apply to him for it. May our countrymen abroad, whether priests or merchants or of any other calling, be firmly convinced that the protection of the German Empire, as represented by the imperial ships, will be constantly afforded them.

Should, however, any one attempt to affront us, or to infringe our good rights, then strike out with mailed fist, and, if God will, weave round your young brow the laurel which nobody in the whole German Empire will begrudge you.

C. Maurice Barrès Exalts French *Revanchisme*, 1902

The generations that will have to bear in history the responsibility for the disaster of 1870–1, and had felt their immediate impact, were not greatly affected by these events; they retained their devotion to words and their insipid sentimentalities. With what execrable literature they have been proposing to amuse us for the last twenty years! They subsided into the mess they had not been able to prevent, boldly putting their feet into the dirt. Their successors, on the other hand, are animated by those violent nationalist passions that are necessary to vanquished peoples. They express them in a dozen doctrines, apparently diverse, but which complement each other: they amount to anti-semitism, anti-protestantism, a protest against the accession of foreigners to high

---

[1] William I and Bismarck; the latter, of course, William II forced from office.

[2] The symbol of Germany

office in the State . . . These movements, these passions must receive their justification and must be raised to the dignity of French truths.

D. Georges Sorel Longs for War or Revolution, 1908

The two methods favoured by official Socialism presuppose this same historical datum. The ideology of a timorous humanitarian middle class professing to have freed its thought from the conditions of its existence is grafted on the degeneration of the capitalist system; and the race of bold captains who made the greatness of modern industry disappears to make way for an ultracivilised aristocracy which asks to be allowed to live in peace. This degeneration fills our Parliamentary Socialists with joy. Their role would vanish if they were confronted with a middle class which was energetically engaged on the paths of capitalistic progress, a class that would look upon timidity with shame, and which would find satisfaction in looking after its class interests. In the presence of a middle class which has become almost as stupid as the nobility of the eighteenth century, their power is enormous. If the stultifying of the upper middle class progresses in a regular manner at the pace it has taken for the last few years, our official Socialists may reasonably hope to reach the goal of their dreams and sleep in sumptuous mansions.

Two accidents alone, it seems, would be able to stop this movement: a great foreign war, which might renew lost energies, and which in any case would doubtless bring into power men with the will to govern; or a great extension of proletarian violence, which would make the revolutionary reality evident to the middle class, and would disgust them with the humanitarian platitudes with which Jaurès lulls them to sleep. It is in view of these two great dangers that the latter displays all his resources as a popular orator. European peace must be maintained at all costs; some limit must be put to proletarian violence.

E. Jean Jaurès Predicts What World War I Will Be Like, 1911

But no matter what we do, gentlemen, we remain surrounded by an atmosphere of suspicion and defiance from which, it seems to me, the clouds of war may descend upon us at any minute. As far as it is our responsibility, as far as it is the responsibility of a great people, we must constantly apply ourselves to dissipate this atmosphere of defiance and to combat the causes of the renewed danger of conflicts. It is our primary duty to reject the pessimism and the fatalism of those who say that war is inevitable.

Gentlemen, I do not disregard the forces for war in this world; but one also has to see and to recognize the forces for peace and to salute them. In its own way, war fosters peace—since the horrors of a modern war are frightening. Gentlemen, when one sometimes speaks lightly of the possibility of this terrible catastrophe one forgets the hitherto unknown extent of the horror and greatness of the disaster that would occur. . . .

The present-day armies of each nation represent entire peoples, as in the times of primitive barbarism; but this time they would be let loose amidst all the complexity and wealth of human civilization. Each of these nations would employ instruments of terrifying destruction created by modern science. Do not imagine that it will be a short war, consisting of a few thunderbolts and flashes of lightning. On the contrary, there will be slow and formidable collisions like the ones which have taken place over there in Manchuria between the Russians and the Japanese. Untold numbers of human beings will suffer from the sickness, the distress, the pain, the ravages of this multiple explosion. The sick will die of fever; commerce will be paralyzed; factories will stop working; oceans, which steamboats nowadays cross in every direction, will again be empty and silent as in former times.

This terrible spectacle will over-stimulate all human passions. Listen to the words of a man who is passionately attached to the ideals of his party and who is convinced that we must revolutionize our form of property holding, but who also believes that it will be the greatness of this movement to proceed in an evolutionary manner, without unleashing the destructive hatreds which have hitherto accompanied all great movements for social reform throughout history. But we must watch out, for it is in the fever of wars that passions for social reform are aroused to a paroxysm of violence. It was during the War of 1870 and the siege of Paris that convulsions seized that city; it was during the Russo-Japanese War that the fever broke out in Russia. Therefore, the conservatives should be the ones who desire peace more than any others, for once peace is broken the forces of chaos will be let loose. . . .

706 DOCUMENT SET 25.4

Document Set 25.4 References

A. Heinrich von Treitschke Teaches a Generation of German Leaders
   Abridged and edited by Hans Kohn, *Politics*, Blanche Dugdale and Torben de Bille, trans. (New York: Harcourt, 1965), 37–38.

B. William II Offers Characteristic Bombast, 1897
   William II, Speech on German World Policy, in James Harvey Robinson and Charles Beard, eds., *Readings in Modern European History* (Boston: Ginn, 1909), 2:193–195.

C. Maurice Barrès Exalts French *Revanchisme*, 1902
   Barrès, in Herbert Tint, *The Decline of French Patriotism, 1870–1914* (London: Weiderfield and Nicholson, 1964), 106.

D. Georges Sorel Longs for War or Revolution, 1908
   Sorel, *Reflections on Violence*, trans. T. E. Hulme (reprinted New York: Peter Smith, 1941), 82–83.

E. Jean Jaurès Predicts What World War I Will Be Like, 1911
   Jaurès, *Oeuvres de Jean Jaurès, Pour la Paix, Europe Incertaine* (Paris: Rieder, 1934), 423–434.

DOCUMENT SET 25.5
July 1914

Historians agree that the assassination of Archduke Francis Ferdinand touched off World War I. They also agree that a chain reaction ended in war: Austria-Hungary felt itself threatened by Serbian nationalism and insisted on either thoroughly humiliating the Serbian government or crushing Serbia in a quick little war; Serbia refused to submit to Habsburg dictation; Russia felt that it must back Slavic Serbia or suffer a devastating loss of face; Germany felt itself encircled and decided to stand by its only reliable ally, Austria-Hungary; France feared more "dynamic" Germany with its growing population and saw no alternative but to back *its* only reliable ally, Russia; Germany's leaders refused to fight Russia without first having knocked out the French with a strike aimed through Belgium; and Great Britain refused to stand passively aside while Germany, having crushed Belgium and France, became the Continent's dominant power. Historians' debate focuses on the extent to which these fears merely rationalized the various nations' determination to use the July 1914 crisis to force rival powers to capitulate or even to precipitate a "short little war" that they expected to win easily. Over the past generation, historians' attention has been directed particularly to the motivations and hour-by-hour conduct of the German leadership. Few scholars now believe that Germany actually plotted to start a war, but many argue that men such as Chancellor Theobald von Bethmann Hollweg were all too ready to accept war once the opportunity opened for a "grab for world power" (*Griff nach der Weltmacht*), to borrow the title of a German study of the 1960s.

The documents of this set represent only a tiny fraction of the sources that historians must sift in trying to determine the truth about the coming of World War I. Read this selection looking for clues to the actors' motivations. Document A is Austria-Hungary's ultimatum to Serbia, dated July 21, 1914; and Document B, Serbia's reply, is dated July 25. In Document C the British ambassador in Berlin reports at midnight on July 28 to his foreign minister, Sir Edward Grey, on his latest conversation with Bethmann Hollweg, who gave assurances that many historians interpret as being intended more to ensure British neutrality than to save the peace. Finally, in Document D, Grey speaks to the House of Commons on August 3, after Austria-Hungary, Germany, Russia, and France have all declared war, and on the eve of Britain's entry.

A. Austria-Hungary Sends Its Ultimatum to Serbia, July 21, 1914

On the 31st of March, 1909, the Serbian Minister in Vienna, on the instructions of the Serbian Government, made the following declaration to the Imperial and Royal Government:

"Serbia recognizes that the fait accompli regarding Bosnia has not affected her rights, and consequently she will conform to the decisions that the Powers may take in conformity with Article 25 of the Treaty of Berlin. In deference to the advice of the Great Powers, Serbia undertakes to renounce from now onwards the attitude of protest and opposition which she has adopted with regard to the annexation since last autumn. She undertakes, moreover, to modify the direction of her policy with regard to Austria-Hungary and to live in future on good neighborly terms with the latter."

The history of recent years, and in particular the painful events of the 28th June last, have shown the existence of a subversive movement with the object of detaching a part of the territories of Austria-Hungary from the Monarchy. The movement which had its birth under the eye of the Serbian Government has gone so far as to make itself manifest on both sides of the Serbian frontier in the shape of acts of terrorism and a series of outrages and murders.

Far from carrying out the formal undertakings contained in the declaration of the 31st March, 1909, the Royal Serbian Government has done nothing to repress these movements. It has permitted the criminal machinations of various societies and associations directed against the Monarchy, and has tolerated unrestrained language on the part of the press, the glorification of the perpetrators of outrages, and the participation of officers and functionaries in subversive agitation. It has permitted an unwholesome propaganda in public instruction, in short, it has permitted all manifestations of a nature to incite the Serbian population to hatred of the Monarchy and contempt of its institutions.

This culpable tolerance of the Royal Serbian Government had not ceased at the moment when the events of the 28th June last proved its fatal consequences to the whole world.

It results from the depositions and confessions of the criminal perpetrators of the outrage of the 28th June that the Sarajevo assassinations were planned in

Belgrade; that the arms and explosives with which the murderers were provided had been given to them by Serbian officers and functionaries belonging to the Narodna Odbrana;[1] and finally that the passage into Bosnia of the criminals and their arms was organized and effected by the chiefs of the Serbian frontier service.

The above-mentioned results of the magisterial investigation do not permit the Austro-Hungarian Government to pursue any longer the attitude of expectant forbearance which they have maintained for years in the face of the machinations hatched in Belgrade, and thence propagated in the territories of the Monarchy. The results, on the contrary, impose on them the duty of putting an end to the intrigues which form a perpetual menace to the tranquillity of the Monarchy.

To achieve this end the Imperial and Royal Government see themselves compelled to demand from the Royal Serbian Government a formal assurance that they condemn this dangerous propaganda against the Monarchy; in other words, the whole series of tendencies, the ultimate aim of which is to detach from the Monarchy territories belonging to it; and that they undertake to suppress by every means this criminal and terrorist propaganda.

In order to give a formal character to this undertaking the Royal Serbian Government shall publish on the front page of their Official Journal of the 13/26 July the following declaration:

"The Royal Government of Serbia condemn the propaganda directed against Austria-Hungary—i.e. the general tendency of which the final aim is to detach from the Austro-Hungarian Monarchy territories belonging to it, and they sincerely deplore the fatal consequences of these criminal proceedings.

"The Royal Government regret that Serbian officers and functionaries participated in the above-mentioned propaganda and thus compromised the good neighborly relations to which the Royal Government were solemnly pledged by their declaration of March 31, 1909.

"The Royal Government, who disapprove and repudiate all idea of interfering or attempting to interfere with the destinies of the inhabitants of any part whatsoever of Austria-Hungary, consider it their duty formally to warn officers and functionaries and the whole population of the kingdom, that henceforward they will proceed with the utmost rigor against persons who may be guilty of such machinations,

which they will use all their efforts to anticipate and suppress."

This declaration shall simultaneously be communicated to the Royal Army as an order of the day by His Majesty the King and shall be published in the Official Bulletin of the Army.

The Royal Serbian Government further undertake:

1. To suppress any publication which incites to hatred and contempt of the Austro-Hungarian Monarchy and the general tendency of which is directed against its territorial integrity;

2. To dissolve immediately the society styled "Narodna Odbrana," to confiscate all its means of propaganda, and to proceed in the same manner against other societies and their branches in Serbia which engage in propaganda against the Austro-Hungarian Monarchy. The Royal Government shall take the necessary measures to prevent the societies dissolved from continuing their activities under another name and form;

3. To eliminate without delay from public instruction in Serbia, both as regards the teaching body and also as regards the methods of instruction, everything that serves, or might serve, to foment the propaganda against Austria-Hungary;

4. To remove from the military service, and from the administration in general, all officers and functionaries guilty of propaganda against the Austro-Hungarian Monarchy whose names and deeds the Austro-Hungarian Government reserve to themselves the right of communicating to the Royal Government;

5. To accept the collaboration in Serbia of representatives of the Austro-Hungarian Government for the suppression of the subversive movement directed against the territorial integrity of the Monarchy;

6. To take judicial proceedings against accessories to the plot of the 28th June who are on Serbian territory; delegates of the Austro-Hungarian Government will take part in the investigation relating thereto;

7. To proceed without delay to the arrest of Major Voija Tankositch and of the individual named Milan Ciganovitch, a Serbian State employee, who have been compromised by the results of the magisterial inquiry at Sarajevo;

8. To prevent by effective measures the cooperation of the Serbian authorities in the illicit traffic in arms and explosives across the frontier, to dismiss and punish severely the officials of the frontier service in Schabatz and Loznica guilty of having assisted the perpetrators of the Sarajevo crime by facilitating their passage across the frontier;

---

[1] "National Defense," a prominent Serbian nationalist organization considered by the Habsburg authorities responsible for promoting anti-Austrian terrorism

9. To furnish the Imperial and Royal Government with explanations regarding the unjustifiable utterances of high Serbian officials, both in Serbia and abroad, who, notwithstanding their official position, have not hesitated since the crime of 28th June to express themselves in interviews in terms of hostility to the Austro-Hungarian Government; and finally,

10. To notify the Imperial and Royal Government without delay of the execution of the measures comprised under the preceding heads.

The Austro-Hungarian Government expect the reply of the Royal Government by 6 o'clock on Saturday evening the 25th of July.

B. Serbia Replies to the Austrian Ultimatum, July 25, 1914

The Royal Servian Government have received the communication of the Imperial and Royal Government of the 10th instant, and are convinced that their reply will remove any misunderstanding which threaten to impair the good neighbourly relations between the Austro-Hungarian Monarchy and the Kingdom of Servia.

Conscious of the fact that the protests which were made both from the tribune of the national Skuptchina[2] and in the declarations and actions of the responsible representatives of the State—protests which were cut short by the declarations made by the Servian Government on the 18th March, 1909—have not been renewed on any occasion as regards the great neighbouring Monarchy, and that no attempt has been made since that time, either by the successive Royal Governments or by their organs, to change the political and legal state of affairs created in Bosnia and Herzegovina, the Royal Government draw attention to the fact that in this connection the Imperial and Royal Government have made no representation except one concerning a school book, and that on that occasion the Imperial and Royal Government received an entirely satisfactory explanation. Servia has several times given proofs of her pacific and moderate policy during the Balkan crisis and it is thanks to Servia and to the sacrifice that she has made in the exclusive interest of European peace that that peace has been preserved. The Royal Government cannot be held responsible for manifestations of a private character, such as articles in the press and the peaceable work of societies—manifestations which take place in nearly all countries in the ordinary course of events, and which, as a general rule, escape

official control. The Royal Government are all the less responsible, in view of the fact that at the time of the solution of a series of questions which arose between Servia and Austria-Hungary they gave proof of a great readiness to oblige, and thus succeeded in settling the majority of these questions to the advantage of the two neighbouring countries.

For these reasons the Royal Government have been pained and surprised at the statements, according to which members of the Kingdom of Servia are supposed to have participated in the preparations for the crime committed at Serajevo; the Royal Government expected to be invited to collaborate in an investigation of all that concerns this crime, and they were ready, in order to prove the entire correctness of their attitude, to take measures against any persons concerning whom representations were made to them. Falling in, therefore, with the desire of the Imperial and Royal Government, they are prepared to hand over for trial any Servian subject, without regard to his situation or rank, of whose complicity in the crime of Serajevo proofs are forthcoming, and more especially they undertake to cause to be published on the first page of the "Journal officiel" on the date of the 13th (26th) July, the following declaration:—

The Royal Government of Servia condemn all propaganda which may be directed against Austria-Hungary, that is to say, all such tendencies as aim at ultimately detaching from the Austro-Hungarian Monarchy territories which form part thereof, and they sincerely deplore the baneful consequences of these criminal movements. The Royal Government regret that, according to the communication from the Imperial and Royal Government, certain Servian officers and officials should have taken part in the above-mentioned propaganda and thus compromised the good neighbourly relations to which the Royal Servian Government was solemnly engaged by the declaration of the 31st March, 1909, which declaration disapproves and repudiates all idea or attempt at interference with the destiny of the inhabitants of any part whatsoever of Austria-Hungary, and they consider it their duty formally to warn the officers, officials, and entire population of the kingdom that henceforth they will take the most rigorous steps against all such persons as are guilty of such acts, to prevent and to repress which they will use their utmost endeavour."

This declaration will be brought to the knowledge of the Royal Army in an order of the day, in the name of His Majesty the King, by his Royal Highness the Crown Prince Alexander, and will be published in the next official army bulletin.

---

[2] The Serbian legislature

The Royal Government further undertake:—

1. To introduce at the first regular convocation of the Skuptchina a provision into the press law providing for the most severe punishment of incitement to hatred or contempt of the Austro-Hungarian Monarchy, and for taking action against any publication the general tendency of which is directed against the territorial integrity of Austria-Hungary. The Government engage at the approaching revision of the Constitution to cause an amendment to be introduced into Article 22 of the Constitution of such a nature that such publication may be confiscated, a proceeding at present impossible under the categorical terms of Article 22 of the Constitution.

2. The Government possess no proof, nor does the note of the Imperial and Royal Government furnish them with any, that the "Narodna Odbrana" and other similar societies have committed up to the present any criminal act of this nature through the proceedings of any of their members. Nevertheless, the Royal Government will accept the demand of the Imperial and Royal Government, and will dissolve the "Narodna Odbrana" Society and every other society which may be directing its efforts against Austria-Hungary.

3. The Royal Servian Government undertake to remove without delay from their public educational establishments in Servia all that serves or could serve to foment propaganda against Austria-Hungary whenever the Imperial and Royal Government furnish them with facts and proofs of this propaganda.

4. The Royal Government also agree to remove from military service all such persons as the judicial inquiry may have proved to be guilty of acts directed against the integrity of the territory of the Austro-Hungarian Monarchy, and they expect the Imperial and Royal Government to communicate to them at a later date the names and the acts of these officers and officials for the purposes of the proceedings which are to be taken against them.

5. The Royal Government must confess that they do not clearly grasp the meaning or the scope of the demand made by the Imperial and Royal Government that Servia shall undertake to accept the collaboration of the organs of the Imperial and Royal Government upon their territory, but they declare that they will admit such collaboration as agrees with the principle of international law, with criminal procedure, and with good neighbourly relations.

6. It goes without saying that the Royal Government consider it their duty to open an inquiry against all such persons as are, or eventually may be, implicated in the plot of the 15th June, and who happen to be within the territory of the kingdom. As regards the participation in this enquiry of Austro-Hungarian agents or authorities appointed for this purpose by the Imperial and Royal Government, the Royal Government cannot accept such an arrangement, as it would be a violation of the Constitution and of the law of criminal procedure; nevertheless, in concrete cases communications as to the results of the investigation in question might be given to the Austro-Hungarian agents.

7. The Royal Government proceeded, on the very evening of the delivery of the note, to arrest Commandant Voislav Tankossitch. As regards Milan Ziganovitch, who is a subject of the Austro-Hungarian Monarchy and who up to the 15th June was employed (on probation) by the directorate of railways, it has not yet been possible to arrest him.

The Austro-Hungarian Government are requested to be so good as to supply as soon as possible, in the customary form, the presumptive evidence of guilt, as well as the eventual proofs of guilt which have been collected up to the present, at the enquiry at Serajevo for the purposes of the later enquiry.

8. The Servian Government will reinforce and extend the measures which have been taken for preventing the illicit traffic of arms and explosives across the frontier. It goes without saying that they will immediately order an enquiry and will severely punish the frontier officials on the Schabatz-Loznitza line who have failed in their duty and allowed authors of the crime of Serajevo to pass.

9. The Royal Government will gladly give explanations of the remarks made by their officials whether in Servia or abroad, in interviews after the crime which according to the statement of the Imperial and Royal Government were hostile towards the Monarchy, as soon as the Imperial and Royal Government have communicated to them the passages in question in these remarks, and as soon as they have shown that the remarks were actually made by the said officials, although the Royal Government will itself take steps to collect evidence and proofs.

10. The Royal Government will inform the Imperial and Royal Government of the execution of the measures comprised under the above heads, in so far as this has not already been done by the present note, as soon as each measure has been ordered and carried out.

If the Imperial and Royal Government are not satisfied with this reply, the Servian Government, considering that it is not to the common interest to precipitate the solution of this question, are ready, as always, to accept a pacific understanding, either by referring this question to the decision of the International Tribunal of The Hague, or to the Great

Powers which took part in the drawing up of the declaration made by the Servian Government on the 18th (31st) March 1909.

Belgrade, July 12 (25), 1914

C. German Chancellor Bethmann-Hollweg Seeks British Neutrality, July 29–30, 1914

Berlin, July 28, 1914
(sent at midnight)

Austria and Servia. At the invitation of Imperial Chancellor, I called upon his Excellency this evening. He said that he wished me to say to you that he was most anxious that Germany should work together with England for maintenance of general peace, as they had done successfully in the last European crisis. He had not been able to accept your proposal for a conference of representatives of the Great Powers, because he did not think that it would be effective and because such a conference would in his opinion have had appearance of an "Areopagus" consisting of two Powers of each group sitting in judgment upon the two remaining Powers; but his inability to accept proposed conference must not be regarded as militating against his strong desire for effective coöperation. You could be assured that he is doing his very best both at Vienna and St. Petersburg to get the two Governments to discuss the situation directly with each other and in a friendly way. He had great hopes that such discussions would take place and lead to a satisfactory result, but if the news were true which he had just read in the papers, namely that Russia had mobilised fourteen army corps in the south, he thought situation was very serious and he himself would be in a very difficult position, as in these circumstances it would be out of his power to continue to preach moderation at Vienna. He added that Austria, who as yet was only partially mobilising, would have to take similar measures and if war were to break out, Russia would be entirely responsible. I ventured to say that if Austria refused to take any notice of Servian note, which, to my mind, gave way in nearly every point demanded by Austria, and which in any case offered a base for discussion, surely a certain portion of responsibility would rest with her. His Excellency said that he did not wish to discuss Servian note, but that Austria's standpoint, and in this he agreed, was that her quarrel with Servia was a purely Austrian concern with which Russia had nothing to do. His Excellency further said that he resented articles in French press which stated that

decision of peace or war rested with German Emperor. This decision rested with Russia and Russia alone. In conclusion his Excellency reiterated his desire to coöperate with England and his intention to do his utmost to maintain general peace. "A war between the Great Powers must be avoided" were his last words.

Austrian colleague said to me today that a general war was most unlikely, as Russia neither wanted nor was in a position to make war. I think that that opinion is shared by many people here.

D. Sir Edward Grey Addresses the House of Commons on the Eve of Britain's Declaration of War, August 3, 1914

In the present crisis, it has not been possible to secure the peace of Europe; because there has been little time, and there has been a disposition—at any rate in some quarters on which I will not dwell—to force things rapidly to an issue, at any rate, to the great risk of peace, and, as we now know, the result of that is that the policy of peace, as far as the Great Powers generally are concerned, is in danger. I do not want to dwell on that, and to comment on it, and to say where the blame seems to us to lie, which powers were most in favor of peace, which were most disposed to risk or endanger peace, because I would like the House to approach this crisis in which we are now, from the point of view of British interests, British honor, and British obligations, free from all passion, as to why peace has not been preserved. . . .

We have great and vital interests in the independence—and integrity is the least part—of Belgium. If Belgium is compelled to submit to allow her neutrality to be violated, of course the situation is clear. Even if by agreement she admitted the violation of her neutrality, it is clear she could only do so under duress. The smaller states in that region of Europe ask but one thing. Their one desire is that they should be left alone and independent. The one thing they fear is, I think, not so much that their integrity but that their independence should be interfered with. If in this war which is before Europe the neutrality of one of those countries is violated, if the troops of one of the combatants violate its neutrality and no action be taken to resist it, at the end of the war, whatever the integrity may be, the independence will be gone.

No, Sir, if it be the case that there has been anything in the nature of an ultimatum to Belgium, asking her to compromise or violate her neutrality, whatever may have been offered to her in return, her independence is gone if that holds. If her independence goes, the independence of Holland will follow. I ask the House from the point of view of British interests, to consider what may be at stake. If France is beaten in a struggle of life or death, beaten to her knees, loses her position as a great power, becomes subordinate to the will and power of one greater than herself—consequences which I do not anticipate, because I am sure that France has the power to defend herself with all the energy and ability and patriotism which she has shown so often—still, if that were to happen, and if Belgium fell under the same dominating influence, and then Holland, and then Denmark, then would not Mr. Gladstone's words come true, that just opposite to us there would be a common interest against the unmeasured aggrandizement of any power? . . .

We are going to suffer, I am afraid, terribly in this war whether we are in it or whether we stand aside. . . .

. . . I do not believe for a moment, that at the end of this war, even if we stood aside and remained aside, we should be in a position, a material position to use our force decisively to undo what had happened in the course of the war, to prevent the whole of the west of Europe opposite to us—if that has been the result of the war—falling under the domination of a single power, and I am quite sure that our moral position would be such as to have lost us all respect. . . .

Document Set 25.5 References

A. Austria-Hungary Sends Its Ultimatum to Serbia, July 21, 1914
Hans Kohn, *The Habsburg Empire, 1804–1918* (Princeton: D. Van Nostrand, 1961), 177–181.

B. Serbia Replies to the Austrian Ultimatum, July 25, 1914
James Brown Scott, ed., *Collected Diplomatic Documents Relating to the Outbreak of the European War* (New York: Oxford University Press, 1916), 1:77–78.

C. German Chancellor Bethmann-Hollweg Seeks British Neutrality, July 29–30, 1914
G. P. Gooch and Harold Temperley, eds., *British Documents on the Origins of the War, 1898–1914* (London: H. M. Stationery Office, 1938), vol. 11, no. 249.

D. Sir Edward Grey Addresses the House of Commons on the Eve of Britain's Declaration of War, August 3, 1914
Hansard's Parliamentary Debates, 5th Series, vol. 65, cols 1809–1827.

26

War, Revolution, and Reconstruction, 1914–1929

DOCUMENT SET 26.1
Making War, 1914–1918

At the outbreak of war, crowds poured into the streets of all the belligerents' major cities to cheer their nation's cause and give their troops a rousing send-off. Everyone expected a glorious victory by Christmas. They got four years of horror, more than 8.5 million dead soldiers (and heavy civilian casualties in some areas), and a destabilization of Europe that would last for the rest of the twentieth century. Use the documents of this set, supplemented by your reading in *The Challenge of the West*, to analyze the war as it was experienced by those who lived through it.

In Document A, a French soldier records in his diary the exaltation and disorientation of mobilization day—August 2, 1914. Document B gives some idea of the war's cost in lives; and in Document C one of those millions of war dead—in this case a German student volunteer—speaks in a letter home shortly before he became one more statistic. One Austro-Hungarian draftee who survived to become a fine writer was the Czech Jaroslav Hasek (1883–1923), whose postwar novel *The Good Soldier Schweik* used comic sarcasm to settle scores with his old officers (Document D).

Women experienced the war as bereaved mothers, wives, and lovers; as workers filling myriad jobs left by men at the front; and as civilians who pulled their families through dreadful privations. One of these was Anna Eisenmenger (Document E), a wealthy Viennese physician's wife who lost her husband and one son, and who learned to scrounge for food for her remaining war-casualty menfolk and for

her malnourished daughter and aunt. Many women realized that the war had changed their lives—and women's opportunities—forever; the English feminist and pacifist Helena Swanwick spoke for them in the extract that forms Document F.

A. Going to War: A Mobilized French Soldier Records His Experiences, August 2, 1914

2 August, Sunday

Mobilized as a reserve lieutenant in the Railway Transport Service, I am posted to [assigned to] Gray. At 6 in the morning, after some painful good-byes, I go to Nogentle-Perreux station. The train service is not yet organized. There are no more passenger or goods trains. The mobilization timetable is now operative but nobody at the station has any idea when a train is due.

Sad day, sad journey. At 7 A.M. a train comes, it arrives at its terminus—Troyes—at 2 P.M. I didn't bring anything to eat, the refreshment room has already sold out. The rush of troops is beginning and consuming everything in its path. Already you find yourself cut off from the world, the newspapers don't come here any more. But, on the other hand, how much news there is! Everyone has his bit of information to tell—and it's true! . . .

At last in the afternoon I catch the first train which comes along: a magnificent row of first-class carriages (a Paris-Vienna de-luxe; all stock is mobilized) which is going no one knows precisely where, except that it is in the direction of the Front. The compartments and corridors are bursting at the seams with people from all classes of society. The atmosphere is friendly, enthusiastic, but the train is already clearly suffering from this influx from every stratum of society! The blinds are torn down, luggage-racks and mirrors broken, and the toilets emptied of their fittings; it's (typical) French destruction.

At midnight, I am at Vesoul; nothing to eat there either; no train for Gray. I go to sleep on a bench in the refreshment room.

The most fantastic rumours are going around; everyone is seeing spies unbolting railway track or trying to blow up bridges.

B. Mobilization and Death in World War I

	dead	mobilised	% dead
Germany	1,950,000	13,250,000	14.7
Russia	1,700,000(?)	15,000,000(?)	11.3
France	1,400,000	8,500,000	16.5
(Frenchmen only	1,322,100	7,935,000	16.6)
Austria-Hungary	1,047,000	9,000,000	11.6
Great Britain and colonies	776,000	6,000,000	12.9
Italy	530,000	5,615,000	9.4
United States	114,000	3,800,000	3.0
Australia	60,000	413,000	14.5

C. A German Soldier Writes from the Trenches, March 1915

Souchez, March 11th, 1915

"So fare you well, for we must now be parting," so run the first lines of a soldier-song which we often sang through the streets of the capital. These words are truer than ever now, and these lines are to bid farewell to you, to all my nearest and dearest, to all who wish me well or ill, and to all that I value and prize.

Our regiment has been transferred to this dangerous spot, Souchez. No end of blood has already flowed down this hill. A week ago the 142nd attacked and took four trenches from the French. It is to hold these trenches that we have been brought here. There is something uncanny about this hill-position. Already, times without number, other battalions of our regiment have been ordered here in support, and each time the company came back with a loss of twenty, thirty or more men. In the days when we had to stick it out here before, we had 22 killed and 27 wounded. Shells roar, bullets whistle; no dug-outs, or very bad ones; mud, clay, filth, shell-holes so deep that one could bathe in them.

This letter has been interrupted no end of times. Shells began to pitch close to us—great English 12-inch ones—and we had to take refuge in a cellar. One such shell struck the next house and buried four men, who were got out from the ruins horribly mutilated. I saw them and it was ghastly!

Everybody must be prepared now for death in some form or other. Two cemeteries have been made up here, the losses have been so great. I ought not to write that to you, but I do so all the same, because the newspapers have probably given you quite a different impression. They tell only of our gains and say nothing about the blood that has been shed, of the cries of agony that never cease. The newspaper doesn't give any description either of *how* the "heroes" are laid to rest, though it talks about "heroes' graves" and writes poems and such-like about them. Certainly in Lens I have attended funeral-parades where a number of dead were buried in one large grave with pomp and circumstance. But up here it is pitiful the way one throws the dead bodies out of the trench and lets them lie there, or scatters dirt over the remains of those which have been torn to pieces by shells.

I look upon death and call upon life. I have not accomplished much in my short life, which has been chiefly occupied with study. I have commended my soul to the Lord God. It bears His seal and is altogether His. Now I am free to dare anything. My future life belongs to God, my present one to the Fatherland, and I myself still possess happiness and strength.

D. Czech Draftee Jaroslav Hasek Recalls His Commanding Officer

Apparently by way of encouraging the rank and file as a whole, he asked where the young recruit came from, how old he was, and whether he had a watch. The young recruit had a watch, but as he thought that he was going to get another one from the old gentleman, he said he hadn't got one, whereupon the aged general gave a fatuous smile, such as Franz Josef used to put on . . . and said, "That's fine, that's fine,'" whereupon he honored a corporal, who was standing near, by asking him whether his wife was well.

"Beg to report, sir," bawled the corporal, "I'm not married."

Whereupon the general, with a patronizing smile, repeated, "That's fine, that's fine."

Then the general, lapsing still further into senile infantility, asked Captain Sagner to show him how the troops number off in twos from the right, and after a while, he heard them yelling, "One—two, one—two, one—two."

The aged general was very fond of this. At home he had two orderlies, and he used to line them up in front of him and make them number off: "One—two, one—two."

Austria had lots of generals like this.

E. A Viennese Woman Remembers Homefront Life

Ten dekagrammes [3 1/2 ounces] of horse-flesh per head are to be given out to-day for the week. The cavalry horses held in reserve by the military authorities are being slaughtered for lack of fodder, and the people of Vienna are for a change to get a few mouthfuls of meat of which they have so long been deprived. Horse-flesh! I should like to know whether my instinctive repugnance to horse-flesh as food is personal, or whether my dislike is shared by many other housewives. My loathing of it is based, I believe, not on a physical but on a psychological prejudice.

I overcame my repugnance, rebuked myself for being sentimental, and left the house. A soft, steady rain was falling, from which I tried to protect myself with galoshes, waterproof, and umbrella. As I left the house before seven o'clock and the meat distribution did not begin until nine o'clock, I hoped to get well to the front of the queue.

No sooner had I reached the neighbourhood of the big market hall than I was instructed by the police to take a certain direction. I estimated the crowd waiting here for a meagre midday meal at two thou-

sand at least. Hundreds of women had spent the night here in order to be among the first and make sure of getting their bit of meat. Many had brought with them improvised seats—a little box or a bucket turned upside down. No one seemed to mind the rain, although many were already wet through. They passed the time chattering, and the theme was the familiar one: What have you had to eat? What are you going to eat? One could scent an atmosphere of mistrust in these conversations: they were all careful not to say too much or to betray anything that might get them into trouble.

At length the sale began. Slowly, infinitely slowly, we moved forward. The most determined, who had spent the night outside the gates of the hall, displayed their booty to the waiting crowd: a ragged, quite freshly slaughtered piece of meat with the characteristic yellow fat. [Others] alarmed those standing at the back by telling them that there was only a very small supply of meat and that not half the people waiting would get a share of it. The crowd became very uneasy and impatient, and before the police on guard could prevent it, those standing in front organized an attack on the hall which the salesmen inside were powerless to repel. Everyone seized whatever he could lay his hands on, and in a few moments all the eatables had vanished. In the confusion stands were overturned, and the police forced back the aggressors and closed the gates. The crowds waiting outside, many of whom had been there all night and were soaked through, angrily demanded their due, whereupon the mounted police made a little charge, provoking a wild panic and much screaming and cursing. At length I reached home, depressed and disgusted, with a broken umbrella and only one galosh.

We housewives have during the last four years grown accustomed to standing in queues; we have also grown accustomed to being obliged to go home with empty hands and still emptier stomachs. Only very rarely do those who are sent away disappointed give cause for police intervention. On the other hand, it happens more and more frequently that one of the pale, tired women who have been waiting for hours collapses from exhaustion. The turbulent scenes which occurred to-day inside and outside the large market hall seemed to me perfectly natural. In my dejected mood the patient apathy with which we housewives endure seemed to me blameworthy and incomprehensible.

F. An English Feminist Foresees an Enlarged Sphere for Postwar Women, 1916

How has the war affected women? How will it affect them? Women, as half the human race, are compelled to take their share of evil and good with men, the other half. The destruction of property, the increase of taxation, the rise of prices, the devastation of beautiful things in nature and art—these are felt by men as well as by women. Some losses doubtless appeal to one or the other sex with peculiar poignancy, but it would be difficult to say whose sufferings are the greater, though there can be no doubt at all that men get an exhilaration out of war which is denied to most women. When they see pictures of soldiers encamped in the ruins of what was once a home, amidst the dead bodies of gentle milch cows, most women would be thinking too insistently of the babies who must die for need of milk to entertain the exhilaration which no doubt may be felt at "the good work of our guns." When they read of miles upon miles of kindly earth made barren, the hearts of men may be wrung to think of wasted toil, but to women the thought suggests a simile full of an even deeper pathos; they will think of the millions of young lives destroyed, each one having cost the travail and care of a mother, and of the millions of young bodies made barren by the premature death of those who should have been their mates. The millions of widowed maidens in the coming generation will have to turn their thoughts away from one particular joy and fulfilment of life. While men in war give what is, at the present stage of the world's development, the peculiar service of men, let them not forget that in rendering that very service they are depriving a corresponding number of women of the opportunity of rendering what must, at all stages of the world's development, be the peculiar service of women. After the war, men will go on doing what has been regarded as men's work; women, deprived of their own, will also have to do much of what has been regarded as men's work. These things are going to affect women profoundly, and one hopes that the reconstruction of society is going to be met by the whole people—men and women—with a sympathetic understanding of each other's circumstances. When what are known as men's questions are discussed, it is generally assumed that the settlement of them depends upon men only; when what are known as women's questions are discussed, there is never any suggestion that they can be settled by women independently of men. Of course they cannot. But, then, neither can "men's questions" be rightly settled so. In fact, life would be far more truly envisaged if we dropped the silly phrases "men's and women's questions"; for, indeed, there are no such matters, and all human questions affect all humanity.

Now, for the right consideration of human questions, it is necessary for humans to understand each other. This catastrophic war will do one good thing if it opens our eyes to real live women as they are, as we know them in workaday life, but as the politician and the journalist seem not to have known them. When war broke out, a Labour newspaper, in the midst of the news of men's activities, found space to say that women would feel the pinch, because their supply of attar of roses would be curtailed. It struck some women like a blow in the face. When a great naval engagement took place, the front page of a progressive daily was taken up with portraits of the officers and men who had won distinction, and the back page with portraits of simpering mannequins in extravagantly fashionable hats; not frank advertisement, mind you, but exploitation of women under the guise of news supposed to be peculiarly interesting to the feeble-minded creatures. When a snapshot was published of the first women ticket collectors in England, the legend underneath the picture ran "Superwomen"! It took the life and death of Edith Cavell[1] to open the eyes of the Prime Minister to the fact that there were thousands of women giving life and service to their country. "A year ago we did not know it," he said, in the House of Commons. Is that indeed so? Surely in our private capacities as ordinary citizens, we knew not only of the women whose portraits are in the picture papers (mostly pretty ladies of the music hall or of society), but also of the toiling millions upon whose courage and ability and endurance and goodness of heart the great human family rests. Only the politicians did not know, because their thoughts were too much engrossed with faction fights to think humanly; only the journalists would not write of them, because there was more money in writing the columns which are demanded by the advertisers of feminine luxuries. Anyone who has conducted a woman's paper knows the steady commercial pressure for that sort of "copy." . . .

The Need for Production

It is often forgotten that for full prosperity a country needs to be producing as much wealth as possible, consistently with the health, freedom, and happiness of its people. To arrive at this desired result, it is quite clear that as many people as possible should be

[1] A British nurse executed by the Germans as an alleged spy

employed productively, and it is one of the unhappy results of our economic anarchy that employers have found it profitable to have a large reserve class of unemployed and that wage-earners have been driven to try and diminish their own numbers and to restrict their own output. To keep women out of the "labour market" (by artificial restrictions, such as the refusal to work with them, or the refusal to allow them to be trained, or the refusal to adapt conditions to their health requirements) is in truth anti-social. But it is easy to see how such anti-social restrictions have been forced upon the workers, and it is futile to blame them. A way must be found out of industrial war before we can hope that industry will be carried on thriftily. Men and women must take counsel together and let the experience of the war teach them how to solve economic problems by co-operation rather than conflict. Women have been increasingly conscious of the satisfaction to be got from economic independence, of the sweetness of earned bread, of the dreary depression of subjection. They have felt the bitterness of being "kept out"; they are feeling the exhilaration of being "brought in." They are ripe for instruction and organisation in working for the good of the whole. . . .

Readjustment of Employment

Most people were astonished in 1914 at the rapidity with which industry and social conditions adapted themselves to the state of war, and there are those who argue that, because the fears of very widespread and continued misery at the outbreak of the war were not justified, we need not have any anxiety about any widespread and continued misery at the establishment of peace. Certainly depression or panic are worse than useless, and a serene and cheerful heart will help to carry the nation beyond difficulties. But comfortable people must beware of seeming to bear the sorrows of others with cheerfulness, and a lack of preparation for easily foreseen contingencies will not be forgiven by those who suffer from carelessness or procrastination. We know quite well what some, at least, of our problems are going to be, and the fool's paradise would lead straight to revolution.

It would be wise to remember that the dislocation of industry at the outbreak of the war was easily met; first, because the people thrown out by the cessation of one sort of work were easily absorbed by the increase of another sort; second, because there was ample capital and credit in hand; third, because the State was prepared to shoulder many risks and to guarantee stability; fourth, because there was an untapped reservoir of women's labour to take the

place of men's. The problems after the war will be different, greater, and more lasting. . . .

Because it will obviously be impossible for all to find work quickly (not to speak of the right kind of work), there is almost certain to be an outcry for the restriction of work in various directions, and one of the first cries (if we may judge from the past) will be to women: "Back to the Home!" This cry will be raised whether the women have a home or not. . . . We must understand the unimpeachable right of the man who has lost his work and risked his life for his country, to find decent employment, decent wages and conditions, on his return to civil life. We must also understand the enlargement and enhancement of life which women feel when they are able to live by their own productive work, and we must realise that to deprive women of the right to live by their work is to send them back to a moral imprisonment (to say nothing of physical and intellectual starvation), of which they have become now for the first time fully conscious. And we must realise the exceeding danger that conscienceless employers may regard women's labour as preferable, owing to its cheapness and its docility, and that women, if unsympathetically treated by their male relatives and fellow workers, may be tempted to continue to be cheap and docile in the hands of those who have no desire except that of exploiting them and the community. The kind of man who likes "to keep women in their place" may find he has made slaves who will be used by his enemies against him. Men need have no fear of free women; it is the slaves and the parasites who are a deadly danger.

The demand for equal wage for equal work has been hotly pressed by men since the war began, and it is all to the good so far as it goes. But most men are still far from realising the solidarity of their interests with those of women in all departments of life, and are still too placidly accepting the fact that women are sweated over work which is not the same as that of men. They don't realise yet that starved womanhood means starved manhood, and they don't enough appreciate the rousing and infectious character of a generous attitude on the part of men, who, in fighting the women's battles unselfishly and from a love of right, would stimulate the women to corresponding generosity. There are no comrades more staunch and loyal than women, where men have engaged their truth and courage. But men must treat them as comrades; they must no longer think only of how they can "eliminate female labour"; they must take the women into their trade unions and other organisations, and they must understand that the complexities of a woman's life are not of her invention or choosing, but are due to her function as mother of men.

The sexual side of a woman's life gravely affects the economic side, and we can never afford to overlook this. As mothers and home-makers women are doing work of the highest national importance and economic value, but this value is one which returns to the nation as a whole and only in small and very uncertain part to the women themselves. The fact that a woman is a wife and mother diminishes her value in the "labour market," and even the fact that she is liable to become a wife and mother has done so in the past. Unless men are prepared to socialise the responsibilities of parenthood, one does not see how women's labour is ever to be organized for the welfare of the whole, nor does one see how women are to perform their priceless functions of motherhood as well as possible if they are to be penalised for them in the future as they have been in the past....

Enfranchisement and Emancipation

The course and conduct of the war, throwing upon women greater and greater responsibilities, bringing home to them how intimately their own lives and all they hold dear and sacred are affected by the government of the country, will tend greatly to strengthen and enlarge their claim for a share in the government. The growth of what was known as "militancy," in the last few years of the British suffrage movement, was the disastrous result of the long denial of justice, the acrid fruit of government which had become coercion, because it was no longer by consent. Now that, for two years past, the women of Great Britain have made common cause with their men in this time of stress, the heat of the internal conflict has died down, and one hears on all sides that prominent anti-suffragists have become ardent suffragists, while others have declared their resolve at any rate never again to *oppose* the enfranchisement of women. The battle of argument was won long ago, but we are not, as a people, much given to theory; custom has a very strong hold over us. The shock of war has loosened that hold, and now almost every one who used to oppose,

when asked whether women should be given votes, would reply: "Why not? They have earned them!" I cannot admit that representation is a thing that people should be called upon to "earn," nor that, if essential contribution to the nation is to count as "earning," the women have not earned the vote for just as long as the men....

What the war has put in a fresh light, so that even the dullest can see, is that if the State may claim women's lives and those of their sons and husbands and lovers, if it may absorb all private and individual life, as at present, then indeed the condition of those who have no voice in the State is a condition of slavery, and Englishmen don't feel quite happy at the thought that their women are still slaves, while their Government is saying they are waging a war of liberation. Many women had long ago become acutely aware of their ignominious position, but the jolt of the war has made many more aware of it.

Document Set 26.1 References

A. Going to War: A Mobilized French Soldier Records His Experiences, August 2, 1914
   Henri Desagneaux, *A French Soldier's War Diary* (Elmsfield Press, 1975), 3–5.
B. Mobilization and Death in World War I
   Colin Dyer, *Population and Society in Twentieth Century France* (New York: Holmes and Meier, 1978), 40.
C. A German Soldier Writes from the Trenches, March 1915
   Alfons Ankenbrand in *German Students' War Letters*, A. F. Wedd, ed. (London: Methuen, 1929), 72–73.
D. Czech Draftee Jaroslav Hasek Recalls His Commanding Officer
   Hasek, *The Good Soldier Schweik*, trans. Paul Selver (Garden City, N.Y.: Doubleday, 1963), 363–364.
E. A Viennese Woman Remembers Homefront Life
   Anna Eisenmenger, *Blockade, The Diary of an Austrian Middle-Class Woman 1914–1924*, trans. Winifred Ray (New York: Ray Long and Richard R. Smith, 1932), 63–68.
F. An English Feminist Foresees an Enlarged Sphere for Postwar Women, 1916
   Excerpt from Helena Swanwick, "The War in Its Effect Upon Women," in Marilyn Shevin-Coetzee and Frans Coetzee, eds., *World War I and European Society* (Lexington, Mass.: D. C. Heath, 1995), 160–164, 166.

DOCUMENT SET 26.2
Making Peace

On January 8, 1918, President Woodrow Wilson announced in a speech before Congress a program for peace immediately known as the Fourteen Points (Document A). Wilson's was not the first attempt to define peace terms. In 1917 a majority in the German Reichstag had passed a non-binding resolution urging peace without annexations on either side, and the pope had tried to negotiate a similar settlement. One of the first acts of the new Bolshevik government in Russia in November 1917 was to propose a peace with no annexations and no indemnities (see Set 26.3, Document B), and when the Allies refused to go along, the Bolsheviks published the secret treaties by which the Allies (including tsarist Russia) had promised each other extensive territorial gains at the Central Powers' expense. On his own initiative Wilson was thus trying to offset the Bolsheviks' appeal to Europe's war-weary population; to what extent do you see his proposals as promising a just end to wartime suffering? Bear in mind, too, that the Central Powers would in March 1918 reveal their own ambitions by forcing upon a prostrate Russia the extremely punitive Treaty of Brest-Litovsk, making all of Russia's western and southern borderlands into German or Turkish satellites.

The price of victory in blood, treasure, and (for France) devastation had been so staggering that few citizens of the allied powers were willing to resist demands that the defeated and—everyone assumed—guilty enemy should pay for it all. Document B gives a sample of the rhetoric of those politicians (in this case a Conservative British MP, running for reelection on December 8, 1918) who demanded vengeance. The British economist John Maynard Keynes, beginning what would become an illustrious and highly controversial career, was one of the relatively few who realized the consequences of trying to make Germany pay (Document C).

German citizens thought that after driving out the Kaiser, declaring a republic, and accepting an armistice on the basis of the Fourteen Points, their country would receive a just peace. Evaluate the reactions of the democratically elected German National Assembly when it faced the allies' demand to ratify the Treaty of Versailles (Document D). Evaluate also the feelings of the German veterans who could not accept the end of the war under such circumstances and joined paramilitary *Freikorps* units—stepping stones for many to what later became the Nazi movement (Document E).

Hopes among colonial peoples that Allied victory would usher in a democratic new world order came to naught. In 1920 an Indian nationalist and feminist, Sarojini Naidu (1879–1949), outraged British public opinion with the speech excerpted in Document F.

Place the documents in this set in the context of the post–World War I peace settlement as you have studied it in *The Challenge of the West*.

A. Woodrow Wilson Proposes a Basis for Peace: The Fourteen Points

1. Open covenants of peace, openly arrived at. Diplomacy shall proceed always frankly and in the public view.

2. Absolute freedom of navigation upon the seas, outside territorial waters.

3. The removal, so far as possible, of all economic barriers and the establishment of an equality of trade conditions.

4. Adequate guarantees given and taken that national armaments will be reduced.

5. A free, open-minded, and absolutely impartial adjustment of all colonial claims. In determining all such questions of sovereignty the interests of the populations concerned must have equal weight with the equitable claims of the Government whose title is to be determined.

6. The evacuation of all Russian territory.

7. Belgium must be evacuated and restored. Without this healing act the whole structure and validity of international law is forever impaired.

8. All French territory should be freed and the invaded portions restored; and the wrong done to France by Prussia in 1871 in the matter of Alsace-Lorraine should be righted.

9. A readjustment of the frontiers of Italy should be effected along clearly recognizable lines of nationality.

10. The peoples of Austria-Hungary, whose place among the nations we wish to see safeguarded and assured, should be accorded the freest opportunity of autonomous development.

11. Rumania, Serbia, and Montenegro should be evacuated; occupied territories restored; Serbia accorded free and secure access to the sea; and international guarantees of the political and economic independence and territorial integrity of the several Balkan states should be entered into.

12. Nationalities which are now under Turkish rule should be assured an unmolested opportunity of autonomous development, and the Dardanelles should be permanently opened as a free passage to the ships and commerce of all nations.

13. An independent Polish state should be erected which should be assured a free and secure access to the sea.

14. A general association of nations must be formed, for the purpose of affording mutual guarantees of political independence and territorial integrity to great and small states alike.

B. Sir Eric Geddes Demands That Germany Pay, 1918

If I am returned [re-elected] Germany is going to pay restitution, reparation, and indemnity, and I have personally no doubt we will get everything out of her that you can squeeze out of a lemon and a bit more, but there are some things I would not take from Germany, because they would hurt our industries. I propose that every bit of German property, movable and immovable, in Allied and neutral countries, whether State property or the private property of Germans, should be surrendered to the Allies, and that Germany pay her precious citizens in her precious paper money. . . . I propose that not only all the gold Germany has got, but all the silver and jewels she has got shall be handed over. All her pictures and libraries and everything of that kind should be sold to the neutral and Allied world, and the proceeds given to pay the indemnity. I would strip Germany as she has stripped Belgium.

C. John Maynard Keynes Dissects *The Economic Consequences of the Peace*

. . . The Treaty includes no provisions for the economic rehabilitation of Europe,—nothing to make the defeated Central Empires into good neighbors, nothing to stabilize the new States of Europe, nothing to reclaim Russia; nor does it promote in any way a compact of economic solidarity amongst the Allies themselves; no agreement was reached at Paris for restoring the disordered finances of France and Italy, or to adjust the systems of the Old World and the New.

The Council of Four paid no attention to these issues, being preoccupied with others,—Clemenceau to crush the economic life of his enemy, Lloyd George to do a deal and bring home something which would pass muster for a week, the President to do nothing that was not just and right. It is an extraordinary fact that the fundamental economic problems of a Europe starving and disintegrating before their eyes, was the one question in which it was impossible to arouse the interest of the Four. Reparation was their main excursion into the economic field, and they settled it as a problem of theology, of politics, of electoral chicane, from every point of view except that of the economic future of the States whose destiny they were handling.

. . . For the immediate future events are taking charge, and the near destiny of Europe is no longer in the hands of any man. The events of the coming year will not be shaped by the deliberate acts of statesmen, but by the hidden currents, flowing continually beneath the surface of political history, of which no one can predict the outcome. In one way only can we influence these hidden currents,—by setting in motion those forces of instruction and imagination which change *opinion*. The assertion of truth, the unveiling of illusion, the dissipation of hate, the enlargement and instruction of men's hearts and minds, must be the means.

In this autumn of 1919, in which I write, we are at the dead season of our fortunes. The reaction from the exertions, the fears, and the sufferings of the past five years is at its height. Our power of feeling or caring beyond the immediate questions of our own material well-being is temporarily eclipsed. The greatest events outside our own direct experience and the most dreadful anticipations cannot move us.

We have been moved already beyond endurance, and need rest. Never in the lifetime of men now living has the universal element in the soul of man burnt so dimly.

D. The German National Assembly Debates the Treaty of Versailles

Bauer [Social Democratic Party, acting chancellor]: Ladies and gentlemen!

The Reich president has entrusted me with the formation of a new cabinet, to replace the Scheidemann government which has resigned. . . . The resignation of the cabinet resulted from its inability to reach an undivided position regarding the peace treaty that has been presented to us. . . . For each of us who were members of the former government it was a bitterly difficult matter to take a position between feelings of indignation and cold rage. And not less difficult was the decision to join this new government whose first and most pressing task it is to conclude this unjust peace.... We are here because of our sense of responsibility, aware that it is our damnable duty to try to salvage what can be salvaged....

No matter how each one of us feels about the question of acceptance or rejection, we are all united about one thing: in strong criticism of this peace treaty (*"Very true!"*) to which we are being forced to affix our signatures! When this draft was first presented to us, it was greeted with a unanimous protest of indignation and rejection from our people. We defied disappointment and hoped for the indignation of the entire world....

Rejection did not mean averting the treaty. (*"Very true!" from the Social Democrats.*) A no vote would only have meant a short delay of the yes vote. (*"Very true!"*) Our ability to resist has been broken; we do not have the capability to avert [signing].... In the name of the national government, ladies and gentlemen, I ask you in view of the circumstances and pending ratification by the National Assembly, to sign the peace treaty laid before you! ...

... The government of the German Republic pledges to fulfill the imposed conditions of the peace. The government, however, wishes during this solemn occasion to express its views quite clearly.... The imposed conditions exceed the limits of Germany's ability to comply....

... Moreover, we emphatically declare that we cannot accept Article 231 of the peace treaty, which demands that Germany accept responsibility for singly initiating the war. (*Applause.*)

Gröber, delegate of the Center Party: Honored Assembly! The Center Party delegation of the National Assembly wishes to acknowledge the government's declaration. We accept this program and will support this government and accept [cabinet] participation.... We say we are prepared to accept the responsibility of fulfilling its terms as far as is humanly possible, but we do not recognize a responsibility for carrying out conditions that are impossible or intolerable. However, although these are oppressive and hardly fulfillable conditions and will have a detrimental effect on the German people, we must also take other facts into account.

First, the peace will shortly bring hundreds of thousands of prisoners back to German families.... Second, the peace will end starvation.... Third, only the peace will give us the possibility of economically rebuilding Germany.... Fourth, the peace also allows us to maintain our German unity....

Schiffer, delegate of the DDP [German Democratic Party]: Contrary to the first two speakers, I wish to declare to this esteemed assembly, that the great majority of my political friends have decided to withhold their approval of the peace treaty laid before us....

Count von Posadowsky, delegate of the DNVP [German National People's Party]: Our Fatherland finds itself in the most difficult hour of its history. The enemy stands before our gates, and in the country there are disconcerting signs of internal breakup.... We in our party are aware of the ramifications for our people which a rejection of the peace treaty will entail. (*"Very true!" from the right.*) The resultant harm, however, will only be temporary, but if we accept this treaty we will abandon countless generations of our people to misery.... For us, acceptance of the treaty is impossible for many reasons.... In addition to making Germany defenseless, there is also the matter of theft of our territory....

Haase, delegate of the USPD [Independent Social Democratic Party]: We know that the peace treaty will bring incredible burdens for our people.... Nonetheless, we have no choice but to accept the treaty. Not only will rejection increase the harm, it will moreover mean sure ruin. (*Agreement from the Independent Social Democrats.*) Our people are in this desperate situation only because of the wicked warmongers and war extenders....

Kahl, delegate of the DVP [German People's Party]: Gentlemen! The German People's Party unanimously rejects this peace.... We reject it because to accept it would mean the destruction of the German state.... We reject because we cannot justify the separation of precious segments of German earth, such as the eastern provinces, from the Motherland.... Yes, if only we had swords in our hands! (*Laughter from the Social Democrats.*) Then we would easily find a response! (*"Very true" from the right.*)....

E. German Veterans Join the Freikorps

I simply can't live without my people ... I can't live without my corps ... I have no other training, no wife or children, only my men ... What place would I have in the world without my soldier's greatcoat; what good would I be in this world without you?

When blood whirled through the brain and pulsed through the veins as before a longed-for night of love, but far hotter and crazier ... The baptism of fire! The air was so charged then with an overwhelming presence of men that every breath was intoxicating, that they could have cried without knowing why. Oh, hearts-of-men, that are capable of this!

F. An Indian Woman Opposes British Imperialism, 1920

I speak to you today as standing arraigned because of the blood-guiltiness of those who have committed murder in my country. I need not go into the details. But I am going to speak to you as a woman about the wrongs committed against my sisters. Englishmen, you who pride yourselves upon your chivalry, you who hold more precious than your imperial treasures the honour and chastity of your women, will you sit still and leave unavenged the dishonour, and the insult and agony inflicted upon the veiled women of the Punjab?

The minions of Lord Chelmsford, the Viceroy, and his martial authorities rent the veil from the faces of the women of the Punjab. Not only were men mown down as if they were grass that is born to wither; but they tore asunder the cherished Purdah,[1] that innermost privacy of the chaste womanhood of India. My sisters were stripped naked, they were flogged, they were outraged. These policies left your British democracy betrayed, dishonored, for no dishonor clings to the martyrs who suffered, but to the tyrants who inflicted the tyranny and pain. Should they hold their Empire by dishonoring the women of another nation or lose it out of chivalry for their honor and chastity? The Bible asked, "What shall it profit a man to gain the whole world and lose his own soul?" You deserve no Empire. You have lost your soul; you have the stain of blood-guiltiness upon you; no nation that rules by tyranny is free; it is the slave of its own despotism.

Document Set 26.2 References

A. Woodrow Wilson Proposes a Basis for Peace: The Fourteen Points
Abridged from Charles F. Horne, ed., *The Great Events of the Great War* (np: National Alumni, 1920), 6:3–6.
B. Sir Eric Geddes Demands That Germany Pay, 1918
Geddes, Speech, in Arno J. Mayer, *Politics and Diplomacy of Peacemaking* (New York: Random House, 1967), 157.
C. John Maynard Keynes Dissects *The Economic Consequences of the Peace*
Keynes, *The Economic Consequences of the Peace* (New York: Harcourt, Brace and Howe, 1920), 226–227, 296–297.
D. The German National Assembly Debates the Treaty of Versailles
Deutsche Parlamentsdebatten in Benjamin Sax and Dieter Kuntz, eds. and trans., *The Making of Modern Germany* (Lexington, Mass.: D. C. Heath, 1992), 45–47.
E. German Veterans Join the Freikorps
Klaus Theweleit, *Male Fantasies* (Minneapolis: University of Minnesota Press, 1987), 1:60.
F. An Indian Woman Opposes British Imperialism, 1920
Sarojini Naidu, Speech, "The Agony and Shame of the Punjab," in *Padmini Sengupta, Sarojini Naidu: A Biography* (London: Asia Publishing House, 1966), 161–162.

---

[1] A practice in which Indian women screen themselves from view through special clothing such as veils and special enclosures in buildings.

DOCUMENT SET 26.3
The Bolshevik Revolution

It is difficult to imagine how the Bolshevik movement could ever have come to power in Russia without the country's virtual disintegration under the strain of World War I, or how the Bolsheviks could have seized and retained power without the leadership of Vladimir Ilych Lenin. When he returned to Russia from exile in Switzerland, the Bolsheviks were a floundering fringe group. In his "April [1917] Theses," excerpted in Document A, Lenin demanded that the Bolsheviks cease cooperating with mainstream liberals and leftists, as most of them had begun doing (including a young Bolshevik who called himself Stalin, or "man of steel"). By November 1917, after Lenin had cajoled and bullied his Bolsheviks into overthrowing the inept, discredited, but democratic Provisional Government, one of his first actions was to have the new Soviet government call for an end to the war (Document B)—not only to revolutionize the workers of other belligerent nations but also to appease ordinary Russians desperate for relief from suffering.

For Western historians, what happened at the grassroots across Russia's vast landmass was long a mystery. Recently accounts have become available of how Bolsheviks took and retained power in provincial towns, and of how local people reacted to the news they heard from Petrograd. One such source is the diary of Alexis Babine, a liberal-leaning physician and university professor at Saratov on the Volga River, a few excerpts from which appear as Document C. Later entries in Babine's diary also record local Bolshevik executions of hostages and opposition elements; such "revolutionary terror" was what Lenin had in mind when even before the Civil War he urged a crackdown on bourgeois enemies of the Revolution (Document D).

The last great conflict of the era of civil war was the uprising in early 1921 of the garrison at Kronstadt, hitherto staunch revolutionaries now disillusioned with the stifling of democracy among Bolshevik supporters and with material suffering. Loyal Red Army troops crushed the revolt even as the Tenth Party Congress was in session, and Lenin demanded that the Congress forbid any factions to form within the Communist Party (as the Bolsheviks had renamed themselves) that would oppose the leadership's policies—groups such as the "Worker's Opposition" that had appeared in 1920 and had sympathized with the Kronstadters. Lenin's "Draft Resolution on Party Unity" (Document E) spelled out the principle of "democratic centralism" by which the Communist Party would be ruled until Mikhail Gorbachev's *perestroika* and *glasnost* policies of the mid-1980s cleared the road to the regime's collapse.

One member of the Workers' Opposition group that demanded democracy within the Party was Alexandra Kollontai (1872–1952). An outspoken feminist, she broke with the traditional Marxist principle that women's rights would come automatically in a socialist revolution; changing women's status would take special efforts, she asserted, and would involve cultural as well as political transformation. In Document F she explains her maverick stand. (Eventually she returned to the Party fold and survived Stalinism by conforming.) That Lenin himself had little patience with talk of effecting a revolution in sexual attitudes—or with Freudian psychology—is apparent from Document G, a 1920 conversation with the Soviet leader recorded by the German Marxist feminist Clara Zetkin (see Set 25.5, Document F).

The extent to which Lenin set the Soviet Union and the Communist Party on the road to totalitarianism has long been debated by Western commentators, and Russian scholars have joined the debate since the fall of Communism. Read the documents in this set—as well as those of Set 26.4—with this question in mind. The questions that Kollontai and Zetkin raise about individual liberation within the socialist revolution also bear on this matter.

A. V. I. Lenin Announces His Basic Strategy, April 1917

I did not arrive in Petrograd until the night of April 3, and therefore at the meeting on April 4 I could, of course, deliver the report on the tasks of the revolutionary proletariat only on my own behalf, and with reservations as to insufficient preparation.

The only thing I could do to make things easier for myself—and for *honest* opponents—was to prepare the theses *in writing*. I read them out, and gave the text to Comrade Tsereteli. I read them *twice* very slowly: first at a meeting of Bolsheviks and then at a meeting of both Bolsheviks and Mensheviks.

I publish these personal theses of mine with only the briefest explanatory notes, which were developed in far greater detail in the report.

Theses

1) In our attitude towards the war, which under the new government of Lvov and Co.[1] unquestionably remains on Russia's part a predatory imperialist war owing to the capitalist nature of that government, not the slightest concession to "revolutionary defencism" is permissible.

The class-conscious proletariat can give its consent to a revolutionary war, which would really justify revolutionary defencism, only on condition: (a) that the power pass to the proletariat and the poorest sections of the peasants aligned with the proletariat; (b) that all annexations be renounced in deed and not in word; (c) that a complete break be effected in actual fact with all capitalist interests. . . .

The most widespread campaign for this view must be organised in the army at the front. . . .

2) The specific feature of the present situation in Russia is that the country is *passing* from the first stage of the revolution—which, owing to the insufficient class-consciousness and organisation of the proletariat, placed power in the hands of the bourgeoisie—to its *second* stage, which must place power in the hands of the proletariat and the poorest sections of the peasants.

This transition is characterised, on the one hand, by a maximum of legally recognised rights (Russia is *now* the freest of all the belligerent countries in the world); on the other, by the absence of violence towards the masses, and, finally, by their unreasoning trust in the government of capitalists, those worst enemies of peace and socialism.

This peculiar situation demands of us an ability to adapt ourselves to the *special* conditions of Party work among unprecedentedly large masses of proletarians who have just awakened to political life.

3) No support for the Provisional Government; the utter falsity of all its promises should be made clear, particularly of those relating to the renunciation of annexations. Exposure in place of the impermissible, illusion-breeding "demand" that *this* government, a government of capitalists, should *cease* to be an imperialist government.

4) Recognition of the fact that in most of the Soviets of Workers' Deputies our Party is in a minority, so far a small minority, as against *a bloc of all* the petty-bourgeois opportunist elements, from the Popular Socialists and the Socialist-Revolutionaries . . . who have yielded to the influence of the bourgeoisie and spread that influence among the proletariat.

[1] The liberal government proclaimed after the fall of tsarism

The masses must be made to see that the Soviets of Workers' Deputies are the *only possible* form of revolutionary government, and that therefore our task is, as long as *this* government yields to the influence of the bourgeoisie, to present a patient, systematic, and persistent *explanation* of the errors of their tactics, an explanation especially adapted to the practical needs of the masses.

As long as we are in the minority we carry on the work of criticising and exposing errors and at the same time we preach the necessity of transferring the entire state power to the Soviets of Workers' Deputies, so that the people may overcome their mistakes by experience.

5) Not a parliamentary republic—to return a parliamentary republic from the Soviets of Workers' Deputies would be a retrograde step—but a Republic of Soviets of Workers', Agricultural Labourers' and Peasants' Deputies throughout the country, from top to bottom.

Abolition of the police, the army and the bureaucracy.

The salaries of all officials, all of whom are elective and displaceable at any time, not to exceed the average wage of a competent worker.

6) The weight of emphasis in the agrarian programme to be shifted to the Soviets of Agricultural Labourers' Deputies.

Confiscation of all landed estates.

Nationalisation of *all* lands in the country, the land to be disposed of by the local Soviets of Agricultural Labourers' and Peasants' Deputies. . . .

7) The immediate amalgamation of all banks in the country into a single national bank, and the institution of control over it by the Soviets of Workers' Deputies.

8) It is not our *immediate* task to "introduce" socialism, but only to bring social production and the distribution of products at once under the *control* of the Soviets of Workers' Deputies. . . .

B. The Bolsheviks Decree Peace, November 8, 1917

The Workers' and Peasants' Government, created by the Revolution of October 24–25 (November 6–7) and supported by the Soviets of Workers', Soldiers' and Peasants' Deputies, proposes to all combatant peoples and to their governments to begin immediate negotiations for an honest democratic peace.

The Government regards as an honest or democratic peace, which is yearned for by the overwhelming majority of the workers and the toiling classes of all the fighting countries, who are exhausted, tormented and tortured by the War, which the Russian workers and peasants demanded most definitely and insistently after the overthrow of the Tsarist monarchy,—an immediate peace without annexations (*i.e.*, without the seizure of foreign land, without the forcible taking over of foreign nationalities) and without contributions.

Such a peace the Government of Russia proposes to all the fighting peoples to conclude immediately, expressing its readiness to take without the least delay immediately all the decisive steps, up to the final confirmation of all the conditions of such a peace by the authorized assemblies of peoples' representatives of all countries and all nations.

As annexation or seizure of alien lands the Government understands, in conformity with the conception of justice, of democracy in general and of the toiling classes in particular, any addition to a large or strong state of a small or weak nationality, without the precisely, clearly and voluntarily expressed agreement and desire of this nationality, irrespective of when this forcible annexation took place, and also irrespective of how advanced or how backward is the nation which is violently annexed or violently held within the frontiers of another state. Irrespective, finally, of whether this nation lives in Europe or in faraway transoceanic countries.

If any nation is kept within the frontiers of another state by violence, if it is not granted the right, despite its expressed desire,—regardless of whether this desire is expressed in the press, in people's meetings, in the decisions of parties or in riots and uprisings against national oppression,—to vote freely, with the troops of the annexationist or stronger nation withdrawn, to decide without the least compulsion the question of the form of its state existence, then the holding of such a nation is annexation, *i.e.*, seizure and violence.

To continue this war in order to decide how to divide between strong and rich nations the weak nationalities which they have seized, the Government considers the greatest crime against humanity; and it solemnly avows its decision immediately to sign conditions of peace which will stop this War on the terms which have been outlined, equally just for all nationalities, without exception.

Along with this the Government states that it does not regard the above mentioned conditions of peace as ultimative, *i.e.*, it is willing to consider any other conditions of peace, insisting only that these be presented as quickly as possible by one of the fighting countries, and on the fullest clarity, on the absolute exclusion of any ambiguity and secrecy in proposing conditions of peace.

The Government abolishes secret diplomacy, announcing its firm intention to carry on all negotiations quite openly before the whole people, proceeding immediately to the full publication of the secret treaties, ratified or concluded by the Government of landlords and capitalists between February and October 25, 1917. All the contents of these secret treaties, inasmuch as they are directed, as usually happened, toward the obtaining of advantages and privileges for Russian landlords and capitalists, toward the maintenance or the increase of Great Russian annexations, the Government declares unconditionally and immediately annulled.

Turning with its proposal to the Governments and peoples of all countries to begin immediately open negotiations for the conclusion of peace, the Government expresses its readiness to carry on these negotiations by means of written communications, by telegraph, by means of negotiations between representatives of different countries or at a conference of such representatives. To facilitate such negotiations the Government will nominate its plenipotentiary representative in neutral countries.

The Government proposes to all Governments and peoples of all combatant countries immediately to conclude an armistice, considering it desirable that this armistice should be concluded for a period of not less than three months, in the course of which time it would be quite possible both to complete negotiations for peace with the participation of representatives of all nationalities or nations which have been drawn into the War or have been forced to participate in it and to convoke authoritative assemblies of peoples' representatives of all countries for the final confirmation of the peace conditions.

Turning with these proposals of peace to the Governments and the peoples of all the combatant countries, the Provisional Workers' and Peasants' Government of Russia also appeals especially to the class-conscious workers of the three leading nations of humanity and the largest states which are participating in the war, England, France and Germany. The workers of these countries rendered the greatest services to the cause of progress and socialism, and the great examples of the Chartist Movement in England, a number of revolutions of world significance, carried out by the French proletariat, finally the heroic struggle against the Exceptional Law in Germany and the long, stubborn, disciplined work of creating mass proletarian organizations in Germany (which was a model for the workers of the whole world),—all these examples of proletarian heroism and historic creation serve us as a guaranty that the workers of the above mentioned countries understand the problems which now fall on them, of liberating humanity from the horrors of war and its consequences, that these workers by their decisive and devotedly energetic activity will help us to bring successfully to its end the cause of peace and, along with this, the cause of freeing the toiling and exploited masses of the population from slavery and exploitation of every kind.

President of the Soviet of Peoples' Commissars,
Vladimir Ulianov-Lenin.

C. At the Grass Roots: A Citizen Chronicles the Bolshevik Seizure of Power in Provincial Saratov

October 27, 1917. An appeal has been published in the local papers to all good citizens to resist the expected Bolshevik attempt to overthrow the existing government in Saratov. Owing to the unpopularity of Kerensky and his rule and to the physical and moral flabbiness of our Christian citizens, only 150 persons are said to have answered the call to defend the city and to have entrenched themselves in the city duma building.

October 28, 1917. Some patriot has written on one of the macadam sidewalks of the Linden Park in chalk: "Down with the Jew Kerensky." It is rumored that the soldiers are planning a Jewish pogrom. Last night and the night before, crowds were gathering around the newsstands awaiting and discussing the latest telegrams. The crowds behaved in an orderly way. This morning streets were full of dirty-looking workers armed with foreign muskets, and of armed soldiers. Soldiers are as opposed to Kerensky as they are to a new monarch. My landlady's lawyer reports that all city banks are closed. She sent her jewelry and other valuables to some poor relations of hers for safekeeping. As a local millionaire, she fears an attack from the Bolshevik mob. She has no weapons and hardly a decent hatchet in the house. The front door was locked for the day, and an order has been given to the janitor to keep the iron yard gate securely barred. In case of need the house could make a good fortress and be defended against any number of the common rabble by spirited, well-armed inhabitants. . . .

From Donald J. Raleigh, ed., *A Russian Civil War Diary: Alexis Babine in Saratov, 1917–1922*, pp. 22–24, 30, 36. Durham, N.C.: Duke University Press, 1988. Reprinted with permission.

November 15, 1917. The Soviet's general and indiscriminate amnesty of all political and criminal prisoners, with all jails thrown open and court records burned, has filled the country with dangerous elements. The younger and the more enterprising jailbirds immediately after their liberation joined the Communist party. In many cases they were given responsible administrative positions and furnished the Bolsheviks with the fittest possible material for fighting and exterminating the enemies of the party, i.e., all idle and flabby lovers of law and order.

December 17, 1917. A peaceful demonstration was announced yesterday by various city and private organizations in favor of the Constituent Assembly, to take place today. The Bolsheviks replied by sponsoring an armed demonstration, turning out all their artillery and infantry, which have just defiled past our house, carrying red flags with the usual inscriptions and howling revolutionary songs as far as today's bitter cold allowed. Many ugly faces turned up toward the upper story of our house. One armed scoundrel shook his fist at the spectators at a window, and another made a show of slipping in a cartridge, with a suggestive gesture.

The peaceful demonstration, under the circumstances, was indefinitely postponed.

D. Lenin Justifies Revolutionary Terror, January 1918

The Paris Commune gave a great example of how to combine initiative, independence, freedom of action and vigour from below with voluntary centralism free from stereotyped forms. Our Soviets are following the same road. But they are still "shy," they have not yet got into their stride, have not yet "bitten into" their new, great, creative task of building the socialist system. The Soviets must set to work more boldly and display greater initiative. Every "commune," every factory, every village, every consumers' society, every committee of supply, must *compete* with its neighbours as a practical organiser of accounting and control of labour and distribution of products. The programme of this accounting and control is simple, clear and intelligible to all; it is: everyone to have bread; everyone to have sound footwear and whole clothing; everyone to have warm dwellings; everyone to work conscientiously; not a single rogue (including those who shirk their work) should be allowed to be at liberty, but kept in prison, or serve his sentence of compulsory labour of the hardest kind; not a single rich man who violates the laws and regulations of socialism to be allowed to escape the fate of the crook, which should, in justice, be the fate of the rich man. "He who does not work, neither shall he eat"—this is the *practical* commandment of socialism. This is how things should be organised *practically*. These are the *practical* successes our "communes" and our worker- and peasant-organisers should be proud of. And this applies *particularly* to the organisers among the intellectuals (*particularly*, because they are *too much, far too much* in the habit of being proud of their general instructions and resolutions).

Thousands of practical forms and methods of accounting and controlling the rich, the rogues and the idlers should be devised and put to a practical test by the communes themselves, by small units in town and country. Variety is a guarantee of vitality here, a pledge of success in achieving the single common aim—to cleanse the land of Russia of all sorts of harmful insects, of crook-fleas, of bedbugs—the rich, and so on and so forth. In one place half a score of rich, a dozen crooks, half a dozen workers who shirk their work (in the hooligan manner in which many compositors in Petrograd, particularly in the Party printing shops, shirk their work) will be put in prison. In another place they will be put to cleaning latrines. In a third place they will be provided with "yellow tickets" after they have served their time, so that all the people shall have them under surveillance, as *harmful* persons, until they reform. In a fourth place, one out of every ten idlers will be shot on the spot. In a fifth place mixed methods may be adopted, and by probational release, for example, the rich, the bourgeois intellectuals, the crooks and hooligans who are corrigible will be given an opportunity to reform quickly. The more variety there will be, the better and richer will be our general experience, the more certain and rapid will be the success of socialism, and the easier will it be for practice to devise—for only practice can devise—the *best* methods and means of struggle.

In what commune, in what district of a large town, in what factory and in what village are there *no* starving people, *no* unemployed, *no* idle rich, *no* scoundrelly lackeys of the bourgeoisie, saboteurs who call themselves intellectuals? Where has most been done to raise the productivity of labour, to build good new houses for the poor, to put the poor in the houses of the rich, to regularly provide a bottle of milk for every child of every poor family? It is on these points that *competition* should unfold itself between the communes, communities, producers-consumers' societies and associations, and Soviets of Workers', Soldiers' and Peasants' Deputies. This is the work in which *organising talent* should reveal itself *in practice* and be promoted to work in the administration of the state. There is a great deal of this talent among the people. It is merely suppressed. It must be given an opportunity to display itself. *It, and it alone,* with the support of the masses, can save Russia and save the cause of socialism.

E. Lenin Demands Party Unity, 1921

1. The Congress calls the attention of all members of the Party to the fact that the unity and cohesion of the ranks of the Party, the guarantee of complete mutual confidence among Party members and truly harmonious work that really embodies the unanimity of will of the vanguard of the proletariat, are particularly essential at the present time, when a number of circumstances are increasing the vacillation among the petty-bourgeois population of the country.

2. Notwithstanding this, even before the general Party discussion on the trade unions, certain signs of factionalism—the formation of groups with separate platforms, striving to a certain degree to segregate and create their own group discipline—had been apparent in the Party. . . .

All class-conscious workers must clearly realise that factionalism of any kind is harmful and impermissible, for no matter how members of individual groups may desire to safeguard Party unity, factionalism in practice inevitably leads to the weakening of harmonious work and to intensified and repeated attempts by the enemies of the governing Party, who have wormed their way into it, to widen the cleavage and to use it for counter-revolutionary purposes.

The way the enemies of the proletariat take advantage of every deviation from a thoroughly consistent communist line was perhaps most strikingly shown in the case of the Kronstadt mutiny, when the bourgeois counter-revolutionaries and whiteguards in all countries of the world immediately expressed their readiness to accept the slogans of the Soviet system, if only they might thereby secure the overthrow of the dictatorship of the proletariat in Russia, and when the Socialist-Revolutionaries and the bourgeois counter-revolutionaries in general resorted in Kronstadt to slogans calling for an insurrection against the Soviet Government of Russia ostensibly in the interest of the Soviet power. These facts fully prove that the whiteguards strive, and are able, to disguise themselves as Communists, and even as the most Left-wing Communists, solely for the purpose of weakening and destroying the bulwark of the proletarian revolution in Russia. Menshevik leaflets distributed in Petrograd on the eve of the Kronstadt mutiny likewise show how the Mensheviks took advantage of the disagreements and certain rudiments of factionalism in the Russian Communist Party actually in order to egg on and support the Kronstadt mutineers, the Socialist-Revolutionaries and the whiteguards, while claiming to be opponents of mutiny and supporters of the Soviet power, only with supposedly slight modifications.

3. In this question, propaganda should consist, on the one hand, in a comprehensive explanation of the harmfulness and danger of factionalism from the standpoint of Party unity and of achieving unanimity of will among the vanguard of the proletariat as the fundamental condition for the success of the dictatorship of the proletariat; and, on the other hand, in an explanation of the peculiar features of the latest tactical devices of the enemies of the Soviet power....

4. In the practical struggle against factionalism, every organisation of the Party must take strict measures to prevent all factional actions. Criticism of the Party's shortcomings, which is absolutely necessary, must be conducted in such a way that every practical proposal shall be submitted immediately, without any delay, in the most precise form possible, for consideration and decision to the leading local and central bodies of the Party. Moreover, every critic must see to it that the form of his criticism takes account of the Party's being surrounded by enemies, and that the content of his criticism is such that, by directly participating in Soviet and Party work, he can test the rectification of the errors of the Party or of individual Party members in practice. Analyses of the Party's general line, estimates of its practical experience, check-ups on the fulfilment of its decisions, studies of methods of rectifying errors, etc., must under no circumstances be submitted for preliminary discussion to groups formed on the basis of "platforms," etc., but must in all cases be submitted for discussion directly to all the members of the Party. For this purpose, the Congress orders ... special symposiums to promote unceasing efforts to ensure that criticism shall be concentrated on essentials and shall not assume a form capable of assisting the class enemies of the proletariat.

5. Rejecting in principle the deviation towards syndicalism and anarchism, which is examined in a special resolution, and instructing the Central Committee to secure the complete elimination of all factionalism, the Congress at the same time declares that every practical proposal concerning questions to which the so-called Workers' Opposition group, for example, has devoted special attention, such as purging the Party of non-proletarian and unreliable elements, combating bureaucratic practices, developing democracy and workers' initiative, etc., must be examined with the greatest care and tested in practice. The Party must know that we have not taken all the necessary measures in regard to these questions because of various obstacles, but that, while ruthlessly rejecting impractical and factional pseudo-criticism, the Party will unceasingly continue—trying out new methods—to fight with all the means at its disposal against the evils of bureaucracy, for the extension of democracy and initiative, for detecting, exposing and expelling from the Party elements that have wormed their way into its ranks, etc.

6. The Congress, therefore, hereby declares dissolved and orders the immediate dissolution of all groups without exception formed on the basis of one platform or another (such as the Workers' Opposition group, the Democratic Centralism group, etc.). Non-observance of this decision of the Congress shall entail unconditional and instant expulsion from the Party.

7. In order to ensure strict discipline within the Party and in all Soviet work and to secure the maximum unanimity in eliminating all factionalism, the Congress authorises the Central Committee, in cases of breach of discipline or of a revival or toleration of factionalism, to apply all Party penalties, including expulsion, and in regard to members of the Central Committee, reduction to the status of alternate members and, as an extreme measure, expulsion from the Party. A necessary condition for the application of such an extreme measure to members of the Central Committee, alternate members of the Central Committee and members of the Control Commission is the convocation of a plenary meeting of the Central Committee, to which all alternate members of the Central Committee and all members of the Control Commission shall be invited. If such a general assembly of the most responsible leaders of the Party deems it necessary by a two-thirds majority to reduce a member of the Central Committee to the status of alternate member, or to expel him from the Party, this measure shall be put into effect immediately.

F. Alexandra Kollontai Promises Women's Emancipation

There were differences of opinion in the Party. I resigned from my post as People's Commissar on the ground of total disagreement with the current policy. Little by little I was also relieved of all my other tasks. I again gave lectures and espoused my ideas on "the new woman" and "the new morality." The revolution was in full swing. The struggle was becoming increasingly irreconcilable and bloodier, much of what was happening did not fit in with my outlook. But after all there was still the unfinished task, women's liberation. Women, of course had received all rights but in practice, of course, they still lived under the old yoke: without authority in family life, enslaved by a thousand menial household chores, bearing the whole burden of maternity, even the material cares, because many women now found life alone as a result of the war and other circumstances.

G. Lenin Talks with Clara Zetkin About Sex and Revolution

"The record of your sins, Clara, is even worse. I have been told that at the evenings arranged for reading and discussion with working women, sex and marriage problems come first. They are said to be the main objects of interest in your political instruction and educational work. I could not believe my ears when I heard that. The first state of proletarian dictatorship is battling with the counter-revolutionaries of the whole world. The situation in Germany itself calls for the greatest unity of all proletarian revolutionary forces, so that they can repel the counter-revolution which is pushing on. But active Communist women are busy discussing sex problems and the forms of marriage—'past, present and future.' They consider it their most important task to enlighten working women on these questions. It is said that a pamphlet on the sex question written by a Communist authoress from Vienna enjoys the greatest popularity. What rot that booklet is! ... The mention of Freud's hypotheses is designed to give the pamphlet a scientific veneer, but it is so much bungling by an amateur. Freud's theory has now become a fad. I mistrust sex theories expounded in articles, treatises, pamphlets, etc.—in short, the theories dealt with in that specific literature which sprouts so luxuriantly on the dung heap of bourgeois society. I mistrust those who are always absorbed in the sex problems, the way an Indian saint is absorbed in the contemplation of his navel. It seems to me that this superabundance of sex theories, which for the most part are mere hypotheses, and often quite arbitrary ones, stems from a personal need. It springs from the desire to justify one's own abnormal or excessive sex life before bourgeois morality and to plead for tolerance towards oneself. ...."

Reprinted from *The Lenin Anthology*, edited by Robert C. Tucker, from pp. 688–689, 692–693. Reprinted with the permission of W. W. Norton & Company, Inc. Copyright © 1975 by W. W. Norton & Company, Inc.

I interposed that where private property and the bourgeois social order prevail, questions of sex and marriage gave rise to manifold problems, conflicts and suffering for women of all social classes and strata. As far as women are concerned, the war and its consequences exacerbated the existing conflicts and suffering to the utmost precisely in the sphere of sexual relations. Problems formerly concealed from women were now laid bare. To this was added the atmosphere of incipient revolution. The world of old emotions and thoughts was cracking up. Former social connections were loosening and breaking. The makings of new relations between people were appearing. Interest in the relevant problems was an expression of the need for enlightnment and a new orientation. . . .

"Youth's altered attitude to questions of sex is of course 'fundamental,' and based on theory. Many people call it 'revolutionary' and 'communist.' They sincerely believe that this is so. I am an old man, and I do not like it. I may be a morose ascetic, but quite often this so-called 'new sex life' of young people— and frequently of the adults too—seems to me purely bourgeois and simply an extension of the good old bourgeois brothel. All this has nothing in common with free love as we Communists understand it. No doubt you have heard about the famous theory that in communist society satisfying sexual desire and the craving for love is as simple and trivial as 'drinking a glass of water.' A section of our youth has gone mad, absolutely mad, over this 'glass-of-water theory.' It has been fatal to many a young boy and girl. Its devotees assert that it is a Marxist theory. I want no part of the kind of Marxism which infers all phenomena and all changes in the ideological superstructure of society directly and blandly from its economic basis, for things are not as simple as all that. A certain Frederick Engels has established this a long time ago with regard to historical materialism.

"I consider the famous 'glass-of-water' theory as completely unMarxist and, moreover, as anti-social. It is not only what nature has given but also what has become culture, whether of a high or low level, that comes into play in sexual life. Engels pointed out in his *Origin of the Family* how significant it was that the common sexual relations had developed into individual sex love and thus became purer. The relations between the sexes are not simply the expression of a mutual influence between economics and a physical want deliberately singled out for physiological examination. It would be rationalism and not Marxism to attempt to refer the change in these relations directly to the economic basis of society in isolation from its connection with the ideology as a whole. To be sure, thirst has to be quenched. But would a normal person normally lie down in the gutter and drink from a puddle? Or even from a glass whose edge has been greased by many lips? But the social aspect is more important than anything else. The drinking of water is really an individual matter. But it takes two people to make love, and a third person, a new life, is likely to come into being. This deed has a social complexion and constitutes a duty to the community. . . .

"Young people are particularly in need of joy and strength. Healthy sports, such as gymnastics, swimming, hiking, physical exercises of every description and a wide range of intellectual interests are what they need, as well as learning, study and research, and as far as possible collectively. This will be far more useful to young people than endless lectures and discussions on sex problems and the so-called living by one's nature. *Mens sana in corpore sano.* Be neither monk nor Don Juan, but not anything in between either, like a German philistine. You know the young comrade X. He is a splendid lad, and highly gifted. For all that, I am afraid that he will never amount to anything. He has one love affair after another. This is not good for the political struggle and for the revolution. I will not vouch for the reliability or the endurance of women whose love affair is intertwined with politics, or for the men who run after every pet-

ticoat and let themselves in with every young female. No, no, that does not go well with revolution."

Lenin sprang to his feet, slapped the table with his hand and paced up and down the room.

Document Set 26.3 References

A. V. I. Lenin Announces His Basic Strategy, April 1917
   Lenin, "April Theses," in Robert C. Tucker, ed., *The Lenin Anthology* (New York: W. W. Norton, 1975), 295–298.
B. The Bolsheviks Decree Peace, November 8, 1917
   Soviet Decree on Peace, in W. C. Langsam, ed., *Documents and Readings in the History of Europe Since 1918*, rev. ed. (Philadelphia: Lippincott, 1951), 743–745.
C. At the Grass Roots: A Citizen Chronicles the Bolshevik Seizure of Power in Provincial Saratov
   Donald J. Raleigh, ed. and trans., *A Russian Civil War Diary: Alexis Babine in Saratov, 1917–1922* (Durham, N.C.: Duke University Press, 1988), 22–24, 30, 36.
D. Lenin Justifies Revolutionary Terror, January 1918
   V. I. Lenin, "How to Organize Competition," in Tucker, 431–432.
E. Lenin Demands Party Unity, 1921
   "Draft Resolution on Party Unity" in Tucker, 500–502.
F. Alexandra Kollontai Promises Women's Emancipation
   Kollontai, *The Autobiography of a Sexually Emancipated Communist Woman*, trans. Salvator Attanasio (New York: Herder and Herder, 1971), 40.
G. Lenin Talks with Clara Zetkin About Sex and Revolution
   Discourse Between V. I. Lenin and Clara Zetkin in Tucker, 688–689, 692–693.

DOCUMENT SET 26.4
Russia Under the NEP

The Kronstadt Revolt was a turning point in more ways than one. Not only did it impel Lenin to tighten Party discipline, but it helped convince him and most other Party leaders that the rigors of "War Communism" ought to be relaxed now that victory had been won on the battlefield. Such were the elements of the New Economic Policy (NEP). But the Party retained control over political life in the U.S.S.R. (the federation of Russia and the other soviet republics created in 1924). And within the Party bureaucracy the authority of Georgian-born Joseph Stalin (1879–1953) was steadily growing despite even Lenin's uneasiness. By the time Lenin died in 1924, Stalin had already begun outmaneuvering rivals like Leon Trotsky (1879–1940), a magnetic orator, capable organizer, and flaming leftist who proved inept at political infighting. One of Stalin's early allies was Nikolai Bukharin (1888–1938), a leading Bolshevik theorist who embraced the NEP and insisted that Soviet industrialization must be financed by a prosperous agrarian economy. After 1929, however, Stalin dumped Bukharin and his "go-slow" approach, launching a radically "leftist" program of collectivization and industrialization. Bukharin would eventually perish in the Great Purges of the 1930s, and Trotsky, exiled to Mexico, would fall to a Stalinist assassin in 1940. Meanwhile Stalin would impose a rigid, unimaginative uniformity on Soviet culture and society, snuffing out most of the innovative trends that had sprung up during the Revolution and the NEP period.

In Document A, Lenin makes his last appearance at a Communist Party Congress (the Eleventh) before a series of strokes incapacitated and eventually killed him. His report conveys his reasoning about the NEP and how it fit into his long-range view of building socialism. By the time he dictated his "Letter to the Congress" (Document B), at the end of 1922 and the beginning of 1923, he was already a dying man. The congress he was addressing had not yet met, and when these documents were eventually transmitted to the Thirteenth Congress, in March 1924, he was dead and Stalin persuaded the other leaders to suppress them. They were not published until 1956, although knowledge of them ("Lenin's Testament") circulated by word of mouth. Needless to say, Lenin's last communication to Stalin, March 6, 1923 (Document C), was not made public, either.

One of the most visible signs of the NEP's change of direction was the freedom that peasants now enjoyed from forced requisitions and to sell their produce at a profit. In 1923 the secret police noted how villagers in the Smolensk region of western Russia were responding to the new incentives (Document D), and in 1925 Bukharin went so far as to envision a permanent place for peasants—even for "rich" ones, or *kulaks*—in the evolving socialist economy (Document E)—a position that would damage him once Stalin embarked on collectivization and the destruction of the *kulaks*.

In their duel to succeed Lenin, Trotsky never really had a chance against Stalin. Until it was too late, Trotsky underestimated the dull, methodical Georgian, who was fully capable of using "Rightists" like Bukharin to destroy the Left and then turning on his former allies. In the biography of his enemy (Document F) that Trotsky was writing at the time of his assassination (the murderer's ax spattered his blood on the manuscript), he analyzed his downfall and the triumph of his enemies.

Although he never went into political opposition, the brilliant Soviet poet Vladimir Mayakovsky (1894–1930)—who had turned his biting wit and jarring, innovative verse into highly literate propaganda throughout the Revolution and the 1920s—realized by 1930 that the times were turning irreversibly against his kind. Some measure of appreciation of the new directions of 1920s Soviet culture and of the despair felt by innovators as the pall of moralistic, didactic, and humorless "socialist realism" descended upon them may be gauged from Mayakovsky's final poem, "Past One O'Clock," which he wrote before losing one of the games of Russian roulette that he had taken to playing with a loaded pistol (Document G).

A. Lenin Justifies the NEP

First, the New Economic Policy is important for us primarily as a means of testing whether we are really establishing a link with the peasant economy. In the preceding period of development of our revolution, when all our attention and all our efforts were concentrated mainly on, or almost entirely absorbed by, the task of repelling invasion, we could not devote the necessary attention to this link; we had other things to think about. To some extent we could and had to ignore this bond when we were confronted by the absolutely urgent and overshadowing task of warding off the danger of being immediately crushed by the gigantic forces of world imperialism. . . .

Retreat is a difficult matter, especially for revolutionaries who are accustomed to advance; especially when they have been accustomed to advance with enormous success for several years; especially if they are surrounded by revolutionaries in other countries who are longing for the time when they can launch an offensive. Seeing that we were retreating, several of them burst into tears in a disgraceful and childish manner, as was the case at the last extended plenary meeting of the Executive Committee of the Communist International. Moved by the best communist sentiments and communist aspirations, several of the comrades burst into tears because—oh horror!—the good Russian Communists were retreating. Perhaps it is now difficult for me to understand this West-European mentality, although I lived for quite a number of years in those marvellous democratic countries as an exile. Perhaps from their point of view this is such a difficult matter to understand that it is enough to make one weep. We, at any rate, have no time for sentiment. It was clear to us that because we had advanced so successfully for many years and had achieved so many extraordinary victories (and all this in a country that was in an appalling state of ruin and lacked the material resources!), to consolidate that advance, since we had gained so much, it was absolutely essential for us to retreat. We could not hold all the positions we had captured in the first onslaught. On the other hand, it was because we had captured so much in the first onslaught, on the crest of the wave of enthusiasm displayed by the workers and peasants, that we had room enough to retreat a long distance, and can retreat still further now, without losing our main and fundamental positions. On the whole, the retreat was fairly orderly, although certain panic-stricken voices, among them that of the Workers' Opposition (this was the tremendous harm it did!), caused losses in our ranks, caused a relaxation of discipline, and disturbed the proper order of retreat. The most dangerous thing during a retreat is panic. When a whole army (I speak in the figurative sense) is in retreat, it cannot have the same morale as when it is advancing. At every step you find a certain mood of depression. We even had poets who wrote that people were cold and starving in Moscow, that "everything before was bright and beautiful, but now trade and profiteering abound." We have had quite a number of poetic effusions of this sort.

Of course, retreat breeds all this. That is where the serious danger lies; it is terribly difficult to retreat after a great victorious advance, for the relations are entirely different. During a victorious advance, even if discipline is relaxed, everybody presses forward on his own accord. During a retreat, however, discipline must be more conscious and is a hundred times more necessary, because, when the entire army is in retreat, it does not know or see where it should halt. It sees only retreat; under such circumstances a few panic-stricken voices are, at times, enough to cause a stampede. The danger here is enormous. When a real army is in retreat, machine-guns are kept ready, and when an orderly retreat degenerates into a disorderly one, the command to fire is given, and quite rightly, too.

B. Lenin Writes His "Testament" to the Communist Party Congress, 1922–1923

I would urge strongly that at this Congress a number of changes be made in our political structure.

I want to tell you the considerations to which I attach most importance.

At the head of the list I set an increase in the number of Central Committee members to a few dozen or even a hundred. It is my opinion that without this reform our Central Committee would be in great danger if the course of events were not quite favourable for us (and that is something we cannot count on).

Then, I intend to propose that the Congress should on certain conditions invest the decisions of the State Planning Commission with legislative force, meeting, in this respect, the wishes of Comrade Trotsky—to a certain extent and on certain conditions.

As for the first point, i.e., increasing the number of C.C. members, I think it must be done in order to raise the prestige of the Central Committee, to do a thorough job of improving our administrative machinery and to prevent conflicts between small sections of the C.C. from acquiring excessive importance for the future of the Party. . . .

. . . Our Party relies on two classes and therefore its instability would be possible and its downfall inevitable if there were no agreement between those two classes. In that event this or that measure, and generally all talk about the stability of our C.C., would be futile. No measures of any kind could prevent a split in such a case. But I hope that this is too remote a future and too improbable an event to talk about.

I have in mind stability as a guarantee against a split in the immediate future, and I intend to deal here with a few ideas concerning personal qualities.

I think that from this standpoint the prime factors in the question of stability are such members of the C.C. as Stalin and Trotsky. I think relations between them make up the greater part of the danger of a split, which could be avoided, and this purpose, in my opinion, would be served, among other things, by increasing the number of C.C. members to 50 or 100.

Comrade Stalin, having become secretary-general, has boundless power concentrated in his hands, and I am not sure whether he will always be capable of using that power with sufficient caution. Comrade Trotsky, on the other hand, as his struggle against the C.C. on the question of the People's Commissariat for Communications has already proved, is distinguished not only by outstanding ability. He is personally perhaps the most capable man in the present C.C., but he has displayed excessive self-assurance and shown excessive preoccupation with the purely administrative side of the work.

These two qualities of the two outstanding leaders of the present C.C. can inadvertently lead to a split, and if our Party does not take steps to avert this, the split may come unexpectedly.

I shall not give any further appraisals of the personal qualities of other members of the C.C. I shall just recall that the October episode with Zinoviev and Kamenev was, of course, no accident, but neither can the blame for it be laid upon them personally, any more than non-Bolshevism can upon Trotsky.

Speaking of the young C.C. members, I wish to say a few words about Bukharin and Pyatakov. They are, in my opinion, the most outstanding figures (among the youngest ones), and the following must be borne in mind about them: Bukharin is not only a most valuable and major theorist of the Party; he is also rightly considered the favourite of the whole Party, but his theoretical views can be classified as fully Marxist only with great reserve, for there is something scholastic about him (he has never made a study of dialectics, and, I think, never fully understood it). . . .

Stalin is too rude and this defect, although quite tolerable in our midst and in dealings among us Communists, becomes intolerable in a secretary-general. That is why I suggest that the comrades think about a way of removing Stalin from that post and appointing another man in his stead who in all other respects differs from Comrade Stalin in having only one advantage, namely, that of being more tolerant, more loyal, more polite and more considerate to the comrades, less capricious, etc. This circumstance may appear to be an insignificant trifle. But I think that from the standpoint of safeguards against a split and from the standpoint of what I wrote above about the relationship between Stalin and Trotsky it is not a trifle, or it is a trifle which can assume decisive significance.

C. Lenin Threatens to Break with Stalin, March 6, 1923

Strictly secret
Personal
Copies to Comrades Kamenev and Zinoviev
Respected Comrade Stalin:

You had the rudeness to call my wife on the telephone and berate her. Although she expressed her willingness to forget what was said, this fact nevertheless became known, through her, to Zinoviev and Kamenev. I do not intend to forget so easily what was done against me, and there is no need to point out that what is done against my wife I consider to be against me also. Therefore, I ask you to consider whether you agree to take back what you said and apologize, or whether you prefer to break relations between us.

With respect,

Lenin

D. Russian Peasants Assess the Bolshevik Regime, 1923

The most important factors regulating the mood of the peasants toward the Soviet are economic relationships such as taxes and prices for industrial goods, and also the attitude of officials toward the peasants. The lowering of the single agricultural tax played an important part in [determining] the mood of the poor peasants and middle peasants. Upon receiving the tax lists, when the peasants see that the agricultural tax has been decreased in comparison with last year, they are convinced that the Soviet government is meeting the peasants half-way. The same thing is observed in regard to lowering prices for industrial goods, which convinces the peasants that the workers in the cities are doing something for them . . . Those peasants who regarded the Soviet government with hostility . . . have changed their minds in view of the destruction of banditry and the general strengthening of Soviet construction; many are beginning in various ways to adjust themselves to the Soviet government.

E. Nikolai Bukharin Expects the Peasant Economy to Stimulate Socialist Construction

[T]he basic network of our cooperative peasant organization will consist of cooperative cells not of a kulak but of a "laboring" type, cells growing into the system of our general state organs and thus becoming *links in a single chain of socialist economy*. On the other hand, the kulak cooperative nests will in exactly the same way, through the banks, etc., grow into this same system; but they will be to a certain extent an alien body. . . . What will become of this type of kulak cooperative in the future? . . . If it wants to prosper, it must inevitably be linked . . . with state economic organs; it . . . will deposit its spare cash in our banks in order to receive a fixed interest. Even if their own banking organizations should arise . . . they unavoidably would have to be linked with the powerful credit institutions of the proletarian state, which have at their disposal the country's basic credit resources. In any event, the kulak and the kulak cooperative will have nowhere to go, for the general pattern of development in our country *has been determined beforehand as the system of the proletarian dictatorship*. . . .

F. Leon Trotsky Analyzes How Stalin Captured Power

The prestige of the leaders as a whole, not only the personal prestige of Lenin, made up in its totality the authority of the Central Committee. The principle of individual leadership was utterly alien to the Party. The Party singled out the more popular figures for leadership, gave them its confidence and admiration, while always adhering to the view that the actual leadership came from the Central Committee as a whole. This tradition was used to tremendous advantage by the triumvirate, which insisted upon the paramountey of the Central Committee over any individual authority. Stalin, schemer, centrist and eclectic par excellence, master of small doses gradually administered, cynically misused that trust [in the Central Committee] for his own advantage.

At the end of 1925 Stalin still spoke of the leaders in the third person and instigated the Party against them. He received the plaudits of the middle layer of the bureaucracy, which refused to bend its neck to any leader. Yet in reality, Stalin himself was already dictator. He was a dictator, but he did not feel yet that he was leader, and no one recognized him as such. He was a dictator not through the force of his personality, but through the power of the political machine that had broken with the old leaders. As late as the Sixteenth Congress, in 1930, Stalin said: "You ask why we expelled Trotsky and Zinoviev? Because we did not want to have aristocrats in the Party, because we have only one law in the Party, and all the Party members are equal in their rights." He reiterated this at the Seventeenth Congress in 1934.

He used the Right as a battering ram against the Left Opposition, for only the Right had a definite platform, interests, and principles, that were jeopardized by a triumph of Left policies. But when he saw that the expulsion of the Left Opposition provoked grave misgivings and dissatisfaction in the Party, and irritation with the triumphant Right, Stalin knew how to utilize this dissatisfaction for a blow against the Rightists. The conflict of class forces in this struggle between Right and Left was of less concern to him than his deceptive role as a conciliator or as the pacifying element which presumably would reduce the inevitable number of victims to a minimum and save the Party from a schism. In his role of super-arbiter, he was able to place the responsibility for the severe measures against certain popular Party members now on one, and now on the other wing of the Party. But classes cannot be fooled. As a maneuver, the pro-*kulak* policy of 1924–1928 was worse than criminal; it was absurd. The *kulak* is nobody's fool. He judges by taxes, prices, profits, not by phrasemongering and declamations: he judges by deeds, not by words. Maneuvering can never replace the action and reaction of class forces; its usefulness is limited at best; and there is nothing so calculated to disintegrate the revolutionary morale of a mass party as clandestine unprincipled maneuvering. Nor is anything deadlier for the morale and the character of the individual revolutionists. Military trickery can never replace major strategy. . . .

G. Vladimir Mayakovsky Ends It All, 1930

Past One O'Clock . . .

Past one o'clock. You must have gone to bed.
The Milky Way streams silver through the night.
I'm in no hurry; with lightning telegrams
I have no cause to wake or trouble you.
And, as they say, the incident is closed.
Love's boat has smashed against the daily grind.
Now you and I are quits. Why bother then
to balance mutual sorrows, pains, and hurts.
Behold what quiet settles on the world.

Night wraps the sky in tribute from the stars.
In hours like these, one rises to address
The ages, history, and all creation.

Document Set 26.4 References

A. Lenin Justifies the NEP
   V. I. Lenin in Robert C. Tucker, ed., *The Lenin Anthology* (New York: W. W. Norton, 1975), 518, 523–524.
B. Lenin Writes His "Testament" to the Communist Party Congress, 1922–1923
   V. I. Lenin in Tucker, 725–728.
C. Lenin Threatens to Break with Stalin, March 6, 1923
   V. I. Lenin in Tucker, 748.
D. Russian Peasants Assess the Bolshevik Regime, 1923
   Merle Fainsod, *Smolensk Under Soviet Rule* (Cambridge, Mass.: Harvard University Press, 1955), 141.
E. Nikolai Bukharin Expects the Peasant Economy to Stimulate Socialist Construction
   Bukharin in Stephen F. Cohen, *Bukharin and the Bolshevik Revolution: A Political Biography* (New York: Alfred A. Knopf, 1973), 198.
F. Leon Trotsky Analyzes How Stalin Captured Power
   Trotsky, *Stalin* (New York: Harper Brothers, 1941), 401–402.
G. Vladimir Mayakovsky Ends It All, 1930
   Mayakovsky, "Past One O'Clock," in Patricia Blake, ed., *The Bedbug and Selected Poetry*, trans. Max Hayward and George Reavey (Cleveland: Meridian, 1960), 237.

The inelegant word *normalcy* was coined by U.S. president Warren G. Harding in his 1921 inaugural address; there was no such word in standard English, and Harding probably meant *normality,* but his malapropism stood as a permanent testimony of postwar Western middle-class longing to put war and social upheaval behind them. But clocks did not turn back. A significant minority of workers and intellectuals continued to demand a democratic socialist reorganization of society, as voiced for example in the British Labour Party's 1918 election manifesto (Document A)—aspirations that would remain largely unfulfilled until the end of the next great war, in 1945. The scholarly president of the new Czechoslovak republic, Thomas G. Masaryk, understood the decade's yearning for stability and consolidation in a far more moralistic and self-critical spirit than conventional conservatives like Harding ever imagined (Document B).

What "normalcy" meant for a staunchly Social-Democratic Berlin working-class couple should be apparent from Document C, one of a series of sketches of their daily lives that the women of a textile union collected in 1930. What do you suppose that this 30-year-old woman would have said of the Dutch physician Theodore van de Velde's *Ideal Marriage,* first published in 1926 (Document D)?

Weave your analysis of the documents of this set into a brief account of the society, culture, and political context of postwar life in democratic Europe, drawing upon *The Challenge of the West* for additional ideas and information.

A. The Labour Party Appeals for Democratic Socialism, 1918

The End of a Civilization

We need to beware of patchwork. The view of the Labour party is that what has to be reconstructed after the war is not this or that government department, or this or that piece of social machinery; but, so far as Britain is concerned, society itself. . . .

What this war is consuming is not merely the security, the homes, the livelihood and the lives of millions of innocent families, and an enormous proportion of all the accumulated wealth of the world, but also the very basis of the peculiar social order in which it has arisen. The individualist system of capitalist production, based on the private ownership and competitive administration of land and capital, which has in the past couple of centuries become the dominant form, with its reckless "profiteering" and wage-slavery; with its glorification of the unhampered struggle for the means of life and its hypocritical pretence of the "survival of the fittest"; with the monstrous inequality of circumstances which it produces and the degradation and brutalization, both moral and spiritual, resulting therefrom, may, we hope, indeed have received a death-blow. With it must go the political system and ideas in which it naturally found expression. We of the Labour party, whether in opposition or in due time called upon to form an administration, will certainly lend no hand to its revival. On the contrary, we shall do our utmost to see that it is buried with the millions whom it has done to death. . . .

The Pillars of the House

We need not here recapitulate, one by one, the different items in the Labour party's program, which successive party conferences have adopted. These proposals, some of them in various publications worked out in practical detail, are often carelessly derided as impracticable, even by the politicians who steal them piecemeal from us! . . . The war, which has scared the old political parties right out of their dogmas, has taught every statesman and every government official, to his enduring surprise, how very much more can be done along the lines that we have laid down than he had ever before thought possible. What we now promulgate as our policy, whether for opposition or for office, is not merely this or that specific reform, but a deliberately thought out, systematic, and comprehensive plan for that immediate social rebuilding which any ministry, whether or not it desires to grapple with the problem, will be driven to undertake. The Four Pillars of the house that we propose to erect, resting upon the common foundation of the democratic control of society in all its activities, may be termed, respectively:

(a) The Universal Enforcement of the National Minimum;
(b) The Democratic Control of Industry;
(c) The Revolution in National Finance; and
(d) The Surplus Wealth for the Common Good.

The Universal Enforcement of a National Minimum

The first principle of the Labour party—in significant contrast with those of the capitalist system, whether expressed by the Liberal or by the Conservative party—is the securing to every member of the community, in good times and bad alike (and not only to the strong and able, the well-born or the fortunate), of all the requisites of healthy life and worthy citizenship. . . .

The Legislative Regulation of Employment

Thus it is that the Labour party to-day stands for the universal application of the policy of the national minimum [wage].

Securing Employment for All

The Labour party insists [that] . . . it is one of the foremost obligations of the government to find, for every willing worker, whether by hand or by brain, productive work at standard rates.

It is accordingly the duty of the government to adopt a policy of deliberately and systematically preventing the occurrence of unemployment, instead of (as heretofore) letting unemployment occur, and then seeking, vainly and expensively, to relieve the unemployed. . . .

Social Insurance Against Unemployment

In so far as the government fails to prevent unemployment—whenever it finds it impossible to discover for any willing worker, man or woman, a suitable situation at the standard rate—the Labour party holds that the government must, in the interest of the community as a whole, provide him or her with adequate maintenance, either with such arrangements for honorable employment or with such useful training as may be found practicable, according to age, health and previous occupation. . . .

The Democratic Control of Industry

. . . Unlike the Conservative and Liberal Parties, the Labour party insists on democracy in industry as well as in government. It demands the progressive elimination from the control of industry of the private capitalist, individual or joint-stock; and the setting free of all who work, whether by hand or by brain, for the service of the community, and of the community only. And the Labour party refuses absolutely to believe that the British people will permanently tolerate any reconstruction or perpetuation of the disor-ganization, waste and inefficiency involved in the abandonment of British industry to a jostling crowd of separate private employers, with their minds bent, not on the service of the community, but—by the very law of their being—only on the utmost possible profiteering. . . .

Immediate Nationalization

The Labour party stands not merely for the principle of the common ownership of the nation's land, to be applied as suitable opportunities occur, but also, specifically, for the immediate nationalization of railways, mines and the production of electrical power. . . .

In quite another sphere the Labour party sees the key to temperance reform in taking the entire manufacture and retailing of alcoholic drink out of the hands of those who find profit in promoting the utmost possible consumption. . . .

Local Government

The Labour party is alive to the evils of centralization and the drawbacks of bureaucracy. To counteract these disadvantages it intends that the fullest possible scope shall be given, in all branches of social reconstruction, to the democratically elected local governing bodies. . . .

A Revolution in National Finance

. . . For the raising of the greater part of the revenue now required the Labour party looks to the direct taxation of the incomes above the necessary cost of family maintenance; and for the requisite effort to pay off the national debt, to the direct taxation of private fortunes both during life and at death. The income tax and super-tax ought at once to be thoroughly reformed in assessment and collection, in abatements and allowances and in graduation and differentiation, so as to levy the required total sum in such a way as to make the real sacrifice of all the taxpayers as nearly as possible equal. . . .

The Street of To-morrow

The house which the Labour party intends to build, the Four Pillars of which have now been described, does not stand alone in the world. Where will it be in the Street of To-morrow? If we repudiate, on the one hand, the imperialism that seeks to dominate other races, or to impose our own will on other parts of the British Empire, so we disclaim equally any conception of a selfish and insular "non-interventionism," unregarding of our special obligations to our fellow-citizens overseas; of the corporate duties of one nation to another; of the moral claims upon us of the non-adult races, and of our own indebtedness to the world of which we are part. We look for an ever increasing intercourse, a constantly developing exchange of commodities, a steadily growing mutual understanding, and a continually expanding friendly co-operation among all the peoples of the world. With regard to that great Commonwealth of all races, all colors, all religions and all degrees of civilization, that we call the British Empire, the Labour party stands for its maintenance and its progressive development on the lines of local autonomy and "Home Rule All Round"; the fullest respect for the rights of each people, whatever its color, to all the democratic self-government of which it is capable, and to the proceeds of its own toil upon the resources of its own territorial home; and the closest possible co-operation among all the various members of what has become essentially not an empire in the old sense, but a Britannic Alliance. . . .

B. Thomas G. Masaryk Calls for Mature, Post-Revolutionary Democracy

Democracy was begotten of revolution. Our own Republic and democracy are no exceptions to this rule. Revolution is justified in self-defense for which the necessity arises when every other means has failed. In revolution, as in war, self-defense is morally permissible. Revolution is permissible when—as during the World War—administrative and political chaos threaten; and it is justified if it brings reform and improvement. But democracy does not mean perpetual revolution. The war, and the upheavals it brought on, stimulated revolutionary fancies. But war fever and the excitement of revolution die down. Men are compelled to resume steady and peaceful work; and, for some of them, it is not easy. Political and social Utopianism, such as the notion that the State is omniscient and all powerful, has swollen the demands upon it so inordinately that disillusionment has entailed dejection and weariness; and, as usual, men are apt to blame others, not themselves, for failure. We shall have to overcome the revolutionary spirit as we overcame militarism. Bloodshed is an evil inheritance of the past. We desire a State, a Europe and a mankind without war and without revolution. In a true democracy, war and revolution will be obsolete and inadequate, for democracy is a system of life. Life means work and a system of work; and work, unostentatious work, is peace. Work, bodily and

mental, will get the better both of the aristocratic and the revolutionary spirit. Even Marx and Engels had to revise the view of revolution which they put forward in 1848, to recognize that machinery, invention, technical progress, applied science and work are the surest and most efficient means of social revolution, and to declare themselves in favor of Parliamentarism.

Democracy, say its opponents contemptuously, consists of perpetual compromise. Its partisans admit the impeachment, and take it as a compliment. Compromise, not of principles but of practice, is necessary in political life as in all fields of human activity. Even the extremest extremists as, for example, Lenin when in power, make compromises. The policy of cultured and conscientious statesmen and parties is not, however, to reach a compromise between opposites but to carry out a program based on knowledge and on the understanding of history and of the situation of their State and nation in Europe and in the world. . . . For the maintenance and development of democracy the thought and cooperation of all are needed; and, as none is infallible, democracy, conceived as tolerant cooperation, signifies the acceptance of what is good no matter from what quarter it may come. What is hateful is the readiness of puny, short-sighted men, without aim or conviction, to make compromise an end in itself, to waver between opinion and opinion, to seek haltingly a middle course which usually runs from one wall to another.

I defend democracy, moreover, against dictatorial absolutism, whether the right to dictate be claimed by the proletariate, the State or the Church. I know the argument that dictatorship is justified, since conscience and right, reason and science, are absolute; and I am not unfamiliar with talk about the dictatorship of "the heart." Logic, mathematics, and some moral maxims may be absolute, that is to say, not relative as they would be if all countries, parties and individuals had a special morality, mathematics and logic of their own; but there is a difference between the epistemological absolutism of theory, and practical, political absolutism. The most scientific policy depends upon experience and induction. It can claim no infallibility. It offers no eternal truths and can form no warrant for absolutism. . . .

C. A Berlin Working Woman Describes Everyday Routines, 1930

At six o'clock my alarm clock wakes me up and thus begins my workday. Washing and dressing are my first jobs; as for grooming, there's not much to do in that regard because I have short hair. Then I put on water for coffee and get some bread and butter ready for my husband and me. With that I'm ready and it's also time to wake my husband because he has a half hour bike ride to his workplace. *While he's getting dressed, I get his bicycle ready.* I pump air in the tires and fasten on his lunchbox. He drinks his coffee and soon he's on his way. I go to the front window and wave him good-bye. Now it's 7:45 and I must quickly bring a little order to the place. I have only a small apartment, but it nonetheless takes some doing in order to make it look right. At 8:15 I also have to leave. I work in the colored-pattern weaving section from 8:30 to 12:30 without stop. I eat my breakfast about 9. *But I don't let my looms stop; they continue working, for when one works by contract, one has to keep going in order to earn something.* At 12:30 it's time for lunch and I return home quickly. After eating, I clean the hall and stairs, and meanwhile it's 1:45 and time to go. Work then goes from 2 to 5 without stop. But when it's five, I go back to my little place with a happy heart. Then my husband soon returns, and I have always taken great pains to have his dinner ready on time. Then I wash the dishes and my husband reads me the newspaper. When I'm ready, we go for a walk. If I had children, I'd probably have to stay home. In addition I go to women's meetings of the union or SPD[1] I never miss a general meeting of the SPD and so it goes one day after another until the weekend.

Saturday I get home from work at about 1 and quickly warm up the soup that I made Friday evening. Today I have to clean thoroughly, because for the rest of the week it only gets done superficially. After we have bathed and had some coffee, my husband goes to perform his union duties, and I help him. He is the first president of the metal workers' union. When he's finished, we go home well satisfied. After dinner we quietly read the union paper. Happy because we don't have to work the next day, we go to bed. I usually wake up at 8:30 Sunday morning and we have a pleasant breakfast. Then I start preparing lunch. Today I have time to make a really elaborate meal. After that we fix ourselves up nicely and go for a walk. We attend unions events or public associations of which my husband is a member. We always return home with the consciousness of having served a good cause. We go to sleep with the intention to struggle further for the trade unions, for trade unions are the stronghold of the workers' movement.

[1] SPD is the abbreviation for the German Social Democratic party.

D. Dr. Theodor van de Velde Advises How to Achieve the *Ideal Marriage*

Sex is the foundation of marriage. Yet most people do not know the A B C of sex. The average husband does not even know that his wife's sexual sensations develop and culminate to a slower rhythm than his own. He does not know *at all* that he must *awaken* her with delicate consideration and adaptation.

If erotic genius does not characterize him, the man needs *explicit knowledge* if he is to be capable of inspiring such desire and imparting such joy.

He must *know how to make love.*

The ensuing chapters may be of help to him here. They can, in certain portions, be read by educated laymen without any difficulty. Other portions, however, need close and careful study. For I aim at giving my instructions and deductions an entirely scientific tone and basis, though keeping free from superfluous pedantry. This manner of treatment, as well as the nature of the theme, make it impossible to avoid the use of many foreign words and technical terms. Readers who do not exactly comprehend any of these words can ask a doctor to explain their precise meaning.

Among civilized races, the urge to reproduce has ceased to "play the lead" among the components of the sexual impulse, which appears as a further stage of evolution; an advance in psychic power and complexity.

We must reflect that sexual activity is not necessarily identical with complete intercourse; that the urge to such activity generally, if not always, exists in children, long before they have any idea of the possibility of intercourse.

The sexual impulse *is an urge or impulse to sexual activity which has its original origin and irradiation not only in the genitals, but in the whole body and the whole psychic personality.* Hence its power is almost supreme.

Document Set 26.5 References

A. The Labour Party Appeals for Democratic Socialism, 1918
Labour Party, *Labour and the New Social Order,* in Walter Arnstein, ed., *The Past Speaks,* 2d ed. (Lexington, Mass.: D. C. Heath, 1993), 2:334–337.

B. Thomas G. Masaryk Calls for Mature, Post-Revolutionary Democracy
Masaryk, *Making of a State* (New York: Stokes Co., 1927), 465–467.

C. A Berlin Working Woman Describes Everyday Routines, 1930
Deutscher Textilarbeitverband, *Mein Arbeitstag—mein Wochenende* (Berlin: Textilpraxis, 1930), 80–81.

D. Dr. Theodor van de Velde Advises How to Achieve the *Ideal Marriage*
Van de Velde, *Ideal Marriage: Its Physiology and Technique,* trans. Stella Browne (New York: Random House, 1957), 8–9, 11–12.

Returning to "normalcy" was emphatically not the aim of Benito Mussolini and his movement when he began creating the Fascist dictatorship in 1923. In what respects does his statement of the "fundamental ideas" of fascism (Document A, which he wrote in 1935) effectively repudiate liberal values and his claim to revolutionize Italy? In what sense does Mussolini use the word *totalitarian* to characterize Fascism? And in what ways does the "Charter of Labor" (Document B), issued by the Fascist government in 1927 as its fundamental socio-economic policy, bear out Mussolini's claims?

The socialist Italian parliamentary deputy Giacomo Matteoti published *The Fascisti Exposed* (Document C) in 1924 and was soon after murdered by a Fascist death-squad. In suppressing the protests of Matteoti's fellow deputies, Mussolini took his first long steps toward consolidating a full-fledged dictatorship. What premonitions of Mussolini's ultimate aims does Matteoti appear to have had?

A. Benito Mussolini Expounds the "Fundamental Ideas" of Fascism

Like all sound political conceptions, Fascism is action and it is thought; action in which doctrine is imminent, and doctrine arising from a given system of historical forces in which it is inserted, and working on them from within. It has therefore a form correlated to contingencies of time and space; but it has also an ideal content which makes it an expression of truth in the higher region of the history of thought. . . . To know men one must know man; and to know man one must be acquainted with reality and its laws. There can be no conception of the State which is not fundamentally a conception of life: philosophy or intuition, system of ideas evolving within the framework of logic or concentrated in a vision or a faith, but always, at least potentially, an organic conception of the world.

Thus many of the practical expressions of Fascism—such as party organisation, system of education, discipline—can only be understood when considered in relation to its general attitude toward life. . . . A spiritual attitude. Fascism sees in the world not only those superficial, material aspects in which man appears as an individual, standing by himself, self-centered, subject to natural law which instinc-tively urges him toward a life of selfish momentary pleasure; it sees not only the individual but the nation and the country; individuals and generations bound together by a moral law, with common traditions and a mission which suppressing the instinct for life closed in a brief circle of pleasure, builds up a higher life, founded on duty, a life free from the limitations of time and space, in which the individual, by self-sacrifice, the renunciation of self-interest, by death itself, can achieve that purely spiritual existence in which his value as a man consists.

The conception is therefore a spiritual one, arising from the general reaction of the century against the placid materialistic positivism of the XIXth century. . . .

In the Fascist conception of history, man is man only by virtue of the spiritual process to which he contributes as a member of the family, the social group, the nation, and in function of history to which all nations bring their contribution. . . . Outside history man is a nonentity. Fascism is therefore opposed to all individualistic abstractions based on eighteenth century materialism; and it is opposed to all Jacobinistic utopias and innovations. . . .

Anti-individualistic, the Fascist conception of life stresses the importance of the State and accepts the individual only in so far as his interests coincide with those of the State, which stands for the conscience and the universal will of man as a historic entity. It is opposed to classical liberalism which arose as a reaction to absolutism and exhausted its historical function when the State became the expression of the conscience and will of the people. Liberalism denied the State in the name of the individual; Fascism reasserts the rights of the State as expressing the real essence of the individual. And if liberty is to be the attribute of living men and not of abstract dummies invented by individualistic liberalism, then Fascism stands for liberty, and for the only liberty worth having, the liberty of the State and of the individual within the State. The Fascist conception of the State is all-embracing; outside of it no human or spiritual values can exist, much less have value. Thus understood, Fascism, is totalitarian, and the Fascist State—a synthesis and a unit inclusive of all values—interprets, develops, and potentiates the whole life of a people. . . .

B. Fascist Italy Creates a Corporative State: The Charter of Labor, 1927

I. The Italian Nation is an organism endowed with a purpose, a life, and means of action transcending those of the individuals composing it. It is a moral, political and economic unit which finds its integral realisation in the Fascist State.

II. Work in all its various forms—intellectual, technical or manual—is a social duty. On these grounds, and on these grounds alone, it is brought under the supervision of the State. . . .

III. There is complete freedom of professional or syndical organisation. But syndicates legally recognised and subject to State control alone have the right to represent legally the whole category for which they are constituted; to protect their interests in their relations with the State or other professional associations; to stipulate collective labour contracts binding on all members of the particular category; to impose dues and to exercise on their account public functions delegated to them.

IV. The concrete expression of the solidarity existing between the various factors of production is represented by the collective labour contract which conciliates the opposing interests of employers of labour and of workers, subordinating them to the higher interests of production. . . .

VI. Legally recognised professional associations ensure legal equality between employers and workers, keep a strict control over production and labour and promote the improvement of both.

The Corporations constitute the unitary organisation of the forces of production and integrally represent their interests.

By virtue of this integral representation, and in view of the fact that the interests of production are the interests of the Nation, the law recognises the Corporations as State organisations.

VII. The Corporative State considers that in the sphere of production private enterprise is the most effective and useful instrument in the interests of the Nation.

In view of the fact that the private organisation of production is a function of national concern, the organiser of the enterprise is responsible to the State for the direction given to production. Collaboration between the forces of production gives rise to reciprocal rights and duties. The worker, whether technician, clerk or labourer, is an active collaborator in the economic enterprise, the responsibility for the direction of which rests with the employer.

VIII. Professional associations of employers are required to promote by all possible means a continued increase in the quantity of production and a reduction of costs. . . .

IX. State intervention in economic production arises only when private initiative is lacking or is inadequate or when political interests of the State are involved. This intervention may take the form of control, assistance or direct management. . . .

XI. Professional associations are required to regulate by means of collective contracts the labour relations existing between the categories of employers of labour and of workers represented by them. . . .

XII. The action of the syndicate, the conciliatory efforts of the Corporations and the decisions of the Labour Courts shall guarantee that wages shall correspond to the normal demands of life, to the possibilities of production and the output of labour.

Wages shall be determined entirely reference to any general rules by agreement between the parties to the collective system.

XIII. The consequences of crises in production and of monetary phenomena should be shared equally by all the different factors of production. . . .

XIV. When the contract concerns piece-work and the payments due thereunder are made at intervals of more than fifteen days, adequate weekly or fortnightly sums on account are due.

Night work, with the exception of ordinary regular night shifts, must be paid at a higher rate than day work.

In cases where the work is paid at piece-rate, the rate must be such that a diligent workman, of a normal working capacity, will be able to earn a minimum amount over and above the basic wage.

XV. The worker has the right to a weekly day of rest which shall fall on Sunday. . . .

XVI. Workers in enterprises of continuous activity shall, after the expiry of a year of uninterrupted service, have the right to an annual period of rest with pay.

XVII. In enterprises of continuous activity the

worker has the right, in the event of a cessation of labour relations on account of discharge without any fault on his part, to an indemnity proportional to his years of service. Similar indemnity is also due in the event of the death of a worker. . . .

XIX. Breaches of discipline or the performance of acts which disturb the normal working of the enterprise on the part of the workers, shall be punished according to the gravity of the offence, by fine, suspension from work, or in certain cases of gravity, by immediate discharge without indemnity.

The cases when the employer can impose fines, suspension from work or immediate discharge without payment of indemnity, shall be specified. . . .

XXII. The State alone can ascertain and control the phenomenon of employment and unemployment of workers, which is a complex of the conditions of production and work.

XXIII. Labour Employment Bureaus founded on a mutual basis are subjected to the control of the Corporations. Employers have the obligation to employ workers whose names are on the register of the said Bureaus and have the right of choice among the names of those who are members of the Party and the Fascist syndicates according to their seniority on the Register.

XXIV. The professional associations of employers are required to exercise a process of selection among the workers with the object of achieving continuous improvement in their technical capacity and moral education.

XXV. The Corporative bodies shall ensure the observance of the laws on the prevention of accidents and the discipline of work on the part of individuals belonging to the federated associations.

XXVI. Insurance is a further expression of the principle of collaboration, and the employer and the worker should both bear a proportional share of its burden. The State, through the medium of Corporations and professional associations, shall see to the coordination and unity, as far as possible, of the system and institutes of insurance.

XXVII. The Fascist State proposes:
1. the perfecting of accident insurance;
2. the improvement and extension of maternity assistance;
3. insurance against industrial diseases and tuberculosis as a step towards insurance against all forms of sickness;
4. the perfecting of insurance against involuntary unemployment;
5. the adoption of special forms of endowment insurance for young workers.

XXVIII. The workers' associations are required to act as guardians of those they represent in administrative and judicial suits arising out of accident and social insurance. . . .

C. Giacomo Matteoti Exposes the Fascists, 1924

The Fascist Government justifies its armed conquest of political power, its use of violence and the risk it incurred of igniting civil war, by the plea of the urgent necessity of restoring the authority of law and the State, and of rescuing the country from economic and financial conditions approaching utter ruin.

The statistical and historical data and documents compiled in this book are a demonstration of the very contrary of this. They show that never as in this last year, during which Fascism has been in power, has the law been so thrust aside in favour of arbitrary action, the State so subjugated by a faction, or the nation so split up into two classes, a dominating and a subject class. The country's economic and financial condition has, on the whole, continued to show the improvement and the slow recovery from the devastation of the war, which had already begun in the preceding years; but had begun thanks to the energies of the people, not the excesses and extravagances of Fascist domination. As to this latter, one thing is demonstrably true: that the profits of the speculators and the capitalists have increased in proportion as the reward of labour and the small resources of the middle classes have diminished, while these two latter classes have lost all freedom and all that is of worth in citizenship.

Part IV.
And the Chronicle of Deeds
May, 1923

Genoa.—At Marassi-Guezzi Fascists strike workmen found in public bars, fire revolver and rifle shots, and set fire to the Friendly Society's premises.
Leonessa.—Fascists command the Marshal of Carabineers to arrest four workers who had sung the "Red Flag."
Rome.—The placarding of manifestoes and of announcements of meetings is prohibited. Workers ordered to resume work on pain of dismissal.

Arzignano (Vicenza).—The manufacturer Pelizzari ordered by Fascists to dismiss immediately twelve workers who had celebrated May-day.

Jesi.—The local silk works ordered to close down because the work-women had celebrated May-day.

Milan.—Chamber of Labour entered during the night and an attempt made to set it on fire.

Naples.—The Chamber of Labour laid waste.

Parma.—The Deputy Picelli insulted and threatened; the worker Maluberto Enrico, a war hero, decorated with one bronze and two silver medals, beaten; Campanini Pietro, a war invalid, seriously wounded.

Document Set 26.6 References

A. Benito Mussolini Expounds the "Fundamental Ideas" of Fascism
   Mussolini, *Fascism: Doctrine and Institutions* (New York: Howard Fertig, 1935), 7–11.
B. Fascist Italy Creates a Corporative State: The Charter of Labor, 1927
   Labour Charter in W. C. Langsam, ed., *Documents and Readings in the History of Europe Since 1918,* rev. ed. (Philadelphia: Lippincott, 1951), 519–525.
C. Giacomo Matteoti Exposes the Fascists, 1924
   Matteoti in Langsam, 510–512.

CHAPTER

27

An Age of Catastrophes, 1929–1945

The Great Depression and the Impotent Democracies

The collapse of the New York stockmarket in October 1929 touched off a chain reaction of economic disasters throughout the capitalist world. Financial panics that spread from nation to nation were nothing new: the nineteenth and early twentieth centuries had seen a string of them, underscoring the interdependence of the West's financial and trading systems. What made the Great Depression of the 1930s truly appalling was its length, depth, and consequences. Self-correcting economic processes that had lifted stricken economies out of previous depressions this time failed to work, forestalled by most governments' wrongheaded monetary and fiscal policies and by their trade-stifling protective tariffs.

Postwar economic recovery had been precarious in Weimar Germany, saddled with enormous reparations obligations that it could pay only with the help of American loans, and whose middle class had lost its savings in the 1923 hyperinflation. When the Great Depression reached Germany in 1930–1931, the ensuing collapse of productivity and employment reached much lower depths than in other industrial nations. Document A captures the despair and impotence of officials in the western Germany city of Mainz in 1931 and 1932. Great Britain slipped into the Depression somewhat more gradually than did either the United States or Germany (the closed trading system of the British Commonwealth and empire afforded some protection), but some of the worst effects of the great contraction were felt in those parts of the United Kingdom that had been economically stag-

nant in the twenties and now sank into seeming hopelessness (Document B).

France was even slower in feeling the full brunt of the Depression. But by the mid-1930s France's centrist cabinets were battered by a combination of economic distress, political scandals, and vicious right-wing attacks on the very idea of democratic government. This discrediting of the center opened the way for two short-lived Popular Front governments under Léon Blum (1872–1950) in 1936 and 1938. A coalition of liberals, socialists, and Communists, the Popular Front promised (Document C) a vigorous assault on economic injustice and a defense of the Third Republic against rightist extremists. Blum's Popular Front governments had only a weak political grip. The first and more promising of them fell apart because it failed to take a resolute stand against the fascist tide in the Spanish Civil War. That bloody conflict (1936–1939) had its roots not in Depression-era distress but in the irreconcilable clash of Spanish rightists and Catholics with the republican, socialist, and anticlerical enthusiasm of the liberals and leftists who were trying to modernize if not radicalize Spain. A sense of the republicans' groping for new social foundations emerges from Document D, the accounts of two republican women who retained their optimism through the dreadful hardships of civil war.

The Great Depression is often blamed for bringing democracy to the brink of repudiation in several Western societies—and over the brink in countries like Germany and Austria. Evaluate this statement on the basis of these documents and of the account in *The Challenge of the West.* (You might want to consider Set 27.2 as well in responding to this question.)

A. The Great Depression Devastates Urban Germany

City of Mainz Chamber of Commerce and Industry, Annual Report for 1931

The year 1931 saw a further rapid decline of the German economy. This downward trend has been in evidence since 1927. . . . No more needs to be said about the desperate condition of the Germany economy. No further proof is required than the findings of the report issued by the Geneva committee of experts, which determined that one-third of the economy and those individuals dependent on it is lying idle, the unemployment figures have reached new, undreamed-of highs, and the number of business failures and shutdowns is growing day by day. . . .

Annual Report for 1932

The catastrophically low level of the German economy which we detailed in the previous annual report persisted during the first half of this reporting year as well. The fourth presidential emergency decree of December 8 [1931] did make the attempt to slow the further decline of the economy, but it soon became clear that the planned artificial and far-reaching encroachment on natural economic relationships could not produce the desired result. The concerns over this encroachment, which we emphatically expressed in our last report, have since proved well founded. Existing contractual agreements in all areas of the market, be it in the area of housing, money and interest, or salaries and wages, were all loosened and changed, while good faith was not taken into account. As a result a considerable insecurity has taken hold not only in the economic sphere, but among the entire population in general. All initiatives falter because of despondent attitudes, and commerce appears to have come to a standstill altogether. This critical situation has been intensified by the failure to solve the reparations problem. . . .

The situation in the field of public finances continues to be of concern. The situation at the community level is hopeless. [Local government finances] bear the main brunt of unemployment, since over the course of time more and more unemployed individuals drift from unemployment insurance to public crisis relief and finally into general welfare recipient status. It is of the utmost urgency to relieve the local communities of this pressure by coordinating the entire system of unemployment relief. The economy in general would stand to benefit from the restoration of the financial health of local communities. . . .

B. A Parliamentary Investigator Reports on the Chronic Depression in Britain's "Special Areas," 1934

25. The Special Areas are in their present unfortunate position owing to the decline of the main industries, coal mining, ship building and iron and steel, which attracted such large numbers of workers to them during the nineteenth century under more prosperous conditions. It seems unlikely that these industries will again employ the numbers engaged in them even up to ten years ago. During the period of prosperity large communities with full equipment of railways, roads, houses, schools and other municipal and social services were created. Many millions of pounds were spent in building up these services. A large proportion of the inhabitants have been associated with the Areas for several generations; they are bound to the Areas by ties of home and family and religion, by local patriotism and, especially in Wales, by a fervent national spirit and, sometimes, a distinctive language. It is natural, therefore, that wherever one goes in these Areas one should be met by the demand that something should be done to attract fresh industries to the Area. This is the general request, and I regard it as at once the most important and the most difficult of my duties to try to satisfy it. I have given more time and personal attention to this side of my work than to any other, but it must be frankly admitted that up to the present the results have been negligible. Many of the negotiations I have initiated with this end in view were necessarily confidential, and it would only prejudice the present slender chances of success if I were to give a full account of them. The following paragraphs will, however, indicate the main lines on which I have been working.

26. In the first place I approached a number of the larger and more prosperous firms in the country in the hope that I might persuade them to open new branches of their industry in one or other of the Special Areas. Without exception they were sympathetic to my representations, but except in one case they had good reasons which made it impossible for them to accede to my request. . . .

29. Some hundreds of new factories have been established in recent years in the Midlands and South, but very few in the Special Areas. Why is this so? The main reasons appear to fall in the following categories:—

(1) Inaccessibility to markets. This applies particularly to Cumberland. . . .

(2) High rates. These probably have a deterrent effect on employers out of proportion to their real significance. . . .

(3) Fear of industrial unrest. This fear is very general and is bred from past disputes mainly in the coal-mining industry. It prevails particularly with regard to South Wales, but the facts scarcely warrant the attitude adopted. Statistics apart from those of coal-mining do not justify the fear which undoubtedly exists in the minds of many employers. . . .

(4) The fact that the areas are, and for some years have been, suffering from industrial depression. This factor, coupled with the common application to them of the term "depressed" or "distressed" areas, has itself a deterrent effect. While it is true that "trade brings trade," the converse unfortunately is equally true. Unemployment undermines business confidence and reduces purchasing power. A vicious circle is thus set up. . . .

(5) Difficulty in obtaining finance to start new industries. . . .

255. . . . Probably the most serious human problem of the Special Areas is that presented by unemployment among young men between 18 and 21. . . .

256. Many of these young persons have done practically no work; they have been brought up in a home where the father has been continuously out of work, and they have little or no conception that a man's ordinary occupation should be such as will provide the means of subsistence for himself and for his family. They have seen their own families and their friends kept for years by the State, and they have come to accept this as a normal condition of life. It is hardly surprising in the circumstances that young persons with this background and upbringing should be ready victims of all manner of demoralizing influences. In short, these young persons present in my view the most tragic aspect of the problem of the Special Areas and one fraught with great danger to the State.

c. The French Popular Front Announces Its Program, 1936

I. Defense of Freedom

1. A general amnesty.
2. Measures against the Fascist Leagues:
   (a) The effective disarmament and dissolution of all semi-military formations, in accordance with the law.
   (b) The enforcement of legal measures in cases of incitement to murder or any attempt against the safety of the State.
3. Measures for the cleansing of public life, especially by forbidding deputies to combine their parliamentary functions with certain other forms of activity.
4. The Press:
   (a) The repeal of the infamous laws and decrees restricting freedom of opinion.
   (b) Reform of the Press by the following legislative measures:
      (i) Measures effectively repressing libel and blackmail.
      (ii) Measures which will guarantee the normal means of existence to newspapers, and compel publication of their financial resources.
      (iii) Measures ending the private monopoly of commercial advertising and the scandals of financial advertising, and preventing the formation of newspaper trusts.
   (c) Organization by the State of radio broadcasts with a view to assuring the accuracy of news and equality of political and social organizations in radio programs.
5. Trade Union Liberties:
   (a) Application and observance of trade-union freedom for all.
   (b) Recognition of women's labor rights.
6. Education and freedom of conscience:
   (a) Measures safeguarding the development of public education by the necessary grants . . .
   (b) Measures guaranteeing to all concerned, pupils and teachers, complete freedom of conscience . . .
7. Colonies: formation of a parliamentary committee of inquiry into the political, economic and cultural situation in France's territories overseas, especially French North Africa and Indo-China.

II. Defense of Peace

. . . 2. International collaboration within the framework of the League of Nations for collective security, by defining the aggressor and by joint application of automatic sanctions in cases of aggression.

3. Ceaseless endeavor to pass from armed peace to disarmed peace, first by a convention of limitation, and then by the general, simultaneous, and effectively controlled reduction of armaments.

4. Nationalization of war industries and suppression of private trade in armaments.

5. Repudiation of secret diplomacy . . .

7. Extension of the system of pacts open to all nations, particularly in eastern Europe, on the lines of the Franco-Soviet Pact.

III. Economic Demands

1. Restoration of purchasing power destroyed or reduced by the crisis. . . . [Proposals follow for unemployment insurance, old age pensions, etc.]
2. Against the robbery of investors and for the better organization of credit. . . . [Proposals follow for banking and stockmarket regulation.]

IV. Financial Purification

Control of the trade in armaments, in conjunction with the nationalization of armaments industries. Prevention of waste in the civil and military departments. . . . [Proposals follow for "democratic reform of the system of taxation so as to relax the fiscal burden blocking economic recovery" and for raising taxes on the wealthy.]

D. Republican Women Respond to the Spanish Civil War

Rosa Vega, a schoolteacher in Madrid: It was so dark that I often bumped into people in the streets. But never once was I molested or in any way made aware that I was a woman. Before the war there would have been remarks of one sort or another—now that was entirely gone. Women were no longer objects, they were human beings, persons on the same level as men.

There were many bad things, no doubt, in the Popular Front zone, but the fact that both sexes were humanly equal was one of the most remarkable social advances of the time.

Maria Solana, a socialist youth member: The war bred a new spirit in people, it was amazing. I was often sent round villages on propaganda missions with other party youth and there wouldn't be enough beds. I, the only woman, would sleep in the same bed with two or three youths and nothing would happen—absolutely nothing. There was a new sense of human relationships.

Document Set 27.1 References

A. The Great Depression Devastates Urban Germany
   From *Rhein-Mainische Wirtschafts-Zeitung 14* (1933) No. 1, in Benjamin Sax and Dieter Kuntz, eds. and trans., *Inside Hitler's Germany* (Lexington, Mass.: D. C. Heath, 1992), 58–59.
B. A Parliamentary Investigator Reports on the Chronic Depression in Britain's "Special Areas," 1934
   First and Second Reports of the Commissioner for the Special Areas [England and Wales], in W. C. Langsam, ed., *Documents and Readings in the History of Europe Since 1918*, rev. and enlarged ed. (Philadelphia: Lippincott, 1951), 303–304, 306.
C. The French Popular Front Announces Its Program, 1936
   The Popular Front Program, 1936, in David Thompson, ed., *France: Empire and Republic, 1850–1940* (New York: Walker and Co., 1968), 293–296.
D. Republican Women Respond to the Spanish Civil War
   Ronald Fraser, *The Blood of Spain: An Oral History of the Spanish Civil War* (New York: Pantheon 1979), 286.

DOCUMENT SET 27.2
Nazi Ideology and Its Mass Appeal

Unquestionably Adolf Hitler (1889–1945) and his National Socialist movement profited greatly from the despair sowed by the Great Depression, though Hitler would not have been appointed chancellor in January 1933 without the intriguing and deal-making of the broader, anti-republican Right. Once in power, the Nazi Party set up its dictatorship by ruthlessly terrorizing opponents. But it is likely that its combination of intimidation, propaganda, and economic recovery through military-oriented investment won at least the passive support of a majority of Germans, and the noisy enthusiasm of a significant minority.

Whatever his intellectual deficiencies and psychopathic hatreds, Hitler was a master demagogue. Document A, an extract from *Mein Kampf* (the combination memoir and political program that he dictated while imprisoned in 1924), spells out with brutal frankness the strategy and tactics that Hitler would follow to the end of his bloody days. Document B, a testimonial written by a worshipful Nazi follower of humble origins during the 1930s, suggests the kind of mind to which Hitler appealed and the circumstances that bred his following. In Document C, the underground network of the now-suppressed Social Democratic Party reports frankly on workers' attitudes toward the Nazi regime in the spring and summer of 1934.

The Nazis took their blood-and-soil ideology very seriously. It is debatable how much it actually impressed the German people; they were more interested in getting jobs. What role do you think that the movement's ideology—a murky mix of romantic mumbo-jumbo and pseudo-scientific racism—played in rationalizing the crimes that individual Nazis would commit? Consider this question in the light of Documents C and D—respectively, propaganda by the Reich Youth Headquarters explaining the purpose and methods of the Nazi Organization of German Girls, and Heinrich Himmler's call to his SS men to help breed the Aryan master-race.

Using these documents and relying on *The Challenge of the West*, weigh the relationship between propaganda and ideology in accounting for the rise of Nazism. To what extent was Nazi ideology simply a propaganda tool? What roots did it spring from, and in what ways might it appeal to ordinary Germans?

A. Hitler Reveals His Thoughts on Propaganda

The psyche of the great masses is not receptive to anything that is half-hearted and weak. . . .

To whom should propaganda be addressed? To the scientifically trained intelligentsia or to the less educated masses?

It must be addressed always and exclusively to the masses. . . .

All propaganda must be popular and its intellectual level must be adjusted to the most limited intelligence among those it is addressed to. Consequently, the greater the mass it is intended to reach, the lower its purely intellectual level will have to be. . . .

The art of propaganda lies in understanding the emotional ideas of the great masses and finding, through a psychologically correct form, the way to the attention and thence to the heart of the broad masses. The fact that our bright boys do not understand this merely shows how mentally lazy and conceited they are.

Once we understand how necessary it is for propaganda to be adjusted to the broad mass, the following rule results:

It is a mistake to make propaganda many-sided, like scientific instruction, for instance.

The receptivity of the great masses is very limited, their intelligence is small, but their power of forgetting is enormous. In consequence of these facts, all effective propaganda must be limited to a very few points and must harp on these in slogans until the last member of the public understands what you want him to understand by your slogan. As soon as you sacrifice this slogan and try to be many-sided, the effect will piddle away, for the crowd can neither digest nor retain the material offered. In this way, the result is weakened and in the end entirely cancelled out. . . .

The broad mass of a nation does not consist of diplomats, or even professors of political law, or even individuals capable of forming a rational opinion; it consists of plain mortals, wavering and inclined to doubt and uncertainty. As soon as our own propaganda admits so much as a glimmer of right on the other side, the foundation for doubt in our own right has been laid. . . .

The people in their overwhelming majority are so feminine by nature and attitude that sober reasoning determines their thoughts and actions far less than emotion and feeling. . . .

But the most brilliant propagandist technique will yield no success unless one fundamental principle is borne in mind constantly and with unflagging attention. It must confine itself to a few points and repeat them over and over. Here, as so often in this world, persistence is the first and most important requirement for success. . . .

The purpose of propaganda is not to provide interesting distraction for blasé young gentlemen, but to convince, and what I mean is to convince the masses. But the masses are slow-moving, and they always require a certain time before they are ready even to notice a thing, and only after the simplest ideas are repeated thousands of times will the masses finally remember them. . . .

[During World War I] at first the claims of the [enemy] propaganda were so impudent that people thought it insane; later, it got on people's nerves; and in the end, it was believed. . . .

B. A Worker Supports the Nazis, 1920s

In the workshops and offices of many large machine factories of the Reich, I became acquainted with Marxism and democracy in both party and labor unions as early as 1904. After the war, once I became aware of the shameful, treasonous action committed by the SPD [Social Democratic Party], Center, Democrats, and so forth against Germany, I instinctively fought against Marxism and its procurers wherever I possibly could. Even in my youth I was antisemitically predisposed and frequently paid for it with house detention because I did not tolerate the impudence and provocations of the Jewish boys. . . .

1922–23 I lived in a small village in the Catholic region near Ellwang. The only Catholic newspaper of that region delighted in tearing this new party and its leader to shreds. That was reason enough for me to connect with what this man wanted. Inflation raced through the land and ruined me, like many others.

As of January 1924 I lived in Ludwigsburg and from August 1924 on in Zuffenhausen, and was better able to follow the proceedings of the people's court of justice in Munich. The manly bearing of Adolf Hitler prompted me to seek out like-minded individuals. At first I made the acquaintance of a young lady who accordingly supplied me with the requisite literature, and who later also procured the *Völkischer Beobachter*[1] for me. Only then did I get a

true picture of the events in Munich and thereby became a fervent follower of Adolf Hitler. . . .

[In 1925] a long period of untiring, nerve-shattering work and stubborn, fanatical struggle began for my comrades and myself. Family life did not exist anymore. I rejected everything that was associated with middle-class clubs. The struggle for the Führer and my job occupied my entire existence.

Ridiculed, laughed at, and scorned by former "friends"; likewise shunned and regarded as abnormal by my closest relatives; those were the immediate consequences. From the day of my entry into the party, there began a boycott of my father's and brothers' business by Jews and their cohorts which reached even into so-called German-Nationalist circles. Adding to this was the age difference that existed between me and my comrades which amounted to more than ten or fifteen years, and which my former friends and acquaintances pointed to as evidence of my stupidity and the inexperience of my comrades.

We began to collect and weld together the few faithful into a local group. Each and every one had to propagandize and persuade; we fought for every single individual with passionate, fanatical zeal. We established ties with other local groups and helped organize new locals in order to protect our meetings. It did not take long for our meetings to grow. They were no longer able to disrupt our meetings, although the attitude of many within the establishment police force was exceedingly deplorable in those days. We held meetings in the vicinity of Neustadt especially in the smaller towns, and on many Sundays I had to pay for the travel costs and provisions out of my own pocket because as speaker for the party I had to have a protection force for the meetings in order to have success. . . .

The first public meeting of the NSDAP in the town of Lambrecht occurred during this period. As the approximately twenty-five-man SA squad of the Neustadt local group marched into the hall, it was already heavily filled with opponents. The Marxists had brought in their heavy cannon—the Reichsbanner[2] leader Schuhmacher from Ludwigshafen. Our now deceased party member K. Faber spoke first, dealing with [Foreign Minister] Stresemann's politics of illusion. I was supposed to make closing remarks. During the discussion period, Schuhmacher stepped up and railed in the most vile manner until finally a brawl broke out. Everything that was not nailed down was used as a missile: beer bottles, glasses, ashtrays, even the pieces of an entire oven were torn off and hurled at us. . . . We barricad-

---

[1] The main Nazi newspaper

[2] The paramilitary unit of Social Democratic War veterans

ed ourselves behind a table and threw everything that had been hurled our way back, toward the mob that was jamming the exit and howling and shrieking. . . .

During working hours I found myself employed as workshop accountant in the reddest factory in Mannheim. For eight years prior to the revolution, I was the only one, of about a one-thousand-man labor force, who openly and without reserve wore the party insignia. I had to endure much in those days. I was hated by those of different political views, ridiculed and mocked by intellectuals, shunned by all, then later feared, fought, slandered, and denounced. . . . It was worse than hell sometimes . . . but nothing was able to turn me away from an intractable belief in the Führer and ultimate victory. . . .

C. The Social Democratic Underground Reports on Worker Attitudes Toward the Nazi Regime, 1934

The reports from the Reich as yet do not provide a uniform picture. . . .

The following report is from southwestern Germany: "Judging by public attitudes, the regime seems to have the most support among workers. This is especially true for those who earlier had not been part of a political organization. . . . It also seems that workers submit more readily [than other social classes] to Nazi terror methods and allow themselves to be easily influenced."

A similar report from Berlin: "Large segments of the working class continue to submit [to the regime]. Faith in Hitler is remarkably strong. The circle of old [Social Democratic] party members is for the most part unshaken and refuses to accept Nazi ideology. . . ."

From northern Bavaria similar sentiments: "The mood among workers has changed abruptly. This is especially so among those large-income earners who were never satisfied with their pay; who were abusive toward Social Democracy and blamed it because they didn't earn more; who never came to a single meeting, and who had no money to spend for a party newspaper. These indifferent egotists actually thought they would effortlessly earn more under Hitler. Now they have got their surprise. They are the ones grumbling the loudest in the factories, because now they earn barely half of their former pay and must make contributions and pay membership dues. . . ."

A different angle sheds light on the situation in southern Bavaria: "A large segment of the work force is indifferent toward the Third Reich. The percentage of workers in this category is changing, however. Much has to do with the ability and quality of the NSBO (Nationalsozialistische Betriebszellenorganisation, National Socialist Factory Cell Organization] people. In general it can be said that in factories where solid union organizations existed earlier the workers have remained skeptical. It is also evident that underground activity will be difficult to get going here. The workers are indecisive; they are not sure of the goal nor of the path toward it. Many are also afraid of losing their jobs. A not inconsiderable number of those not 'coordinated' [gleichgeschaltet] are discouraged and resigned to their fate."

Much more optimistic is a report from western Saxony: "The situation here has changed markedly since Christmas. The change is a very unfavorable one for the National Socialists. Within factories, at construction sites and other workplaces, there is now much discussion during breaks. One can surmise from this that the workers are basically opposed to the regime. Even [National Socialist] party members are expressing their dissatisfaction and disappointment. . . ."

A Berlin report analyzes the reasons for the more confident mood of the workers: "Workers today are not as afraid of unemployment. They do not have to fear losing their jobs from one day to the next because the regime, in its effort to provide work, is exerting heavy pressure on employers to retain even their surplus work force as long as possible. . . .

. . . The reports from the period of June 30 almost all express the opinion that of all segments of German society, the working class is most submissive toward the regime, and it is presenting the least opposition.

From East Saxony: The workers in the factories are, without exception, adopting a wait-and-see attitude toward the regime and do not believe the things the Nazis are prophesying. Doubts about the accuracy of the Marxist ideological basis surfaced during this past year amid the ranks of former low-level [Social Democratic] party functionaries. The reports of rapid dwindling of the masses of unemployed were not believed by all. Many are doubting the authenticity of the figures released publicly. In any case, the fact that it was possible to obtain large sums on credit, to create new jobs and new work projects without having serious difficulties surface during the first year has shaken the opinion of many who believed that the National Socialist economic program would collapse. . . .

The matter-of-fact way in which factory workers are accepting everything that is being thrust on them is frightening. They only grumble when the dozens of different collecting lists and the contribution collectors approach them. There is not even an inner resistance to the Hitler greeting. The fact that one has to greet others by raising the hand [and saying "Heil Hitler"] is regarded as an insignificant act, as is participating in the May 1 events. The number of those who could have excluded themselves from the beginning could have been much higher. There is a fear throughout the ranks that one will have difficulties at work and possibly lose one's job. This fear induces the workers to act in a certain way. Moreover, these things are probably only demanded of the workers in order to gauge their response. I have encountered only a few who have said, "I can't stand this rubbish anymore, I'd rather sacrifice my job."

D. The League of German Girls Runs a Summer Camp

We are a political Organization of Girls and acknowledge herewith the task which has been set for us by the National Socialist State: to remain alert and ready for our duty and to help with all our strength in the building of a National Socialist *Volk*. Politics today means to us not only the consideration of daily political occurrences, but Politics means to us also the ideological, spiritual, and cultural forming of the entire German people in the sense of National Socialist Demands. Our educational work is determined by this great political task. It has to readjust itself continually to these demands. Then there will emerge from the community where such work is done the person who is the embodiment of our way, healthy and capable, inwardly strong and womanly, consciously German and consciously National Socialistic.

These recreation camps, where our community becomes closely cemented, are an essential expression of our way. Our chief work in the summer month is therefore consciously the holding of recreation camps in which our political education pattern takes shape. Recreation camps force a cementing of community. Girls from all walks of life, from overpopulated cities as well as the wide open country, stand together under our flag for days and weeks, leaving behind all their ordinary interests in life—school and machine, lecture hall and household—and finding a vigorous and healthful life.

Political education in the recreation camp is not synonymous with scientific discussions, but is rather determined by the experiences shared by the camp community and is shaped accordingly. Our recreation camps are organized more loosely than the leadership schools [Führerinnenschulungen], but in spite of all fun, rigid discipline prevails. Our girls

should really be able to leave their daily troubles and cares behind during this week to ten days.

Many who have not yet found us inwardly, acquaint themselves here with the life and the forms of the National Socialist League of Girls and become so attached to it that they cannot dissolve this bond upon their return to everyday life. . . .

Everything the girls experience here takes on a clear, visible pattern in their joint discussions, in which knowledge of their mission in our state, our educational pattern, and the National Socialist Ideology is imparted. During the domestic evenings [Heimabende] the work done during the forenoon, and the work of the Führer and his assistants, the work of the young creative forces in our ranks, is brought closer to them. During the forenoons devoted to reading, they acquaint themselves with the literature of National Socialism and so absorb lasting values. . . .

In clear recognition we created these recreation camps not only for the girls already in our ranks, but also for all the others. We want to do our work with a joyful sense of responsibility, with loyal performance of our duty, and with industry. In order not to become tired and sluggish under the burden of work which each working girl carries however, we need a time which permits quiet collection of strength—free time: Our recreation camps, in which the girls are schooled and prepared for their responsibility and duty to the people and the State, are a political necessity.

Borderland

The circular which called us to camps stated: each junior girl leader will give a survey of the historical and native development of her subdistrict [Untergau] and will consider how she would work this out with junior girls [Jungmädel].

Each of us then realized anew how many living witnesses of ancient history, memorials, walls and bulwarks, legends, tales and jokes, songs and old customs are still alive in her subdistrict.

We had been in camps for three days now. We had penetrated deeper and deeper into National Socialist ideology, emphasized especially the cultural desire of National Socialism; we had discussed our junior girl activities and had worked on the arrangement of our home; we had sung, gone on a short trip, and participated in practical junior girl sports. Today in our domestic evening we want to hear something about Pomeranian customs and Pomeranian History.[3]

---

[3] Pomerania was one of Germany's eastern provinces along the Baltic coast. Since 1945 it has been part of Poland.

After supper we march silently down to the sea. . . .

Our Pomeranian coast lies before our eyes. Now Traute, from the village of Leba up on the Polish border, tells us about the immensity of the shore and on the sea. . . .

Then she suddenly becomes serious: "In our subdistrict we have 200 kilometers of border. Consider what that means: 200 kilometers of border. The Versailles Treaty separates German soil from German soil, blocks our access to the nearest port, and cuts off traffic to the east. Our border city of Lauenburg is flooded with agricultural products. One farm after another in our country gets into great difficulties since, because of the demarcation of the border, there is no longer a market outlet for agricultural products. In Lauenburg itself the greatest amount of unemployment in Pomerania prevails. The Winter relief work tries to alleviate the worst conditions of misery and distress during the winter. Everything is shut down—the factories, the brickyards, and all large plants. These are the effects of the demarcation of the border on our Homeland. . . ."

"And the border itself; visualize a forest, through which a road leads to a railroad station. The road is neutral, the forest is German on the right and Polish on the left. I cannot tell you how one feels on this road; you would have to come and experience it all yourselves."

"But we know that we are on outpost duty there. You can rely on us." Traute is silent. We all get up, grasp each other's hand, and our song is solemn now: "Holy Fatherland, in danger thy sons will flock around thee. . . ." And then we stand around the flag and look silently toward the East.

E. Himmler Demands That SS Men Apply Themselves to "Selective Breeding"

As early as December 13, 1934, I wrote to all SS leaders and declared that we have fought in vain if political victory was not to be followed by victory of births of good blood. The question of multiplicity of children is not a private affair of the individual, but his duty towards his ancestors and our people.

The SS has taken the first step in this direction long ago with the engagement and marriage decree of December 1931. However, the existence of sound marriage is futile if it does not result in the creation of numerous descendants.

I expect that here, too, the SS and especially the SS leader corps, will serve as a guiding example.

The minimum amount of children for a good sound marriage is four. Should unfortunate circumstances deny a married couple their own children, then every SS leader should adopt racially and hereditarily valuable children, educate them in the spirit of National Socialism, let them have education corresponding to their abilities.

The organization "Lebensborn eingetragener Verein [Spring of Life, registered society]" serves the SS leaders in the selection and adoption of qualified children. The organization "Lebensborn e. V." is under my personal direction, is part of the Central Office for Race and Resettlement bureau of the SS, and has the following obligations:

1. Support racially, biologically, and hereditarily valuable families with many children.

2. Place and care for racially and biologically and hereditarily valuable pregnant women, who, after thorough examination of their and the progenitor's families by the Central Office for Race and Resettlement central bureau of the SS, can be expected to produce equally valuable children.

3. Care for the children.

4. Care for the children's mothers.

It is the honorable duty of all leaders of the central office to become members of the organization "Lebensborn e. V." The application for admission must be filed prior to September 23, 1936.

The dues of the SS leaders of the central office, from the Hauptsturmfuehrer [rank of captain] on are determined in the enclosed tables.

I shall personally keep myself informed of the success of my appeal.

Let me remind every SS leader one more that only sacrifices of a personal and material nature have brought us success in the times of the battle, and that the further construction of Germany, to last hundreds and thousands of years, will not be possible unless each and every one of us is ready to keep doing his share in the fulfillment of his obvious duty.

Reichsführer SS
[signed] H. HIMMLER

Document Set 27.2 References

A. Hitler Reveals His Thoughts on Propaganda
Adolf Hitler, *Mein Kampf*, trans. Ralph Mannheim (Boston:
Houghton-Mifflin, 1943), 42, 179–185.

B. A Worker Supports the Nazis, 1920s
Nationalsozialistische Deutsche Arbeiter-Partei, Hauptarchiv
1919–1945 (Stanford: Hoover Institution on War, Revolution,
and Peace), in Benjamin Sax and Dieter Kuntz, eds. and trans.
Inside Hitler's Germany (Lexington, Mass.: D. C. Heath,
1992), 82–84.

C. The Social Democratic Underground Reports on Worker
Attitudes Toward the Nazi Regime, 1934
*Deutschland-Berichte de Sozialdemokratischen Partei
Deutschlands (Sopade), 1934–1940* (Frankfurt: Verlag Petra
Nettelbeck, 1980). April/May, June/July 1934, 29–31, 207–208.
Translated by Dieter Kuntz.

D. The League of German Girls Runs a Summer Camp
U.S. Chief of Counsel for the Prosecution of Axis
Criminality, *Nazi Conspiracy and Aggression* (Washington,
D.C.: U.S. Government Printing Office, 1946), vol. 5, doc. no.
2439-PS, 136–138.

E. Himmler Demands That SS Men Apply Themselves to
"Selective Breeding"
U.S. Chief of Counsel for the Prosecution of Axis
Criminality, vol. 5, doc. no. 2825-PS, 465–466.

DOCUMENT SET 27.3
The Nazi Regime

Whatever its mass appeal, the Nazi regime ultimately rested on force. Document A is the postwar confession of Rudolf Diels, the first Gestapo (secret police) chief, who in 1934 was demoted to relatively low positions; in his deposition to American interrogators he gives an insider's view of how Nazi *Gleichschaltung*—the transformation of normal civil institutions into the agencies of totalitarian power—worked in practice.

An early example of Nazi legislation intended to "cleanse" the Aryan race of "unhealthy stock" was the July 1933 Law to Prevent the Perpetuation of Heritable Diseases (Document B). And Document C reproduces key provisions of the most notorious of Nazi legislation, the 1935 Nuremberg Laws defining who was a Jew.

Write a brief essay analyzing the implications of these documents.

A. *Gleichshaltung*: The Nazis Take Over Germany's Local Police Apparatus, 1933

I, Rudolf Diels, 45 years of age, testify under oath as follows: When Hitler became Chancellor of the Reich on January 30th 1933, I was a Superior Government Councillor [Oberregierungsrat] in the police section of the Prussian Ministry of Interior. There I was in the section: Political Police. Therefore I know the happenings within the police, as they occurred during the time after Hitler's seizure of power, from my own experience.

When Hitler became Chancellor of the Reich, Hermann Goering became provisional [Kommissarischer] Prussian Minister of the Interior and thereby my superior. As such he was the head of the centralized Prussian police administration. This organization constituted the strongest power [Machtfaktor] aside from the army.

The perfectly primitive Nazi conception of the conduct of a state was, that one had to annihilate or render harmless all adversaries or suspected adversaries. The inferiority complex of the Nazis towards everything they did not know, e.g. legal institutions, experts and so on has much to do with that.

As for that, it was a natural matter for the new Nazi Government and the party, which had come into power, to annihilate their adversaries by all possible means. These actions started after the Reichstag fire. They were executed by various party groups, especially by the SA; for such criminal purposes the government also tried to make the most of certain official government agencies. The methods applied were as follows: Human beings, who deprived of their freedom [were] subjected to severe bodily mistreatment or killed. These illegal detentions [Freiheitsberaubungen] took place in camps, often old military barracks, storm-troop quarters or fortresses. Later on these places became known as concentration camps, such as Oranienburg, near Berlin, Lichtenburg, Papenburg, Dachau in Bavaria, Columbiahouse Berlin, etc.

During this period of time, numerous politicians, deputies, writers, doctors, lawyers and other personalities of leading circles were arrested illegally, tortured and killed. Among the killed, there were the Social Democrat Stelling, Ernst Heilmann, the former Police President of Altona Otto Eggerstedt, the communist Schehr from the Ruhr territory, and numerous parties and denominations, amongst them Conservatives, Democrats, Catholics, Jews, Communists and Pacifists.

These murders were camouflaged by the expression: "shot while trying to escape" or "resisting arrest" or similar things. Approximately 5[00]–700 people perished during this first wave of terror (from March until October 1933 approximately).

I myself and co-workers, old civil servants, Not-Nazis, tried to resist this wave of terror.

There was no legal possibility left any more, to undertake anything in order to stop these illegal arrests, because the Reich Cabinet had suspended Civil Rights by decree of February 28th 1933. On account of this fact, it was also impossible for the inmates of the concentration camps to appeal to any court. Such a state of affairs had never existed before, not even during extraordinary times. The word "protective custody" as used at that time for concentration camps etc. was an irony. There were a few cases of real protective custody, in which I put people behind safe walls, in order to protect them against terrible excesses.

The number of illegal cases attained an ever-increasing extent. When Heinrich Himmler took over the reins of power as the highest Chief of police in Prussia under Goering, these actions were really organized by the State proper. The first, great, state-organized terror project under his leadership was the blood purge of June 30th, 1934, at that time SA leaders, Generals, leading Catholics and others were murdered. He also arrested people again, who had been released from concentrations camps before that time. This at a time, when actually a certain tranquillity in the country had set in already.

Read by myself, approved, signed and sworn to:
[signed] RUDOLF DIELS

B. Sterilization Is Legalized for "The Unfit," 1933

1

(1) Whoever suffers from a heritable disease may be made unfruitful (sterilized) through surgical means if, in the experience of medical science, it may, with great likelihood, be expected that his descendants will suffer from serious heritable physical or mental defects.

(2) Whoever suffers from one of the following ailments is considered to be heritably diseased within the meaning of this law:
1. congenital feeble-mindedness
2. schizophrenia
3. manic-depression
4. congenital epilepsy
5. heritable St. Vitus's dance (Huntington's Chorea)
6. hereditary blindness
7. hereditary deafness
8. serious heritable malformations.

(3) Further, anyone suffering from chronic alcoholism may also be made unfruitful.

2

(1) Entitled to request [sterilization], is he who is to be made unfruitful. If he should be incapacitated or under guardianship because of feeble-mindedness or not yet 18 years of age, then his legal representative is empowered to make the motion. In the other cases of limited capacity the request must be consented to by the legal representative. If the person is of age and has a nurse, the consent of the latter is necessary.

(2) The request is to be accompanied by a certificate from a physician accredited by the German Reich stating that the one to be sterilized has been enlightened regarding the nature and consequences of sterilization.

(3) The request for sterilization is subject to recall.

3

Sterilization may also be recommended by
1. the official physician,
2. the official in charge of the institution in the case of inmates of a hospital, sanitarium, or prison.

4

The request is to be presented in writing to, or put into writing by the business office of, the Health-Inheritance Court (Erbgesundheitigericht). The facts underlying the request are to be certified to by a medical document or in some other way authenticated. The business office of the court must notify the official physician. . . .

7

(1) The proceedings before the Health-Inheritance Courts are secret. . . .

10

. . . (3) The Supreme Health-Inheritance Court has final jurisdiction.

11

(1) The surgical operation necessary for sterilization may be performed only in a hospital and by a physician accredited by the German Reich. . . .

18

This law becomes effective January 1, 1934.

C. The Nuremberg Laws Differentiate Germans and Jews, 1935

Article 5.

1. A Jew is anyone who descended from at least three grandparents who were racially full Jews. Article 2, par. 2, second sentence will apply.

2. A Jew is also one who descended from two full Jewish parents, if: (a) he belonged to the Jewish religious community at the time this law was issued, or who joined the community later; (b) he was married to a Jewish person, at the time the law was issued, or married one subsequently; (c) he is the offspring from a marriage with a Jew, in the sense of Section 1, which was contracted after the Law for the Protection of German Blood and German Honor became effective . . . ; (d) he is the offspring of an extramarital relationship, with a Jew, according to Section 1, and will be born out of wedlock after July 31, 1936. . . .

Law for the Protection of German Blood and German Honor of 15 September 1935

Thoroughly convinced by the knowledge that the purity of German blood is essential for the further existence of the German people and animated by the inflexible will to safe-guard the German nation for the entire future, the Reichstag has resolved upon the following law unanimously, which is promulgated herewith:

Section 1

1. Marriages between Jews and nationals of German or kindred blood are forbidden. Marriages concluded in defiance of this law are void, even if, for the purpose of evading this law, they are concluded abroad. . . .

Section 2

Relation outside marriage between Jews and nationals of German or kindred blood are forbidden.

Section 3

Jews will not be permitted to employ female nationals of German or kindred blood in their household.

Section 4

1. Jews are forbidden to hoist the Reich and national flag and to present the colors of the Reich. . . .

Section 5

1. A person who acts contrary to the prohibition of section 1 will be punished with hard labor.

2. A person who acts contrary to the prohibition of section 2 will be punished with imprisonment or with hard labor.

3. A person who acts contrary to the provisions of sections 3 or 4 will be punished with imprisonment up to a year and with a fine or with one of these penalties. . . .

Document Set 27.3 References

A. *Gleichschaltung:* The Nazis Take Over Germany's Local Police Apparatus, 1933
Rudolf Diels, in U.S. Chief of Counsel for the Prosecution of Axis Criminality, *Nazi Conspiracy and Aggression* (Washington, D.C.: U.S. Government Printing Office, 1946), vol. 5, doc. no. 2544-PS, 288–290.

B. Sterilization Is Legalized for "The Unfit," 1933
Germany, *Reichsgesetzblatt,* in W. C. Langsam, ed., *Documents and Readings in the History of Europe Since 1918,* rev. and enlarged ed. (Philadelphia: Lippincott, 1951), 683–684.

C. The Nuremberg Laws Differentiate Germans and Jews, 1935
U.S. Chief of Counsel for the Prosecution of Axis Criminality, *Nazi Conspiracy and Aggression* (Washington, D.C.: U.S. Government Printing Office, 1946), vol. 4, doc. no. 1417-PS, 8–10; vol. 4, doc. no. 2000-PS, 636–638.

DOCUMENT SET 27.4
The Stalin Revolution: Collectivization and Industrialization

As noted in Set 26.4, Stalin embarked upon the "left" policy of crash industrialization in 1929, having just used the pro-NEP "right" faction within the Soviet leadership to defeat his opponents on the left. The documents in Set 27.4 show how Stalin carried out industrialization and its agrarian foundation, collectivization, with a ferocity that not even his "left" opponents in the "industrialization debate" of the 1920s, had suggested would be necessary.

The first three documents illustrate aspects of the collectivization drive, which in Ukraine alone cost several million lives as the authorities engineered a famine to break the peasantry's will to resist. Document A records the opposition to collective farming by peasants in the west Russian Smolensk district[1] in 1930. It is not likely that villagers would have been so naive as to write a letter of complaint to the local newspaper at a later date—in 1934, for example, when the secret police in the same region reported on continued grass-roots opposition (Document B). Document C, from the Smolensk archives in 1932, reports the problems of running the new collective farms.

The last two documents offer insights into the 1930s industrialization drive. In Document D, the secret police watch textile workers in Smolensk who are protesting increased norms. Demands for greater productivity were common both in old industries like the Smolensk textile mills and in the new industrial plants built under the Five Year Plans. Conditions in a new Soviet industry are described in a very interesting and generally objective book by a contemporary American eyewitness and participant, John Scott, published in the United States in 1942 and excerpted as Document E. Scott, the son of a prominent U.S. left-wing intellectual, in 1932–1935 worked at the blast furnaces at Magnitogorsk, a new industrial city constructed in the Ural Mountains; he married a Russian woman and appears to have lived at about the same level as other skilled Soviet workers.

Analyze these documents to ascertain the "class basis" (as the Soviets would put it) of the attitudes of the individuals involved. What evidence do you see of "poor peasants" and "kulaks" in the collectivization documents? What can you say about the industrial workers? What light do these documents shed on the processes of collectivization and industrialization and their impact on various individuals and social groups? What opportunities did the "Stalin Revolution" open up?

A. A Smolensk Peasant Protests Collectivization, 1930

For a long time I have wanted to write you about what you have written on collectivization in your newspaper *Nasha Derevnya.*

In the first place I will give you my address so that you will not suspect that I am a kulak or one of his parasites. I am a poor peasant. I have one hut, one barn, one horse, 3 dessyatins[2] of land, and a wife and three children. Dear Comrades, as a subscriber to your newspaper . . . I found in No. 13/85 for February 15 a letter from a peasant who writes about the life of kolkhoz construction. I, a poor peasant, reading this letter, fully agreed with it. This peasant described life in the kolkhoz completely correctly. Isn't it true that all the poor peasants and middle peasants do not want to go into the kolkhoz at all, but that you drive them in by force? For example, I'll take my village soviet of Yushkovo. A brigade of soldiers came to us. This brigade went into all the occupied homes, and do you think that they organized a kolkhoz? No, they did not organize it. The hired laborers, and the poor peasants came out against it and said they did not want corvée, they did not want serfdom . . . I'll write more of my village soviet. When the Red Army brigade left, they sent us a kolkhoz organizer from Bryansk okrug. And whom do you think this Comrade signed up? Not poor peasants, not hired laborers, but kulaks, who, sensing their own ruin, enter the kolkhoz. And your organizer . . . takes to evil deeds. At night, together with the Komsomolites, he takes everything away from the peasants, both surpluses and taxes, which you fleece from the peasants of course agricultural taxes are necessary, self-taxation is necessary, fire taxes are necessary, tractorization is necessary. But where can the toiling peasant get this money if not from the seeds of

---

[1] The Smolensk district is particularly well documented because the local Soviet secret police archives fell into German hands during World War II; after the war these materials were analyzed and published by American scholars. Until the fall of the U.S.S.R. in 1991, which began the process of opening many Communist-era archives, the Smolensk documents provided an exceptionally rare glimpse of the Soviet system at work day-to-day.

[2] About 8.1 acres

his products? And these Party people stay up all night and rob the peasants. If he brings a pud, if he brings 5, it's all the same. I would propose that you let the peasant live in greater freedom than he does now, and then we won't beg you to get rid of such a gang, for we ourselves will eliminate them.

B. The Soviet Secret Police Report on Resistance to Collectivization, 1934

In analyzing the reasons why whole villages of individual farmers do not enter a kolkhoz we receive the following picture (we cite the most characteristic and typical reasons from the majority of such settlements in the raion): The village of Nivki, Konnovsk village soviet, consists of nineteen farms, four of them prosperous ones. In this village there is an anti-Soviet group who keep the entire village under their thumb. The leader of this group is Roman Chervyakov. A one-time chairman of a village soviet, he enjoys great respect and confidence among his fellow-villagers. His closest assistant is Yegor Kovalev, a fiery agitator against the kolkhozes. He leads five farms. In the spring in this village there were many who wanted to join the kolkhoz, but under the influence of this group the organization of the kolkhoz did not take place. Now among the peasants there is a mutual guarantee (an agreement that no one will join the kolkhoz). Two poor peasants tried to violate this agreement because of a bread shortage, and they wanted to enter the kolkhoz. But [the anti-kolkhoz fraction] bargained with them, hired them to pasture the cattle of the village, gave them as much bread as they asked for, and persuaded them in no case to enter the kolkhoz.

In another village—Galnevo—a group of sectarians read the Bible collectively, predict that "there is not much longer to live; do not succumb to temptation, brothers" (i.e., do not enter the kolkhoz).

We find the same things in a number of other settlements.

C. The Authorities Try to Organize Kolkhoz Life, 1930s

In the kolkohz "Stalin," Markovsk village soviet, Krasnyi raion, which includes more than 40 households, there exists the most complete negligence. Some members of the board of the kolkhoz systematically engage in drinking and abuses ... The chairman of the board ... a former middle peasant, systematically gets drunk and does not guide the work

of the kolkhoz at all ... about 20 hectares[3] of oats lie cut down, which, as a result of the fact that they were not harvested, almost completely rotted ... There remained unmowed 1 1/2 hectares of oats, which were completely spoiled. The winter wheat, which was mowed on time, remained lying in the fields, thanks to which it rotted. Almost all the pulled flax is still lying in the field and is rotting, as a result of which the flaxseed is almost completely ruined. There are about 100 hectares of as yet unmown meadows, while the socialized livestock in the kolkhoz are not supplied with fodder for the winter, and according to calculations [feed] is about 4,000 puds [72 tons] short. With the funds of the kolkhoz 4 former kulak homes were bought for the reconstruction of a cattle yard which the kolkhoz greatly needed, but these buildings are being pilfered by the kolkhozniks and burned as firewood. The equipment and harnesses of the kolkhoz are not repaired on time, as a result of which future use has been made impossible ... Up to the present time no income has been earned by the kolkhoz. At present, as a result of mismanagement and abuses on the part of the board of the kolkhoz, certain kolkhozniks ... talk of leaving ...

D. Soviet Textile Workers React to Demands for Greater Output, 1929

As soon as the meeting opened, the weavers made their way to the exit, and, as a result, of all the weavers working in the second shift, not more than 100 remained ... The weavers as they were leaving, shouted: "You well-fed devils have sucked the juices out of us enough. You hypocritical wall-eyes are pulling the wool over our eyes. For twelve years already you have driveled and agitated and stuffed our heads. Before you shouted that the factory owners exploited us, but the factory owners did not force us to work in 4 shifts, and there was enough of everything in the shops. Now we work in 4 shifts. Where before 4 men worked, now only one works. You are bloodsuckers, and that's not all, you still want to draw blood out of our veins. If you go to a shop now and want to buy something, the shops are empty; there are no shoes, no clothing; there is nothing the worker needs. But the [cost of] shares in the coöperative increase every day. Before we got along without any shares, and there was enough of everything. When the administration had to transfer the factory to an uninterrupted shift, they built refreshment stands, sold rolls, did everything for the worker so

---

[3] A hectare is about 2.5 acres

that he would support the proposal, but as soon as this project was put into effect what happened? They closed the refreshment stands, stopped selling rolls, again everything was as before. After 8 hours of work at the benches you are so worn out that your eyes are dimmed, and then they come to drown your senses completely. They have found a gimmick which they can keep using—you comrades are the managers of the factory. But when you look at the managers, you will see how they throw hundreds of us out of the factory onto the labor market. Here are managers for you! Before the bourgeoisie during a strike used to fire two or three participants and then let it go at that, and now not a year goes by without their cutting down. . . .

E. An American Works at the Magnitogorsk Blast Furnaces, 1932–1935

I spent two days stumbling around the immense iron mine which was producing upwards of five million tons of ore a year—nearly twenty-five per cent of the Soviet Union's total output. Twenty-five imported electric locomotives were at work pulling modern fifty-ton dump cars from cutting to crusher and thence to the agglomeration plant. I watched the electric excavators shoveling ore at the rate of fifty tons per minute, or else standing with their arms extended awaiting the arrival of empty cars to fill—a sight which always reminded me of a man surprised while eating, frozen with his fork halfway to his open mouth.

The mine did not appeal to me as a place to work. I went back to the blast furnaces to survey the possibilities there.

I had seldom seen any but the seedy side of the blast furnaces. Our gang of construction workers was called in only to do repair work when something went wrong.

During the winters of 1933 and 1934 the whole blast-furnace department was periodically shut down. The cold winds played havoc with the big furnaces. Gas lines, air lines, water pipes, all froze. Tons of ice hung down all around, sometimes collapsing steel structures with their weight. One of the four furnaces was shut down for general repairs most of the time.

One job we all remembered vividly was the demolition work after the disastrous explosion on No. 2 in 1934. We were kept busy night and day for two months. Owing to incorrect handling of the tapping hole a water jacket burned through and several cubic yards of water came into contact with the molten iron. The resultant blast blew the roof off the cast house, badly damaged the side of the furnace, and seriously injured everybody who was near-by at the time. No. 2 was shut down for two months for repairs, which cost the country some fifty thousand tons or iron. The repairs themselves cost a million and a half roubles, and occupied construction workers who could have been doing other things. Several people were tried in an attempt to fix responsibility for this accident, but there was no convictions. For two weeks previous to the disaster everybody connected with the furnace had known that the tapping hole was in bad shape. The foreman told the superintendent, who told the director, who told Zavenyagin, who telephoned Ordjonokidze, the People's Commissar of the USSR for the whole industry. Nobody realized the dangers of a bad tapping hole, and no one wanted to take the responsibility for shutting down the furnace prematurely at a time when the country needed pig iron very badly.

Inexperience and carelessness took a heavy toll in the blast-furnace transport system also. There were never enough ladles, mainly because of the fact that the railroad workers failed to put them squarely under the iron spouts or else neglected to take them away in time. In either case the ladles were inundated with hot iron, which ate through axles, wheels, and rails. . . .

By 1935 conditions were much improved. When I went scouting for a job I was struck by the appearance of No. 2. It was clean as a billiard table, the walls were whitewashed, tools hung neatly in their places. The gang went about its work quietly and efficiently.

The personnel was getting enough to eat. Everybody had given up trying to idolize proletarian labor on a komsomol[4] blast furnace (work on any blast furnace in any country is hot, unhealthy, dangerous, and gruelingly hard). The workers were enjoying some of the good things of life outside the mill. Their living conditions had improved, so that their attention could be focused on these things and their work regarded more realistically, as necessary labor which must be done efficiently and well in order to make possible the sunnier side of life. This point of view made possible strict labor discipline and efficient work. . . .

I knew a number of people working on the rolling mills, and one afternoon I set out to visit some of them. I walked down the immense blooming mill, where eight-ton ingots were tossed and shot around

---

[4] Communist Youth League, to which many Magnitogorsk workers belonged

by mechanized cranes and power-driven rollers, and entered the operator's cabin where a close friend of Masha's [Scott's Russian wife] worked.

Shura was an operator. She sat in a white cabin with large double glass windows directly over the rolls of the mill, and operated a score of control buttons and a dozen foot pedals. One set in motion the rolls which brought the ingots to the mill; another regulated their speed; several more controlled the large mechanical fingers which turned the ingot over; others reversed the direction, and so on. Shura had under her control a ten-thousand-horsepower direct-current motor which reversed its direction of rotation every ten or fifteen seconds and which had received the full benefit of several decades of the best electrical engineering experience in the United States, and a score of auxiliary motors of various kinds. The place was as clean as the operating room of a good hospital, and before I was fairly inside the door an electrician came up and told me no one was supposed to come in because it might upset the operator. They were trying to make a record, he told me. According to the project they should roll an ingot in less than a minute. Actually it took 3.2 minutes on the average and the record for an eight-hour shift was only two minutes, and an average of fifteen per cent of their production was not up to specifications. The electrician made a whole speech until a shortage of ingots caused a shutdown and Shura left her levers and came and talked to me.

She was a village girl who had been very sick, which had been the cause of her taking the operators' course instead of doing more active work. She was twenty-three, had the high cheekbones and open features of peasant stock, and the rather pale, nervous expression which had come as a result of her months in the hospital and subsequent work as blooming-mill operator. She came to work always with a red kerchief around her head, and the same serious, high-strung expression. She was never late, did not have to take off for a smoke like many of the men, and never came with a hang-over. Moreover, she had learned the technique of operating the blooming mill. She understood the electrical controls which she operated, and while her knowledge of theoretical physics was not extensive (she had gone to school only seven years), she knew enough to be a thoroughly competent operator. Beyond this it was a question of a simple mechanical and nervous dexterity, and at this she was a master. She was one of the best operators in Magnitogorsk. . . .

The Party Cell in Mill 500 included fifty-six members and candidates and twenty-one sympathizers. (Before one can become a full-fledged party member, it is necessary to go through the preliminary stages of sympathizer and candidate.) Weissberg, two of his assistants, three of the four shift engineers, four foremen, and the general foreman were all members of the party. Party members were privileged in that it was easier for them to get scholarships to schools, obtain new apartments, or get vacations in August instead of November.

But, on the other hand, a great deal more responsibility was put on them. If something went wrong and the brigade spoiled a job, a worker who was a party member was held as much or more responsible than the non-party brigadier. In case of vacancies in administrative posts, a party member was usually advanced faster than a non-party member of the same capabilities.

Mitya, as party organizer, probably more than any one person was responsible for the production successes in Mill 500. He had an efficient tongue, and knew how to talk to the workers, making them ashamed of bad work; getting them to try harder by making them understand what they were working for. He was fired with such tangible ardor for the construction of Socialism and everything connected with it that it impressed and influenced everyone with whom he came in contact.

Administrative and technical questions were discussed at regular closed party meetings, and inasmuch as most of the administrators were party members, important decisions could be, and were, made.

The development of 'vigilance' was a major party task. All party members had to be on the watch all the time for sabotage, spying, propaganda of the class enemy, counter-revolution, and similar phenomena. This boiled down to a rather abnormal interest of party members in other people's business and continual 'tattletaling,' and resultant suspicion and distrust particularly among the administrative personnel.

Document Set 27.4 References

A. A Smolensk Peasant Protests Collectivization, 1930
   Ivan Trofimovich Chuyunkov, in Merle Fainsod, *Smolensk Under Soviet Rule* (Cambridge, Mass.: Harvard University Press, 1955), 251–252.
B. The Soviet Secret Police Report on Resistance to Collectivization, 1934
   Report from Belyi, in Fainsod, 129.
C. The Authorities Try to Organize Kolkhoz Life, 1930s
   OGPU Report, 1932, in Fainsod, 265–266.
D. Soviet Textile Workers React to Demands for Greater Output, 1929
   OGPU Report, in Fainsod, 311.
E. An American Works at the Magnitogorsk Blast Furnaces, 1932–1935
   John Scott, *Behind the Urals*, enlarged ed., prepared by Stephen Kotkin (Bloomington: Indiana University Press, 1973, 1989), 139–144, 151–152.

DOCUMENT SET 27.5
The Stalin Revolution: Terror and Totalitarianism

The terror that Stalin unleashed on the Communist party and the Soviet people raged with particular ferocity between early 1935 and mid-1938, claiming millions of lives—many executed, many more vanished into forced-labor camps, the *Gulag*. Very few victims ever recorded their experiences, though every Soviet citizen experienced the fear of vulnerability. Document A, dating from June 1936, provides a rare glimpse of a lonely woman named Zinaida Cherkovskaya caught in the cycle of suspicion and denunciation that the Great Terror bred. Her letter to a local Party official was preserved in the Smolensk secret police files with the official's cryptic query whether a mistake might have been made "in regard to [her lover] Melnikov"; but the fate of all individuals involved is unknown except for the official to whom she wrote: he was later purged. Vladimir Tchernavin, a specialist in the fishing industry and the author of *I Speak for the Silent* (published in the United States in 1935), was relatively lucky: arrested in 1930 and sent to work on the White Sea Canal project that cost the lives of tens of thousands of political prisoners, he managed to escape to neighboring Finland. His account (Document B) of being interrogated meshes with later revelations about the secret police's methods of extracting confessions. Such procedures, along with actual torture and threats against relatives, almost certainly broke the prominent Communists whose cases were heard at the great purge trials. Document C is an extract from one of those trials, in 1937, dominated by Soviet Procurator-General Andrei Vyshinsky (1883–1954) and climaxed with the abject confessions of Karl Radek (1885–1939?) and other "Trotskyites." (Unlike the other defendants, who were shot, Radek drew a ten-year sentence but probably died in the *Gulag* in 1939.)

Many Western observers (including the American ambassador to the U.S.S.R.) refused to believe that these trials were hoaxes. In Document D the veteran socialists Sidney and Beatrice Webb (1859–1947; 1858–1943), who had lived all their lives in law-abiding Britain, defended the essential justice of the trials. Why? What is your explanation (informed by studying the documents and by reading *The Challenge of the West*) for why the Great Terror was unleashed and sustained? What does it say—or not say—for the reality of that much-debated phenomenon, *totalitarianism,* a system of dictatorial rule under which the state supposedly seeks (and achieves?) total control over the lives of its people?

A. A Woman Pleads That Her Lover Not Be Purged on Her Account

To the secretary of the Western Oblast Committee of the CPSU(b), Comrade Rumyantsev
Ivan Petrovich:

The matter about which I have decided to write you concerns the CPSU(b) member Melnikov, who works with you in the Obkom. In the investigation of Party documents he received a reprimand because of me, and because of this my life has been completely shattered, and therefore I cannot remain silent. I feel that I should write you everything frankly and honestly.

I am the daughter of a railroad employee. My father worked on the railroad for 35 years, 25 years at Pochinok Station, Western Oblast. A few years ago, at the age of 17, I married a veterinarian, who, upon finishing the institute, was assigned to Pochinok. It may have been because he was twice as old as I, or for another reason, but from the first days of our life together it became obvious that we had nothing in common, we were different types of people, strangers. At first I did not have enough resoluteness to speak of divorce, and than a baby came and I lived for the greater part of a year with my parents in Pochinok. When my husband was transferred to the Brasov stud farm, I started to study at the Brasov technical school, and he at the same time found himself a more suitable woman and began to live with her, although unofficially. I did not finish the technical school, because I did not want to live where he was, and I went to Moscow for a half-year course, leaving my daughter with my mother. After finishing the course, I returned to Pochinok and remained there to take care of my sick mother, who died within a year. From the moment I left Brasov I had no correspondence with my former husband. He lived openly with another woman, but no one in Pochinok, except my parents knew that we had separated. I was ashamed to talk about it. In 1932 I learned that he had been arrested for participation in a wreckers' organization and was exiled for 3 years. When things went badly with him he remembered me and our daughter and began to write, to beg forgiveness, etc. I never loved him, and after all this he didn't mean anything to me at all, but for the sake of our daughter I agreed to write him once in a while about her. After the death of my mother I continued to live with my daughter and my father in Pochinok. I began to work as a proofreader in the editorial office of the *Pochinok Kolkhoznik*. I worked enthusiastically, felt free, independent, wanted very much to live, wanted happiness, which I had never known. After a time Melnikov was appointed editor of the *P.K.* We became acquainted and liked each other. We began to see each other. On the first night I told him everything about myself, so that there would be no misunderstandings afterwards. I'm not going to begin to speak about him, but I fell head over heels in love with him. After some time we became intimate. Soon he was appointed assistant secretary of the raikom of the CPSU(b), and under the pretext that he had a great deal of work, we began to see each other less often, and after a time I was dismissed from work. It was Melnikov who did this, since there was not a new editor. It is impossible to express in words how I suffered. I had put my whole soul into my work, heard only approval from those around me, and the man who knew me best of all dismissed me from work. Often I was insistently pursued by the thought of suicide. This is cowardice, I know, but I felt that it was easier to die than to live without the man in whom I saw all happiness, all joy for myself. My little daughter forced me to dispel these thoughts.

I went to Smolensk and got a job as a proofreader in the House of the Press, and although I was the youngest proofreader, they soon appointed me copy editor on the kolkhoz newspaper. Soon Melnikov began to study in the Institute of Marxism-Leninism, and we met and spent our free time together, but he lived in the dormitory and I with my sister, since it was difficult to find a room in which to live together, and furthermore, it was easier and better for him to study while living with his fellow students. We lived in the hope that after he finished his studies we would finally settle things. But in the fall of 1935 I learned that they had created a whole case against Melnikov because he was seeing me. We began to see each other less frequently, and finally parted. Later I learned that they had reprimanded him because of me. I do not know to this day of what I was accused—nobody told me. But I was completely devoted to Melnikov, lived for his interests, and the fact that he had unpleasantness on account of me was painful and incomprehensible to me. My position was desperate.

After working a year in the House of the Press, I left work in August, as Melnikov had suggested. When I learned of his reprimand, I went to pieces. It seemed to me that not only had I no right to work, but that I could not live with people. I left my sister without telling her the reason, and I did not want to live with my father. I feared that there would be

unpleasantness for him on account of me, although he was in the decline of life.

In January 1936 I received a letter from my former husband, in which he wrote that they had freed him before his term was up and that he had worked for a year in the system of the NKVD in Kazakhstan. At the end he wrote: if during these four years you did not get married, during your vacation come to visit me with your daughter, to see Kazakhstan. At that time I could not reason sensibly. I decided that my life was at an end anyway, and I went to him with my daughter, but I could not live with him for one day. I told him I had loved somebody else for three years now, and that only despair could have pushed me to this rash journey. He decided that I had sacrificed myself for the sake of my daughter. He really does not know the situation, and I did not want to tell him. He hopes that sometime I will "quiet down" and will be able to live with him. In April he went to a health resort and I went to my relatives in Smolensk. I am not deceived in regard to him. I am not a young girl. I am 24 years old and have lived through many adversities of life, and things were good with me only with Melnikov. I will not be able to fall out of love with him or forget him, and I never want to build my life without him. I met him accidentally in Smolensk, told him how much I had suffered without him, and he told me that I should live only in my work, but that we should not see each other.

But I think I shall go mad. I don't want to be reconciled to it. I cannot get it through my head that in our free country, where the children of kulaks are not responsible for the crimes of their parents, I should be tortured my whole life because my former husband was once sentenced, and I do not have the right to be the wife of the man I love. Though he is a Party member, I am not an alien. I have concealed nothing, I have deceived no one, and I do not want to be a criminal without a crime.

I have recounted my whole life and all my "crimes" to you, Ivan Petrovich, more frankly than to my own father. At the cost of my life I would be happy to prove to you the truthfulness of my words.

I trust you implicitly, and whatever your opinion will be on this problem, it will be law for me.

ZINAIDA CHERKOVSKAYA

B. An Arrested "Wrecker" Is Interrogated, 1930

It was my second day in prison—my second cross-examination. I was called before the tea ration was given out and had only time to eat an apple.

"How do you do?" the examining officer asked, scanning me attentively to see if I showed signs of a sleepless night.

"All right."

"It isn't so good in your cell. You are in 22?"

"A cell like any other."

"Well, did you do any thinking? Are you going to tell the truth *today?*"

"Yesterday I told only the truth."

He laughed. "What will it be today—not the truth?"

Then he returned to the subject of the cell.

"I tried to choose a better cell for you, but we are so crowded. I hope we will come to an understanding and that I will not be forced to change the regime I have ordered for you. The third category is the mildest: exercise in the yard, permission to receive food parcels from outside, a newspaper and books. The first two categories are much stricter. Remember, however, that it depends entirely on me; any minute you may be deprived of everything and transferred to solitary confinement. Or rather, this depends not on me but on your own behavior, your sincerity. The more frank your testimony, the better will be the conditions of your imprisonment. . . ."

He spoke slowly, looking me straight in the eye, emphasizing his words with evident pleasure and relish, watching for their effect.

"Did you know Scherbakoff? He was a strong man, but I broke him and forced him to confess."

With great difficulty I controlled myself before replying.

"I don't doubt for a minute that you use torture, and if you believe that this assists in discovering the truth and speeding up the investigation, and since Soviet laws permit its use, I would suggest that you don't give up mediaeval methods: a little fire is a wonderful measure. Try it! I am not afraid of you. Even with that you can't get anything out of me."

"Well, we will see about that later. Now let's get down to business. Let's talk about your acquaintances. Did you know V. K. Tolstoy, the wrecker, executed in connection with the case of the '48'?"

"Yes, I knew him. How could I not know him when he was the director of the fishing industry in the north?" I replied in frank astonishment. "We both worked in it for more than twenty years."

"And did you knew him well?"

"Very well."

"How long did you know him?"

"From childhood."

His manner changed completely; he hurriedly picked up a statement sheet and placed it in front of me.

"Write down your confession."

"What confession?"

"That you knew Tolstoy, that you were in friendly relation with him from such and such a time. I see that we will come to an understanding with you; your frankness will be appreciated. Write."

He evidently was in a hurry, did not quite know what he was saying, afraid that I might reverse my statements.

I took the sheet and wrote down what I had said.

"Excellent. Let's continue."

Then followed a barrage of questions about Tolstoy, about Scherbakoff and other people that I had known. He did not find me quite so tractable and we launched into a battle of wits that kept up hour after hour. He questioned me with insistence and in great detail, trying without success to make me give dates.

"You'll not succeed in outwitting me," he snapped sharply. "I advise you not to try. I am going home to dinner now and you will stay here till evening. This examination will continue—not for a day or two, but for months and, if necessary, for years. Your strength is equal to mine. I will force you to tell what we need."

After threatening me still further he handed me some sheets of paper.

"You are going to state in writing your opinion regarding the building of a fertilization factory in Murmansk, its equipment and work in the future. I'll soon be back; when I return, your comments on these questions must be completed."

He put on his overcoat and left. His assistant took his place, and I busied myself with my writing. It was three or four hours before he returned, already evening.

Although I had eaten almost nothing for three days. I was still in good fighting form. He questioned me about the buying of a ship from abroad, trying to make me say that here was "wrecking," because the price had been exorbitant and the ship itself had proved unsatisfactory. It was most confusing and his questions far-fetched. We talked and we argued, but I would not give the answers he wanted.

He began on another tack. . . .

"All right," he said. "And what is your attitude regarding the subject of the fish supply in the Sea of Barents in connection with the construction of trawlers as provided for by the Five-Year Plan?"

Now he had broached a subject with which I *could* have a direct connection. The evening was already changing into night, but I was still sitting in the same chair. I was becoming unconscious of time: was it my second day in prison or my tenth? In spite of the depressing weariness, mental and physical, which was taking hold of me, I told him that I thought the fresh fish supply should be minutely and thoroughly investigated. I tried to make him see the hazards of the fishing industry in Murmansk and the enormous equipment that would be necessary to meet the proposals of the Five-Year Plan.

"And thus you confess that you doubted the practicability of the Five-Year Plan? he said with a smile of smug satisfaction.

What could one say? I believed, as did everybody, that the plan was absurd, that it could not be fulfilled. For exactly such statements—no, for only a suspicion of having such thoughts—forty-eight men had been shot. . . .

C. The Trial of the Seventeen, 1937: Andrei Vishinsky Prosecutes; Karl Radek Confesses

The President: The session is resumed. Comrade Vyshinsky, Procurator of the U.S.S.R., will speak for the Prosecution.
Vyshinsky: Comrade Judges and members of the Supreme Court of the Union of Soviet Socialist Republics. In proceeding to perform my last duty in the present case I cannot but deal with several highly important specific features of the present trial.

In my opinion these specific features are, first of all, that the present trial, in a certain sense, sums up the criminal activities of the Trotskyite conspirators who for many years have systematically, and with the assistance of the most repulsive and despicable weapons, fought against the Soviet system, against the Soviet state, against the Soviet power and against our Party. This trial sums up the struggle waged against the Soviet state and the Party by these people, who started it long before the present time, started it during the life of our great teacher and organizer of the Soviet state, Lenin. While Lenin was alive these people fought against Lenin; and after his death they fought against his great disciple, that loyal guardian of Lenin's behests and the continuator of his cause—Stalin.

Another specific feature of this trial is that it, like a searchlight, illuminates the most remote recesses, the secret byways, the disgusting hidden corners of the Trotskyite underground.

This trial has revealed and proved the stupid obstinacy, the reptile cold-bloodedness, the cool calculation of professional criminals with which the Trotskyite bandits have been waging their struggle against the U.S.S.R. They stuck at nothing—neither wrecking, nor diversions, nor espionage, nor terrorism, nor treason to their country.

When several months ago, in this very hall, in this very dock, the members of the so-called united Trotskyite-Zinovievite terrorist centre were sitting; when the Supreme Court, represented by the Military Collegium, was trying those criminals, all of us listened to the story of their crimes that unfolded itself like a nightmare scene before us, with horror and revulsion.

Every honest man in our country, every honest man in every country in the world could not then but say:

This is the abyss of degradation!

This is the limit, the last boundary of moral and political decay!

This is the diabolical infinitude of crime!

Every honest son of our country thought to himself: such hideous crimes cannot be repeated. There cannot be in our country any more people who have fallen so low and who have so despicably betrayed us.

But now we are again overcome with the sentiments that we felt not long ago! Once again across our anxious and wrathful vision pass frightful scenes of monstrous crime, of monstrous treachery, of monstrous treason. . . .

Many years ago our Party, the working class, our whole people, rejected the Trotskyite-Zinovievite platform as an anti-Soviet, anti-socialist platform. Our people banished Trotsky from our country; his accomplices were expelled from the ranks of the Party as traitors to the cause of the working class and socialism. Trotsky and Zinoviev were routed, but they did not subside; they did not lay down their arms.

The Trotskyites went underground, they donned the mask of repentance and pretended that they had disarmed. Obeying the instructions of Trotsky, Pyatakov and the other leaders of this gang of criminals, pursuing a policy of duplicity, camouflaging themselves, they again penetrated into the Party, again penetrated into Soviet offices, here and there they even managed to creep into responsible positions of state, concealing for a time, as has now been established beyond a shadow of doubt, their old Trotskyite, anti-Soviet wares in their secret apartments, together with arms, codes, passwords, connections and cadres.

Beginning with the formation of an anti-Party faction, passing to sharper and sharper methods of struggle against the Party, becoming, after their expulsion from the Party, the principal mouthpiece of all anti-Soviet groups and trends, they became transformed into the vanguard of the fascists operating on the direct instructions of foreign intelligence services....

The President: Accused Radek.

Radek: Citizen Judges, after I have confessed to the crime of treason to the country there can be no question of a speech in defence. There are no arguments by which a grown man in full possession of his senses could defend treason to his country. Neither can I plead extenuating circumstances. A man who has spent 35 years in the labour movement cannot extenuate his crime by any circumstances when he confesses to a crime of treason to the country. I cannot even plead that I was led to err from the true path by Trotsky. I was already a grown man with fully formed views when I met Trotsky. And while in general Trotsky's part in the development of these counter-revolutionary organizations is tremendous, at the time I entered this path of struggle against the Party, Trotsky's authority for me was minimal.

I joined the Trotskyite organization not for the sake of Trotsky's petty theories, the rottenness of which I realized at the time of my first exile, and not because I recognized his authority as a leader, but because there was no other group upon which I could rely in those political aims which I had set myself. I had been connected with this group in the past, and therefore I went with this group. I did not go because I was drawn into the struggle, but as a result of my own appraisal of the situation, as the result of a path I had voluntarily chosen. And for this I bear complete and sole responsibility—a responsibility which you will measure according to the letter of the law and according to your conscience as judges of the Soviet Socialist Republic.

And with this I might conclude my last plea, if I did not consider it necessary to object to the view of the trial—as regards a partial, not the main, point—which was given here and which I must reject, not from my own personal standpoint, but from a political standpoint. I have admitted my guilt and I have given full testimony concerning it, not from the simple necessity of repentance—repentance may be an internal state of mind which one need not necessarily share with or reveal to anybody—not from love of the truth is general—the truth is a very bitter one, and I have already said that I would prefer to have been shot thrice rather than to have had to admit it—but I must admit my guilt from motives of the general benefit that this truth must bring....

... this trial has revealed two important facts. The intertwining of the counter-revolutionary organizations with all the counter-revolutionary forces in the country—that is one fact. But this fact is tremen-dous objective proof. Wrecking work can be established by technical experts; the terrorists activities were connected with so many people that the testimony of these people, apart from material evidence, presents an absolute picture. But the trial is bicentric, and it has another important significance. It has revealed the smithy of war, and has shown that the Trotskyite organization became an agency of the forces which are fomenting a new world war....

And finally, we must say to the whole world, to all who are struggling for peace: Trotskyism is the instrument of the warmongers. We must say that with a firm voice, because we have learned it by our own bitter experience. It has been extremely hard for us to admit this, but it is a historical fact, for the truth of which we shall pay with our heads....

D. Sidney and Beatrice Webb Report *The Truth About Soviet Russia*, 1942

... During the three or four years from the autumn of 1917 to 1922, the Bolshevik Government had established itself in Moscow and had succeeded in repelling the German, British, French, American and Japanese invasion, of that part of the territory of Tsarist Russia which the Bolsheviks thought themselves capable of defending. For some time after they had made a formal peace with their recent enemies they were confronted not only by local rebellions but by continuous and extensive underground sabotage in the newly established plants and factories, mines and means of communication, workers' flats and hospitals, by the remnant of the upholders of the old Tsarist régime, all of which had to be summarily suppressed. But this obviously necessary use of force was not the only task awaiting the revolutionary government. History proves that in all violent revolutions, those who combine to destroy an old social order seldom agree as to what exactly should be the political and economic pattern of the new social organization to be built up to replace it. Even our own limited revolution of 1689 in Great Britain, whereby a Protestant king by Parliamentary statute was substituted for a Catholic king by Divine Right, was followed, for nearly a hundred years, by generation after generation of conspirators to whom treason and rebellion, spying and deceit, with or without the connivance of a foreign power, were only part of what they deemed to be a rightful effort to overturn an even worse state of home and foreign affairs than they had joined as rebels to destroy. Thus, when we published the second edition of *Soviet Communism* in 1937, the outstanding scandal, so hostile critics of the Soviet Union declared, were the Treason Trials which took place in the thirties, not only of old Bolshevik comrades of Lenin and opponents of Stalin's subsequent policy, but also of the best known commanding officers of the Red Army, many of whom had been Tsarist generals, transferring their allegiance to the Bolshevik Government in order to defend their native land from invasion by German, British, American, French and Japanese armies; but who, it was alleged and I think proved, had begun to intrigue with the German Army against the new social order of the Soviet Union. The most important of these conspiracies was the Trotsky movement against the policy of building up socialism in one country as impracticable and insisting that the Bolshevik Party should abide by what was held to be the Marx-Lenin policy of promoting proletarian revolutions throughout the world. The success of the Soviet Government in instituting not only a political but an industrial democracy, and thereby enormously increasing the health, wealth and culture of the inhabitants, and the consequent recognition of the USSR as a Great Power, discredited the Trotsky movement, which I think was finally liquidated by the murder of Trotsky in Mexico by one of his own followers.[1] Today, and for some time, there has been no sign of conspiracies or faked conspiracies within the Soviet Union. The fear of German invasion and the consequent dominance of the Nazi system of racial oppression has made clear to all the *bona fide* citizens of the USSR the overwhelming desirability of keeping out of world war as long as possible, meanwhile devoting their energies to increasing their means of livelihood and their defensive power; whilst the capitalist democracies and Axis powers were engaged in mutual mass murder and the destruction of property. When the German attack plunged Russian into war it was immediately apparent that the inhabitants of the USSR, whether soldiers or civilians, men, women and young people, were so convinced of the benefits yielded to the Socialist Fatherland that they resisted not only with reckless courage, but with considerable skill and ingenuity the powerful onslaught of the highly mechanized German Army hitherto victorious conquerors of one country after another....

Far more repugnant to our western political habits is the absolute prohibition within the USSR of any propaganda advocating the return to capitalist profit-making or even to any independent thinking on the fundamental social issues about possible new ways of organizing men in society, new forms of social activity, and new development of the socially established code of conduct. It is upon this power to think new thoughts, and to formulate even the most unexpected fresh ideas, that the future progress of mankind depends. This disease of orthodoxy in a milder form is not wholly absent in the capitalist political democracies. No one suggests that Switzerland is not a political democracy, and yet, as I have already noted, members of the Society of Jesus are not only refused citizenship but are actually banished from their native land, a penalization which has been extended of late years to the members of the Third International, assuredly a strangely discordant couple to be linked together in the dock of Swiss Courts of Justice accused of the propaganda of living philosophy incompatible with the public safety. Likewise the U.S.A., in some of the constituent States, through the device of Primaries, has excluded the Communist Party, and today even the Socialist Party, from selecting the candidates for election to the legislature of those states; while in one or two state being a member of the Communist Party is punished by penal servitude....

Whenever a country is threatened with foreign invasion or revolutionary upheaval, the suppression of sects advocating disobedience to the law, sabotage or giving information to the enemy is a necessary use of force on the part of a government, however democratically representative of the majority of the inhabitants it may be....

Document Set 27.5 References

A. A Woman Pleads That Her Lover Not Be Purged on Her Account
   Zinaida Cherkovskaya, in Merle Fainsod, *Smolensk Under Soviet Rule* (Cambridge, Mass.: Harvard University Press, 1955), 225, 228–229.

B. An Arrested "Wrecker" Is Interrogated, 1930
   Vladimir Tchernavin, *I Speak for the Silent* (Newton Center, Mass.: Charles T. Branford, 1935).

C. The Trial of the Seventeen, 1937: Andrei Vishinsky Prosecutes; Karl Radek Confesses
   Andrei Vyshinsky and Karl Radek, court proceedings, in Thomas Riha, ed., *Readings in Russian Civilization* (Chicago: University of Chicago Press, 1964),3:662–663, 667–668, 671.

D. Sidney and Beatrice Webb Report *The Truth About Soviet Russia*, 1942.
   Sidney and Beatrice Webb, *The Truth About Soviet Russia, 1942* (New York: Longman's, 1942), 66–69, 71–73.

---

[1] In reality, Trotsky was assassinated by a Stalinist agent.

DOCUMENT SET 27.6
The Coming of World War II

Unlike the causes of World War I, over which scholars continue to debate trying to assign blame for the outbreak of that conflict, the responsibility for World War II rests by universal informed agreement upon Adolf Hitler. Document A, extracts from the so-called Hossbach Memorandum, records the Führer's monologue (taken down by an underling named Hossbach) before high-ranking Nazi party, diplomatic, and military leaders in November 1937. In it Hitler declares his intention of going to war to win "living space" for Germany by 1943–1945 at the latest. At about the same time Hitler ousted most of the surviving old-fashioned conservative nationalists from leadership posts in the army and the foreign office, installing fervent Nazis or compliant toadies in their place. Knowing this, what other signs of Hitler's strategy does this document suggest to you?

Austria and Czechoslovakia, which figured prominently in the Hossbach Memorandum, both fell to Germany in 1938 without a shot being fired. Sheer bullying, aided by strong Nazi sentiment among many of Austria's non-Jewish citizenry, allowed the Führer to grab Austria in March 1938. Next, Czechoslovakia was forced to cede its strategically critical but German-inhabited (and fervently pro-Nazi) borderland, the Sudetenland—the key pressure being exerted by Czechoslovakia's western friends, France and Britain, at the Munich conference in late September 1938. When British prime minister Neville Chamberlain (1869–1940) got a hero's welcome for bringing home "peace in our time," one of his relatively few public critics was Conservative member of Parliament Winston Churchill (1874–1965, Document B).

The greatest shock on the road to war, however, came in August 1939, when the Soviet Union and Nazi Germany ended six years of ceaseless mutual vilification by signing a nonaggression pact (Document C). A "Secret Additional Protocol" divided up eastern Europe. The consternation of western communists, who had seen the U.S.S.R. as the world's bulwark against fascism as well as the homeland of socialism, may be grasped from Document D, a letter from the French correspondent of *Izvestia*, addressed to one of the French Communist party leaders.

Having conquered Poland in the *Blitzkrieg* of September 1939, Hitler turned his armies westward in the spring of 1940. Denmark and Norway fell in April; between May 20 and June 18 he overran the Low Countries and had so thoroughly hammered the French that by the latter date Paris had been evacu-

ated and a collaboration-minded cabinet was offering the Germans peace. June 18 was also the date on which Britain's new prime minister (since May 10), Winston Churchill, announced that his country would stand alone against the Nazi war machine (Document E).

What had brought the western democracies to the edge of this debacle?

A. Hitler Makes His Plans, 1937

The Führer began by stating that the subject of the present conference was of such importance that its discussion would, in other countries, certainly be a matter for a full Cabinet meeting, but he—the Führer—had rejected the idea of making it a subject of discussion before the wider circle of the Reich Cabinet just because of the importance of the matter. His exposition to follow was the fruit of thorough deliberation and the experiences of his 4 1/2 years of power. He wished to explain to the gentlemen present his basic ideas concerning the opportunities for the development of our position in the field of foreign affairs and its requirements, and he asked, in the interests of a long-term German policy, that his exposition be regarded, in the event of his death, as his last will and testament.

The Führer then continued:

The aim of German policy was to make secure and to preserve the racial community [*Volksmasse*] and to enlarge it. It was therefore a question of space. . . .

Germany's problem could only be solved by means of force and this was never without attendant risk. The campaigns of Frederick the Great for Silesia and Bismarck's wars against Austria and France had involved unheard-of risk, and the swiftness of the Prussian action in 1870 had kept Austria from entering the war. If one accepts as the basis of the following exposition the resort to force with its attendant risks, then there remain still to be answered the questions "when" and "how." In this matter there were three cases [*Fälle*] to be dealt with:

Case 1: Period 1943–1945

After this date only a change for the worse, from our point of view, could be expected.

The equipment of the army, navy, and *Luftwaffe*, as well as the formation of the officer corps, was nearly completed. Equipment and armament were modern; in further delay there lay the danger of their obsolescence. In particular, the secrecy of "special weapons" could not be preserved forever. The recruiting of reserves was limited to current age groups; further drafts from older untrained age groups were no longer available.

Our relative strength would decrease in relation to the rearmament which would by then have been carried out by the rest of the world. If we did not act by 1943–1945, any year could, in consequence of a lack of reserves, produce the food crisis, to cope with which the necessary foreign exchange was not available, and this must be regarded as a "waning point of the regime." Besides, the world was expecting our attack and was increasing its counter-measures from year to year. It was while the rest of the world was still preparing its defenses [*sich abriegele*] that we were obliged to take the offensive.

Nobody knew today what the situation would be in the years 1943–1945. One thing only was certain, that we could not wait longer.

On the one hand there was the great *Wehrmacht*, and the necessity of maintaining it at its present level, the aging of the movement and of its leaders; and on the other, the prospect of a lowering of the standard of living and of a limitation of the birth rate, which left no choice but to act. If the Führer was still living, it was his unalterable resolve to solve Germany's problem of space at the latest by 1943–1945. The necessity for action before 1943–1945 would arise in cases 2 and 3.

Case 2

If internal strife in France should develop into such a domestic crisis as to absorb the French Army completely and render it incapable of use for war against Germany, then the time for action against the Czechs had come.

Case 3

If France is so embroiled by a war with another state that she cannot "proceed" against Germany.

For the improvement of our politico-military position our first objective, in the event of our being embroiled in war, must be to overthrow Czechoslovakia and Austria simultaneously in order to remove the threat to our flank in any possible operation against the West. In a conflict with France it was hardly to be regarded as likely that the Czechs would declare war on us on the very same day as France. The desire to join in the war would, however, increase among the Czechs in proportion to any weakening on our part and then her participation could clearly take the form of an attack toward Silesia, toward the north or toward the west.

If the Czechs were overthrown and a common German-Hungarian frontier achieved, a neutral attitude on the part of Poland could be the more certainly counted on in the event of a Franco-German conflict. Our agreements with Poland only retained their force as long as Germany's strength remained unshaken. In the event of German setbacks a Polish action against East Prussia, and possibly against Pomerania and Silesia as well, had to be reckoned with.

On the assumption of a development of the situation leading to action on our part as planned, in the years 1943–1945, the attitude of France, Britain, Italy, Poland, and Russia could probably be estimated as follows:

Actually, the Führer believed that almost certainly Britain, and probably France as well, had already tacitly written off the Czechs and were reconciled to the fact that this question would be cleared up in due course by Germany. Difficulties connected with the Empire, and the prospect of being once more entangled in a protracted European War, were decisive considerations for Britain against participation in a war against Germany. Britain's attitude would certainly not be without influence on that of France. An attack by France without British support, and with the prospect of the offensive being brought to a standstill on our western fortifications, was hardly probable. . . . It would of course be necessary to maintain a strong defense [*eine Abriegelung*] on our western frontier during the prosecution of our attack on the Czechs and Austria. And in this connection it had to be remembered that the defense measures of the Czechs were growing in strength from year to year, and that the actual worth of the Austrian Army also was increasing in the course of time. Even though the populations concerned, especially of Czechoslovakia, were not sparse, the annexation of Czechoslovakia and Austria would mean an acquisition of footstuffs for 5 to 6 million people, on the assumption that the compulsory emigration of 2 million people from Czechoslovakia and 1 million people from Austria was practicable. The incorporation of these two States with Germany meant, from the politico-military point of view, a substantial advantage because it would mean shorter and better frontiers, the freeing of forces for other purposes, and the possibility of creating new units up to a level of about twelve divisions, that is, one new division per million inhabitants.

Italy was not expected to object to the elimination of the Czechs, but it was impossible at the moment to estimate what her attitude on the Austrian question would be; that depended essentially upon whether the Duce were still alive.

The degree of surprise and the swiftness of our action were decisive factors for Poland's attitude. Poland—with Russia at her rear—will have little inclination to engage in war against a victorious Germany.

Military intervention by Russia must be countered by the swiftness of our operations; however, whether such an intervention was a practical contingency at all was, in view of Japan's attitude, more than doubtful. . . .

B. Winston Churchill Attacks the Munich Agreement, 1938

MR. CHURCHILL. . . . I will therefore, begin by saying the most unpopular and most unwelcome thing. I will begin by saying what everybody would like to ignore or forget but which must nevertheless be stated, namely, that we have sustained a total and unmitigated defeat, and that France has suffered even more than we have.

VISCOUNTESS ASTOR. Nonsense!

MR. CHURCHILL. When the noble Lady cries "Nonsense," she could not have heard the Chancellor of the Exchequer admit in his illuminating and comprehensive speech just now that Herr Hitler had gained in this particular leap forward in substance all he set out to gain. The utmost my right hon. Friend, the prime minister, has been able to secure by all his immense exertions, by all the great efforts and mobilization which took place in this country, and by all the anguish and strain through which we have passed in this country, the utmost he has been able to gain [*Hon. Members: "Is Peace"*]. I thought I might be allowed to make that point in its due place, and I propose to deal with it. The utmost he has been able to gain for Czechoslovakia and in the matters which were in dispute has been that the German dictator, instead of snatching his victuals from the table has been content to have them served to him course by course.

The Chancellor of the Exchequer said it was the first time Herr Hitler has been made to retract (I think that was the word) in any degree. We really must not waste time, after all this long debate, upon the difference between the positions reached at Berchtesgaden, at Godesberg and at Munich. They can be very simply epitomized, if the House will permit me to vary the metaphor. One pound was demanded at the pistol's point. When it was given, two pounds were demanded at the pistol's point. Finally, the dictator consented to take one pound, seventeen shillings and six pence, and the rest in promises of good will for the future.

Now I come to the point, which was mentioned to me just now from some quarters of the House, about the saving of peace. No one has been a more resolute and uncompromising struggler for peace than the prime minister. Everyone knows that. Never

has there been such intense and undaunted determination to maintain and to secure peace. This is quite true. Nevertheless, I am not quite clear why there was so much danger of Great Britain or France being involved in a war with Germany at this juncture if, in fact, they were ready all along to sacrifice Czechoslovakia. . . .

There never can be any absolute certainty that there will be a fight if one side is determined that it will give way completely. . . .

I have always held the view that the maintenance of peace depends upon the accumulation of deterrents against the aggressor, coupled with a sincere effort to redress grievances. Herr Hitler's victory, like so many of the famous struggles that have governed the fate of the world, was won upon the narrowest of margins. After the seizure of Austria in March, we faced this problem in our debates. I ventured to appeal to the government to go a little further than the prime minister went, and to give a pledge that in conjunction with France and other powers they will guarantee the security of Czechoslovakia, while the Sudeten Deutsch question was being examined either by a League of Nations commission, or some other impartial body, and I still believe that if that course had been followed events would not have fallen into this disastrous state. . . .

France and Great Britain together, especially if they had maintained a close contact with Russia, which certainly was not done, would have been able in those days in the summer, when they had the prestige, to influence many of the smaller states of Europe. . . . Such a combination, prepared at the time when the German dictator was not deeply and irrevocably committed to his new adventure, would, I believe, have given strength to all those forces in Germany which resisted this departure, this new design. . . .

All is over. Silent, mournful, abandoned, broken, Czechoslovakia recedes into the darkness. She has suffered in every respect by her association with the Western democracies and with the League of Nations, of which she has always been an obedient servant. . . . We in this country, as in other liberal and democratic countries, have a perfect right to exalt the principle of self-determination, but it comes ill out of the mouths of those in totalitarian states who deny even the smallest element of toleration to every section and creed within their bounds. But, however you put it, this particular block of land, this mass of human beings to be handed over, has never expressed the desire to go into the Nazi rule. I do not believe that even now—if their opinion could be asked, they would exercise such an option. . . .

I venture to think that in the future the

Czechoslovak state cannot be maintained as an independent entity. You will find that in a period of time which may be measured by years, but may be measured only by months, Czechoslovakia will be engulfed in the Nazi regime. . . . It is the most grievous consequence which we have yet experienced of what we have done and of what we have left undone in the last five years: five years of futile good intention, five years of eager search for the line of least resistance, five years of uninterrupted retreat of British power, five years of neglect of our air defenses. . . .

C. The Nazi-Soviet Pact, 1939

Guided by the desire to strengthen the cause of peace between Germany and the Union of Soviet Socialist Republics, and basing themselves on the fundamental stipulations of the Neutrality Agreement concluded between Germany and the Union of Soviet Socialist Republics in April, 1926, the German Government and the Government of the Union of Soviet Socialist Republics have come to the following agreement:

Article 1.

The two contracting parties undertake to refrain from any act of force, any aggressive act, and any attacks against each other undertaken either singly or in conjunction with any other Powers.

Article 2.

If one of the contracting parties should become the object of war-like action on the part of a third Power, the other contracting party will in no way support the third Power.

Article 3.

The Governments of the two contracting parties will in future remain in consultation with one another in order to inform each other about questions which touch their common interests.

Article 4.

Neither of the two contracting parties will join any group of Powers which is directed, mediately or immediately, against the other party.

Article 5.

In case disputes or conflicts on questions of any kind should arise between the two contracting parties, the two partners will solve these disputes or conflicts exclusively by friendly exchange of views or if necessary by arbitration commissions.

Article 6.

The present agreement is concluded for the duration of ten years with the stipulation that unless one of the contracting partners denounces it one year before its expiration, it will automatically be prolonged by five years.

Article 7.

The present agreement shall be ratified in the shortest possible time. The instruments of ratification are to be exchanged in Berlin. The treaty comes into force immediately after is has been signed

[The "secret protocol"]. . . .

1. In the event of a territorial-political restructuring in the territories belonging to the Baltic States (Finland, Estonia, Latvia and Lithuania), the northern border of Lithuania shall also constitute the border of the spheres of interest between Germany and the USSR. In this connection the interest of Lithuania in the Vilna district is recognized by both sides.

2. In the event of a territorial-political restructuring of the territories belonging to the Polish state, the spheres of interest of the USSR and Germany shall be defined approximately by the line of the rivers Pissa, Narew, Weichsel [Vistula] and San. The question of whether the interests of both sides make the maintenance of an independent Polish state appear desirable, and how this state's borders should be defined, can ultimately by determined only in the course of further political developments. In any case, the two governments will resolve this question by way of amicable agreement.

3. In regard to southeastern Europe, the Soviet side emphasizes that it has interests in Bessarabia. The German side declares that it has no political interest at all in these territories.

4. This protocol is to be treated as top secret by both sides.

Moscow, August 23, 1939 [signed] VON RIBBENTROP
W. MOLOTOV

D. A French Communist Is Baffled by the Hitler-Stalin Pact

How is it possible to appraise without rage and indignation the fact that our newspapers celebrate the German-Soviet pact as a providential event for the French people and that they present it as the most precious instrument of peace, as the most powerful obstacle to the outbreak of the war? All this at the very moment when thousands of French citizens are called to the colors, when almost all of them, if not all, are leaving for the frontiers altogether convinced that they are drafted precisely because Stalin refused to sign a defensive pact with France and England and instead signed an agreement with Hitlerite Germany. . .

To the man in the street it appears that the approaching war is a direct result of the German-Soviet pact. And at this very moment *L'Humanité* and *Ce Soir* [French Communist newspapers] choose to shout 'The peace is saved, long live Stalin,' without even attempting to give a serious explanation for their extraordinary jubilation.

E. Britain Stands Alone, 1940

The military events which have happened during the past fortnight have not come to me with any sense of surprise. Indeed, I indicated a fortnight ago as clearly as I could to the House that the worst possibilities were open, and I made it perfectly clear then that whatever happened in France would make no difference to the resolve of Britain and the British Empire to fight on, "if necessary for years, if necessary alone." During the last few days we have successfully brought off the great majority of the troops we had on the lines of communication in France—a very large number, scores of thousands—and seven-eighths of the troops we have sent to France since the beginning of the war, that is to say, about 350,000 out of 400,000 men, are safely back in this country. Others are still fighting with the French, and fighting with considerable success in their local encounters with the enemy. We have also brought back a great mass of stores, rifles and munitions of all kinds which had been accumulated in France during the last nine months.

We have, therefore, in this island to-day a very large and powerful military force. . . .

This brings me, naturally, to the great question of invasion from the air and of the impending struggle between the British and German air forces. It seems quite clear that no invasion on a scale beyond the capacity of our land forces to crush speedily is likely to take place from the air until our air force has been definitely overpowered. In the meantime, there may be raids by parachute troops and attempted descents of airborne soldiers. We should be able to give those gentry a warm reception both in the air and if they reach the ground in any condition to continue the dispute. But the great question is, can we break Hitler's air weapon? Now, of course, it is a very great pity that we have not got an air force at least equal to that of the most powerful enemy within striking distance of these shores. But we have a very powerful air force which has proved itself far superior in quality, both in men and in many types of machine, to what we have met so far in the numerous fierce air battles which have been fought. In France, where we were at a considerable disadvantage and lost many machines on the ground, we were accustomed to inflict losses of as much as two to two and a half to one. In the fighting over Dunkirk, which was a sort of no man's land, we undoubtedly beat the German air force, and this gave us the mastery locally in the air, and we inflicted losses of three or four to one. . . .

There remains the danger of bombing attacks, which will certainly be made very soon upon us by the bomber forces of the enemy. It is true that the German bomber force is superior in numbers to ours, but we have a very large bomber force also which we shall use to strike at military targets in Germany without intermission. I do not at all underrate the severity of the ordeal which lies before us, but I believe our countrymen will show themselves capable of standing up to it. . . .

What General Weygand called the "Battle of France" is over. I expect that the battle of Britain is about to begin. Upon this battle depends the survival of Christian civilization. Upon it depends our own British life and the long continuity of our institutions and our empire. The whole fury and might of the enemy must very soon be turned on us. Hitler knows that he will have to break us in this island or lose the war. If we can stand up to him all Europe may be free, and the life of the world may move forward into broad, sunlit uplands, but if we fail then the whole world, including the United States, and all that we have known and cared for, will sink into the abyss of a new dark age made more sinister, and perhaps more prolonged, by the lights of a perverted science. Let us therefore brace ourselves to our duty and so bear ourselves that if the British Commonwealth and Empire lasts for a thousand years men will still say, "This was their finest hour."

Document Set 27.6 References

A. Hitler Makes His Plans, 1937
  "The Hossbach Memorandum," in Keith Eubank, ed., *World War II: Roots and Causes,* 2d ed. (Lexington, Mass.: D. C. Heath, 1992), 110, 115–117.
B. Winston Churchill Attacks the Munich Agreement, 1938
  Hansard's Parliamentary Debates, 5th Series, vol. 339, cols. 359–371, 373, in Walter Arnstein, ed., *The Past Speaks,* 2d ed. (Lexington, Mass.: D. C. Heath, 1993), 2:373–375.
C. The Nazi-Soviet Pact, 1939
  German Library of Information, *Documents on the Events Preceding the Outbreak of War,* compled and published by the German Foreign Office (Berlin, 1939; New York, 1940), 370–371.
D. A French Communist Is Baffled by the Hitler-Stalin Pact
  Henry W. Ehrmann, *French Labor from the Popular Front to Liberation* (New York: Oxford University Press, 1947), 142.
E. Britain Stands Alone, 1940
  Winston Churchill, June 18, 1940 Speech Before House of Commons, in Walter Arnstein, ed., *The Past Speaks,* 2d ed. (Lexington, Mass.: D. C. Heath, 1993), 2:376–378.

The documents in this set focus not on high policy but on the wartime experiences of ordinary people, military and civilian. As you read them, ask what kinds of social ties the war disrupted and forged.

Breaking the 1939 nonaggression pact, Hitler invaded the U.S.S.R. in June 1941, enormously escalating the stakes of the European conflict but at last making the bid for eastern "living space" that had always obsessed him. The war on Soviet territory was waged with exceptional ferocity. The Nazis openly aimed (albeit with a good deal of internal squabbling over the division of spoils) at creating in the east a vast colonial empire: the Jews and gypsies exterminated, the Slavs reduced to helots, and the Germans as the master race. Not surprisingly, the German army gave no quarter to Communists, and even ordinary Soviet prisoners (who at the outset had surrendered in droves) often received barbaric treatment. The hated collective farms remained in place. A formidable guerrilla movement arose in the U.S.S.R. in 1942. Yet the three extracts collected as Document A suggest that even under such circumstances many Soviet citizens tried to lie low and sit out the war. (Number 1 is a proclamation by the partisans to Soviet soldiers and civilians caught behind German lines; number 2 is from a memoir by a committed guerrilla fighter; number 3 is a German army order for rooting out the partisans.)

The turning point of the war, most authorities believe, came at the end of 1942 and the beginning of 1943, when the Red Army stopped the Germans at Stalingrad and counterattacked, capturing an entire, starving German army. Document B is an anonymous letter from a German soldier that was among the final mailbags waiting to be airlifted out of Stalingrad before the German capitulation; it was never delivered, and the writer's fate is unknown.

Civilians lived through—and died in—the horrors of mass air bombardment, making Warsaw, Rotterdam, London, Hamburg, Dresden, and hundreds of other cities truly front-line battlefields. In Document C an upper-middle-class woman recalls such raids on London in February 1944, after a three-year respite from bombing after the 1940–1941 "Blitz." A similar air of trying to maintain a semblance of normality appears in the diary of a journalist in Berlin in the late spring of 1944, just as the Allies were invading the Continent and the Germans were unleashing the first guided-missile (V-1) raids on London. Yet notice the difference in tone and in public morale.

Underground resistance was always nerve-wracking and dangerous. Precise numbers are impossible to calculate (and postwar claims of participation are often hard to verity), but the ranks of actual resistance fighters must have been low in most places. Document E, a set of guidelines distributed surreptitiously to Communist activists in wartime Germany, suggests why.

Use these documents and the account in *The Challenge of the West* to prepare a brief analysis of the kinds of ways in which war and its political context reshaped private lives, and of how personal experiences or memories helped individuals to endure, even to prevail.

A. Soviet Partisans Fight the Germans

1. All members of the armed forces who escaped . . . and are at home, also all men in the class of 1925 [i.e. born in that year], report to your regular units or join the partisan units. Those who remain in hiding and continue to sit at home in order to save their skins, and those who do not join in the patriotic war to help destroy the German robbers, also those who desert to the Fascist army and help the latter to carry on a robber war against the Soviet people, are traitors to the homeland and will be liquidated by us sooner or later.

2. But there were all kinds of men among the escaped prisoners-of-war. Some had voluntarily surrendered to the Germans. Later, when they had been eaten up by lice in the camps and had become sick and tired of being punched in the jaw, they repented and escaped to join the partisans. Not all of them by any means told us the whole truth. And, of course, very few of them admitted they had surrendered of their own free will.

These men joined the partisans only because there was nothing else for them to do. They didn't want to go back to the Germans but, on the other hand, they didn't fight them any too energetically either.

Some of the formerly encircled men who joined us had been "hubbies" [stragglers who had married local girls]. These were soldiers who for one reason or another had fallen behind the army . . . . Among the "hubbies" there were specimens who would have been glad to sit out the war behind a woman's skirt, but the Hitlerites would either drive them off to work in Germany or else make them join the police. After turning this over in his mind such a man would come to the conclusion that, after all, joining the partisans was more advantageous.

3. The combating of the enemy behind the front line is still not being taken seriously enough. Treacherous, cruel partisans and unnatural women are still being made prisoners-of-war, and guerrilla fighters dressed partly in uniforms or plain clothes, and vagabonds, are still being treated as proper soldiers and sent to prisoner-of-war camps. . . . Such an attitude by the troops can only be explained as complete thoughtlessness. . . . If isolated partisans are found using firearms in the rear of the army, drastic measures are to be taken. These measures will be extended to that part of the male population who were in a position to hinder or report the attacks. . . . The fear of German counter-measures must be stronger than the threats of the wandering Bolshevik remnants.

B. A German Soldier Writes His Last Letter from Stalingrad, 1942

. . . Dearest, I think of you all the time. Today, standing in the chow line I thought of you again. Of the wonderful food you used to cook. My socks are in shreds, too, and I can't get rid of my cough any more. No pills are available for it. You could send me cough syrup, but don't use any glass bottles. Have you caught cold too? Always put on something good and warm. Do you have enough coal? Just go and see A—, he got lumber from me for his furniture. Let him give you coal for it now. I hope Uncle Paul has nailed the weather stripping to your windows; otherwise it will be too late for it this year. I did not celebrate Christmas here. I was on the road with the car, and we got stuck in the snow because we went the wrong way. But we soon got out again. I have decided that next year we will celebrate a real Christmas, and I am going to give you a beautiful present.

It is not my fault that I can't give it to you now. The Russians are all around us, and we won't get out again until Hitler gets us out. But you must not tell that to anyone. It is supposed to be a surprise.

C. Mrs. Robert Henrey Recalls the Bombing Raids on London, February 1944

The sharp raids of February 1944 broke a lull of nearly three years. The weather was bitterly cold, with

occasional snow, but it was gone by morning, leaving a hard frost in the Green Park and a thin coating of ice on the sump.

Nobody was surprised to hear the sirens again, because the newspapers were filled with stories about the Allied raids on Germany. The unknown factor was the extent to which the enemy could go and the improvements he had made in his technique. This uncertainty, added to tiredness and war strain, made many people more nervous than during the battle of London [1940–1941], and when the bombs began to drop near the centre of town, one saw again the early evening trek towards the tube stations. As soon as it became dark a great hush fell over the city.

This mantle of silence was one of the strangest phenomena. One could hear it, yes, actually hear it. On several occasions when I was at home with the curtains drawn, this sudden blanketing fell upon my ears and made me aware that it was now officially night. It was most impressive on the evening following a big raid, when people were still under the domination of fear. One felt a shudder down the spine. There was something about it which was not of this world.

These raids were not at all like those of 1940–1. They were noisier but seldom lasted more than an hour, at any rate in their intensity, whereas in the old days, or rather, in the old nights, the sirens wailed regularly at dusk and did not sound the all clear until half an hour before dawn.

London itself had also changed. It was now crowded with American soldiers, many of whom, only a few months earlier, were pursuing peaceful occupations in city or farm. In addition to this great army from across the Atlantic, there had come into London a tremendous number of people of every sort and kind who had not been through any of the previous raids. The population had therefore to be welded together and tempered before attaining that hardness and stoicism with which it faced the much more terrifying raids of May 1941.

The bombs did not really hit the heart of the town until Sunday, 20th February. Before that we had only seen fires round the perimeter. But on this occasion there was quite a large conflagration in Pall Mall, and one saw other patches of deep red seemingly quite near but more difficult to locate.

D. Journalist Ursula von Kardorff Chronicles Life in Berlin, June 1944

Berlin, 31 May 1944 Pessimism is increasing. The Russian front is drawing closer. Where should my flight take me, I often ask myself, because I am prepared to flee. But for the time being we are still dancing on a stage that grows smaller and smaller and is surrounded by an abyss.

Spent the day before yesterday with Ulrich Dörtenbach in the Rose Theater. [Saw] Lessing's *Miss Sara Simpson*, starring Inge of Austria. This theater in the eastern section of the city, in the midst of the destroyed but, even in earlier times, desolate Frankfurter Allee, is one of the cheeriest showplaces in Berlin. Workers, craftsmen, housewives, and the businessmen who live in this section have had season tickets for decades. Here one is able to find a piece of the Berlin of old, no "class-conscious proletarians," no KdF [*Kraft durch Freude*, Strength Through Joy] functions, no termites, only individual human beings. Hauptmann, Ibsen, Schiller, Shakespeare, and good old burlesque are on the program. Never trash and never hokum. In the refreshment room—a well-proportioned room with mirrors built in 1877—a small orchestra played during intermission. I could have caressed them all, musicians as well as audience; these people, with their tired faces and stooping posture, who in spite of difficult conditions, poor nourishment, and the constant threat of air raids, come here to find release from tension.

6 June 1944 It began tonight. The invasion. Excitement among the editorial staff. We have received instructions to write rejoicingly about this long-desired event. Hurrah, the time is finally here; now we will show them how we will chase them out again. Finally, we are moving toward the ultimate victory!

However, all 'round [there is] only skepticism and fear of air raids. Great doubt if the Atlantic fortifications will hold.

10 June 1944 As a substitute [for the editor] I was charged with composing the front page, and had to carry a photograph from the *Times* which showed the invasion. Incredible that it was cleared by the censors. It is a frightening sight—hundreds of little dots, paratroopers and tiny boats; it looks like a swarm of grasshoppers attacking the coast. The defense appears meager. In any case, they have gotten a foothold, and "Fortress Europe" is now besieged from two sides as well as by air. Maybe now things will move rapidly.

Berlin is in a curious mood. A mixture of apathy and inordinate pleasure-seeking. The janitor's wife, who cleans at my place, warningly raises her index finger [and proclaims]: "So, soon it'll be over with little Adolf, maybe it'll go fast." No one saves these days. . . . Witnessed ordinary soldiers leaving gratuities as high as half a month's pay. The waiter at a small pub at the Gendarme Market bought himself a small farm—purely from the tips he received by procuring a bottle of Mosel [wine]. Money flows through hands like water.

16 June 1944 I arrive at the editor's office, Willy looks at me, he seems disturbed. In front of him lies the blue page containing the secret news reports: the apocalypse has begun, we are shooting at London with long-distance weapons that are supposed to destroy the city. The new weapon is called V-I. By noon the reports are publicly aired. According to Goebbels, V-II, V-III, and V-IV are soon to follow. The whole world will blow up by the time V-V rolls around.

In all the pubs, places where usually no one speaks his mind, there is much talk of vengeance, Allied vengeance, that is. A soldier who boasted that soon we would have the war won was contradicted. It is hard to fool Berliners. Goebbels has it nowhere so tough as here. Lately everyone speaks of gas warfare. That would really crown all of this horror.

During warm evenings when friends come over, we sit with them on the roof, which is flat. Several benches are up there, covered with dust. . . . All 'round one sees burned-out houses without roofs and lofts.

E. "How a Communist Must Conduct Himself When Engaging in Underground Activities"

1. You are no longer to have a good, reliable friend or acquaintance with whom you can discuss your activity.
2. Therefore, do not tell anything to someone who might know; instead tell only him who must know.
3. It is not necessary for a friend to know more about personal and internal organizational matters than is absolutely necessary in order to do one's work.
4. If when walking you slouch and shuffle along, behave conspicuously on the street, and talk a lot with your hands, you will give police an opportunity to describe you quickly and ultimately track you down.
5. The shortest way is not always the best; that is, arrange to meet your friends with whom you are working so that on the way there you will have enough time to shake possible pursuers. Allow enough time for the next rendezvous, and set an example by being punctual.
6. It is best not to talk at all about our activities in public places, public transportation, or taverns; but if you do, do it in the form of an everyday conversation.

7. At our meetings, remember to agree beforehand what you will say if the Gestapo raids the meeting.

8. Carry potential evidence on your person only if it cannot be avoided, and then only for as brief a time as possible. Keep your apartment devoid of evidence.

9. Carefully check all apartments, operative meeting places, and addresses necessary in carrying out your work.

10. No matter what, all contacts gone awry should be broken off. Make arrangements with your associates beforehand so that you will find each other again later, even without knowing names or each other's place of residence.

11. Organize the exchange of informational materials on short notice and between only two individuals. Therefore, consider well beforehand the distribution numbers and the locations.

12. Terminate normal relationships with each other. As a private person you should also have nothing to do with other friends, even if you know that they can be trusted. This is precisely why you should not burden them needlessly. If you should happen to meet on the street, walk past each other. No one but the Gestapo is interested in whether or not you are acquainted.

13. Do not make [an] habitual haunt out of any one tavern, cinema, or park. You do not need to be known to more people than necessary.

14. Fight hard and with conviction against rumors and general feelings of panic on certain occasions. No one is to pass on unverified messages. Everyone must immediately attempt to determine the author of such things. . . .

15. Remember, carelessness is not synonymous with courage. Our work requires skill, so that by applying all measures of caution and paying heed to the smallest detail we can be maximally effective in our work for the masses. Through the proper distribution of energy and application of flexible tactics we can succeed. . . .

It is obvious that in conspiratorial matters new situations and variations will always present themselves. Therefore, you should periodically discuss the methods of the opponent and determine your own course of action accordingly. That way you will have the advantage of always being one step ahead, because in the meantime the opponent must first adjust to our tactics. Ruthlessly, but in a comradely spirit, make the guilty party accountable if the rules are broken. Through truly solid political activity you can establish the basis of such mass support that, regardless of how bloody the terror is, it will not be capable of harming you.

Let these words of Lenin guide you in your organizational activity: "Whosoever, during this period of illegality, breaches Bolshevik discipline even ever so slightly—he aids, willingly or not, our enemy, the bourgeoisie."

Document Set 27.7 References

A. Soviet Partisans Fight the Germans
   Matthew Cooper, *The Nazi War Against Soviet Partisans, 1941–1944* (New York: Stein and Day, 1979), 71–72, 52.
B. A German Soldier Writes His Last Letter from Stalingrad, 1942
   Last Letters from Stalingrad, Franz Schneider and Charles Gullans, trans. (New York: Signet, 1961), 78–79.
C. Mrs. Robert Henrey Recalls the Bombing Raids on London, February 1944
   Mrs. Robert Henrey, *London Under Fire*, 1940–1945 (London: J. M. Dent, 1969), 174–175.
D. Journalist Ursula von Kardorff Chronicles Life in Berlin, June 1944
   Ursula von Kardorff, *Berliner Aufzeichnungen* (Munich: Biederstein Verlag, 1962), 156–160, 163, 262. Translated by Dieter Kuntz.
E. "How a Communist Must Conduct Himself When Engaging in Underground Activities"
   Nationalsozialistische Deutsche Arbeiter-Partei, Hauptarchiv 1919–1945 (Stanford: Hoover Institution on War, Revolution, and Peace), in Benjamin Sax and Dieter Kuntz, eds. and trans., *Inside Hitler's Germany* (Lexington, Mass.: D. C. Heath, 1992), 477–478.

DOCUMENT SET 27.8
The Holocaust

No "smoking gun" has ever been found in the form of a direct written order from Adolf Hitler to exterminate the Jews under Nazi control. Most likely no such order was ever put down in writing; in your opinion, why not? Only a kind of spoken consensus apparently developed among the high Nazi leadership as to what was to be done. Document A—an extract from a speech by Heinrich Himmler (1900–1945) to his SS leaders in October 1943—suggests something of the mentality with which the top Nazis pursued their ultimate war aim. On this evidence, how would you analyze Himmler's psychological makeup? How would you explain the 1941 account (Document B) of Traian Popovici, the mayor of the Romanian city (now in Ukraine) of Czernowitz, who witnessed the confinement of the local Jews in a ghetto? Why were there so few in positions of influence who spoke out? Why did so many collaborate?

Ever since the Holocaust, Jews have somberly debated whether they could—or should—have offered more effective resistance to genocide. (A determination never again to be passive victims is, for example, part of the ethos of the State of Israel, founded by Holocaust survivors in 1948.) Nevertheless, scattered Jewish resistance did take place. Around Vilnius (today the capital of Lithuania), some Jews managed to escape being rounded up and fought as partisans in the countryside; and within the Vilnius ghetto a desperate attempt at resistance resulted in the distribution of the January 1942 manifesto excerpted in Document C.

Almost none of the Vilnius Jews survived the ghetto and the death camps. What arrival in such a camp—in this case, Auschwitz—was like can be inferred from the harrowing account (Document D) of a Transylvanian Jewish women, Olga Lengyel, who survived most likely because she came late. (The Hungarian and Transylvanian Jews were spared deportation until late 1944.)

It is sobering to turn from such accounts to the confession of Rudolf Hoess, the Auschwitz commandant, who was convicted and executed by the Polish authorities in March 1947 (Document E). Remember that Hoess wrote this account while in British custody, awaiting being turned over to the Poles. What do you make of his attempt to exculpate himself? Compare his confession to Himmler's 1943 attempt to swathe the extermination campaign in robes of unspoken glory (Document A). Why did this horror happen?

A. Heinrich Himmler Commends His Men on Carrying Out Their "Unpleasant Duty," 1943

I also want to talk to you, quite frankly, on a very grave matter. Among ourselves it should be mentioned quite frankly, and yet we will never speak of it publicly. Just as we did not hesitate on June 30th, 1934 to do the duty we were bidden, and stand comrades who had lapsed, up against the wall and shoot them, so we have never spoken about it and will never speak of it. It was that tact which is a matter of course and which I am glad to say, is inherent in us, that made us never discuss it among ourselves, never to speak of it. It appalled everyone, and yet everyone was certain that he would do it the next time if such orders are issued and if it is necessary.

I mean the clearing out of the Jews, the extermination of the Jewish race. It's one of those things it is easy to talk about—"The Jewish race is being exterminated," says one party member, "that's quite clear, it's in our program—elimination of the Jews, and we're doing it, exterminating them." And then they come, 80 million worthy Germans, and each one has his decent Jew. Of course the others are vermin, but this one is an A-1 Jew. Not one of all those who talk this way has witnessed it, not one of them has been through it. Most of *you* must know what it means when 100 corpses are lying side by side, or 500 or 1,000. To have stuck it out and at the same time—apart from exceptions caused by human weakness—to have remained decent fellows, that is what has made us hard. This is a page of glory in our history which has never been written and is never to be written, for we know how difficult we should have made it for ourselves, if—with the bombing raids, the burdens and the deprivations of war—we still had Jews today in every town as secret saboteurs, agitators and trouble-mongers. We would now probably have reached the 1916/17 stage when the Jews were still in the German national body.

We have taken from them what wealth they had. I have issued a strict order, which SS-Lieutenant General Pohl has carried out, that this wealth should, as a matter of course, be handed over to the Reich without reserve. We have taken none of it for ourselves. Individual men who have lapsed will be punished in accordance with an order I issued at the beginning, which gave this warning: Whoever takes so much as a mark of it, is a dead man. A number of SS men—there are not very many of them—have fallen short, and they will die, without mercy. We had the moral right, we had the duty to our people, to destroy this people which wanted to destroy us. But we have not the right to enrich ourselves with so much as a fur, a watch, a mark, or a cigarette or anything else. Because we have exterminated a bacterium we do not want, in the end, to be infected by the bacterium and die of it. I will not see so much as a small area of sepsis appear here or gain a hold. Wherever it may form, we will cauterize it. Altogether, however, we can say, that we have fulfilled this most difficult duty for the love of our people. And our spirit, our soul, our character has not suffered injury from it.

B. A Romanian Official Describes the Czernowitz Ghetto

On the morning of October 11 . . . I looked out the window. It was snowing and—I could not believe my eyes: on the street in front of my window long columns of people were hurrying by. Old people supported by children, women with infants in their arms, invalids dragging their maimed bodies along, all with their luggage in wagons or on their backs, with hastily packed suitcases, bedding, bundles, clothes; they all made silent pilgrimage into the city's valley of death, the ghetto. . . .

Great activity in the city hall. . . . The "abandoned" wealth of the Jews was to be inventoried and their dwellings sealed. Romanianization departments were to be formed and with police assistants to be distributed throughout the city neighborhoods.

It first dawned on me then that the procedure had been a long time in the planning. I hurried to military headquarters where General Jonescu informed me of events. He let me see the promulgated ordinances. . . . I paged through the instructions in haste and read the regulations for the functioning of the ghetto. The bakeries were to be under city hall control, as were the [food] markets. Then I hurried again to the city hall in order to see to the measures necessary for the uninterrupted provisioning of bread, food, and especially milk for the children. For the time being, this was the role that providence allotted to me, thanks to the military cabinet.

Only those who know the topography of the city can measure how slight was the space for the ghetto to which the Jewish population was confined and in which, under pain of death, they had to be by six o'clock.

In this part of the city, even with the greatest crowding, ten thousand people could be housed at most. Fifty thousand had to be brought in, not counting the Christian population already living there. Then, and even today, I compare the ghetto to a cattle pen.

The accommodation possibilities were minimal. Even if the available rooms were to receive thirty or more people, a great number would have to seek shelter from the snow and rain in corridors, attics, cellars, and similar sorts of places. I would rather not speak of the demands of hygiene. Pure drinking water was lacking; the available public fountains did not suffice. I noted that the city already suffered from a water shortage since two of the three pumping stations had been destroyed. The strong odors of sweat, urine, and human waste, of mold and mildew, distinguished the quarter from the rest of the city. . . . It was a miracle that epidemics that would endanger the whole city did not break out. With surprising speed the ghetto was nearly hermetically sealed with barbed wire. At the main exits, wooden gates were erected and military guards posted. I do not know whether it was intentional, but the effect was clear: the despised were being intimidated. . . .

Although . . . the regulation concerning the ghetto categorically stated that no one could enter without the authorization of the governor, no one observed this rule. As early as the second day after the erection of the ghetto, there began a pilgrimage consisting of ladies of all social strata and intellectual jobbers, well known to the Czernowitz public. Persons of "influence" from all strata and professions—hyenas all—caught the scent of cadaverous souls among the unfortunates. Under the pretext that they were in the good graces of the governor, the military cabinet, or the mayor, they began the high-level pillaging of all that was left to the unfortunates. Their gold coins, jewelry, precious stones, furs, and valuable foodstuffs (tea, coffee, chocolate, cocoa) were supposedly to be used to bribe others or to compensate [the interlopers] for putting in a good word to save someone from deportation. Trading in influence was in full bloom. Another category of hyena was the so-called friend who volunteered to protect all these goods from theft or to deliver them to family members and acquaintances elsewhere in the country. Individuals never previously seen in the city of Czernowitz streamed in from all corners of the country in order to draw profit from a human tragedy. If the deportation with all its premeditation was in itself monstrous, then the exploitation of despair surpassed even this. . . .

C. A Jewish Manifesto Calls for Resistance to the Holocaust

Let us not be led like sheep to the slaughter!

I. Let us defend ourselves during a deportation!

For several months now, day and night, thousands and tens of thousands have been torn away from our midst. . . . The illusion still lives within us that they are still alive somewhere, in an undisclosed concentration camp, in a ghetto.

In the face of the next day which arrives with the horror of deportation and murder, the hour has struck to dispel the illusion: There is no way out of the ghetto, except the way of death!

No illusion greater than that our dear ones are alive.

II. On guard over national honor and dignity

We work for Germans and Lithuanians. Everyday we come face to face with our employers, the murderers of our brothers. Great the shame and pain, observing the conduct of Jews, stripped of the awareness of human dignity.

Comrades!

Don't give the foe the chance to ridicule you!

When a German ridicules a Jew—don't help him laugh!

Don't play up to your murderers!

Denounce the bootlickers at work!

Denounce the girls who flirt with Gestapo men!

Work slowly, don't speed!

Show solidarity! If misfortune befalls one of you—don't be vile egotists—all of you help him.

Jewish agents of the Gestapo and informers of all sorts walk the streets. If you get hold of one such, sentence him—to be beaten until death!

D. A Transylvanian Woman Arrives at Auschwitz

When I learned that our barrack chief, a Polish woman named Irka, had been in the camp for four years, I felt reassured.

However, when I hinted at these thoughts to Irka, she made short work of my illusions.

"You think they are going to let you live?" she jeered. "You are burying your head in the sand. All of you will be killed, except a few rare cases, who will have, perhaps, a few months. Have you a family?"

I told her the circumstances under which I had taken my parents and my children with me, and how we had been separated from one another when we arrived at camp.

She shrugged her shoulders with an air of indifference, and told me coldly:

"Well, I can assure you that neither your mother, your father, nor your children are in this world any more. They were liquidated and burned the same day you arrived."

I listened, petrified.

"No, no, that's impossible," I mumbled. This timid protest made the block chief beside herself with impatience.

"Since you don't believe me, look for yourself!" she cried, and dragged me to the door with hysterical gestures. "You see those flames? That's the crematory oven. It would go bad with you if you let on that you knew. Call it by the name we use: the bakery. Perhaps it is your family that is being burned this moment."

[Olga Lengyel hears that someone has seen her husband and finds him on the other side of the barbed wire fence.]

Though I had lost my sensitivity after the first experiences in the camp, I still was painfully shocked when I saw my husband again. He, too, stared at me with unbelieving eyes. In my tattered dress, in which I was half exposed, in my stripped drawers, and with my clipped head, I must have shocked him even worse than he did me.

We stood there silently, clocking our emotions.

As briefly as I could, I told him about the deaths of our two sons and of my parents. I spoke without expression in a tone that rang strangely in my own ears.

I said: "I cannot believe that human beings, even Germans, would be capable of killing little children. Can you believe it? If it is true, then there is no longer any reason for living."

E. The Commandant at Auschwitz Confesses, 1946

This mass extermination, with all its attendant circumstances, did not, as I know, fail to affect those who took part in it. . . .

Many of the men involved approached me as I went my rounds through the extermination buildings, and poured out their anxieties and impressions to me, in the hope that I could allay them.

Again and again during these confidential conversations I was asked: is it necessary that we do all this? Is it necessary that hundreds of thousands of women and children be destroyed? And I, who in my innermost being had on countless occasions asked myself exactly this question, could only fob them off and attempt to console them by repeating that it was done on Hitler's order. I had to tell them that this extermination of Jewry had to be, so that Germany and our posterity might be freed forever from their relentless adversaries.

There was no doubt in the mind of any of us that Hitler's order had to be obeyed regardless, and that it was the duty of the SS to carry it out. Nevertheless we were all tormented by secret doubts.

I myself dared not admit to such doubts. In order to make my subordinates carry on with their task, it was psychologically essential that I myself appear convinced of the necessity for this gruesomely harsh order. . . .

On one occasion two small children were so absorbed in some game that they quite refused to let their mother tear them away from it. Even the Jews of the Special Detachment were reluctant to pick the children up. The imploring look in the eyes of the mother, who certainly knew what was happening, is something I shall never forget. The people were already in the gas chamber and becoming restive, and I had to act. Everyone was looking at me. I nodded to the junior noncommissioned officer on duty and he picked up the screaming, struggling children in his arms and carried them into the gas chamber, accompanied by their mother who was weeping in the most heart-rending fashion. My pity was so great that I longed to vanish from the scene; yet I might not show the slightest trace of emotion.

I had to see everything. I had to watch hour after hour, by day and by night, the removal and burning of the bodies, the extraction of the teeth, the cutting of the hair, the whole grisly, interminable business. I had to stand for hours on end in the ghastly stench, while the mass graves were being opened and the bodies dragged out and burned.

I had to look through the peephole of the gas chambers and watch the process of death itself, because the doctors wanted me to see it.

I had to do all this because I was the one to whom everyone looked, because I had to show them all that I did not merely issue the orders and make the regulations but was also prepared myself to be present at whatever task I had assigned to my subordinates.

Even Mildner and [Adolf] Eichmann, who were certainly tough enough, had no wish to change places with me. This was one job which nobody envied me.

I had many detailed discussions with Eichmann concerning all matters connected with the "final solu-

tion of the Jewish question," but without ever disclosing my inner anxieties. I tried in every way to discover Eichmann's innermost and real convictions about this "solution."

Yes, every way. Yet even when we were quite alone together and the drink had been flowing freely so that he was in his most expansive mood, he showed that he was completely obsessed with the idea of destroying every single Jew that he could lay his hands on. Without pity and in cold blood we must complete this extermination as rapidly as possible. Any compromise, even the slightest, would have to be paid for bitterly at a later date.

In the face of such grim determination I was forced to bury all my human considerations as deeply as possible. . . .

My family, to be sure, were well provided for in Auschwitz. Every wish that my wife or children expressed was granted them. The children could live a free and untrammeled life. My wife's garden was a paradise of flowers. The prisoners never missed an opportunity for doing some little act of kindness to my wife or children and thus attracting their attention.

No former prisoner can ever say that he was in any way or at any time badly treated in our house. My wife's greatest pleasure would have been to give a present to every prisoner who was in any way connected with our household. . . .

The children always kept animals in the garden, creatures the prisoners were forever bringing them. Tortoises, martens, cats, lizards: there was always something new and interesting to be seen there. In summer they splashed in the wading pool in the garden, or in the Sola. But their greatest joy was when Daddy bathed with them. He had, however, so little time for all these childish pleasures. Today I deeply regret that I did not devote more time to my family. I always felt that I had to be on duty the whole time. This exaggerated sense of duty has always made life more difficult for me than it actually need have been. Again and again my wife reproached me and said: "You must think not only of the service always, but of your family too."

Document Set 27.8 References

A. Heinrich Himmler Commends His Men on Carrying Out
   Their "Unpleasant Duty," 1943
   U.S. Chief of Counsel for the Prosecution of Axis
   Criminality, *Nazi Conspiracy and Aggression* (Washington,
   D.C.: U.S. Government Printing Offfice, 1946), vol. 4, doc.
   no. 1919-PS, 563–564.

B. A Romanian Official Describes the Czernowitz Ghetto
   Traian Popovici, "Mein Bekenntnis," in Richard Levy, ed. and
   trans., *Antisemitism in the Modern World* (Lexington, Mass.:
   D.C. Heath, 1991), 243–244.

C. A Jewish Manifesto Calls for Resistance to the Holocaust
   Lucy S. Dawidowicz, ed., *A Holocaust Reader* (New York:
   Behrman House, 1976), 334–336.

D. A Transylvanian Woman Arrives at Auschwitz
   Olga Lengyel, *Five Chimneys: The Story of Auschwitz*
   (Chicago: Ziff-Davis, 1947), 31–34.

E. The Commandant at Auschwitz Confesses, 1946
   Rudolph Hoess, *Commandant of Auschwitz*, trans.
   Constantine FitzGibbons (New York: Weidenfeld and
   Nicolson, 1959), 169–174.

28

The Atomic Age, 1945–1962

DOCUMENT SET 28.1
The Atomic Age Begins

Discovery of the atom's internal structure and of the tremendous energy that it stores dates back to work in the 1890s by the New Zealand-born British physicist Lord Rutherford (1871–1931). Throughout the 1920s and 1930s scientists around the world labored to clarify the mysteries of the atom, culminating at the end of 1938 with the discovery of fission in uranium by the Austrian Jewish physicist Lise Meitner (1878–1968)—soon to flee Nazi Germany—and her German colleague Otto Hahn (1879–1968). Realization of this breakthrough's potential implications led a small group of Central European émigré physicists, headed by Albert Einstein, to warn President Franklin D. Roosevelt in March 1939 that Nazi Germany must not be allowed to build the world's first atomic bomb. Similar warnings and further scientific evidence from Great Britain, as well as alarm generated by Hitler's initially successful invasion of the Soviet Union, led the U.S. government in 1941 secretly to launch the most elaborate and expensive research-and-development undertaking ever organized, code-named the Manhattan Project. Led by the project's scientific director, the American J. Robert Oppenheimer, many of the world's most brilliant physicists and chemists managed to overcome the technical hurdles that were baffling the scientists in Germany, Japan, and the Soviet Union who had also begun experimenting with nuclear weaponry. On July 16, 1945, the world's first nuclear device was successfully tested at Almogordo, New Mexico. Two days later the Manhattan Project's military director, General Leslie Groves, wrote the report to U.S. Secretary of War Henry Stimson that is excerpted as Document A. Less than a month later, on August 6 and 9, the United States detonated atom bombs over the Japanese cities of Hiroshima and Nagasaki, bringing World War II to an end.

The postwar generation realized that humanity must either learn to control atomic energy or be destroyed by it. A few years after Hiroshima, Einstein (1879–1955), who had discovered relativity theory in 1905 and who had been a pacifist most of his life, spoke out on the implications of releasing atomic energy (Document B). Nuclear energy was, indeed, widely understood to offer a cheap and inexhaustible source of electrical power, as can be seen in the 1955 British government report excerpted as Document C. Yet simultaneously there arose in the West a passionate protest movement demanding unilateral nuclear disarmament, even at the price of allowing the Soviet Union a monopoly on atomic weaponry. Great Britain's Bertrand Russell (1872–1970), one of the twentieth century's great philosophers and mathematicians, in his old age became a leader of the ban-the-bomb movement (Document D); ironically, as Lord Russell explains in this extract dating from 1959, before the U.S.S.R. exploded its own nuclear device in 1949, he had advocated using the threat of atomic bombardment to force the Soviet Union to behave more reasonably.

Evaluate the reasoning of Einstein and Russell in the light of the other two documents in this set and of what you have learned from *The Challenge of the West* about the advent of the nuclear age.

A. Two American Generals Witness the First Atomic Test, July 18, 1945

18 July 1945

TOP SECRET
MEMORANDUM FOR THE SECRETARY OF WAR.
SUBJECT: The Test.

1. This is not a concise, formal military report but an attempt to recite what I would have told you if you had been here on my return from New Mexico.

2. At 0530, 16 July 1945, in a remote section of the Alamogordo Air Base, New Mexico, the first full scale test was made of the implosion type atomic fission bomb. For the first time in history there was a nuclear explosion. And what an explosion! It resulted from the atomic fission of about 13-1/2 pounds of plutonium which was compressed by the detonation of a surrounding sphere of some 5000 pounds of high explosives. The bomb was not dropped from an airplane but was exploded on a platform on top of a 100-foot high steel tower.

3. The test was successful beyond the most optimistic expectations of anyone. . . . There were tremendous blast effects. For a brief period there was a lighting effect within a radius of 20 miles equal to several suns in midday; a huge ball of fire was formed which lasted for several seconds. This ball mushroomed and rose to a height of over ten thousand feet before it dimmed. The light from the explosion was seen clearly at Albuquerque, Santa Fe, Silver City, El Paso and other points generally to about 180 miles away. The sound was heard to the same distance in a few instances but generally to about 100 miles. Only a few windows were broken although one was some 125 miles away. A massive cloud was formed which surged and billowed upward with tremendous power, reaching the substratosphere at an elevation of 41,000 feet, 36,000 feet above the ground, in about five minutes. . . . Huge concentrations of highly radioactive materials resulted from the fission and were contained in this cloud.

4. A crater from which all vegetation had vanished, with a diameter of 1200 feet and a slight slope toward the center, was formed. In the center was a shallow bowl 130 feet in diameter and 6 feet in depth. The material within the crater was deeply pulverized dirt. The material within the outer circle is greenish and can be distinctly seen from as much as 5 miles away. The steel from the tower was evaporated. 1500 feet away there was a four-inch iron pipe 16 feet high set in concrete and strongly guyed. It disappeared completely. . . .

11. Brigadier General Thomas F. Farrell was at the control shelter located 10,000 yards south of the point of explosion. His impressions are given below:

"The scene inside the shelter was dramatic beyond words. In and around the shelter were some twenty-odd people concerned with last minute arrangements prior to firing the shot. Included were: Dr. Oppenheimer, the Director who had borne the great scientific burden of developing the weapon from the raw materials made in Tennessee and Washington and a dozen of his key scientists. . . .

"For some hectic two hours preceding the blast, General Groves stayed with the Director, walking with him and steadying his tense excitement. Every time the Director would be about to explode because of some untoward happening, General Groves would take him off and walk with him in the rain, counselling with him and reassuring him that everything would be all right. . . .

"Just after General Groves left, announcements began to be broadcast of the interval remaining before the blast. They were sent by radio to the other groups participating in and observing the test. As the time interval grew smaller and changed from minutes to seconds, the tension increased by leaps and bounds. Everyone in that room knew the awful potentialities of the thing that they thought was about to happen. The scientists felt that their figuring must be right and that the bomb had to go off but there was in everyone's mind a strong measure of doubt. The feeling of many could be expressed by "Lord, I believe; help Thou mine unbelief." We were reaching into the unknown and we did not know what might come of it. It can be safely said that most of those present—Christian, Jew and Atheist—were praying and praying harder than they had ever prayed before. If the shot were successful, it was a justification of the several years of intensive effort of tens of thousands of people—statesmen, scientists, engineers, manufacturers, soldiers, and many others in every walk of life.

"In that brief instant in the remote New Mexico desert the tremendous effort of the brains and brawn of all these people came suddenly and startling to the fullest fruition. Dr. Oppenheimer, on whom had rested a very heavy burden, grew tenser as the last seconds ticked off. He scarcely breathed. He held on to a post to steady himself. For the last few seconds, he stared directly ahead and then when the announcer shouted "Now!" and there came this tremendous burst of light followed shortly thereafter by the deep growling roar of the explosion, his face relaxed into an expression of tremendous relief. Several of the observers standing back of the shelter to watch the lighting effects were knocked flat by the blast.

"The tension in the room let up and all started congratulating each other. Everyone sensed "This is it!" No matter what might happen now all knew that the impossible scientific job had been done. Atomic fission would no longer be hidden in the cloisters of the theoretical physicists' dreams. It was almost full grown at birth. It was a great new force to be used for good or for evil. There was a feeling in that shelter that those concerned with its nativity should dedicate their lives to the mission that it would always be used for good and never for evil. . . .

"The effects could well be called unprecedented, magnificent, beautiful, stupendous and terrifying. No man-made phenomenon of such tremendous power had ever occurred before. The lighting effects beggared description. The whole country was lighted by a searing light with the intensity many times that of the midday sun. It was golden, purple, violet, gray and blue. It lighted every peak, crevasse and ridge of the nearby mountain range with a clarity and beauty that cannot be described but must be seen to be imagined. It was that beauty the great poets dream about but describe most poorly and inadequately. Thirty seconds after the explosion came first, the air blast pressing hard against the people and things, to be followed almost immediately by the strong, sustained, awesome roar which warned of doomsday and made us feel that we puny things were blasphemous to dare tamper with the forces heretofore reserved to The Almighty. Words are inadequate tools for the job of acquainting those not present with the physical, mental and psychological effects. It had to be witnessed to be realized." . . .

B. Albert Einstein Discusses His Responsibility for the Atomic Bomb, 1946

I do not consider myself the father of the release of atomic energy. My part in it was quite indirect. I did not, in fact, foresee that it would be released in my time. I believed only that it was theoretically possible. It became practical through the accidental discovery of chain reaction, and this was not something I could have predicted. It was discovered by Hahn in Berlin, and he himself misinterpreted what he discovered. It was Lize [sic] Meitner who provided the correct interpretation, and escaped from Germany to place the information in the hands of Niels Bohr.

I do not believe that a great era of atomic science is to be assured by organizing science, in the way large corporations are organized. One can organize to apply a discovery already made, but not to make one. Only a free individual can make a discovery. There can be a kind of organizing by which scientists are assured their freedom and proper conditions of work. Professors of science in American universities, for instance, should be relieved of some of their teaching so as to have time for more research. Can you imagine an organization of scientists making the discoveries of Charles Darwin?. . .

To give any estimate when atomic energy can be applied to constructive purposes is impossible. What now is known is only how to use a fairly large quantity of uranium. The use of small quantities, sufficient, say, to operate a car or an airplane, so far is impossible, and one cannot predict when it will be achieved. No doubt, it will be achieved, but nobody can say when. Nor can one predict when materials more common than uranium can be used to supply atomic energy. Presumably all materials used for this purpose will be among the heavier elements of high atomic weight. Those elements are relatively scarce due to their lesser stability. Most of these materials may have already disappeared by radio-active disintegration. So though the release of atomic energy can be, and no doubt will be, a great boon to mankind, that may not be for some time.

I myself do not have the gift of explanation with which I am able to persuade large numbers of people of the urgency of the problems the human race now faces. Hence I should like to commend someone who has this gift of explanation, Emery Reves, whose book, *The Anatomy of the Peace,* is intelligent, clear, brief, and, if I may use the abused term, dynamic on the topic of war and need for world government.

Since I do not foresee that atomic energy is to be a great boon for a long time, I have to say that for the present it is a menace. Perhaps it is well that it should be. It may intimidate the human race to bring order into its international affairs, which, without the pressure of fear, it undoubtedly would not do.

C. The British Government Reports on Nuclear Power, 1955

1. An important stage has been reached in the development of nuclear energy for peaceful purposes. Hitherto the work in this country has consisted of a military programme, a broadly based research and development programme, and the production and use of radioisotopes. The military programme continues to be of great importance but the peaceful applications of nuclear energy now demand attention.

Nuclear energy is the energy of the future. Although we are still only at the edge of knowledge of its peaceful uses, we know enough to assess some of its possibilities.

2. Our future as an industrial country depends both on the ability of our scientists to discover the secrets of nature and on our speed in applying the new techniques that science places within our grasp. The exact lines of future development in nuclear energy are uncertain, but this must not deter us from pressing on with its practical application wherever it appears promising. It is only by coming to grips with the problems of the design and building of nuclear plant that British industry will acquire the experience necessary for the full exploitation of this new technology.

3. The application that now appears practicable on a commercial scale is the use of nuclear fission as a source of heat to drive electric generating plant. This comes moreover at a time when the country's great and growing demand for energy, and especially electric power, is placing an increasing strain on our supplies of coal and makes the search for supplementary sources of energy a matter of urgency. Technical developments in nuclear energy are taking place so fast that no firm long-term programme can yet be drawn up. But if progress is to be made some indication must be given of the probable lines of development so that the necessary preparations can be made in good time. A large power station may take five or more years to complete, including finding the site, designing the station and building it. . . .

15. It is expected that it will be possible to extract as much as 3,000 megawatt-days of heat from every ton of fuel. This is the equivalent of the heat from 10,000 tons of coal. There is as yet no practical experience of this level of irradiation at high temperatures and the metallurgical behaviour of the fuel elements is uncertain. But there are many lines of development which should overcome such metallurgical defects as may appear. . . .

19. . . . Taking what appears to be a reasonable value for the plutonium, the cost of electricity from the first commercial nuclear station comes to about $0.6d$ a unit. This is about the same as the probable future cost of electricity generated by new coal-fired power stations. . . . If no credit were allowed for the plutonium the cost of nuclear power would be substantially more than $0.6d$ a unit. Later stations should show a great improvement in efficiency, but the value of plutonium would probably fall considerably during their lifetime. Even so their higher efficiency should enable them to remain competitive with other power stations.

20. These estimates assume that all the plutonium is used for civil purposes, as would be most desirable. No allowance has been made for any military credits. . . .

D. Bertrand Russell Explains His Anti-Nuclear Position, 1959

Opponents of my recent activities in the campaign against H-bomb warfare have brought up what they consider to be an inconsistency on my part and have used statements that I made ten years ago to impair the force of the statements that I have made more recently. I should like to clear up this matter once for all.

At a time when America alone possessed the atom bomb and when the American Government was advocating what was known as the Baruch Proposal, the aim of which was to internationalize all the uses of atomic energy, I thought the American proposal both wise and generous. It seemed to me that the Baruch scheme, if adopted, would prevent an atomic arms race, the appalling dangers of which were evident to all informed opinion in the Western World. For a time it seemed possible that the USSR would agree to this scheme, since Russia had everything to gain by agreeing and nothing to lose. Unfortunately, Stalin's suspicious nature made him think that there was some trap, and Russia decided to produce her own atomic weapons. I thought, at that time, that it would be worth while to bring pressure to bear upon Russia and even, if necessary, to go so far as to threaten war on the sole issue of the internationalizing of atomic weapons. My aim, then as now, was to prevent a war in which both sides possessed the power of producing worldwide disaster. Western statesmen, however, confident of the supposed technical superiority of the West, believed that there was no danger of Russia achieving equality with the non-Communist world in the field of nuclear warfare. Their confidence in this respect has turned out to have been mistaken. It follows that, if nuclear war is now to be prevented, it must be by new methods and not by those which could have been employed ten years ago.

My critics seem to think that, if you have once advocated a certain policy, you should continue to advocate it after all the circumstances have changed. This is quite absurd. If a man gets into a train with a view to reaching a certain destination and on the way the train breaks down, you will not consider the man

Text from *Common Sense and Nuclear Warfare*, Bertrand Russell, Simon & Schuster, 1959, pp. 89–92.

guilty of an inconsistency if he gets out of the train and employs other means of reaching his destination. In like manner, a person who advocates a certain policy in certain circumstances will advocate a quite different policy in different circumstances.

I have never been a complete pacifist and have at no time maintained that all who wage war are to be condemned. I have held the view, which I should have thought was that of common sense, that some wars have been justified and others not. What makes the peculiarity of the present situation is that, if a great war should break out, the belligerents on either side and the neutrals would be all, equally, defeated. This is a new situation and means that war cannot still be used as an instrument of policy. It is true that the threat of war can still be used, but only by a lunatic. Unfortunately, some people *are* lunatics, and, not long ago, there were such lunatics in command of a powerful State. We cannot be sure this will not happen again and, if it does, it will produce a disaster compared with which the horrors achieved by Hitler were a flea-bite. The world at present is balanced in unstable equilibrium upon a sharp edge. To achieve stability, new methods are required, and it is these new methods that those who think as I do are attempting to urge upon the East and upon the West.

I do not deny that the policy that I have advocated has changed from time to time. It has changed as circumstances have changed. To achieve a single purpose, sane men adapt their policies to the circumstances. Those who do not are insane.

Though I do not admit inconsistency, I should not be wholly sincere if I did not admit that my mood and feelings have undergone a change somewhat deeper than that resulting from strategic considerations alone. The awful prospect of the extermination of the human race, if not in the next war, then in the next but one or the next but two, is so sobering to any imagination which has seriously contemplated it as to demand very fundamental fresh thought on the whole subject not only of international relations but of human life and its capabilities. If you were quarrelling with a man about some issue that both you and he had thought important just at the moment when a sudden hurricane threatened to destroy you both and the whole neighbourhood, you would probably forget the quarrel. I think what is important at present is to make mankind aware of the hurricane and forgetful of the issue which had been producing strife. I know it is difficult after spending many years and much eloquence on the evils of Communism or Capitalism, as the case may be, to see this issue as one of relative unimportance. But, although this is difficult, it is what both the Communist Rulers and the men who shape the policy of the West will have to achieve if mankind is to survive. To make sure a realization possible is the purpose of the policy which I now advocate.

Document Set 28.1 References

A. Two American Generals Witness the First Atomic Test, July 18, 1945
   Martin Sherwin, *A World Destroyed* (New York: Vintage Books, 1976), 308–312.
B. Albert Einstein Acknowledges His Responsibility for the Atomic Bomb, 1946
   Albert Einstein, *Out of My Later Years* (Secaucus, N.J.: Citadel Press, 1956), 188–190.
C. The British Government Reports on Nuclear Power, 1955
   "A Progamme of Nuclear Power," *B. P. P.*, 1954–1955, 13:1, 4–6, in B. W. Clapp, ed., *Documents in English Economic History* (London: G. Bell, 1977), 2:168–169.
D. Bertrand Russell Explains His Anti-Nuclear Position, 1959
   Bertrand Russell, *Common Sense and Nuclear Warfare* (New York: Simon and Schuster, 1959), 89–92.

DOCUMENT SET 28.2
The Cold War

Why the World War II anti-fascist alliance broke up, giving way to over forty years of East-West confrontation known as the Cold War, is a subject that has kindled vigorous debate among historians. Was this a case of one expansive totalitarian power replacing another as the sworn enemy of western democracy? Was the West ultimately to blame for not heeding the Soviet Union's legitimate security demands and by overestimating Stalin's potential for aggression? Were both sides equally at fault because they viewed the world through ideological hazes and thus failed to understand each other's objective interests and behavior? Read the documents of this set with these questions in mind.

No one disputes Stalin's suspiciousness and basic ignorance of the outside world. In 1962 the by-then ex-Communist Milovan Djilas (1911–1995) published a memoir of his wartime visits to the Kremlin at the head of Yugoslav Partisan delegations, extracts from which form Document A. Compare Djilas's testimony with the evident anger in Franklin D. Roosevelt's communications with Stalin and Churchill in the very last days of the president's life (Document B), occasioned by Stalin's accusations of bad faith upon learning of contacts between the commanders of western and soon-to-be-defeated German troops in northern Italy. Bear in mind that in February 1945 Roosevelt and Churchill had met Stalin at Yalta and attempted—among other goals—to secure his promise to use free elections in establishing the "friendly" government that the Soviets demanded in Poland; these Soviet assurances were already being broken by the end of Roosevelt's life, causing the president to rethink his wartime optimism about securing the peace through mutual understandings among the American, British, and Soviet leaders.

By 1946, mutual suspicion and disillusionment were clearly causing the wartime alliance to sunder, although it was not yet clear how deep the East-West division would become. George F. Kennan, an American professional diplomat well versed in history and long experienced in dealing with the Kremlin, in 1946 sent to Washington from Moscow his "Long Telegram" (Document C) analyzing Soviet conduct and outlining a policy that would become known as "containment." Do you detect any differences between Kennan's recommendations—which, of course, were meant only for the eyes of policymakers—and the solemn warning that the out-of-office Winston Churchill uttered to Americans in his famous "Iron Curtain" speech at Fulton, Missouri, in the same year (Document D)? Keep in mind Kennan's purpose of countering what he regarded as misguidedly idealistic American hopes of counting on "goodwill" in maintaining the wartime alliance, and Churchill's hope of forestalling a reversion to prewar American isolationism. In turn, compare both statements with the other "long telegram" that we now know was sent in 1946—in this case from Washington to Moscow, by Soviet ambassador Nikolai Novikov, analyzing the motives of American conduct toward the U.S.S.R. (Document E).

In spring 1947 came what many regard as the plunge into full-scale Cold War, precipitated by the British government's realization that its resources were stretched too thin to permit it to continue propping up struggling anti-Communist regimes in Greece and Turkey. By asking the United States to assume this burden, the U.K. helped escalate its effort to maintain its influence in the eastern Mediterranean, where it had long been the dominant power, into an East-West confrontation between the United States and the international Communist movement. In responding to Britain's appeal, U.S. President Harry S Truman felt that he had "to scare the hell out of the American people," in the words of one advisor. Evaluate the March 12, 1947, presidential speech to Congress announcing what became known as the Truman Doctrine (Document F). Compare Truman's statement to another famous declaration of western purpose, delivered before a crowd that "shook itself and rose and roared like an animal" at the height of the Cold War in 1961—President John F. Kennedy's "Ich bin ein Berliner" address in front of the Berlin Wall (Document G).

What evidence do you see in these pronouncements of geopolitical "realism," and what signs of an ideological challenge to an elusive, worldwide threat to the western way of life? Supplementing these documents with the account of the Cold War in *The Challenge of the West*, evaluate the onset of the postwar East-West conflict from these two perspectives.

A. Milovan Djilas Recalls Conversations with Stalin, June 1944 and April 1945

[1. June 1944. *Stalin:*] . . . "Perhaps you think that just because we are the allies of the English that we have forgotten who they are and who Churchill is. They find nothing sweeter than to trick their allies. During the First World War they constantly tricked the Russians and the French. And Churchill? Churchill is the kind who, if you don't watch him, will slip a kopeck out of your pocket. Yes, a kopeck out of your pocket! By God, a kopeck out of your pocket! And Roosevelt? Roosevelt is not like that. He dips in his hand only for bigger coins. But Churchill? Churchill—even for a kopeck." . . .

[2. April 1945] Stalin presented his views on the distinctive nature of the war that was being waged: "This war is not as in the past; whoever occupies a territory also imposes on it his own social system. Everyone imposes his own system as far as his army can reach. It cannot be otherwise."

He also pointed out, without going into long explanations, the meaning of his Panslavic policy. "If the Slavs keep united and maintain solidarity, no one in the future will be able to move a finger. Not even a finger!" he repeated, emphasizing his thought by cleaving the air with his forefinger.

Someone expressed doubt that the Germans would be able to recuperate within fifty years. But Stalin was of a different opinion. "No, they will recover, and very quickly. That is a highly developed industrial country with an extremely qualified and numerous working class and technical intelligentsia. Give them twelve to fifteen years and they'll be on their feet again. And this is why the unity of the Slavs is important. But even apart from this, if the unity of the Slavs exists, no one will dare move a finger."

At one point he got up, hitched up his pants as though he was about to wrestle or to box, and cried out almost in a transport, "The war shall soon be over. We shall recover in fifteen or twenty years, and then we'll have another go at it."

There was something terrible in his words: a horrible war was still going on. Yet there was something impressive, too, about his cognizance of the paths he had to take, the inevitability that faced the world in which he lived and the movement that he headed.

The rest of what was said that evening was hardly worth remembering. There was much eating, even more drinking, and countless senseless toasts were raised. . . .

B. Franklin D. Roosevelt Rejects Stalin's Charge of Bad Faith, April 1945

[1. To Stalin]
I have received with astonishment your message of April 3 containing an allegation that arrangements which were made between Field Marshals [Harold] Alexander [British] and [Albert] Kesselring [German] at Berne [Switzerland] "permitted the Anglo-American troops to advance to the East and the Anglo-Americans promised in return to ease for the Germans the peace terms."

In my previous messages to you in regard to the attempts made in Berne to arrange a conference to discuss a surrender of the German army in Italy I have told you that: (1) No negotiations were held in Berne, (2) The meeting had no political implications whatever, (3) In any surrender of the enemy army in Italy there would be no violation of our agreed principle of unconditional surrender, (4) Soviet officers would be welcomed at any meeting that might be arranged to discuss surrender.

For the advantage of our common war effort against Germany, which today gives excellent promise of an early success in a disintegration of the German armies, I must continue to assume that you have the same high confidence in my truthfulness and reliability that I have always had in yours.

I have also a full appreciation of the effect your gallant army has had in making possible a crossing of the Rhine by the forces under General [Dwight D.] Eisenhower and the effect that your forces will have hereafter on the eventual collapse of the German resistance to our combined attacks.

I have complete confidence in General Eisenhower and know that he certainly would inform me before entering into any agreement with the Germans. He is instructed to demand and will demand unconditional surrender of enemy troops that may be defeated on his front. Our advances on the Western Front are due to military action. Their speed has been attributable mainly to the terrific impact of our air power resulting in destruction of German communications, and to the fact that Eisenhower was able to cripple the bulk of the German forces on the Western Front while they were still west of the Rhine.

I am certain that there were no negotiations in Berne at any time and I feel that your information to that effect must have come from German sources which have made persistent efforts to create dissension between us in order to escape in some measure responsibility for their war crimes. If that was [General Karl] Wolff's purpose in Berne, your message proves that he has had some success.

With a confidence in your belief in my personal reliability and in my determination to bring about, together with you, an unconditional surrender of the Nazis, it is astonishing that a belief seems to have reached the Soviet Government that I have entered into an agreement with the enemy without first obtaining your full agreement.

Finally I would say this, it would be one of the great tragedies of history if at the very moment of the victory, now within our grasp, such distrust, such lack of faith should prejudice the entire undertaking after the colossal losses of life, material and treasure involved.

Frankly I cannot avoid a feeling of bitter resentment toward your informers, whoever they are, for such vile misrepresentations of my actions or those of my trusted subordinates.

[2. To Churchill]

I would minimize the general Soviet problem as much as possible because these problems, in one form or another, seem to arise every day and most of them straighten out as in the case of the Berne meeting.

We must be firm, however, and our course thus far is correct.

C. George F. Kennan Analyzes Soviet Policy and Recommends a Western Response, 1946

At bottom of Kremlin's neurotic view of world affairs is traditional and instinctive Russian sense of insecurity. Originally, this was insecurity of a peaceful agricultural people trying to live on vast exposed plain in neighborhood of fierce nomadic peoples. To this was added, as Russia came into contact with economically advanced West, fear of more competent, more powerful, more highly organized societies in that area. But this latter type of insecurity was one which afflicted rather Russian rulers than Russian people; for Russian rulers have invariably sensed that their rule was relatively archaic in form, fragile and artificial in its psychological foundation, unable to stand comparison or contact with political systems of Western countries. For this reason they have always feared foreign penetration, feared direct contact between Western world and their own, feared what

From "Long Telegram" 1946, Reprinted by permission of the translator, Kenneth M. Jensen.

would happen if Russians learned truth about world without or if foreigners learned truth about world within. And they had learned to seek security only in patient but deadly struggle for total destruction of rival power, never in compacts and compromises with it.

It was no coincidence that Marxism, which had smouldered ineffectively for half a century in Western Europe, caught hold and blazed for first time in Russia. Only in this land which had never known a friendly neighbor or indeed any tolerant equilibrium of separate powers, either internal or international, could a doctrine thrive which viewed economic conflicts of society as insoluble by peaceful means. After establishment of Bolshevist regime, Marxist dogma, rendered even more truculent and intolerant by Lenin's interpretation, became a perfect vehicle for sense of insecurity with which Bolsheviks, even more than previous Russian rulers, were afflicted. In this dogma, with its basic altruism of purpose, they found justification for their instinctive fear of outside world, for the dictatorship without which they did not know how to rule, for cruelties they did not dare not to inflict, for sacrifices they felt bound to demand. In the name of Marxism they sacrificed every single ethical value in their methods and tactics. Today they cannot dispense with it. It is fig leaf of their moral and intellectual respectability. Without it they would stand before history, at best, as only the last of that long succession of cruel and wasteful Russian rulers who have relentlessly forced country on to ever new heights of military power in order to guarantee external security of their internally weak regimes. This is why Soviet purposes must always be solemnly clothed in trappings of Marxism, and why no one should underrate importance of dogma in Soviet affairs. Thus Soviet leaders are driven [by?] necessities of their own past and present position to put forward a dogma which [apparent omission] outside world as evil, hostile and menacing, but as bearing within itself germs of creeping disease and destined to be wracked with growing internal convulsions until it is given final *coup de grace* by rising power of socialism and yields to new and better world. This thesis provides justification for the increase of military and police power of Russian state, for that isolation of Russian population from outside world, and for that fluid and constant pressure to extend limits of Russian police power which are together the natural and instinctive urges of Russian rulers. Basically this is only the steady advance of uneasy Russian nationalism, a centuries old movement in which conceptions of offense and defense are inextricably confused. But in new guise of international Marxism, with its honeyed promises to a desperate and war torn outside world, it is more dangerous and insidious than ever before. . . .

In summary, we have here a political force committed fanatically to the belief that with US there can be no permanent *modus vivendi*, that it is desirable and necessary that the internal harmony of our society be disrupted, our traditional way of life be destroyed, the international authority of our state be broken, if Soviet power is to be secure. This political force has complete power of disposition over energies of one of world's greatest peoples and resources of world's richest national territory, and is borne along by deep and powerful currents of Russian nationalism. In addition, it has an elaborate and far flung apparatus for exertion of its influence in other countries, an apparatus of amazing flexibility and versatility, managed by people whose experience and skill in underground methods are presumably without parallel in history. Finally, it is seemingly inaccessible to considerations of reality in its basic reactions. For it, the vast fund of objective fact about human society is not, as with us, the measure against which outlook is constantly being tested and re-formed, but a grab bag from which individual items are selected arbitrarily and tendenciously to bolster an outlook already preconceived. This is admittedly not a pleasant picture. . . . But I would like to record my conviction that problem is within our power to solve—and that without recourse to any general military conflict. And in support of this conviction there are certain observations of a more encouraging nature I should like to make:

1. Soviet power, unlike that of Hitlerite Germany, is neither schematic nor adventuristic. It does not work by fixed plans. It does not take unnecessary risks. Impervious to logic of reason, and it is highly sensitive to logic of force. For this reason it can easily withdraw—and usually does—when strong resistance is encountered at any point. Thus, if the adversary has sufficient force and makes clear his readiness to use it, he rarely has to do so. If situations are properly handled there need be no prestige-engaging showdowns.

2. Gauged against Western World as a whole, Soviets are still by far the weaker force. Thus, their success will really depend on degree of cohesion, firmness and vigor which Western World can muster. And this is factor which it is within our power to influence.

3. Success of Soviet system, as form of internal power, is not yet finally proven. It has yet to be demonstrated that it can survive supreme test of suc-

cessive transfer of power from one individual or group to another. Lenin's death was first such transfer, and its effects wracked Soviet state for 15 years. After Stalin's death or retirement will be second. But even this will not be final test. Soviet internal system will now be subjected, by virtue of recent territorial expansions, to series of additional strains which once proved severe tax on Tsardom. We here are convinced that never since termination of civil war have mass of Russian people been emotionally farther removed from doctrines of Communist Party than they are today. In Russia, party has now become a great and—for the moment—highly successful apparatus of dictatorial administration, but it has ceased to be a source of emotional inspiration. Thus, internal soundness and permanence of movement need not yet be regarded as assured.

4. All Soviet propaganda beyond Soviet security sphere is basically negative and destructive. It should therefore be relatively easy to combat it by any intelligent and really constructive program.

D. Churchill Warns of the Iron Curtain, 1946

The United States stands at this time at the pinnacle of world power. It is a solemn moment for the American democracy. With primacy in power is also joined an awe-inspiring accountability to the future. As you look around you, you feel not only the sense of duty done but also feel anxiety lest you fall below the level of achievement. Opportunity is here now, clear and shining, for both our countries. To reject it or ignore it or fritter it away will bring upon us all the long reproaches of the after-time. It is necessary that constancy of mind, persistency of purpose, and the grand simplicity of decision shall guide and rule the conduct of the English speaking peoples in peace as they did in war. . . .

A shadow has fallen upon the scenes so lately lighted by the Allied victory. Nobody knows what Soviet Russia and its Communist international organization intends to do in the immediate future, or what are the limits, if any, to their expansive and proselytizing tendencies. I have a strong admiration and regard for the valiant Russian people and for my wartime comrade, Marshal Stalin. There is sympathy and good will in Britain—and I doubt not here also—toward the peoples of all the Russias and a resolve to persevere through many differences and rebuffs in establishing lasting friendships.

We understand the Russian need to be secure on her western frontiers from all renewal of German aggression. We welcome her to her rightful place among the leading nations of the world. Above all, we welcome constant, frequent, and growing contacts between Russian people and our own people on both sides of the Atlantic. It is my duty, however, to place before you certain facts about the present position in Europe.

From Stettin in the Baltic to Trieste in the Adriatic, an iron curtain has descended across the continent. Behind that line lie all the capitals of the ancient states of Central and Eastern Europe. Warsaw, Berlin, Prague, Vienna, Budapest, Belgrade, Bucharest, and Sofia, all these famous cities and the populations around them lie in the Soviet sphere and all are subject, in one form or another, not only to Soviet influence but to a very high and increasing measure of control from Moscow. Athens alone, with its immortal glories, is free to decide its future at an election under British, American, and French observation. . . .

If now the Soviet government tries, by separate action, to build up a pro-Communist Germany in their areas, this will cause new serious difficulties in the British and American zones, and will give the defeated Germans the power of putting themselves up to auction between the Soviets and the Western democracies. Whatever conclusions may be drawn from these facts—and facts they are—this is certainly not the liberated Europe we fought to build up. Nor is it one which contains the essentials of permanent peace.

In front of the iron curtain which lies across Europe are other causes for anxiety. In Italy the Communist party is seriously hampered by having to support the Communist-trained Marshall Tito's claims to former Italian territory at the head of the Adriatic. Nevertheless, the future of Italy hangs in the balance. Again, one cannot imagine a regenerated Europe without a strong France. . . .

However, in a great number of countries, far from the Russian frontiers and throughout the world, Communist fifth columns are established and work in complete unity and absolute obedience to the directions they receive from the Communist center. Except in the British Commonwealth, and in the United States, where communism is in its infancy, the Communist parties or fifth columns constitute a growing challenge and peril to Christian civilization. These are somber facts for anyone to have to recite on the morrow of a victory gained by so much splendid comradeship in arms and in the cause of freedom and democracy, and we should be most unwise not to face them squarely while time remains. . . .

Our difficulties and dangers will not be removed by closing our eyes to them; they will not be removed by mere waiting to see what happens; nor will they be relieved by a policy of appeasement. What is needed is a settlement, and the longer this is delayed, the more difficult it will be and the greater our dangers will become. From what I have seen of our Russian friends and allies during the war, I am convinced that there is nothing they admire so much as strength, and there is nothing for which they have less respect than for military weakness. For that reason the old doctrine of a balance of power is unsound. We cannot afford, if we can help it, to work on narrow margins, offering temptations to a trial of strength. If the Western democracies stand together in strict adherence to the principles of the United Nations Charter, their influence for furthering these principles will be immense and no one is likely to molest them. If, however, they become divided or falter in their duty, and if these all-important years are allowed to slip away, then indeed catastrophe may overwhelm us all.

E. Soviet Ambassador Nikolai Novikov Detects an American Drive for World Domination, 1946

The foreign policy of the United States, which reflects the imperialist tendencies of American monopolistic capital, is characterized in the postwar period by a striving for world supremacy. This is the real meaning of the many statements by President Truman and other representatives of American ruling circles: that the United States has the right to lead the world. All the forces of American diplomacy—the army, the air force, the navy, industry and science—are enlisted in the service of this foreign policy. For this purpose broad plans for expansion have been developed and are being implemented through diplomacy and the establishment of a system of naval and air bases stretching far beyond the boundaries of the United States, through the arms race, and through the creation of ever newer types of weapons. . . .

Europe has come out of the war with a completely dislocated economy, and the economic devastation that occurred in the course of the war cannot be overcome in a short time. All of the countries of Europe and Asia are experiencing a colossal need for consumer goods, industrial and transportation equipment, etc. Such a situation provides American monopolistic capital with prospects for enormous shipments of goods and the importation of capital into these countries—a circumstance that would permit it to infiltrate their national economies.

Such a development would mean serious

strengthening of the economic position of the United States in the whole world and would be a stage on the road to world domination by the United States.

On the other hand, we have seen a failure of calculations on the part of U.S. circles which assumed that the Soviet Union would be destroyed in the war or would come out of it so weakened that it would be forced to go begging to the United States for economic assistance. Had that happened, they would have been able to dictate conditions permitting the United States to carry out its expansion in Europe and Asia without hindrance from the USSR. . . .

F. President Harry S Truman Announces the Truman Doctrine, 1947

The United States has received from the Greek Government an urgent appeal for financial and economic assistance. Preliminary reports from the American Economic Mission now in Greece and reports from the American Ambassador in Greece corroborate the statement of the Greek Government that assistance is imperative if Greece is to survive as a free nation. . . .

The British Government has informed us that, owing to its own difficulties, it can no longer extend financial or economic aid to Turkey.

As in the case of Greece, if Turkey is to have the assistance it needs, the United States must supply it. We are the only country able to provide that help.

I am fully aware of the broad implications involved if the United States extends assistance to Greece and Turkey, and I shall discuss these implications with you at this time.

One of the primary objectives of the foreign policy of the United States is the creation of conditions in which we and other nations will be able to work out a way of life free from coercion. This was a fundamental issue in the war with Germany and Japan. Our victory was won over countries which sought to impose their will, and their way of life, upon other nations.

To ensure the peaceful development of nations, free from coercion, the United States has taken a leading part in establishing the United Nations. The United Nations is designed to make possible lasting freedom and independence for all its members. We shall not realize our objectives, however, unless we are willing to help free peoples to maintain their free institutions and their national integrity against aggressive movements that seek to impose upon them totalitarian regimes. This is no more than a frank recognition that totalitarian regimes imposed upon

free peoples, by direct or indirect aggression, undermine the foundations of international peace and hence the security of the United States.

The peoples of a number of countries of the world have recently had totalitarian regimes forced upon them against their will. The Government of the United States has made frequent protests against coercion and intimidation, in violation of the Yalta agreement, in Poland, Rumania, and Bulgaria. I must also state that in a number of other countries there have been similar developments.

At the present moment in world history nearly every nation must choose between alternative ways of life. The choice is too often not a free one.

One way of life is based upon the will of the majority, and is distinguished by free institutions, representative government, free elections, guarantees of individual liberty, freedom of speech and religion, and freedom from political oppression.

The second way of life is based upon the will of a minority forcibly imposed upon the majority. It relies upon terror and oppression, a controlled press and radio, fixed elections, and the suppression of personal freedoms.

I believe that it must be the policy of the United States to support free peoples who are resisting attempted subjugation by armed minorities or by outside pressures.

I believe that we must assist free peoples to work out their own destinies in their own way.

I believe that our help should be primarily through economic and financial aid which is essential to economic stability and orderly political processes.

The world is not static, and the *status quo* is not sacred. But we cannot allow changes in the *status quo* in violation of the Charter of the United Nations by such methods as coercion, or by such subterfuges as political infiltration. In helping free and independent nations to maintain their freedom, the United States will be giving effect to the principles of the Charter of the United Nations.

It is necessary only to glance at a map to realize that the survival and integrity of the Greek nation are of grave importance in a much wider situation. If Greece should fall under the control of an armed minority, the effect upon its neighbor, Turkey, would be immediate and serious. Confusion and disorder might well spread throughout the entire Middle East.

Moreover, the disappearance of Greece as an independent state would have a profound effect upon those countries in Europe whose peoples are struggling against great difficulties to maintain their freedoms and their independence while they repair the damages of war. . . .

Should we fail to aid Greece and Turkey in this fateful hour, the effect will be far reaching to the West as well as to the East.

We must take immediate and resolute action.

I therefore ask the Congress to provide authority for assistance to Greece and Turkey is the amount of $400,000,000 for the period ending June 30, 1948. In requesting these funds, I have taken into consideration the maximum amount of relief assistance which would be furnished to Greece out of the $350,000,000 which I recently requested that the Congress authorize for the prevention of starvation and suffering in countries devastated by the war.

In addition to funds, I ask the Congress to authorize the detail of American civilian and military personnel to Greece and Turkey, at the request of those countries, to assist in the tasks of reconstruction, and for the purpose of supervising the use of such financial and material assistance as may be furnished. I recommend that authority also be provided for the instruction and training of selected Greek and Turkish personnel. . . .

This is a serious course upon which we embark.

I would not recommend it except that the alternative is much more serious. The United States contributed $341,000,000,000 toward winning World War II. This is an investment in world freedom and world peace.

The assistance that I am recommending for Greece and Turkey amounts to little more than 1/10 of 1 percent of this investment. It is only common sense that we should safeguard this investment and make sure that it was not in vain.

The seeds of totalitarian regimes are nurtured by misery and want. They spread and grow in the evil soil of poverty and strife. They reach their full growth when the hope of a people for a better life has died.

We must keep that hope alive.

The free peoples of the world look to us for support in maintaining their freedoms.

If we falter in our leadership, we may endanger the peace of the world—and we shall surely endanger the welfare of this Nation.

Great responsibilities have been placed upon us by the swift movement of events.

I am confident that the Congress will face these responsibilities squarely.

G. President John F. Kennedy Declares, "Ich bin ein Berliner," 1961

There are some people in the world who really don't understand, or say they don't, what is the great issue between the free world and the Communist world.

Let them come to Berlin!

There are some who say that Communism is the wave of the future.

Let them come to Berlin!

And there are some who say in Europe and elsewhere we can work with the Communists.

Let them come to Berlin!

And there are even a few who say that it is true that Communism is an evil system, but it permits us to make economic progress.

Lass sie nach Berlin kommen! Let them come to Berlin!

I know of no town, no city, that has been besieged for eighteen years, that still lives with the vitality and the force and the determination of the city of West Berlin.

When all are free the people of West Berlin can take sober satisfaction in the fact that they were in the front lines for almost two decades.

All free men, wherever they may live, are citizens of Berlin. And, therefore, as a free man, I take pride in the words: "Ich bin ein Berliner."

Document Set 28.2 References

A. Milovan Djilas Recalls Conversations with Stalin, June 1944 and April 1945
Milovan Djilas, *Conversations with Stalin*, trans. Michael B. Petrovich (New York: Harcourt Brace, 1962), 73, 114–115.
B. Franklin D. Roosevelt Rejects Stalin's Charge of Bad Faith, April 1945
Roosevelt, Letters to Stalin and to Churchill, in Thomas G. Paterson and Dennis Merrill, eds., *Major Problems in American Foreign Relations*, 4th ed. (Lexington, Mass.: D. C. Heath, 1995), 2:201–202.
C. George F. Kennan Analyzes Soviet Policy and Recommends a Western Response, 1946
Kennan, "Long Telegram," in Paterson and Merrill, 2:244–247.
D. Churchill Warns of the Iron Curtain, 1946
Winston Churchill, Speech in Fulton, Missouri, in Paterson and Merrill, 2:247–249.
E. Soviet Ambassador Nikolai Novikov Detects an American Drive for World Domination, 1946
Kenneth M. Jensen, ed., *Origins of the Cold War: The Novikov, Kennan and Roberts "Long Telegram" of 1946* (Washington: United States Institute of Peace, 1991).
F. President Harry S Truman Announces the Truman Doctrine, 1947
Truman, in Paterson and Merrill, 259–261.
G. President John F. Kennedy Declares, "Ich bin ein Berliner," 1961
Kennedy, Speech in Berlin, in Walter Henry Nelson, *The Berliners: Their Saga and Their City* (New York: David McKay, 1969), 181–182.

DOCUMENT SET 28.3
Stalinism and De-Stalinization

The Soviet Union emerged from "The Great Patriotic War" horribly devastated. Wartime losses may have totaled 20 million citizens killed or missing, including those who had been deported or captured, or who had fled. The survivors longed desperately for recognition of their sacrifices in the form of relaxed ideological vigilance by the Soviet government and greater attention to consumer needs. Such a "normal" postwar life was not what Stalin meant to give the Soviet and East European peoples. (Why not?) Document A is a 1947 condemnation of the "liberalizing" trends that appeared in Soviet literature at the end of the war, delivered by Stalin's spokesman in cultural matters, Andrei Zhdanov, a hard-liner who looked like a potential successor to Stalin until his premature death in 1949. What evidence and motives do you see here for a turn to the ideological hard line?

Stalinism bred internal enemies within the Communist system, although for obvious reasons critics could speak out only under certain conditions. The 1948 break between the Kremlin and the Yugoslav communists led by Josip Broz (Tito) impelled the latter to define the special road to socialism that they proposed to follow once the U.S.S.R. had for them ceased to be the ideological lodestar. Djilas, whose wartime recollections of Stalin we have already encountered (Set 28.2, Document A), was an idealistic communist revolutionary of Montenegrin origin whose growing disenchantment with bureaucracy eventually led him to challenge not only Stalin's but also Tito's authoritarian system in the celebrated book *The New Class* (Document B), for which he was expelled from the Yugoslav Communist Party in 1954 and imprisoned at hard labor. Stalin's attack on Tito was deplored by the man who eventually rose to the top of the Soviet leadership after Stalin's death. Nikita Khrushchev (1894–1977) not only tried (for the most part in vain) to heal the Moscow-Belgrade breach but also, in early 1956, after Stalin's death, set out to "demythologize" the leader who since 1928 had been regarded by orthodox Communists everywhere as "the supreme teacher of progressive mankind." Attempts to keep under wraps Khrushchev's "secret" speech to the Twentieth Party Congress (Document C) failed, causing perhaps the greatest shock to international Communism since the Hitler-Stalin Pact of 1939. One immediate result was to so thoroughly undermine the self-confidence of the Communist regimes in Poland and Hungary that popular resis-

tance erupted in October and November 1956. A "national communist" who in 1949 had been deposed as a "Titoist," Władysław Gomułka, barely managed to keep Poland within the Soviet fold, but a full-fledged anti-communist revolt swept Hungary, impelling the Soviets to crush it with great brutality (Document D).

Khrushchev sincerely believed that Marxism-Leninism, if applied with the right mixture of firmness and concessions to popular sentiment, would unleash tremendous human productivity and one day bury capitalism. Even the Hungarian debacle did not deter him from continuing to tolerate new trends "within the system." One such experiment was the permission he granted in 1962 to publish the novel *One Day in the Life of Ivan Denisovich* (Document E) by a hitherto unknown writer, Alexander Solzhenitsyn (born 1918). For the first time a writer described to Soviet readers some of the realities of Stalinist-era hard-labor camps—experiences that Solzhenitsyn himself had undergone as a result of having written some mildly disrespectful comments about Stalin in an intercepted private letter while serving as an army officer late in World War II.

To the end of his political life—he was deposed by his colleagues in 1964 for "hare-brained scheming" and for having humiliated the Soviet Union by blundering into the 1962 Cuban Missile Crisis—Khrushchev never ceased to promise "goulash communism," the material abundance that he insisted was Marxism's ultimate goal. Document F represents the kind of statistics that Khrushchev and his successors liked to boast of as they continued to insist that the Marxist-Leninist system was fundamentally humanitarian and represented the wave of the future.

Pulling these documents together, and considering what you have already learned from *The Challenge of the West* about the Soviet Union, evaluate why it proved impossible to maintain the full rigor of Stalinism.

A. Andrei Zhdanov Defines Politically Correct Soviet Literature, 1947

It is clear from the Central Committee's decision that *Zvezda*'s worst mistake has been that of allowing the writings of [Nikolai] Zoshchenko and [Anna]

Akhmatova to appear in its pages. It is, I think, hardly necessary for me to instance Zoshchenko's "work" *The Adventures of a Monkey.* You have certainly all read it and know it better than I do. The point of this "work" of Zoshchenko's is that in it he portrays Soviet people as lazy, unattractive, stupid and crude. He is in no way concerned with their labour, their efforts, their heroism, their high social and moral qualities. He never so much as mentions these. He chooses, like the cheap philistine he is, to scratch about in life's basenesses and pettinesses. This is no accident. It is intrinsic in all cheap philistine writers, of whom Zoshchenko is one....

Is it possible to fall morally and politically lower than this? How can the people of Leningrad tolerate such rubbish and vulgarity in the pages of their journals?

The Leningraders in charge of *Zvezda* must indeed be lacking in vigilance if a "work" of this sort is offered to the journal's Soviet readers, if it is found possible to publish works steeped in the venom of bestial enmity towards the Soviet order. Only the scum of the literary world could write such "works," and only the blind, the apolitical could allow them to appear....

Zoshchenko's thoroughly rotten and corrupt social, political and literary attitude does not result from any recent transformation. There is nothing accidental about his latest "works." They are simply the continuation of his literary "legacy" dating from the twenties....

What is the cause of these errors and failings [by the Leningrad literary journals]?

It is that the editors of the said journals, our Soviet men of letters, and the leaders of our ideological front in Leningrad, have forgotten some of the principal tenets of Leninism as regards literature. Many writers, and many of those working as responsible editors, or holding important posts in the Writers' Union, consider politics to be the business of the Government or of the Central Committee. When it comes to men of letters, engaging in politics is no business of theirs. If a man has done a good, artistic, fine piece of writing, his work should be published even though it contains vicious elements liable to confuse and poison the minds of our young people.

We demand that our comrades, both practising writers and those in positions of literary leadership, should be guided by that without which the Soviet order cannot live, that is to say, by politics, so that our young people may be brought up not in the spirit of do-nothing and don't care, but in an optimistic revolutionary spirit....

Lenin was the first to state clearly what attitude towards art and literature advanced social thought should take. Let me remind you of the well-known article, *Party Organisation and Party Literature,* which he wrote at the end of 1905, and in which he demonstrated with characteristic forcefulness that literature cannot but have a partisan adherence and that it must form an important part of the general proletarian cause. All the principles on which the development of our Soviet literature is based are to be found in this article....

The lack of ideological principles shown by leading workers on *Zvezda* and *Leningrad* has led to a second serious mistake. Certain of our leading workers have, in their relations with various authors, set personal interests, the interests of friendship, above those of the political education of the Soviet people or these authors' political tendencies. It is said that many ideologically harmful and from a literary point of view weak productions are allowed to be published because the editor does not like to hurt the author's feelings. In the eyes of such workers it is better to sacrifice the interests of the people and of the state than to hurt some author's feelings. This is an entirely wrong and politically dangerous principle. It is like swapping a million roubles for a kopeck....

However fine may be the external appearance of the work of the fashionable modern bourgeois writers in America and Western Europe, and of their film directors and theatrical producers, they can neither save nor better their bourgeois culture, for its moral basis is rotten and decaying. It has been placed at the service of capitalist private ownership, of the selfish and egocentric interests of the top layer of bourgeois society. A swarm of bourgeois writers, film directors and theatrical producers are trying to draw the attention of the progressive strata of society away from the acute problems of social and political struggle and to divert it into a groove of cheap meaningless art and literature, treating of gangsters and show-girls and glorifying the adulterer and the adventures of crooks and gamblers.

Is it fitting for us Soviet patriots, the representatives of advanced Soviet culture, to play the part of admirers or disciples of bourgeois culture? Our literature, reflecting an order on a higher level than any bourgeois-democratic order and a culture manifoldly superior to bourgeois culture, has, it goes without saying, the right to teach the new universal morals to others....

B. Milovan Djilas Defines the "New Class," 1955

The greatest illusion [of Communism] was that industrialization and collectivization in the U.S.S.R., and destruction of capitalist ownership, would result in a classless society. In 1936, when the new Constitution was promulgated, Stalin announced that the "exploiting class" had ceased to exist. The capitalist and other classes of ancient origin had in fact been destroyed, but a new class, previously unknown to history, had been formed.

It is understandable that this class, like those before it, should believe that the establishment of its power would result in happiness and freedom for all men. The only difference between this and other classes was that it treated the delay in the realization of its illusions more crudely. It thus affirmed that its power was more complete than the power of any other class before in history, and its class illusions and prejudices were proportionally greater.

This new class, the bureaucracy, or more accurately the political bureaucracy, has all the characteristics of earlier ones as well as some new characteristics of its own.

C. Nikita Khrushchev Denounces Stalin's Crimes

At the present we are concerned with a question which has immense importance for the party now and for the future—[we are concerned] with how the cult of the person of Stalin has been gradually growing, the cult which became at a certain specific stage the source of a whole series of exceedingly serious and grave perversions of party principles, of party democracy, of revolutionary legality. . . .

When we analyze the practice of Stalin in regard to the direction of the party and of the country, when we pause to consider everything which Stalin perpetrated, we must be convinced that Lenin's fears were justified. The negative characteristics of Stalin, which, in Lenin's time, were only incipient, transformed themselves during the last years into a grave abuse of power by Stalin, which caused untold harm to our Party. . . .

Stalin acted not through persuasion, explanation, and patient co-operation with people, but by imposing his concepts and demanding absolute submission to his opinion. Whoever opposed this concept or tried to prove his viewpoint, and the correctness of his position, was doomed to removal from the leading collective and to subsequent moral and physical

annihilation. This was especially true during the period following the XVIIth Party Congress [1934], when many prominent party leaders and rank-and-file party workers, honest and dedicated to the cause of Communism, fell victim to Stalin's despotism.

We must affirm that the party had fought a serious fight against the Trotskyites, rightists and bourgeois nationalists, and that it disarmed ideologically all the enemies of Leninism. This ideological fight was carried on successfully, as a result of which the Party became strengthened and tempered. Here Stalin played a positive role. . . .

It was precisely during this period (1935–1937–1938) that the practice of mass repression through the government apparatus was born, first against the enemies of Leninism—Trotskyites, Zinovievites, Bukharinites, long since politically defeated by the party, and subsequently also against many honest Communists, against those party cadres who had borne the heavy load of the Civil War and the first and most difficult years of industrialization and collectivization, who actively fought against the Trotskyites and the rightists for the Leninist Party line. . . .

This led to glaring violations of revolutionary legality, and to the fact that many entirely innocent persons, who in the past had defended the party line, became victims.

We must assert that in regard to those persons who in their time had opposed the party line, there were often no sufficiently serious reasons for their physical annihilation. The formula, "enemy of the people," was specifically introduced for the purpose of physically annihilating such individuals. . . .

. . . Many party, soviet and economic activists who were branded in 1937–1938 as "enemies" were actually never enemies, spies, wreckers, etc., but were always honest Communists; they were only so stigmatized, and often, no longer able to bear barbaric tortures, they charged themselves (at the order of the investigative judges—falsifiers) with all kinds of grave and unlikely crimes. The commission [for investigation of the purge] has presented to the Central Committee Presidium lengthy and documented materials pertaining to mass repressions against the delegates to the XVIIth Party Congress and against members of the Central Committee elected at that Congress. These materials have been studied by the Presidium of the Central Committee.

It was determined that of the 139 members and candidates of the Party's Central Committee who were elected at the XVIIth Congress, 98 persons. i.e., 70 percent were arrested and shot (mostly in 1937–1938). (*Indignation in the hall*) . . .

Facts prove that many abuses were made on Stalin's orders without reckoning with any norms of party and Soviet legality. Stalin was a very distrustful man, sickly suspicious; we knew this from our work with him. He could look at a man and say: "Why are your eyes so shifty today?" or "Why are you turning so much today and avoiding to look me directly in the eyes?" The sickly suspicion created in him a general distrust even toward eminent party workers whom he had known for years. Everywhere and in everything he saw "enemies," "two-facers" and "spies."

Possessing unlimited power he indulged in great willfulness and choked a person morally and physically. A situation was created where one could not express one's own will.

When Stalin said that one or another should be arrested, it was necessary to accept on faith that he was an "enemy of the people." Meanwhile, Beria's gang, which ran the organs of state security, outdid itself in proving the guilt of the arrested and the truth of materials which it falsified. And what proofs were offered? The confessions of the arrested, and the investigative judges accepted these "confessions." And how is it possible that a person confesses to crimes which he has not committed? Only in one way—because of application of physical methods of pressuring him, tortures, bringing him to a state of unconsciousness, deprivation of his judgment, taking away of his human dignity. In this manner were "confessions" acquired. . . .

I recall the first days when the conflict between the Soviet Union and Yugoslavia began artificially to be blown up. Once, when I came from Kiev to Moscow, I was invited to visit Stalin who, pointing to the copy of a letter lately sent to Tito, asked me, "Have you read this?" Not waiting for my reply he answered, "I will shake my little finger—and there will be no more Tito. He will fall." . . .

But this did not happen to Tito. No matter how much or how little Stalin shook, not only his little finger but everything else that he could shake, Tito did not fall. Why? The reason was that, in this case of disagreement with the Yugoslav comrades, Tito had behind him a state and a people who had gone through a severe school of fighting for liberty and independence, a people which gave support to its leaders.

You see to what Stalin's mania for greatness led. He had completely lost consciousness of reality; he demonstrated his suspicion and haughtiness not only in relation to individuals in the USSR, but in relation to whole parties and nations. . . .

Some comrades may ask us: Where were the members of the Political Bureau of the Central Committee? Why did they not assert themselves against the cult of the individual in time? And why is this being done only now?

First of all we have to consider the fact that the members of the Political Bureau viewed these matters in a different way at different times. Initially, many of them backed Stalin actively because Stalin was one of the strongest Marxists and his logic, his strength and his will greatly influenced the cadres and party work. . . .

Later, however, Stalin, abusing his power more and more, began to fight eminent party and government leaders and to use terroristic methods against honest Soviet people. . . .

In the situation which then prevailed I have talked often with Nikolai Alexandrovich Bulganin; once when we two were traveling in a car, he said, "It has happened sometimes that a man goes to Stalin on his invitation as a friend. And when he sits with Stalin, he does not know where he will be sent next, home or to jail."

It is clear that such conditions put every member of the Political Bureau in a very difficult situation. And when we also consider the fact that in the last years the Central Committee plenary sessions were not convened and that the sessions of the Political Bureau occurred only occasionally, from time to time, then we will understand how difficult it was for any member of the Political Bureau to take a stand against one or another injust or improper procedure, against serious errors and shortcomings in the practices of leadership. . . .

Comrades: We must abolish the cult of the individual decisively, once and for all; we must draw the proper conclusions concerning both ideological-theoretical and practical work.

It is necessary for this purpose: . . . to return to and actually practice in all our ideological work the most important theses of Marxist-Leninist science about the people as the creator of history and as the creator of all material and spiritual good of humanity, about the decisive role of the Marxist Party in the revolutionary fight for the transformation of society, about the victory of Communism. . . .

We are absolutely certain that our party, armed with the historical resolutions of the XXth Congress, will lead the Soviet people along the Leninist path to new successes, to new victories. (*Tumultuous, prolonged applause*)

Long live the victorious banner of our party— Leninism! (*Tumultuous, prolonged applause ending in ovation. All rise.*)

D. A British Journalist Witnesses the Hungarian Revolution, 1956

In the Stalin square the next morning [late October, 1956], the people of Budapest had not only pulled down the dictator's statue, they were feverishly chopping it up into little bits, so that not a trace should remain. Outside the Communist Party headquarters was a mountain of cinders, consisting of burnt communist books and pamphlets. A ceaseless hail of these came hurtling out of the windows, together with paintings and photographs of Stalin, Lenin and Rákosi [the Hungarian Communist leader], to keep the fires alight. Even gramophone records of the leaders' speeches added to the blaze.

When these busy people realized who we were, they clustered around, beseeching us to let our countrymen know the truth, suggesting that we should take photographs of a big oil painting of Stalin which had just been hideously defaced. They slapped us on the back and shook our hands a dozen times, until we felt that we, not they, had liberated their city. An old woman in tears kissed my hand as if I were a Monsignore; and one of the Austrians suddenly found himself clasping two babies.

Meanwhile inside the building, a grim AVO [Allamvedelmi Osztaly, State Security Department] hunt was in progress. A number of AVO men had just been caught in the sewers and hanged, I was told. Would I care to step inside and take some photographs of them, for the benefit of the West? But the sight of the hanged men the night before had been enough, and I refused this invitation. The AVO men had evidently imagined that their Russian masters would quickly dominate the situation, and they had been waiting underground (literally) for this to happen. But when the lull came and they appeared in public again, they found to their dismay not the Russians, but the population of Budapest, in control. Their cruelties of the past were now expiated. After execution, their bodies were left hanging for an hour or so, for all to see; then the dust-carts came and took them away, and more were displayed. The Hungarians never seemed to tire of looking at the corpses of their late masters. To see the hate combined with glee on the faces of some of these people as they gazed on them was to realize what communism had done in ten years to the Hungarian mind. . . .

[On November 2] I was standing near the Chain bridge watching [the Soviets'] families leave, when an English journalist I had met the day before ran up to me and said, "If you want the story of your life, come to the Parliament buildings now! Nagy is about to make an important declaration about the Warsaw Pact."

I followed him to this building where, by showing his journalist's pass, he was able to take me upstairs, through salons and corridors full of the Biedermeyer furnishings, marble-mounted and ormolu mirrors from the last century, to the door of the cabinet room. Here, he said, the government had been in session for two hours, arguing about the weighty decision they are about to take.

On the first landing we were told to wait in a reception room, in which other journalists were walking up and down with notebooks. Suddenly the big doors opposite opened and we saw, for a moment, Kádár the new first secretary of the Communist Party, seated at a table, and at his shoulder the Prime Minister, Imre Nagy. Near the wall was the President, Tildy, whose voice seemed raised in argument. On the other side of the table, out of view, sat (we did not know it at the time), the Russian ambassador [Yuri] Andropov.[1]

A quarter of an hour later, an official from the Hungarian Foreign Office, whom my friend evidently knew, came out of the cabinet room quickly. Taking him by the arm he said in English, "Have you a motorcar? Well, leave Budapest immediately! Don't waste time here asking for more news. When it comes, you won't be able to leave."

He said that the government had decided to withdraw from the Warsaw Pact, and had appealed for help to the United Nations. Whatever Nagy might feel personally about the wisdom of this step, he felt it was the will of the Hungarian people. Some of the cabinet, and of course the Soviet ambassador, were trying to dissuade him; "And the pro-Russian forces in the cabinet will finally win," he said. "Nagy is now going to the radio building to make the announcement. But you see what will happen afterwards."

Five minutes later we saw the Russian ambassador leave hurriedly; and a half an hour later, Nagy went to make the courageous statement about withdrawing from the Warsaw Pact, which meant that Hungary was no longer a satellite—which was responsible virtually, too, for the second Russian intervention. But in the streets that evening the Hungarians were elated. "Nagy has cleaned his slate," they said. "We can support him, he's our man now." . . .

[The British Legation soon ordered all British journalists and non-essential personnel to leave the

---

[1] In 1982–1983 Andropov would serve as General Secretary of the Soviet Communist Party.

country, sensing what was about to happen. Rhodes and others in his party drove westward, toward the Austrian frontier.]

A wintry gale from the south-east was now blowing, stripping off the leaves and sweeping them along in slanting squalls of snow and sleet. Not far from Györ, we ran into a heavy snow-storm and then, through the falling flakes, we saw ahead a large tank going in our direction. "A 50-ton Stalin," said one of the British officials in our party learnedly. "What splendid tanks the Russians have left the insurgents!"

It was difficult to pass this tank because it was moving west too: I blew the horn impatiently, to get it to withdraw to the side of the road. At length we managed to squeeze past, only to find ahead of it another Stalin tank of the same size. Again I blew the horn in irritation—and again at last we managed to pass. But there was yet another tank in front of this and then, as we rounded a corner, a whole line of them running out ahead, about fifteen, trundling along, wagging their guns and antennae.

"Really! These insurgent tanks ought to get off the roads to let us pass," said the British official again. But then as we passed one of them, a face appeared at the turret and looked down—a Mongolian face. ". . . they are Russians!" he finished lamely.

Our car was in fact sandwiched in a long column of Russian tanks. More Mongoloid faces peered down at us as we passed, blank, expressionless, slit-eyed, beneath bell-shaped helmets. The Russians were bringing up their eastern troops. With these not particularly reassuring road companions we remained for nearly three-quarters of an hour, trying to pass. It is understandable that to men in such machines the ordinary, standard motor-horn means little or nothing.

After Györ, we saw more Russians in a maize field at the side of the road—armoured cars with tents around them, soldiers eating their midday meal out of mess-tins in the snow. Young for the most part, the term "simple soldier" applied to these men admirably. Of the thirty or so I saw, twenty at least were Mongoloid, almost Chinese, in appearance; several had taken off their helmets and were scratching their shaven heads. These were the troops who were gathering around Budapest for the assault due to take place in two days' time. Although dirty and slovenly in appearance, there was a businesslike air about their equipment and vehicles. They could clearly move, fire and communicate with one another by wireless. And what more can you ask of the modern soldier?

We later learned that we were one of the last Western convoys these Russian troops allowed through. A few hours later, their tanks fanned out along the Austrian frontier, closing it completely, in preparation for the assault. To travellers from Budapest, Red Cross personnel, or journalists wishing to "file" their cables in Vienna, they repeated the two words, "*Niet Wien!*" stubbornly, and forced them to return to Györ, Magyaróvár, or Budapest itself. In this way we came to Nickelsdorf again, and left the people, who, by liberating themselves, were soon to liberate Eastern Europe from the excesses of communism.

E. Solzhenitsyn's Ivan Denisovich Survives One More Day

At that very moment the door bolt rattled to break the calm that now reigned in the barracks. From the corridor ran two of the prisoners . . .

"Second count," they shouted.

On their heels came a guard.

"All out to the other half." . . .

"Damn them," said Shukhov. Mildly, because he hadn't gone to sleep yet.

Tsezar raised a hand and gave him two biscuits, two lumps of sugar, and a slice of sausage.

"Thank you, Tsezar Markovich," said Shukhov, leaning over the edge of his bunk. . . .

Then he waited a little till more men had been sent out—he wouldn't have to stand barefoot so long in the corridor. But the guard scowled at him and shouted: "Come on, you there in the corner." . . .

"Do you want to be carried out, you shits?" the barracks commander shouted.

They shoved them all into the other half of the barracks . . . Shukhov stood against the wall near the bucket. The floor was moist underfoot. An icy draft crept in from the porch.

They had them all out now, and once again the guard and the orderly did their round, looking for any who might be dozing in dark corners. There'd be trouble if they counted short. . . .

Shukhov managed to squeeze in eighteenth. He ran back to his bunk . . .

All right. Feet back into the sleeve of his jacket. Blanket on top. Then the coat. . . .

Now for that slice of sausage. Into the mouth. Getting your teeth into it. Your teeth. The meaty taste. And the meaty juice, the real stuff. Down it goes, into your belly.

Gone. . . .

Shukhov went to sleep fully content. He'd had many strokes of luck that day: they hadn't put him in the cells; they hadn't sent his squad to the settlement; he'd swiped a bowl of kasha at dinner. . . .

F. Socialist Czechoslovakia Provides Maternal and Infant Health Care Services, 1948–1978

	1948	1957	1967	1976	1978
Resources					
Prenatal clinics	434	1,625	1,812	1,840	1,840
Obstetrical/gynecological beds	6,531	12,624	14,856	15,932	15,935
Specialized obstetricians	326	1,030	1,865	2,341	2,407
Midwives	2,643	4,648	5,570	6,387	6,510
Activities					
Deliveries in maternity homes (%)	41	86	99.2	99.8	99.8
Average number of visits to prenatal clinics per woman	0.6	3.9	7.1	9.2	9.4
Outcome					
Maternal mortality rate per 100,000 deliveries	137	63	28	15	13
Cases of eclampsia per 100,000 deliveries		122	68	35	34
Perinatal mortality rate per 1,000 live births	51	26.3	20.9	20.3	18.5
Stillbirth rate per 1,000 live births	19	11.6	7.1	6.8	6.0
Early neonatal mortality rate per 1,000 live births	32	14.7	13.8	13.5	12.5

Document Set 28.3 References

A. Andrei Zhdanov Defines Politically Correct Soviet Literature, 1947
   Zhdanov, in Thomas Riha, ed., *Readings in Russian Civilization* (Chicago: University of Chicago Press, 1964), 3:685–691.
B. Milovan Djilas Defines the "New Class," 1955
   Djilas, *The New Class: An Analysis of the Communist System* (New York: Praeger, 1963), 37–38.
C. Nikita Khrushchev Denounces Stalin's Crimes
   Khrushchev, "De-Stalinization," in Robert V. Daniels, ed., *A Documentary History of Communism* (New York: Vintage Press, 1962), 2:224–231.

D. A British Journalist Witnesses the Hungarian Revolution, 1956
   Anthony Rhodes, "Hungary 1956" in Tamas Aczel, ed., *Ten Years After: The Hungarian Revolution in the Perspective of History* (New York: Holt, Rinehart & Winston, 1967), 83–85, 88–92.
E. Solzhenitsyn's Ivan Denisovich Survives One More Day
   Alexander Solzhenitsyn, *One Day in the Life of Ivan Denisovich*, trans. Max Hayward and Ronald Hingley (New York: Praeger, 1963), 206–210.
F. Socialist Czechoslovakia Provides Maternal and Infant Health Care Services, 1948–1978
   Alena Heitlinger, *Reproduction, Medicine and the Socialist State* (London: Macmillan, 1987), 79.

DOCUMENT SET 28.4
Rebuilding Western Europe

George C. Marshall (1880–1959), the U.S. Army's chief of staff during World War II, became Truman's secretary of state in the first years of the Cold War, 1947–1949. His name will be forever associated with the Marshall Plan, the program of economic assistance for reconstruction that the United States offered to Europe after the war and that was accepted by the nations of western Europe. (Stalin rejected it, determined that the emerging Soviet Bloc would rebuild without capitalist assistance.) Document A, Marshall's brief commencement speech at Harvard in 1947 in which he unveiled the plan, conveys the rationale and the essence of the American policy. Document B, taken from an official British report on conditions in occupied Germany in the autumn of 1947, suggests something of the needs to which the Marshall Plan responded.

West Europeans dedicated to the humane reconstruction of their war-shattered societies nevertheless debated vigorously among themselves over the extent to which the state should actively direct recovery and distribute scarce resources. The liberal British economist William Beveridge (1879–1963), later named Lord Beveridge, headed an official commission that in 1941–1942 outlined the future policies of what would become known as the "welfare state," which included a good measure of Keynesian economic theory aiming at preventing future depressions by maintaining "full employment" (Document C). The equally distinguished Austrian-born British economist Friedrich von Hayek (1899–1993), a liberal in the nineteenth-century sense rather than in Beveridge's twentieth-century sense, responded to the prospect of a postwar socialist Britain by writing *The Road to Serfdom* (1945; Document D) as a warning against any "statist" solution to Europe's postwar problems. Hayek lived to win a Nobel Prize for economics in the neo-conservative 1990s, although he was widely condemned in the 1940s as an economic reactionary. In the immediate postwar years, public opinion in Britain and other west European countries strongly endorsed the welfare state in terms generally along the lines of the woman quoted in Document E. One reason for this widespread support was the continuing presence of women in the work force—and in non-agricultural sectors, which involved daily work outside the household and created an ever-growing need for government-sponsored child-care and old-age support programs. Document F, a statistical table of female employment in Germany, demonstrates the long-range trends.

Using these documents and the coverage of postwar Europe in *The Challenge of the West,* assess the impact of the Marshall Plan and the European's debate over the welfare state.

A. American Secretary of State George C. Marshall Calls for American Assistance in Rebuilding a War-Shattered World, 1947

I need not tell you, gentlemen, that the world situation is very serious. That must be apparent to all intelligent people. I think one difficulty is that the problem is one of such enormous complexity that the very mass of facts presented to the public by press and radio make it exceedingly difficult for the man in the street to reach a clear appraisement of the situation. Furthermore, the people of this country are distant from the troubled areas of the earth and it is hard for them to comprehend the plight and consequent reactions of the long-suffering peoples, and the effect of those reactions on their governments in connection with our efforts to promote peace in the world.

In considering the requirements for the rehabilitation of Europe the physical loss of life, the visible destruction of cities, factories, mines and railroads was correctly estimated, but it has become obvious during recent months that this visible destruction was probably less serious than the dislocation of the entire fabric of European economy. For the past ten years conditions have been highly abnormal.

The feverish preparation for war and the more feverish maintenance of the war effort engulfed all aspects of national economies. Machinery has fallen into disrepair or is entirely obsolete. Under the arbitrary and destructive Nazi rule, virtually every possible enterprise was geared into the German war machine. Long-standing commercial ties, private institutions, banks, insurance companies and shipping companies disappeared, through loss of capital, absorption through nationalization or by simple destruction.

In many countries, confidence in the local currency has been severely shaken. The breakdown of the business structure of Europe during the war was complete. Recovery has been seriously retarded by the fact that two years after the close of hostilities a peace settlement with Germany and Austria has not been agreed upon. But even given a more prompt solution of these difficult problems, the rehabilitation of the economic structure of Europe quite evidently will require a much longer time and greater effort than had been foreseen.

There is a phase of this matter which is both interesting and serious. The farmer has always produced the foodstuffs to exchange with the city dweller for the other necessities of life. This division of labor is the basis of modern civilization. At the present time it is threatened with breakdown. The town and city industries are not producing adequate goods to exchange with the food-producing farmer. Raw materials and fuel are in short supply. Machinery is lacking or worn out.

The farmer or the peasant cannot find the goods for sale which he desires to purchase. So the sale of his farm produce for money which he cannot use seems to him an unprofitable transaction. He, therefore, has withdrawn many fields from crop cultivation and is using them for grazing. He feeds more grain to stock and finds for himself and his family an ample supply of food, however short he may be on clothing and the other ordinary gadgets of civilization. Meanwhile, people in the cities are short of food and fuel. So the governments are forced to use their foreign money and credits to procure these necessities abroad. This process exhausts funds which are urgently needed for reconstruction. Thus a very serious situation is rapidly developing which bodes no good for the world. The modern system of the division of labor upon which the exchange of products is based is in danger of breaking down.

The truth of the matter is that Europe's requirements for the next three or four years of foreign food and other essential products—principally from America—are so much greater than her present ability to pay that she must have substantial additional help, or face economic, social and political deterioration of a very grave character.

The remedy lies in breaking the vicious circle and restoring the confidence of the European people in the economic future of their own countries and of Europe as a whole. The manufacturer and the farmer throughout wide areas must be able and willing to exchange their products for currencies, the continuing value of which is not open to question.

Aside from the demoralizing effect on the world at large and the possibilities of disturbances arising as a result of the desperation of the people concerned, the consequences to the economy of the United States should be apparent to all. It is logical that the United States should do whatever it is able to do to assist in the return of normal economic health in the world, without which there can be no political stability and no assured peace.

Our policy is directed not against any country or doctrine but against hunger, poverty, desperation and chaos. Its purpose should be the revival of a working economy in the world so as to permit the emergence of political and social conditions in which free institutions can exist. Such assistance, I am convinced, must not be on a piecemeal basis as various crises develop. Any assistance that this Government may render in the future should provide a cure rather than a mere palliative.

Any government that is willing to assist in the task of recovery will find full cooperation. I am sure, on the part of the United States Government. Any government which maneuvers to block the recovery of other countries cannot expect help from us. Furthermore, governments, political parties or groups which seek to perpetuate human misery in order to profit therefrom politically or otherwise will encounter the opposition of the United States.

It is already evident that, before the United States Government can proceed much further in its efforts to alleviate the situation and help start the European world on its way to recovery, there must be some agreement among the countries of Europe as to the requirements of the situation and the part those countries themselves will take in order to give proper effect to whatever action might be undertaken by this Government. It would be neither fitting nor efficacious for this Government to undertake to draw up unilaterally a program designed to place Europe on its feet economically. This is the business of the Europeans. The initiative, I think, must come from Europe. The role of this country should consist of friendly aid in the drafting of a European program and of later support of such a program so far as it may be practical for us to do so. The program should be a joint one, agreed to by a number, if not all European nations.

An essential part of any successful action on the part of the United States is an understanding on the part of the people of America of the character of the problem and the remedies to be applied. Political passion and prejudice should have no part. With foresight, and a willingness on the part of our people to face up to the vast responsibility which history has clearly placed upon our country, the difficulties I have outlined can and will be overcome.

B. British Officials Report on Conditions in the British Zone in Germany, October 1947

. . . The situation in Germany has been affected by certain outstanding events. First, there was the Agreement, signed in New York in December, 1946, for the fusion of the British and American Zones. The principal objects of the Agreement were the improved administration of the economy of the two Zones and the provision of money for their economic rehabilitation. This entailed the setting up of a bipartite administration and the hastening of the transfer of power to the Germans in the British Zone, which was not so advanced in this matter as the American Zone. The second event was the transfer of considerable powers of local government to the German Governments at *Land* [state] level and below. Among the powers transferred were responsibility for education, public health and the police. Thirdly, in chronological order, was the severity of last winter. Its effects are still being felt. Great hardships were suffered, industry almost came to a standstill and the fusion agreement had a bad start. Fourthly, there was the failure of the Foreign Ministers' Conference in Moscow, which had serious effects for Germany, and made quadripartite agreement even more difficult. A direct result of this failure was the fifth major event, the strengthening of the fusion agreement and the setting up of a central bizonal economic organization at Frankfurt. Lastly, there was the breakdown in the food supply in the spring, which led to a severe shortage from the latter part of March until well into June. The basic ration which was nominally fixed at 1,550 calories fell to below 1,000. As a result, coal production, on which the prosperity of the Zone depends, dropped disastrously at a time when it had just reached a new high level of 233,000 tons a day. In addition, this shortage had a great effect on the morale of the Germans, whose feelings hardened towards those whom they were bound to hold responsible for their conditions.

7. The situation at present may be summarised briefly as follows:—

(1) Disarmament is virtually complete, but demilitarisation by the removal of industrial plant as reparations has hardly begun. . . .

(2) Denazification has almost finished. At the beginning of October responsibility for it was handed over to the Germans, with instruction that it was to be completed by the end of the year.

(3) In the political sphere, some progress has been made in the democratisation of the German system, such as the introduction of an electoral system by which an elector votes for a candidate and not a party list; but the German Civil Service is still far from being non-political.

(4) The labour problem is acute. Out of a total population in the Zone of about 22 1/4 million, only some 9 million are in employment. To put it in another way, before the war over 47 per cent. of the population was employed. In order to reach this percentage to-day, it would be necessary to increase the labour force by 2 million. The explanation is largely to be found in the present lack of balance in the age groups. Apart from the absence of prisoners of war, the additions to the population of refugees from eastern Germany have aggravated the position. At least 75 per cent. of the 1 1/2 million refugees accepted into the Zone have been old and infirm or children. One result is that there is practically no unemployment of fit men, although there is undoubtedly some underemployment.

(5) The food situation remains extremely serious. The basic ration for the normal consumer is now 1,550 calories, but it is not by any means always honoured. The stocks of bread-grains and meat are better than they were at this time last year, but the drought during the summer has reduced the supply of fats and has caused a poor potato harvest. The immediate aim is to increase the ration to at least 1,800 calories, but the prospects for such an increase during the next year are not promising.

(6) The level of coal production, vital to German recovery, follows the level of the food ration. By last March production had risen to 233,000 tons a day, but the shortage of food in the spring caused it to fall to little over 210,000. By September, the figure had reached 240,000 tons.

(7) The volume of industrial production in the British Zone has only increased from 33 per cent. to 34 per cent. of the 1936 figure.[1] The factors which are preventing industrial recovery are lack of food, lack of coal, and lack of incentive, especially the lack of any real purchasing power in the Reichsmark.

(8) Transport is in a very bad state, owing to the lack of steel and timber for the repair of locomotives, rolling stock and permanent was Road transport and the inland waterways are in little better condition. In fact it is difficult to see how it is going to be possible to move any extra coal which the miners may produce. The position is aggravated by the fact that repairs scarcely keep pace with wastage and no new construction is being carried out; and by the delay in

[1] The figure for the combined Zones is 37 per cent.

the return of a large number of wagons which have travelled outside the Zone, carrying exported coal.

(9) The export trade reflects the general low level of the economy of the combined Zone. . . .

C. William Beveridge Explains "The Nature of Full Employment Policy"

As unemployment has three distinct sources, action against unemployment must be taken on three lines—of maintaining at all times adequate total outlay; of controlling the location of industry; of securing the organized mobility of labour. The first of these is the main attack: the others are subsidiary—mopping-up operations. Employment depends on outlay, that is to say on the spending of money on the products of industry; when employment falls off, this means that someone is spending less; when employment increases, this means that in total more is being spent. The first condition of full employment is that total outlay should always be high enough to set up a demand for products of industry which cannot be satisfied without using the whole man-power of the country: only so can the number of vacant jobs be always as high as or higher than the number of men looking for jobs. Who is to secure that the first condition is satisfied? The answer is that this must be made a responsibility of the State. No one else has the requisite powers; the condition will not get satisfied automatically. It must be a function of the State in future to ensure adequate total outlay and by consequence to protect its citizens against mass unemployment, as definitely as it is now the function of the State to defend the citizens against attack from abroad and against robbery and violence at home. Acceptance of this new responsibility of the State, to be carried out by whatever Government may be in power, marks the line which we must cross, in order to pass from the old Britain of mass unemployment and jealousy and fear to the new Britain of opportunity and service for all.

D. Friedrich von Hayek Warns Against Taking the *Road to Serfdom*

[Socialism] may mean, and is often used to describe, merely the ideals of social justice, greater quality, and security, which are the ultimate aims of socialism. But it means also the particular method by which most socialists hope to attain these ends and which many competent people regard as the only methods by which they can be fully and quickly attained. In this sense socialism means the abolition of private enter-prise, of private ownership of the means of production, and the creation of a system of "planned economy" in which the entrepreneur working for profit is replaced by a central planning body.

There are many people who call themselves socialists, although they care only about the first, who fervently believe in those ultimate aims of socialism but neither care nor understand how they can be achieved, and who are merely certain that they must be achieved, whatever the cost. But to nearly all those to whom socialism is not merely a hope but an object of practical politics, the characteristic methods of modern socialism are as essential as the ends themselves. Many people, on the other hand, who value the ultimate ends of socialism no less than the social-ists refuse to support socialism because of the dangers to other values they see in the methods proposed by the socialists. The dispute about socialism has thus become largely a dispute about means and not about ends—although the question whether the different ends of socialism can be simultaneously achieved is also involved.

This would be enough to create confusion. And the confusion has been further increased by the common practice of denying that those who repudiate the means value the ends. But this is not all. The situation is still more complicated by the fact that the same means, the "economic planning" which is the prime instrument of socialist reform, can be used for many other purposes. We must centrally direct economic activity if we want to make the distribution of income conform to current ideas of social justice. "Planning," therefore, is wanted by all those who demand that "production for use" be substituted for production for profit. But such planning is no less indispensable if the distribution of incomes is to be regulated in a way which to us appears to be the opposite of just. Whether we should wish that more of the good things of this world should go to some racial élite, the Nordic men, or the members of a party or an aristoc-racy, the methods which we shall have to employ are the same as those which could insure an equalitarian distribution. . . .

. . . Nearly all the points which are disputed between socialists and liberals concern the methods common to all forms of collectivism and not the par-ticular ends for which socialists want to use them; and all the consequences with which we shall be con-cerned in this book follow from the methods of col-lectivism irrespective of the ends for which they are used. It must also not be forgotten that socialism is not only by far the most important species of collec-tivism of "planning" but that it is socialism which has persuaded liberal-minded people to submit once more to that regimentation of economic life which they had overthrown because, in the words of Adam Smith, it puts governments in a position where "to support themselves they are obliged to be oppressive and tyrannical."

... "Planning" owes its popularity largely to the fact that everybody desires, of course, that we should handle our common problems as rationally as possible and that, in so doing, we should use as much foresight as we can command. In this sense everybody who is not a complete fatalist is a planner, every political act is (or ought to be) an act of planning, and there can be differences only between good and bad, between wise and foresighted and foolish and shortsighted planning. An economist, whose whole task is the study of how men actually do and how they might plan their affairs, is the last person who could object to planning in this general sense. But it is not in this sense that our enthusiasts for a planned society now employ this term, nor merely in this sense that we must plan if we want the distribution of income or wealth to conform to some particular standard. According to the modern planners, and for their purposes, it is not sufficient to design the most rational permanent framework within which the various activities would be conducted by different persons according to their individual plans. This liberal plan, according to them, is no plan—and it is, indeed, not a plan designed to satisfy particular views about who should have what. What our planners demand is a central direction of all economic activity according to a single plan, laying down how the resources of society should be "consciously directed" to serve particular ends in a definite way.

The dispute between the modern planners and their opponents is, therefore, *not* a dispute on whether we ought to choose intelligently between the various possible organizations of society; it is not a dispute on whether we ought to employ foresight and systematic thinking in planning our common affairs. It is a dispute about what is the best way of so doing. The question is whether for this purpose it is better that the holder of coercive power should confine himself in general to creating conditions under which the knowledge and initiative of individuals are given the best scope so that *they* can plan most successfully; or whether a rational utilization of our resources requires *central* direction and organization of all our activities according to some consciously constructed "blueprint." The socialists of all parties have appropriated the term "planning" for planning of the latter type. ...

E. A British Woman Praises the Welfare State

The 1950s was a time when state intervention in children's lives was highly visible, and experienced, by me at least, as entirely beneficent. The calculated, dictated fairness of the ration book went on into the new decade, and we spent a lot of time ... picking up medicine bottles of orange juice and jars of Virol from the baby clinic for my sister. I think I would be a very different person now if orange juice and milk and dinners at school hadn't told me, in a covert way, that I had a right to exist, was worth something. ... I think that had I grown up with my parents only twenty years before, I would not now believe this. ... Being a child when the state was practically engaged in making children healthy and literate was a support against my own circumstances. ...

It was a considerable achievement for a society to pour so much milk and so much orange juice, so many vitamins, down the throats of its children, and for the height and weight of those children to outstrip the measurements of only a decade before. ... Within that period of time more children were provided with the goods of the earth than had any generation been before. What my mother lacked, I was given; and though vast inequalities remained between me and others of my generation, the sense that a benevolent state bestowed on me, that of my own existence and the worth of that existence ... demonstrates in some degree what a fully material culture might offer in terms of physical comfort and the structures of care and affection that it symbolizes, to all its children.

F. The Rise of Female Employment in Germany, 1882–1970

Sector	1882	1895	1907	1925	1933	1939	1950	1961	1970
Agricultural	34.8%	31.9%	28.2%	17.0%	13.7%	11.0%	8.0%	1.7%	0.9%
Household service	40.0	34.4	26.2	21.7	19.0	18.4	12.4	4.9	1.7
Trade	1.6	2.4	4.9	9.0	12.5	11.2	11.9	16.7	17.5
Old service[2]	3.4	5.6	6.2	6.1 ⎫	18.6	11.5	12.1	15.8	15.8
New service[3]	3.0	3.7	5.4	8.8 ⎭		10.3	14.6	20.1	23.4
Clerk	0.1	0.2	1.2	5.2	5.1	6.3	6.7	10.4	13.4
No permanent post or not indicated	2.5	1.3	0.9	1.3	0.7	0.1	5.2	0.3	—
Industry	14.5	20.5	27.0	30.8	30.4	31.2	29.1	30.1	27.4
Number in millions	3.494	4.351	5.08	6.264	6.398	7.321	4.8	6.999	7.638

[2] Old service occupations: public administration and military, church, culture, personal service (innkeeping, beautician), cleaning.
[3] New service occupations: education, health, hygiene, welfare, legal, transport and commerce, banks and insurance, architecture and laboratory.

Document Set 28.4 References

A. American Secretary of State George C. Marshall Calls for American Assistance in Rebuilding a War-Shattered World, 1947
"The Address of Secretary Marshall at Harvard," *The New York Times*, Friday, June 6, 1947.

B. British Officials Report on Conditions in the British Zone in Germany, October 1947
Beate Ruhm von Oppen, ed., *Documents on Germany Under Occupation* (Oxford: Oxford University Press, 1955), 251–253.

C. William Beveridge Explains "The Nature of Full Employment Policy"
Beveridge, *Full Employment in a Free Society* (New York: W. W. Norton, 1945), 29.

D. Friedrich von Hayek Warns Against Taking the *Road to Serfdom*
Friedrich A. von Hayek, *The Road to Serfdom* (Chicago: University of Chicago Press, 1945), 32–35.

E. A British Woman Praises the Welfare State
Carolyn Kay Steedman, *Landscape for a Good World: A Story of Two Lives* (New Brunswick, N.J.: Rutgers University Press, 1987), 121–123.

F. The Rise of Female Employment in Germany, 1882–1970
Walter Müller, Angelika Willms, and Johann Handl, *Strukturwandel der Frauenarbeit, 1880–1980* (Frankfurt/New York: Campus Verlag, 1983), 176.

DOCUMENT SET 28.5
Postwar Survivors Take Stock of Their Values

Liberation from Nazi oppression was greeted ecstatically by every European except those who had reason to worry about being branded a collaborationist (a not-inconsiderable number) and Germans fearful of what the conquerors had in store for them. But soon the stark realities sank in, creating deep pessimism and cynicism. Document A and B record the impressions of two British writers of democratic-socialist leanings who visited, respectively, France in late 1945 and "darkest Germany" in 1947.

The philosophical school that captured the postwar European imagination was existentialism, a body of thought with roots in nineteenth-century cultural despair and that was capable of being interpreted to fit a wide range of political stances, from fascism to liberal democracy and communism. The central existentialist idea was that human beings had no predetermined "essence" or meaning, but were free—some said "condemned"—to create their own values, to define themselves in terms of the actual fact of their "existence." (Did this core idea give existentialism its capacity for adapting to *any* political ideology?) The foremost existentialist of postwar Europe was Jean-Paul Sartre (1905–1980), a French intellectual of middle-class origin and communist sympathies who rocketed to fame after 1945 as an inspired playwright and novelist—and as the author of ponderous philosophical essays that every "with-it" undergraduate of the day felt obliged to attempt. (Sartre even became a "must-see" celebrity as postwar American tourists in Paris dutifully sought a glimpse of him haunting his favorite Montmartre cafés.) A relatively lucid exposition of Sartre's brand of atheistic existentialism is excerpted as Document C. Sartre's reputation faded in the 1960s, just as the influence of his long-time companion Simone de Beauvoir (1908—1986) was growing enormously as the philosophical inspirer of the women's liberation movement. Beauvoir's feminist manifesto *The Second Sex,* published in 1949, was infused by the existentialist conviction that women could define and therefore free themselves only by emancipation from their male-defined "otherness" (Document D). Hers was to prove probably the most enduring legacy of postwar existentialism.

One reason for Sartre's decline as an intellectual prophet was his never-broken connection with the French Communist Party, which increasingly made him an apologist for Stalinism. His fellow-existentialist and one-time co-editor of the French left-wing paper *Combat,* Albert Camus (1913–1960), broke with the Communists in 1948 and thereafter made his way as a gadfly: a novelist, playwright, and essayist committed to finding human values in what he considered an inherently meaningless world. The Hungarian revolution of 1956 (ended by a bloodbath that Sartre refused to condemn) elicited from Camus the passionate outburst against knee-jerk leftism quoted as Document E. Camus died "meaninglessly" in an auto crash in 1960, at the dawn of the decade in which his writings would find their widest reverberation among young people struggling for idealistic commitment.

Against the background of Europe's—particularly Germany's—recovery, of systematic "de-Nazification" and "re-education" campaigns, and of intellectuals' search for meaning in human existence, it is instructive to follow German public opinion as it was repeatedly polled on the question of who "really" caused World War II. What conclusions do you draw, particularly from the trend in the responses "Germany," "other states," and "do not know"?

Persistent cultural pessimism and—from 1948 onward—steady economic recovery seemed to go hand-in-hand in western Europe. Drawing on this document set and on your reading of *The Challenge of the West,* how do you account for this?

A. A Journalist Records the Mood in Liberated Paris, November 1945

. . . Except for the row between de Gaulle and the Communists, nobody seems much interested in politics. Much more interested in food conditions. . . . Black market in full swing—sugar, wine, coffee, cigarettes. . . . Life in Paris not quite normal yet. Taxis very hard to get. In principle, they are only for pregnant women. Lots of silly jokes about it. . . . Lot of metro stations still closed. . . . They don't seem to sweep even the parks. Walked through the Tuileries today over a rustling eight-inch carpet of red leaves. . . . Talk with Bidault at the Quai. Rhineland, Ruhr, Ruhr coal are his chief worries. . . . Furious with Molotov for failing to support France. . . . To my question about how the Communists fitted into the government, he made a face, and said: "*Hm . . .enfin, ça va . . . à peu près. . . .*" Wretched "black market" dinner in a "workmen's bistrot", Batignolles way— 300 francs for two: 30s at the present preposterous rate; they say there's going to be devaluation—480 to the £—even that will be far too little.... Streets badly lit at night. Lots of robberies and burglaries.... GI's responsible for some of them. *France-Soir* came out with big headline; "CHICAGO-SUR-SEINE," telling about misdeeds by the GI's.

Some anti-American feeling almost everywhere; strong anti-Russian feeling among the *nice* people, but still some vestiges of previous admiration for the Red Army, Stalingrad, etc. Good deal of anti-Russian stuff in the popular press.... Half the people I meet claim to have been "in the Resistance." But they also say: "Most unfair to have shot Laval. He did his best. We wouldn't be here but for him. . ." . . . Economic *collabos* (met one who made a fortune building bits of the Atlantic Wall) running around freely and living in luxury. They also talk in a starry-eyed way of Sartre and "existentialism"; very fashionable these days. Called on Jean-Richard Bloch at *Ce Soir*. Found him very pessimistic. "Everything going to hell; all the old (and new) reactionaries coming up on top again.". . . *Daily X* chap (eyes popping out): "We must, must, MUST get the Communists thrown out of the Government . . . Fifth Column . . ." and so on. Same attitude among the rest of the Anglo-American press, who eat beastly American-canned-food lunches (mostly bully-beef hash) at the Scribe. . . . Quite different attitude *chez* Duff Cooper [British politician], who thinks it's *very sensible* of de Gaulle to keep them in the Government. Thinks Thorez [French Communist leader] a tremendous chap "with great charm" (has asked him to the Embassy to lunch), and thinks that several of the others are "very able and earnest fellows," especially Croizat.

Spent a week in Normandy. The peasants, who made fortunes during the war and had no trouble to speak of, all claim to have been "in the Resistance." Like hell they were. They continue to make fortunes, selling meat to the black market in Paris. Except for a privileged minority, Paris is hungry and down-at-heel; but in Normandy—in the countryside—I was served steaks that hung over the sides of the plate.... The peasants are for de Gaulle and against the Communists. Most of them seem to have voted MRP which they consider "de Gaulle's Party". But what interests them most is the attitude of the parties to the *bouilleurs de crû* [the private distiller of tax-free apple brandy].... Railways running, but slowly, and very few trains. Took nearly ten hours, with a change at Le Mans, to get to Alençon. . . . The curator of the "museum" attached to one of the Norman *châteaux*—a dusty little old man, like something out of Courteline—treated me to a long discourse on *la*

crise morale which, he said, was *quite* general in France. Even small children were crooks. . . .

B. A British Editor Travels "In Darkest Germany," 1947

The worst thing in Germany—worse than the malnutrition, the overcrowding, the gaping footwear in the schools—is the spiritual condition of the youth. I thought I had touched bottom in Jülich, where in cellar after cellar I found 5, 6, 9 people—fathers, mothers, children, adult daughters and sons—all jumbled together without light or air, and lacking even the pretence of any decent privacy. But a conference with young people at Düsseldorf a day later, and then another, were still more horrible; and what I learned then confirmed similar experiences with university students at Kiel and Hamburg.

The attitude of the youth varies from one of a puzzled bewilderment, still friendly to the British— these are in a minority—to bitterness, cynicism and a growing hostility to us and all our works. The mood is not (yet) pro-Nazi: it shows rather a nihilistic contempt for government and governments of every kind. They contrast our promises with our deeds: the B.B.C. told us, they say, that you were coming to liberate us, but what has it all amounted to? I mention democracy; and they ask whether democracy means starvation rations and lack of the barest necessities, or turning people out of their homes and seizing their furniture, or blowing up shipyards, closing down factories, and throwing tens of thousands of men out of employment. I risk a question about Nuremberg; and they say—at the very best—yes, they were guilty, but so are the Allies: look at the expellees, sick, starving and robbed, not thousands of them but millions. Many jeer openly at Nuremberg. I met no single young person who denied the Nazi guilt; but I met very few who thought it in any way special, or different in kind from that of all politicians everywhere. They talk a good deal about justice; and they want to know whether it is just to hale a man off to internment without trial and release him as innocent a year later. They talk, too, about their ostracism by the British on the one hand, and the behaviour of our troops to German girls on the other.

At the root is despair about the future. Time after time I was told "We don't mind how hard life is if only we can have something to hope for". But they see their factories being dismantled; they know that hundreds of other factories are on the list; and the majority are convinced that we are determined to ruin them, partly by way of punishment but mainly as commercial rivals. The minority wonders.

And yet—I am convinced of it after contact with them—they had, and perhaps still have, the makings in them of good democrats. After Belsen, the worst of all my experiences was when a university student at Hamburg said in an agonized voice "For God's sake don't make us Nazis." If we are to save them we must (1) stop doing the things they justly criticise, and give instead a living example of the liberal tradition; (2) put a little psychological understanding into our propaganda, which, on such subjects as war guilt or the world food situation, has been contemptible when it has not been non-existent; (3) increase the establishment of the education and youth section of the C.C.G., which is doing devoted work, but is as grotesquely understaffed as Trade and Industry is overstaffed, and is frustrated at every turn into the bargain; (4) remove the nightmare of uncertainty from the German future—which is to say, abandon Potsdam.

C. Jean-Paul Sartre Defines Atheistic Existentialism

[Existentialism] has been reproached as an invitation to people to dwell in quietism of despair. For if every way to a solution is barred, one would have to regard any action in this world as entirely ineffective, and one would arrive finally at a contemplative philosophy. Moreover, since contemplation is a luxury, this would be only another bourgeois philosophy. This is, especially, the reproach made by the Communists.

From another quarter we are reproached for having underlined all that is ignominious in the human situation...

From the Christian side, we are reproached as people who deny the reality and seriousness of human affairs. For since we ignore the commandments of God and all values prescribed as eternal, nothing remains but what is strictly voluntary. Everyone can do what he likes, and will be incapable, from such a point of view, of condemning either the point of view or the action of anyone else.

It is to these various reproaches that I shall endeavor to reply . . . [W]e can begin by saying that existentialism, in our sense of the word, is a doctrine that does render human life possible; a doctrine, also, which affirms that every truth and every action imply both an environment and a human subjectivity. . . .

Atheistic existentialism, of which I am a representative, declares with greater consistency that if God does not exist there is at least one being whose existence comes before its essence, a being which exists before it can be defined by any conception of it. That being is man . . . What do we mean by saying that existence precedes essence? We mean that man first of all exists, encounters himself, surges up in the world—and defines himself afterwards . . . [T]here is no human nature, because there is no God to have a conception of it. . . .

D. Simone de Beauvoir Calls for Women's Liberation, 1952

According to French law, obedience is no longer included among the duties of a wife, and each woman citizen has the right to vote; but these civil liberties remain theoretical as long as they are unaccompanied by economic freedom. A woman supported by a man—wife or courtesan—is not emancipated from the male because she has a ballot in her hand; if custom imposes less constraint upon her than formerly, the negative freedom implied has not profoundly modified her situation; she remains bound in her condition of vassalage. It is through gainful employment that woman has traversed most of the distance that separated her from the male; and nothing else can guarantee her liberty in practice. Once she ceases to be a parasite, the system based on her dependence crumbles; between her and the universe there is no longer any need for a masculine mediator.

The curse that is upon woman as vassal consists, as we have seen, in the fact that she is not permitted to do anything; so she persists in the vain pursuit of her true being through narcissism, love, or religion. . . .

It is quite understandable, also, that the milliner's apprentice, the shopgirl, the secretary, will not care to renounce the advantages of masculine support. I have already pointed out that the existence of a privileged caste, which she can join by merely surrendering her body, is an almost irresistible temptation to the young woman; she is fated for gallantry by the fact that her wages are minimal while the standard of living expected of her by society is very high. If she is content to get along on her wages, she is only a pariah: ill lodged, ill dressed, she will be denied all amusement and even love. Virtuous people preach asceticism to her, and, indeed, her dietary regime is often as austere as that of a Carmelite [nun]. Unfortunately, not everyone can take God as a lover;

From *The Second Sex* by Simone de Beauvoir, trans. H. M. Parshley, pp. 679, 681, 696–7, 715. Copyright 1952 and renewed 1980 by Alfred A. Knopf Inc. Reprinted by permission of the publisher.

she has to please men if she is to succeed in her life as a woman. She will therefore accept assistance, and this is what her employer cynically counts on in giving her starvation wages. This aid will sometimes allow her to improve her situation and achieve a real independence; in other cases, however, she will give up her work and become a kept woman. She often retains both sources of income and each serves more or less as an escape from the other; but she is really in double servitude: to job and to protector. For the married woman her wages represent only pin money as a rule; for the girl who "makes something on the side" it is the masculine contribution that seems extra; but neither of them gains complete independence through her own efforts.

There are, however, a fairly large number of privileged women who find in their professions a means of economic and social autonomy. These come to mind when one considers woman's possibilities and her future. This is the reason why it is especially interesting to make a close study of their situation, even though they constitute as yet only a minority; they continue to be a subject of debate between feminists and antifeminists. The latter assert that the emancipated women of today succeed in doing nothing of importance in the world and that furthermore they have difficulty in achieving their own inner equilibrium. The former exaggerate the results obtained by professional women and are blind to their inner confusion. . . .

There is one feminine function that is actually almost impossible to perform in complete liberty. It is maternity. In England and America and some other countries a woman can at least decline maternity at will, thanks to contraceptive techniques. We have seen that in France she is often driven to painful and costly abortion or she frequently finds herself responsible for an unwanted child that can ruin her professional life. If this is a heavy charge, it is because inversely, custom does not allow a woman to procreate when she pleases. The unwed mother is a scandal to the community, and a illegitimate birth is a stain on the child; only rarely is it possible to become a mother without accepting the chains of marriage or losing caste. If the idea of artificial insemination interests many women, it is not because they wish to avoid intercourse with a male, it is because they hope that freedom of maternity is going to be accepted by society at last. It must be said in addition that in spite of convenient day nurseries and kindergartens, having a child is enough to paralyze a woman's activity entirely; she can go on working only if she abandons it to relatives, friends, or servants. She is forced to choose between sterility, which is often felt as a

painful frustration, and burdens hardly compatible with a career.

Thus the independent woman of today is torn between her professional interests and the problems of her sexual life; it is difficult for her to strike a balance between the two; if she does, it is at the price of concessions, sacrifices, acrobatics, which require her to be in a constant state of tension. . . .

The free woman is just being born; when she has won possession of herself perhaps Rimbaud's prophecy will be fulfilled: "There shall be poets! When women's unmeasured bondage shall be broken, when she shall live for and through herself, man—hitherto detestable—having let her go, she, too, will be poet! Woman will find the unknown! Will her ideational worlds be different from ours? She will come upon strange, unfathomable, repellent, delightful things; we shall take them, we shall comprehend them." It is not sure that her "ideational worlds" will be different from those of men, since it will be through attaining the same situation as theirs that she will find emancipation; to say in what degree she will remain different, in what degree these differences will retain their importance—this would be to hazard bold predictions indeed. What is certain is that hitherto woman's possibilities have been suppressed and lost to humanity, and that it is high time she be permitted to take her chances in her own interest and in the interest of all.

E. Albert Camus Announces That "Conformity Is on the Left," 1957

. . . [W]e must hope for a common rallying. But first our Leftist intellectuals, who have swallowed so many insults and may well have to begin doing so again, would have to undertake a critique of the reasonings and ideologies to which they have hitherto subscribed, which have wreaked the havoc they have seen in our most recent history. That will be the hardest thing. We must admit that today conformity is on the Left. To be sure, the Right is not brilliant. But the Left is in complete decadence, a prisoner of words, caught in its own vocabulary, capable merely of stereotyped replies, constantly at a loss when faced with the truth, from which it nevertheless claimed to derive its laws. The Left is schizophrenic and needs doctoring through pitiless self-criticism, exercise of the heart, close reasoning, and a little modesty. Until such an effort at re-examination is well under way, any rallying will be useless and even harmful. Meanwhile, the intellectual's role will be to say that the king is naked when he is, and not to go into raptures over his imaginary trappings.

In order to strike a constructive note, however, I shall propose as one of the preliminaries to any future gathering the unqualified acceptance of the following principle: none of the evils that totalitarianism (defined by the single party and the suppression of all opposition) claims to remedy is worse than totalitarianism itself.

In conclusion, I believe (as people say: I believe in God, creator of heaven and earth) that the indispensable conditions for intellectual creation and historical justice are liberty and the free confronting of differences. Without freedom, no art; art lives only on the restraints it imposes on itself, and dies of all others. But without freedom, no socialism either, except the socialism of the gallows.

F. West Germans Ponder Their Country's Responsibility for World War II, 1951–1964

Question: *"It may be hard to say, but who do you think was really responsible for the outbreak of war in 1939?"*

	Oct. 1951 %	May 1955 %	April 1956 %	May 1959 %	Aug. 1962 %	May 1964 %
Germany	32	43	47	50	53	51
Other states	24	14	12	11	9	9
Both sides	18	15	11	10	10	7
International capitalism	6	5	5	6	3	2
Fate, the circumstances of that time	4	3	3	3	5	2
Other factors	1	1	2	2	1	2
Do not know	15	19	20	19	20	28
	100	100	100	101	101	101

Document Set 28.5 References

A. A Journalist Records the Mood in Liberated Paris, November 1945
Alexander Werth, *France 1940–1955* (New York: Henry Holt, 1956), 276–277.

B. A British Editor Travels "In Darkest Germany," 1947
Victor Gollancz, *In Darkest Germany* (Hinsdale, Ill.: Regnery, 1947), 230–232.

C. Jean-Paul Sartre Defines Atheistic Existentialism
Sartre, *Existentialism*, in Walter Kaufmann, ed., *Existentialism from Dostoevsky to Sartre* (New York: Meridian, 1974), 345–368 passim.

D. Simone de Beauvoir Calls for Women's Liberation, 1952
Simone de Beauvoir, *The Second Sex*, H. M. Parshley, ed. and trans. (New York: Alfred A. Knopf, 1952), 679, 681, 696–697, 715.

E. Albert Camus Announces That "Conformity Is on the Left," 1957
Camus, *Resistance, Rebellion, and Death*, trans. Justin O'Brien (New York: Modern Library, 1960), 128–129.

F. West Germans Ponder Their Country's Responsibility for World War II, 1951–1964
Public Opinion Poll, in Elizabeth Noelle and Erich Peter Neumann, eds., *The Germans* (Allensbach and Bonn: Verlag für Demoskopie, 1967), 199.

Contemporary Voices, The 1960s to the Present

DOCUMENT SET 29.1
Voices of Anger and Frustration

Unlike other document sets in *Connecting with the Past*, those in Chapter 29 are tied not to one but to two chapters in *The Challenge of the West*, Chapters 29 and 30. The selections have been made to challenge you to use your textbook and your understanding of your own times to look for historical linkages in events and trends that are still unfolding.

How, for example, do you interpret the Francophone African Frantz Fanon's 1960s cry for the Third World to utterly reject the West as inherently racist, imperialist, and capitalist (Document A)? Has his demand been superseded by events since the 1960s, and in particular by contemporary "globalizing" trends? Conversely, perhaps, does it take on new relevance now that the East-West clash of the Cold War may be giving way to a North-South struggle of "have-nots" against "haves," or even of Islamic fundamentalism against the Western world? Does the term *Third World* still have much meaning? Did it ever?

Now that one of Europe's longest-running guerrilla wars may be ending, it is instructive to recall Irish Republican Army leader Gerry Adams's 1979 pronouncement (Document B) on his movement's ultimate aims. In retrospect, do you see Adams's rhetoric as post-1960s flamboyance? Was the I.R.A. a genuinely revolutionary movement? How would you place it in the context of nationalist movements of the nineteenth and early twentieth centuries? Does reading this document cause you to modify whatever impression you may have of the I.R.A. and Sinn Fein based on current news reports?

Recent accounts of racist attacks on Europe's new ethnic minorities should put Document C into perspective. Considering the question in historical perspective, why has it been so difficult for Europeans—particularly but not exclusively for the French and Germans—to accept racial pluralism and ethnic minorities? Do you hear echoes of earlier anti-assimilationist sentiments? (Which ones, and why?) Is there something inherently or historically exclusionist about all—or certain—Western societies? Is there any reason why anti-"outsider" emotions should run so high at the present time?

A. Third World Revolutionary Frantz Fanon Analyzes the Self-Identity of Colonized Peoples

I propose nothing short of the liberation of the man of color from himself. . . .

The black shoolboy in the Antilles, who in his lessons is forever talking about "our ancestors, the [French]," identifies himself with the explorer, the bringer of civilization, the white man who carries truth to savages—an all-white truth. There is identification—that is, the young Negro subjectively adopts a white man's attitude. . . .

Little by little, one can observe in the young Antillean the formation and crystallization of an attitude and a way of thinking and seeing that are essentially white. When in school he has to read stories of savages told by white men, he always thinks of the

[African]. . . . The Negro lives in Africa. Subjectively, intellectually, the Antillean conducts himself like a white man. But he is a Negro. That he will learn once he goes to Europe; and when he hears Negroes mentioned he will recognize that the word includes himself.

B. Terrorist Gerry Adams Reveals the IRA's Ultimate Aims, 1979

The task that we, as republicans, have set ourselves, and the ills affecting our people and our country are too complex to be satisfied merely by a British withdrawal or by the establishment of a 32 county neo-colonial Free State.[1] We are not, and never have been, merely a 'Brits Out' movement. . . . We stand opposed to all forms and all manifestations of imperialism and capitalism. We stand for an Ireland free, united, socialist and Gaelic . . . . Our movement needs constructive and thoughtful self-criticism. We also require links with those oppressed by economic and social pressures. Today's circumstances and our objectives dictate the need for building an agitational struggle in the 26 Counties, an economic resistance movement, linking up republicans with other sections of the working class. It needs to be done now because to date our most glaring weakness lies in our failure to develop revolutionary politics and to build an alternative to so-called constitutional politics.

C. Germany's Turks Face Racism

As the Turkish workers were recruited and later, as their families came, they discovered at first that they were welcome as workers but despised as human beings. Where they sought a dwelling, which they often only found with great difficulty, they had the experience that Germans moved out, because they did not want to live under the same roof as Turks. Where they were provided with dwellings by the state or their employers, these were often dwellings in which Germans no longer wanted to live because there was a lack of sanitary facilities, etc. The different culture of the Turks, their different socialisation,

was unilaterally rejected by the majority of the German population as backward or even uncivilised. Even members of the German left put emphasis on issues like the severe repression of Turkish women, without knowing its causes through their own experience, while ignoring for instance the significance of mutual neighbourly help. This meant that foreign citizens were not treated humanely by the Germans, and were forced into a ghetto situation. At the same time, such treatment created the desire among Turkish citizens of at least maintaining a degree of national and cultural identity. The process of withdrawal from a society in which foreigners were only welcome as workers began. Turkish associations and tea-rooms were set up, in which it was possible to find some part of that emotional security which had been lost through emigration to an alien and hostile country. But exclusion from German society also created the conditions for the spread of mistaken nationalist feelings and even fascist ideas among foreigners. The idea that all Germans were bad arose for many people from the shattering experiences of daily life in Germany. Today German racist nationalism is therefore matched by nationalism on the part of the foreigners. Nationalism is in principle a mistaken and harmful idea, but it is necessary to differentiate between the nationalism of the oppressor and the nationalism of the oppressed which arises in response. The nationalism of the oppressed is wrong and harmful and must therefore be overcome through joint struggle, the nationalism of the oppressor is a crime.

Document Set 29.1 References

A. Third World Revolutionary Frantz Fanon Analyzes the Self-Identity of Colonized Peoples
Fanon, *Black Skin, White Masks*, trans. Charles Lam Markmann (New York: Grove, 1967), 8, 147–148.
B. Terrorist Gerry Adams Reveals the IRA's Ultimate Aims, 1979
Adams, Bodenstown oration, in Kevin J. Kelley, *The Longest War: Northern Ireland and the I.R.A.* (London: Zed Books, 1982, 1988), 303.
C. Germany's Turks Face Racism
Stephen Castles, *Here for Good: Western Europe's New Ethnic Minorities* (London: Pluto Press, 1984), 221–222.

[1] Historically, Ireland is divided into thirty-two counties; of these, twenty-six today constitute the Republic of Ireland and six remain part of the United Kingdom.

DOCUMENT SET 29.2
Voices of Hope

Document A, taken from an address by the Indian prime minister Jawaharlal Nehru (1889–1964) to a congress of Asian historians in 1961, deserves to be read alongside Frantz Fanon's protest (Set 29.1, Document A). Is this statement by Mohandas Gandhi's successor as India's paramount leader an example of the historic convergence of West and non-West? An instance of the West's fruitful influence upon the Third World? Or a manifestation of the West's successful cultural imperialism, which may prove more persistent than the relatively short-lived political imperialism of recent centuries? And, incidentally, what has awareness of the distant western past (which evidently made a powerful impression on Nehru) offered people of the twentieth century, particularly those descended from other cultural traditions?

The convocation of the Roman Catholic church's ecumenical council Vatican II in 1961 marked a great turning point in that ancient institution's history. Out of this gathering came the abandonment of many church practices, including the exclusive use of Latin in the liturgy, rules on fasting, and the prohibition against giving the laity communion "in both kinds"— practices that the church's refusal to modify in past centuries had led to heresies and even martyrs. (Review the medieval and early modern chapters of *The Challenge of the West* for examples.) More important still, Vatican II produced a profound questioning within the ranks of Catholic laypeople and clergy, and it marked a willingness by the papacy "to dialogue" with non-Catholic and non-Christian faiths unprecedented in its history. What was the significance of these changes, and why did they occur only in the late twentieth century—rather than, for example, in the late nineteenth or late eighteenth century? To what changes in the twentieth-century world did the Roman Catholic church respond?

In retrospect, the 1975 Helsinki Conference on European Security may also be assuming great historic significance. It gave final confirmation to the border changes of postwar Europe, promised the Soviet Bloc that the West harbored no "revanchist" ambitions to upset the continental balance of power, created a mechanism for the peaceful resolution of disputes, encouraged ongoing disarmament negotiations, and enunciated basic human rights that all signatories pledged to respect. In what ways can you connect these promises with the slow unraveling of Europe's communist dictatorships over the next fif-

teen years? Do you see any parallels to attempts in previous centuries (particularly the early nineteenth century) to create a "concert of Europe"? And why is it that changes in Europe's borders began to occur only after the fall of Communism, and may not yet be completed?

A. Jawaharlal Nehru Takes a Long View of History, 1961

The old idea of writing a history of any one country has become progressively out of date. It is impossible today to think of the history of a country isolated from the rest of the world. The world is getting integrated. We have really to consider history today in a world perspective.

What is the basic philosophy of history? I try to think of history as a process that leads man to higher and better stages of progress. Then I find to my surprise that those higher stages have been represented by great men in the long past. Having been fascinated by the scientific and technological civilization which has been built in Europe and in America, I gradually come to a stage when it seems to me to have stopped. I begin seeking for something deeper than merely the physical aspect of civilization. I find that my mind is more interested in what Plato or the Buddha said, which has a timelessness about it. So I wonder if our present-day history, having fulfilled its destiny in so far as science and technology are concerned, is at all moving on to a higher plane of human existence. I do not presume that the average historian will be able to answer such a question unless he himself becomes a great seer who can pierce the veil of the future. But he can help in putting things in proper perspective.

B. Pope John XXIII Convokes the Second Vatican Council, 1961

Painful Considerations

Today the Church is witnessing a crisis under way within society. While humanity is one the edge of a new era, tasks of immense gravity and amplitude await the Church, as in the most tragic periods of its history. It is a question in fact of bringing the modern world into contact with the vivifying and perennial energies of the gospel, a world which exalts itself with its conquests in the technical and scientific fields, but which brings also the consequences of a temporal order which some have wished to reorganize excluding God. This is why modern society is earmarked by a great material progress to which there is not a corresponding advance in the moral field.

Hence there is a weakening in the aspiration toward the values of the spirit. Hence an urge for the almost exclusive search for earthly pleasures, which progressive technology places with such ease within the reach of all. And hence there is a completely new and disconcerting fact: the existence of a militant atheism which is active on a world level.

Reasons for Confidence

These painful considerations are a reminder of the duty to be vigilant and to keep the sense of responsibility awake. Distrustful souls see only darkness burdening the face of the earth. We, instead, like to reaffirm all our confidence in our Savior, who has not left the world which He redeemed.

Indeed, we make ours the recommendation of Jesus that one should know how to distinguish the "signs of the times" (Mt. 16:4), and we seem to see now, in the midst of so much darkness, a few indications which auger well for the fate of the Church and of humanity.

The bloody wars that have followed one on the other in our times, the spiritual ruins caused by many ideologies, and the fruits of so many bitter experiences have not been without useful teachings. Scientific progress itself, which gave man the possibility of creating catastrophic instruments for his destruction, has raised questions. It has obliged human beings to become thoughtful, more conscious of their own limitations, desirous of peace, and attentive to the importance of spiritual values. And it has accelerated that progress of closer collaboration and of mutual integration toward which, even though in the midst of a thousand uncertainties, the human family seems to be moving. And this facilitates, no doubt, the apostolate of the Church, since many people who did not realize the importance of its mission in the past are, taught by experience, today more disposed to welcome its warnings.

Present Vitality of the Church

Then, if we turn our attention to the Church, we see that it has not remained a lifeless spectator in the face of these events, but has followed step by step the evolution of peoples, scientific progress, and social revolution. It has opposed decisively the materialistic ideologies which deny faith. Lastly, it has witnessed the rise and growth of the immense energies of the apostolate of prayer, of action in all fields. It has seen the emergence of a clergy constantly better equipped in learning and virtue for its mission; and of a laity which has become ever more conscious of its responsibilities within the bosom of the Church, and, in a special way, of its duty to collaborate with the Church hierarchy.

To this should be added the immense suffering of entire Christian communities, through which a multitude of admirable bishops, priests, and laymen seal their adherence to the faith, bearing persecutions of all kinds and revealing forms of heroism which certainly equal those of the most glorious periods of the Church. . . .

. . . [W]elcoming as from above the intimate voice of our spirit, we considered that the times now were right to offer to the Catholic Church and to the world the gift of a new Ecumenical Council, as an addition to, and continuation of, the series of the twenty great councils, which have been through the centuries a truly heavenly providence for the increase of grace and Christian progress. . . .

The forthcoming Council will meet therefore and at a moment in which the Church finds very alive the desire to fortify its faith, and to contemplate itself in its own awe-inspiring unity. In the same way, it feels more urgent the duty to give greater efficiency to its sound vitality and to promote the sanctification of its members, the diffusion of revealed truth, the consolidation of its agencies. . . .

And, finally, to a world, which is lost, confused, and anxious under the constant threat of new frightful conflicts, the forthcoming Council must offer a possibility for all men of good will to turn their thoughts and their intentions toward peace, a peace which can and must, above all, come from spiritual and supernatural realities, from human intelligence and conscience, enlightened and guided by God the Creator and Redeemer of humanity.

Working Program of the Council

These fruits that we expect so much from the Council, and on which we like so often to dwell, entail a vast program of work which is now being prepared. This concerns the doctrinal and practical problems which correspond more to the requirements of perfect conformity with Christian teaching, for the edification and in the service of the Mystical Body and of its supernatural mission, and, therefore, the sacred books, venerable tradition, the sacraments, prayer, ecclesiastical discipline, charitable and relief activities, the lay apostolate, and mission horizons.

This supernatural order must, however, reflect its

efficiency in the other order, the temporal one, which on so many occasions is unfortunately ultimately the only one that occupies and worries man. In this field, the Church also has shown that it wishes to be *Mater et Magistra*—Mother and Teacher—according to the words of our distant and glorious predecessor, Innocent III, spoken on the occasion of the Fourth Lateran Council [in 1215]. . . .

C. The Helsinki Final Act Puts Human Rights on the International Agenda, 1975

VII. Respect for human rights and fundamental freedoms, including the freedom of thought, conscience, religion or belief

The participating States will respect human rights and fundamental freedoms, including the freedom of thought, conscience, religion or belief, for all without distinction as to race, sex, language or religion.

They will promote and encourage the effective exercise of civil, political, economic, social, cultural and other rights and freedoms all of which derive from the inherent dignity of the human person and are essential for his free and full development.

Within this framework the participating States will recognize and respect the freedom of the individual to profess and practice, alone or in community with others, religion or belief acting in accordance with the dictates of his own conscience.

The participating States on whose territory national minorities exist will respect the right of persons belonging to such minorities to equality before the law, will afford them the full opportunity for the actual enjoyment of human rights and fundamental freedoms and will, in this manner, protect their legitimate interests in this sphere.

The participating States recognize the universal significance of human rights and fundamental freedoms, respect for which is an essential factor for the peace, justice and well-being necessary to ensure the development of friendly relations and co-operation among themselves as among all States.

They will constantly respect these rights and freedoms in their mutual relations and will endeavour jointly and separately, including in cooperation with the United Nations, to promote universal and effective respect for them.

They confirm the right of the individual to know and act upon his rights and duties in this field.

In the field of human rights and fundamental freedoms, the participating States will act in conformity with the purposes and principles of the Charter of the United Nations and with the Universal Declaration of Human Rights. They will also fulfill their obligations as set forth in the international declarations and agreements in this field, including, *inter alia*, the International Covenants on Human Rights, by which they may be bound.

VIII. Equal rights and self-determination of peoples

The participating States will respect the equal rights of peoples and their right to self-determination, acting at all times in conformity with the purposes and principles of the Charter of the United Nations and with the relevant norms of international law, including those relating to territorial integrity of States.

By virtue of the principle of equal rights and self-determination of peoples, all peoples always have the right, in full freedom, to determine, when and as they wish, their internal and external political status, without external interference, and to pursue as they wish their political, economic, social and cultural development.

The participating States reaffirm the universal significance of respect for and effective exercise of equal rights and self-determination of peoples for the development of friendly relations among themselves as among all States; they also recall the importance of the elimination of any form of violation of this principle.

Document Set 29.2 References

A. Jawaharlal Nehru Takes a Long View of History, 1961
   Nehru, address, in Sarvepalli Gopal, ed., *Jawaharlal Nehru: An Anthology* (Delhi: Oxford University Press, 1980), 538–539.
B. Pope John XXIII Convokes the Second Vatican Council, 1961
   John XXIII, in Walter M. Abbott, S. J., ed. and trans., *The Documents of Vatican II: All Sixteen Official Texts Promulgated by the Ecumenical Council 1963–1965* (New York: Herder and Herder, 1966), 703–707.
C. The Helsinki Final Act Puts Human Rights on the International Agenda, 1975
   Helsinki Final Act, human rights provision, in John Fry, *The Helsinki Process: Negotiating Security and Cooperation in Europe* (Washington: National Defense University Press, 1993), 186–187.

DOCUMENT SET 29.3
Voices of Reason

Willy Brandt (1913–1992), the mayor of West Berlin when the Wall was erected in 1961 (see Set 28.2, Document F), went on to become federal chancellor and the author of West Germany's *Ostpolitik,* an attempt beginning in 1969 to open up the German Democratic Republic, Eastern Europe, and the Soviet Union to West German influence by building economic ties and abandoning previous efforts to reverse the postwar territorial divisions. In pursuing this policy, Brandt aroused no little suspicion among the other Western powers that he was flirting with neutralism and undercutting American efforts to speak for NATO. How would you evaluate the justification for his policy, which he described in his 1991 memoirs (Document A)? Was he taking the first steps that would lead to Helsinki in 1975 (see Set 29.2, Document C)? What did his alliance partners have to fear in the specter of West German neutrality, and what historical echoes did such a prospect touch off? Can you compare his policy to Bismarckian *Realpolitik*? What has been the long-term pattern of Germany's relationship with Central and Eastern Europe, down to the present day? And what does Brandt's account say for United States policy toward the Soviet Union in the era of those self-professed *Realpolitikers* Richard Nixon and Henry Kissinger?

Kissinger (born 1923 in Fürth, Germany, and as a young man a Jewish refugee from Nazism) was a discerning student of history; before he became a shaper of American foreign policy he was known for his admiring study of Metternich's diplomacy in restoring Europe's balance of power after 1815. The extract that serves as Document B, from an interview after his service as secretary of state, shows him in typical form reflecting on international relations from a historical viewpoint. What, in your opinion, had such Old World conservatives as Metternich and Bismarck to teach Americans in the art of diplomacy? Given their political views, were they appropriate role models for American policy makers, or for other shapers of foreign policy in democratic nations? What is the relative weight of ideology and "realism" in the thinking that Kissinger here displays? How do you react to Kissinger's historical perspective, and has your study of history given you other insights? Did thinking such as Kissinger's play any role in ending the Cold War, and is it still appropriate in the post-Cold War world?

The Club of Rome was an informal organization of world business leaders formed to ponder the impli-

cations of the energy and raw-materials shortages that so rudely shocked the West in 1973. Using elaborate computer models, it concluded that the world was not only running dangerously low on resources but was also adding population at a dangerous rate and recklessly polluting the environment. What earlier demographic pessimist, from the end of the eighteenth century, does this scenario recall? In Document C, the Club of Rome's experts in 1977 grimly warn the western world to modify drastically its lifestyle or risk global doom. Almost two decades later, do you find these warnings still valid? What would be the implications of implementing these recommendations? How do you react to the Club's warnings about technology? Is it fair to say that the Club of Rome is calling for a restructuring of Western values themselves? If so, what values does it attack, and what are their historical roots? To what extent do the Club's recommendations reflect a genuinely global perspective?

Michel Foucault (1926–1984), an extract from whose *Madness and Civilization* (1961) appears as Document D, appears here as a representative of the important contemporary philosophical trend known variously as post-structuralism or post-modernism. On the evidence of Foucault's claim that all cultures reflect codes embedded in their languages, thought processes, and values, would you place this school in the western philosophical tradition as it has been traced in *The Challenge of the West*? Is it fair, specifically, to see this trend in the succession of basically rationalist attempts to understand the world? Or does it seem to represent a new departure by reducing culture to a series of codes? Does it seem to confine cultures and the people who comprise them to deterministic paths of thought and action? Do you see any political implications in Foucault's argument?

A. Willy Brandt Explains the Evolution of His Ostpolitik

I was not happy about the concept of *Ostpolitik* as it was first ascribed to me and then identified with me. But how can you capture a term which has acquired a life of its own and been swiftly adopted into foreign languages? Why did I dislike the label? Because I was afraid it suggested that I regarded foreign policy as a chest from which you might pull out now one drawer, now another. Together with my colleagues, and not least my Foreign Minister and Deputy Chancellor, I assumed that we needed two things at the same time, and co-ordinated with each other: reliable partnership with the West, and the understanding with the East that was laboriously taking shape and must then be extended. I was aware that our national interests simply would not allow us to oscillate between West and East.

Reduced to basics, this meant that our efforts in *Ostpolitik* must be attuned to our Western partners and rooted in the political structure of the Atlantic Alliance. Even more simply: our *Ostpolitik* had to begin in the West. But developments since the Western treaties of 1955 meant that relations as normal and productive as possible were also called for with the Soviet Union and the other Warsaw Pact countries. Normalizing those relations was necessary for the Federal Republic to be able to protect its own interests in European co-operation on anything like an equal footing. We were therefore determined to do what we could to encourage peace on a basis of the utmost possible security—'in awareness of our special responsibility in Europe and to the best of our ability, which we do not, however, overestimate.'

At the time, in the autumn of 1969, a West European summit conference of the six Common Market countries was imminent. It took place in The Hague at the beginning of December. We said that this conference could and perhaps would decide whether Western Europe took a brave step forward or plunged into a dangerous crisis. My government assumed that the European Economic Community would have to be made deeper and broader, and needed both the United Kingdom and the other countries that were willing to join. It must also find appropriate forms of co-operation with those European states which could not or would not join. We determined that German and French unanimity could be the deciding factor in this process. We would try to give our close contractual ties with France a steadiness which would be a model for the nature of relations between European partners. We declared our readiness to encourage closer co-operation in foreign policy, with the aim of helping the Western European states, step by step, to adopt a common stance on international political questions.

Another important point of departure was our assumption that the North Atlantic Alliance would continue to guarantee our security. Its firm coherence was the prerequisite for the kind of solidarity of conduct which could lead to détente in Europe. Safeguarding peace was the first essential, whether we were concerned with a serious and tenacious effort to bring about proportional arms limitation, or with the

guaranteeing of our own security policy. As part of the Western Alliance, we wanted to help bring equilibrium between West and East. We saw our contribution as defensive, which was how the Western Alliance soon came to see itself. The Bundeswehr, we said, was not suitable for offensive strategy, by virtue either of its training and structure or of its arms and equipment. At no price would I be moved from the defensive principle that lay at the heart of our defence policy.

It has sometimes been suggested, not always kindly, that my policies may have been motivated by doubts about the intentions of the United States. They were not. However, it is true that I took an evaluation of the interests and special problems of the United States into consideration, and assumed that American commitment to Europe would be reduced rather than increased over the years. But I stated with the utmost clarity that our close ties with the United States excluded any doubt about the binding nature of the duties they had undertaken towards Europe, the Federal Republic and West Berlin. Our common interest required neither additional assurances nor repeated declarations. They supported a more independent German policy in a more active partnership. . . .

And what about keeping the Western powers informed? What about consulting them, in so far as their rights in connection with 'Germany as a whole' were affected? It is true that we wanted to represent ourselves—that goes for the East as well—and to that extent we wanted to be 'more equal' than before. We did observe the principle of regularly furnishing accurate information. However, Henry Kissinger was correct in saying that Brandt had not asked for permission, but for American co-operation in a political course whose direction was already determined.

You do not need to have read Kissinger's memoirs to know that there was ill-concealed suspicion in the Western capitals—as far as I could see, it was least felt in London; in Paris, there were marked swings between friendly understanding and wild speculation; the Washington attitude was quite simple—Nixon's security adviser told my eminent colleague Paul Frank in 1970 that any détente with the Soviet Union would be America's doing.

Before our meeting in April 1970 Nixon invited me to spend a few days of relaxation at Camp David. . . . Henry Kissinger turned up at the President's retreat, and did not trouble to hide his suspicions. In later years, however, he set the record straight by several times 'congratulating' me on the achievements of German *Ostpolitik*. He was once heard to say that all we got in return for accepting the division of Germany was 'improvements in the political atmosphere.' Kissinger, powerful as a security adviser, and later Secretary of State under Presidents Nixon and Ford, thought in terms of the Concert of Powers and the classic secret diplomacy of the nineteenth century. He saw Europeans as pawns in the great game of the superpowers.

B. Henry Kissinger Reflects on the Balance of Power

[Walter] Laqueur: There are interesting lessons to be learned about the relationship between legitimacy, equilibrium, and peace. But I am sure you will agree that the modern period in the history of diplomacy starts with Bismarck.

Kissinger: Of course. Without going into the specifics of his diplomacy, Bismarck essentially believed that an international system can be based entirely on the balance of power. The restraints that had been imposed by the common adherence to legitimate principles, along with the convictions that had developed since the eighteenth century, were so much baggage for him. Every state should be free to conduct its own policy based on its own conception of national interest. If it calculated correctly it would understand that there are inherent limits to its strength, and it would produce a rather moderate foreign policy. But at the same time it placed all its energies on the balance of power. Through extraordinarily skillful and extremely moderate foreign policy, Bismarck managed to create a united Germany and maintain the peace for about forty years, even after upsetting the previous system.

Contrary to popular belief, a policy based on pure balance of power is the most difficult foreign policy to conduct. It requires, first of all, a constantly correct assessment of the elements of power. Secondly, it demands a total ruthlessness and means that statesmen must be able to ignore friendship, loyalty, and anything other than the national interest. Third, it requires a domestic structure that will tolerate if not support this strategy. Fourth, it requires the absence of both permanent friends and permanent enemies, because as soon as a permanent enemy exists, freedom of maneuver is immediately reduced.

After Germany defeated France in 1871, the German generals insisted on the annexation of Alsace-Lorraine, which caused Bismarck to say, "I have achieved much more than I thought desirable in this war." He was correct: France became a permanent German enemy, and Germany's freedom of maneuver was greatly reduced. Indeed, the paradox of the German victory was that it, along with the German unification which followed, produced the very structural dangers that Bismarck sought to avoid. A united Germany was a threat to each of its neighbors; its very existence forced them into an alliance. Subsequent German leaders tried to be "reliable" and consistent in foreign affairs, but this only compounded their problems, for the more rigid their policy, the more united their neighbors became.

All of this is crucial in understanding the great tragedy in Western history: the outbreak of the First World War. . . .

C. The Club of Rome Proposes World Economic Goals, 1977

The population of the developed world makes up about 30 percent of the world population, and may shrink to no more than 10 percent in the next century, unless war, famine, and disease slow down the growth of human numbers in developing countries. Less than one-third of the world population controls more than two-thirds of its wealth, possesses 95 percent of existing scientific and technological research and development facilities, consumes some 40 percent of the world's nonrenewable resources, and contributes the lion's share of its pollution.

These conditions impose special responsibilities on the people of the developed world. They must take the initiative in specifying and pursuing global security, food, energy, and resource goals. They must work together with the poor nations to create a more just and sustainable international order. And they must also take care that their own lives are not locked into pathways of alienation, meaninglessness, and stress. There is, we believe, a set of feasible policy alternatives available to developed countries which responds to all these needs. They can improve the national quality of life and at the same time bring about more equity and justice in the world.

The already discussed goals related to security, food, energy, and resources need to be vigorously pursued in the developed world. Combined with them are goals to overcome the worst side effects of technological civilization without demanding unrealistic sacrifices from individuals and leaders.

Present conditions in the developed world arose from historical processes that resulted in significant achievements in the spheres of industry, agriculture, and social organization. These achievements are closely associated with efficient applications of science and technology and the creation of great national and corporate wealth. Discoveries in science led to rapid advances in technology, and these permitted the creation of large-scale production systems with decreasing unit costs. Higher productivity gave rise to increases in real income which, in turn, created a demand for more and more production in an ongoing spiral. The resultant economic process was self-reinforcing, product-proliferating, and energy- and materials-hungry. This pattern continued almost without interruption from the end of World War II to the early 1970s, despite fluctuations of the business cycle. . . .

During the 1970s many governmental and business leaders began to wonder whether the exponential growth of industries had begun to deplete stocks of nonrenewable natural resources. Since industry depends for continued growth on large stocks of reasonably priced natural resources as well as on cheap and abundant energies, more and more people began to question whether the industrial system would undermine itself by depleting its essential stocks.

The growth-no growth debates, triggered by *Limits to Growth,* the famous first report to the Club of Rome, are now history. Without rehashing well-worn arguments, it is enough to say that the issue for the economy is not whether to grow or not to grow; it is *how* to grow, and for what *purpose.* Growth for its own sake often proves to be contrary to human interests—it can depress, rather than enhance, the quality of life. Economic growth should serve human ends—and should occur only when it can fulfill this function. Further growth in pollution, traffic jams, urban conglomerations, mindless automation, and impersonal bureaucracy is contrary to human interests, although it might register as a contribution to economic growth when measured by such overall quantitative indicators as gross national product, national income, and international trade. But growth can occur in many areas where human needs are truly served—where the quality of life within developed countries is enhanced, and where world development and justice are promoted. Such growth is not undifferentiated but selective, and responds to social and cultural needs. The fact is that notwithstanding pockets of poverty, the basic material needs of people in affluent countries can already be fully met; the problem is better distribution, not more material growth. Further material growth would merely create increasing gaps between rich and poor. Hence rather than emphasizing overall growth, problems of distri-

bution and injustice need to be addressed, and ways and means found to reduce, and eventually eliminate, the alienation, isolation, and impersonal tenor of life in affluent urban environments. . . .

To improve the quality of life in developed countries, policies must be geared to reducing the undesirable side effects of economic growth—such as unemployment and inflation—and promoting the satisfaction of material, social, and cultural needs. Major goals must be to place less emphasis on material- and energy-wasteful modes of production and more on conservation and recycling; less emphasis on automated machines and more on human services. Industrialized societies can progress by improving education, health and social services, cultural activities, and recreational opportunities.

There is a great need to improve educational systems. . . .

Communication in the political sphere needs to be expanded. . . .

In most of the free market economies, health and social services are insufficiently funded. . . .

While there is much room for progress in such services areas, a linear increase in materials- and energy-wasteful production systems would worsen rather than improve the overall quality of life. The artificial inculcation of demand for certain types of products is a disservice to the public, as illustrated by advertising designed to sell gas-guzzling private automobiles. Continued increase in the number of such automobiles would produce serious health hazards, create transportation breakdowns, and increase energy and raw material costs.

A trend toward the standard concept of a "postindustrial" society, however, is not without its grave dangers. Technologies should not be put in use simply because they are available—not even automated production systems or electronic communication technologies. Employment could be much reduced, and there could be a decline in face-to-face communication. Privacy could be invaded, and extensive data files used to control behavior. People could be exposed to information overload. Indeed, wide use of electronic communication systems could be a bane as well as a blessing. On the one hand people could be freed from many manual chores, could have much leisure time, and could have the cultural and environmental facilities to fill such time with enjoyment; on the other hand such societies could become impersonal technocracies, subject to a high degree of surveillance, saturated with services, and plagued by unsolved problems of unemployment and alienation. . . .

D. Michel Foucault Describes the "Fundamental Codes of a Culture," 1961

The fundamental codes of a culture—those governing its language, its schemas of perception, its exchanges, its techniques, its values, the hierarchy of its practices—establish for every man, from the very first, the empirical orders with which he will be dealing and within which he will be at home. At the other extremity of thought, there are the scientific theories or the philosophical interpretations which explain why order exists in general, what universal law it obeys, what principle can account for it, and why this particular order has been established and not some other. But between these two regions, so distant from one another, lies a domain which, even though its role is mainly an intermediary one, is nonetheless fundamental: it is more confused, more obscure, and probably less easy to analyse. It is here that a culture, imperceptibly deviating from the empirical orders prescribed for it by its primary codes, instituting an initial separation from them, causes them to lose their original transparency, relinquishes its immediate and invisible powers, frees itself sufficiently to discover that these orders are perhaps not the only possible ones or the best ones; this culture then finds itself faced with the stark fact that there exist, below the level of its spontaneous orders, things that are in themselves capable of being ordered, that belong to a certain unspoken order; the fact, in short, that order *exists*. As though emancipating itself to some extent from its linguistic, perceptual, and practical grids, the culture superimposed on them another kind of grid which neutralized them, which by this superimposition both revealed and excluded them at the same time, so that the culture, by this very process, came face to face with order in its primary state. It is on the basis of this newly perceived order that the codes of language, perception, and practice are criticized and rendered partially invalid. It is on the basis of this order, taken as a firm foundation, that general theories as to the ordering of things, and the interpretation that such an ordering involves, will be constructed. Thus, between the already "encoded" eye and reflexive knowledge there is a middle region which liberates order itself: it is here that it appears, according to the culture and the age in question, continuous and graduated or discontinuous and piecemeal, linked to space or constituted anew at each instant by the driving force of time, related to a series of variables or defined by separate systems of coherences, composed of resemblances which are either successive or corresponding, organized around increasing differences, etc. This middle region, then, in so far as it makes manifest the modes of being of order, can be posited as the most fundamental of all: anterior to words, perceptions, and gestures, which are then taken to be more or less exact, more or less happy, expressions of it (which is why this experience of order in its pure primary state always plays a critical role); more solid, more archaic, less dubious, always more "true" than the theories that attempt to give those expressions explicit form, exhaustive application, or philosophical foundation. Thus, in every culture, between the use of what one might call the ordering codes and reflections upon order itself, there is the pure experience of order and its modes of being.

Document Set 29.3 References

A. Willy Brandt Explains the Evolution of His Ostpolitik
Brandt, *My Life in Politics* (New York: Viking Press, 1991), 172–175.

B. Henry Kissinger Reflects on the Balance of Power
Kissinger, *For the Record: Selected Statements, 1977–1980* (Boston: Little, Brown, 1977–1981), 119–120.

C. The Club of Rome Proposes World Economic Goals, 1977
Ervin Laszlo et al., eds., *Goals for Mankind: A Report to the Club of Rome on the New Horizons of Global Community* (New York: E. P. Dutton, 1977), 302–305.

D. Michel Foucault Describes the "Fundamental Codes of a Culture," 1961
Foucault, *The Order of Things* (New York: Random House, 1970).

DOCUMENT SET 29.4
Voices of Youth

A generation after students in the United States and France attempted to revolutionize their respective societies—and in the case of France briefly came close to toppling the Fifth Republic—how do the "Revolutions of 1968" appear to you? As students, are you sympathetic to your predecessors' demands on society, as expressed in Documents A and B? Is it fair to compare these uprisings to those of 1848? What evidence can you find at earlier moments in the history of Western society of students, as a group, emerging as an organized force for change? And do you find any prior evidence of the existence of youth cultures or subcultures manifesting themselves in a phenomenon such as rock music, as described in Document C? What is your reaction, as a western student familiar with the contemporary youth culture, to the solemn analysis that it received at Soviet hands in the 1980s (Document D)? In what ways does this youth culture "encode" (to use Foucault's terminology) liberating impulses? Do you see similar impulses imbedded in other aspects of the Western tradition?

A. French Students Complain That They "Come to Everything Too Late," 1966–1967

In their ideological existence French students come to everything too late. All the values and illusions that are the pride of their cloistered world are already doomed as untenable illusions which history has long ago made ridiculous.

Because they share a little of the University's crumbling prestige, students are still pleased to be students. Too late. The mechanical, specialized teaching they receive has fallen as abysmally low (in comparison with the former level of bourgeois general culture)[1] as their own intellectual level at the time they enter it, due to the single fact that the reality that dominates it all, the economic system, calls for mass production of untutored students incapable of thinking. Being unaware that the University has become institutionalized organization of ignorance, that "higher education" itself is disintegrating at the same tempo that mass production of professors progresses, and that *all* of these professors are morons, most of

whom would set any high school student body into an uproar, students continue, therefore, to listen respectfully to their teachers, with the conscious determination to rid themselves of all spirit of criticism, the better to commune in the mystic illusion of having become "students," i.e., persons who are seriously occupied with acquiring *serious* knowledge in the hope that they will be entrusted with ultimate truths. This is a menopause of the mind. Everything that is taking place today in school and faculty amphitheatres will be condemned in the future revolutionary society as just so much socially harmful *noise*. From now on, students make people laugh.

Students don't even realize that history is also changing their absurd, "cloistered" world. The famous "crisis of the University," which is a detail of the more general crisis of modern capitalism, remains the subject of a deaf men's dialogue between different specialists. It expresses quite simply the difficulties of belated adjustment by this special production sector to overall transformation of the production apparatus. The leftovers of the old ideology of the liberal bourgeois University become commonplaces as its social basis disappears. The University could consider that it was an autonomous power at the time of free-trade capitalism and liberal government, which left it a certain marginal freedom.

It was in fact closely dependent on the needs of this type of society which were: to give a privileged minority who were pursuing studies an adequate general culture before they joined the ranks of the ruling class, which they had hardly left. Hence the ridiculous position of certain nostalgic[2] professors, embittered at having lost their former function of watchdogs of future leaders for the much less honorable one of sheep dogs leading flocks of "white collar" workers, according to the planified needs of the economic system, along the path to their respective factories and offices. They are the ones who oppose their archaic ideas to technocratization of the University and continue imperturbedly to impact scraps of the culture called "general" to future specialists who won't know what to do with it.

More serious, and therefore more dangerous, are the modernists on the left and those in the UNEF led by the "ultras" of the FGEL, who demand "structural

---

[1] We do not mean the culture of the *Ecole normale supérieure* or of the "Sorboniqueurs," but that of the Encyclopaedists, or of Hegel.

[2] Not daring to claim kinship with philistine liberalism, they invent references for themselves to the academic freedoms of the Middle Ages, which was the time of "non-freedom democracy."

reform of the University," "re-introduction of the University into social and economic life," that is to say, its adaptation to the needs of modern capitalism. From having been the dispensers of "general culture" for the use of the ruling classes, the various *facultés* and schools, still draped in anachronistic prestige, have been turned into quick-breeding factories for lower and medium cadres. So far from protesting against this historical process that directly subordinates one of the last relatively autonomous sectors of social life to the demands of the mercantile system, our progressives protest against the delays and lapses that beset its realization. They are the champions of the future cybernetically run University, which is already apparent here and there. The mercantile system and its modern hirelings are the real enemy.

B. Jean-Paul Sartre Interviews Daniel Cohn-Bendit, 1968

J.-P.S.: You have said that the student movement is now on the crest of a wave. But the vacation is coming, and with it a deceleration, probably a retreat. The government will take the opportunity to put through reforms. It will invite students to participate and many will accept, saying either 'Reformism is all we want,' or 'It is only reformism, but it is better than nothing, and we have obtained it by force.' So you will have a transformed university, but the changes may be merely superficial ones, dealing particularly with the development of material facilities, lodgings, university restaurants. These things would make no basic changes in the system. They are demands that the authorities could satisfy without bringing the regime into question. Do you think that you could obtain any 'adjustments' that would really introduce revolutionary elements into the bourgeois university—for example, that would make the education given at the university contradictory to the basic function of the university in the present regime: the training of cadres who are well integrated into the system?

D.C.-B.: First, purely material demands may have a revolutionary content. On university restaurants we have a demand which is basic. We demand their abolition as university restaurants. They must become youth restaurants in which all young people, whether students or not, can eat for one franc forty. No one can reject this demand: if young workers are working during the day, there seems no reason why they should not dine for one franc forty in the evening. Similarly with the *Cités Universitaires* [campuses]. There are many young workers and apprentices who would rather live away from their parents but who cannot take a room because that would cost them 30,000 francs per month; let us welcome them to the *Cités*, where the rent is from 9,000 to 10,000 francs per month. And let the well-to-do students in law and *sciences-po* [political science] go elsewhere.

Basically, I don't think that any reforms the government might make would be enough to demobilize the students. There obviously will be a retreat during the vacation, but they will not 'break' the movement. Some will say, 'We have lost our chance', without any attempt to explain what has happened. Others will say, 'The situation is not yet ripe.' But many militants will realize that we must capitalize on what has just taken place, analyse it theoretically and prepare to resume our action next term. For there will be an explosion then, whatever the government's reforms. And the experience of disorderly, unintentional, authority-provoked action we have just been through will enable us to make any action launched in the autumn more effective. The vacation will enable students to come to terms with the disarray they showed during the fortnight's crisis, and to think about what they want to do and can do.

As to the possibility of making the education given at the university a 'counter-education' manufacturing not well-integrated cadres but revolutionaries, I am afraid that that seems to me a somewhat idealistic hope. Even a reformed bourgeois education will still manufacture bourgeois cadres. People will be caught in the wheels of the system. At best they will become members of a *bien-pensant* ["right-thinking"] left, but objectively they will remain cogs ensuring the functioning of society.

Our aim is to pursue successfully a 'parallel education' which will be technical and ideological. We must launch a university ourselves, on a completely new basis, even if it only lasts a few weeks. We shall call on left-wing and extreme left-wing teachers who are prepared to work with us in seminars and assist us with their knowledge—renouncing their 'professional' status—in the investigations which we shall undertake.

In all faculties we shall open seminars—not lectures courses, obviously—on the problems of the workers' movement, on the use of technology in the interests of man, on the possibilities opened up by automation. And all this not from a theoretical viewpoint (every sociological study today opens with the words 'Technology must be made to serve man's interests'), but by posing concrete problems. Obviously this education will go in the opposite direction to the education provided by the system and the experiment could not last long; the system would quickly react and the movement give way. But what matters is not working out a reform of capitalist society, but launching an experiment that completely breaks with that society, an experiment that will not last, but which allows a glimpse of a possibility: something which is revealed for a moment and then vanishes. But that is enough to prove that the something could exist.

We do not hope to make some kind of socialist university in our society, for we know that the function of the university will stay the same so long as the system is unchanged as a whole. But we believe that there can be moments of rupture in the system's cohesion and that it is possible to profit by them to open breaches in it.

C. Rock Music as Fun: The Rolling Stones Give a Concert

Fifty police and a squad of first aid attendants were called in to deal with the crowds. . . . Many girls fainted and were treated.

From my third row seat I had to lip-read on many occasions to find out what song was being performed! The screams from the audience completely drowned the Stones.

The long-haired ones began with "Beautiful Delilah" and were met with a torrent of gifts which plummeted onto the stage from all parts of the theatre. To their credit, the Stones carried on even though they were hit several times. Mick's dancing was grade one and served to incite fresh attacks of frenzy from the fans.

Even though "You Better Move On" is a slow number, the screams continued, but you should have heard what happened during "I'm Alright." From the moment Mick picked up his maracas and the Stones burst into action it was a battle between them and the teenagers as to who could make the most noise. . . .

It was over ten minutes after the act finished . . . before the fans stopped chanting, "We want the Stones."

D. Rock Music as a Serious Issue: Glasnost-Era Sociologists Discuss the Rise of Soviet Rock, 1987

Rock music is thirty-five years old. For quite a long time it was held back by all sorts of official cultural prohibitions, but can one really establish any reliable obstacles against something that stirs the interest of millions? Regardless of all bans, rock music increas-

ingly defines the music scene in our country. In the 1970s in the pages of newspapers and magazines the following words began to appear: "rock ensemble," "rock group," "rock star," and "rock opera." Among the musical preferences of the young, this movement became dominant. It continues to remain so to this day. For example, according to the data of the Estonian sociologist N. Meinert, of nine genres of music the most popular with young people is rock music: 79 percent of those polled liked it (statistics are from 1984).

Experts state that the attraction to rock is declining. However, for a dozen years it was a mass phenomenon, and so it deserves the serious attention of sociologists. By the way, the music community has repeatedly addressed such bothersome questions to sociologists. For example, in a conversation with an *Izvestiya* correspondent, A. Rybnikov, author of the famous operas *Yunona* and *Avos,* proposed to investigate such questions as "Do we need rock or not?" and "Do we need classical music or not?" The lack of sociological interpretations for the process of the formation of the musical tastes of the young is obvious. This is a professional "debt" that sociologists owe to the readers of this magazine and to the society as a whole. We have decided to present the theme of rock culture as a social phenomenon at this "round table" discussion.

N. D. Sarkitov: Rock music exists in the USSR in two forms, foreign and indigenous. The audience that accepts this music is also heterogeneous. The fans of indigenous amateur rock music are, as a rule, highly educated connoisseurs. In sharp contrast to them are the fans of foreign "metal" music. Among the latter one doesn't find intellectuals. Many of the functions of Western and Soviet rock music do not correspond.

It is necessary to elaborate one point: Rock music has experienced three stages of development and is now beginning a fourth. The first stage lasted from the mid-1960s to the mid-1970s. In the beginning, the majority of ensembles followed the best Western rock groups and performers, more often than not faithfully reproducing their best compositions. That was natural. At the beginning of the last century a very similar period was experienced in the development of Russian classical music.

The second stage was also characterized by the formation of a new kind of rock within the youth music culture. By the beginning of the 1980s so-called amateur rock music had been born, in contrast to the "commercial" professional rock.

The third stage began in the late 1970s and early 1980s and has continued to this day. It is differentiated from the first two stages first, by rock's sharp divergence by 1983 into two ideologically distinct entities (professional and amateur) and, second, by the unusually successful blossoming of "heavy metal" on both the amateur and the professional stage. (Amateur groups worked during this period in rock clubs and rock laboratories.) The second half of this stage has been marked by the formation of a third center of Soviet rock music, in the Urals (Yuri Shevchuk and DDT, Urfin Juice, Nautilus). These groups have defined the philosophical and aesthetic positions of Soviet rock music.

Now, the third period is finished (by 1986). A new time has arrived, and it is too early to discern its characteristic features. . . .

V. Ovchinsky: . . . Soviet youth does not live in an isolated world. The broadening of contacts with foreigners has intensified the exchange of information. Rock rather quickly entered our lives through unofficial channels. The makers of Soviet music policy simply ignored the real situation. Four generations of youths (1950s, 1960s, 1970s, and the 1980s) confronted the mass media's angry condemnation of any variety of rock music. The fear of the further spread of "rock mania" as a source of antisocial phenomena brought forth a "forbid-o-mania." Even now you can occasionally hear authoritative statements such as: "Today you listen to rock, tomorrow you will betray your motherland." As a result, our youth has had to decide alone (or with the aid of Western radio broadcasts) whom to select as a musical idol. Thus the homemade "rock underground" was brought to life with all its negative aspects: fashionable violence, sexual promiscuity, drunkenness, and drug abuse.

Sweet is the forbidden fruit, and prohibition removes the situation from any kind of social control. This happened with "heavy metal." Barriers placed in front of this rock movement brought about a "natural" market for "metallists" where speculation in albums and video and tape recordings flourishes, and "*samizdat*" hand-typed rock magazines such as *Urlait* and *Ucho* [Ear] are disseminated. All sorts of "bunkers" (attics and basements so named by teenagers) have appeared, where they listen to "metal rock." Often this listening is accompanied by the use of toxic substances and misdemeanors. Outside of the professional stage several rock groups, devotees of "heavy metal," strut their semi-legal condition, actively promoting the worst examples of punk rock. The media have reported the hooliganism and pornographic escapades of the group Chudo-yudo [Miracle] at the festival of the Moscow rock laboratory in the spring of 1987. . . .

M. Manuilsky: . . . Rock music is not the only passion of the young. Many young men and women, follow-ing fashion, consider themselves fans of "heavy metal" without fearing ostracism, especially since the official ban has been lifted. In reality, a considerable part of the youth (exactly what part remains to be determined) associates rock with any composition that is performed with a heavy beat on ultramodern instruments.

Rock music is quite heterogeneous and controversial. It encompasses commercial music, *shlyager* [coarse popular tunes], and *razvlekashki* [empty entertainment]. There are musicians and music oriented toward "getting high" and being shocking. Distorted faces, wild whistling and screaming, torn clothing, shattered furniture, and doses of drugs—all of this has happened and still occurs right here in the performance hall. This is not somewhere in California, but in Moscow or in Ufa. . . .

To a great extent, the situation described above explains the unusualness, the "differentness" of rock music. With a relative sparseness of musical means of expression, its works are distinguished by complex emotional images and the broad use of symbols and metaphors. It is not simply a search for "one's own values," but rather an attempt to uncover the diversity and polyphony of humanitarian ideals and bring them to everyday life. Polysemy is the fundamental feature of rock music. In contrast to the cheap stylized rock tunes, rock refutes standards. The world is diverse. Every young person is bothered by the eternal problems (love, friendship, obligation) in his own way. Rock music provides an opportunity to grapple with the depth and breadth of life, to develop a unique perception. This is the attraction of rock.

Rock music is a position. To enter the world and affirm yourself, to discover one's "self" and present it to other people—this is the highest goal of rock culture.

Document Set 29.4 References

A. French Students Complain That They "Come to Everything Too Late," 1966–1967.
   Extract from pamphlet "On student wretchedness in its economic, political, psychological, sexual, and particularly its intellectual aspects, and several means for remedying it," in Alain Schnapp, ed., *The French Student Uprising* (Boston: Beacon Press, 1971), 67–69.

B. Jean-Paul Sartre Interviews Daniel Cohn-Bendit, 1968
   The Student Revolt: The Activists Speak (London: Jonathan Cape, 1968), 104–106.

C. Rock Music as Fun: The Rolling Stones Give a Concert
   The New Musical Express, in Carey Schofield, *Jagger* (London: Metheun, 1983), 65–66.

D. Rock Music as a Serious Issue: Glasnost-Era Sociologists Discuss the Rise of Soviet Rock, 1987
   J. Tarasulo, ed., *Gorbachev and Glasnost: Viewpoints from the Soviet Press* (Wilmington, Del.: Scholarly Resources, 1989), 154–156, 158–161.

DOCUMENT SET 29.5
The Decline and Fall of Communism

It now seems fairly clear that one of the great revolutionary transformations in modern history began in the mid-1980s when the new Soviet leader Mikhail Gorbachev set in motion the processes he called *glasnost* (openness) and *perestroika* (restructuring). Within six years of his accession to power, Communist power collapsed in the U.S.S.R. and its satellites in Eastern Europe. What may ultimately emerge from the wreckage is by no means certain; the history of revolutions in Western civilization is littered with false starts, missed turns, and unexpected outcomes that seem "inevitable" only in hindsight. The documents selected for this set suggest an optimistic interpretation that may not seem justified some years from now. They do, however, connect the history of dissent against Communist dictatorship with the Western tradition of honoring human rights, if necessary sacrificing one's life to advance the cause of liberty, and working steadily to advance the arena of unfettered behavior. The manifesto "2000 Words" and the self-sacrifice of activist Jan Palach (Documents A and B) date from the "Prague Spring" of 1968 and its subsequent stifling by Warsaw Pact tanks. How do you evaluate the analysis of the young Soviet historian Andrei Amalryk, who in 1969 predicted that the U.S.S.R. would collapse by 1984—as the result of a war with China more than from internal dissent (Document C)? The first relatively successful challenge to Soviet-style rule, although it took almost a decade to prevail, was mounted by the Polish movement Solidarity (Document D); unlike dissidents in the Soviet Union and Czechoslovakia, Solidarity enjoyed *organized* mass support. Do you see any historical precedents for such a movement?

Gorbachev's aim, it seems clear, was not to destroy Marxism-Leninism and the Soviet Union, but to revitalize them (Document E). Was he realistic? Have you seen other attempts in history to reform an autocratic system from above that led to unintended outcomes? What has been the historical experience of reformers in Russia, from the time of Peter the Great onward?

The last two documents in the set offer retrospective comments on the Revolution of 1989, both by individuals well acquainted with the Western tradition and with Western values. In the opinion of these now-successful activists, what remains to be accomplished in the "civil societies" they helped to restore? In view of the far darker outcome (so far) of the revolution unleashed by the fall of Communism in, for

example, former Yugoslavia, what explains the relatively hopeful results in former East Germany and former Czechoslovakia?

A. Seventy Czechoslovak Intellectuals Issue the Manifesto "2000 Words," 1968

First, the life of our nation was threatened by the war. Then came blacker days, which threatened our spiritual and national character. Most of the nation accepted and had faith in the new program of socialism, which was taken over by the wrong people. It would not have mattered so much that they lacked the experience of statesmen, the knowledge of scholars or the training of philosophers, if they had allowed themselves to be replaced by more capable persons.

The communist party betrayed the great trust the people put in it after the war. It preferred the glories of office, until it had those and nothing more. The disappointment was great among communists as well as noncommunists. The leadership of the party changed it from a political and ideological group into a power-hungry organization, attracting egotists, cowards, and crooks.

They influenced the party's operations to such an extent that honest people could not gain a foothold without debasement, much less make it a modern political instrument. There were many communists who fought this deterioration but they could not prevent what happened.

The situation in the party led to a similar situation in the state, resulting in the linkage of party and state. There was no criticism of the state and economic organizations. Parliament forgot how to deliberate, the government forgot how to rule and managers how to manage. Elections had no significance and the laws lost their value. We could not trust any of our representatives, and when we could it was impossible to ask them for anything because they were powerless. What made things even worse was that we could not trust each other.

The Decline of Honesty

Personal and collective honor deteriorated. Honesty led nowhere, and it was useless to speak of rewards according to ability. As a result, most citizens lost interest in public affairs. They were concerned only with themselves and with accumulating money. The situation got so bad that now one cannot even rely on money. Relations among people were undermined and joy in work was lost. To sum up, the nation was in a morass that threatened its spiritual health and character. . . .

In all justice, we can say that some of them did realize what was happening. We know that now because they are redressing wrongs, correcting mistakes, bringing decisions to the membership and the citizens, and limiting the authority and the size of the official apparatus. They no longer support the conservative viewpoint in the party. But there are still many officials opposed to change who exercise the instruments of power, particularly in the districts and in the communities.

Since the beginning of the year we have been in the process of reviving democratization. It began in the communist party. We must say this. And those noncommunists among us who, until recently, expected no good to come from the communists also know it. We must add, however, that this process could not have begun elsewhere. After twenty years, only the communists had an actual political life; only communist criticism was in a position to assess things as they were; only the opposition in the communist party had the privilege of being in contact with the enemy.

The Basis of Democratization

The present effort of the democratic communists is only an installment in the repayment of the debt the entire party owes the people outside the party, who had no political rights. No gratitude is due to the communist party, although it should probably be acknowledged that it is honestly striving to use this last opportunity to save its own honor and the nation's. . . .

Therefore, let us not overestimate the significance of the criticism from the ranks of writers and students. The source of social change is in the economy. The right word is significant only if it is spoken under conditions which have been duly prepared. "Duly prepared conditions in our country"—unfortunately, this cliché means our general level of poverty and the complete disintegration of the old system of rule, under which certain types of politicians calmly and peacefully compromised themselves at our expense.

Truth does not prevail. It only remains when everything else fails. . . .

Yet, we have not spoken up. All we have to do is complete what we started out to do—humanize this regime. Otherwise the revenge of the old forces will be cruel. We turn to those who have been waiting.

The days immediately ahead of us will determine our future course for many years to come. . . .

B. Czech Student Jan Palach Immolates Himself, 1969

Seeing that our nations [Czechs and Slovaks] are on the brink of despair we have decided to make our protest and arouse the people of this country in the following way.

Our group consists of volunteers who have resolved to let themselves be burned alive for our cause.

I have the honor to draw the first lot and thus obtain the right to draft this first letter and become the first torch.

Our demands are: (1) The immediate abolition of censorship. (2) A ban on the distribution of *Zpravy*.[1]

Unless our demands are met within five days, i.e. by 21 January, and unless the public demonstrates adequate support (i.e. by an indefinite strike), further torches will burst into flames.

Signed: Torch Number 1

P.S. Remember August! Czechoslovakia has obtained room for manoeuvre in international affairs: let us exploit the fact.

C. Andrei Amalyk Questions the Soviet Middle Class's Willingness to Support Dissent, 1969

. . . [T]here exists an influential class, or stratum of society, on which the Democratic Movement could seemingly base itself. But there are at least three interrelated factors that militate strongly against such a development.

Two of these factors spring to mind immediately. First, the planned elimination from society of the most independent-minded and active of its members, which has been going on for decades, has left an imprint of grayness and mediocrity on all strata of society—and this could not fail to be reflected in the "middle class" which is once again taking shape. This elimination, whether through emigration or exile from the country or through imprisonment or physical annihilation, affected all strata of our people.

Second, that section of the "middle class" which most clearly recognizes the need for democratic reforms is also the section that is most imbued with

---

1 *Zpravy* was a Soviet-controlled occupation newspaper with scurilous attacks on reformers.

the defensive thought, "Well, there's nothing I can do anyway" or "You can't break down the wall by beating your head against it." In reaction to the power of the regime, it practices a cult of its own impotence.

The third factor, although less obvious, is most interesting. As is well known, in any country the stratum of society least inclined toward change or any sort of independent action is that composed of state employees. This is natural, because every government worker considers himself too insignificant in comparison with the power apparatus of which he is only a small cog to demand of that apparatus any kind of change. At the same time, he has been relieved of all social responsibility, since his job is simply to carry out orders. Thus he always has the feeling of having performed his duty even though he has done things that he would not have done had he been given a choice.

(On the other hand, the person who issues the orders is equally freed from a sense of responsibility inasmuch as the officials on the level beneath him regard his orders as "good" because they come from above. This creates the illusion among the authorities that everything they do is good.)

For the government worker, the notion of work is narrowed to the notion of a "job." He is an automaton at his post and passive when he leaves it. The government worker's psychology is therefore the one that is most convenient both for the government and for himself.

In our country, since all of us work for the state, we all have the psychology of government workers. Writers who are members of the Union of Writers, scholars employed in government institutions, common laborers or collective farmers are creatures of this psychology just as much as are officials of the KGB or the Interior Ministry.

Therefore, much of the overt and covert protest in the Soviet Union has the character of the dissatisfaction of a junior clerk with the attitude of his superior. This can be seen clearly in the attitude of a number of writers whose names are used in the West as yardsticks of "Soviet liberalism." They are inclined to regard their rights and duties not so much as the rights and duties of a *writer* as those of an "official in the literary department," to use the expression of a character in Dostoevsky.

For example, after Alexander Solzhenitsyn wrote his famous letter about the situation of the Soviet writer, the Moscow correspondent of the *Daily Telegraph* of London, John Miller, asked a well-known Soviet poet in a private conversation whether he intended to join in Solzhenitsyn's protest. The poet said no.

"You must understand," he said, "that this is our internal affair, a question of our relations with the state."

In other words, he regarded the matter not as a question of the writer's conscience and his moral right and duty to write what he thinks, but as a question of internal relations within the Soviet "literary department." He may also protest, but in the manner of a petty clerk, not against the "department" as such but against his rather low salary or against his rude boss. Naturally, this is an "internal matter" and should be of no interest to those who do not belong to the "department."

This curious conversation took place in one of the shops in Moscow where those privileged to have foreign currency are allowed to buy goods not available on the Soviet market.

It goes without saying that the "middle class" is no exception in adopting this government-employee attitude; indeed, this psychology is particularly typical of it by virtue of its position in the middle of the social scale. Many members of this class are simply functionaries of the Communist Party or governmental apparatus. They regard the regime as a lesser evil than the painful process of changing it.

Consequently we are faced with an interesting phenomenon. Although there exists in our country a social class capable of comprehending the principles of personal freedom, rule of law and democratic government, a class that needs those principles and provides the emerging Democratic Movement with its basic contingent of supporters, the vast majority of this class is so mediocre, its ways of thinking are so much those of the government employee, and its intellectually most independent members are so passive that the success of a Democratic Movement based on it seems to me to be gravely in doubt.

D. Solidarity Issues Its 21 Demands, 1980

1. Acceptance of Free Trade Unions independent of both the Party and employers, in accordance with the International Labor Organization's Convention number 87 on the freedom to form unions, which was ratified by the Polish government.

2. A guarantee of the right to strike and guarantees of security for strikers and their supporters.

3. Compliance with the freedoms of press and publishing guaranteed in the Polish constitution. A halt to repression of independent publications and access to the mass media for representatives of all faiths.

4. (a) Reinstatement to their former positions for: people fired for defending workers' rights, in particular those participating in the strikes of 1970 and 1976; students dismissed from school for their convictions. (b) The release of all political prisoners . . . (c) A halt to repression for one's convictions.

5. The broadcasting on the mass media of information about the establishment of the Interfactory Strike Committee (MKS) and publication of the list of demands.

6. The undertaking of real measures to get the country out of its present crisis by:
(a) providing comprehensive, public information about the socio-economic situation;
(b) making it possible for people from every social class and stratum of society to participate in open discussions concerning the reform program.

7. Compensation of all workers taking part in the strike for its duration with holiday pay from the Central Council of Trade Unions.

8. Raise the base pay of every worker 2,000 złotys per month to compensate for price rises to date.

9. Guaranteed automatic pay raises indexed to price inflation and to decline in real income.

10. Meeting the requirements of the domestic market for food products: only surplus goods to be exported.

11. The rationing of meat and meat products through food coupons (until the market is stabilized).

12. Abolition of "commercial prices" and hard currency sales in so-called "internal export" shops.

13. A system of merit selection for management positions on the basis of qualifications rather than Party membership. Abolition of the privileged status of MO [police], SB [Internal Security Police], and the party apparatus through: equalizing all family subsidies; eliminating special stores, etc.

14. Reduction of retirement age for women to 50 and for men to 55. Anyone who has worked in the PRL [Polish People's Republic] for 30 years, for women, or 35 years for men, without regard to age, should be entitled to retirement benefits.

15. Bringing pensions and retirement benefits of the "old portfolio" to the level of those paid currently.

16. Improvement in the working conditions of the Health Service, which would assure full medical care to working people.

17. Provision for sufficient openings in daycare nurseries and preschools for the children of working people.

18. Establishment of three-year paid maternity leaves for the raising of children.

19. Reduce the waiting time for apartments.

20. Raise per diem [for work-related travel] from 40 złotys to 100 złotys and provide cost-of-living increases.

21. Saturdays to be days off from work. Those who work on round-the-clock jobs or three-shift systems should have the lack of free Saturdays compensated by increased holiday leaves or through other paid holidays off from work.

E. Mikhail Gorbachev Discusses Perestroika and Glasnost

. . . Perestroika is an urgent necessity arising from the profound processes of development in our socialist society. This society is ripe for change. It has long been yearning for it. Any delay in beginning perestroika could have led to an exacerbated internal situation in the near future, which, to put it bluntly, would have been fraught with serious social, economic and political crises. . . .

. . . In the latter half of the seventies—something happened that was at first sight inexplicable. The country began to lose momentum. Economic failures became more frequent. Difficulties began to accumulate and deteriorate, and unresolved problems to multiply. Elements of what we call stagnation and other phenomena alien to socialism began to appear in the life of society. A kind of "braking mechanism" affecting social and economic development formed. And all this happened at a time when scientific and technological revolution opened up new prospects for economic and social progress. . . .

An absurd situation was developing. The Soviet Union, the world's biggest producer of steel, raw materials, fuel and energy, has shortfalls in them due to wasteful or inefficient use. One of the biggest producers of grain for food, it nevertheless has to buy millions of tons of grain a year for fodder. We have the largest number of doctors and hospital beds per thousand of the population and, at the same time, there are glaring shortcomings in our health services.

Our rockets can find Halley's comet and fly to Venus with amazing accuracy, but side by side with these scientific and technological triumphs is an obvious lack of efficiency in using scientific achievements for economic needs, and many Soviet household appliances are of poor quality.

This, unfortunately, is not all. A gradual erosion of the ideological and moral values of our people began.

It was obvious to everyone that the growth rates were sharply dropping and that the entire mechanism of quality control was not working properly; there was a lack of receptivity to the advances in science and technology; the improvement in living standards was slowing down and there were difficulties in the supply of foodstuffs, housing, consumer goods and services.

On the ideological plane as well, the braking mechanism brought about ever greater resistance to the attempts to constructively scrutinize the problems that were emerging and to the new ideas. Propaganda of success—real or imagined—was gaining the upper hand. Eulogizing and servility were encouraged; the needs and opinions of ordinary working people, of the public at large, were ignored. . . .

The presentation of a "problem-free" reality backfired: a breach had formed between word and deed, which bred public passivity and disbelief in the slogans being proclaimed. It was only natural that this situation resulted in a credibility gap: everything that was proclaimed from the rostrums and printed in newspapers and textbooks was put in question. Decay began in public morals; the great feeling of solidarity with each other that was forged during the heroic times of the Revolution, the first five-year plans, the Great Patriotic War and postwar rehabilitation was weakening; alcoholism, drug addiction and crime were growing; and the penetration of the stereotypes of mass culture alien to us, which bred vulgarity and low tastes and brought about ideological barrenness increased. . . .

An unbiased and honest approach led us to the only logical conclusion that the country was verging on crisis. . . .

I would like to emphasize here that this analysis began a long time before the April Plenary Meeting and that therefore its conclusions were well thought out. It was not something out of the blue, but a balanced judgment. It would be a mistake to think that a month after the Central Committee Plenary Meeting in March 1985, which elected me General Secretary, there suddenly appeared a group of people who understood everything and knew everything, and

that these people gave clear-cut answers to all questions. Such miracles do not exist.

The need for change was brewing not only in the material sphere of life but also in public consciousness. People who had practical experience, a sense of justice and commitment to the ideals of Bolshevism criticized the established practice of doing things and noted with anxiety the symptoms of moral degradation and erosion of revolutionary ideals and socialist values. . . .

Perestroika is closely connected with socialism as a system. That side of the matter is being widely discussed, especially abroad, and our talk about perestroika won't be entirely clear if we don't touch upon that aspect.

Does perestroika mean that we are giving up socialism or at least some of its foundations? Some ask this question with hope, others with misgiving.

There are people in the West who would like to tell us that socialism is in a deep crisis and has brought our society to a dead end. That's how they interpret our critical analysis of the situation at the end of the seventies and beginning of the eighties. We have only one way out, they say: to adopt capitalist methods of economic management and social patterns, to drift toward capitalism.

They tell us that nothing will come of perestroika within the framework of our system. They say we should change this system and borrow from the experience of another socio-political system. To this they add that, if the Soviet Union takes this path and gives up its socialist choice, close links with the West will supposedly become possible. They go so far as to claim that the October 1917 Revolution was a mistake which almost completely cut off our country from world social progress.

To put an end to all the rumors and speculations that abound in the West about this, I would like to point out once again that we are conducting all our reforms in accordance with the socialist choice. We are looking within socialism, rather than outside it, for the answers to all the questions that arise. We assess our successes and errors alike by socialist standards. Those who hope that we shall move away from the socialist path will be greatly disappointed. Every part of our program of perestroika—and the program as a whole, for that matter—is fully based on the principle of more socialism and more democracy. . . .

We will proceed toward better socialism rather than away from it. We are saying this honestly, without trying to fool our own people or the world. Any hopes that we will begin to build a different, nonsocialist society and go over to the other camp are unrealistic and futile. Those in the West who expect us to give up socialism will be disappointed. It is high time they understood this, and, even more importantly, proceeded from that understanding in practical relations with the Soviet Union. . . .

We want more socialism and, therefore, more democracy. . . .

F. A Woman Activist Helps Bring Down the German Democratic Republic

So much has happened lately that I haven't thought about me and my development for a long time. . . .

I am a woman who has been interested in political issues as far back as I can remember. I always had a desire to have influence. Of course, one would have to reflect on the question as to what it means to "have influence," but it represented a basic motivation to become active politically; otherwise, I could have continued to live a normal life, like most others. I already wanted to have this influence as a child. I was very active in the Pioneer [Communist children's] organization, but quickly began to feel very exploited by them. I just felt treated unfairly, having to do things and being exploited for things that I did not agree with, that I did not support. . . .

I had a pretty high position within the structure of the Pioneer organization; I was chairperson of the friendship council. And in this position you had quite a few privileges and responsibilities. I remember at one time we participated in the so-called Weltjugendspiele [World Youth Games]. That was in 1973; Walter Ulbricht [first secretary of the Socialist Unity Party until 1971] had just died. We had to stay in one of those camps, guarded and everything, and we were not allowed to move around freely, to go places and meet young people from other countries. I perceived that as an outrageous restriction at the time. And then we were told to go to an official demonstration—not to participate, but to stand on the sidelines and to sort of "fill in." They did not tell us what this was all about, why we could not participate actively, or anything. We were just puppets being moved around according to their plans. I was so angry that I got sick and did not participate, which, of course, was considered to be a disciplinary offense for someone in my position. . . .

From Dirk Philipson, *We Were the People: Voices from East Germany; Revolutionary Autumn of 1989*, pp. 67–95. Durham, N.C.: Duke University Press, 1993. Reprinted with prmission.

During my training at the university I began to seek contact with grassroots groups here in Leipzig and with the ESG [Evangelical Student Community]. In November of 1985 I organized a presentation on the fortieth anniversary of the victory over fascism within the context of the Protestant Peace Decade that was held in Leipzig at the time. Before that, I had only had sporadic contacts with the church. . . .

My problem had always been to find a way to express myself politically, to find a context or people with whom I could work. . . .

Actually, I was trying to find the women's movement, except that I had not yet quite realized that at the time. . . .

You see, the church was the only possible alternative for any kind of political activism. There was absolutely nothing else. . . .

Had you heard about the group "Women for Peace" that was founded in Berlin in 1983?

Yes, I had heard about it, but I did not know much about them. It was very difficult to find out things like that. We did not have any contacts with them; the linkages were simply missing. It was very difficult to obtain certain pieces of information in the GDR; one always depended on personal contacts. Only afterward did I find out that there was a group "Women for Peace" in Leipzig as well. I don't know how they came into existence, but very few people knew about them. . . .

It was very difficult in the GDR to realize that your problems as a woman might not have personal causes, but instead were indicative of a larger problem, of gender antagonisms permeating all of society. As you know, the official ideology claimed that emancipation and equal rights had already been achieved in the GDR—in short, they claimed that there were no gender-related problems.

What helped me a great deal was when I met a woman from Marburg who was active in the West German feminist movement. Only by talking to her did I realize how much was going on out there in terms of women's issues, how large the women's movement was, and for how long they had been organizing. Of course, discrimination against women was probably also not as clear-cut as it is in the West. I could not claim, for example, that I was discriminated against in terms of my own education or job in the GDR. It had more to do with smaller things, with things that were not as tangible. I had always perceived disadvantages or unfair treatment as my private matter, as a problem that had only to do with me, but not as something that might perhaps be tied into the larger issue of gender relations in the GDR. . . .

Why exactly did they arrest you?

Well, at the end they pretty much picked up people at random in front of the Thomas Church. Of course, they were particularly looking for people who they already knew were engaged in "subversive activities" and those who somehow looked conspicuously "alternative." I did not particularly look "alternative," and I could probably have avoided arrest. But first of all I thought that it was time for me to go through this experience as well, and second of all I figured it would be important for them also to arrest people once who did not fit into their preconceptions of who was and who was not opposed to the regime they were serving.

How long did they keep you in detention?
Until about 2:30 at night.
How did they treat you?
Not too badly. The guy who interrogated me was talking about "enemies of the state" and things like that, but that was normal. Surprisingly, I was also not scared at all. We knew, for example, that they were eavesdropping on us, but that did not matter to us at all; we talked to one another completely freely. There was a mood among us—the kind of mood that prevailed until October and, I think, that goes a long way in explaining the mass demonstrations of October—that it did not matter anymore. Things were so bad, it really no longer mattered. Something just *had* to happen, and people were increasingly willing to take risks in order to bring about change. That so many people took the tremendous risks they did on 9 October, even though they knew what the state apparatus could potentially do to us, and even though it was absolutely unclear as to what would happen, I think can only be explained by people having reached a tremendous degree of alienation and resignation. In retrospect, after we have found out what some of their plans were . . . it was really quite scary.

Anyway, I did not get treated badly, but I think that mostly had to do with the fact that there were so many of us. But after I had gotten out, I was severely depressed, and my partner Matthias and I concluded that it was time for us to become more active ourselves. We decided to play the role of the naive citizen who had seen innocent people being arrested. So we wrote three official letters inquiring about what had happened and wondering as to why the state was conducting itself in this fashion. We sent one letter to the city councilman for cultural affairs, one we sent to the editor in chief of the *FAZ* [West German daily in Frankfurt], and the third to Kurt Masur [director of the Leipzig orchestra]. We got no answer to the first letter; the second was answered in a very unresponsive fashion, which depressed us even more. But

Professor Masur wrote back, telling us that he had taken notice of this and that he was surprised how the police had apparently treated people and so on. And then he wrote that he would plan a session on 28 August in which he would invite all the people who were interested in street music.

You can imagine what a big success this was for us. A high-ranking personality and connections to [Erich] Honecker [the East German leader] was actually paying attention to us and responding to us. In fact, from then on he became active as a sort of mediator in critical events—before that he had not done anything. . . .

Many things happened after this meeting in August, the wave of emigration through Hungary and such. What also seemed important to me at the time was the fact that Honecker was sick, and that the entire party leadership simply came across as desolate. They seemed no longer capable of any real decisions. All of this, of course, left the impression that this "power"—this party and state leadership that we had come to know simply as "the power"—that this power had disintegrated so much primarily because Honecker was sick. It was somehow encouraging, because if that was true, it could not be all that great a "power" after all. I at least experienced it that way, and I believe many others did as well. It just signified that such power cannot be infinite.

I well remember a meeting we had in September among opposition activists and church members, and one person said "the whole system is so well organized, so stable, that it will certainly defend itself to the last man." Particularly older citizens, due to all their experiences, thought that this entire party apparatus could never be broken.

Many thought that inertia, or a kind of self-perpetuating dynamic would keep the apparatus in place indefinitely. How wrong everybody was.

G. President Václav Havel Addresses Czechoslovakia on New Year's Day, 1991

Dear Fellow Citizens,
There was a time when each New Year the president could deliver the same speech as he had the year before and no one would know the difference. Fortunately, that time is past. Time and history have come back into our lives. The gloomy skies of bore-

Vaclav Havel, "The New Year in Prague," March 7, 1991. Reprinted from *The New York Review of Books.* Copyright © 1991 Nyrev, Inc.

dom and stultifying inaction have cleared, and we can only marvel at the vast range of possibilities a truly free political climate can offer, and at how it continues to astonish us, in both the good and the bad sense of the word.

Let me first talk about the unpleasant surprises the last year has brought us. In the first place, the heritage of the past few decades has proven worse than we could possibly have anticipated in the joyous atmosphere of those first few weeks of freedom. Each day brings new problems, and each day we realize how interrelated they are, how long they will take to solve, and how difficult it is to establish the proper order in which to deal with them.

We knew that the house we had inherited was not in order: the plaster was cracking and falling off, the roof looked as though it might leak, and we had doubts about other parts of it as well. After a year of careful inspection, we are shocked to discover that all the pipes are rusting, the beams are rotten, the wiring is in terrible shape, and the reconstruction we had planned for and looked forward to will take longer and cost far more than we first thought. What a year ago appeared to be a rundown house is in fact a ruin. This is not a pleasant discovery, and not surprisingly it has made us all feel disappointed and out of sorts.

Many of you are asking why we have settled so few accounts with the past, why we have failed to rehabilitate all its victims, right all the wrongs, and justly punish all the guilty ones. Many of you are asking why the "aristocracy" of the former regime, who grew rich at the society's expense, are still the aristocracy and why they have been able to find their feet so quickly in the new conditions. Many of you are surprised that the broad transformation of our economy is still only being talked about, and that you cannot see any changes for the better in your everyday lives. People are anxious because all that planned reforms have brought so far are higher prices and the threat of a loss of social security and jobs. We are all upset by the serious increase in crime. Our hopes for a better future are increasingly mixed with a feeling of the opposite kind: fear of the future.

In this atmosphere of general impatience, anxiety, disappointment, and doubt, elements of spitefulness, suspicion, mistrust, and mutual recrimination are creeping into public life. Surprisingly, freedom has opened the door to many of our negative qualities and has revealed the depth of the moral decline infecting our souls. We have clearly defeated the monolithic, visible, and easily identifiable enemy and now—driven by our discontent and our need to find a living culprit—we are seeking the enemy in each other. Each of us feels let down, even cheated by the other.

A year ago we were all united by the joy of having liberated ourselves from the totalitarian system; today we have all become somewhat neurotic from the burden of freedom. Our society is still in a state of shock. It could have been predicted, but no one predicted that the shock would be so profound. The old system has collapsed, the new one is not yet built, and our life together is marked by a subconscious uncertainty about what kind of system we want, how to build it, and whether we have the know-how to build it in the first place. The distance, the vagueness, and the uncertainty of the new order leads many of us to seek substitute, partial solutions and to forget that our success as individuals or groups is only possible with the general success of our whole community.

The unpleasant surprise of 1990, then, is this rather uncertain, if not stultifying, atmosphere that surrounds us at the end of the year. . . .

[Havel goes on to list some of the "good things" that also happened in 1990, including the withdrawal of Soviet forces and the restoration of political democracy and civil liberties, and creation of a framework for free-market economic reforms.]

Dear fellow citizens,
I am saying nothing new if I tell you that a difficult time lies ahead, and that the year which begins today will be the most difficult. It is most important that we not lose hope, no matter how difficult the trials we face may be. Were we to become dispirited, these trials would no longer be a test of our mettle, but merely the occasion for suffering and want. We will meet these challenges, I believe, and pass the test with flying colors. It all depends on the degree of hope we can keep alive in our souls. We must safeguard this hope both in ourselves, and in those around us. . . .

After so many years, we have got rid of the evil landlord, and no matter how desolate the state of our house after so many years of his rule, it now belongs to us, and what we do with it is up to us alone. Therefore I ask you all, Czechs, Slovaks, and people of other nationalities, to respect our new state, to treat it as your own, and to make a contribution to its overall success. We have already undergone the first difficult test of our ability to coexist as different nations in the same state, and the Czechs and Slovaks have passed the test.[1]

I wish all Slovaks success in building an autonomous and economically independent republic. I believe that it will be a republic of love and pride for

---

[1] In the course of 1991, however, Slovakia seceded and formed an independent republic.

all its citizens. I wish the same to all Czechs. I believe that their republic will be a republic of wisdom and tolerance for all its citizens. . . .

I appeal to all who, through their work, create things of value for the whole society. Once again you will be creating these things for yourselves and those close to you, not for those who rule over you or for the abstract future of a utopian ideology. I appeal to all those who quickly find their feet in the new economic system to be mindful of those who do not find immediate success, to use their skills to help them. . . . I ask them not to forget that the profit they create is not an end in itself, but a means to enhance the common wealth of society, and to create conditions for a genuinely dignified and full human life.

Dear fellow citizens, dear friends,
The time when New Year's addresses were the same each year has definitely come to an end. I firmly believe that the coming year will contain more pleasant surprises than unpleasant ones. I believe that I will be able to announce to you that the reconstruction of our house has been successfully begun, and that its foundations once more rest firmly in this land and its best traditions.

A year ago I finished my New Year's address by paraphrasing a well-known quotation from Comenius[2]: "People, your government has been returned to you!" Today, I would add: "And it is up to you to show that the return of your government into your own hands has not been in vain."

Document Set 29.5 References

A. Seventy Czechoslovak Intellectuals Issue the Manifesto "2000 Words," 1968
   "2000 Words: A Statement on Democratization," from *East Europe* (August 1968), 25–28.
B. Czech Student Jan Palach Immolates Himself, 1969
   David Caute, *Sixty-eight* (London: Hamilton, 1988), 380.
C. Andrei Amalyk Questions the Soviet Middle Class's Willingness to Support Dissent, 1969
   Amalyk, *Will the Soviet Union Survive Until 1984?* (New York: Harper and Row, 1969), 18–21.
D. Solidarity Issues Its 21 Demands, 1980
   "The Twenty-one Demands," in Lawrence Weschler, *The Passion of Poland* (New York: Pantheon, 1984), 206–208.
E. Mikhail Gorbachev Discusses Perestroika and Glasnost
   Mikhail Gorbachev, *Perestroika: New Thinking for Our Country and the World* (New York: Harper & Row, 1987).
F. A Woman Activist Helps Bring Down the German Democratic Republic
   Cornelia Matzke, interview, in Dirk Philipsen, *We Were the People: Voices From East Germany's Revolutionary Autumn of 1989* (Durham, N.C.: Duke University Press, 1993), 68–75.
G. President Václav Havel Addresses Czechoslovakia on New Year's Day, 1991
   Havel, "New Year in Prague," in *New York Review of Books*, March 7, 1991.

---

[2] Comenius (Jan Amos Komenský, 1592–1670), was a notable Czech educational reformer and Protestant leader, active not only in Bohemia but also in Puritan England.